T0181505

Lecture Notes in Computer Science

Lecture Notes in Artificial Intelligence   14281

Founding Editor

Jörg Siekmann

Series Editors

Randy Goebel, *University of Alberta, Edmonton, Canada*
Wolfgang Wahlster, *DFKI, Berlin, Germany*
Zhi-Hua Zhou, *Nanjing University, Nanjing, China*

The series Lecture Notes in Artificial Intelligence (LNAI) was established in 1988 as a topical subseries of LNCS devoted to artificial intelligence.

The series publishes state-of-the-art research results at a high level. As with the LNCS mother series, the mission of the series is to serve the international R & D community by providing an invaluable service, mainly focused on the publication of conference and workshop proceedings and postproceedings.

Sarah Gaggl · Maria Vanina Martinez ·
Magdalena Ortiz
Editors

Logics in Artificial Intelligence

18th European Conference, JELIA 2023
Dresden, Germany, September 20–22, 2023
Proceedings

 Springer

Editors
Sarah Gaggl ⓘ
TU Dresden
Dresden, Germany

Maria Vanina Martinez ⓘ
Artificial Intelligence Research Institute -
IIIA CSIC
Barcelona, Spain

Magdalena Ortiz ⓘ
Umeå University
Umeå, Sweden

TU Wien
Vienna, Austria

ISSN 0302-9743   ISSN 1611-3349 (electronic)
Lecture Notes in Artificial Intelligence
ISBN 978-3-031-43618-5   ISBN 978-3-031-43619-2 (eBook)
https://doi.org/10.1007/978-3-031-43619-2

LNCS Sublibrary: SL7 – Artificial Intelligence

Preface

This volume contains the proceedings of the 18th European Conference on Logics in Artificial Intelligence, which took place at TU Dresden, Germany, during September 20–22, 2023.

The European Conference on Logics in Artificial Intelligence (or Journées Européennes sur la Logique en Intelligence Artificielle–JELIA) began back in 1988, as a workshop, in response to the need for a European forum for the discussion of emerging work in this field. Since then, JELIA has been organized biennially, with proceedings published in the Springer series Lecture Notes in Artificial Intelligence. Previous meetings took place in Roscoff, France (1988), Amsterdam, The Netherlands (1990), Berlin, Germany (1992), York, UK (1994), Évora, Portugal (1996), Dagstuhl, Germany (1998), Málaga, Spain (2000), Cosenza, Italy (2002), Lisbon, Portugal (2004), Liverpool, UK (2006), Dresden, Germany (2008), Helsinki, Finland (2010), Toulouse, France (2012), Madeira, Portugal (2014), Larnaca, Cyprus (2016), and Rende, Italy (2019). Due to the COVID-19 pandemic, the 2021 edition was held online, instead of the University of Klagenfurt, Austria. But in 2023, the conference could return to its traditional in-person format, as an engaging and inspiring meeting in the beautiful city of Dresden.

The aim of JELIA is to bring together active researchers interested in all aspects concerning the use of logics in artificial intelligence to discuss current research, results, problems, and applications of either a theoretical and practical nature. JELIA strives to foster links and facilitate cross-fertilization of ideas among researchers from various disciplines, among researchers from academia and industry, and between theoreticians and practitioners. The scientific community has been increasingly showing interest in JELIA, which during the years featured the growing participation of researchers from outside Europe and a very high overall technical quality of contributions; hence, the conference turned into a major biennial forum and a reference for the discussion of logic-based approaches to artificial intelligence.

JELIA 2023 received 112 submissions in two different formats: long and short papers. Each submission was reviewed by three Program Committee members. Out of the 112 submissions, 41 were accepted as long papers and 11 as short papers. Of the 55 submissions which were declared to have a student as a leading author, 26 were included in the program. All of the accepted submissions were given a slot for oral presentation at the conference.

This year's conference included a Special Track on *Logics for Explainable and Trustworthy* AI, focusing on logic-based approaches to making AI more transparent, safer, and more trustable. Of the 112 submissions, 14 were submitted to this special track. They went through the same reviewing process, and 7 papers were accepted and presented in a dedicated session at the conference.

The conference program also featured four wonderful invited talks by Mario Alviano, Katie Atkinson, Franz Baader, and Vaishak Belle. The abstracts of these talks—and in most cases also an accompanying paper—can be found in these proceedings.

JELIA 2023 recognized and awarded two prizes to contributions that the Program Committee deemed to be of exceptional quality. The *Best Paper Award* was given to Stéphane Demri and Karin Quaas for their work entitled *First Steps Towards Taming Description Logics with Strings*, while the *Best Student Paper Award* was given to Bartosz Bednarczyk for his paper *Beyond $\mathcal{ALC}_{reg}$: Exploring Non-Regular Extensions of Propositional Dynamic Logic with Description-Logics Features*. Each award was accompanied by a prize of 500 €, kindly offered by Springer.

We would like to thank the members of the Program Committee and the additional reviewers for their efforts to produce fair and thorough evaluations of the submitted papers, which is essential for a successful scientific conference. Thank you also to the authors of the scientific papers, including those not accepted for publication. The number of high-quality submissions on relevant and exciting topics was substantial, and unfortunately, not all could be included in the program. We want to extend our gratitude to the local organization committee for their hard work in making JELIA 2023 a wonderful event.

We are very grateful to all the sponsors for their generous support of JELIA 2023: School of Embedded Composite Artificial Intelligence (SECAI), Center for Perspicuous Computing (CPEC), Center for Scalable Data Analytics and Artificial Intelligence (ScaDS.AI), compl3te, Springer, and Potassco Solutions. Last, but not least, we thank the people behind EasyChair for the useful conference management system.

August 2023   Magdalena Ortiz
Sarah Gaggl
Maria Vanina Martinez

Organization

General Chair

Sarah Gaggl   TU Dresden, Germany

Program Committee Chairs

Maria Vanina Martinez   Artificial Intelligence Research Institute, IIIA -
                                CSIC, Spain
Magdalena Ortiz   Umeå University, Sweden and TU Wien, Austria

Program Committee

Sergio Abriola   Universidad de Buenos Aires, Argentina
Shqiponja Ahmetaj   TU Wien, Austria
Gianvincenzo Alfano   University of Calabria, Italy
Jose Julio Alferes   Universidade NOVA de Lisboa, Portugal
Mario Alviano   University of Calabria, Italy
Grigoris Antoniou   University of Huddersfield, UK
Carlos Areces   Universidad Nacional de Córdoba, Argentina
Peter Baumgartner   CSIRO, Australia
Bartosz Bednarczyk   TU Dresden, Germany & University of Wrocław,
                                Poland
Leopoldo Bertossi   SKEMA Business School Canada inc., Canada
Alexander Bochman   Holon Institute of Technology, Israel
Gerhard Brewka   Leipzig University, Germany
Pedro Cabalar   University of A Coruña, Spain
Marco Calautti   University of Milano, Italy
Francesco Calimeri   University of Calabria, Italy
Giovanni Casini   ISTI - CNR, Italy
Lukáš Chrpa   Czech Technical University in Prague, Czechia
Gianluca Cima   Sapienza University of Rome, Italy
Mehdi Dastani   Utrecht University, The Netherlands
Thomas Eiter   TU Wien, Austria
Esra Erdem   Sabanci University, Turkey
Wolfgang Faber   Alpen-Adria-Universität Klagenfurt, Austria
Eduardo Fermé   Universidade da Madeira, Portugal

Johannes K. Fichte	Linköping University, Sweden
Michael Fisher	University of Manchester, UK
Tommaso Flaminio	Artificial Intelligence Research Institute, IIIA - CSIC, Spain
Gerhard Friedrich	Alpen-Adria-Universitaet Klagenfurt, Austria
Maurice Funk	Universität Leipzig, Germany
Marco Garapa	Universidade da Madeira, Portugal
Martin Gebser	University of Klagenfurt, Austria
Tobias Geibinger	TU Wien, Austria
Laura Giordano	Università del Piemonte Orientale, Italy
Lluis Godo	Artificial Intelligence Research Institute, IIIA - CSIC, Spain
Markus Hecher	MIT, USA
Tomi Janhunen	Tampere University, Finland
Gabriele Kern-Isberner	Technische Universität Dortmund, Germany
Sébastien Konieczny	CRIL - CNRS, France
Roman Kontchakov	Birkbeck, University of London, UK
Davide Lanti	Free University of Bozen-Bolzano, Italy
Joao Leite	Universidade NOVA de Lisboa, Portugal
Vladimir Lifschitz	University of Texas at Austin, USA
Anela Lolic	TU Wien, Austria
Emiliano Lorini	IRIT, France
Thomas Lukasiewicz	TU Wien, Austria
Sanja Lukumbuzya	TU Wien, Austria
Quentin Manière	Universität Leipzig, Germany
Marco Maratea	University of Calabria, Italy
Pierre Marquis	CRIL, U. Artois & CNRS - Institut Universitaire de France, France
Andrea Mazzullo	University of Trento, Italy
Loizos Michael	Open University of Cyprus, Cyprus
Angelo Montanari	University of Udine, Italy
Michael Morak	University of Klagenfurt, Austria
Manuel Ojeda-Aciego	University of Malaga, Spain
Cem Okulmus	Umeå University, Sweden
Nina Pardal	University of Sheffield, UK
Xavier Parent	TU Wien, Austria
Francesco Parisi	University of Calabria, Italy
David Pearce	Universidad Politécnica de Madrid, Spain
Rafael Peñaloza	University of Milano-Bicocca, Italy
Andreas Pieris	University of Edinburgh, UK and University of Cyprus, Cyprus
Nico Potyka	Cardiff University, UK

Antonio Rago   Imperial College London, UK
Anna Rapberger   TU Wien, Austria
Maurício Reis   Universidade da Madeira, Portugal
Francesco Ricca   University of Calabria, Italy
Ricardo Oscar Rodriguez   University of Buenos Aires, Argentina
Sebastian Rudolph   TU Dresden, Germany
Chiaki Sakama   Wakayama University, Japan
Zeynep Saribatur   TU Wien, Austria
Kai Sauerwald   FernUniversität in Hagen, Germany
Torsten Schaub   University of Potsdam, Germany
Stefan Schlobach   Vrije Universiteit Amsterdam, The Netherlands
Paulo Shakarian   Arizona State University, USA
Gerardo Simari   Universidad Nacional del Sur (UNS) and
                                   CONICET, Argentina

Mantas Simkus   TU Wien, Austria
Michael Thielscher   University of New South Wales, Australia
Matthias Thimm   FernUniversität in Hagen, Germany
Mirek Truszczynski   University of Kentucky, USA
Sara Ugolini   Artificial Intelligence Research Institute, IIIA -
                                   CSIC, Spain
Mauro Vallati   University of Huddersfield, UK
Leon van der Torre   University of Luxembourg, Luxembourg
Ivan Varzinczak   Université Paris 8, France
Joost Vennekens   KU Leuven, Belgium
Amanda Vidal Wandelmer   Artificial Intelligence Research Institute, IIIA -
                                   CSIC, Spain

Carlos Viegas Damásio   Universidade NOVA de Lisboa, Portugal
Johannes P. Wallner   Graz University of Technology, Austria
Toby Walsh   University of New South Wales, Australia
Frank Wolter   University of Liverpool, UK
Stefan Woltran   TU Wien, Austria
Jessica Zangari   University of Calabria, Italy

Additional Reviewers

Alrabbaa, Christian   Collenette, Joe
Arndt, Doerthe   Cruchten, Mike
Belardinelli, Francesco   De Rose, Edoardo
Bengel, Lars   Diéguez, Martín
Bernreiter, Michael   Dvořák, Wolfgang
Blümel, Lydia   Fernandes, Renan L.
Chafik, Anasse   Feyzbakhsh Rankooh, Masood

Friedrich, Gerhard
Gabelaia, David
Gladyshev, Maksim
Gonçalves, Ricardo
Hahn, Susana
He, Yifan
Herrmann, Luisa
Higuera, Nelson
Hunther, Anthony
Ielo, Antonio
Jaakkola, Reijo
Knorr, Matthias
Kohlhase, Michael
König, Matthias
Laferriere, François
Mastria, Elena
Mazzotta, Giuseppe

Meier, Arne
Morak, Michael
Motamed, Nima
Oetsch, Johannes
Opitz, Juri
Pan, Wei
Petrova, Iliana M.
Ribeiro, Jandson S.
Ricioppo, Aldo
Rühling, Nicolas
Schaerf, Andrea
Strauch, Klaus
Tarzariol, Alice
Turhan, Anni-Yasmin
Vilander, Miikka
Yilmaz, Baturay

Organizing Committee

Marcos Cramer	TU Dresden, Germany
Martin Diller	TU Dresden, Germany
Stefan Borgwardt	TU Dresden, Germany
Stefan Ellmauthaler	TU Dresden, Germany
Lucía Gómez Alvarez	TU Dresden, Germany
Dominik Rusovac	TU Dresden, Germany
Hannes Straß	TU Dresden, Germany
Piotr Gorczyca	TU Dresden, Germany

Combining Symbolic and Machine Learning Approaches for Automating Legal Reasoning (Abstract of Invited Talk)

Katie Atkinson

University of Liverpool
katie@liverpool.ac.uk

Abstract. The need for AI applications to be explainable and trustworthy is eminently clear in domains where AI-supported decisions can have significant real-world consequences. The field of law is one such characteristic domain. In this talk I will present an overview of recent research investigating how different AI techniques can be combined to provide support for automating reasoning about legal cases in an efficient and explainable manner. Symbolic, logic-based techniques are used to represent the legal knowledge of a domain in a structured manner and machine learning techniques are used to identify the inputs to the symbolic model. The hybrid approach enables the different techniques to be targeted towards the particular tasks where they are most effective, within the overall automation pipeline. I will provide an overview of the hybrid system along with the first sets of results of experiments evaluating the performance of the hybrid system where the domain used is legal cases from the European Court of Human Rights.

References

1. Collenette, J., Atkinson, K., Bench-Capon, T.J.M.: Explainable AI tools for legal reasoning about cases: a study on the European Court of Human Rights. Artif. Intell. **317**, 103861 (2023). https://doi.org/10.1016/j.artint.2023.103861
2. Mumford, J., Atkinson, K., Bench-Capon, T.J.M.: Combining a legal knowledge model with machine learning for reasoning with legal cases. In: Proceedings of 19th International Conference on Artificial Intelligence and Law (ICAIL 2023). pp. 167–176 (2023)

Contents

Argumentation

Answer Set Programming

Description Logics and Ontological Reasoning

Logics of Knowledge and Belief

Non-monotonic Reasoning

Planning

xviii   Contents

Invited Papers

Generative Datalog and Answer Set Programming – Extended Abstract

Mario Alviano[✉][iD]

DEMACS, University of Calabria, Via Bucci 30/B, 87036 Rende, CS, Italy
`mario.alviano@unical.it`

Abstract. Generative Datalog is an extension of Datalog that incorporates constructs for referencing parameterized probability distributions. This augmentation transforms the evaluation of a Generative Datalog program into a stochastic process, resulting in a declarative formalism suitable for modeling and analyzing other stochastic processes. This work provides an introduction to Generative Datalog through the lens of Answer Set Programming (ASP), demonstrating how Generative Datalog can explain the output of ASP systems that include @-terms referencing probability distributions. From a theoretical point of view, extending the semantics of Generative Datalog to stable negation proved to be challenging due to the richness of ASP relative to Datalog in terms of linguistic constructs. On a more pragmatic side, the connection between the two formalisms lays the foundation for implementing Generative Datalog atop efficient ASP systems, making it a practical solution for real-world applications.

Keywords: Answer Set Programming · Datalog · probabilistic reasoning · non-measurable sets · stable model semantics

Extended Abstract

Generative Datalog [4,5] extends Datalog with Δ-*terms*, which are primitive constructs representing *probability distributions* [13,17]. Δ-terms can occur in rule heads to represent that specific conditions encoded by rule bodies trigger random phenomena. The conventional bottom-up evaluation of Datalog programs is then naturally extended by sampling outcomes for Δ-terms when needed, with the probability given by the associated probability distributions. If all the events of such probability distributions are independent, as it is commonly assumed, the probability that a model is produced by the bottom-up evaluation of a Generative Datalog program is the product of the probabilities of the sampled Δ-term outcomes. It turns out that models of a Generative Datalog program define a probabilistic space, and lay the foundation of a declarative specification language for stochastic processes.

Recall that a *probability space* is a triple $(\Omega, \mathcal{F}, P)$ satisfying the following conditions:

© The Author(s), under exclusive license to Springer Nature Switzerland AG 2023
S. Gaggl et al. (Eds.): JELIA 2023, LNAI 14281, pp. 3–10, 2023.
https://doi.org/10.1007/978-3-031-43619-2_1

- Ω is the *sample space*, a nonempty set comprising all possible outcomes (of the modeled stochastic process).
- $\mathcal{F} \subseteq 2^{\Omega}$ is the *event space*, a collection of all the *events* to consider, where an event is a set of possible outcomes. $\mathcal{F}$ must be a σ-algebra, i.e.,
  - $\mathcal{F}$ contains the sample space: $\Omega \in \mathcal{F}$;
  - $\mathcal{F}$ is closed under complement: if $E \in \mathcal{F}$, then $(\Omega \setminus E) \in \mathcal{F}$;
  - $\mathcal{F}$ is closed under countable unions: if $E_i \in \mathcal{F}$ for $i \in \mathbb{N}$, then $\left(\bigcup_{i \in \mathbb{N}} E_i\right) \in \mathcal{F}$.
- $P : \mathcal{F} \to [0, 1]$ is the *probability measure*, a function on events such that
  - P is countably additive: if $E_i \in \mathcal{F}$ (for all $i \in \mathbb{N}$) are pairwise disjoint sets, then $P(\bigcup_{i \in \mathbb{N}} E_i) = \sum_{i \in \mathbb{N}} P(E_i)$;
  - the measure of the sample space is equal to one: $P(\Omega) = 1$.

A *discrete probability distribution* over a *countable* sample space Ω is a function $P : \Omega \to [0, 1]$ such that $\sum_{o \in \Omega} P(o) = 1$; it is essentially a probability space whose event space includes all elementary events (i.e., singletons of Ω).

One strength of Generative Datalog is the fact that random phenomena are not necessarily fixed a priori, but materialized when some conditions are met. To clarify this aspect of Generative Datalog, let us consider the stochastic process resulting from flipping an unbiased coin multiple times. Let $s = s_1 \cdots s_n$ $(n \geq 1)$ be a string with each $s_i \in \{h, t\}$, so that $o_s := \{\mathsf{Flip}(i) = s_i \mid i = 1, \ldots, n\}$ denotes one possible outcome of flipping the coin n times. As a first example, the stochastic process of flipping the coin two times is associated with the probabilistic space having four possible outcomes, namely o_{hh}, o_{ht}, o_{th} and o_{tt}. On the other hand, if the coin is flipped a second time only when the first flipping resulted tails, then the probabilistic space only has three possible outcomes, namely o_h, o_{th} and o_{tt}. If random phenomena are necessarily fixed a priori, the second stochastic process must be associated with a probabilistic space with four possible outcomes, two of which (o_{hh} and o_{ht}) associated with the event $\{o_{hh}, o_{ht}\}$ and no singletons are in the event space; intuitively, such a modeling of the stochastic process ignores the outcome of the second flip, rather than not flipping the coin a second time. While this is reasonable when the number of random phenomena is bounded by a small constant, it practically fails in general, for example, if the coin is flipped until heads is obtained. In this case, the number of random phenomena is unbounded, still there are several possible outcomes $o_{t^n h}$ of finite size, for $n \geq 0$ and with probability 0.5^{n+1}.

In order to materialize the sampled outcomes of the random phenomena involved in computing a minimal model of a Generative Datalog program, rules with Δ-terms are rewritten by introducing fresh predicates that collect the sampled values from probability distributions. For example, the program

$$\top \to side(1, \mathsf{Flip}(1)) \tag{1}$$

$$side(I, tails) \to side(I + 1, \mathsf{Flip}(I + 1)) \tag{2}$$

is rewritten as

$$\top \to \exists Y \; Result^{\mathsf{Flip}}(1, Y) \tag{3}$$

$$Result^{\mathsf{Flip}}(1, Y) \to side(1, Y) \tag{4}$$

$$side(I, tails) \to \exists Y \; Result^{\mathsf{Flip}}(I+1, Y) \tag{5}$$

$$side(I, tails) \wedge Result^{\mathsf{Flip}}(I+1, Y) \to side(I+1, Y) \tag{6}$$

where the existential variable Y takes values from the probability distribution Flip, i.e., Y is replaced by either *heads* or *tails* with probability $\frac{1}{2}$ whenever the bodies of (3) and (5) are true. It turns out that minimal models of the rewritten program have the form $\{Result^{\mathsf{Flip}}(i, tails), side(i, tails) \mid i = 1, \ldots, n\} \cup \{Result^{\mathsf{Flip}}(n+1, heads), side(n+1, heads)\}$, for all $n \geq 0$ with probability 0.5^{n+1} (beside an additional infinite model $\{Result^{\mathsf{Flip}}(i, tails), side(i, tails) \mid i \geq 1\}$). It can be observed that the probability of an outcome can be computed by multiplying the probabilities of the atoms in the extension of predicate $Result^{\mathsf{Flip}}$.

Interestingly, the semantics of Generative Datalog can be used to measure the probability of the possible outcomes of Answer Set Programming (ASP) engines [1,11] processing programs of a specific form. In fact, the language of ASP extends Datalog with several constructs, among them @-terms in CLINGO [10] to represent interpreted function symbols; the interpretation of @-terms is given by functions implemented in Python or Lua, and can easily refer probability distributions. It turns out that the evaluation of a Datalog program using such @-terms in rule heads is essentially a stochastic process analogous to the one associated with Generative Datalog programs. For example, the repeated flipping of a coin can be encoded as follows in CLINGO:

```
1 #script(python)

2 import functools
3 import random

4 @functools.lru_cache(maxsize=None)
5 def flip(signature):
6     return "tails" if random.uniform(0, 1) <= 0.5 else "heads"

7 #end.

8 side(  1, @flip(  1)).
9 side(I+1, @flip(I+1))  :- side(I, "tails").
```

Note that function `flip` is decorated by a caching mechanism so that multiple calls with the same argument returns the same value, which is randomly determined on the first call (at line 8).

Given the many linguistic extensions of ASP supported by mainstream engines, a natural question arises: *What is the probability space associated with the possible outcomes of ASP engines processing programs using @-terms that refer probability distributions?* One important step in answering such a question is to extend Generative Datalog with nonmonotonic negation under stable model semantics [12]; some other common constructs, among them constraints and choice rules, can be seen as shortcuts for rules with nonmonotonic negation.

Intuitively, stable models are minimal models under the assumption they provide for false literals. An important point here is that a program is associated with zero or several stable models. While this is very convenient for representing combinatorial search and optimization problems, whose instances are typically associated with several solutions, it also makes the understanding of the underlying stochastic process, in case @-terms refer to probability distributions, more challenging.

First of all, in general a possible outcome of the stochastic process cannot be simply a model anymore, as asking an ASP engine to search for a single stable model normally results in one stable model of the program in input (if any), which is non-deterministically selected; here the adjective non-deterministically is slightly abused, as ASP engines in fact implement repeatable computation, but the exact stable model produced in output depends on many internals that are almost impossible to track, among them the branching heuristic and its parameters, the order of atoms in memory, and so on. Such non-determinism essentially disappears when the ASP engine is asked to compute *all* stable models of a program, and the order in which they are enumerated is ignored. On the other hand, even sets of stable models may have insufficient information regarding the stochastic process that produced them; in the extreme case in which the program has no stable models, the (empty) set of stable models carries indeed no information at all. The lack of information is an insight that a previous computational step of the stochastic process should be considered, where all required information is still present. In mainstream ASP engines, stable model enumeration is preceded by intelligent grounding, a form of bottom-up computation similar to the one implemented by Datalog engines and that produces a portion of the Herbrand expansion sufficient to compute all stable models of the input program. It is actually at grounding time that @-terms are processed, and this is particularly important when they refer to probability distributions, as indeed the stochastic part of the process is precisely the intelligent grounding: once all @-terms are processed, the subsequent stable model enumeration does not involve any other random phenomena.

For example, let us consider a simple game, which can be played or not, consisting in flipping a coin; a played game is won if the coin shows heads. Such a scenario is captured by

```
10 {play}.      % equivalent to   play :- not play'.   play' :- not play.
11 side(@flip(1)) :- play.
12 :- play, not side("heads").
```

where the @-term `flip` is defined in lines 4–6. The choice rule in line 10 gives the possibility to take `play` as true, without enforcing it; when `play` is true, line 11 can support the truth of one instance of `side/1` obtained by sampling a value between *heads* and *tails*, each one with probability $\frac{1}{2}$. Finally, the constraint in line 12 checks that the game is won if played. All in all, there are two possible outcomes: when `@flip(1)= "heads"`, there are two stable models, namely $\{Result^{Flip}(heads)\}$ (i.e., the game is not played) and $W := \{Result^{Flip}(heads),$ `play, side("heads")`$\}$ (i.e., the game is played and won); when `@flip(1)= "tails`

", the only stable model is $\{Result^{\mathsf{Flip}}(tails)\}$ (i.e., the game is not played), as indeed adding `play` would raise an inconsistency with line 12. Note that, in both cases, the set of stable models must be considered as a whole when measuring probabilities. Moreover, if line 10 is replaced by the fact `play.`, then the only stable model is W; for `@flip(1)= "tails"` the program has no stable models, and the empty set carries no information about its $\frac{1}{2}$ probability of being computed.

Based on the above observations, in order to preserve the information about the sampled Δ-terms, a possible outcome of the evaluation of a Generative Datalog program with nonmonotonic negation by an ASP engine must be the program produced by the intelligent grounder, with the probability given by multiplying the probabilities of all sampled Δ-terms. However, ground programs are just *intermediate artifacts* that mainstream ASP engines use to compute stable models, and the interest of ASP programmers is usually on stable models rather than ground programs. Such an interest can be represented in the probability space by means of the event space: all finite ground programs in the sample space that are associated with the same set of stable models are part of the same indivisible event, whose probability is given by the sum of the probabilities of the ground programs. Note that we considered finite ground programs so far, but in fact there is also the possibility that the intelligent grounder does not terminate, which pragmatically implies that the subsequent stable model enumeration does not even start. All such infinite ground programs are collected in an error event, whose probability is obtained as the complement of the event comprising all finite ground programs.

For a broader example, let us consider a network of routers, possible failures, and zero budget for replacements and reconfiguration. A router is expected to have one failure every ten years on average. We are interested in understanding the probability that the network is still connected after five years; hence, every router has $\frac{1}{2}$ failure probability. Using again the `flip` @-term from lines 4–6, such a scenario can be encoded as follows:

```
13 side(X, @flip(X)) :- router(X).
14 fail(X) :- side(X, "heads").

15 reach(X) :- X = #min{Y : router(Y), not fail(Y)}.
16 reach(Y) :- reach(X), connection(X,Y), not fail(Y).
17 disconnected :- router(X), not fail(X), not reach(X).

18 :- not disconnected.
```

Note that the atom `disconnected` must be true in any stable model of the above program because of the constraint in line 18. Therefore, the *no stable models event* is associated with possible outcomes representing a network that is still connected after removing failing routers.

While by now the tiles of the puzzle have been identified, there is still one big obstacle in defining the probability space of a Generative Datalog program with nonmonotonic negation evaluated by an ASP engine: possible outcomes are ground programs obtained by the intelligent grounder of the ASP engine. The obstacle lies in the fact that intelligent grounders implement many sophisticated algorithms to simplify the program in input in order to reduce the number of iterations, and to reduce the size of the join operations. An abstraction of the process is thus crucial to obtain something understandable. The idea is to parameterize the probability space by the adopted intelligent grounder in order to obtain an underestimate of the probabilities of the events associated with sets of stable models. Intuitively, a more sophisticated grounder is expected to produce less ground rules in output, and therefore reduce the size (and the probability) of the error event; the probability subtracted from the error event is distributed among the events associated with stable models.

A *perfect grounder*, intended as one that always returns a minimal set of ground rules sufficient to compute the stable models of the program in input, does not exist in general. However, there are fragments of the language for which such perfect grounders actually do exist. A prominent example is Datalog: if the program in input is a Datalog program, then the intelligent grounder essentially mimics the bottom-up evaluation of Datalog engines; nothing more than the rules sufficient to derive the minimal model of the input program is actually produced in this case, and every atom in the model is in the head of exactly one of such rules. There is another important fragment for which a perfect grounder does exist: if the program in input is *stratified with respect to negation*, then it can be evaluated one stratum at time, starting from facts and concluding falsity of all atoms belonging to already processed strata and that have not been derived as true. In this case, the ground program produced in output is associated with a unique stable model, which comprises all rule heads. The program shown in lines 13–17 (hence, excluding the constraint) is indeed stratified with respect to negation. Predicates `router` and `connection` are given by facts, the other predicates can be processed one by one in the order `side`, `fail`, `reach`, `disconnected`. When predicate `reach` is processed in line 16, the extension of predicate `fail` is already known and can be used to obtain a two-valued evaluation of the rule body: ground atoms with predicate `fail` occurring in rule heads are true, and any other ground atom with predicate `fail` is false.

The reader is referred to our recent PODS'23 paper on Generative Datalog with Stable Negation [2] for a more detailed description of the language and the formalization of its semantics, as well as for some of its properties. For the sake of completeness, we mention here that there are other probabilistic logic languages in the literature. Some of them attach probabilities to database facts [7,18,26,27, 29] or to rules [8,19,21,22] whereas other provide constructs similar to Δ-terms [3,6,16,20,23,28]. The reader is referred to [5] for a detailed comparison between these languages and Generative Datalog. Other frameworks related to our work are (Hybrid) ProbLog [9,15,24], probabilistic extensions of Prolog where rules can be annotated with probability values and distributions; Probabilistic Answer Set Programming [7], adding probabilistic facts to ASP in order to obtain upper and lower probability bounds for true atoms; (Hybrid) Markov Logic Networks (MLNs) [19,25,30], adding weights and probability distributions to first-order constraints and ASP rules. As a final note, there are extensions of Generative Datalog to deal with continuous distributions [14].

Acknowledgments. This work is about some ongoing research with Matthias Lanzinger, Michael Morak, and Andreas Pieris [2]. This work was partially supported by Italian Ministry of Research (MUR) under PNRR project FAIR "Future AI Research", CUP H23C22000860006, under PNRR project Tech4You "Technologies for climate change adaptation and quality of life improvement", CUP H23C22000370006, and under PNRR project SERICS "SEcurity and RIghts in the CyberSpace", CUP H73C22000880001; by the LAIA lab (part of the SILA labs) and by GNCS-INdAM.

References

1. Alviano, M., et al.: The ASP system DLV2. In: Balduccini, M., Janhunen, T. (eds.) LPNMR 2017. LNCS (LNAI), vol. 10377, pp. 215–221. Springer, Cham (2017). https://doi.org/10.1007/978-3-319-61660-5_19
2. Alviano, M., Lanzinger, M., Morak, M., Pieris, A.: Generative datalog with stable negation. In: PODS. ACM (2023). https://arxiv.org/abs/2206.12247
3. Baral, C., Gelfond, M., Rushton, J.N.: Probabilistic reasoning with answer sets. Theory Pract. Log. Program. **9**(1), 57–144 (2009)
4. Bárány, V., ten Cate, B., Kimelfeld, B., Olteanu, D., Vagena, Z.: Declarative probabilistic programming with datalog. In: ICDT. LIPIcs, vol. 48, pp. 7:1–7:19. Schloss Dagstuhl - Leibniz-Zentrum für Informatik (2016)
5. Bárány, V., ten Cate, B., Kimelfeld, B., Olteanu, D., Vagena, Z.: Declarative probabilistic programming with datalog. ACM Trans. Database Syst. **42**(4), 22:1–22:35 (2017)
6. Santos Costa, V., Page, D., Cussens, J.: CLP($\mathcal{BN}$): constraint logic programming for probabilistic knowledge. In: De Raedt, L., Frasconi, P., Kersting, K., Muggleton, S. (eds.) Probabilistic Inductive Logic Programming. LNCS (LNAI), vol. 4911, pp. 156–188. Springer, Heidelberg (2008). https://doi.org/10.1007/978-3-540-78652-8_6
7. Cozman, F.G., Mauá, D.D.: The joy of probabilistic answer set programming: semantics, complexity, expressivity, inference. Int. J. Approx. Reason. **125**, 218–239 (2020)
8. Domingos, P.M., Lowd, D.: Markov Logic: An Interface Layer for Artificial Intelligence. Synthesis Lectures on Artificial Intelligence and Machine Learning. Morgan & Claypool Publishers (2009)
9. Fierens, D., et al.: Inference and learning in probabilistic logic programs using weighted Boolean formulas. Theory Pract. Log. Program. **15**(3), 358–401 (2015)
10. Gebser, M., Kaminski, R., Kaufmann, B., Schaub, T.: Multi-shot ASP solving with clingo. Theory Pract. Log. Program. **19**(1), 27–82 (2019). https://doi.org/10.1017/S1471068418000054
11. Gebser, M., Kaufmann, B., Kaminski, R., Ostrowski, M., Schaub, T., Schneider, M.: Potassco: the Potsdam answer set solving collection. AI Commun. **24**(2), 107–124 (2011)
12. Gelfond, M., Lifschitz, V.: Classical negation in logic programs and disjunctive databases. New Gener. Comput. **9**(3/4), 365–386 (1991)
13. Goodman, N.D.: The principles and practice of probabilistic programming. In: POPL, pp. 399–402. ACM (2013)
14. Grohe, M., Kaminski, B.L., Katoen, J., Lindner, P.: Generative datalog with continuous distributions. In: PODS, pp. 347–360. ACM (2020)

15. Gutmann, B., Jaeger, M., De Raedt, L.: Extending ProbLog with continuous distributions. In: Frasconi, P., Lisi, F.A. (eds.) ILP 2010. LNCS (LNAI), vol. 6489, pp. 76–91. Springer, Heidelberg (2011). https://doi.org/10.1007/978-3-642-21295-6_12
16. Gutmann, B., Thon, I., Kimmig, A., Bruynooghe, M., Raedt, L.D.: The magic of logical inference in probabilistic programming. Theory Pract. Log. Program. 11(4–5), 663–680 (2011)
17. Jones, C., Plotkin, G.D.: A probabilistic powerdomain of evaluations. In: LICS, pp. 186–195. IEEE Computer Society (1989)
18. Kimelfeld, B., Senellart, P.: Probabilistic XML: models and complexity. In: Ma, Z., Yan, L. (eds.) Advances in Probabilistic Databases for Uncertain Information Management. Studies in Fuzziness and Soft Computing, vol. 304, pp. 39–66. Springer, Heidelberg (2013). https://doi.org/10.1007/978-3-642-37509-5_3
19. Lee, J., Talsania, S., Wang, Y.: Computing LPMLN using ASP and MLN solvers. Theory Pract. Log. Program. 17(5–6), 942–960 (2017)
20. Nitti, D., Laet, T.D., Raedt, L.D.: Probabilistic logic programming for hybrid relational domains. Mach. Learn. 103(3), 407–449 (2016)
21. Niu, F., Ré, C., Doan, A., Shavlik, J.W.: Tuffy: scaling up statistical inference in Markov logic networks using an RDBMS. Proc. VLDB Endow. 4(6), 373–384 (2011)
22. Niu, F., Zhang, C., Ré, C., Shavlik, J.W.: DeepDive: web-scale knowledge-base construction using statistical learning and inference. In: VLDS. CEUR Workshop Proceedings, vol. 884, pp. 25–28. CEUR-WS.org (2012)
23. Poole, D.: The independent choice logic and beyond. In: De Raedt, L., Frasconi, P., Kersting, K., Muggleton, S. (eds.) Probabilistic Inductive Logic Programming. LNCS (LNAI), vol. 4911, pp. 222–243. Springer, Heidelberg (2008). https://doi.org/10.1007/978-3-540-78652-8_8
24. Raedt, L.D., Kimmig, A., Toivonen, H.: Problog: a probabilistic prolog and its application in link discovery. In: IJCAI, pp. 2462–2467 (2007)
25. Richardson, M., Domingos, P.M.: Markov logic networks. Mach. Learn. 62(1–2), 107–136 (2006)
26. Sato, T., Kameya, Y.: PRISM: a language for symbolic-statistical modeling. In: IJCAI, pp. 1330–1339. Morgan Kaufmann (1997)
27. Suciu, D., Olteanu, D., Ré, C., Koch, C.: Probabilistic Databases. Synthesis Lectures on Data Management. Morgan & Claypool Publishers (2011)
28. Vennekens, J., Denecker, M., Bruynooghe, M.: CP-logic: a language of causal probabilistic events and its relation to logic programming. Theory Pract. Log. Program. 9(3), 245–308 (2009)
29. Vieira, T., Francis-Landau, M., Filardo, N.W., Khorasani, F., Eisner, J.: Dyna: toward a self-optimizing declarative language for machine learning applications. In: MAPL@PLDI, pp. 8–17. ACM (2017)
30. Wang, J., Domingos, P.M.: Hybrid Markov logic networks. In: AAAI, pp. 1106–1111. AAAI Press (2008)

Optimal Repairs in the Description Logic $\mathcal{EL}$ Revisited

Franz Baader[1,2]([⊠]) [iD], Patrick Koopmann[1] [iD], and Francesco Kriegel[1] [iD]

[1] Theoretical Computer Science, Technische Universität Dresden, Dresden, Germany
{patrick.koopmann,francesco.kriegel}@tu-dresden.de
[2] Center for Scalable Data Analytics and Artificial Intelligence (ScaDS.AI)
Dresden/Leipzig, Dresden, Germany
franz.baader@tu-dresden.de

Abstract. Ontologies based on Description Logics may contain errors, which are usually detected when reasoning produces consequences that follow from the ontology, but do not hold in the modelled application domain. In previous work, we have introduced repair approaches for $\mathcal{EL}$ ontologies that are optimal in the sense that they preserve a maximal amount of consequences. In this paper, we will, on the one hand, review these approaches, but with an emphasis on motivation rather than on technical details. On the other hand, we will describe new results that address the problems that optimal repairs may become very large or need not even exist unless strong restrictions on the terminological part of the ontology apply. We will show how one can deal with these problems by introducing concise representations of optimal repairs.

1 Introduction

Description Logics (DLs) [4,5] are a prominent family of logic-based knowledge representation formalisms, which offer a good compromise between expressiveness and the complexity of reasoning and are the formal basis for the Web ontology language OWL.[1] In a DL ontology, the important notions of the application domain are introduced as background knowledge in the *terminology (TBox)*, and then these notions are used to represent a specific application situation in the *ABox*. The DLs of the $\mathcal{EL}$ family have drawn considerable attention since their reasoning problems are tractable [3], but they are nevertheless expressive enough to represent ontologies in many application domains, such as biology and medicine.[2] For instance, the medical ontology SNOMED CT employs $\mathcal{EL}$ and contains the following *concept inclusion (CI)* in its TBox:

$$Common\_cold \sqsubseteq Disease \sqcap \exists causative\_agent.\,Virus$$
$$\sqcap \exists finding\_site.\,Upper\_respiratory\_tract\_structure$$
$$\sqcap \exists pathological\_process.\,Infectious\_process,$$

---

[1] https://www.w3.org/TR/owl2-overview/.
[2] see. e.g., https://bioportal.bioontology.org and https://www.snomed.org/.

S. Gaggl et al. (Eds.): JELIA 2023, LNAI 14281, pp. 11–34, 2023.
https://doi.org/10.1007/978-3-031-43619-2_2

which says that a common cold is a disease that is caused by a virus, can be found in the upper respiratory tract, and has as pathological process an infectious process. A GP can then employ this concept to store in the ABox that patient Alice is diagnosed with common cold using the *concept assertion* $(\exists has\_diagnosis.Common\_cold)(alice)$. The GP's ABox may also contain the information that Charles is Alice's father, expressed as *role assertion* $has\_father(alice, charles)$, which might be of interest in the context of hereditary diseases.

Like all large human-made digital artefacts, the ontologies employed in such applications may contain errors, and this problem gets even worse if parts of the ontology (usually the ABox) are automatically generated by inexact methods based on information retrieval or machine learning. Errors in ontologies are often detected when the reasoner generates a consequence that formally follows from the knowledge base, but is incorrect in the sense that it does not hold in the application domain that is supposed to be modelled. For example, in a previous version of SNOMED CT, the concept "Amputation of finger" was classified as a subconcept of "Amputation of hand," which is fortunately wrong in the real world. To correct such errors in large ontologies, the *knowledge engineer (KE)* should be supported by an appropriate *repair tool*. Such a tool receives as input one or more consequences of the given ontology that are unwanted, and it should return one or more repaired ontologies that no longer have these consequences (called *repairs*). The KE can then choose one of the computed repairs and either use it as the new ontology, or continue the repair process from it if other unwanted consequences are detected. Of course, it makes no sense to use as a repair an arbitrary ontology that does not have the unwanted consequences. The repaired ontology should (a) not introduce new information and (b) be as close as possible to the original ontology. There are different possibilities for how to formalize these conditions.

The *classical approaches* for ontology repair return maximal subsets of the ontology that do not have the unwanted consequence, and employ methods inspired by model-based diagnosis [33] to compute these sets [17,32,34]. Thus, these approaches interpret the above conditions in a syntactic way: (a) is read as "no new axioms" and (b) is realized by the maximality condition. In [15] we called classical repairs that satisfy this maximality condition *optimal classical repairs*. While these approaches preserve as many of the axioms in the ontology as possible, they need not preserve a maximal amount of consequences, and they are syntax-dependent. For example, consider the ABoxes $\mathcal{A} := \{(A \sqcap B)(a)\}$ and $\mathcal{B} := \{A(a), B(a)\}$, which both say that individual a belongs to the concepts A and B, and are thus equivalent. However, with respect to the unwanted consequence $A(a)$, the ABox $\mathcal{A}$ has the empty ABox as only optimal classical repair, whereas $\mathcal{B}$ has the optimal classical repair $\{B(a)\}$. Thus, the latter repair retains the consequence $B(a)$, whereas the former does not. To overcome this problem, more gentle repair approaches have been introduced, e.g., in [15,21,23,26,35]. The basic idea underlying these approaches is to replace some axioms of the ontology by weaker ones, rather than just removing them, as in the classical approach. In our example, one can replace the axiom $(A \sqcap B)(a)$ in the ABox $\mathcal{A}$ with the weaker axiom $B(a)$, and thus retain the consequence $B(a)$ even if one starts with $\mathcal{A}$ rather than $\mathcal{B}$. However, these *gentle repairs* are still dependent on the syntactic structure of the axioms in the ontology, and how well they realize condition (b) depends on the employed weakening relation between axioms and the strategy used to apply it.

Providing the KE with syntax-dependent repair tools is not in line with the *functional approach* to knowledge representation [18,27] adopted by DLs. In this approach, the syntactic structure of the axioms in the ontology is supposed to be irrelevant. What counts is what queries are entailed by the ontology, which in DLs are usually *instance queries (IQ)* or *conjunctive queries (CQ)*. In this functional setting, (a) should be read as "no new consequences" (expressed in the adopted query formalism) and (b) as preserving a maximal set of such consequences. This leads us to the definition of an *optimal repair* [7,15], which is an ontology that does not have the unwanted consequences, is entailed by the original ontology (thus realizing property (a)), and preserves a maximal amount of consequences in the sense that there is no repair (i.e., no ontology satisfying the first two properties) that strictly entails it (property (b)). Entailment can be IQ-*entailment* or CQ-*entailment*, depending on whether we are interested only in instance queries, or also in conjunctive queries [28]. Maximizing the retained consequences is also motivated by the following observation. All the repair tool knows is the original ontology and the consequences that should be removed, which are specified in what we call a *repair request*. If it were to remove more consequences than are strictly needed to satisfy the repair request, then the decision which additional consequences to remove would be a random choice by the tool, not based on any application knowledge, which is held by the KE. In case the optimal repair retains consequences that should be removed, the KE needs to specify this in a subsequent repair request.

If a *repair problem* consisting of an ontology and a repair request does not have a repair, then it cannot have an optimal one. In general, however, optimal repairs of repair problems that have a repair need not exist either, even in the simple setting of $\mathcal{EL}$ ABoxes without a TBox. This is illustrated in the following example, where the ABox $\mathcal{A} = \{V(n), \ell(n, n)\}$ says that Narcissus is a vain individual that loves itself, and the repair request $\mathcal{R} = \{V(n)\}$ wants us to remove the consequence that Narcissus is vain. Intuitively, to obtain a repair, we must remove $V(n)$. However, since all assertions of the form $\exists \ell.(V \sqcap (\exists \ell.)^k \top)(n)$, saying that Narcissus loves a vain individual that is the starting point of a loves-chain of length k, are consequences of $\mathcal{A}$ and can be added to $\{\ell(n, n)\}$ without entailing $V(n)$, it is easy to see that there is no finite $\mathcal{EL}$ ABox that is an optimal repair. In fact, since Narcissus is no longer vain, the retained cycle $\ell(n, n)$ cannot be used to generate the loves-chains of arbitrary length starting from a vain individual. Even if a given repair problem has optimal repairs, they may not *cover all repairs* in the sense that every repair is entailed by an optimal one. To see this, we can look at a modified version of the above example. Consider the ABox $\mathcal{B} = \{k(t, n), V(n), \ell(n, n)\}$, which contains the additional information that Tiresias knows Narcissus, and the repair request $Q = \{(\exists k.V)(t)\}$. Removing $k(t,n)$ from B yields an optimal repair. However, there are also repairs that retain this assertion, but there is no optimal one among them for the same reason as in the previous example. Thus, if the KE is only offered the optimal repair $\{V(n), \ell(n,n)\}$ by the repair tool, the repair options that retain the assertion $k(t,n)$ are missed. This illustrates that the use of optimal repairs in a repair tool requires a setting where the optimal repairs always cover all repairs.

This can be achieved by using a more general notion of ABoxes, called *quantified ABoxes (qABoxes)* [16], where in addition to the usual named individuals we also have anonymous objects, which are represented as (existentially quantified) variables. In our Narcissus example, an optimal repair of A for R is obtained by removing $V(n)$ and introducing an anonymous vain and self-loving lover of Narcissus, which yields the qABox $\exists \{x\}. \{\ell(n,n), \ell(n,x), \ell(x,n), \ell(x,x), V(x)\}$. Note that we could not have used a named individual b instead of the variable x since then the resulting ABox would have entailed instance relationships for b, such as $V(b)$, that are not entailed by A. One might think that retaining a consequence like $(\exists \ell.V)(n)$ is not justified since one of the reasons for this being a consequence of A, namely $V(n)$, has been removed. However, with this argument, we would be back at the classical repair approach. As argued above, since the repair request only specifies that $V(n)$ should no longer be a consequence, other consequences like $(\exists \ell.V)(n)$ should not be lost unless this is needed to remove $V(n)$.

In [16] we consider a setting where ontologies are qABoxes and the repair requests consist of entailed $\mathcal{EL}$ instance relationships.[3] Given such a repair problem, we show how to construct a finite set of repairs, called the *canonical repairs*, which cover all repairs. The canonical repairs are of exponential size, and there may be exponentially many of them. Not every canonical repair is optimal, but due to the covering property, the set of them contains all optimal repairs up to equivalence. The set of optimal repairs can thus be obtained by removing non-optimal canonical repairs, i.e., ones that are strictly entailed by another canonical repair, and this set covers all repairs. The construction of the canonical repairs is actually the same for the CQ and the IQ case. The only difference is that, when removing non-optimal canonical repairs, the respective entailment relation must be used. Since CQ-entailment implies IQ-entailment, but not vice versa, more canonical repairs may be removed as non-optimal in the IQ setting. In addition, since CQ-entailment is NP-complete and IQ-entailment is tractable, the complexity of removing non-optimal repairs is higher in the CQ case.

The differences between the CQ and the IQ case get more pronounced if we add an $\mathcal{EL}$ TBox. In [7], we assume that this *TBox is correct*, and thus should not be changed in the repair process. In order to adapt the approach and the results of [16] to this setting, the first step is to *saturate* the given qABox w.r.t.

---

[3] The paper [16] actually calls repairs "compliant anonymisations" and repair requests "privacy policies" since it considers a situation where consequences are to be removed not because they are incorrect, but since this information should be hidden.

the TBox, to reduce entailment with TBox to entailment without TBox. For the IQ case, such a saturation always exists and can be computed in polynomial time. For the CQ case, a finite saturation need not exist in general. However, for *cycle-restricted TBoxes* [2], it always exists, but may be of exponential size. Continuing the repair process with the saturated qABox, we still need to take the TBox into account when defining canonical repairs, to ensure that consequences that have been removed from the qABox cannot be reintroduced by the TBox. With this adapted notion of canonical repairs, we obtain the same results as for the case without TBox. The canonical repairs cover all repairs and can be computed in exponential time. From them the set of all optimal repairs can be obtained by removing non-optimal ones using entailment test [7]. This works both for the IQ and the CQ case, but in the latter only if we can compute a finite saturation, which is always the case if the TBox is cycle-restricted. For TBoxes that are not cycle-restricted, optimal repairs need not exist in the CQ case. For example, with respect to the TBox $\{V \sqsubseteq \exists \ell. V, \exists \ell. V \sqsubseteq V\}$, which says that vain individuals are exactly the ones that love a vain individual, the qABox $\{V(n)\}$ does not have an optimal repair for the repair request $\mathcal{R} = \{V(n)\}$. Intuitively, the reason is that the qABox together with the TBox implies the existence of arbitrarily long loves-chains starting from n, which are no longer entailed by the TBox if $V(n)$ is removed (see Example 9 in [11] for a more detailed argument). One might think that the first GCI $V \sqsubseteq \exists \ell. V$ is enough to destroy existence of an optimal repair. This is, however, not the case. Without the second GCI one can introduce an anonymous vain individual x that is loved by n and loves itself to obtain an optimal repair.

In the *first part* of the paper (Sect. 2 and Sect. 3), we will describe the repair approaches developed in our previous work [7,16], but with an emphasis on motivation rather than on technical details. The *second part* of the paper (Sect. 4 and Sect. 5) describes new result. We will consider more *concise representations* of optimal repairs, to deal both with the exponential size of canonical repairs in the IQ case and the non-existence problem w.r.t. cyclic TBoxes in the CQ case.

The former problem is due to the fact that the canonical repairs employed in our approach are by construction of exponential size. To alleviate this problem, we have, on the one hand, developed in [7] an optimized algorithm for computing repairs, which yields *optimized repairs* that are equivalent to the canonical ones, but in most cases considerably smaller, though in the worst case they may still be exponential. On the other hand, each canonical repair is induced by a so-called *repair seed*, whose size is polynomial in the size of the TBox and the repair request. We have seen in [13] that, for the IQ case, one can compute consequences of canonical repairs and check IQ-entailment between them by working only with the seed functions inducing them. This way, the exponential blow-up due to the construction of the canonical repair can be avoided. In Sect. 4, we report on experimental results that compare the performance on answering instance queries between the optimized repairs and the canonical ones represented by seed functions.

In Sect. 5, we show that, also in the CQ case, optimal repairs always exist and cover all repairs if we allow for certain infinite, but finitely represented qABoxes. To be more precise, we introduce the notion of a *shell unfolding* of a given qABox, which basically unravels parts of the qABox into (possibly infinite) trees. The shell unfoldings of IQ-saturations turn out to be CQ-saturations, and this also works for cyclic TBoxes. If we then consider the canonical IQ-repairs for a given repair problem, then we can prove that their shell unfoldings yields a set of (possibly infinite) CQ-repairs that cover all CQ-repairs. In addition, consequences from such shell unfolded repairs and entailment between them can be decided based on their finite representation without an increase in complexity. Thus, one can work with them as if they were finite.

2   Preliminaries

We recall the definition of the DL $\mathcal{EL}$ and then introduce quantified ABoxes as well as the two entailment relations we employ for them.

The Description Logic $\mathcal{EL}$. As usual in DL, knowledge about an application domain is represented in $\mathcal{EL}$ using classes (called concepts), relationships (called roles), and objects (called individuals), which are collected in the signature Σ, consisting of pairwise disjoint sets of *concept names* Σ_C, *role names* Σ_R, and *individual names* Σ_I. *Concept descriptions* C of $\mathcal{EL}$ are then constructed using the grammar rule $C ::= \top \mid A \mid C \sqcap C \mid \exists r. C$, where A ranges over concept names and r over role names. An *atom* is a concept name A or an *existential restriction* $\exists r. C$. Each concept description C is a conjunction of atoms, with $\top$ corresponding to the empty conjunction. We denote the set of these atoms as $\mathsf{Conj}(C)$.

An $\mathcal{EL}$ TBox can be used to state subconcept-superconcept relationships between such concept descriptions, i.e., it is a finite set of *concept inclusions (CIs)* $C \sqsubseteq D$, where C, D are $\mathcal{EL}$ concept descriptions. In the ABox one can then relate individuals with concepts and with other individuals, i.e., it is a finite set of *concept assertions* $C(a)$ and *role assertions* $r(a, b)$, where a, b are individual names, r is a role name, and C is an $\mathcal{EL}$ concept description. An $\mathcal{EL}$ *ontology* is a pair consisting of an $\mathcal{EL}$ ABox and an $\mathcal{EL}$ TBox.

The semantics of $\mathcal{EL}$ is defined as usual [5] based on the notion of an *interpretation* $\mathcal{I} = (\mathsf{Dom}(\mathcal{I}), \cdot^{\mathcal{I}})$, which assigns subsets $A^{\mathcal{I}}$ of the non-empty set $\mathsf{Dom}(\mathcal{I})$ to concept names A, binary relations $r^{\mathcal{I}}$ on $\mathsf{Dom}(\mathcal{I})$ to role names r, and elements $a^{\mathcal{I}}$ of $\mathsf{Dom}(\mathcal{I})$ to individual names a. This mapping is extended to concept descriptions according to the semantics of the constructors. The interpretation $\mathcal{I}$ is a model of the TBox $\mathcal{T}$ if it satisfies all its CIs, i.e., $C^{\mathcal{I}} \subseteq D^{\mathcal{I}}$ holds for all CIs $C \sqsubseteq D$ in $\mathcal{T}$. Similarly, $\mathcal{I}$ is a model of the ABox $\mathcal{A}$ if it satisfies its assertions, i.e., $a^{\mathcal{I}} \in C^{\mathcal{I}}$ and $(a^{\mathcal{I}}, b^{\mathcal{I}}) \in r^{\mathcal{I}}$ holds for all concept assertions $C(a)$ and role assertion $r(a, b)$ in $\mathcal{A}$. It is a model of the ontology $(\mathcal{T}, \mathcal{A})$ if it is a model of both $\mathcal{T}$ and $\mathcal{A}$.

Reasoning makes implicit consequences of an ontology explicit. For instance, we say that a concept assertion $C(a)$ is *entailed* by an ABox $\mathcal{A}$ w.r.t. a TBox $\mathcal{T}$

if $C(a)$ is satisfied in all models of $\mathcal{A}$ and $\mathcal{T}$; this is abbreviated as $\mathcal{A} \models^{\mathcal{T}} C(a)$ and we also say that a is an *instance* of C w.r.t. $\mathcal{A}$ and $\mathcal{T}$. Similarly, a CI $C \sqsubseteq D$ is *entailed* by $\mathcal{T}$ if $C \sqsubseteq D$ is satisfied in every model of $\mathcal{T}$; we then write $C \sqsubseteq^{\mathcal{T}} D$ and also say that C is *subsumed* by D w.r.t. $\mathcal{T}$. In case $\mathcal{T} = \emptyset$, we may omit the superscript $\emptyset$ and just write $\models$ instead of $\models^{\emptyset}$. Both the instance and the subsumption problem are decidable in polynomial time in $\mathcal{EL}$ [3].

Quantified ABoxes. Quantified ABoxes were first introduced in [16], but they were also considered, as relational datasets with labelled nulls, in [20], and their existentially quantified variables correspond to the "anonymous individuals" in the OWL 2 standard [31]. Also, as explained in [16], quantified ABoxes are basically the same as Boolean conjunctive queries. Informally, a quantified ABox is an $\mathcal{EL}$ ABox where concept assertions are restricted to concept names and in addition to individuals one can use variables in assertions. To indicate that the names of these variables are irrelevant, we quantify them existentially.

More formally, a *quantified ABox (qABox)* $\exists X. \mathcal{A}$ consists of a finite set X of *variables*, which is disjoint with the signature Σ, and of a *matrix* $\mathcal{A}$, which is a finite set of assertions $A(u)$ and $r(u, v)$, where A is a concept name, r a role name, and u, v individual names or variables. We call the individual names and variables occurring in $\exists X. \mathcal{A}$ its *objects*, and denote the set of them by $\mathrm{Obj}(\exists X. \mathcal{A})$. Regarding the semantics of a qABox $\exists X. \mathcal{A}$, we can translate it in an obvious way into a first-order formula by taking the conjunction of the assertions in $\mathcal{A}$ (viewed as atomic formulas) and prefacing it with an existential quantifier prefix containing exactly the variables in X. The models of $\exists X. \mathcal{A}$ are then the first-order models of this formula.

Based on this semantics, we can now define when a qABox entails another qABox or a concept assertion in the usual way. If α is an $\mathcal{EL}$ concept assertion or a qABox, then $\exists X. \mathcal{A}$ entails α w.r.t. the $\mathcal{EL}$ TBox $\mathcal{T}$ (written $\exists X. \mathcal{A} \models^{\mathcal{T}} \alpha$) if every model of $\exists X. \mathcal{A}$ and $\mathcal{T}$ is a model of α. Again, we may omit the superscript $\emptyset$ if $\mathcal{T}$ is empty. If α is a concept assertion, then entailment $\models^{\mathcal{T}}$ can be decided in polynomial time whereas it is NP-complete if α is a qABox [7, 16]. NP-hardness already holds without a TBox.

From a syntactic point of view, $\mathcal{EL}$ ABoxes that use compound concept descriptions in concept assertions are not qABoxes, but it is easy to see that every $\mathcal{EL}$ ABox can be transformed into an equivalent qABox (i.e., one having the same models) [16]. Conversely, not every qABox has an equivalent $\mathcal{EL}$ ABox, the simplest example being $\exists \{y\}. \{r(y, y)\}$, which enforces an r-loop in every model, but without naming the element that has this loop. In contrast, $\mathcal{EL}$ ABoxes can only enforce loops for named individuals, i.e., elements of Σ_I. Also note that a qABox cannot entail $C(x)$ for a variable x since this is not a well-formed concept assertion. We can, however, view the matrix $\mathcal{A}$ as a normal ABox (where the variables are treated as individuals), and then one can derive concept assertions for elements of X from $\mathcal{A}$. The following lemma, which gives a recursive characterization of the instance relationship for the case of an empty TBox is relevant for our construction of canonical repairs.

Lemma 1 ([16]). *Let $\exists X.\mathcal{A}$ be a qABox, D an $\mathcal{EL}$ concept description, and $u \in \mathrm{Obj}(\exists X.\mathcal{A})$. Then $\mathcal{A} \models D(u)$ iff the following statements are satisfied for every $C \in \mathrm{Conj}(D)$:*

1. *if $C = A$ is a concept name, then $\mathcal{A}$ contains $A(u)$,*
2. *if $C = \exists r.E$ is an existential restriction, then $\mathcal{A}$ contains a role assertion $r(u,v)$ such that $\mathcal{A} \models E(v)$.*

Two Entailment Relations Between qABoxes. As motivated in the introduction, it makes sense to compare qABoxes w.r.t. the queries they entail rather than w.r.t. the models they have. Instance queries (IQ) are just concept assertions whereas (Boolean) conjunctive queries (CQ) are just qABoxes. The qABox $\exists X.\mathcal{A}$ *IQ-entails* the qABox $\exists Y.\mathcal{B}$ w.r.t. $\mathcal{T}$ (written $\exists X.\mathcal{A} \models^{\mathcal{T}}_{\mathsf{IQ}} \exists Y.\mathcal{B}$) if $\exists Y.\mathcal{B} \models^{\mathcal{T}} C(a)$ implies $\exists X.\mathcal{A} \models^{\mathcal{T}} C(a)$ for every $\mathcal{EL}$ concept assertion $C(a)$. The definition of CQ-entailment considers all qABoxes $\exists Z.\mathcal{C}$ in place of concept assertions $C(a)$. It is easy to see that the CQ-entailment relation $\models^{\mathcal{T}}_{\mathsf{CQ}}$ actually coincides with the model-based entailment relation $\models^{\mathcal{T}}$ introduced above [7, 16]. Since every concept assertion can be translated into an equivalent qABox, CQ-entailment is a stronger requirement that IQ-entailment.

With respect to the empty TBox, these query-based entailment relations have structural characterizations by means of simulations and homomorphisms [16]. In the IQ case, $\exists X.\mathcal{A} \models_{\mathsf{IQ}} \exists Y.\mathcal{B}$ iff there is a *simulation* from $\exists Y.\mathcal{B}$ to $\exists X.\mathcal{A}$, which is a relation $\mathfrak{S} \subseteq \mathrm{Obj}(\exists Y.\mathcal{B}) \times \mathrm{Obj}(\exists X.\mathcal{A})$ satisfying the following:

(S1) If a is an individual name, then $(a,a) \in \mathfrak{S}$.
(S2) If $(u,u') \in \mathfrak{S}$ and $A(u) \in \mathcal{B}$, then $A(u') \in \mathcal{A}$.
(S3) If $(u,u') \in \mathfrak{S}$ and $r(u,v) \in \mathcal{B}$, then $(v,v') \in \mathfrak{S}$ and $r(u',v') \in \mathcal{A}$ for some v'.

A *homomorphism* from $\exists Y.\mathcal{B}$ to $\exists X.\mathcal{A}$ is a function $h: \mathrm{Obj}(\exists Y.\mathcal{B}) \to \mathrm{Obj}(\exists X.\mathcal{A})$ for which the relation $\{\, (u,h(u)) \mid u \in \mathrm{Obj}(\exists Y.\mathcal{B}) \,\}$ is a simulation. In the CQ case, entailment is characterized as follows: $\exists X.\mathcal{A} \models_{\mathsf{CQ}} \exists Y.\mathcal{B}$ iff there is a homomorphism from $\exists Y.\mathcal{B}$ to $\exists X.\mathcal{A}$.

To extend these characterizations of the entailment relations to the case of non-empty TBoxes, we must first saturate the qABox on the left-hand side. We defer describing saturation to the second part of the next section, where we extend our repair approach from the setting without TBox to the one with a TBox.

3   Canonical and Optimal Repairs

We start with introducing (optimal) repairs in the general setting, but then concentrate first on the CQ case without a TBox for didactic reasons, before considering the IQ case and explaining how non-empty TBoxes can be tackled.

As unwanted consequences we consider $\mathcal{EL}$ concept assertions. Whereas it would be useful to be able to specify unwanted consequences via CQs, this may cause non-existence of optimal repairs unless one considers a strongly restricted class of CQs [11]. For this reason, a *repair request* will in the following be a finite set of concept assertions, both in the IQ and in the CQ case.

Definition 2. *Let $\mathcal{T}$ be an $\mathcal{EL}$ TBox, $\exists X.\mathcal{A}$ a qABox, $\mathcal{R}$ a repair request, and QL $\in \{IQ, CQ\}$.*

- *The qABox $\exists Y.\mathcal{B}$ is a QL-repair of $\exists X.\mathcal{A}$ for $\mathcal{R}$ w.r.t. $\mathcal{T}$ if $\exists X.\mathcal{A} \models_{QL}^{\mathcal{T}} \exists Y.\mathcal{B}$ and $\exists Y.\mathcal{B} \not\models^{\mathcal{T}} C(a)$ for each $C(a) \in \mathcal{R}$.*
- *Such a repair $\exists Y.\mathcal{B}$ is optimal if there is no QL-repair $\exists Z.\mathcal{C}$ such that $\exists Z.\mathcal{C} \models_{QL}^{\mathcal{T}} \exists Y.\mathcal{B}$, but $\exists Y.\mathcal{B} \not\models_{QL}^{\mathcal{T}} \exists Z.\mathcal{C}$.*
- *We say that a set $\mathfrak{R}$ of QL-repairs of $\exists X.\mathcal{A}$ for $\mathcal{R}$ w.r.t. $\mathcal{T}$ covers all QL-repairs if every QL-repair of $\exists X.\mathcal{A}$ for $\mathcal{R}$ w.r.t. $\mathcal{T}$ is QL-entailed by an element of $\mathfrak{R}$.*

Since CQ-entailment implies IQ-entailment, every CQ-repair is also an IQ-repair, but the converse need not hold. The latter can be illustrated by the second version of our Narcissus example from the introduction. Consider the TBox $\mathcal{T} = \{V \sqsubseteq \exists \ell.V, \exists \ell.V \sqsubseteq V\}$, the qABox $\exists \emptyset.\{V(n)\}$ and the repair request $\mathcal{R} = \{V(n)\}$. Then $\exists \{x\}.\{\ell(n,x), \ell(x,x)\}$ is an IQ-repair, but not a CQ-repair. In fact, this qABox is not CQ-entailed w.r.t. $\mathcal{T}$ by $\exists \emptyset.\{V(n)\}$ since there are models of $\exists \emptyset.\{V(n)\}$ and $\mathcal{T}$ that do not contain an individual with a loop. It is IQ-entailed, basically since all $\mathcal{EL}$ concept assertions of the form $(\exists \ell.)^k \top(n)$ are entailed by $\exists \emptyset.\{V(n)\}$ w.r.t. $\mathcal{T}$.

The question is now how one can actually compute all optimal repairs of a given repair problem, consisting of an $\mathcal{EL}$ TBox, a qABox, and a query language QL $\in \{IQ, CQ\}$. We start with the case where the TBox is empty and QL $=$ CQ.

Blind Search. A first idea could be to start with the input qABox and then generate a chain of qABoxes with entailment relationships between them, until a qABox that does not entail any element of $\mathcal{R}$ has been found. Such a chain can be generated by applying the following rules successively to the current qABox $\exists X.\mathcal{A}$:

Copy Rule. Choose an object u of $\exists X.\mathcal{A}$ as well as a fresh variable $y \notin$ $\mathsf{Obj}(\exists X.\mathcal{A})$, and return the qABox $\exists (X \cup \{y\}).(\mathcal{A} \cup \{A(y) \mid A(u) \in \mathcal{A}\} \cup \{r(t,y) \mid r(t,u) \in \mathcal{A}\} \cup \{r(y,y) \mid r(u,u) \in \mathcal{A}\} \cup \{r(y,v) \mid r(u,v) \in \mathcal{A}\})$.

Delete Rule. Choose an assertion α in $\mathcal{A}$ and return the qABox $\exists X.(\mathcal{A} \setminus \{\alpha\})$, or choose a variable $x \in X$ that does not occur in $\mathcal{A}$ and return the qABox $\exists (X \setminus \{x\}).\mathcal{A}$.

It is easy to see that the qABox obtained from $\exists X.\mathcal{A}$ by application of ones of these rules is CQ-entailed by $\exists X.\mathcal{A}$. The following proposition shows that these rules indeed cover the whole search space of entailed qABoxes.

Proposition 3. *If $\exists X.\mathcal{A} \models_{CQ} \exists Y.\mathcal{B}$, then there is a finite chain of applications of the Copy and Delete Rules that starts with $\exists X.\mathcal{A}$ and ends with $\exists Y.\mathcal{B}$.*

Proof sketch. If $\exists X.\mathcal{A} \models_{\mathsf{CQ}} \exists Y.\mathcal{B}$, then there is a homomorphism from $\exists Y.\mathcal{B}$ to $\exists X.\mathcal{A}$. If this homomorphism is not injective, then we can make it injective by adding copies of individuals that are images of several elements of $\mathsf{Obj}(\exists Y.\mathcal{B})$ to $\exists X.\mathcal{A}$. After that, we can remove assertions that are in the image, but not in the pre-image. Finally, we can rename variables and remove variables that do not have a pre-image (see [6] for a more detailed proof).   □

If one starts with the input qABox $\exists X.\mathcal{A}$ and generates a search tree by applying the above rules, this process need not terminate since one can generate an arbitrary number of copies of objects. But now Proposition 11 in [11] comes to the rescue: if $\exists X.\mathcal{A}$ contains m objects and $\mathcal{R}$ contains n atoms, then any repair of $\exists X.\mathcal{A}$ for $\mathcal{R}$ is CQ-entailed by a repair that has at most $m \cdot 2^n$ objects. Thus, we can restrict the search to qABoxes that have at most this many objects, which makes the search tree finite. We can be sure that the repairs found this way cover all repairs. The optimal repair can be obtained from this covering set by removing non-optimal elements, i.e., elements that are strictly entailed by another element.

Canonical Repairs. Obviously, the blind search approach for computing optimal repairs sketched above is very inefficient. However, it provides us with several interesting ideas for how to construct, in a more direct way, a set of repairs that covers all repairs. First, we notice that we must generate copies of objects, and then may need to remove assertions for these copies. Second, the cited result from [11] tells us that creating at most exponentially many copies of each object is sufficient.

In our canonical repairs, each object u of the input qABox $\exists X.\mathcal{A}$ receives copies of the form $\langle\!\langle u, \mathcal{K} \rangle\!\rangle$, where the second component specifies which assertions $C(u)$ that are entailed by $\mathcal{A}$ must *not* hold for this copy. More formally, $\mathcal{K}$ is a *repair type* for u, i.e., a subset of the set of atoms occurring in $\mathcal{R}$ that satisfies the following two properties:

(RT1) $\mathcal{A} \models C(u)$ for each atom $C \in \mathcal{K}$,
(RT2) $C \not\sqsubseteq^\emptyset D$ for each pair of distinct atoms C, D in $\mathcal{K}$.

The first condition is due to the fact that we only need to remove instance relationships that hold in $\mathcal{A}$. The second reduces the number of different repair types. It is justified by the fact that requiring to remove $D(u)$ ensures that also $C(u)$ must be removed if $C \sqsubseteq^\emptyset D$.

The canonical repairs have the same set of objects and the same matrix. They have all tuples $\langle\!\langle u, \mathcal{K} \rangle\!\rangle$ as their objects, where $u \in \mathsf{Obj}(\exists X.\mathcal{A})$ and $\mathcal{K}$ is a repair type for u. Using these objects, the matrix $\mathcal{B}$ of the canonical repairs consists of the following assertions:

(CR1) $A(\langle\!\langle u, \mathcal{K} \rangle\!\rangle) \in \mathcal{B}$ if $A(u) \in \mathcal{A}$ and $A \notin \mathcal{K}$,
(CR2) $r(\langle\!\langle u, \mathcal{K} \rangle\!\rangle, \langle\!\langle v, \mathcal{L} \rangle\!\rangle) \in \mathcal{B}$ if $r(u,v) \in \mathcal{A}$ and, for each $\exists r.C \in \mathcal{K}$
with $\mathcal{A} \models C(v)$, there is an atom $D \in \mathcal{L}$ such that $C \sqsubseteq^\emptyset D$.

To understand this definition, one needs to consider Lemma 1. Regarding concept names $A \in \mathcal{K}$, not adding the concept assertion $A(\langle\!\langle u, \mathcal{K} \rangle\!\rangle)$ to $\mathcal{B}$ ensures that this assertion is not entailed by $\mathcal{B}$. For existential restrictions $\exists r.C \in \mathcal{K}$, we can only have the role assertion $r(\langle\!\langle u, \mathcal{K} \rangle\!\rangle, \langle\!\langle v, \mathcal{L} \rangle\!\rangle)$ in $\mathcal{B}$ if $\mathcal{B}$ does not entail $C(\langle\!\langle v, \mathcal{L} \rangle\!\rangle)$. This non-entailment is ensured by having an atom $D \in \mathcal{L}$ that satisfies $C \sqsubseteq^\emptyset D$. In fact, $\mathcal{B} \models C(\langle\!\langle v, \mathcal{L} \rangle\!\rangle)$ would otherwise imply $\mathcal{B} \models D(\langle\!\langle v, \mathcal{L} \rangle\!\rangle)$, which is forbidden due to $D \in \mathcal{L}$.

To determine a concrete canonical repair, we choose, for each individual a of $\exists X.\mathcal{A}$, one of its copies as representative of a in $\mathcal{B}$. Of course, this choice must be made such that the obtained qABox really is a repair, i.e., does not entail any of the unwanted consequences in $\mathcal{R}$. Formally, this is realized by fixing a *repair seed* $\mathcal{S}$, which maps each individual name a to a repair type $\mathcal{S}_a$ for a such that the following condition is satisfied:

(RS) If $C(a) \in \mathcal{R}$ and $\mathcal{A} \models C(a)$, then there is an atom D in $\mathcal{S}_a$ s.t. $C \sqsubseteq^\emptyset D$.

Given such a repair seed $\mathcal{S}$, the *canonical repair* $\mathsf{rep}(\exists X.\mathcal{A}, \mathcal{S})$ *induced by* $\mathcal{S}$ is the qABox $\exists Y.\mathcal{B}$, where individual names a and their copies $\langle\!\langle a, \mathcal{S}_a \rangle\!\rangle$ are used as synonyms, and Y consists of the other objects of $\mathcal{B}$. This construction works both in the CQ and in the IQ case, and yields a set of repairs that covers all repairs.

Proposition 4 ([16]). *Consider a qABox $\exists X.\mathcal{A}$, an $\mathcal{EL}$ repair request $\mathcal{R}$, and a query language* $\mathsf{QL} \in \{\mathsf{IQ}, \mathsf{CQ}\}$. *For each repair seed $\mathcal{S}$, the induced canonical repair* $\mathsf{rep}(\exists X.\mathcal{A}, \mathcal{S})$ *is a* QL-*repair of $\exists X.\mathcal{A}$ for $\mathcal{R}$. Conversely, if $\exists Z.\mathcal{C}$ is a* QL-*repair of $\exists X.\mathcal{A}$ for $\mathcal{R}$, then there is a repair seed $\mathcal{S}$ such that* $\mathsf{rep}(\exists X.\mathcal{A}, \mathcal{S}) \models_{\mathsf{QL}} \exists Z.\mathcal{C}$.

The set of all canonical repairs can obviously be computed in exponential time. To obtain the optimal repairs, one needs to employ entailment tests to remove the non-optimal ones from it. Since IQ-entailment is in P and CQ-entailment is NP-complete, this yields the complexity results stated in the following theorem. Obviously, after removing redundant elements, the obtained set still covers all repairs.

Theorem 5 ([16]). *The set of optimal* QL-*repairs of $\exists X.\mathcal{A}$ for $\mathcal{R}$ covers all* QL-*repairs. There is a (deterministic) algorithm that computes this set and runs in exponential time. If* $\mathsf{QL} = \mathsf{CQ}$, *then this algorithm needs access to an NP oracle, whereas no such oracle is required for* $\mathsf{QL} = \mathsf{IQ}$.

Let us come back to the first variant of the Narcissus example from the introduction, where the input qABox is $\exists \emptyset.\mathcal{A}$ for $\mathcal{A} = \{V(n), \ell(n, n)\}$ and the repair request is $\mathcal{R} = \{V(n)\}$. The only atom in $\mathcal{R}$ is V, and both $\emptyset$ and $\{V\}$ is a repair type for n. The only repair seed is $\mathcal{S}$ with $\mathcal{S}_n = \{V\}$. If we denote $\langle\!\langle n, \mathcal{S}_n \rangle\!\rangle$ with n and $\langle\!\langle n, \emptyset \rangle\!\rangle$ with x, then the qABox $\exists \{x\}.\{\ell(n, n), \ell(n, x), \ell(x, n), \ell(x, x), V(x)\}$ is the only canonical repair, which thus is an optimal repair both in the CQ and in the IQ case.

Adding a Static TBox. As mentioned before, we restrict the attention to the case where the TBox is assumed to be correct, and thus is static in the sense that it must not be changed in the repair process. Our main idea for dealing with an $\mathcal{EL}$ TBox $\mathcal{T}$ is to extend the given qABox $\exists X.\mathcal{A}$ with consequences entailed by the CIs in $\mathcal{T}$. We call this extension process *saturation* [7].

Intuitively, if $C \sqsubseteq D \in \mathcal{T}$, then saturation adds the assertion $D(u)$ to the matrix $\mathcal{A}$ if $\mathcal{A} \models C(u)$, but $\mathcal{A} \not\models D(u)$. However, if D is a compound concept description, then this does not generate a well-formed new qABox. For this reason, one must express $D(u)$ by atomic assertions. Obviously, for each concept name $A \in \mathsf{Conj}(D)$, we must add the assertion $A(u)$ to $\mathcal{A}$. For each existential restriction $\exists r.E \in \mathsf{Conj}(D)$, we add a new variable x to X and the assertions $r(u, x)$ and $E(x)$ to $\mathcal{A}$. In case E is still compound, we apply the process of expressing such an assertion by atomic ones recursively. To be more precise, the treatment of existential restrictions differs depending on whether we are in the CQ or the IQ case. In the former, we always need to use a new variable x. In the IQ case, for each concept description E occurring in an existential restriction $\exists r.E$ in $\mathcal{T}$, we introduce the variable x_E, and reuse this variable whenever we encounter an existential restriction with E in the second position. Let us call this process of expressing a concept assertion $D(u)$ for a compound concept description D the QL-*unfolding of* $D(u)$, for QL $\in \{\mathsf{IQ}, \mathsf{CQ}\}$. QL-*saturation* is the process of applying the following saturation rule exhaustively:

QL-Saturation Rule. Choose an object u of $\exists X.\mathcal{A}$ as well as a CI $C \sqsubseteq D$ in $\mathcal{T}$ with $\mathcal{A} \models C(u)$, but $\mathcal{A} \not\models D(u)$, and add $D(u)$ to $\mathcal{A}$. Then apply QL-unfolding to $D(u)$.

Example 6. Consider again the TBox $\mathcal{T} = \{V \sqsubseteq \exists \ell.V, \exists \ell.V \sqsubseteq V\}$ and the qABox $\exists \emptyset. \{V(n)\}$. The first application of the IQ-saturation rule to n adds the assertion $(\exists \ell.V)(n)$ to the qABox. The IQ-unfolding of this assertion introduces one new variable x_V, adds the assertions $\ell(n, x_V)$ and $V(x_V)$, and removes the compound assertion. The IQ-saturation rule now applies to x_V, adding $(\exists \ell.V)(x_V)$. The IQ-unfolding of this assertion reuses the variable x_V, and adds the assertion $\ell(x_V, x_V)$. This completes the IQ-saturation process with the IQ-saturated qABox $\exists \{x_V\}. \{V(n), \ell(n, x_V), V(x_V), \ell(x_V, x_V)\}$.

This qABox is IQ-entailed by $\exists \emptyset. \{V(n)\}$ w.r.t. $\mathcal{T}$, but it is not CQ-entailed. The reason for the latter non-entailment is that there are models of $\exists \emptyset. \{V(n)\}$ and $\mathcal{T}$ where no element has a loop. To avoid introducing a loop or a cycle, we must use a new variable in each CQ-unfolding of an assertion of the form $(\exists \ell.V)(x)$. But this clearly leads to non-termination of the CQ-saturation process. To ensure termination for the CQ case, we restrict the attention in [7] to cycle-restricted TBoxes, where an $\mathcal{EL}$ TBox $\mathcal{T}$ is *cycle-restricted* if there are no role names $r_1, \ldots, r_n$ and no $\mathcal{EL}$ concept description C such that $C \sqsubseteq^{\mathcal{T}} \exists r_1. \cdots \exists r_n.C$.

Proposition 7 ([7]). *Let* QL $\in \{\mathsf{IQ}, \mathsf{CQ}\}$, $\exists X.\mathcal{A}$ *a qABox, and* $\mathcal{T}$ *an* $\mathcal{EL}$ *TBox, which is cycle-restricted if* QL $=$ CQ. *Then* QL-*saturation always terminates* with a qABox $\mathsf{sat}^{\mathcal{T}}_{\mathsf{QL}}(\exists X.\mathcal{A})$ that satisfies $\exists X.\mathcal{A} \models^{\mathcal{T}}_{\mathsf{QL}} \exists Y.\mathcal{B}$ iff $\mathsf{sat}^{\mathcal{T}}_{\mathsf{QL}}(\exists X.\mathcal{A}) \models_{\mathsf{QL}}$ $\exists Y.\mathcal{B}$ for all qABoxes $\exists Y.\mathcal{B}$. The IQ-saturation $\mathsf{sat}^{\mathcal{T}}_{\mathsf{IQ}}(\exists X.\mathcal{A})$ can be computed in polynomial time, whereas the computation of $\mathsf{sat}^{\mathcal{T}}_{\mathsf{CQ}}(\exists X.\mathcal{A})$ may require exponential time in the worst case.

The idea is now to apply the repair process described above to the saturated qABox rather than the original one. This ensures that, in RT1, the entailment is then w.r.t. the TBox. However, without additional changes to our construction of canonical repairs, the obtained qABox would not be a repair. In our example, a canonical repair of $\exists\{x_V\}.\{V(n), \ell(n, x_V), V(x_V), \ell(x_V, x_V)\}$ for $\mathcal{R} = \{V(n)\}$ could choose as synonym for n the copy $\langle\!\langle n, \{V\}\rangle\!\rangle$ that does not belong to V, but still has an ℓ-successor that belongs to V. Together with the CI $\exists\ell.V \sqsubseteq V$, this qABox would then still entail $V(n)$.

To avoid this problem, we amend the definition of repair types as follows. First, we now consider subsets of the atoms occurring in $\mathcal{R}$ or $\mathcal{T}$ as possible repair types. Second, we add an additional condition to the definition:

(RT3) If C is an atom in $\mathcal{K}$ and $E \sqsubseteq F$ is a CI in $\mathcal{T}$ with $\mathcal{A} \models E(u)$ and $F \sqsubseteq^{\emptyset} C$, then there is an atom D in $\mathcal{K}$ such that $E \sqsubseteq^{\emptyset} D$.[4]

In our example, $\mathcal{K} = \{V\}$ does not satisfy RT3 since the saturated qABox entails $\exists\ell.V(n)$, there is a CI that has $\exists\ell.V$ as left-hand side and $V \in \mathcal{K}$ as right-hand side, but $\mathcal{K}$ does not contain an atom that subsumes $\exists\ell.V(n)$. In fact, with the additional condition RT3, any repair type for n that contains V must also contain $\exists\ell.V$. The copy $\langle\!\langle n, \{V, \exists\ell.V\}\rangle\!\rangle$ of n does not belong to V in the canonical repair, and also does not have an ℓ-successor that belongs to V.

Overall, for $\mathcal{T} = \{V \sqsubseteq \exists\ell.V, \exists\ell.V \sqsubseteq V\}$, the qABox $\exists X.\mathcal{A} = \exists\emptyset.\{V(n)\}$, and the repair request $\mathcal{R} = \{V(n)\}$, we obtain the following canonical IQ-repair induced by the (unique) repair seed $\mathcal{S}$ with $\mathcal{S}_n = \{V, \exists\ell.V\}$:

$\mathsf{rep}^{\mathcal{T}}_{\mathsf{IQ}}(\exists X.\mathcal{A}, \mathcal{S}):$

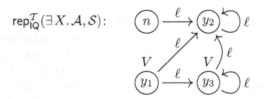

where y_1 stands for $\langle\!\langle n, \emptyset\rangle\!\rangle$, y_2 for $\langle\!\langle x_N, \{N, \exists\ell.N\}\rangle\!\rangle$, and y_3 for $\langle\!\langle x_N, \emptyset\rangle\!\rangle$.

In general, let $\mathsf{rep}^{\mathcal{T}}_{\mathsf{QL}}(\exists X.\mathcal{A}, \mathcal{S})$ be the canonical repairs obtained by first QL-saturating $\exists X.\mathcal{A}$ w.r.t. $\mathcal{T}$ and then applying the amended repair approach that takes RT3 into account. Then Proposition 4 and Theorem 5 hold accordingly in the presence of a static TBox $\mathcal{T}$ if we replace $\mathsf{rep}(\exists X.\mathcal{A}, \mathcal{S})$ with $\mathsf{rep}^{\mathcal{T}}_{\mathsf{QL}}(\exists X.\mathcal{A}, \mathcal{S})$ and in the CQ case add the assumption that $\mathcal{T}$ is cycle-restricted (see [7]).

---

[4] This condition differs from the one given in [7]. However, this third condition is only employed in Lemma XIII in [8] to show that the canonical repairs are saturated, for which the simpler condition given here suffices.

4   Concise Representations of Canonical IQ-Repairs

Canonical IQ-repairs are of exponential size, not only in the worst case, but also in the best case. In this section, we consider two approaches for alleviating this problem. One approach produces considerably smaller repairs in practice, which may, however, still be exponential in the worst case. The second approach uses the polynomial-sized repair seeds as representations for the exponentially large canonical repairs.

Optimized IQ-Repairs. To avoid generating exponential-sized repairs also in the best case, we have developed in [7] an optimized algorithm for computing repairs induced by repair seeds. Intuitively, these *optimized repairs* do not contain all the objects occurring in the canonical repair, but only those that are really needed. We have shown that the optimized IQ-repair induced by a repair seed S is IQ-equivalent to the canonical one induced by S, and thus the set of optimized IQ-repairs can be used in place of the set of canonical ones when computing the optimal repairs. The experiments described in [7] show that the optimized repairs are in most cases considerably smaller than the canonical ones. For example, in the canonical IQ-repair we have just computed for our Narcissus example, the objects y_1 and y_3 are not needed since they are not reachable from n. IQ-equivalence of the optimized repair $\exists\{y_2\}.\{\ell(n, y_2), \ell(y_2, y_2)\}$ with the canonical one can be seen by using the identity on the objects n and y_2 as simulation in both directions.

Note, however, that in general an exponential blow-up cannot be avoided, as already shown in [12] for a restricted class of qABoxes without a TBox. This blow-up is not only a problem when computing the repair, but also when using it later on to answer queries. While answering IQs is polynomial for the original (unrepaired) qABox, it may become exponential after the repair if we measure the complexity in the size the repair problem, consisting of the original qABox, the TBox, and the repair request.

Representing Canonical IQ-Repairs by Repair Seeds. The size of a repair seed S is polynomial in the size of the repair problem, and it uniquely determines the induced canonical repair $\text{rep}_{\text{IQ}}^{\mathcal{T}}(\exists X.\mathcal{A}, S)$. To take advantage of this more concise representation of canonical repairs, we must be able to work directly with this representation when comparing the repairs w.r.t. IQ-entailment and when answering IQs w.r.t. them. The following proposition shows how this can be realized.

Proposition 8 ([10,13]). *Let $\mathcal{T}$ be an $\mathcal{EL}$ TBox, $\exists X.\mathcal{A}$ a qABox, $\mathcal{R}$ a repair request, S, S' repair seeds, and $E(b)$ an $\mathcal{EL}$ concept assertion. Then,*

1. $\text{rep}_{\text{IQ}}^{\mathcal{T}}(\exists X.\mathcal{A}, S) \models_{\text{IQ}}^{\mathcal{T}} \text{rep}_{\text{IQ}}^{\mathcal{T}}(\exists X.\mathcal{A}, S')$ *iff for each individual name a and for each atom $C \in S_a$, there is an atom $D \in S'_a$ with $C \sqsubseteq^{\emptyset} D$.*
2. $\text{rep}_{\text{IQ}}^{\mathcal{T}}(\exists X.\mathcal{A}, S) \models^{\mathcal{T}} E(b)$ *iff $\exists X.\mathcal{A} \models^{\mathcal{T}} E(b)$ and S_b does not contain any atom D with $E \sqsubseteq^{\mathcal{T}} D$.*

The conditions formulated in this proposition are clearly decidable in time polynomial in the size of the repair problem. Thus, from a theoretical point of view, representing canonical repairs using repair seeds is preferable to using optimized repairs since the worst-case complexity of the relevant inference problems is polynomial for the former, whereas it is exponential for the latter. Comparing the worst-case complexity of two algorithms does not always tell us which algorithm will perform better in practice. To investigate the advantages and disadvantages of our two concise representations of canonical IQ-repairs in practice, we performed experiments on real-world ontologies.

Experimental Evaluation. The goal of the experiments was to evaluate the performance of the two representations with respect to the time needed for answering instance queries. To this end, we created a benchmark consisting of $\mathcal{EL}$ ontologies, instance queries, and repair requests. As in the experiments in [7], which mainly compared the sizes of the optimized repairs with that of the canonical ones, we took the ontologies from the OWL EL Materialization track of the OWL Ontology Reasoner Evaluation 2015 [30], filtering out axioms that cannot be expressed in $\mathcal{EL}$. To test the limits of both approaches, we this time included all 109 ontologies from this corpus, instead of considering only ontologies of up to 100,000 axioms as in [7]. Table 1 provides information on how large the employed ontologies were.

For each ontology, we randomly generated 100 IQs. To generate repair requests, we used the approach employed in [7], which generates requests where the concept assertions involve only concept names. In addition, we this time also generated repair requests containing assertions with compound concept descriptions. The repair requests generated in these two ways are respectively denoted RR1 and RR2 in the following. We attempted to compute 10 repair seeds per ontology based on the generated repair requests, which was, however, not always possible within a timeout of 10 min. For each tuple of ontology, repair request, and repair seed, we first computed the induced optimized IQ-repair, which was possible in most, but not all, cases within a timeout of 1 h. Then we compared the performance of answering IQs from the optimized repairs and from the repair seeds. Any required $\mathcal{EL}$ reasoning was performed using ELK [24]. More information on the experimental setup can be found in [6].

Figure 1 shows the results of this comparison, where each point corresponds to a tuple of ontology, repair request, and seed function, the x-axis to the runtime of evaluating all 100 IQs using the repair seed, and the y-axis of evaluating all IQs using the optimized repair, where the red color denotes that we also count the computation time of the optimized repair, and the blue color denotes that we do not. For RR1 with the simple repair requests, using the repair seed instead of the precomputed repair was faster in 98.7% of cases if we also count the time for computing the repair, and otherwise in 17.9% of cases. As we can see however in Fig. 1, using the optimized repair was almost never significantly faster, and there were many cases in which using the repair seed instead of the repair was significantly faster even if we do not count the time for computing the

Table 1. Statistics of the used corpus of $\mathcal{EL}$ ontologies after filtering out non-$\mathcal{EL}$ axioms.

Size Ontology				Size ABox				Size TBox			
min.	max.	med.	avg.	min.	max.	med.	avg.	min.	max.	med.	avg.
154	891,452	6,751	77,761.5	103	747,998	2,089	46,625.7	61	473,254	2,706	31,135.8

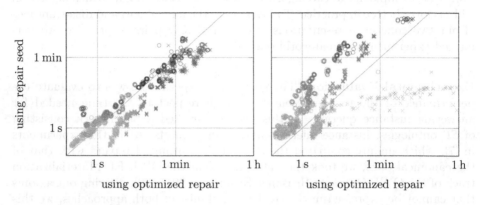

Fig. 1. Run times of evaluating 100 instance queries on repairs using the seed function (x-axis) vs. using the optimized repairs (y-axis). Color intensity corresponds to size of the input ontology. Orange-red crosses include times for computing the repair, whereas cyan-blue circles do not. Results of **RR1** on the left, and for **RR2** on the right. (Color figure online)

repair. For **RR2** with the complex repair requests, using the repair seed was faster in 64.6% of cases if we count the time for computing the repair, and otherwise almost never (0.13% of cases). The reason for this was that after obtaining the query answers from ELK, we still have to do a subsumption check for each individual in the answer when using the repair seed only (see the condition in Proposition 8). In **RR2**, each of these tests was more expensive, since we were comparing complex $\mathcal{EL}$ concepts. When using the precomputed optimized repair, no additional subsumption tests are necessary.

The results show that computing the optimized repair explicitly rather than using the repair seed is only advisable if this repair is considered to be the final one, which is then used for many instance tests. This is not the case for intermediate repairs in a setting where the KE iteratively repairs the ontology by (a) choosing a repair seed, then (b) checking out the induced canonical repair by looking at some of its consequences, and based on this inspection deciding whether (c) to choose a different repair seed or (d) to use this repair seed, but maybe repair the obtained ontology further by formulating a new repair request. It then makes sense to compute the optimized repair only after the iterative repair process is finished.

If the repair is assumed to be the final one, a good indicator for when computing the optimized repair does not pay off is the size of the original ontology. If we consider RR1 and do not count the time for computing the repair, for ontologies with at most 404,509 axioms (85% of the corpus), using the repair seed was faster in only 6.8% of the cases, while for the larger ontologies, it was faster in 80.5% of the cases. The numbers are similar if we look at the size increase of the repair: if the repair contained at most 132,622 axioms more than the original ontology (85% of the corpus), then using the repair seed was faster in 5.5% of the cases, and otherwise in 87.5% of the cases.

5   Finite Representations of Optimal CQ-Repairs

The results concerning optimal CQ-repairs of [7] recalled in Sect. 3 assume that the TBox is cycle-restricted. We have seen an example (the version of our Narcissus example with a TBox) that for TBoxes not satisfying this restriction, optimal repairs need not exist. To overcome this problem, we allow for infinite qABoxes as repairs, but require that they have an appropriate finite representation. In our construction of optimal CQ-repairs, cycle-restrictedness of the TBox is needed to ensure that CQ-saturation terminates. For IQ-saturation, cycles in the TBox do not lead to non-termination since the saturation process can reuse variables. This is not possible for CQ-saturation since it may generate cycles in the saturated qABox that are not CQ-entailed by the original qABox. Whereas IQs cannot distinguish such cycles from their unfoldings, CQs obviously can. The idea is now to use appropriate unfoldings of IQ-saturations and canonical IQ-repairs in the CQ case.

Infinite qABoxes. An *infinite qABox* is still of the form $\exists X. \mathcal{A}$, but now both the variable set X and the matrix $\mathcal{A}$ may be infinite. The model-based semantics can straightforwardly be extended from finite qABoxes to infinite ones, and the correspondence between (model-based) entailment and the existence of a homomorphism is still easy to show. However, the equivalence between entailment and CQ-entailment no longer holds. While the existence of a homomorphism is still sufficient for CQ-entailment, it is no longer necessary, as illustrated by the following example.

Example 9. As left-hand side of the entailment, we consider the qABox representing the natural numbers with their usual order relation: $\exists X. \mathcal{A}$ with variables $X := \mathbb{N}$ and matrix $\mathcal{A} := \{\, r(m, n) \mid m < n \,\}$. As right-hand side, we take the real numbers: $\exists Y. \mathcal{B}$ with variables $Y := \mathbb{R}$ and matrix $\mathcal{B} := \{\, r(x, y) \mid x < y \,\}$. Each finite qABox entailed by $\exists Y. \mathcal{B}$ is also entailed by $\exists X. \mathcal{A}$, i.e., $\exists X. \mathcal{A} \models_{\mathsf{CQ}} \exists Y. \mathcal{B}$. However, there is no homomorphism from $\exists Y. \mathcal{B}$ to $\exists X. \mathcal{A}$. In fact, no mapping from $\mathbb{R}$ (the objects of $\exists Y. \mathcal{B}$) to $\mathbb{N}$ (the objects of $\exists X. \mathcal{A}$) can be injective. Thus, if h was a homomorphism, then it would send two real numbers $x < y$ to the same natural number n, which would be a contradiction since $\mathcal{B}$ contains the role assertion $r(x, y)$, whereas $\mathcal{A}$ does not contain its image $r(n, n)$.

A slightly more complicated example can be used to show that this problem persists even if we consider only countable qABoxes [6]. The intuitive reason for the difference between entailment and CQ-entailment is that CQs (which are finite) cannot capture differences of infinite qABoxes that manifest themselves only "in the infinite." Fortunately, the problem goes away if we restrict the attention to shell unfoldings of finite ABoxes. Shell unfolding are similar to what is called unraveling in the DL literature [5], but it is applied to ABoxes rather than to interpretations.

Shell Unfoldings and Homomorphisms. Consider a (finite) quantified ABox $\exists X.\mathcal{A}$, the objects of which are divided into *kernel objects* and *shell objects*, such that each individual name is a kernel object, each shell object is reachable from some kernel object, but no kernel object is reachable from any shell object. Later on, we will apply the shell unfolding operation to the IQ-saturation $\exists X.\mathcal{A}$ of a given finite qABox $\exists Y.\mathcal{B}$. In this setting, the kernel objects of $\exists X.\mathcal{A}$ are the objects of $\exists Y.\mathcal{B}$, and the shell objects are the additional objects introduced during the saturation process. It is easy to see that this division into kernel and shell objects satisfies the requirements we have just formulated.

A *shell path* is a sequence $u_0 \xrightarrow{r_1} u_1 \xrightarrow{r_2} \cdots \xrightarrow{r_n} u_n$ that starts with a kernel object u_0 but otherwise only contains shell objects $u_1, \ldots, u_n$ such that $\mathcal{A}$ contains $r_i(u_{i-1}, u_i)$ for all $i \in \{1, \ldots, n\}$. We call $n \geq 0$ its *length*, u_0 its *source*, and u_n its *target*. Note that kernel objects, and thus also individuals, can be seen as shell paths of length 0. The target of such a shell path representing a kernel object is this object itself.

Definition 10. *The* shell unfolding *of $\exists X.\mathcal{A}$ is defined as the qABox $\exists X'.\mathcal{A}'$ with the following components:*

$$X' := \{\, p \mid p \text{ is a shell path where } p \notin \Sigma_\mathsf{I} \,\},$$
$$\mathcal{A}' := \{\, A(p) \mid p \text{ is a shell path with target } u \text{ and } A(u) \in \mathcal{A} \,\} \cup$$
$$\{\, r(u,v) \mid u,v \text{ are kernel objects and } r(u,v) \in \mathcal{A} \,\} \cup$$
$$\{\, r(p,q) \mid p,q \text{ are shell paths such that } q = p \xrightarrow{r} u \text{ for a shell object } u \,\}.$$

Note that a finite qABox can be seen as the shell unfolding of itself where all objects are assumed to be kernel objects. If the matrix $\mathcal{A}$ contains cycles among shell objects, then the shell unfolding $\exists X'.\mathcal{A}'$ of $\exists X.\mathcal{A}$ is infinite. However, since $\exists X'.\mathcal{A}'$ is uniquely determined by the finite qABox $\exists X.\mathcal{A}$ and the division of its objects into kernel and shell objects, we can use this as a finite representation of the infinite qABox $\exists X'.\mathcal{A}'$.

We can show [6] that, for shell unfoldings, CQ-entailment can again be characterized by the existence of a homomorphism, and thus coincides with (model-based) entailment.

Proposition 11 ([6]). *If $\exists X'.\mathcal{A}'$ and $\exists Y'.\mathcal{B}'$ are shell unfoldings, then $\exists X'.\mathcal{A}' \models_{\mathsf{CQ}} \exists Y'.\mathcal{B}'$ iff there is a homomorphism from $\exists Y'.\mathcal{B}'$ to $\exists X'.\mathcal{A}'$.*

If we want to work with (finitely represented) shell unfoldings in the context of CQ-repairs, we must be able to decide CQ-entailment, and thus the existence of a homomorphism between shell unfoldings. This is possible in non-deterministic polynomial time in the size of the finite representation.

Theorem 12 ([6]). *Let $\exists X.\mathcal{A}$ and $\exists Y.\mathcal{B}$ be two finite qABoxes whose object sets are partitioned into kernel objects and shell objects as introduced above, and let $\exists X'.\mathcal{A}'$ and $\exists Y'.\mathcal{B}'$ be their shell unfoldings. Then the problem of deciding whether there is a homomorphism from $\exists X'.\mathcal{A}'$ to $\exists Y'.\mathcal{B}'$ is NP-complete in the size of the input $\exists X.\mathcal{A}$ and $\exists Y.\mathcal{B}$.*

Since a finite qABox can be seen as the shell unfolding of itself (with empty set of shell objects), this theorem also shows that answering CQs for shell unfoldings is NP-complete in the size of their finite representations.

Infinite CQ-Saturation and CQ-Repair. The idea is now to extend the notion of a CQ-repair to a setting where qABoxes need not be finite, but must be finitely representable as the shell unfoldings of finite qABoxes. We call such qABoxes *rational qABoxes* since they consist of a finite part (the kernel) out of which grow (possibly) infinite trees, which are however rational [19]. We start with showing that, in this setting, finite qABoxes always have a CQ-saturation, even if the TBox is not cycle-restricted.

Given a finite qABox $\exists X.\mathcal{A}$ and an $\mathcal{EL}$ TBox $\mathcal{T}$, we consider the shell unfolding of the IQ-saturation $\mathsf{sat}_{\mathsf{IQ}}^{\mathcal{T}}(\exists X.\mathcal{A})$, where all objects of the sub-qABox $\exists X.\mathcal{A}$ are kernel objects and all other objects (added by applications of the IQ-Saturation Rule) are shell objects. We can show that this rational qABox CQ-entails exactly those rational qABoxes that are CQ-entailed by $\exists X.\mathcal{A}$ and $\mathcal{T}$. It can thus replace the finite CQ-saturation from [7], but is not limited to cycle-restricted TBoxes. For this reason, we denote this shell unfolding by $\mathsf{sat}_{\mathsf{CQ}}^{\mathcal{T}}(\exists X.\mathcal{A})$ and call it the CQ-*saturation* of $\exists X.\mathcal{A}$ w.r.t. $\mathcal{T}$.

Proposition 13 ([6]). *Let $\exists X.\mathcal{A}$ be a finite qABox and $\mathcal{T}$ an $\mathcal{EL}$ TBox. Then $\exists X.\mathcal{A} \models_{\mathsf{CQ}}^{\mathcal{T}} \exists Z.\mathcal{C}$ iff $\mathsf{sat}_{\mathsf{CQ}}^{\mathcal{T}}(\exists X.\mathcal{A}) \models_{\mathsf{CQ}} \exists Z.\mathcal{C}$ for each rational qABox $\exists Z.\mathcal{C}$.*

Coming back to Example 6, where we constructed the IQ-saturation with kernel object n and shell object x_N, we now obtain as shell unfolding the CQ-saturation $\mathsf{sat}_{\mathsf{CQ}}^{\mathcal{T}}(\exists X.\mathcal{A}) = \exists\{x_1, x_2, \dots\}.\{N(n), \ell(n, x_1), N(x_1), \ell(x_1, x_2), N(x_2), \dots\}$, where $x_k := n \overset{\ell}{\to} \underbrace{x_N \overset{\ell}{\to} \cdots \overset{\ell}{\to} x_N}_{k \text{ times}}$.

$$\mathsf{sat}_{\mathsf{CQ}}^{\mathcal{T}}(\exists X.\mathcal{A}): \quad \overset{N}{\textcircled{n}} \overset{\ell}{\longrightarrow} \overset{N}{\textcircled{x_1}} \overset{\ell}{\longrightarrow} \overset{N}{\textcircled{x_2}} \overset{\ell}{\longrightarrow} \overset{N}{\textcircled{x_3}} \overset{\ell}{\longrightarrow} \cdots$$

Regarding repairs, we now allow them to be rational qABoxes, i.e., in Definition 2 the qABoxes $\exists Y.\mathcal{B}$ and $\exists Z.\mathcal{C}$ are allowed to be rational qABoxes rather than just finite one. We call such repairs *rational* CQ-*repairs*. But note that the input qABox is still assumed to be finite.

In this setting, the rôle of canonical CQ-repairs is now taken on by shell unfoldings of canonical IQ-repairs. In such an IQ-repair $\text{rep}^{\mathcal{T}}_{\text{IQ}}(\exists X.\mathcal{A}, \mathcal{S})$, an object $\langle\!\langle u, \mathcal{K} \rangle\!\rangle$ is a kernel object if u is a kernel object in the underlying IQ-saturation, and otherwise it is a shell object. We denote the shell unfolding of $\text{rep}^{\mathcal{T}}_{\text{IQ}}(\exists X.\mathcal{A}, \mathcal{S})$ as $\text{rep}^{\mathcal{T}}_{\text{CQ}}(\exists X.\mathcal{A}, \mathcal{S})$, and call it again the *canonical* CQ-*repair induced by* $\mathcal{S}$. The following proposition shows that using this notation is justified.

Proposition 14 ([6]). *Consider a finite qABox* $\exists X.\mathcal{A}$, *an* $\mathcal{EL}$ *TBox* $\mathcal{T}$, *and an* $\mathcal{EL}$ *repair request* $\mathcal{R}$. *For each repair seed* $\mathcal{S}$, *the induced canonical repair* $\text{rep}^{\mathcal{T}}_{\text{CQ}}(\exists X.\mathcal{A}, \mathcal{S})$ *is a rational* CQ-*repair of* $\exists X.\mathcal{A}$ *for* $\mathcal{R}$. *Conversely, if* $\exists Z.\mathcal{C}$ *is a rational* CQ-*repair of* $\exists X.\mathcal{A}$ *for* $\mathcal{R}$, *then there is a repair seed* $\mathcal{S}$ *such that* $\text{rep}^{\mathcal{T}}_{\text{CQ}}(\exists X.\mathcal{A}, \mathcal{S}) \models_{\text{CQ}} \exists Z.\mathcal{C}$.

Note that the canonical CQ-repair must be constructed as shell unfolding of the *full* canonical IQ-repair, not from the optimized IQ-repair or any another qABox that is IQ-equivalent to it. In our Narcissus example with TBox, the canonical IQ-repair contains objects belonging to N, which are, however, not reachable from n. The optimized IQ-repair no longer contains such objects. Thus, the shell unfolding of the optimized repair does not entail $\exists\{x\}.\{N(x)\}$, but there are CQ-repairs that do, such as the shell unfolding of the canonical IQ-repair.

As an immediate consequence of the previous proposition, we obtain the main result of this section.

Theorem 15 ([6]). *Let* $\exists X.\mathcal{A}$ *be a finite qABox,* $\mathcal{T}$ *an* $\mathcal{EL}$ *TBox, and* $\mathcal{R}$ *an* $\mathcal{EL}$ *repair request. Then we can compute, in (deterministic) exponential time using an* NP-*oracle, a finite set of repair seeds* $\{\mathcal{S}_1, \ldots, \mathcal{S}_m\}$ *such that the set* $\{\text{rep}^{\mathcal{T}}_{\text{CQ}}(\exists X.\mathcal{A}, \mathcal{S}_1), \ldots, \text{rep}^{\mathcal{T}}_{\text{CQ}}(\exists X.\mathcal{A}, \mathcal{S}_m)\}$ *consists of all optimal rational* CQ-*repairs of* $\exists X.\mathcal{A}$ *for* $\mathcal{R}$ *w.r.t.* $\mathcal{T}$ *(up to* CQ-*equivalence). This set covers all rational* CQ-*repairs of* $\exists X.\mathcal{A}$ *for* $\mathcal{R}$ *w.r.t.* $\mathcal{T}$.

Also note that the optimal repairs $\text{rep}^{\mathcal{T}}_{\text{CQ}}(\exists X.\mathcal{A}, \mathcal{S}_i)$ are saturated w.r.t. $\mathcal{T}$ in the sense that they CQ-entail a rational qABox w.r.t. $\mathcal{T}$ if they already entail it without $\mathcal{T}$. By Theorem 12, this implies that conjunctive queries can be answered for $\text{rep}^{\mathcal{T}}_{\text{CQ}}(\exists X.\mathcal{A}, \mathcal{S}_i)$ in non-deterministic polynomial time in the size of $\text{rep}^{\mathcal{T}}_{\text{IQ}}(\exists X.\mathcal{A}, \mathcal{S}_i)$ and the query.

6   Conclusion

In the first part of this paper we have mainly recalled the approaches and results from [7,16]. In other work, we have extended these results in several directions. The paper [11] extends the expressivity of the underlying DL considerably, by adding nominals, inverse roles, regular role inclusions and the bottom concept to $\mathcal{EL}$, which yields a fragment of the well-known DL Horn-$\mathcal{SROIQ}$ [29]. In [9], we investigate whether and how one can obtain optimal repairs if one restricts the output of the repair process to being ABoxes rather than qABoxes. In general, such optimal ABox repairs need not exist. The main contribution of the paper is an approach that can decide the existence of optimal ABox repairs in exponential time, and can compute all such repairs in case they exist. The papers [13, 14] consider error-tolerant reasoning based on optimal repairs and [1] compares optimal repairs with contractions from the area of belief change. Moreover, an approach to computing optimal repairs of $\mathcal{EL}$ TBoxes is developed in [25].

In the second part of this paper we have presented new results on how to represent exponentially large repairs in a polynomial way and infinite repairs in a finite way. It would be interesting to see whether such approaches can also be extended to other settings. We conjecture that non-cycle-restricted TBoxes can still be tackled by using shell-unfoldings for the DLs considered in [11]. However, in [11] we also show that optimal repairs need not exist if the role inclusions are not regular. It is unclear whether this problem can be overcome by an appropriate finite representation of infinite repairs. Another interesting topic for future research is to investigate whether finitely represented rational repairs can be used in practice.

Acknowledgements. This work has been supported by Deutsche Forschungsgemeinschaft (DFG) in projects 430150274 (Repairing Description Logic Ontologies) and 389792660 (TRR 248: Foundations of Perspicuous Software Systems).

Author contributions. FB and FK contributed equally to the paper. PK ran the experiments and wrote the description of them. He also wrote a first version of the proof of the last proposition in Sect. 5 of [6].

References

1. Baader, F.: Optimal repairs in ontology engineering as pseudo-contractions in belief change. In: Proceedings of the 38th ACM/SIGAPP Symposium on Applied Computing (SAC 2023), Tallinn, Estonia, 27–31 March 2023, pp. 983–990. Association for Computing Machinery (2023). https://doi.org/10.1145/3555776.3577719
2. Baader, F., Borgwardt, S., Morawska, B.: SAT encoding of unification in $\mathcal{ELH}_{R^+}$ w.r.t. cycle-restricted ontologies. In: Gramlich, B., Miller, D., Sattler, U. (eds.) IJCAR 2012. LNCS (LNAI), vol. 7364, pp. 30–44. Springer, Heidelberg (2012). https://doi.org/10.1007/978-3-642-31365-3_5
3. Baader, F., Brandt, S., Lutz, C.: Pushing the $\mathcal{EL}$ envelope. In: Kaelbling, L.P., Saffiotti, A. (eds.) IJCAI 2005, Proceedings of the Nineteenth International Joint Conference on Artificial Intelligence, Edinburgh, Scotland, UK, 30 July–5 August 2005, pp. 364–369. Professional Book Center (2005). http://ijcai.org/Proceedings/05/Papers/0372.pdf
4. Baader, F., Calvanese, D., McGuinness, D., Nardi, D., Patel-Schneider, P.F. (eds.): The Description Logic Handbook: Theory, Implementation, and Applications. Cambridge University Press (2003)
5. Baader, F., Horrocks, I., Lutz, C., Sattler, U.: An Introduction to Description Logic. Cambridge University Press (2017). https://doi.org/10.1017/9781139025355
6. Baader, F., Koopmann, P., Kriegel, F.: Optimal repairs in the description logic $\mathcal{EL}$ revisited (extended version). LTCS-Report 23-03, Chair of Automata Theory, Institute of Theoretical Computer Science, Technische Universität Dresden, Dresden, Germany (2023). https://doi.org/10.25368/2023.121

7. Baader, F., Koopmann, P., Kriegel, F., Nuradiansyah, A.: Computing optimal repairs of quantified ABoxes w.r.t. static $\mathcal{EL}$ TBoxes. In: Platzer, A., Sutcliffe, G. (eds.) CADE 2021. LNCS (LNAI), vol. 12699, pp. 309–326. Springer, Cham (2021). https://doi.org/10.1007/978-3-030-79876-5_18

8. Baader, F., Koopmann, P., Kriegel, F., Nuradiansyah, A.: Computing optimal repairs of quantified ABoxes w.r.t. static $\mathcal{EL}$ TBoxes (extended version). LTCS-Report 21-01, Chair of Automata Theory, Institute of Theoretical Computer Science, Technische Universität Dresden, Dresden, Germany (2021). https://doi.org/10.25368/2022.64

9. Baader, F., Koopmann, P., Kriegel, F., Nuradiansyah, A.: Optimal ABox repair w.r.t. static $\mathcal{EL}$ TBoxes: from quantified ABoxes back to ABoxes. In: Groth, P., et al. (eds.) ESWC 2022. LNCS, vol. 13261, pp. 130–146. Springer, Cham (2022). https://doi.org/10.1007/978-3-031-06981-9_8

10. Baader, F., Koopmann, P., Kriegel, F., Nuradiansyah, A.: Optimal ABox repair w.r.t. static $\mathcal{EL}$ TBoxes: from quantified ABoxes back to ABoxes (extended version). LTCS-Report 22-01, Chair of Automata Theory, Institute of Theoretical Computer Science, Technische Universität Dresden, Dresden, Germany (2022). https://doi.org/10.25368/2022.65

11. Baader, F., Kriegel, F.: Pushing optimal ABox repair from $\mathcal{EL}$ towards more expressive Horn-DLs. In: Kern-Isberner, G., Lakemeyer, G., Meyer, T. (eds.) Proceedings of the 19th International Conference on Principles of Knowledge Representation and Reasoning, KR 2022, Haifa, Israel, 31 July–5 August 2022, pp. 22–32 (2022). https://doi.org/10.24963/kr.2022/3

12. Baader, F., Kriegel, F., Nuradiansyah, A.: Privacy-preserving ontology publishing for $\mathcal{EL}$ instance stores. In: Calimeri, F., Leone, N., Manna, M. (eds.) JELIA 2019. LNCS (LNAI), vol. 11468, pp. 323–338. Springer, Cham (2019). https://doi.org/10.1007/978-3-030-19570-0_21

13. Baader, F., Kriegel, F., Nuradiansyah, A.: Error-tolerant reasoning in the description logic $\mathcal{EL}$ based on optimal repairs. In: Governatori, G., Turhan, A. (eds.) RuleML+RR 2022. LNCS, vol. 13752, pp. 227–243. Springer, Cham (2022). https://doi.org/10.1007/978-3-031-21541-4_15

14. Baader, F., Kriegel, F., Nuradiansyah, A.: Treating role assertions as first-class citizens in repair and error-tolerant reasoning. In: Proceedings of the 38th ACM/SIGAPP Symposium on Applied Computing (SAC 2023), Tallinn, Estonia, 27–31 March 2023, pp. 974–982. Association for Computing Machinery (2023). https://doi.org/10.1145/3555776.3577630

15. Baader, F., Kriegel, F., Nuradiansyah, A., Peñaloza, R.: Making repairs in description logics more gentle. In: Thielscher, M., Toni, F., Wolter, F. (eds.) Principles of Knowledge Representation and Reasoning: Proceedings of the Sixteenth International Conference, KR 2018, Tempe, Arizona, 30 October–2 November 2018, pp. 319–328. AAAI Press (2018). https://aaai.org/ocs/index.php/KR/KR18/paper/view/18056

16. Baader, F., Kriegel, F., Nuradiansyah, A., Peñaloza, R.: Computing compliant anonymisations of quantified ABoxes w.r.t. $\mathcal{EL}$ policies. In: Pan, J.Z., et al. (eds.) ISWC 2020. LNCS, vol. 12506, pp. 3–20. Springer, Cham (2020). https://doi.org/10.1007/978-3-030-62419-4_1

17. Baader, F., Suntisrivaraporn, B.: Debugging SNOMED CT using axiom pinpointing in the description logic $\mathcal{EL}^+$. In: Cornet, R., Spackman, K.A. (eds.) Proceedings of the Third International Conference on Knowledge Representation in Medicine,

Phoenix, Arizona, USA, 31st May–2nd June 2008. CEUR Workshop Proceedings, vol. 410. CEUR-WS.org (2008). http://ceur-ws.org/Vol-410/Paper01.pdf

18. Brachman, R.J., Fikes, R., Levesque, H.J.: Krypton: a functional approach to knowledge representation. Computer **16**(10), 67–73 (1983). https://doi.org/10. 1109/MC.1983.1654200

19. Colmerauer, A.: Prolog and infinite trees. In: Clark, K., Tarnlund, S.A. (eds.) Logic Programming, pp. 231–251. Academic Press, New York (1982)

20. Cuenca Grau, B., Kostylev, E.V.: Logical foundations of linked data anonymisation. J. Artif. Intell. Res. **64**, 253–314 (2019). https://doi.org/10.1613/jair.1.11355

21. Du, J., Qi, G., Fu, X.: A practical fine-grained approach to resolving incoherent OWL 2 DL terminologies. In: Proceedings of the 23rd ACM International Conference on Information and Knowledge Management (CIKM 2014), pp. 919–928 (2014). http://doi.acm.org/10.1145/2661829.2662046

22. Greiner, R., Smith, B.A., Wilkerson, R.W.: A correction to the algorithm in Reiter's theory of diagnosis. Artif. Intell. **41**(1), 79–88 (1989). https://doi.org/ 10.1016/0004-3702(89)90079-9

23. Horridge, M., Parsia, B., Sattler, U.: Laconic and precise justifications in OWL. In: Sheth, A., et al. (eds.) ISWC 2008. LNCS, vol. 5318, pp. 323–338. Springer, Heidelberg (2008). https://doi.org/10.1007/978-3-540-88564-1_21

24. Kazakov, Y., Krötzsch, M., Simancik, F.: The incredible ELK - from polynomial procedures to efficient reasoning with $\mathcal{EL}$ ontologies. J. Autom. Reason. **53**(1), 1–61 (2014). https://doi.org/10.1007/s10817-013-9296-3

25. Kriegel, F.: Optimal fixed-premise repairs of $\mathcal{EL}$ TBoxes. In: Bergmann, R., Malburg, L., Rodermund, S.C., Timm, I.J. (eds.) KI 2022. LNCS, vol. 13404, pp. 115–130. Springer, Cham (2022). https://doi.org/10.1007/978-3-031-15791-2_11

26. Lam, J.S.C., Sleeman, D.H., Pan, J.Z., Vasconcelos, W.W.: A fine-grained approach to resolving unsatisfiable ontologies. J. Data Semant. **10**, 62–95 (2008). https:// doi.org/10.1007/978-3-540-77688-8_3

27. Levesque, H.J.: Foundations of a functional approach to knowledge representation. Artif. Intell. **23**(2), 155–212 (1984). https://doi.org/10.1016/0004-3702(84)90009-2

28. Lutz, C., Wolter, F.: Deciding inseparability and conservative extensions in the description logic $\mathcal{EL}$. J. Symb. Comput. **45**(2), 194–228 (2010). https://doi.org/ 10.1016/j.jsc.2008.10.007

29. Ortiz, M., Rudolph, S., Šimkus, M.: Worst-case optimal reasoning for the Horn-DL fragments of OWL 1 and 2. In: Lin, F., Sattler, U., Truszczynski, M. (eds.) Principles of Knowledge Representation and Reasoning: Proceedings of the Twelfth International Conference, KR 2010 (2010). http://aaai.org/ocs/index.php/KR/ KR2010/paper/view/1296

30. Parsia, B., Matentzoglu, N., Gonçalves, R.S., Glimm, B., Steigmiller, A.: The OWL reasoner evaluation (ORE) 2015 competition report. J. Autom. Reason. **59**(4), 455–482 (2017). https://doi.org/10.1007/s10817-017-9406-8

31. Parsia, B., Rudolph, S., Hitzler, P., Krötzsch, M., Patel-Schneider, P.: OWL 2 web ontology language primer (second edition). W3C recommendation (2012). http:// www.w3.org/TR/2012/REC-owl2-primer-20121211/

32. Parsia, B., Sirin, E., Kalyanpur, A.: Debugging OWL ontologies. In: Ellis, A., Hagino, T. (eds.) Proceedings of the 14th International Conference on World Wide Web, WWW 2005, Chiba, Japan, 10–14 May 2005, pp. 633–640. ACM (2005). https://doi.org/10.1145/1060745.1060837

33. Reiter, R.: A theory of diagnosis from first principles. Artif. Intell. **32**(1), 57–95 (1987). https://doi.org/10.1016/0004-3702(87)90062-2. See the erratum [22]

34. Schlobach, S., Huang, Z., Cornet, R., van Harmelen, F.: Debugging incoherent terminologies. J. Autom. Reason. **39**(3), 317–349 (2007). https://doi.org/10.1007/s10817-007-9076-z

35. Troquard, N., Confalonieri, R., Galliani, P., Peñaloza, R., Porello, D., Kutz, O.: Repairing ontologies via axiom weakening. In: McIlraith, S.A., Weinberger, K.Q. (eds.) Proceedings of the Thirty-Second AAAI Conference on Artificial Intelligence, (AAAI 2018), The 30th Innovative Applications of Artificial Intelligence (IAAI-18), and the 8th AAAI Symposium on Educational Advances in Artificial Intelligence (EAAI 2018), New Orleans, Louisiana, USA, 2–7 February 2018, pp. 1981–1988. AAAI Press (2018). https://www.aaai.org/ocs/index.php/AAAI/AAAI18/paper/view/17189

Excursions in First-Order Logic and Probability: Infinitely Many Random Variables, Continuous Distributions, Recursive Programs and Beyond

Vaishak Belle[1,2](✉)(iD)

[1] University of Edinburgh, Edinburgh, UK
vbelle@ed.ac.uk
[2] Alan Turing Institute, London, UK

Abstract. The unification of the first-order logic and probability has been seen as a long-standing concern in philosophy, AI and mathematics. In this talk, I will briefly review our recent results on revisiting that unification. Although there are plenty of approaches in communities such as statistical relational learning, automated planning, and neuro-symbolic AI that leverage and develop languages with logical and probabilistic aspects, they almost always restrict the representation as well as the semantic framework in various ways which do not fully explain how to combine first-order logic and probability theory in a general way. In many cases, this restriction is justified because it may be necessary to focus on practicality and efficiency. However, the search for a restriction-free mathematical theory remains ongoing. In this article, we discuss our recent results regarding the development of languages that support arbitrary quantification, possibly infinitely many random variables, both discrete and continuous distributions, as well as programming languages built on top of such features to include recursion and branching control.

Keywords: First-order logic · Probabilistic logic · Programs

1 Introduction

The unification of the logic and probability has been seen as a long-standing concern in philosophy and mathematical logic, going back to Carnap [14] and Gaifman [23], at least in terms of early rigorous algebraic studies. In artificial intelligence, starting from Nilsson [47], Bacchus [2] and Halpern [25], a wide range of formalisms encompassing various first-order logical features have been proposed. A probabilistic underpinning provides the gateway for incorporating probabilistic induction, and so areas such as statistical relational learning [50], inductive logic programming [45] and neuro-symbolic AI [27] are promising candidates for unifying deduction, noisy sensory observations and association-based pattern learning.

This material introduces the topic of my keynote at the *18th Edition of the European Conference on Logics in Artificial Intelligence* (**JELIA**), September 20–22, 2023. This research was partly supported by a Royal Society University Research Fellowship, UK, and partly supported by a grant from the UKRI Strategic Priorities Fund, UK to the UKRI Research Node on Trustworthy Autonomous Systems Governance and Regulation (EP/V026607/1, 2020–2024).

S. Gaggl et al. (Eds.): JELIA 2023, LNAI 14281, pp. 35–46, 2023.
https://doi.org/10.1007/978-3-031-43619-2_3

1.1   What's Missing from a First-Order Viewpoint?

From a knowledge representation viewpoint, however, especially in the context of reasoning about first-order knowledge—which by design must resolve issues around quantification, and an arbitrary (possibly infinite) domain of discourse—there is very little work beyond the initial study by Halpern [25]. This is despite the fact that first-order logic is widely acknowledged to be very important for capturing common sense and reasoning about generalized assertions [37,38] in a way that humans intuitively seem to be able to do.

There are many practical dimensions to this concern. For example, even though data that automated systems would encounter is finite, we still want knowledge such as "the father of a father is a grandfather" to be applicable to all humans in the universe. A robot might encounter an object and it is reasonable to assume that there are objects that are potentially occluded by the first object, and behind it. So the mental model of the robot should allow for the possibility that an unknown number of objects are behind the first object. More generally, a thinking system should have a model of the world that is not purely restricted to direct sensory inputs.

This issue, of course, has not gone unnoticed by the community. There are plenty of works that explore concepts such as open-world modeling—in contrast to the **closed-world assumption** that assumes the set of objects is fixed and finite in advance [4, 42]. But most solutions in the literature make a number of assumptions in terms of the modeling and the reasoning capabilities of the frameworks. This is justified from the point of view of practicality, but it leaves open what **a general mathematical theory for first-order logic and probability** looks like. Such a theory should allow, in the least:

1. infinite domains and arbitrary quantification from a first-order viewpoint;
2. discrete, continuous and mixed discrete-continuous distributions from a probability theory viewpoint.

The logical framework, understandably, should provide a calculus where we can express sentences that mix logical and probabilistic assertions. Moreover, these may be provided at any level of specificity by the modeler [3,9] such that the model theory allows one to reason about entailments in a way that adheres to the axioms of first-order logic as well as probability theory.

1.2   The Story Does Not Get Easier with Actions

The world is constantly in motion and objects, as well as their properties, are subject to change. Therefore, a static representation of the world is insufficient, as it does not allow for the possibility of changes occurring as a result of actions. Some of these actions may be initiated by the agent by choice, for example, whereas others may be caused by external factors that the agent cannot control but only perceive and react to. We might then complement (1) and (2) above, with (3):

3 The theory should enable the modeling of actions, effects, and sensors, even those that are error-prone, with a probabilistic model. It should also provide a mechanism

for reasoning about how all of these entities impact the way knowledge about the world is evolving.

The above desideratum is virtually ignored in probabilistic modelling languages, at least in a general way that permits a comprehensive account of actions and sensing, and its complications such as the frame and ramification problem [43]. Indeed, probabilistic graphical models [49] and Kalman filters [56] are used for temporal phenomena, but under strict assumptions about how distributions are affected to capture a changing world. Although decision-theoretic [30] and probabilistic-planning languages allow the modelling of actions and effects [59], they are neither logics (in allowing for arbitrary connectives and quantifiers) nor general models of actions in terms of being able to reason about past and future histories. Relational probabilistic models [57], including dynamic ones [17], offer some logical features (such as clausal reasoning), but are not usually embedded in a theory of action and so do not provide a framework to reason about unbounded sequences of actions. This is not to say that such a framework could not designed starting from one of the more practical options—and indeed, there are many that come close [48]—but just that the search for a general and restriction-free option is still ongoing.

It is also not the case that these problems are completely solved by the knowledge representation community either. Consider, for example, that Reiter's [52] reconsideration of the situation calculus has proven enormously useful for the design of logical agents, essentially paving the way for cognitive robotics [34]. Among other things, it incorporates a simple monotonic solution to the frame problem, leading Reiter to define the notion of regression for basic action theories. The situation calculus has enjoyed numerous extensions for time, processes, concurrency, exogeneity, reactivity, sensing and knowledge. Nevertheless, one criticism levelled at this line of work, and indeed at much of the work in cognitive robotics and reasoning about actions, is that the theory is far removed from the kind of probabilistic uncertainty and noise seen in typical robotic applications [56] and machine learning [46]. In fact, for many years, this criticism applied broadly to almost every knowledge representation language for reasoning about actions including dynamic epistemic logic [58] and fluent calculus [55], among others [5,53].

As discussed above, many recent attempts do come close to our desiderata, but often fall short in addressing (1) and (3) fully. For example, [48] unifies probabilistic relational languages, (not necessarily finite) discrete and continuous distributions, and a model of time to capture change to object properties. But it does not support arbitrary first-order logic or a full model of actions and unbounded sequences of actions. Analogously, [54] is a dynamic version of [42]—a probabilistic relational model with open-world features—but it does not support all of first-order logic or even arbitrary connectives. It also restricts how we can reason about sequences of past and future histories.

1.3   The Case for Meta-Beliefs

A final ingredient ignored by almost all statistical relational learning and machine learning frameworks is the lack of a construct that can reason about meta-beliefs [22]. In areas from game theory [1] to distributed systems [44] to computer science [26], epistemic notions play an important role because we can easily distinguish between what is known versus what is true. For instance, we might be wanting to say that the box is red, but the robot **believes** it is blue, until it comes close to it and senses the **true** color. The notion of knowledge becomes even more important in a distributed and multi-agent setting [7] where we need to reason about the beliefs of many agents at the same time. Moreover, each agent may need to hold beliefs about other agents so that they can collaborate, communicate and/or compete in a systematic way. Epistemic notions may also be useful for explaining automated systems [6, 32].

1.4   Our Results

In this talk, I will briefly review our recent results on revisiting the unification of first-order logic and probability theory. In particular, we discuss the development of languages that support arbitrary quantification, possibly infinitely many random variables, both discrete and continuous distributions, as well as programming languages built on top of such features to include recursion and branching control. All of these languages are epistemic logics, and thus support reasoning about beliefs and meta-beliefs as a bonus. In particular, we refer to the following results:

1. first-order logic for actions and continuous distributions [9], but with finitely many random variables. (This model, however, is not a very convenient approach to reason about meta-beliefs.)
2. Query rewriting results for that logic that reduce an action sequence to some formula about the initial (static) knowledge base [10]. We may instead update the knowledge base [11].
3. A programming model with recursion for that logic [13].
4. A reconstruction of the logic with infinitely many random variables but with discrete distributions [8]. This model, in contrast, is an epistemic modal logic and permits reasoning about meta-beliefs in the usual way.
5. A model of program abstraction based on this epistemic modal logic [28]. This allows one to abstract the stochasticity away so that probabilistic programs can be mapped onto ones that mention no probabilities at all.
6. A refinement of the modal logic with infinitely many random variables and both discrete and continuous distributions [41].

2   A Brief Overview of Results

Although it would be impossible to provide all the details of these contributions, we will give a quick overview of the key ideas behind these results here.

2.1   Language

We are interested in a first-order language. That is, it includes a set of predicates, function symbols, equality, first-order quantifiers (both universal quantification and existential quantification) and the usual connectives for conjunction, disjunction and negation.

It will be simpler to often assume a fixed domain of discourse, say the set of natural numbers: ℕ, which serves as a domain of quantification.

Of course, if we want the language to also capture continuous distributions, we will also need to allow the domain to include the set of reals. The idea is that when we reason about objects (such as places, things and people), we will be quantifying over the countable domain of discourse. And when we need to reason about real-valued quantities, we will be using variable maps to go over the real numbers. The most general introduction to this can be found in [41].

2.2 Beliefs

If we simply want to talk about probabilities and how they change, our language can remain "objective". That is, we would need to only write down probabilistic expressions in our language and reason about them, as seen in [21]. However, since our aim here is to capture the beliefs of the robot, we will need epistemic operators. In particular, we will consider a "degrees of belief" modal operator that can be used as follows:

- $B(mass < 20) > 0.9$;
- $B(mass \neq 0 \wedge mass \neq 1) > 0.8$; and
- $K(mass^2 > 5 \vee mass^2 > 6)$, where $K\alpha \doteq (B\alpha = 1)$.

The first formula says that the agent believes the mass of an object being less than 20 units (say, kilograms) is greater than 0.9. We are dealing with normalized probabilities here so probabilities range between 0 and 1 inclusive. The second formula is saying that the agent believes the mass of the object not being 0 and not being 1 is greater than 0.8. Finally, the third one is saying that the square of the mass of this object being greater than 5 or being greater than 6 is believed with a degree of 1. The last formula is interesting because although it provides a probability for the disjunction, it does not quite say what exactly is a degree of belief for each of the disjuncts. This is the power of providing a general way to combine logic and probability because it allows one to express and quantify over arbitrary first-order formulas without specifying how exactly the probabilities should be assigned to the (ground) atoms in those formulas. This then raises the question: what does the semantics look like?

2.3 Semantics

The semantics for epistemic logics is usually given in terms of possible worlds [22]. The idea being that the agent considers some worlds possible and is said to know things only when those things are true in all the worlds considered possible. Ordinarily, when dealing with degrees of belief [20], we would say that the worlds are also assigned weights. This allows us to then say that some formula is believed with a degree of belief r if and only if the sum of the weights of the worlds that satisfy this formula comes up to r.

How then do we generalize this idea to deal with first order formulas, as well as the assigning of probabilities to complex formulas without providing the probabilities of atoms, as seen in the example of the disjunction above? For starters, we would say that each world is a first-order structure that interprets the predicates and the functions over the constants and the domain of discourse in the usual way [19]. But because there are uncountably many worlds, we need to ensure that distributions are defined so as to obey the usual axioms of probability theory. There are a number of different ways to do this. We could either provide an appropriate analogue to the classical concept of defining a measure over an uncountable space [41]. Or, we could set up the probability of formulas based on countable additivity and convergence of the weights of worlds [8].

Such a framework, however, only accounts for a single distribution over the formulas. But because we are permitting situations where there may not be a unique distribution for formulas, we define an epistemic state as a set of distributions.

Once the semantics is set up this way, we can reason about disjunctions with the appropriate interpretation. For example: $B(p \lor q) = r$ for $r \neq 0$ does not imply $B(p) = n$ for any n. Note that, of course, in each of the distributions in the epistemic state, $B(p)$ will be equal to some n, but there is no single value agreed upon by all distributions in an epistemic state where $B(p \lor q) \neq 0$. In other words, the only obvious consequence of $B(p \lor q) \neq 0$ is $B(\neg p \land \neg q) \neq 1$.

Moreover, with the same semantical setup, we will now be able to reason about meta-beliefs and meta-knowledge very much in the spirit of introspective epistemic logics [15]:

- $(B(\alpha) = r) \supset K(B(\alpha) = r)$;
- $(\neg K\alpha) \supset K(\neg K\alpha)$;
- $(\alpha \equiv \beta) \supset (B\alpha = B\beta)$;
- $(B(\alpha) = r) \land (B(\beta) = r') \land (B(\alpha \land \beta) = r'')$ implies $B(\alpha \lor \beta) = (r + r' - r'')$.

The first formula says that if the agent believes a formula with degree r, then it knows (degree = 1) that it believes this. The second says that not knowing something means that the agent knows what it does not know. The third formula says that if two formulas are logically equivalent then the degree of belief for these formulas has to be the same. Finally the last formula is about the additive rule of probability.

2.4 Actions

To extend the model to actions [8], we can consider a language where a subset of the function symbols are reserved for actions. These function symbols could be things like $move(x)$ which might say that the agent should move to x, and $pick(x)$ which says that the agent should pick up the object x, and so on. To include these actions in the language, we will introduce two modal operators: $[a]$ and $\Box$, such that if ϕ is a formula, then so are $[a]\phi$ and $\Box\phi$. The first one says that ϕ is true after doing a. The second one says that after every sequence of actions, ϕ is true.

To extend the semantics, now we have to think of every world as a tree of first-order structures, because the world would be interpreting what is true initially as well as what is true after sequences of actions. (We allow for arbitrary sequences of actions, so the tree will also be infinite.) The agent language is actually based on the situation calculus [52], but recast in a modal logic [33].

2.5   Basic Action Theories

To capture an application domain, we define a set of axioms which describes how the domain works: what actions are available, what sensors are available and what effects these have on the world and on the agent's knowledge. For example, consider [28]:

- $\Sigma_0 = at(near) \lor at(midpos) \lor at(far)$;
- $\Box Poss(a) \equiv \exists l.a = goto(l) \land \neg at(l)$; and
- $\Box[a]at(l) \equiv a = goto(l) \lor at(l) \land \neg \exists l' a = goto(l')$.

This says that initially the robot might believe to be close to an object (say, a wall), or at mid-distance from the object, or far away. The second one says that doing a go-to action is only possible when the robot is not already at the location. And finally the third sentence captures a monotonic solution to the frame problem [39] and basically says that the robot is at a location either if it executed a go-to action previously to that particular location, or it was already at this location and it did not go to some other location. Notice the box operator for the second and the third sentence. These conditions—the precondition and the effect of actions—is something that we want the worlds to obey after every action. So these are axioms that hold for all possible action histories.

A programming language can be defined on such axiomisations for high-level control [36]. For example, a program to get close to the wall and move away from the wall could be:

if $\neg At(near)$ **then** $goto(near)$ **endif**; $goto(far)$

Classically, most action languages have made a number of serious assumptions: noiseless sensors without measurement error and exact actions that always have the desired effect. In practice, both assumptions are idealistic: The sonar sensor may measure with an error, e.g., ± 1, or even have a continuous noise profile [56]. The robot may get stuck or fail with some probability. Most seriously, the robot may not be able to observe those errors.

2.6   Revisiting the Axiomatisation

To address these assumptions, we need to revisit how we capture the domain. It may be too simplistic to simply say we can go to some location as an atomic action. And to say that we are either close or far from the wall might be too coarse to work with for a probabilistic representation. So we might end up using the following symbols in our language to capture the domain:

- $loc(x)$ is true if the distance to the wall is x;
- An action $move(x, y)$, where
    - x is the distance the robot intends to move;
    - y is the distance that the robot actually moves;
    - but y may not be observed by the robot; and
    - so, we will write $move(x)$ for $\pi y. move(x, y)$.

Here, πy is a nondeterministic pick operator for programs, the idea being that nature nondeterministically chooses y. Analogously, if $sonar(x)$ measures the distance to the wall and returns x, we let $sonar()$ be short for $\pi x.\ sonar(x)$ (where nature chooses x). Let us also assume that if a move by x units is intended, then the actual outcome is within one unit of the intended value. Likewise, whenever the sensor reads x, the true value is within one unit of that number. The probabilities accorded to these alternatives does not really matter for our informal discussion below, but for the sake of concreteness, say that each of $\{x - 1, x, x + 1\}$ taken on a probability of 1/3. (That is, the possible values are taken from a discrete uniform distribution.) Note that, by way of the language, we do not have to commit to a single distribution for the outcomes, much like how we did not need to commit to a single distribution for the robot's initial knowledge.

2.7 A Revised Program

With all of this machinery, the simple program from above, understandably, gets a lot more complicated and would look something like this:

sonar()
  while $\neg K(\exists x.loc(x) \land x \le 2)$ **do** $move(-1)$; *sonar()* **end while**
  while $\neg K(\exists x.loc(x) \land x \ge 5)$ **do** $move(1)$; *sonar()* **end while**

So, while the robot does not know that it is close, move towards the wall (using a negative argument). But because the move action is noisy, the robot needs to sense. And the sense-act loop needs to repeat until the robot has full certainty that it is actually close. It then exits the first while-loop and enters the second while-loop. Here, as long as it does not believe that is far, it moves away from the wall and senses to counter the noisy action. This repeats until it is actually away from the wall.

3   Abstraction at Play

Probabilistic belief programs seem to capture the intuitions perfectly, and they corresponding to cyclic policies [35], but they present several challenges, at least when written down by hand. Firstly, correctly designing these programs is a complex task. The incorporation of probabilities into the program structure requires a careful assessment of how sensed values, which are not in the robot's control, need to determine what to do next. Secondly, reasoning about probabilities can be a difficult endeavor for the modeler. It is challenging to accurately assess the likelihood of different outcomes or events, especially over long histories. Lastly, comprehending how and why a probabilistic belief program works is nontrivial.

So, ideally, we would like to write high-level programs without having to deal with probabilities. And, by doing so, one can obtain models and execution traces that are easy to understand. This is where abstraction comes in. The (low-level) action theory includes stochastic actions as usual, but then a high-level action theory is defined that abstracts away stochasticity [28]. For example, it is possible to show that there is a mapping for predicates and actions for the numeric example above such that the above programming involving two while-loops has the same behavior as the one with if-then-endif (the first program introduced above)! This is because the goto action in the if-then-endif program maps to a sense-act while-loop for the low-level action theory, allowing us to establish that formally the two programs are equivalent for a particular mapping. Obviously, this has a huge advantage because it is very easy to design the first program. It almost corresponds to how we might describe the instructions in natural language. In contrast, the second program is much harder and requires an understanding of probability theory and dynamics.

3.1   A Note About Continuous Noise

The discussion above was largely based on a discrete model of probability theory embedded in first-order logic. This is why we were able to consider the degree of belief taking a value of exactly one. The sensor model, moreover, also introduced an error within one unit of the actual value. In reality, in continuous models, this becomes far more complex. Beliefs about the initial situation may take on uncountably many values. Both the sensor and effector can have, say, Gaussian error profiles [56]. What this means is that we still require sense-act loops, but it is highly unlikely that the degree of belief in a formula of interest would be exactly one. We might have to contend with a degree of belief greater than, say, 0.9 as conditions in the programs. It would even make sense to involve the expected values of the probabilistic variables, as discussed in [13].

4   Future Work

Much of this discussion has largely been on a theoretical front in terms of searching for general-purpose languages where restrictions are not placed purely for computational reasons. We are interested in developing the semantics and the mathematical theory that allows us to reason about properties in languages that allow a full fragment of first-order logic + all of probability. As argued, this is a much needed mathematical exercise, but in reality we would want to work with robots and virtual agents. So the obvious question here is how can we make any of this tractable, scalable or efficient?

To do that, we need to revisit areas such as statistical relation learning and neurosymbolic AI, which have achieved considerable success in developing concise languages [51]. These languages not only capture interesting probability distributions described over symbolic artifacts but also provide implementations and, in some cases, tractability guarantees [16]. However, as we have argued, these areas do not offer a complete understanding of how probability theory integrates with first-order logic over a general theory of actions. Hence, our above exercise sets the stage. With that in hand, we may now strive to find a middle ground, where we can explore fragments that are slightly more expressive than existing proposals in statistical relation learning. These fragments should retain certain features mentioned earlier, including the ability to define recursive programs and reason about hypothetical events and future histories, much like in temporal logic [18].

To some extent we have some early results that do exactly this. For example, in [12], we showed how reasoning about actions can be reduced to a formula about the initial situation, after which we can use any existing reasoning module for the initial situation, including Bayesian networks and relational probabilistic models. Interestingly, this type of reduction strategy was explored independently for the practical problem of robot task and motion planning [31]. In [13], we showed that the kinds of belief-based programs discussed above, involving degrees of beliefs as conditions in the program, can be implemented using a particle-filtering strategy provided the language was appropriately restricted. By extension, it would be interesting to also develop fragments where it is possible to combine discrete and continuous distributions in natural way, and reason about things like abstraction. There is some recent work on verifying such programs [40].

It might be also possible to connect these advances in knowledge representation to exciting work in ML on probabilistic programming [24], where the topic of synthesis and learning are also embraced. For example, there is already work on synthesizing (recursion-free) probabilistic program abstractions [29] and perhaps it is possible to leverage such ideas for the programs discussed above.

More broadly, despite the advances of deep learning, it is now becoming increasingly clear that symbolic artifacts play an important role from the perspective of explainability, domain adaptation, domain knowledge inclusion, as well as reasoning. Neuro-symbolic AI is a representative example for the scientific need for this type of unification [27]. However, ad-hoc or otherwise limited combinations of logic and probability are likely to only take us so far: we need to think more carefully about how general-purpose open-ended agents might reason with quantifiers and how they might reason about past histories and future outcomes. All of these latter features are precisely what motivates many expressive knowledge representation languages. By embracing probability theory, we are now in a position to draw concrete connections between expressive KR languages and learning, and offer capabilities, including reasoning about meta-beliefs and belief-based program verification, that are out of reach for standard machine learning theory based on probability theory alone.

References

1. Aumann, R.J.: Interactive epistemology II: probability. Int. J. Game Theory **28**(3), 301–314 (1999)
2. Bacchus, F.: Representing and Reasoning with Probabilistic Knowledge. MIT Press, Cambridge (1990)
3. Bacchus, F., Halpern, J.Y., Levesque, H.J.: Reasoning about noisy sensors and effectors in the situation calculus. Artif. Intell. **111**(1–2), 171–208 (1999)
4. Banko, M., Cafarella, M.J., Soderland, S., Broadhead, M., Etzioni, O.: Open information extraction from the web. In: IJCAI, vol. 7, pp. 2670–2676 (2007)
5. Baral, C., Gelfond, M.: Logic programming and reasoning about actions. In: Handbook of Temporal Reasoning in Artificial Intelligence, pp. 389–426. Elsevier (2005)
6. Belle, V.: Counterfactual explanations as plans. In: The 39th International Conference on Logic Programming. Open Publishing Association (2023)
7. Belle, V., Bolander, T., Herzig, A., Nebel, B.: Epistemic planning: perspectives on the special issue (2022)
8. Belle, V., Lakemeyer, G.: Reasoning about probabilities in unbounded first-order dynamical domains. In: IJCAI (2017)

9. Belle, V., Levesque, H.J.: Reasoning about continuous uncertainty in the situation calculus. In: Proceedings of the IJCAI (2013)
10. Belle, V., Levesque, H.J.: Reasoning about probabilities in dynamic systems using goal regression. In: Proceedings of the UAI (2013)
11. Belle, V., Levesque, H.J.: How to progress beliefs in continuous domains. In: Proceedings of the KR (2014)
12. Belle, V., Levesque, H.J.: PREGO: an action language for belief-based cognitive robotics in continuous domains. In: Proceedings of the AAAI (2014)
13. Belle, V., Levesque, H.J.: Allegro: belief-based programming in stochastic dynamical domains. In: IJCAI (2015)
14. Carnap, R.: Logical Foundations of Probability. Routledge and Kegan Paul London (1951)
15. Chellas, B.: Modal Logic. Cambridge University Press, Cambridge (1980)
16. Choi, A., Darwiche, A.: On relaxing determinism in arithmetic circuits. arXiv preprint arXiv:1708.06846 (2017)
17. Choi, J., Guzman-Rivera, A., Amir, E.: Lifted relational Kalman filtering. In: Proceedings of the IJCAI, pp. 2092–2099 (2011)
18. Dixon, C., Fisher, M., Konev, B.: Tractable temporal reasoning. In: IJCAI, vol. 7, pp. 318–323 (2007)
19. Enderton, H.: A Mathematical Introduction to Logic. Academic Press, New York (1972)
20. Fagin, R., Halpern, J.Y.: Reasoning about knowledge and probability. J. ACM 41(2), 340–367 (1994)
21. Fagin, R., Halpern, J.Y., Megiddo, N.: A logic for reasoning about probabilities. Inf. Comput. 87(1–2), 78–128 (1990)
22. Fagin, R., Halpern, J.Y., Moses, Y., Vardi, M.Y.: Reasoning About Knowledge. MIT Press, Cambridge (1995)
23. Gaifman, H.: Concerning measures in first order calculi. Israel J. Math. 2(1), 1–18 (1964)
24. Gordon, A.D., Henzinger, T.A., Nori, A.V., Rajamani, S.K.: Probabilistic programming. In: Proceedings of the International Conference on Software Engineering (2014)
25. Halpern, J.: An analysis of first-order logics of probability. Artif. Intell. 46(3), 311–350 (1990)
26. Halpern, J.Y., Pass, R., Raman, V.: An epistemic characterization of zero knowledge. In: TARK, pp. 156–165 (2009)
27. Hitzler, P.: Neuro-symbolic artificial intelligence: the state of the art (2022)
28. Hofmann, T., Belle, V.: Abstracting noisy robot programs. In: AAMAS (2023)
29. Holtzen, S., Broeck, G., Millstein, T.: Sound abstraction and decomposition of probabilistic programs. In: International Conference on Machine Learning, pp. 1999–2008. PMLR (2018)
30. Kaelbling, L.P., Littman, M.L., Cassandra, A.R.: Planning and acting in partially observable stochastic domains. Artif. Intell. 101(1–2), 99–134 (1998)
31. Kaelbling, L.P., Lozano-Pérez, T.: Integrated task and motion planning in belief space. I. J. Robot. Res. 32(9–10), 1194–1227 (2013)
32. Kambhampati, S.: Challenges of human-aware AI systems. AI Mag. 41(3) (2020)
33. Lakemeyer, G., Levesque, H.J.: Situations, Si! situation terms, No! In: Proceedings of the KR, pp. 516–526 (2004)
34. Lakemeyer, G., Levesque, H.J.: Cognitive robotics. In: Handbook of Knowledge Representation, pp. 869–886. Elsevier (2007)
35. Lang, J., Zanuttini, B.: Knowledge-based programs as plans - the complexity of plan verification. In: Proceedings of the ECAI, pp. 504–509 (2012)
36. Levesque, H., Reiter, R., Lespérance, Y., Lin, F., Scherl, R.: GOLOG: a logic programming language for dynamic domains. J. Log. Program. 31, 59–84 (1997)
37. Levesque, H.J.: Common Sense, the Turing Test, and the Quest for Real AI. MIT Press, Cambridge (2017)

38. Levesque, H.J., Lakemeyer, G.: The Logic of Knowledge Bases. The MIT Press, Cambridge (2001)
39. Levesque, H.J., Pirri, F., Reiter, R.: Foundations for the situation calculus. Electron. Trans. Artif. Intell. **2**, 159–178 (1998)
40. Liu, D.: Projection in a probabilistic epistemic logic and its application to belief-based program verification. Ph.D. thesis, RWTH Aachen University (2023)
41. Liu, D., Feng, Q., Belle, V., Lakemeyer, G.: Concerning measures in a first-order logic with actions and meta-beliefs. In: 20th International Conference on Principles of Knowledge Representation and Reasoning (2023)
42. Milch, B., Marthi, B., Russell, S.J., Sontag, D., Ong, D.L., Kolobov, A.: BLOG: probabilistic models with unknown objects. In: Proceedings of the IJCAI, pp. 1352–1359 (2005)
43. Morgenstern, L., McIlraith, S.A.: John McCarthy's legacy. Artif. Intell. **175**(1), 1–24 (2011)
44. Moses, Y., Dolev, D., Halpern, J.Y.: Cheating husbands and other stories: a case study of knowledge, action, and communication. Distrib. Comput. **1**(3), 167–176 (1986)
45. Muggleton, S., et al.: ILP turns 20. Mach. Learn. **86**(1), 3–23 (2012)
46. Murphy, K.: Machine Learning: A Probabilistic Perspective. The MIT Press, Cambridge (2012)
47. Nilsson, N.J.: Probabilistic logic. Artif. Intell. **28**(1), 71–87 (1986)
48. Nitti, D.: Hybrid probabilistic logic programming. Ph.D. thesis, KU Leuven (2016)
49. Pearl, J.: Graphical models for probabilistic and causal reasoning. In: Smets, P. (ed.) Quantified Representation of Uncertainty and Imprecision. HDRUMS, vol. 1, pp. 367–389. Springer, Dordrecht (1998). https://doi.org/10.1007/978-94-017-1735-9_12
50. Poole, D.: Logic, probability and computation: foundations and issues of statistical relational AI. In: Delgrande, J.P., Faber, W. (eds.) LPNMR 2011. LNCS (LNAI), vol. 6645, pp. 1–9. Springer, Heidelberg (2011). https://doi.org/10.1007/978-3-642-20895-9_1
51. Raedt, L.D., Kersting, K., Natarajan, S., Poole, D.: Statistical relational artificial intelligence: logic, probability, and computation. Synth. Lect. Artif. Intell. Mach. Learn. **10**(2), 1–189 (2016)
52. Reiter, R.: Knowledge in Action: Logical Foundations for Specifying and Implementing Dynamical Systems. MIT Press, Cambridge (2001)
53. Scherl, R.B., Son, T.C., Baral, C.: State-based regression with sensing and knowledge. Int. J. Softw. Inform. **3**(1), 3–30 (2009)
54. Srivastava, S., Russell, S.J., Ruan, P., Cheng, X.: First-order open-universe POMDPs. In: UAI, pp. 742–751 (2014)
55. Thielscher, M.: From situation calculus to fluent calculus: state update axioms as a solution to the inferential frame problem. Artif. Intell. **111**(1–2), 277–299 (1999)
56. Thrun, S., Burgard, W., Fox, D.: Probabilistic Robotics. MIT Press, Cambridge (2005)
57. Van den Broeck, G., Meert, W., Davis, J.: Lifted generative parameter learning. In: Statistical Relational Artificial Intelligence, AAAI Workshop (2013)
58. van Ditmarsch, H., van der Hoek, W., Kooi, B.: Dynamic Epistemic Logic, 1st edn. Springer, Heidelberg (2007). https://doi.org/10.1007/978-1-4020-5839-4
59. Yoon, S.W., Fern, A., Givan, R.: FF-Replan: a baseline for probabilistic planning. In: Boddy, M.S. Fox, M., Thiébaux, S. (eds.) ICAPS, p. 352. AAAI (2007)

Special Track: Logics for Explainable and Trustworthy AI

Efficient Computation of Shap Explanation Scores for Neural Network Classifiers via Knowledge Compilation

Leopoldo Bertossi[1(✉)] and Jorge E. León[2]

[1] SKEMA Business School, Montreal, Canada
leopoldo.bertossi@skema.edu
[2] Universidad Adolfo Ibáñez (UAI), Santiago, Chile
jorgleon@alumnos.uai.cl

Abstract. The use of Shap scores has become widespread in Explainable AI. However, their computation is in general intractable, in particular when done with a black-box classifier, such as neural network. Recent research has unveiled classes of open-box Boolean Circuit classifiers for which Shap can be computed efficiently. We show how to transform binary neural networks into those circuits for efficient Shap computation. We use logic-based knowledge compilation techniques. The performance gain is huge, as we show in the light of our experiments.

1 Introduction

In recent years, there has been a growing demand for methods to explain and interpret the results from machine learning (ML) models. Explanations come in different forms, and can be obtained through different approaches. A common one assigns *attribution scores* to the features values associated to an input that goes through an ML-based model, to *quantify* their relevance for the obtained outcome. We concentrate on *local* scores, i.e. associated to a particular input, as opposed to a global score that indicated the overall relevance of a feature. We also concentrate on explanations for binary classification models that assign labels 0 or 1 to inputs.

A popular local score is Shap [18], which is based on the Shapley value that was introduced in coalition game theory and practice [29,31]. Shap scores can be computed with a black-box or an open-box model [30]. With the former, we do not know or use its internal components, but only its input/output relation. This is the most common approach. In the latter case, we can have access to its internal structure and components, and we can use them for score computation. It is common to consider neural-network-based models as black-box models, because their internal gates and structure may be difficult to understand or process when it comes to explaining classification outputs. However, a decision-tree model, due to its much simpler structure and use, is considered to be open-box for the same purpose.

Even for binary classification models, the complexity of Shap computation is provably hard, actually #P-hard for several kinds of binary classification models, independently from whether the internal components of the model are used when computing

---

L. Bertossi—Member of the Millennium Institute for Foundational Research on Data (IMFD, Chile).

S. Gaggl et al. (Eds.): JELIA 2023, LNAI 14281, pp. 49–64, 2023.
https://doi.org/10.1007/978-3-031-43619-2_4

Shap [1,2,4]. However, there are classes of classifiers for which, using the model components and structure, the complexity of Shap computation can be brought down to polynomial time [2,19,37].

A polynomial time algorithm for Shap computation with *deterministic and decomposable Boolean circuits* (dDBCs) was presented in [2]. From this result, the tractability of Shap computation can be obtained for a variety of Boolean circuit-based classifiers and classifiers that can be represented as (or compiled into) them. In particular, this holds for *Ordered Binary Decision Diagrams* (OBDDs) [8], decision trees, and other established classification models that can be compiled into (or treated as) OBDDs [11,23,33]. This applies, in particular, to *Sentential Decision Diagrams* (SDDs) [14] that form a convenient *knowledge compilation* target language [12,36].

In this work, we show how to use logic-based knowledge compilation techniques to attack, and -to the best of our knowledge- for the first time, the important and timely problem of efficiently computing explanations scores in ML, which, without these techniques, would stay intractable.

More precisely, we concentrate on explicitly developing the compilation-based approach to the computation of Shap for *binary (or binarized) neural networks* (BNNs) [17,23,27,35]. For this, a BNN is transformed into a dDBC using techniques from *knowledge compilation* [12], an area that investigates the transformation of (usually) propositional theories into an equivalent one with a canonical syntactic form that has some good computational properties, e.g. tractable model counting. The compilation may incur in a relatively high computational cost [12,13], but it may still be worth the effort when a particular property is checked often, as is the case of explanations for the same BNN.

More specifically, we describe in detail how a BNN is first compiled into a propositional formula in Conjunctive Normal Form (CNF), which, in its turn, is compiled into an SDD, which is finally compiled into a dDBC. Our method applies at some steps established transformations that are not commonly illustrated or discussed in the context of real applications, which we do here. The whole compilation path and the application to Shap computation are new. We show how Shap is computed on the resulting circuit via the efficient algorithm in [2]. This compilation is performed once, and is independent from any input to the classifier. The final circuit can be used to compute Shap scores for different input entities.

We also make experimental comparisons of computation times between this open-box and circuit-based Shap computation, and that based directly on the BNN treated as a black-box, i.e. using only its input/output relation. For our experiments, we consider real estate as an application domain, where house prices depend on certain features, which we appropriately binarize[1]. The problem consists in classifying property blocks, represented as entity records of thirteen feature values, as *high-value* or *low-value*, a binary classification problem for which a BNN is used.

To the best of our knowledge, our work is the first at using knowledge compilation techniques for efficiently computing Shap scores, and the first at reporting experiments with the polynomial time algorithms for Shap computation on binary circuits. We confirm that Shap computation via the dDBC vastly outperforms the direct Shap

---

[1] California Housing Prices dataset: https://www.kaggle.com/datasets/camnugent/california-housing-prices.

computation on the BNN. It is also the case that the scores obtained are fully aligned, as expected since the dDBC represents the BNN. The same probability distribution associated to the Shapley value is used with all the models.

Compilation of BNNs into OBDDs was done in [11,33] for other purposes, not for Shap computation or any other kind of attribution score. In this work we concentrate only on explanations based on Shap scores. There are several other explanations mechanisms for ML-based classification and decision systems in general, and also specific for neural networks. See [16] and [28] for surveys.

This paper is structured as follows. Section 2 contains background on Shap and Boolean circuits (BCs). Section 3 shows in detail, by means of a running example, the kind of compilation of BNNs into dDBCs we use for the experiments. Section 4 presents the experimental setup, and the results of our experiments with Shap computation. In Sect. 5 we draw some conclusions.

2 Preliminaries

In coalition game theory and its applications, the Shapley value is a established measure of the contribution of a player to a shared wealth that is modeled as a game function. Given a set of players S, and a game function $G : \mathcal{P}(S) \rightarrow \mathbb{R}$, mapping subsets of players to real numbers, the Shapley value for a player $p \in S$ quantifies its contribution to G. It emerges as the only measure that enjoys certain desired properties [29]. In order to apply the Shapley value, one has to define an appropriate game function.

Now, consider a fixed entity $\mathbf{e} = \langle F_1(\mathbf{e}), \dots, F_N(\mathbf{e}) \rangle$ subject to classification. It has values $F_i(\mathbf{e})$ for features in $\mathcal{F} = \{F_1, \dots, F_N\}$. These values are 0 or 1 for binary features. In [18,19], the Shapley value is applied with $\mathcal{F}$ as the set of players, and with the game function $\mathcal{G}_\mathbf{e}(s) := \mathbb{E}(L(\mathbf{e}') \mid \mathbf{e}'_s = \mathbf{e}_s)$, giving rise to the Shap score. Here, $s \subseteq \mathcal{F}$, and $\mathbf{e}_s$ is the projection (or restriction) of $\mathbf{e}$ on (to) the s. The label function L of the classifier assigns values 0 or 1. The $\mathbf{e}'$ inside the expected value is an entity whose values coincide with those of $\mathbf{e}$ for the features in s. For feature $F \in \mathcal{F}$:

$$\mathsf{Shap}(\mathcal{F}, \mathcal{G}_\mathbf{e}, F) = \sum_{s \subseteq \mathcal{F} \setminus \{F\}} \frac{|s|!(|\mathcal{F}| - |s| - 1)!}{|\mathcal{F}|!} \, [\tag{1}$$
$$\mathbb{E}(L(\mathbf{e}') \mid \mathbf{e}'_{s \cup \{F\}} = \mathbf{e}_{s \cup \{F\}}) - \mathbb{E}(L(\mathbf{e}') \mid \mathbf{e}'_s = \mathbf{e}_s) \,].$$

The expected value assumes an underlying probability distribution on the entity population. Shap quantifies the contribution of feature value $F(\mathbf{e})$ to the outcome label.

In order to compute Shap, we only need function L, and none of the internal components of the classifier. Given that all possible subsets of features appear in its definition, Shap is bound to be hard to compute. Actually, for some classifiers, its computation may become $\#P$-hard [2]. However, in [2], it is shown that Shap can be computed in polynomial time for every *deterministic and decomposable Boolean circuit* (dDBC) used as a classifier. The circuit's internal structure is used in the computation.

Figure 1 shows a Boolean circuit that can be used as a binary classifier, with binary features x_1, x_2, x_3, whose values are input at the bottom nodes, and then propagated upwards through the Boolean gates. The binary label is read off from the top node. This circuit is *deterministic* in that, for every $\vee$-gate, at most one of its inputs is 1 when the output is 1. It is *decomposable* in that, for every ∧-gate, the inputs do not share features. The dDBC in the Figure is also *smooth*, in that sub-circuits that feed a same ∨-gate share the same features. It has a *fan-in* at most two, in that every ∧-gate and ∨-gate have at most two inputs. We denote this subclass of dDBCs with dDBCSFi(2).

Fig. 1. A dDBC.   **Fig. 2.** A BNN.

More specifically, in [2] it is established that Shap can be computed in polynomial time for dDBCSFi(2)-classifiers, assuming that the underlying probability distribution is the uniform, P^u, or the product distribution, $P^\times$. They are as follows for binary features: $P^u(\mathbf{e}) := \frac{1}{2^N}$ and $P^\times(\mathbf{e}) := \Pi_{i=1}^N p_i(F_i(\mathbf{e}))$, where $p_i(v)$ is the probability of value $v \in \{0, 1\}$ for feature F_i.

3   Compiling BNNs into dDBCs

In order to compute Shap with a BNN, we convert the latter into a dDBC, on which Shap scores will be computed with the polynomial time algorithm in [2]. The transformation goes along the the following path that we describe in this section:

$$\text{BNN} \underset{(a)}{\longmapsto} \text{CNF} \underset{(b)}{\longmapsto} \text{SDD} \underset{(c)}{\longmapsto} \text{dDBC} \tag{2}$$

A BNN can be converted into a CNF formula [23,34], which, in its turn, can be converted into an SDD [14,25]. It is also known that SDDs can be compiled into a formula in d-DNNF (deterministic and decomposable negated normal form) [12], which forms a subclass of dDBCs. More precisely, the resulting dDBC in (2) is finally compiled in polynomial time into a dDBCSFi(2).

Some of the steps in (2) may not be polynomial-time transformations, which we will discuss in more technical terms later in this section. However, we can claim at this stage that: (a) Any exponential cost of a transformation is kept under control by a usually small parameter. (b) The resulting dDBCSFi(2) is meant to be used multiple times, to explain different and multiple outcomes; and then, it may be worth taking a one-time, relatively high transformation cost. A good reason for our transformation path is the availability of implementations we can take advantage of[2].

---

[2] The path in (2) is not the only way to obtain a dDBC. For example, [33] describe a conversion of BNNs into OBDDs, which can also be used to obtain dDBCs. However, the asymptotic time complexity is basically the same.

We will describe, explain and illustrate the conversion path (2) by means of a running example with a simple BNN, which is not the BNN used for our experiments. For them, we used a BNN with one hidden layer with 13 gates.

Example 1. The BNN in Fig. 2 has hidden neuron gates h_1, h_2, h_3, an output gate o, and three input gates, x_1, x_2, x_3, that receive binary values. The latter represent, together, an input entity $\bar{x} = \langle x_1, x_2, x_3 \rangle$ that is being classified by means of a label returned by o. Each gate g is activated by means of a *step function* $\phi_g(\bar{i})$ of the form:

$$sp(\bar{w}_g \bullet \bar{i} + b_g) := \begin{cases} 1 & \text{if } \bar{w}_g \bullet \bar{i} + b_g \geq 0, \\ -1 & \text{otherwise and } g \text{ is hidden}, \\ 0 & \text{otherwise and } g \text{ is output}, \end{cases} \tag{3}$$

which is parameterized by a vector of binary weights $\bar{w}_g$ and a real-valued constant bias $b_g{}^3$. The $\bullet$ is the inner vector product. For technical, non-essential reasons, for a hidden gate, g, we use 1 and -1, instead of 1 and 0, in $\bar{w}_g$ and outputs. Similarly, $\bar{x} \in \{-1, 1\}^3$. Furthermore, we assume we have a single output gate, for which the activation function does return 1 or 0, for *true* or *false*, respectively.

For example, h_1 is *true*, i.e. outputs 1, for an input $\bar{x} = (x_1, x_2, x_3)$ iff $\bar{w}_{h_1} \bullet \bar{x} + b_{h_1} = (-1) \times x_1 + (-1) \times x_2 + 1 \times x_3 + 0.16 \geq 0$. Otherwise, h_1 is *false*, i.e. it returns -1. Similarly, output gate o is *true*, i.e. returns label 1 for a binary input $\bar{h} = (h_1, h_3, h_3)$ iff $\bar{w}_o \bullet \bar{h} = 1 \times h_1 + 1 \times h_2 + (-1) \times h_3 - 0.01 \geq 0$, and 0 otherwise. □

The first step, (a) in (2), represents the BNN as a CNF formula, i.e. as a conjunction of disjunctions of *literals*, i.e. atomic formulas or their negations.

Each gate of the BNN is represented by a propositional formula, initially not necessarily in CNF, which, in its turn, is used as one of the inputs to gates next to the right. In this way, we eventually obtain a defining formula for the output gate. The formula is converted into CNF. The participating propositional variables are logically treated as *true* or *false*, even if they take numerical values 1 or -1, resp.

3.1 Representing BNNs as Formulas in CNF

Our conversion of the BNN into a CNF formula is inspired by a technique introduced in [23], in their case, to verify properties of BNNs. In our case, the NN is fully binarized in that inputs, parameters (other than bias), and outputs are always binary, whereas they may have real values as parameters and outputs. Accordingly, they have to binarize values along the transformation process. They also start producing logical constraints that are later transformed into CNF formulas. Furthermore, [23] introduces auxiliary variables during and at the end of the transformation. With them, in our case, such a BC could not be used for Shap computation. Furthermore, the elimination of auxiliary variables, say via *variable forgetting* [26], could harm the determinism of the final circuit. In the following we describe a transformation that avoids introducing auxiliary variables[4]. However, before describing the method in general, we give an example, to convey the main ideas and intuitions.

---

[3] We could also used binarized *sigmoid* and *softmax* functions.

[4] At this point is where using 1, -1 in the BNN instead of 1, 0 becomes useful.

Example 2. (Example 1 cont.) Consider gate h_1, with parameters $\bar{w} = \langle -1, -1, 1 \rangle$ and $b = 0.16$, and input $\bar{i} = \langle x_1, x_2, x_3 \rangle$. An input x_j is said to be *conveniently instantiated* if it has the same sign as w_j, and then, contributing to having a larger number on the LHS of the comparison in (3). E.g., this is the case of $x_1 = -1$. In order to represent as a propositional formula its output variable, also denoted with h_1, we first compute the number, d, of conveniently instantiated inputs that are necessary and sufficient to make the LHS of the comparison in (3) greater than or equal to 0. This is the (only) case when h_1 becomes *true*; otherwise, it is *false*. This number can be computed in general by [23]:

$$d = \left\lceil \left(-b + \sum_{j=1}^{|\bar{i}|} w_j \right)/2 \right\rceil + \# \text{ of negative weights in } \bar{w}. \tag{4}$$

For h_1, with 2 negative weights: $d(h_1) = \lceil (-0.16 + (-1 - 1 + 1))/2 \rceil + 2 = 2$. With this, we can impose conditions on two input variables with the right sign at a time, considering all possible convenient pairs. For h_1 we obtain its condition to be true:

$$h_1 \longleftrightarrow (-x_1 \wedge -x_2) \vee (-x_1 \wedge x_3) \vee (-x_2 \wedge x_3). \tag{5}$$

This DNF formula is directly obtained -and just to convey the intuition- from considering all possible convenient pairs (which is already better that trying all cases of three variables at a time). However, the general iterative method presented later in this subsection, is more expedite and compact than simply listing all possible cases; and still uses the number of convenient inputs. Using this general algorithm, we obtain, instead of (5), this equivalent formula defining h_1:

$$h_1 \longleftrightarrow (x_3 \wedge (-x_2 \vee -x_1)) \vee (-x_2 \wedge -x_1). \tag{6}$$

Similarly, we obtain defining formulas for h_2, h_3, and o: (for all of them, $d = 2$)

$$h_2 \longleftrightarrow (-x_3 \wedge (-x_2 \vee -x_1)) \vee (-x_2 \wedge -x_1),$$
$$h_3 \longleftrightarrow (x_3 \wedge (x_2 \vee x_1)) \vee (x_2 \wedge x_1),$$
$$o \longleftrightarrow (-h_3 \wedge (h_2 \vee h_1)) \vee (h_2 \wedge h_1). \tag{7}$$

Replacing the definitions of h_1, h_2, h_3 into (7), we finally obtain:

$$o \longleftrightarrow (-[(x_3 \wedge (x_2 \vee x_1)) \vee (x_2 \wedge x_1)] \wedge ([[(-x_3 \wedge (-x_2 \vee -x_1)) \vee (-x_2 \wedge -x_1)]$$
$$\vee [(x_3 \wedge (-x_2 \vee -x_1)) \vee (-x_2 \wedge -x_1)]])) \vee ([[(-x_3 \wedge (-x_2 \vee -x_1)) \vee$$
$$(-x_2 \wedge -x_1)] \wedge [(x_3 \wedge (-x_2 \vee -x_1)) \vee (-x_2 \wedge -x_1)]). \tag{8}$$

The final part of step (a) in path (2), requires transforming this formula into CNF. In this example, it can be taken straightforwardly into CNF. For our experiments, we implemented and used the general algorithm presented right after this example. It guarantees that the generated CNF formula does not grow unnecessarily by eliminating some redundancies along the process. The resulting CNF formula is, in its turn, simplified into a shorter and simpler new CNF formula by means of the *Confer* SAT solver [20]. For this example, the simplified CNF formula is as follows:

$$o \longleftrightarrow (-x_1 \vee -x_2) \wedge (-x_1 \vee -x_3) \wedge (-x_2 \vee -x_3). \tag{9}$$

Having a CNF formula will be convenient for the next steps along path (2).   □

In more general terms, consider a BNN with L layers, numbered with $Z \in [L] := \{1, \ldots, L\}$. W.l.o.g., we may assume all layers have M neurons (a.k.a. gates), except for the last layer that has a single, output neuron. We also assume that every neuron receives an input from every neuron at the preceding layer. Accordingly, each neuron at the first layer receives the same binary input $\bar{i}_1 = \langle x_1, \ldots, x_N \rangle$ containing the values for the propositional input variables for the BNN. Every neuron at a layer Z to the right receives the same binary input $\bar{i}_Z = \langle i_1, \ldots, i_M \rangle$ formed by the output values from the M neurons at layer $Z - 1$. Variables $x_1, \ldots, x_N$ are the only variables that will appear in the final CNF representing the BNN[5].

To convert the BNN into a representing CNF, we iteratively convert every neuron into a CNF, layerwise and from input to output (left to right). The CNFs representing neurons at a given layer Z are used to build all the CNFs representing the neurons at layer $Z + 1$.

Now, for each neuron g, at a layer Z, the representing CNF, φ^g, is constructed using a matrix-like structure M^g with dimension $M \times d_g$, where M is the number of inputs to g (and N for the first layer), and d_g is computed as in (4), i.e. the number of inputs to conveniently instantiate to get output 1. Formula φ^g represents g's activation function $sp(\bar{w}_g \bullet \bar{i} + b_g)$. The entries c_{ij} of M^g contain terms of the form $w_k \cdot i_k$, which are not interpreted as numbers, but as propositions, namely i_k if $w_k = 1$, and $\neg i_k$ if $w_k = -1$ (we recall that i_k is the k-th binary input to g, and w_k is the associated weight).

Each M^g is iteratively constructed in a row-wise manner starting from the top, and then column-wise from left to right, as follows: (in it, the c_{ik} are entries already created in the same matrix)

$$
M^g = \begin{bmatrix}
w_1 \cdot i_1 & false & false & \cdots & false \\
\begin{array}{c} w_2 \cdot i_2 \\ \vee c_{11} \end{array} & \begin{array}{c} w_2 \cdot i_2 \\ \wedge c_{11} \end{array} & false & \cdots & false \\
\begin{array}{c} w_3 \cdot i_3 \\ \vee c_{21} \end{array} & \begin{array}{c} (w_3 \cdot i_3 \\ \wedge c_{21}) \\ \vee c_{22} \end{array} & \begin{array}{c} w_3 \cdot i_3 \\ \wedge c_{22} \end{array} & false & \\
\cdots & \cdots & \cdots & & \cdots \\
\begin{array}{c} w_M \cdot i_M \vee \\ c_{(M-1)1} \end{array} & \begin{array}{c} (w_M \cdot i_M \\ \wedge c_{(M-1)1}) \\ \vee c_{(M-1)2} \end{array} & \begin{array}{c} (w_M \cdot i_M \\ \wedge c_{(M-1)2}) \\ \vee c_{(M-1)3} \end{array} & \cdots & \begin{array}{c} (w_M \cdot i_M \wedge \\ c_{(M-1)(d_g-1)}) \\ \underline{\vee c_{(M-1)d_g}} \end{array}
\end{bmatrix} \tag{10}
$$

The k-th row represents the first $k \in [M]$ inputs considered for the encodings, and each column, the threshold $t \in [d_g]$ to surpass, meaning that at least t inputs should be instantiated conveniently. For every component $c_{k,t}$ with $k < t$, the threshold cannot be reached, which makes every component in the upper-right triangle $false$.

The propositional formula of interest, namely the one that represents neuron g and will be passed over as an "input" to the next layer to the right, is the bottom-right most, c_{Md_g} (underlined). Notice that it is not necessarily a CNF; nor does the construction of M^g requires using CNFs. It is also clear that, as we construct the components of matrix M^g, they become formulas that keep growing in size. Accordingly, before passing over this formula, it is converted into a CNF φ^g that has also been simplified by means of a SAT solver (this, at least experimentally, considerably reduces the size of the CNF).

---

[5] We say "a CNF" meaning "a formula in CNF". Similarly in plural.

The vector $\langle \varphi^{g_1}, \ldots, \varphi^{g_M} \rangle$ becomes the input for the construction of the matrices $M^{g'}$, for neurons g' in layer $Z+1$. Reducing the sizes of these formulas is important because the construction of $M^{g'}$ will make the the formula sizes grow further.

Example 3. (Example 2 cont.) Let us encode neuron h_1 using the matrix-based construction. Since $d_{h_1} = 2$, and it has 3 inputs, matrix M^{h_1} will have dimension 3×2. Here, $\bar{w}_{h_1} = \langle -1, -1, 1 \rangle$ and $\bar{i}_{h_1} = \langle x_1, x_2, x_3 \rangle$. Accordingly, M_{h_1} has the following structure:

$$\begin{bmatrix} w_1 \cdot i_1 & false \\ w_2 \cdot i_2 \vee c_{11} & w_2 \cdot i_2 \wedge c_{11} \\ w_3 \cdot i_3 \vee c_{21} & (w_3 \cdot i_3 \wedge c_{21}) \vee c_{22} \end{bmatrix}$$

Replacing in its components the corresponding values, we obtain:

$$\begin{bmatrix} -x_1 & false \\ -x_2 \vee -x_1 & -x_2 \wedge -x_1 \\ x_3 \vee -x_2 \vee -x_1 & (x_3 \wedge (-x_2 \vee -x_1)) \vee (-x_2 \wedge -x_1) \end{bmatrix}$$

The highlighted formula coincides with that in (6). □

In our implementation, and this is a matter of choice and convenience, it turns out that each component of M^g is transformed right away into a simplified CNF before being used to build the new components. This is not essential, in that we could, in principle, use (simplified) propositional formulas of any format all long the process, but making sure that the final formula representing the whole BNN is in CNF. Notice that all the M^g matrices for a same layer $Z \in L$ can be generated in parallel and without interaction. Their encodings do not influence each other. With this construction, no auxiliary propositional variables other that those for the initial inputs are created.

Departing from [23], our use of the M^g arrays helps us directly build (and work with) CNF formulas without auxiliary variables all along the computation. The final CNF formula, which then contains only the input variables for the BNN, is eventually transformed into a dDBC. The use of a SAT solver for simplification of formulas is less of a problem in [23] due to the use of auxiliary variables. Clearly, our simplification steps make us incur in an extra computational cost. However, it helps us mitigate the exponential growth of the CNFs generated during the transformation of the BNN into the representing CNF.

Overall, and in the worst case that no formula simplifications are achieved, having still used the SAT solver, the time complexity of building the final CNF is exponential in the initial input. This is due to the growth of the formulas along the process. The number of operations in which they are involved in the matrices construction is quadratic.

3.2 Building an SDD Along the Way

Following with step (b) along path (2), the resulting CNF formula is transformed into a *Sentential Decision Diagram* (SDD) [14, 36], which, as a particular kind of *decision diagram* [6], is a directed acyclic graph. So as the popular OBDDs [8], that SDDs generalize, they can be used to represent general Boolean formulas, in particular, propositional formulas (but without necessarily being *per se* propositional formulas).

Example 4. (Example 2 cont.) Figure 3(a) shows an SDD, $\mathcal{S}$, representing our CNF formula on the RHS of (9). An SDD has different kinds of nodes. Those represented with encircled numbers are *decision nodes* [36], e.g. ① and ③, that consider alternatives for the inputs (in essence, disjunctions). There are also nodes called *elements*. They are labeled with constructs of the form $[\ell_1|\ell_2]$, where ℓ_1, ℓ_2, called the *prime* and the *sub*, resp., are Boolean literals, e.g. x_1 and $\neg x_2$, including $\top$ and $\perp$, for 1 or 0, resp. E.g. $[\neg x_2|\top]$ is one of them. The *sub* can also be a pointer, •, with an edge to a decision node. $[\ell_1|\ell_2]$ represents two conditions that have to be satisfied simultaneously (in essence, a conjunction). An element without • is a *terminal*. (See [7,22] for a precise definition of SDD.)

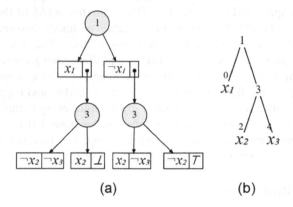

Fig. 3. An SDD (a) and a vtree (b).

An SDD represents (or defines) a total Boolean function $F_{\mathcal{S}}$: $\langle x_1, x_2, x_3 \rangle \in \{0,1\}^3 \mapsto \{0,1\}$. For example, $F_{\mathcal{S}}(0,1,1)$ is evaluated by following the graph downwards. Since $x_1 = 0$, we descent to the right; next via node ③ underneath, with $x_2 = 1$, we reach the instantiated leaf node labeled with $[1|0]$, a "conjunction", with the second component due to $x_3 = 1$. We obtain $F_{\mathcal{S}}(0,1,1) = 0$. □

In SDDs, the orders of occurrence of variables in the diagram must be compliant with a so-called *vtree* (for "variable tree")[6]. The connection between a vtree and an SDD refers to the compatibility between the partitions $[prime|sub]$ and the tree structure (see Example 5 below). Depending on the chosen vtree, substructures of an SDD can be better reused when representing a Boolean function, e.g. a propositional formula, which becomes important to obtain a compact representation. SDDs can easily be combined via propositional operations, resulting in a new SDD [14].

A vtree for a set of variables $\mathcal{V}$ is binary tree that is full, i.e. every node has 0 or 2 children, and ordered, i.e. the children of a node are totally ordered, and there is a bijection between the set of leaves and $\mathcal{V}$ [7].

Example 5. (Example 4 cont.) Figure 3(b) shows a vtree, $\mathcal{T}$, for $\mathcal{V} = \{x_1, x_2, x_3\}$. Its leaves, $0, 2, 4$, show their associated variables in $\mathcal{V}$. The SDD $\mathcal{S}$ in Fig. 3(a) is

---

[6] Extending OBDDs, whose vtrees make variables in a path always appear in the same order. This generalization makes SDDs much more succinct than OBDDs [6,7,36].

compatible with $\mathcal{T}$. Intuitively, the variables at $\mathcal{S}$'s terminals, when they go upwards through decision nodes ⓝ, also go upwards through the corresponding nodes n in $\mathcal{T}$. (See [6,7,22] for a precise, recursive definition.)

The SDD S can be straightforwardly represented as a propositional formula by interpreting decision points as disjunctions, and elements as conjunctions, obtaining $[x_1 \wedge ((-x_2 \wedge -x_3) \vee (x_2 \wedge \perp))] \vee [-x_1 \wedge ((x_2 \wedge -x_3) \vee (-x_2 \wedge \top))]$, which is logically equivalent to the formula on the RHS of (9) that represents our BNN.   □

For the running example and experiments, we used the *PySDD* system [21]: Given a CNF formula ψ, it computes an associated vtree and a compliant SDD, both optimized in size [9,10]. This compilation step, the theoretically most expensive along path (2), takes exponential space and time only in $TW(\psi)$, the *tree-width* of the *primal graph* $\mathcal{G}$ associated to ψ [14,25]. $\mathcal{G}$ contains the variables as nodes, and undirected edges between any of them when they appear in a same clause. The tree-width measures how close the graph is to being a tree. This is a positive *fixed-parameter tractability* result [15], in that $TW(\psi)$ is in general smaller than $|\psi|$. For example, the graph $\mathcal{G}$ for the formula ψ on the RHS of (9) has x_1, x_2, x_3 as nodes, and edges between any pair of variables, which makes $\mathcal{G}$ a complete graph. Since every complete graph has a tree-width equal to the number of nodes minus one, we have $TW(\psi) = 2$. Overall, this step in the transformation process has a time complexity that, in the worst case, is exponential in the size of the tree-width of the input CNF.

3.3   The Final dDBC

Our final dDBC is obtained from the resulting SDD: An SDD corresponds to a d-DNNF Boolean circuit, for which decomposability and determinism hold, and has only variables as inputs to negation gates [14]. And d-DNNFs are also dDBCs. Accordingly, this step of the whole transformation is basically for free, or better, linear in the size of the SDD if we locally convert decision nodes into disjunctions, and elements into conjunctions (see Example 5).

The algorithm in [1] for efficient Shap computation needs the dDBC to be a dDBCSFi(2). To obtain the latter, we use the transformation Algorithm 1 below, which is based on [1, sec. 3.1.2]. In a bottom-up fashion, fan-in 2 is achieved by rewriting every ∧-gate (resp. and ∨-gate) of fan-in $m > 2$ with a chain of $m - 1$ ∧-gates (resp. ∨-gates) of fan-in 2. After that, to enforce smoothness, for every disjunction gate (now with a fan-in 2) of subcircuits C_1 and C_2, find the set of variables in C_1, but not in C_2 (denoted V_{1-2}), along with those in C_2, but not in C_1 (denoted V_{2-1}). For every variable $v \in V_{2-1}$, redefine C_1 as $C_1 \wedge (v \vee -v)$. Similarly, for every variable $v \in V_{1-2}$, redefine C_2 as $C_2 \wedge (v \vee -v)$. For example, for $(x_1 \wedge x_2 \wedge x_3) \vee (x_2 \wedge -x_3)$, becomes $((x_1 \wedge x_2) \wedge x_3) \vee ((x_2 \wedge -x_3) \wedge (x_1 \vee -x_1))$. This algorithm takes quadratic time in the size of the dDBC, which is its number of edges [1, sec. 3.1.2], [32].

Example 6. (Example 4 cont.) By interpreting decision points and elements as disjunctions and conjunctions, resp., the SDD in Fig. 3(a) can be easily converted into d-DNNF circuit. Only variables are affected by negations. Due to the children of node ③, that do not have the same variables, the resulting dBBC is not smooth (but it has fan-in 2). Algorithm 1 transforms it into the dDBCSFi(2) in Fig. 1.   □

Algorithm 1:   From dDBC to dDBCSFi(2)

Input   : Original $dDBC$ (starting from root node).
Output: A $dDBCSFi(2)$ equivalent to the given $dDBC$.

---

1 **function** FIX_NODE($dDBC\_node$)
2 $\quad$ **if** $dDBC\_node$ is a disjunction **then**
3 $\quad\quad$ $c_{new} = false$
4 $\quad\quad$ **for** each subcircuit sc in $dDBC\_node$
5 $\quad\quad\quad$ sc_{fixed} = FIX_NODE(sc)
6 $\quad\quad\quad$ **if** sc_{fixed} is a $true$ value or is equal to $\neg c_{new}$ **then**
7 $\quad\quad\quad\quad$ **return** $true$
8 $\quad\quad\quad$ **else if** sc_{fixed} is not a $false$ value **then**
9 $\quad\quad\quad\quad$ **for** each variable v in c_{new} and not in sc_{fixed}
10 $\quad\quad\quad\quad\quad$ $sc_{fixed} = sc_{fixed} \wedge (v \vee \neg v)$
11 $\quad\quad\quad\quad$ **for** each variable v in sc_{fixed} and not in c_{new}
12 $\quad\quad\quad\quad\quad$ $c_{new} = c_{new} \wedge (v \vee \neg v)$
13 $\quad\quad\quad\quad$ $c_{new} = c_{new} \vee sc_{fixed}$
14 $\quad\quad$ **return** c_{new}
15 $\quad$ **else if** $dDBC\_node$ is a conjunction **then**
16 $\quad\quad$ $c_{new} = true$
17 $\quad\quad$ **for** each subcircuit sc in $dDBC\_node$
18 $\quad\quad\quad$ sc_{fixed} = FIX_NODE(sc)
19 $\quad\quad\quad$ **if** sc_{fixed} is a $false$ value or is equal to $\neg c_{new}$ **then**
20 $\quad\quad\quad\quad$ **return** $false$
21 $\quad\quad\quad$ **else if** sc_{fixed} is not a $true$ value **then**
22 $\quad\quad\quad\quad$ $c_{new} = c_{new} \wedge sc_{fixed}$
23 $\quad\quad$ **return** c_{new}
24 $\quad$ **else if** $dDBC\_node$ is a negation **then**
25 $\quad\quad$ **return** $\neg$FIX_NODE($\neg dDBC\_node$)
26 $\quad$ **else**
27 $\quad\quad$ **return** $dDBC\_node$
28 $dDBCSFi(2)$ = FIX_NODE($root\_node$)

---

4   Shap Computation: Experiments

The "California Housing Prices" dataset was used for our experiments (it can be down-loaded from Kaggle [24]). It consists of 20,640 observations for 10 features with infor-mation on the block groups of houses in California, from the 1990 Census. Table 1 lists and describes the features, and the way they are binarized, actually by considering if the value is above the average or not[7] to better The categorical feature #1 is one-hot encoded, giving rise to 5 binary features: #1_a, ..., #1_e. Accordingly, we end up with 13 binary input features, plus the binary output feature, #10, representing whether the median price at each block is high or low, i.e. above or below the average of the original #10. We used the "Tensorflow" and "Larq" Python libraries to train a BNN with one

---

[7] Binarization could be achieved in other ways, depending on the feature, for better interaction with the feature independence assumption.

hidden layer, with as many neurons as predictors, i.e. 13, and one neuron for the output. For the hidden neurons, the activation functions are step function, as in (3).

Table 1. Features of the "California Housing Prices" dataset.

Id #	Feature Name	Description	Original Values	Binarization
#1	*ocean_proximity*	A label of the location of the house w.r.t sea/ocean	Labels *1h_ocean, inland, island, near_bay* and *near_ocean*	Five features (one representing each label), for which 1 means a match with the value of *ocean_proximity*, and -1 otherwise
#2	*households*	The total number of households (a group of people residing within a home unit) for a block	Integer numbers from 1 to 6,082	1 (above average of the feature) or -1 (below average)
#3	*housing_median_age*	The median age of a house within a block (lower numbers means newer buildings)	Integer numbers from 1 to 52	1 (above average of the feature) or -1 (below average)
#4	*latitude*	The angular measure of how far north a block is (the higher value, the farther north)	Real numbers from 32.54 to 41.95	1 (above average of the feature) or -1 (below average)
#5	*longitude*	The angular measure of how far west a block is (the higher value, the farther west)	Real numbers from -124.35 to -114.31	1 (above average of the feature) or -1 (below average)
#6	*median_income*	The median income for households within a block (measured in tens of thousands of US dollars)	Real numbers from 0.50 to 15.00	1 (above average of the feature) or -1 (below average)
#7	*population*	The total number of people residing within a block	Integer numbers from 3 to 35,682	1 (above average of the feature) or -1 (below average)
#8	*total_bedrooms*	The total number of bedrooms within a block	Integer numbers from 1 to 6,445	1 (above average of the feature) or -1 (below average)
#9	*total_rooms*	The total number of rooms within a block	Integer numbers from 2 to 39,320	1 (above average of the feature) or -1 (below average)
#10	*median_house_value*	The median house value for households within a block (measured in US dollars)	Integer numbers from 14,999 to 500,001	1 (above average of the feature) or 0 (below average)

According to the transformation path (2), the constructed BNN was first represented as a CNF formula with 2,391 clauses. It has a tree-width of 12, which makes sense having a middle layer of 13 gates, each with all features as inputs. The CNF was transformed, via the SDD conversion, into a dDBCSFi(2), $\mathcal{C}$, which ended up having 18,671 nodes (without counting the negations affecting only input gates). Both transformations were programmed in Python. For the intermediate simplification of the CNF, the *Riss* SAT solver was used [20]. The initial transformation into CNF took 1.3 hrs. This is the *practically* most expensive step, as was explained at the end of Sect. 3.1. The conversion of the simplified CNF into the dDBCSFi(2) took 0.8276 s.

With the resulting BC, we computed Shap, for each input entity, in three ways:

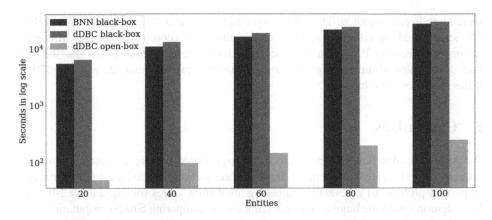

Fig. 4. Seconds taken to compute all Shap scores on 20, 40, 60, 80 and 100 input entities; using the BNN as a black-box (blue bar), the dDBC as a black-box (red bar), and the dDBC as an open-box (orange bar). Notice the logarithmic scale on the vertical axis. (Color figure online)

(a) Directly on the BNN as a black-box model, using formula (1) and its input/output relation for multiple calls;
(b) Similarly, using the circuit $\mathcal{C}$ as a black-box model; and
(c) Using the efficient algorithm in [1, page 18] treating circuit $\mathcal{C}$ as an open-box model.

These three computations of Shap scores were performed for sets of 20, 40, 60, 80, and 100 input entities, for *all* 13 features, and *all* input entities in the set. In all cases, using the uniform distribution over population of size 2^{13}. Since the dDBC faithfully represents the BNN, we obtained exactly the same Shap scores under the modes of computation (a)–(c) above. The *total* computation times were compared. The results are shown in Fig. 4. Notice that these times are represented *in logarithmic scale*. For example, with the BNN, the computation time of all Shap scores for 100 input entities was 7.7 hrs, whereas with the open-box dDBC it was 4.2 min. We observe a huge gain in performance with the use of the efficient algorithm on the open-box dDBC. Those times do not show the one-time computation for the transformation of the BNN into the dDBC. If the latter was added, each red and orange bar would have an increase of 1.3 hrs. For reference, even considering this extra one-time computation, with the open-box approach on the dDBC we can still compute all of the Shap scores for 100 input entities in less time than with the BNN with just 20 input entities[8].

For the cases (a) and (b) above, i.e. computations with black-box models, the classification labels were first computed for all input entities in the population $\mathcal{E}$. Accordingly, when computing the Shap scores for a particular input entity e, the labels for all the other entities related to it via a subset of features S as specified by the game function

---

[8] The experiments were run on *Google Colab* (with an NVIDIA Tesla T4 enabled). Algorithm 1 was programmed in Python. The complete code for *Google Colab* can be found at: https://github.com/Jorvan758/dDBCSFi2.

were already precomputed. This allows to compute formula (1) much more efficiently[9]. The specialized algorithm for (c) does not require this precomputation. The difference in time between the BNN and the black-box dDBC, cases (a) and (b), is due the fact that BNNs allow some batch processing for the label precomputation; with the dDBC it has to be done one by one.

5   Conclusions

We have showed in detail the practical use of logic-based knowledge compilation techniques in a real application scenario. Furthermore, we have applied them to the new and important problem of efficiently computing attribution scores for explainable ML. We have demonstrated the huge computational gain, by comparing Shap computation with a BNN classifier treated as an open-box vs. treating it as a black-box. The performance gain in Shap computation with the circuit exceeds by far both the compilation time and the Shap computation time for the BNN as a black-box classifier.

We emphasize that the effort invested in transforming the BNN into a dDBC is something we incur once. The resulting circuit can be used to obtain Shap scores multiple times, and for multiple input entities. Furthermore, the circuit can be used for other purposes, such as *verification* of general properties of the classifier [11,23], and answering explanation queries about a classifier [3]. Despite the intrinsic complexity involved, there is much room for improving the algorithmic and implementation aspects of the BNN compilation. The same applies to the implementation of the efficient Shap computation algorithm.

We computed Shap scores using the uniform distribution on the entity population. There are a few issues to discuss in this regard. First, it is computationally costly to use it with a large number of features. One could use instead the *empirical distribution* associated to the dataset, as in [4] for black-box Shap computation. This would require appropriately modifying the applied algorithm, which is left for future work. Secondly, and more generally, the uniform distribution does not capture possible dependencies among features. The algorithm is still efficient with the *product distribution*, which also suffers from imposing feature independence (see [4] for a discussion of its empirical version and related issues). It would be interesting to explore to what extent other distributions could be used in combination with our efficient algorithm.

Independently from the algorithmic and implementation aspects of Shap computation, an important research problem is that of bringing *domain knowledge* or *domain semantics* into attribution scores and their computations, to obtain more meaningful and interpretable results. This additional knowledge could come, for example, in declarative terms, expressed as *logical constraints*. They could be used to appropriately modify the algorithm or the underlying distribution [5]. It is likely that domain knowledge can be more easily be brought into a score computation when it is done on a BC classifier.

In this work we have considered only binary NNs. It remains to be investigated to what extent our methods can be suitably modified for dealing with non-binary NNs.

---

[9] As done in [4], but with only the entity sample.

Acknowledgments. Special thanks to Arthur Choi, Andy Shih, Norbert Manthey, Maximilian Schleich and Adnan Darwiche, for their valuable help. Work was funded by ANID - Millennium Science Initiative Program - Code ICN17002; CENIA, FB210017 (Financiamiento Basal para Centros Científicos y Tecnológicos de Excelencia de ANID), Chile; SKEMA Business School, and NSERC-DG 2023-04650. L. Bertossi is a Professor Emeritus at Carleton University, Canada.

References

1. Arenas, M., Barceló, P., Bertossi, L., Monet, M.: On the complexity of SHAP-score-based explanations: tractability via knowledge compilation and non-approximability results. J. Mach. Learn. Res. **24**(63), 1–58 (2023). Extended version of [2]
2. Arenas, M., Barceló, P., Bertossi, L., Monet, M.: The tractability of SHAP-score-based explanations for classification over deterministic and decomposable Boolean circuits. In: Proceedings of the 35th AAAI Conference on Artificial Intelligence, pp. 6670–6678 (2021)
3. Audemard, G., Koriche, F., Marquis, P.: On tractable XAI queries based on compiled representations. In: Proceedings KR 2020, pp. 838–849 (2020)
4. Bertossi, L., Li, J., Schleich, M., Suciu, D., Vagena, Z.: Causality-based explanation of classification outcomes. In: Proceedings of the 4th International Workshop on "Data Management for End-to-End Machine Learning" (DEEM) at ACM SIGMOD/PODS, pp. 1–10 (2020). Posted as Corr arXiv Paper arXiv:2003.06868
5. Bertossi, L.: Declarative approaches to counterfactual explanations for classification. Theory Pract. Logic Program. **23**(3), 559–593 (2023)
6. Bollig, B., Buttkus, M.: On the relative succinctness of sentential decision diagrams. Theory Comput. Syst. **63**(6), 1250–1277 (2019)
7. Bova, S.: SDDs are exponentially more succinct than OBDDs. In: Proceedings of the 30th AAAI Conference on Artificial Intelligence, pp. 929–935 (2016)
8. Bryant, R.E.: Graph-based algorithms for Boolean function manipulation. IEEE Trans. Comput. **C-35**(8), 677–691 (1986)
9. Choi, A., Darwiche, A.: Dynamic minimization of sentential decision diagrams. In: Proceedings of the 27th AAAI Conference on Artificial Intelligence, pp. 187–194 (2013)
10. Choi, A., Darwiche, A.: SDD Advanced-User Manual Version 2.0. Automated Reasoning Group, UCLA (2018)
11. Darwiche, A., Hirth, A.: On the reasons behind decisions. In: Proceedings of the 24th European Conference on Artificial Intelligence, pp. 712–720 (2020)
12. Darwiche, A., Marquis, P.: A knowledge compilation map. J. Artif. Intell. Res. **17**(1), 229–264 (2002)
13. Darwiche, A.: On the tractable counting of theory models and its application to truth maintenance and belief revision. J. Appl. Non-Classical Logics **11**(1–2), 11–34 (2011)
14. Darwiche, A.: SDD: a new canonical representation of propositional knowledge bases. In: Proceedings of the 22th International Joint Conference on Artificial Intelligence (IJCAI 2011), pp. 819–826 (2011)
15. Flum, J., Grohe, M.: Parameterized Complexity Theory. Springer, Heidelberg (2006). https://doi.org/10.1007/3-540-29953-X
16. Guidotti, R., Monreale, A., Ruggieri, S., Turini, F., Giannotti, F., Pedreschi, D.: A survey of methods for explaining black box models. ACM Comput. Surv. **51**(5), 1–42 (2018)
17. Hubara, I., Courbariaux, M., Soudry, D., El-Yaniv, R., Bengio, Y.: Binarized neural networks. In: Proceedings of the NIPS 2016, pp. 4107–4115 (2016)
18. Lundberg, S.M., Lee, S.-I.: A unified approach to interpreting model predictions. In: Proceedings of the 31st International Conference on Neural Information Processing Systems, pp. 4768–4777 (2017). arXiv Paper arXiv:1705.07874

19. Lundberg, S., et al.: From local explanations to global understanding with explainable AI for trees. Nat. Mach. Intell. **2**(1), 56–67 (2020). arXiv Paper arXiv:1905.04610
20. Manthey, N.: RISS tool collection (2017). https://github.com/nmanthey/riss-solver
21. Meert, W., Choi, A.: Python Wrapper Package to Interactively Use Sentential Decision Diagrams (SDD) (2018). https://github.com/wannesm/PySDD
22. Nakamura, K., Denzumi, S., Nishino, M.: Variable shift SDD: a more succinct sentential decision diagram. In: Proceedings of the 18th International Symposium on Experimental Algorithms (SEA 2020). Leibniz International Proceedings in Informatics, vol. 160, pp. 22:1–22:13 (2020)
23. Narodytska, N., Kasiviswanathan, S., Ryzhyk, L., Sagiv, M., Walsh, T.: Verifying properties of binarized deep neural networks. In: Proceedings of the 32nd AAAI Conference on Artificial Intelligence, pp. 6615–6624 (2018)
24. Nugent, C.: California Housing Prices (2018). https://www.kaggle.com/datasets/camnugent/california-housing-prices
25. Oztok, U., Darwiche, A.: On compiling CNF into decision-DNNF. In: O'Sullivan, B. (ed.) CP 2014. LNCS, vol. 8656, pp. 42–57. Springer, Cham (2014). https://doi.org/10.1007/978-3-319-10428-7_7
26. Oztok, U., Darwiche, A.: On compiling DNNFs without determinism (2017). arXiv:1709.07092
27. Qin, H., Gong, R., Liu, X., Bai, X., Song, J., Sebe, N.: Binary neural networks: a survey. Pattern Recogn. **105**, 107281 (2020)
28. Ras, G., Xie, N., van Gerven, M., Doran, D.: Explainable deep learning: a field guide for the uninitiated. J. Artif. Intell. Res. **73**, 329–396 (2022)
29. Roth, A.: The Shapley Value: Essays in Honor of Lloyd S. Shapley. Cambridge University Press (1988)
30. Rudin, C.: Stop explaining black box machine learning models for high stakes decisions and use interpretable models instead. Nat. Mach. Intell. **1**, 206–215 (2019). arXiv Paper arXiv:1811.10154
31. Shapley, L.S.: A value for n-person games. In: Contributions to the Theory of Games (AM-28), vol. 2, pp. 307–318 (1953)
32. Shih, A., Van den Broeck, G., Beame, P., Amarilli, A.: Smoothing structured decomposable circuits. In: Proceedings of the NeurIPS (2019)
33. Shi, W., Shih, A., Darwiche, A., Choi, A.: On tractable representations of binary neural networks. In: Proceedings of the 17th International Conference on Principles of Knowledge Representation and Reasoning, pp. 882–892 (2020)
34. Shih, A., Darwiche, A., Choi, A.: Verifying binarized neural networks by Angluin-Style learning. In: Janota, M., Lynce, I. (eds.) SAT 2019. LNCS, vol. 11628, pp. 354–370. Springer, Cham (2019). https://doi.org/10.1007/978-3-030-24258-9_25
35. Simons, T., Lee, D.-J.: A review of binarized neural networks. Electronics **8**(6), 661 (2019)
36. Van den Broeck, G., Darwiche, A.: On the role of canonicity in knowledge compilation. In: Proceedings of the 29th AAAI Conference on Artificial Intelligence, pp. 1641–1648 (2015)
37. Van den Broeck, G., Lykov, A., Schleich, M., Suciu, D.: On the tractability of SHAP explanations. In: Proceedings of the 35th AAAI Conference on Artificial Intelligence, pp. 6505–6513 (2021)

Logic, Accountability and Design: Extended Abstract

Pedro Cabalar[1] and David Pearce[2(✉)]

[1] University of Corunna, A Coruña, Spain
cabalar@udc.es
[2] Universidad Politécnica de Madrid, Madrid, Spain
david.pearce@upm.es

1 Introduction

This note is a contribution to the methodology of applied, computational logics in light of their potential role in securing the accountability of Artificial Intelligence (AI) systems. A key feature of the idea of accountability is that solutions, actions and decisions made by intelligent systems should ultimately be explainable to the end user in a comprehensible manner. In view of this, explainable AI has recently become a hot topic of research. Much of symbolic AI is supported by logic-based system whose reasoning mechanisms are, or should be, transparent and comprehensible. But is it really the case that a logic-based system can provide convincing explanations accessible to the non-expert? In practice this is doubtful as such systems may contain many lines of code and numerous computational reasoning steps. Even the expert user or developer may not be able to survey and assimilate the entire reasoning process for a given outcome.

This point has been recognised for quite some time. Already [5] contains an extensive survey of approaches to adding explanations or justifications to answer set programs. Recently the XLoKR workshop series on Explainable Logic-Based Knowledge Representation has featured systems such as ASP, description logics, default logics, argumentation theory and more. However until now attention has mainly focused on how to add human-understandable explanations to the reasoning steps computed by a primary logic-based systems. While these works are valuable, for the most part they implicitly take for granted the adequacy of the primary reasoning formalism that they aim to extend.

If logic is to play a significant role in making AI systems explainable, then logic itself needs to be accountable. Many logics applied in AI systems are in competition with one another. Since logics are an integral part of our approaches to knowledge representation and reasoning, they can no longer be considered as a kind of 'theory-neutral' component, as logic was often treated by philosophers

Supported by project LIANDA - BBVA Foundation Grants for Scientific Research Projects; additional support from the Spanish Ministry of Science and Innovation, Spain, MCIN/AEI/10.13039/501100011033 (grant PID2020-116201GB-I00), and by Xunta de Galicia, Spain and the European Union (grant GPC ED431B 2022/33).

S. Gaggl et al. (Eds.): JELIA 2023, LNAI 14281, pp. 65–72, 2023.
https://doi.org/10.1007/978-3-031-43619-2_5

of science in the past. In light of this we should ask ourselves, what kinds of adequacy conditions should applied logics fulfil in order to be candidates to support accountable and ultimately trustworthy AI. In doing so we hope to dispel the idea that *anything goes*, ie that the engineer has a free hand just to pick off the shelf any reasoning mechanism that appeals to her. Instead we argue for a principled approach to designing applied logics and formal reasoning tools for uptake in AI; an approach that complies with suitable adequacy conditions and respects a sound methodology. One consequence will be to attempt to rule out *ad hoc* solutions to formal reasoning problems.[1]

2   Conceptual Analysis and Explication

The formal analysis of concepts was a major component of the work of logical empiricist philosophers in the 20th Century, and Rudolf Carnap was perhaps in this respect its most illustrious representative. Carnap's method of *explication* is probably the clearest account of how logic and formal methods should be applied to the rational reconstruction of scientific concepts. Carnap's method is most clearly articulated in the introduction to his *Logical Foundations of Probability* [2]. As he explains, the method

> consists in transforming a more or less inexact concept into an exact one or, rather, in replacing the first by the second. We call the given concept the **explicandum**, and the exact concept proposed to take the place of the first the **explicatum**. The explicandum may belong to everyday language or to a previous stage in the development of scientific language. The explicatum must be given by explicit rules for its use, for example, by a definition which incorporates it into a well-constructed system of scientific either logico-mathematical or empirical concepts [2].

Part of the task consists in specifying adequacy conditions that the explicatum should satisfy: a pre-formal analysis of the explicandum may suggest a series of properties desirable for the explicatum.

> If a concept is given as explicandum, the task consists in finding another concept as its explicatum which fulfils the following requirements to a sufficient degree.
> 1. The explicatum is to be *similar to the explicandum* in such a way that, in most cases in which the explicandum has so far been used, the explicatum can be used; however, close similarity is not required, and considerable differences are permitted.
> 2. The characterization of the explicatum, that is, the rules of its use (for instance in the form of a definition), is to be given in an *exact* form, so as to introduce the explicatum into a well-connected system of scientific concepts.

---

[1] The full version of the paper elaborates more on this issue and includes a case study of the adequacy of logics underlying ASP. In this abridged version, we focus just on adequacy conditions for logics in KR.

3. The explicatum is to be a *fruitful* concept, that is, useful for the formulation of many universal statements (empirical laws in the case of a nonlogical concept, logical theorems in the case of a logical concept).
4. The explicatum should be as *simple* as possible; this means as simple as the more important requirements (1), (2), and (3) permit [2].

Ultimately the question whether the explicatum is or is not correct is not a factual one, but a question of methodological adequacy [2].

Although logic has formed a prominent part of the design of intelligent systems, most developers of logic-based systems have shied away from specifying a clear methodology of the type that Carnap has proposed. One exception is the programme proposed by Michael Gelfond, a founder of answer set programming and a leading contributor to logic-based AI. The aim of his programme is to reconstruct some of the most basic forms of human knowledge and to exploit this knowledge for practical problem solving. It combines scientific and engineering knowledge of real systems with practical human skills and abilities and commonsense reasoning. It deals with both static and dynamic domains. Gelfond's programme combines the physicalist language of engineering and physical systems with epistemic notions such as belief, agency and action. The new programme of rational reconstruction is much less self-conscious than its predecessor and is less well known. Nevertheless it has clear goals and methodology, even if they are sometimes buried in technical articles and lectures.

Gelfond's programme for KR has two main objectives [6]. First, achieving an understanding of "basic commonsense notions we use to think about the world: beliefs, knowledge, defaults, causality, intentions, probability, etc., and to learn how one ought to reason about them." Secondly it aims "to understand how to build software components of agents – entities which observe and act upon an environment and direct its activity towards achieving goals" ([6]).

These goals shape the criteria used to evaluate and select languages for KR. In particular, Gelfond [6] endorses four main adequacy criteria: clarity, elegance, expressiveness and relevance. These are further elaborated in [7]:

- *Naturalesness*: Constructs of a formal language L should be close to formal constructs used in the parts of natural language that L is designed to formalize. The language should come with a methodology of using these constructs for knowledge representation and programming.
- *Clarity*: The language should have simple syntax and clear intuitive semantics based on understandable informal principles.
- *Mathematical Elegance*: Formal description of syntax and semantics of the language should be mathematically elegant. Moreover, the language should come with mathematical theory facilitating its use for knowledge representation and programming.
- *Stability*: Informally equivalent transformations of a text should correspond to formally equivalent ones.
- *Elaboration Tolerance*: It should be possible to expand a language by new relevant constructs without substantial changes in its syntax and semantics.

Gelfond's first criterion is close to Carnap's first condition of *similarity*, while his second criterion echoes Carnaps's fourth condition of *simplicity*. Gelfond's third criterion is close to Carnap's second requirement of *exactness*, while elaboration tolerance and Gelfond's other criterion of relevance (from [6]) clearly relate to Carnap's requirements 2 and 3.

One condition that Gelfond does not entertain is the requirement of *efficiency* understood in a computational sense. Efficiency is evidently an aim in designing computational systems and a requirement of any KR language is that it can eventually be processed by a computer. But Gelfond's methodology suggests that conceptual adequacy should initially at least take preference over computational efficiency.

A similar point has been recently made by Jones, Artikis and Pitt in their proposed methodology for the design of socio-technical systems [11]. They are concerned with the way in which social concepts are reconstructed and represented in computational, socio-technical systems. [11] deals mainly with social concepts such as *trust*, *role* and *normative power*. But their reconstruction in computational systems will typically involve a strongly logical component. [11] proposes a multi-stage process of representing and implementing these concepts. The first stage involves theory construction, passing from some observed social phenomena S to pre-formal representations. Then, Step2-Phase1 representations provide an analysis of conceptual structure "constrained primarily by considerations of expressive capacity, not those of computational tractability" [11]. Later we come to the stage of implementation where simplifications may have to be made to achieve comptational tractability. For [11], a primary requirement for assessing the adequacy of a conceptual characterisation is expressive capacity. As criteria, they list the capacity to (i) identify the principle elements; (ii) test for consistency; (iii) articulate specific, characteristic aspects of the concept; (iv) 'place' the concept in relation to its near relatives. (iv) is clearly related to Carnap's second and third requirements, and also to Gelfond's criteria of *naturalness* and *relevance*.

These three approaches to the formal analysis of concepts come from very different backgrounds and yet display important commonalities. They each urge a principled approach to formal reconstructions, based on a clear methodology. They propose a preliminary, informal analysis of concepts, preferably informed by scientific or philosophical reflection, suggesting that this may lead to specifying criteria of adequacy that the formal concepts should satisfy. Then there is the shared idea that the formal characterisations fit into the broader scheme of scientific concepts covering related domains. Lastly, there is the idea of fruitfulness or relevance for problem solving, as well as the aim of expressive capacity. These are all considerations that we may bring to bear on the study of possible conditions for the adequacy of logical systems in AI. We will focus on applied logics for KR, trying to extract some formal adequacy conditions.

3   Nonmonotonic Reasoning and Strong Equivalence

Logic-based systems for KR in AI are typically *nonmonotonic* in character, to allow for the representation of defaults and to be able to express exceptions to general rules. Since these systems depart considerably from ordinary, bread and butter logics, classical or otherwise, it is not immediately obvious that they fulfil the needs of explainability and accountability for AI in practical cases. Can all such systems really be considered logics? Do they lend themselves to support explainable AI? How can we choose between rival solutions to specific kinds of reasoning?

One way to approach these questions is by way of some concepts that were studied already in the early years of nonmonotonic reasoning (NMR). In particular, to ask what constitutes a (monotonic) logical basis for an NMR system. If our logic for KR, despite nonmonotonicity, is clearly anchored to a standard, monotonic logic, this may help to clarify and even legitimate its reasoning mechanism. This suggests that we might focus initially on how an NMR system extends and relates to a given, underlying monotonic logic. To consider what it means saying that a logic L forms a well-behaved monotonic basis for a given nonmonotonic consequence relation, three main conditions come to light.[2]

Definition 1. *Let C be a (possibly nonmonotonic) consequence relation and let C_L be the consequence relation for a monotonic logic L. We say that L forms a deductive base for C if the following conditions hold:*

$$Sublogic: \quad C_L \leq C \quad (ie \quad C_L(\Gamma) \subseteq C(\Gamma) \quad forall \quad \Gamma) \tag{1}$$

$$Left\ absorption: \quad C_L C = C \tag{2}$$

$$right\ absorption: \quad C C_L = C \tag{3}$$

Absorption guarantees that if theories are equivalent in L they remain equivalent at the nonmonotonic level (i.e. under C). Moreover closing the nonmonotonic consequences of a theory under L-consequence does not produce anything new. One characteristic of standard, monotonic logics is the presence of replacement theorems that guarantee when equivalent formulas or theories are interchangeable *salva veritate* in any context. In nonmonotonic logics, replacement properties are more complex, since equivalence may also be derived from the absence of information. For instance, two theories Π_1 and Π_2 may yield the same C-consequences but these may differ after adding new information Γ. This motivates:

Definition 2. *In the context of a nonmomontonic consequence relation C, two theories Π_1 and Π_2 are said to be strongly equivalent if for all Γ, $C(\Pi_1 \cup \Gamma) = C(\Pi_2 \cup \Gamma)$.*

In other words, Π_1 and Π_2 remain equivalent in whatever context Γ they are embedded. One property of deductive bases is immediate but very powerful: if L

---

[2] The term deductive base defined below is taken from [3,4]; however similar ideas can be found in [12] and elsewhere.

is a deductive base for C, then L-equivalence of Π_1 and Π_2 is a sufficient condition for strong equivalence. A given nonmonotonic relation C may have several monotonic deductive bases and equivalence in any of them is a sufficient condition for strong equivalence, but not always a necessary condition. To guarantee a suitable replacement property one can add a further refinement and say that a deductive base is *strong* if it satisfies:

$$C_L(\Pi_1) \neq C_L(\Pi_2) \Rightarrow \quad \text{there exists } \Gamma \text{ such that } C(\Pi_1 \cup \Gamma) \neq C(\Pi_2 \cup \Gamma).$$

If a deductive base is strong we obtain what is known as a strong equivalence theorem, namely that two theories are interchangeable in any context under the nonmonotonic inference *if an only if* they are equivalent in the monotonic base.[3] This has important consequences for simplifying nonmonotonic theories and programs and studying their properties. For example if the base logic has a suitable proof theory we can use it to test for program equivalences.

4   Methodologies for Applied Logics

Given the discussion above, let us try to compile some guidelines for the design and development of logic-based systems for KR and AI. We propose an initial list of criteria that we group in the following three kinds of conditions.

Type I. General Requirements for Good Design and Sound Methodology

1. Is it logic?
2. Is the reasoning based on a known underlying logic?
3. Is it a combination of known logics?

The first condition may at first sight appear to be circular. But if understood correctly, it does make sense. In KR there are formal reasoning methods that appear to be logic-based yet fail some natural properties that one would expect to hold. Computational logics have vastly extended the boundaries of what the repertoire of logic, in its mathematical paradigm, was formerly supposed to include. Nevertheless, some properties seem to be constitutive and basic to logic, especially if we consider the KR context. We sometimes find formalisms defined only for syntactic fragments or under syntax restrictions and with *ad hoc* semantic definitions that do not rely on any standard method for defining a logic. So we keep Condition 1 as an imprecise but useful first test of adequacy.

Condition 2 is inspired by the discussion of the previous section. If our system is based on a known logic whose reasoning mechanisms are well understood and appropriate for the domain, we have advanced on the path to verifying its adequacy. Condition 3 is related to Carnap's third and Gelfond's fifth requirements. Much work has been done on combining logics, and in KR many opportunities

---

[3] Equivalence usually means same intended models; but if consequence is defined in terms of intended models, then this will imply equivalence wrt C.

arise for their application. One may think of combinations such as knowledge with belief, tense and modality, space and time, nonmonotonicity combined with epistemic reasoning, and others. A primary logic that can be combined with other logics to gain new functionalities can be a very fruitful conceptual tool. Criteria for combining logics are also important. For instance, a combined formalism should have a clear connection to its constituent logics – for instance, a modal extension of ASP should collapse to ASP when no modal operators are used. Also, the combined formalism should inherit and generalise recognisable properties from its constituent logics.

Type II. Specific Adequacy Conditions for the Logical Concepts to be Formalised. These include adequacy conditions that pertain to a specific concept and context, perhaps based on a pre-formal analysis of the concept.

1. Does it adequately reconstruct/formalise the intended concepts?
2. Does it offer suitable reasoning mechanisms for those concepts?
3. Does it accommodate new cases in a clear and natural manner?
4. Does it possess desirable metatheoretic properties?

The first of these may include for instance the expressive capacity of the formal language and be based on prior analysis of the concept. The second condition relates to semantics and inference. The third requirement relates to Carnap's and Gelfond's ideas of simplicity and clarity. A successful formalisation should yield a general approach that goes beyond just a few isolated cases of reasoning. Moreover, it should handle new examples in a natural manner without needing *ad hoc* adjustments and revisions. 4 may include matters of tractability of reasoning, properties that are generally regarded as 'good' for a logic, or properties that are desirable in a given KR context. These will tend to change from domain to domain and so can best be made precise given a specific context.

Type III. Methods of Reasoning that May Lead to Explainable AI and Support the Rational Acceptability of Conclusions. Lastly we may consider requirements that will allow for reasoning steps to be displayed in a way that can explain the outcome of a logic-based, computational system in practical cases.

1. Can it be combined with methods of explanation?
2. Can explanations be broken down into simple steps for human comprehension and rational acceptance?

This is currently an very active field of inquiry. It may involve the ability to apply a secondary type of logic that can add justification steps, or perhaps argumentation trees, to computations carried out in the primary logical system. Such methods should be convincing to a rational agent and, if possible, graspable by a human user.

5   Related and Future Work and Conclusions

We have argued that for logic to play a key role in making AI systems more accountable, we also have to analyse and question the adequacy of the primary reasoning system itself. Here there is much territory still to be explored. As examples of works that *have* initiated a critical analysis and discussion of the adequacy of logical systems in AI, we can mention [8–10], focused on epistemic reasoning and multi-agent systems in particular.

We have tried to raise awareness of the need to take a principled approach to the design of logical systems, to reject the assumption that *anything goes* when proposing a new reasoning formalism, and to avoid *ad hoc* solutions designed to 'save the phenomena'. We have also looked at some general requirements for the formal reconstruction of concepts and proposed some preliminary desiderata for logics to be applied in AI systems.

There is much more to be done. This is the first of a three-part work in progress. The second part will treat extensions of logic programming, such as those dealing with aggregates, temporal logic or epistemic reasoning. The third part will extend work already started on explanatory ASP [1].

References

1. Cabalar, P., Fandinno, J., Muñiz, B.: A system for explainable answer set programming. In: Ricca, F., et al. (eds.) Proceedings 36th International Conference on Logic Programming (Technical Communications), ICLP Technical Communications 2020, UNICAL, Rende (CS), Italy, 18–24th September 2020. EPTCS, vol. 325, pp. 124–136 (2020)
2. Carnap, R.: Logical Foundations of Probability. University of Chicago Press (1950)
3. Dietrich, J.: Deductive bases of nonmonotonic inference operations. NTZ report, University of Leipzig (1994)
4. Dietrich, J.: Inferenzframes, University of Leipzig. Ph.D. thesis (1995)
5. Fandinno, J., Schulz, C.: Answering the "why" in answer set programming - a survey of explanation approaches. Theory Pract. Log. Program. **19**(2), 114–203 (2019). https://doi.org/10.1017/S1471068418000534
6. Gelfond, M.: Personal perspective on the development of logic programming based KR languages (2011). http://www.depts.ttu.edu/cs/research/krlab/papers.php. unpublished draft, available online at
7. Gelfond, M., Zhang, Y.: Vicious circle principle and logic programs with aggregates. Theory Pract. Log. Program. **14**(4–5), 587–601 (2014)
8. Herzig, A.: Logics of knowledge and action: critical analysis and challenges. Auton. Agent Multi-Agent Syst. **29**(5), 719–753 (2014). https://doi.org/10.1007/s10458-014-9267-z
9. Herzig, A.: Dynamic epistemic logics: promises, problems, shortcomings, and perspectives. J. Appl. Non-Classical Log. **27**, 1–14 (2018)
10. Herzig, A., Lorini, E., Perrussel, L., Xiao, Z.: Bdi logics for bdi architectures: old problems, new perspectives. KI - Künstliche Intelligenz **31**(1), 73–83 (2017)
11. Jones, A.J.I., Artikis, A., Pitt, J.: The design of intelligent socio-technical systems. Artif. Intell. Rev. **39**(1), 5–20 (2013)
12. Makinson, D.: General patterns in nonmonotonic reasoning. In: Handbook of Logic in Artificial Intelligence and Logic Programming (Vol. 3): Nonmonotonic Reasoning and Uncertain Reasoning, vol. III, pp. 35–110. Clarendon Press, Oxford (1994)

Contrastive Explanations for Answer-Set Programs

Thomas Eiter🄳, Tobias Geibinger(✉)🄳, and Johannes Oetsch🄳

Knowledge-based Systems Group, Institute for Logic and Computation, TU Wien, Vienna,
Austria
{thomas.eiter,tobias.geibinger,johannes.oetsch}@tuwien.ac.at

Abstract. Answer-Set Programming (ASP) is a popular declarative reasoning
and problem solving formalism. Due to the increasing interest in explainability,
several explanation approaches have been developed for ASP. However, while
those formalisms are correct and interesting on their own, most are more technical
and less oriented towards philosophical or social concepts of explanation. In this
work, we study the notion of contrastive explanation, i.e., answering questions
of the form "Why P instead of Q?", in the context of ASP. In particular, we are
interested in answering why atoms are included in an answer set, whereas others
are not. Contrastive explainability has recently become popular due to its strong
support from the philosophical, cognitive, and social sciences and its apparent
ability to provide explanations that are concise and intuitive for humans. We formally define contrastive explanations for ASP based on counterfactual reasoning
about programs. Furthermore, we demonstrate the usefulness of the concept on
example applications and give some complexity results. The latter also provide a
guideline as to how the explanations can be computed in practice.

1 Introduction

Historically, symbolic artificial intelligence (AI) systems have had integrated explanation components, but over time the interest in those features has had died down. The
growing need and usage of AI has lead to a demand of transparency and explainability.
This has rejoiced the interest in explanation components in symbolic systems again.

Answer-Set Programming (ASP) is a symbolic, rule-based reasoning formalism that
has been employed for various AI applications in numerous domains [13,15], among
them planning [29], scheduling [1,2,46], product configuration [8], life sciences [14],
health insurance [3], and psychology [23], to mention a few. ASP allows for a declarative encoding of problems in a succinct manner. Solutions to a problem instance are
obtained from *answer sets*, which result from the evaluation of the encoding using an
ASP solver.

While ASP is a declarative AI approach, there is still a need for providing concise
and understandable explanations as to why certain facts are, or are not, in a computed
answer set. For this reason, a number of explanation approaches for ASP have been
developed; we refer to the comprehensive survey by Fandinno and Schulz [17] for further reading. Recently, Miller [32] has questioned the practicability of common formal

ⓒ The Author(s), under exclusive license to Springer Nature Switzerland AG 2023
S. Gaggl et al. (Eds.): JELIA 2023, LNAI 14281, pp. 73–89, 2023.
https://doi.org/10.1007/978-3-031-43619-2_6

approaches and the understanding of what constitutes an explanation from the view of theoretical computer science. One of his criticisms is that simply providing static justifications, which are a common theme in explanation approaches for ASP, are not well-aligned with research from the philosophical, cognitive, and social sciences on what humans really request from an explanation. In his analysis, he argues that contrastive explanation, which is due to Lipton [30], is a suited approach for explainable AI. Simply put, contrastive explanation seeks to answer questions of the form "Why P instead of Q?" by providing a *meaningful difference* as to why P happened instead of Q. This is notably different from providing individual explanations for "Why P?" and "Why not Q?". In fact, Miller argues that research has shown that humans seeking explanation might ask "Why P?" but actually have some implicit contrast Q in mind. For example, suppose a system classifies an animal as a crow but the user expected it to be a magpie. Here, we refer to "crow" as the *fact*, while "magpie" is the *foil*; we shall expound on this example later. The argument is that people are surprised by the occurrence of the fact and actually expected something different, namely the foil or contrast.

In this work, we provide a formal notion of contrastive explanation for ASP programs which, to the best of our knowledge, is still lacking. Intuitively, contrastive explanations include rules which allow to derive the fact and highlight the difference to the contrastive case by identifying rules which would have derived the foil in some alternative scenario, where some hypothetical additional assumptions may be adopted. Furthermore, contrastive explanations also include rules from the program which would need to be removed to enable this scenario. Notably, such explanations may be given in an interactive setting, allowing the user to ask multiple questions which take previously given answers into account.

Our main contributions can be summarised as follows.

- We provide a formalisation of contrastive explanation for ASP programs based on counterfactual reasoning, where the counterfactual is essentially an alternative program producing the desired answer set. Additionally, certain assumptions can be made or rules may be dropped. Our contrastive explanations are concise and per design do not necessarily include full length derivations, which existing explanation approaches often amount to, and which may be hard to parse for the user.
- We show that contrastive explanations are adequate by giving several examples as well as example applications, like rule-based classifiers and AI planning.
- We analyse the computational complexity of problems related to the novel notions of contrastive explanation for ASP. Deciding the existence of such explanations is Σ_2^p-complete in general and NP-complete for normal programs, while recognising them is D_2^p-complete, resp., DP-complete. Computing contrastive explanations is feasible in polynomial time with a witness oracle for Σ_2^p, resp., NP, and in fact complete under polynomial-time reductions when logarithmically many oracle calls are allowed.

As research suggests, our notion of contrastive explanation is closer to what humans expect from an explanation than just presenting rules that allow to derive facts. It serves building advanced explanation components of AI systems, which will in particular be important for combinations of ASP with sub-symbolic AI systems such as (deep) neural networks.

2 Preliminaries

2.1 Answer-Set Programming

We consider *Answer-Set Programming* (ASP) with (disjunctive) logic programs, which are finite sets of rules of the following form

$$a_1 \vee \cdots \vee a_l \leftarrow a_{l+1}, \ldots, a_m, not\ a_{m+1}, \ldots, not\ a_n, \qquad (1)$$

where $l \leq m \leq n$, $a_1, \ldots, a_n$ are from a denumerable set $\mathcal{A}$ of *atoms*, and *not* denotes *default negation*. We call a rule *normal* if $l = 1$; a *fact* if $l = 1$ and $m = n = 0$, a *constraint* if $l = 0$; and *positive* if $m = n$. We call a program *normal*, resp., *positive*, if all of its rules are normal, resp., positive. Note that in practice rules generally contain variables, which are removed during a process called *grounding*. Hence, rules with variables can be seen as shorthands for propositional rules, which we tacitly consider.

For a rule r of the form (1), $H(r) := \{a_1, \ldots, a_l\}$ is the *head* of the rule, whereas $B^+(r) := \{a_{l+1}, \ldots, a_m\}$ and $B^-(r) := \{a_{m+1}, \ldots, a_n\}$ is the *positive* and, resp., *negative body*. Furthermore, $B(r) := B^+(r) \cup not\ B^-(r)$, where $not\ S := \{not\ a \mid a \in S\}$ for any set of atoms $S \subseteq \mathcal{A}$. The set of all propositional atoms appearing in program P is denoted by $\mathcal{A}_P$. Furthermore, a *literal* is either an atom or a default negated atom. We will also prefix rules with labels, i.e., write $l : r$ where l is the label and r is a rule as defined above, to give names to rules.

The semantics of logic programs is based on *interpretations*, which are sets of atoms. An atom a is *satisfied* by interpretation $I \subseteq \mathcal{A}$, denoted by $I \models a$, if $a \in I$. Analogously, for a default negated atom $not\ a$, $I \models not\ a$ if $I \not\models a$. Furthermore, for a set of literals L, $I \models L$ if $I \models l$ for every $l \in L$.

A rule r is satisfied by an interpretation I, denoted by $I \models r$, if $I \models H(r)$ whenever $I \models B(r)$. For a program P, $I \models P$ if each $r \in P$ is satisfied by I. The formalisation of answer-set semantics is generally achieved via program reducts [18]. Here, we will use the reduct due to Wang et al. [45], which for a program P and an interpretation I is defined as $P^I := \{H(r) \cap I \leftarrow B^+(r) \mid r \in P, I \models B(r)\}$. An interpretation I is an *answer set* of a program P if I is the subset-least model of P^I. Notably, for each atom $a \in I$, $P^I \models a$ if I is an answer set of P. For any disjunctive program, this reduct leads to the same answer sets as the original *Gelfond-Lifschitz reduct* [18]. With $AS(P)$ we denote the set of all answer sets of P.

2.2 Contrastive Explanations

Contrastive explanations [30] answer why a decision has been reached in contrast to a different one, i.e., they answer questions of the form "Why P rather than Q?". It has been argued that contrastive explanations are intuitive for humans to understand and to produce and also that standard why questions contain a hidden *contrast case*, e.g., "Why P?" represents "Why P rather than not P?" [32]. Lipton [30] define an answer to a question of the form "Why P rather than Q?" as the *difference condition*, which states that the answer should contain a cause for P that is missing in the causal history of not Q. More formally, an answer consists of a cause c of P and a cause c' of Q such that $c \neq c'$ and c did occur whereas c' did not. One of the benefits of contrastive explanation is that the question includes partial information about the explainee. Namely, the contrast case reveals which parts of the causal history are clear to them. To illustrate, let us look at the following example by Miller.

Example 1 ([33]). Consider a classifier of animals in pictures. Given a picture of a bird, the answer of the classifier is "crow". A user might now ask why the result was "crow" and one could list all of the features of a crow, like "beak", "feathers", "dark wings", and so forth. However, another way to ask would be why is it classified a "crow" instead of a "magpie", which implicitly suggests that the user agrees that the animal in the image is a bird, and thus this part of the classification needs no explanation. Now, a contrastive explanation simply highlights why the bird is a crow instead of a magpie by, for example, noting that a crow has dark wings, whereas a magpie has white ones.

3 Contrastive Explanations for ASP

We start by introducing a formal object encompassing the setting of our intended explanation process, which might be interactive.

Definition 1. *An* explanation frame *is a tuple* (P, S, A), *where (i)* P *is a program, (ii)* $S \subseteq P$ *is a set of fixed rules, and (iii)* $A \subseteq \mathcal{A}_P$ *is a set of assumable atoms.*

Intuitively, an explanation frame describes the setting of an explanation process, where P is the program in question, S is the *common knowledge* of the explainee and the explanation system, i.e., S is the set of rules the explainee is sure on and considers fixed, and A is the set of *assumables*. The latter can be seen as hypothetical facts the explainee is willing to consider.

The overall setting we are considering is that the user obtained an answer set from a program and now seeks explanation. As stated, we are interested in questions of the form "Why P instead of Q?", where P and Q amount to sets of atoms, the former being the *facts* or the *explanandum*, contained in the given answer set, and the latter is the *foil*, which are atoms not in the answer.

Definition 2. *A* contrastive explanation (CE) problem *for an explanation frame* $\mathcal{F} = (P, S, A)$ *is a tuple* $\langle I, E, F \rangle$, *where* $I \in AS(P)$, $E \subseteq I$ *is the* explanandum *and* $F \cap I = \emptyset$ *is the* foil.

While the explanation frame and the CE problem are static objects, one can imagine an explanation system were the explainee is essentially in a dialogue with the explainer and the system uses evolving frames and the explainee presents different CE problems.

Our solutions for such CE problems will be based on counterfactuals, which contain alternative programs that adhere to the common knowledge of the explainee and what they accept as hypothetical facts.

Definition 3. *Let* $\mathcal{F} = (P, S, A)$ *be an explanation frame and* $\mathcal{P} = \langle I, E, F \rangle$ *be a CE problem for* $\mathcal{F}$. *Then, a program* $P' \subseteq P$, *an interpretation* I', *and a set* $A' \subseteq A$ *of assumptions are a* counterfactual account (CA) *for* $\mathcal{P}$ *if*

(i) $S \subseteq P'$,
(ii) $F \cap A' = I \cap A' = \emptyset$,
(iii) $I' \in AS(P' \cup A')$,
(iv) $F \subseteq I'$ and $E \not\subseteq I'$, and
(v) P' is $\subseteq$-maximal, i.e., there is no CA P'', I'', A'' for $\mathcal{P}$ where $P'' \supset P'$.

Program P' constitutes an assumption of the explainer regarding the epistemic state of the explainee, (i) assures that this state contains the common knowledge, (ii) ensures that A' are counterfactual assumptions (not true in the current answer set) and they do not contain any part of the foil, (iii) expresses that I' represents an answer set that is obtained from P' and A' and contains the foil while some fact is no longer satisfied (iv). The program P' is maximal in order to ensure that the divergence from the original program is minimal. This reflects that the explainee wants to diverge from the original program as little as possible. Note that maximality of P' entails that $P \cap A' = \emptyset$, i.e., no atom can be assumed in A' that is already present as a fact in P.

Example 2. Suppose we have the following program $P_1 = \{r_1 : a \leftarrow not\ b,\ r_2 : b \leftarrow c\}$ with the only answer set $I_1 = \{a\}$. Furthermore, suppose we have the explanation frame $\mathcal{F}_1 = (P_1, \emptyset, \{c\})$ and a CE problem $\mathcal{P}_1 = \langle I_1, \{a\}, \{b\} \rangle$. Then, a CA for $\mathcal{P}_1$ is $P'_1 = P_1$, $I'_2 = \{b\}$, and $A' = \{c\}$. Intuitively, in the CA, the original rules are preserved, but we additionally have to assume c to derive b.

Example 3. Consider the program $P_2 = \{r_3 : a \vee b,\ r_4 : b \leftarrow a\}$ with the only answer set $I_2 = \{b\}$ and the explanation frame $\mathcal{F}_2 = (P_2, \emptyset, \emptyset)$. The only CA for $\mathcal{P}_2 = \langle I_2, \{b\}, \{a\} \rangle$ under $\mathcal{F}_2$ is $P'_2 = P_2 \setminus \{r_4\}$, $I'_2 = \{a\}$, and $A' = \emptyset$, since as long as r_4 is there, it is not possible to have a in an answer set.

The following example illustrates that a CA does not always exist.

Example 4 (Ex. 2 cont.). The explanation frame $\mathcal{F}_1$ and CE problem $\langle I_1, \{a\}, \{c\} \rangle$ have no CA, since having c in some answer set would require $c \in A'$ which is prohibited by condition (ii) of Definition 3.

Counterfactual accounts play an important role in our definition of contrastive explanation, but first we introduce the concept of a counterfactual explanation.

Definition 4. Let $\mathcal{F} = (P, S, A)$ be an explanation frame and $\mathcal{P} = \langle I, E, F \rangle$ a CE problem for $\mathcal{F}$. A counterfactual explanation for $\mathcal{P}$ is any tuple $\langle Q_1, Q_2, Q_\Delta \rangle$ such that

(i) there is some CA P', I', A' for $\langle I, E, F \rangle$ under $\mathcal{F}$,
(ii) $Q_1 \subseteq P$ and $Q_1^I \models a$ for every $a \in E$,
(iii) $Q_2 \subseteq P' \cup A'$ and $Q_2^{I'} \models a$ for every $a \in F$,
(iv) $Q_\Delta = P \setminus P'$,
(v) Q_1 is lexicographic $\subseteq$-minimal w.r.t. (P', Q_Δ) satisfying (ii), and
(vi) Q_2 is $\subseteq$-minimal satisfying (iii).

Here, Q_1 is lexicographic $\subseteq$-smaller than Q_1' if either $(Q_1 \cap P') \subset (Q_1' \cap P')$ or $(Q_1 \cap P') = (Q_1' \cap P')$ and $(Q_1 \cap Q_\Delta) \subseteq (Q_1' \cap Q_\Delta)$. The intuition behind this definition is as follows: Q_1 are rules that allow to derive the explanandum concisely, where we give preference to derivations that use few rules from the program P' that the explanation system assumes is known to the explainee, and thus involve rather rules that have to change for establishing the foil. Similarly, Q_2 are rules that can derive the foil in the counterfactual account. Both Q_1 and Q_2 are required to be subset-minimal to ensure the the focus is on rules which are relevant. The set Q_Δ simply contains all rules that have to change for the counterfactual account, and it allows to assess which rules have to be discarded in order to achieve the contrast. Note that we do not explicitly provide the set A', as the set of used assumptions can always be extracted from Q_2.

Example 5 (Ex. 2 cont.). Recall explanation frame $\mathcal{F}_1 = (P_1, \emptyset, \{c, d\})$, CE problem $\mathcal{P}_1 = \langle I_1, \{a\}, \{b\} \rangle$, and CA $P_1' = P_1$, $I_1' = \{b\}$, $A_1' = \{c\}$.

A counterfactual explanation is thus $\langle \{r_1\}, \{r_2, c\}, \emptyset \rangle$, since r_1 can derive a under P_1 and I_1, whereas rules r_2 and c derive b under P' and I_1'.

Definition 5. *Given an explanation frame $\mathcal{F} = (P, S, A)$ and a CE problem $\mathcal{P} = \langle I, E, F \rangle$ for $\mathcal{F}$, a tuple $\langle C_1, C_2, C_\Delta \rangle$ is a* contrastive explanation (CE) *for $\mathcal{P}$ if there is a counterfactual explanation $\langle Q_1, Q_2, Q_\Delta \rangle$ for $\mathcal{P}$ such that (i) $C_1 = Q_1 \setminus (Q_2 \cup S)$, (ii) $C_2 = Q_2 \setminus (Q_1 \cup S)$, and (iii) $C_\Delta = Q_\Delta \setminus S$.*

The idea is that in accordance with Lipton's difference condition (cf. Sect. 2.2), a contrastive explanation cites a difference between the casual derivation of the explanandum and the counterfactual casual derivation of the foil, i.e., rules which derive the explanandum under P and I and rules which derive the foil under the counterfactual without the rules shared by Q_1 and Q_2. Furthermore, the explanation also includes which rules differ in the original program and the counterfactual account (C_Δ). The set of fixed rules S further projects away information which should not be presented to the explainee.

Example 6 (Ex. 3 cont.). For the explanation frame $\mathcal{F}_2 = (P_2, \emptyset, \emptyset)$ and answer set $I_2 = \{b\}$, the only CA for $\mathcal{P}_2 = \langle I_2, \{b\}, \{a\} \rangle$ is $P_2' = P_2 \setminus \{r_4\}$, $I_2' = \{a\}$, and $A_2' = \emptyset$. The single CE for $\mathcal{P}_2$ under $\mathcal{F}_2$ is $\langle \emptyset, \emptyset, \{r_4\} \rangle$. Intuitively, this explanation says that a is true instead of b since we have r_4 in the program P_2.

Example 7. Consider the program $P_3 = \{r_5 : a \leftarrow c, \ r_6 : a \leftarrow d, \ r_7 : b \leftarrow e, \ r_8 : c, \ r_9 : d\}$ with answer set $I_3 = \{a, c, d\}$, and suppose we have $\mathcal{F}_3 = (P_3, \emptyset, \mathcal{A}_{P_3})$. For the CE problem $\langle I_3, \{a\}, \{b\} \rangle$, we have four potential CAs, as there are two ways to derive a where each requires two rules. This results in the following CEs: $\langle \{r_6, r_9\}, \{r_7, \ e\}, \{r_9\} \rangle$, $\langle \{r_5, r_8\}, \{r_7, \ e\}, \{c\} \rangle$, $\langle \{r_6, r_9\}, \{r_7, \ e\}, \{r_6\} \rangle$, and $\langle \{r_5, r_8\}, \{r_7, \ e\}, \{r_5\} \rangle$.

Even though removing one of four rules is enough to hinder the derivation of a, requiring Q_1 to be minimal forces the explanations to include both rules needed for the derivation.

Those examples nicely demonstrate some basic properties of our notion. However, its adequacy is better illustrated by the following example.

Example 8. Let us revisit the crow/magpie example from the preliminaries. Encoding the classifier and the instance as an ASP program, we obtain

$$P_4 = \{\ r_{10} : bird \leftarrow feathers, beak, shape,\ r_{11} : crow \leftarrow bird, darkwings,$$
$$r_{12} : magpie \leftarrow bird, whitewings,\ r_{13} : feathers,\ r_{14} : beak,$$
$$r_{15} : shape,\ r_{16} : darkwings\ \}$$

with the single answer set $I = \{\ crow,\ feathers,\ beak,\ shape,\ darkwings\}$ indicating that the bird is a crow.

Suppose now our current explanation frame is $\mathcal{F}_0 = (P_4, S_0, A_0)$ where $S_0 = \emptyset$, $A_0 = \{whitewings\}$, i.e., the common knowledge is empty, and the potential alternative fact is that the bird in the scene has white wings. Furthermore, the question "Why crow instead of magpie?" can be encoded as the CE problem $\langle I, \{crow\}, \{magpie\}\rangle$. For example, we could obtain the following contrastive explanation:

$$\langle\{r_{10}, r_{16}\}, \{r_{11}, whitewings\}, \{r_{16}\}\rangle$$

Intuitively, this can be read as "The animal was classified as a crow instead of a magpie, since it is a crow if it is a bird and has dark wings, and there are dark wings, whereas it would have been a magpie if it is a bird and has white wings, but there were dark wings".

Let us consider $\mathcal{F}_1 = (P_4, S_1, A_0)$, where S_1 is P_4 without all facts. The intuition is that the explainee is sure the classifier works correctly and wants an explanation based on the feature instances alone. This yields the contrastive explanation

$$\langle\{r_{16}\}, \{whitewings\}, \{r_{16}\}\rangle$$

which can be read as "The animal was classified as a crow instead of a magpie, since there are dark wings, whereas it would have been a magpie, if there were white wings".

As can be seen from the above example, there is some intuitive reading of the provided explanations. It is also worth studying how our contrastive explanations could be automatically translated into natural language to make them readable to non-experts. *Controlled natural language* [41] or large-language models might be useful in this regard. Furthermore, incorporating domain-specific knowledge or rule labeling, like it is done in xclingo [6], could be of use.

The existence of CEs depends on the existence of counterfactual accounts.

Theorem 1. *A CE problem* $\mathcal{P} = \langle I, E, F\rangle$ *for an explanation frame* $\mathcal{F} = (P, S, A)$ *has some contrastive explanation iff there is a CA for* $\mathcal{P}$.

Proof. Clearly, by Definition 5, if a contrastive explanation exists then some counterfactual account exists. So assume we have some CA P', I', A'. By definition of the reduct, it follows that $P^I \models a$ for every $a \in E$ and $(P' \cup A')^{I'} \models b$ for every $b \in F$. Hence, there are Q_1, Q_2, Q_Δ satisfying Definition 4, and thus they form a counterfactual explanation which means that a contrastive explanation exists. □

We have mentioned earlier that we image the explanation process to be a potential dialogue, where the explanation frame, i.e., the set of fixed rules S and assumptions

A, is evolving. This can mean that the explainee discards assumables after seeing an explanation utilising them or it can refer to an update in S. The latter for example being the inclusion of rules which were already presented in a CE. The relationship between the possible CEs and the set S is described by the following property.

Proposition 1. *Let $\mathcal{F}_1 = (P, S_1, A)$ and $\mathcal{F}_2 = (P, S_2, A)$ be explanation frames such that $S_1 \subseteq S_2$, and P be a CE problem for $\mathcal{F}_1$ and $\mathcal{F}_2$. If $\mathcal{X}$ is a CE for P w.r.t. $\mathcal{F}_2$, then $\mathcal{X}$ is a CE for P w.r.t. $\mathcal{F}_1$.*

4   Applications

We next describe how CEs can be utilised in example applications. In particular, we cover CEs for ASP-based classifiers and planning.

4.1   Decision Sets

Decision sets [28] are rule-based classifiers, which given an instance of certain features assign a class. We only consider discrete classifiers which can be expressed using ASP.

We assume a denumerable set of features $F = \{1, \ldots, n\}$ and a denumerable set (called domain) D_f for each feature $f \in F$. Now, an instance I is an assignment of features to a value in their domain. Formally, $I \subseteq \{(f, v) \mid f \in F, v \in D_f\}$ such that for any feature $f \in F$, $|\{(f, v) \mid v \in D_f\}| = 1$. The set of all possible instances is denoted by $\mathcal{I}$. A discrete classifier is a function $c : \mathcal{I} \to \mathcal{C}$, where $\mathcal{C}$ is a denumerable set of classes. A rule-based classifier implements such an abstract classifier as follows. An instance I is expressed as a set M_I of facts, where for each $(f, v) \in I$ there is a corresponding fact $feat(f, v)$ in M_I. Furthermore, the function c is represented as a stratified ASP program R which, in conjunction with M_I, yields the single answer set A, i.e., $AS(R \cup M_I) = A$, where $class(c) \in A$ for exactly one $c \in \mathcal{C}$ representing the result of the classification. A common question arising in this setting is "Why was instance I classified as c_1 instead of c_2?". A potential answer is to provide alternative feature assignments such that the set of features taking on a different value is minimal. The question can be expressed as the CE problem $\langle A, \{c_1\}, \{c_2\}\rangle$ for the explanation frame $(R \cup M_I, R, \{feature(f, v) \mid (f, v) \in J, J \in \mathcal{I}\})$. The assumables are simply all possible instances of the features, and the common knowledge includes all the rules of the classifier. Any contrastive explanation will now be of the form $\langle F^e, F^a, F^d\rangle$, where F^d are facts corresponding to the features instances responsible for c_1, and F^a are the hypothetical instances which would need to be assumed to flip the classification.

We have already seen the crow/magpie example which is a particular instantiation of the pattern described above. As another use case, consider the following rule used to decide which trauma patients do not require cervical spine imaging. A trauma patient does not require imaging, if the patient is alert and stable, there is no focal neurological deficit, there is no altered level of consciousness, the patient is not intoxicated, there is no midline spinal tenderness, and there is no distracting injury. To compose this rule into a classifier, we extract the following Boolean features: (1) alert and stable, (2) focal neurological deficit, (3) altered level of consciousness, (4) intoxication, (5) midline spinal tenderness, and (6) distracting injury.

An ASP-based classifier (data integrity constraints omitted) is given by

$$R = \left\{ \begin{array}{l} r_{17} : class(req) \leftarrow not\ class(nreq) \\ r_{18} : class(nreq) \leftarrow feat(1,1), feat(2,0), \ldots, feat(6,0) \end{array} \right\},$$

where the classes req and $nreq$ represent whether imaging is, resp., is not, required.

Furthermore, consider the instance $I = \{(1,1),(2,0),(3,0),(4,1),(5,0),(6,0)\}$ describing an alert and stable but intoxicated trauma patient. The corresponding ASP representation is given by $M_I = \{feat(1,1), feat(2,0), feat(3,0), feat(4,1), feat(5,0), feat(6,0)\}$ and $AS(R \cup M_I) = \{A\}$ where $class(req) \in A$ indicating that spinal imaging is required.

Naturally, one might ask why this is the case. This task can be formalised using the schema from above resulting in the CE $\langle C_1, C_2, C_\Delta \rangle$, where $C_1 = \emptyset$, $C_\Delta = \{feat(4,0)\}$ and $C_2 = \{feat(4,1)\}$. The explanation can be read as saying that the imaging would not be required if the patient was not intoxicated.

4.2 Planning

Another application we are going to show case is AI planning. For this purpose, consider the following ASP encoding of a simplistic STRIPS planning problem with time horizon $t = 2$, fluents p, q, and actions a, b, c. Furthermore, the actions have the following pre- and postconditions: action a has precondition p and postconditions q and $\neg p$, b has precondition q and postconditions $\neg q$ and r, and c has preconditions p and q and postcondition r. The planning goal is r, i.e., we need a plan ending in a state in which r holds. The planning problem can be encoded as an ASP program P consisting of the following rules:

- $occ(a,i) \lor occ(b,i) \lor occ(c,i) \leftarrow$ for $0 < i \leq t$ stating that at each point in time i some action (a,b or c) has to occur,
- $\leftarrow occ(x,i), pre(y,i), not\ holds(y, i-1)$ for $0 < i \leq t$ and $x, y \in \{a, b, c\}$ which says that an action can only occur after its preconditions hold,
- $holds(x,i) \leftarrow holds(x, i-1), not\ occdel(x,i)$ for $0 < i \leq t$ and $x \in \{a, b, c\}$ encoding that fluents have inertia unless they have been removed,
- $holds(x,i) \leftarrow occ(x,i), add(x,y)$ for $0 < i \leq t$, $x \in \{a, b, c\}$ and $y \in \{p, q\}$ enforcing that positive postconditions are upheld,
- $occdel(x,i) \leftarrow occ(x,i), del(x,y)$ for $0 < i \leq t$, $x \in \{a, b, c\}$ and $y \in \{p, q\}$ enforcing that negative postconditions are upheld,
- $\leftarrow holds(r,t)$ formalising the goal, and
- facts encoding the pre- and postconditions $pre(a,p)$, $pre(b,q)$, $pre(c,p)$, $pre(c,q)$, $add(a,q)$, $del(a,p)$, $add(b,r)$, $del(b,q)$, and $add(c,r)$.

The program has exactly one answer set I containing $occ(a,1)$ and $occ(b,2)$. The user might now ask the planner why b was chosen as the second action instead of c? This can be formalised as the CE problem $\langle I, \{occ(b,2)\}, \{occ(c,2)\} \rangle$. Suppose we have the explanation frame $(P, S_0, \emptyset)$ where $S_0 = \emptyset$, and the user does not consider any potential assumptions. Then, a possible contrastive explanation is $\langle C_1^1, C_2^1, C_\Delta^1 \rangle$ where $C_1^1 = C_2^1 = \emptyset$, and $C_\Delta^1 = \{\leftarrow occ(c,2), pre(c,p), not\ holds(p,1)\}$, which intuitively states that c cannot occur at time point 2 as its precondition p does not hold at 1. There is more than one contrastive explanation, another one is $\langle C_1^2, C_2^2, C_\Delta^2 \rangle$, where $C_1^2 = C_2^2 = \emptyset$, and $C_\Delta^2 = \{occdel(p, 1) \leftarrow occ(a, 1), del(a, p)\}$, stating that b occurs instead of c, since p gets removed by a after time point 1.

For these explanations, we have assumed that the explainee has to interpret the presented rules. In practice, an explanation system could also use a translation of ASP into the already mentioned *controlled natural language* [41], potentially enhanced with domain specific preprocessing, to produce more readable contrastive explanations.

It is also possible to fix the rules of the planning problem leaving only the facts. We thus consider a new explanation frame $(P, S_1, \emptyset)$, where S_1 are the non-facts of P. Any contrastive explanation consists of facts only now which potentially makes them easier to parse for the explainee. In our case, the explanations are $\langle \{\emptyset, \emptyset, \{pre(c, p)\} \rangle$ and $\langle \emptyset, \emptyset, \{del(a, p)\} \rangle$. The former is saying that b occurs instead of c since c has precondition p, and the latter states that the reason is that $\neg p$ is a postcondition of a.

5   Computational Complexity

We assume basic familiarity with complexity theory [37] and start by investigating the complexity of deciding whether a contrastive explanation exists.

Theorem 2. *Given an explanation frame* $\mathcal{F} = (P, S, A)$ *and a CE problem* $\mathcal{P} = \langle I, E, F \rangle$ *for* $\mathcal{F}$, *deciding whether there is some contrastive explanation for* $\mathcal{P}$ *under* $\mathcal{F}$ *is (i)* Σ_2^p-complete in general and (ii) NP-complete for normal programs.

Proof. (Sketch) By Theorem 1, the problem amounts to checking whether some CA P', I', A' for $\mathcal{P}$ exists. We start by showing membership, which is obtained by the following procedure. First guess P', I', and A', and then check whether conditions (i)–(iv) of Definition 3 are satisfied. Note that verifying condition (iii) needs an NP-oracle in general but can be done in polynomial time if P is normal. Furthermore, we do not need to check condition (v), since even if it were violated, there would exist some CA P'', I'', A'' such that $P'' \supset P'$.

The hardness parts can be shown by a simple reduction from brave reasoning on logic programs, where we want to know whether an atom p occurs in some answer set of a given program P_0, which is Σ_2^p-hard (resp., NP-hard) to decide for general (resp., normal) programs. We construct $P = \{H(r) \leftarrow B(r), q' \mid r \in P_0\} \cup \{q \leftarrow not\ q',\ q' \leftarrow not\ q\}$, where q, q' are fresh atoms, and let $I = \{q\}, S = P, A = \emptyset$. Furthermore, we let $E = \{q\}$ and $F = \{q'\}$. Clearly, $I \in AS(P)$ and some CA exists for $\mathcal{P}$ iff some $I' \in AS(P)$ exists such that $q' \in I'$, which by construction is equivalent to $q' \in I''$ for some $I'' \in AS(P_0)$. $\square$

For recognising a counterfactual account, we have the following result which will be helpful for showing the corresponding result for CEs.

Theorem 3. *Given an explanation frame* $\mathcal{F} = (P, S, A)$ *and a CE problem* $\mathcal{P} = \langle I, E, F \rangle$ *for* $\mathcal{F}$, *deciding whether* P', A', I' *is a CA for* $\mathcal{P}$ *is (i)* Π_2^p-complete in general and (ii) coNP-complete for normal programs.

Proof. (Sketch) For membership, consider the following procedure. Since we have P', A', and I' checking conditions (i), (ii), and (iv) of Definition 3 can be done in polynomial time. Checking (iii) requires a call to a coNP oracle. Assuming all of those conditions hold, it remains to check condition (v). The complementary problem can be solved by guessing a larger program and checking the conditions (i)–(iv). Hence, this is in Π_2^p and so is the overall problem. For normal programs, condition (iii) can be checked in polynomial time and thus the problem is in coNP.

For hardness, suppose we are given a program P_1 and want to check whether it has some answer set, which is Π_2^p-hard (resp., coNP-hard) to decide for general (resp., normal) programs. To this end, we construct a program P with rules

- $q \leftarrow not\ q'$,
- $q' \leftarrow not\ q$,
- q'', and
- $H(r) \leftarrow B(r), q', q''$, for each $r \in P_0$,

where q'' is a fresh atom. We then let $I = \{q, q''\}$, $S = P \setminus \{q''\}$, $A = \emptyset$. By construction, $I \in AS(P)$. Now, let $E = \{q\}$ and $F = \{q'\}$. Then, $P' = P \setminus \{q''\}$, $I' = \{q'\}$, and $A' = \emptyset$ are a CA iff P_1 has no answer set. $\square$

Now for recognising a contrastive explanation, we have the following result, where DP denotes the class of problems decidable using single calls to an NP and coNP-oracle respectively, and the class D_2^p is defined—mutatis mutandis—using oracles one level higher on the polynomial hierarchy.

Theorem 4. *Given an explanation frame $\mathcal{F} = (P, S, A)$ and a CE problem $\mathcal{P} = \langle I, E, F \rangle$, deciding whether $\langle C_1, C_2, C_\Delta \rangle$ is a contrastive explanation for $\mathcal{P}$ is (i) D_2^p-complete in general and (ii) DP-complete for normal programs.*

Proof. (Sketch) We start with membership. Note that $P' = P \setminus C_\Delta$ and $A' = C_2 \setminus P$. Checking whether both are part of some CA amounts to testing conditions (i)–(v) of Definition 3, where (iii) requires a call to a Σ_2^p oracle (resp., NP oracle) and (iv) a call to a Π_2^p oracle (resp., coNP oracle). Checking whether a counterfactual explanation exists from which C_1 and C_2 can be obtained can also be included in the first oracle call. Hence, we have D_2^p-membership in general and DP-membership for normal programs.

We recall the instances of deciding CE existence constructed from P_0 and P_1 in Theorem 2 and 3. We merge those constructions to check whether it holds for given P_0 and P_1 that P_0 has some answer set containing p, whereas P_1 has no answer set. To this end, we simply take P to be the union of both. We then let $I = \{q, q''\}$, $S = P \setminus \{q''\}$, and $A = \emptyset$. Furthermore, we define $E = \{q\}$ and $F = \{p\}$. Then, $\langle \emptyset, \emptyset, \{q''\} \rangle$ is a contrastive explanation iff P_0 has some answer set that contains p and P_1 has no answer set. $\square$

Finally, we consider the problem of computing some contrastive explanation. For our complexity characterisations, we are going to rely on the notion of *witness oracles* [5,24] and their generalisation to the polynomial hierarchy [42]. We recall that $\mathsf{FP}^{\Sigma_k^p}[log, wit]$ is the class of search problems for which some solution can be computed with logarithmically many calls to a Σ_k^p oracle, $k \geq 1$, in polynomial time; here a witness oracle returns, on input of an instance of a problem in Σ_k^p, in case it is a yes-instance also a "witness", i.e., a polynomial size proof (or certificate) that can be checked with an Σ_{k-1}^p oracle in polynomial time. In particular, for $k = 1$ the class is $\mathsf{FP}^{\mathsf{NP}}[log, wit]$ and a witness oracle for SAT would return a satisfying assignment.

Theorem 5. *Given an explanation frame $\mathcal{F} = (P, S, A)$ and a CE problem $\mathcal{P} = \langle I, E, F\rangle$, computing a CE for $\mathcal{P}$ is (i) $\mathsf{FP}^{\Sigma_2^p}[log, wit]$-complete for general programs and (ii) $\mathsf{FP}^{\mathsf{NP}}[log, wit]$-complete for normal programs.*

Proof. (Sketch) For membership, we can compute some CA P', A', I' using a Σ_2^p witness oracle for the conditions (i)–(iii) of Definition 3 with binary search on the size $|P'|$ of a largest P' over the range $|S|, \ldots, |P|$. (To test whether a CE exists, we can make an initial oracle call whether some P' of size greater or equal to $|S|$ exists.) Similarly, a counterfactual explanation $\mathcal{X} = \langle Q_1, Q_2, Q_\Delta\rangle$ can be computed with the oracle and binary search on the sizes $|Q_1 \cap P'|, |Q_1 \cap Q_\Delta|, |Q_2|$ over $0, \ldots, |P'|$, resp., $|Q_\Delta|, |P|$. From $\mathcal{X}$, a CE is then easily obtained, which shows membership in $\mathsf{FP}^{\Sigma_2^p}[log, wit]$. In case of normal programs, an NP witness oracle is sufficient, and we obtain membership in $\mathsf{FP}^{\mathsf{NP}}[log, wit]$.

The hardness proof is is by reduction of the following $\mathsf{FP}^{\Sigma_2^p}[log, wit]$-complete variant of QBF Solving [5,42]. Given a QBF $\Phi = \exists X \forall Y E(X, Y)$ where $X = X_1 \cup X_2$, compute some assignment σ to X_1 such that (i) $\Phi_\sigma = \exists X_2 \forall Y E(X_1\sigma, X_2, Y)$ evaluates to true, and (ii) σ is minimal, i.e., no $\sigma' \neq \sigma$ satisfies (i) such that $\sigma'(x_i) = 1$ implies $\sigma(x_i) = 1$, for each $x_i \in X_1$; seen as a Boolean vector, σ is pointwise minimal. For the reduction, we may look at the saturation encoding of Eiter and Gottlob [10] that proved the Σ_2^p-hardness of brave reasoning via an encoding of a QBF. Briefly, in that encoding, for each assignment σ to X the model $M_\sigma = \{x_i \in X \mid \sigma(x_i) = 1\} \cup \{x_i' \in X \mid \sigma(x_i) = 0\} \cup Y \cup Y' \cup \{w\}$ is a minimal model of the logic program P_0 constructed containing w iff $\forall Y E(X\sigma, Y)$ evaluates to true; furthermore, every minimal model containing w is of this form. The program P_0 contains a guessing rule $x_i \vee x_i'$ for each variable $x_i \in X$, while the rest are rules defining atoms in $Y \cup Y' \cup \{w\}$. If we set the foil to $F = Y \cup Y' \cup \{w\}$, then none of these atoms can be in A'. So only atoms in $X \cup X'$ can be assumed. To avoid that both x_i and x_i' are assumed, we then add to the program P that we constructed above from P_0 the rule $\leftarrow x_i, x_i'$ for all $x_i \in X$. Then, for S consisting of the latter rules, $I = \{q\}, A = \mathcal{A}_P, E = \{q\}, F = Y \cup Y' \cup \{w\}$, some contrastive explanation exists iff Φ evaluates to true. Furthermore, we can add the constraint $r_{x_i} : \leftarrow x_i$ for each $x_i \in X_1$ to P. Its effect is that whenever the answer set I' of $P' \cup A'$ encodes that x_i is assigned true, then the rule r_{x_i} must not be in P', and hence is in C_Δ. Thus, a contrastive explanation encodes a minimal assignment σ.

For normal programs, $\mathsf{FP}^{\mathsf{NP}}[log, wit]$-hardness can be shown by a reduction from the QBF problem above where $\forall Y$ is void and E is a conjunction of clauses $\gamma_i, i = 1, \ldots, m$ on X; this is known as computing some X_1-minimal model, which is well-known to be $\mathsf{FP}^{\mathsf{NP}}[log, wit]$-complete [5,7,24]. Let P contain the following rules:

- $q \leftarrow not\ s$,
- $c_j \leftarrow x, not\ q$, for each $x \in \gamma_j$, $c_j \leftarrow x', not\ q$, for each $\neg x \in \gamma_j$,
- $x_i' \leftarrow not\ x_i$, for each $x_i \in X$,

- r_{sat} : $s \leftarrow c_1, \ldots, c_m$,
- r_{x_i} : $f_{x_i} \leftarrow x_i$, not f_{x_i}, for each $x_i \in X_1$ (recall that $X = X_1 \cup X_2$) where f_{x_i} is a fresh atom.

Then $I = \{q, x_1', \ldots, x_n'\}$ is an answer set of P. Let $S = P \setminus \{r_{x_i} \mid x_i \in X_1\}$ and $A = X$, and set $E = \{q\}$ and $F = \{s\}$. Any CA for $\langle I, E, F \rangle$ assumes some subset $X' \subseteq X$ such that in P' some rule with head c_j fires (clause γ_j is satisfied) and also the rule r_{sat} fires. Furthermore, by construction, $r_{x_i} \notin P'$ must hold for each $x_i \in X'$. As P' is maximal, the part $X' \cap X_1$ must be minimal. In any counterfactual explanation $\langle Q_1, Q_2, Q_\Delta \rangle$, Q_Δ must contain all r_{x_i} for $x_i \in X_1$; then in any CE $\langle C_1, C_2, C_\Delta \rangle$ induced by it, C_Δ encodes the minimal assignment σ to X_1.   □

6 Related Work

To the best of our knowledge, the first explicit formalisations of contrastive explanation in a logical setting were given by Kean [26] and Ignatiev et al. [22,31]. The former considered propositional knowledge bases under classical semantics which are obviously monotonic and thus quite different from ASP. An explanation there is first defined through finding sentences that entail the fact and the foil, respectively. A partial model of each sentence is then extracted, which is a smallest set of literals describing the entailment. Kean's contrastive explanation is then the symmetric difference of a partial model for the entailment of the fact and foil, respectively.

On the other hand, Ignatiev et al. [22] considered contrastive explanation in the setting of machine learning like, for example, decision trees and other discrete classifiers. In their definition, a contrastive explanation is a minimal set of feature instances which, if having taken another value, would have changed the prediction outcome. This differs from our explanations in Sect. 4.1, as they do not support specifying a particular foil.

Recently, Eiter et al. [11] presented a use-case of contrastive explanation for *visual question answering* using ASP. Their approach uses counterfactual scenes to answer why an answer was provided instead of a foil. While similar, their work is not problem independent but engineered for this single application.

Another formalisation of contrastive explanation was given by Miller [33] for Halpern and Pearl's *structural causal models* [19,21]. This formalism is not as expressive as ASP but already has well established notions of what constitutes an explanation [20]. The main difference between the approach of Miller and ours is that for Miller, the internals of the model are never part of any explanation.

Contrastive explanation also has been studied for planning [27]. However, there the questions are answered by contrasting the current plan with one where the foil is necessarily included. This differs from our notion where we highlight which parts of the model would need to be changed.

Other related work is on *model-based diagnosis* which, in one incarnation, also employs abductive reasoning to find out which components of a system might be malfunctioning [9]. The underlying idea of "deactivating" some components in a counterfactual setting and then checking the outcome in this setting is quite similar to our usage of counterfactual accounts. However, the result of diagnosis is generally just the assumptions which have to be made to "fix" the system, whereas our contrastive explanations also include relevant rules needed for the derivation of fact and foil, respectively.

In logic programming and specifically the ASP community, we would like to mention related work on explainability [16,38,40,44] and also *debugging* [4,35,36], cf. Fandinno and Schulz [17] for a survey. As mentioned in the introduction, those ASP explanation approaches generally try to answer non-contrastive questions by providing justifications, whereas debugging aims to give answers to the question of why a program has no answer set at all or not the one the programmer intended. Some debugging approaches are even interactive [36]. However, the salient differences between contrastive explanation and debugging are that explanation is not necessarily aimed at an engineer and that the program in question is mostly likely working as it is supposed to. The goal is more to "convince" and provide further insights for the explainee regarding the program's reasoning and less to point out potential flaws in the program.

At first glance, *model reconciliation* [34,43] in ASP seems quite similar to the problem we consider here, but there are several differences. Informally, in model reconciliation, one is given two programs P_1, P_2 and a formula that is (bravely) entailed by P_1 but not by P_2. The goal is then to find a minimal way to adapt P_2 such that it also entails the formula. The motivating use case here is that P_1 is the model of some system, whereas P_2 is the—potentially incomplete or flawed—model of a human. The main difference between model reconciliation and our contrastive explanation is that the former only considers a single formula and not a pair of fact and foil. Furthermore, as P_1 already entails the formula, rules deriving it can be extracted and added to the second program, making computation somewhat easier.

Further related work in the area of logic programming are *view updates* [39] and *belief revision* [47]. The former tries to update a logic program through abduction, incorporating new information that is needed to entail (or not entail) a given literal. Belief revision in the context of ASP is even more general and aimed at updating a program with new rules in such a way that the program is still consistent.

7   Conclusion and Future Work

In this work, we have provided a formalisation of contrastive explanation for ASP which aims to highlight why an explanandum (or fact) P is in a given answer set instead of a particular contrast or foil Q based on counterfactual reasoning over the underlying program. Our explanations are sets of rules which aim at emphasising which rules were required for the fact and foil, respectively. Inspired by Lipton's difference condition [30], the respective rule sets are disjoint thus hiding any shared causes and providing concise explanations. We illustrated the usefulness of or notions on example applications, and we characterised their computational complexity.

For future work, we intend to provide a prototypical implementation of an explanation system based on our definitions and see whether they can be made user-friendly using translations to controlled natural language and/or connecting them with large language models. Ideally, those implementations will be achieved using ASP itself. Investigating abductive logic programming [12,25] in this regard also seems promising. Another worthwhile direction is to generalise our definitions for more fine-tuned selections of counterfactuals to consider and which sets of rules to return by imposing suitable preferences. Finally, it would be interesting to develop stateful notions of contrastive explanations in which a history of CE problems over an evolving explanation frame may be considered to provide more useful explanations, which might also be presented in an interactive setting.

Acknowledgments. This work was supported by funding from the Bosch Center for Artificial Intelligence. Furthermore, Tobias Geibinger is a recipient of a DOC Fellowship of the Austrian Academy of Sciences at the Institute of Logic and Computation at the TU Wien.

References

1. Abels, D., Jordi, J., Ostrowski, M., Schaub, T., Toletti, A., Wanko, P.: Train scheduling with hybrid ASP. In: Balduccini, M., Lierler, Y., Woltran, S. (eds.) LPNMR. LNCS, vol. 11481, pp. 3–17. Springer, Cham (2019). https://doi.org/10.1007/978-3-030-20528-7_1
2. Ali, R., El-Kholany, M.M.S., Gebser, M.: Flexible job-shop scheduling for semiconductor manufacturing with hybrid answer set programming (application paper). In: Hanus, M., Inclezan, D. (eds.) PADL 2023. LNCS, pp. 85–95. Springer, Cham (2023). https://doi.org/10.1007/978-3-031-24841-2_6
3. Beierle, C., Dusso, O., Kern-Isberner, G.: Using answer set programming for a decision support system. In: Baral, C., Greco, G., Leone, N., Terracina, G. (eds.) LPNMR 2005. LNCS (LNAI), vol. 3662, pp. 374–378. Springer, Heidelberg (2005). https://doi.org/10.1007/11546207_30
4. Brain, M., Gebser, M., Pührer, J., Schaub, T., Tompits, H., Woltran, S.: Debugging ASP programs by means of ASP. In: Baral, C., Brewka, G., Schlipf, J. (eds.) LPNMR 2007. LNCS (LNAI), vol. 4483, pp. 31–43. Springer, Heidelberg (2007). https://doi.org/10.1007/978-3-540-72200-7_5
5. Buss, S.R., Krajıcek, J., Takeuti, G.: On provably total functions in bounded arithmetic theories. In: Clote, P., Krajıcek, J. (eds.) Arithmetic, Proof Theory and Computational Complexity, pp. 116–161. Oxford University Press (1993)
6. Cabalar, P., Fandinno, J., Muñiz, B.: A system for explainable answer set programming. In: Technical Communications of the 36th International Conference on Logic Programming (ICLP 2020). EPTCS, vol. 325, pp. 124–136 (2020). https://doi.org/10.4204/EPTCS.325.19
7. Chen, Z., Toda, S.: The complexity of selecting maximal solutions. Inf. Comput. **119**(2), 231–239 (1995). https://doi.org/10.1006/inco.1995.1087
8. Comploi-Taupe, R., Francescutto, G., Schenner, G.: Applying incremental answer set solving to product configuration. In: Proceedings o the 26th ACM International Systems and Software Product Line Conference (SPLC 2022), pp. 150–155. ACM (2022). https://doi.org/10.1145/3503229.3547069
9. Console, L., Torasso, P.: A spectrum of logical definitions of model-based diagnosis. Comput. Intell. **7**, 133–141 (1991). https://doi.org/10.1111/j.1467-8640.1991.tb00388.x
10. Dantsin, E., Eiter, T., Gottlob, G., Voronkov, A.: Complexity and expressive power of logic programming. ACM Comput. Surv. **33**(3), 374–425 (2001). https://doi.org/10.1145/502807.502810
11. Eiter, T., Geibinger, T., Ruiz, N.H., Oetsch, J.: A logic-based approach to contrastive explainability for neurosymbolic visual question answering. In: Proceedings of the 32rd International Joint Conference on Artificial Intelligence (IJCAI 2023) (2023). https://www.ijcai.org/proceedings/2023/408

12. Eiter, T., Gottlob, G., Leone, N.: Abduction from logic programs: semantics and complexity. Theor. Comput. Sci. **189**(1), 129–177 (1997). https://doi.org/10.1016/S0304-3975(96)00179-X
13. Erdem, E., Gelfond, M., Leone, N.: Applications of answer set programming. AI Mag. **37**(3), 53–68 (2016). https://doi.org/10.1609/aimag.v37i3.2678
14. Erdem, E., Oztok, U.: Generating explanations for biomedical queries. Theory Pract. Logic Program. **15**(1), 35–78 (2015). https://doi.org/10.1017/S1471068413000598
15. Falkner, A., Friedrich, G., Schekotihin, K., Taupe, R., Teppan, E.C.: Industrial applications of answer set programming. KI - Künstliche Intell. **32**(2), 165–176 (2018). https://doi.org/10.1007/s13218-018-0548-6
16. Fandinno, J.: Deriving conclusions from non-monotonic cause-effect relations. Theory Pract. Logic Program. **16**(5–6), 670–687 (2016). https://doi.org/10.1017/S1471068416000466
17. Fandinno, J., Schulz, C.: Answering the "why" in answer set programming - A survey of explanation approaches. Theory Pract. Logic Program. **19**(2), 114–203 (2019). https://doi.org/10.1017/S1471068418000534
18. Gelfond, M., Lifschitz, V.: Classical negation in logic programs and disjunctive databases. New Gener. Comput. **9**, 365–385 (1991)
19. Halpern, J.Y.: A modification of the Halpern-pearl definition of causality. In: Yang, Q., Wooldridge, M.J. (eds.) Proceedings of the 24th International Joint Conference on Artificial Intelligence (IJCAI 2015), pp. 3022–3033. AAAI Press (2015). https://ijcai.org/Abstract/15/427
20. Halpern, J.Y., Pearl, J.: Causes and explanations: a structural-model approach - part II: explanations. In: Proceedings of the 17th International Joint Conference on Artificial Intelligence (IJCAI 2001), pp. 27–34. Morgan Kaufmann (2001)
21. Halpern, J.Y., Pearl, J.: Causes and explanations: a structural-model approach: Part 1: causes. In: Proceedings of the 17th Conference in Uncertainty in Artificial Intelligence (UAI 2001), pp. 194–202. Morgan Kaufmann (2001)
22. Ignatiev, A., Narodytska, N., Asher, N., Marques-Silva, J.: From contrastive to abductive explanations and back again. In: Baldoni, M., Bandini, S. (eds.) AIxIA 2020. LNCS (LNAI), vol. 12414, pp. 335–355. Springer, Cham (2021). https://doi.org/10.1007/978-3-030-77091-4_21
23. Inclezan, D.: An application of answer set programming to the field of second language acquisition. Theory Pract. Logic Program. **15**(1), 1–17 (2015). https://doi.org/10.1017/S1471068413000653
24. Janota, M., Marques-Silva, J.: On the query complexity of selecting minimal sets for monotone predicates. Artif. Intell. **233**, 73–83 (2016). https://doi.org/10.1016/j.artint.2016.01.002
25. Kakas, A.C., Kowalski, R.A., Toni, F.: Abductive logic programming. J. Logic Comput. **2**(6), 719–770 (1992). https://doi.org/10.1093/logcom/2.6.719
26. Kean, A.: A characterization of contrastive explanations computation. In: Lee, H.-Y., Motoda, H. (eds.) PRICAI 1998. LNCS, vol. 1531, pp. 599–610. Springer, Heidelberg (1998). https://doi.org/10.1007/BFb0095304
27. Krarup, B., Krivic, S., Magazzeni, D., Long, D., Cashmore, M., Smith, D.E.: Contrastive explanations of plans through model restrictions. J. Artif. Intell. Res. **72**, 533–612 (2021). https://doi.org/10.1613/jair.1.12813
28. Lakkaraju, H., Bach, S.H., Leskovec, J.: Interpretable decision sets: a joint framework for description and prediction. In: Proceedings of the 22nd ACM SIGKDD International Conference on (KDD 2016), pp. 1675–1684. ACM (2016). https://doi.org/10.1145/2939672.2939874
29. Lifschitz, V.: Answer set programming and plan generation. Artif. Intell. **138**(1–2), 39–54 (2002). https://doi.org/10.1016/S0004-3702(02)00186-8

30. Lipton, P.: Contrastive explanation. R. Inst. Philos. Suppl. **27**, 247–266 (1990). https://doi. org/10.1017/S1358246100005130
31. Marques-Silva, J.: Logic-based explainability in machine learning. In: Bertossi, L., Xiao, G. (eds.) Reasoning Web. Causality, Explanations and Declarative Knowledge. LNCS, pp. 24–104. Springer, Cham (2023). https://doi.org/10.1007/978-3-031-31414-8_2
32. Miller, T.: Explanation in artificial intelligence: insights from the social sciences. Artif. Intell. **267**, 1–38 (2019). https://doi.org/10.1016/j.artint.2018.07.007
33. Miller, T.: Contrastive explanation: a structural-model approach. Knowl. Eng. Rev. **36**, e14 (2021). https://doi.org/10.1017/S0269888921000102
34. Nguyen, V., Stylianos, V.L., Son, T.C., Yeoh, W.: Explainable planning using answer set programming. In: Proceedings of the 17th International Conference on Principles of Knowledge Representation and Reasoning (KR 2020). pp. 662–666 (2020). https://doi.org/10.24963/kr. 2020/66
35. Oetsch, J., Pührer, J., Tompits, H.: Catching the ouroboros: on debugging non-ground answer-set programs. Theory Pract. Log. Program. **10**(4–6), 513–529 (2010). https://doi.org/10. 1017/S1471068410000256
36. Oetsch, J., Pührer, J., Tompits, H.: Stepwise debugging of answer-set programs. Theory Pract. Logic Program. **18**(1), 30–80 (2018). https://doi.org/10.1017/S1471068417000217
37. Papadimitriou, C.H.: Computational Complexity. Addison-Wesley, Boston (1994)
38. Pontelli, E., Son, T.C., Elkhatib, O.: Justifications for logic programs under answer set semantics. Theory Pract. Logic Program. **9**(1), 1–56 (2009). https://doi.org/10.1017/ S1471068408003633
39. Sakama, C., Inoue, K.: Updating extended logic programs through abduction. In: Gelfond, M., Leone, N., Pfeifer, G. (eds.) LPNMR 1999. LNCS (LNAI), vol. 1730, pp. 147–161. Springer, Heidelberg (1999). https://doi.org/10.1007/3-540-46767-X_11
40. Schulz, C., Toni, F.: Justifying answer sets using argumentation. Theory Pract. Logic Program. **16**(1), 59–110 (2016). https://doi.org/10.1017/S1471068414000702
41. Schwitter, R.: Specifying and verbalising answer set programs in controlled natural language. Theory Pract. Logic Program. **18**(3–4), 691–705 (2018). https://doi.org/10.1017/ S1471068418000327
42. Shen, Y., Eiter, T.: Determining inference semantics for disjunctive logic programs. Artif. Intell. **277**, 103165 (2019). https://doi.org/10.1016/j.artint.2019.103165
43. Son, T.C., Nguyen, V., Vasileiou, S.L., Yeoh, W.: Model reconciliation in logic programs. In: Faber, W., Friedrich, G., Gebser, M., Morak, M. (eds.) JELIA 2021. LNCS (LNAI), vol. 12678, pp. 393–406. Springer, Cham (2021). https://doi.org/10.1007/978-3-030-75775-5_26
44. Viegas Damásio, C., Analyti, A., Antoniou, G.: Justifications for logic programming. In: Cabalar, P., Son, T.C. (eds.) LPNMR 2013. LNCS (LNAI), vol. 8148, pp. 530–542. Springer, Heidelberg (2013). https://doi.org/10.1007/978-3-642-40564-8_53
45. Wang, Y., Eiter, T., Zhang, Y., Lin, F.: Witnesses for answer sets of logic programs. ACM Trans. Comput. Logic (2022). https://doi.org/10.1145/3568955
46. Yli-Jyrä, A., Rankooh, M.F., Janhunen, T.: Pruning redundancy in answer set optimization applied to preventive maintenance scheduling. In: Hanus, M., Inclezan, D. (eds.) PADL 2023. LNCS, pp. 279–294. Springer, Cham (2023). https://doi.org/10.1007/978-3-031-24841-2_18
47. Zhuang, Z., Delgrande, J.P., Nayak, A.C., Sattar, A.: Reconsidering AGM-style belief revision in the context of logic programs. In: Proceedings of the 22nd European Conference on Artificial Intelligence (ECAI 2016). Frontiers in Artificial Intelligence and Applications, vol. 285, pp. 671–679. IOS Press (2016). https://doi.org/10.3233/978-1-61499-672-9-671

Short Boolean Formulas as Explanations in Practice

Reijo Jaakkola[1], Tomi Janhunen[1], Antti Kuusisto[1,2](✉),
Masood Feyzbakhsh Rankooh[1], and Miikka Vilander[1]

[1] Tampere University, Tampere, Finland
antti.kuusisto@tuni.fi
[2] University of Helsinki, Helsinki, Finland

Abstract. We investigate explainability via short Boolean formulas in the data model based on unary relations. As an explanation of length k, we take a Boolean formula of length k that minimizes the error with respect to the target attribute to be explained. We first provide novel quantitative bounds for the expected error in this scenario. We then also demonstrate how the setting works in practice by studying three concrete data sets. In each case, we calculate explanation formulas of different lengths using an encoding in Answer Set Programming. The most accurate formulas we obtain achieve errors similar to other methods on the same data sets. However, due to overfitting, these formulas are not necessarily ideal explanations, so we use cross validation to identify a suitable length for explanations. By limiting to shorter formulas, we obtain explanations that avoid overfitting but are still reasonably accurate and also, importantly, human interpretable.

Keywords: Boolean formula size · Explainability · Interpretable AI · Overfitting error · Answer Set Programming · Boolean optimization

1 Introduction

In this article we investigate explainability and classification via short Boolean formulas. As the data model, we use multisets of propositional assignments. This is one of the simplest data representations available—consisting simply of data points and properties—and corresponds precisely to relational models with unary relations. The data is given as a model M with unary relations $p_1, \ldots, p_k$ over its domain W, and furthermore, there is an additional *target predicate* $q \subseteq W$. As classifiers for recognizing q, we produce Boolean formulas φ over $p_1, \ldots, p_k$, and the corresponding error is then the percentage of points in W that disagree on φ and q over W. For each formula length ℓ, a formula producing the minimum error is chosen as a candidate classifier. Longer formulas produce smaller errors, and ultimately the process is halted based on cross validation which shows that the classifier formulas φ begin performing significantly better on training data in comparison to test data, suggesting overfitting.

© The Author(s) 2023
S. Gaggl et al. (Eds.): JELIA 2023, LNAI 14281, pp. 90–105, 2023.
https://doi.org/10.1007/978-3-031-43619-2_7

Importantly, the final classifier formulas φ tend to be short and therefore *explicate* the global behavior of the classifier φ itself in a transparent way. This leads to *inherent interpretability* of our approach. Furthermore, the formulas φ can *also* be viewed as *explanations* of the target predicate q. By limiting to short formulas, we obtain explanations (or classifiers) that avoid overfitting but are still reasonably accurate and also—importantly—human interpretable.

Our contributions include theory, implementation and empirical results. We begin with some theory on the errors of Boolean formulas as explanations. We first investigate general reasons behind overfitting when using Boolean formulas. We also observe, for example, that if all distributions are equally likely, the expected *ideal theoretical error* of a distribution is 25%. The ideal theoretical error is the error of an ideal Boolean classifier for the entire distribution. We proceed by proving novel, quantitative upper and lower bounds on the expected *ideal empirical error* on a data set sampled from a distribution. The ideal empirical error is the smallest error achievable on the data set. Our bounds give concrete information on sample sizes required to avoid overfitting.

We also compute explanation formulas in practice. We use three data sets from the UCI machine learning repository: Statlog (German Credit Data), Breast Cancer Wisconsin (Original) and Ionosphere. We obtain results comparable to other experiments in the literature. In one set of our experiments, the empirical errors for the obtained classifiers for the credit, breast cancer and ionosphere data are 0.27, 0.047 and 0.14. The corresponding formulas are surprisingly short, with lengths 6, 8 and 7, respectively. This makes them highly interpretable. The length 6 formula for the credit data (predicting if a loan will be granted) is

$$\neg(a[1,1] \wedge a[2]) \vee a[17,4],$$

where $a[1,1]$ means negative account balance; $a[2]$ means above median loan duration; and $a[17,4]$ means employment on managerial level. Our errors are comparable to those obtained for the same data sets in the literature. For example, [25] obtains an error 0.25 for the credit data where our error is 0.27. Also, all our formulas are immediately interpretable. See Sect. 5 for further discussion.

On the computational side, we deploy answer set programming (ASP; see, e.g., [6,14]) where the solutions of a search problem are described declaratively in terms of rules such that the *answer sets* of the resulting logic program correspond to the solutions of the problem. Consequently, dedicated search engines, known as *answer-set solvers*, provide means to solve the problem via the computation of answer sets. The CLASP [8] and WASP [1] solvers represent the state-of-the art of native answer set solvers, providing a comparable performance in practice. These solvers offer various reasoning modes—including prioritized optimization—which are deployed in the sequel, e.g., for the minimization of error and formula length. Besides these features, we count on the flexibility of rules offered by ASP when describing explanation tasks. More information on the technical side of ASP can be found from the de-facto reference manual [9] of the CLINGO system.

The efficiency of explanation is governed by the number of hypotheses considered basically in two ways. Firstly, the search for a plausible explanation requires the exploration of the hypothesis space and, secondly, the exclusion of better explanations becomes a further computational burden, e.g., when the error with respect to data is being minimized. In computational learning approaches (cf. [17]), such as *current-best-hypothesis search* and *version space learning*, a hypothesis in a normal form is maintained while minimizing the numbers of false positive/negative examples. However, in this work, we tackle the hypothesis space somewhat differently: we rather specify the form of hypotheses and delegate their exploration to an (optimizing) logic solver. In favor of interpretability, we consider formulas based on negations, conjunctions, and disjunctions, not necessarily in a particular normal form. By changing the form of hypotheses, also other kinds of explanations such as decision trees [19] or lists could alternatively be sought.

Concerning further related work, our bounds on the difference between theoretical and expected empirical error are technically related to results in statistical learning theory [24] and PAC learning [15,23]. In PAC learning, the goal is to use a sample of labeled points drawn from an unknown distribution to find a hypothesis that gives a small true error with high probability. The use of hypotheses with small descriptions has also been considered in the PAC learning in relation to the Occam's razor principle [3–5]. One major difference between our setting and PAC learning is that in the latter, the target concept is a (usually Boolean) function of the attribute values, while in our setting we only assume that there is a probability distribution on the propositional types over the attributes.

Explanations relating to minimality notions in relation to different Boolean classifiers have been studied widely, see for example [20] for *minimum-cardinality* and *prime implicant* explanations, also in line with Occam's razor [3]. Our study relates especially to global (or general [11]) explainability, where the full behavior of a classifier is explained instead of a decision concerning a particular input instance. Boolean complexity—the length of the shortest equivalent formula—is promoted in the prominent article [7] as an empirically tested measure of the subjective difficulty of a concept. On a conceptually related note, intelligibility of various Boolean classifiers are studied in [2]. While that study places, e.g., DNF-formulas to the less intelligible category based on the complexity of explainability queries performed on classifiers, we note that with genuinely small bounds for classifier length, asymptotic complexity can sometimes be a somewhat problematic measure for intelligibility. In our study, the bounds arise already from the overfitting thresholds in real-life data. In the scenarios we studied, overfitting indeed sets natural, small bounds for classifier length. In inherently Boolean data, such bounds can be fundamental and cannot be always ignored via using different classes of classifiers. The good news is that while a length bound may be *necessary* to avoid overfitting, *shorter length increases interpretability*. This is important from the point of theory as well as applications.

We proceed as follows. After the preliminaries in Sect. 2, we present theoretical results on errors in Sect. 3. Then, Sect. 4 explains our ASP implementation. Next, we present and interpret empirical results in Sect. 5 and conclude in Sect. 6.

2   Preliminaries

The syntax of propositional logic PL[σ] over the vocabulary $\sigma = \{p_1, \ldots, p_m\}$ is given by $\varphi :: = p \mid \neg\varphi \mid \varphi \wedge \varphi \mid \varphi \vee \varphi$ where $p \in \sigma$. We also define the exclusive or $\varphi \oplus \psi := (\varphi \vee \psi) \wedge \neg(\varphi \wedge \psi)$ as an abbreviation. A σ-**model** is a structure $M = (W, V)$ where W is a finite, non-empty set referred to as the **domain** of M and $V : \sigma \to \mathcal{P}(W)$ is a **valuation** function that assigns each $p \in \sigma$ the set $V(p)$ (also denoted by p^M) of points $w \in W$ where p is considered to be true.

A σ-valuation V can be extended in the standard way to a valuation $V : \mathrm{PL}[\sigma] \to \mathcal{P}(W)$ for all $\mathrm{PL}[\sigma]$-formulas. We write $w \models \varphi$ if $w \in V(\varphi)$ and say that w **satisfies** φ. We denote by $|\varphi|_M$ the *number* of points $w \in W$ where $\varphi \in \mathrm{PL}[\sigma]$ is true. For σ-formulas φ and ψ, we write $\varphi \models \psi$ iff for all σ-models $M = (W, V)$ we have $V(\psi) \subseteq V(\varphi)$. Let $lit(\sigma)$ denote the set of σ-**literals**, i.e., formulas p and $\neg p$ for $p \in \sigma$. A σ-**type base** is a set $S \subseteq lit(\sigma)$ such that for each $p \in \sigma$, precisely one of the literals p and $\neg p$ is in S. A σ-**type** is a conjunction $\bigwedge S$. We assume some fixed bracketing and ordering of literals in $\bigwedge S$ so there is a one-to-one correspondence between type bases and types. The set of σ-types is denoted by T_σ. Note that in a σ-model $M = (W, V)$, each element w satisfies precisely one σ-type, so the domain W is partitioned by some subset of T_σ. The **size** $size(\varphi)$ of a formula $\varphi \in \mathrm{PL}[\sigma]$ is defined such that $size(p) = 1$, $size(\neg\psi) = size(\psi) + 1$, and $size(\psi \wedge \vartheta) = size(\psi \vee \vartheta) = size(\psi) + size(\vartheta) + 1$.

We will use short propositional formulas as *explanations* of target attributes in data. Throughout the paper, we shall use the vocabulary $\tau = \{p_1, \ldots, p_k\}$ for the language of explanations, while $q \notin \tau$ will be the target attribute (or target proposition) to be explained. While the set of τ-types will be denoted by T_τ, we let $T_{\tau,q}$ denote the set of $(\tau \cup \{q\})$-types in the extended language $\mathrm{PL}[\tau \cup \{q\}]$.

By a probability distribution over a vocabulary σ, or simply a σ-distribution, we mean a function $\mu_\sigma : T_\sigma \to [0, 1]$ that gives a probability to each type in T_σ. We are mainly interested in such distributions over τ and $\tau \cup \{q\}$. For notational convenience, we may write $\mu_{\tau,q}$ or simply μ instead of $\mu_{\tau \cup \{q\}}$. In the theoretical part of the paper, we assume that the studied data (i.e., $(\tau \cup \{q\})$-models) are sampled using such a distribution μ.

We then define some notions of error for explanations. Let $\tau = \{p_1, \ldots, p_k\}$. Fix a probability distribution $\mu : T_{\tau,q} \to [0, 1]$. Let φ and ψ be $(\tau \cup \{q\})$-formulas. The **probability of** φ **over** μ is defined as

$$\mathrm{Pr}_\mu(\varphi) := \sum_{t \in T_{\tau,q}, \, t \models \varphi} \mu(t).$$

The **probability of** ψ **given** φ **over** μ is defined as $\mathrm{Pr}_\mu(\psi \mid \varphi) := \frac{\mathrm{Pr}_\mu(\psi \wedge \varphi)}{\mathrm{Pr}_\mu(\varphi)}$ (and 0 if $\mathrm{Pr}_\mu(\varphi) = 0$). For simplicity, we may write $\mu(\varphi)$ for $\mathrm{Pr}_\mu(\varphi)$ and $\mu(\psi \mid \varphi)$ for $\mathrm{Pr}_\mu(\psi \mid \varphi)$. Let $M = (W, V)$ be a $(\tau \cup \{q\})$-model. The **probability of** φ **over** M is $\mathrm{Pr}_M(\varphi) := \frac{1}{|W|}|\varphi|_M$, and the **probability of** ψ **given** φ **over** M is defined as $\mathrm{Pr}_M(\psi \mid \varphi) := \frac{|\psi \wedge \varphi|_M}{|\varphi|_M}$ (and 0 if $\mathrm{Pr}_M(\varphi) = 0$). The disjunction $\varphi_{id}^M := \bigvee\{t \in T_\tau \mid \mathrm{Pr}_M(q \mid t) \le \frac{1}{2}\}$ is the **ideal classifier** w.r.t. M, and the disjunction $\varphi_{id}^\mu := \bigvee\{t \in T_\tau \mid \mu(q \mid t) \le \frac{1}{2}\}$ is the **ideal classifier** w.r.t. μ.

Now, let $\psi \in \mathrm{PL}[\tau]$. The **theoretical error** (or **true error**) of ψ with respect to μ is $\mathrm{err}_\mu(\psi) := \Pr_\mu(\psi \oplus q)$. The **ideal theoretical error** of μ is

$$\mathrm{err}(\mu) := \min_{\psi \in \mathrm{PL}[\tau]} \mathrm{err}_\mu(\psi) = \Pr_\mu(\varphi_{id}^\mu) = \sum_{t \in T_\tau} \min\{\mu(t \wedge q), \mu(t \wedge \neg q)\}.$$

Let M be a $(\tau \cup \{q\})$-model. The **empirical error** of ψ with respect to M is $\mathrm{err}_M(\psi) := \Pr_M(\psi \oplus q)$. The **ideal empirical error** of M is

$$\mathrm{err}(M) := \min_{\psi \in \mathrm{PL}[\tau]} \mathrm{err}_M(\psi) = \Pr_M(\varphi_{id}^M) = \frac{1}{|W|} \sum_{t \in T_\tau} \min\{|t \wedge q|_M, |t \wedge \neg q|_M\}.$$

For a τ-type t, the **ideal error over** t **w.r.t.** μ is $\min\{\mu(q\,|\,t), \mu(\neg q\,|\,t)\}$. The **ideal error over** t **w.r.t.** M is $\min\{\Pr_M(q\,|\,t), \Pr_M(\neg q\,|\,t)\}$.

The main problem studied in this paper is the following: over a $(\tau \cup \{q\})$-model M, given a bound ℓ on formula length, find ψ with $size(\psi) \leq \ell$ and with minimal empirical error w.r.t. M. This can be formulated as a *general explanation problem* (GEP) in the sense of [11]; see in particular the extended problems in [12]. The goal in GEP is to explain the *global* behavior of a classifier rather than a reason why a particular instance was accepted or rejected.

Finally, we define $cut : [0,1] \to [0, \frac{1}{2}]$ to be the function such that $cut(x) = x$ if $x \leq \frac{1}{2}$ and otherwise $cut(x) = 1 - x$.

3   Expected Errors

In this section we consider the errors given by Boolean classifiers, including the phenomena that give rise to the errors. With no information on the distribution $\mu : T_{\tau,q} \to [0,1]$, it is difficult to predict the error of a classifier φ in $PL[\tau]$. However, some observations can be made. Consider the scenario where all distributions μ are equally likely, meaning that we consider the flat Dirichlet distribution $Dir(\alpha_1, \ldots, \alpha_{|T_{\tau,q}|})$ with each α_i equal to 1, i.e., the distribution that is uniform over its support which, in turn, is the $(|T_{\tau,q}| - 1)$-simplex. For more on Dirichlet distributions, see [16]. We begin with the following observation.

Proposition 1. *Assuming all distributions over $\tau \cup \{q\}$ are equally likely, the expected value of the ideal theoretical error is 0.25. Also, for any type $t \in T_\tau$ and any μ_τ with $\mu_\tau(t) > 0$, if all extensions μ of μ_τ to a $(\tau \cup \{q\})$-distribution are equally likely, the expectation of the ideal error over t w.r.t. μ is likewise 0.25.*

Proof. We prove the second claim first. Fix a μ and t. If $x = \mu(q\,|\,t)$, then the ideal error over t w.r.t. μ is given by $cut(x)$. Therefore the corresponding expected value is given by $\frac{1}{1-0} \int_0^1 cut(x)\,dx = \int_0^{\frac{1}{2}} x\,dx + \int_{\frac{1}{2}}^1 (1-x)\,dx = \frac{1}{4}$. This proves the second claim. Based on this, it is not difficult to show that the also the first claim holds; the full details are given in the full version [13]. $\square$

One of the main problems with Boolean classifiers is that the number of types is exponential in the vocabulary size, i.e., the curse of dimensionality. This leads to overfitting via overparameterization; even if the model M is faithful to an underlying distribution μ, classifiers φ_{id}^M tend to give empirical errors that are significantly smaller than the theoretical ones for μ. To see why, notice that in the extreme case where $|t|_M = 1$ for each $t \in T_{\tau,q}$, the ideal empirical error of M is zero. In general, when the sets $|t|_M$ are small, ideal classifiers φ_{id}^M benefit from that. Let us consider this issue quantitatively. Fix μ and $t \in T_\tau$. For a model M, let $\text{err}(M, t)$ refer to the ideal error over t w.r.t. M. Consider models M sampled according to μ, and let $m \in \mathbb{N}$ and $\mu(q \mid t) = p$. Now, the expected value $E(m, p)$ of $\text{err}(M, t)$ over those models M where $|t|_M = m$ is given by

$$\Big(\sum_{0 < k \leq m/2} \binom{m}{k} p^k (1-p)^{m-k} \cdot \frac{k}{m} \Big) + \Big(\sum_{m/2 < k < m} \binom{m}{k} p^k (1-p)^{m-k} \cdot \frac{(m-k)}{m} \Big).$$

Now for example $E(4, 0.7) = 0.2541$ and $E(2, 0.7) = 0.21$, both significantly lower than $cut(p) = cut(0.7) = 0.3$ which is the expected value of $\text{err}(M, t)$ when the size restriction $|t|_M = m$ is lifted and models of increasing size are sampled according to μ. Similarly, we have $E(4, 0.5) = 0.3125$ and $E(2, 0.5) = 0.25$, significantly lower than $cut(p) = cut(0.5) = 0.5$. A natural way to avoid this phenomenon is to limit formula size, the strategy adopted in this paper. This also naturally leads to shorter and thus more interpretable formulas.

We next estimate empirical errors for general Boolean classifiers (as opposed to single types). The **expected ideal empirical error of** μ is simply the expectation $\mathbb{E}(\text{err}(M))$ of $\text{err}(M)$, where M is a model of size n sampled according to μ. One can show that $\mathbb{E}(\text{err}(M)) \leq \text{err}(\mu)$ and that $\mathbb{E}(\text{err}(M)) \to \text{err}(\mu)$ as $n \to \infty$. Thus it is natural to ask how the size of the difference $\text{err}(\mu) - \mathbb{E}(\text{err}(M))$, which we call the **bias** of empirical error, depends on n.

In the remaining part of this section we establish bounds on the expected ideal empirical error, which in turn can be used to give bounds on the bias of empirical error. Since expectation is linear, it suffices to give bounds on

$$\frac{1}{n} \sum_{t \in T_\tau} \mathbb{E} \min\{|t \wedge q|_M, |t \wedge \neg q|_M\}, \tag{1}$$

where M is a model of size n which is sampled according to μ. Here, for each type $t \in T_\tau$, $|t \wedge q|_M$ and $|t \wedge \neg q|_M$ are random variables that are distributed according to $\text{Binom}(n, \mu(t \wedge q))$ and $\text{Binom}(n, \mu(t \wedge \neg q))$ respectively. Since $|t \wedge q|_M + |t \wedge \neg q|_M = |t|_M$, we can replace $|t \wedge \neg q|_M$ with $|t|_M - |t \wedge q|_M$.

To simplify (1), we will first use the law of total expectation to write it as

$$\frac{1}{n} \sum_{t \in T_\tau} \sum_{m=0}^{n} \mathbb{E}(\min\{|t \wedge q|_M, m - |t \wedge q|_M\} \mid |t|_M = m) \cdot \Pr(|t|_M = m). \tag{2}$$

For each $0 \leq m \leq n$ and $t \in T_\tau$ we fix a random variable $X_{m,t,q}$ distributed according to $\text{Binom}(m, \mu(q|t))$, where $\mu(q|t) := \mu(t \wedge q)/\mu(t)$. In the full version

[13] we show that (2) equals

$$\frac{1}{n} \sum_{t \in T_\tau} \sum_{m=0}^{n} \mathbb{E} \min\{X_{m,t,q},\ m - X_{m,t,q}\} \cdot \Pr(|t|_M = m). \tag{3}$$

To avoid dealing directly with the expectation of a minimum of two Binomial random variables, we simplify it via the identity $\min\{a, b\} = \frac{1}{2}(a + b - |a - b|)$. In the full version [13] we show that using this identity on (3) gives the form

$$\frac{1}{2} - \frac{1}{n} \sum_{t \in T_\tau} \sum_{m=0}^{n} \mathbb{E} \left| X_{m,t,q} - \frac{m}{2} \right| \cdot \Pr(|t|_M = m). \tag{4}$$

In the above formula the quantity $\mathbb{E}|X_{m,t,q} - \frac{m}{2}|$ is convenient since we can bound it from above using the standard deviation of $X_{m,t,q}$. Some further estimates and algebraic manipulations suffice to prove the following result.

Theorem 1. *Expected ideal empirical error is bounded from below by*

$$\mathrm{err}(\mu) - \frac{1}{\sqrt{n}} \sum_{t \in T_\tau} \sqrt{\mu(q|t)(1 - \mu(q|t))\mu(t)}.$$

We note that Theorem 1 implies immediately that the bias of the empirical error is bounded from above by $\frac{1}{\sqrt{n}} \sum_{t \in T_\tau} \sqrt{\mu(q|t)(1 - \mu(q|t))\mu(t)} \leq \frac{1}{2}\sqrt{\frac{|T_\tau|}{n}}$. This estimate yields quite concrete sample bounds. For instance, if we are using three attributes to explain the target attribute (so $|T_\tau| = 8$) and we want the bias of the empirical error to be at most 0.045, then a sample of size at least 1000 suffices. For the credit data set with 1000 data points, this means that if three attributes are selected, then the (easily computable) ideal empirical error gives a good idea of the ideal theoretical error for those three attributes.

Obtaining an upper bound on the expected ideal empirical error is much more challenging, since in general it is not easy to give good lower bounds on $\mathbb{E}|X - \lambda|$, where X is a binomial random variable and $\lambda > 0$ is a real number. Nevertheless we were able to obtain the following result.

Theorem 2. *Expected ideal empirical error is bounded from above by*

$$\frac{1}{2} - \frac{1}{\sqrt{8n}} \sum_{n\mu(t) \geq 1} \sqrt{\mu(t)} + \frac{1}{2\sqrt{8n}} \sum_{n\mu(t) \geq 1} \frac{1 - \mu(t)}{\sqrt{n\mu(t)}} - \frac{1}{\sqrt{8}} \sum_{n\mu(t) < 1} \mu(t)(1 - \mu(t))^n.$$

The proof of Theorem 2 — which can be found in the full version [13] — can be divided into three main steps. First, we observe that the expected ideal empirical error is maximized when $\mu(q|t) = 1/2$, for every $t \in T_\tau$, in which case $\mathbb{E}(X_{m,t,q}) = \frac{m}{2}$. Then, we use a very recent result of [18] to obtain a good lower bound on the value $\mathbb{E}|X_{m,t,q} - \mathbb{E}(X_{m,t,q})|$. Finally, after some algebraic manipulations, we are left with the task of bounding $\mathbb{E}(\sqrt{|t|_M})$ from below, which we achieve by using an estimate that can be obtained from the Taylor expansion of $\sqrt{x}$ around 1.

To get a concrete feel for the lower bound of Theorem 2, consider the case where $\mu(q|t) = 1/2$, for every $t \in T_\tau$. In this case a *rough* use of Theorem 2 implies that the bias of the empirical error is bounded from below by

$$\frac{1}{\sqrt{8}} \sum_{n\mu(t)<1} \mu(t)(1-\mu(t))^n \geq \frac{1}{\sqrt{8}e} \cdot \frac{(n-1)}{n} \cdot \sum_{n\mu(t)<1} \mu(t),$$

where we used the fact that $(1-1/n)^{n-1} \geq 1/e$, which holds provided that $n > 1$. This lower bound very much depends on the properties of the distribution μ, but one can nevertheless make general remarks about it. For instance, if $|T_\tau|$ is much larger than n and μ is not concentrated on a small number of types (i.e., its Shannon entropy is not small), then we except $\sum_{n\mu(t)<1} \mu(t)$ to be close to one. Thus the above bound would imply that in this scenario the generalization gap is roughly $1/(\sqrt{8} \cdot e) \approx 0.13$, which is a significant deviation from zero.

4 An Overview of the Implementation in ASP

In this section, we describe our proof-of-concept implementation of the search for short formulas explaining data sets. Our implementation presumes Boolean attributes only and *complete* data sets having no missing values. In the following, we highlight the main ideas behind our ASP encoding in terms of code snippets in the Gringo syntax [9]. The complete encoding will be published under the ASPTOOLS collection[1] along with some preformatted data sets for testing purposes. Each data set is represented in terms of a predicate val(D,A,V) with three arguments: D for a data point identifier, A for the name of an attribute, and V for the value of the attribute A at D, i.e., either 0 or 1 for Boolean data.

Given a data set based on attributes $a_0, \ldots, a_n$ where a_n is the target of explanation, the hypothesis space is essentially the propositional language $\mathrm{PL}[\tau]$ with the vocabulary $\tau = \{a_0, \ldots, a_{n-1}\}$. Thus, the goal is to find a definition $a_n \leftrightarrow \varphi$ where $\varphi \in \mathrm{PL}[\tau]$ with the least error. To avoid obviously redundant hypotheses, we use only propositional connectives from the set $C = \{\neg, \wedge, \vee\}$ and represent formulas in the so-called *reversed Polish notation*. This notation omits parentheses altogether and each formula φ is encoded as a sequence $s_1, \ldots, s_k$ of symbols where $s_i \in \tau \cup C$ for each s_i. Such a sequence can be transformed into a formula by processing the symbols in the given order and by pushing formulas on a *stack* that is empty initially. If $s_i \in \tau$, it is pushed on the stack, and if $s_i \in C$, the arguments of s_i are popped from the stack and the resulting formula is pushed on the stack using s_i as the connective. Eventually, the result appears as the only formula on top of stack. For illustration, consider the sequence $a_2, a_1, \wedge, \neg, a_0, \vee$ referring to attributes a_0, a_1, and a_2. The stack evolves as follows: $a_2 \mapsto a_2, a_1$ $\mapsto (a_1 \wedge a_2) \mapsto \neg(a_1 \wedge a_2) \mapsto \neg(a_1 \wedge a_2), a_0 \mapsto a_0 \vee \neg(a_1 \wedge a_2)$. Thus, the formula is

---

[1] https://github.com/asptools/benchmarks.

Listing 1. Encoding the syntactic structure of hypotheses

```
1   % Domains
2   #const l=10.
3   node(1..l).   root(l).    op(neg;and;or).
4   data(D) :- val(D,A,B).
5   attr(A) :- val(D,A,B).
6
7   % Choose the actual length
8   {used(N)} :- node(N).
9   used(N+1) :- used(N), node(N+1).
10  used(N) :- root(N).
11
12  %  Choose leaf nodes and inner nodes, and label them
13  {leaf(N)} :- used(N).
14  inner(N) :- used(N), not leaf(N).
15  { op(N,O): op(O) } = 1 :- inner(N).
16  { lat(N,A): attr(A) } = 1 :- leaf(N).
```

Listing 2. Checking the syntax using a stack

```
1   % Check the size of the stack
2   count(N,0) :- used(N), not used(N-1).
3   count(N+1,K+1) :- leaf(N), count(N,K), node(N), K>=0, K<=2.
4   count(N+1,K) :- count(N,K), node(N), op(N,neg).
5   count(N+1,K-1) :- count(N,K), node(N), op(N,O), O!=neg.
6   :- not count(l+1,1).
7
8   % The step-by-step evolution of the stack
9   stack(N+1,K+1,N) :- leaf(N), count(N,K), K>=0, K<=2.
10  stack(N+1,K, N) :- op(N,neg), count(N,K), K>0, K<=3.
11  stack(N+1,K-1,N) :- op(N,O), O!=neg, count(N,K), K>=2, K<=3.
12
13  stack(N+1,I, M) :- leaf(N), count(N,K), I>=0, I<=K, stack(N,I,M).
14  stack(N+1,I, M) :- op(N,neg), count(N,K), I>0, I<K, stack(N,I,M).
15  stack(N+1,1, M) :- op(N,O), O!=neg, count(N,3), stack(N,1,M).
```

$a_0 \vee \neg(a_1 \wedge a_2)$. For a formula φ, the respective sequence of symbols can be found by traversing the syntax tree of φ in the *post order*. There are also malformed sequences not corresponding to any formula.

Based on the reverse Polish representation, the first part of our encoding concentrates on the generation of hypotheses whose syntactic elements are defined in Listing 1. In Line 2, the maximum length of the formula is set, as a global parameter l of the encoding, to a default value 10. Other values can be issued by the command-line option -cl=<number>. Based on the value chosen, the respective number of *nodes* for a syntax tree is defined in Line 3, out of which the last one is dedicated for the *root*. The three Boolean *operators* are introduced using the predicate op/1. The data points and attributes are extracted from data in Lines 4 and 5, respectively. To allow explanations shorter than l, the choice rule in Line 8 may take any node into use (or not). The rule in Line 9 ensures that all nodes with higher index values up to l are in use. The root node is always in

Listing 3. Evaluating the hypothesis at data points

```
1  true(D,N) :- data(D), leaf(N), lat(N,A), val(D,A,1).
2  {true(D,N)} :- data(D), used(N), inner(N).
3
4  % Constraints for disjunctions
5  :- data(D), op(N,or), count(N,I), stack(N,I-1,N3),
6     true(D,N), not true(D,N-1), not true(D,N3).
7  :- data(D), op(N,or), not true(D,N), true(D,N-1).
8  :- data(D), op(N,or), count(N,I), stack(N,I-1,N2),
9     not true(D,N), true(D,N2).
```

Listing 4. Encoding the objective function

```
1  % Compute error
2  error(D) :- data(D), val(D,A,0), expl(A), true(D,N), root(N).
3  error(D) :- data(D), val(D,A,1), expl(A), not true(D,N), root(N).
4
5  #minimize { 1@1,D: error(D);   1@0,N: used(N), node(N) }.
```

use by Line 10. The net effect is that the nodes i..l taken into use determine the actual length of the hypothesis. Thus the length may vary between 1 and l. In a valid syntax tree, the nodes are either *leaf* or *inner* nodes, see Lines 13 and 14, respectively. Each inner node is assigned an operator in Line 15 whereas each leaf node is assigned an attribute in Line 16, to be justified later on.

The second part of our encoding checks the syntax of the hypothesis using a stack, see Listing 2. Line 2 resets the size of the stack in the first used node. The following rules in Lines 3–5 take the respective effects of attributes, unary operators, and binary operators into account. The constraint in Line 6 ensures that the count reaches 1 after the root node. Similar constraints limit the size of the stack: at most two for leaf nodes and at least one/two for inner nodes with a unary/binary connective. The predicate stack/3 propagates information about arguments to operators, i.e., the locations N where they can be found. Depending on node type, the rules in Lines 9–11 create a new reference that appears on top of the stack at the next step N+1 (cf. the second argument K+1, K, or K-1). The rules in Lines 13–15 copy the items under the top item to the next step N+1.

The third part of our encoding evaluates the chosen hypothesis at data points D present in the data set given as input. For a leaf node N, the value is simply set based on the value of the chosen attribute A at D, see Line 1. For inner nodes N, we indicate a choice of the truth value in Line 2, but the choice is made deterministic in practice by the constraints in Lines 5–9, illustrating the case of the **or** operator. The constraints for the operators **neg** and **and** are analogous.

Finally, Listing 4 encodes the objective function. Lines 2 and 3 spot data points D that are incorrect with respect to the attribute A being explained and the selected hypothesis rooted at N. For a false positive D, the hypothesis is true at D while the value of A is 0. In the opposite case, the hypothesis is false while the value of A at D is 1. The criteria for minimization are given in Line 5. The number of errors is the first priority (at level 1) whereas the length of the hypothesis is the secondary objective (at level 0). Also, recall that the maximum length has been set as a parameter earlier. The optimization proceeds *lexicographically* as follows: a formula that minimizes the number of errors is sought first and, once such an explanation has been found, the length of the formula is minimized additionally. So, it is not that crucial to set the (maximum) length parameter l to a particular value: the smaller values are feasible, too, based on the nodes in use. The performance of our basic encoding can be improved by adding constraints to prune redundant hypotheses, sub-optimal answer sets, and candidates.

5   Results from Data and Interpretation

To empirically analyze short Boolean formulas as explanations and classifiers, we utilize three data sets from the UCI machine learning repository: Statlog (German Credit Data), Breast Cancer Wisconsin (Original) and Ionosphere. The target attributes are given as acceptance of a loan application, benignity of a tumor and "good" radar readings, respectively. The breast cancer data contains a small number of instances with missing attribute values (16 out of 699), which are excluded from the analysis. The original data sets contain categorical and numerical attributes, as well as Boolean ones. To convert a categorical attribute into Boolean format, we treat the inclusion of instances in each corresponding category as a separate Boolean attribute. For numerical attributes, we use the median across all instances as the threshold. Thus the Booleanized credit, breast cancer and ionosphere data sets consist of 1000, 683 and 351 instances, respectively, with 68, 9 and 34 Boolean attributes each, plus the target attribute. To evaluate the obtained formulas as classifiers, we randomly divide each data set into two equal parts: one serving as the training data and the other as the test data. For the training data M, target predicate q and increasing formula length bounds ℓ, we produce formulas ψ not involving q with $size(\psi) \leq \ell$ that minimize the empirical error $\mathrm{err}_M(\psi)$. We also record the error on the test data (i.e., the complement of the training data). We repeated this process 10 times. For each data set, Figs. 1, 2 and 3 record both the first experiment as an example and the average over 10 experiments on separately randomized training and test data sets. We employed CLINGO (v. 5.4.0) as the answer-set solver in all experiments.

For the ionosphere data, the Booleanization via median is rough for the real-valued radar readings. Thus we expect larger errors compared to methods using real numbers. This indeed happens, but the errors are still surprisingly low.

Overfitting and Choice of Explanations. The six plots show how the error rates develop with formula length. In all plots, the error of the test data eventually stays roughly the same while the error of the training data keeps decreasing. This illustrates how the overfitting phenomenon ultimately arises. We can use these results to find a *cut-off point* for the length of the formulas to be used as explanations. Note that this should be done on a case-by-case basis and we show the average plots only to demonstrate trends. For the single tests given on the left in Figs. 1, 2 and 3, we might choose the lengths 6, 8 and 7 for the credit, breast cancer and ionosphere data sets, respectively. The errors of the chosen

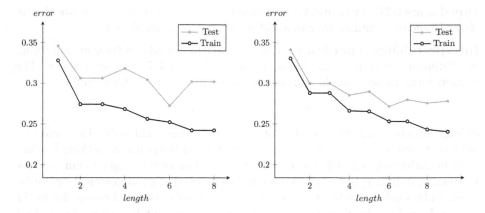

Fig. 1. Credit data set – first test (left) and average (right)

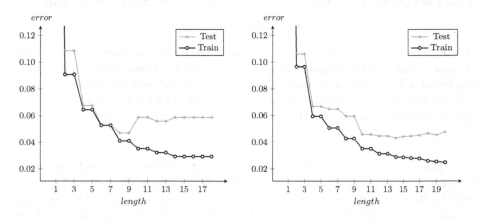

Fig. 2. Breast cancer data set – first test (left) and average (right)

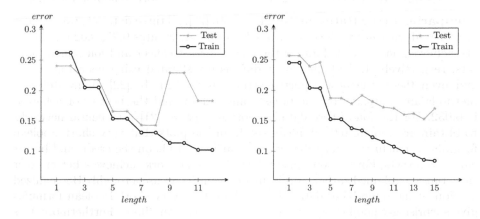

Fig. 3. Ionosphere data set – first test (left) and average (right)

formulas are 0.27, 0.047 and 0.14, respectively. We conclude that by sticking to short Boolean formulas, we can avoid overfitting in a simple way.

Interpretability. A nice feature of short Boolean formulas is their interpretability. Suppose we stop at the formula lengths 6, 8 and 7 suggested above. The related formulas are simple and indeed readable. Consider the formula

$$\neg(a[1,1] \wedge a[2]) \vee a[17,4]$$

of length 6 and a test error of 0.27 obtained from the credit data. The meanings of the attributes are as follows: $a[1,1]$ means the applicant has a checking account with negative balance, $a[2]$ means that the duration of the applied loan is above median, and $a[17,4]$ means the applicant is employed at a management or similar level. (The second number in some attributes refers to original categories in the data.) Therefore the formula states that if an applicant is looking for a short term loan, has money on their account or has a management level job, then they should get the loan. For the breast cancer data set, we choose the formula

$$\neg(((a[1] \wedge a[6]) \vee a[5]) \wedge a[3])$$

of length 8 with test error 0.047. The meanings of the attributes in the order of appearance in the formula are given as clump thickness, bare nuclei, single epithelial cell size and uniformity of cell shape. The full power of Boolean logic is utilized here, in the form of both negation and alternation between conjunction and disjunction. Finally, for the ionosphere data set, the formula

$$((a[8] \wedge a[12]) \vee a[15]) \wedge a[1]$$

of length 7 and test error 0.14 is likewise human readable as a formula. However, it must be mentioned again that the data was used here for technical reasons, and the Booleanized attributes related to radar readings are difficult to explicate.

Using the power of Boolean logic (i.e., including all the connectives $\neg$, $\wedge$, $\vee$) tends to compress the explanations suitably in addition to giving flexibility in explanations. We observe that our experiments gave short, readable formulas.

Comparing Error Rates on Test Data. In [25], all three data sets we consider are treated with *naive Bayesian classifiers* and error rates 0.25, 0.026 and 0.10 are achieved on the test data for the credit, breast cancer and ionosphere data sets, respectively. In [10], the credit data is investigated using neural networks and even there, the best reported error rate is 0.24. In [22], many different methods are compared on the breast cancer data, and the best error achieved is 0.032. For the ionosphere data, the original paper [21] uses neural networks to obtain an error of 0.04. We can see from the plots that very short Boolean formulas can achieve error rates of a similar magnitude on the credit and breast cancer data sets. For the ionosphere data, neural networks achieve a better error rate, but as explained earlier, this is unsurprising as we use a roughly Booleanized version of the underlying data. We conclude that very short Boolean formulas give surprisingly good error rates compared to other methods. Furthermore, this approach seems inherently interpretable for many different purposes.

Runtime Behavior. When computing explanations, no strict timeout was set and the runs were finished only when the optimum was found. Figure 4 depicts the average runtime (over the 10 runs) as a function of formula length. The number of attributes (i.e., 68, 34 and 9 in the order of the curves) appears to be a key factor affecting the performance. Maximum runtimes (approx. 10 hours) indicate the feasibility of our approach, as demonstrated here for realistic data sets previously explored in the literature. Besides minimal explanations, intermediate ones may also be useful.

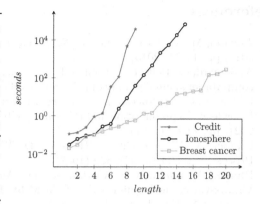

Fig. 4. Average runtimes for data sets

6 Conclusion

We have studied short Boolean formulas as a platform for producing explanations and interpretable classifiers. We have investigated the theoretical reasons behind overfitting and provided related quantitative bounds. Also, we have tested the approach with three different data sets, where the resulting formulas are indeed interpretable—all being genuinely short—and relatively accurate. In general, short formulas may sometimes be necessary to avoid overfitting, and moreover, shorter length leads to increased interpretability.

Our approach need not limit to Boolean formulas only, as we can naturally extend our work to general relational data. We can use, e.g., description logics and compute concepts $C_1, \ldots, C_k$ and then perform our procedure using $C_1, \ldots, C_k$, finding short Boolean combinations of concepts. This of course differs from the approach of computing minimal length formulas in the original description logic, but can nevertheless be fruitful and interesting. We leave this for future work. Further future directions include, e.g., knowledge discovery via computing all formulas up to some short length ℓ with errors smaller than a given threshold.

Acknowledgments. T. Janhunen, A. Kuusisto, M. F. Rankooh and M. Vilander were supported by the Academy of Finland consortium project *Explaining AI via Logic* (XAILOG), grant numbers 345633 (Janhunen) and 345612 (Kuusisto). A. Kuusisto was also supported by the Academy of Finland project *Theory of computational logics*, grant numbers 352419, 352420, 353027, 324435, 328987. The author names have been ordered on the basis of alphabetical order.

References

1. Alviano, M., Dodaro, C., Leone, N., Ricca, F.: Advances in WASP. In: LPNMR 2015, pp. 40–54 (2015)
2. Audemard, G., Bellart, S., Bounia, L., Koriche, F., Lagniez, J., Marquis, P.: On the computational intelligibility of Boolean classifiers. In: Bienvenu, M., Lakemeyer, G., Erdem, E. (eds.) Proceedings of the 18th International Conference on Principles of Knowledge Representation and Reasoning, KR 2021, Online event, 3–12 November 2021, pp. 74–86 (2021)
3. Blumer, A., Ehrenfeucht, A., Haussler, D., Warmuth, M.K.: Occam's razor. Inf. Process. Lett. **24**(6), 377–380 (1987)
4. Blumer, A., Ehrenfeucht, A., Haussler, D., Warmuth, M.K.: Learnability and the Vapnik-Chervonenkis dimension. J. ACM **36**(4), 929–965 (1989)
5. Board, R.A., Pitt, L.: On the necessity of Occam algorithms. Theor. Comput. Sci. **100**(1), 157–184 (1992)
6. Brewka, G., Eiter, T., Truszczynski, M.: Answer set programming at a glance. Commun. ACM **54**(12), 92–103 (2011)
7. Feldman, J.: Minimization of Boolean complexity in human learning. Nature **407**(6804), 630–633 (2022)
8. Gebser, M., Kaminski, R., Kaufmann, B., Romero, J., Schaub, T.: Progress in clasp series 3. In: LPNMR 2015, pp. 368–383 (2015)
9. Gebser, M., Kaminski, R., Kaufmann, B., Schaub, T.: Answer Set Solving in Practice. Synthesis Lectures on Artificial Intelligence and Machine Learning. Morgan & Claypool Publishers, Williston (2012)
10. Griffith, J., O'Dea, P., O'Riordan, C.: A neural net approach to data mining: classification of users to aid information management. In: Szczepaniak, P.S., Segovia, J., Kacprzyk, J., Zadeh, L.A. (eds.) Intelligent Exploration of the Web. Studies in Fuzziness and Soft Computing, vol. 111, pp. 389–401. Physica, Heidelberg (2003). https://doi.org/10.1007/978-3-7908-1772-0_23
11. Jaakkola, R., Janhunen, T., Kuusisto, A., Rankooh, M.F., Vilander, M.: Explainability via short formulas: the case of propositional logic with implementation. In: RCRA 2022. CEUR Workshop Proceedings, vol. 3281, pp. 64–77. CEUR-WS.org (2022)
12. Jaakkola, R., Janhunen, T., Kuusisto, A., Rankooh, M.F., Vilander, M.: Explainability via short formulas: the case of propositional logic with implementation. CoRR abs/2209.01403 (2022)
13. Jaakkola, R., Janhunen, T., Kuusisto, A., Rankooh, M.F., Vilander, M.: Short boolean formulas as explanations in practice. CoRR abs/2307.06971 (2023)
14. Janhunen, T., Niemelä, I.: The answer set programming paradigm. AI Mag. **37**(3), 13–24 (2016)
15. Kearns, M.J., Vazirani, U.: An Introduction to Computational Learning Theory. The MIT Press, Cambridge (1994)
16. Kotz, S., Balakrishnan, N., Johnson, N.: Continuous Multivariate Distributions, Volume 1: Models and Applications. Continuous Multivariate Distributions, Wiley, Hoboken (2004)
17. Mitchell, T.M.: Generalization as search. Artif. Intell. **18**(2), 203–226 (1982)
18. Pelekis, C., Ramon, J.: A lower bound on the probability that a binomial random variable is exceeding its mean. Stat. Probab. Lett. **119**, 305–309 (2016)
19. Quinlan, J.R.: Induction of decision trees. Mach. Learn. **1**(1), 81–106 (1986)

20. Shih, A., Choi, A., Darwiche, A.: A symbolic approach to explaining Bayesian network classifiers. In: Lang, J. (ed.) IJCAI, pp. 5103–5111 (2018)
21. Sigillito, V.G., Wing, S.P., Hutton, L.V., Baker, K.B.: Classification of radar returns from the ionosphere using neural networks. J. Hopkins APL Tech. Dig. **10**, 262–266 (1989)
22. Šter, B., Dobnikar, A.: Neural networks in medical diagnosis: comparison with other methods. In: Proceedings of the International Conference on Engineering Applications of Neural Networks (1996)
23. Valiant, L.G.: A theory of the learnable. Commun. ACM **27**(11), 1134–1142 (1984)
24. Vapnik, V.: The Nature of Statistical Learning Theory. Springer, New York (2013). https://doi.org/10.1007/978-1-4757-3264-1
25. Yang, Y., Webb, G.I.: Proportional k-interval discretization for Naive-Bayes classifiers. In: De Raedt, L., Flach, P. (eds.) ECML 2001. LNCS (LNAI), vol. 2167, pp. 564–575. Springer, Heidelberg (2001). https://doi.org/10.1007/3-540-44795-4_48

A New Class of Explanations
for Classifiers with Non-binary Features

Chunxi Ji$^{(\boxtimes)}$ ⓘ and Adnan Darwiche ⓘ

University of California, Los Angeles, Los Angeles, CA 90095, USA
{jich,darwiche}@cs.ucla.edu

Abstract. Two types of explanations have been receiving increased attention in the literature when analyzing the decisions made by classifiers. The first type explains why a decision was made and is known as a sufficient reason for the decision, also an abductive explanation or a PI-explanation. The second type explains why some other decision was not made and is known as a necessary reason for the decision, also a contrastive or counterfactual explanation. These explanations were defined for classifiers with binary, discrete and, in some cases, continuous features. We show that these explanations can be significantly improved in the presence of non-binary features, leading to a new class of explanations that relay more information about decisions and the underlying classifiers. Necessary and sufficient reasons were also shown to be the prime implicates and implicants of the complete reason for a decision, which can be obtained using a quantification operator. We show that our improved notions of necessary and sufficient reasons are also prime implicates and implicants but for an improved notion of complete reason obtained by a new quantification operator that we also define and study.

Keywords: Explainable AI · Decision Graphs · Prime Implicants/Implicates

1   Introduction

Explaining the decisions of classifiers has been receiving significant attention in the AI literature recently. Some explanation methods operate directly on classifiers, e.g., [43,44], while some other methods operate on symbolic encodings of their input-output behavior, e.g., [8,25,37,40], which may be compiled into tractable circuits [5,11,21,45–47]. When explaining the decisions of classifiers, two particular notions have been receiving increased attention in the literature: The sufficient and necessary reasons for a decision on an instance.

A *sufficient reason* for a decision [17] is a minimal subset of the instance which is guaranteed to trigger the decision. It was first introduced under the name *PI-explanation* in [46] and later called an *abductive explanation* [25].[1] Consider the classifier in Fig. 1a and a patient, Susan, with the following characteristics: AGE ≥55, BTYPE=A and WEIGHT=over. Susan is judged as susceptible to disease

---

[1] We will use sufficient reasons and PI/abductive explanations interchangeably.

S. Gaggl et al. (Eds.): JELIA 2023, LNAI 14281, pp. 106–122, 2023.
https://doi.org/10.1007/978-3-031-43619-2_8

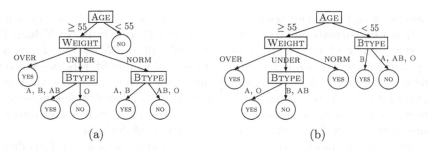

Fig. 1. Two classifiers of patients susceptible to a certain disease. The classifier in (b) will be discussed later in the paper.

by this classifier, and a sufficient reason for this decision is $\{\text{AGE} \geq 55, \text{BTYPE}=\text{A}\}$. Hence, the classifier will judge Susan as susceptible to disease as long as she has these two characteristics, regardless of how the feature WEIGHT is set.[2]

A *necessary reason* for a decision [18] is a minimal subset of the instance that will flip the decision if changed appropriately. It was formalized earlier in [24] under the name *contrastive explanation* which is discussed initially in [33,39].[3] Consider again the patient Susan and the classifier in Fig. 1a. A necessary reason for the decision on Susan is $\{\text{AGE} \geq 55\}$, which means that she would not be judged as susceptible to disease if she were younger than 55. The other necessary reason is $\{\text{WEIGHT}=\text{OVER}, \text{BTYPE}=\text{A}\}$ so the decision on Susan can be flipped by changing these two characteristics (and this cannot be achieved by changing only one of them). Indeed, if Susan had WEIGHT=NORM and BTYPE=AB, she will not be judged as susceptible. However, since WEIGHT and BTYPE are discrete variables, there are multiple ways for changing them and some changes may not flip the decision (e.g., WEIGHT=UNDER and BTYPE=B).

The notion of a *complete reason* behind a decision was introduced in [17] and its prime implicants were shown to be the sufficient reasons for the decision. Intuitively, the complete reason is a particular condition on the instance that is both necessary and sufficient for the decision on that instance; see [16]. A declarative semantics for complete reasons was given in [19] which showed how to compute them using *universal literal quantification*. Furthermore, the prime implicates of a complete reason where shown to be the necessary reasons for the decision in [18]. Given these results, one would first use universal literal quantification to obtain the complete reason for a decision and then compute its prime implicates and implicants to obtain necessary and sufficient explanations.

---

[2] See, e.g., [13,44,49] for some approaches that can be viewed as approximating sufficient reasons and [26] for a study of the quality of some of these approximations.

[3] We will use necessary reasons and contrastive explanations interchangeably in this paper. Counterfactual explanations are related but have alternate definitions in the literature. For example, as defined in [5], they correspond to length-minimal necessary reasons; see [18]. But according to some other definitions, they include contrastive explanations (necessary reasons) as a special case; see Sect. 5.2 in [34]. See also [1] for counterfactual explanations that are directed towards Bayesian network classifiers and [2] for a relevant recent study and survey.

Necessary and sufficient reasons are *subsets* of the instance being explained so each reason corresponds to a set of variable settings (Feature=Value), like WEIGHT=UNDER and BTYPE=B, which we shall call *simple literals*. Since necessary and sufficient reasons correspond to sets of simple literals, we will refer to them as *simple* or *classical* explanations. We will show next that these simple explanations can be significantly improved if the classifier has non-binary features, leading to more general notions of necessary, sufficient and complete reasons that provide more informative explanations of decisions.

Consider again the decision on Susan discussed above which had the sufficient reason {AGE $\geq$55, BTYPE=A}. Such an explanation can be viewed as a *property* of the instance which guarantees the decision. The property has a specific form: a conjunction of feature settings (i.e., instance characteristics) which leaves out characteristics of the instance that are irrelevant to the decision (WEIGHT=OVER). However, the following is a weaker property of the instance which will also trigger the decision: {AGE $\geq$55, BTYPE $\in$ {A, B}}. This property tells us that not only is WEIGHT=OVER irrelevant to the decision, but also that BTYPE=A is not particularly relevant since BTYPE could have been B and the decision would have still been triggered. In other words, what is really relevant is that BTYPE $\in$ {A, B} or, alternatively, BTYPE $\notin$ {AB, O}. Clearly, this kind of explanation reveals more information about why the classifier made its decision. We will later formalize and study a new class of explanations for this purpose, called *general sufficient reasons*, which arise only when the classifier has non-binary features.

A necessary reason for a decision can also be understood as a property of the instance, but one that will flip the decision if violated in a *certain* manner [18]. As mentioned earlier, {WEIGHT=OVER, BTYPE=A} is a necessary reason for the decision on Susan. This reason corresponds to the property (WEIGHT=OVER or BTYPE=A). We can flip the decision by violating this property through changing the values of WEIGHT and BTYPE in the instance. Since these variables are non-binary, there are multiple changes (six total) that will violate the property. Some violations will flip the decision, others will not (we are only guaranteed that at least one violation will flip the decision). For example, WEIGHT=NORM, BTYPE=O and WEIGHT=UNDER, BTYPE=AB will both violate the property but only the first one will flip the decision. However, the following weaker property is guaranteed to flip the decision regardless of how it is violated: (WEIGHT=OVER or BTYPE $\in$ {A, B, AB}). We can violate this property using two different settings of WEIGHT and BTYPE, both of which will flip the decision. This property corresponds to the *general necessary reason* {WEIGHT=OVER, BTYPE $\in$ {A, B, AB}}, a new notion that we introduce and study later. Similar to general sufficient reasons, general necessary reasons provide more information about the behavior of a classifier and arise only when the classifier has non-binary features.

We stress here that using simple explanations in the presence of non-binary features is quite prevalent in the literature; see, e.g., [4,6,8,18,23,28,36]. Two notable exceptions are [12,27] which we discuss in more detail later.[4]

---

[4] Interestingly, the axiomatic study of explanations in [3] allows non-binary features, yet Axiom 4 (*feasibility*) implies that explanations must be simple.

Our study of general necessary and sufficient reasons follows a similar structure to recent developments on classical necessary and sufficient reasons. In particular, we define a new quantification operator like the one defined in [19] and show how it can be used to compute the *general reason* of a decision, and that its prime implicates and implicants contain the general necessary and sufficient reasons. Complete reasons are known to be monotone formulas. We show that general reasons are *fixated formulas* which include monotone ones. We introduce the fixation property and discuss some of its (computational) implications.

This paper is structured as follows. We start in Sect. 2 by discussing the syntax and semantics of formulas with discrete variables which are needed to capture the input-output behavior of classifiers with non-binary features. We then introduce the new quantification operator in Sect. 3 where we study its properties and show how it can be used to formulate the new notion of general reason. The study of general necessary and sufficient reasons is conducted in Sect. 4 where we also relate them to their classical counterparts and argue further for their utility. Section 5 provides closed-form general reasons for a broad class of classifiers and Sect. 6 discusses the computation of general necessary and sufficient reasons based on general reasons. We finally close with some remarks in Sect. 7. Proofs of all results are in Appendix A of [30].

2 Representing Classifiers Using Class Formulas

We now discuss the syntax and semantics of *discrete formulas,* which we use to represent the input-output behavior of classifiers. Such symbolic formulas can be automatically compiled from certain classifiers, like Bayesian networks, random forests and some types of neural networks; see [16] for a summary.

We assume a finite set of variables Σ which represent classifier features. Each variable $X \in \Sigma$ has a finite number of *states* $x_1, \ldots, x_n$, $n > 1$. A *literal* ℓ for variable X, called X-literal, is a set of states such that $\emptyset \subset \ell \subset \{x_1, \ldots, x_n\}$. We will often denote a literal such as $\{x_1, x_3, x_4\}$ by x_{134} which reads: the state of variable X is either x_1 or x_3 or x_4. A literal is *simple* iff it contains a single state. Hence, x_3 is a simple literal but x_{134} is not. Since a simple literal corresponds to a state, these two notions are interchangeable.

A *formula* is either a constant $\top$, $\bot$, literal ℓ, negation $\overline{\alpha}$, conjunction $\alpha \cdot \beta$ or disjunction $\alpha + \beta$ where α, β are formulas. The set of variables appearing in a formula Δ are denoted by $vars(\Delta)$. A *term* is a conjunction of literals for distinct variables. A *clause* is a disjunction of literals for distinct variables. A *DNF* is a disjunction of terms. A *CNF* is a conjunction of clauses. An *NNF* is a formula without negations. These definitions imply that terms cannot be inconsistent, clauses cannot be valid, and negations are not allowed in DNFs, CNFs, or NNFs. Finally, we say a term/clause is *simple* iff it contains only simple literals.

A *world* maps each variable in Σ to one of its states and is typically denoted by ω. A world ω is called a *model* of formula α, written $\omega \models \alpha$, iff α is satisfied by ω (that is, α is true at ω). The constant $\top$ denotes a valid formula (satisfied by every world) and the constant $\bot$ denotes an unsatisfiable formula (has no models). Formula α implies formula β, written $\alpha \models \beta$, iff every model of α is also a model of β. A term τ_1 subsumes another term τ_2 iff $\tau_2 \models \tau_1$. A clause σ_1 subsumes another clause σ_2 iff $\sigma_1 \models \sigma_2$. Formula α is weaker than formula β iff $\beta \models \alpha$ (hence β is stronger than α).

The *conditioning* of formula Δ on simple term τ is denoted $\Delta|\tau$ and obtained as follows. For each state x of variable X that appears in term τ, replace each X-literal ℓ in Δ with $\top$ if $x \in \ell$ and with $\bot$ otherwise. Note that $\Delta|\tau$ does not mention any variable that appears in term τ. A *prime implicant* for a formula Δ is a term α such that $\alpha \models \Delta$, and there does not exist a distinct term β such that $\alpha \models \beta \models \Delta$. A *prime implicate* for a formula Δ is a clause α such that $\Delta \models \alpha$, and there does not exist a distinct clause β such that $\Delta \models \beta \models \alpha$.

An *instance* of a classifier will be represented by a simple term which contains exactly one literal for each variable in Σ. A classifier with n classes will be represented by a set of mutually exclusive and exhaustive formulas $\Delta^1, \ldots, \Delta^n$, where the models of formula Δ^i capture the instances in the ith class. That is, instance $\mathcal{I}$ is in the ith class iff $\mathcal{I} \models \Delta^i$. We refer to each Δ^i as a *class formula*, or simply a *class,* and say that instance $\mathcal{I}$ is in class Δ^i when $\mathcal{I} \models \Delta^i$.

Consider the decision diagram on the right which represents a classifier with three ternary features (X, Y, Z) and three classes c_1, c_2, and c_3. This classifier can be represented by the class formulas $\Delta^1 = x_{12} + x_3 \cdot y_1 \cdot z_{13}$, $\Delta^2 = x_3 \cdot z_2$ and $\Delta^3 = x_3 \cdot y_{23} \cdot z_{13}$. This classifier has 27 instances, partitioned as follows: 20 instances in class c_1, 3 in class c_2 and 4 in class c_3. For example, instance $\mathcal{I} = x_3 \cdot y_2 \cdot z_2$ belongs to class c_2 since $\mathcal{I} \models \Delta^2$.

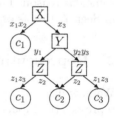

3 The General Reason for a Decision

An operator $\forall x$ which eliminates the state x of a Boolean variable X from a formula was introduced and studied in [19]. This operator, called universal literal quantification, was also generalized in [19] to the states of discrete variables but without further study. Later, [18] studied this discrete generalization, given next.

Definition 1. *For variable X with states $x_1, \ldots, x_n$, the universal literal quantification of state x_i from formula Δ is defined as $\forall x_i \cdot \Delta = \Delta|x_i \cdot \prod_{j \neq i}(x_i + \Delta|x_j)$.*

The operator $\forall$ is commutative so we can equivalently write $\forall x \cdot (\forall y \cdot \Delta)$, $\forall y \cdot (\forall x \cdot \Delta)$, $\forall x, y \cdot \Delta$ or $\forall \{x, y\} \cdot \Delta$. It is meaningful then to quantify an instance $\mathcal{I}$ from its class formula Δ since $\mathcal{I}$ is a set of states. As shown in [19], the quantified formula $\forall \mathcal{I} \cdot \Delta$ corresponds to the complete reason for the decision on instance $\mathcal{I}$. Hence, the prime implicants of $\forall \mathcal{I} \cdot \Delta$ are the sufficient reasons for the decision [17] and its prime implicates are the necessary reasons [18].

We next define a new operator $\overline{\forall}$ that we call a *selection operator* for reasons that will become apparent later. This operator will lead to the notion of a general reason for a decision which subsumes the decision's complete reason, and provides the basis for defining general necessary and sufficient reasons.

Definition 2. *For variable X with states $x_1, \ldots, x_n$ and formula Δ, we define $\overline{\forall} x_i \cdot \Delta$ to be $\Delta | x_i \cdot \Delta$.*

The selection operator $\overline{\forall}$ is also commutative, like $\forall$.

Proposition 1. $\overline{\forall} x \cdot (\overline{\forall} y \cdot \Delta) = \overline{\forall} y \cdot (\overline{\forall} x \cdot \Delta)$ *for states x, y.*

Since a term τ corresponds to a set of states, the expression $\overline{\forall} \tau \cdot \Delta$ is well-defined just like $\forall \tau \cdot \Delta$. We can now define our first major notion.

Definition 3. *Let $\mathcal{I}$ be an instance in class Δ. The general reason for the decision on instance $\mathcal{I}$ is defined as $\overline{\forall} \mathcal{I} \cdot \Delta$.*

The complete reason $\forall \mathcal{I} \cdot \Delta$ can be thought of as a property/abstraction of instance $\mathcal{I}$ that justifies (i.e., can trigger) the decision. In fact, it is equivalent to the weakest NNF Γ whose literals appear in the instance and that satisfies $\mathcal{I} \models \Gamma \models \Delta$ [18,19]. The next result shows that the general reason is a weaker property and, hence, a further abstraction that triggers the decision.

Proposition 2. *For instance $\mathcal{I}$ and formula Δ where $\mathcal{I} \models \Delta$, we have $\mathcal{I} \models \forall \mathcal{I} \cdot \Delta \models \overline{\forall} \mathcal{I} \cdot \Delta \models \Delta$. ($\mathcal{I} \not\models \Delta$ only if $\forall \mathcal{I} \cdot \Delta = \overline{\forall} \mathcal{I} \cdot \Delta = \bot$)*

The next result provides further semantics for the general reason and highlights the key difference with the complete reason.

Proposition 3. *The general reason $\overline{\forall} \mathcal{I} \cdot \Delta$ is equivalent to the weakest NNF Γ whose literals are implied by instance $\mathcal{I}$ and that satisfies $\mathcal{I} \models \Gamma \models \Delta$.*

The complete and general reasons are abstractions of the instance that explain why it belongs to its class. The former can only reference simple literals in the instance but the latter can reference any literal that is implied by the instance. The complete reason can be recovered from the general reason and the underlying instance. Moreover, the two types of reasons are equivalent when all variables are binary since $\forall x \cdot \Delta = \overline{\forall} x \cdot \Delta$ when x is the state of a binary variable.

We next provide a number of results that further our understanding of general reasons, particularly their semantics and how to compute them. We start with the following alternative definition of the operator $\overline{\forall} x_i$.

Proposition 4. *For formula Δ and variable X with states $x_1, \ldots, x_n$, $\overline{\forall} x_i \cdot \Delta$ is equivalent to $(\Delta | x_i) \cdot \prod_{j \neq i} (\ell_j + (\Delta | x_j))$, where ℓ_j is the literal $\{x_1, \ldots, x_n\} \setminus \{x_j\}$.*

According to this definition, we can always express $\overline{\forall} x_i \cdot \Delta$ as an NNF in which every X-literal includes state x_i (recall that $\Delta | x_i$ and $\Delta | x_j$ do not mention variable X). This property is used in the proofs and has a number of implications.[5]

---

[5] For example, we can use it to provide *forgetting* semantics for the dual operator $\overline{\exists} x_i \cdot \Delta = \overline{\overline{\forall} x_i \cdot \overline{\Delta}}$. Using Definition 2, we get $\overline{\exists} x_i \cdot \Delta = \Delta + \Delta | x_i$. Using Proposition 4, we get $\overline{\exists} x_i \cdot \Delta = \Delta | x_i + \sum_{j \neq i} (x_j \cdot \Delta | x_j)$. We can now easily show that (1) $\Delta \models \overline{\exists} x_i \cdot \Delta$ and (2) $\overline{\exists} x_i \cdot \Delta$ is equivalent to an NNF whose X-literals do not mention state x_i. That is, $\overline{\exists} x_i$ can be understood as forgetting the information about state x_i from Δ. This is similar to the dual operator $\exists x_i \cdot \Delta = \overline{\forall x_i \cdot \overline{\Delta}}$ studied in [19,32] except that $\overline{\exists} x_i$ erases less information from Δ since one can show that $\Delta \models \overline{\exists} x_i \cdot \Delta \models \exists x_i \cdot \Delta$.

When Δ is a class formula, [19] showed that the application of $\forall x$ to Δ can be understood as *selecting* a specific set of instances from the corresponding class. This was shown for states x of Boolean variables. We next generalize this to discrete variables and provide a selection semantics for the new operator $\overline{\forall}$.

Proposition 5. *Let τ be a simple term, Δ be a formula and ω be a world. Then $\omega \models \forall \tau \cdot \Delta$ iff $\omega \models \Delta$ and $\omega' \models \Delta$ for any world ω' obtained from ω by changing the states of some variables that are set differently in τ. Moreover, $\omega \models \overline{\forall} \tau \cdot \Delta$ iff $\omega \models \Delta$ and $\omega' \models \Delta$ for any world ω' obtained from ω by setting some variables in ω to their states in τ.*

That is, $\forall \tau \cdot \Delta$ selects all instances in class Δ whose membership in the class does not depend on characteristics that are inconsistent with τ. These instances are also selected by $\overline{\forall} \tau \cdot \Delta$ which further selects instances that remain in class Δ when any of their characteristics are changed to agree with τ.

The complete reason is monotone which has key computational implications as shown in [17–19]. The general reason satisfies a weaker property called *fixation* which has also key computational implications as we show in Sect. 6.

Definition 4. *An NNF is locally fixated on instance $\mathcal{I}$ iff its literals are consistent with $\mathcal{I}$. A formula is fixated on instance $\mathcal{I}$ iff it is equivalent to an NNF that is locally fixated on $\mathcal{I}$.*

We also say in this case that the formula is $\mathcal{I}$-fixated. For example, if $\mathcal{I} = x_1 \cdot y_1 \cdot z_2$ then the formula $x_{12} \cdot y_1 + z_2$ is (locally) $\mathcal{I}$-fixated but $x_{12} \cdot z_1$ is not. By the selection semantic we discussed earlier, a formula Δ is $\mathcal{I}$-fixated only if for every model ω of Δ, changing the states of some variables in ω to their states in $\mathcal{I}$ guarantees that the result remains a model of Δ. Moreover, if Δ is $\mathcal{I}$-fixated, then $\mathcal{I} \models \Delta$ but the opposite does not hold (e.g., $\Delta = x_1 + y_1$ and $\mathcal{I} = x_1 \cdot y_2$). We now have the following corollary of Proposition 3.

Corollary 1. *The general reason $\overline{\forall} \mathcal{I} \cdot \Delta$ is $\mathcal{I}$-fixated.*

The next propositions show that the new operator $\overline{\forall}$ has similar computational properties to $\forall$ which we use in Sect. 5 to compute general reasons.

Proposition 6. *For state x and literal ℓ of variable X, $\overline{\forall} x \cdot \ell = \ell$ if $x \in \ell$ ($x \models \ell$); else $\overline{\forall} x \cdot \ell = \bot$. Moreover, $\overline{\forall} x \cdot \Delta = \Delta$ if X does not appear in Δ.*

Proposition 7. *For formulas α, β and state x_i of variable X, we have $\overline{\forall} x_i \cdot (\alpha \cdot \beta) = (\overline{\forall} x_i \cdot \alpha) \cdot (\overline{\forall} x_i \cdot \beta)$. Moreover, if variable X does not occur in both α and β, then $\overline{\forall} x_i \cdot (\alpha + \beta) = (\overline{\forall} x_i \cdot \alpha) + (\overline{\forall} x_i \cdot \beta)$.*

An NNF is $\vee$-decomposable if its disjuncts do not share variables. According to these propositions, we can apply $\overline{\forall} \mathcal{I}$ to an $\vee$-decomposable NNF in linear time, by simply applying $\overline{\forall} \mathcal{I}$ to each literal in the NNF (the result is $\vee$-decomposable).

4   General Necessary and Sufficient Reasons

We next introduce generalizations of necessary and sufficient reasons and show that they are prime implicates and implicants of the general reason for a decision. These new notions have more explanatory power and subsume their classical counterparts, particularly when explaining the behavior of a classifier beyond a specific instance/decision. For example, when considering the classifier in Fig. 1b, which is a variant of the one in Fig. 1a, we will see that the two classifiers will make identical decisions on some instances, leading to identical simple necessary and sufficient reasons for these decisions but distinct general necessary and sufficient reasons. Moreover, we will see that general necessary and sufficient reasons are particularly critical when explaining the behavior of classifiers with (discretized) numeric features.

4.1   General Sufficient Reasons (GSRs)

We start by defining the classical notion of a (simple) sufficient reason but using a different formulation than [46] which was the first to introduce this notion under the name of a PI-explanation. Our formulation is meant to highlight a symmetry with the proposed generalization.

Definition 5 (SR). *A sufficient reason for the decision on instance $\mathcal{I}$ in class Δ is a weakest simple term τ s.t. $\mathcal{I} \models \tau \models \Delta$.*

This definition implies that each literal in τ is a variable setting (i.e., characteristic) that appears in instance $\mathcal{I}$. That is, the (simple) literals of sufficient reason τ are a subset of the literals in instance $\mathcal{I}$. We now define our generalization.

Definition 6 (GSR). *A general sufficient reason for the decision on instance $\mathcal{I}$ in class Δ is a term τ which satisfies (1) τ is a weakest term s.t. $\mathcal{I} \models \tau \models \Delta$ and (2) no term τ' satisfies the previous condition if $vars(\tau') \subset vars(\tau)$.*

This definition does not require the GSR τ to be a simple term, but it requires that it has a minimal set of variables. Without this minimality condition, a GSR will be redundant in the sense of the upcoming Proposition 8. For a term τ and instance $\mathcal{I}$ s.t. $\mathcal{I} \models \tau$, we will use $\mathcal{I} \dot\cap \tau$ to denote the smallest subterm in $\mathcal{I}$ that implies τ. For example, if $\mathcal{I} = x_2 \cdot y_1 \cdot z_3$ and $\tau = x_{12} \cdot y_{13}$, then $\mathcal{I} \dot\cap \tau = x_2 \cdot y_1$.

Proposition 8. *Let $\mathcal{I}$ be an instance in class Δ and τ be a weakest term s.t. $\mathcal{I} \models \tau \models \Delta$. If τ' is a weakest term s.t. $\mathcal{I} \models \tau' \models \Delta$ and $vars(\tau') \subset vars(\tau)$, then $\mathcal{I} \dot\cap \tau \models \mathcal{I} \dot\cap \tau' \models \Delta$. Also, $\mathcal{I} \dot\cap \tau$ is a SR iff such a term τ' does not exist.*

According to this proposition, the term τ is redundant as an explanation in that the subset of instance $\mathcal{I}$ which it identifies as being a culprit for the decision ($\mathcal{I} \dot\cap \tau$) is dominated by a smaller subset that is identified by the term τ' ($\mathcal{I} \dot\cap \tau'$).

Consider the classifiers in Figs. 1a and 1b and the patient Susan: AGE $\geq$55, BTYPE=A and WEIGHT=OVER. Both classifiers will make the same decision YES on

Susan with the same SRs: $(\text{AGE} \geq 55 \cdot \text{BTYPE=A})$ and $(\text{AGE} \geq 55 \cdot \text{WEIGHT=OVER})$. The GSRs are different for these two (equal) decisions. For the first classifier, they are $(\text{AGE} \geq 55 \cdot \text{BTYPE} \in \{A, B\})$ and $(\text{AGE} \geq 55 \cdot \text{WEIGHT=OVER})$. For the second, they are $(\text{AGE} \geq 55 \cdot \text{BTYPE} \in \{A, O\})$ and $(\text{AGE} \geq 55 \cdot \text{WEIGHT} \in \{\text{OVER}, \text{NORM}\})$. GSRs encode all SRs and contain more information.[6]

Proposition 9. *Let τ be a simple term. Then τ is a SR for the decision on instance $\mathcal{I}$ iff $\tau = \mathcal{I} \,\hat{\cap}\, \tau'$ for some GSR τ'.*

Consider the instance Susan again, $\mathcal{I} = (\text{AGE} \geq 55) \cdot (\text{BTYPE=A}) \cdot (\text{WEIGHT=OVER})$ and the classifier in Fig. 1b. As mentioned, the GSRs for the decision on Susan are $\tau_1' = (\text{AGE} \geq 55 \cdot \text{BTYPE} \in \{A, O\})$ and $\tau_2' = (\text{AGE} \geq 55 \cdot \text{WEIGHT} \in \{\text{OVER}, \text{NORM}\})$ so $\tau_1 = \mathcal{I} \,\hat{\cap}\, \tau_1' = (\text{AGE} \geq 55 \cdot \text{BTYPE=A})$ and $\tau_2 = \mathcal{I} \,\hat{\cap}\, \tau_2' = (\text{AGE} \geq 55 \cdot \text{WEIGHT=OVER})$, which are the two SRs for the decision on Susan.

The use of general terms to explain the decision on an instance $\mathcal{I}$ in class Δ was first suggested in [12]. This work proposed the notion of a general PI-explanation as a prime implicant of Δ that is consistent with instance $\mathcal{I}$. This definition is equivalent to Condition (1) in our Definition 6 which has a second condition relating to variable minimality. Hence, the definition proposed by [12] does not satisfy the desirable properties stated in Propositions 8 and 9 which require this minimality condition. The merits of using general terms were also discussed when explaining decision trees in [27], which introduced the notion of an *abductive path explanation (APXp)*. In a nutshell, each path in a decision tree corresponds to a general term τ that implies the formula Δ of the path's class. Such a term is usually used to explain the decisions made on instances that follow that path. As observed in [27], such a term can often be shortened, leading to an APXp that still implies the class formula Δ and hence provides a better explanation. An APXp is an implicant of the class formula Δ but not necessarily a prime implicant (or a variable-minimal prime implicant). Moreover, an APXp is a property of the specific decision tree (syntax) instead of its underlying classifier (semantics). See Appendix B in [30] for further discussion of these limitations.[7]

4.2   General Necessary Reasons (GNRs)

We now turn to simple necessary reasons and their generalizations. A necessary reason is a property of the instance that will flip the decision if violated in a certain way (by changing the instance). As mentioned earlier, the difference between the classical necessary reason and the generalized one is that the latter comes with stronger guarantees. Again, we start with a definition of classical necessary reasons using a different phrasing than [24] which formalized them under the name of contrastive explanations [33]. Our phrasing, based on [18], highlights a symmetry with the generalization and requires the following notation.

---

[6] Unlike SRs, two GSRs may mention the same set of variables. Consider the class formula $\Delta = (x_1 \cdot y_{12}) + (x_{12} \cdot y_1)$ and instance $\mathcal{I} = x_1 \cdot y_1$. There are two GSRs for the decision on $\mathcal{I}$, $x_1 \cdot y_{12}$ and $x_{12} \cdot y_1$, and both mention the same variables X, Y.

[7] A dual notion, contrastive path explanation (CPXp), was also proposed in [27].

For a clause σ and instance $\mathcal{I}$ s.t. $\mathcal{I} \models \sigma$, we will use $\mathcal{I}\backslash\!\backslash\sigma$ to denote the largest subterm of $\mathcal{I}$ that does not imply σ. For example, if $\mathcal{I} = x_2 \cdot y_1 \cdot z_3$ and $\sigma = x_{12} + y_{13}$ then $\mathcal{I}\backslash\!\backslash\sigma = z_3$. We will also write $\mathcal{I} \overset{\cdot}{\models} \sigma$ to mean that instance $\mathcal{I}$ implies every literal in clause σ. For instance $\mathcal{I} = x_2 \cdot y_1 \cdot z_3$, we have $\mathcal{I} \overset{\cdot}{\models} x_{12} + y_{13}$ but $\mathcal{I} \overset{\cdot}{\not\models} x_{12} + y_{23}$ even though $\mathcal{I} \models x_{12} + y_{23}$.

Definition 7 (NR). *A necessary reason for the decision on instance $\mathcal{I}$ in class Δ is a strongest simple clause σ s.t. $\mathcal{I} \overset{\cdot}{\models} \sigma$ and $(\mathcal{I}\backslash\!\backslash\sigma) \cdot \overline{\sigma} \not\models \Delta$ (if we minimally change the instance to violate σ, it is no longer guaranteed to stay in class Δ).*

A necessary reason guarantees that *some* minimal change to the instance which violates the reason will flip the decision. But it does not guarantee that *all* such changes will. A general necessary reason comes with a stronger guarantee.

Definition 8 (GNR). *A general necessary reason for the decision on instance $\mathcal{I}$ in class Δ is a strongest clause σ s.t. $\mathcal{I} \overset{\cdot}{\models} \sigma$, $(\mathcal{I}\backslash\!\backslash\sigma) \cdot \overline{\sigma} \models \overline{\Delta}$, and no clause σ' satisfies the previous conditions if $vars(\sigma') \subset vars(\sigma)$.*

The key difference between Definitions 7 and 8 are the conditions $(\mathcal{I}\backslash\!\backslash\sigma) \cdot \overline{\sigma} \not\models \Delta$ and $(\mathcal{I}\backslash\!\backslash\sigma) \cdot \overline{\sigma} \models \overline{\Delta}$. The first condition guarantees that *some* violation of a NR will flip the decision (by placing the modified instance outside class Δ) while the second condition guarantees that *all* violations of a GNR will flip the decision.

The next proposition explains why we require GNRs to be variable-minimal. Without this condition, the changes identified by a GNR to flip the decision may not be minimal (we can flip the decision by changing a strict subset of variables).

For instance $\mathcal{I}$ and clause σ s.t. $\mathcal{I} \models \sigma$, we will use $\mathcal{I} \overset{\cdot}{\cap} \sigma$ to denote the disjunction of states that appear in both $\mathcal{I}$ and σ (hence, $\mathcal{I} \overset{\cdot}{\cap} \sigma \models \sigma$). For example, if $\mathcal{I} = x_1 \cdot y_1 \cdot z_1$ and $\sigma = x_{12} + y_{23} + z_1$, then $\mathcal{I} \overset{\cdot}{\cap} \sigma = x_1 + z_1$.

Proposition 10. *Let $\mathcal{I}$ be an instance in class Δ and let σ be a strongest clause s.t. $\mathcal{I} \overset{\cdot}{\models} \sigma$ and $(\mathcal{I}\backslash\!\backslash\sigma) \cdot \overline{\sigma} \models \overline{\Delta}$. If σ' is another strongest clause satisfying these conditions and $vars(\sigma') \subset vars(\sigma)$, then $\mathcal{I}\backslash\!\backslash\sigma' \models \mathcal{I}\backslash\!\backslash\sigma$. Moreover, $\mathcal{I} \overset{\cdot}{\cap} \sigma$ is a NR iff such a clause σ' does not exist.*

That is, if violating σ requires changing some characteristics C of instance $\mathcal{I}$, then σ' can be violated by changing a strict subset of these characteristics C.

Consider the classifiers in Figs. 1a and 1b which make the same decision, YES, on Susan (AGE $\geq$55, BTYPE=A, WEIGHT=OVER). The NRs for these equal decisions are the same: (AGE $\geq$55) and (WEIGHT=OVER + BTYPE=A). The GNRs for the classifier in Fig. 1a are (AGE $\geq$55), (BTYPE $\in\{$A, B, AB$\}$+ WEIGHT=OVER$\}$) and (BTYPE $\in\{$A, B$\}$ + WEIGHT $\in\{$UNDER, OVER$\}$). If the instance is changed to violate any of them, the decision will change. For example, if we set BTYPE to AB and WEIGHT to NORM, the third GNR will be violated and the decision on Susan becomes NO. For the classifier in Fig. 1b, the GNRs for the decision are different: (AGE $\geq$55) and (BTYPE $\in\{$A, O$\}$ + WEIGHT $\in\{$NORM, OVER$\}$). However, both sets of GNRs contain more information than the NRs since the minimal changes they identify to flip the decision include those identified by the NRs.

Proposition 11. *Let σ be a simple clause. Then σ is a NR for the decision on instance $\mathcal{I}$ iff $\sigma = \mathcal{I} \dot{\cap} \sigma'$ for some GNR σ'.*

Consider the instance Susan again, $\mathcal{I} = (\text{AGE} \geq 55) \cdot (\text{BTYPE}=A) \cdot (\text{WEIGHT}=\text{OVER})$ and the classifier in Fig. 1b. As mentioned earlier, the GNRs for the decision on Susan are $\sigma_1' = (\text{AGE} \geq 55)$ and $\sigma_2' = (\text{BTYPE} \in \{A, O\} + \text{WEIGHT} \in \{\text{NORM}, \text{OVER}\})$. Then $\sigma_1 = \mathcal{I} \dot{\cap} \sigma_1' = (\text{AGE} \geq 55)$ and $\sigma_2 = \mathcal{I} \dot{\cap} \sigma_2' = (\text{WEIGHT}=\text{OVER} + \text{BTYPE}=A)$, which are the two NRs for the decision on Susan.

GSRs and GNRs are particularly significant when explaining the decisions of classifiers with numeric features, a topic which we discuss in Appendix C of [30].

We next present a fundamental result which allows us to compute GSRs and GNRs using the general reason for a decision (we use this result in Sect. 6).

Definition 9. *A prime implicant/implicate c of formula Δ is variable-minimal iff there is no prime implicant/implicate c' of Δ s.t. $vars(c') \subset vars(c)$.*

Proposition 12. *Let $\mathcal{I}$ by an instance in class Δ. The GSRs/GNRs for the decision on instance $\mathcal{I}$ are the variable-minimal prime implicants/implicates of the general reason $\bar{\forall} \mathcal{I} \cdot \Delta$.*

The disjunction of SRs is equivalent to the complete reason which is equivalent to the conjunction of NRs. However, the disjunction of GSRs implies the general reason but is not equivalent to it, and the conjunction of GNRs is implied by the general reason but is not equivalent to it; see Appendix D in [30]. This suggests that more information can potentially be extracted from the general reason beyond the information provided by GSRs and GNRs.

5   The General Reasons of Decision Graphs

Decision graphs are DAGs which include decision trees [7,9], OBDDs [10], and can have discrete or numeric features. They received significant attention in the work on explainable AI since they can be compiled from other types of classifiers such as Bayesian networks [47], random forests [12] and some types of neural networks [45]. Hence, the ability to explain decision graphs has a direct application to explaining the decisions of a broad class of classifiers. Moreover, the decisions undertaken by decision graphs have closed-form complete reasons as shown in [18]. We provide similar closed forms for the general reasons in this section. We first review decision graphs to formally state our results.

Each leaf node in a decision graph is labeled with some class c. An internal node T that *tests* variable X has outgoing edges $\xrightarrow{X, S_1} T_1, \ldots, \xrightarrow{X, S_n} T_n, n \geq 2$. The children of node T are $T_1, \ldots, T_n$ and $S_1, \ldots, S_n$ is a partition of *some* states of variable X. A decision graph will be represented by its root node. Hence, each node in the graph represents a smaller decision graph. Variables can be tested more than once on a path if they satisfy the *weak test-once property* discussed next [18,22]. Consider a path $\ldots, T \xrightarrow{X, S_j} T_j, \ldots, T' \xrightarrow{X, R_k} T_k, \ldots$ from the root to a leaf (nodes T and T' test X). If no nodes between T and T' on the path test variable X, then $\{R_k\}_k$ must be a partition of states S_j. Moreover, if T is the first node that tests X on the path, then $\{S_j\}_j$ must be a partition of *all* states for X. Discretized numeric variables are normally tested more than once while satisfying the weak test-once property; see Appendix C in [30] for an illustration.

Proposition 13. *Let T be a decision graph, $\mathcal{I}$ be an instance in class c, and $\mathcal{I}[X]$ be the state of variable X in instance $\mathcal{I}$. Suppose $\Delta^c[T]$ is the class formula of T and class c. The general reason $\overline{\forall}\mathcal{I} \cdot \Delta^c[T]$ is given by the NNF circuit:*[8]

$$
\Gamma^c[T] = \begin{cases}
\top & \text{if } T \text{ is a leaf with class } c \\
\bot & \text{if } T \text{ is a leaf with class } c' \neq c \\
\prod_j (\Gamma^c[T_j] + \ell) & \text{if } T \text{ has outgoing edges } \xrightarrow{X, S_j} T_j
\end{cases}
$$

Here, ℓ is the X-literal $\{x_i \mid x_i \notin S_j\}$ if $\mathcal{I}[X] \notin S_j$, else $\ell = \bot$.

The following proposition identifies some properties of the above closed form, which have key computational implications that we exploit in the next section.

Proposition 14. *The NNF circuit in Proposition 13 is locally fixated on instance $\mathcal{I}$. Moreover, every disjunction in this circuit has the form $\ell + \Delta$ where ℓ is an X-literal, and for every X-literal ℓ' in Δ we have $\ell' \neq \ell$ and $\ell \models \ell'$.*

6   Computing Prime Implicants and Implicates

Computing the prime implicants/implicates of Boolean formulas was studied extensively for decades; see, e.g., [29,31,48]. The classical methods are based on *resolution* when computing the prime implicates of CNFs, and *consensus* when computing the prime implicants of DNFs; see, e.g., [15,20]. More modern approaches are based on passing encodings to SAT-solvers; see, e.g., [28,35,41]. In contrast, the computation of prime implicants/implicates of discrete formulas has received very little attention in the literature. One recent exception is [12] which showed how an algorithm for computing prime implicants of Boolean formulas can be used to compute simple prime implicants of discrete formulas given an appropriate encoding. Computing prime implicants/implicates of NNFs also received relatively little attention; see [14,18,42] for some exceptions. We next provide methods for computing variable-minimal prime implicants/implicates of some classes of discrete formulas that are relevant to GSRs and GNRs.

A set of terms S will be interpreted as a DNF $\sum_{\tau \in S} \tau$ and a set of clauses S will be interpreted as a CNF $\prod_{\sigma \in S} \sigma$. If S_1 and S_2 are two sets of terms, then $S_1 \times S_2 = \{\tau_1 \cdot \tau_2 \mid \tau_1 \in S_1, \tau_2 \in S_2\}$. For a set of terms/clauses S, $\ominus(S)$ denotes the result of removing subsumed terms/clauses from S.

---

[8] An NNF circuit is a DAG whose leaves are labeled with $\bot$, $\top$, or literals; and whose internal nodes are labelled with $\cdot$ or $+$.

Algorithm 1. GSR(Δ) — without Line 10, this is **Algorithm 2** PI(Δ)

Input: NNF circuit Δ which satisfies the properties in Proposition 14

1: **if** CACHE(Δ) $\neq$ NIL **then return** CACHE(Δ)
2: **else if** $\Delta = \top$ **then return** $\{\top\}$
3: **else if** $\Delta = \bot$ **then return** $\emptyset$
4: **else if** Δ is a literal **then return** $\{\Delta\}$
5: **else if** $\Delta = \alpha \cdot \beta$ **then**
6:     $S \leftarrow \ominus(\mathrm{GSR}(\alpha) \times \mathrm{GSR}(\beta))$
7: **else if** $\Delta = \alpha + \beta$ **then**
8:     $S \leftarrow \ominus(\mathrm{GSR}(\alpha) \cup \mathrm{GSR}(\beta))$
9: **end if**
10: $S \leftarrow \boxtimes(S, ivars(\Delta))$
11: CACHE(Δ) $\leftarrow S$
12: **return** S

6.1 Computing General Sufficient Reasons

Our first result is Algorithm 1 which computes the variable-minimal prime implicants of an NNF circuit that satisfies the properties in Proposition 14 and, hence, is applicable to the general reasons of Proposition 13. If we remove Line 10 from Algorithm 1, it becomes Algorithm 2 which computes all prime implicants instead of only the variable-minimal ones. Algorithm 2 is the same algorithm used to convert an NNF into a DNF (i.e., no consensus is invoked), yet the resulting DNF is guaranteed to be in prime-implicant form. Algorithm 2 is justified by the following two results, where the first result generalizes Proposition 40 in [38].

In the next propositions, pi(Δ) denotes the prime implicants of formula Δ.

Proposition 15. $pi(\alpha \cdot \beta) = \ominus(pi(\alpha) \times pi(\beta))$.

Proposition 16. *For any disjunction $\alpha + \beta$ that satisfies the property of Proposition 14, $pi(\alpha + \beta) = \ominus(pi(\alpha) \cup pi(\beta))$.*

We will next explain Line 10 of Algorithm 1, $S \leftarrow \boxtimes(S, ivars(\Delta))$, which is responsible for pruning prime implicants that are not variable-minimal (hence, computing GSRs). Here, Δ is a node in the NNF circuit passed in the first call to Algorithm 1, and $ivars(\Delta)$ denotes variables that appear only in the sub-circuit rooted at node Δ. Moreover, $\boxtimes(S, V)$ is the set of terms obtained from terms S by removing every term $\tau \in S$ that satisfies $vars(\tau) \supset vars(\tau')$ and $V \cap (vars(\tau) \setminus vars(\tau')) \neq \emptyset$ for some other term $\tau' \in S$.[9] That is, term τ will be removed only if some variable X in $vars(\tau) \setminus vars(\tau')$ appears only in the sub-circuit rooted at node Δ (this ensures that term τ will not participate in constructing any variable-minimal prime implicant). This incremental pruning technique is enabled by the local fixation property (Definition 4).

---

[9] The condition $V \cap (vars(\tau) \setminus vars(\tau')) \neq \emptyset$ is trivially satisfied when Δ is the root of the NNF circuit since V will include all circuit variables in this case.

Proposition 17. *Algorithm 1, $GSR(\Delta)$, returns the variable-minimal prime implicants of NNF circuit Δ.*

6.2 Computing General Necessary Reasons

We can convert an NNF circuit into a CNF using a dual of Algorithm 2 but the result will not be in prime-implicate form, even for ciruits that satisfy the properties Proposition 14.[10] Hence, we next propose a generalization of the Boolean resolution inference rule to discrete variables, which can be used to convert a CNF into its prime-implicate form. Recall first that Boolean resolution derives the clause $\alpha + \beta$ from the clauses $x + \alpha$ and $\overline{x} + \beta$ where X is a Boolean variable.

Definition 10. *Let $\alpha = \ell_1 + \sigma_1$, $\beta = \ell_2 + \sigma_2$ be two clauses where ℓ_1 and ℓ_2 are X-literals s.t. $\ell_1 \not\models \ell_2$ and $\ell_2 \not\models \ell_1$. If $\sigma = (\ell_1 \cdot \ell_2) + \sigma_1 + \sigma_2 \neq \top$, then the X-resolvent of clauses α and β is defined as the clause equivalent to σ.*

We exclude the cases $\ell_1 \models \ell_2$ and $\ell_2 \models \ell_1$ to ensure that the resolvent is not subsumed by clauses α and β. If $\sigma = \top$, it cannot be represented by clause since a clause is a disjunction of literals over distinct variables so it cannot be trivial.

Proposition 18. *Closing a (discrete) CNF under resolution and removing subsumed clauses yields the CNF's prime implicates.*

The following proposition shows that we can incrementally prune clauses that are not variable-minimal after each resolution step. This is significant computationally and is enabled by the property of local fixation (Definition 4) which is satisfied by the general reasons in Proposition 13 and their CNFs.

Proposition 19. *Let S be a set of clauses (i.e., CNF) that is locally fixated. For any clauses σ and σ' in S, if $vars(\sigma') \subset vars(\sigma)$, then the variable-minimal prime implicates of S are the variable-minimal prime implicates of $S \setminus \{\sigma\}$.*

In summary, to compute GNRs, we first convert the general reason in Proposition 13 into a CNF, then close the CNF under resolution while removing subsumed clauses and ones that are not variable-minimal after each resolution step.

7   Conclusion

We considered the notions of sufficient, necessary and complete reasons which have been playing a fundamental role in explainable AI recently. We provided generalizations of these notions for classifiers with non-binary features (discrete or discretized). We argued that these generalized notions have more explanatory power and reveal more information about the underlying classifier. We further provided results on the properties and computation of these new notions.

Acknowledgments. This work has been partially supported by NSF grant ISS-1910317.

---

[10] The number of clauses in this CNF will be no more than the number of NNF nodes if the NNF is the general reason of a decision tree (i.e., the NNF has a tree structure).

References

1. Albini, E., Rago, A., Baroni, P., Toni, F.: Relation-based counterfactual explanations for Bayesian network classifiers. In: IJCAI, pp. 451–457 (2020). https://www.ijcai.org/
2. Amgoud, L.: Explaining black-box classifiers: properties and functions. Int. J. Approx. Reason. **155**, 40–65 (2023)
3. Amgoud, L., Ben-Naim, J.: Axiomatic foundations of explainability. In: IJCAI, pp. 636–642 (2022). https://www.ijcai.org/
4. Audemard, G., Bellart, S., Bounia, L., Koriche, F., Lagniez, J., Marquis, P.: On the explanatory power of Boolean decision trees. Data Knowl. Eng. **142**, 102088 (2022)
5. Audemard, G., Koriche, F., Marquis, P.: On tractable XAI queries based on compiled representations. In: KR, pp. 838–849 (2020)
6. Audemard, G., Lagniez, J., Marquis, P., Szczepanski, N.: Computing abductive explanations for boosted trees. CoRR abs/2209.07740 (2022)
7. Belson, W.A.: Matching and prediction on the principle of biological classification. J. R. Stat. Soc. Ser. C (Appl. Stat.) **8**(2), 65–75 (1959). https://www.jstor.org/stable/2985543
8. Boumazouza, R., Alili, F.C., Mazure, B., Tabia, K.: ASTERYX: a model-agnostic sat-based approach for symbolic and score-based explanations. In: CIKM, pp. 120–129. ACM (2021)
9. Breiman, L., Friedman, J.H., Olshen, R.A., Stone, C.J.: Classification and Regression Trees. Wadsworth (1984)
10. Bryant, R.E.: Graph-based algorithms for Boolean function manipulation. IEEE Trans. Comput. **35**(8), 677–691 (1986)
11. Chan, H., Darwiche, A.: Reasoning about Bayesian network classifiers. In: UAI, pp. 107–115. Morgan Kaufmann (2003)
12. Choi, A., Shih, A., Goyanka, A., Darwiche, A.: On symbolically encoding the behavior of random forests. CoRR abs/2007.01493 (2020)
13. Choi, A., Xue, Y., Darwiche, A.: Same-decision probability: a confidence measure for threshold-based decisions. Int. J. Approx. Reason. **53**(9), 1415–1428 (2012)
14. de Colnet, A., Marquis, P.: On the complexity of enumerating prime implicants from decision-DNNF circuits. In: IJCAI, pp. 2583–2590 (2022). https://www.ijcai.org/
15. Crama, Y., Hammer, P.L.: Boolean functions - theory, algorithms, and applications. In: Encyclopedia of Mathematics and Its Applications (2011)
16. Darwiche, A.: Logic for explainable AI. In: 38th Annual ACM/IEEE Symposium on Logic in Computer Science, LICS, pp. 1–11. IEEE (2023). CoRR abs/2305.05172
17. Darwiche, A., Hirth, A.: On the reasons behind decisions. In: ECAI. Frontiers in Artificial Intelligence and Applications, vol. 325, pp. 712–720. IOS Press (2020)
18. Darwiche, A., Ji, C.: On the computation of necessary and sufficient explanations. In: AAAI, pp. 5582–5591. AAAI Press (2022)
19. Darwiche, A., Marquis, P.: On quantifying literals in Boolean logic and its applications to explainable AI. J. Artif. Intell. Res. **72**, 285–328 (2021)
20. Gurvich, V., Khachiyan, L.: On generating the irredundant conjunctive and disjunctive normal forms of monotone Boolean functions. Discrete Appl. Math. **96**, 363–373 (1999)
21. Huang, X., Izza, Y., Ignatiev, A., Cooper, M.C., Asher, N., Marques-Silva, J.: Efficient explanations for knowledge compilation languages. CoRR abs/2107.01654 (2021)

22. Huang, X., Izza, Y., Ignatiev, A., Marques-Silva, J.: On efficiently explaining graph-based classifiers. In: KR, pp. 356–367 (2021)
23. Ignatiev, A., Izza, Y., Stuckey, P.J., Marques-Silva, J.: Using MaxSAT for efficient explanations of tree ensembles. In: AAAI, pp. 3776–3785. AAAI Press (2022)
24. Ignatiev, A., Narodytska, N., Asher, N., Marques-Silva, J.: From contrastive to abductive explanations and back again. In: Baldoni, M., Bandini, S. (eds.) AIxIA 2020. LNCS (LNAI), vol. 12414, pp. 335–355. Springer, Cham (2021). https://doi.org/10.1007/978-3-030-77091-4_21
25. Ignatiev, A., Narodytska, N., Marques-Silva, J.: Abduction-based explanations for machine learning models. In: Proceedings of the Thirty-Third Conference on Artificial Intelligence (AAAI), pp. 1511–1519 (2019)
26. Ignatiev, A., Narodytska, N., Marques-Silva, J.: On validating, repairing and refining heuristic ML explanations. CoRR abs/1907.02509 (2019)
27. Izza, Y., Ignatiev, A., Marques-Silva, J.: On tackling explanation redundancy in decision trees. J. Artif. Intell. Res. **75**, 261–321 (2022)
28. Izza, Y., Marques-Silva, J.: On explaining random forests with SAT. In: IJCAI, pp. 2584–2591 (2021). https://www.ijcai.org/
29. Jackson, P.: Computing prime implicates. In: Proceedings of the 1992 ACM Annual Conference on Communications, CSC 1992, pp. 65–72. Association for Computing Machinery, New York, NY, USA (1992). https://doi.org/10.1145/131214.131223
30. Ji, C., Darwiche, A.: A new class of explanations for classifiers with non-binary features. CoRR abs/2304.14760 (2023)
31. Kean, A., Tsiknis, G.: An incremental method for generating prime implicants/implicates. J. Symbolic Comput. **9**(2), 185–206 (1990)
32. Lang, J., Liberatore, P., Marquis, P.: Propositional independence: formula-variable independence and forgetting. J. Artif. Intell. Res. **18**, 391–443 (2003)
33. Lipton, P.: Contrastive explanation. Roy. Inst. Philos. Suppl. **27**, 247–266 (1990). https://doi.org/10.1017/S1358246100005130
34. Liu, X., Lorini, E.: A unified logical framework for explanations in classifier systems. J. Log. Comput. **33**(2), 485–515 (2023)
35. Luo, W., Want, H., Zhong, H., Wei, O., Fang, B., Song, X.: An efficient two-phase method for prime compilation of non-clausal Boolean formulae. In: 2021 IEEE/ACM International Conference On Computer Aided Design (ICCAD), pp. 1–9 (2021). https://doi.org/10.1109/ICCAD51958.2021.9643520
36. Marques-Silva, J., Gerspacher, T., Cooper, M.C., Ignatiev, A., Narodytska, N.: Explanations for monotonic classifiers. In: ICML. Proceedings of Machine Learning Research, vol. 139, pp. 7469–7479. PMLR (2021)
37. Marques-Silva, J., Ignatiev, A.: Delivering trustworthy AI through formal XAI. In: AAAI, pp. 12342–12350. AAAI Press (2022)
38. Marquis, P.: Consequence finding algorithms. In: Kohlas, J., Moral, S. (eds.) Handbook of defeasible reasoning and uncertainty management systems, pp. 41–145. Springer, Cham (2000). https://doi.org/10.1007/978-94-017-1737-3_3
39. Miller, T.: Explanation in artificial intelligence: insights from the social sciences. Artif. Intell. **267**, 1–38 (2019)
40. Narodytska, N., Kasiviswanathan, S.P., Ryzhyk, L., Sagiv, M., Walsh, T.: Verifying properties of binarized deep neural networks. In: Proceedings of AAAI 2018, pp. 6615–6624 (2018)
41. Previti, A., Ignatiev, A., Morgado, A., Marques-Silva, J.: Prime compilation of non-clausal formulae. In: IJCAI, pp. 1980–1988. AAAI Press (2015)
42. Ramesh, A., Becker, G., Murray, N.V.: CNF and DNF considered harmful for computing prime implicants/implicates. J. Autom. Reason. **18**(3), 337–356 (1997)

43. Ribeiro, M.T., Singh, S., Guestrin, C.: "Why should I trust you?": explaining the predictions of any classifier. In: KDD, pp. 1135–1144. ACM (2016)

44. Ribeiro, M.T., Singh, S., Guestrin, C.: Anchors: high-precision model-agnostic explanations. In: AAAI, pp. 1527–1535. AAAI Press (2018)

45. Shi, W., Shih, A., Darwiche, A., Choi, A.: On tractable representations of binary neural networks. In: KR, pp. 882–892 (2020)

46. Shih, A., Choi, A., Darwiche, A.: A symbolic approach to explaining Bayesian network classifiers. In: IJCAI, pp. 5103–5111 (2018). https://www.ijcai.org/

47. Shih, A., Choi, A., Darwiche, A.: Compiling Bayesian network classifiers into decision graphs. In: AAAI, pp. 7966–7974. AAAI Press (2019)

48. Slagle, J., Chang, C.L., Lee, R.: A new algorithm for generating prime implicants. IEEE Trans. Comput. C- **19**(4), 304–310 (1970). https://doi.org/10.1109/T-C.1970.222917

49. Wang, E., Khosravi, P., den Broeck, G.V.: Probabilistic sufficient explanations. In: IJCAI, pp. 3082–3088 (2021). https://www.ijcai.org/

Stable Normative Explanations: From Argumentation to Deontic Logic

Cecilia Di Florio[1] , Antonino Rotolo[1(✉)] , Guido Governatori[2] ,
and Giovanni Sartor[1,3]

[1] ALMA AI and Department of Legal Studies, University of Bologna, Bologna, Italy
{cecilia.diflorio2,antonino.rotolo,giovanni.sartor}@unibo.it
[2] Cooroibah QLD 4565, Australia
guido@governatori.net
[3] EUI, Fiesole, Italy

Abstract. This paper reconstructs in the context of formal argumentation the notion of stable explanation developed elsewhere in Defeasible Logic. With this done, we discuss the deontic meaning of this notion and show how to build from argumentation neighborhood structures for deontic logic where a stable explanation can be characterised.

1 Introduction

Developing explainable AI systems is important in the law since '*transparency*' and '*justification*' of legal decision-making require formalising normative explanations [1, 4, 6, 15]. A normative explanation is an explanation where norms are crucial: in the context of legal decision-making, this means to explain why a legal conclusion ought to be the case on the basis of certain norms and facts [2, 10, 13, 14, 18, 19].

Legal proceedings are adversarial in nature: if a judge or a litigant aim at predicting possible outcomes, this fact must be taken into account, and formal tools to make such predictions understandable should allow for checking if a certain legal outcome is *stable* [9, 10, 16]. In such a perspective, given some facts, the proceeding aims at determining what legal requirements hold, and whether such legal requirements have been fulfilled. (In)Stability means that, if more/new facts were presented, the outcome of a case might be quite different or can even be modified. How to ensure a specific outcome for a case? How to ensure that the facts presented by a party are 'resilient' to the attacks from the opponent? In this paper we adopt [9, 10]'s definition of stability and elaborate it in the argumentation setting of Defeasible Logic [3].

What is the deontic meaning of stable normative explanation as developed in an argumentation setting? In legal argumentation, a typical outcome of judicial decisions are obligations and permissions. In moving to the deontic domain, we notice that deontic argumentation can be developed in various ways [12, 21]. We assume that legal norms are rules having the form $\phi_1, \ldots, \phi_n \Rightarrow \psi$ and we follow the intuition that, if

Antonino Rotolo and Giovanni Sartor were partially supported by the Project PE01 "Future AI Research" (FAIR, PNRR, CUP: J33C22002830006).

AF is an argumentation framework where arguments are built using rules, then **OBL**ψ holds in AF iff ψ is justified w.r.t. AF [20]. Once this is done and we have defined the notion of normative explanation, we adapt [11]'s method and show how *this machinery can be reconstructed in neighborhood semantics for classical deontic logics* [7] *and how the notion of explanation can be semantically characterised.*

The layout of article is as follows[1]. Section 2 offers a variant of the idea of argumentation framework based on Defeadible Logic. Section 3 presents the definition of stable normative explanation. Section 4 illustrates how to move from argumentation structures to neighbourhood semantics for deontic logic. Section 5 applies the ideas of Sects. 3 and 4 to semantically reconstruct the concept of stable normative explanation.

2   Background: Logic and Argumentation

Our framework is Defeasible Logic (DL) [3]. The basic language consists of a set Lit of literals. The *complementary* of a literal ϕ is denoted by $\sim\phi$: if ϕ is positive then $\sim\phi$ is $\neg\phi$, if ϕ is negative then $\sim\phi$ is ϕ. Let Lab be a set of labels to represent names of rules. A rule r has the form $r: A(r) \Rightarrow C(r)$, where: (i) $r \in$ Lab is the unique name of the rule, (ii) $A(r) \subseteq$ Lit is r's (set of) antecedents, (iii) $C(r) = \phi \in$ Lit is its conclusion. Unlike standard DL, *we only use defeasible rules*, in which, if the premises are the case, then typically the conclusion holds unless we have contrary evidence.

We also use a special type of logical theory in DL:

Definition 1 (Argumentation theory). *An argumentation theory D is a tuple $(F, R, >)$ where (a) $F \subseteq$ Lit is a finite and consistent set of facts (indisputable statements), (b) R is a finite rule set, and (c) a binary superiority relation over R (which is used to solve rule conflicts). We state that $\forall \phi \in F, R[\phi] \cup R[\sim\phi] = \emptyset.$*

As a convention, $R[\phi]$ denotes the set of all rules in R whose conclusion is ϕ.

A *conclusion* of D is a *tagged literal* with the following form: $+\partial\phi$ (resp. $-\partial\phi$) means that ϕ is *defeasibly proved* (resp. *defeasibly refuted*) in D, i.e., there is a defeasible proof for ϕ in D (resp. a proof does not exist). A proof P of length n in D is a finite sequence $P(1), P(2), \ldots, P(n)$ of tagged literals for which specific proof conditions are defined [3]. $P(1..n)$ denotes the first n steps of P. We present only the positive one for defeasible conclusions.

$+\partial\phi$: If $P(n+1) = +\partial\phi$ then either
    (1) $\phi \in F$, or
    (2.1) $\exists r \in R[\phi]$ s.t. $\forall \psi \in A(r). +\partial\psi \in P(1..n)$ and
    (2.2) $\forall s \in R[\sim\phi]$ either
        (2.2.1) $\exists \psi \in A(s). -\partial\psi$, or
        (2.2.2) $\exists t \in R[\phi]$ s.t. $\forall \psi \in A(t). +\partial\psi \in P(1..n)$ and $t > s$.

Argumentation frameworks for DL have been studied in [8]. Here, we present a variant of it, which is based on the above fragment of DL [9, 10].

---

[1] A full version of this paper with some proofs is here: http://arxiv.org/abs/2307.05156.

Definition 2 (Argument). *Let* $D = (F, R, >)$ *be an argumentation theory. An argument* A *constructed from D has either the the form* $\Rightarrow_F \phi$ *(factual argument), where* $\phi \in F$, *or the form* $A_1, \ldots, A_n \Rightarrow_r \phi$ *(plain argument), where* $1 \leq k \leq n$, *and*

- A_k *is an argument constructed from D, and*
- $r : \text{Conc}(A_1), \ldots, \text{Conc}(A_n) \Rightarrow \phi$ *is a rule in R.*

For a given argument A, Conc *returns its conclusion,* Sub *returns all its subarguments, and* TopRule *returns the last rule in the argument.*

Any argument A is a tree whose root is labelled by $\text{Conc}(A)$, and for every node x labelled by any ϕ, its children $x_1, \ldots, x_n$ are labelled by $\phi_1, \ldots, \phi_n$ (except its leaves, which can be also labelled by $\emptyset$) and the arcs are labeled by a rule $r : \phi_1, \ldots, \phi_n \Rightarrow \phi$. Arguments of height 1 are called *atomic arguments*; for any argument A, the set of its atomic sub-arguments is denoted by $\text{ASub}(A)$.

The notions of *attack*, *support*, and *undercut* are the standard ones for DL (see [8]). We can now define the argumentation framework.

Definition 3 (Argumentation Framework). *Let D be an argumentation theory. The argumentation framework* $\text{AF}(D)$ *determined by D is* $(\mathscr{A}, \gg)$ *where* $\mathscr{A}$ *is the set of all arguments constructed from D, and* $\gg$ *is the attack relation.*

The core of argumentation semantics are the notions of *acceptable* and *rejected* *argument*. An argument is acceptable with respect to a set of arguments that undercut any attacks. Then, we can define recursively the *extension of an argumentation theory D* and of the corresponding framework $\text{AF}(D)$, which is the set of *justified arguments* w.r.t. $\text{AF}(D)$. The definitions of the set $JArgs^D$ of *justified arguments* and of the set $RArgs^D$ of *rejected arguments* are a fix-point construction. For the details see [8].

Theorem 1. *Let D be an argumentation theory and A be an argument in* $\text{AF}(D)$ *such that* $\text{Conc}(A) = \phi$. *Then, (a)* $A \in JArgs^D$ *iff* $D \vdash +\partial\phi$; *(b)* $A \in RArgs^D$ *iff* $D \vdash -\partial\phi$.

3   Stable Normative Explanations

We define the idea of *normative explanation* for ϕ, which is a normative decision or any piece of normative knowledge that justifies ϕ and that is minimal [9, 10, 14].

Definition 4 (Normative explanation). *Let* $D = (F, R, >)$ *be an argumentation theory and* $\text{AF}(D) = (\mathscr{A}, \gg)$ *be the argumentation framework determined by D. The set* arg $\subseteq$ $\mathscr{A}$ *is a normative explanation* $\text{Expl}(\phi, \text{AF}(D))$ *in* $\text{AF}(D)$ *for* ϕ *iff*

- $A \in$ arg *is an argument for* ϕ *and A is justified w.r.t.* $\text{AF}(D)$;
- arg *is a minimal set in* $\text{AF}(D)$ *such that A is acceptable w.r.t to* arg.

Example 1. Consider the following fragment of an argumentation theory:

$$R = \{s_1 : \Rightarrow \neg\alpha, s_2 : \lambda \Rightarrow \alpha, s_3 : \beta, \pi \Rightarrow \alpha, s_4 : \delta \Rightarrow \neg\alpha, s_5 : \iota \Rightarrow \delta\}$$
$$>= \{\langle s_2, > s_1 \rangle, \langle s_3 > s_1 \rangle, \langle s_4 > s_3 \rangle, \langle s_4 > s_2 \rangle\}.$$

Assume an argumentation theory $D = (F, R, >)$ where $F = \{\iota, \lambda\}$. Then, $\mathsf{AF}(D) = (\mathscr{A}, \gg)$ is as follows:

$$\mathscr{A} = \{A_1: \ \Rightarrow_F \iota, A_2: \ \Rightarrow_F \lambda, A_3: A_1 \Rightarrow_{s_5} \delta, A_4: A_3 \Rightarrow_{s_4} \neg\alpha, A_5: A_2 \Rightarrow_{s_2} \alpha\}$$
$$\gg = \{\langle A_4, A_5 \rangle\}.$$

It is easy to see that $\{A_1, A_4\} = \mathsf{Expl}(\neg\alpha, \mathsf{AF}(D))$.

An explanation for a normative conclusion ϕ is stable when adding new elements to that explanation does not affect its power to explain ϕ [9, 10].

Definition 5. *Let R a finite set of rules. We define the set of literals $\mathrm{Lit}(R)$ as $\{\phi, \sim\phi \mid \forall r \in R : \phi \in A(r) \ or \sim\phi \in A(r), R[\phi] \cup R[\sim\phi] = \emptyset\}$.*

Definition 6 (Stable Normative Explanation). *Let $\mathsf{AF}(D) = (\mathscr{A}, \gg)$ be an argumentation framework determined by the argumentation theory $D = (F, R, >)$. We say that $\arg = \mathsf{Expl}(\phi, \mathsf{AF}(D))$ is a stable normative explanation for ϕ in $\mathsf{AF}(D)$ iff for all $\mathsf{AF}(D') = (\mathscr{A}', \gg')$ where $D' = (F', R, >)$ s.t. $F \subseteq F' \subseteq \mathrm{Lit}(R)$, we have that $\arg = \mathsf{Expl}(\phi, \mathsf{AF}(D'))$.*

Example 2. Let us consider Example 1. Then, $\{A_1, A_4\}$ is stable normative explanation for $\neg\alpha$ in $\mathsf{AF}(D)$, whereas, e.g., $\{A_2, A_5\}$ is not a stable normative explanation for α.

4 From Argumentation to Deontic Logic

To move to deontic logic we follow [11] by stating that defeasible provability (and justification) of any ϕ corresponds to the obligatoriness of ϕ, and—if **PERM** is the dual of **OBL**—the non-provability (and non-justification) of ϕ means that $\sim\phi$ is permitted.

Definition 7 (Modal language and logic). *Let Lit be the set of literals of our language $\mathscr{L}$. The language $\mathscr{L}(\mathrm{Lit})$ of $\mathbf{E}_{\mathscr{L}}$ is defined as follows:*

$$p :: = l \mid \neg p \mid \mathbf{OBL}\phi \mid \mathbf{PERM}\phi,$$

where l ranges over PROP and ϕ ranges over Lit.
   The logical system $\mathbf{E}_{\mathscr{L}}$ is based on $\mathscr{L}(\mathrm{Lit})$ and is closed under logical equivalence.

Proposition 1. *The system $\mathbf{E}_{\mathscr{L}}$ is a fragment of system $\mathbf{E}$ [7].*

To introduce an appropriate semantics for our fragment, the following is needed.

Definition 8. *Let $D = (F, R, >)$ be any argumentation theory, $\mathsf{AF}(D) = (\mathscr{A}, \gg)$ be the argumentation framework determined by D, and $\mathrm{Lit}(D)$ be the set of literals occurring in D. The D-extension $E(D)$ of a theory D is the smallest set of literals such that, for all $\phi \in \mathrm{Lit}(D)$: (a) $\phi \in E(D)$ iff ϕ is justified w.r.t. $\mathsf{AF}(D)$, (b) $\sim\phi \in E(D)$ iff ϕ is not justified w.r.t. $\mathsf{AF}(D)$.*

Definition 9. *Let L be a consistent set of literals. A defeasible rule theory is a structure $D = (R, >)$. The D-extension of L is the extension of the argumentation theory $(L, R, >)$; we denote it with $E_L(D)$.*

Definition 10 (Dependency graph). *Let D be any argumentation theory and* $\mathrm{Lit}(D)$ *be literals occurring in D. The* dependency graph *of D is the directed graph* (V,A) *where:*

- $V = \{p \mid p \in \mathrm{PROP}, \{p, \neg p\} \cap \mathrm{Lit}(D) \neq \emptyset\}$;
- *A is the set such that* $(n,m) \in A$ *iff*
  - $n = \phi$ *and* $\exists r \in R[\phi] \cup R[\sim\phi]$;
  - $m = \psi$ *and* $\exists r \in R[\psi] \cup R[\sim\psi]$ *such that* $\{n, \sim n\} \cap A(r) \neq \emptyset$.

Proposition 2. *Let L be a set of literals,* $D = (R, >)$ *be a defeasible rule theory such that the transitive closure of* $>$ *is acyclic and* $D' = (L, R, >)$ *be the corresponding argumentation theory such that the dependency graph of* D' *is acyclic. Then, the D-extension of L is consistent iff L is consistent.*

Definition 11. (Neighbourhood D-frame, neighbourhood D-model, and truth). *Let* $D = (F, R, >)$ *be an argumentation theory such that the transitive closure of* $>$ *is acyclic and the dependency graph of D is acyclic. Let* $R' = R \cup \{r :\Rightarrow \phi \mid \phi \in F\}$. *A neighbourhood D-frame is a structure* $\langle W, \mathcal{N} \rangle$ *where*

- $W = \{w \mid w \in (2^{E(D)} - \{\emptyset\})\}$;
- $\mathcal{N}$ *is a function with signature* $W \mapsto 2^{2^W}$ *defined as follows:*
  - $xS_j y$ *iff* $\exists r_j \in R'$ *such that* $A(r_j) \subseteq x$ *and* $C(r_j) \in y$
  - $\forall s \in R'[\sim C(r_j)]$ *either*
    1. $\exists a \in A(s), a \notin x$; *or*
    2. $\exists t \in R'[C(r_j)]$ *such that* $t > s$, $A(t) \subseteq x$
  - $S_j(w) = \{x \in W : wS_j x\}$
  - $\mathscr{S}_j(w) = \bigcup_{C(r_k)=C(r_j)} S_k(w)$
  - $\mathcal{N}(w) = \{\mathscr{S}_j(w)\}_{r_j \in R'}$.

A neighbourhood *D*-model $\mathcal{M}$ is obtained by adding an evaluation function $v : \mathrm{PROP} \mapsto 2^W$ to a neighbourhood *D*-frame such that, for any $p \in \mathrm{PROP}$, $v(p) = \{w \mid p \in w\}$.

To build canonical structures, we consider all possible defeasible rule theories and, for each of them, all possible maximal consistent sets of facts that can be generated.

Lemma 1 (Lindenbaum's Lemma). *Let D any defeasible rule theory. Any consistent set* $w_{EL(D)}$ *of formulae in the language* $\mathscr{L}(\mathrm{Lit})$ *consisting of a D-extension of any L can be extended to a consistent* $\mathscr{L}(\mathrm{Lit})$-*maximal set* $w^+_{EL(D)}$.

Definition 12. (Canonical neighbourhood D-model). *Given the language* $\mathscr{L}$, *let* $\mathscr{D}$ *be the set of all defeasible rule theories that can be obtained from* $\mathscr{L}$. *For all* $D_i = (R_i, >_i) \in \mathscr{D}$, *define* $R'_i = R_i \cup \{r :\Rightarrow \phi \mid \phi \in L\}$ *for each* $(L, R_i, >_i)$, $L \in 2^{\mathrm{Lit}(D_i)}$. *The canonical neighbourhood model is the structure* $\mathcal{M}_{\mathscr{D}} = (W, \mathcal{N}, v)$ *where*

- $W = \bigcup_{\forall D_i \in \mathscr{D}} W_i$ *where* $W_i = \{w_L \mid \forall L \in 2^{\mathrm{Lit}(D_i)}, w_L = w^+_{EL(D_i)}\}$.
- $\mathcal{N}$ *is a function with signature* $W \mapsto 2^{2^W}$ *defined as follows:*
  - $xS^i_j y$ *where* **OBL**$\phi \in x$ *iff* $\exists r_j \in R'_i$ *such that* $C(r_j) = \phi$, $A(r_j) \subseteq x$ *and* $C(r_j) \in y$ *where* $x, y \in W_i$;
  - $\forall s \in R'_i[\sim C(r_j)]$ *either*

    1. $\exists a \in A(s), a \notin x$; or
    2. $\exists t \in R'_i[C(r_j)]$ such that $t > s$, $A(t) \subseteq x$
- $S^i_j(w) = \{x \in W_i : wS^i_j x\}$,
- $\mathscr{S}^i_j(w) = \bigcup_{C(r_k)=C(r_j)} S^i_k(w)$,
- $\mathscr{N}(w) = \{\mathscr{S}^i_j(w)\}_{r_j \in R'_i}$;

– for each $\phi \in$ Lit and any $w \in W$, v is an evaluation function such that $w \in v(\phi)$ iff $\phi \in w$, and $w \notin v(\phi)$ iff $\sim\phi \in w$.

Lemma 2 (Truth Lemma). *If $\mathscr{M} = (W, \mathscr{N}, v)$ is canonical for S, where $S \supseteq E_{\mathscr{L}}$, then for any $w \in W$ and for any formula ϕ, $\phi \in w$ iff $\mathscr{M}, w \models \phi$.*

Corollary 1. (Completeness of $E_{\mathscr{L}}$). *The system $E_{\mathscr{L}}$ is sound and complete with respect to the class of neighbourhood D-frames.*

Corollary 2. *Let $\mathscr{M}$ be any neighbourhood D-model. Then (a) $\mathscr{M} \models$ **OBL**ϕ iff there exists an argumentation theory $D = (F, R, >)$ such that ϕ is justified w.r.t. AF(D); (b) (b) $\mathscr{M} \models$ **PERM**ϕ iff there exists an argumentation theory $D = (F, R, >)$ such that $\neg\phi$ is not justified w.r.t. AF(D).*

5   Stable Explanations in Neighbourhood Semantics

The definition of normative explanation of Sect. 3 can be appropriately captured in our deontic logic setting. First of all, we have to formulate the modal version of an argument.

Proposition 3 (Neighbourhood D-model for an argument). *Let $D = (F, R, >)$ be an argumentation theory, AF(D) $= (\mathscr{A}, \gg)$ be the argumentation framework determined by D, and $\mathscr{M}_D = (W, \mathscr{N}, v)$ be the corresponding neighbourhood D-model. An argument $A \in \mathscr{A}$, where $\text{Conc}(A) = \phi_0$, is justified w.r.t. AF(D) iff, if h is the height of A and $\mathscr{A} = \{A_x | A_x \in \text{ASub}(A), \forall x \in \{(h-1)_1, \ldots, (h-1)_m, \ldots, 1_1, \ldots, 1_p, 0\}, \text{Conc}(A_x) = \phi_x\}$, then the following condition holds in $\mathscr{M}_D$: if $y \in \{h_1, \ldots, h_m, (h-1)_1, \ldots, (h-1)_m, \ldots, 1_1, \ldots, 1_p, 0\}$*

$$\exists w_y \in W \begin{cases} \forall (h-1)_z \in \{(h-1)_1, \ldots, (h-1)_m\}, (\ldots (||\phi_{(h-1)_z}|| \in \mathscr{N}(w_{h_z})) \\ \& \\ \forall (h-2)_z \in \{(h-2)_1, \ldots, (h-2)_j\}, (w_{(h-1)_z} \in ||\phi_{(h-1)_z}|| \Rightarrow \\ \Rightarrow ||\phi_{(h-2)_z}|| \in \mathscr{N}(w_{(h-1)_z})) \\ \& \\ \vdots \\ \& \\ \forall 2_z \in \{2_1, \ldots 2_k\}, (w_{2_z} \in ||\phi_{2_z}|| \Rightarrow ||\phi_{1_z}|| \in \mathscr{N}(w_{2_z})) \\ \& \\ \forall 1_z \in \{1_1, \ldots 1_j\}, (w_{1_z} \in ||\phi_{1_z}|| \Rightarrow ||\phi_0|| \in \mathscr{N}(w_{1_z})) \ldots) \end{cases}$$

The model $\mathscr{M}_D$ is called a neighbourhood D-model for A.

The concept of normative explanation directly follows from Proposition 3.

Proposition 4 (Neighbourhood D-model for a normative explanation). *Let $D = (F, R, >)$ be an argumentation theory, $\mathsf{AF}(D) = (\mathscr{A}, \gg)$ be the argumentation framework determined by D, and $\mathscr{M}_D = (W, \mathscr{N}, v)$ be the corresponding neighbourhood D-model.*

If $\mathsf{Expl}(\psi, \mathsf{AF}(D)) = \{A_1, \ldots, A_n\}$ then $\mathscr{M}_D$ is neighbourhood D-model for each argument A_k, $1 \leq k \leq n$.

The model $\mathscr{M}_D$ is called a neighbourhood D-model for $\mathsf{Expl}(\psi, \mathsf{AF}(D))$.

We can semantically isolate the arguments in a normative explanation by using Proposition 3 as well as by resorting to the notion of generated sub-model [5, 17].

Definition 13 (Generated submodel [5, 17]). *Let $\mathscr{M} = (W, \mathscr{N}, v)$ be any neighbourhood model. A generated submodel $\mathscr{M}_X = (X, \mathscr{N}_X, v_X)$ of $\mathscr{M}$ is neighbourhood model where $X \subseteq W$, $\forall Y \subseteq W, \forall w \in X, Y \in \mathscr{N}(w) \Leftrightarrow Y \cap X \in \mathscr{N}_X(w)$.*

Proposition 5 (Generated D-submodel for a normative explanation). *Let $D = (F, R, >)$ be an argumentation theory, $\mathsf{AF}(D) = (\mathscr{A}, \gg)$ be the argumentation framework determined by D, $\mathscr{X} = \mathsf{Expl}(\psi, \mathsf{AF}(D))$, $\mathscr{M}_D = (W, \mathscr{N}, v)$ be a neighbourhood D-model for $\mathscr{X}$, and $\mathscr{M}_{D_{\mathscr{X}}} = (W_{\mathscr{X}}, \mathscr{N}_{\mathscr{X}}, v_{\mathscr{X}})$ be a generated submodel of $\mathscr{M}_D$.*
$\mathscr{X} = \{A_1, \ldots, A_n\}$ iff $W_{\mathscr{X}} = W - X$ where

$$X = \{w \mid w \in W, \forall \phi \in w : \phi \in F \,\&\, A_x \in \mathscr{A}, A_x \notin \mathscr{X} \text{ and } A_x :\Rightarrow_F \phi\}$$

The model $\mathscr{M}_{D_{\mathscr{X}}}$ is called the generated D-submodel for $\mathscr{X}$.

Corollary 3 (Stable normative explanation in neighbourhood D-models). *Let $D = (F, R, >)$ be an argumentation theory and $\mathsf{AF}(D) = (\mathscr{A}, \gg)$ be the argumentation framework determined by D.*

If $\mathscr{X} = \mathsf{Expl}(\psi, \mathsf{AF}(D)) = \{A_1, \ldots, A_n\}$ is a stable normative explanation for ψ in $\mathsf{AF}(D)$ and $D^+ = (F^+, R, >)$ is the argumentation theory where $F^+ = \{\phi \mid \forall r \in R : \phi \in A(r) \text{ and } R[\phi] \cup R[\sim\phi] = \emptyset\}$, then $\mathsf{Expl}(\psi, \mathsf{AF}(D^+))$, and $\mathscr{M}_{D_{\mathscr{X}}} = \mathscr{M}_{D^+_{\mathscr{X}}}$ such that $\mathscr{M}_{D_{\mathscr{X}}}$ and $\mathscr{M}_{D^+_{\mathscr{X}}}$ are, respectively, the generated D-submodel and generated D^+-submodel for $\mathscr{X}$.

A stable explanation considers a neighbourhood model where all possibile facts of a theory D are the case and requires that in such a model the conclusion ψ is still justified.

6 Summary

In this paper we investigated the concept of stable normative explanation in argumentation. Then we have devised in a deontic logic setting a new method to construct appropriate neighborhood models from argumentation frameworks and we have characterised accordingly the notion of stable normative explanation. The problem of determining a stable normative explanation for a certain legal conclusion means to identify a set of facts, obligations, permissions, and other normative inputs able to ensure that such a conclusion continues to hold when new facts are added to a case. This notion is interesting from a logical point of view—think about the classical idea of inference to the best explanation—and we believe it can also pave the way to develop symbolic models for XAI when applied to the law.

References

1. Akata, Z., et al.: A research agenda for hybrid intelligence: augmenting human intellect with collaborative, adaptive, responsible, and explainable artificial intelligence. Computer **53**(8), 18–28 (2020). https://doi.org/10.1109/MC.2020.2996587
2. Alexy, R.: A Theory of Legal Argumentation: The Theory of Rational Discourse as Theory of Legal Justification. Clarendon (1989)
3. Antoniou, G., Billington, D., Governatori, G., Maher, M.: Representation results for defeasible logic. ACM Trans. Comput. Logic **2**(2), 255–287 (2001). https://doi.org/10.1145/371316.371517
4. Atkinson, K., Bench-Capon, T., Bollegala, D.: Explanation in AI and law: past, present and future. Artif. Intell. **289**, 103387 (2020) https://doi.org/10.1016/j.artint.2020.103387, https://www.sciencedirect.com/science/article/pii/S0004370220301375
5. van Benthem, J., Pacuit, E.: Dynamic logics of evidence-based beliefs. Studia Logica: Int. J. Symbol. Logic **99**(1/3), 61–92 (2011). https://www.jstor.org/stable/41475196
6. Bex, F., Prakken, H.: On the relevance of algorithmic decision predictors for judicial decision making. In: Maranhão, J., Wyner, A.Z. (eds.) Eighteenth International Conference for Artificial Intelligence and Law, ICAIL 2021, São Paulo Brazil, 21–25 June 2021, pp. 175–179. ACM (2021). https://doi.org/10.1145/3462757.3466069
7. Chellas, B.F.: Modal Logic: An Introduction. Cambridge University Press, Cambridge (1980)
8. Governatori, G., Maher, M.J., Antoniou, G., Billington, D.: Argumentation semantics for defeasible logic. J. Log. Comput. **14**(5), 675–702 (2004)
9. Governatori, G., Olivieri, F., Rotolo, A., Cristani, M.: Inference to the stable explanations. In: Gottlob, G., Inclezan, D., Maratea, M. (eds.) LPNMR 2022. LNCS, pp. 245–258. Springer, Cham (2022). https://doi.org/10.1007/978-3-031-15707-3_19
10. Governatori, G., Olivieri, F., Rotolo, A., Cristani, M.: Stable normative explanations. In: Francesconi, E., Borges, G., Sorge, C. (eds.) Legal Knowledge and Information Systems - JURIX 2022: The Thirty-fifth Annual Conference, Saarbrücken, Germany, 14–16 December 2022. Frontiers in Artificial Intelligence and Applications, vol. 362, pp. 43–52. IOS Press (2022). https://doi.org/10.3233/FAIA220447
11. Governatori, G., Rotolo, A., Calardo, E.: Possible world semantics for defeasible deontic logic. In: Ågotnes, T., Broersen, J., Elgesem, D. (eds.) DEON 2012. LNCS (LNAI), vol. 7393, pp. 46–60. Springer, Heidelberg (2012). https://doi.org/10.1007/978-3-642-31570-1_4
12. Governatori, G., Rotolo, A., Riveret, R.: A deontic argumentation framework based on deontic defeasible logic. In: Miller, T., Oren, N., Sakurai, Y., Noda, I., Savarimuthu, B.T.R., Cao Son, T. (eds.) PRIMA 2018. LNCS (LNAI), vol. 11224, pp. 484–492. Springer, Cham (2018). https://doi.org/10.1007/978-3-030-03098-8_33
13. Liao, B., van der Torre, L.: Explanation semantics for abstract argumentation. In: Prakken, H., Bistarelli, S., Santini, F., Taticchi, C. (eds.) Computational Models of Argument - Proceedings of COMMA 2020, Perugia, Italy, 4–11 September 2020. Frontiers in Artificial Intelligence and Applications, vol. 326, pp. 271–282. IOS Press (2020). https://doi.org/10.3233/FAIA200511
14. Liu, X., Lorini, E., Rotolo, A., Sartor, G.: Modelling and explaining legal case-based reasoners through classifiers. In: Francesconi, E., Borges, G., Sorge, C. (eds.) Legal Knowledge and Information Systems - JURIX 2022: The Thirty-fifth Annual Conference, Saarbrücken, Germany, 14–16 December 2022. Frontiers in Artificial Intelligence and Applications, vol. 362, pp. 83–92. IOS Press (2022). https://doi.org/10.3233/FAIA220451
15. Medvedeva, M., Vols, M., Wieling, M.: Using machine learning to predict decisions of the European court of human rights. Artif. Intell. Law **28**(2), 237–266 (2020). https://doi.org/10.1007/s10506-019-09255-y

16. Odekerken, D., Bex, F., Borg, A., Testerink, B.: Approximating stability for applied argument-based inquiry. Intell. Syst. Appl. **16**, 200110 (2022). https://doi.org/10.1016/j.iswa.2022.200110
17. Pacuit, E.: Neighborhood Semantics for Modal Logic. Springer, Cham, Switzerland (2017)
18. Peczenik, A.: On Law and Reason. Kluwer, Dordrecht (1989)
19. Prakken, H., Ratsma, R.: A top-level model of case-based argumentation for explanation: formalisation and experiments. Argument Comput. **13**(2), 159–194 (2022). https://doi.org/10.3233/AAC-210009
20. Prakken, H., Sartor, G.: Law and logic: a review from an argumentation perspective. Artif. Intell. **227**, 214–245 (2015). https://doi.org/10.1016/j.artint.2015.06.005
21. Riveret, R., Rotolo, A., Sartor, G.: A deontic argumentation framework towards doctrine reification. FLAP **6**(5), 903–940 (2019). https://collegepublications.co.uk/ifcolog/?00034

Declarative Reasoning on Explanations Using Constraint Logic Programming

Laura State[1,2(✉)] ⓘ, Salvatore Ruggieri[1] ⓘ, and Franco Turini[1] ⓘ

[1] University of Pisa, Pisa, Italy
laura.state@di.unipi.it
[2] Scuola Normale Superiore, Pisa, Italy

Abstract. Explaining opaque Machine Learning (ML) models is an increasingly relevant problem. Current explanation in AI (XAI) methods suffer several shortcomings, among others an insufficient incorporation of background knowledge, and a lack of abstraction and interactivity with the user. We propose REASONX, an explanation method based on Constraint Logic Programming (CLP). REASONX can provide declarative, interactive explanations for decision trees, which can be the ML models under analysis or global/local surrogate models of any black-box model. Users can express background or common sense knowledge using linear constraints and MILP optimization over features of factual and contrastive instances, and interact with the answer constraints at different levels of abstraction through constraint projection. We present here the architecture of REASONX, which consists of a Python layer, closer to the user, and a CLP layer. REASONX's core execution engine is a Prolog meta-program with declarative semantics in terms of logic theories.

1 Introduction

Artificial Intelligence (AI) systems are increasingly being adopted for taking critical decisions impacting society, such as loan concession in bank systems. The acceptance and trust of applications based on AI is hampered by the opaqueness and complexity of the Machine Learning (ML) models adopted, possibly resulting in biased or socially discriminatory decision-making [33].

For these reasons, there has recently been a flourishing of proposals for explaining the decision rationale of ML models [18,27,29,31], coined eXplanation in AI (XAI) methods. These approaches lack sufficient abstraction for reasoning over the decision rationale of the ML model. By reasoning, we mean the possibility for the user to define any number of conditions over factual and contrastive instances, which would codify both background knowledge and what-if analyses, and then looking at answers at the symbolic and intensional level.

To close this gap, we present REASONX (*reason to explain*), an explanation tool built in two layers. The first is in Python, closer to users, where decision tree (DT) models and user queries are parsed and translated. The DT can be the ML model itself, or a surrogate of other ML models at global/local level. The

S. Gaggl et al. (Eds.): JELIA 2023, LNAI 14281, pp. 132–141, 2023.
https://doi.org/10.1007/978-3-031-43619-2_10

second is in Constraint Logic Programming (CLP), where embedding of DTs and background knowledge are reasoned about, using a Prolog meta-program.

We display an exemplary dialogue between a fictional user and REASONX below. It is situated in the context of a credit application scenario, i.e. the user is a person whose credit application has been rejected by an automated decision-making system. Please note that while the information content is exactly what REASONX can provide, we enhanced the dialogue by translating the interaction into natural language, to mimic better a realistic interaction.

USER: Can I see the rule that led to the denial of my credit application?

REASONX: Your credit application was rejected, because your income is lower than 60,000 EUR/year, and you still have to pay back the lease of your car.

USER: Ok. Can you present me two options that will lead to a change of the decision outcome? Please take into consideration that I need a credit of at least 10,000 EUR. I would like to see options that require as little change as necessary.

REASONX: You have the following two options: You pay back the lease on the car, or you increase your age by 10 years (from 35 to 45 years).

USER: The second option presented is a bit strange. I am wondering whether this is salient in the model. Can I please see the options to obtain credit for an individual with the same properties as me, for a credit of at least 10,000 EUR, but with the feature age at 35 years or less (i.e. young applicant), instead of fixed?

REASONX: For the given profile, the credit is always rejected.

USER: Given this profile, how can the decision reversed, under as little changes as possible?

REASONX: Credit can be obtained, if the feature age is set to higher than 35 years.

USER: This interesting and worth investigating further. There could be bias w.r.t. the age of the person that applies for credit.

Adding background knowledge to explanations has the potential to significantly improve their quality [2,46]. Ignoring it can lead to explanations that disregard the needs of the user, or do not fit the reality of our world - depending on its purpose. An example is the minimum credit amount ("a credit of at least 10,000 EUR"). Further, interactivity arises naturally in REASONX: the user can flexibly query it, choosing queries that best fit to her questions, e.g., by adding constraints, and thereby building an own, personalized explanation.

Here, we focus on the CLP layer of REASONX. The Python layer and case studies at the user level are thoroughly presented in a companion paper [47].

The paper is structured as follows. In Sect. 2, we discuss background and related work. Section 3 describes the syntax, semantics, and meta-programming features of CLP that REASONX builds on. The architecture of REASONX is described in Sect. 4. We summarize contributions and future work in Sect. 5.

2 Background and Related Work

Logic and Knowledge in XAI. Several XAI approaches have used (propositional) logic rules as forms of model-agnostic explanations both locally [17,28,36] and globally [41]. Such approaches, however, do not allow for reasoning over produced explanations. Surveys on work at the intersection between symbolic and sub-symbolic methods (incl. argumentation and abduction) are [10,14,20].

Contrastive Explanations. Contrastive explanations[1] (CEs), i.e., instances similar to those to explain but with different labels assigned by the black-box (BB) classifier, are a key element in causal approaches to interpretability [11, 48]. [49] introduces contrastive explanations to the field of XAI, with several extensions [21,39]. Moreover, while [9] argues in favor of CEs from a psychological point of view, [27,30] make clear that explanations in a contrastive form are highly desirable for (lay) end-users.

Interactivity. Interactivity aligns closely with our working definition of an explanation: "[...] an interaction, or an exchange of information", where it crucially matters to *whom* the explanation is given, and for *what* purpose [46]. [45] convincingly arguments for interactivity by presenting the glass-box tool [43]. [25] confirms the relevance of interactivity via an interview study with practitioners.

Explanations and Decision Trees. Closely linked work is presented by a series of papers of Sokol et al., introducing explanations for DTs [42], generalizing it to local surrogate models [44], and exploiting interactivity [43]. Again, the main difference to our work is our reliance on CLP, and thus reasoning capabilities. Another related work is [4], providing CEs via (actual) causality.

Embedding Decision Trees into Constraints. In this paper, we assume that the DT is already available. We reason over the DT by encoding it as a set of linear constraints. This problem, known as embedding [6], requires to satisfy $c(x,y) \Leftrightarrow f(x) = y$, where $f(x)$ is the class as predicted by the DT, x the input vector consisting of discrete and/or continuous variables, and c is a constraint of some type. We adopt a rule-based encoding, which takes space in $O(N \log N)$ where N is the number of nodes in the DT. Other encodings, such as Table and MDD [6], require discretization of continuous features, thus losing the power of reasoning over linear constraints over reals.

3   Preliminaries: Constraint Logic Programming

Logic programming (LP) is a declarative approach to problem-solving based on logic rules in the form of Horn clauses [1]. It supports reasoning under various settings, e.g., deductive, inductive, abductive, and meta-reasoning [13,40]. Starting with Prolog [12], LP has been extended in several directions, as per expressivity and efficiency [24]. Constraint logic programming (CLP) augments logic programming with the ability to solve constrained problems [19]. The CLP

---

[1] To avoid confusion with the concept of counterfactuals as understood in the statistical causality literature, and following [27], we use the term contrastive explanations.

scheme defines a family of languages, CLP($\mathcal{C}$), that is parametric in the constraint domain $\mathcal{C}$. We are interested in CLP($\mathcal{R}$), namely the constraint domain over the reals. We use the SWI Prolog system [50] implementation.

We rely on meta-programming, a powerful technique that allows a LP to manipulate programs encoded as terms. This is extended in CLP by encoding constraints as terms.

Further, CLP($\mathcal{R}$) offers mixed integer linear programming (MILP) optimization functionalities [26]. Common predicates include the calculation of the supremum and the infimum of an expression w.r.t. the solutions of the constraint store. Complex constraint meta-reasoning procedures are based on such predicates, some examples are [3,38].

4   Explaining via Reasoning: REASONX

REASONX consists of two layers. The top layer in Python is designed for integration with the **pandas** and **scikit-learn** standard libraries for data storage and model construction. Meta-data, models, and user constraints specified at this level are parsed and transformed into Prolog facts. The bottom layer is in CLP($\mathcal{R}$) and it is written in SWI Prolog [50].

REASONX relies on a DT, the *base model*. Such a tree can be: (a) the model to be explained/reasoned about[2]; (b) a global surrogate of an opaque ML model; (c) a local surrogate trained to mimic a BB model in the neighborhood of the (local) instance to explain. In cases (b) and (c), the surrogate model is assumed to have good fidelity in reproducing the decisions of the black-box. This is reasonable for local models, i.e., in case (c). Learning the tree over a local neighborhood has been a common strategy in perturbation-based XAI methods such as LIME [35]. Following, we present an excerpt of the initialization code:

```
> r = reasonx.ReasonX(...)
> r.model(clf)
```

where the meta-data about the features are passed to the object r during its creation, and the DT clf is passed over. There can be more than one base model to account for different ML models, e.g., Neural Networks vs ensembles. The user can declare and reason about one or more instances, factual or contrastive, by specifying their class value. Each instance refers to a specific base model. The instance does not need to be fully specified, as in existing XAI methods. For example, an instance F can be declared with only the following characteristics:

```
> r.instance('F', label=1)
> r.constraint('F.age = 30, F.capitalloss >= 1000')
```

to intensionally denote a persons with age of 30 and capital loss of at least $1,000$. Background knowledge can be expressed through linear constraints over features of instances. E.g., by declaring another instance CE classified differently by the

---

[2] While DTs are generally thought interpretable, it depends on their size/depth. Large DTs are hard to reason about, especially in a contrastive explanation scenario.

base model (the contrastive instance), the following constraints require that the contrastive instance must not be younger, and has a larger capital loss:

```
> r.instance('CE', label=0)
> r.constraint('F.age <= CE.age, CE.capitalloss >= F.capitalloss + 500')
```

The output of REASONX consists of constraints for which the declared instances are classified as expected by the DT(s) and such that user and implicit constraints on feature data types are satisfied. The output can be projected on only some of the instances or of the features:

```
> r.solveopt(project=['CE'])
> ---
> Answer: 30 <= CE.age, F.capitalloss >= 1500, CE.hoursperweek >= 40.0
```

where $30 <= CE.age, F.capitalloss >= 1500$ are entailed by the constraints and $CE.hoursperweek >= 40.0$ is due to conditions in the DT. Moreover, the user can specify a distance function for the minimization problem to derive the closest contrastive example, e.g., as in `solveopt(minimize='l1norm(F, CE)')`.

4.1   Embeddings into CLP

We are agnostic about the learning algorithm that produces the base model(s). Features can be nominal, ordinal, or continuous. Ordinal features are coded as consecutive integer values (some preprocessing is offered in REASONX). Nominal features can be one-hot encoded or not. When embedding the DT into CLP, we force one-hot encoding of nominal features anyway, and silently decode back when returning the answer constraints to the user. A nominal feature x_i is one-hot encoded into $x_i^{v_1}, \ldots, x_i^{v_k}$ with $v_1, \ldots, v_k$ being the distinct values in the domain of x_i. We assume that the split conditions from a parent node to a child node are of the form $\mathbf{a}^T \mathbf{x} \simeq b$, where $\mathbf{x}$ is the vector of features x_i's. The following common split conditions are covered by such an assumption:

- axis-parallel splits for continuous and ordinal features, i.e., $x_i \leq b$ or $x_i > b$;
- linear splits for continuous features: $\mathbf{a}^T \mathbf{x} \leq b$ or $\mathbf{a}^T \mathbf{x} > b$;
- (in)equality splits for nominal features: $x_i = v$ or $x_i \neq v$; in terms of one-hot encoding, they respectively translate into $x_i^v = 1$ or $x_i^v = 0$.

Axis parallel and equality splits are used in CART [7] and C4.5 [34]. Linear splits are used in oblique [32] and optimal decision trees [5]. Linear model trees combine axis parallel splits at nodes and linear splits at leaves [16].

Embedding Base Model(s) into Prolog Facts. Each path (root to the leaf in the DT), is translated into a fact, a conjunction of linear split conditions:

$$\text{path}(m, [\mathbf{x}], [\mathbf{a}_1^T \mathbf{x} \simeq b_1, \ldots, \mathbf{a}_k^T \mathbf{x} \simeq b_k], c, p).$$

where m is an id of the decision tree, $[\mathbf{x}]$ a list of (Prolog) variables representing the features, c the class predicted at the leaf, p the confidence of the prediction, and $[\mathbf{a}_1^T \mathbf{x} \simeq b_1, \ldots, \mathbf{a}_k^T \mathbf{x} \simeq b_k]$ the list of the k split conditions.

Encoding Instances. Each instance is represented by a list of Prolog variables. The mapping between names and variables is positional, and decoding is stored in a predicate feature(i, *varname*) where i is a natural number and *varname* a constant symbol, e.g., vAge. All instances are collectively represented by a list of lists of variables *vars*. Further, REASONX is defining a utility predicate data_instance with instance's meta-data.

Encoding Implicit Constraints (Ψ). Constraints on the features **x** of each instance derive from their data types. We call them "implicit" because the system can generate them from meta-data:

- for continuous features: $x_i \in \mathcal{R}$;
- for ordinal features: $x_i \in \mathcal{Z}$ and $m_i \leq x_i \leq M_i$ where $dom(x_i) = \{m_i, \ldots, M_i\}$;
- for one-hot encoded nominal features: $x_i^{v_1}, \ldots, x_i^{v_k} \in \mathcal{Z}$ and $\wedge_{j=1}^{k} 0 \leq x_i^{v_j} \leq 1$ and $\sum_{j=1}^{k} x_i^{v_j} = 1$;

Constraints for ordinal and nominal features are computed by the Prolog predicates ord_constraints(*vars*, COrd) and cat_constraints(*vars*, CCat) respectively. We denote by Ψ the conjunction of all implicit constraints.

Encoding User Constraints (Φ). The following background knowledge, loosely categorized as in [23], can be readily expressed in REASONX:

Feasibility. Constraints concerning the possibility of feature changes, and how these depend on previous values or (changes of) other features:
  - *Immutability*: a feature cannot/must not change.
  - *Mutable but not actionable*: the change is only a result of changes in features it depends upon.
  - *Actionable but constrained*: the feature can be changed only under some condition.
Consistency. Constraints aiming at specific domain values a feature can take.

Constraints specified in Python are parsed and transformed into a list of CLP constraints. An interpreter of expressions is provided which returns a list of linear constraints over variables. The only non-linear constraint is equality of nominal values and is translated exploiting one-hot-encoding of nominal features.

Encoding Distance Functions. We simplify the optimization proposed in [49] by the assumption that declared instances have a class label[3]. The distance function is defined as a linear combination of L_1 and L_∞ norms for ordinal and continuous features and of a simple matching distance for nominal features:

$$\min \sum_{i \text{ nominal}} \mathbb{1}(x_{cf,i} \neq x_{f,i}) + \beta \sum_{i \text{ ord., cont.}} |x_{cf,i} - x_{f,i}| + \gamma \max_{i \text{ ord., cont.}} |x_{cf,i} - x_{f,i}| \quad (1)$$

---

[3] The split conditions from root to leaf do not necessarily lead to the same class label with 100% probability. REASONX includes a parameter in the declaration of an instance to require a minimum confidence value of the required class.

where β and γ denote parameters. L_1 and L_∞ norms are calculated over max-min normalized values to account for different units of measures. See [22,49] for a discussion. To solve the MILP problem, we need to linearize the minimization. This leads to additional constraints and slack variables.

4.2 The Core Meta-Interpreter of REASONX

We reason on constraints as theories and design operators for composing such theories. The core engine of REASONX is implemented as a Prolog meta-interpreter of expressions over those operators.

A (logic) theory is a set of formulas, from which one is interested to derive implied formulas, and a logic program is itself a theory [8]. In our context, a theory consists of a set of linear constraints $\{c_i\}_i$ to be interpreted as the disjunction $\vee_i c_i$. Theories are coded in LP by exploiting its non-deterministic computational model, i.e., each c_i's is returned by a clause in the program. The language of expressions over theories is closed: operators map one or more theories into a theory. The following theories are included:

typec the theory with only the conjunction $\wedge_{c \in \Psi} c$ of the implicit constraints;
userc the theory with only the conjunction $\wedge_{c \in \Phi} c$ of the user constraints;
inst(I) the theory of constraints $\wedge_i \mathbf{a}_i^T \mathbf{x} \simeq b_i$ where $\mathbf{x}$ are features of the instance I, and primitive constraints $\mathbf{a}_i^T \mathbf{x} \simeq b_i$ are those in the path of the decision tree M the instance refers to.

We provide the following operators on theories: the cross-product of constraints of theories, the subset of constraints in a theory that are satisfiable, the projection of constraints in a theory over a set of variables, and the subset of constraints in a theory that minimize a certain (distance) function.

The queries to the CLP layer of REASONX can be answered by a Prolog query over the predicates instvar (building *vars*), proj_vars (computing which of those variables are to be projected in the output), and solve (evaluating expressions over the cross-product of typec, userc, and the theories inst(I) for all instances I).

5 Conclusion

We presented REASONX, a declarative XAI tool that relies on linear constraint reasoning, solving for background knowledge, and for interaction with the user at a high abstraction and intensional level. These features make it a unique tool when compared to instance-level approaches commonly adopted for explaining ML models. We aim at extending REASONX along three directions: *i)* the implementation of additional constraints, possibly with non-linear solvers, *ii)* an extensive evaluation based on some theoretical measures, as well as through user-studies [37] and real-world data, and *iii)* extension to non-structured data, such as images and text, e.g., through the integration of concepts [15].

Software. REASONX is released open source at https://github.com/lstate/REASONX.

Acknowledgments. Work supported by the European Union's Horizon 2020 research and innovation programme under Marie Sklodowska-Curie Actions for the project NoBIAS (g.a. No. 860630), and by the NextGenerationEU program within the PNRR-PE-AI scheme (M4C2, investment 1.3, line on Artificial Intelligence) for the project FAIR (Future Artificial Intelligence Research). This work reflects only the authors' views and the European Research Executive Agency (REA) is not responsible for any use that may be made of the information it contains.

References

1. Apt, K.: From Logic Programming to Prolog. Prentice Hall, London New York (1997)
2. Beckh, K., et al.: Explainable machine learning with prior knowledge: An overview. CoRR abs/2105.10172 (2021)
3. Benoy, F., King, A., Mesnard, F.: Computing convex hulls with a linear solver. Theory Pract. Log. Program. 5(1–2), 259–271 (2005)
4. Bertossi, L.E.: Declarative approaches to counterfactual explanations for classification. CoRR abs/2011.07423 (2020)
5. Bertsimas, D., Dunn, J.: Optimal classification trees. Mach. Learn. **106**(7), 1039–1082 (2017). https://doi.org/10.1007/s10994-017-5633-9
6. Bonfietti, A., Lombardi, M., Milano, M.: Embedding decision trees and random forests in constraint programming. In: Michel, L. (ed.) CPAIOR 2015. LNCS, vol. 9075, pp. 74–90. Springer, Cham (2015). https://doi.org/10.1007/978-3-319-18008-3_6
7. Breiman, L., Friedman, J.H., Olshen, R.A., Stone, C.J.: Classification and Regression Trees. Wadsworth (1984)
8. Brogi, A., Mancarella, P., Pedreschi, D., Turini, F.: Theory construction in computational logic. In: Jacquet, J. (ed.) Constructing Logic Programs, pp. 241–250. Wiley (1993)
9. Byrne, R.M.J.: Counterfactuals in explainable artificial intelligence (XAI): evidence from human reasoning. In: IJCAI, pp. 6276–6282. ijcai.org (2019)
10. Calegari, R., Ciatto, G., Omicini, A.: On the integration of symbolic and subsymbolic techniques for XAI: a survey. Intelligenza Artificiale **14**(1), 7–32 (2020)
11. Chou, Y., Moreira, C., Bruza, P., Ouyang, C., Jorge, J.A.: Counterfactuals and causability in explainable artificial intelligence: theory, algorithms, and applications. Inf. Fusion **81**, 59–83 (2022)
12. Clocksin, W.F., Mellish, C.S.: Programming in Prolog. Using the ISO Standard. Springer, Heidelberg (2003)
13. Cropper, A., Dumancic, S.: Inductive logic programming at 30: a new introduction. J. Artif. Intell. Res. **74**, 765–850 (2022)
14. Dietz, E., Kakas, A.C., Michael, L.: Argumentation: a calculus for human-centric AI. Front. Artif. Intell. **5**, 955579 (2022)
15. Donadello, I., Dragoni, M.: SeXAI: introducing concepts into black boxes for explainable Artificial Intelligence. In: XAI.it@AI*IA. CEUR Workshop Proceedings, vol. 2742, pp. 41–54. CEUR-WS.org (2020)
16. Frank, E., Wang, Y., Inglis, S., Holmes, G., Witten, I.H.: Using model trees for classification. Mach. Learn. **32**(1), 63–76 (1998)
17. Guidotti, R., Monreale, A., Giannotti, F., Pedreschi, D., Ruggieri, S., Turini, F.: Factual and counterfactual explanations for black box decision making. IEEE Intell. Syst. **34**(6), 14–23 (2019)

18. Guidotti, R., Monreale, A., Ruggieri, S., Turini, F., Giannotti, F., Pedreschi, D.: A survey of methods for explaining black box models. ACM Comput. Surv. **51**(5), 93:1–93:42 (2019)
19. Jaffar, J., Michaylov, S., Stuckey, P.J., Yap, R.H.C.: The CLP(R) language and system. ACM Trans. Program. Lang. Syst. **14**(3), 339–395 (1992)
20. Kakas, A.C., Michael, L.: Abduction and argumentation for explainable machine learning: a position survey. CoRR abs/2010.12896 (2020)
21. Kanamori, K., Takagi, T., Kobayashi, K., Arimura, H.: DACE: distribution-aware counterfactual explanation by mixed-integer linear optimization. In: IJCAI, pp. 2855–2862. ijcai.org (2020)
22. Karimi, A., Barthe, G., Balle, B., Valera, I.: Model-agnostic counterfactual explanations for consequential decisions. In: AISTATS. Proceedings of Machine Learning Research, vol. 108, pp. 895–905. PMLR (2020)
23. Karimi, A., Barthe, G., Schölkopf, B., Valera, I.: A survey of algorithmic recourse: definitions, formulations, solutions, and prospects. CoRR abs/2010.04050 (2020)
24. Körner, P., et al.: Fifty years of Prolog and beyond. Theory Pract. Log. Program. **22**(6), 776–858 (2022)
25. Lakkaraju, H., Slack, D., Chen, Y., Tan, C., Singh, S.: Rethinking explainability as a dialogue: a practitioner's perspective. CoRR abs/2202.01875 (2022)
26. Magatão, L.: Mixed integer linear programming and constraint logic programming: towards a unified modeling framework. Ph.D. thesis, Federal University of Technology - Paraná, Brazil (2010)
27. Miller, T.: Explanation in artificial intelligence: insights from the social sciences. Artif. Intell. **267**, 1–38 (2019)
28. Ming, Y., Qu, H., Bertini, E.: Rulematrix: Visualizing and understanding classifiers with rules. IEEE Trans. Vis. Comput. Graph. **25**(1), 342–352 (2019)
29. Minh, D., Wang, H.X., Li, Y.F., Nguyen, T.N.: Explainable artificial intelligence: a comprehensive review. Artif. Intell. Rev. **55**(5), 3503–3568 (2022)
30. Mittelstadt, B.D., Russell, C., Wachter, S.: Explaining explanations in AI. In: FAT, pp. 279–288. ACM (2019)
31. Molnar, C.: Interpretable Machine Learning. A Guide for Making Black Box Models Explainable (2019). https://christophm.github.io/interpretable-ml-book
32. Murthy, S.K., Kasif, S., Salzberg, S.: A system for induction of oblique decision trees. J. Artif. Intell. Res. **2**, 1–32 (1994)
33. Ntoutsi, E., et al.: Bias in data-driven artificial intelligence systems - an introductory survey. WIREs Data Min. Knowl. Discov. **10**(3), e1356 (2020)
34. Quinlan, J.R.: C4.5: Programs for Machine Learning. Morgan Kaufmann, Burlington (1993)
35. Ribeiro, M.T., Singh, S., Guestrin, C.: "Why should I trust you?": Explaining the predictions of any classifier. In: KDD, pp. 1135–1144. ACM (2016)
36. Ribeiro, M.T., Singh, S., Guestrin, C.: Anchors: high-precision model-agnostic explanations. In: AAAI, pp. 1527–1535. AAAI Press (2018)
37. Rong, Y., Leemann, T., Nguyen, T., Fiedler, L., Seidel, T., Kasneci, G., Kasneci, E.: Towards human-centered explainable AI: user studies for model explanations. CoRR abs/2210.11584 (2022)
38. Ruggieri, S.: Deciding membership in a class of polyhedra. In: ECAI. Frontiers in Artificial Intelligence and Applications, vol. 242, pp. 702–707. IOS Press (2012)
39. Russell, C.: Efficient search for diverse coherent explanations. In: FAT, pp. 20–28. ACM (2019)
40. Russell, S.J., Norvig, P.: Artificial Intelligence: A Modern Approach, 2nd edn. Pearson Education, London (2003)

41. Setzu, M., Guidotti, R., Monreale, A., Turini, F., Pedreschi, D., Giannotti, F.: Glocalx - from local to global explanations of black box AI models. Artif. Intell. **294**, 103457 (2021)
42. Sokol, K.: Towards Intelligible and Robust Surrogate Explainers: A Decision Tree Perspective. Ph.D. thesis, School of Computer Science, Electrical and Electronic Engineering, and Engineering Maths, University of Bristol (2021)
43. Sokol, K., Flach, P.A.: Glass-box: explaining AI decisions with counterfactual statements through conversation with a voice-enabled virtual assistant. In: IJCAI, pp. 5868–5870. ijcai.org (2018)
44. Sokol, K., Flach, P.A.: LIMEtree: interactively customisable explanations based on local surrogate multi-output regression trees. CoRR abs/2005.01427 (2020)
45. Sokol, K., Flach, P.A.: One explanation does not fit all. Künstliche Intell. **34**(2), 235–250 (2020)
46. State, L.: Logic programming for XAI: a technical perspective. In: ICLP Workshops. CEUR Workshop Proceedings, vol. 2970. CEUR-WS.org (2021)
47. State, L., Ruggieri, S., Turini, F.: Reason to explain: interactive contrastive explanations (REASONX). CoRR abs/2305.18143 (2023)
48. Stepin, I., Alonso, J.M., Catalá, A., Pereira-Fariña, M.: A survey of contrastive and counterfactual explanation generation methods for explainable artificial intelligence. IEEE Access **9**, 11974–12001 (2021)
49. Wachter, S., et al.: Counterfactual explanations without opening the black box. Harv. JL Tech. **31**, 841 (2017)
50. Wielemaker, J., Schrijvers, T., Triska, M., Lager, T.: SWI-Prolog. Theory Pract. Log. Program **12**(1–2), 67–96 (2012)

Argumentation

On the Expressive Power
of Assumption-Based Argumentation

Matti Berthold[1]([⊠]), Anna Rapberger[2]([⊠]), and Markus Ulbricht[1]([⊠])

[1] ScaDS.AI Dresden/Leipzig, Universität Leipzig, Leipzig, Germany
{berthold,ulbricht}@informatik.uni-leipzig.de
[2] TU Wien, Vienna, Austria
anna.rapberger@tuwien.ac.at

Abstract. The expressiveness of any given formalism lays the theoretical foundation for more specialized topics such as investigating dynamic reasoning environments. The modeling capabilities of the formalism under investigation yield immediate (im)possibility results in such contexts. In this paper we investigate the expressiveness of assumption-based argumentation (ABA), one of the major structured argumentation formalisms. In particular, we examine so-called *signatures*, i.e., sets of extensions that can be realized under a given semantics. We characterize the signatures of common ABA semantics for flat, finite frameworks with and without preferences. We also give several results regarding conclusion-based semantics for ABA.

1 Introduction

Within the last decades, AI research has witnessed an increasing demand for knowledge representation systems that are capable of handling inconsistent beliefs. Research in computational argumentation has addressed this issue by developing numerous sophisticated methods to representing and analyzing conflicting information [22]. A key player in this field are abstract argumentation frameworks (AFs) as proposed by Dung in 1995 [15]. In AFs, arguments are interpreted as atomic entities and conflicts as a binary relation; consequently, an AF represents a given debate as a directed graph F. Research on AFs is driven by various *semantics* which strive to formalize what reasonable viewpoints F entails. That is, if $E \in \sigma(F)$ for a semantics σ, then E is interpreted as a jointly acceptable set of arguments. These sets E are called σ-*extensions* of F.

In the research area of *structured argumentation*, an AF is constructed from a given knowledge base in order to explicate arising conflicts in a comprehensible graph. One highly influential approach in this area is *assumption-based argumentation* (ABA) [8,12]. *Assumptions* provide the foundation for arguments and determine their conflicts. ABA frameworks (ABAFs) are also evaluated under so-called semantics; in contrast to many other argumentation formalisms, the native ABA semantics output sets of assumptions rather than arguments.

S. Gaggl et al. (Eds.): JELIA 2023, LNAI 14281, pp. 145–160, 2023.
https://doi.org/10.1007/978-3-031-43619-2_11

Within the last years, researchers have studied the modeling capabilities of different AF semantics extensively [6,16,33]. To this end the notion of the *signature* Σ_σ of a semantics σ has been coined. This concept formalizes what can be the set of σ-extensions of an AF, i.e., $\Sigma_\sigma = \{\sigma(F) \mid F \text{ is a finite AF}\}$. Some properties of important semantics are folklore within the AF community. For example, the empty set is always *admissible* and the *stable* extensions of an AF are incomparable[1]. However, establishing the precise characterizations for the common AF semantics is a challenging endeavor [16].

The signatures of argumentation semantics are an important formal tool underlying several applications as well as theoretical results building upon them. Recent years witnessed significant developments in the construction of explanations based on formal argumentation [13,34]. Key to obtain argumentative explanations are translations of the given (rule-based) knowledge base into a suitable abstract argumentation formalism [21]. Such formalisms differ in their expressive power and thus in their ability to provide semantics-preserving translations. Signature characterizations for different abstract and structured formalisms thus pave the way for developing suitable translations, facilitating the extraction of argumentative explanations. Precise characterizations of the modeling capacities of semantics furthermore play a central role in the context of dynamic reasoning environments, i.e., knowledge bases that evolve over time [22]. Many research questions on dynamics heavily rely on insights as to how the models of a given AF can be manipulated in order to reach a certain goal. A noteworthy example is the current hot topic of forgetting [2,5,7,25] where the goal is oftentimes to cut arguments out of or remove extensions entirely. Whether the target modification is attainable can be decided by studying the signatures of the semantics.

While signatures have been investigated for various abstract argumentation formalisms [16,17,20], this line of research has mostly been neglected in the realm of structured argumentation. In this paper, we tackle this issue and present various results regarding the expressive power of ABA. We first consider the most common ABA fragment and fully characterize the signatures of all standard semantics commonly studied in the literature. We achieve this by building upon previous results from abstract argumentation research. We then study various aspects, adding to our investigation by shifting the focus to the conclusions of the extensions or incorporating preferences.

2   Background

We recall assumption-based argumentation (ABA) [12], argumentation frameworks with collective attacks (SETAFs) [27], and their relation [24].

Assumption-Based Argumentation. We consider a *deductive system*, i.e., a tuple $(\mathcal{L}, \mathcal{R})$, where $\mathcal{L}$ is a set of atoms and $\mathcal{R}$ is a set of inference rules over $\mathcal{L}$. A rule $r \in \mathcal{R}$ has the form $a_0 \leftarrow a_1, \ldots, a_n$, s.t. $a_i \in \mathcal{L}$ for all $0 \le i \le n$; $head(r) = a_0$ is the *head* and $body(r) = \{a_1, \ldots, a_n\}$ is the (possibly empty) *body* of r.

---

[1] We refer to Sect. 2 for a formal introduction of the semantics we consider.

Definition 1. *An ABA framework (ABAF) is a tuple* $(\mathcal{L}, \mathcal{R}, \mathcal{A}, ^-)$, *where* $(\mathcal{L}, \mathcal{R})$ *is a deductive system,* $\mathcal{A} \subseteq \mathcal{L}$ *a set of assumptions, and* $^- : \mathcal{A} \to \mathcal{L}$ *a contrary function.*

In this work, we focus on frameworks which are *flat*, i.e., $head(r) \notin \mathcal{A}$ for each rule $r \in \mathcal{R}$, and *finite*, i.e., $\mathcal{L}$, $\mathcal{R}$, $\mathcal{A}$ are finite. By $\mathcal{A}(\mathcal{D})$ and $\mathcal{L}(\mathcal{D})$ we denote the assumptions and atoms occurring in $\mathcal{D}$, respectively.

An atom $p \in \mathcal{L}$ is tree-derivable from assumptions $S \subseteq \mathcal{A}$ and rules $R \subseteq \mathcal{R}$, denoted by $S \vdash_R p$, if there is a finite rooted labeled tree t *s.t.* i) the root of t is labeled with p, ii) the set of labels for the leaves of t is equal to S or $S \cup \{\top\}$, and iii) for each node v that is not a leaf of t there is a rule $r \in R$ such that v is labeled with $head(r)$ and labels of the children correspond to $body(r)$ or $\top$ if $body(r) = \emptyset$. We write $S \vdash p$ iff there exists $R \subseteq \mathcal{R}$ such that $S \vdash_R p$. Moreover, we let $Th_{\mathcal{D}}(S) = \{p \in \mathcal{L} \mid S \vdash p\}$.

A set of assumptions S *attacks* a set of assumptions T if there are $S' \subseteq S$ and $a \in T$ *s.t.* $S' \vdash \bar{a}$; The set S is conflict-free $(S \in cf(\mathcal{D}))$ if it does not attack itself; S *defends* $a \in \mathcal{A}$ if for each attacker T of $\{a\}$, we have S attacks T. A conflict-free set S is admissible $(S \in ad(\mathcal{D}))$ iff S defends each $a \in S$. We recall grounded, complete, preferred, and stable ABA semantics (abbr. *gr*, *co*, *pr*, *stb*).

Definition 2. *Let* $\mathcal{D}$ *be an ABAF and let* $S \in ad(\mathcal{D})$. *Then*

- $S \in co(\mathcal{D})$ *iff* S *contains every assumption it defends;*
- $S \in gr(\mathcal{D})$ *iff* S *is* $\subseteq$-*minimal in* $co(\mathcal{D})$;
- $S \in pr(\mathcal{D})$ *iff* S *is* $\subseteq$-*maximal in* $ad(\mathcal{D})$;
- $S \in stb(\mathcal{D})$ *iff* S *attacks each* $\{x\} \subseteq \mathcal{A}(\mathcal{D}) \backslash S$.

Example 1. We consider an ABAF $\mathcal{D} = (\mathcal{L}, \mathcal{R}, \mathcal{A}, ^-)$ with $\mathcal{L} = \{a, b, c, a_c, b_c, c_c\}$, assumptions $\mathcal{A} = \{a, b, c\}$, their contraries a_c, b_c, and c_c, respectively, and rules

$$a_c \leftarrow b, c \qquad\qquad b_c \leftarrow a \qquad\qquad c_c \leftarrow a, b$$

Then the set $\{a\}$ is admissible: it defends itself against its only attacker $\{b, c\}$, by attacking b. The set $\{a\}$ is not complete, however, since it also defends the assumption c. The sets $\{a, c\}$ and $\{b, c\}$ are complete, preferred and stable. Moreover, $\emptyset$ is complete and the unique grounded extension of $\mathcal{D}$. ◇

SETAFs. We recall *argumentation frameworks with collective attacks* [27].

Definition 3. *A SETAF is a pair* $F = (A, R)$ *where* A *is a finite set of arguments and* $R \subseteq (2^A \backslash \{\emptyset\}) \times A$ *encodes attacks.*

SETAFs generalize Dung's *abstract argumentation frameworks (AFs)* [15]. In AFs, each attacking set is a singleton, i.e., $|T| = 1$ for each $(T, h) \in R$. The SETAF semantics are defined in a way that they naturally generalize Dung's AF semantics. They are, however, even closer in spirit to ABA semantics.

A set of arguments S *attacks* an argument $a \in A$ if there is some $S' \subseteq S$ such that $(S', a) \in R$; S attacks a set of arguments T if there are $S' \subseteq S$ and $t \in T$ such that $(S', t) \in R$; S is conflict-free $(S \in cf(F))$ if it does not attack itself.

A set S *defends* an argument $a \in A$ if for each attacker T of a, it holds that S attacks T; S defends $T \subseteq A$ iff it defends each $t \in T$. A conflict-free set S is admissible ($S \in ad(F)$) iff S defends each $a \in S$. We recall grounded, complete, preferred, and stable SETAF semantics (abbr. *gr*, *co*, *pr*, and *stb*).

Definition 4. *Let F be a SETAF and let $S \in ad(F)$. Then,*

- *$S \in co(F)$ iff S contains each argument it defends;*
- *$S \in gr(F)$ iff S is $\subseteq$-minimal in $co(F)$;*
- *$S \in pr(F)$ iff S is $\subseteq$-maximal in $ad(F)$;*
- *$S \in stb(F)$ iff S attacks all $a \in A(F) \backslash S$.*

Relating ABAFs and SETAFs. For our first main result we exploit the close connection of ABAFs and SETAFs. The key idea is to identify assumptions in ABAFs with arguments in SETAFs; moreover, attacks between assumption-sets can be viewed as collective attacks between arguments in SETAFs and vice versa. The following translations are due to [24].

Definition 5. *For an ABAF $\mathcal{D} = (\mathcal{L}, \mathcal{R}, \mathcal{A}, ^-)$, the corresponding SETAF $F_\mathcal{D} = (A_\mathcal{D}, R_\mathcal{D})$ is defined by $A_\mathcal{D} = \mathcal{A} \backslash \{a \mid \overline{a} \in Th_\mathcal{D}(\emptyset)\}$ and for $S \cup \{a\} \subseteq A_\mathcal{D}$ we let $(S, a) \in R_\mathcal{D}$ iff $S \vdash \overline{a}$.[2] For a SETAF $F = (A, R)$, the corresponding ABAF $\mathcal{D}_F = (\mathcal{L}_F, \mathcal{R}_F, \mathcal{A}_F, ^-)$ is defined by $\mathcal{L}_F = A \cup \{p_x \mid x \in A\}$, $\mathcal{A}_F = A$, $\overline{x} = p_x$ for all $x \in A$, and for each $(T, h) \in R$, we add a rule $p_h \leftarrow T$ to $\mathcal{R}_F$.*

Example 2. Consider the ABAF $\mathcal{D}$ from Example 1. The corresponding SETAF $F_\mathcal{D}$ has the arguments $A_\mathcal{D} = \{a, b, c\}$; moreover, the arguments determine the collective attacks. For instance, from $\{b, c\} \vdash a_c$ we obtain that $\{b, c\}$ collectively attacks a. Below, we depict all attacks between the assumption-sets as usually done in the literature (left) and the corresponding SETAF (right). Left, we omit the (irrelevant) $\emptyset$ and (self-attacking) $\mathcal{A}$.

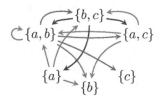 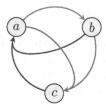

Attacks obtained from $\{a\} \vdash b_c$ are in cyan, from $\{b, c\} \vdash a_c$ in violet, and attacks obtained from $\{a, b\} \vdash c_c$ are depicted in red. Overall, we observe that the SETAF representation is significantly smaller: in contrast to the traditional ABA set representation, it requires only a single node for each assumption.   ◊

We recall the close relation between ABAFs and SETAFs.

Proposition 1. *Given a semantics $\sigma \in \{ad, gr, co, pr, stb\}$. For an ABAF $\mathcal{D}$ and its associated SETAF $F_\mathcal{D}$, it holds that $\sigma(\mathcal{D}) = \sigma(F_\mathcal{D})$. For a SETAF F and its associated ABAF $\mathcal{D}_F$, it holds that $\sigma(F) = \sigma(\mathcal{D}_F)$.*

---

[2] We note that the original translation slightly deviates from this version.

In [24], the result has only been stated for gr, co, pr, stb semantics; however, the adaption to admissible semantics can be easily obtained.

3   Signatures of ABA Frameworks

The investigation of the *signature* of a semantics is driven by properties of a given set $\mathbb{S}$ of sets, in order to assess whether it is conceivable that there is some knowledge base (in our case: some ABAF) $\mathcal{D}$ s.t. $\sigma(\mathcal{D}) = \mathbb{S}$. Let us familiarize with this setting by considering the following example.

Example 3. Let $\mathbb{S} = \{\{a\}, \{a, b\}, \{a, c\}\}$. We can actually already infer a lot about this set.

- It is impossible that $\mathbb{S}$ corresponds to the ad sets of an ABA knowledge base, i.e., $ad(\mathcal{D}) = \mathbb{S}$; the reason is that $\emptyset \in ad(\mathcal{D})$ for any ABAF $\mathcal{D}$, but $\emptyset \notin \mathbb{S}$;
- $\mathbb{S}$ cannot correspond to gr since $|gr(\mathcal{D})| = 1$ for any ABAF $\mathcal{D}$;
- it is also impossible that $stb(\mathcal{D}) = \mathbb{S}$ or $pr(\mathcal{D}) = \mathbb{S}$, because stable and preferred sets are always incomparable; however, in $\mathbb{S}$ we have $\{a\} \subsetneq \{a, b\}$;
- it is however possible to construct $\mathcal{D}$ with $co(\mathcal{D}) = \mathbb{S}$. The set $\{a\}$ could be the grounded extension and b and c in a mutual attack, yielding the complete extensions $co(\mathcal{D}) = \{\{a\}, \{a, b\}, \{a, c\}\}$.   ◇

We now formally define ABA signatures.

Definition 6. *Given a semantics σ, the signature of σ is*

$$\Sigma_\sigma^{ABA} = \{\sigma(\mathcal{D}) \mid \mathcal{D} \text{ is a flat, finite ABAF}\}.$$

Signatures are sets of sets of assumptions, i.e., $\Sigma_\sigma^{ABA} \subseteq 2^{2^{\mathcal{U}}}$ where $\mathcal{U}$ denotes the set of all possible (countably infinitely many) assumptions. We call a set $\mathbb{S} \subseteq 2^{\mathcal{U}}$ an *extension-set*. An extension-set $\mathbb{S}$ is *realizable* under the given semantics σ, if there exists a ABAF $\mathcal{D}$ that *realizes* it, i.e., $o(\mathcal{D}) = \mathbb{S}$.

We will infer Σ_σ^{ABA} by exploiting the close relation to SETAFs. To this end we recall the concept of their signatures, given as

$$\Sigma_\sigma^{SF} = \{\sigma(F) \mid F \text{ is a SETAF}\}.$$

Analogously, signatures for SETAFs are sets of sets of arguments. The concepts of *extension-sets* and *realizations* naturally transfer to this setting.

We are now ready to study the ABA signatures. Before we can delve into our results, however, we need to introduce some theoretical machinery (cf. [16,17]).

Definition 7. *Let $\mathbb{S}$ be a set of sets. We let*

$$\mathbb{A}_\mathbb{S} = \bigcup \mathbb{S}, \quad \mathbb{P}_\mathbb{S} = \{S \subseteq \bigcup \mathbb{S} \mid \nexists S' \in \mathbb{S} : S \subseteq S'\}, \quad dcl(\mathbb{T}) = \{S' \subseteq S \mid S \in \mathbb{T}\}.$$

Thereby, $\mathbb{P}_\mathbb{S}$ is the set of potential conflicts *in $\mathbb{S}$ and $dcl(\mathbb{T})$ the downward closure of $\mathbb{T}$. The* completion-sets *of a set of assumptions T in $\mathbb{S}$ are given by*

$$\mathbb{C}_\mathbb{S}(T) = \{S \in \mathbb{S} \mid T \subseteq S, \nexists S' \in \mathbb{S} : T \subseteq S' \subseteq S\}.$$

Let us illustrate these concepts in the following example.

Example 4. Let $\mathbb{S} = \{\{a\}, \{a, b\}, \{a, c\}\}$. We have the following sets:

- $\mathbb{A}_\mathbb{S} = \{a, b, c\}$ intuitively corresponding to credulously accepted assumptions;
- $\mathbb{P}_\mathbb{S} = \{\{b, c\}, \{a, b, c\}\}$ since b and c never occur in the same extension;
- $\mathbb{C}_\mathbb{S}(\{a\})$ is only $\{a\}$ itself; on the other hand, $\mathbb{C}_\mathbb{S}(\{b\}) = \{\{a, b\}\}$ since $\{a, b\}$ is a (the only) minimal set containing $\{b\}$.
- The downward closure of $\mathbb{S}$ is the set $dcl(\mathbb{S}) = \{\emptyset, \{a\}, \{b\}, \{c\}, \{a, b\}, \{a, c\}\}$. Intuitively, if $\mathbb{S}$ are the extensions of some ABA $\mathcal{D}$, we can be certain that each set in $dcl(\mathbb{S})$ if conflict-free.   ◇

Having established the sets we require, let us now consider relevant properties.

Definition 8. *Given an ABAF $\mathcal{D} = (\mathcal{L}, \mathcal{R}, \mathcal{A}, {}^-)$. A set $\mathbb{S} \subseteq 2^\mathcal{A}$ is*

- *incomparable if for $S, S' \in \mathbb{S}$, $S \subseteq S'$ implies $S = S'$;*
- *set-conflict-sensitive if for all $S, S' \in \mathbb{S}$ with $S \cup S' \notin \mathbb{S}$ it holds that there is some $p \in S$ such that $S' \cup \{p\} \in \mathbb{P}_\mathbb{S}$;*
- *set-com-closed if for all $\mathbb{T}, \mathbb{U} \subseteq \mathbb{S}$, the following holds: if their elements $T = \bigcup \mathbb{T}$ and $U = \bigcup \mathbb{U}$ are both contained in the downward closure of $\mathbb{S}$ and satisfy $|\mathbb{C}_\mathbb{S}(T \cup U)| \neq 1$ then there is an assumption $u \in U$ such that $T \cup \{u\} \in \mathbb{P}_\mathbb{S}$.*

Example 5. We continue the above example with $\mathbb{S} = \{\{a\}, \{a, b\}, \{a, c\}\}$:

- $\mathbb{S}$ is not incomparable since $\{a\} \subsetneq \{a, b\}$;
- $\mathbb{S}$ is set-conflict-sensitive. The only sets with $S, S' \in \mathbb{S}$ with $S \cup S' \notin \mathbb{S}$ are $\{a, b\}$ and $\{a, c\}$. Now consider $b \in S$. Indeed, $S' \cup \{b\} = \{a, b, c\} \in \mathbb{P}_\mathbb{S}$. Intuitively, this formalizes that the union $S \cup S'$ is not an extension, i.e., not contained in $\mathbb{S}$, since b and c cause a conflict.
- $\mathbb{S}$ is set-com-closed. Take for example $\mathbb{T} = \{\{a\}, \{a, b\}\}$ and $\mathbb{U} = \{\{a, c\}\}$. We thus have $T = \{a, b\}$ and $U = \{a, c\}$. Both T and U are contained in the downward closure $dcl(\mathbb{S})$ we calculated before. For the union $T \cup U = \{a, b, c\}$ we have $\mathbb{C}_\mathbb{S}(T \cup U) = \emptyset$ since no superset of $T \cup U$ occurs in $\mathbb{S}$. Therefore, the condition $|\mathbb{C}_\mathbb{S}(T \cup U)| \neq 1$ fires and we need to find $u \in U$ s.t. $T \cup \{u\} \in \mathbb{P}_\mathbb{S}$. Indeed, c occurs in U and $T \cup \{c\} = \{a, b, c\}$ is a potential conflict.
  The rationale behind this property is the following: Suppose we consider complete semantics. Then, $\mathbb{C}_\mathbb{S}(\emptyset)$ is the grounded extension and we thus have $|\mathbb{C}_\mathbb{S}(\emptyset)| = 1$. This does not only apply to the empty set; given some admissible extension E, there is also always a unique minimal complete extension containing E. The set-com-closed property extracts situations where $|\mathbb{C}_\mathbb{S}(\cdot)| = 1$ must hold; if not, then we need to find a corresponding "reason", i.e., some $u \in U$ causing the conflict, i.e., $T \cup \{u\} \in \mathbb{P}_\mathbb{S}$.   ◇

We are ready to state the main result of this section.

Theorem 1. *It holds that*

$$\Sigma_{gr}^{ABA} = \{\mathbb{S} \mid |\mathbb{S}| = 1\},$$

$$\Sigma_{ad}^{ABA} = \{\mathbb{S} \neq \emptyset \mid \mathbb{S} \text{ is set-conflict-sensitive and } \emptyset \in \mathbb{S}\},$$

$$\Sigma_{co}^{ABA} = \{\mathbb{S} \neq \emptyset \mid \mathbb{S} \text{ is set-com-closed and } \bigcap \mathbb{S} \in \mathbb{S}\},$$

$$\Sigma_{stb}^{ABA} = \{\mathbb{S} \mid \mathbb{S} \text{ is incomparable}\}, \text{ and}$$

$$\Sigma_{pr}^{ABA} = \Sigma_{stb}^{ABA} \backslash \{\emptyset\}.$$

We obtain the result by (1) exploiting the connection between SETAFs and ABAFs [24] (cf. Definition 5 and Proposition 1) in order to (2) transfer signature results for SETAF semantics [17] to the associated ABAF semantics.

4   Compact Realizability in ABA

In the previous section we could establish the plain ABA signatures by exploiting the close relation to SETAFs. In the remainder of this paper we will study further aspects which require more specialized techniques. In the context of AF signatures it was observed that there are extension-sets that can only be realized by the use of auxiliary arguments that are never accepted. An AF F is *compact w.r.t. a semantics* σ iff each argument in F is credulously accepted [4]. This notion can be translated to ABA and be employed to prove certain unsatisfiability results.

Definition 9. *Given* σ, *an ABAF* $\mathcal{D}$ *is compact w.r.t.* σ *iff* $\mathcal{A}(\mathcal{D}) = \bigcup \sigma(\mathcal{D})$.

We term a semantics σ to be *compactly realizable*, iff for any $\mathcal{D}$ there exists a $\mathcal{D}'$ that is equivalent to $\mathcal{D}$ under σ such that $\mathcal{D}'$ is compact. In the remainder of this section, we prove the following theorem.

Theorem 2. *For ABA, the semantics gr and pr are compactly realizable, whereas ad and co are not. The semantics stb is compactly realizable if we limit ourselves to non-empty extension-sets.*

The empty extension-set $\mathbb{S} = \emptyset$ is not compactly realizable under stable semantics since an ABAF with no assumption has the unique stable extension $\emptyset$. To prove the compact realizability of *gr* and *pr*, and *stb* (for non-empty extension-sets) we employ canonical constructions for ABAFs[3] that are similar in spirit to SETAF constructions for these semantics [17]. We first show compactness of *gr* semantics. For this, we construct a canonical ABA $\mathcal{D}$ with no rule at all.

Definition 10. *Given an extension-set* $\mathbb{S}$ *with* $|\mathbb{S}| = 1$, *i.e.,* $\mathbb{S} = \{S\}$, *we let* $\mathcal{D}_{\mathbb{S}}^{gr} = (\mathcal{L}, \mathcal{R}, \mathcal{A}, {}^{-})$, *where* $\mathcal{L} = \mathcal{A} \cup \{a_c \mid a \in \mathcal{A}\}$, $\mathcal{R} = \emptyset$, $\mathcal{A} = S$, *and* $\bar{a} = a_c$ *for each* $a \in \mathcal{A}$.

---

[3] Implementation of the canonical constructions for all semantics considered in this paper are available at https://pyarg.npai.science.uu.nl/ [28].

It is easy to see that $gr(\mathcal{D}_{\mathbb{S}}^{gr}) = \{S\}$ if $\{S\} = \mathbb{S}$; thus, this construction realizes $\mathbb{S}$ under gr semantics. For pr and stb semantics, we proceed as follows.

Definition 11. *Given an incomparable, non-empty extension-set $\mathbb{S}$, we define $\mathcal{D}_{\mathbb{S}}^{inc} = (\mathcal{L}, \mathcal{R}, \mathcal{A}, {}^-)$, where $\mathcal{L} = \mathcal{A} \cup \{a_c \mid a \in \mathcal{A}\}$, $\mathcal{R} = \{a_c \leftarrow S \mid a \notin S, S \in \mathbb{S}\}$, $\mathcal{A} = \bigcup \mathbb{S}$, and $\bar{a} = a_c$ for each $a \in \mathcal{A}$.*

Example 6. Let $\mathbb{S} = \{\{a,b\}, \{a,c\}, \{b,c\}\}$. We construct the ABAF $\mathcal{D}$ with assumptions $\mathcal{A} = \{a,b,c\}$ and rules $\mathcal{R} = \{a_c \leftarrow b, c; \ b_c \leftarrow a, c; \ c_c \leftarrow a, b\}$. Note that $\mathcal{L}$ and $^-$ are now also determined. Indeed, $\mathcal{D}$ realizes our desired assumption-set under stable and preferred semantics, e.g., $\sigma(\mathcal{D}) = \{\{a,b\}, \{a,c\}, \{b,c\}\}$. ◊

The compact realizability of gr, pr and stb holds due to the constructions in Definitions 10 and 11 not employing unaccepted assumptions.

Proposition 2. *The semantics gr and pr are compact realizable. The semantics stb is compactly realizable if we limit ourselves to non-empty extension-sets.*

In contrast, admissible and complete semantics are not compact realizable. We give corresponding counter-examples.

Example 7. (admissible) Consider $\mathcal{D} = (\mathcal{L}, \mathcal{R}, \mathcal{A}, {}^-)$ with

$$\mathcal{L} = \{a, b, c, a_c, b_c, c_c\} \qquad \mathcal{R} = \{a_c \leftarrow b; \ b_c \leftarrow c\}$$
$$\mathcal{A} = \{a, b, c\} \qquad {}^- = \{(a, a_c), (b, b_c), (c, c_c)\}$$

Then $ad(\mathcal{D}) = \{\emptyset, \{c\}, \{a,c\}\}$, but there is no ABAF $\mathcal{D}'$ with $\mathcal{A}(\mathcal{D}') = \{a,c\}$, s.t. $ad(\mathcal{D}') = \{\emptyset, \{c\}, \{a,c\}\}$. It is impossible to express c supporting a without the presence of a third assumption.

(complete). Consider $\mathcal{D} = (\mathcal{L}, \mathcal{R}, \mathcal{A}, {}^-)$, with

$$\mathcal{L} = \{a, b, a_c, b_c\} \qquad \mathcal{R} = \{b_c \leftarrow a; \ a_c \leftarrow b; \ a_c \leftarrow a\}$$
$$\mathcal{A} = \{a, b\} \qquad {}^- = \{(a, a_c), (b, b_c)\}$$

Then $co(\mathcal{D}) = \{\emptyset, \{b\}\}$, but there is no ABAF $\mathcal{D}'$ with $\mathcal{A}(\mathcal{D}') = \{b\}$, s.t. $co(\mathcal{D}') = \{\emptyset, \{b\}\}$, because if b is the only assumption, then there is only one complete extension as there is nothing against b could defend itself. ◊

From these observations, Theorem 2 follows.

5   Claims, Preferences and Beyond

So far, we put our focus on the most common ABA fragment. In particular, we considered semantics in terms of assumption-sets only. There are, however, several other aspects of ABA that can also be taken into account. In this section, we present several results for realizing extension sets in ABA$^+$ which extends the basic setting by allowing for preferences between assumptions. Moreover, we outline some insights regarding signatures for conclusion sets, i.e., we evaluate $\mathcal{D}$ in terms of accepted conclusions, not just the underlying assumptions.

Signatures for Conclusion Extensions

Let us now also consider the set of all atoms derivable from an assumption-set. Recall that by

$$Th_{\mathcal{D}}(S) = \{p \mid \exists S' \subseteq S : S' \vdash p\}$$

we denote the set of all conclusions derivable from an assumption-set S in an ABAF $\mathcal{D}$. Observe that $S \subseteq Th_{\mathcal{D}}(S)$ since per definition, each assumption $a \in \mathcal{A}$ is derivable from $\{a\} \vdash_{\emptyset} a$. We define the conclusion-based semantics for ABA by considering the derivable conclusions of acceptable assumption sets.

Definition 12. *Let* $\mathcal{D} = (\mathcal{L}, \mathcal{R}, \mathcal{A}, ^{-})$ *be an ABAF and let* σ *be a semantics. We define its* conclusion-based variant *as* $\sigma_c(\mathcal{D}) = \{ Th_{\mathcal{D}}(E) \mid E \in \sigma(\mathcal{D})\}$.

We write $\Sigma_{\sigma_c}^{ABA}$ to denote the conclusion-based signatures. In this section, we compare the conclusion-based signatures with the standard ABA signatures from above. Since deriving the conclusions as well gives more fine-grained extensions, the attentive reader might expect that this setting is more expressive, i.e., $\Sigma_{\sigma}^{ABA} \subseteq \Sigma_{\sigma_c}^{ABA}$. It turns out, however, that in general the opposite is the case. Let us start with the simple case of gr, where both notions indeed coincide (due to the simplicity of gr).

Proposition 3. $\Sigma_{gr}^{ABA} = \Sigma_{gr_c}^{ABA}$.

Proof. Each extension-set of size 1 can be realized for gr semantics in ABA. Our above construction does not require any rules, thus $\sigma(\mathcal{D}) = \sigma_c(\mathcal{D})$ □

Now, in general it is the case that assumption-extensions are more flexible in their modeling capabilities in the sense that $\Sigma_{\sigma_c}^{ABA} \subseteq \Sigma_{\sigma}^{ABA}$. To achieve this result we require a detour to so-called claim-augmented AFs [19] and their relation to SETAFs [18] and ABAFs [24]. We omit the proof details.

Proposition 4. *For all semantics* σ *in this paper,* $\Sigma_{\sigma_c}^{ABA} \subseteq \Sigma_{\sigma}^{ABA}$.

Interestingly, the other direction fails. For all semantics except gr, there are sets which are realizable as assumption-extensions, but not as conclusion extensions.

Proposition 5. *For all semantics* $\sigma \neq gr$ *in this paper,* $\Sigma_{\sigma_c}^{ABA} \subsetneq \Sigma_{\sigma}^{ABA}$.

Proof. (*stb* and *pr*) Let $\mathbb{S} = \{\{a\}, \{b\}, \{c\}\}$. We remark that $\{a\}, \{b\}, \{c\}$ can of course be realized by means of the usual assumption-extensions $\sigma(\mathcal{D})$ for *pr* and *stb* semantics, as our signatures results show. Now suppose $\sigma_c(\mathcal{D}) = \{\{a\}, \{b\}, \{c\}\}$.

We first argue that each of the three elements a, b, and c has to be an assumption: Supposing, e.g., that $a \notin \mathcal{A}$ holds yields that $a \in Th_{\mathcal{D}}(\emptyset)$, because otherwise $\{a\}$ could not be a conclusion-extension. However, in this case a would occur in each extension, but it does not. By symmetry, $\{a, b, c\} \subseteq \mathcal{A}$ must hold.

Thus $Th_{\mathcal{D}}(\{a\}) = \{a\}$, $Th_{\mathcal{D}}(\{b\}) = \{b\}$, and $Th_{\mathcal{D}}(\{c\}) = \{c\}$ for otherwise the conclusion-extensions would be larger. Since $\{a, b\}$, $\{a, c\}$ and $\{b, c\}$ are no extension, we deduce that these sets are not conflict-free or not capable of defending themselves. However, the latter can be excluded since each single assumption a, b, c defends itself. So they have to be conflicting.

We distinguish several cases. (1) Suppose $\bar{a} = b$. But then a can only defend itself if $\bar{b} = a$ holds as well. Since $\{a, c\}$ is conflicting, it must also be the case that (a) $\bar{c} = a$ or (b) $\bar{a} = c$. Supposing (a), then $\{c\}$ can only defend itself if $\bar{a} = c$, i.e., this case yields (b). Supposing (b) implies $b = c$ since $^-$ is a function. But $b = c$ implies the extensions are actually $\{\{a\}, \{b\}\}$, a contradiction.

Other cases like, e.g., $\bar{b} = a$ yield analogous contradictions.

(*ad* and *co*) Now consider $\mathbb{S} = \{\emptyset, \{a\}, \{b\}, \{c\}\}$. Now, $\mathbb{S}$ can be realized by assumption-extensions *w.r.t.* *ad* and *co* semantics. Regarding σ_c, the same reasoning as above applies: $Th_{\mathcal{D}}(\{a\}) = \{a\}$, $Th_{\mathcal{D}}(\{b\}) = \{b\}$, and $Th_{\mathcal{D}}(\{c\}) = \{c\}$ can be inferred analogously and consequently, we find again that, e.g., $\{a\}$ cannot defend itself, yielding the same contradiction.   □

Signatures for ABA with Preferences

Let us now head back to assumption-extensions. ABA$^+$ has been introduced in [14]; it generalizes ABA by incorporating preferences between the assumptions. We recall the necessary background.

Definition 13. *An ABA$^+$ framework is a tuple $(\mathcal{L}, \mathcal{R}, \mathcal{A}, ^-, \leq)$, where $(\mathcal{L}, \mathcal{R}, \mathcal{A}, ^-)$ is an ABAF and $\leq$ is a transitive binary relation on $\mathcal{A}$.*

As usual, we write $a < b$ if $a \leq b$ and $b \not\leq a$. Attacks are generalized as follows.

Definition 14. *Given an ABA$^+$ framework $(\mathcal{L}, \mathcal{R}, \mathcal{A}, ^-, \leq)$. A set of assumptions $S \subseteq \mathcal{A}$ attacks a set of assumptions $T \subseteq \mathcal{A}$ iff*

- *there is $S' \subseteq S$, $t \in T$ s.t. $S' \vdash \bar{t}$, and there is no $s \in S'$ with $s < t$; or*
- *there is $T' \subseteq T$, $s \in S$ s.t. $T' \vdash \bar{s}$, and there is $t \in T'$ with $t < s$.*

For ABA without preferences, only the first item matters: a set of assumptions S attacks another set of assumptions T iff (a subset of) S derives a contrary of some assumption in T. Taking preferences into account might cause an attack reversal, as formalized in item two. The semantics are defined as in Definition 2, but with the generalized attack notion as stated above. That is, S is *admissible* iff i) S does not attack itself and ii) if T attacks S, then S attacks T as well; S is *complete* iff it also contains each a it defends; S is *grounded* iff it is minimal complete and S *preferred* iff it is maximal admissible; S is stable iff S attacks each singleton $\{a\} \subseteq \mathcal{A} \backslash S$.

We let $\Sigma_\sigma^{ABA^+}$ denote the signature of semantics σ for ABA$^+$, i.e.,

$$\Sigma_\sigma^{ABA^+} = \{\sigma(\mathcal{D}) \mid \mathcal{D} \text{ is a flat, finite ABA}^+ \text{ framework}\}.$$

In this section, we establish the following main theorem.

Theorem 3. *It holds that*

$$\Sigma_{gr}^{ABA^+} = \{\mathbb{S} \mid |\mathbb{S}| \leq 1\},$$

$$\Sigma_{ad}^{ABA^+} = \{\mathbb{S} \mid \emptyset \in \mathbb{S}\},$$

$$\Sigma_{stb}^{ABA^+} = \{\mathbb{S} \mid \mathbb{S} \text{ is incomparable}\}, \text{ and}$$

$$\Sigma_{pr}^{ABA^+} = \Sigma_{stb}^{ABA}\backslash\{\emptyset\}.$$

We first note that each extension-set $\mathbb{S}$ which is contained in Σ_{σ}^{ABA} is also contained in $\Sigma_{\sigma}^{ABA^+}$; it suffices to consider the empty preference relation.

Proposition 6. *For all semantics considered in this paper* $\Sigma_{\sigma}^{ABA^+} \supseteq \Sigma_{\sigma}^{ABA}$.

For preferred and stable semantics, we even have a stronger result. Below, we show that the signatures for ABA^+ corresponds to the signatures for ABA without preferences. For preferred semantics, we obtain this result because the semantics operate on maximizing the assumption-sets. For stable semantics, we additionally rely on the monotonicity of the range function.

Proposition 7. *For* $\sigma \in \{stb, pr\}$ *we have* $\Sigma_{\sigma}^{ABA^+} = \Sigma_{\sigma}^{ABA}$.

Proof. Let $\sigma \in \{stb, pr\}$. According to Proposition 6, $\Sigma_{\sigma}^{ABA^+} \supseteq \Sigma_{\sigma}^{ABA}$ holds. On the other hand, $\Sigma_{pr}^{ABA^+} \subseteq \Sigma_{pr}^{ABA}$ since preferred extensions are incomparable by definition. For $\Sigma_{stb}^{ABA^+} \subseteq \Sigma_{stb}^{ABA}$ suppose $\mathcal{D}$ is an ABA^+ framework with stable extensions $S \subsetneq S'$. Even with preferences, the range is monotonic, i.e., we have that $Th_{\mathcal{D}}(S) \subseteq Th_{\mathcal{D}}(S')$. Consequently, if S is stable, then S' is not conflict-free; contradiction. $\square$

In contrast, admissible semantics in ABA^+ are significantly more powerful than their counterpart in ABA without preferences. We observe that each extension set that contains the empty set can be realized.

Proposition 8. $\Sigma_{ad}^{ABA^+} = \{\mathbb{S} \mid \emptyset \in \mathbb{S}\}$.

Proof. Let $\mathbb{S} \neq \emptyset$ with $\emptyset \in \mathbb{S}$. Moreover, let $A_{\mathbb{S}} = \bigcup_{S \in \mathbb{S}} S$ and let $N_{\mathbb{S}} = 2^{A_{\mathbb{S}}}\backslash\mathbb{S}$. We construct the corresponding ABAF $\mathcal{D} = (\mathcal{L}, \mathcal{A}, \mathcal{R}, \overline{}, \leq)$ with

$$\mathcal{L} = \mathcal{A} \cup \{a^c \mid a \in \mathcal{A}\}, \ \mathcal{A} = A_{\mathbb{S}} \cup \{v_N \mid N \in N_{\mathbb{S}}\}, \ \overline{a} = a^c \text{ for each } a \in \mathcal{A},$$

$$\mathcal{R} = \{v_N{}^c \leftarrow N; v_N{}^c \leftarrow v_N \mid N \in N_{\mathbb{S}}\} \cup \{v_N{}^c \leftarrow S\backslash N \mid S \in \mathbb{S}, N \in N_{\mathbb{S}}, N \subseteq S\},$$

and preference relation as follows: for each $N \in N_{\mathbb{S}}$, we let $v_N > n$ for some $n \in N$. An example of the construction is given in Fig. 1.

We observe that the set $A_{\mathbb{S}}$ itself is conflict-free(no assumption is a contrary). Each set N that is *not* contained in $\mathbb{S}$ receives an attack from v_N: The attack from the rule $v_N{}^c \leftarrow N$ is reversed because N contains some $n \in N$ with $n < v_N$. However, each set $S \in \mathbb{S}$ that is attacked by some v_N defends itself: v_N is counter-attacked by $S\backslash N$ (and there is no $s < v_N$ for any $s \in S\backslash N$ since $(S\backslash N)\cap N = \emptyset$). Based on these observations, we can show that $ad(\mathcal{D}) = \mathbb{S}$.

$$\mathcal{L} = \mathcal{A} \cup \{a^c \mid a \in \mathcal{A}\}$$
$$\mathcal{A} = \{a, b, c, v_{\{b\}}, v_{\{c\}}, v_{\{a,b,c\}}\}$$
$$\mathcal{R} = \{v_{\{b\}}{}^c \leftarrow b; \quad v_{\{c\}}{}^c \leftarrow c;$$
$$\qquad v_{\{a,b,c\}}{}^c \leftarrow a, b, c;$$
$$\qquad v_{\{b\}}{}^c \leftarrow a; \quad v_{\{b\}}{}^c \leftarrow c;$$
$$\qquad v_{\{c\}}{}^c \leftarrow a; \quad v_{\{c\}}{}^c \leftarrow b;$$
$$\qquad v_{\{b\}}{}^c \leftarrow v_{\{b\}}; \quad v_{\{c\}}{}^c \leftarrow v_{\{c\}};$$
$$\qquad v_{\{a,b,c\}}{}^c \leftarrow v_{\{a,b,c\}}\},$$

$$v_{\{b\}} > b, v_{\{c\}} > c, v_{\{a,b,c\}} > a$$

(a) Resulting ABA$^+$.

(b) Attacks between assumption-sets.

Fig. 1. Example of the construction from the proof of Proposition 8 for $\mathbb{S} = \{\emptyset, \{a,b\}, \{a,c\}, \{b,c\}, \{a\}\}$. We get $A_{\mathbb{S}} = \{a, b, c\}$ and $N_{\mathbb{S}} = \{\{b\}, \{c\}, \{a,b,c\}\}$. The corresponding ABA$^+$ is depicted left (1a), sets between assumption-sets are depicted right (1b) (supersets of $\{v_N\}$ are omitted since they are self-attacking).

First, we show that $ad(\mathcal{D}) \subseteq \mathbb{S}$. We note that $\emptyset \in ad(\mathcal{D})$ by definition. Now let $S \in \mathbb{S}$ with $S \neq \emptyset$. As observed above, $S \in cf(\mathcal{D})$. We show that S defends itself: let $X \subseteq \mathcal{A}$ be an assumption-set that attacks S. That is, either (a) there is $X' \subseteq X$, $s \in S$ such that $X' \vdash s$ and none of the elements in X' is strictly weaker than s, or (b) there is $S' \subseteq S$, $x \in X$ such that $S' \vdash x$ and there is $s \in S'$ such that $s < x$. By construction, no contrary of an assumption $a \in A_{\mathbb{S}}$ can be derived. Hence, case (a) cannot occur. Now, suppose (b) is the case. Then there are $S' \subseteq S$ and $x \in X$ such that $S' \vdash x$ and there is $s \in S'$ such that $s < x$. By construction, this can only be the case if S' is not contained in $\mathbb{S}$ (i.e., $S' \in N_{\mathbb{S}}$), S' derives the contrary of $v_{S'}$, and the direction of the attack is reversed by the preference relation $v_{S'} > n$ for some $n \in S'$. It is clear that S' is a *proper* subset of S. Otherwise we obtain $S \in N_{\mathbb{S}}$, contradicting our assumption. Hence, the set $S \backslash S'$ is not empty. By construction, the assumption $v_{S'}$ is attacked by $S \backslash S'$ (via the rule $v_{S'} \leftarrow S \backslash S'$). Hence, we obtain that S defends itself against the attack from X, as desired.

It remains to show that no other set is admissible, i.e., $ad(\mathcal{D}) \supseteq \mathbb{S}$. This is ensured by construction since each $N \in N_{\mathbb{S}}$ is attacked by v_N and is not defended against this assumption. We obtain $ad(\mathcal{D}) = \mathbb{S}$, as desired.   □

Regarding grounded semantics, we require some auxiliary observations. We define the characteristic function for an ABA$^+$ framework $\mathcal{D} = (\mathcal{L}, \mathcal{R}, \mathcal{A}, ^-, \leq)$ as usual, i.e., we let $\Gamma_{\mathcal{D}}(S) = \{a \in \mathcal{A} \mid S \text{ defends } a\}$. The more involved attack notion does not alter the fact that Γ is monotonic.

Proposition 9. *Let $\mathcal{D} = (\mathcal{L}, \mathcal{R}, \mathcal{A}, ^-, \leq)$ be an ABA$^+$ framework. If $S \subseteq S' \subseteq \mathcal{A}$, then $\Gamma_{\mathcal{D}}(S) \subseteq \Gamma_{\mathcal{D}}(S')$.*

Monotonicity of the characteristic function is one of the key ingredients for showing that the grounded extension is unique (for the most common argumentation formalisms). Consequently, we can infer a similar result: The only candidate for the grounded extension is $\bigcup_{i\geq 1} \Gamma_{\mathcal{D}}^i(\emptyset)$, i.e., iterating the characteristic function. Perhaps somewhat surprising we can only derive $|gr(\mathcal{D})| \leq 1$, since complete extensions do not necessarily exist.

Proposition 10. *For any ABA$^+$ framework* $\mathcal{D} = (\mathcal{L}, \mathcal{R}, \mathcal{A},^-, \leq)$, $|gr(\mathcal{D})| \leq 1$.

As the following example shows, the case $co(\mathcal{D}) = \emptyset$ (and thus $gr(\mathcal{D}) = \emptyset$) is indeed possible. Consider the following simple ABA$^+$ framework.

Example 8. Let $\mathcal{D}$ be the ABA$^+$ framework with $\mathcal{A} = \{a, b, c\}$, the rule $\bar{c} \leftarrow a, b$, and let $c > a$. Then $\{c\}$ attacks $\{a, b\}$ since $\{a, b\} \vdash \bar{c}$ and $a < c$.

In $\mathcal{D}$, all assumptions a, b, and c are unattacked; however, the set $\{a, b, c\}$ is conflicting. Hence, no grounded extension exist in $\mathcal{D}$. Therefore, also complete semantics return the empty set.   ◇

Consequently, the grounded ABA$^+$ signature is given as follows.

Proposition 11. $\Sigma_{gr}^{ABA^+} = \{\mathbb{S} \mid |\mathbb{S}| \leq 1\}$

Thereby, the above examples shows how to realize $\mathbb{S} = \emptyset$, and if $|\mathbb{S}| = 1$, then the construction given for usual ABAFs suffices. From the propositions we inferred within this section, the desired Theorem 3 follows.

6 Conclusion

In this paper, we investigated several aspects of ABA expressiveness. We characterized the signatures of ABA semantics by connecting two recent developments in the field of formal argumentation: we used the close relation to SETAFs presented in [24] in order to benefit from the established SETAF signatures [17]. We amplified our investigation with several aspects which are central for understanding the expressiveness of ABA. In particular, we discussed the relation to conclusion-based ABA semantics and signatures for ABA with preferences.

Our notion of signatures is inspired by research on expressiveness in abstract argumentation formalisms [16,17,20]. We are not aware of any comprehensive investigation of signatures in structured argumentation in the literature.

Searching for Suitable Translations. Semantics-preserving translations between non-monotonic reasoning formalisms are well-studied [10,11,24,29]. They are useful for several reasons. First, they enable access to solvers and other tools that have been developed for the target formalism (see e.g., [32]). Second, translations from structured to abstract argumentation formalisms have gained increasing attention in the context of explainability. Abstract graph-based representations are intuitive and easy-to-understand by design; moreover, they are central for extracting argumentative explanations. Since AFs are particularly well-studied, they are oftentimes considered as the default target formalism. However, many translations to AFs often require auxiliary arguments which may cause an exponential blowup; moreover, they often preserve semantics only under projection.

The underlying issue becomes clear when looking at the signatures in the different formalisms: it turns out that many argumentation formalisms are more expressive than AFs [17,20]. In particular, our results show that flat ABAFs are closer in their nature to SETAFs than to Dung's AFs. Moreover, we show that the more advanced ABA fragments that we consider admit a higher expressiveness than flat ABA for most of the semantics. Building upon our insights, we identify the search for suitable abstract formalisms with matching expressiveness that capture ABA with preferences, conclusion-semantics of ABA, or even more general fragments like non-flat ABA as a challenging future work direction. Generally speaking, it would be interesting to put more emphasis on abstract formalisms with higher expressiveness, e.g., in order to obtain competitive instantiation-based ABA solvers or to extract argumentative explanations.

The Role of Signatures in Dynamics in Argumentation. In particular in order to push forward dynamics research in structured argumentation, understanding the modeling capabilities of a formalism is crucial: oftentimes dynamics research is driven by a certain goal like, e.g., enforcing a target set of conclusions or forgetting given elements of a knowledge base [1,2,5,7,9,25].

Example 9. Suppose we want to develop a forgetting operator that removes from each extension the element that should be forgotten. This notion is known as *persistence.* Our signature results indicate whether it is possible so satisfy such constraints. For instance, it becomes clear that we cannot construct a forgetting operator that satisfies persistence for stable semantics: for an ABAF $\mathcal{D}$ with $stb(\mathcal{D}) = \{\{a, b\}, \{b, c\}\}$, we run into an issue if we aim to forget the assumption a. The set $\{\{b\}, \{b, c\}\}$ is not incomparable and hence it cannot be realized, as we have shown.[4] $\Diamond$

Recent studies on dynamics in structured argumentation show that we cannot rely on the corresponding results for AFs [30,31]. Hence, our results provide a solid theoretical foundation in order to understand what can be attained and what not. Moreover, understanding expressiveness is indispensable in order to extend this line of research to further dynamic tasks like belief revision [3].

Open Problems. The present work characterizes the expressiveness of ABA semantics in several aspects. Nonetheless, certain questions in this context remain open: i) precise signature characterizations for admissible, complete, preferred, and stable semantics for conclusion-based ABA semantics; ii) precise signature characterizations of complete semantics for ABA$^+$; and iii) signature characterizations for semantics in non-flat ABAFs. We view closing these gaps as a natural future work directions. Moreover, our research was focusing on ABAFs, but there a several other structured argumentation formalisms worth investigating, for instance defeasible logic programming [23] or ASPIC+ [26].

---

[4] We refer the interested reader to [7] for an in-depth study on forgetting in flat ABA.

Acknowledgements. This research has been supported by the Federal Ministry of Education and Research of Germany and by Sächsische Staatsministerium für Wissenschaft, Kultur und Tourismus in the programme Center of Excellence for AI-research "Center for Scalable Data Analytics and Artificial Intelligence Dresden/Leipzig", project identification number: ScaDS.AI. Anna Rapberger was partially funded by the Vienna Science and Technology Fund (WWTF) through project ICT19-065, by the Austrian Science Fund (FWF) through project P32830, and by the European Research Council (ERC) under the European Union's Horizon 2020 research and innovation programme (grant agreement No. 101020934).

References

1. Baumann, R.: What does it take to enforce an argument? Minimal change in abstract argumentation. In: Proceeding of (ECAI-12), pp. 127–132 (2012)
2. Baumann, R., Berthold, M.: Limits and possibilities of forgetting in abstract argumentation. In: Proceedings of (IJCAI-22), pp. 2539–2545. ijcai.org (2022)
3. Baumann, R., Brewka, G.: AGM meets abstract argumentation: Expansion and revision for dung frameworks. In: Proceedings of (IJCAI-15), pp. 2734–2740 (2015)
4. Baumann, R., Dvořák, W., Linsbichler, T., Strass, H., Woltran, S.: Compact argumentation frameworks. In: Proceedings of (ECAI-14). FAIA, vol. 263, pp. 69–74. IOS Press (2014)
5. Baumann, R., Gabbay, D.M., Rodrigues, O.: Forgetting an argument. In: Proceedings of (AAAI-20), pp. 2750–2757. AAAI Press (2020)
6. Baumann, R., Strass, H.: On the maximal and average numbers of stable extensions. In: Black, E., Modgil, S., Oren, N. (eds.) TAFA 2013. LNCS (LNAI), vol. 8306, pp. 111–126. Springer, Heidelberg (2014). https://doi.org/10.1007/978-3-642-54373-9_8
7. Berthold, M., Rapberger, A., Ulbricht, M.: Forgetting aspects in assumption-based argumentation. In: Proceedings of (KR-23) (2023)
8. Bondarenko, A., Toni, F., Kowalski, R.A.: An assumption-based framework for non-monotonic reasoning. In: Proceedings of (LPNMR-93), pp. 171–189. MIT Press (1993)
9. Borg, A., Bex, F.: Enforcing sets of formulas in structured argumentation. In: Proceedings of (KR-21), pp. 130–140 (2021)
10. Caminada, M., Sá, S., Alcântara, J., Dvořák, W.: On the difference between assumption-based argumentation and abstract argumentation. IFCoLog J. Logic Appl. **2**(1), 15–34 (2015)
11. Caminada, M., Sá, S., Alcântara, J., Dvořák, W.: On the equivalence between logic programming semantics and argumentation semantics. Int. J. Approximate Reasoning **58**, 87–111 (2015)
12. Čyras, K., Fan, X., Schulz, C., Toni, F.: Assumption-based argumentation: disputes, explanations, preferences. In: Handbook of Formal Argumentation, vol. 1, chap. 7, pp. 365–408. College Publications (2018)
13. Čyras, K., Rago, A., Albini, E., Baroni, P., Toni, F.: Argumentative XAI: a survey. In: Proceedings of (IJCAI-21), pp. 4392–4399. ijcai.org (2021)
14. Čyras, K., Toni, F.: ABA+: assumption-based argumentation with preferences. CoRR abs/1610.03024 (2016)
15. Dung, P.M.: On the acceptability of arguments and its fundamental role in non-monotonic reasoning, logic programming and n-person games. Artif. Intell. **77**(2), 321–357 (1995)

16. Dunne, P.E., Dvořák, W., Linsbichler, T., Woltran, S.: Characteristics of multiple viewpoints in abstract argumentation. Artif. Intell. **228**, 153–178 (2015)
17. Dvořák, W., Fandinno, J., Woltran, S.: On the expressive power of collective attacks. Argument Comput. **10**(2), 191–230 (2019)
18. Dvořák, W., Rapberger, A., Woltran, S.: On the relation between claim-augmented argumentation frameworks and collective attacks. In: Proceedings of (ECAI-20). FAIA, vol. 325, pp. 721–728. IOS Press (2020)
19. Dvořák, W., Woltran, S.: Complexity of abstract argumentation under a claim-centric view. Artif. Intell. **285**, 103290 (2020)
20. Dvořák, W., Rapberger, A., Woltran, S.: Argumentation semantics under a claim-centric view: Properties, expressiveness and relation to SETAFs. In: Proceedings of (KR-20), pp. 341–350 (2020)
21. Fan, X., Toni, F.: On computing explanations in argumentation. In: Proceedings of (AAAI-15), pp. 1496–1502. AAAI Press (2015)
22. Gabbay, D., Giacomin, M., Simari, G.R., Thimm, M. (eds.): Handbook of Formal Argumentation, vol. 2. College Publications (2021)
23. García, A.J., Simari, G.R.: Defeasible logic programming: an argumentative approach. Theory Pract. Logic Program. **4**(1–2), 95–138 (2004)
24. König, M., Rapberger, A., Ulbricht, M.: Just a matter of perspective. In: Proceedings of (COMMA-22). FAIA, vol. 353, pp. 212–223. IOS Press (2022)
25. Lin, F., Reiter, R.: Forget it. In: Working Notes of AAAI Fall Symposium on Relevance, pp. 154–159 (1994)
26. Modgil, S., Prakken, H.: The ASPIC$^+$ framework for structured argumentation: a tutorial. Argument Comput. **5**(1), 31–62 (2014)
27. Nielsen, S.H., Parsons, S.: A generalization of dung's abstract framework for argumentation: arguing with sets of attacking arguments. In: Maudet, N., Parsons, S., Rahwan, I. (eds.) ArgMAS 2006. LNCS (LNAI), vol. 4766, pp. 54–73. Springer, Heidelberg (2007). https://doi.org/10.1007/978-3-540-75526-5_4
28. Odekerken, D., Borg, A., Berthold, M.: Accessible algorithms for applied argumentation. In: Proceedings of (Arg&App@KR-23) (2023)
29. Polberg, S.: Developing the Abstract Dialectical Framework. Phd thesis, Vienna University of Technology, Institute of Information Systems (2017)
30. Prakken, H.: Formalising an aspect of argument strength: Degrees of attackability. In: Proceedings of (COMMA-22), vol. 353, pp. 296–307. IOS Press (2022)
31. Rapberger, A., Ulbricht, M.: On dynamics in structured argumentation formalisms. J. Artif. Intell. Res. **77**, 563–643 (2023)
32. Tuomo, L., Rapberger, A., Ulbricht, M., Wallner, J.P.: Argumentation frameworks induced by assumption-based argumentation: relating size and complexity. In: Proceedings of (KR-23) (2023)
33. Ulbricht, M.: On the maximal number of complete extensions in abstract argumentation frameworks. In: Proceedings of (KR-21), pp. 707–711 (2021)
34. Vassiliades, A., Bassiliades, N., Patkos, T.: Argumentation and explainable artificial intelligence: a survey. Knowl. Eng. Rev. **36**, e5 (2021)

Weak Argumentation Semantics and Unsafe Odd Cycles: Results and a Conjecture

Sjur K Dyrkolbotn[(✉)]

Department of Civil Engineering, Western Norway University of Applied Sciences,
Bergen, Norway
sdy@hvl.no

Abstract. Some semantics for argumentation, including the newly introduced weakly admissible semantics, allow us to ignore attacks from arguments that are perceived as problematic. A key intuition motivating such semantics is that arguments that indirectly attack themselves may be problematic in such a way that this is justified. In this paper, we formalise this intuition and provide a class of semantics that are weakly admissible, coincide with the stable semantics on a large class of argumentation frameworks that admit stable sets, and only ignore attacks from arguments on unsafe cycles of odd length. We also show that no member of our class of semantics coincide with the semantics that takes all ⊆-maximal weakly admissible sets as extensions. However, we show that this semantics satisfies an even stronger property, if the following conjecture is true: if an argumentation framework has no non-empty weakly admissible sets, then every argument lies on an unsafe odd cycle.

1 Introduction

Abstract argumentation based on argumentation frameworks in the style of [8] 'has become a popular modelling paradigm in knowledge representation and artificial intelligence. Several different semantics for argumentation have been proposed in this tradition, catering to various intuitions, applications and modelling requirements. One key issue that arises concerns the semantic status of arguments that directly or indirectly attack themselves: when should such possibly problematic arguments be regarded as capable of defeating other arguments? The traditional semantics for argumentation arguably fail to provide satisfactory answers to this question, but in [4], the authors provide a new class of semantics that looks very promising on examples. It is explicitly motivated by the idea that we should be able to ignore attacks from self-defeating arguments. But what exactly does this mean? The authors provide an informal answer, writing that "self-defeat occurs if an argument attacks itself either directly or indirectly via

---

Thanks to the anonymous reviewers for pointing out some relevant references and making suggestions that greatly improved the presentation of the paper.

S. Gaggl et al. (Eds.): JELIA 2023, LNAI 14281, pp. 161–175, 2023.
https://doi.org/10.1007/978-3-031-43619-2_12

an odd attack loop, unless the loop is broken up by some argument attacking the loop from outside." In this paper, we propose a formal definition based on the same intuition. We clarify what we mean by an argument attacking itself directly or indirectly and note that loops/cycles may also be broken up from the "inside", when there are additional attacks between arguments on the cycle. We then investigate what semantics for argumentation are *justified* by the key intuition at work, when formalised as a requirement that a semantics may or may not satisfy. We show that while the most permissive semantics based on weak admissibility is not justified, it is possible to define, for any well-behaved admissible semantics, a corresponding weakly admissible semantics that is justified. We show that these semantics extend the stable semantics in a reasonable way, returning only stable sets as extensions for a large class of argumentation frameworks that have no problematic odd cycles. However, we also show that no semantics in the class we define is equivalent to the weakly preferred semantics, obtained by taking all $\subseteq$-maximal weakly admissible sets as extensions. Despite this negative result, we conjecture that the weakly preferred semantics is also justified. We show that if this is true, then the weakly preferred semantics satisfies an even stronger property, whereby for every extension, every argument not included or attacked by it lies on an unbroken odd cycle.

2   Background

The basic notion is that of an argumentation framework, which mathematically speaking is nothing but a directed graph, usually assumed to be finite.

Definition 1. *An* argumentation framework *(AF) is a directed graph $AF = (A, R)$ where $R \subseteq A \times A$ is referred to as an attack relation over a finite set of arguments A.*

For any $AF = (A, R)$ and $S \subseteq A$, the subframework of AF induced by S is $AF\!\downarrow_S = (S, R \cap (S \times S))$. Moreover, for any $a \in A$ we denote by $R(a) = \{b \in A \mid (a, b) \in R\}$ the set of arguments attacked by a and by $R^-(a) = \{b \in A \mid (b, a) \in R\}$ the set of arguments that attack a. We extend the notation to sets $S \subseteq A$, so that $R(S) = \bigcup_{a \in S} R(a)$ and $R^-(S) = \bigcup_{a \in S} R^-(a)$. If $S, Q \subseteq A$, we say that S attacks Q just in case $S \cap R^-(Q) \neq \emptyset$. For any $AF = (A, R)$ and $S \subseteq A$ we let $[S]_{AF} = S \cup R(S)$. We omit the subscript when it is clear from the context. Furthermore, we denote by AF^S the subframework of AF induced by $A \backslash [S]_{AF}$, called the *reduct* of AF by S. Given S, an odd cycle in AF^S can be regarded as an odd cycle that is not broken up from the outside by S.

An (attack) walk of length n in AF is a sequence of arguments $W_{a_0, a_n} = (a_0, a_1, \ldots, a_n)$ such that $a_i \in R(a_{i-1})$ for all $1 \leq i \leq n$. If $i \neq j \Rightarrow a_i \neq a_j$ for all $0 \leq i \leq n$, the walk is an (attack) path. If $a_0 = a_n$ and $i \neq j \Rightarrow a_i \neq a_j$ for all $1 \leq i \leq n$, the walk is an (attack) cycle of length n. When n is even, the cycle is even, and when n is odd, the cycle is odd. Notice that (a, a) is an odd cycle consisting of a single argument attacking itself.

If $W_{a_0,a_n} = (a_0, a_1, \ldots, a_n)$ is a walk and $W_{a_n,a_m} = (a_n, a_{n+1}, \ldots, a_m)$ is a walk of length $m - n$, then $W_{a_0,a_n} + W_{a_n,a_m} = (a_0, a_1, \ldots, a_n, a_{n+1}, \ldots, a_m)$ is a walk of length $n + (m - n) = m$. Beware that if $P_{a,b}$ is a path ending at b and $P_{b,c}$ is a path beginning at b, then $P_{a,b} + P_{b,c}$ is a walk, but not necessarily a path, since $P_{a,b}$ and $P_{b,c}$ might intersect internally. Given a set $B \subseteq A$ and a walk $W = (a_0, a_1, \ldots, a_n)$ we say that W is B-alternating if $a_i \in B \Leftrightarrow a_{i+1} \notin B$ for all $0 \leq i < n$. That is, W is B-alternating just in case every other argument on W is in B. So, for instance, if $B = \{a, c\}$, then the paths (a, b, c) and (a, b, c, d) are B-alternating, while (a, b, d) is not. Notice that a B-alternating path from B to B always has even length.

If $P = (a_0, a_1, \ldots, a_n)$ is a path, then $P_{a_i,a_{i+j}} = (a_i, a_{i+1}, \ldots, a_{i+j})$ is a subpath of P for all $0 \leq i < n$ and $j \leq n - i$. Moreover, an attack $(a_i, a_j) \in R$ with $0 \leq i, j \leq n$ and $j \neq i + 1$ is called a *chord* on P. We say that a chord (a_i, a_j) on $P = (a_0, a_1, \ldots, a_n)$ *breaks* P if i and j are both even. If $C = (a_0, \ldots, a_n = a_0)$ is an odd cycle and (a_i, a_j) is a chord that breaks $P = (a_0, \ldots, a_{n-1})$, then we say that C is *safe* at a_0. It is *unsafe* at a_0 otherwise.

An argumentation semantics ς assigns, to any $AF = (A, R)$, a set of subsets of the arguments, also called ς-*extensions*, $\varsigma : A \to 2^{2^A}$. A semantics is typically defined in terms of requirements on the sets of arguments it returns as extensions. Many different semantics have been defined using various combinations of different requirements. Hence, different requirements and how they may be understood, motivated and justified in different contexts, as well as how they relate to one another mathematically, has become an important research topic in argumentation theory. Following [1], requirements are also often used to classify and compare different argumentation semantics. In this context, underlying mathematical requirements arc lifted from sets of arguments to semantics and referred to as semantic *principles*. A principle corresponds to a whole class of different semantics, consisting of all semantics that only return extensions that satisfy the underlying requirement.

The most widely endorsed argumentation principle is that a semantics for argumentation should only return *conflict free* sets of arguments as extensions. Given $AF = (A, R)$ and $S \subseteq A$, we say that S is conflict free if $(S \times S) \cap R = \emptyset$. That is, S is conflict free if there are no attacks between any two elements of S. Lifting the requirement to define a class of semantics, we say that a semantics ς for argumentation is conflict free – meaning that it satisfies the principle of conflict-freeness – if for all $AF = (A, R)$ and all $S \in \varsigma(AF)$, S is conflict free.

Many semantics for argumentation, including the original ones presented in [8], satisfy another principle, namely that they only return extensions that defend themselves. Formally, a set $S \subseteq A$ defends itself just in case it attacks everything that attacks it, $R^-(S) \subseteq R(S)$. Lifting this notion from sets to semantics, we say that a semantics ς is *defensive* if for all $AF = (A, R)$ and $S \in \varsigma(AF)$, S defends itself. A set that is conflict free and defends itself is *admissible*. Lifting this notion to semantics ς, if ς is conflict free and defensive, it is an admissible semantics. Hence, notice that with this terminology there are several admissible semantics, not just the most permissive one that always returns all admissible sets as extensions (often called the admissible semantics in the literature).

Notice that if S is admissible, $a \in S$, and $P_{a,b}$ is broken by a chord, then since S is conflict free, $P_{a,b}$ is not S-alternating. Intuitively, an S-alternating path starting at S is an unbroken path of semantic dependencies that arise when we regard S as an extension, so such paths can have no chords that break them. This also explains why an odd cycle can be broken from the inside and why we say that $C = (a_0, a_1 \ldots, a_n)$ is safe at a when the path $P = (a_0, \ldots, a_{n-1})$ is broken: attempting to include a in some extension S could not produce a sequence of semantic dependencies along C that would end up defeating a. Hence, C does not indicate that a is actually self-defeating, regardless of S and whether or not C is broken by it from the outside.

The most permissive admissible semantics is not very reasonable, most notably because it always returns $\emptyset$ as a possible extension of any AF. However, the notion of admissibility is still fundamental, since it forms the basis for a range of other semantics, often arrived at by stipulating additional principles.

Semantics that are conflict free but not defensive, allowing us to sometimes ignore attacks, are *weaker* than admissible semantics. Such semantics are not new. In fact, a whole class of semantics weaker than the admissible semantics has been introduced based on computing (maximal) conflict free sets [2]. These semantics generally do not quite match the desiderata explored in this paper, however, as they typically allow us to ignore attacks also from arguments that do not indirectly attack themselves. This is shown with examples and discussed at length in [4], so we do not go into detail. Instead, we will focus on a new class of semantics which is explicitly motivated by the intuition we formalise in this paper. The key notion is that of weak admissibility, defined as follows.

Definition 2. *Given any* $AF = (A, R)$, *a set of arguments* $S \subseteq A$ *is weakly admissible when it is conflict free and there is no set* $Q \subseteq A \backslash [S]$ *that attacks* S *in* AF *and is weakly admissible in* AF^S.

We will also lift this notion from sets to semantics and regard it as a principle, by saying that a semantics ς is *weakly admissible* if for all $AF = (A, R)$, if $S \in \varsigma(AF)$, then S is weakly admissible. So a semantics is said to be weakly admissible if it only returns weakly admissible sets as extensions. Notice that if S defends itself, then there is no set attacking S in AF that is also present in AF^S. Hence, every admissible S is also weakly admissible. At the level of semantics, adopting our terminology, it follows that all admissible semantics are weakly admissible.

3   Perfect Extensions of the Stable Semantics

If a semantics ς seems too permissive, for instance because $\emptyset$ is always a ς-extension, one may impose additional principles to arrive at a more restricted semantics. The most straightforward approach is to restrict ς by taking as extensions only those $S \in \varsigma(AF)$ that are $\subseteq$-maximal. This scheme yields what we call ς-preferred semantics, which is referred to simply as the preferred semantics when ς is the most permissive admissible semantics. When ς is the most permissive weakly admissible semantics, then the ς-preferred semantics is referred to as the weakly preferred semantics.

A stronger principle than $\subseteq$-maximality is to demand that S must attack every argument not in S. Formally, for any $AF = (A, R)$ we say that $S \subseteq A$ is *dominating* if $S \cup R(S) = A$. As before, a semantics ς such that for all $AF = (A, R)$, any $S \in \varsigma(AF)$ is dominating, is called a dominating semantics.

A set that is conflict free and dominating is called a *stable set* in the literature, and the semantics that returns all stable sets in AF as extensions is called the stable semantics. A stable set unambiguously determines the semantic status of every argument in the AF, partitioning them into those arguments we accept and those we reject, which are all attacked by some argument we accept. Unfortunately, stable sets may not exist, as illustrated by the AF consisting of a single self-attacking argument.

The fact that stable sets may not exist is a key motivation for introducing weaker semantics that tolerate partial semantic verdicts. Hence, it may seem natural to require that weaker semantics are *conservative extensions* of the stable semantics, in the sense that whenever stable sets exist, the weaker semantics only returns stable sets as extensions. One way of ensuring this is to define some class of sets that include all stable sets and then choose as extensions all sets from the class that have minimal reducts. Then the stable sets are the only extensions whenever they exist, because their reducts are always empty. Following this approach starting with admissible sets yields a trivially equivalent formulation of the so-called semi-stable semantics [5], which returns as extensions all admissible sets S for which $[S] = S \cup R(S)$ is $\subseteq$-maximal.

It is not clear, however, that conservative extensions of the stable semantics yield reasonable results. Consider, for instance, the following AF:

$$a \mathrel{\rlap{\raise0.5ex{\leftarrow}}{\raise-0.5ex{\rightarrow}}} b \longrightarrow c \mathbin{\reflectbox{$\circlearrowleft$}} d$$

The only stable set is $\{b\}$, which is also the only semi-stable set, having an empty reduct. It is also a preferred set, of course, but it is not the only one. The set $\{a, d\}$ is also preferred, being $\subseteq$-maximal among the admissible sets. Is it reasonable to say that d (and a) must be rejected because a prevents b from defeating the self-defeating c? This is far from obvious and will depend on what the AF is intended to model (or how it is instantiated by less abstract arguments).

Clearly, the preferred semantics is not a conservative extension, so how does it relate to the stable semantics? This can be answered formally using a concept from graph theory [11] that appears to have been largely neglected by the argumentation community. Adapting the terminology to the present setting, we say that $AF = (A, R)$ is *perfectly stable* if for all $S \subseteq A$, the subframework induced by S, $AF\!\downarrow_S$, has a stable set. Then we define a new argumentation principle as follows.

Definition 3. *A semantics ς is a* perfect extension *of the stable semantics if for all $AF = (A, R)$ such that AF is perfectly stable, we have*

$$\forall S \in \varsigma(AF) : R(S) = A \backslash S$$

That is, a semantics is a perfect extension of the stable semantics if it only returns stable sets as extensions for perfectly stable AFs.[1] Several sufficient conditions for the existence of stable sets in AF are known, most notably that a (finite) AF has a stable set if it has no odd cycles (a result that originally appeared in [13], published in 1953). This and most other sufficient conditions for the existence of stable sets ensure that AF is perfectly stable, so they also ensure that any perfect extension of the stable semantics only returns stable sets as extensions on AF. Moreover, it follows from [11] that a minimal AF that is not perfectly stable satisfies a property that is particularly interesting in the present context: all arguments a on AF lie on odd cycles. This suggests that it should be possible to define a semantics that satisfies the desiderata explored in the present paper, although how exactly to do it remains a non-trivial open question.

Before we move on, we note that the definition of a perfect extension is well matched to the concept of modularity, explored in [4] and defined as follows.

Definition 4. *An argumentation semantics ς is* modular *if for every $AF = (A, R)$ and $S \subseteq A$, if $S \in \varsigma(AF)$ and $S' \in \varsigma(AF^S)$, then $S \cup S' \in \varsigma(AF)$.*

Admissible sets are modular, so if S is preferred, then AF^S has no admissible set [4]. In the terminology from [4], it has a "meaningless reduct". From this it follows that the preferred semantics is a perfect extension of the stable semantics, as we now prove.

Theorem 5. *Given any $AF = (A, R)$, if AF is perfectly stable, then every preferred set in AF is a stable set. Hence, the preferred semantics is a perfect extension of the stable semantics.*

Proof. Assume AF is perfectly stable and let S be a preferred set in AF. We must show that S is stable. Assume towards contradiction that it is not. Since S is conflict free, it follows that S is not dominating, so that AF^S is non-empty. Since S is perfectly stable, AF^S must then have a non-empty stable set S'. Since stable sets are admissible, S' is admissible in AF^S. Hence, by the fact that preferred sets are admissible and admissible sets are modular, it follows that $S \cup S'$ is admissible in AF, contradicting $\subseteq$-maximality of S.

---

[1] The notion of a perfect extension could be made more general by explicitly taking the principle that is perfectly extended as a parameter, defining an AF to be perfectly X if all induced subdigraphs of the AF has an extension satisfying X. Then we could say that a semantics perfectly extends X, or that it satisfies the perfect extension principle for X, whenever it satisfies X for all AFs that are perfectly X. However, we only consider perfect extensions of the stable semantics in this paper, so we prefer to avoid the additional notation and terminology that the generalisation entails.

Since weakly admissible sets are modular, as shown in [4], it follows from essentially the same argument used to establish Theorem 5 that the weakly preferred semantics is *also* a perfect extension of the stable semantics. We regard this as a desirable property for an argumentation semantics to satisfy, and record it as a theorem.

Theorem 6. *The weakly preferred semantics is a perfect extension of the stable semantics.*

4   A Formal Justification for Ignoring Attacks

The informal motivation for weak admissibility presented in [3] is to provide a class of semantics that allow us to sometimes ignore attacks from arguments that attack themselves, directly or indirectly, on cycles that are not broken from the outside. On simple examples, it is verified that weakly admissible sets do indeed allow us to do this, as in the two AFs on the left below:

In the two leftmost AFs, it is easy to see that $\{d\}$ is weakly admissible, since there is no weakly admissible set from $AF^{\{d\}}$ that attacks it. Hence, we can disregard the attack from the self-defeating a, which lies on an unbroken odd cycle. By telling us to look for weakly admissible sets in the reduct AF^S, the definition of weak admissibility also seems to capture roughly the idea that we only ignore attacks from odd cycles that are not broken from the "outside" by S. However, in the rightmost AF above, $\{d\}$ is not weakly admissible, even though the odd cycle in $AF^{\{d\}}$ is not broken from the outside. It is broken from the inside, however, since it is safe at a, so we might no longer feel entitled to ignore the attack on d. Indeed, $\{a\}$ is the only non-empty weakly admissible set of this AF, despite being on an odd cycle that is not broken from the outside. It is also stable, so by Theorem 13, the weakly preferred semantics still behaves reasonably on examples like these, but not in a way that is fully explained by the informal explanation provided in [3].

Examples like these illustrate that it is hardly intended that we should *always* ignore attacks from odd cycles that are unbroken by the outside. On the other hand, it seems quite reasonable to interpret the authors of [3] as intending that we should *only* disregard attacks from such arguments. This, at any rate, would be a very interesting descriptive property for a weak semantics to satisfy, as it would indicate that we have weakened the notion of admissibility only as much as our informal intuition warrants us to do. Based on this idea, we propose the following two semantic principles, corresponding to two possible justifications for ignoring attacks.

Definition 7. *An argumentation semantics ς is said to be*

- *justified (by unsafe odd cycles) if it is conflict free and for all $AF = (A, R)$ and all $S \in \varsigma(AF)$, every argument $a \in A\backslash[S]$ that attacks S in AF lies on an odd cycle in AF^S that is unsafe at a.*
- *strongly justified (by unsafe odd cycles) if it is conflict free and for all $AF = (A, R)$ and all $S \in \varsigma(AF)$, every argument $a \in A\backslash[S]$ lies on an odd cycle in AF^S that is unsafe at a.*

Notice that a semantics is justified whenever it is strongly justified, while the converse does not hold in general. In particular, notice that if ς is strongly justified and AF has only the empty extension under ς, then every argument in AF lies on an odd cycle. So if ς is strongly justified, then whenever there is some argument not indirectly attacking itself, there is a non-empty extension. Also notice that if ς is strongly justified and a does not lie on an odd cycle in AF, then if $S \in \varsigma(AF)$ and $R^-(a) \cap S = \emptyset$, we must have $a \in S$, since otherwise $a \in A\backslash[S]$ without being on an odd cycle in AF^S. In view of this, being strongly justified is a stronger property than being strongly complete outside odd cycles, as defined in [6], whereby $a \in S$ is only required when there is also no argument in $R^-(a)$ that lies on an odd cycle.

While being (strongly) justified is a strong property that seems desirable, it is not clear whether weakly admissible and (strongly) justified semantics exist. In the next section, we provide a class of weakly admissible semantics that are justified, before showing that they are not strongly justified. First we note that the most permissive weakly admissible semantics, taking all weakly admissible sets as extensions, is not justified. This can be shown, for instance, by the following example:

$$\circlearrowleft x \longrightarrow y \longrightarrow z \longrightarrow w$$

In this AF, it is clear that $\{w\}$ is weakly admissible. This follows since there is no weakly admissible set containing z, which in turn follows from the fact that there *is* a weakly admissible set containing y, since x – its only attacker – attacks itself. The fact that weakly admissible sets are not necessarily justified should not come as a great surprise. A similar phenomenon is observed for admissibility, whereby we quickly conclude that the most permissive admissible semantics is not very reasonable, despite admissibility being a fundamental notion that forms a basis for other semantics. The situation is similar, we believe, with respect to weak admissibility.

5 A Class of Justified Semantics Based on Admissible Sets

To arrive at a class of justified semantics, we will start by defining a class of semantics that is *more* permissive than weakly admissible semantics. Then we will define a restrictive class of weakly admissible semantics that ignore attacks only from arguments that are not acceptable under the corresponding permissive semantics. We will then prove that the more restrictive class of semantics is weakly admissible and that taking its $\subseteq$-maximal sets yields a justified semantics that is also a perfect extension of the stable semantics. The first definition, giving rise to the permissive class of semantics, is the following.

Definition 8. *Given any $AF = (A, R)$ and a semantics ς, we say that $S \subseteq A$ is ς-plausible if it is conflict free and there is no $Q \in \varsigma(AF^S)$ that attacks S.*

Notice that if $S \subseteq A$ is admissible, then S is also ς-plausible. This is trivial, since S is conflict free and is not attacked by *any* argument from AF^S, since it defends itself. Also notice that if we take ς to be the most permissive weakly admissible semantics, consisting of all weakly admissible sets, then S is ς-plausible if, and only if, it is weakly admissible. So for the weakly admissible semantics, there is no difference between being a ς-extension and being ς-plausible. This is not true for semantics based on admissible sets. In fact, since weakly admissible sets are admissible, it follows that if ς is admissible, then S is ς-plausible whenever S is weakly admissible. So ς-plausibility behaves similarly to the weakly admissible semantics on simple motivating examples. It also seems to have independent interest as a natural dual of ς. However, ς-plausibility for admissible ς is too permissive to be justified. This is illustrated by the fact that both $\{b\}$ and $\{c\}$ is ς-plausible in the following AF, whenever ς is admissible:

$$\circlearrowright a \longrightarrow b \longrightarrow c$$

This example also demonstrates that ς-plausible sets are not modular, so they will fail to provide justified and perfect extensions of the stable semantics. However, as it turns out, the doubly dual notion obtained by demanding non-existence of ς-plausible attackers *does* yield such semantics.

Definition 9. *For any semantics ς and any $AF = (A, R)$: if $S \subseteq A$ is conflict free and S is not attacked in AF by any ς-plausible set from AF^S, we say that S is ς-reasonable.*

A ς-reasonable semantics is any semantics that only returns ς-reasonable sets as extensions. As before, if S is admissible, then it is trivially ς-reasonable, for any ς. We also note the following property.

Proposition 10. *For any admissible ς and any $AF = (A, R)$, if $S \subseteq A$ is ς-reasonable, then it is ς-plausible.*

Proof. Let $S \subseteq A$ be ς-reasonable and assume towards contradiction that it is not ς-plausible. Then there is some admissible set S' in AF^S that attacks S in AF. Since S' is admissible, it is not attacked in AF^S by any set from $(AF^S)^{S'}$. Hence, S' is trivially ς-plausible, contradicting the fact that S is ς-reasonable.

So for admissible ς, we have that every admissible set it ς-reasonable and that every ς-reasonable set is ς-plausible. Moreover, it is easy to show that any ς-reasonable set is weakly admissible.

Proposition 11. *For any admissible semantics ς and any $AF = (A, R)$, if $S \subseteq A$ is ς-reasonable, then S is weakly admissible.*

Proof. Let $S \subseteq A$ be ς-reasonable and assume towards contradiction that S is not weakly admissible. Then there is some weakly admissible set S' in AF^S such that S' attacks AF^S. However, since S is ς-reasonable, there is some admissible set S'' in $(AF^S)^{S'}$ that attacks S' in AF^S. But then S'' is also a weakly admissible set in $(AF^S)^{S'}$ that attacks S' in AF^S, contradicting the fact that S' is weakly admissible.

We now show the less obvious result that ς-reasonable sets are in fact modular whenever ς is admissible and modular.

Proposition 12. *For any admissible and modular ς and any $AF = (A, R)$, if $S \subseteq A$ is ς-reasonable in AF and S' is ς-reasonable in AF^S, then $S \cup S'$ is ς-reasonable in AF.*

Proof. Assume towards contradiction that $S \cup S'$ is not conflict free. Since $S' \subseteq (A\backslash[S])$ is not attacked by S, it follows that S' attacks S in AF. Since S is ς-reasonable, this means that S' is not ς-plausible, but since S' is ς-reasonable, this contradicts Proposition 10. So $S \cup S'$ is conflict free. Assume towards contradiction that there is some conflict free Q that is ς-plausible in $AF^{S \cup S'} = (AF^S)^{S'}$ and attacks $S \cup S'$ in AF. If Q attacks S', this contradicts the fact that S' is ς-reasonable in AF^S. Hence, Q does not attack S'. It follows that $Q \cup S'$ is a conflict free set from AF^S that attacks S in AF. Since S is ς-reasonable, there is a ς-extension K in $(AF^S)^{Q \cup S'} = (AF^{S \cup S'})^Q$ that attacks $Q \cup S'$ in AF^S. Since Q is ς-plausible in $(AF^{S \cup S'})$, K does not attack Q. Hence, $K \cup Q$ is a conflict free set from $AF^{S \cup S'}$ that attacks S' in AF^S. Assume towards contradiction that there is some ς-extension L in $(AF^{S \cup S'})^{K \cup Q} = ((AF^{S \cup S'})^Q)^K$ that attacks $K \cup Q$. Then since K is a ς-extension in $(AF^{S \cup S'})^Q$ and ς is modular, it follows that $K \cup L$ is a ς-extension in $(AF^{S \cup S'})^Q$ that attacks Q, contradicting the fact that Q is ς-plausible. Hence, $K \cup Q$ is ς-plausible in $AF^{S \cup S'} = (AF^S)^{S'}$, contradicting the fact that S' is ς-reasonable.

As with the preferred and weakly preferred semantics, modularity of ς implies that the ς-reasonable preferred semantics is a perfect extension of the stable semantics.

Theorem 13. *When ς is admissible and modular, then the ς-reasonable preferred semantics is a perfect extension of the stable semantics.*

Next, we will need a non-trivial graph-theoretic property of admissible sets, namely that if Q is a minimal such set containing a, then all arguments in Q have Q-alternating paths to a. To our knowledge, the following statement and proof of this fact is new, but the result is a variation of theorems from [11], regarding the closely related concepts of kernels and semi-kernels from graph theory (for more on the link between argumentation and kernel theory, see [10]). We remark that minimal non-empty admissible sets have also been studied independently in argumentation theory [14, 16], where such sets are referred to as *initial sets*. Hence, the following graph-theoretic result may well be of broader interest to the argumentation community.

Theorem 14. *For any $AF = (A, R)$ and any admissible set $S \subseteq A$ with $a \in S$: if Q is a $\subseteq$-minimal admissible set such that $Q \subseteq S$ and $a \in Q$, then for all $b \in Q$ there is a Q-alternating path $P_{b,a}$ from b to a in AF.*

Proof. Assume that Q is a $\subseteq$-minimal admissible set satisfying $Q \subseteq S$ and $a \in Q$. Let K be the set of all $b \in Q$ such that there is a Q-alternating path $P_{b,a}$ from b to a in AF. Clearly, we have $a \in K$, witnessed by the empty path. We are done if we can show that K is admissible, since then $K = Q$ by $\subseteq$-minimality of Q. Since Q is conflict free, K is conflict free. To show that K defends itself, assume c attacks K in AF at $d \in K \cap R(c)$. We must show that K defends d against c. Since $d \in K$, there is a Q-alternating path $P_{d,a}$ from d to a. Since Q is admissible and $d \in Q$, there must be some $e \in Q$ attacking c. Then $(e, c) + (c, d) + P_{d,a}$ is a walk from e to a. There are three cases. Case i) e occurs on $P_{d,a}$. In this case, the sub-path of $P_{d,a}$ from e to a is a Q-alternating path from e to a, so $e \in K$ as desired. Case ii) e does not occur on $P_{d,a}$, but c occurs on $P_{d,a}$. In this case, let $P_{c,a}$ denote the sub-path of $P_{d,a}$ from c to a. Then $(e, c) + P_{c,a}$ is a Q-alternating path from e to a, so $e \in K$ as desired. Case iii) neither e nor c occurs on $P_{d,a}$. Then $(e, c) + (c, d) + P_{d,a}$ is a Q-alternating path from e to a, so $e \in K$ in this case as well.

Notice that all Q-alternating paths from Q to Q have even length, since every other argument from such a path is from Q. It follows that we are now in a position to prove that the ς-reasonable preferred semantics is in fact justified by unsafe odd cycles.

Theorem 15. *For any admissible and modular ς and any $AF = (A, R)$: if $S \subseteq A$ is a $\subseteq$-maximal ς-reasonable set and $a \in A \backslash [S]$ attacks S, then a lies on an odd cycle that is unsafe at a.*

Proof. Assume $S \subseteq A$ is ς-reasonable and that $a \in A \backslash [S]$ attacks S. Since S is ς-reasonable, $\{a\}$ is not ς-plausible. If $(a, a) \in R$, the proof is done, so assume this is not the case. Then since $\{a\}$ is conflict free but not ς-plausible, there is a ς-extension $K \in (AF^S)^{\{a\}}$ with some $b \in K$ that attacks a. Since K is ς-plausible and S is ς-reasonable, K does not attack S. Since ς is admissible, K is an admissible set. Hence, we let Q be a $\subseteq$-minimal admissible set in $(AF^S)^{\{a\}}$ with $Q \subseteq K$ and $b \in Q$. Note that Q does not attack S and that Q is trivially ς-reasonable in $(AF^S)^{\{a\}}$, since it is admissible there. Since S is a $\subseteq$-maximal ς-reasonable set, it then follows from Proposition 12 that Q is not admissible in AF^S. Hence, there is some $c \in R(a)$ that attacks some $d \in Q$. By Theorem 14, there is a Q-alternating path $P_{d,b}$ from d to b in $(AF^S)^{\{a\}}$. Let f be the first occurrence of an argument from Q on $P_{d,b}$ that attacks a. Then $P_{d,f}$ is a path from d to f that is also a Q-alternating path from $(AF^S)^{\{a\}}$. Since a and c do not occur on $P_{d,f}$, $C = (a, c) + (c, d) + P_{d,f} + (f, a)$ is an odd cycle. If C is unsafe at a we are done, so assume C is safe at a. Then let $P_{a,f}$ be the sub-path of C from a to f. Since C is safe at a, there is a chord (x,y) on $P_{a,f}$ such that the sub-paths from a to x and from a to y along $P_{a,b}$ are both even. Assume towards contradiction that $x \neq y$. Since $Q \subseteq A\backslash[S \cup \{a\}]$ and x attacks y, $x \neq a$. Moreover, by our choice of f there is no argument from Q on $P_{d,f}$ that attacks a. Hence, $y \neq a$. So both x and y are in Q, contradicting the fact that Q is conflict free. So $x = y = a$. Then a attacks itself and we are done.

5.1   A Remark on Strongly Undisputed Sets

As pointed out by one of the reviewers, there is a close connection between ς-plausible and ς-reasonable sets and so-called *undisputed* and *strongly undisputed* sets, as recently introduced in [15]. In fact, when ς is the most permissive admissible semantics, then it is easy to see that the undisputed sets of AF are its ς-plausible preferred sets while the strongly undisputed sets are its ς-reasonable preferred sets. Hence, the present paper generalises the two notions, while showing how to define them without having $\subseteq$-maximality built in from the start. Moreover, the results proven about strongly undisputed sets in [15], including results on complexity which we have not addressed, carry over to preferred ς-reasonable preferred semantics when ς is the most permissive admissible semantics. Conversely, it follows from Theorem 15 that the strongly undisputed semantics is justified by unsafe odd cycles.

6   A Counterexample and a Conjecture

It is natural to ask about the relationship between ς-reasonable preferred sets and weakly preferred sets for admissible and modular ς. On simple examples, they behave the same way, so it is tempting to think that they might be equivalent for some admissible and modular ς. If this was true, it would mean that the recursive scheme of weak admissibility is redundant and that the nature of $\subseteq$-maximal weakly admissible sets could be described in a more succinct way in terms of admissible sets. However, the following example shows that this is not the case:

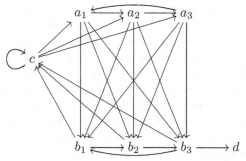

In this AF, we have two odd cycles of length 3, namely $C_a = (a_1, a_2, a_3, a_1)$ and $C_b = (b_1, b_2, b_3, b_4)$, as well as a self-attacking c and a much more innocent-looking d. All arguments on C_a attack all arguments on C_b, all arguments on

C_b attack c, and c attacks all arguments on C_a. The argument d, meanwhile, is only attacked by b_3 and attacks no argument. What is its semantic status? It is only attacked by b_3, which is on an odd cycle, so a justified semantics is entitled to ignore the attack on d, making $\{d\}$ a possible extension. However, no ς-reasonable semantics allows us to accept d when ς is admissible.

To verify that d cannot be accepted, notice that b_3 is not attacked by any admissible set from the reduct, $AF^{\{b_3\}}$:

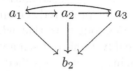

Clearly, $AF^{\{b_3\}}$ has no admissible set, so it has no admissible set attacking b_3. This means that $\{b_3\}$ is ς-plausible in $AF^{\{d\}}$ for all admissible ς, which in turn implies that $\{d\}$ is not ς-reasonable. In fact, AF has no non-empty ς-reasonable extension for any admissible ς, as the reader can verify. The weakly preferred semantics, by contrast, provides $\{d\}$ as the unique weakly preferred extension of the AF above. This is because b_3 is attacked by a weakly admissible set from $AF^{\{b_3\}}$, namely $\{b_2\}$. Hence, we have proven the following result about the weakly preferred semantics.

Proposition 16. *The weakly preferred semantics is not equivalent to any ς-reasonable semantics for which ς is admissible.*

The counterexample also shows that while ς-reasonable semantics for admissible ς are justified, they are not strongly justified: the counterexample has no non-empty ς-reasonable set, yet it has an argument that is not on any (odd) cycle. We believe the weakly preferred semantics *is* in fact strongly justified, but we have been unable to prove it so far. Hence, we leave it as a conjecture.

Conjecture 17. *The weakly preferred semantics is strongly justified.*

The challenging part is to prove that the weakly preferred semantics is justified. If it is, then it is not hard to prove that it is also strongly justified, using the following simple lemma.

Lemma 18. *If the weakly preferred semantics is justified and AF has no non-empty weakly preferred set, then every argument a in AF lies on an odd cycle that is unsafe at a.*

Proof. Assume $AF = (A, R)$ has no non-empty weakly preferred set and let $a \in A$ be arbitrary. We must show that a lies on an odd cycle from AF that is unsafe at a. So define the AF $M = (A \cup \{b\}, R \cup \{(a, b)\})$ for some fresh $b \notin A$. Clearly, $\{b\}$ is weakly preferred since $M^{\{b\}} = AF$ has no non-empty weakly admissible set. Hence, if the weakly preferred semantics is justified, then a is on an odd cycle in AF that is unsafe at a.

The difficulty comes when we try to prove that an argument from the reduct attacking a weakly preferred set must be on an odd cycle. This is made challenging by the fact that we need to keep track of the parity of paths, without having Theorem 14 to help us. So we think the best proof strategy is to first try to establish its analogue for weakly admissible sets, if possible. Note that we could weaken the definition of a strongly justified semantics by saying that ς is weakly justified when for all $AF = (A, R)$, if $\varsigma(AF) = \{\emptyset\}$, then for all $a \in A$ there is an odd *walk* from a to a. Then it is relatively straightforward to prove by induction on the size of AF that the weakly preferred semantics is weakly justified. We omit the details for space reasons, but note that while this property goes some way towards justifying the weakly preferred semantics in formal terms, it is a much weaker property than being strongly justified.

7   Conclusion

We have provided a formal definition of the intuition that if we ignore an attack from argument a then a should be part of an unbroken odd cycle. We provided a class of semantics satisfying this requirement, showing that they are also weakly admissible and agree with the stable semantics on a large class of AFs that have stable sets. We also conjectured that the weakly preferred semantics satisfies an even stronger property, namely that whenever S is weakly preferred and $a \notin [S]$, then a is part of an unbroken odd cycle.

In future work, we would like to prove our conjecture, or find a counterexample to it. We would also like to explore the new class of semantics introduced here in further depth, as they seem to be of independent interest. It seems clear, for instance, that our notion of ς-plausibility is closely related to the labelling-based semantics explored in [9]. These labelling-based semantics should also be investigated further, not just as argumentation semantics, but as systems of three-valued logic and theories in such systems. They seem to arise from introducing an interesting conditional, whereby $a \to b$ is true just in case a is neither true nor undecided when b is false, in which case $(a \to b) \to (\neg b \to \neg a)$ is no longer valid in the presence of undecidedness. It is also interesting to explore applications of the new semantics we introduce, for instance in the context of legal argumentation, by combining them with the work done on modelling shifting proof burdens in [12]. Moreover, it would be natural to classify the new semantics in a more comprehensive way with respect to the principles investigated in [7]. Finally, we would like to generalise our results to infinite AFs, where absence of odd cycles is no longer sufficient for the existence of stable sets.

References

1. Baroni, P., Giacomin, M.: On principle-based evaluation of extension-based argumentation semantics. Artif. Intell. **171**(10–15), 675–700 (2007)
2. Baroni, P., Giacomin, M., Guida, G.: SCC-recursiveness: a general schema for argumentation semantics. Artif. Intell. **168**(1–2), 162–210 (2005)

3. Baumann, R., Brewka, G., Ulbricht, M.: Revisiting the foundations of abstract argumentation - semantics based on weak admissibility and weak defense. In: The Thirty-Fourth AAAI Conference on Artificial Intelligence (AAAI-20), pp. 2742–2749. AAAI Press (2020)
4. Baumann, R., Brewka, G., Ulbricht, M.: Shedding new light on the foundations of abstract argumentation: Modularization and weak admissibility. Artif. Intell. **310**, 103742 (2022)
5. Caminada, M.W.A., Carnielli, W.A., Dunne, P.E.: Semi-stable semantics. J. Log. Comput. **22**(5), 1207–1254 (2012)
6. Cramer, M., van der Torre, L.: SCF2 - an argumentation semantics for rational human judgments on argument acceptability. In: Beierle, C., Ragni, M., Stolzenburg, F., Thimm, M. (eds.) Proceedings of the 8th Workshop on Dynamics of Knowledge and Belief (DKB-2019) and the 7th Workshop KI & Kognition (KIK-2019)co-located with 44nd German Conference on Artificial Intelligence (KI 2019), Kassel, Germany, September 23, 2019. CEUR Workshop Proceedings, vol. 2445, pp. 24–35. CEUR-WS.org (2019). https://ceur-ws.org/Vol-2445/paper_3.pdf
7. Dauphin, J., Rienstra, T., van der Torre, L.: A principle-based analysis of weakly admissible semantics. In: Prakken, H., Bistarelli, S., Santini, F., Taticchi, C. (eds.) Computational Models of Argument - Proceedings of COMMA 2020, Perugia, Italy, September 4–11, 2020. Frontiers in Artificial Intelligence and Applications, vol. 326, pp. 167–178. IOS Press (2020)
8. Dung, P.M.: On the acceptability of arguments and its fundamental role in non-monotonic reasoning, logic programming and n-person games. Artif. Intell. **77**(2), 321–357 (1995)
9. Dvořák, W., Rienstra, T., van der Torre, L., Woltran, S.: Non-admissibility in abstract argumentation. In: Toni, F., Polberg, S., Booth, R., Caminada, M., Kido, H. (eds.) Computational Models of Argument - Proceedings of COMMA 2022, Cardiff, Wales, UK, 14–16 September 2022. Frontiers in Artificial Intelligence and Applications, vol. 353, pp. 128–139. IOS Press (2022)
10. Dyrkolbotn, S.K., Walicki, M.: Propositional discourse logic. Synthese **191**(5), 863–899 (2014)
11. Galeana-Sánchez, H., Neumann-Lara, V.: On kernels and semikernels of digraphs. Discret. Math. **48**(1), 67–76 (1984)
12. Kampik, T., Gabbay, D.M., Sartor, G.: A comprehensive account of the burden of persuasion in abstract argumentation. J. Log. Comput. **33**(2), 257–288 (2023)
13. Richardson, M.: Solutions of irreflexive relations. Ann. Math. **58**(3), 573–590 (1953). http://www.jstor.org/stable/1969755
14. Thimm, M.: Revisiting initial sets in abstract argumentation. Argument Comput. **13**(3), 325–360 (2022)
15. Thimm, M.: On undisputed sets in abstract argumentation. In: The Thirty-Seventh AAAI Conference on Artificial Intelligence (AAAI-23), pp. 6550–6557. AAAI Press (2023)
16. Xu, Y., Cayrol, C.: Initial sets in abstract argumentation frameworks. In: Ågotnes, T., Liao, B., Wáng, Y.N. (eds.) Proceedings of the 1st Chinese Conference on Logic and Argumentation (CLAR 2016), Hangzhou, China, April 2–3, 2016. CEUR Workshop Proceedings, vol. 1811, pp. 72–85. CEUR-WS.org (2016). https://ceur-ws.org/Vol-1811/paper6.pdf

Computing Stable Extensions of Argumentation Frameworks using Formal Concept Analysis

Sergei Obiedkov[1]([⊠]) [iD] and Barış Sertkaya[2] [iD]

[1] Knowledge-Based Systems Group, Faculty of Computer Science/cfaed/ScaDS.AI,
TU Dresden, Germany
`sergei.obiedkov@tu-dresden.de`
[2] Frankfurt University of Applied Sciences, Frankfurt, Germany
`sertkaya@fb2.fra-uas.de`

Abstract. We propose an approach based on Formal Concept Analysis (FCA) for computing stable extensions of Abstract Argumentation Frameworks (AFs). To this purpose, we represent an AF as a formal context in which stable extensions of the AF are closed sets called concept intents. We make use of algorithms developed in FCA for computing concept intents in order to compute stable extensions of AFs. Experimental results show that, on AFs with a high density of the attack relation, our algorithms perform significantly better than the existing approaches. The algorithms can be modified to compute other types of extensions, in particular, preferred extensions.

1 Introduction

Abstract argumentation is a field of Artificial Intelligence (AI) dealing with formal representation of arguments and relations between arguments. Its aim is, among others, to provide methods for resolving conflicts collaboratively. The most prominent approach in this field, Argumentation Frameworks (AFs), has attracted increasing attention in the AI and particularly in the Knowledge Representation communities since its introduction by Dung in [10]. In AFs, arguments are abstracted away from their actual contents and conflicts are modelled in form of attacks between arguments. This abstraction allows an intuitive formalization using directed graphs. The semantics is defined through sets of arguments called extensions. Several different types of extensions of AFs have been proposed in the literature [3], which gave rise to interesting computational problems such as, for instance, deciding whether a given argument appears in at least one extension of a certain type (credulous reasoning), or deciding whether it appears in all extensions of a certain type (skeptical reasoning), or enumerating all extensions of a certain type.

The computational complexity of these and related decision, enumeration, and counting problems have by now been well investigated [11,21]. There are also highly optimized solvers that can handle large problem instances. In the

S. Gaggl et al. (Eds.): JELIA 2023, LNAI 14281, pp. 176–191, 2023.
https://doi.org/10.1007/978-3-031-43619-2_13

bi-annually organized International Competition on Computational Models of Argumentation (ICCMA), these solvers compete in different tracks on several different reasoning tasks. Typically, they encode these tasks as problems from other formalisms such as, for instance, the constraint satisfaction problem or the satisfiability problem of propositional logic, and benefit from existing highly optimized solvers developed there. There are also algorithms specifically tailored for computational problems in AFs that directly solve these problems without reducing them to another formalism. A detailed survey of both types of approaches can be found in [8].

In the present work, we propose an approach for computing extensions of AFs based on Formal Concept Analysis (FCA) [15]. To this purpose, we characterize an AF as a formal context. Such a characterization was first noted in [2]. We exploit the similarity between an AF and a formal context and employ algorithms from FCA to compute stable extensions. Our algorithms can be modified to compute extensions of other types, such as preferred extensions.

The paper is organized as follows. In Sect. 2, we introduce basic notions of AFs and FCA. In Sect. 3, we present a translation from AF to FCA and show that stable extensions are closed sets (called concept intents) in this translation with some special properties. We then modify two well-known algorithms from FCA to compute stable extensions. In Sect. 4, we present an evaluation of our algorithms on randomly generated AFs and provide a comparison with existing tools. In Sect. 5, we conclude with a summary and future work.

2 Preliminaries

2.1 Abstract Argumentation Frameworks

We recall some basic notions from abstract argumentation frameworks as introduced in [10]. An AF is a directed graph $F = (A, R)$, where A is a finite set of *arguments* and $R \subseteq A \times A$ is the *attack relation*. An edge $(a, b) \in R$ denotes that the argument a *attacks* the argument b (in the AF F). A set of arguments $S \subseteq A$ *attacks* b if there is $a \in S$ such that $(a, b) \in R$, and b *attacks* S if $(b, a) \in R$ for some $a \in S$. We say that $S \subseteq A$ *defends* $a \in A$ if every argument attacking a is attacked by S.

Figure 1 gives an example of an argumentation framework over arguments $A = \{a, b, c, d, e\}$. Here, for example, a attacks b and c; the set $\{b, c\}$ attacks a and d; the argument d attacks the set $\{a, e\}$ and, in fact, every set containing c or e; and $\{a, e\}$ defends d, since it attacks both its attackers, c and e.

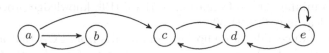

Fig. 1. Example of an argumentation framework.

Given an AF $F = (A, R)$, a set $S \subseteq A$ is said to be *conflict-free* (in F) if S does not attack any of its elements. We denote the set of conflict-free subsets of A as $cf(F)$. That is, $cf(F) = \{S \subseteq A \mid \forall a, b \in S : (a, b) \notin R\}$.

Several different types of semantics expressing different properties of sets of arguments have been considered in the literature [3,10]. We introduce only those of them that are relevant for our work.

Let $F = (A, R)$ be an argumentation framework and $S \in cf(F)$. Then S is called

- an *admissible extension* if every $a \in S$ is defended by S;
- a *preferred extension* if it is a maximal (w.r.t. set inclusion) admissible extension;
- a *stable extension* if S attacks every $a \in A \setminus S$.

Since a stable extension S attacks all other elements including all those that attack S, every stable extension is also a preferred extension.

The preferred extensions of the AF from Fig. 1 are $\{a, d\}$, $\{b, c\}$, and $\{b, d\}$, and its stable extensions are $\{a, d\}$ and $\{b, d\}$.

Several interesting decision, counting, and enumeration problems in abstract argumentation have been considered in the literature [4,11,21]. Here we list only two of them that are relevant for us. For an AF $F = (A, R)$, an argument $a \in A$, and a semantic σ:

- Find a σ-extension of F if there is one.
- Enumerate all σ-extensions of F.

It is known that these problems are intractable for many of the interesting semantics [11,21]. Existing approaches typically solve these problems by reducing them to other formalisms such as constraint-satisfaction problem (CSP), propositional logic, or answer-set programming, and benefit from highly optimized solvers developed for these formalisms. To name a few, μ-toksia [27] encodes these problems as the Boolean satisfiability problem and makes use of a SAT-solver; pyglaf [1] reduces these problems to circumscription and employs an existing solver for circumscription; and ConArg [5] reduces them to constraints and uses a CSP-solver.

2.2   Formal Concept Analysis

Formal Concept Analysis [15] is a field of mathematics used for identifying clusters in data and for building a hierarchy of these clusters with tools originating from lattice theory. It has found application in several domains including biology [18], data mining [26], information retrieval [19], knowledge processing [31], and machine learning [6,9,24,30].

We will introduce only those notions and results from FCA that are relevant for our purposes. In FCA, one represents data using a *formal context* specifying which objects have which attributes. A formal context is usually denoted by $\mathbb{K} = (G, M, I)$, where G is a set of *objects*, M is a set of *attributes*, and $I \subseteq G \times M$

is an *incidence* relation between the objects and the attributes. A finite context can be visualized as a cross table, where the rows represent the objects and the columns represent the attributes of the context. A cross in column m of row g means that the object g has the attribute m, and the absence of a cross means that g does not have the attribute m.

For a set of objects $A \subseteq G$, the *derivation operator* $(\cdot)^\uparrow$ applied to A produces the set of attributes that are common to all objects in A:

$$A^\uparrow = \{m \in M \mid \forall g \in A \colon (g, m) \in I\}.$$

Similarly, for a set of attributes $B \subseteq M$, the *derivation operator* $(\cdot)^\downarrow$ applied to B yields the set of objects that have all attributes in B:

$$B^\downarrow = \{g \in G \mid \forall m \in B \colon (g, m) \in I\}.$$

We sometimes abuse the notation and write $x^\uparrow$ (resp. $x^\downarrow$) instead of $\{x\}^\uparrow$ (resp. $\{x\}^\downarrow$) for an object (resp. attribute) x.

Proposition 1. *For $A_1 \subseteq A_2 \subseteq G$ (resp. $B_1 \subseteq B_2 \subseteq M$), it holds that*

- $A_2^\uparrow \subseteq A_1^\uparrow$ *(resp. $B_2^\downarrow \subseteq B_1^\downarrow$);*
- $A_1 \subseteq A_1^{\uparrow\downarrow}$ *and* $A_1^\uparrow = A_1^{\uparrow\downarrow\uparrow}$ *(resp. $B_1 \subseteq B_1^{\downarrow\uparrow}$ and $B_1^\downarrow = B_1^{\downarrow\uparrow\downarrow}$).*

As a consequence of this, the combined operator $(\cdot)^{\uparrow\downarrow}$ is a *closure operator* on G and $(\cdot)^{\downarrow\uparrow}$ is a closure operator on M. Using these closure operators, one can describe "natural clusters" in data, which are called formal concepts. A *formal concept* of $\mathbb{K} = (G, M, I)$ is a pair (A, B), where $A \subseteq G$ and $B \subseteq M$, such that $A^\uparrow = B$ and $B^\downarrow = A$. A is called the *extent*, and B is called the *intent* of the formal concept (A, B).

When ordered w.r.t. subset inclusion of their extents (or, equivalently, w.r.t. inverse inclusion of their intents), formal concepts yield a complete lattice called the *concept lattice* of $\mathbb{K}$. The concept lattice obtained from a dataset allows an intuitive visualization of the data and enables domain experts to spot dependencies between clusters in the data.

For $A \subseteq G$, the set $A^\uparrow$ is the intent of some formal concept, since $(A^{\uparrow\downarrow}, A^\uparrow)$ is always a formal concept. $A^{\uparrow\downarrow}$ is the smallest extent containing A. Consequently, a set $A \subseteq G$ is an extent if and only if $A = A^{\uparrow\downarrow}$. The same applies to intents. The intersection of any number of extents (respectively, intents) is always an extent (intent). Hence, the set of all extents forms a closure system on G, and the set of all intents forms a closure system on M [15].

It is well known that the set of all formal concepts of a context can be exponential in the size of the context and determining the number of formal concepts is #P-complete [23]. There are several algorithms for enumerating formal concepts [7,12,13,17,22,28,29,32], some of which do this with a polynomial delay [20]. For an analysis and evaluation of such algorithms, see [25].

3   An FCA Characterization of AF Semantics

We consider semantics of AFs from the viewpoint of FCA and make use of algorithms developed there for solving the above mentioned problems. To this purpose, we formulate argumentation frameworks as formal contexts, following the connection first noted in [2].

Definition 1. *Let (A, R) be an argumentation framework. The induced formal context of (A, R) is $\mathbb{K}(A, R) = (A, A, (A \times A) \setminus R)$.*

Note that such induced contexts are special in that their sets of objects and attributes coincide, which is not the case in general. Figure 2 shows the induced formal context of the argumentation framework from Fig. 1.

$\mathbb{K}(A, R)$	a	b	c	d	e
a	×			×	×
b		×	×	×	×
c	×	×	×		×
d	×	×		×	
e	×	×	×		

Fig. 2. The induced formal context of the argumentation framework in Fig. 1. Its concept intents are $\varnothing$, $\{e\}$, $\{d\}$, $\{d,e\}$, $\{b\}$, $\{b,d\}$, $\{b,c\}$, $\{b,c,e\}$, $\{b,c,d,e\}$, $\{a\}$, $\{a,e\}$, $\{a,d\}$, $\{a,d,e\}$, $\{a,b\}$, $\{a,b,d\}$, $\{a,b,c\}$, $\{a,b,c,e\}$, and $\{a,b,c,d,e\}$.

Following the definitions from Sect. 2.2, an application of the derivation operators of $\mathbb{K}(A, R)$ to $S \subseteq A$ yields the following sets:

$$S^\uparrow = \{a \in A \mid \forall s \in S \colon (s, a) \notin R\}$$

and

$$S^\downarrow = \{a \in A \mid \forall s \in S \colon (a, s) \notin R\}.$$

Obviously, for $a, b \in A$, a attacks b if and only if $b \notin a^\uparrow$ or, equivalently, $a \notin b^\downarrow$. More generally, for $S \subseteq A$, the set $S^\uparrow$ consists of arguments not attacked by S, and $S^\downarrow$ is the set of arguments that do not attack S.

For example, in the context shown in Fig. 2, we have $\{a, b\}^\uparrow = \{d, e\}$ and $\{a, b\}^\downarrow = \{c, d, e\}$. Indeed, d and e are the only arguments attacked neither by a nor by b in the AF from Fig. 1, while c, d, and e are the only arguments that attack neither a nor b.

Proposition 2. *Let (A, R) be an AF. A set $S \subseteq A$ defends $c \in A$ if and only if $S^\uparrow \subseteq c^\downarrow$ holds in $\mathbb{K}(A, R)$.*

Proof. By definition, $S^\uparrow \subseteq c^\downarrow$ reads as follows: every $a \in A$ not attacked by S does not attack c, which is equivalent to S defending c.

More formally, let $b, c \in A$ and $(b, c) \in R$. Then, by definition, $b \notin c^{\downarrow}$. Assuming $S^{\uparrow} \subseteq c^{\downarrow}$, we have $b \notin S^{\uparrow}$ and S attacks b. Thus, S attacks all attackers of c, or, in other words, S defends c.

Conversely, suppose that S defends c. Take $b \in S^{\uparrow}$, i.e., some b not attacked by S. Since S defends c, we have $(b, c) \notin R$, which is equivalent to $b \in c^{\downarrow}$. Consequently, $S^{\uparrow} \subseteq c^{\downarrow}$ holds in $\mathbb{K}(A, R)$.   □

Proposition 3. *Given an AF* (A, R), *a set* $S \subseteq A$ *is conflict-free if and only if* $S \subseteq S^{\uparrow}$ *(or, equivalently,* $S \subseteq S^{\downarrow}$*) holds in* $\mathbb{K}(A, R)$. *S is a maximal conflict-free set if and only if* $S = S^{\uparrow} \cap S^{\downarrow} \cap \{a \in A \mid a \in a^{\downarrow}\}$.

Proof. The first statement holds by definition. To prove the second one, assume that S is a conflict-free set and there is some $b \in (S^{\uparrow} \cap S^{\downarrow} \cap \{a \in A \mid a \in a^{\downarrow}\}) \setminus S$. It holds that $b \in S^{\uparrow}$, $b \in S^{\downarrow}$, and b does not attack itself. Then $S \cup \{b\}$ is also conflict-free, and S cannot be a maximal conflict-free set. Conversely, if $S = S^{\uparrow} \cap S^{\downarrow} \cap \{a \in A \mid a \in a^{\downarrow}\}$, then, for every $b \notin S$, either $b \notin S^{\uparrow}$ and b is attacked by S, or $b \notin S^{\downarrow}$ and b attacks S, or $b \notin b^{\downarrow}$ and b attacks itself. In none of these case, $S \cup \{b\}$ is conflict-free. Hence, S is a maximal conflict-free set.   □

Proposition 4. *Given an AF* (A, R), *a set* $S \subseteq A$ *is an admissible extension if and only if* $S \subseteq S^{\uparrow} \subseteq S^{\downarrow}$. *A preferred (i.e., maximal admissible) extension S is always a concept intent of* $\mathbb{K}(A, R)$, *i.e.,* $S = S^{\downarrow\uparrow}$.

Proof. The first statement follows from Propositions 3 and 2. In particular, since $S^{\downarrow} = \bigcap \{c^{\downarrow} \mid c \in S\}$, Proposition 2 implies that $S^{\uparrow} \subseteq S^{\downarrow}$ is equivalent to S defending all its elements.

To prove the second statement, assume that S is admissible. Then it holds that $S \subseteq S^{\uparrow} \subseteq S^{\downarrow}$. Due to Proposition 1, this implies $S^{\downarrow\uparrow} \subseteq S^{\uparrow}$. Now, suppose that $S \neq S^{\downarrow\uparrow}$, and take any $b \in (S^{\downarrow\uparrow} \setminus S)$. It holds that $b \in S^{\uparrow}$ and thus $b \in S^{\downarrow}$, i.e., S and b do not attack each other. Additionally, $b \in S^{\downarrow} = S^{\downarrow\uparrow\downarrow} \subseteq b^{\downarrow}$, the last inclusion holding due to $\{b\} \subseteq S^{\downarrow\uparrow}$ and Proposition 1. Therefore, b does not attack itself and $S \cup \{b\}$ is conflict-free.

To see that S defends b, take an $a \in A$ that attacks b, i.e., $b \notin a^{\uparrow}$. If S does not attack a, then $a \in S^{\uparrow} \subseteq S^{\downarrow}$. Hence, $S^{\downarrow\uparrow} \subseteq a^{\uparrow}$ and $b \in a^{\uparrow}$, which is a contradiction. Thus, S attacks a.

We have shown that S does not attack, is not attacked by, and defends every element of $S^{\downarrow\uparrow}$. No such element a can attack another such element b, since, otherwise, a would have been attacked by S, which defends b. Therefore, if S is an admissible set, then so is $S^{\downarrow\uparrow}$. This means that preferred extensions are concept intents (the reverse is not necessarily true).   □

Indeed, the three preferred extensions of the argumentation framework in Fig. 1, $\{a, d\}$, $\{b, c\}$, and $\{b, d\}$, are among concept intents of the induced context from Fig. 2. Since every stable extension S is also a preferred extension, from Proposition 4, we have

Corollary 1. *Given an AF* (A, R), *a stable extension* $S \subseteq A$ *is always a concept intent of* $\mathbb{K}(A, R)$, *i.e.,* $S = S^{\downarrow\uparrow}$.

It turns out that we can give a compact and precise characterization of stable extensions in terms of derivation operators of the induced formal context. Note that $S = S^{\uparrow}$ reads as follows: "The set of elements not attacked by S is equal to S," which is the definition of a stable extension. Thus, we have

Proposition 5. *Given an AF (A, R), a set $S \subseteq A$ is a stable extension if and only if $S = S^{\uparrow}$.*

It is easy to see that no proper subset of a stable extension can be a stable extension; therefore, stable extensions form an antichain (a subset of incomparable elements) in the lattice of concept intents.

3.1   Enumerating Stable Extensions Using Next-Closure Algorithm

Proposition 5 suggests that we can enumerate stable extensions of an AF (A, R) by computing concept intents of the induced context $\mathbb{K}(A, R)$ and outputting only those intents S for which $S = S^{\uparrow}$. One well-known way of enumerating concept intents in FCA is enumerating them in a so-called lectic order, which helps avoiding multiple computation of the same intent. The lectic order is defined as follows:

Definition 2. *Let $\mathbb{K} = (G, M, I)$ be a formal context. Fix some some linear order $m_1 < m_2 < \cdots < m_n$ on the set of attributes $M = \{m_1, \ldots, m_n\}$. This order induces a linear order on the power set of M, called the* lectic *order, which we also denote by $<$. For $m_i \in M$ and $A, B \subseteq M$, we define:*

$$A <_i B \quad \text{iff} \quad m_i \in B, \ m_i \notin A \ \text{and} \ \forall j < i \ (m_j \in A \Leftrightarrow m_j \in B).$$

The order $<$ is the union of these orders $<_i$, i.e.,

$$A < B \quad \text{iff} \quad A <_i B \ \text{for some} \ i \in M.$$

Note this is the same order as the one obtained when we map sets to binary numbers in a standard way, so that attribute m_i adds 2^{i-1} to the number. Obviously, $<$ extends the strict subset order, and thus $\varnothing$ is the smallest and M is the largest set w.r.t. $<$. The following proposition from [12,14] shows how to compute the lectically next concept intent set for a given set.

Proposition 6. *Given a formal context $\mathbb{K} = (G, M, I)$ and a set $A \subsetneq M$, the smallest concept intent greater than A w.r.t. the lectic order is*

$$((A \cap \{m_1, \ldots, m_{j-1}\}) \cup \{m_j\})^{\downarrow\uparrow},$$

where j is the maximal attribute satisfying $A <_j ((A \cap \{m_1, \ldots, m_{j-1}\}) \cup \{m_j\})^{\downarrow\uparrow}$.

In order to enumerate all concept intents of $\mathbb{K}$, one starts with the lectically smallest intent $\varnothing^{\downarrow\uparrow}$ and applies the proposition successively until the lectically largest intent M is reached. This algorithm, known as the *next-closure algorithm*, enumerates all concept intents of a given context with polynomial delay [12], and, although the proposition may suggest otherwise, the algorithm is quite easy to understand and implement.

Roughly speaking, the algorithm follows a computation tree, where a node corresponds to an intent and a child is formed by adding an attribute to the intent, computing the closure of the resulting set, and keeping it only if it does not contain an attribute smaller than the one that was added. Along every branch of the tree, attributes are added in the increasing order; that is, if an intent S results from adding an attribute m_i to its parent, its children are formed by adding only attributes m_j, where $j > i$, to S. For a more detailed explanation and analysis of the algorithm, see [14].

To enumerate stable extensions of an argumentation framework, we can compute the concept intents of the induced context with the next-closure algorithm, cutting a computation branch as soon as we reach an intent that is not conflict-free. Algorithm 1 enumerates all stable extensions of a given AF using this idea.

Algorithm 1 ALL STABLE EXTENSIONS(A, R)

Input: Argumentation framework (A, R) with $A = \{a_1, \ldots a_n\}$.
Output: Stable extensions of (A, R) in the lectic order.
1: Construct the induced context $\mathbb{K}(A, R)$
2: Fix a total order $a_1 < a_2 < \ldots < a_n$ on A
3: $S = \varnothing^{\downarrow\uparrow}$ {lectically smallest intent}
4: **while** $S \neq A$ **do**
5:     **if** $S = S^\uparrow$ **then**   {Check if S is a stable extension}
6:         output S
7:     $S := $ NEXT-CONFLICT-FREE-INTENT$(\mathbb{K}(A, R),\ S)$

Termination of Algorithm 1 is guaranteed since A is finite. It is correct due to Proposition 5. Termination and correctness of Algorithm 2 is guaranteed due to Proposition 6 [14]. The only modification we have done is checking for conflicts in line 6 of Algorithm 2, which does not influence termination and correctness.

Algorithm 1 computes all conflict-free concept intents $S \subseteq A$ of the induced context $\mathbb{K}(A, R)$ with polynomial delay. However, only those that are stable extensions are output. Between two stable extensions there can potentially be exponentially many concept intents S that do not satisfy the criteria $S = S^\uparrow$ and, hence, are not stable extensions. The runtime of our algorithm heavily depends on the number of concept intents of $\mathbb{K}(A, R)$, which can be exponential in the size of $\mathbb{K}(A, R)$. It is known that determining the number of concept intents is #P-complete [23]. It was shown in [21] that enumerating stable extensions is not output-polynomial unless P = NP; thus we cannot expect to enumerate them efficiently. On a positive side, it is easy to see that the memory requirements of the algorithm depend only linearly on the number of arguments, since it needs to store a constant number of sets and maintain a constant number of indices.

Algorithm 2 NEXT CONFLICT FREE INTENT($\mathbb{K}(A, R), S$)

Input: Induced context $\mathbb{K}(A, R)$ with a total order $a_1 < a_2 < \ldots < a_n$ on A and a set $S \subseteq A$.

Output: Lectically next conflict-free intent of $\mathbb{K}$ coming after S.

1: **for** $a_i := a_n$ **to** $a_i := a_1$ **do**   {iterate in reverse order}
2:     **if** $a_i \in S$ **then**
3:         remove a_i from S
4:     **else**
5:         $T := (S \cup \{a_i\})^{\downarrow\uparrow}$
6:         **if** $T \subseteq T^\downarrow$ **then**   {check for conflict}
7:             **if** $a_j \notin (T \setminus S)$ holds for every $a_j < a_i$ **then**   {lectic-order check}
8:                 **return** T {lectically next conflict-free intent}

3.2   Norris-Based Algorithm for Stable Extensions

Next, we present an adaptation of an algorithm that was originally developed by E.M. Norris for computing the maximal rectangles in a binary relation [28]. This algorithm, being used in the FCA community for enumerating concept intents, has proven to be fast for different types of formal contexts in practice [25]. Similar to the next-closure algorithm, it uses the lectic-order check to avoid multiple generation of the same intent. Unlike next-closure, it keeps a list of candidates from which intents are incrementally computed, which makes closure computation more efficient.

Algorithm 3 is an adaptation of this approach. It iteratively processes subcontexts $(A, B, (A \times B) \setminus R)$, where $B \subseteq A$, of the context $\mathbb{K}(A, R)$, starting with $B = \varnothing$ and adding one argument at a time in an arbitrary order. The algorithm maintains a list of 4-tuples of the form $(S^\downarrow, S, S^\uparrow, S^\downarrow \cap S^\uparrow)$, where S is potentially a subset of a stable extension and the derivation operators are taken with respect to the current subcontext.

Algorithm 3 INCREMENTAL STABLE EXTENSIONS(A, R)

Input: Argumentation framework (A, R).

Output: Stable extensions of (A, R) yielded by the ADD subrprocedure.

1: $B := \varnothing$
2: $\mathcal{C} := \{(A, \varnothing, A, A)\}$
3: **for all** $a \in A$ **do**
4:     ADD$((A, R), B, a, \mathcal{C})$ {ADD modifies $\mathcal{C}$}
5:     $B := B \cup \{a\}$

When processing an argument a, the algorithm attempts to extend every set S on the list with a if this does not cause a conflict (see line 1 of Algorithm 4). Two cases are possible then. If arguments not attacking S do not attack a either, then every stable extension containing S must contain a, and the algorithm simply updates the components of the tuple corresponding to S (lines 2–11). Otherwise (lines 12–22), the algorithm generates a new tuple corresponding to $S \cup \{a\}$ and, unless it cannot be further extended without introducing conflicts, the algorithm adds the new tuple to the list (lines 21–22). This new tuple is not further processed in the current call to Algorithm 4. Note also the lectic-order check in line 14. In both cases, if $S \cup \{a\}$ turns out to be a stable extension, it is reported as such (lines 6 and 18) and the corresponding tuple is removed from (or not added to) the list since, in this case, supersets of $S \cup \{a\}$ cannot be stable extensions.

Algorithm 4 $\mathrm{ADD}((A, R), B, a, C)$

Input: Argumentation framework (A, R), $B \subseteq A$, $a \in A \setminus B$, and set C,
    which, at the point of the call, must be equal to
$$\{(S^{\downarrow}, S, S^{\uparrow}, S^{\downarrow} \cap S^{\uparrow}) \mid S^{\downarrow\uparrow} \cap B = S \subseteq B \text{ and } S \subsetneq S^{\downarrow} \cap S^{\uparrow}\}.$$
Output: Stable extensions $S \subseteq B \cup \{a\}$ of (A, R) containing a and updated C.

1: **for all** $(X, S, Y, Z) \in C$ such that $a \in Z$ **do** $\{S \cup \{a\}$ is conflict-free$\}$
2:     **if** $X \subseteq a^{\downarrow}$ **then** $\{$arguments not attacking S do not attack $a\}$
3:         $S := S \cup \{a\}$ $\{$update the components of the existing tuple$\}$
4:         $Y := Y \cap a^{\uparrow}$
5:         **if** $Y = S$ **then** $\{S$ attacks everything but itself$\}$
6:             **output** S
7:             remove (X, S, Y, Z) from C
8:         **else**
9:             $Z := Z \cap a^{\uparrow}$
10:            **if** $Z = S$ **then**
11:                remove (X, S, Y, Z) from C
12:     **else**
13:         $U := X \cap a^{\downarrow}$ $\{$arguments not attacking $S \cup \{a\}\}$
14:         **if** $U \subseteq b^{\downarrow}$ for no $b \in B \setminus S$ **then** $\{(S \cup \{a\})^{\downarrow\uparrow} \cap B = S \cup \{a\}\}$
15:             $T := S \cup \{a\}$
16:             $V := Y \cap a^{\uparrow}$ $\{$arguments not attacked by $T\}$
17:             **if** $T = V$ **then** $\{T$ attacks everything but itself$\}$
18:                **output** T
19:             **else**
20:                $W := U \cap V$
21:                **if** $W \neq T$ **then** $\{T$ can be extended$\}$
22:                   add (U, T, V, W) to C

Termination of Algorithm 4 is guaranteed, since C is finite. Termination of Algorithm 3 is guaranteed, since Algorithm 4 is invoked exactly once for every $a \in A$.

Algorithm 4 differs from the original algorithm for computing concept intents in several aspects. It stores additional information in the last two components of tuples in list $\mathcal{C}$; however, if memory is an issue, this information can be recomputed from the second component and the original framework. In line 1, it is checked if adding a to S causes a conflict. In line 5, it is checked whether S is a stable extension; in this case, it is removed from the list, since its supersets cannot be stable extensions. Finally, a new tuple generated after line 12 is added to the list only if the corresponding intent is not a stable extension (which is checked in line 17) and there remain arguments that can be added to it without causing conflicts (which is checked in line 21). Apart from these changes, the algorithm acts as the original algorithm. Therefore, Algorithm 3 generates all conflict-free intents, which guarantees its correctness.

3.3   Preferred Extensions

With some effort, the Algorithms 1 and 3 can be adapted to other semantics. In this subsection, we outline a possible adaptation to preferred semantics.

As shown in Proposition 4, every preferred (i.e., maximal admissible) extension is a concept intent. Each of the two presented algorithms implicitly builds a tree of intents, from small to large, cutting a branch as soon as it stumbles upon a maximal conflict-free set, which may or may not be a stable extension. While doing so, it necessarily generates all preferred extensions. To identify them among generated intents, one can check admissibility for every generated intent and keep track of the largest generated admissible extension on each branch. If a branch terminates with a stable extension, it is the only preferred extension on this branch. The other preferred extensions are among admissible extensions that are either terminal nodes in the tree or intermediate nodes with no admissible extensions among descendants. Let us call nodes satisfying this condition *preferred candidates*. They have to be checked for subset-maximality (unless they are stable).

If the goal is to compute a single preferred extension, the maximality check can be avoided. Traversing the tree of intents in the left-to-right depth-first-order, we can be sure that the first preferred candidate S is, in fact, a maximal admissible extension. This is so, because all intents containing S as a subset are either among its descendants in the tree or precede S in this order. Neither of the two presented algorithms follows this left-to-right depth-first-order when computing intents; so, some care should taken when implementing this trick with them. Alternatively, it is possible to modify the algorithms so that they follow this order (resulting in an algorithm similar to what is known as Close by One in the FCA community [22]), and then the first preferred candidate as computed by the algorithm will be a preferred extension.

If the goal is to enumerate all preferred extensions, we do need to check for maximality. A simple way to do this is as follows: we start with an empty list $\mathcal{L}$ of potentially preferred extensions and, as soon as we obtain a new preferred candidate S, we check if it is a subset of any set from $\mathcal{L}$ (in which case we ignore S; otherwise, we add S to $\mathcal{L}$) or a superset of some sets from $\mathcal{L}$ (in which case, these sets are removed from $\mathcal{L}$). Upon the termination of the algorithm, $\mathcal{L}$ will be the set of all preferred extensions.

4   Experimental Results

Most of the available tools for argumentation frameworks do no support enumerating all stable extensions, but only allow finding a single extension. The latter problem is called "SE-ST" at the ICCMA competitions, and, in this section, we evaluate the performance of our algorithms on this problem. This means that we terminate our algorithms as soon as they produce the first extension or allow them to run to completion if the AF contains no stable extensions.

We have evaluated the runtime performance of Algorithms 1 and 3 from Sect. 3 on randomly generated AFs with different sizes and densities. By the size of an AF (A, R), we mean the number of arguments of the AF, i.e., $|A|$. By its density, we mean the proportion $|R|/|A|^2$. We have generated test frameworks containing 200, 600, 800, 1k, 2k, 3k, 4k, 5k, 6k, 7k, 8k, 9k, and 10k arguments, each with densities ranging from 0.1 to 0.9. Thus we have generated altogether 117 test files.[1] While generating the test frameworks, we did not allow arguments to attack themselves. Our implementation[2] supports the new input format introduced for ICCMA 2023. The tools used for the comparison accept input in the apx-format. Therefore, the test data contains each framework in both formats.

The tests were performed under Ubuntu Linux on a hardware with a 32 core-CPU running at 2.9 GHz and 256 GB of main memory. For comparing our approach with the existing ones, we have evaluated three other tools from the ICCMA competitions with the same test frameworks. These are μ-toksia[3], pyglaf[4], and a-folio-dpdb[5]. As time limit, we fixed five minutes for all the five approaches. We did not put any constraints on their memory usage.

The results of the experiments on frameworks with densities from 0.2 to 0.9 are shown in Fig. 3, which refers to Algorithm 1 as affca-nc and to Algorithm 3 as affca-norris. For density 0.1, all approaches failed with a timeout on almost all framework sizes. In the diagrams, discontinued lines are due to timeouts for some framework sizes. For instance, for density 0.9, pyglaf terminated within the time limit for frameworks of sizes 200, 600, 2k, 3k, 4k, and 5k but not for frameworks of sizes 800, 1k, and greater than 5k. Therefore, there is a gap in the corresponding line between the framework sizes 600 and 2k.

The results of the evaluation show that Algorithm 3 performs significantly better than all other four approaches on test frameworks with density of 0.5 and above (the exceptions being the 4k-framework with density 0.6, and the 2k-framework with density 0.5, which only μ-toksia was able to process within the time limit). The performance difference is most visible on frameworks with large densities. For instance, for density 0.9 and size 9k, Algorithm 3 is almost ten times faster than μ-toksia and two times faster than Algorithm 1; the other tools get timeout. As the density of the frameworks decreases, the performance

---

[1] The test frameworks are available via the GitHub Repository of the project.
[2] https://github.com/sertkaya/afca.
[3] https://bitbucket.org/andreasniskanen/mu-toksia/src/master/.
[4] https://alviano.com/software/pyglaf.
[5] https://github.com/gorczyca/dp_on_dbs.

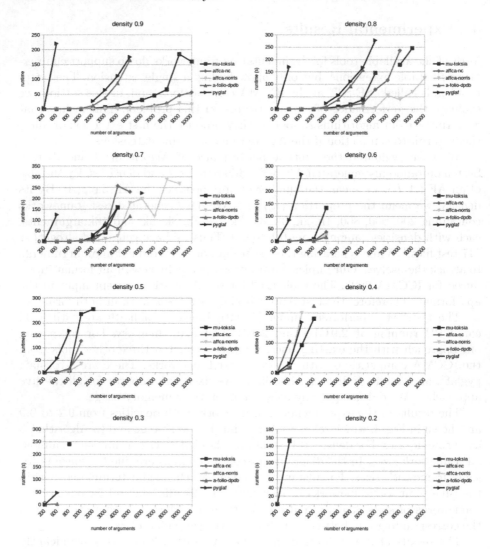

Fig. 3. Experimental results

of our algorithms deteriorates. For density 0.3 and below, they terminate within the time limit only for the framework with the smallest number of arguments, namely, 200 arguments. For such test frameworks, μ-toksia is the only tool that still terminates within the time limit.

The reason why our algorithms perform better on AFs with denser attack relations is, in fact, clear: for such AFs, the induced context representing the not-attack relation is sparser, and the number of concepts in a sparse context is usually small.

5   Conclusion and Future Work

We have presented a characterization of AFs as formal contexts and adapted two algorithms from FCA for computing stable extensions of AFs. Experimental results with randomly generated test data show that our approach performs significantly better than the existing approaches for AFs with dense attack relations. Our Algorithm 1, based on the Next Closure algorithm, has the advantage that its memory requirements depend linearly on the number of arguments and do not depend on any other parameters of the argumentation framework. The other one, Algorithm 3, can more efficiently prune the search tree and, therefore, often has the best performance among all approaches we have evaluated. However, it has the disadvantage that it stores all stable-extension candidates and, because of this, has a high memory requirement, in the worst case, exponential in the number of arguments.

We plan to improve the algorithms so that they could skip larger number of intents when searching for stable extensions and, in particular, prune larger parts of the search tree that will not lead to stable extensions. Various heuristics could be used to speed up the computation [16]. One heuristic that could work for both algorithms when run on frameworks with self-attacking arguments would be to fix the linear order on arguments so that such arguments (which cannot be part of any stable extension) are easily skipped. Another option would be to fix an order where arguments that are more likely to appear in stable extensions are used first. These can be, for instance, arguments that are attacked by a small number of arguments but attack a large number of other arguments. This heuristic can especially be useful for the problem of finding a single stable extension.

Acknowledgements. This work is partly supported by Deutsche Forschungsgemeinschaft (DFG, German Research Foundation) in project 389792660 (TRR 248, Center for Perspicuous Systems), by the Bundesministerium für Bildung und Forschung (BMBF, Federal Ministry of Education and Research) in the Center for Scalable Data Analytics and Artificial Intelligence (ScaDS.AI), and by BMBF and DAAD (German Academic Exchange Service) in project 57616814 (SECAI, School of Embedded Composite AI).

References

1. Alviano, M.: The PYGLAF argumentation reasoner (ICCMA2021). CoRR abs/2109.03162 (2021). https://arxiv.org/abs/2109.03162
2. Amgoud, L., Prade, H.: A formal concept view of abstract argumentation. In: van der Gaag, L.C. (ed.) ECSQARU 2013. LNCS (LNAI), vol. 7958, pp. 1–12. Springer, Heidelberg (2013). https://doi.org/10.1007/978-3-642-39091-3_1
3. Baroni, P., Caminada, M., Giacomin, M.: An introduction to argumentation semantics. Knowl. Eng. Rev. **26**(4), 365–410 (2011). https://doi.org/10.1017/S0269888911000166

4. Baroni, P., Dunne, P.E., Giacomin, M.: On extension counting problems in argumentation frameworks. In: Baroni, P., Cerutti, F., Giacomin, M., Simari, G.R. (eds.) Computational Models of Argument: Proceedings of COMMA 2010, Desenzano del Garda, Italy, 8–10, September 2010. Frontiers in Artificial Intelligence and Applications, vol. 216, pp. 63–74. IOS Press (2010). https://doi.org/10.3233/978-1-60750-619-5-63

5. Bistarelli, S., Santini, F.: ConArg: a constraint-based computational framework for argumentation systems. In: IEEE 23rd International Conference on Tools with Artificial Intelligence, ICTAI 2011, Boca Raton, FL, USA, 7–9 November 2011, pp. 605–612. IEEE Computer Society (2011). https://doi.org/10.1109/ICTAI.2011.96

6. Borchman, D., Hanika, T., Obiedkov, S.: Probably approximately correct learning of Horn envelopes from queries. Discret. Appl. Math. **273**, 30–42 (2020). https://doi.org/10.1016/j.dam.2019.02.036

7. Bordat, J.P.: Calcul pratique du treillis de Galois d' une correspondance. Mathématiques, Informatique et Sciences Humaines **96**, 31–47 (1986)

8. Cerutti, F., Gaggl, S.A., Thimm, M., Wallner, J.P.: Foundations of implementations for formal argumentation. FLAP **4**(8), 2623–2705 (2017). http://www.collegepublications.co.uk/downloads/ifcolog00017.pdf

9. Cimiano, P., Hotho, A., Staab, S.: Learning concept hierarchies from text corpora using formal concept analysis. J. Artif. Intell. Res. **24**(1), 305–339 (2005)

10. Dung, P.M.: On the acceptability of arguments and its fundamental role in non-monotonic reasoning, logic programming and n-person games. Artif. Intell. **77**(2), 321–358 (1995). https://doi.org/10.1016/0004-3702(94)00041-X

11. Dunne, P.E., Wooldridge, M.J.: Complexity of abstract argumentation. In: Simari, G.R., Rahwan, I. (eds.) Argumentation in Artificial Intelligence, pp. 85–104. Springer, Boston (2009). https://doi.org/10.1007/978-0-387-98197-0_5

12. Ganter, B.: Two basic algorithms in concept analysis. Technical report Preprint-Nr. 831, Technische Hochschule Darmstadt, Darmstadt, Germany (1984)

13. Ganter, B.: Two basic algorithms in concept analysis. In: Kwuida, L., Sertkaya, B. (eds.) ICFCA 2010. LNCS (LNAI), vol. 5986, pp. 312–340. Springer, Heidelberg (2010). https://doi.org/10.1007/978-3-642-11928-6_22

14. Ganter, B., Obiedkov, S.: Conceptual Exploration. Springer, Heidelberg (2016). https://doi.org/10.1007/978-3-662-49291-8

15. Ganter, B., Wille, R.: Formal Concept Analysis: Mathematical Foundations. Springer, Heidelberg (1999). https://doi.org/10.1007/978-3-642-59830-2

16. Geilen, N., Thimm, M.: Heureka: a general heuristic backtracking solver for abstract argumentation. In: Black, E., Modgil, S., Oren, N. (eds.) TAFA 2017. LNCS (LNAI), vol. 10757, pp. 143–149. Springer, Cham (2018). https://doi.org/10.1007/978-3-319-75553-3_10

17. Godin, R., Missaoui, R., Alaoui, H.: Incremental concept formation algorithms based on Galois (concept) lattices. Comput. Intell. **11**(2), 246–267 (1995)

18. Grissa, D., Comte, B., Pétéra, M., Pujos-Guillot, E., Napoli, A.: A hybrid and exploratory approach to knowledge discovery in metabolomic data. Discrete Appl. Math. **273**, 103–116 (2020). https://doi.org/10.1016/j.dam.2018.11.025. Advances in Formal Concept Analysis: Traces of CLA 2016

19. Ignatov, D.I.: Introduction to formal concept analysis and its applications in information retrieval and related fields. CoRR abs/1703.02819 (2017). http://arxiv.org/abs/1703.02819

20. Johnson, D.S., Yannakakis, M., Papadimitriou, C.H.: On generating all maximal independent sets. Inf. Process. Lett. **27**(3), 119–123 (1988)

21. Kröll, M., Pichler, R., Woltran, S.: On the complexity of enumerating the extensions of abstract argumentation frameworks. In: Sierra, C. (ed.) Proceedings of the Twenty-Sixth International Joint Conference on Artificial Intelligence, IJCAI 2017, Melbourne, Australia, 19–25 August 2017, pp. 1145–1152. ijcai.org (2017). https://doi.org/10.24963/ijcai.2017/159

22. Kuznetsov, S.O.: A fast algorithm for computing all intersections of objects in a finite semi-lattice. Autom. Documentation Math. Linguist. **27**(5), 11–21 (1993)

23. Kuznetsov, S.O.: On computing the size of a lattice and related decision problems. Order **18**(4), 313–321 (2001). https://doi.org/10.1023/A:1013970520933

24. Kuznetsov, S.O.: Machine learning and formal concept analysis. In: Eklund, P. (ed.) ICFCA 2004. LNCS (LNAI), vol. 2961, pp. 287–312. Springer, Heidelberg (2004). https://doi.org/10.1007/978-3-540-24651-0_25

25. Kuznetsov, S.O., Obiedkov, S.: Comparing performance of algorithms for generating concept lattices. J. Exp. Theor. Artif. Intell. **14**(2–3), 189–216 (2002)

26. Lakhal, L., Stumme, G.: Efficient mining of association rules based on formal concept analysis. In: Ganter, B., Stumme, G., Wille, R. (eds.) Formal Concept Analysis. LNCS (LNAI), vol. 3626, pp. 180–195. Springer, Heidelberg (2005). https://doi.org/10.1007/11528784_10

27. Niskanen, A., Järvisalo, M.: μ-toksia: an efficient abstract argumentation reasoner. In: Calvanese, D., Erdem, E., Thielscher, M. (eds.) Proceedings of the 17th International Conference on Principles of Knowledge Representation and Reasoning, KR 2020, Rhodes, Greece, 12–18 September 2020, pp. 800–804 (2020). https://doi.org/10.24963/kr.2020/82

28. Norris, E.M.: An algorithm for computing the maximal rectangles in a binary relation. Rev. Roumaine Math. Pures Appl. **23**(2), 243–250 (1978)

29. Nourine, L., Raynaud, O.: A fast algorithm for building lattices. Inf. Process. Lett. **71**(5–6), 199–204 (1999)

30. Obiedkov, S.: Learning implications from data and from queries. In: Cristea, D., Le Ber, F., Sertkaya, B. (eds.) ICFCA 2019. LNCS (LNAI), vol. 11511, pp. 32–44. Springer, Cham (2019). https://doi.org/10.1007/978-3-030-21462-3_3

31. Poelmans, J., Ignatov, D.I., Kuznetsov, S.O., Dedene, G.: Formal concept analysis in knowledge processing: a survey on applications. Expert Syst. Appl. **40**(16), 6538–6560 (2013)

32. Valtchev, P., Missaoui, R.: Building concept (Galois) lattices from parts: generalizing the incremental methods. In: Delugach, H.S., Stumme, G. (eds.) ICCS-ConceptStruct 2001. LNCS (LNAI), vol. 2120, pp. 290–303. Springer, Heidelberg (2001). https://doi.org/10.1007/3-540-44583-8_21

Reasoning in Assumption-Based Argumentation Using Tree-Decompositions

Andrei Popescu[ID] and Johannes P. Wallner[✉][ID]

Institute of Software Technology, Graz University of Technology, Graz, Austria
{andrei.popescu,wallner}@ist.tugraz.at

Abstract. We address complex reasoning tasks in assumption-based argumentation (ABA) by developing dynamic programming algorithms based on tree-decompositions. As one of the prominent approaches in computational argumentation, our focus is on NP-hard reasoning in ABA. We utilize tree-width, a structural measure describing closeness to trees, for an approach to handle computationally complex tasks in ABA. We contribute to the state of the art by first showing that many reasoning tasks in ABA are fixed-parameter tractable w.r.t. tree-width using Courcelle's theorem, informally signaling wide applicability of dynamic programming algorithms for ABA. Secondly, we develop such algorithms operating on tree-decompositions of given ABA frameworks. We instantiate the algorithms in the recent D-FLAT framework allowing for declarative and extensible specification of dynamic programming algorithms. In an experimental evaluation on a resulting prototype, we show promise of the approach in particular for complex counting tasks.

1 Introduction

Computational approaches to arguing in favour or against statements under scrutiny are a main research theme in the field of computational argumentation [4,38], within Artificial Intelligence (AI). Placed in the area of knowledge representation and reasoning and non-monotonic reasoning, computational argumentation features a diverse set of application avenues, such as legal reasoning, medical reasoning, and e-government [3].

Approaches to formalize argumentative reasoning are studied in the field of structured argumentation [5]. Formalisms in structured argumentation usually follow the so-called argumentation workflow [14] to prescribe ways of finding arguments and their relationships. A starting point are knowledge bases, oftentimes assumed to be in a rule-based form. Arguments are then instantiated as derivations applicable within the knowledge base. Reasoning based on the arguments and their relations is carried out by using argumentation semantics, through which one can specify acceptable sets of arguments. Several approaches to structured argumentation have been studied, e.g., assumption-based argumentation (ABA) [12,20], ASPIC$^+$ [50,51], defeasible logic programming (DeLP) [40,41], and deductive argumentation [6,7].

S. Gaggl et al. (Eds.): JELIA 2023, LNAI 14281, pp. 192–208, 2023.
https://doi.org/10.1007/978-3-031-43619-2_14

Computationally speaking, argumentative reasoning in these approaches to structured argumentation is hard: in almost all cases reasoning defined in these formalisms is NP-hard, see, e.g., the survey by Dunne and Dvořák [32]. To address the complexity barrier, several algorithmic approaches were developed [15,16], and in a biannual International Competition on Computational Models of Argumentation (ICCMA) [8,39,46,53], which this year is being held for the fifth time, systems compete in terms of runtime performance.

An approach to tackle high complexity is the utilization of structural properties of instances, such as viewing instances in a graph-like manner and considering, e.g., acyclicity or other graph properties. A prominent such property is tree-width [10], informally measuring closeness of instances to trees. The milder complexity of many problems on trees oftentimes transfers to problems on graphs of low tree-width. Algorithms following dynamic programming can then operate on a tree-decomposition of the initial instance, with which one confines the combinatorial explosion of complex problems into subproblems, whose size can be bounded by the tree-width of the original instance. Tree-based forms, or forms close to trees, appear appealing to computational argumentation, since, e.g., dialogues might be represented in a tree-like structure. Indeed, tree-width has been studied in several works in argumentation [27–31,34,47]. These studies focus on the field of abstract argumentation, i.e., on formalisms where arguments are given in an abstracted form such as the well-known argumentation framework (AF) [26], and a form of deductive argumentation. To the best of our knowledge, there is no current account of the utilization of tree-width for rule-based structured argumentation formalisms such as ABA, ASPIC$^+$, or DeLP.

Recent works show that lifting computational approaches in abstract argumentation to structured argumentation is not immediate, and seems to involve dedicated research on the structured formalisms [48,49]. We follow this line and take up this opportunity to study algorithmic approaches utilizing tree-width for ABA, as one of the prominent structured argumentation approaches with applications in medical decision making [19,22] and in multi-agent contexts [33].

Our main contributions are as follows.

- We first show wide applicability of algorithms using tree-width by showing fixed-parameter tractability of reasoning tasks in ABA, under the parameter tree-width. We show these results by making use of Courcelle's theorem [17] and expressing reasoning in ABA in monadic second order logic (MSO).
- We develop tree-decomposition-based algorithms for ABA. Towards wider extensibility, we first give a detailed account of a dynamic programming algorithm for the stable semantics and instantiate algorithms for admissible, complete, and stable semantics in the framework of D-FLAT [1,2,9], which enables declarative specification of such algorithms in answer set programming (ASP) [13,43,52]. Together with expressing ABA reasoning in MSO, the declarative approach of D-FLAT leads to a system that has potential for adaptation to other forms of structured argumentation, further semantics, or other modes of reasoning.

– Finally, we present an experimental evaluation of a prototype using D-FLAT, showing promise of our approach for complex counting tasks involving in particular a high number of solutions.

Further material, including ASP encodings used within D-FLAT, can be found at https://gitlab.tugraz.at/krr/astra.

2   Background

We recall assumption-based argumentation (ABA) [12,20], monadic second order logic, and tree-width and tree-decompositions [10], next.

Assumption-Based Argumentation. We assume a deductive system $(\mathcal{L}, \mathcal{R})$, where $\mathcal{L}$ is a set of atoms and $\mathcal{R}$ a set of inference rules over $\mathcal{L}$. A rule $r \in \mathcal{R}$ has the form $a_0 \leftarrow a_1, \ldots, a_n$ with each $a_i \in \mathcal{L}$. We denote the head of rule r by $head(r) = a_0$ and the (possibly empty) body of r with $body(r) = \{a_1, \ldots, a_n\}$.

Definition 1. *An ABA framework is a tuple $F = (\mathcal{L}, \mathcal{R}, \mathcal{A}, ^-)$, where $(\mathcal{L}, \mathcal{R})$ is a deductive system, $\mathcal{A} \subseteq \mathcal{L}$ a non-empty set of assumptions, and $^-$ a function mapping assumptions $\mathcal{A}$ to atoms $\mathcal{L}$.*

In words, an ABA framework includes a deductive system, a distinction between assumptions and non-assumptions, and a contrary function that assigns contraries to assumptions. In this work, we focus on the commonly used logic programming fragment of ABA [12]. We assume that all sets and rules in an ABA framework are finite, and no assumption occurs in the head of a rule. The last condition means that the ABA frameworks are flat. As a slight generalization, we allow the contrary function to be partial.

Derivability in ABA can be defined in multiple ways, we recall the so-called forward-derivations, here called simply derivations. An atom $a \in \mathcal{L}$ is derivable from a set $X \subseteq \mathcal{A}$ using rules $\mathcal{R}$, denoted by $X \vdash_{\mathcal{R}} a$, if $a \in X$ or there is a sequence of rules $(r_1, \ldots, r_n)$ such that $head(r_n) = a$ and for each rule r_i we have $r_i \in \mathcal{R}$ and each atom in the body of r_i is derived from rules earlier in the sequence or is in X, i.e., $body(r_i) \subseteq X \cup \bigcup_{j<i}\{head(r_j)\}$. The deductive closure for an assumption set X w.r.t. rules $\mathcal{R}$ is defined as $Th_{\mathcal{R}}(X) = \{a \in \mathcal{L} \mid X \vdash_{\mathcal{R}} a\}$.

Example 1. Our running example ABA framework $F = (\mathcal{L}, \mathcal{R}, \mathcal{A}, ^-)$ is given with $\mathcal{A} = \{a, b\}$, $\mathcal{L} = \mathcal{A} \cup \{x, y, z\}$, the rules $r_1 = (x \leftarrow a)$, $r_2 = (y \leftarrow x)$, $r_3 = (z \leftarrow b)$, and contraries $\bar{a} = z$ and $\bar{b} = y$.

The contrary function is used to define attacks between assumption sets.

Definition 2. *Let $F = (\mathcal{L}, \mathcal{R}, \mathcal{A}, ^-)$ be an ABA framework, and $A, B \subseteq \mathcal{A}$ be two sets of assumptions. Assumption set A attacks assumption set B in F if $A' \vdash_{\mathcal{R}} \bar{b}$ for some $A' \subseteq A$ and $b \in B$.*

Conflict-free assumption sets and defense are defined, as follows.

Definition 3. *Let $F = (\mathcal{L}, \mathcal{R}, \mathcal{A}, ^-)$ be an ABA framework. An assumption set $A \subseteq \mathcal{A}$ is conflict-free in F iff A does not attack itself. Set A defends assumption set $B \subseteq \mathcal{A}$ in F iff for all $C \subseteq \mathcal{A}$ that attack B it holds that A attacks C.*

The ABA semantics we focus on in this work are then defined next.

Definition 4. *Let $F = (\mathcal{L}, \mathcal{R}, \mathcal{A}, ^-)$ be an ABA framework. Further, let $A \subseteq \mathcal{A}$ be a conflict-free set of assumptions in F. In F, set A is*

- admissible *iff A defends itself,*
- complete *iff A is admissible and contains all assumption sets defended by A,*
- preferred *iff A is admissible and there is no admissible set of assumptions B with $A \subset B$, and*
- stable *iff each $\{x\} \subseteq \mathcal{A} \setminus A$ is attacked by A.*

Reasoning tasks on ABA include verifying whether a given set of assumptions is a σ-assumption set, and enumerating or counting σ-assumption sets. In addition, often a relevant question is to find out whether a given atom is acceptable under a semantics. To answer this question, two prominent reasoning modes are credulous and skeptical acceptance of atoms in an ABA framework. A given atom $s \in \mathcal{L}$ is credulously accepted in F under semantics σ iff there is a σ-assumption set A such that $s \in Th_{\mathcal{R}}(A)$, and skeptically accepted in F under semantics σ iff $s \in Th_{\mathcal{R}}(A)$ for all σ-assumption sets A. Credulous reasoning under admissible, complete, stable, and preferred semantics is NP-complete and skeptical acceptance under stable is coNP-complete, and Π_2^P-complete under preferred semantics [21, 24].

Example 2. Continuing Example 1, there are two stable assumption sets $\{a\}$ and $\{b\}$, with deductive closures $Th_{\mathcal{R}}(\{a\}) = \{a, x, y\}$ and $Th_{\mathcal{R}}(\{b\}) = \{b, z\}$, respectively. In this example, atoms x, y, and z are credulously accepted under stable semantics, and no atom is skeptically accepted under stable semantics.

Monadic Second Order Logic and Tree-Decompositions. We recap monadic second order logic and tree-decompositions, following Gottlob et al. [44].

Monadic second order logic (MSO) extends first order logic by allowing set variables, which range over sets of domain variables, and quantification over these set variables. We write individual variables as lowercase letters x and set variables as uppercase letters X. For a set $\tau = \{R_1, \dots, R_k\}$ of predicate symbols, a finite structure I over τ, also called a τ-structure, has a finite domain $D = dom(I)$ and relations $R_i^I \subseteq D^{r_i}$ of arity r_i for each predicate symbol $R_i \in \tau$. Evaluation of an MSO formula ϕ over a τ-structure I is defined, as usual. For our purposes, it is sufficient to only consider unary and binary predicates.

A tree-decomposition of a τ-structure I is a pair $(T, (D_t)_{t \in T})$, with T being a rooted tree and each $D_t \subseteq D = dom(I)$, satisfying the following properties.

1. Every domain element $x \in D$ is part of some D_t, i.e., $x \in D_t$ for some $t \in T$.
2. For every $R_i \in \tau$ and tuple $(a_1, \dots, a_{r_i}) \in R_i^I$ it holds that there is some node $t \in T$ with $\{a_1, \dots, a_{r_i}\} \subseteq D_t$.
3. The set $\{t \mid a \in D_t\}$ induces a subtree of T, for each $a \in D$.

In brief terms, a tree-decomposition is a tree formed of so-called bags D_t consisting of sets of domain elements. The second condition ensures that each relation is fully part of at least one bag. The third condition, often referred to as the connectedness condition, states that whenever two bags D_t and $D_{t'}$ both contain an a, then on the path between those two bags, we encounter a in the bags.

The width of a tree-decomposition $(T, (D_t)_{t \in T})$ is the maximum number of domain elements in bags minus one, i.e., $max\{|D_t| \mid t \in T\} - 1$. The tree-width of a τ-structure I is the minimum width of all tree-decompositions of I.

Complexity-wise, MSO and tree-width are connected, as stated by Courcelle's theorem.

Theorem 1 ([17]). *Let ϕ be an MSO formula over a structure τ, and I be a τ-structure of tree-width w. It holds that evaluating ϕ over I can be achieved in $\mathcal{O}(f(|\phi|, w) \cdot |I|)$, for some function f.*

In brief, a problem expressible in MSO is then said to be fixed-parameter tractable (FPT) for the parameter tree-with of the underlying τ-structure. For an overview on parametrized complexity (including FPT), see the book by Downey and Fellows [25].

3   Complexity of ABA Under the Lens of Tree-Width

In this section, we show that a large range of problems in ABA can be addressed algorithmically via utilizing tree-width, formally by stating that these problems are FPT with the parameter tree-width.

Towards these results, we represent reasoning in ABA in MSO. We make use of the following set of predicate symbols: $\tau_{ABA} = \{atom/1, asm/1, rule/1, head/2, body/2, contrary/2, query/1\}$, together with the arities of the predicates. The intention of the predicates is formalized next.

Definition 5. *Let $F = (\mathcal{L}, \mathcal{R}, \mathcal{A}, ^-)$ be an ABA framework. The associated τ_{ABA} structure, denoted by I_F, is defined by $atom(x)$ for each $x \in \mathcal{L}$, $asm(a)$ for each $a \in \mathcal{A}$, $rule(r)$, $head(r, h)$, and $body(r, b_1), \ldots, body(r, b_k)$ for each rule $r = h \leftarrow b_1, \ldots, b_k$, and $contrary(a, x)$ for each $a \in \mathcal{A}$ and $x \in \mathcal{L}$ s.t. $\overline{a} = x$.*

The remaining *query* predicate is used to indicate what to query for credulous or skeptical reasoning.

Example 3. Consider again the ABA framework from Example 1, which can be written as a τ_{ABA} structure containing $atom(a)$, $atom(b)$, $atom(x)$, $atom(y)$, $atom(z)$, $asm(a)$, $asm(b)$, $rule(r_1)$, $rule(r_2)$, and $rule(r_3)$ for the unary predicates, and $contrary(a, z)$, $contrary(b, y)$, $head(r_1, x)$, $head(r_2, y)$, $head(r_3, z)$, $body(r_1, a)$, $body(r_2, x)$, and $body(r_3, b)$ for the binary predicates. Part of a tree-decomposition of this ABA framework is depicted in Fig. 1. This decomposition is a so-called "nice" tree-decomposition, which has to satisfy further constraints useful for algorithms operating on such a nice tree-decomposition. We recall the formal definition of nice tree-decompositions in the next section. In this tree-decomposition there are 22 nodes. For instance, r_1 and a are together in the bag

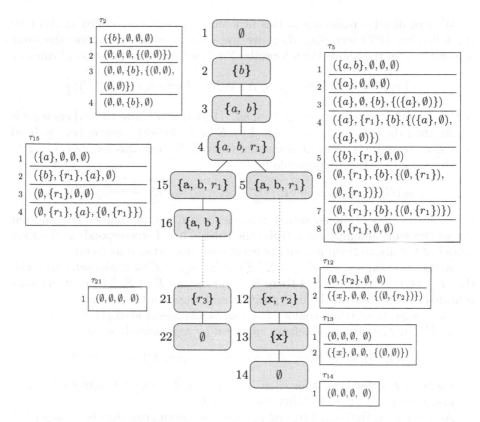

Fig. 1. Part of an example tree-decomposition of the ABA framework of Example 1. (Color figure online)

of node 15, satisfying the condition that these two have to be together in one bag because $body(r_1, a)$ holds.

We move on to expressing ABA semantics in terms of MSO. We make use of several common shortcuts, as defined next, in addition to "$x \in X$" to denote that a domain element is in the set.

$$x \notin X := \neg(x \in X) \qquad\qquad X \subseteq Y := \forall x(x \in X \to x \in Y)$$
$$X \subsetneq Y := (X \subseteq Y) \wedge \neg(Y \subseteq X) \qquad X \subseteq_{\mathcal{A}} Y := \forall x((x \in X \wedge asm(x)) \to x \in Y)$$
$$X \subsetneq_{\mathcal{A}} Y := (X \subseteq_{\mathcal{A}} Y) \wedge \neg(Y \subseteq_{\mathcal{A}} X) \quad X =_{\mathcal{A}} Y := (X \subseteq_{\mathcal{A}} Y) \wedge (Y \subseteq_{\mathcal{A}} X)$$

First, we encode derivability. For a given ABA framework F and $A \subseteq \mathcal{A}$, there is a direct connection between $Th_{\mathcal{R}}(A)$ and the unique $\subseteq$-minimal classical model of the propositional Horn formula $\bigwedge_{a \in A} a \wedge \bigwedge_{r \in \mathcal{R}} \left(\bigwedge_{b \in body(r)} b \to head(r)\right)$, that is, the Horn theory consisting of each assumption in A as facts and rules in $\mathcal{R}$ as implications. It holds that $M \subseteq \mathcal{L}$ is the $\subseteq$-minimal model of this formula iff $M = Th_{\mathcal{R}}(A)$.

We can directly make use of this fact and represent derivability in ABA by the following MSO formula, where we use quantification to express the same reasoning as in the above Horn formula. First, we define satisfaction of rules by

$$\forall r\Big(rule(r) \rightarrow \exists s\big((head(r,s) \wedge s \in E) \vee (body(r,s) \wedge s \notin E)\big)\Big).$$

In this formula the set variable E is open. The formula states that whenever r is a rule, then the rule has to be satisfied by E in the logical sense: either the head is in E or some body element is missing from E. We call this formula $\phi_{Sat}(E)$.

Derivability is then expressible by

$$\phi_{Th}(E) = \phi_{Sat}(E) \wedge \forall E'\big((E' \subsetneq E \wedge E' =_\mathcal{A} E) \rightarrow \neg\phi_{Sat}(E')\big),$$

which states that E should satisfy the rules and no proper subset $E' \subsetneq E$ that shares the same assumptions satisfies the rules. Then E corresponds to the least model of the above Horn formula (with assumptions stated as facts).

Attacks are expressible via $\phi_{att}(E,S) = \exists x, a\big(x \in E \wedge a \in S \wedge contrary(a,x)\big)$, that is, set E attacks set S if there is a contrary in E of S. The contrary only contains assumptions in the first position and atoms in the second.

The property of being conflict-free can be expressed as $\phi_{cf}(E) = \phi_{Th}(E) \wedge \neg\phi_{att}(E,E)$. The notion of defense can then be represented, as follows.

$$\phi_{def}(E,A) = \forall S\big((S \subseteq \mathcal{L} \wedge \phi_{Th}(S) \wedge \phi_{att}(S,A)) \rightarrow \phi_{att}(E,S)\big)$$

In words, if E defends A if for each S attacking A we find E attacks S (for S we also need to check derivability via $\phi_{Th}(S)$).

Admissibility, the complete, and preferred semantics can then be represented, as stated next.

$$\phi_{adm}(E) = \phi_{cf}(E) \wedge \phi_{def}(E,E)$$
$$\phi_{com}(E) = \phi_{adm}(E) \wedge \forall S\big((\phi_{def}(E,S) \wedge \phi_{Th}(S)) \rightarrow S \subseteq E\big)$$
$$\phi_{prf}(E) = \phi_{adm}(E) \wedge \forall E'\neg\big(E' \subseteq \mathcal{L} \wedge E \subsetneq E' \wedge \phi_{adm}(E')\big)$$

Finally, the stable semantics can be expressed by formula $\phi_{stb}(E)$, given as $\phi_{cf}(E) \wedge \forall a(asm(a) \rightarrow a \in E \vee \exists x(x \in E \wedge contrary(a,x)))$, capturing directly the definition of stable semantics.

Credulous and skeptical reasoning can then be specified by stating

$$\phi_\sigma^{Cred} = \exists E\big(E \subseteq \mathcal{L} \wedge \phi_{query}(E) \wedge \phi_\sigma(E)\big) \text{ and}$$
$$\phi_\sigma^{Skept} = \forall E\Big((E \subseteq \mathcal{L} \wedge \phi_\sigma(E)) \rightarrow (\phi_{query}(E))\Big).$$

with $\phi_{query}(E) = (\forall x(query(x) \rightarrow x \in E))$. The formula $\phi_{query}(E)$ directly states that the atoms defined by query are in E. We tacitly assume that queries defined by $query$ refer only to atoms and not to rules.

By utilizing Courcelle's results (Theorem 1), we can directly infer the following FPT result. The proof of this theorem directly follows from the previous formulas, declaratively representing the definitions of ABA, and Theorem 1.

Theorem 2. *Deciding credulous or skeptical acceptance of atoms in a given ABA framework under admissible, complete, stable, or preferred semantics is FPT w.r.t. tree-width.*

4 Dynamic Programming Algorithms for ABA

In this section, we present our approach to compute reasoning tasks in ABA using dynamic programming (DP) algorithms. Due to page limitations, we present a DP algorithm using tree-decompositions for computing stable assumption sets, and discuss changes needed for admissible and complete assumption sets. We explain how to instantiate our algorithms in the D-FLAT [1,2,9] framework, allowing for a declarative specification of the DP algorithms, and give full declarative encodings in the online supplementary material.

On a high level, DP algorithms operating on tree-decompositions of a given instance usually work bottom-up, by computing tables for each bag in post-order. The tables computed for each bag represent current partial solution candidates that can be inferred from the information encountered "so far". In a final step, partial solutions are then combined into full solutions. We delegate this step to D-FLAT, which follows so called extension pointers in a top-down fashion, and combines compatible partial solutions.

For the sake of clarity, we present our DP algorithm for stable semantics by requiring that the tree-decomposition is nice and has empty bags as leaves and as the root. Our implementation in D-FLAT does not require nice tree-decompositions, however. In nice tree-decompositions each node has a type and is either a *leaf*, the *root*, an *introduction* node, a *removal* node, or a *join* node. Except for leaves and join nodes, the nodes have exactly one child, and join nodes have exactly two children. Bags of introduction nodes have all objects of the child bag and one additional object, while bags of removal nodes have exactly one object less. Join nodes and their children have exactly the same bags. These conditions allow for a more compact algorithm representation. One can efficiently compute a nice tree-decomposition from a given tree decomposition [11].

Our algorithm is inspired by concepts for DP algorithms [35] for answer set programming [43]. For a given ABA framework $F = (\mathcal{L}, \mathcal{R}, \mathcal{A}, ^-)$, we define a partial stable assumption set as a quadruple (I, R, D, CW), where $I \subseteq \mathcal{L}$ is called a witness, $R \subseteq \mathcal{R}$, $D \subseteq \mathcal{A}$, and CW is a set of so-called counterwitnesses, which are pairs (C, R_C) with $C \subseteq I$ and $R_C \subseteq \mathcal{R}$. We utilize the concepts of witnesses counterwitnesses, as presented by Fichte et al. [35], in our DP algorithms. Intuitively, each partial stable assumption set consists of a witness set I of atoms that is a candidate for a stable assumption set and all atoms that can be derived from the stable assumption set, while D contains the assumptions attacked ("defeated") by I. That is, I can be seen as atoms and assumptions we "assume" to be part of a stable assumption set. Since we might encounter components of rules in various places in the tree-decomposition, we view the rules as Boolean Horn clauses and store in R all rules that are satisfied by I (similar as in Sect. 3). Finally, a counterwitness represents pairs (C, R_C) where

C shares the same assumptions as in I, i.e., $I \cap \mathcal{A} = C \cap \mathcal{A}$, but has strictly fewer atoms (i.e., represents proper a subset) and R_C the associated satisfied rules. A counterwitness testifies that one can satisfy the rules R_C with fewer atoms, and, thus, is a counter to derivability of the atoms in I from the assumptions in I if both I and C satisfy all rules in the root node. During bottom-up computation, partial stable assumption sets and their counterwitnesses are modified, added, or removed, depending on the objects encountered in the bags. A partial stable assumption set contains only components of the current bag (and may use information from child bags).

Let us go over Algorithm 1 and Algorithm 2 for stable assumption sets. We show here the case for enumerating stable assumption sets, but credulous and skeptical reasoning can be achieved via small modifications: enumerating only stable assumption sets containing or not containing a query.

In Algorithm 1 we call Algorithm 2 for each node in the tree-decomposition of the given ABA instance and store the result in a table (Tab). Algorithm 2 computes these tables, given the tables of the children nodes. We store partial stable assumption sets computed in Res (initially empty). In Line 3 we merge the tables of the two children tables, by combining compatible partial stable assumption sets. Two such sets are compatible if they coincide on their first components I, i.e., for two sets τ_i and τ_j of partial stable assumptions sets, the function $merge$ returns $\{(I, R_i \cup R_j, D_i \cup D_j, C_i \sqcup C_j) \mid (I, R_i, D_i, C_i) \in \tau_i, (I, R_j, D_j, C_j) \in \tau_j\}$. For merging the counterwitnesses, we use $C_i \sqcup C_j = \{(C, R \cup R') \mid (C, R) \in C_i, (C, R') \in C_j\}$. If we are not in a join node, there is only one child and we go over all previous partial stable assumption sets (loop beginning with Line 5, after extracting the single table in the line before).

For the root node, there is a simple check: if there are no counterwitnesses ($C = \emptyset$, Line 6), we have found an entry leading to stable assumption set.

Line 7 considers bags in which an atom a is introduced. In this case, the set of partial stable assumption sets for this bag is obtained by utilizing each partial stable assumption set in the child partial solution I, and creating two partial stable assumption sets I_{out} and I_{in}, the former by not adding the introduced atom a (Line 8), and the latter by adding it (Line 13). Note that the partial stable assumption set with introduced atom a is only constructed if not conflicting (Line 12). This can be seen in Fig. 1 at node 13 which introduces x, resulting in two witnesses on lines 1 and 2 of τ_{13}. In the figure, witnesses are shown in blue and counterwitnesses are in red.

Algorithm 1. Compute partial stable assumption sets on T

Require: ABA framework $F = (\mathcal{L}, \mathcal{R}, \mathcal{A}, {}^-)$ and a nice tree-decomposition T of F.
Out: Function $Tab(t)$ assigning each node T a set of partial solutions.
1: **for** t **in** post-order(T) **do**
2:     $childTables := \{Tab(t') \mid t' \text{ child of } t \text{ in } T\}$
3:     $Tab(t) := ComputeTable_{stb}(T, t, childTables)$

The *Sat* function is used to compute satisfied rules, for a given node t, and set I of atoms by defining $Sat(t, I, R) = \{r \in R \mid head(r) \in I$ or $body(r) \cap bag(t) \not\subseteq I\}$, following a similar line of reasoning as in Sect. 3.

To construct new sets of counterwitnesses for each newly constructed partial stable assumption set, an analogous process occurs (Line 10 and Line 15). In the most trivial case, that of a new witness I_{out} constructed by not adding the

---

Algorithm 2. *ComputeTable$_{stb}$ (t, childTables)*

Require: node t, and set of sets of partial stable assumption sets *childTables*
Out: Return partial stable assumption sets
1: $Res := \emptyset$
2: **if** $type(t) = leaf$ **then return** $\emptyset$
3: **if** $type(t) = join$ **then return** $merge_{ST}(childTables)$
4: Let $\tau \in childTables$ ▷ *childTables* is a singleton
5: **for** $(I, R, D, C) \in \tau$ **do**
6:       **if** $type(t) = root \wedge C = \emptyset$ **then** $Res := Res \cup \{(I, R, D, C)\}$
7:       **if** $type(t) = intro \wedge a$ is the introduced atom
8:             $I_{out} := I$, $R_{out} := R \cup Sat(t, I_{out}, Rules(t))$
9:             **if** $\bar{a} \in I_{out}$ **then** $D_{out} := D \cup \{a\}$ **else** $D_{out} := D$
10:            $C_o = \{(I_{Co}, R_{Co} \cup Sat(t, I_{Co}, Rules(t))) \mid (I_{Co}, R_{Co}) \in C\}$
11:            $Res := Res \cup \{(I_{out}, R_{out}, D_{out}, C_o)\}$
12:            **if** $\bar{a} \notin I \cup \{a\}$ ▷ Conflict-free check
13:                  $I_{in} := I \cup \{a\}$
14:                  $R_{in} := Sat(t, I_{in}, Rules(t))$ ▷ New rules can become satisfied.
15:                  $C_{in} := \{(I_c \cup \{a\}, Sat(t, I_c \cup \{a\}, Rules(t))) \mid (I_c, R_c) \in C\}$
16:                  **if** $a \notin \mathcal{A}$ **then** $C_{in} := C_{in} \cup C$
17:                  $Res := Res \cup \{(I_{in}, R_{in}, D, C_{in})\} \cup \{(I, Sat(t, I, Rules(t)))\}$
18:      **if** $type(t) = rem \wedge a$ is the removed atom
19:            **if** $a \in \mathcal{A}$
20:                  **if** $a \in I \vee a \in D$ ▷ Stable check: only preserve if either In or Def.
21:                        $R' := Sat(t, I \setminus \{a\}, Rules(t))$
22:                        $C' := \{(I_c \setminus \{a\}, Sat(t, I_c \setminus \{a\}, Rules(t))) \mid (I_c, R_c) \in C\}$
23:                        $Res := Res \cup \{(I \setminus \{a\}, R', D \setminus \{a\}, C')\}$
24:                  **else**
25:                        $R' := Sat(t, I \setminus \{a\}, Rules(t))$
26:                        $C' := \{(I_c \setminus \{a\}, Sat(t, I_c \setminus \{a\}, Rules(t))) \mid (I_c, R_c) \in C\}$
27:                        $Res := Res \cup \{(I \setminus \{a\}, R', D, C')\}$
28:      **if** $type(t) = intro \wedge r$ is the introduced rule
29:            $R' := R \cup Sat(t, I, \{r\})$
30:            $C' := \{(I_c, R_c \cup Sat(t, I_c, \{r\})) \mid (I_c, R_c) \in C\}$
31:            $Res := Res \cup \{(I, R', D, C')\}$
32:      **if** $type(bag) = rem \wedge r$ is the removed rule
33:            **if** $r \in R$ ▷ only keep an answer if r sat
34:                  $R' := R \setminus \{r\}$
35:                  $C' := \{(I_c, R_c \setminus \{r\}) \mid (I_c, R_c) \in C\}$
36:                  $Res := Res \cup \{(I, R', D, C')\}$
37: **return** Res

---

introduced atom a, the set C_o is given by preserving the counterwitnesses from the child partial solution, with an updated set of satisfied bag rules (Line 10).

In the case of a witness constructed by the addition of a to a child witness, if a is an introduced assumption, we require a to be part of the constructed counterwitnesses, and thus we do not preserve all the child counterwitnesses C. On the contrary, if the introduced atom is not an assumption (Line 16), we add to our set of newly created counterwitnesses C_{in} the child counterwitnesses C. In intuitive terms, for a witness constructed by the addition of an introduced atom $a \notin A$, there can be counterwitnesses, subsets of the witness, such that the introduced atom has not been derived.

To enforce the return of stable assumption sets only, Algorithm 2 ensures that when an atom is removed at node t, only those child assumption sets that were stable are preserved as partial stable assumption sets in t. This is achieved through the check for stable assumption sets in Line 20. In case an atom $a \notin \mathcal{A}$ is removed, this check is not required, and partial stable assumption sets are preserved with updated sets I and R. With respect to Fig 1, node 2 removes a, and row 2 in τ_2 is the result of preserving a witness from τ_3 (not shown) s.t. $a \in D$, and $b \notin I$, $b \notin D$.

Finally, consider the two possibilities of a bag either introducing or removing a rule r (Line 28 and Line 32 respectively). When a rule is introduced, witnesses and counterwitnesses are preserved, both with an updated set of satisfied rules accounting for the status of the introduced rule. On the contrary, when a rule is removed, by the connectedness property we have visited all atoms in the rule, hence the rule could not become satisfied elsewhere. Algorithm 2 enforces the satisfiability of the removed rule by not preserving partial stable assumption sets for which the removed rule has not been satisfied. Figure 1 depicts the case for an introduced rule in table τ_{12}, which introduces rule r_2. In this case, counterwitnesses that have been preserved, e.g., on line 2 of τ_{12}, must have an updated set of satisfied rules.

Admissibility and Complete Semantics. To verify whether an assumption set defends itself against all attacks, one can ensure that all its attackers are attacked by the set, or inversely, that there are no undefeated attackers. One can adapt Algorithm 2 as follows: (i) we track derivability for undefeated atoms, (ii) we check its correctness by ensuring that undefeated atoms are not attacked by the set of supported assumptions, i.e. by the candidate admissible set I, (iii) we track the set of atoms that are defeated, (iv) we require an assumption to be either undefeated or defeated, and (v) we add the admissibility check by not preserving those assumption sets that are attacked by some undefeated atom.

For complete semantics, one can ensure that the supported set of assumptions I includes all those assumptions that are undefeated and not attacked by some undefeated set of assumptions, i.e., those assumptions that are *defended*. In an algorithm for the complete semantics we can track an additional set AU of assumptions that are attacked by undefeated. The algorithm then avoids preserving assumption sets that do not include undefeated assumptions that are not attacked by an undefeated assumption set.

Instantiating Our DP Algorithms. D-FLAT is a problem solving framework based on the DP paradigm that was specifically developed to provide means for declarative specification of algorithms operating on tree-decompositions of given problem instances. The framework allows prototyping an algorithm to solve a given problem by means of the ASP language.

We utilize D-FLAT to instantiate our algorithms for admissible, complete, and stable assumption sets, and associated reasoning tasks, in the ASP language. In the D-FLAT workflow, one can delegate the burden of computing a tree decomposition of the problem instance, and of combining partial solutions to D-FLAT itself. In this workflow, one specifies how partial solutions look like (for stable semantics, our Algorithm 2), and how they can be validly combined, also referred to as extended in D-FLAT terms. D-FLAT then takes care of the storage and actual combination of partial solutions. More concretely, at each node of the tree decomposition, D-FLAT performs a call to an ASP solver, and computes a partial solution. Finally, D-FLAT combines partial solutions by following external pointers, which intuitively specify which partial solutions can be appropriately combined into a complete solution of the problem instance.

5   Experiments

In this section, we present an empirical evaluation of our prototype implementation using D-FLAT. The encodings, instances, and an instance generator used in our evaluation are available with the online material.

Our prototype supports enumeration and counting of σ-assumption sets, for $\sigma \in \{adm, com, stb\}$, and checking skeptical and credulous acceptance for these semantics. Due to a potential high number of assumption sets, we considered counting admissible, complete, and stable assumption sets in two modes, similar to previous works [18,48]. First, counting all σ-assumption sets and second counting all σ-assumption sets with a given atom being derivable.

We observed that previous random generation methods for ABA instances often result in instances with high tree-width. To explore the potential of our tree decomposition-based approach, we generated ABA frameworks exhibiting a (controlled) low tree-width. For general undirected graphs, $k \times n$ grids (with vertices connected only to vertical and horizontal neighbours) have a controlled tree-width of $min(k, n)$. We adapted this behavior, by constructing $k \times n$ grids of $k \cdot n$ atoms. A third of these are randomly and uniformly chosen as assumptions. For each non-assumption atom in the grid, this atom is used as a head in a predefined number rph (rules per head) of rules. The rph number is randomly picked in a restricted range (0–3). The number of body elements for each rule is picked randomly between 0 and the number of cross neighbours of an atom. The selected amount of body elements are then randomly picked from the cross neighbourhood. This process is repeated an rph number of times, and during the first iteration only assumptions are allowed as body elements. Contraries are generated based on the flip of a coin from the two steps cross neighbourhood of an assumption in the grid. While the contraries might lead to a higher tree-width, we observed that the resulting tree-width is sufficiently bounded. A randomly chosen query atom is generated for each instance (uniform probability).

Our experiments were conducted on a Linux machine with 64-bit architecture, powered by an Intel i5 CPU with 8 cores and 8 GB of memory. We imposed a timeout limit of 600 s per run, and a memory limit of 8192 MB.

We compared our approach against the current state-of-the-art ASP-based approach [48,49] using Clingo [42] (version 5.4.1) as the ASP solver. Table 1 shows an overview of the results, computed over a total of 81 instances generated by four instances for each $k \in \{2,3,5\}$ and $n \in \{10, 20, 100, 200, 400, 500, 700\}$, excluding 3 instances that resulted in errors for D-FLAT.

The results indicate that for solving the counting tasks, the semantics plays a major role: our prototype had fewer timeouts than when using clingo when counting admissible assumption sets (the case with query denoted by appending "-q"). For stable semantics, both approaches are somewhat on-par with Clingo having an edge over the D-FLAT based approach. For complete semantics, Clingo outperforms the D-FLAT approach.

We hypothesize that the number of solutions (assumption sets) plays a major role, together with the fact that the D-FLAT encoding of stable semantics is simpler, in explaining the runtime. There are more admissible and complete assumption sets than for stable semantics, and in particular, the number of admissible assumption sets might be high.

6 Discussions

In this work we looked at complex computational tasks arising in assumption-based argumentation, and showed that many such reasoning tasks are fixed-parameter tractable w.r.t. the parameter tree-width, of a given graph representation of ABA frameworks. We showed these results by using monadic second order logic (MSO) and Courcelle's theorem. We developed DP algorithms for reasoning in ABA and implemented these in the D-FLAT framework, allowing for declarative specification of such algorithms.

Table 1. Median running time and timeouts per task (in seconds)

Task	Clingo		D-FLAT	
	Median	Timeouts	Median	Timeouts
count-adm	600.0	55	287.179	29
count-co	0.039	16	254.624	30
count-st	0.034	0	5.97	0
count-adm-q	600.0	46	98.24	27
count-co-q	0.039	11	98.39	28
count-st-q	0.034	0	5.30	2

Taken together, our MSO and D-FLAT encodings can be useful for the extension of our work to other structured argumentation formalisms: the MSO encodings suggest wide applicability of FPT results, and our D-FLAT encodings have the potential for direct adaptations to related computational problems arising in structured argumentation, e.g., for the ASPIC$^+$ formalism [51].

An interesting direction for future work is to utilize recent findings [36, 47] of developing theoretical upper and lower runtime bounds by encoding problems in quantified Boolean logic, instead of using MSO, under certain constraints. These allow for showing more tight bounds in terms of running time (e..g, include also lower bounds). Moreover, decomposition-guided reductions were recently shown to be viable for problems in abstract and logic-based argumentation [34]. These reductions are guided by tree-decompositions and result in (quantified) Boolean formulas which linearly preserve tree-width. In contrast to these works, our approach uses D-FLAT, enabling ASP encodings of the DP algorithms. Our theoretical result (Theorem 2) complements existing results for abstract argumentation [27–31, 34, 47] and logic-based argumentation [34].

Performance of our prototype relies on the performance of D-FLAT. Recent works [23, 37] show that one can specify DP algorithms using database management systems (DBMS), which give another interesting route for extending our work with a different declarative framework for specifications of DP algorithms. Developing systems for ABA based on DP algorithms using DBMS and decomposition-guided reductions to quantified Boolean logic appear as a natural next step for further evaluating strengths of these approaches, also comparing them to D-FLAT.

Our empirical results indicate strength of our approach for complex counting tasks. We believe this could also be interesting for computationally intensive tasks in probabilistic argumentation [45], where counting or weighted summation problems arise naturally. Investigating possibilities for applying our approach to probabilistic argumentation appears to be a natural avenue for future work.

Acknowledgements. This work was supported by the Austrian Science Fund (FWF) P35632.

References

1. Abseher, M., Bliem, B., Charwat, G., Dusberger, F., Hecher, M., Woltran, S.: The D-FLAT system for dynamic programming on tree decompositions. In: Fermé, E., Leite, J. (eds.) JELIA 2014. LNCS (LNAI), vol. 8761, pp. 558–572. Springer, Cham (2014). https://doi.org/10.1007/978-3-319-11558-0_39
2. Abseher, M., Bliem, B., Hecher, M., Moldovan, M., Woltran, S.: Dynamic programming on tree decompositions with D-FLAT. Künstliche Intell. **32**(2–3), 191–192 (2018)
3. Atkinson, K., et al.: Towards artificial argumentation. AI Mag. **38**(3), 25–36 (2017)
4. Baroni, P., Gabbay, D., Giacomin, M., van der Torre, L. (eds.): Handbook of Formal Argumentation. College Publications (2018)
5. Besnard, P., et al.: Introduction to structured argumentation. Argument Comput. **5**(1), 1–4 (2014)

6. Besnard, P., Hunter, A.: Elements of Argumentation. MIT Press, Cambridge (2008)
7. Besnard, P., Hunter, A.: A review of argumentation based on deductive arguments. In: Baroni, P., Gabbay, D., Giacomin, M., van der Torre, L. (eds.) Handbook of Formal Argumentation, chap. 9, pp. 437–484. College Publications (2018)
8. Bistarelli, S., Kotthoff, L., Santini, F., Taticchi, C.: Summary report for the third international competition on computational models of argumentation. AI Mag. **42**(3), 70–73 (2021)
9. Bliem, B., Charwat, G., Hecher, M., Woltran, S.: D-FLAT^2: Subset minimization in dynamic programming on tree decompositions made easy. Fundam. Informaticae **147**(1), 27–61 (2016)
10. Bodlaender, H.L.: A tourist guide through treewidth. Acta Cybern. **11**(1–2), 1–21 (1993)
11. Bodlaender, H.L., Koster, A.M.C.A.: Combinatorial optimization on graphs of bounded treewidth. Comput. J. **51**(3), 255–269 (2007)
12. Bondarenko, A., Dung, P.M., Kowalski, R.A., Toni, F.: An abstract, argumentation-theoretic approach to default reasoning. Artif. Intell. **93**, 63–101 (1997)
13. Brewka, G., Eiter, T., Truszczynski, M.: Answer set programming at a glance. Commun. ACM **54**(12), 92–103 (2011)
14. Caminada, M., Amgoud, L.: On the evaluation of argumentation formalisms. Artif. Intell. **171**(5–6), 286–310 (2007)
15. Cerutti, F., Gaggl, S.A., Thimm, M., Wallner, J.P.: Foundations of implementations for formal argumentation. In: Baroni, P., Gabbay, D., Giacomin, M., van der Torre, L. (eds.) Handbook of Formal Argumentation, chap. 15, pp. 688–767. College Publications (2018)
16. Charwat, G., Dvořák, W., Gaggl, S.A., Wallner, J.P., Woltran, S.: Methods for solving reasoning problems in abstract argumentation - a survey. Artif. Intell. **220**, 28–63 (2015)
17. Courcelle, B.: Graph rewriting: an algebraic and logic approach. In: van Leeuwen, J. (ed.) Handbook of Theoretical Computer Science, Volume B: Formal Models and Semantics, pp. 193–242. Elsevier and MIT Press (1990)
18. Craven, R., Toni, F.: Argument graphs and assumption-based argumentation. Artif. Intell. **233**, 1–59 (2016)
19. Craven, R., Toni, F., Cadar, C., Hadad, A., Williams, M.: Efficient argumentation for medical decision-making. In: Brewka, G., Eiter, T., McIlraith, S.A. (eds.) Proceedings of the KR, pp. 598–602. AAAI Press (2012)
20. Čyras, K., Fan, X., Schulz, C., Toni, F.: Assumption-based argumentation: disputes, explanations, preferences. In: Baroni, P., Gabbay, D., Giacomin, M., van der Torre, L. (eds.) Handbook of Formal Argumentation, chap. 7, pp. 365–408. College Publications (2018)
21. Cyras, K., Heinrich, Q., Toni, F.: Computational complexity of flat and generic assumption-based argumentation, with and without probabilities. Artif. Intell. **293**, 103449 (2021)
22. Cyras, K., Oliveira, T., Karamlou, A., Toni, F.: Assumption-based argumentation with preferences and goals for patient-centric reasoning with interacting clinical guidelines. Argument Comput. **12**(2), 149–189 (2021)
23. Dewoprabowo, R., Fichte, J.K., Gorczyca, P.J., Hecher, M.: A practical account into counting Dung's extensions by dynamic programming. In: Gottlob, G., Inclezan, D., Maratea, M. (eds.) LPNMR 2022. LNCS, vol. 13416, pp. 387–400. Springer, Cham (2022). https://doi.org/10.1007/978-3-031-15707-3_30

24. Dimopoulos, Y., Nebel, B., Toni, F.: On the computational complexity of assumption-based argumentation for default reasoning. Artif. Intell. **141**(1/2), 57–78 (2002)
25. Downey, R.G., Fellows, M.R.: Parameterized Complexity. Monographs in Computer Science. Springer, New York (1999)
26. Dung, P.M.: On the acceptability of arguments and its fundamental role in non-monotonic reasoning, logic programming and n-person games. Artif. Intell. **77**(2), 321–358 (1995)
27. Dunne, P.E.: Computational properties of argument systems satisfying graph-theoretic constraints. Artif. Intell. **171**(10–15), 701–729 (2007)
28. Dvořák, W., Hecher, M., König, M., Schidler, A., Szeider, S., Woltran, S.: Tractable abstract argumentation via backdoor-treewidth. In: Proceedings of the AAAI, pp. 5608–5615. AAAI Press (2022)
29. Dvořák, W., Morak, M., Nopp, C., Woltran, S.: dynPARTIX - a dynamic programming reasoner for abstract argumentation. In: Tompits, H., et al. (eds.) INAP/WLP -2011. LNCS (LNAI), vol. 7773, pp. 259–268. Springer, Heidelberg (2013). https://doi.org/10.1007/978-3-642-41524-1_14
30. Dvořák, W., Pichler, R., Woltran, S.: Towards fixed-parameter tractable algorithms for abstract argumentation. Artif. Intell. **186**, 1–37 (2012)
31. Dvořák, W., Szeider, S., Woltran, S.: Abstract argumentation via monadic second order logic. In: Hüllermeier, E., Link, S., Fober, T., Seeger, B. (eds.) SUM 2012. LNCS (LNAI), vol. 7520, pp. 85–98. Springer, Heidelberg (2012). https://doi.org/10.1007/978-3-642-33362-0_7
32. Dvořák, W., Dunne, P.E.: Computational problems in formal argumentation and their complexity. In: Baroni, P., Gabbay, D., Giacomin, M., van der Torre, L. (eds.) Handbook of Formal Argumentation, chap. 14. College Publications (2018)
33. Fan, X., Toni, F., Mocanu, A., Williams, M.: Dialogical two-agent decision making with assumption-based argumentation. In: Bazzan, A.L.C., Huhns, M.N., Lomuscio, A., Scerri, P. (eds.) Proceedings of the AAMAS, pp. 533–540. IFAAMAS/ACM (2014)
34. Fichte, J.K., Hecher, M., Mahmood, Y., Meier, A.: Decomposition-guided reductions for argumentation and treewidth. In: Zhou, Z. (ed.) Proceedings of the IJCAI, pp. 1880–1886. ijcai.org (2021)
35. Fichte, J.K., Hecher, M., Morak, M., Woltran, S.: Answer set solving with bounded treewidth revisited. In: Balduccini, M., Janhunen, T. (eds.) LPNMR 2017. LNCS (LNAI), vol. 10377, pp. 132–145. Springer, Cham (2017). https://doi.org/10.1007/978-3-319-61660-5_13
36. Fichte, J.K., Hecher, M., Pfandler, A.: Lower bounds for QBFs of bounded treewidth. In: Hermanns, H., Zhang, L., Kobayashi, N., Miller, D. (eds.) Proceedings of the LICS, pp. 410–424. ACM (2020)
37. Fichte, J.K., Hecher, M., Thier, P., Woltran, S.: Exploiting database management systems and treewidth for counting. Theory Pract. Log. Program. **22**(1), 128–157 (2022)
38. Gabbay, D., Giacomin, M., Simari, G.R., Thimm, M. (eds.): Handbook of Formal Argumentation, vol. 2. College Publications (2021)
39. Gaggl, S.A., Linsbichler, T., Maratea, M., Woltran, S.: Summary report of the second international competition on computational models of argumentation. AI Mag. **39**(4), 77–79 (2018)
40. García, A.J., Simari, G.R.: Defeasible logic programming: an argumentative approach. Theory Pract. Log. Program. **4**(1–2), 95–138 (2004)

41. García, A.J., Simari, G.R.: Argumentation based on logic programming. In: Baroni, P., Gabbay, D., Giacomin, M., van der Torre, L. (eds.) Handbook of Formal Argumentation, chap. 8, pp. 409–435. College Publications (2018)
42. Gebser, M., Kaminski, R., Kaufmann, B., Schaub, T.: Multi-shot ASP solving with clingo. Theory Pract. Log. Program. **19**(1), 27–82 (2019)
43. Gelfond, M., Lifschitz, V.: The stable model semantics for logic programming. In: Kowalski, R.A., Bowen, K.A. (eds.) Proceedings of the ICLP, pp. 1070–1080. MIT Press (1988)
44. Gottlob, G., Pichler, R., Wei, F.: Bounded treewidth as a key to tractability of knowledge representation and reasoning. Artif. Intell. **174**(1), 105–132 (2010)
45. Hunter, A., Polberg, S., Potyka, N., Rienstra, T., Thimm, M.: Probabilistic argumentation: a survey. In: Gabbay, D., Giacomin, M., Simari, G.R., Thimm, M. (eds.) Handbook of Formal Argumentation, vol. 2, chap. 7. College Publications (2021)
46. Lagniez, J., Lonca, E., Mailly, J., Rossit, J.: Introducing the fourth international competition on computational models of argumentation. In: Gaggl, S.A., Thimm, M., Vallati, M. (eds.) Proceedings of the SAFA. CEUR Workshop Proceedings, vol. 2672, pp. 80–85. CEUR-WS.org (2020)
47. Lampis, M., Mengel, S., Mitsou, V.: QBF as an alternative to Courcelle's theorem. In: Beyersdorff, O., Wintersteiger, C.M. (eds.) SAT 2018. LNCS, vol. 10929, pp. 235–252. Springer, Cham (2018). https://doi.org/10.1007/978-3-319-94144-8_15
48. Lehtonen, T., Wallner, J.P., Järvisalo, M.: Declarative algorithms and complexity results for assumption-based argumentation. J. Artif. Intell. Res. **71**, 265–318 (2021)
49. Lehtonen, T., Wallner, J.P., Järvisalo, M.: An answer set programming approach to argumentative reasoning in the ASPIC+ framework. In: Calvanese, D., Erdem, E., Thielscher, M. (eds.) Proceedings of the KR, pp. 636–646 (2020)
50. Modgil, S., Prakken, H.: A general account of argumentation with preferences. Artif. Intell. **195**, 361–397 (2013)
51. Modgil, S., Prakken, H.: Abstract rule-based argumentation. In: Baroni, P., Gabbay, D., Giacomin, M., van der Torre, L. (eds.) Handbook of Formal Argumentation, chap. 6, pp. 287–364. College Publications (2018)
52. Niemelä, I.: Logic programs with stable model semantics as a constraint programming paradigm. Ann. Math. Artif. Intell. **25**(3–4), 241–273 (1999)
53. Thimm, M., Villata, S.: The first international competition on computational models of argumentation: results and analysis. Artif. Intell. **252**, 267–294 (2017)

A Principle-Based Analysis of Bipolar Argumentation Semantics

Liuwen Yu[1](✉)(iD), Caren Al Anaissy[2](✉)(iD), Srdjan Vesic[3](✉)(iD), Xu Li[1](iD),
and Leendert van der Torre[1](iD)

[1] University of Luxembourg, Esch-sur-Alzette, Luxembourg
{liuwen.yu,xu.li,leendert.torre}@uni.lu
[2] CRIL Université d'Artois & CNRS, Lens, France
alanaissy@cril.fr
[3] CRIL CNRS Univ. Artois, Lens, France
vesic@cril.fr

Abstract. In this paper, we introduce and study seven types of semantics for bipolar argumentation frameworks, each extending Dung's interpretation of attack with a distinct interpretation of support. First, we introduce three types of defence-based semantics by adapting the notions of defence. Second, we examine two types of selection-based semantics that select extensions by counting the number of supports. Third, we analyse two types of traditional reduction-based semantics under deductive and necessary interpretations of support. We provide full analysis of twenty-eight bipolar argumentation semantics and ten principles.

Keywords: Bipolar argumentation semantics · Support · Principle-based approach · Knowledge representation and reasoning

1 Introduction

In this paper, we consider so-called bipolar argumentation frameworks [13–15] containing not only attacks but also supports among arguments. While there is general agreement in the formal argumentation literature on how to interpret attack, even when different kinds of semantics have been defined, there is much less consensus on how to interpret support [18]. There exist very few results and studies about the role of support in abstract argumentation. Consequently, the principle-based approach is used to bring structure to the field [16,42]. In this paper, we address the following research questions: In which ways can support affect attack, defence and argumentation semantics? Which principles can be introduced to distinguish between, and characterise, these semantics?

There exist different approaches to extending Dung's abstract theory by taking into consideration the support relation. The relation between support and attack has been studied extensively in reduction-based approaches, in the sense that deductive and necessary interpretations of support give rise to various notions of indirect attack [16], thus, they typically give opposite results. Deductive support [8] captures the intuition that if

---

L. Yu and C. Al Anaissy—Contributed equally to this work.

S. Gaggl et al. (Eds.): JELIA 2023, LNAI 14281, pp. 209–224, 2023.
https://doi.org/10.1007/978-3-031-43619-2_15

a supports b, then the acceptance of a implies the acceptance of b. This intuition is characterised by the so-called closure principle [16]. Necessary support [29] captures the intuition that if a supports b, then the acceptance of a is necessary to obtain the acceptance of b, or equivalently, the acceptance of b implies the acceptance of a. It has been characterised by the inverse closure principle [33]. Another approach to handling support is the evidence-based approach [31] where the notion of evidential support is introduced. An argument cannot stand unless it is supported by evidential support. Support can also be seen as an inference relation between the premises and the conclusion of the argument itself [35]. Moreover, in selection-based approaches [23], support is used only to select some of the extensions provided in Dung's semantics, and thus does not change the definition of attack, or defence.

Despite the relevance and significance of all the mentioned approaches, we think that there is still the need to explore other approaches that have not been yet considered for bipolar argumentation frameworks. The aim of our research is not to replace other approaches but rather to point to the existence of other interesting ones that can be applied depending on the chosen application. Note that our approach is novel in its methodology. On one hand, reduction-based approaches can be seen as a kind of pre-processing step for Dung's theory of abstract argumentation (i.e. adding the complex attacks and then applying Dung's semantics). On the other hand, selection-based approaches can be seen as a kind of post-processing step (i.e. applying Dung's semantics and then applying the approach to select some of the extensions). Differently from those two groups of approaches, our approach (i.e. the defence-based approach) does not affect the concept of attack and conflict-freeness, but rather changes the definition of defence.

Most of the principles we introduce and use for analysing bipolar argumentation are in the same spirit as the principles used in the principle-based analysis of Dung's semantics [40]. For example, the robustness of argumentation semantics when adding or removing attacks plays a central role [39]. In this paper, we consider robustness when adding or removing support relations. We also introduce some principles specifically defined for support, such as to which extent an argument is accepted while receiving support from others.

The layout of this paper is as follows. We first introduce three defence-based semantics, then two selection-based ones, and we study two traditional reduction-based ones. Then, we introduce ten principles, and we analyse which properties are satisfied by which semantics, before concluding and introducing the ideas for future work.

2   Bipolar Argumentation Framework

Bipolar argumentation frameworks extend the argumentation frameworks introduced by Dung (1995) with a binary support relation among the arguments.

Definition 1 (Bipolar Argumentation Framework [15]**).** *A bipolar argumentation framework (BAF) is a triple $\langle Ar, att, sup \rangle$ where Ar is a finite set called arguments, and $att, sup \subseteq Ar \times Ar$ are binary relations over Ar called attack and support respectively.*

Figure 1 illustrates three BAFs, where attack relations are depicted by solid arrows, and support relations are depicted by dashed arrows. Given a, b in Ar, $(a, b) \in att$ standing for a attacks b, and $(a, b) \in sup$ standing for a supports b, the definitions of conflict-freeness and defence provided by Dung are called conflict-free$_0$ and defended$_0$.

Definition 2 (Conflict-free$_0$ and Defended$_0$ [21]). *Let $\mathcal{F} = \langle Ar, att, sup \rangle$ be a BAF. A set of arguments $E \subseteq Ar$ is conflict-free$_0$, written as $cf_0(\mathcal{F}, E)$, iff there are no arguments a and b in E such that a attacks b. The set of arguments defended$_0$ by E, written as $d_0(\mathcal{F}, E)$, is the set of a arguments such that for every argument b attacking a, there is an argument c in E attacking b.*

2.1   Defence-Based Semantics

We first define three new types of defence-based semantics, which are based on conflict-free$_0$ and the new definitions of defended$_1$, defended$_2$ and defended$_3$. To have a generic definition of defence-based semantics (Definition 5), we also define conflict-free$_1$, confli-ct-free$_2$, and conflict-free$_3$, for each of the new types of semantics. The three notions of defended have stronger requirements than defended$_0$. Defended$_1$ requires that the argument defending$_0$ another argument also supports it. Defended$_2$ requires that a defender is supported. Moreover, defended$_3$ requires not only that the attackers are attacked, but also that all supporters of the attackers are attacked as well.

Definition 3 (Conflict-free$_{1-3}$ and Defended$_{1-3}$). *Let $\mathcal{F} = \langle Ar, att, sup \rangle$ be a BAF. We use the same definition as Dung for conflict-free, i.e. $cf_1 \equiv cf_2 \equiv cf_3 \equiv cf_0$. Moreover:*

- *the set of arguments defended$_1$ by E, written as $d_1(\mathcal{F}, E)$, is the set of arguments a in Ar such that for each argument b in Ar attacking a, there exists an argument c in E attacking b and supporting a (supporting-defence);*
- *the set of arguments defended$_2$ by E, written as $d_2(\mathcal{F}, E)$, is the set of arguments a in Ar such that for all arguments b in Ar attacking a, there exists an argument c in E attacking b, and there is an argument d in E supporting c (supported-defence);*
- *the set of arguments defended$_3$ by E, written as $d_3(\mathcal{F}, E)$, is the set of arguments a in Ar such that for all arguments b in Ar attacking a, there exists an argument c in E attacking b, and for all arguments d in Ar supporting b, there is an argument e in E attacking d (attacking-defence).*

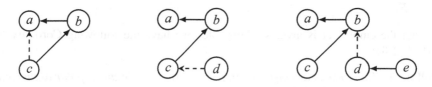

Fig. 1. Three BAFs illustrating the three new defence notions, for the lefthand figure, $d_1(\mathcal{F}, \{c\}) = \{a, c\}$; for the middle figure, $d_2(\mathcal{F}, \{c, d\}) = \{a, c, d\}$; for the righthand figure, $d_3(\mathcal{F}, \{c, e\}) = \{a, c, e\}$

Following Dung's approach, we say the characteristic function $d_i(\mathcal{F}, E)$ of a bipolar argumentation framework BAF is as follows:

- $d_i(\mathcal{F}, E) : 2^{Ar} \to 2^{Ar}$,
- $d_i(\mathcal{F}, E) = \{A \mid A \text{ is defended}_i \text{ by } E\}$, for $i \in \{0, 1, 2, 3\}$.

Definition 4 (Admissibility$_{0-3}$). *A set of arguments E in BAF $\mathcal{F} = \langle Ar, att, sup \rangle$, is said to be admissible$_i$ iff E is conflict-free$_i$ and $E \subseteq d_i(\mathcal{F}, E)$, for $i \in \{0, 1, 2, 3\}$.*

To define the complete (abbreviated as c), preferred (p), and stable (s) semantics of bipolar argumentation frameworks, the following definition is generic and can be used with any kind of conflict-freeness and defence.

Definition 5 (Semantics$_{0-3}$). *An extension-based semantics σ is a function that maps a BAF $\mathcal{F} = \langle Ar, att, sup \rangle$ onto a set of subsets of Ar, written as $\sigma_i^x(\mathcal{F})$, where $i \in \{0, 1, 2, 3\}$, $x \in \{c, p, s\}$ as follows:*

- $\sigma_i^c(\mathcal{F}) = \{E \subseteq Ar \mid cf_i(\mathcal{F}, E) \text{ and } d_i(\mathcal{F}, E) = E\}$;
- $\sigma_i^p(\mathcal{F}) = \{E \subseteq Ar \mid E \text{ is admissible}_i, \text{ and for all admissible}_i \text{ set } E', E \not\subseteq E'\}$;
- $\sigma_i^s(\mathcal{F}) = \{E \subseteq Ar \mid E \text{ is admissible}_i, \text{ and for all arguments } a \text{ not in } E, \text{ there is an argument } b \text{ in } E \text{ attacking } a\}$.

Most of the following propositions were introduced and proved for semantics$_0$ by Dung (1995). We prove that the above three new defence semantics are able to conserve the relations among complete$_i$, preferred$_i$, and grounded$_i$ for $i \in \{1, 2, 3\}$ and stable$_i$ for $i = 3$.

Lemma 1 (Fundamental Lemma). *Let E be an admissible$_i$ set of arguments, and A_1 and A_2 be two arguments which are defended$_i$ by E. Then for $i \in \{0, 1, 2, 3\}$, we have the following:*

- $E' = E \cup \{A_1\}$ *is admissible$_i$.*
- A_2 *is defended$_i$ by E'.*

The following theorem follows directly from the Fundamental Lemma.

Theorem 1. *Let $\mathcal{F}$ be a BAF, for $i \in \{0, 1, 2, 3\}$:*

- *The set of all admissible$_i$ sets of $\mathcal{F}$ forms a complete partial order with respect to set inclusion.*
- *For each admissible$_i$ set S of $\mathcal{F}$, there exists a preferred$_i$ extension E of $\mathcal{F}$ such that $S \subseteq E$.*

Note that the empty set is always admissible$_i$, we have the following Corollary for $i \in \{0, 1, 2, 3\}$:

Corollary 1. *There exists at least one preferred$_i$ extension in any bipolar argumentation framework for $i \in \{0, 1, 2, 3\}$.*

Proposition 1. *For $i \in \{0, 1, 2, 3\}$, we have the following: every complete$_i$ extension is also admissible$_i$; every preferred$_i$ extension is also complete$_i$; every stable$_i$ extension is also preferred$_i$.*

Proposition 2. *The characteristic function $d_i(\mathcal{F}, E)$ is monotonic (with respect to set inclusion) for $i \in \{0, 1, 2, 3\}$.*

Proposition 3. *Any BAF $\mathcal{F}$ induces a complete lattice which is the power set of all the arguments in $\mathcal{F}$. The characteristic function $d_i(\mathcal{F}, E)$, $i \in \{0, 1, 2, 3\}$, is monotonic (with respect to set inclusion). Therefore, from Knaster-Tarski theorem:*

- *The set of fixed points of $d_i(\mathcal{F}, E)$ is a complete lattice.*
- *$d_i(\mathcal{F}, E)$ has a unique least fixed point which can be obtained either by doing the intersection of all the fixed points of $d_i(\mathcal{F}, E)$, or by iteratively applying $d_i(\mathcal{F}, E)$, to the empty set.*

Definition 6 (Grounded$_{0-3}$ semantics). *The grounded$_i$ extension of a BAF $\mathcal{F} = \langle Ar, att, sup \rangle$, is the least fixed point of the characteristic function $d_i(\mathcal{F}, E)$, for $i \in \{0, 1, 2, 3\}$. We denote the grounded$_i$ semantics by $\sigma_i^g(\mathcal{F})$.*

Proposition 4. *The grounded$_i$ extension of $\mathcal{F}$ for $i \in \{0, 1, 2, 3\}$ is the minimal (with respect to set inclusion) complete extension of $\mathcal{F}$.*

We now give a real legal example to illustrate the intuition behind semantics$_1$. This example deals with a neighbor's quarrel over a row of conifers and was used to explain how the judge defends the claimant's interest [32].

Example 1 (Neighbours' quarrel over conifers). (...) The defendant argues that the conifers have been planted to reduce draught in his house, but this argument is absolutely unsound since most of the window posts are closed and the window that does open is located on a point higher than the tops of the conifers and has not been fitted with any anti-draught facilities. (...) Whereas the defendant has no considerable interest in these conifers, removal is of significant concern to the claimant since they block his view and take away the light. (...) (2981. Country court Enschede 6 October 1988)

The judge defends the standpoint that the claimant's interest in the removal of the conifers is greater than the defendant's interest in leaving them untouched. In the judge's preceding remarks, he mentions the defendant's argument: he does have a considerable interest in the conifers since they reduce draught in his house, thus he wants to keep the conifers. To support the standpoint of the claimant and against the defendant, the judge argues that the conifers block the view and take away the light, most of the window posts are closed and the opening window, which has no anti-draught facilities whatsoever, is located higher than the tops of the conifers.

As stated by Plug: "the judge's argumentation consists of a pro-argument and the refutation of a counter-argument which, in conjunction, form sufficient support for his standpoint." This type of defence inspires semantics$_1$.

We now give an example to illustrate the intuition behind semantics$_2$.

Example 2 (Twelve Angry Men play using Semantics$_2$). We consider an example extracted from the NoDE benchmark [10], which consists of annotated datasets extracted from a variety of sources (Debatepedia, Procon, Wikipedia web pages and the script of "Twelve Angry Men" play), where the aim of this benchmark is to analyse the support and attack relations between the arguments. We explore the Twelve Angry

Men dataset, this play is about a jury consisting of twelve men who must decide whether a young man is guilty or not for murdering his father. Consider the following arguments extracted from this dataset.

- a_1: I think we proved that the old man couldn't have heard the boy say, "I'm going to kill you" but supposing he really did hear it? This phrase: how many times has each of you used it? Probably hundreds. "If you do that once more, Junior, I'm going to murder you." "Come on, Rocky, kill him!" We say it every day. This doesn't mean that we're going to kill someone.
- e_1: The phrase was "I'm going to kill you" and the kid screamed it out at the top of his lungs. Anybody says a thing like that the way he said it-they mean it.
- g_1: Do you really think the boy would shout out a ["I'm going to kill you"] so the whole neighbourhood would hear it? I don't think so. He's much too bright for that.

The example above is shown in Fig. 2. In this example, argument g_1 attacks argument e_1 by raising some doubt about it. In the same manner, argument e_1 attacks argument a_1. We can see that the argument g_1 defends argument a_1 in Dung's sense. Just because argument g_1 is not attacked, argument a_1 is accepted.

In a legal case, any given argument must be evaluated based on the evidence provided to support it. In the absence of such evidence, the presence of at least a support, even if it is challenged, seems necessary. Therefore, one can ask themselves whether Dung's notion of defence seems enough, in this case, to say that the argument g_1 defends the argument a_1. Hence, for this kind of application, one might want to use a stronger notion of defence. An example of such a notion is our semantics$_2$, where an argument must be supported in order to be able to defend another argument. The idea behind this semantics is to provide a stronger and more restrictive defence notion than Dung's defence notion, by taking into account the support relation.

We consider now the following arguments extracted from the same dataset, to illustrate semantics$_2$.

- f: Maybe he didn't hear [the boy yelling "I'm going to kill you"]. I mean with the el noise.
- g: [The old man cannot be a liar, he must have heard the boy yelling "I'm going to kill you"].
- h: It stands to reason, [the old man can be a liar].
- i: Attention, maybe [the old man is a liar].

Contrary to the previous example, we see that argument i is supported by another one, hence it might be seen as having a better capacity to defend f. Formally, the set of arguments $\{h, i\}$ defends$_2$ the argument f.

Example 3 (Recruitment using semantics$_3$). Consider the following arguments.

- a: Alice should be hired as a professor.
- b: Alice lacks many essential qualifications to become a professor.
- c: Alice has few publications.
- d: Alice has recently got her PhD, she does not have enough teaching experience.

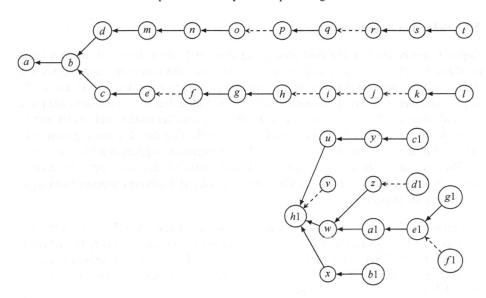

Fig. 2. The BAF illustrating the Twelve Angry Men dataset - Act 2.

- e: All of Alice's publications are in top conferences. When it comes to publications, quality beats quantity.
- f: Alice has taught 64 h of practical works during every year of her PhD, which is considered enough as teaching experience.
- g: Alice is good at team work, she also has an excellent academic carrier, these two enable her to become a professor.

This example can be represented with the BAF depicted on the left-hand side of Fig. 3. g fails to reinstate a because g does not attack b's supporters c and d. The set of arguments $\{e, g, f\}$ reinstates a because it attacks all the supporters of b. $\sigma_3^{c,g,p,s}(\mathcal{F}) = \{\{a, e, g, f\}\}$.

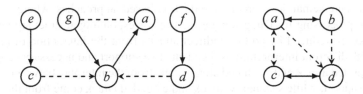

Fig. 3. A BAF illustrating recruitment case (on the left) and a BAF illustrating semantics$_4$ and semantics$_5$ (on the right)

2.2   Selection-Based Semantics

Support can be used in the post-processing step for Dung's theory of abstract argumentation [23]. Semantics$_4$ and semantics$_5$ are two selection-based approaches, i.e. they select extensions from semantics$_0$. Semantics$_4$ selects the extensions that have the largest number of internal supports, reflecting the idea that for a coalition, the more internal supports they have, the more cohesive they are. Semantics$_5$ selects the extensions that receive the most support from outside, reflecting the idea that the more support a coalition receives, the stronger it is. It thus interprets support as a kind of voting.

We say that argument b in E is internally supported if b receives support from arguments in E. Argument b in E is externally supported if b receives support from arguments that are outside E.

Definition 7 (Number of Internal and External Supports). *Let $\mathcal{F} = \langle Ar, att, sup \rangle$ be a BAF. For an extension $E \in \sigma_0^x$, the number of internal supports is written as NS_I, such that $NS_I(\mathcal{F}, E) =| \{(a,b) \in sup \mid a,b \in E\} |$, and the number of external supports is written as NS_O, such that $NS_O(\mathcal{F}, E) =| \{(a,b) \in sup \mid b \in E, a \in Ar \setminus E\} |$.*

Definition 8 (Semantics$_{4-5}$). *For each $\mathcal{F} = \langle Ar, att, sup \rangle$, for $x \in \{c, g, p, s\}$:*

- $\sigma_4^x(\mathcal{F}) = \arg\max_{E \in \sigma_0^x(\mathcal{F})} \{NS_I(\mathcal{F}, E)\}$*; and*
- $\sigma_5^x(\mathcal{F}) = \arg\max_{E \in \sigma_0^x(\mathcal{F})} \{NS_O(\mathcal{F}, E)\}$*.*

We use Example 4 to illustrate the difference between semantics$_4$ and semantics$_5$.

Example 4 (Semantics$_{4-5}$). Consider the bipolar argumentation framework on the right-hand side of Fig. 3, $\sigma_0^c(\mathcal{F}) = \{\{a\}, \{b\}, \{c\}, \{d\}, \{a,d\}, \{a,c\}, \{b,d\}, \{b,c\}\}$, $\sigma_0^{ps}(\mathcal{F}) = \{\{a,d\}, \{a,c\}, \{b,d\}, \{b,c\}\}$. Then, $\sigma_4^{cps}(\mathcal{F}) = \{\{a,c\}\}$, because $\{a,c\}$ has the biggest number of internal supports. Then, $\sigma_5^c(\mathcal{F}) = \{\{d\}, \{a,d\}\}$, and $\sigma_5^{ps}(\mathcal{F}) = \{\{a,d\}\}$, because they receive the biggest number of external supports.

2.3   Reduction-Based Semantics

Reduction-based approaches have been studied extensively in the literature [13–15]. Semantics$_6$ and semantics$_7$ are two reduction-based approaches where support is used as pre-processing for Dung semantics. The corresponding abstract argumentation frameworks are reduced by adding indirect attacks from the interaction of attack and support with different interpretations, i.e. deductive support and necessary support. So-called supported attack and mediated attack come from the interplay between attack and deductive support, while secondary attack and extended attack come from the interplay between attack and necessary support.

Definition 9 *(Four Indirect Attacks [15]).* *Let $\mathcal{F} = \langle Ar, att, sup \rangle$ be a BAF, and let arguments $a, b, c \in Ar$. There is:*

- *a supported attack from a to b in $\mathcal{F}$ iff there exists an argument c such that there is a sequence of supports from a to c and c attacks b, represented as $(a, b) \in att^{supp}$;*

- *a mediated attack from a to b in $\mathcal{F}$ iff there exists an argument c such that there is a sequence of supports from b to c and a attacks c, represented as $(a, b) \in att^{med}$;*
- *a super-mediated attack from a to b in $\mathcal{F}$ iff there exists an argument c such that there is a sequence of supports from b to c and a directly or supported-attacks c, represented as $(a, b) \in att^{med}_{att^{supp}}$;*
- *a secondary attack from a to b in $\mathcal{F}$ iff there exists an argument c such that there is a sequence of supports from c to b and a attacks c, so that $(a, b) \in att^{sec}$;*
- *an extended attack from a to b in $\mathcal{F}$ iff there exists an argument c such that there is a sequence of supports from c to a and c attacks b, so that $(a, b) \in att^{ext}$.*

Definition 10 (Semantics$_{6-7}$ [15]). *Let $\mathcal{F} = \langle Ar, att, sup \rangle$ be a BAF:*

- *let $att' = \{att^{supp}, att^{med}_{att^{supp}}\}$ be the collection of supported and super-mediated attacks in $\mathcal{F}$, and we have $RD(\mathcal{F}) = (Ar, att \cup \bigcup att')$, and $\sigma_6^x(\mathcal{F}) = \sigma_0^x(RD(\mathcal{F}))$;*
- *let $att' = \{att^{sec}, att^{ext}\}$ be the collection of secondary and extended attacks in $\mathcal{F}$, and we have $RN(\mathcal{F}) = (Ar, att \cup \bigcup att')$, and $\sigma_7^x(\mathcal{F}) = \sigma_0^x(RN(\mathcal{F}))$.*

We use Example 5 to illustrate semantics$_6$ and semantics$_7$.

Example 5 (Semantics$_{6-7}$). Consider the bipolar argumentation framework in Fig. 4.1. If the interpretation of support from a to d is deductive, a supported-attacks c, c mediated-attacks a. We have $RD(\mathcal{F}) = \langle Ar, att \cup \{(a, c), (c, a)\} \rangle$ as visualised in Fig. 4.2. $\sigma_6^g = \{\emptyset\}$, $\sigma_6^c = \{\{b\}, \{d\}, \{a, d\}, \{b, d\}, \{b, c\}\}$, and $\sigma_6^p = \sigma_6^s = \{\{a, d\}, \{b, d\}, \{b, c\}\}$. If the interpretation of support from a to d is necessary, then b secondary-attacks d, and d extended-attacks b. We have $RN(\mathcal{F}) = \langle Ar, att \cup \{\{b, d\}, \{d, b\}\} \rangle$ as visualised in Fig. 4.3. $\sigma_7^g = \{\emptyset\}$, $\sigma_7^c = \{\{a\}, \{c\}, \{a, d\}, \{a, c\}, \{b, c\}\}$, $\sigma_7^p = \sigma_7^s = \{\{a, d\}, \{a, c\}, \{b, c\}\}$.

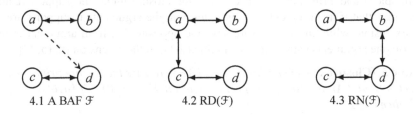

4.1 A BAF $\mathcal{F}$ 4.2 RD($\mathcal{F}$)   4.3 RN($\mathcal{F}$)

Fig. 4. Deductive and necessary interpretations give different corresponding AFs

3 Principles

In this section, we present ten principles. Due to the space limitation, we only present some interesting proofs, others can be found in additional supplement. The first principle concerns the support relation alone. It expresses transitivity of support.

Principle 1 (Transitivity). *A semantics σ_i^x for $BAFs$ satisfies the transitivity principle iff for all $BAFs$ $\mathcal{F} = \langle Ar, att, sup \rangle$, if a supports b, and b supports c, then $\sigma_i^x \langle Ar, att, sup \rangle = \sigma_i^x \langle Ar, att, sup \cup \{a, c\} \rangle$.*

Principle 2 states that supports can be used to select extensions.

Principle 2 (Extension Selection). *A semantics σ_i^x for $BAFs$ satisfies the extension selection principle iff for all BAFs where $\mathcal{F} = \langle Ar, att, sup \rangle$, that $\sigma_i^x (Ar, att, sup) \subseteq \sigma_i^x (Ar, att, \emptyset)$.*

Principle 3 and Principle 4 are robustness principles that distinguish between semantics$_4$ and semantics$_5$. The set of robustness principles was proposed by Rienstra et al. [38]. Here, we adapt their idea to bipolar argumentation in order to investigate the robustness of bipolar argumentation semantics when removing and adding support. Principle 3 states that if two arguments a and b are in an extension E such that a supports b, then E is still an extension after we remove the support from a to b.

Principle 3 (Internal Support Removal Robustness). *A semantics σ_i^x for BAFs satisfies the internal support removal robustness principle iff for all BAFs $\mathcal{F} = \langle Ar, att, sup \rangle$, for every extension $E \in \sigma_i^x(\mathcal{F})$, if arguments $a, b \in E$ and a supports b, then $E \in \sigma_i^x (Ar, att, sup \setminus \{(a, b)\})$.*

Principle 4 states that if argument a is not in an extension E and argument b is in this extension E such that a supports b, then E is still an extension after we remove the support from a to b.

Principle 4 (External Support Removal Robustness). *A semantics σ_i^x for BAFs satisfies the external support removal robustness principle iff for all BAFs $\mathcal{F} = \langle Ar, att, sup \rangle$, for every extension $E \in \sigma_i^x(\mathcal{F})$, if argument $a \in Ar \setminus E$ supports argument $b \in E$, then $E \in \sigma_i^x (Ar, att, sup \setminus \{(a, b)\})$.*

Principle 5 and Principle 6 both concern the closure under the support relation. Closure says that if an argument is in an extension, the arguments it supports are also in the extension, while inverse closure says the opposite, i.e. if an argument is in an extension, the arguments supporting it should also be in the extension [8, 15, 33].

Principle 5 (Closure). *A semantics σ_i^x for $BAFs$ satisfies the closure principle iff for all $BAFs$ $\mathcal{F} = \langle Ar, att, sup \rangle$, for every extension $E \in \sigma_i^x(\mathcal{F})$, if $(a, b) \in sup$ and $a \in E$, then $b \in E$.*

Principle 6 (Inverse Closure). *A semantics σ_i^x for $BAFs$ satisfies the inverse closure principle iff for all $BAFs$ $\mathcal{F} = \langle Ar, att, sup \rangle$, for every extension $E \in \sigma_i^x(\mathcal{F})$, if $(a, b) \in sup$ and $b \in E$, then $a \in E$.*

Principle 7 reflects the idea that if there is no support relation, the extensions under semantics σ_i^x are equivalent to the ones in Dung semantics.

Principle 7 (Extension Equivalence). *A semantics σ_i^x for $BAFs$ satisfies the extension equivalence principle iff for all $BAFs$ $\mathcal{F} = \langle Ar, att, sup \rangle$, $\sigma_i^x(Ar, att, \emptyset) = \sigma_0^x(Ar, att, \emptyset)$.*

Principle 8 and Principle 9 both state the positive effect of supports on the supported arguments. We first present the definition of the status of arguments as introduced by Baroni and Giacomin [3]. Extension-based semantics classifies arguments into three statuses, namely sceptically accepted, credulously accepted, and rejected.

Definition 11 *(Status of an Argument* [3]*). Let* $\mathcal{F} = \langle Ar, att, sup \rangle$ *be a BAF. If the set of extensions is empty, all the arguments are declared to be rejected. Otherwise, we say that an argument is: (1) sceptically accepted if it belongs to all extensions; (2) credulously accepted if it is not sceptically accepted and it belongs to at least one extension; (3) rejected if it does not belong to any extension.*

Gargouri et al. [23] write $\text{Status}(a, \mathcal{F}) = sk(resp. \, cr, rej)$, and they define the order $\leqslant$ on the set of statuses as expected: $sk > cr > rej$. We denote the set of sceptically accepted (resp. credulously accepted, rejected) arguments of a BAF by $Sk(Ar, att, sup)$ (resp. $Cr(Ar, att, sup)$, $Rej(Ar, att, sup)$. Principle 8 states that adding supports to arguments does not change their status into a lower order. Gargouri et al. [23] call this monotony, but we prefer to use a more specific name (i.e. monotony of status) to make it more precise and avoid ambiguity.

Principle 8 (Monotony of Status). *A semantics* σ_i^x *for* $BAFs$ *satisfies the monotony of status principle iff for all* $BAFs$ $\mathcal{F} = \langle Ar, att, sup \rangle$, *for every extension* $E \in \sigma_i^x(\mathcal{F})$, *for all* $a, b \in Ar$, *we have* $\text{Status}\,(a, \langle Ar, att, sup \rangle) \leqslant \text{Status}(a, \langle Ar, att, sup \cup \{(b, a)\} \rangle)$.

Principle 9 shows a skeptically accepted argument stays skeptically accepted when supports are added [25].

Principle 9 (Extension Growth). *A semantics* σ_i^x *for* $BAFs$ *satisfies the extension growth principle iff for all* $BAFs$ $\mathcal{F} = \langle Ar, att, sup \rangle$, *for every extension* $E \in \sigma_i^x(\mathcal{F})$, *it holds that* $Sk(Ar, att, sup) \subseteq Sk(Ar, att, sup \cup sup\prime)$.

Directionality is introduced by Baroni, Giacomin, and Guida [4]. It reflects the idea that we can decompose an argumentation framework into sub-frameworks so that the semantics can be defined locally. For the directionality principle, they first introduce the definition of an unattacked and unsupported set.

Definition 12 (Unattacked and unsupported arguments in BAF). *Given a BAF* $\mathcal{F} = \langle Ar, att, sup \rangle$, *a set* U *is unattacked and unsupported if and only if there exists no* $a \in Ar \backslash U$ *such that* a *attacks* U *or* a *supports* U. *The set unattacked and unsupported sets in* $\mathcal{F}$ *is denoted* $US(\mathcal{F})$ *(U for short).*

Principle 10 (BAF Directionality). *A semantics* σ_i^x *for* $BAFs$ *satisfies the BAF directionality principle iff for every* BAF $\mathcal{F} = \langle Ar, att, sup \rangle$, *for every* $U \in US(\mathcal{F})$, *it holds that* $\sigma_i^x(\mathcal{F}_{\downarrow U}) = \{E \cap U | E \in \sigma_i^x(\mathcal{F})\}$, *where* $\mathcal{F}_{\downarrow U} = (U, att \cap U \times U, sup \cap U \times U)$ *is a projection, and* $\sigma_i^x(\mathcal{F}_{\downarrow U})$ *are the extensions of the projection.*

Table 1 compares the semantics with respect to the principles. For the defence-based semantics, semantics$_1$ and semantics$_2$ can be classified by the same principles, and they can be distinguished from semantics$_3$ by Principles 3, 7 and 9. Semantics$_4$ and semantics$_5$ are selected from semantics$_0$, they can be distinguished by Principle 3 and Principle 4. However, Table 1 indicates it is not the case that if semantics$_0$ satisfies a principle implies semantics$_4$ and semantics$_5$ also satisfy it, e.g. the results regarding Principle 10. Reduction-based semantics can be distinguished from others by Principles 1, 5, 6 and 8. More precisely, they themselves can be further distinguished by Principle 5 and 6, and surprisingly, only semantics$_7$ satisfies Principle 8. One thing worth noting is that, in the literature, there are two other reductions based on necessary interpretation of support, i.e. one introduces only secondary attacks and the other introduces only extended attacks. Both of them do not satisfy directionality [42]. However, the result in this paper shows when the necessary reduction induces both secondary and extended attacks, semantics$_7$ (except for stable$_7$) satisfy directionality.

Table 1. Comparison of semantics and principles. We refer to the semantics as follows: complete ($\mathbb{C}$), grounded ($\mathbb{G}$), preferred ($\mathbb{P}$) and stable ($\mathbb{S}$). When a principle is never satisfied by a certain reduction for all semantics, we use the × symbol. P1 refers to Principle 1, and the same holds for the others.

	P1	P2	P3	P4	P5	P6	P7	P8	P9	P10
σ_0^x	CGPS	CGPS	CGPS	CGPS	×	×	CGPS	CGPS	CGPS	CGP
σ_1^x	×	×	×	CGPS	×	×	×	CGPS	CGPS	CGP
σ_2^x	×	×	×	CGPS	×	×	×	CGPS	CGPS	CGP
σ_3^x	×	×	CGPS	CGPS	×	×	CGPS	CGPS	×	CGP
σ_4^x	×	CGPS	×	CGPS	×	×	CGPS	CGPS	CGPS	×
σ_5^x	×	CGPS	CGPS	×	×	×	CGPS	CGPS	CGPS	×
σ_6^x	CGPS	×	CGPS	CGPS	CGPS	×	CGPS	CGPS	×	×
σ_7^x	CGPS	×	CGPS	CGPS	×	CGPS	CGPS	×	×	CGP

4   Related Work

The notion of support has drawn the attention of many scholars in argumentation theory, including the role of support in argumentation, whether attack and support should be treated as equals, the link between the abstract approaches and ASPIC+, and also higher-order abstract bipolar argumentation frameworks [11,24,36,37]. We now review and comment on the three approaches to define semantics studied in this paper. For the defence-based approach, we adapted the core notions in Dung's theory. There are other variants of semantics that adapt these notions, such as weak defence for weak admissibility semantics [7,20], but it is not related to the notion of support. For selection-based approach, semantics$_4$ and semantics$_5$ select extensions based on the number of internal (or external) supports received respectively. Such an approach has already been used in some previous work, and most of them are based on preference [2,25] or weight of arguments and relations [19,26]. More recently, Gargouri et al. proposed an approach to select the best extensions to BAFs by comparing the number of received supports with scores for each extension [23]. The reduction-based approach allows a BAF to be transformed into an argumentation graph that has been already discussed in the literature [11, 16, 30, 36]. There is a striking similarity at the abstract level between support in bipolar argumentation and preference-based argumentation, as both can be seen as reductions, as well as both can be used to select extensions [25]. For other approaches to bipolar argumentation semantics, Cayrol et al. proposed some properties of gradual semantics for bipolar argumentation [12], after which Evripidou and Toni provided a concrete definition of gradual semantics for bipolar argumentation [22] and introduced the quantitative argumentation debate (QuAD) framework [6]. Concerning aggregating bipolar argumentation frameworks, Chen considered how to cope with different opinions on support relations and analyse which properties can be preserved by desirable aggregation rules during aggregation of support relations [17]. Lauren et al. also considered aggregating bipolar assumption-based argumentation frameworks under the assumption that agents propose the same set of arguments, different sets of attacks and different interpretations of supporting arguments [28].

Baroni and Giacomin are the first to adopt a principle-based approach for classifying argumentation semantics [3], which was followed by other papers axiomatising abstract argumentation [40], preference-based argumentation [25] and agent argumentation [41]. There are papers that propose principles for bipolar ranking-based/gradual semantics [1], and their generalisations [5]. However, there is a lack of such work for extension-based semantics. Cayrol et al. compared bipolar argumentation semantics, they discussed the semantics based on deductive and necessary interpretations, and provided a few properties, e.g. closure, coherence and safe [16]. Inspired by this work, Yu and van der Torre analysed reduction-based semantics with more properties [42], however, they have only considered reduction-based semantics, without comparing them with others.

5   Summary and Future Work

In this paper, we gave an axiomatic analysis of bipolar argumentation semantics. We considered three approaches, namely defence-based, selection-based, and reduction-based approaches. In total, we introduced seven different types of semantics and studied them together with Dung semantics, which is the baseline and does not take into account supports. Semantics$_{1-3}$ are defence-based, i.e. they are defined by generalising the new notions of defence. Such an approach allows us to treat attack and support at the same level. Semantics$_4$ and semantics$_5$ are not only based on admissibility, but also borrow the idea from another field, i.e. social voting, to use the number of supports as a way of voting or selecting to derive extensions. Semantics$_6$ and semantics$_7$ are based on the notions of necessary and deductive support respectively. We evaluated those semantics against the set of ten principles. The results are shown in Table 1. Given the diversity of interpretations of support, such axiomatic analysis can provide us an overview and systematic assessment of different approaches. It can help us to choose a semantics for a given task or a particular application in function of the desirable properties. One can look at the table and see if there exists a semantics that satisfies the given desiderata.

An interesting question for future work is how to relate semantics defined by various approaches, e.g. can we define a new defence with attacks and supports indicating the deductive, necessary or evidential interpretation of support? We have semantics$_2$ stating that only a supported argument can defend others, which also reflects the idea of evidential support [30,34]. In this paper, we use dynamic properties, e.g. the robustness of semantics when adding and removing support. This could be further developed by analyzing labelling-based semantics of bipolar argumentation. The distinction between arguments labelled out and undecided makes the principles more precise. We also consider that the approaches to the dynamics of argumentation can be used as a source for principles [9,25]. Another possible direction is to study the relation between the principles, for example, to verify whether one principle implies another one, or if there is a set of principles such that no semantics satisfies all of them. Lastly, in the same spirit of this paper, another future work is the principle-based analysis of higher-order bipolar argumentation frameworks [27].

Acknowledgements. We extend our gratitude to all the anonymous reviewers for their insightful comments. Caren Al Anaissy and Srdjan Vesic benefited from the support of the project AGGREEY (ANR-22-CE23-0005) from the French National Research Agency (ANR). Xu Li and Leendert van der Torre are financially supported by Luxembourg's National Research Fund (FNR) through the project Deontic Logic for Epistemic Rights (OPEN O20/14776480). Leendert van der Torre is also financially supported by the (Horizon 2020 funded) CHIST-ERA grant CHIST-ERA19-XAI (G.A.INTER/CHIST/19/14589586). Liuwen Yu received funding from the European Union's Horizon 2020 research and innovation program under the Marie Skłodowska-Curie ITN EJD grant agreement. No 814177.

References

1. Amgoud, L., Ben-Naim, J.: Evaluation of arguments in weighted bipolar graphs. Int. J. Approximate Reasoning **99**, 39–55 (2018)
2. Amgoud, L., Vesic, S.: Rich preference-based argumentation frameworks. Int. J. Approximate Reasoning **55**(2), 585–606 (2014)
3. Baroni, P., Giacomin, M.: On principle-based evaluation of extension-based argumentation semantics. Artif. Intell. **171**(10–15), 675–700 (2007)
4. Baroni, P., Giacomin, M., Guida, G.: SCC-recursiveness: a general schema for argumentation semantics. Artif. Intell. **168**(1–2), 162–210 (2005)
5. Baroni, P., Rago, A., Toni, F.: How many properties do we need for gradual argumentation? In: Thirty-Second AAAI Conference on Artificial Intelligence (2018)
6. Baroni, P., Romano, M., Toni, F., Aurisicchio, M., Bertanza, G.: Automatic evaluation of design alternatives with quantitative argumentation. Argument Comput. **6**(1), 24–49 (2015)
7. Baumann, R., Brewka, G., Ulbricht, M.: Comparing weak admissibility semantics to their Dung-style counterparts-reduct, modularization, and strong equivalence in abstract argumentation. In: International Conference on Principles of Knowledge Representation and Reasoning, vol. 17, pp. 79–88 (2020)
8. Boella, G., Gabbay, D.M., van der Torre, L., Villata, S.: Support in abstract argumentation. In: Proceedings of the Third International Conference on Computational Models of Argument (COMMA 2010), pp. 40–51. Frontiers in Artificial Intelligence and Applications, IOS Press (2010)
9. Booth, R., Kaci, S., Rienstra, T., van der Torre, L.: A logical theory about dynamics in abstract argumentation. In: Liu, W., Subrahmanian, V.S., Wijsen, J. (eds.) SUM 2013. LNCS (LNAI), vol. 8078, pp. 148–161. Springer, Heidelberg (2013). https://doi.org/10.1007/978-3-642-40381-1_12

10. Cabrio, E., Villata, S.: Node: A benchmark of natural language arguments. In: Computational Models of Argument, pp. 449–450. IOS Press (2014)

11. Cayrol, C., Cohen, A., Lagasquie-Schiex, M.C.: Higher-order interactions (bipolar or not) in abstract argumentation: A state of the art. In: Gabbay, D., Giacomin, M., Simari, G.R., Thimm, M. (eds.) Handbook of Formal Argumentation, vol. 2, pp. 15–130. College Publications, Norcross (2021)

12. Cayrol, C., Lagasquie-Schiex, M.C.: Gradual valuation for bipolar argumentation frameworks. In: Godo, L. (ed.) ECSQARU 2005. LNCS (LNAI), vol. 3571, pp. 366–377. Springer, Heidelberg (2005). https://doi.org/10.1007/11518655_32

13. Cayrol, C., Lagasquie-Schiex, M.C.: On the acceptability of arguments in bipolar argumentation frameworks. In: Godo, L. (ed.) ECSQARU 2005. LNCS (LNAI), vol. 3571, pp. 378–389. Springer, Heidelberg (2005). https://doi.org/10.1007/11518655_33

14. Cayrol, C., Lagasquie-Schiex, M.C.: Bipolar abstract argumentation systems. In: Simari, G., Rahwan, I. (eds.) Argumentation in Artificial, pp. 65–84. Springer, Boston (2009). https://doi.org/10.1007/978-0-387-98197-0_4

15. Cayrol, C., Lagasquie-Schiex, M.C.: Bipolarity in argumentation graphs: towards a better understanding. Int. J. Approximate Reasoning 54(7), 876–899 (2013)

16. Cayrol, C., Lagasquie-Schiex, M.-C.: An axiomatic approach to support in argumentation. In: Black, E., Modgil, S., Oren, N. (eds.) TAFA 2015. LNCS (LNAI), vol. 9524, pp. 74–91. Springer, Cham (2015). https://doi.org/10.1007/978-3-319-28460-6_5

17. Chen, W.: Aggregation of support-relations of bipolar argumentation frameworks. In: Proceedings of the 19th International Conference on Autonomous Agents and MultiAgent Systems, pp. 1804–1806 (2020)

18. Cohen, A., Gottifredi, S., García, A.J., Simari, G.R.: A survey of different approaches to support in argumentation systems. Knowl. Eng. Rev. 29(5), 513–550 (2014)

19. Coste-Marquis, S., Konieczny, S., Marquis, P., Ouali, M.A.: Selecting extensions in weighted argumentation frameworks. COMMA 12, 342–349 (2012)

20. Dauphin, J., Rienstra, T., van der Torre, L.: New weak admissibility semantics for abstract argumentation. In: Baroni, P., Benzmüller, C., Wáng, Y.N. (eds.) CLAR 2021. LNCS (LNAI), vol. 13040, pp. 112–126. Springer, Cham (2021). https://doi.org/10.1007/978-3-030-89391-0_7

21. Dung, P.M.: On the acceptability of arguments and its fundamental role in nonmonotonic reasoning, logic programming, and n-person games. Artif. Intell. 77(2), 321–357 (1995)

22. Evripidou, V., Toni, F.: Quaestio-it.com: a social intelligent debating platform. J. Decis. Syst. 23(3), 333–349 (2014)

23. Gargouri, A., Konieczny, S., Marquis, P., Vesic, S.: On a notion of monotonic support for bipolar argumentation frameworks. In: 20th International Conference on Autonomous Agents and MultiAgent Systems (2020)

24. Gordon, T.F.: Towards requirements analysis for formal argumentation. In: Baroni, P., Gabbay, D., Giacomin, M., van der Torre, L. (eds.) Handbook of formal argumentation, vol. 1, pp. 145–156. College Publications, Norcross (2018)

25. Kaci, S., van der Torre, L., Vesic, S., Villata, S.: Preference in abstract argumentation. In: Gabbay, D., Giacomin, M., Simari, G.R., Thimm, M. (eds.) Handbook of Formal Argumentation, vol. 2, pp. 211–248. College Publications, Norcross (2021)

26. Konieczny, S., Marquis, P., Vesic, S.: On supported inference and extension selection in abstract argumentation frameworks. In: Destercke, S., Denoeux, T. (eds.) ECSQARU 2015. LNCS (LNAI), vol. 9161, pp. 49–59. Springer, Cham (2015). https://doi.org/10.1007/978-3-319-20807-7_5

27. Lagasquie-Schiex, M.C.: Handling support cycles and collective interactions in the logical encoding of higher-order bipolar argumentation frameworks. J. Log. Comput. 33(2), 289–318 (2023)

28. Lauren, S., Belardinelli, F., Toni, F.: Aggregating bipolar opinions. In: Proceedings of the 20th International Conference on Autonomous Agents and MultiAgent Systems, pp. 746–754 (2021)
29. Nouioua, F., Risch, V.: Bipolar argumentation frameworks with specialized supports. In: 2010 22nd IEEE International Conference on Tools with Artificial Intelligence, vol. 1, pp. 215–218. IEEE (2010)
30. Oren, N., Luck, M., Reed, C.: Moving between argumentation frameworks. In: Proceedings of the 2010 International Conference on Computational Models of Argument. IOS Press (2010)
31. Oren, N., Norman, T.J.: Semantics for evidence-based argumentation. In: Proceedings of the 2008 conference on Computational Models of Argument: Proceedings of COMMA 2008, pp. 276–284 (2008)
32. Plug, J.: Complex argumentation in judicial decisions. Analysing conflicting arguments. In: FAPR, pp. 464–479 (1996)
33. Polberg, S.: Intertranslatability of abstract argumentation frameworks. Technical report, Technical Report DBAI-TR-2017-104, Institute for Information Systems (2017)
34. Polberg, S., Oren, N.: Revisiting support in abstract argumentation systems. In: Computational Models of Argument - Proceedings of COMMA. Frontiers in Artificial Intelligence and Applications, vol. 266, pp. 369–376. IOS Press (2014)
35. Prakken, H.: An abstract framework for argumentation with structured arguments. Argument Comput. 1(2), 93–124 (2010)
36. Prakken, H.: On support relations in abstract argumentation as abstractions of inferential relations. In: ECAI 2014, pp. 735–740. IOS Press (2014)
37. Prakken, H.: Historical overview of formal argumentation. In: Baroni, P., Gabbay, D., Giacomin, M., van der Torre, L. (eds.) Handbook of formal argumentation, vol. 1, pp. 75–143. College Publications, Norcross (2018)
38. Rienstra, T., Sakama, C., van der Torre, L.: Persistence and monotony properties of argumentation semantics. In: Black, E., Modgil, S., Oren, N. (eds.) TAFA 2015. LNCS (LNAI), vol. 9524, pp. 211–225. Springer, Cham (2015). https://doi.org/10.1007/978-3-319-28460-6_13
39. Rienstra, T., Sakama, C., van der Torre, L., Liao, B.: A principle-based robustness analysis of admissibility-based argumentation semantics. Argument Comput. 11(3), 305–339 (2020)
40. van der Torre, L., Vesic, S.: The principle-based approach to abstract argumentation semantics. In: Baroni, P., Gabbay, D., Giacomin, M., van der Torre, L. (eds.) Handbook of Formal Argumentation, vol. 1, pp. 797–838. College Publications, Norcross (2018)
41. Yu, L., Chen, D., Qiao, L., Shen, Y., van der Torre, L.: A principle-based analysis of abstract agent argumentation semantics. In: Proceedings of the International Conference on Principles of Knowledge Representation and Reasoning, vol. 18, pp. 629–639 (2021)
42. Yu, L., van der Torre, L.: A principle-based approach to bipolar argumentation. In: 18th International Workshop on Non-monotinic Reasoning Notes, p. 227 (2020)

Answer Set Programming

Comparing Planning Domain Models Using Answer Set Programming

Lukáš Chrpa[1]([⊠]), Carmine Dodaro[2], Marco Maratea[2], Marco Mochi[3], and Mauro Vallati[4]

[1] Czech Technical University in Prague, Prague, Czechia
chrpaluk@cvut.cz
[2] University of Calabria, Arcavacata, Italy
{carmine.dodaro,marco.maratea}@unical.it
[3] University of Genova, Genova, Italy
marco.mochi@edu.unige.it
[4] University of Huddersfield, Huddersfield, UK
m.vallati@hud.ac.uk

Abstract. Automated planning is a prominent area of Artificial Intelligence, and an important component for intelligent autonomous agents. A critical aspect of domain-independent planning is the domain model, that encodes a formal representation of domain knowledge needed to reason upon a given problem. Despite the crucial role of domain models in automated planning, there is lack of tools supporting knowledge engineering process by comparing different versions of the models, in particular, determining and highlighting differences the models have.

In this paper, we build on the notion of *strong equivalence* of domain models and formalise a novel concept of *similarity* of domain models. To measure the similarity of two models, we introduce a directed graph representation of lifted domain models that allows to formulate the domain model similarity problem as a variant of the graph edit distance problem. We propose an Answer Set Programming approach to optimally solve the domain model similarity problem, that identifies the minimum number of modifications the models need to become strongly equivalent, and we demonstrate the capabilities of the approach on a range of benchmark models.

Keywords: Automated Planning · Answer Set Programming · Domain Model

1 Introduction

Automated planning is a research discipline that addresses the problem of generating a totally- or partially-ordered sequence of actions that transforms the environment from an initial state to a desired goal state. It has matured to such a degree that there exists a wide range of applications utilising planning, including UAV manoeuvring [21], space exploration [1], and train dispatching [7].

A critical aspect of domain-independent planning is the domain knowledge that must be fed into a planning engine that comes under the form of a domain model, a symbolic representation of the environment and actions, that has to be engineered prior its use [16]. The importance of good quality domain models in planning, and of

© The Author(s), under exclusive license to Springer Nature Switzerland AG 2023
S. Gaggl et al. (Eds.): JELIA 2023, LNAI 14281, pp. 227–242, 2023.
https://doi.org/10.1007/978-3-031-43619-2_16

the corresponding knowledge engineering process, has been well-argued [17,27,28]. However, there is a lack of approaches to support the knowledge engineering process. In particular, there is no "diff" tool that compares different versions of a domain model and highlights differences among them. Tools such as D-VAL [25] or a recent work of Coulter et al. [10] provide some limited support to compare domain models focusing on the state space they can generate, and the model reconciliation problem focuses on explaining why two models cannot create the same optimal plans [8].

To address the highlighted research gap, we propose a novel concept of domain model similarity and present a theoretical framework underlying the concept, which employs an extension of the notion of *strong equivalence* informally introduced by Shoeeb and McCluskey [24], which determines whether domain models are the same except naming. We propose a directed graph representation of lifted domain models and we show that domain models are strongly equivalent if and only if the graphs representing them are isomorphic. Then, we define *distance* between domain models as the minimum number of modifications that have to be made to both models to make them strongly equivalent. It corresponds to the notion of *edit distance* between two graphs (representing the domain models). The introduced theoretical framework gives us the notion of *similarity* by measuring the distance between domain models and enumerating the modifications that need to be done to make the models (strongly) equivalent. Then, we present an approach based on Answer Set Programming (ASP) [3,5,14,20] that allows to compare planning domain models to assess their similarity. This is not the first time that declarative programming, in particular ASP, is employed in this context, but considering either different problems in the planning domain (the already mentioned [25]), or not focused on planning [26]. Our solution relies on a directed graph representation of the lifted domain models, and is capable of providing optimally minimal sets of changes to transform one model into the other. Beside providing the first concrete approach to assess if two domain models are strongly equivalent, the proposed notion of similarity, and the ASP-based approach to measure it, have several practical implications: (i) it can be incorporated into a "diff" tool for highlighting differences between two versions of a domain model, to help knowledge engineers in understanding modifications; (ii) it can support the evaluation of tools for automated domain model acquisition (e.g., LOCM [11]) by comparing acquired domain models to the reference domain models; (iii) it can be exploited as an advanced plagiarism checker, where it can provide a "similarity" score to flag potential cases of plagiarism, and (iv) it can support the evaluation of models in competitions on domain modelling such as ICKEPS [9] and provide useful insights into how groups of experts differ in developing models.

We evaluate the approach on well-known benchmark domains from international competitions, of different size with regards to the number of models' predicates and operators. We present a fully declarative approach, which is able to compare a number of planning domains, except the largest, and an improved solution, that exploits a preprocessor via imperative programming that acts as a sort of "problem-aware pregrounder", which complements the declarative encoding. The related empirical evaluation shows that, by employing the improved solution, the comparison can be performed in less than a CPU-time second for all evaluated models, hence suggesting that it can be fruitfully exploited to support the knowledge engineering process of domain models in real time.

2 Background

In this section we present, in two separate subsections, needed preliminaries about automated planning and graph similarity, respectively.

Automated Planning. In the STRIPS representation, the environment is represented by *propositions*. *States* are defined as sets of these propositions (or *atoms*). An *action* is a quadruple $a = (name(a), pre(a), del(a), add(a))$, where $name(a)$ represents a unique action name, $pre(a)$, $del(a)$ and $add(a)$ are sets of atoms representing the *precondition* of a, the *delete* and *add effects* of a, respectively. We assume a is always *well defined*, i.e., $add(a) \neq \varnothing$ (as an action without any add effect would be useless). We say that an action a is *applicable* in a state s if and only if $pre(a) \subseteq s$. Application of a in s (if possible) results in a state $(s \setminus del(a)) \cup add(a)$.

In the lifted STRIPS representation, the environment is represented by first-order logic *predicates*. A *planning operator* $o = (name(o), pre(o), del(o), add(o))$ is specified such that $name(o) = op\_name(x_1, \dots, x_k)$ (op_name represents a unique operator name and $x_1, \dots x_k$ are variable symbols (parameters) appearing in the operator), $pre(o)$ is a set of predicates representing the operator's *preconditions*, $del(o)$ and $add(o)$ are sets of predicates representing the operator's *delete* and *add* effects, respectively. Again, we assume o is always *well defined*, i.e., $add(o) \neq \varnothing$. A *(lifted) domain model* $\mathcal{D} = (P, O)$ is specified via a set of predicates P and a set of operators O. A *problem instance* $\mathcal{P} = (Obj, I, G)$ for a lifted domain model $\mathcal{D}$ is specified via a set of objects Obj, the initial state I and a set of atoms representing the goal G. Atoms are obtained by grounding of the predicates from P, i.e., by substituting objects for predicates' variables. Actions are grounded instances of planning operators.

A *planning task* $(\mathcal{D}, \mathcal{P})$ consists of a domain model $\mathcal{D}$ and a problem instance $\mathcal{P}$. A *solution plan* for a planning task is a sequence of actions such that consecutive application of the actions in the plan (starting in the initial state) results in a state in which all the goal atoms are true. We say that predicates are *equal* if they have the same name and their parameters including their order are identical. We define a function $pars(\cdot)$ that returns the set of variable symbols of a predicate or an operator. We also define a function $arity(\cdot)$ that returns the number of variable symbols of a predicate or an operator. With regards to *substitution mappings* that map free variables into terms (variables or constants in our case), we use a specific notation in order to disambiguate with other types of mappings. In particular, for a substitution mapping χ and a predicate (or an operator) $p(x_1, \dots, x_n)$, $(p|\chi)$ refers to substituting $x_1, \dots, x_n$ for terms according to χ, i.e., $(p|\chi) \equiv p(\chi(x_1), \dots, \chi(x_n))$.

Graph Similarity. Comparing graphs, in terms of how similar they are, belongs under of the umbrella of *graph matching* [4]. For our purpose, we will consider (labelled) directed graphs with different types of edges. Let $\mathcal{G}_1 = (V_1, E_1^1, E_1^2, \dots, E_1^k)$ and $\mathcal{G}_2 = (V_2, E_2^1, E_2^2, \dots, E_2^k)$ be directed graphs with k different types of edges, and $\mathcal{L}_1$ and $\mathcal{L}_2$ be the sets of their edge labels. We say that $\mathcal{G}_1$ and $\mathcal{G}_2$ are *isomorphic* if and only if there exist bijective mappings $\xi : V_1 \to V_2$ and $\nu : \mathcal{L}_1 \to \mathcal{L}_2$ such that for each $1 \leqslant i \leqslant k : (x, l, y) \in E_1^i \Leftrightarrow (\xi(x), \nu(l), \xi(y)) \in E_2^i$. Note that for unlabelled directed graphs it is the case that $\mathcal{G}_1$ and $\mathcal{G}_2$ are *isomorphic* if and only if there exist a bijective mapping $\xi : V_1 \to V_2$ such that for each $1 \leqslant i \leqslant k : (x, y) \in E_1^i \Leftrightarrow (\xi(x), \xi(y)) \in E_2^i$.

Let $\mathcal{G}_1'$ and $\mathcal{G}_2'$ be subgraphs of $\mathcal{G}_1$ and $\mathcal{G}_2$, respectively. We say that $\mathcal{G}_1'$ and $\mathcal{G}_2'$ are *common isomorphic subgraphs* of $\mathcal{G}_1$ and $\mathcal{G}_2$ if and only if $\mathcal{G}_1'$ and $\mathcal{G}_2'$ are isomorphic.

Let *elem* denote the number of elements in a graph (with k different types of edges), i.e., for $\mathcal{G} = (V, E^1, \ldots, E^k)$, $elem(\mathcal{G}) = |V| + \sum_{i=1}^{k} |E^i|$. We say that $\mathcal{G}_1'$ and $\mathcal{G}_2'$ are *maximum common isomorphic subgraphs* of $\mathcal{G}_1$ and $\mathcal{G}_2$ if and only if (i) $\mathcal{G}_1'$ and $\mathcal{G}_2'$ are common isomorphic subgraphs of $\mathcal{G}_1$ and $\mathcal{G}_2$ and (ii) for every pair $\mathcal{G}_1''$ and $\mathcal{G}_2''$ being also common isomorphic subgraphs of $\mathcal{G}_1$ and $\mathcal{G}_2$ it is the case that $elem(\mathcal{G}_1') \geqslant elem(\mathcal{G}_1'')$ (and $elem(\mathcal{G}_2') \geqslant elem(\mathcal{G}_2'')$). Then, we define a function *dist* representing a *distance* between graphs $\mathcal{G}_1$ and $\mathcal{G}_2$ as $dist(\mathcal{G}_1, \mathcal{G}_2) = elem(\mathcal{G}_1) + elem(\mathcal{G}_2) - 2*elem(\mathcal{G}_1')$ with $\mathcal{G}_1'$ and $\mathcal{G}_2'$ being maximum common isomorphic subgraphs of $\mathcal{G}_1$ and $\mathcal{G}_2$. Note that our notion of distance is a variant of *Graph Edit Distance* [22] in which vertex and edge substitutions are not explicitly counted.

3 Strong Equivalence of Domain Models

Equivalence of domain models can be understood in a similar fashion as equivalence of grammars, i.e., two domain models are equivalent if a planning task specified in one model can be also specified in the other model and both models generate same plans for the corresponding planning tasks [24]. An alternative understanding of domain model equivalence, "functional equivalence", compares corresponding state-transition systems such that two domain models are (functionally) equivalent if and only if for corresponding planning tasks the sets of reachable states are equivalent [25]. In this paper, we focus on *strong equivalence* of domain models that has been informally defined in [24] as models being logically identical up to naming. It assumes that there exist bijective mappings between particular elements (e.g., atoms, action names).

To formally define *strong equivalence* for lifted domain models, we have to make sure that for each corresponding grounded instance of two strongly equivalent lifted domain models it is the case that those instances are strongly equivalent too. Whereas the (bijective) mapping between predicates needs to consider only naming and arity (without loss of generality we assume that free variables in each predicate are distinct), the (bijective) mapping between planning operators has to take into account ordering of their parameters (free variables). We formally define *strong equivalence* for two lifted domain models as follows.

Definition 1. *Let $\mathcal{D} = (P, O)$ and $\mathcal{D}' = (P', O')$ be lifted domain models. If there exist bijective mappings $\mathcal{P} : P \rightarrow P'$ and $\mathcal{O} : \{name(o) \mid o \in O\} \rightarrow \{name(o') \mid o' \in O'\}$ such that*

- *for each $p \in P$, $arity(p) = arity(\mathcal{P}(p))$*
- *for each $o \in O$, $arity(name(o)) = arity(\mathcal{O}(name(o)))$ and there exists $o' \in O'$ and a bijective substitution mapping $\chi^o : pars(o) \rightarrow pars(o')$, where*
  - *$name(o') = \mathcal{O}(name(o))$*
  - *$pre(o') = \{(\mathcal{P}(p)|\chi^o) \mid p \in pre(o)\}$*
  - *$del(o') = \{(\mathcal{P}(p)|\chi^o) \mid p \in del(o)\}$*
  - *$add(o') = \{(\mathcal{P}(p)|\chi^o) \mid p \in add(o)\}$*

*then $\mathcal{D}$ and $\mathcal{D}'$ are **strongly equivalent**.*

Next, we will construct a *Lifted Domain Model Graph* (LDMG) which is a labelled directed graph connecting operators with predicates in a given lifted domain model. LDMG has vertices standing for both predicates and operator names, and three types of edges referring to preconditions, delete, and add effects, respectively. Edge labels represent matchings between operators' and predicates' variables. To show that two domain models are strongly equivalent their respective LDMGs have to be isomorphic.

Definition 2. *Let $\mathcal{D} = (P, O)$ be a lifted domain model. We assume, without loss of generality, that all variable symbols defined in $\mathcal{D}$ are distinct. We say that $\mathcal{G} = (V, E_{pre}, E_{del}, E_{add})$ is a **Lifted Domain Model Graph (LDMG)** of $\mathcal{D}$, where $V = P \cup \{name(o) \mid o \in O\}$ is a set of vertices, $E_{pre} = \{(name(o), \Theta^o, p) \mid p \in (pre(o|\Theta^o)), o \in O, p \in P\}$, $E_{del} = \{(name(o), \Theta^o, p) \mid p \in (del(o|\Theta^o)), o \in O, p \in P\}$ and $E_{add} = \{(name(o), \Theta^o, p) \mid p \in ((add(o|\Theta^o)), o \in O, p \in P\}$ are sets of labelled directed edges, where Θ^o is the substitution mapping from $pars(o)$ to $\bigcup_{p \in P} pars(p)$ for each operator o.*

Theorem 1. *Let $\mathcal{D} = (P, O)$ and $\mathcal{D}' = (P', O')$ be lifted domain models. We assume, without loss of generality, that all variable symbols defined in both $\mathcal{D}$ and $\mathcal{D}'$ are distinct. Let $\mathcal{G} = (V, E_{pre}, E_{del}, E_{add})$ and $\mathcal{G}' = (V', E'_{pre}, E'_{del}, E'_{add})$ be LDMGs of $\mathcal{D}$ and $\mathcal{D}'$, respectively. $\mathcal{D}$ and $\mathcal{D}'$ are strongly equivalent if and only if $\mathcal{G}$ and $\mathcal{G}'$ are isomorphic with a bijective mapping $\xi : V \rightarrow V'$ such that for each $x \in V : arity(x) = arity(\xi(x))$.*

Proof. The "if" part: If $\mathcal{D}$ and $\mathcal{D}'$ are strongly equivalent, then there exist bijective mappings $\mathcal{P}$ and $\mathcal{O}$ between atoms and operator names of both domain models as in Definition 1. We can combine $\mathcal{P}$ and $\mathcal{O}$ into ξ such that for each $f \in P : \xi(f) = \mathcal{P}(f)$ and for each $o \in O : \xi(name(o)) = \mathcal{O}(name(o))$. Hence, ξ is a bijective mapping from V to V'. Then, we can observe that for each $o \in O$ there exists $o' \in O'$ such that $\xi(name(o)) = name(o')$, $arity(\xi(name(o))) = arity(name(o'))$. There also exist substitution mappings χ^o for each $o \in O$ as in Definition 1 and $\Theta^o : pars(o) \rightarrow \bigcup_{p \in P} pars(p)$ and $\Theta^{o'} : pars(o') \rightarrow \bigcup_{p' \in P'} pars(p')$ for each $o \in O$ and $o' \in O'$ as in Definition 2. Now we can define a bijective substitution mapping $\nu : \bigcup_{o \in O} pars(o) \times \bigcup_{p \in P} pars(p) \rightarrow \bigcup_{o' \in O'} pars(o') \times \bigcup_{p' \in P'} pars(p')$ (since variable symbols are distinct) such that for all $o \in O$ and $x \in pars(o)$, $((x, (x|\Theta^o))|\nu) = ((x|\chi^o), ((x|\chi^o)|\Theta^{o'})$. Then, if for $o \in O$ and $p \in P$ it is the case that $p \in (pre(o|\Theta^o))$, then there exists $o' \in O'$ such that $(\xi(p)|\chi^o) \in (pre(o'|\Theta^{o'}))$. Hence, if $(name(o), \Theta^o, p) \in E_{pre}$, then $(\xi(name(o)), (\Theta^o|\nu), \xi(p)) \in E'_{pre}$. For E_{del} and E_{add}, it can be proven analogously.

The "only if" part: From Definition 2 and the fact that every operator is well defined, we can derive that $X = \{x \mid (x, y) \in E_{add}\} = \{name(o) \mid o \in O\}$. If $\mathcal{G}$ and $\mathcal{G}'$ are isomorphic, then there exist a bijective mapping $\xi : V \rightarrow V'$ and a bijective substitution mapping $\nu : \bigcup_{o \in O} pars(o) \times \bigcup_{p \in P} pars(p) \rightarrow \bigcup_{o' \in O'} pars(o') \times \bigcup_{p' \in P'} pars(p')$. Hence, we can "split" ξ into two bijective mappings $\mathcal{P}$ and $\mathcal{O}$ such that for each $x \in X : \mathcal{O}(x) = \xi(x)$ and for each $y \in (V \setminus X) : \mathcal{P}(y) = \xi(y)$. Also, with $\forall x \in V : arity(x) = arity(\xi(x))$ we can derive $arity(p) = arity(\mathcal{P}(p))$ and $arity(name(o)) = arity(\mathcal{O}(name(o)))$. We can also observe (from the isomorphism of $\mathcal{G}$ and $\mathcal{G}'$) that for each $o \in O$ and $x \in pars(o)$, $((x, (x|\Theta^o))|\nu) = (y, (y|\Theta^{o'}))$ for some $o' \in O'$ and $y \in pars(o')$. Since Θ^o and $\Theta^{o'}$ are substitution mappings, then we can define a substitution mapping $\chi^o : pars(o) \to pars(o')$ such that $(x|\chi^o) = y$ (with $((x, (x|\Theta^o))|\nu) = (y, (y|\Theta^{o'})))$ and χ^o is bijective. Hence, we can derive for each $o \in O$ and $p \in pre(o)$ that there exists $o' \in O'$ such that $(\mathcal{P}(p)|\chi^o) \in pre(o')$. For $del(o')$ and $add(o')$, it can be proven analogously.   □

Example 1 (Running example). We consider as running example a simplified version of the well-known Logistics domain, originally introduced in the IPC 2000. In the simplified version, a number of trucks are used to deliver packages from a location of origin to a destination location. The domain model includes 4 predicates: (at-truck ?Loc ?Truck), (at-package ?Loc ?Pkg), (in-package ?Pkg ?Truck), (in-city ?Cty ?Loc) and 3 operators: load(?Loc ?Pkg ?Truck), unload(?Loc ?Pkg ?Truck), and move(?Cty ?Loc1 ?Loc2 ?Truck).

We can define another domain model that concerns transporting passengers from one location to another by shuttles. The domain model includes 4 predicates: (at-shuttle ?Loc ?Shtl), (at-passenger ?Loc ?Psg), (in-passenger ?Psg ?Shtl), (in-city ?Cty ?Loc) and 3 operators: embark(?Loc ?Psg ?Shtl), debark(?Loc ?Psg ?Shtl), and move(?Cty ?Loc1 ?Loc2 ?Shtl). We can observe that the structure of the domain model is identical to the Logistics model apart of naming of (most of) predicates and operators. Hence, the domain models are strongly equivalent.

4   Domain Model Similarity

Informally speaking, *domain model similarity* stands for quantifying how close domain models are to each other, in terms of how many manipulations (adding/modifying an element in either of the models) are needed to make the models strongly equivalent.

Initially, we define the notion of *submodel* that describes the relation between domain models based on the subgraph relation between their LDMGs.

Definition 3. *Let $\mathcal{D}$ and $\mathcal{D}'$ be domain models. We say that $\mathcal{D}'$ is a **submodel** of $\mathcal{D}$ if the LDMG of $\mathcal{D}'$ is a subgraph of the LDMG of $\mathcal{D}$. We say that a domain model $\mathcal{D}''$ is a **strongly equivalent submodel** of $\mathcal{D}$ if $\mathcal{D}''$ is strongly equivalent with $\mathcal{D}'$ (being a submodel of $\mathcal{D}$).*

In more general cases, domain models share the same structure only partially. In other words, they share common (strongly equivalent) submodels.

Definition 4. *Let $\mathcal{D}_1$ and $\mathcal{D}_2$ be domain models. We say that submodels $\mathcal{D}'_1$ and $\mathcal{D}'_2$ of $\mathcal{D}_1$ and $\mathcal{D}_2$, respectively, are **common strongly equivalent submodels** of $\mathcal{D}_1$ and $\mathcal{D}_2$ if and only if $\mathcal{D}'_1$ and $\mathcal{D}'_2$ are strongly equivalent. We say that $\mathcal{D}'_1$ and $\mathcal{D}'_2$ are **maximum common strongly equivalent submodels** of $\mathcal{D}_1$ and $\mathcal{D}_2$ if and only if they are common strongly equivalent submodels and the value of elem is maximum for their LDMGs compared to other common strongly equivalent submodels of $\mathcal{D}_1$ and $\mathcal{D}_2$.*

Proposition 1. *Let $\mathcal{D}'_1$ and $\mathcal{D}'_2$ be submodels of domain models $\mathcal{D}_1$ and $\mathcal{D}_2$, respectively. It holds that $\mathcal{D}'_1$ and $\mathcal{D}'_2$ are (maximum) common strongly equivalent submodels of $\mathcal{D}_1$ and $\mathcal{D}_2$ if and only if the LDMG of $\mathcal{D}'_1$ and the LDMG of $\mathcal{D}'_2$ are (maximum) common isomorphic subgraphs of the LDMGs of $\mathcal{D}_1$ and $\mathcal{D}_2$, respectively.*

Proof. The claim of the proposition is directly implied from the definition of (maximum) common isomorphic subgraphs (see the Background Section) and Theorem 1.
□

The above proposition connects our variant of edit distance of graphs and the distance of domain models. The definition below summarizes the concept.

Definition 5. *Let $\mathcal{D}_1$ and $\mathcal{D}_2$ be domain models and $\mathcal{G}_1$ and $\mathcal{G}_2$ be their LDMGs, respectively. We define a dist function representing the* **distance** *between $\mathcal{D}_1$ and $\mathcal{D}_2$ as $dist(\mathcal{D}_1, \mathcal{D}_2) = dist(\mathcal{G}_1, \mathcal{G}_2)$.*

The notion of distance between two domain models determines a minimum number of *elementary operations* to modify these two models to make them strongly equivalent. That corresponds to adding vertices and edges to the LDMGs of these two models. Let $\mathcal{D} = (P, O)$ be a domain model and $\mathcal{G} = (V, E_{pre}, E_{del}, E_{add})$ its LDMG. The *elementary operations* over $\mathcal{D}$ and $\mathcal{G}$ are defined as follows:

(1) Add p into $pre(o)$ (resp. $del(o)$, resp. $add(o)$) iff (o, p) is added into E_{pre} (resp. E_{del}, resp. E_{add}).
(2) Add o into O iff o is added into V and (o, p) is added into E_{add} for some p.
(3) Add p into P iff p is added into V and no edge from p is added to E_{add}.

We would like to emphasise that we do not explicitly distinguish operator and predicate nodes. We can observe that a well defined operator has to have at least one add effect and hence the corresponding vertex in the underlying LDMG has to have at least one outgoing "add" edge. Note, again, that we assume that all operators are well defined. On the other hand, each predicate node has no outgoing edge.

It is known that the problem of graph edit distance is NP-hard [29]. Due to specific structure of LDMGs, again, the question whether determining distance between domain models is NP-hard is still open.

Example 2 (Example 1 cont'd). Let us simplify the model introduced in Example 1 by removing the (in-city ?Cty ?Loc) predicate. The simplified model is a submodel of the original one. Now, let us add a macro-operator move-load(?Pkg ?Truck ?Loc1 ?Loc2 ?Cty) encapsulating the sequence of move and load operators into the simplified model. The simplified model is a submodel of the "macro" model. Finally, we can compare the "macro" Logistics model with the "passenger" model from Example 1. The models are not strongly equivalent. We can, on the other hand, find their maximum common strongly equivalent submodels, i.e., the simplified Logistic model and the "passenger" model which is simplified by removing (in-city ?Cty ?Loc).

5   Comparing Domain Models via ASP

In this section, we describe our approach based on Answer Set Programming (ASP), and its results. Note that the ASP terminology may be not perfectly aligned to the one of planning in the usage of some terms, e.g., atoms and predicates.

Algorithm 1: Comparing Domain Models

Input : A graph $\mathcal{G}_1$ and graph $\mathcal{G}_2$.
Output: Differences between $\mathcal{G}_1$ and $\mathcal{G}_2$

1   $\Pi := preprocessing(\mathcal{G}_1, \mathcal{G}_2)$;
2   $\Pi := \Pi \cup \Pi'$;   // Π' reported in Figure 1
3   $A := ASPSolver(\Pi)$;
4 **for** $p \in A$ **do**
5   **if** p is $ver(,add, g, name, \ldots)$ **then**
6   Print("Add vertex " + $name$ + " in " + g);

7   **if** p is $edge(add, g, n1, n2, t, l)$ **then**
8   Print("Add " + t + " edge with label " + l + " from vertex " + $n1$ + " to " + $n2$ + " in " + g);

9   **if** p is $map(n1, n2, e1, e2)$ **then**
10   Print("Map vertex " + $n1$ + " of g_2 to vertex " + $n2$ + "of g_1");
11   **if** $e1 \neq e2$ **then**
12   Print("Remapping " + $e1$ + " to " + $e2$);

```
r1 {map(ID1, ID2, N1, N2) : ver(ID2, _, gr1, _, T, P, N1), ver(ID1, _, gr2, _, T, P,
      N2)} = 1 :- ver(ID2, _, gr2, _, T, _, _).
r2 :- ver(ID, _, gr1, _, _, _, _), #count{X: map(X, ID, _, _)} != 1.
r3 :- #sum{1,ID: ver(ID, _, gr2, _, _, _, _); -1,ID: ver(ID, _, gr1, _, _, _, _)} !=
      0.
r4 edge(add, gr1, X2, X4, L, R) :- map(X1, X2, _, _), map(X3, X4, _, _), edge(orig,
      gr2, X1, X3, L, R), not edge(orig, gr1, X2, X4, L, R).
r5 edge(add, gr2, X1, X3, L, R) :- map(X1, X2, _, _), map(X3, X4, _, _), edge(orig,
      gr1, X2, X4, L, R), not edge(orig, gr2, X1, X3, L, R).
r6 :~ ver(ID, orig, G, _, _, _, N1), ver(ID, orig, G, _, _, _, N2), N1 != N2.
      [1@1,ID]
r7 :~ ver(ID, add, G, _, _, _, _). [1@2, ID, G]
r8 :~ edge(add, G, N1, N2, L, R). [1@2, ID, G, N1, N2, L, R]
```

Fig. 1. ASP Program Π'.

Answer Set Programming. ASP is a well-known declarative language. An ASP program [6] is made of (a combination of): (1) facts of the form head.; (2) rules of the form head :- body.; (3) choice rules of the form tomsatoms = 1 :- body.; (4) constraints of the form :- body.; and (5) weak constraints of the form :~ body. [weight@level,terms]; where head is an atom, atoms is a set of atoms, and body is a set of (possibly negated) atoms, also including aggregate functions, such as #sum, and terms is a sequence of terms, i.e., variables (strings starting with uppercase letter) or constants (non-negative integers or strings starting with lowercase letters). Atoms can be made over terms. The semantics is given in terms of its *answer sets*, that is, sets A of ground atoms, where atoms in A are said to be true (false, otherwise), such that: (1) head is in A; (2) whenever the body is true (i.e., all positive atoms are in A and all negated atoms are not in A), head is in A; (3) exactly one of the atoms in atoms is in A whenever the body is true; or if = 1 is omitted then one of the atoms in atoms can be in A whenever the body is true; (4) the body must be false. Moreover, weak constraints of the form (5) allow expressing preferences among answer sets, where level represents the priority and `weight` is a numerical cost that is paid whenever the body of a weak constraint is true w.r.t. an answer set. Overall, the preferred weak constraints are the ones with the lowest costs at the highest levels. For formal details about syntax and semantics of ASP programs, the reader is referred to [5,6].

ASP-based Comparison. Following the theory presented in previous sections, we implemented an ASP-based approach depicted in Algorithm 1. The algorithm receives two LDMGs (referred to as $\mathcal{G}_1$ and $\mathcal{G}_2$) as input, and prints a minimal number of changes to the graphs to make them isomorphic as output. In the following, we assume that the number of vertices representing an operator (resp. a predicate) of $\mathcal{G}_1$ is less than or equal to the number of vertices representing an operator (resp. a predicate) of $\mathcal{G}_2$. The idea of the algorithm is as follows: Firstly, a processing step creates an ASP program Π starting from the input graphs; then, Π is combined with the ASP encoding reported in Fig. 1, and an ASP solver is invoked on the resulting program. Finally, the output of the ASP solver is processed by a postprocessing part which produces human-readable instructions to make the two graphs isomorphic. In more detail, the ASP program operates on atoms over the predicates *ver*, *edge*, and *map*, as follows. Atoms of the form *ver(id, status, graph, name, type, parameters, changes)* denote the vertices of the input graphs, where *id* is a unique identifier of the vertex, *status* denotes if the vertex was in the input graph (*orig*) or if it must be added (*add*), *graph* indicates the graph of the vertex (between $\mathcal{G}_1$ and $\mathcal{G}_2$), *name* is the name of the vertex, *type* indicates if vertex is a predicate or an operator, *parameters* is a string representing the parameters of the predicate, and *changes* indicates if (and how) the parameters of the vertex must be changed for a correct match. Atoms of the form *edge(status, graph, id_ver1, id_ver2, type, label)* denote the edges of the input graphs, where *status* and *graph* are as the ones of *ver*, *id_ver1* and *id_ver2* are the identifiers of the vertices connected by the edges, *type* denotes if the edge is in E_{pre}, E_{del}, or E_{add}, respectively, and *label* is the label of the edge. Atoms of the form *map(id_ver1,id_ver2,params1,params2)* denote the mapping from vertices of the different graphs, where *id_ver1* and *id_ver2* belong to $\mathcal{G}_2$ and $\mathcal{G}_1$, respectively, *params1* and *params2* denote the parameters of the two matched vertices, respectively. The preprocessing step creates the rules:

(1) $ver(id,\ orig,\ gr_i,\ name,\ t,\ \text{“}x_1,\ldots,x_k\text{”},\text{“}x_1,\ldots,x_k\text{”}).$
for each vertex $name(x_1,\ldots,x_k)$ in $\mathcal{G}_i (i \in \{1,2\})$ representing a vertex of type t, where t is *predicate* or *operator*, and *id* is an identifier of the vertex;

(2) $edge(orig,\ gr_i,\ v_1,\ v_2,\ x,\ label).$
for each edge (v_1, v_2) in $E_x (x \in \{pre, del, add\})$ of the graph $\mathcal{G}_i (i \in \{1,2\})$, where *label* is the label of the edge;

(3) $\{ver(id,\ add,\ gr_1,\ name,\ t,\ \text{“}x_1,\ldots,x_k\text{”},\text{“}x_1,\ldots,x_k\text{”})\}.$
for each vertex $name(x_1,\ldots,x_k)$ in $\mathcal{G}_2$ of type t such that there is no vertex $name(x_1,\ldots,x_k)$ of type t in $\mathcal{G}_1$, where t can be either *predicate* or *operator*;

(4) $\{ver(id,orig,gr_1,name,t,\text{“}x_1,\ldots,x_k\text{”},\text{“}y_1,\ldots,y_z\text{”})\}.$
for each vertex $name(x_1,\ldots,x_k)$ in $\mathcal{G}_1$ of type t and for each vertex $name(y_1,\ldots,y_z)$ in $\mathcal{G}_2$ of type t, with the set of the parameters $x_1,\ldots,x_k$ different from the set of the parameters $y_1,\ldots,y_z$, where t can be either *predicate* or *operator*.

The program Π produced by the preprocessing is combined with the ASP encoding of Fig. 1, whose behaviour is described in the following. Rules r_1 and r_2 associate each vertex of $\mathcal{G}_2$ to exactly one vertex of the same type of $\mathcal{G}_1$. Rule r_3 ensures that the number of vertices of the two graphs are the same. Rules r_4 and r_5 generate missing edges between the vertices after the mapping. Finally, weak constraints r_6, r_7, and r_8 minimise the number of vertices with different parameters, i.e., the number of added vertices, and the number of added edges, respectively. Observe that weak constraints r_7, and r_8 have a higher level than r_6, that is, preserving the same number of vertices and edges has a higher priority than changing the parameters of the vertices.

An ASP solver is then executed on the resulting program, and its output is processed to produce human-readable instructions on how to make the two graphs isomorphic.

Example 3 (Example 2 cont'd). Let $\mathcal{G}_1$ and $\mathcal{G}_2$ be the LDMGs of the Logistics domains considered in Example 1 and the "macro" variant with the *incity* predicate (see Example 2), respectively. For the sake of compactness, we shorten the name of variables of STRIPS predicates and operators to a single capital letter. Thus, $\mathcal{G}_2$ consists of the vertices of $\mathcal{G}_1$ extended with a vertex of the form $moveload(?P, ?T, ?L1, ?L2, ?C)$. Moreover, $E_t^2 = E_t^1 \cup E_t'$ ($t \in \{pre, del, add\}$), where E_{pre}' is

$$\{(moveload, ?T = ?T, ?L1 = ?L, attruck),$$
$$(moveload, ?L1 = ?L, ?C = ?C, incity),$$
$$(moveload, ?L2 = ?L, ?C = ?C, incity),$$
$$(moveload, ?P = ?P, ?L1 = ?L, atpackage)\}$$

E_{add}' is $\{(moveload, ?T = ?T, ?L1 = ?L, atpackage), (moveload, ?P = ?P, ?T = ?T, inpackage)\}$ and E_{del}' is $\{(moveload, ?T = ?T, ?L1 = ?L, attruck), (moveload, ?P = ?P, ?L1 = ?L, atpackage)\}$. Note that rules (1) and (2) produced by the preprocessing step of Algorithm 1 encode the vertices and the edge, for instance $ver(0, orig, gr_1, load, operator, "L, P, T", "L, P, T")$ represents the vertex *load* of $\mathcal{G}_1$, where 0 is a unique identifier of the vertex, and "L, P, T" corresponds to the (ordered) parameters. Moreover, there is only one rule of type (3), i.e., $\{ver(7, add, gr_1, moveload, operator, "C, L, L, P, T", "C, L, L, P, T")\}$, since there is only one vertex in $\mathcal{G}_2$ that is not in $\mathcal{G}_1$. Finally, an excerpt of the rules of type (4), are the following (where *or*, *o*, and *p* stand for *orig*, *operator*, and *predicate*, respectively):

$\{ver(0, or, gr_1, load, o, "L, P, T", "C, L, L, T")\}.$
$\{ver(0, or, gr_1, load, o, "L, P, T", "C, L, L, P, T")\}.$
$\{ver(1, or, gr_1, unload, o, "L, P, T", "C, L, L, T")\}.$
$\{ver(1, or, gr_1, unload, o, "L, P, T", "C, L, L, P, T")\}.$
$\{ver(2, or, gr_1, move, o, "C, L, L, T", "L, P, T")\}.$
$\{ver(2, or, gr_1, move, o, "C, L, L, T", "C, L, L, P, T")\}.$
$\{ver(3, or, gr_1, attruck, p, "L, T", "L, P")\}.$
$\{ver(3, or, gr_1, attruck, p, "L, T", "P, T")\}.$
$\{ver(3, or, gr_1, attruck, p, "L, T", "C, L")\}.$
$\{ver(4, or, gr_1, atpackage, p, "L, P", "L, T")\}.$
$\{ver(4, or, gr_1, atpackage, p, "L, P", "P, T")\}.$
$\{ver(4, or, gr_1, atpackage, p, "L, P", "C, L")\}.$
$\{ver(5, or, gr_1, inpackage, p, "P, T", "L, P")\}.$
$\{ver(5, or, gr_1, inpackage, p, "P, T", "L, T")\}.$
$\{ver(5, or, gr_1, inpackage, p, "P, T", "C, L")\}.$
$\{ver(6, or, gr_1, incity, p, "C, L", "L, P")\}.$
$\{ver(6, or, gr_1, incity, p, "C, L", "L, T")\}.$
$\{ver(6, or, gr_1, incity, p, "C, L", "P, T")\}.$

The preprocessing step allows generating only the meaningful combinations of vertices and terms in a graph via imperative programming. These combinations are added as choice rules, which can then be utilised by the solver as possible newly added vertices. Without preprocessing, all choice rules for mapping all terms/operator combinations are instead generated, and is left to the solver to derive new vertices by combining original vertices with every choice to potentially change terms. After the preprocessing (line 1 of Algorithm 1), the ASP solver is executed (line 3) on the resulting program extended with Π' (line 2). Then, Algorithm 1 analyses its output (from line 4 on) and produces the following instructions:

– Add vertex *moveload* in g_1.
– Add *pre* edge with label T=T,L1=L from vertex *moveload* to vertex *attruck* in g_1.
– Add *pre* edge with label L1=L,C=C from vertex *moveload* to vertex *incity* in g_1.
– Add *pre* edge with label L2=L,C=C from vertex *moveload* to vertex *incity* in g_1.
– Add *pre* edge with label P=P,L1=L from vertex *moveload* to vertex *atpackage* in g_1.
– Add *add* edge with label T=T,L1=L from vertex *moveload* to vertex *attruck* in g_1.
– Add *add* edge with label P=P,T=T from vertex *moveload* to vertex *inpackage* in g_1.
– Add *del* edge with label T=T,L1=L from vertex *moveload* to vertex *attruck* in g_1.
– Add *del* edge with label P=P,L1=L from vertex *moveload* to vertex *atpackage* in g_1.
– Map vertex v of g_2 to vertex v of g_1, where $v \in \{load, unload, move, attruck, atpackage, inpackage, incity, moveload\}$.

Finally, note how Algorithm 1 can be easily extended in order to deal with the generation of multiple answer sets, corresponding to minimal sets of changes.

Evaluation. We selected 7 different domain models from well-known international competitions. In particular, we considered the domains of Barman, Blocksworld, (simplified) Logistics, Rovers, Satellite, and Sokoban from various editions of the International Planning Competition (IPC), and the RPG domain from the 2016 International Competition on Knowledge Engineering for Planning and Scheduling (ICKEPS).[1] The number of operators ranges between 2 and 12, and the number of predicates between 4 and 25. To obtain a different model for each benchmark domain, but RPG, we reformulated the original models by considering a mix of entanglements and macro-actions, and by modifying preconditions and effects of original operators. For the RPG domain, we compared two models crafted by two of the teams that took part in the competition: Such models present significant differences in terms of predicates and operators as they embody very different interpretations of the domain at hand. Details of the LDMGs corresponding to the models are shown in the left part of Table 1. Year indicates when the model was introduced. Finally, to perform a stress test of the proposed approach, we compared models designed for diverse domains too. Table is divided horizontally in two parts: The top part considering cases where a model has been reformulated, while the bottom part focuses on comparing very different models (RPG, Barman vs Logistics, Rovers vs Satellite). We performed experiments on an Intel Core i5-10210U machine with 1.6 GHz, 8 GB of RAM and Linux operating system. Each system run was given an overall memory limit of 6 GB and 5 CPU-time minutes. As ASP system we used the state-of-the-art tool CLINGO [13], configured with the option --parallel-mode=4, which enables the use of multiple threads (with different solving strategies). We used 4 threads and in our experiments this helps improve the performance of Clingo compared to the default configuration. Moreover, we used the open-source python library PYSPEL [2] which simplifies the implementation of Algorithm 1. We tested two approaches: The first one is the implementation of Algorithm 1 as described in Sect. 5, and the second one is the same implementation where rules (3) and (4) of the preprocessing (line 1 of Algorithm 1) are produced using plain ASP rules. We preliminary tested, on Logistics and Rover domains, the ability of our solution to compare models that are exactly the same but for the names of the involved operators and predicates, i.e., if they are strongly equivalent. The results indicate that the ASP solution employing preprocessing always identifies the compared graphs as isomorphic, and provides an appropriate mapping between the nodes of the compared LDMGs, in less than 0.5 CPU-time seconds.

Then, we move to the general case and the results of the experimental analysis are shown in the right part of Table 1 where, for each domain and tested approach, we report the number of optimal models found, the CPU time, and the number of rules generated by the grounding. Square brackets indicate that an optimal solution has been found in the reported CPU time (checked manually), but has not been proved by CLINGO. As a first observation, the approach employing preprocessing is extremely fast, since for all the tested benchmarks we are able to find an optimal solution (through not proved) in less than 1 CPU-time second. Instead, plain ASP encoding exceeds the memory limits when executed on large domains (Barman and Rovers) or in the presence of significant difference between the compared domains, showing that preprocessing is

---

[1] Encoding and benchmarks are available at: https://github.com/MarcoMochi/jelia-planning.

Table 1. Size of the generated graphs for each benchmark domain model (Left) and performance of the proposed ASP-based approach without/with preprocessing (Right). Vertices and Edges give information of the size of the graphs to compare, G_1 is the graph obtained by considering the original domain model, G_2 is obtained from the reformulated model for all the domains but RPG, where two original models independently crafted are compared. RPG is the only domain presented at ICKEPS, while other domains have been used as IPC benchmarks. Results are presented in terms of seconds needed to enumerate all the optimal solutions, and the number of optimal models (Opt. Mod.). Square brackets indicate that the optimal solution was not proved. (# Rules) shows the size of the ASP program.

Domain	Year	Vertices		Edges		Opt. Mod.	No preprocessing		Preprocessing	
		G_1	G_2	G_1	G_2		CPU Time	# Rules	CPU Time	# Rules
Sokoban	2008	6	7	16	18	1	0.1	1,411	0.1	636
Logistics	1998	7	8	13	21	1	0.1	832	0.1	697
Blocksworld	2000	9	11	27	29	2	0.1	3,219	0.1	2,446
Satellite	2002	13	16	23	44	2	2.7	2,132,131	0.1	10,666
Barman	2011	27	29	97	123	1	–	–	0.3	98,676
Rovers	2002	34	39	75	103	4	–	–	0.4	146,857
RPG	2016	13	34	23	74	[1]	[1.9]	849,732	[0.4]	44,601
Barman_Log	–	–	–	–	–	[1]	–	–	[0.1]	93,893
Rovers_Sat	–	–	–	–	–	[1]	–	–	[0.8]	37,251

indeed necessary in challenging cases. Note that even the mid-size Satellite leads to more than 2 Million rules, whereas the approach using preprocessing produces only around 10 thousands rules. In models where differences are limited, (i.e., modification of 2-3 vertices and a few tens of edges), there is no substantial difference between finding one optimal solution and finding all of them. This result can be explained by the fact that the number of optimal solutions is rather small (maximum 4) and this paves the way for the development of more comparison techniques, e.g., by proposing preferences among the possible solutions.

Turning our attention more on the stress test, it is easy to notice that despite the fact that the optimal solution for models of different domains required over 100 modifications/additional elements (nodes and edges) and for the RPG domain required 4 additional nodes and 78 edges, the proposed solution was able to generate an optimal result in less than 1 CPU-time second. However, differently from the other tests, in these cases the approach was able to generate a single optimal solution and not to enumerate all the optimal ones. On the one hand, this result confirms that ASP is a viable tool to be used; on the other hand, it may suggest that additional optimisation could be beneficial for fully enumerate all optimal cases.

Summarising, the performed experimental analysis indicates that the presented ASP system, enhanced with the preprocessing step, is very efficient in generating optimally minimal sets of modifications that allows to transform a model into the compared one, on the basis of the corresponding LDMGs. Considering that results are generated efficiently, the proposed tool can also be exploited during the domain encoding step, for comparing alternative representations of a domain's dynamics.

6 Related Work and Discussion

The notion of strong domain model equivalence has been informally introduced in [24]. On a similar note, [25] proposed an automated approach, D-VAL, to check the functional equivalence of two domain models, i.e., their ability to parse the same set of problems. D-VAL focuses on comparing models of the same domain that has been reformulated, to ensure that the reformulation process did not undermine the domain model capabilities. The approach proposed in this paper is more general, and allows to compare even very different models in terms of their corresponding solution spaces, and to obtain a measure of their similarity.

An application-specific investigation of the engineering of different models has been proposed in [23], and ICKEPS introduced metrics to manually compare models [9].

Notably, an approach based on ASP has been proposed also for the MRP in planning [19], while [26] deals with the MRP but specifically defined on two logic programs and their answer sets. Some authors of [26] followed a similar direction in [18], but in the context of (numerical) scheduling and employing CLINGO-DL language, which is an extension of ASP enriched with a limited form of arithmetic [15].

7 Conclusion

This paper contributes to theory and practice of the problem of comparing planning domain models: We defined the concept of similarity of domain models, which builds on the notion of strong equivalence of domain models, also introduced in the paper. We proposed an approach based on Answer Set Programming for specifying and solving the problem – with particular attention given to the identification of optimal minimal sets of modifications that allows to transform one model into the compared one. Experiments on well-known planning benchmarks of different size show that the approach can find a minimal set of corrections in very short time. Future work will focus on extending the approach to more expressive planning representation languages, such as PDDL+ [12], that can also consider hybrid discrete-continuous numeric changes, and to improve the explanations provided as output.

Acknowledgements. L. Chrpa was funded by the Czech Science Foundation (project no. 23-05575S). M. Vallati was supported by the UKRI Future Leaders Fellowship [grant number MR/T041196/1]. C. Dodaro was supported by Italian Ministry of Research (MUR) under PNRR projects FAIR "Future AI Research", CUP H23C22000860006, and Tech4You "Technologies for climate change adaptation and quality of life improvement", CUP H23C22000370006;

References

1. Ai-Chang, M., et al.: MAPGEN: mixed-initiative planning and scheduling for the mars exploration rover mission. IEEE Intell. Syst. **19**(1), 8–12 (2004)
2. Alviano, M., Dodaro, C., Previti, A.: Python Specification Language (2021). https://github.com/dodaro/pyspel
3. Baral, C.: Knowledge Representation, Reasoning and Declarative Problem Solving. Cambridge University Press, Cambridge (2003). https://doi.org/10.1017/CBO9780511543357

4. Bengoetxea, E.: Inexact Graph Matching Using Estimation of Distribution Algorithms. Ph.D. thesis, Ecole Nationale Supérieure des Télécommunications, Paris, France, December 2002
5. Brewka, G., Eiter, T., Truszczynski, M.: Answer set programming at a glance. Commun. ACM **54**(12), 92–103 (2011)
6. Calimeri, F., et al.: ASP-Core-2 input language format. Theory Pract. Log. Program. **20**(2), 294–309 (2020)
7. Cardellini, M., Maratea, M., Vallati, M., Boleto, G., Oneto, L.: In-station train dispatching: a PDDL+ planning approach. In: Proceedings of ICAPS, pp. 450–458 (2021)
8. Chakraborti, T., Sreedharan, S., Zhang, Y., Kambhampati, S.: Plan explanations as model reconciliation: moving beyond explanation as soliloquy. In: Proceedings of the Twenty-Sixth International Joint Conference on Artificial Intelligence, IJCAI, pp. 156–163 (2017)
9. Chrpa, L., McCluskey, T.L., Vallati, M., Vaquero, T.: The fifth international competition on knowledge engineering for planning and scheduling: summary and trends. AI Mag. **38**(1), 104–106 (2017)
10. Coulter, A., Ilie, T., Tibando, R., Muise, C.: Theory alignment via a classical encoding of regular bisimulation. In: Workshop on Knowledge Engineering for Planning and Scheduling (KEPS) (2022)
11. Cresswell, S., McCluskey, T.L., West, M.M.: Acquiring planning domain models using LOCM. Knowl. Eng. Rev. **28**(2), 195–213 (2013)
12. Fox, M., Long, D.: Modelling mixed discrete-continuous domains for planning. J. Artif. Intell. Res. **27**, 235–297 (2006)
13. Gebser, M., Kaminski, R., Kaufmann, B., Ostrowski, M., Schaub, T., Wanko, P.: Theory solving made easy with Clingo 5. In: ICLP (Technical Communications). OASICS, vol. 52, pp. 2:1–2:15 (2016)
14. Gelfond, M., Lifschitz, V.: Classical negation in logic programs and disjunctive databases. N. Gener. Comput. **9**(3/4), 365–386 (1991)
15. Janhunen, T., Kaminski, R., Ostrowski, M., Schellhorn, S., Wanko, P., Schaub, T.: Clingo goes linear constraints over reals and integers. Theory Pract. Log. Program. **17**(5–6), 872–888 (2017)
16. McCluskey, T.L., Porteous, J.M.: Engineering and compiling planning domain models to promote validity and efficiency. Artif. Intell. **95**(1), 1–65 (1997)
17. McCluskey, T.L., Vaquero, T.S., Vallati, M.: Engineering knowledge for automated planning: towards a notion of quality. In: Proceedings of K-CAP, pp. 14:1–14:8 (2017)
18. Nguyen, V., Son, T.C., Yeoh, W.: Explainable problem in clingo-dl programs. In: Ma, H., Serina, I. (eds.) Proceedings of the Fourteenth International Symposium on Combinatorial Search (SOCS 2021), pp. 231–232. AAAI Press (2021)
19. Nguyen, V., Stylianos, V.L., Son, T.C., Yeoh, W.: Explainable planning using answer set programming. In: Proceedings of the 17th International Conference on Principles of Knowledge Representation and Reasoning, KR, pp. 662–666 (2020)
20. Niemelä, I.: Logic programs with stable model semantics as a constraint programming paradigm. Ann. Math. Artif. Intell. **25**(3–4), 241–273 (1999)
21. Ramírez, M., et al.: Integrated hybrid planning and programmed control for real time UAV maneuvering. In: Proceedings of the AAMAS, pp. 1318–1326 (2018)
22. Sanfeliu, A., Fu, K.: A distance measure between attributed relational graphs for pattern recognition. IEEE Trans. Syst. Man Cybern. **13**(3), 353–362 (1983). https://doi.org/10.1109/TSMC.1983.6313167
23. Shah, M.M.S., Chrpa, L., Kitchin, D.E., McCluskey, T.L., Vallati, M.: Exploring knowledge engineering strategies in designing and modelling a road traffic accident management domain. In: Proceedings of the 23rd International Joint Conference on Artificial Intelligence, pp. 2373–2379 (2013)

24. Shoeeb, S., McCluskey, T.: On comparing planning domain models. In: PlanSIG Workshop (2011)
25. Shrinah, A., Long, D., Eder, K.: D-VAL: an automatic functional equivalence validation tool for planning domain models. arXiv preprint arXiv:2104.14602 (2021)
26. Son, T.C., Nguyen, V., Vasileiou, S.L., Yeoh, W.: Model reconciliation in logic programs. In: Faber, W., Friedrich, G., Gebser, M., Morak, M. (eds.) JELIA 2021. LNCS (LNAI), vol. 12678, pp. 393–406. Springer, Cham (2021). https://doi.org/10.1007/978-3-030-75775-5_26
27. Vallati, M., Chrpa, L.: On the robustness of domain-independent planning engines: the impact of poorly-engineered knowledge. In: Proceedings of K-CAP, pp. 197–204 (2019)
28. Vallati, M., McCluskey, T.L.: A quality framework for automated planning knowledge models. In: Proceedings of the 13th International Conference on Agents and Artificial Intelligence, ICAART, pp. 635–644 (2021)
29. Zeng, Z., Tung, A.K.H., Wang, J., Feng, J., Zhou, L.: Comparing stars: on approximating graph edit distance. Proc. VLDB Endow. 2(1), 25–36 (2009)

Hybrid ASP-Based Multi-objective Scheduling of Semiconductor Manufacturing Processes

Mohammed M. S. El-Kholany[1,2] , Ramsha Ali[1] , and Martin Gebser[1,3](✉)

[1] University of Klagenfurt, Klagenfurt am Wörthersee, Austria
{mohammed.el-kholany,ramsha.ali}@aau.at
[2] Cairo University, Giza, Egypt
[3] Graz University of Technology, Graz , Austria
martin.gebser@aau.at

Abstract. Modern semiconductor manufacturing involves intricate production processes consisting of hundreds of operations, which can take several months from lot release to completion. The high-tech machines used in these processes are diverse, operate on individual wafers, lots, or batches in multiple stages, and necessitate product-specific setups and specialized maintenance procedures. This situation is different from traditional job-shop scheduling scenarios, which have less complex production processes and machines, and mainly focus on solving highly combinatorial but abstract scheduling problems. In this work, we address the scheduling of realistic semiconductor manufacturing processes by modeling their specific requirements using hybrid Answer Set Programming with difference logic, incorporating flexible machine processing, setup, batching and maintenance operations. Unlike existing methods that schedule semiconductor manufacturing processes locally with greedy heuristics or by independently optimizing specific machine group allocations, we examine the potentials of large-scale scheduling subject to multiple optimization objectives.

Keywords: Hybrid Answer Set Programming · Semiconductor manufacturing scheduling · Difference logic · Multi-objective optimization

1 Introduction

Scheduling semiconductor manufacturing processes imposes a complex challenge due to the variety of products, operations, and high-tech machines with diverse capabilities and characteristics. Effective scheduling aims at allocating jobs to machines in a manner that satisfies production needs, optimizes factory throughput, and guarantees punctual delivery [34]. In view of the steadily increasing demand [24], semiconductor manufacturers are forced to optimize their throughput, decrease cycle times, and enhance the on-time delivery of products to customers [28]. To reduce the required investments into costly machines [22], constant utilization and idleness prevention are important goals.

A typical wafer fabrication plant encompasses a variety of process flows, which are designated production routes for wafer lots within the factory. Each route consists of several hundred operations to be processed by machines belonging to about one hundred separate tool groups with specific functionalities and characteristics. Sophisticated

© The Author(s), under exclusive license to Springer Nature Switzerland AG 2023
S. Gaggl et al. (Eds.): JELIA 2023, LNAI 14281, pp. 243–252, 2023.
https://doi.org/10.1007/978-3-031-43619-2_17

process steps are iterated in several stages, resulting in a re-entrant flow where lots revisit machines in the same tool group multiple times. Hence, the manufacturing environment is different from traditional flow-shop and job-shop scenarios [15]. A crucial consequence of this re-entrant flow is that wafers at different stages in their manufacturing cycle can compete for the same machines, and dispatching strategies to resolve such competing demands have a noticeable impact on the overall production efficiency.

While lacking specific features of the semiconductor manufacturing process such as, e.g., re-entrant flow, batching, setup and maintenance operations, as well as varying processing times and sudden machine disruptions, the Flexible Job-Shop Scheduling Problem (FJSP) [7,32] along with the optimization methods devised for it are related approaches. Meta-heuristic algorithms for FJSP solving incorporate local search methods, such as Genetic Programming [25,35], Tabu Search [25], Simulated Annealing [35], Harmony Search [31], Particle Swarm Optimization [20], and Ant Colony Optimization [37]. Exact solving methods are based on FJSP models in Mixed Integer Programming (MIP) [8,18,19], Constraint Programming (CP) [10,19], or Answer Set Programming (ASP) with difference logic [13,17,21].

Beyond FJSP, ASP [26] has been successfully used to schedule printing devices [5], specialist teams [30], work shifts [2], course timetables [6], medical treatments [11], and aircraft routes [33]. The hybrid framework of ASP with difference logic [9] particularly supports a compact representation and reasoning with quantitative resources like time, which has also been exploited in domains such as lab resource [14], train connection [1], and parallel machine [12] scheduling.

Unlike these scheduling domains, the semiconductor manufacturing process is typically controlled by handcrafted [29] or machine-learned [36] dispatching rules at the execution level, or (re-)scheduling is localized to specific tool groups [27], e.g., for optimizing the allocation of lots queuing in front of a group of batching machines. While such local decision making approaches are tuned to specific fab settings, their scope is generally too narrow to guarantee overall efficiency in terms of optimization objectives such as the factory throughput or makespan as well as setup and batching criteria.

Our work goes beyond local decision making and constitutes a step towards large-scale scheduling by modeling the production processes of a modern wafer fab, represented by the SMT2020 simulation scenario [22]. We extend our preliminary approach [3] to semiconductor fab scheduling with support for batching machines, partially flexible machine allocation strategies, and multi-objective optimization functionalities. Section 2 introduces the scheduling problem including crucial features of the SMT2020 scenario, an experimental evaluation examining the potentials of large-scale scheduling subject to multiple optimization objectives is performed in Sect. 3, and Sect. 4 concludes with a brief summary and outlook on future work. The extended version [4] of this paper in addition elaborates our hybrid ASP with difference logic encoding enabling the large-scale scheduling of semiconductor manufacturing processes.

2   Semiconductor Manufacturing Scheduling

We consider a *Semiconductor Manufacturing Scheduling Problem* (SMSP) inspired by the SMT2020 simulation scenario. Given a set P of available *products* (the producible types of wafers), the production *route* for each product $p \in P$ is a finite sequence $p[1], \ldots, p[n_p]$ of production *operations*, where n_p denotes the length of the production route for p. Each operation $p[i]$ needs to be performed by some machine belonging to a *tool group* $M(p[i])$ and requires a *setup* $s(p[i]) \in \mathbb{N}$, with $s(p[i]) = 0$ indicating the special case that any (positive) setup can be in place when performing $p[i]$. Each setup $s \in \mathbb{N}$ has an associated parameter $\min(s) \in \mathbb{N}$ specifying a minimum number of production operations that should be processed by a machine before changing from s to another setup. Moreover, *batching* capacities for operations $p[i]$ are expressed by the parameters $\min(p[i]) \in \mathbb{N}$ and $\max(p[i]) \in \mathbb{N}$, denoting a minimum and a maximum batch size in terms of wafer lots. While the maximum batch size is a hard limit on the number of lots that can be processed simultaneously, the minima on batch size and setup changes reflect desiderata for a regular process flow but are not strictly necessary process limitations. Furthermore, each tool group M has associated *maintenance* operations $c(M)$ and $d(M)$, which must be performed periodically based on the number of processed lots or accumulated processing time, respectively. That is, for each $c \in c(M)$ (or $d \in d(M)$), the parameters $\min(c) \in \mathbb{N}$ and $\max(c) \in \mathbb{N}$ (or $\min(d) \in \mathbb{N}$ and $\max(d) \in \mathbb{N}$) denote the minimum and maximum number of lots (or processing time) after which the maintenance operation has to be performed. Finally, for any production operation $p[i]$, setup s, and maintenance operation c or d, $\text{time}(p[i]) \in \mathbb{N}, \text{time}(s) \in \mathbb{N}$, $\text{time}(c) \in \mathbb{N}$ or $\text{time}(d) \in \mathbb{N}$ provide the time required for performing the respective operation or changing to the machine setup, respectively.

The general properties above describe production routes and features of machines, and a set L of wafer lots represents the requested products, where each lot $l \in L$ belongs to some product $p(l) \in P$. A *machine assignment* $m(l[1]) \in M(p(l)[1]), \ldots,$ $m(l[n_{p(l)}]) \in M(p(l)[n_{p(l)}])$ determines a specific machine to perform each operation $l[i]$ in the production route for a lot l. The *schedule* for a machine m in the tool group M is a finite sequence $m[1], \ldots, m[n_m]$ of sets of operations, where for each $1 \leq j \leq n_m$:

$$
m[j] = \begin{cases}
\{l_1[i], \ldots, l_k[i]\} & \text{for lots } \{l_1, \ldots, l_k\} \subseteq L \text{ with } p(l_1) = \ldots = p(l_k) = p, \\
& i \leq n_p, m(l_1[i]) = \ldots = m(l_k[i]) = m, k \leq \max(p[i]); \\
\{s\} & \text{for some setup } s > 0; \\
\{c\} & \text{for some maintenance operation } c \in c(M); \text{ or} \\
\{d\} & \text{for some maintenance operation } d \in d(M).
\end{cases}
$$

Starting from the initial machine setup $s(m)[1] = 0$, we define the successor setups for $1 < j \leq n_m$ by $s(m)[j] = \{s\}$ if $m[j-1] = \{s\}$ indicates a change to the setup $s \in \mathbb{N}$, or $s(m)[j] = s(m)[j-1]$ otherwise. Moreover, let $l(m[j]) = \{l_1[i], \ldots, l_k[i]\}$ if $m[j] = \{l_1[i], \ldots, l_k[i]\}$ for lots $\{l_1, \ldots, l_k\} \subseteq L$ whose i-th operation is processed in batch, or $l(m[j]) = \emptyset$ otherwise. The schedule for m is *feasible* if each $l[i]$ with $m(l[i]) = m$ belongs to exactly one set $m[j]$ of operations, and for each $1 \leq j \leq n_m$:

- $s(m)[j] = s(p(l)[i])$ if $s(p(l)[i]) > 0$ for some lot $l \in L$ with $l[i] \in l(m[j])$,
- $\sum_{\max(\{0\} \cup \{j_c < j | m[j_c] = \{c\}}) < j' \leq j} |l(m[j'])| \leq \max(c)$ for each $c \in c(M)$,
- $\min(c) \leq \sum_{\max(\{0\} \cup \{j_c < j | m[j_c] = \{c\}}) < j' < j} |l(m[j'])|$ if $m[j] = \{c\}$ for $c \in c(M)$,
- $\sum_{\max(\{0\} \cup \{j_d < j | m[j_d] = \{d\}}) < j' \leq j, l[i] \in l(m[j'])} (\text{time}(p(l)[i]) \div |l(m[j'])|) \leq \max(d)$ for each $d \in d(M)$, and

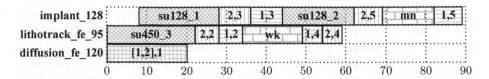

Fig. 1. The chart illustrates an optimal schedule for an example SMSP instance with two lots of the same product, indicated by the labels 1 and 2 followed by respective production operation numbers from 1 to 5. The production operations are performed by machines in three tool groups, called *implant_128*, *lithotrack_fe_95*, and *diffusion_fe_120*, with 1 machine in each. The *diffusion_fe_120* machine starts by processing the first operation for the batch of both lots, while the remaining four operations per lot are performed sequentially by the *lithotrack_fe_95* and *implant_128* machines. The *su450_3*, *su128_1*, and *su128_2* slots indicate the equipping of machines with required setups, and the additional *wk* and *mn* slots denote maintenance operations.

$$- \min(d) \leq \sum\nolimits_{\max(\{0\}\cup\{j_d<j|m[j_d]=\{d\}\})<j'<j, l[i]\in l(m[j'])}(\text{time}(p(l)[i]) \div |l(m[j'])|)$$
if $m[j] = \{d\}$ for $d \in d(M)$.

That is, the required (positive) setup must be in place when performing a production operation, and the number of lots (or processing time) between maintenance operations $c \in c(M)$ (or $d \in d(M)$) must lie in the range $[\min(c), \max(c)]$ (or $[\min(d), \max(d)]$).

Given a feasible schedule for each machine m, for each $1 \leq j \leq n_m$, we denote the *operation time* of $m[j]$ by $o(m[j]) = \text{time}(p(l)[i])$ if there is some $l[i] \in l(m[j])$, or $o(m[j]) = \text{time}(o)$ if $m[j] \setminus l(m[j]) = \{o\}$. Then, starting from $o(m[0]) = 0$ and $t(m[0]) = 0$, the earliest *start time* of $m[j]$ is

$$t(m[j]) = \max \left(\begin{matrix} \{t(m[j-1]) + o(m[j-1])\} \cup \\ \{t(m'[j']) + o(m'[j']) \mid l[i] \in l(m[j]), 1 < i, l[i-1] \in l(m'[j'])\} \end{matrix} \right).$$

The start time $t(m[j])$ thus reflects the earliest time at which $m[j-1]$ is completed by machine m and the predecessor operations $l[i-1]$ (if any) of all $l[i] \in l(m[j])$ have been finished as well. Note that start times become infinite when the schedules for machines induce circular waiting dependencies between the production operations for lots, and we say that the (global) schedule of machine assignments for lots and feasible schedules for machines is *globally feasible* if all start times are finite.

The *makespan* of a globally feasible schedule is the maximum completion time $t(m[n_m]) + o(m[n_m])$ over all machines m. An operation $m[j_s] = \{s\}$ constitutes a *setup violation* for $s \in \mathbb{N}$ if $m[j] \in \mathbb{N}$ for some $j > j_s$ indicates a setup change such that $|\{j_s < j' < j \mid l(m[j']) \neq \emptyset\}| < \min(s)$. Moreover, $m[j]$ amounts to a *batch violation* if we have that $|l(m[j])| < \min(p(l)[i])$ for some $l[i] \in l(m[j])$. The makespan, setup and batch violations provide optimization objectives to be minimized for globally feasible schedules.

For example, an (optimal) schedule for an SMSP instance is displayed in Fig. 1. The machine in the *diffusion_fe_120* tool group is capable of batching and processes the first operation in the route of two lots of the same product simultaneously. Meanwhile, the setups *su450_3* and *su128_1*, required for sequential successor operations on machines in the tool groups *lithotrack_fe_95* and *implant_128*, are brought in place before processing the second and third production operations for each lot. The machine in the *lithotrack_fe_95* group undergoes a maintenance operation labeled *wk* and then continues with the fourth operation in the production route for both lots. The fifth and last operation per lot is processed by the machine in the tool group *implant_128*, where a switch to setup *su128_2* as well as a maintenance operation labeled *mn* need to be performed in addition. The makespan 89 of this schedule is optimal, and likewise the setup and batch operations, the machine assignment of operations is fixed for simplicity, yet revisits of the *lithotrack_fe_95* and *implant_128* machines illustrate re-entrant flow.

3   Experiments

Experiments with our prototypical SMSP encoding [3] showed that fixing the machine assignment of operations upfront sacrifices optimality, while a fully flexible assignment leads to plenty ground rules slowing down the optimization when a tool group contains many machines. To enable trade-offs between the fixed and fully flexible machine allocation strategies, a novel encoding part, detailed in the extended version [4] of this paper, introduces the constant `sub_size` that allows for limiting the number of assignable machines per operation. That is, when `sub_size` is 0, the machine assignment remains fully flexible, gets fixed if the value is 1, or is limited to some *subgroup* of a tool group with at most `sub_size` many machines for values greater than one. Moreover, the allocation of operations to subgroups can be configured by the constant `lot_step`: if its value is 0, all operations of a lot are mapped to the same subgroup, or to successive subgroups in case of value 1. The rationale for these two strategies is that operations performed on the same lot succeed one another and will thus never compete for a machine. On the other hand, the operations may require different setups so that changes are needed when reusing the same machine. In fact, the strategy with `lot_step` value 1 is likely to map operations of a lot to separate subgroups, as they get allocated in a round robin fashion.

As subordinate machine allocation criterion within each subgroup, the setups of operations are inspected when the constant `by_setup` is set to a value other than 0. The idea is to order setups by the sum of processing times for their operations, where setups requiring more processing time come first. Following this order, setups and the respective operations are successively mapped to specific machines, always picking the machine with the least load so far for the next setup to allocate. The rationale of this approach is to reduce the problem size and combinatorics by fixing the machine assignment of operations upfront, while grouping similar operations to make setup changes less likely.

Our novel multi-objective optimization approach combines minimization at the level of difference logic variable values, as already used in [3,13], with native ASP optimization capacities, as applied in [1,12,14] w.r.t. the satisfaction of difference logic constraints, by means of multi-shot solving functionalities [16]. To this end, we utilize a custom control script on top of the Python interface of clingo[DL]. Its first stage concerns makespan minimization, where the value of a difference logic variable representing the makespan is decremented and thus minimized over iterative solving rounds.

Once an unsatisfiable solving attempt yields that the makespan of the schedule obtained last is optimal or a time limit is exceeded, we switch to the second stage using weak constraints for minimizing setup and batch violations by native ASP optimization. Here we take setup violations, where a setup gets changed before performing the intended minimum number of production operations using it, as strictly more significant than violations of the minimum batch size, considering that equipping a machine with a setup takes extra time and effort. The second solving stage can also be restricted by setting a (separate) time limit, and an optimal or best schedule found in time constitutes the final result. Notably, our preliminary approach [3] incorporated neither setup violations nor batching (and its violations) and used only the `--minimize-variable` option of clingo[DL] for makespan minimization, while our novel multi-objective optimization functionalities take advantage of the multi-shot solving interface offered by clingo[DL].

We constructed a scalable set of benchmark instances, focusing on sub-routes of 10 production operations for two product types from the SMT2020 simulation scenario [22]. The 10 operations in both sub-routes are processed by machines belonging to three tool groups and do thus involve re-entrant flow, as a lot visits the same tool group multiple times. Moreover, the operations incorporate batching and specific setups, and machines undergo periodic maintenance operations. In the following, we concentrate on instances with 9 machines, i.e., 3 per tool group, and gradually increasing number of lots. Further smaller- and larger-scale instances along with our implementation are available online.[1]

We ran our experiments with clingo[DL] (version 1.4.0) on an Intel® Core™ i7-8650U CPU Dell Latitude 5590 machine under Windows 10, imposing two time limits per run: the first stage for makespan minimization is aborted at 450 s, in which case the best schedule found so far is taken as upper bound on the makespan for proceeding to minimize setup and batch violations with another 150 s time limit.

Table 1 reports the quality of best schedules obtained within the time limits for both optimization stages, split into 'Makespan' and 'Setup/Batch' values, while two runtimes or 'TO' for a timeout, respectively, are given in the '1 st/2 nd Stage' rows, only listing a single 'TO' entry in case both stages timed out. The 'Size' column provides the value taken for the constant `sub_size`, limiting the number of machines in subgroups to which the operations are preallocated. For the latter, the 'Lot' columns include results with value 0 for the constant `lot_step`, where a common subgroup takes all operations for a lot, or for value 1 in the 'Step' columns, leading to their distribution among subgroups.

The 'Size' value 1 necessarily leads to a fixed machine assignment, for which the quality indicators clearly show that the 'Step' strategy yields better schedules, although it incurs more timeouts and thus fewer certain optima because operations on different lots increase the flexibility of execution sequences and thus search complexity. While flexibility within subgroups by setting their 'Size' to 2 or 3 in principle allows for improved schedules, we observe a deterioration due to sharply increasing instantiation size and search effort, as already observed in [3]. The setup strategy to differentiate operations and machines within subgroups, activated by changing the constant `by_setup`, aims to cut down the scheduling complexity in line with the optimization objectives by reducing the need for setup changes. This leads to significantly improved schedules with 'Size' 3, where the 'Lot' and 'Step' preallocation strategies are indifferent and

---

[1] https://github.com/prosysscience/FJSP-SMT2020.

Table 1. Preallocation strategy results with 3 machines per tool group and 10 operations per lot

9 Machines			70 Operations		80 Operations		90 Operations		100 Operations	
	Size		Lot	Step	Lot	Step	Lot	Step	Lot	Step
Fixed	1	Makespan	483	428	489	440	486	531	592	553
		Setup/Batch	6/12	2/12	5/14	0/13	5/14	3/12	3/12	0/16
		1 st/2 nd Stage	2/1	TO/27	6/2	TO/13	11/13	TO	TO/78	TO
Flexible	2	Makespan	483	475	592	592	592	539	745	698
		Setup/Batch	2/8	0/9	1/8	1/8	1/10	0/11	0/12	0/15
		1 st/2 nd Stage	5/1	TO	TO/114	TO/1	TO/130	TO	TO	TO
	3	Makespan	559	–	815	–	1357	–	1486	–
		Setup/Batch	0/8	–	0/8	–	0/10	–	10/18	–
		1 st/2 nd Stage	TO	–	TO/140	–	TO/79	–	TO	–
Setup	2	Makespan	483	475	592	592	592	536	745	683
		Setup/Batch	2/8	0/9	1/8	1/8	1/10	0/12	0/13	0/16
		1 st/2 nd Stage	2/1	TO	TO/21	TO/25	TO/22	TO	TO/76	TO
	3	Makespan	334	–	345	–	434	–	555	–
		Setup/Batch	0/8	–	0/8	–	0/11	–	0/12	–
		1 st/2 nd Stage	TO/20	–	TO/123	–	TO	–	TO/73	–

redundant results for the latter are omitted, up to a critical size reached with 100 operations.

With our preliminary approach [3], using a more naive and less feature-rich encoding of either fixed or fully flexible machine assignments, the threshold at which problem size and combinatorics get prohibitive was reached at less than 50 operations already. Despite gearing up to double that size, our benchmark instances still represent small excerpts of the large-scale semiconductor fabs with more than 100 tool groups and from 242 to 543 production operations per lot modeled by [22]. The elevated complexity in comparison to basic settings like the traditional FJSP is mainly due to sophisticated setup and maintenance operations, requiring a detailed analysis of execution sequences on machines for SMSP. We conjecture that similar scalability limits would also be encountered with MIP or CP encodings, yet the first-order modeling language of ASP with difference logic facilitates rapid prototyping and experimentation. In fact, our performance evaluation aims to explore the feasibility of search and optimization, in order to come up with strategies for breaking down large SMSP instances into more manageable portions, e.g., focusing on some bottleneck tool groups or re-entrant flow of operations.

4   Conclusion

This work extends our preliminary SMSP approach [3] with crucial features, namely, scalable and informed preallocation strategies to reduce the instantiation size and search complexity, as well as batch processing and multiple optimization objectives. While we enhance the scheduling scalability and coverage of real-world features, our mid-term goal is to incorporate scheduling into the real or simulated management of semiconductor manufacturing processes. As next step into this direction, we aim to use scheduling for improving the decision making in the PySCFabSim simulator [23], where methods available so far, i.e., handcrafted dispatching rules or black-box machine learning models, function locally and do not take the global impact of their decisions into account.

Acknowledgments. This work was funded by FFG project 894072 (SwarmIn) as well as KWF project 28472, cms electronics GmbH, FunderMax GmbH, Hirsch Armbänder GmbH, incubed IT GmbH, Infineon Technologies Austria AG, Isovolta AG, Kostwein Holding GmbH, and Privatstiftung Kärntner Sparkasse. We are grateful to the anonymous reviewers for their helpful comments.

References

1. Abels, D., Jordi, J., Ostrowski, M., Schaub, T., Toletti, A., Wanko, P.: Train scheduling with hybrid ASP. Theory Pract. Logic Program. **21**(3), 317–347 (2021). https://doi.org/10.1017/S1471068420000046
2. Abseher, M., Gebser, M., Musliu, N., Schaub, T., Woltran, S.: Shift design with answer set programming. Fund. Inform. **147**(1), 1–25 (2016). https://doi.org/10.3233/FI-2016-1396
3. Ali, R., El-Kholany, M., Gebser, M.: Flexible job-shop scheduling for semiconductor manufacturing with hybrid answer set programming (application paper). In: Hanus, M., Inclezan, D. (eds.) PADL. LNCS, vol. 13880, pp. 85–95. Springer, Cham (2023). https://doi.org/10.1007/978-3-031-24841-2_6
4. Ali, R., El-Kholany, M., Gebser, M.: Hybrid ASP-based multi-objective scheduling of semiconductor manufacturing processes (extended version) (2023). https://doi.org/10.48550/arXiv.2307.14799
5. Balduccini, M.: Industrial-size scheduling with ASP+CP. In: Delgrande, J.P., Faber, W. (eds.) LPNMR 2011. LNCS (LNAI), vol. 6645, pp. 284–296. Springer, Heidelberg (2011). https://doi.org/10.1007/978-3-642-20895-9_33
6. Banbara, M., et al.: teaspoon: Solving the curriculum-based course timetabling problems with answer set programming. Ann. Oper. Res. **275**(1), 3–37 (2019). https://doi.org/10.1007/s10479-018-2757-7
7. Brucker, P., Schlie, R.: Job-shop scheduling with multi-purpose machines. Computing **45**(4), 369–375 (1990). https://doi.org/10.1007/BF02238804
8. Ceylan, Z., Tozan, H., Bulkan, S.: A coordinated scheduling problem for the supply chain in a flexible job shop machine environment. Oper. Res. Int. Journal **21**(2), 875–900 (2021). https://doi.org/10.1007/s12351-020-00615-0
9. Cotton, S., Maler, O.: Fast and flexible difference constraint propagation for DPLL(T). In: Biere, A., Gomes, C.P. (eds.) SAT 2006. LNCS, vol. 4121, pp. 170–183. Springer, Heidelberg (2006). https://doi.org/10.1007/11814948_19
10. Da Col, G., Teppan, E.C.: Industrial size job shop scheduling tackled by present day CP solvers. In: Schiex, T., de Givry, S. (eds.) CP 2019. LNCS, vol. 11802, pp. 144–160. Springer, Cham (2019). https://doi.org/10.1007/978-3-030-30048-7_9
11. Dodaro, C., Galatà, G., Grioni, A., Maratea, M., Mochi, M., Porro, I.: An ASP-based solution to the chemotherapy treatment scheduling problem. Theory Pract. Logic Program. **21**(6), 835–851 (2021). https://doi.org/10.1017/S1471068421000363
12. Eiter, T., Geibinger, T., Musliu, N., Oetsch, J., Skocovský, P., Stepanova, D.: Answer-set programming for lexicographical makespan optimisation in parallel machine scheduling. In:

Proceedings of the Eighteenth International Conference on Principles of Knowledge Representation and Reasoning (KR 2021), pp. 280–290. AAAI Press (2021). https://doi.org/10.24963/kr.2021/27

13. El-Kholany, M., Gebser, M., Schekotihin, K.: Problem decomposition and multi-shot ASP solving for job-shop scheduling. Theory Pract. Logic Program. **22**(4), 623–639 (2022). https://doi.org/10.1017/S1471068422000217

14. Francescutto, G., Schekotihin, K., El-Kholany, M.M.S.: Solving a multi-resource partial-ordering flexible variant of the job-shop scheduling problem with hybrid ASP. In: Faber, W., Friedrich, G., Gebser, M., Morak, M. (eds.) JELIA 2021. LNCS (LNAI), vol. 12678, pp. 313–328. Springer, Cham (2021). https://doi.org/10.1007/978-3-030-75775-5_21

15. Garey, M., Johnson, D., Sethi, R.: The complexity of flowshop and jobshop scheduling. Math. Oper. Res. **1**(2), 117–129 (1976). https://doi.org/10.1287/moor.1.2.117

16. Gebser, M., Kaminski, R., Kaufmann, B., Schaub, T.: Multi-shot ASP solving with clingo. Theory Pract. Logic Program. **19**(1), 27–82 (2019). https://doi.org/10.1017/S1471068418000054

17. Gebser, M., Kaminski, R., Kaufmann, B., Ostrowski, M., Schaub, T., Wanko, P.: Theory solving made easy with clingo 5. In: Technical Communications of the Thirty-second International Conference on Logic Programming (ICLP 2016), pp. 2:1–2:15. Schloss Dagstuhl (2016). https://doi.org/10.4230/OASIcs.ICLP.2016.2

18. Gran, S., Ismail, I., Ajol, T., Ibrahim, A.: Mixed integer programming model for flexible job-shop scheduling problem (FJSP) to minimize makespan and total machining time. In: Proceedings of the International Conference on Computer, Communications, and Control Technology (I4CT), pp. 413–417. IEEE (2015). https://doi.org/10.1109/I4CT.2015.7219609

19. Ham, A., Park, M., Kim, K.: Energy-aware flexible job shop scheduling using mixed integer programming and constraint programming. Math. Probl. Eng. 2021(Article ID 8035806), 1–12 (2021). https://doi.org/10.1155/2021/8035806

20. Hassanzadeh, A., Rasti-Barzoki, M., Khosroshahi, H.: Two new meta-heuristics for a bi-objective supply chain scheduling problem in flow-shop environment. Appl. Soft Comput. **49**, 335–351 (2016). https://doi.org/10.1016/j.asoc.2016.08.019

21. Janhunen, T., Kaminski, R., Ostrowski, M., Schellhorn, S., Wanko, P., Schaub, T.: Clingo goes linear constraints over reals and integers. Theory Pract. Logic Program. **17**(5–6), 872–888 (2017). https://doi.org/10.1017/S1471068417000242

22. Kopp, D., Hassoun, M., Kalir, A., Mönch, L.: SMT2020-A semiconductor manufacturing testbed. IEEE Trans. Semicond. Manuf. **33**(4), 522–531 (2020). https://doi.org/10.1109/TSM.2020.3001933

23. Kovács, B., Tassel, P., Ali, R., El-Kholany, M., Gebser, M., Seidel, G.: A customizable simulator for artificial intelligence research to schedule semiconductor fabs. In: Proceedings of the Thirty-third Annual SEMI Advanced Semiconductor Manufacturing Conference (ASMC 2022), pp. 106–111. IEEE (2022). https://doi.org/10.1109/ASMC54647.2022.9792520

24. Leslie, M.: Pandemic scrambles the semiconductor supply chain. Engineering **9**, 10–12 (2022). https://doi.org/10.1016/j.eng.2021.12.006

25. Li, X., Gao, L.: An effective hybrid genetic algorithm and tabu search for flexible job shop scheduling problem. Int. J. Prod. Econ. **174**, 93–110 (2016). https://doi.org/10.1016/j.ijpe.2016.01.016

26. Lifschitz, V.: Answer Set Programming. Springer, Cham (2019). https://doi.org/10.1007/978-3-030-24658-7

27. Mönch, L., Fowler, J., Dauzère-Pérès, S., Mason, S., Rose, O.: A survey of problems, solution techniques, and future challenges in scheduling semiconductor manufacturing operations. J. Sched. **14**(6), 583–599 (2011). https://doi.org/10.1007/s10951-010-0222-9

28. Pfund, M., Balasubramanian, H., Fowler, J., Mason, S., Rose, O.: A multi-criteria approach for scheduling semiconductor wafer fabrication facilities. J. Sched. **11**(1), 29–47 (2008). https://doi.org/10.1007/s10951-007-0049-1

29. Pfund, M., Mason, S., Fowler, J.: Semiconductor manufacturing scheduling and dispatching. In: Herrmann, J.W. (ed.) Handbook of Production Scheduling. International Series in Operations Research and Management Science, vol. 89, pp. 213–241. Springer, Boston (2006). https://doi.org/10.1007/0-387-33117-4_9

30. Ricca, F., et al.: Team-building with answer set programming in the Gioia-Tauro seaport. Theory Pract. Logic Program. **12**(3), 361–381 (2012). https://doi.org/10.1017/S147106841100007X

31. Sahraeian, R., Rohaninejad, M., Fadavi, M.: A new model for integrated lot sizing and scheduling in flexible job shop problem. J. Ind. Syst. Eng. **10**(3), 72–91 (2017). https://www.jise.ir/article_44919.html

32. Taillard, E.: Benchmarks for basic scheduling problems. Eur. J. Oper. Res. **64**(2), 278–285 (1993). https://doi.org/10.1016/0377-2217(93)90182-M

33. Tassel, P., Rbaia, M.: A multi-shot ASP encoding for the aircraft routing and maintenance planning problem. In: Faber, W., Friedrich, G., Gebser, M., Morak, M. (eds.) JELIA 2021. LNCS (LNAI), vol. 12678, pp. 442–457. Springer, Cham (2021). https://doi.org/10.1007/978-3-030-75775-5_30

34. Upasani, A., Uzsoy, R., Sourirajan, K.: A problem reduction approach for scheduling semiconductor wafer fabrication facilities. IEEE Trans. Semicond. Manuf. **19**(2), 216–225 (2006). https://doi.org/10.1109/TSM.2006.873510

35. Wang, L., Zheng, D.: An effective hybrid optimization strategy for job-shop scheduling problems. Comput. Oper. Res. **28**(6), 585–596 (2001). https://doi.org/10.1016/S0305-0548(99)00137-9

36. Waschneck, B., et al.: Deep reinforcement learning for semiconductor production scheduling. In: Proceedings of the Twenty-ninth Annual SEMI Advanced Semiconductor Manufacturing Conference (ASMC 2018), pp. 301–306. IEEE (2018). https://doi.org/10.1109/ASMC.2018.8373191

37. Xing, L., Chen, Y., Wang, P., Zhao, Q., Xiong, J.: A knowledge-based ant colony optimization for flexible job shop scheduling problems. Appl. Soft Comput. **10**(3), 888–896 (2010). https://doi.org/10.1016/j.asoc.2009.10.006

On Heuer's Procedure for Verifying Strong Equivalence

Jorge Fandinno[1]($\boxtimes$) and Vladimir Lifschitz[2]

[1] University of Nebraska at Omaha, Omaha, USA
jfandinno@unomaha.edu
[2] University of Texas at Austin, Austin, USA

Abstract. In answer set programming, two groups of rules are considered strongly equivalent if replacing one group by the other within any program does not affect the set of stable models. Jan Heuer has designed and implemented a system that verifies strong equivalence of programs in the ASP language mini-GRINGO. The design is based on the syntactic transformation τ^* that converts mini-GRINGO programs into first-order formulas. Heuer's assertion about τ^* that was supposed to justify this procedure turned out to be incorrect, and in this paper we propose an alternative justification for his algorithm. We show also that if τ^* is replaced by the simpler and more natural translation ν then the algorithm will still produce correct results.

1 Introduction

In answer set programming (ASP), two groups of rules are considered strongly equivalent if replacing one group by the other within any program does not affect the set of stable models [21]. This equivalence relation has been extensively studied in the literature because of its interesting theoretical properties and its usefulness for the practice of answer set programming [1–6,8,10,11,15,16, 19,20,22–24,27]. Jan Heuer designed and implemented a system that verifies strong equivalence of programs in the ASP language mini-GRINGO. The system is described in his Bachelor Thesis [12], presented to the University of Potsdam.

The design of the system is based on the syntactic transformation τ^* [20], which converts mini-GRINGO rules and programs into first-order formulas. Mini-GRINGO programs Π_1, Π_2 are strongly equivalent whenever the formulas $\tau^*\Pi_1$ and $\tau^*\Pi_2$ can be derived from each other in the deductive system HTA ("here-and-there with arithmetic") [17].

To use a resolution theorem prover as a proof engine for HTA, Heuer needed an additional translation that would relate HTA to a classical first-order theory. The translation that he implemented is a straightforward generalization of the process proposed by Pearce et al. [25] for propositional formulas.

Unfortunately, the claim that is supposed to justify this additional translation [12, Theorem 3] is incorrect as stated, because it disregards the existence of interpretations that treat arithmetical symbols in nonstandard ways.[1] For

---

[1] Lifschitz et al. [20] made the same mistake in their Proposition 6.

S. Gaggl et al. (Eds.): JELIA 2023, LNAI 14281, pp. 253–261, 2023.
https://doi.org/10.1007/978-3-031-43619-2_18

example, the facts $p(2 + 3)$ and $p(5)$ are strongly equivalent, but we cannot assert that they get the same truth value under any interpretation. Indeed, the expressions $2 + 3$ and 5 can have different values if the symbols 2, 3, 5 and + are not interpreted as usual in arithmetic.

In this paper we show that, in spite of this difficulty, Heuer's procedure is in fact correct. Second, we show that the procedure will produce correct results if we modify it by replacing $\tau^* R$ with the simpler translation νR when the rule R is regular [18]. The paper begins with a review of the mini-GRINGO language and of the target language of the translations τ^* and ν (Sects. 2 and 3). The main results of this paper are stated in Sect. 4. In Sect. 5 we give examples of their use. In Sect. 6 we describe an extension HTA$^\omega$ of the deductive system HTA, which plays an important role in our proofs of the main results.

2   Review: Programs

We assume that three countably infinite sets of symbols are selected: *numerals*, *symbolic constants*, and *variables*. We assume that a 1–1 correspondence between numerals and integers is chosen; the numeral corresponding to an integer n is denoted by $\overline{n}$. *Precomputed terms* are numerals and symbolic constants. We assume that a total order on precomputed terms is chosen such that for all integers m and n, $\overline{m} < \overline{n}$ iff $m < n$.

Terms allowed in a mini-GRINGO program are formed from precomputed terms and variables using the six operation names

$$+ \quad - \quad \times \quad / \quad \backslash \quad ..$$

(the last three serve to represent integer division, remainder and intervals). An *atom* is a symbolic constant optionally followed by a tuple of terms in parentheses. A *literal* is an atom possibly preceded by one or two occurrences of *not*. A *comparison* is an expression of the form $t_1 \prec t_2$, where t_1, t_2 are terms and $\prec$ is $=$ or one of the comparison symbols

$$\neq \quad < \quad > \quad \leq \quad \geq \tag{1}$$

A *rule* is an expression of the form $Head \leftarrow Body$, where

- *Body* is a conjunction (possibly empty) of literals and comparisons, and
- *Head* is either an atom (then the rule is *basic*), or an atom in braces (then this is a *choice rule*), or empty (then this is a *constraint*).

A *(mini-GRINGO) program* is a finite set of rules.

The semantics of ground terms is defined by assigning to every ground term t the finite set $[t]$ of its *values* [20, Section 3]. Values of a ground term are precomputed terms. For instance,

$$[\overline{2}/\overline{3}] = \{\overline{0}\}, \quad [\overline{2}/\overline{0}] = \emptyset, \quad [\overline{0}..\overline{2}] = \{\overline{0}, \overline{1}, \overline{2}\}.$$

A *predicate symbol* is a pair p/n, where p is a symbolic constant, and n is a nonnegative integer. About a predicate symbol p/n we say that it *occurs* in a program Π if a rule of Π contains an atom of the form $p(t_1, \ldots, t_n)$.

Stable models of a program are defined as stable models of the set of propositional formulas obtained from it by the syntactic transformation τ [20, Section 3]. Atomic parts of these formulas are *precomputed atoms*—atoms $p(\mathbf{t})$ such that the members of $\mathbf{t}$ are precomputed terms. For example, τ transforms the rule

$$\{q(X)\} \leftarrow p(X) \tag{2}$$

into the set of formulas $p(t) \rightarrow (q(t) \vee \neg q(t))$ for all precomputed terms t. The rule

$$q(\overline{0}\,..\,\overline{2}) \leftarrow p \tag{3}$$

is transformed into $p \rightarrow (q(\overline{0}) \wedge q(\overline{1}) \wedge q(\overline{2}))$. Thus stable models of mini-GRINGO programs are sets of precomputed atoms.

Mini-GRINGO programs Π_1 and Π_2 are *strongly equivalent* to each other if, for every set Ω of propositional combinations of precomputed atoms, $\tau\Pi_1 \cup \Omega$ has the same stable models as $\tau\Pi_2 \cup \Omega$.

3   Review: Two-Sorted Formulas

The target language of the translations τ^* [20, Section 6] and ν [18, Sections 4, 5] is a first-order language with the sort *general* and its subsort *integer*.[2] Variables of the first sort are meant to range over arbitrary precomputed terms, and we identify them with variables used in mini-GRINGO rules. Variables of the second sort are meant to range over numerals (or, equivalently, integers). This is made precise in the definition of a standard interpretation at the end of this section.

The signature σ_0 of the language includes

- all precomputed terms as object constants; an object constant is assigned the sort *integer* iff it is a numeral;
- the symbols $+$, $-$ and $\times$ as binary function constants; their arguments and values have the sort *integer*;[3]
- predicate symbols p/n as n-ary predicate constants; their arguments have the sort *general*;
- comparison symbols (1) as binary predicate constants; their arguments have the sort *general*.

---

[2] The need to use a language with two sorts is explained by the fact that function symbols in a first-order language are supposed to represent total functions, and arithmetic operations are not defined on symbolic constants.

[3] The symbols $/$ and $\backslash$ are not included because the corresponding functions are not total on the set of integers. The symbol $..$ is not included because intervals do not belong to the domain of precomputed terms.

An atomic formula $(p/n)(t_1,\ldots,t_n)$ can be abbreviated as $p(t_1,\ldots,t_n)$. An atomic formula of the form $\prec(t_1,t_2)$, where $\prec$ is a comparison symbol, can be written as $t_1 \prec t_2$. A conjunction of the form $t_1 \leq t_2 \wedge t_2 \leq t_3$ can be written as $t_1 \leq t_2 \leq t_3$, and similarly for other chains of inequalities.

For example, the translation ν converts rule (2) into

$$\forall X(p(X) \rightarrow (q(X) \vee \neg q(X))). \tag{4}$$

Rule (3) is transformed into

$$p \rightarrow \forall N(\overline{0} \leq N \leq \overline{2} \rightarrow q(N)),$$

where N is an integer variable. The result of applying ν to the rule

$$q(X, Y + \overline{1}) \leftarrow p(X, Y) \tag{5}$$

is

$$\forall X N(p(X, N) \rightarrow q(X, N + \overline{1})). \tag{6}$$

An interpretation of the signature σ_0 is *standard* if

- its domain of the sort *general* is the set of all precomputed terms;
- its domain of the sort *integer* is the set of all numerals;
- it interprets every precomputed term t as t;
- it interprets $\overline{m} + \overline{n}$ as $\overline{m+n}$, and similarly for subtraction and multiplication;
- it interprets every atomic sentence $t_1 \prec t_2$, where t_1 and t_2 are precomputed terms, as true iff the relation $\prec$ holds for the pair (t_1, t_2).

4   Translation γ and Its Properties

By σ_0' we denote the extension of the signature σ_0 obtained by adding, for every predicate symbol p/n, a new n-ary predicate constant $(p/n)'$. An atomic formula $(p/n)'(\mathbf{t})$ can be abbreviated as $p'(\mathbf{t})$. For the signature σ_0', the definition of a standard interpretation is the same as for the signature σ_0 above.

For any formula F over the signature σ_0, by F' we denote the formula over σ_0' obtained from F by replacing every occurrence of every predicate symbol p/n by $(p/n)'$.

The translation γ, which relates logic of here-and-there with arithmetic to classical logic, maps formulas over σ_0 to formulas over σ_0'.[4] It is defined recursively:

- $\gamma F = F$ if F is atomic,
- $\gamma(\neg F) = \neg F'$,
- $\gamma(F \wedge G) = \gamma F \wedge \gamma G$,
- $\gamma(F \vee G) = \gamma F \vee \gamma G$,

---

[4] Heuer [12, Sections 2.2.3 and 3.3] denotes this translation by σ^*. We switched to γ to avoid confusion with the symbols denoting signatures.

- $\gamma(F \to G) = (\gamma F \to \gamma G) \wedge (F' \to G')$,
- $\gamma(\forall X\, F) = \forall X\, \gamma F$,
- $\gamma(\exists X\, F) = \exists X\, \gamma F$.

Our justification of Heuer's procedure is given by Theorem 1 below. In the statement of the theorem, $\mathcal{A}(p/n)$ stands for the formula $\forall \mathbf{X}(p(\mathbf{X}) \to p'(\mathbf{X}))$, where $\mathbf{X}$ is an n-tuple of distinct general variables.

Theorem 1. *Mini-*GRINGO *programs* Π_1, Π_2 *are strongly equivalent iff all standard interpretations of* σ_0' *satisfy the formula*

$$\left(\bigwedge_{p/n} \mathcal{A}(p/n) \right) \to (\gamma \tau^* \Pi_1 \leftrightarrow \gamma \tau^* \Pi_2), \tag{7}$$

where the conjunction extends over all predicate symbols p/n *that occur in* Π_1 *or in* Π_2.

This theorem differs from the incorrect assertion mentioned in the introduction [12, Theorem 3] by requiring the interpretations to be standard. It shows that strong equivalence between Π_1 and Π_2 can be established by proving formula (7) in a first-order theory such that its axioms are satisfied by all standard interpretations. This is how Heuer's procedure operates. It translates formula (7) into the TPTP language [26] using the algorithm implemented earlier as part of the proof assistant ANTHEM [7]. Then the theorem prover VAMPIRE [14] is invoked to find a proof.

Results similar to the theorem above are due to Lin [23] (his Theorem 1 is about strong equivalence of propositional programs), to Pearce et al. [25] (their Theorem 6(iii) is about strong equivalence of propositional formulas), and to Ferraris et al. [9] (their Theorem 9 is about strong equivalence of first-order formulas without arithmetic).

Theorem 2 below shows that the assertion of Theorem 1 will remain true if we replace τ^* by the simpler and more natural translation ν when a "regular" rule [18, Section 2] is translated. (The two main distinctive features of regular rules are that they do not use function symbols / and \, and do not apply arithmetical operations to intervals, as in $X \times (Y\,..\,Z)$.)

For any mini-GRINGO program Π, by $\mu\Pi$ we denote the set consisting of

- the formulas νR for all rules R of Π that are regular [18, Section 2], and
- the formulas $\tau^* R$ for all rules R of Π that are not regular.

The assertion of Theorem 1 will remain true if we replace τ^* in its statement by μ:

Theorem 2. *Mini-*GRINGO *programs* Π_1, Π_2 *are strongly equivalent iff all standard interpretations of* σ_0' *satisfy the formula*

$$\left(\bigwedge_{p/n} \mathcal{A}(p/n) \right) \to (\gamma \mu \Pi_1 \leftrightarrow \gamma \mu \Pi_2), \tag{8}$$

where the conjunction extends over all predicate symbols p/n that occur in Π_1 or in Π_2.

5 Examples

Example 1. Let Π_1 be rule (2), and let Π_2 be the rule

$$q(X) \leftarrow p(X) \wedge not\ not\ q(X). \tag{9}$$

Both rules are regular, so that $\mu\Pi_1$ is (4), and $\mu\Pi_2$ is

$$\forall X (p(X) \wedge \neg\neg q(X) \rightarrow q(X)).$$

Then $\gamma\mu\Pi_1$ is

$$\forall X ((p(X) \rightarrow (q(X) \vee \neg q'(X))) \wedge (p'(X) \rightarrow (q'(X) \vee \neg q'(X)))),$$

which is (classically) equivalent to

$$\forall X (p(X) \rightarrow (q(X) \vee \neg q'(X))); \tag{10}$$

$\gamma\mu\Pi_2$ is

$$\forall X ((p(X) \wedge \neg\neg q'(X) \rightarrow q(X)) \wedge (p'(X) \wedge \neg\neg q'(X) \rightarrow q'(X))),$$

which is equivalent to

$$\forall X (p(X) \wedge q'(X) \rightarrow q(X)))$$

and furthermore to (10). Thus the consequent of (8) is in this case logically valid, and the programs are strongly equivalent by Theorem 2.

Example 2. Let Π_1 be rule (5), and let Π_2 be the rule

$$q(X,Y) \leftarrow p(X, Y - \bar{1}). \tag{11}$$

Both rules are regular, so that $\mu\Pi_1$ is (6), and $\mu\Pi_2$ is

$$\forall XN (p(X, N - \bar{1}) \rightarrow q(X,N)).$$

Then $\gamma\mu\Pi_1$ is

$$\forall XN ((p(X,N) \rightarrow q(X, N + \bar{1})) \wedge (p'(X,N) \rightarrow q'(X, N + \bar{1}))),$$

and $\gamma\mu\Pi_2$ is

$$\forall XN ((p(X, N - \bar{1}) \rightarrow q(X,N)) \wedge (p'(X, N - \bar{1}) \rightarrow q'(X,N))).$$

The equivalence $\gamma\mu\Pi_1 \leftrightarrow \gamma\mu\Pi_2$ is a logical consequence of the formulas

$$\forall N ((N - \bar{1}) + \bar{1} = N) \text{ and } \forall N ((N + \bar{1}) - \bar{1} = N),$$

which are satisfied by all standard interpretations. The programs are strongly equivalent by Theorem 2.

In both examples above, we did not refer to the antecedent of implication (8); in each case, all standard interpretations satisfy the consequent. Strong equivalence between the program

$$q \leftarrow p,$$
$$\leftarrow p \wedge \neg q$$

and its first rule is a case when the presence of the antecedents in implications (7) and (8) is essential. This example is due to Lin [23, Section 2].

6   Logic of Here-and-there with Arithmetic

Proofs of Theorems 1 and 2 are derived from a lemma that refers to an extension of the deductive system HTA. This extension, denoted by HTA^ω, can be described as the result of adding a few axiom schemas and inference rules to intuitionistic logic with equality for the signature σ_0.

The list of additional axioms includes the Hosoi axiom schema [13]

$$F \vee (F \to G) \vee \neg G$$

and the schema SQHT [22]

$$\exists X (F(X) \to \forall X\, F(X)).$$

It includes also the formulas

$$t_1 \prec t_2$$

where $\prec$ is one of comparison symbols (1), and t_1, t_2 are precomputed terms that satisfy the condition $t_1 \prec t_2$;

$$\neg(t_1 \prec t_2)$$

where $\prec$ is $=$ or one of comparison symbols (1), and t_1, t_2 are precomputed terms that do not satisfy the condition $t_1 \prec t_2$; and

$$\overline{m + n} = \overline{m} + \overline{n}, \qquad \overline{m - n} = \overline{m} - \overline{n}, \qquad \overline{m \cdot n} = \overline{m} \times \overline{n}$$

for all integers m, n.

The additional inference rules are "omega-rules" with infinitely many premises:

$$\frac{F(t) \text{ for all precomputed terms } t}{\forall X\, F(X)}$$

where X is a general variable, and

$$\frac{F(\overline{n}) \text{ for all integers } n}{\forall N\, F(N)} \tag{12}$$

where N is an integer variable [6, Section 5.3].

Main Lemma. *Let Π_1, Π_2 be mini-GRINGO programs, and let F_i $(i = 1, 2)$ be a sentence over σ_0 that is equivalent to $\tau^* \Pi_i$ in HTA^ω. Programs Π_1, Π_2 are strongly equivalent iff every standard model of $\mathcal{A}$ satisfies $\gamma F_1 \leftrightarrow \gamma F_2$, where $\mathcal{A}$ denotes the set of formulas $\mathcal{A}(p/n)$ for all predicate symbols p/n.*

Conclusion

Theorem 2 shows that Heuer's procedure can be modified by replacing $\tau^* R$ with the simpler translation νR when the rule R is regular. We expect that this modification will make the system easier to use, and we plan to verify this conjecture in collaboration with researchers at the University of Potsdam.

References

1. Bochman, A., Lifschitz, V.: Yet another characterization of strong equivalence. In: Technical Communications of the 27th International Conference on Logic Programming (ICLP), pp. 11–15 (2011)
2. Cabalar, P., Ferraris, P.: Propositional theories are strongly equivalent to logic programs. Theory Pract. Logic Program. **7**, 745–759 (2007)
3. Chen, Y., Lin, F., Li, L.: SELP – a system for studying strong equivalence between logic programs. In: Proceedings of International Conference on Logic Programming and Nonmonotonic Reasoning, pp. 442–446 (2005)
4. De Jongh, D., Hendriks, L.: Characterization of strongly equivalent logic programs in intermediate logics. Theory Pract. Logic Program. **3**, 259–270 (2003)
5. Eiter, T., Fink, M., Tompits, H., Woltran, S.: Strong and uniform equivalence in answer-set programming: characterizations and complexity results for the non-ground case. In: Proceedings of AAAI Conference on Artificial Intelligence (AAAI), pp. 695–700 (2005)
6. Fandinno, J., Lifschitz, V.: Omega-completeness of the logic of here-and-there and strong equivalence of logic programs. In: Proceedings of International Conference on Principles of Knowledge Representation and Reasoning (to appear) (2023)
7. Fandinno, J., Lifschitz, V., Lühne, P., Schaub, T.: Verifying tight logic programs with anthem and vampire. Theory Pract. Logic Program. **20**, 735–750 (2020)
8. Ferraris, P.: On modular translations and strong equivalence. In: Proceedings of International Conference on Logic Programming and Nonmonotonic Reasoning (LPNMR), pp. 79–91 (2005)
9. Ferraris, P., Lee, J., Lifschitz, V.: Stable models and circumscription. Artif. Intell. **175**, 236–263 (2011)
10. Harrison, A., Lifschitz, V., Pearce, D., Valverde, A.: Infinitary equilibrium logic and strong equivalence. In: Proceedings of International Conference on Logic Programming and Nonmonotonic Reasoning (LPNMR), pp. 398–410 (2015)
11. Harrison, A., Lifschitz, V., Pearce, D., Valverde, A.: Infinitary equilibrium logic and strongly equivalent logic programs. Artif. Intell. **246**, 22–33 (2017)
12. Heuer, J.: Automated verification of equivalence properties in advanced logic programs (2020). Bachelor Thesis, University of Potsdam

13. Hosoi, T.: The axiomatization of the intermediate propositional systems S_n of Gödel. J. Faculty Sci. Univ. Tokyo **13**, 183–187 (1966)
14. Kovács, L., Voronkov, A.: First-order theorem proving and VAMPIRE. In: Sharygina, N., Veith, H. (eds.) CAV 2013. LNCS, vol. 8044, pp. 1–35. Springer, Heidelberg (2013). https://doi.org/10.1007/978-3-642-39799-8_1
15. Lee, J., Palla, R.: Yet another proof of the strong equivalence between propositional theories and logic programs. In: Working Notes of the Workshop on Correspondence and Equivalence for Nonmonotonic Theories (2007)
16. Lierler, Y., Lifschitz, V.: Termination of grounding is not preserved by strongly equivalent transformations. In: Proceedings of International Conference on Logic Programming and Nonmonotonic Reasoning (LPNMR) (2011)
17. Lifschitz, V.: Here and there with arithmetic. Theory Pract. Logic Program. **21**, 735–749 (2021)
18. Lifschitz, V.: Transforming gringo rules into formulas in a natural way. In: Faber, W., Friedrich, G., Gebser, M., Morak, M. (eds.) JELIA 2021. LNCS (LNAI), vol. 12678, pp. 421–434. Springer, Cham (2021). https://doi.org/10.1007/978-3-030-75775-5_28
19. Lifschitz, V.: Strong equivalence of logic programs with counting. Theory Pract. Logic Program. **22**, 573–588 (2022)
20. Lifschitz, V., Lühne, P., Schaub, T.: Verifying strong equivalence of programs in the input language of gringo. In: Balduccini, M., Lierler, Y., Woltran, S. (eds.) LPNMR 2019. Lecture Notes in Computer Science, vol. 11481, pp. 270–283. Springer, Cham (2019). https://doi.org/10.1007/978-3-030-20528-7_20
21. Lifschitz, V., Pearce, D., Valverde, A.: Strongly equivalent logic programs. ACM Trans. Comput. Log. **2**, 526–541 (2001)
22. Lifschitz, V., Pearce, D., Valverde, A.: A characterization of strong equivalence for logic programs with variables. In: Baral, C., Brewka, G., Schlipf, J. (eds.) LPNMR 2007. LNCS (LNAI), vol. 4483, pp. 188–200. Springer, Heidelberg (2007). https://doi.org/10.1007/978-3-540-72200-7_17
23. Lin, F.: Reducing strong equivalence of logic programs to entailment in classical propositional logic. In: Proceedings of International Conference on Principles of Knowledge Representation and Reasoning (KR), pp. 170–176 (2002)
24. Lin, F., Chen, Y.: Discovering classes of strongly equivalent logic programs. In: Proceedings of International Joint Conference on Artificial Intelligence (IJCAI) (2005)
25. Pearce, D., Tompits, H., Woltran, S.: Characterising equilibrium logic and nested logic programs: reductions and complexity. Theory Pract. Logic Program. **9**, 565–616 (2009)
26. Sutcliffe, G.: The TPTP problem library and associated infrastructure. J. Autom. Reason. **59**(4), 483–502 (2017)
27. Turner, H.: Strong equivalence made easy: nested expressions and weight constraints. Theory Pract. Logic Program. **3**(4–5), 609–622 (2003)

Hamiltonian Cycle Reconfiguration
with Answer Set Programming

Takahiro Hirate[1], Mutsunori Banbara[1]([✉]) [iD], Katsumi Inoue[2] [iD],
Xiao-Nan Lu[3] [iD], Hidetomo Nabeshima[4] [iD], Torsten Schaub[5] [iD],
Takehide Soh[6] [iD], and Naoyuki Tamura[6] [iD]

[1] Nagoya University, Furo-cho, Chikusa-ku, Nagoya 464-8601, Japan
{hirate310,banbara}@nagoya-u.jp
[2] National Institute of Informatics, Hitotsubashi, Chiyoda-ku, Tokyo 101-8430, Japan
inoue@nii.ac.jp
[3] Gifu University, Yanagido, Gifu 501-1193, Japan
xnlu@gifu-u.ac.jp
[4] University of Ymanashi, Takeda, Kofu, Yamanashi 400-8511, Japan
nabesima@yamanashi.ac.jp
[5] Universität Potsdam, An der Bahn 2, 14476 Potsdam, Germany
torsten@cs.uni-potsdam.de
[6] Kobe University, Rokkodai-cho, Nada-ku, Kobe 657-8501, Japan
soh@lion.kobe-u.ac.jp, tamura@kobe-u.ac.jp

Abstract. The Hamiltonian cycle reconfiguration problem is defined as
determining, for a given Hamiltonian cycle problem and two among its
feasible solutions, whether one is reachable from another via a sequence
of feasible solutions subject to certain transition constraints. We develop
an approach to solving the Hamiltonian cycle reconfiguration problem
based on Answer Set Programming (ASP). Our approach relies on a
high-level ASP encoding and delegates both the grounding and solving
tasks to an ASP-based solver. To show the effectiveness of our approach,
we conduct experiments on the benchmark set of Flinders Hamiltonian
Cycle Project.

Keywords: Answer Set Programming · Hamiltonian Cycle
Reconfiguration · Combinatorial Reconfiguration

1 Introduction

The motivation of *combinatorial reconfiguration* [13,15,27] is to understand the
solution spaces of combinatorial problems and to decide whether or not there
are sequences of feasible solutions that have special properties. *Combinatorial
Reconfiguration Problems* (CRPs) are defined in general as determining, for a
given combinatorial problem and two among its feasible solutions, whether one
is reachable from another via a reconfiguration sequence of feasible solutions
subject to certain transition constraints. The theoretical aspect of combinatorial

S. Gaggl et al. (Eds.): JELIA 2023, LNAI 14281, pp. 262–277, 2023.
https://doi.org/10.1007/978-3-031-43619-2_19

reconfiguration problems has rapidly grown in the field of theoretical computer science over the last decade. For many NP-complete problems, their reconfigurations have been shown to be PSPACE-complete, such as SAT reconfiguration [9,25], independent set reconfiguration [15,17,19], dominating set reconfiguration [10,30], graph coloring reconfiguration [4–6,16], clique reconfiguration [18], and many others.

The Hamiltonian Cycle Reconfiguration Problem (HCRP; [31]) is one of the combinatorial reconfiguration problems based on the well-known *Hamiltonian Cycle Problem* (HCP; [21]). Theoretically, this problem is known to be PSPACE-complete when two edges are flipped in each transition [31]. On the other hand, little attention has been paid so far to the practical aspect of Hamiltonian cycle reconfiguration problem as well as many other combinatorial reconfiguration problems. To overcome this situation and to provide the state-of-the-art of CRP solving, the first combinatorial reconfiguration challenge (CoRe Challenge 2022; [29]) has been held very recently.[1]

This paper describes an approach to solving the Hamiltonian cycle reconfiguration problem based on Answer Set Programming (ASP; [2,8,26]). We first revisit traditional ASP encodings for HCP solving and develop two new encodings. Then, we conduct experiments with the encodings on an HCP benchmark set. Based on these performance comparisons, we adapt the best performing encoding for efficient HCRP solving. The resulting solver reads an HCRP instance and converts it into ASP facts. In turn, these facts are combined with an ASP encoding for HCRP solving, which can subsequently be solved by an ASP-based CRP solver *recongo*. In this paper, we focus on HCP and HCRP on undirected graphs.

The declarative approach of ASP has obvious advantages. First, ASP provides a rich language and is well suited for modeling combinatorial problems. Second, ASP allows for easy extensions of encodings to their reconfiguration problems. And finally, combinatorial reconfiguration problems can be solved by a general-purpose CRP solver, viz. *recongo*, rather than dedicated implementations. The *recongo* solver is an award-winning solver at the CoRe Challenge 2022; it is built upon an efficient ASP solver *clingo* [7].

The main contributions of this paper are as follows.

(1) We present two ASP encodings for undirected HCP solving. Especially, *the bidirectional encoding* is based on the idea of a SAT encoding [28] that transforms undirected graph problems into directed ones by mapping each edge $u - v$ to one of its directional edges $u \rightarrow v$ and $v \rightarrow u$.
(2) We extend the bidirectional encoding to solving the Hamiltonian cycle reconfiguration problem by utilizing *clingo*'s multi-shot ASP solving capabilities [20].
(3) We create a new benchmark set of the Hamiltonian cycle reconfiguration problem. In detail, the new benchmark set consists of 948 HCRP instances, in which 431 are reachable and 517 are unreachable.

---

[1] https://core-challenge.github.io/2022/.

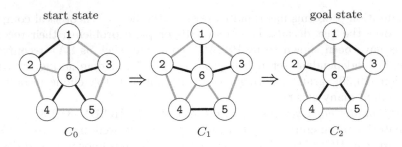

Fig. 1. Example of 3-opt HCRP

For (1), our empirical analysis considers all 1,001 HCP instances, which are publicly available from the Flinders Hamiltonian Cycle Project (FHCP [11]). The bidirectional encoding performs better compared with traditional encodings [7,22,24]. Furthermore, we establish the competitiveness of our declarative approach by contrasting it to other approaches, including the award-winning solvers of the FHCP challenge and XCSP competition [1], and a state-of-the-art SAT encoding for HCP solving [12]. For (2) and (3), the proposed encoding for HCRP solving managed to determine the reachability of 882 out of 948 instances. Furthermore, it was able to find shortest reconfiguration sequences of length 28 in about 200 s in average.

All in all, the proposed declarative approach can represent a significant contribution to the state-of-the-art for HCRP. In addition, our study also contributes to HCP solving, since to the best of our knowledge there have not been any research papers that have compared ASP encodings for HCP solving and have contrasted them with other different approaches.

In this paper, we assume some familiarity with ASP, its semantics as well as its language and multi-shot ASP solving capabilities [20]. Our encodings are given in the language of *clingo*.

2 Background

2.1 Hamiltonian Cycle Reconfiguration Problem

The Hamiltonian cycle problem (HCP) is the task of deciding whether there is a cycle that visits each node in a graph exactly once. The Hamiltonian cycle reconfiguration problem (HCRP) is defined as determining, for a given HCP instance and two of its feasible solutions C_s and C_g (viz., Hamiltonian cycles), whether C_g is reachable from C_s via a sequence of feasible solutions $C_s = C_0, C_1, \ldots, C_\ell = C_g$, subject to the transition constraint k-opt [31]. The symbol ℓ indicates the length of the reconfiguration sequence, and we refer to C_s and C_g as start and goal states, respectively. The transition constraint k-opt enforces that C_t and C_{t+1} differ in exact k edges for each step $0 \leq t < \ell$. This constraint corresponds to a well-know k-opt heuristic for the Traveling Salesman Problem (TSP; [23]).

```
node(1).    node(2).    node(3).    node(4).    node(5).    node(6).
edge(1,2). edge(1,3). edge(1,6). edge(2,4). edge(2,6).
edge(3,5). edge(3,6). edge(4,5). edge(4,6). edge(5,6).
```

Listing 1.1. ASP fact format of HCP in Fig. 1

```
1 | { in(X,Y) } :- edge(X,Y).
2 | :- not 2 { in(X,_) ; in(_,X) } 2, node(X).
3 |
4 | reached(s).
5 | reached(Y) :- reached(X), in(X,Y).   reached(Y) :- reached(X), in(Y,X).
6 | :- not reached(X), node(X).
```

Listing 1.2. ASP encoding for undirected HCP solving

Figure 1 shows an example of 3-opt HCRP. In each step $0 \leq t \leq 2$, Hamiltonian cycles are highlighted in red. We can observe that the goal state is reached from the start state with step length $\ell = 2$. For instance, in the transition from C_0 to C_1, three edges 1–6, 2–6, and 4–5 are removed.

2.2 ASP Encoding for HCP Solving

Let us first consider solving undirected HCPs with ASP. Listing 1.1 shows an ASP fact format of the undirected graph in Fig. 1. The nodes and edges are represented by the predicates node/1 and edge/2 in a standard way, respectively. A typical ASP encoding for undirected HCP solving is shown in Listing 1.2. This encoding can be considered as an undirected version of a traditional encoding for directed HCP solving shown below. The rule in Line 1 introduces the atom in(X,Y) for each edge X–Y, which is intended to represent that the edge X–Y is in a Hamiltonian cycle. The rule in Line 2 enforces that, for each node X, its degree is equal to 2 (*the degree constraints*). The rules in Lines 4–5 introduce the auxiliary atom reached(X), which represents that the node X can be reachable from the start node s. The rule in Line 6 enforces that each node X is reachable from the start node (*the connectivity constraints*). As can be seen, ASP can elegantly represent the constraints of HCP. We refer to the encoding of Listing 1.2 as *the undirected encoding*.

Second, directed HCPs can be solved in the same way. The fact format of directed graphs is the same as in Listing 1.1 except that the atom edge(X,Y) represents the directed edge X→Y. Listing 1.3 shows a traditional ASP encoding for directed HCP solving, which is essentially equivalent to encodings in the literature [7,22,24]. The major difference from the undirected encoding is that the degree constraint is split into in-degree and out-degree constraints represented by exact-one constraints in Line 2. We refer to this encoding as *the directed encoding*. And finally, we note that the directed encoding can be extended to

```
1  { in(X,Y) } :- edge(X,Y).
2  :- not 1 { in(X,_) } 1, node(X).   :- not 1 { in(_,X) } 1, node(X).
3
4  reached(s).  reached(Y) :- reached(X), in(X,Y).
5  :- not reached(X), node(X).
```

Listing 1.3. ASP encoding for directed HCP solving

```
1  { in(X,Y) ; in(Y,X) } 1 :- edge(X,Y).
2  :- not 1 { in(X,_) } 1, node(X).   :- not 1 { in(_,X) } 1, node(X).
3
4  reached(s).  reached(Y) :- reached(X), in(X,Y).
5  :- not reached(X), node(X).
6
7  :- not X < Y, in(s,X), in(Y,s).
```

Listing 1.4. Bidirectional encoding for undirected HCP solving

undirected HCP solving. The extension can be easily done by adding a simple preprocessing rule "`edge(Y,X) :- edge(X,Y).`" and a symmetry breaking constraint like "`:- not X < Y, in(s,X), in(Y,s).`".

3 New Encodings for HCP Solving

For the first step toward efficient HCRP solving, we present two ASP encodings for undirected HCP solving: *the bidirectional encoding* and *the acyclic encoding*. The bidirectional encoding is shown in Listing 1.4. The main difference from directed encoding in Listing 1.3 is that the rule in Line 1 introduces two bidirectional edges `in(X,Y)` and `in(Y,X)` for each edge X–Y and enforces that at most one of them is included in a resulting Hamiltonian cycle. The rule in Line 7 removes symmetric solutions, since each Hamiltonian cycle in a undirected graph has two corresponding directed cycles. The acyclic encoding is shown in Listing 1.5. The only difference from bidirectional encoding is that the connectivity constraint is replaced with acyclic constraints by utilizing *clingo*'s `#edge` directive in Line 4 [3].

Both bidirectional and acyclic encodings are based on the idea of a SAT encoding technique [28] that transforms undirected graph problems into directed ones. The technique can be applied to a wide range of graph problems. The effectiveness of the technique has been empirically confirmed in our preliminary results on power distribution network problems [14] and circuit wiring problems. In the case of HCP, the essential difference of the bidirectional encoding from the directed encoding is enforcing at-most-one constraints in Line 1. Although those are implied constraints, they gain some performance improvement for HCP solving, as can be seen from Table 1 and Fig. 2 below.

```
1  { in(X,Y) ; in(Y,X) } 1 :- edge(X,Y).
2  :- not 1 { in(X,_) } 1, node(X).   :- not 1 { in(_,X) } 1, node(X).
3
4  #edge (X,Y): in(X,Y), X != s, Y != s.
5
6  :- not X < Y, in(s,X), in(Y,s).
```

Listing 1.5. Acyclic encoding for undirected HCP solving

Table 1. The number of solved HCP instances

#Nodes	#Instances	Traditional Encoding		Proposed Encoding	
		undirected	directed	bidirectional	acyclic
$0 \leq |V| < 1000$	171	155	**171**	**171**	157
$1000 \leq |V| < 2000$	165	120	**165**	**165**	118
$2000 \leq |V| < 3000$	177	124	176	**176**	78
$3000 \leq |V| < 4000$	185	107	166	**167**	51
$4000 \leq |V| < 5000$	128	94	112	**113**	28
$5000 \leq |V| < 6000$	80	64	71	**74**	23
$6000 \leq |V| < 7000$	55	40	45	**46**	22
$7000 \leq |V| < 8000$	28	11	**15**	**15**	4
$8000 \leq |V| < 9000$	10	2	**5**	**5**	1
$9000 \leq |V| < 10000$	2	**2**	**2**	**2**	1
Total	1,001	719	928	**934**	483

Experiments. Our empirical analysis considers all 1,001 HCP instances from the Flinders Hamiltonian Cycle Project (FHCP; [11]).[2] The FHCP benchmark set has been used in an international HCP competition named FHCP Challenge. In the FHCP benchmark set, all of the instances are designed to be hard to solve by using standard HCP heuristics [11]. Every instance is satisfiable (viz., Hamiltonian). The number of nodes ranges from 66 to 9,528. The number of nodes and edges, in average, is 3,099 and 7,309 respectively. We compare the proposed bidirectional (Listing 1.4) and acyclic (Listing 1.5) encodings with the traditional undirected (Listing 1.2) and directed (Listing 1.3) encodings. We note that the directed encoding implements the additional preprocessing and symmetry breaking mentioned in the previous section. For each instance, we select the node of the minimum degree as the start node represented by the constant s. We ran our experiments on a Mac OS with Intel Core i7 3.2 GHz processor and 64 GB memory. We used *clingo* version 5.5.0 with the *trendy* option. We imposed a time limit of 30 min for each instance.

First, Table 1 shows the number of solved instances. The columns display in order the range of nodes, the number of instances, and the number of solved

---

[2] https://sites.flinders.edu.au/flinders-hamiltonian-cycle-project/.

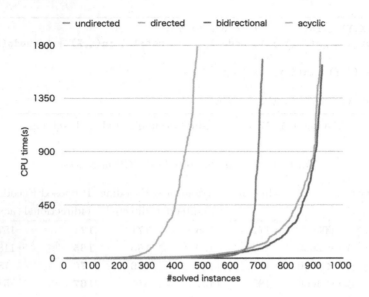

Fig. 2. Cactus plot of HCP solving

Table 2. The top-ranked solvers of the FHCP Challenge [11]

Rank	Team	#Solved	Method
1	INRIA, France	985	CPLEX
2	IBM, United Kingdom	614	SAT
3	King Saud University, Saudi Arabia	488	unknown
4	TU Darmstadt, Germany	464	unknown
5	Independent Researcher	385	unknown

instances for each encoding. The best results in the last four columns are highlighted in bold. The bidirectional encoding solved the most, namely 934 instances. It is followed by 928 of directed, 719 of undirected, and 483 of acyclic encoding. The bidirectional encoding provides better results in every range of nodes compared with the other encodings.

Figure 2 shows a cactus plot where the vertical axis indicates CPU times in seconds, and the horizontal axis indicates the number of solved instances. We can observe that the bidirectional encoding based on directed edges, as well as the directed encoding, performs well compared with the undirected encoding. In contrast, the acyclic encoding using the #edge directive can solve less instances, and we will investigate this issue in future work.

Second, we compare our proposed encoding with the top-ranked solvers of the FHCP Challenge held in 2015–2016. In the challenge, competitors compete on the number of solved instances in the FHCP benchmark set. There are no restrictions on solvers used, time limits, or execution environments.

Table 3. Comparison with other different approaches

Instances	ASP (proposal)	*PicatSAT*	SAT encoding
graph48	**0.752**	68.718	62.920
graph162	**7.500**	45.849	44.440
graph171	**10.383**	15.809	10.390
graph197	**0.342**	78.241	12.970
graph223	125.580	201.394	**22.600**
graph237	**0.306**	121.177	16.580
graph249	**0.956**	75.776	1.380
graph252	266.701	95.879	**9.950**
graph254	2.717	73.901	**2.660**
graph255	83.760	87.443	**6.110**
Average ratio	1.00	83.33	18.54

Table 2 shows the results of the top-ranked solvers in the FHCP Challenge [11]. The first-place team solved 985 instances with the CPLEX solver; the second-place team solved 614 with a SAT solver. The details of the other are unknown except the number of solved instances. We note that the first-place team analyzes each HCP instance and utilizes its structural properties.[3] Our declarative approach can be highly competitive in performance, since the bidirectional encoding solved 934 instances that corresponds to the second place in Table 2.

Finally, we contrast our proposed encoding to other approaches. Our comparison considers a state-of-the-art SAT encoding for HCP solving [12] and the award-winning CSP solver *PicatSAT* [32] of XCSP competition [1]. The former SAT encoding is based on the Chinese remainder theorem, and performs well compared to existing SAT encodings [12].[4] We use *cadical* version 1.5.2[5] as a back-end SAT solver. For the latter CSP solver, we use *PicatSAT* version 2.8 (*xcsp_picat*[6]). We ran them on the same environment as before.

Table 3 shows the CPU times in seconds on all HCP instances used in the XCSP 2019 competition. This benchmark set consists of 10 instances in total; it is a subset of the FHCP benchmark set. The columns display in order the instance name and the CPU time of finding a Hamiltonian cycle for each. The better time of the last three columns are highlighted in bold. As can be seen in Table 3, our bidirectional encoding is 83 times faster in average than *PicatSAT* and 18 times faster than the SAT encoding. On the other hand, Heule's SAT encoding performs well for graph223, graph252, and graph255 that have relatively small average degrees.

---

[3] https://interstices.info/le-defi-des-1001-graphes/.
[4] https://github.com/marijnheule/ChineseRemainderEncoding.
[5] https://github.com/arminbiere/cadical.
[6] https://github.com/nfzhou/xcsp.

```
start(1,3).  start(1,6).  start(2,4).  start(2,6).  start(3,5).  start(4,5).
goal(1,2).   goal(1,6).   goal(2,4).   goal(3,5).   goal(3,6).   goal(4,5).
```

Listing 1.6. ASP fact format of the start and goal states in Fig. 1

```
1   #program base.
2   :- not 1 { in(X,Y,0) ; in(Y,X,0) } 1, start(X,Y).
3
4   #program step(t).
5   { in(X,Y,t) ; in(Y,X,t) } 1 :- edge(X,Y).
6   :- not 1 { in(X,_,t) } 1, node(X).   :- not 1 { in(_,X,t) } 1, node(X).
7
8   reached(s,t).   reached(Y,t) :- reached(X,t), in(X,Y,t).
9   :- not reached(X,t), node(X).
10
11  :- not X < Y, in(s,X,t), in(Y,s,t).
12
13  removed(X,Y,t) :- in(X,Y,t-1), not in(X,Y,t), not in(Y,X,t), t>0.
14  :- not k { removed(_,_,t) } k, t>0.
15
16  #program check(t).
17  :- not 1 { in(X,Y,t) ; in(Y,X,t) } 1, goal(X,Y), query(t).
```

Listing 1.7. hcrp-bidirectional encoding for k-opt HCRP solving

4   Hamiltonian Cycle Reconfiguration Problem

We now extend our best bidirectional encoding in Listing 1.4 to the Hamiltonian
cycle reconfiguration problem. The extension can be easily done by utilizing
clingo's multi-shot solving capabilities [20].

Fact Format. The input of HCRP are an HCP instance, a start state, and a goal
state. The fact format of HCP instances is the same as before (cf. Listing 1.1).
Listing 1.6 shows an ASP fact format of the start and goal states in Fig. 1. The
predicates start/2 and goal/2 represent the edges of the start and goal states,
respectively. For instance, start(1,3) represents that the edge 1–3 is included
in the Hamiltonian cycle of the start state.

ASP Encoding. Listing 1.7 shows an ASP encoding for HCRP solving. The
encoding consists of three sub-programs base, step(t), and check(t). The
argument t is a constant parameter representing each step in a reconfiguration sequence. The main difference from the bidirectional encoding is that the
constant t is added to the predicate in/2. The extended atom in(X,Y,t) is
intended to represent that the directed edge X→Y is in a Hamiltonian cycle at
step t. We refer to the encoding of Listing 1.7 as *the hcrp-bidirectional encoding*.

The subprogram base specifies the constraints that must be satisfied at the
start state. The rule in Line 2 enforces that either in(X,Y,0) or in(Y,X,0)
holds for each edge X–Y in the start state. The subprogram step(t) specifies the

```
#program step(t).
:- not #sum { 1,X,Y: start(X,Y), not in(X,Y,t), not in(Y,X,t) } k*t.
```

Listing 1.8. Distance constraints (d1)

```
#program step(t).
:- not { not in(X,Y,T) : goal(X,Y), not in(Y,X,T) } k*(t-T), T = 0..t-1,
   query(t).
```

Listing 1.9. Distance constraints (d2)

constraints that must be satisfied at each step t. The rules in Line 4–11 represent the constraints of HCP. The rules in Line 13–14 represent the k-opt transition constraints. The auxiliary atom removed(X,Y,t) in Line 13 represents that the directed edge X→Y is removed from a Hamiltonian cycle in the transition from step t-1 to t. The rule in Line 14 enforces that exactly k edges in a Hamiltonian cycle are removed at each step t by using cardinality constraints. The subprogram check(t) specifies the termination condition that must be satisfied at the goal state. The query rule in Line 17 enforces that either in(X,Y,t) or in(Y,X,t) holds for each X–Y in the goal state. We note that switching between activation and deactivation of the query is realized by making it subject to the truth assignment to the external atom query(t).

Reachability Checking. We here explain how the reachability checking is realized by the hcrp-directed encoding and the *clingo* solver. For a given HCRP instance I of ASP fact format and length ℓ, we consider a logic program $\varphi_\ell = I \cup$ base $\cup \bigcup_{t=0}^{\ell}$ step(t) $\cup$ check(ℓ) where base, step(t), and check(ℓ) are the subprograms of the hcrp-directed encoding. We can check the reachability of I by solving φ_ℓ with *clingo*. If φ_ℓ is satisfiable, then we obtain a reconfiguration sequence of length ℓ. Otherwise, we reconstruct a logic program $\varphi_{\ell+1}$ and repeat the execution by *clingo*. Indeed, this procedure is incomplete and can not prove unreachability, but it can decide both reachability and unreachability when there exists an upper bound of length (e.g., the diameter of solution space). The *recongo* solver incrementally constructs φ_ℓ rather than the full reconstruction of it. More precisely, *recongo* incrementally constructs φ_ℓ not only by adding step(ℓ) and check(ℓ) to the previous logic program $\varphi_{\ell-1}$, but also by deactivating check($\ell-1$) by setting the external atom query($\ell-1$) to false. Therefore, *recongo* can reduce the cost of expensive grounding and can efficiently check the reachability.

Hint Constraints. We present three hint constraints for the hcrp-directed encoding to accelerate HCRP solving.

- *The distance constraint* (d1) is shown in Listing 1.8. It enforces that, for each step t, there are at most k×t edges that are in the start state but not in step t.

```
#program step(t).
:- in(X,Y,t): removed(X,Y,t-1); t>1.
```

Listing 1.10. No restoring constraints (n)

Table 4. The number of solved HCRP instances

Reachability	#Instance	hcrp-bidirectional encoding							
		no hint	d1	d2	n	d1+d2	d1+n	d2+n	d1+d2+n
Reachable	431	376	414	422	373	422	403	408	**423**
Unreachable	517	431	456	**460**	430	458	435	441	457
Total	948	807	870	**882**	803	880	838	849	880

- *The distance constraint* (d2) is shown in Listing 1.9. It enforces that, for each step t and T∈ {0...t-1}, there are at most k*(t-T) edges that are in the goal state but not in step T.
- *The no restoring constraint* (n) is shown in Listing 1.10. It forbids that the edges removed in step t-1 are all restored in step t.

The hint constraints are independent of each other and can be used in any combination.

Generating HCRP Instances. There has been no benchmark set for the Hamiltonian cycle reconfiguration problem so far. We therefore generated a new benchmark set for HCRP. The benchmark set consists of 948 instances in total, of which 431 are reachable and 517 are unreachable. Regarding the transition constraint, 867 instances are designed for 3-opt and 81 for 4-opt.

The procedure of generating HCRP instances is as follows:

(1) We conducted experiments on the FHCP benchmark instances (1001 instances in total) for enumerating all solutions. The time limit is 5 min for each. As a result, *clingo* was able to enumerate all solutions of 309 instances. Among them, 101 instances have more than two solutions.

(2) For each of the 101 instances, we attempted to construct its solution space by breadth-first search. A solution space is a graph in which a node corresponds to a feasible solution, and the adjacency relation on nodes corresponds to the *k*-opt constraint. As a result, we obtained the solution spaces of 56 instances, of which 49 instances are 3-opt and 7 instances are 4-opt.

(3) For each solution space of the 56 HCP instances, we attempted to generate both at most 10 reachable HCRP instances and at most 10 unreachable ones. As a result, we succeeded in generating 948 instances in total, of which 431 are reachable and 517 are unreachable.

For reachable instances in (3), we selected the start and goal states such that the length of the shortest sequence between them is maximum. The resulting lengths

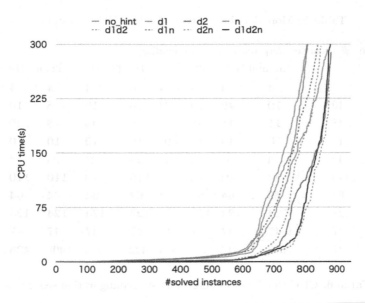

Fig. 3. Cactus plot of HCRP solving

range from 1 to 28. For unreachable instances, we selected the start and goal states respectively from different connected components of the solution space.

Experiments. We conducted experiments on the newly generated HCRP instances for evaluating the effectiveness of our proposed encoding. Our evaluation considers the hcrp-bidirectional encoding (Listing 1.7) with the combination of hint constraints (Listing 1.8–1.10). We use *recongo* version 0.3 and *clingo* version 5.5.0 as its back-end. The time limit is 5 min for each. The experimental environment is the same as before.

Table 4 shows the number of solved instances. The columns display in order reachability (reachable or unreachable), and the number of solved instances for each encoding. The best results in the last eight columns are highlighted in bold. For reachable instances, the hcrp-bidirectional encoding with all hints (d1+d2+n) solved the most 423 instances. For unreachable instances, the encoding with (d2) solved the most 460 instances. In total, the encoding with (d2) solved the most, namely 882 instances out of 948. Regarding single hint constraint, as can be seen in Table 4, the distance constraint (d2) is the most effective in performance. In contrast, the no restoring constraint (n) is less effective, and we will investigate this issue in future work. Figure 3 shows a cactus plot of solved instances. We can observe that the hcrp-bidirectional encoding with (d2) performs well with respect to not only the number of solved instances but also CPU time. Table 5 shows a more detailed analysis of the solved instances. The columns display in order the length, the number of instances, and the number of solved instances for each. The best results in the last eight columns are high-

Table 5. More detailed analysis of solved HCRP instances

Length	#Instance	hcrp-bidirectional encoding							
		no hint	d1	d2	n	d1+d2	d1+n	d2+n	d1+d2+n
28	4	**4**	**4**	**4**	**4**	**4**	**4**	**4**	**4**
14	10	**10**	**10**	**10**	**10**	**10**	**10**	8	**10**
8	18	**11**	**11**	10	10	9	10	8	10
7	10	**10**	**10**	**10**	**10**	**10**	**10**	**10**	**10**
6	44	24	38	43	24	**44**	34	33	**44**
4	110	83	106	**110**	82	**110**	100	**110**	**110**
3	64	63	**64**	**64**	62	**64**	**64**	**64**	**64**
2	124	**124**	**124**	**124**	**124**	**124**	**124**	**124**	**124**
1	47	**47**	**47**	**47**	**47**	**47**	**47**	**47**	**47**
Total	431	376	414	422	373	422	403	408	**423**

Table 6. CPU time(s) of finding shortest reconfiguration sequences

Length	#Instance	CPU time(s)		
		average	maximum	minimum
28	4	200.725	290.375	130.622
14	10	148.754	209.782	119.712
8	10	141.659	293.491	74.568
7	10	2.304	2.652	1.994
6	44	26.723	67.564	8.663
4	110	14.200	83.747	0.889
3	64	6.048	25.496	1.100
2	124	1.343	2.207	0.274
1	47	0.669	2.036	0.434

lighted in bold. We can see that there is a significant gap between the encodings in the sequence lengths 4 and 6.

Finally, Table 6 shows the CPU times in seconds of finding shortest reconfiguration sequences. The columns display in order the step length, the number of instances, and the average, the maximum, and the minimum CPU times. Our encoding succeeded in finding the solutions of step length 28 in about 200 s in average. Basically, the longer the length, the more time is required. We noticed that the 10 instances of length 7 required relatively less CPU time than the others. This is because those instances were generated from the same small HCP instance of 546 nodes.

5 Conclusion

We presented an ASP-based approach to solving the Hamiltonian cycle reconfiguration problem. The problem is a combinatorial reconfiguration problem based on the well-known Hamiltonian cycle problem. Our approach relies on high-level ASP encodings presented in Sect. 4 and delegates both the grounding and solving tasks to an ASP-based CRP solver *recongo*. All source code including *recongo* is available from https://github.com/banbaralab/hcr.

Combinatorial reconfiguration [13,15,27] aims at analyzing properties of the solution space of source combinatorial problem, which can be exponential size with respect to the input size. A great deal of theoretical research has been done in recent years. However, little attention has been paid so far to its practical aspects. On the other hand, recent advances in ASP, especially the incremental ASP solving open up a successful direction to apply ASP to bounded model checking and automated planning. Those research fields are strongly related to combinatorial reconfiguration in the sense of transforming a given state to another state. Our declarative approach therefore can be applied to a wide range of combinatorial reconfiguration problems, such as independent set reconfiguration, dominating set reconfiguration, graph coloring reconfiguration, and clique reconfiguration. We will investigate the possibilities, and the results will be applied to realizing more practical combinatorial reconfiguration.

Acknowledgements. The research was supported by JSPS KAKENHI Grant Number JP20H05964, ROIS NII Open Collaborative Research 2023 (23FP04), JST CREST Grant Number JPMJCR22D3.

References

1. Audemard, G., Boussemart, F., Lecoutre, C., Piette, C., Roussel, O.: XCSP^3 and its ecosystem. Constraints **25**(1–2), 47–69 (2020)
2. Baral, C.: Knowledge Representation, Reasoning and Declarative Problem Solving. Cambridge University Press, Cambridge (2003)
3. Bomanson, J., Gebser, M., Janhunen, T., Kaufmann, B., Schaub, T.: Answer set programming modulo acyclicity. In: Calimeri, F., Ianni, G., Truszczynski, M. (eds.) LPNMR 2015. LNCS (LNAI), vol. 9345, pp. 143–150. Springer, Cham (2015). https://doi.org/10.1007/978-3-319-23264-5_13
4. Bonsma, P.S., Cereceda, L.: Finding paths between graph colourings: PSPACE-completeness and superpolynomial distances. Theoret. Comput. Sci. **410**(50), 5215–5226 (2009)
5. Brewster, R.C., McGuinness, S., Moore, B.R., Noel, J.A.: A dichotomy theorem for circular colouring reconfiguration. Theoret. Comput. Sci. **639**, 1–13 (2016)
6. Cereceda, L., van den Heuvel, J., Johnson, M.: Finding paths between 3-colorings. J. Graph Theory **67**(1), 69–82 (2011)
7. Gebser, M., et al.: Potassco User Guide, 2nd edn. University of Potsdam (2015). http://potassco.org
8. Gelfond, M., Lifschitz, V.: The stable model semantics for logic programming. In: Kowalski, R., Bowen, K. (eds.) Proceedings of the Fifth International Conference

and Symposium of Logic Programming (ICLP 1988), pp. 1070–1080. MIT Press (1988)

9. Gopalan, P., Kolaitis, P.G., Maneva, E.N., Papadimitriou, C.H.: The connectivity of Boolean satisfiability: computational and structural dichotomies. SIAM J. Comput. **38**(6), 2330–2355 (2009)

10. Haddadan, A., et al.: The complexity of dominating set reconfiguration. Theoret. Comput. Sci. **651**, 37–49 (2016)

11. Haythorpe, M.: FHCP challenge set: the first set of structurally difficult instances of the Hamiltonian cycle problem. Bulletin ICA **83**, 98–107 (2018)

12. Heule, M.J.H.: Chinese remainder encoding for Hamiltonian cycles. In: Li, C.-M., Manyà, F. (eds.) SAT 2021. LNCS, vol. 12831, pp. 216–224. Springer, Cham (2021). https://doi.org/10.1007/978-3-030-80223-3_15

13. van den Heuvel, J.: The complexity of change. In: Blackburn, S.R., Gerke, S., Wildon, M. (eds.) Surveys in Combinatorics 2013, London Mathematical Society Lecture Note Series, vol. 409, pp. 127–160. Cambridge University Press (2013)

14. Inoue, T., et al.: Distribution loss minimization with guaranteed error bound. IEEE Trans. Smart Grid **5**(1), 102–111 (2014)

15. Ito, T., et al.: On the complexity of reconfiguration problems. Theoret. Comput. Sci. **412**(12–14), 1054–1065 (2011)

16. Ito, T., Kaminski, M., Demaine, E.D.: Reconfiguration of list edge-colorings in a graph. Discret. Appl. Math. **160**(15), 2199–2207 (2012)

17. Ito, T., Kamiński, M., Ono, H., Suzuki, A., Uehara, R., Yamanaka, K.: On the parameterized complexity for token jumping on graphs. In: Gopal, T.V., Agrawal, M., Li, A., Cooper, S.B. (eds.) TAMC 2014. LNCS, vol. 8402, pp. 341–351. Springer, Cham (2014). https://doi.org/10.1007/978-3-319-06089-7_24

18. Ito, T., Ono, H., Otachi, Y.: Reconfiguration of cliques in a graph. In: Jain, R., Jain, S., Stephan, F. (eds.) TAMC 2015. LNCS, vol. 9076, pp. 212–223. Springer, Cham (2015). https://doi.org/10.1007/978-3-319-17142-5_19

19. Kaminski, M., Medvedev, P., Milanic, M.: Complexity of independent set reconfigurability problems. Theoret. Comput. Sci. **439**, 9–15 (2012)

20. Kaminski, R., Romero, J., Schaub, T., Wanko, P.: How to build your own asp-based system?! Theory Pract. Logic Program. **23**(1), 299–361 (2023)

21. Karp, R.M.: Reducibility among combinatorial problems. In: Miller, R.E., Thatcher, J.W. (eds.) Proceedings of a Symposium on the Complexity of Computer Computations, pp. 85–103. Plenum Press, New York (1972)

22. Lifschitz, V.: Answer Set Programming. Springer, Heidelberg (2019)

23. Lin, S., Kernighan, B.W.: An effective heuristic algorithm for the traveling-salesman problem. Oper. Res. **21**(2), 498–516 (1973)

24. Liu, L., Truszczynski, M.: Encoding selection for solving Hamiltonian cycle problems with ASP. In: Proceedings of the 35th International Conference on Logic Programming (ICLP 2019), Technical Communications. EPTCS, vol. 306, pp. 302–308 (2019)

25. Mouawad, A.E., Nishimura, N., Pathak, V., Raman, V.: Shortest reconfiguration paths in the solution space of Boolean formulas. SIAM J. Discret. Math. **31**(3), 2185–2200 (2017)

26. Niemelä, I.: Logic programs with stable model semantics as a constraint programming paradigm. Ann. Math. Artif. Intell. **25**(3–4), 241–273 (1999)

27. Nishimura, N.: Introduction to reconfiguration. Algorithms **11**(4), 52 (2018)

28. Soh, T., Le Berre, D., Roussel, S., Banbara, M., Tamura, N.: Incremental SAT-based method with native Boolean cardinality handling for the Hamiltonian cycle

problem. In: Fermé, E., Leite, J. (eds.) JELIA 2014. LNCS (LNAI), vol. 8761, pp. 684–693. Springer, Cham (2014). https://doi.org/10.1007/978-3-319-11558-0_52

29. Soh, T., Okamoto, Y., Ito, T.: Core challenge 2022: solver and graph descriptions. CoRR abs/2208.02495 (2022)

30. Suzuki, A., Mouawad, A.E., Nishimura, N.: Reconfiguration of dominating sets. J. Comb. Optim. **32**(4), 1182–1195 (2016)

31. Takaoka, A.: Complexity of Hamiltonian cycle reconfiguration. Algorithms **11**(9), 140 (2018)

32. Zhou, N.-F., Kjellerstrand, H., Fruhman, J.: Constraint Solving and Planning with Picat. SIS, Springer, Cham (2015). https://doi.org/10.1007/978-3-319-25883-6

Recongo: Bounded Combinatorial Reconfiguration with Answer Set Programming

Yuya Yamada[1], Mutsunori Banbara[1]([⊠]) [iD], Katsumi Inoue[2] [iD], and Torsten Schaub[3] [iD]

[1] Nagoya University, Furo-cho, Chikusa-ku, Nagoya 464-8601, Japan
{yuya.yamada,banbara}@nagoya-u.ac.jp
[2] National Institute of Informatics, Hitotsubashi, Chiyoda-ku, Tokyo 101-8430, Japan
inoue@nii.ac.jp
[3] Universität Potsdam, An der Bahn 2, 14476 Potsdam, Germany
torsten@cs.uni-potsdam.de

Abstract. We develop an approach called *bounded combinatorial reconfiguration* for solving combinatorial reconfiguration problems based on Answer Set Programming. The general task is to study the solution spaces of source combinatorial problems and to decide whether or not there are sequences of feasible solutions that have special properties. The resulting *recongo* solver covers all metrics of the solver track in the most recent international competition on combinatorial reconfiguration (CoRe Challenge 2022). *recongo* ranked first in the shortest metric of the single-engine solvers track.

Keywords: Answer Set Programming · Multi-shot ASP solving · Combinatorial Reconfiguration · Independent Set Reconfiguration

1 Introduction

Combinatorial reconfiguration [11,12,22] aims at analyzing the structure and properties (e.g., connectivity and reachability) of the solution spaces of source combinatorial problems. Each solution space has a graph structure in which each node represents an individual feasible solution, and the edges are defined by a certain adjacency relation. *Combinatorial Reconfiguration Problems* (CRPs) are defined in general as the task of deciding, for a given source problem and two among its feasible solutions, whether or not one is reachable from another via a sequence of adjacent feasible solutions in the solution space. A CRP is *reachable* if there exists such a sequence, otherwise it is *unreachable*. *CRP solvers* are programs solving combinatorial reconfiguration problems. The solvers output a reconfiguration sequence as a solution if reachable.

A great effort has been made to investigate the theoretical aspects of CRPs in the field of theoretical computer science over the last decade. For many NP-complete source problems, their reconfigurations have been shown to be PSPACE-complete, including SAT reconfiguration [9,20], independent set reconfiguration [12,14,16], dominating set reconfiguration [10,24], graph coloring

S. Gaggl et al. (Eds.): JELIA 2023, LNAI 14281, pp. 278–286, 2023.
https://doi.org/10.1007/978-3-031-43619-2_20

reconfiguration [3–5,13], clique reconfiguration [15], Hamiltonian cycle reconfiguration [25,27], and set covering reconfiguration [12]. However, little attention has been paid so far to its practical aspects. To stimulate research and development on practical CRP solving, the first international combinatorial reconfiguration competition (CoRe Challenge 2022; [23]) has been held last year.

In this paper, we present an approach for solving combinatorial reconfiguration problems based on Answer Set Programming (ASP; [1,8,21]). Our declarative approach is inspired by bounded model checking (BMC; [2]), which is widely used in formal verification of finite state transition systems. We develop an ASP-based CRP solver *recongo* using multi-shot ASP solving [17]. *recongo* ranked first at the shortest metric of the single-engine solvers track in the CoRe Challenge 2022, and ranked second or third in the other four metrics. We present an ASP encoding for solving the independent set reconfiguration problem. This problem is one of the most studied combinatorial reconfiguration problems that has been shown to be PSPACE-complete [12]. Finally, we discuss the competitiveness of our approach by empirically contrasting it to the top-ranked solvers of the CoRe Challenge 2022 [23].

In the sequel, we assume some familiarity with ASP's basic language constructs and its extension to multi-shot ASP solving. A comprehensive introduction to ASP can be found in [7]. Our encodings are given in the language of *clingo* [6].

2 Background

The combinatorial reconfiguration problem (CRP) is defined as the task of deciding, for a given source combinatorial problem and two of its feasible solutions X_s and X_g, whether or not there are sequences of transitions:

$$X_s = X_0 \rightarrow X_1 \rightarrow X_2 \rightarrow \cdots \rightarrow X_\ell = X_g, \tag{1}$$

where X_s and X_g are optional. Each state X_i represents a feasible solution of the source problem. We refer to X_s and X_g as the start and the goal states, respectively. We write $X \rightarrow X'$ if state X at step t can be followed by state X' at step $t+1$ subject to a certain *adjacency relation*. We refer to the sequence (1) as a *reconfiguration sequence*. The *length* of the reconfiguration sequence, denoted by ℓ, is the number of transitions. Regarding the reconfiguration sequences, CRPs can be classified into three categories: *existent*, *shortest*, and *longest*. The existent-CRP is to decide whether or not there are reconfiguration sequences. The shortest-CRP is to find the shortest reconfiguration sequences. The longest-CRP is to find the longest reconfiguration sequences that cannot include any loop.

Let us consider the independent set reconfiguration problem (ISRP). Its source is *the independent set problem*, that is, to decide whether or not there are independent sets in G of size k, for a given graph $G = (V, E)$ and an integer k. A subset $V' \subseteq V$ is called an *independent set* in G of size k if $(u, v) \notin E$ for all $u, v \in V'$ and $|V'| = k$. In the ISRP, each state X in (1) represents an

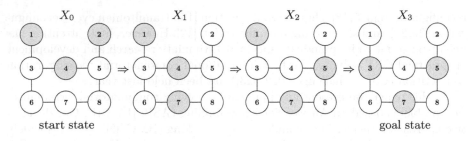

Fig. 1. An ISRP example

independent set. Regarding adjacency relations, we focus on one of the most studied relations called *token jumping* [12]. Suppose that a *token* is placed on each node in an independent set. The token jumping meaning of $X \to X'$ is that a single token "jumps" from one node in X to any other node in X'.

Figure 1 shows an example of ISRP. The example consists of a graph having 8 nodes and 8 edges, and the size of independent sets is $k = 3$. The independent sets (tokens) are highlighted in yellow. We can observe that the goal state can be reachable from the start state with length $\ell = 3$. For instance, in the transition from X_0 to X_1, a token jumps from node 2 in X_0 to node 7 in X_1.

3   The *recongo* Approach

Basic Design. Combinatorial reconfiguration problems can be readily expressed as satisfiability problems. Let $x = \{x_1, x_2, \ldots, x_n\}$ and $C(x)$ be the variables and the constraints of a source combinatorial problem, respectively. For its reconfiguration problem, each state X at step t can be represented by a set of variables $x^t = \{x_1^t, x_2^t, \ldots, x_n^t\}$. Each adjacent relation can be represented by a set of constraints $T(x^{t-1}, x^t)$ that must be satisfied. Optionally, additional constraints $S(x^0)$ and $G(x^\ell)$ can be added to specify conditions on the start state X_s and/or the goal state X_g, respectively, as well as any other constraints that we want to enforce. Then, the existence of a reconfiguration sequence (1) of bounded length ℓ is equivalent to the following satisfiability problem

$$\varphi_\ell = S(x^0) \wedge \bigwedge_{t=0}^{\ell} C(x^t) \wedge \bigwedge_{t=1}^{\ell} T(x^{t-1}, x^t) \wedge G(x^\ell). \tag{2}$$

We use φ_ℓ to check properties of a reconfiguration relation (a transition relation) between the possible feasible solutions of the source combinatorial problem. We call this general framework "bounded combinatorial reconfiguration", because we consider only reconfiguration sequences that have a bounded length ℓ.

For reachability checking, if φ_ℓ is satisfiable, there is a reconfiguration sequence of length ℓ. Otherwise, we keep on reconstructing a successor (e.g., $\varphi_{\ell+1}$) and checking its satisfiability until a reconfiguration sequence is found.

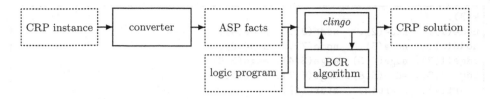

Fig. 2. The architecture of *recongo*

Bounded combinatorial reconfiguration is an incomplete method, because it can find reconfiguration sequences if they exist, but cannot prove unreachability in general. However, it can be a complete method if the diameters of solution spaces are given. Any off-the-shelf satisfiability solvers, such as SAT solvers and CSP solvers, can be used as back-end. In this paper, we make use of ASP solvers, in our case *clingo*.

Implementation. Bounded combinatorial reconfiguration (BCR) can be easily implemented using *clingo*'s Python API.[1] The resulting *recongo* solver is a general-purpose CRP solver. *recongo* covers all metrics of the solver track in the most recent international competition on combinatorial reconfiguration (CoRe Challenge 2022): *existent*, *shortest*, and *longest*. The architecture of *recongo* is shown in Fig. 2. *recongo* reads an CRP instance and converts it into ASP facts. In turn, these facts are combined with an ASP encoding for CRP solving, which are afterward solved by the BCR algorithm powered by *clingo*. Further details of *recongo* can be found in [26].

4   ASP Encoding for Independent Set Reconfiguration

We present an ASP encoding for solving the independent set reconfiguration problem (ISRP).

Fact Format. The input of ISRP is an independent set problem, a start state, and a goal state. Listing 1.1 shows an ASP fact format of the ISRP instance in Fig. 1. The predicate k/1 represents the size of independent sets. The predicates node/1 and edge/2 represent the nodes and edges, respectively. The predicates start/1 and goal/1 represent the independent sets of the start and goal states, respectively. For instance, the atom start(4) means that node 4 is in an independent set at the start state.

First Order Encoding. Listing 1.2 shows an ASP encoding for ISRP solving. The encoding consists of three parts: base, step(t), and check(t). The parameter t represents each step in a reconfiguration sequence. The atom in(X,t) is intended to represent that the node X is in an independent set at step t. The base part specifies the constraints on the start state $S(x^0)$. The rule in Line 3 enforces that in(X,0) holds for each node X in the start state. The step(t)

---

[1] https://potassco.org/clingo/python-api/current/.

```
k(3).
node(1).    node(2).    node(3).    node(4).
node(5).    node(6).    node(7).    node(8).
edge(1,3). edge(2,5). edge(3,4). edge(3,6).
edge(4,5). edge(5,8). edge(6,7). edge(7,8).
start(1).   start(2).   start(4).
goal(3).    goal(5).    goal(7).
```

Listing 1.1. ASP fact format of ISRP instance in Fig. 1

```
1   #program base.
2   % start state
3   :- not in(X,0), start(X).
4
5   #program step(t).
6   % independent set constraints
7   K { in(X,t): node(X) } K :- k(K).
8   :- in(X,t), in(Y,t), edge(X,Y).
9
10  % adjacency relation: token jumping
11  moved_from(X,t) :- in(X,t-1), not in(X,t), t > 0.
12  :- not 1 { moved_from(X,t) } 1, t > 0.
13
14  #program check(t).
15  % goal state
16  :- not in(X,t), goal(X), query(t).
```

Listing 1.2. ASP encoding for ISRP solving

part specifies the constraints that must be satisfied at each step t. The rules in Lines 7–8 represent the constraints of independent set $C(x^t)$. The rule in Line 7 generates a candidate independent set with size K. The rule in Line 8 enforces that no two nodes connected by an edge are in an independent set. The rules in Lines 11–12 represent the adjacency relation $T(x^{t-1}, x^t)$. The auxiliary atom moved_from(X,t) in Line 11 represents that a token jumps from node X to any other node, from step $t-1$ to t. The rule in Line 12 enforces that exactly one token jumps at each step t. The check(t) part specifies the termination condition that must be satisfied at the goal state $G(x^t)$. The rule in Line 16 enforces that in(X,t) holds for each node X in the goal state. The volatility of this rule is handled by a truth assignment to the external atom query(t) via *clingo*'s API.

5 CoRe Challenge 2022

We discuss the competitiveness of our approach by empirically contrasting it to the top-ranked solvers of the CoRe Challenge 2022 [23]. The competition consists

Table 1. The result of the single-engine solver track in CoRe Challenge 2022

metric		1st	2nd	3rd
existent	solver name	*PARIS single*	***recongo***	@toda5603
	method	planning	ASP	greedy search/BMC
	score	299 (275/24)	244 (238/6)	207 (207/0)
shortest	solver name	***recongo***	@tigrisg	*PARIS single*
	method	ASP	brute force/SARSA	planning
	score	238	232	213
longest	solver name	*PARIS single*	***recongo***	*ReconfAIGERation*
	method	planning	ASP	SAT/BMC
	score	144	115	54

of two tracks: solver track and graph track. The solver track is divided into the following three metrics.

(1) *existent*: This metric is to decide the reachability of ISRP. Its evaluation index is the number of instances that contestants can solve.

(2) *shortest*: This metric is to find reconfiguration sequences as short as possible of ISRP. Its evaluation index is the number of instances that contestants can find the shortest sequence among all contestants.

(3) *longest*: This metric is to find reconfiguration sequences of as long as possible of ISRP. Its evaluation index is the number of instances that contestants can find the longest sequence among all contestants.

Each metric is evaluated by two indices: single-engine solvers and overall solvers. The former index can be applied only to sequential solvers. The latter index can be applied to all solvers, including portfolio solvers as well as sequential solvers. The benchmark instances (369 in a total) are publicly available.[2] The ISRP instances are classified into seven families. The benchmark family `color04` consists of 202 instances, `grid` of 49 instances, `handcraft` of 6 instances, `power` of 17 instances, `queen` of 48 instances, `sp` of 30 instances, and `square` of 17 instances. The number of nodes ranges from 7 to 40,000. There are no restrictions on solvers used, time limits, or execution environments. Eight solvers (from seven groups) participated in the solver track of CoRe Challenge 2022.

Table 1 shows the results of the top-ranked solvers of single-engine solvers track. The columns display in order the metric, the solver name, the implementation method, and the score for each solver. Our proposed solver *recongo* ranked first in the shortest metric, ranked second both in the existent and longest metrics of single-engine solvers track. In addition, it also ranked second in the longest metric and ranked third in the shortest metric of overall solvers track. Overall, our declarative approach can be highly competitive in performance.

---

[2] https://core-challenge.github.io/2022/.

Discussion. We discuss some more details of the results from a practical point of view. *recongo* showed good performance for the `color04` and `queen` families for all metrics. In particular, *recongo* was able to find the shortest reconfiguration sequences for all instances of `color04`. The `color04` family contains many instances that have relatively short reconfiguration sequences. In contrast, *recongo* is less effective to the `power`, `sp`, and `square` families. They contain many instances for which the shortest sequences are relatively long. The current implementation of *recongo* relied on simple linear search, and this issue can be improved by utilize different search strategies such as exponential search. *recongo* is also less effective for the `grid` family since most instances are unreachable. To resolve this issue, we will investigate the possibility of incorporating *the numeric abstraction* used in the *PARIS* solver to our declarative approach.

6   Conclusion

We presented an ASP-based approach called bounded combinatorial reconfiguration to solving combinatorial reconfiguration problems. We also presented an ASP encoding of the independent set reconfiguration problem. We discussed the competitiveness of our approach by empirically contrasting it to other approaches based on the results of CoRe Challenge 2022. The resulting *recongo* system is an ASP-based CRP solver, which is available from https://github.com/banbaralab/recongo.

Perhaps the most relevant related fields are bounded model checking [2] and classical planning [18,19], in the sense of transforming a given state to another state. Bounded model checking in general is to study properties (e.g., safety and liveness) of finite state transition systems and to decide whether there is no sequence $X_s = X_0 \to X_1 \to X_2 \to \cdots \to X_\ell = X_g$, for which X_s is a start state and X_g is an error state expressed by rich temporal logic. Classical planning in general is to develop action plans for more practical applications and to decide whether there are sequences of actions for which X_s is a start state and X_g is a goal state. In contrast, combinatorial reconfiguration is to study the structure and properties of solution spaces (e.g., connectivity, reachability, and diameters) of source combinatorial problems and to decide whether there are reconfiguration sequences, but X_s and X_g are optional. From a broader perspective, combinatorial reconfiguration can involve the task of constructing problem instances that have the maximum length of shortest reconfiguration sequences. Such a distinctive task has been used at the graph track of CoRe Challenge 2022. On the other hand, combinatorial reconfiguration is a relatively new research field. Therefore, the relationship between those fields has not been well investigated, both from theoretical and practical points of view. We will investigate the relationship and will explore the possibility of synergy between techniques independently developed in those closely related research fields.

Acknowledgements. The research was supported by JSPS KAKENHI Grant Number JP20H05964, ROIS NII Open Collaborative Research 2023 (23FP04), JST CREST Grant Number JPMJCR22D3.

References

1. Baral, C.: Knowledge Representation, Reasoning and Declarative Problem Solving. Cambridge University Press, Cambridge (2003)
2. Biere, A.: Bounded model checking. In: Handbook of Satisfiability, pp. 457–481. IOS Press, Amsterdam (2009)
3. Bonsma, P.S., Cereceda, L.: Finding paths between graph colourings: PSPACE-completeness and superpolynomial distances. Theor. Comput. Sci. **410**(50), 5215–5226 (2009)
4. Brewster, R.C., McGuinness, S., Moore, B.R., Noel, J.A.: A dichotomy theorem for circular colouring reconfiguration. Theor. Comput. Sci. **639**, 1–13 (2016)
5. Cereceda, L., van den Heuvel, J., Johnson, M.: Finding paths between 3-colorings. J. Graph Theory **67**(1), 69–82 (2011)
6. Gebser, M., et al.: Potassco User Guide. 2 edn. University of Potsdam (2015). http://potassco.org
7. Gebser, M., Kaminski, R., Kaufmann, B., Schaub, T.: Answer Set Solving in Practice. Morgan and Claypool Publishers, San Rafael (2012)
8. Gelfond, M., Lifschitz, V.: The stable model semantics for logic programming. In: Kowalski, R., Bowen, K. (eds.) Proceedings of the Fifth International Conference and Symposium of Logic Programming (ICLP 1988), pp. 1070–1080. MIT Press (1988)
9. Gopalan, P., Kolaitis, P.G., Maneva, E.N., Papadimitriou, C.H.: The connectivity of Boolean satisfiability: Computational and structural dichotomies. SIAM J. Comput. **38**(6), 2330–2355 (2009)
10. Haddadan, A., et al.: The complexity of dominating set reconfiguration. Theor. Comput. Sci. **651**, 37–49 (2016)
11. van den Heuvel, J.: The complexity of change. In: Blackburn, S.R., Gerke, S., Wildon, M. (eds.) Surveys in Combinatorics 2013, London Mathematical Society Lecture Note Series, vol. 409, pp. 127–160. Cambridge University Press (2013)
12. Ito, T., et al.: On the complexity of reconfiguration problems. Theor. Comput. Sci. **412**(12–14), 1054–1065 (2011)
13. Ito, T., Kaminski, M., Demaine, E.D.: Reconfiguration of list edge-colorings in a graph. Discrete Appl. Math. **160**(15), 2199–2207 (2012)
14. Ito, T., Kamiński, M., Ono, H., Suzuki, A., Uehara, R., Yamanaka, K.: On the parameterized complexity for token jumping on graphs. In: Gopal, T.V., Agrawal, M., Li, A., Cooper, S.B. (eds.) TAMC 2014. LNCS, vol. 8402, pp. 341–351. Springer, Cham (2014). https://doi.org/10.1007/978-3-319-06089-7_24
15. Ito, T., Ono, H., Otachi, Y.: Reconfiguration of cliques in a graph. In: Jain, R., Jain, S., Stephan, F. (eds.) TAMC 2015. LNCS, vol. 9076, pp. 212–223. Springer, Cham (2015). https://doi.org/10.1007/978-3-319-17142-5_19
16. Kaminski, M., Medvedev, P., Milanic, M.: Complexity of independent set reconfigurability problems. Theor. Comput. Sci. **439**, 9–15 (2012)
17. Kaminski, R., Romero, J., Schaub, T., Wanko, P.: How to build your own ASP-based system?! Theory Pract. Logic Program. **23**(1), 299–361 (2023)
18. Kautz, H.A., Selman, B.: Planning as satisfiability. In: Proceedings of the 10th European Conference on Artificial Intelligence (ECAI 1992), pp. 359–363 (1992)
19. Kautz, H.A., Selman, B.: Pushing the envelope: planning, propositional logic and stochastic search. In: Proceedings of the 13th National Conference on Artificial Intelligence (AAAI 1996), pp. 1194–1201 (1996)

20. Mouawad, A.E., Nishimura, N., Pathak, V., Raman, V.: Shortest reconfiguration paths in the solution space of Boolean formulas. SIAM J. Discrete Math. **31**(3), 2185–2200 (2017)
21. Niemelä, I.: Logic programs with stable model semantics as a constraint programming paradigm. Ann. Math. Artif. Intell. **25**(3–4), 241–273 (1999)
22. Nishimura, N.: Introduction to reconfiguration. Algorithms **11**(4), 52 (2018)
23. Soh, T., Okamoto, Y., Ito, T.: Core challenge 2022: solver and graph descriptions. CoRR abs/2208.02495 (2022)
24. Suzuki, A., Mouawad, A.E., Nishimura, N.: Reconfiguration of dominating sets. J. Comb. Optim. **32**(4), 1182–1195 (2016)
25. Takaoka, A.: Complexity of Hamiltonian cycle reconfiguration. Algorithms **11**(9), 140 (2018)
26. Yamada, Y., Banbara, M., Inoue, K., Schaub, T.: Bounded combinatorial reconfiguration with answer set programming. CoRR abs/2307.10688 (2023)
27. Hirate T., et al.: Hamiltonian cycle reconfiguration with answer set programming. JELIA 2023. to appear

Description Logics and Ontological Reasoning

Beyond $\mathcal{ALC}_\mathsf{reg}$: Exploring Non-Regular Extensions of PDL with Description Logics Features

Bartosz Bednarczyk[1,2](✉) [iD]

[1] Computational Logic Group, Technische Universität Dresden, Dresden, Germany
bartosz.bednarczyk@cs.uni.wroc.pl
[2] Institute of Computer Science, University of Wrocław, Wrocław, Poland

Abstract. We investigate the impact of non-regular path expressions on the decidability of satisfiability checking and querying in description logics. Our primary object of interest is $\mathcal{ALC}_\mathsf{vpl}$, an extension of $\mathcal{ALC}$ with path expressions using visibly-pushdown languages, which was shown to be decidable by Löding et al. in 2007. The paper present a series of undecidability results. We prove undecidability of $\mathcal{ALC}_\mathsf{vpl}$ with the seemingly innocent Self operator. Then, we consider the simplest non-regular (visibly-pushdown) language $r^\# s^\# := \{r^n s^n \mid n \in \mathbb{N}\}$. We establish undecidability of the concept satisfiability problem for $\mathcal{ALC}_\mathsf{reg}$ extended with nominals and $r^\# s^\#$, as well as of the query entailment problem for $\mathcal{ALC}$-TBoxes, where such non-regular atoms are present in queries.

1 Introduction

Formal ontologies play a crucial role in artificial intelligence, serving as the backbone of various applications such as the Semantic Web, ontology-based information integration, and peer-to-peer data management. In reasoning about graph-structured data, a significant role is played by *description logics* (DLs) [2], a robust family of logical formalisms serving as the logical foundation of contemporary standardised ontology languages, including OWL 2 by the W3C [16,23]. Among many features present in extensions of the basic description logic $\mathcal{ALC}$, an especially useful one is $\cdot_\mathsf{reg}$, supported by popular $\mathcal{Z}$-family of description logics [10]. With $\cdot_\mathsf{reg}$ one can specify regular path constraints, allowing the user to navigate graph-structured data. In recent years many extensions of $\mathcal{ALC}_\mathsf{reg}$ for ontology-engineering were proposed, see *e.g.* [6,11,30], and the complexity landscape of their reasoning problems is now mostly well-understood [4,5,10]. In fact, the logic $\mathcal{ALC}_\mathsf{reg}$ was already studied in 1979 by the formal-verification community [13], under the name of Propositional Dynamic Logic (PDL). Consult [12] for a discussion on relationship between (extensions of) PDL and $\mathcal{ALC}_\mathsf{reg}$.

Due to wideness of the spectrum of recognizable word languages, the question of whether regularity constraints in path expressions of $\mathcal{ALC}_\mathsf{reg}$ can be lifted to more expressive classes of languages received a lot of attention from researchers.

S. Gaggl et al. (Eds.): JELIA 2023, LNAI 14281, pp. 289–305, 2023.
https://doi.org/10.1007/978-3-031-43619-2_21

We call such extensions *non-regular*. After the first undecidability proof of satisfiability of $\mathcal{ALC}_{reg}$ with context-free languages [20], several decidable cases were identified. For instance, Koren and Pnueli [25] proved that $\mathcal{ALC}_{reg}$ extended with the simplest non-regular language $r^{\#} s^{\#} := \{r^n s^n \mid n \in \mathbb{N}\}$ for *fixed* roles r, s is decidable; while combining it with $s^{\#} r^{\#}$ leads to undecidability [19]. This surprises at first glance, but as it was shown later [29], PDL extended with a broad class of input-driven context-free languages, called *visibly pushdown languages* [1], remain decidable. This generalises all previously known decidability results, and partially explains the reason behind known failures (*e.g.* the languages $r^{\#} s^{\#}$ and $s^{\#} r^{\#}$ cannot be both visibly-pushdown under the same partition of the alphabet).

Our motivation and contribution. Despite the presence of a plethora of various results concerning non-regular extensions of PDL [8,18,21,22,25], no one considered their extensions with popular features supported by W3C ontology languages. Such extensions are, *e.g.* *nominals* (constants), *inverse roles* (inverse programs), *functionality* (deterministic programs), and Self operator (self-loops). The honourable exception is the unpublished undecidability result for $\mathcal{ALC}_{reg}$ extended with the language $r^{\#} s(r^-)^{\#}$ (with r^- denoting the converse of r) from Göller's thesis [15]. The lack of results on entailment of non-regular queries over ontologies is also intriguing, taking into account positive results for conjunctive visibly-pushdown queries in the setting of relational-databases [28].

In this paper we contribute to a further understanding of the aforementioned questions. Our results are negative. For the first part of the paper, we investigate $\mathcal{ALC}_{reg}$ extended with $r^{\#} s^{\#}$. In Sect. 3 we prove that its extension with nominals has an undecidable satisfiability problem. In Sect. 4 we show that, already for $\mathcal{ALC}$, the query entailment problem of queries involving $r^{\#} s^{\#}$, is also undecidable. For the second part of the paper, we study $\mathcal{ALC}_{vpl}$, the extension of $\mathcal{ALC}_{reg}$ with visibly pushdown languages (that generalise $r^{\#} s^{\#}$). We show that adding the seemingly innocent Self renders the logic undecidable.

Because of lack of space, the journal version of this paper contains
all missing proofs, extra pictures and expanded definitions.

2   Preliminaries

We assume familiarity with basics on description logic $\mathcal{ALC}$ [2, Sec. 2.1–2.3], regular and context-free languages, Turing machines and computability [33, Sec. 1–5]. As usual, $\mathbb{N}$ denotes non-negative integers, and $\mathbb{Z}_n$ denotes the set $\{0, 1, \ldots, n-1\}$.

Basics on $\mathcal{ALC}$. We fix countably infinite pairwise disjoint sets of *individual names* $\mathbf{N_I}$, *concept names* $\mathbf{N_C}$, and *role names* $\mathbf{N_R}$ and introduce the description logic $\mathcal{ALC}$. Starting from $\mathbf{N_C}$ and $\mathbf{N_R}$, the set $\mathbf{C}_{\mathcal{ALC}}$ of $\mathcal{ALC}$-*concepts* is built using the following concept constructors: *negation* ($\neg C$), *conjunction* ($C \sqcap D$), *existential restriction* ($\exists r.C$), and the *top concept* $\top$ with the grammar:

$$C, D ::= \top \mid A \mid \neg C \mid C \sqcap D \mid \exists r.C,$$

where $C, D \in \mathbf{C}_{\mathcal{ALC}}$, $A \in \mathbf{N_C}$ and $r \in \mathbf{N_R}$. We employ the following abbreviations: $C \sqcup D := \neg(\neg C \sqcap \neg D)$, $\forall r.C := \neg \exists r.\neg C$, $\bot := \neg \top$, and $C \to D := \neg C \sqcup D$. The semantics of $\mathcal{ALC}$ is defined via *interpretations* $\mathcal{I} := (\Delta^{\mathcal{I}}, \cdot^{\mathcal{I}})$ composed of a non-empty set $\Delta^{\mathcal{I}}$ called the *domain of* $\mathcal{I}$ and an *interpretation function* $\cdot^{\mathcal{I}}$ mapping individual names to elements of $\Delta^{\mathcal{I}}$, concept names to subsets of $\Delta^{\mathcal{I}}$, and role names to subsets of $\Delta^{\mathcal{I}} \times \Delta^{\mathcal{I}}$. This mapping is then extended to concepts.

Name	Syntax	Semantics
top concept	$\top$	$\Delta^{\mathcal{I}}$
concept negation	$\neg C$	$\Delta^{\mathcal{I}} \setminus C^{\mathcal{I}}$
concept intersection	$C \sqcap D$	$C^{\mathcal{I}} \cap D^{\mathcal{I}}$
existential restriction	$\exists r.C$	$\{d \mid \exists e \in C^{\mathcal{I}}\ (d, e) \in r^{\mathcal{I}}\}$

An interpretation $\mathcal{I}$ *satisfies* a concept C (or $\mathcal{I}$ is a *model* of C, written: $\mathcal{I} \models C$) if $C^{\mathcal{I}} \neq \emptyset$. A concept is *satisfiable* if it has a model. In the *satisfiability problem* we ask, whether an input concept has a model. We consider three popular description-logics features: *nominals* ($\mathcal{O}$), *functionality* ($\mathcal{F}$), and the Self *operator* ($\cdot^{\mathsf{Self}}$). Their semantics is recalled in the table below, assuming that $r, s \in \mathbf{N_R}$, and $a \in \mathbf{N_I}$.

Name	Syntax	Semantics
functionality	$\mathsf{func}(r)$	$\mathcal{I} \models \mathsf{func}(r)$ if $\forall d \forall e_1 \forall e_2 \left((d, e_1) \in r^{\mathcal{I}} \wedge (d, e_2) \in r^{\mathcal{I}} \Rightarrow e_1 = e_2 \right)$
nominal	$\{a\}$	$\{a^{\mathcal{I}}\}$
self-operator	$\exists r.\mathsf{Self}$	$\{d \mid (d, d) \in r^{\mathcal{I}}\}$

A path ρ in an interpretation $\mathcal{I}$ is a finite word in $(\Delta^{\mathcal{I}})^*$. We usually enumerate its components with $\rho_1, \ldots, \rho_{|\rho|}$, where the number $|\rho| - 1$ is called the *length* of ρ. We say that ρ *starts from* (resp. *ends in*) d if $\rho_1 = d$ holds (resp. $\rho_{|\rho|} = d$). If $N \subseteq \mathbf{N_I}$ is given, we call an element $d \in \Delta^{\mathcal{I}}$ N-*named* if $d = a^{\mathcal{I}}$ holds for some $a \in N$.

$\mathcal{ALC}$ with Path Expressions. We treat $\Sigma_{\text{all}} := \mathbf{N_R} \cup \{A? \mid A \in \mathbf{N_C}\}$ as an infinite alphabet. Let $\mathbb{ALL}$ and $\mathbb{REG}$ denote classes of all recognizable (resp. regular) finite-word languages over finite subsets of Σ_{all}. For a language $\mathcal{L}$ and a path $\rho := \rho_1 \rho_2 \cdots \rho_n \rho_{n+1}$ in an interpretation $\mathcal{I}$, we say that ρ is an $\mathcal{L}$-*path*, if there exists a word $w := w_1 w_2 \ldots w_n \in \mathcal{L}$ such that for all $i \leq n$ we have either (i) $w_i \in \mathbf{N_R}$ and $(\rho_i, \rho_{i+1}) \in (w_i)^{\mathcal{I}}$, or (ii) w_i has the form $A?$, $\rho_i = \rho_{i+1}$ and $\rho_i \in A^{\mathcal{I}}$. Intuitively w either traverses roles or loops at an element to check the satisfaction of concepts. We say that $e \in \Delta^{\mathcal{I}}$ is $\mathcal{L}$-*reachable from* $d \in \Delta^{\mathcal{I}}$ (or that d $\mathcal{L}$-*reaches* e) if there is an $\mathcal{L}$-path ρ that starts from d and ends in e. The logic $\mathcal{ALC}_{\text{all}}$ extends $\mathcal{ALC}$ with concept constructors of the form $\exists \mathcal{L}.C$, where $\mathcal{L} \in \mathbb{ALL}$ and C is an $\mathcal{ALC}_{\text{all}}$-concept. Their semantics is as follows: $(\exists \mathcal{L}.C)^{\mathcal{I}}$ is the set of all $d \in \Delta^{\mathcal{I}}$ that can $\mathcal{L}$-reach some $e \in C^{\mathcal{I}}$, and $\forall \mathcal{L}.C$ stands for $\neg \exists \mathcal{L}.\neg C$. The logic $\mathcal{ALC}_{\text{reg}}$ (a.k.a. PDL [13]) is a restriction of $\mathcal{ALC}_{\text{all}}$ to regular languages.

VPLs. The class of *Visibly-pushdown languages* (VPLs) [1] is a well-behaved family of context-free languages, in which the usage of the stack in the underlying pushdown automata model is input-driven. A *pushdown alphabet* Σ is an alphabet equipped with a partition $(\Sigma_c, \Sigma_i, \Sigma_r)$. The elements of Σ_c, Σ_i, and Σ_r are called, respectively, *call* letters, *internal* letters, and *return* letters. A *visibly-pushdown automaton* (VPA) $\mathcal{A}$ over a pushdown alphabet Σ is a deterministic pushdown automaton that can push (resp. pop) a letter from its stack only after reading a call (resp. return) symbol. A *visibly one-counter automaton* [3] (VOCA) is a VPA that can use only a single stack letter. Given a VPA $\mathcal{A}$, we speak about words *accepted* by $\mathcal{A}$, and the language $\mathcal{L}(\mathcal{A})$ of $\mathcal{A}$ defined in the usual way. As an example, suppose that $r \in \Sigma_c$ and $s \in \Sigma_r$. Then the language $r^{\#}s^{\#} := \{r^n s^n \mid n \in \mathbb{N}\}$ is visibly-pushdown, but the language $s^{\#}r^{\#}$ over the same alphabet is not. What is more, every regular language is visibly-pushdown.

We present Σ_{all} as a pushdown alphabet $((\mathbf{N_R})_c, (\mathbf{N_R})_i \cup \{A? \mid A \in \mathbf{N_C}\}, (\mathbf{N_R})_r)$. The logic $\mathcal{ALC}_{\text{vpl}}$ is defined as the restriction of $\mathcal{ALC}_{\text{all}}$ to visibly-pushdown languages over finite subsets of Σ_{all} (note that the letters are equally partitioned for all the languages). It is known that $\mathcal{ALC}_{\text{vpl}}$ has 2ExpTime-complete [29] satisfiability problem. Finally, $\mathcal{ALC}_{\text{reg}}^{r^{\#}s^{\#}}$ denotes the restriction of $\mathcal{ALC}_{\text{vpl}}$ in which the only allowed non-regular language is $r^{\#}s^{\#}$ for *fixed* call r and return s.

3   Nominals Lead to Undecidability

We first establish undecidability of the satisfiability problem for $\mathcal{ALCO}_{\text{reg}}^{r^{\#}s^{\#}}$.

A *domino tiling system* is a triple $\mathcal{D} := (\text{Col}, \text{T}, \square)$, where Col is a finite set of *colours*, $\text{T} \subseteq \text{Col}^4$ is a finite set of 4-sided *tiles*, and $\square \in$ Col is a distinguished colour called *white*. For brevity, we call a tile $(c_l, c_d, c_r, c_u) \in \text{T}$ (i) *left-border* if $c_l = \square$, (ii) *down-border* if $c_d = \square$, (iii) *right-border* if $c_r = \square$, and (iii) *up-border* if $c_u = \square$. We say that $\text{t} := (c_l, c_d, c_r, c_u)$ and $\text{t}' := (c_l', c_d', c_r', c_u')$ from T are (i) *H-compatible* if $c_r = c_l'$, and (ii) *V-compatible* if $c_u = c_d'$. We say that $\mathcal{D}$ *covers* $\mathbb{Z}_n \times \mathbb{Z}_m$ (where n, m are positive integers) if there is a mapping $\xi \colon \mathbb{Z}_n \times \mathbb{Z}_m \to \text{T}$ such that for all pairs $(x, y) \in \mathbb{Z}_n \times \mathbb{Z}_m$ with $\xi(x, y) := (c_l, c_d, c_r, c_u)$ we have:

(TBor) $x = 0$ iff $c_l = \square$; $x = n-1$ iff $c_r = \square$; $y = 0$ iff $c_d = \square$; $y = m-1$ iff $c_u = \square$
(THori) If $(x+1, y) \in \mathbb{Z}_n \times \mathbb{Z}_m$ then $\xi(x, y)$ and $\xi(x+1, y)$ are H-compatible.
(TVerti) If $(x, y+1) \in \mathbb{Z}_n \times \mathbb{Z}_m$ then $\xi(x, y)$ and $\xi(x, y+1)$ are V-compatible.

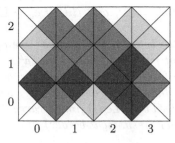

(a) Visualization of ξ.

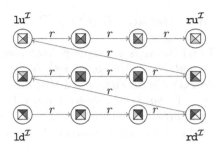

(b) The encoding of ξ as a $\mathcal{D}$-snake $\mathcal{I}$.

Fig. 1. If Col $= \{\blacksquare, \blacksquare, \square, \square\}$ and $T = \text{Col}^4$, the map $\xi := \{(0,0) \mapsto \boxtimes, (1,0) \mapsto \boxtimes, (2,0) \mapsto \boxtimes, (3,0) \mapsto \boxtimes, (0,1) \mapsto \boxtimes, (1,1) \mapsto \boxtimes, (2,1) \mapsto \boxtimes, (3,1) \mapsto \boxtimes, (0,2) \mapsto \boxtimes, (1,2) \mapsto \boxtimes, (2,2) \mapsto \boxtimes, (3,2) \mapsto \boxtimes\}$ covers $\mathbb{Z}_4 \times \mathbb{Z}_3$.

Intuitively, $\xi : \mathbb{Z}_n \times \mathbb{Z}_m$ can be seen as a rectangle of size $n \times m$ coloured by unit 4-sided tiles (with coordinates corresponding to the left, down, right, and upper colour) from T, where sides of tiles of consecutive squares have matching colours, and borders of the rectangle are white. Consult Fig. 1a for more intuitions.

W.l.o.g. we will always assume that T does not contain tiles having more than two white sides. A system $\mathcal{D}$ is *solvable* if there exist positive $n, m \in \mathbb{N}$ for which $\mathcal{D}$ covers $\mathbb{Z}_n \times \mathbb{Z}_m$. The problem of deciding if an input domino tiling system is solvable is undecidable, which can be shown by a minor modification of classical undecidability proofs for tilling problems, see *e.g.* [32, Lemma 3.9].

For a tiling system $\mathcal{D} := (\text{Col}, T, \square)$ we encode mappings ξ from some $\mathbb{Z}_n \times \mathbb{Z}_m$ to T in interpretations $\mathcal{I}$ as certain r^+-paths ρ from $\mathtt{ld}^\mathcal{I}$ to $\mathtt{ru}^\mathcal{I}$ passing through $\mathtt{rd}^\mathcal{I}$ and $\mathtt{lu}^\mathcal{I}$ (using fresh names from $\mathsf{N}^{\mathsf{T}}_{\clubsuit} := \{\mathtt{ld}, \mathtt{rd}, \mathtt{lu}, \mathtt{ru}\}$) composed of elements labelled with fresh concepts names from $\mathsf{C}^{\mathsf{T}}_{\clubsuit} := \{\mathsf{C}_\mathsf{t} \mid \mathsf{t} \in \mathsf{T}\}$, see Fig. 1b.

Definition 1. *An interpretation $\mathcal{I}$ is a $\mathcal{D}$-snake for a tiling system $\mathcal{D}$ if:*

(SPath) *There is an r^+-path ρ that starts in $\mathtt{ld}^\mathcal{I}$, then passes through $\mathtt{rd}^\mathcal{I}$, then passes through $\mathtt{lu}^\mathcal{I}$ and finishes in $\mathtt{ru}^\mathcal{I}$.*

(SNoLoop) *No $\mathsf{N}^{\mathsf{T}}_{\clubsuit}$-named element can r^+-reach itself.*

(SUniqTil) *For every $\mathtt{d}$ r^*-reachable from $\mathtt{ld}^\mathcal{I}$ there is precisely one tile $\mathsf{t} \in \mathsf{T}$ such that $\mathtt{d} \in \mathsf{C}^\mathcal{I}_\mathsf{t}$ (we say that $\mathtt{d}$ is labelled by a tile t or that it carries t).*

(SSpecTil) *The $\mathsf{N}^{\mathsf{T}}_{\clubsuit}$-named elements are unique elements r^*-reachable from $\mathtt{ld}^\mathcal{I}$ that are labelled by tiles with two white sides. Moreover, we have that (a) $\mathtt{ld}^\mathcal{I}$ carries a tile that is left-border and down-border, (b) $\mathtt{rd}^\mathcal{I}$ carries a tile that is right-border and down-border, (c) $\mathtt{lu}^\mathcal{I}$ carries a tile that is left-border and up-border, (d) $\mathtt{ru}^\mathcal{I}$ carries a tile that is right-border and up-border.*

(SHori) *For all elements $\mathtt{d}$ different from $\mathtt{ru}^\mathcal{I}$ that are r^*-reachable from $\mathtt{ld}^\mathcal{I}$ and labelled by some tile $\mathsf{t} := (c_l, c_d, c_r, c_u)$, there exists a tile $\mathsf{t}' := (c'_l, c'_d, c'_r, c'_u)$ for which all r-successors $\mathtt{e}$ of $\mathtt{d}$ carry the tile t' and: (i) t, t' are*

H-*compatible, (ii) if* $c_d = \square$ *then* $(c_l \neq \square$ *iff* $c'_d = \square)$, *and (iii) if* $c_u = \square$ *then* $c'_u = \square$.

(SLen) *There is a unique* N *such that all* r^+-*paths between* $ld^{\mathcal{I}}$ *and* $rd^{\mathcal{I}}$ *are of length* N-1. *Moreover,* $rd^{\mathcal{I}}$ *is the only element* r^{N-1}-*reachable from* $ld^{\mathcal{I}}$.

(SVerti) *For all elements* d *that are* r^*-*reachable from* $ld^{\mathcal{I}}$ *and labelled by some* t $\in$ T *that is not up-border, we have that (a) there exists a tile* t$'$ $\in$ T *such that all elements* e r^N-*reachable (for* N *guaranteed by (SLen)) from* d *carry* t$'$, *(b)* t *and* t$'$ *are* V-*compatible, (c)* t *is left-border (resp. right-border) iff* t$'$ *is.*

If $\mathcal{I}$ satisfy all but the last two conditions, we call it a $\mathcal{D}$-*pseudosnake*. The key property of our encoding is summarised in the following lemma.

Lemma 2. *A domino tiling system* $\mathcal{D}$ *is solvable iff there exists a* $\mathcal{D}$-*snake.*

While $\mathcal{D}$-snakes are not directly axiomatizable in $\mathcal{ALCO}_{\mathrm{reg}}^{r\#s\#}$, we at least see how to express $\mathcal{D}$-pseudosnakes. See full version of the paper for the proof.

Lemma 3. *For every tiling system* $\mathcal{D} := (\mathrm{Col}, \mathrm{T}, \square)$, *there is an* $\mathcal{ALCO}_{\mathrm{reg}}^{r\#s\#}$-*concept* $C_{\mathcal{S}}^{\mathcal{D}}$, *that employs the role* r, *individual names from* $\mathsf{N}_{\mathbf{I}}^{\mathrm{T}}$ *and concept names from* $C_{\mathbf{I}}^{\mathrm{T}}$, *such that for all* $\mathcal{I}$ *we have that* $\mathcal{I}$ *is a* $\mathcal{D}$-*pseudosnake iff* $\mathcal{I} \models C_{\mathcal{S}}^{\mathcal{D}}$.

Note that the property that pseudosnakes are missing in order to be proper snakes, is the ability to measure. We tackle this issue by introducing "yardsticks".

Definition 4. *Let* T *be a finite and non-empty set, and let* $\mathsf{N}_{\mathbf{I}}^{\mathrm{T}} := \{st, md, md_t, end_t \mid t \in T\}$ *be composed of (pairwise different) individual names. A* T-*yardstick is any interpretation* $\mathcal{I}$ *that satisfies all the conditions listed below.*

(YDifNom) $\mathsf{N}_{\mathbf{I}}^{\mathrm{T}}$-*named elem. are pairwise-diffr. and* $(r + s)^*$-*reach. from* $st^{\mathcal{I}}$.

(YNoLoop) *No* $\mathsf{N}_{\mathbf{I}}^{\mathrm{T}}$-*named element can* $(r + s)^+$-*reach itself.*

(YMid) $md^{\mathcal{I}}$ *is the* unique *elem. with an* s-*successor that is* r^*-*reachable from* $st^{\mathcal{I}}$.

(YSuccOfMid) s-*successors of* $md^{\mathcal{I}}$ *are precisely* $\{md_t \mid t \in T\}$-*named elems.*

(YReachMidT) *For every* t $\in$ T *we have that* $md_t^{\mathcal{I}}$ *can* s^*-*reach* $end_t^{\mathcal{I}}$ *but it cannot* s^*-*reach* $end_{t'}^{\mathcal{I}}$ *for all* t$'$ $\neq$ t.

(YEqDst) *The* $\{end_t \mid t \in T\}$-*named elements are precisely the elements* $r^\#s^\#$-*reachable from* $st^{\mathcal{I}}$.

(YNoEqDst) *No* $\{end_t \mid t \in T\}$-*named element is* $r^\#s^\#$-*reachable from an element* $(s + r)^+$-*reachable from* $st^{\mathcal{I}}$.

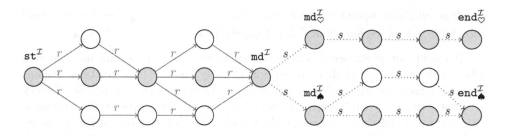

An example $\{\heartsuit, \spadesuit\}$-yardstick is depicted above. A "minimal" yardstick would contain the grey nodes only. Lemma 5 justifies the name "yardstick". Intuitively it says that in any T-yardstick $\mathcal{I}$, all s^*-paths from $\mathbf{md}^{\mathcal{I}}$ to all $\mathbf{end}_t^{\mathcal{I}}$ have equal length, to which we refer as the *length* of $\mathcal{I}$.

Lemma 5. *Let $\mathcal{I}$ be a T-yardstick. Then there exists a unique positive integer* N *such that: (i) for all* $t \in T$ *we have that* $\mathbf{end}_t^{\mathcal{I}}$ *is* s^N-*reachable from* $\mathbf{md}^{\mathcal{I}}$, *and (ii) for all* $t \in T$ *we have that* $\mathbf{end}_t^{\mathcal{I}}$ *is* s^{N-1}-*reachable from* $\mathbf{md}_t^{\mathcal{I}}$.

Proof. Fix $t_* \in T$. By (YEqDst) we know that $\mathbf{st}^{\mathcal{I}}$ $r^{\#}s^{\#}$-reaches $\mathbf{end}_{t_*}^{\mathcal{I}}$, and let $\rho := \rho_1 \ldots \rho_{2N+1}$ be a path witnessing it. We claim that N is the desired length of $\mathcal{I}$. First, note that N is greater than 0 by (YDifNom). Second, by the semantics of $r^{\#}s^{\#}$, for all $i \leq N$ we have $(\rho_i, \rho_{i+1}) \in r^{\mathcal{I}}$ and $(\rho_{N+i}, \rho_{N+i+1}) \in s^{\mathcal{I}}$. Thus ρ_{N+1} is r^*-reachable from $\mathbf{st}^{\mathcal{I}}$ and has an s-successor. These two facts imply (by (YMid)) that ρ_{N+1} is equal to $\mathbf{md}^{\mathcal{I}}$. It remains to show that all the paths leading from $\mathbf{md}^{\mathcal{I}}$ to some $\mathbf{end}_t$ are of length N. Towards a contradiction, assume that there is $t' \in T$ and an integer $M \neq N$ such that $\mathbf{md}^{\mathcal{I}}$ s^M-reaches $\mathbf{end}_{t'}^{\mathcal{I}}$ via a path $\rho' := \rho'_1 \ldots \rho'_M$. We stress that $\rho'_1 = \mathbf{md}^{\mathcal{I}}$ and $\rho'_M = \mathbf{end}_{t'}^{\mathcal{I}}$ (by design of ρ'), and $\rho'_2 = \mathbf{md}_{t'}^{\mathcal{I}}$ (by a conjunction of (YSuccOfMid) and (YReachMidT)). To conclude the proof, it suffices to resolve the following two cases.

- Suppose that $M < N$. Then ρ_{N+1-M} $(r^M s^M)$-reaches (thus $r^{\#}s^{\#}$-reaches) $\mathbf{end}_{t'}^{\mathcal{I}}$, as witnessed by the path $\rho_{N+1-M} \ldots \rho_N \rho'$. Moreover ρ_{N+1-M} is r^+-reachable from $\mathbf{st}^{\mathcal{I}}$, witnessed by the path $\rho_1 \ldots \rho_{N+1-M}$ (note that its length is positive by the inequality $M < N$). This contradicts (YNoEqDst).
- Suppose that $M > N$. Consider the path $\rho_1 \ldots \rho_N \rho'_1 \ldots \rho'_N$. By design, such a path witnesses that $\mathbf{st}^{\mathcal{I}}$ $(r^N s^N)$-reaches (and thus also $r^{\#}s^{\#}$-reaches) ρ'_N. By (YEqDst) we infer that ρ'_N is then $\{\mathbf{end}_t \mid t \in T\}$-named. As $\rho'_2 = \mathbf{md}_{t'}^{\mathcal{I}}$ s^+-reaches ρ'_N, we infer that $\rho'_N = \mathbf{end}_{t'}^{\mathcal{I}}$ (otherwise we would have a contradiction with (YReachMidT)). But then $\mathbf{end}_{t'}^{\mathcal{I}}$ s^+-reaches itself via a path $\rho'_N \ldots \rho_M$, which is of positive length due to $M > N$. A contradiction with (YNoLoop).

This establishes Property (i). The satisfaction of Property (ii) is now immediate.

As the next step of our construction, we establish existence of arbitrary long yardsticks, and axiomatise them with an $\mathcal{ALCO}_{\text{reg}}^{r^{\#}s^{\#}}$-concept. Indeed:

Lemma 6. *For every finite non-empty set* T *and a positive integer* N, *there exists a* T-*yardstick of length* N. *Moreover, there exists an* $\mathcal{ALCO}_{\text{reg}}^{r^{\#}s^{\#}}$-*concept* $\mathbf{C}_{\blacksquare}^{T}$, *that* *employs only role names r, s and individual names from* $\mathbf{N_I^T}$*, such that for all interpretations $\mathcal{I}$ we have that $\mathcal{I}$ is a T-yardstick if and only if $\mathcal{I} \models \mathbf{C_i^T}$.*

We next put pseudosnakes and yardsticks together, obtaining metricobras. The intuition behind their construction is fairly simple: (i) we take a disjoint union of a pseudosnake and a yardstick, (ii) we then connect (via the role s) every element carrying a tile t with the interpretation of the corresponding nominal $\mathtt{md_t}$, and finally (iii) we synchronise the length of the underlying yardstick, say N, with the length of the path between the interpretations of $\mathtt{ld}$ and $\mathtt{rd}$. After such "merging", retrieving (SHori) is relatively easy: rather than testing if every N-reachable element from some d carries a suitable tile t (for an a priori unknown N) we can check instead whether d can $r^\# s^\#$-reach the interpretation of $\mathtt{end_t}$.

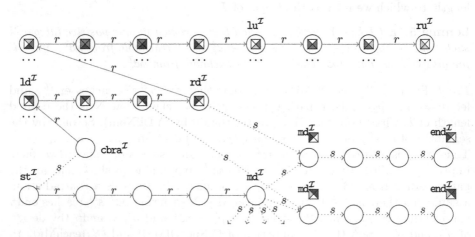

Fig. 2. A fragment of an example $\mathcal{D}$-metricobra representing ξ from Fig. 1. The upper part corresponds to a $\mathcal{D}$-snake, and the lower part corresponds to a T-yardstick. The distances between named elements are important.

Definition 7. *Let* $\mathcal{D} := (\mathrm{Col}, \mathrm{T}, \square)$ *be a domino tiling system and* $\mathtt{cbra}$ *be an individual name. An interpretation $\mathcal{I}$ is a $\mathcal{D}$-metricobra if it satisfies:*

(MInit) *$\mathcal{I}$ is a $\mathcal{D}$-pseudosnake and a T-yardstick, and $\mathtt{cbra}^\mathcal{I}$ has precisely two successors: one r-successor, namely $\mathtt{ld}^\mathcal{I}$, and one s-successor, namely $\mathtt{st}^\mathcal{I}$.*

(MTile) *For every tile $t \in \mathrm{T}$ and every element $d \in \Delta^\mathcal{I}$ that is r^*-reachable from $\mathtt{ld}^\mathcal{I}$ we have that d carries a tile $t \in \mathrm{T}$ if and only if d has a unique s-successor and such a successor is equal to $\mathtt{md_t^\mathcal{I}}$.*

(MSync) *Let t be the tile of $\mathtt{rd}^\mathcal{I}$. Then (a) $\mathtt{cbra}^\mathcal{I}$ $r^\# s^\#$-reaches $\mathtt{end_t^\mathcal{I}}$ and cannot $r^\# s^\#$-reach any of $\mathtt{end_{t'}^\mathcal{I}}$ for $t' \neq t$, (b) $\mathtt{cbra}^\mathcal{I}$ cannot $r^\# s^\#$-reach an elem. that s^+-reaches $\mathtt{end_t^\mathcal{I}}$, (c) no elem. r^*-reachable from $\mathtt{ld}^\mathcal{I}$ $r^\# s^\#$-reaches $\mathtt{end_t^\mathcal{I}}$.*

(MVerti) *For all elements d that are r^*-reachable from $\mathtt{ld}^\mathcal{I}$ and carry a tile $t \in \mathrm{T}$ that is not up-border, we have that there exists a tile $t' \in \mathrm{T}$ such that* *(a)* t *and* t′ *are* V-*compatible, (b)* t *is left-border (resp. right-border) iff* t′ *is, and (c)* d *can* $r^{\#}s^{\#}$-*reach* $\mathbf{end}_{t'}$ *but cannot reach* $r^{\#}s^{\#}$-*reach* $\mathbf{end}_{t''}$ *for all* t″ ≠ t′.

We first provide an $\mathcal{ALCO}_{reg}^{r^{\#}s^{\#}}$-axiomatization of $\mathcal{D}$-metricobras.

Lemma 8. *There exists an* $\mathcal{ALCO}_{reg}^{r^{\#}s^{\#}}$-*concept* $C_{\clubsuit}^{\mathcal{D}}$ *such that for all interpretations* $\mathcal{I}$ *we have that* $\mathcal{I}$ *is a* $\mathcal{D}$-*metricobra if and only if* $(C_{\clubsuit}^{\mathcal{D}})^{\mathcal{I}} = \{\mathbf{cbra}^{\mathcal{I}}\}$.

Second, we relate $\mathcal{D}$-snakes and $\mathcal{D}$-metricobras as follows.

Lemma 9. *Every* $\mathcal{D}$-*metricobra is also a* $\mathcal{D}$-*snake. Moreover, if a* $\mathcal{D}$-*snake exists then so does a* $\mathcal{D}$-*metricobra.*

By collecting all previous lemmas we infer the main theorem of the paper:

Theorem 10. *A tiling system* $\mathcal{D}$ *is solvable iff the* $\mathcal{ALCO}_{reg}^{r^{\#}s^{\#}}$-*concept* $C_{\clubsuit}^{\mathcal{D}}$ *is satisfiable. Thus, the concept satisfiability problem of* $\mathcal{ALCO}_{reg}^{r^{\#}s^{\#}}$ *is undecidable.*

4   Querying in $\mathcal{ALC}_{vpl}$

We next address the problem of query entailment under logical constraints. The $\mathbb{C}$-*enriched Positive Existential Queries* (abbreviated as $\mathbb{C}$-PEQs) are defined with:

$$q, q' ::= \bot \mid A(x) \mid r(x,y) \mid \mathcal{L}(x,y) \mid q \vee q' \mid q \wedge q',$$

where $A \in \mathbf{N_C}$, $r \in \mathbf{N_R}$, $\mathcal{L} \in \mathbb{C}$, and x, y are variables from a countably infinite set $\mathbf{N_V}$. The semantics is defined as expected, *e.g.* $\mathcal{L}(x,y)$ evaluates to true under a variable assignment η if and only if $\eta(x)$ can $\mathcal{L}$-reach $\eta(y)$ in $\mathcal{I}$. The ∅-PEQs (or Positive Existential Queries) are well-known generalizations of (unions of) *conjunctive queries, e.g.* PEQs in which disjunction is allowed only at the outermost level. The REG-PEQs (or Positive Regular Path Queries) are among the most popular query languages nowadays [14,31]. Finally, VPL-PEQs recently received some attention in [28]. An interpretation $\mathcal{I}$ *satisfies* a query q (written $\mathcal{I} \models q$), if there exists an assignment η of variables (a *match*) from q to $\Delta^{\mathcal{I}}$ under which q evaluates to true. A concept C *entails* a query q (written $C \models q$) if all models of C satisfy q. In the $\mathbb{C}$-*PEQ entailment problem* for a DL $\mathcal{L}$ we ask, given an $\mathcal{L}$-concept C and a $\mathbb{C}$-PEQ q, whether $C \models q$ holds.

By existing results on querying $\mathcal{ALC}$ [17, Lemma 8] and by the tree model property of $\mathcal{ALC}_{vpl}$ [29, Sec. 4.1], we obtain:

Corollary 11. *The entailment problem of* REG-*PEQs over* $\mathcal{ALC}_{vpl}$-*concepts is complete for* 2ExpTime.

Unfortunately, the relatively positive results of Corollary 11 do not transfer beyond the class of REG-PEQs, especially if atoms of the form $r^{\#}s^{\#}(x,y)$ are present in the query. To justify this claim, we are going to provide a reduction

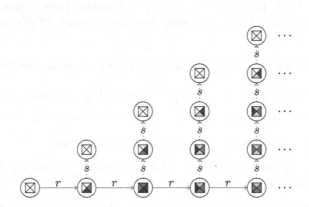

Fig. 3. Visualisation of an octant-based interpretation.

from the *Octant Tiling Problem* [7, Sec 3.1]. Roughly speaking, the ontology in our reduction will define a grid labelled with tiles, while the query counterpart will serve as a tool to detect mismatches in its lower triangle (a.k.a. octant) part. Let $\mathcal{D} := (\mathrm{Col}, \mathrm{T}, \square)$ be a domino tiling system (defined as in Sect. 3), and let us call the set $\mathbb{O} := \{(x, y) \mid x, y \in \mathbb{N}, 0 \leq y \leq x\}$ *the octant*. It is convenient for our reduction to assume that T contains an all-border white tile $\boxtimes$, and all other tiles from T are not right-border and not down-border. We say that $\mathcal{D}$ *covers* $\mathbb{O}$ if there exists a mapping $\xi \colon \mathbb{O} \to \mathrm{T}$ such that for all pairs $(x, y) \in \mathbb{O}$ satisfy:

(OBord) $\xi(0,0) = \boxtimes$, and $\xi(1,0) \neq \boxtimes$.
(OHori) The tiles $\xi(x,y)$ and $\xi(x+1,y)$ are H-compatible. In addition, whenever $\xi(x,y) = \boxtimes$ holds, the tile $\xi(x+1,y)$ is left- and up-border.
(OVerti) If $(x, y+1) \in \mathbb{O}$ then $\xi(x,y)$ and $\xi(x,y+1)$ are V-compatible.

Note that $\mathcal{D}$ covers $\mathbb{O}$ if and only if it covers $\mathbb{N} \times \mathbb{N}$, which is a consequence of (OBord) and the specific use of white colour by tiles in T. The *octant tiling problem* asks to decide, for an input domino tiling system $\mathcal{D}$, whether $\mathcal{D}$ covers the octant. This problem can easily be shown undecidable, as discussed in [7].

We again employ concepts from $\mathrm{C}^{\mathrm{T}}_{\text{\tiny\#}}$, and the non-regular language $r^{\#} s^{\#}$. We call a pointed interpretation $(\mathcal{I}, (0,0))$ *octant-based* if (i) $\Delta^{\mathcal{I}} = \mathbb{O}$, (ii) $r^{\mathcal{I}} = \{((n,0), (n{+}1,0)) \mid n \in \mathbb{N}\}$, (iii) $s^{\mathcal{I}} = \{((n,m), (n,m{+}1)) \mid n, m \in \mathbb{N}, m < n\}$, and (iv) for every $\mathrm{e} \in \Delta^{\mathcal{I}}$ there is a unique $\mathrm{t} \in \mathrm{T}$ for which $\mathrm{e} \in \mathrm{C}^{\mathcal{I}}_{\mathrm{t}}$. Consult Fig. 3 for a visualization. An octant-based $\mathcal{I}$ naturally encodes a mapping $\xi \colon \mathbb{O} \to \mathrm{T}$ defined as $(n, m) \mapsto \mathrm{t}$ for the unique tile carried by (n, m). For convenience, we say that $\mathcal{I}$ $\mathcal{D}$-*semicovers* (resp. $\mathcal{D}$-*covers*) the octant if such a map ξ satisfies (OBord) and (OVerti) (resp. all (OBord), (OVerti), and (OHori)). We analogously speak about *grid-based* pointed interpretations, which are defined similarly to octant-based interpretations above, with the exception that their domains are $\mathbb{N} \times \mathbb{N}$ and the condition $m < n$ is removed from Item (iii).

Violations of the condition (OHori) by an octant-based interpretation will be detected with a $\mathbb{VPL}$-PEQ $q_{\blacktriangle}^{\mathcal{D}}$ (to be defined next), which we visualise as follows.

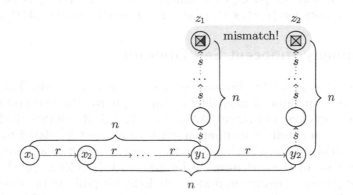

Fig. 4. Visualisation of the query $q_{\blacktriangle}^{\mathcal{D}}(x_1, x_2, y_1, y_2, z_1, z_2)$. The variables z_1, z_2 are mapped to elements that carry tiles violating (OHori); the fact that x_1 and x_2 lie in consecutive columns is handled by means of r-connectedness of y_1, y_2; finally, equi-height of z_1 and z_2 is ensured with non-regular atoms $r^{\#}s^{\#}(x_i, z_i)$.

After the informal explanation, we provide the formal definition of $q_{\blacktriangle}^{\mathcal{D}}$.

$$q_{\blacktriangle}^{\mathcal{D}} := \bigvee_{\substack{t,t' \text{ violating (OHori)}}} \big[r(x_1, x_2) \wedge r^*(x_2, y_1) \wedge r(y_1, y_2) \wedge s^*(y_1, z_1) \wedge s^*(y_2, z_2)$$

$$\wedge r^{\#}s^{\#}(x_1, z_1) \wedge r^{\#}s^{\#}(x_2, z_2) \wedge C_t(z_1) \wedge C_{t'}(z_2) \big]$$

By routine case analysis with a bit of calculations, we can show that:

Lemma 12. *Let $\mathcal{D} := (\text{Col}, T, \square)$ be a domino tilling system. If $\mathcal{D}$ covers the octant, then there exist octant-based and grid-based interpretations $\mathcal{D}$-covering the octant. Moreover, for all octant-based or grid-based $\mathcal{I}$ that $\mathcal{D}$-semicover the octant, $\mathcal{I} \not\models q_{\blacktriangle}^{\mathcal{D}}$ if and only if $\mathcal{I}$ actually $\mathcal{D}$-covers the octant.*

It is routine to define a $\mathcal{ALC}_{reg}$-concept $C_{semicov}^{T}$ stating that the starting element carries $\boxtimes$, that every element carries exactly one tile, and that the tiles of s-connected elements are V-compatible. Expanding $C_{semicov}^{T}$ with an $\mathcal{ALC}_{reg}$-concept expressing that any element has an r-successor and an s-successor, leads to a concept $C_{\blacksquare}^{\mathcal{D}}$. This concept is especially useful as it defines grids that $\mathcal{D}$-semicovers the octant. (We note that the use of grids is crucial here, as $\mathcal{ALC}_{reg}$ cannot define octant-based structures but our queries look only at octants.)

The main property of our reduction is established below.

Lemma 13. *Let $\mathcal{D} := (\text{Col}, T, \square)$ be a domino tilling system. Then $C_{\blacksquare}^{\mathcal{D}} \not\models q_{\blacktriangle}^{\mathcal{D}}$ if and only if there is a grid-based interpretation $\mathcal{I}$ such that $\mathcal{I} \models C_{\blacksquare}^{\mathcal{D}}$ and $\mathcal{I} \not\models q_{\blacktriangle}^{\mathcal{D}}$. Thus $C_{\blacksquare}^{\mathcal{D}} \not\models q_{\blacktriangle}^{\mathcal{D}}$ if and only if $\mathcal{D}$ covers the octant.*

The concept $C_{\blacksquare}^{\mathcal{Q}}$ can be equivalently expressed as an $\mathcal{ALC}$-TBox (*cf.* [2, Sec. 2.2.1]). By a combination of previously presented lemmas we thus infer:

Theorem 14. *The* $\mathbb{VPL}$-*PEQs entailment problem for* $\mathcal{ALC}_{reg}$ *is undecidable. This holds already for* $\{r, r^*, s, s^*, r^{\#}s^{\#}\}$-*PEQ entailment over* $\mathcal{ALC}$-*TBoxes.*

5   Seemingly Innocent **Self** Operator

We conclude the paper by showing yet another negative result. This time we tackle the Self operator, a modelling feature supported by two profiles of the OWL 2 Web Ontology Language [24, 26] and $\mathcal{SROIQ}$. Recall that the Self operator allows us to specify the situation when an element is related to it*self* by a binary relationship, *e.g.* we interpret the concept $\exists r.\mathsf{Self}$ in an interpretation $\mathcal{I}$ as the set of all those elements d for which (d, d) belongs to $r^{\mathcal{I}}$. In what follows, we provide a reduction from an undecidable problem of non-emptiness of the intersection of deterministic one-counter automata (DOCA) [34, p. 75]. Such an automata model is similar to pushdown automata, but its stack alphabet is single-letter only. The Self operator will be especially useful to introduce "disjunction" to paths.

Let Σ be an alphabet and $\mathbf{w} := (\mathsf{a}_1, \star_1) \ldots (\mathsf{a}_n, \star_n)$ be a word over $\Sigma \times \{c, r, i\}$. We call the word $\pi_1(\mathbf{w}) := \mathsf{a}_1 \ldots \mathsf{a}_n$ the *projection* of $\mathbf{w}$. An important property of DOCA is that they can be made visibly one-counter in the following sense.

Lemma 15. *For any DOCA* $\mathcal{A}$ *over* Σ, *we can construct a VOCA* $\tilde{\mathcal{A}}$ *over* $\tilde{\Sigma} := (\Sigma \times \{c\}, (\Sigma \times \{i\}) \cup \{\mathsf{x}\}, \Sigma \times \{r\})$ *where* x *is a fresh internal letter, such that all words in* $\mathcal{L}(\tilde{\mathcal{A}})$ *have the form* $\tilde{\mathsf{a}}_1 \mathsf{x} \tilde{\mathsf{a}}_2 \mathsf{x} \ldots \mathsf{x} \tilde{\mathsf{a}}_n$ *for* $\tilde{\mathsf{a}}_1, \ldots, \tilde{\mathsf{a}}_n \in \Sigma \times \{c, i, r\}$, *and* $\mathcal{L}(\mathcal{A}) = \{\pi_1(\tilde{\mathsf{w}}) \mid \tilde{\mathsf{w}} := \tilde{\mathsf{a}}_1 \ldots \tilde{\mathsf{a}}_n, \ \tilde{\mathsf{a}}_1 \mathsf{x} \ldots \mathsf{x} \tilde{\mathsf{a}}_n \in \mathcal{L}(\tilde{\mathcal{A}})\}$ *holds.*

We fix a finite alphabet $\Sigma \subseteq \mathbf{N_R}$. Moreover, fix two deterministic one-counter automata $\mathcal{A}_1$ and $\mathcal{A}_2$ over Σ, as well as deterministic one-counter automata $\mathcal{C}_1$ and $\mathcal{C}_2$ recognizing the complement of their languages (they can be constructed as DOCA are closed under complement). Finally, we construct their visibly-one-counter counterparts $\tilde{\mathcal{A}}_1, \tilde{\mathcal{A}}_2, \tilde{\mathcal{C}}_1, \tilde{\mathcal{C}}_2$ over the pushdown alphabet $\tilde{\Sigma}$, as provided by Lemma 15. We stress that the letter x, playing the role of a "separator", is identical for all of the aforementioned visibly-one-counter automata. We also point out that the non-emptiness of $\mathcal{L}(\tilde{\mathcal{A}}_1) \cap \mathcal{L}(\tilde{\mathcal{A}}_2)$ is not equivalent to the non-emptiness of $\mathcal{L}(\mathcal{A}_1) \cap \mathcal{L}(\mathcal{A}_1)$, as the projection of a letter $\mathsf{a} \in \tilde{\Sigma}$ may be used by $\mathcal{A}_1$ and $\mathcal{A}_2$ in different contexts (*e.g.* both as a call or as a return).

We are going to encode words accepted by one-counter automata by means of word-like interpretations. A pointed interpretation $(\mathcal{I}, d)$ is Σ-*friendly* if for every element $e \in \Delta^{\mathcal{I}}$ that is x^*-reachable from d in $\mathcal{I}$ there exists a unique letter $\mathsf{a} \in \Sigma$ so that e carries $\tilde{\mathsf{a}}$-self-loops for all $\tilde{\mathsf{a}} \in \tilde{\Sigma}$ with $\pi_1(\tilde{\mathsf{a}}) = \mathsf{a}$, and no self-loops for all other letters in $\tilde{\Sigma}$ (also including the "separator letter" x). Σ-friendly interpretations can easily be axiomatised with an $\mathcal{ALC}^{\mathsf{Self}}$-concept C_{fr}^{Σ}:

$$C_{\mathrm{fr}}^{\Sigma} := \forall \mathsf{x}^*. \bigsqcup_{\mathsf{a} \in \Sigma} \bigcap_{\mathsf{b} \neq \mathsf{a}, \mathsf{b} \in \Sigma, \pi_1(\tilde{\mathsf{a}}) = \mathsf{a}, \pi_1(\tilde{\mathsf{b}}) = \mathsf{b}} \left([\exists \tilde{\mathsf{a}}.\mathsf{Self}] \sqcap \neg [\exists \tilde{\mathsf{b}}.\mathsf{Self}] \sqcap \neg [\exists \mathsf{x}.\mathsf{Self}] \right).$$

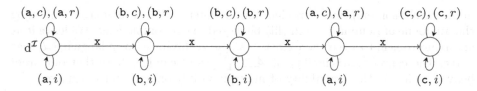

Fig. 5. An example Σ-friendly pointed $(\mathcal{I}, d)$ encoding the word **abbac**.

Moreover, every x^*-path ρ in a Σ-friendly $\mathcal{I}$ *represents* a word in Σ^* in the following sense: the i-th letter of such a word is a if and only if the i-th element of the path carries an (a, c)-self-loop. This is well-defined, as every element in Σ-friendly $\mathcal{I}$ carries a (a, c)-self-loop for a unique letter $a \in \Sigma$. Consult Fig. 5.

As a special class of Σ-friendly interpretations we consider Σ-metawords. We say that $(\mathcal{I}, d)$ is a Σ-*metaword* if it is a Σ-friendly interpretation of the domain $\mathbb{Z}_n$ for some positive $n \in \mathbb{N}$, the role name x is interpreted as the set $\{(i, i{+}1) \mid 0 \le i \le n{-}2\}$, and all other role names are either interpreted as $\emptyset$ or are subsets of the diagonal $\{(i, i) \mid i \in \mathbb{Z}_n\}$ (or, put differently, they appear only as self-loops). The example Σ-friendly $\mathcal{I}$ from Fig. 5 is actually a Σ-metaword. It is not too hard to see that for every word $\mathbf{w} \in \Sigma^+$ there is a Σ-metaword representing $\mathbf{w}$. A crucial observation regarding Σ-metawords is as follows. If an element starting a Σ-metaword can $\{\tilde{w}\}$-reach some element (for some $\tilde{w}$ in the language of $\tilde{\mathcal{A}}_1$), then the path ρ witnessing this fact satisfies $\rho_i = \rho_{i+1}$ for all odd indices i and $\rho_i + 1 = \rho_{i+1}$ for all even indices i. Similar remarks apply to Σ-friendly interpretations but the correspondence is not as elegant anymore.

As the next step of the construction, we are going to decorate Σ-friendly interpretations with extra information on whether or not words represented by paths are accepted by $\mathcal{A}_1$. This is achieved by means of the following concept

$$C_{\mathcal{A}_1} := C_{\text{fr}}^{\Sigma} \sqcap \forall \mathcal{L}(\tilde{\mathcal{A}}_1).\text{Acc}_{\mathcal{A}_1} \sqcap \forall \mathcal{L}(\tilde{\mathcal{C}}_1).\neg\text{Acc}_{\mathcal{A}_1},$$

for a fresh concept name $\text{Acc}_{\mathcal{A}_1}$. We define $C_{\mathcal{A}_2}$ analogously. We have that:

Lemma 16. *If* $C_{\mathcal{A}_1}$ *is satisfied by a Σ-friendly pointed interpretation* $(\mathcal{I}, d)$, *then for every element* $e \in \Delta^{\mathcal{I}}$ *that is x^*-reachable from d via a path ρ we have that* $e \in (\text{Acc}_{\mathcal{A}_1})^{\mathcal{I}}$ *iff the Σ-word represented by ρ belongs to* $\mathcal{L}(\mathcal{A}_1)$. *Moreover, after reinterpreting the concept* $\text{Acc}_{\mathcal{A}_1}$, *every Σ-metaword becomes a model of* $C_{\mathcal{A}_1}$.

Lemma 17. $C_{\mathcal{A}_1} \sqcap C_{\mathcal{A}_2} \sqcap \exists x^*.(\text{Acc}_{\mathcal{A}_1} \sqcap \text{Acc}_{\mathcal{A}_2})$ *is satisfiable iff* $\mathcal{L}(\mathcal{A}_1) \cap \mathcal{L}(\mathcal{A}_2) \ne \emptyset$.

By the undecidability of the non-emptiness problem for intersection of one-counter languages [34, p. 75], we conclude the last theorem of the paper.

Theorem 18. *The concept satisfiability problem for* $\mathcal{ALC}_{\text{vpl}}^{\text{Self}}$ *is undecidable, even if only visibly-one-counter languages are allowed in concepts.*

We stress that there is nothing special about DOCA used in the proof. In fact, any automata model would satisfy our needs as long as it would (i) have undecidable non-emptiness problem for the intersection of languages, (ii) enjoy the analogue of Lemma 15, and (iii) be closed under complement. We leave it as an open problem to see if there exists a *single* visibly-pushdown language $\mathcal{L}$ that makes the concept satisfiability of $\mathcal{ALC}^{\mathsf{Self}}_{\mathsf{reg}+\mathcal{L}}$ undecidable. Note that our proof heavily relied on the availability of multiple visibly-one-counter languages.

6 Conclusions

We investigated the decidability status of extensions of $\mathcal{ALC}_{\mathsf{vpl}}$ (also known as Propositional Dynamic Logic with Visibly Pushdown Programs) with popular features supported by W3C ontology languages. Our results are negative: we established undecidability of (fragments of) $\mathcal{ALC}_{\mathsf{vpl}}$ with nominals or self-loops, and of the query entailment of non-regular queries even in the case of $\mathcal{ALC}$-TBoxes. We conclude with a list of open problems.

– Our undecidability proof for $\mathcal{ALC}_{\mathsf{vpl}}$ with Self relied on the availability of multiple visibly-one-counter languages. Can this undecidability result be improved? Is satisfiability of $\mathcal{ALC}^{r\#s\#}_{\mathsf{reg}}$ with Self already undecidable?
– Positive results regarding $\mathcal{ALC}_{\mathsf{vpl}}$ concern the concept satisfiability problem, rather than the knowledge-base satisfiability problem. Is the later decidable for $\mathcal{ALC}_{\mathsf{vpl}}$? Classical techniques [12, p. 210] for incorporating ABoxes inside concepts do not work, as the class of visibly-pushdown languages is not compositional (of "infinite memory"). The problem already occurs for $\mathcal{ALC}^{r\#s\#}_{\mathsf{reg}}$.
– Is the extension of $\mathcal{ALC}_{\mathsf{vpl}}$ (or even $\mathcal{ALC}^{r\#s\#}_{\mathsf{reg}}$) with functionality or counting decidable? Once more, classical techniques [12, p. 210] do not seem to be applicable due to the lack of "compositionality" in visibly-pushdown languages. A good idea would be to investigate a model of *graded* visibly pushdown tree automata, obtained by marrying graded alternating tree automata [27, Sec. 3.1] and visibly pushdown tree automata [29, p. 55].
– Existing positive results on non-regular extensions of $\mathcal{ALC}_{\mathsf{reg}}$, especially these of Löding et al [29, Thm. 18], rely on the use of (potentially infinite) tree-like models. Is the *finite* satisfiability problem for $\mathcal{ALC}_{\mathsf{vpl}}$ decidable? We stress that already the case of $\mathcal{ALC}^{r\#s\#}_{\mathsf{reg}}$ is open.

Acknowledgements. This work was supported by the ERC Consolidator Grant No. 771779 (DeciGUT). Snake and cobra icons were downloaded from Icons8 and Flaticon.

The author would like to thank Reijo Jaakkola for many inspiring discussions; Sebastian Rudolph for pinpointing [9] and suggesting many improvements, especially related to the previous versions of Sect. 4; Witold Charatonik for very careful proof-reading and his pedantic approach to writing; as well as Alessio Mansutti and Emanuel Kieroński for their help polishing the introduction.

References

1. Alur, R., Madhusudan, P.: Adding nesting structure to words. J. ACM **56**(3) (2009)
2. Baader, F., Horrocks, I., Lutz, C., Sattler, U.: An Introduction to Description Logic. Cambridge University Press, Cambridge (2017)
3. Bárány, V., Löding, C., Serre, O.: Regularity problems for visibly pushdown languages. In: Durand, B., Thomas, W. (eds.) STACS 2006. LNCS, vol. 3884, pp. 420–431. Springer, Heidelberg (2006). https://doi.org/10.1007/11672142_34
4. Bednarczyk, B., Kieronski, E.: Finite entailment of local queries in the Z family of description logics. In: Thirty-Sixth AAAI Conference on Artificial Intelligence, AAAI 2022, Thirty-Fourth Conference on Innovative Applications of Artificial Intelligence, IAAI 2022, The Twelveth Symposium on Educational Advances in Artificial Intelligence, EAAI 2022 Virtual Event, February 22–1 March 2022, pp. 5487–5494. AAAI Press (2022)
5. Bednarczyk, B., Rudolph, S.: Worst-case optimal querying of very expressive description logics with path expressions and succinct counting. In: Kraus, S. (ed.) Proceedings of the Twenty-Eighth International Joint Conference on Artificial Intelligence, IJCAI 2019, Macao, China, 10–16 August 2019, pp. 1530–1536. ijcai.org (2019)
6. Bienvenu, M., Calvanese, D., Ortiz, M., Simkus, M.: Nested regular path queries in description logics. In: Baral, C., De Giacomo, G., Eiter, T. (eds.) Principles of Knowledge Representation and Reasoning: Proceedings of the Fourteenth International Conference, KR 2014, Vienna, Austria, 20–24 July 2014. AAAI Press (2014)
7. Bresolin, D., Della Monica, D., Goranko, V., Montanari, A., Sciavicco, G.: Undecidability of the logic of overlap relation over discrete linear orderings. Electron. Notes Theor. Comput. Sci. **262**, 65–81 (2010). proceedings of the 6th Workshop on Methods for Modalities (M4M–6 2009)
8. Bruse, F., Lange, M.: A decidable non-regular modal fixpoint logic. In: Haddad, S., Varacca, D. (eds.) 32nd International Conference on Concurrency Theory, CONCUR 2021, 24–27 August 2021, Virtual Conference. LIPIcs, vol. 203, pp. 23:1–23:18. Schloss Dagstuhl - Leibniz-Zentrum für Informatik (2021)
9. Calvanese, D., De Giacomo, G., Rosati, R.: A note on encoding inverse roles and functional restrictions in ALC knowledge bases. In: Franconi, E., De Giacomo, G., MacGregor, R.M., Nutt, W., Welty, C.A. (eds.) Proceedings of the 1998 International Workshop on Description Logics (DL'98), IRST, Povo - Trento, Italy, 6–8 June 1998. CEUR Workshop Proceedings, vol. 11. CEUR-WS.org (1998)
10. Calvanese, D., Eiter, T., Ortiz, M.: Regular path queries in expressive description logics with nominals. In: Boutilier, C. (ed.) IJCAI 2009, Proceedings of the 21st International Joint Conference on Artificial Intelligence, Pasadena, California, USA, 11–17 July 2009, pp. 714–720 (2009)
11. Calvanese, D., Ortiz, M., Simkus, M.: Verification of evolving graph-structured data under expressive path constraints. In: Martens, W., Zeume, T. (eds.) 19th International Conference on Database Theory, ICDT 2016, Bordeaux, France, 15–18 March 2016. LIPIcs, vol. 48, pp. 15:1–15:19. Schloss Dagstuhl - Leibniz-Zentrum für Informatik (2016)
12. De Giacomo, G., Lenzerini, M.: Boosting the correspondence between description logics and propositional dynamic logics. In: Hayes-Roth, B., Korf, R.E. (eds.) Proceedings of the 12th National Conference on Artificial Intelligence, Seattle, WA, USA, July 31–4 August 1994, vol. 1, pp. 205–212. AAAI Press/The MIT Press (1994)

13. Fischer, M.J., Ladner, R.E.: Propositional dynamic logic of regular programs. J. Comput. Syst. Sci. **18**(2), 194–211 (1979)
14. Florescu, D., Levy, A.Y., Suciu, D.: Query containment for conjunctive queries with regular expressions. In: Mendelzon, A.O., Paredaens, J. (eds.) Proceedings of the Seventeenth ACM SIGACT-SIGMOD-SIGART Symposium on Principles of Database Systems, 1–3 June 1998, Seattle, Washington, USA, pp. 139–148. ACM Press (1998)
15. Göller, S.: Computational Complexity of Propositional Dynamic Logics. Ph.D. thesis, University of Leipzig (2008). https://d-nb.info/99245168X
16. Grau, B.C., Horrocks, I., Motik, B., Parsia, B., Patel-Schneider, P., Sattler, U.: OWL 2: the next step for OWL. J. Web Semant. **6**(4), 309–322 (2008)
17. Gutiérrez-Basulto, V., Ibáñez-García, Y., Jung, J.C., Murlak, F.: Answering regular path queries mediated by unrestricted SQ ontologies. Artif. Intell. **314**, 103808 (2023)
18. Harel, D., Paterson, M.: Undecidability of PDL with $L = \{a^{2^i} \mid i \geq 0\}$. J. Comput. Syst. Sci. **29**(3), 359–365 (1984)
19. Harel, D., Pnueli, A., Stavi, J.: Further results on propositional dynamic logic of nonregular programs. In: Kozen, D. (ed.) Logic of Programs 1981. LNCS, vol. 131, pp. 124–136. Springer, Heidelberg (1982). https://doi.org/10.1007/BFb0025779
20. Harel, D., Pnueli, A., Stavi, J.: Propositional dynamic logic of context-free programs. In: 22nd Annual Symposium on Foundations of Computer Science (SFCS 1981), pp. 310–321. IEEE (1981)
21. Harel, D., Raz, D.: Deciding properties of nonregular programs. SIAM J. Comput. **22**(4), 857–874 (1993)
22. Harel, D., Singerman, E.: More on nonregular PDL: finite models and Fibonacci-like programs. Inf. Comput. **128**(2), 109–118 (1996)
23. Hitzler, P., Krötzsch, M., Parsia, B., Patel-Schneider, P.F., Rudolph, S.: OWL 2 Web Ontology Language Primer (Second Edition). World Wide Web Consortium (W3C), December 2012
24. Horrocks, I., Kutz, O., Sattler, U.: The even more irresistible SROIQ. In: Doherty, P., Mylopoulos, J., Welty, C.A. (eds.) Proceedings, Tenth International Conference on Principles of Knowledge Representation and Reasoning, Lake District of the United Kingdom, 2–5 June 2006, pp. 57–67. AAAI Press (2006)
25. Koren, T., Pnueli, A.: There exist decidable context free propositonal dynamic logics. In: Clarke, E., Kozen, D. (eds.) Logic of Programs 1983. LNCS, vol. 164, pp. 290–312. Springer, Heidelberg (1984). https://doi.org/10.1007/3-540-12896-4_369
26. Krötzsch, M., Rudolph, S., Hitzler, P.: ELP: tractable rules for OWL 2. In: Sheth, A., et al. (eds.) ISWC 2008. LNCS, vol. 5318, pp. 649–664. Springer, Heidelberg (2008). https://doi.org/10.1007/978-3-540-88564-1_41
27. Kupferman, O., Sattler, U., Vardi, M.Y.: The complexity of the graded μ-calculus. In: Voronkov, A. (eds.) Automated Deduction—CADE-18. CADE 2002. LNCS, vol. 2392, pp. 423–437. Springer, Berlin, Heidelberg (2002). https://doi.org/10.1007/3-540-45620-1_34
28. Lange, M., Lozes, E.: Conjunctive visibly-pushdown path queries. In: Kosowski, A., Walukiewicz, I. (eds.) FCT 2015. LNCS, vol. 9210, pp. 327–338. Springer, Cham (2015). https://doi.org/10.1007/978-3-319-22177-9_25
29. Löding, C., Lutz, C., Serre, O.: Propositional dynamic logic with recursive programs. J. Log. Algebraic Methods Program. **73**(1–2), 51–69 (2007)

30. Ortiz, M.: Query Answering in Expressive Description Logics: Techniques and Complexity Results. Ph.D. thesis, Technische Universität Wien (2010)
31. Ortiz, M., Šimkus, M.: Reasoning and query answering in description logics. In: Eiter, T., Krennwallner, T. (eds.) Reasoning Web 2012. LNCS, vol. 7487, pp. 1–53. Springer, Heidelberg (2012). https://doi.org/10.1007/978-3-642-33158-9_1
32. Pratt-Hartmann, I.: Fragments of First-Order Logic. Oxford University Press, Oxford (2023)
33. Sipser, M.: Introduction to the Theory of Computation, third edn. Course Technology, Boston, MA (2013)
34. Valiant, L.: Decision Procedures for Families of Deterministic Pushdown Automata. Ph.D. thesis, University of Warwick (1973)

Non-Normal Modal Description Logics

Tiziano Dalmonte[1], Andrea Mazzullo[2(✉)], Ana Ozaki[3,4],
and Nicolas Troquard[1]

[1] Free University of Bozen-Bolzano, Bolzano, Italy
{tiziano.dalmonte,nicolas.troquard}@unibz.it
[2] University of Trento, Trento, Italy
andrea.mazzullo@unitn.it
[3] University of Oslo, Oslo, Norway
anaoz@ifi.uio.no
[4] University of Bergen, Bergen, Norway

Abstract. Modal logics are widely used in multi-agent systems to reason about actions, abilities, norms, or epistemic states. Combined with description logic languages, they are also a powerful tool to formalise modal aspects of ontology-based reasoning over an object domain. However, the standard relational semantics for modalities is known to validate principles deemed problematic in agency, deontic, or epistemic applications. To overcome these difficulties, weaker systems of so-called *non-normal* modal logics, equipped with *neighbourhood semantics* that generalise the relational one, have been investigated both at the propositional and at the description logic level. We present here a family of *non-normal modal description logics*, obtained by extending $\mathcal{ALC}$-based languages with non-normal modal operators. For formulas interpreted on neighbourhood models over varying domains, we provide a modular framework of terminating, correct, and complete tableau-based satisfiability checking algorithms in NExpTime. For a subset of these systems, we also consider a reduction to satisfiability on constant domain relational models. Moreover, we investigate the satisfiability problem in fragments obtained by disallowing the application of modal operators to description logic concepts, providing tight ExpTime complexity results.

1 Introduction

Modal logics are powerful tools used to represent and reason about actions and abilities [10,16], coalitions [31,39], knowledge and beliefs [1,8,26,40], obligations and permissions [2,20,42], etc. In combination with *description logics*, they give rise to *modal description logics* [18,43], knowledge representation formalisms used for modal reasoning over an object domain and with a good trade-off between expressive power and decidability.

The standard *relational semantics* for modal operators is given in terms of *frames* consisting of a set of *possible worlds* equipped with binary *accessibility relations*. The foundations of modal description logics, so far, have also mostly

S. Gaggl et al. (Eds.): JELIA 2023, LNAI 14281, pp. 306–321, 2023.
https://doi.org/10.1007/978-3-031-43619-2_22

been studied with relational semantics. However, all the modal systems interpreted with respect to this semantics, known as *normal*, validate principles that have been considered problematic or debatable for agency-based, coalitional, epistemic, or deontic applications, in that they lead to unacceptable conclusions, e.g., *logical omniscience* in epistemic settings [40], as well as *agency* or *deontic paradoxes* in the representation of agents' abilities [16] and obligations [3, 17, 32].

To overcome these problems, a generalisation of relational semantics, known as *neighbourhood semantics*, was introduced by Scott [34] and Montague [27]. Since it avoids in general the problematic principles validated by relational semantics, it has been used to interpret a number of *non-normal* modal logics, first studied by C.I. Lewis [25], Lemmon [24], Kripke [23], Segerberg [35], and Chellas [11], among others. A *neighbourhood frame* consists of a set of worlds, each one associated with a "neighbourhood", i.e., a set of subsets of worlds. Intuitively, a subset of worlds can be thought of as representing a fact in a model, namely, those worlds where that fact holds. Hence, the idea is that every world is assigned to a collection of facts, those that are brought about, known, obligatory, etc., in that world of the model.

These are the neighbourhood semantics ingredients for *propositional* non-normal modal logics. A further line of research focuses on the behaviour of modal operators interpreted on neighbourhood frames in combination with *first-order* logic. In this direction, completeness results for first-order non-normal modal logics have been provided [4, 5]. In addition, *non-normal modal description logics*, extending standard description logics, with modal operators interpreted on neighbourhood frames, have been considered for knowledge representation applications [13, 14, 36], also in multi-agent coalitional settings [37, 38].

To illustrate the expressivity of non-normal modal description logic languages, as well some of the limitations of relational frames behind adoption of neighbourhood semantics, we provide an example based on a classic multi-agent purchase choreography scenario [28] (see [15] for a detailed version). Our multi-agent setting involves a customer c and a seller s, as well as agency operators $\mathbb{D}_i$ and $\mathbb{C}_i$, for $i \in \{c, s\}$, read as 'agent i does/makes' and 'agent i can do/make', respectively [16, 21]. The formula $\mathsf{Ord} \equiv \mathbb{D}_c \exists \mathsf{req}.(\mathsf{Prod} \sqcap \mathsf{InCatal})$ defines an order Ord as a request made by customer c of an in-catalogue product.

By stating $\exists \mathsf{req}.(\mathsf{Prod} \sqcap \mathsf{InCatal}) \sqsubseteq \mathsf{Confirm} \sqcup \neg\mathsf{Confirm}$, we can also enforce that any request of an in-catalogue product is either confirmed or not confirmed. However, relational semantics validates the so-called **M**-*principle* (often called *monotonicity*) as well, according to which $C \sqsubseteq D$ always entails $\mathbb{D}_i C \sqsubseteq \mathbb{D}_i D$, for any concepts C, D and any agent i. Thus, from the **M**-principle and Ord definition, we obtain $\mathsf{Ord} \sqsubseteq \mathbb{D}_c(\mathsf{Confirm} \sqcup \neg\mathsf{Confirm})$, meaning that any order is made confirmed or not confirmed by c. This is an unwanted conclusion in our agency-based scenario, since customers' actions should be unrelated to order confirmation aspects.[1]

---

[1] Other approaches (out of the scope of this paper) to avoid such consequences would involve rejecting the principle of *excluded middle*, as done e.g. in *intuitionistic description logics* [9, 30, 33].

Moreover, the formula $\mathsf{SubmitOrd} \sqsubseteq \mathbb{C}_s\mathsf{Confirm} \sqcap \mathbb{C}_s\mathsf{PartConf} \sqcap \mathbb{C}_s\mathsf{Reject}$ states that a submitted order can be confirmed, can be partially confirmed, and can be rejected by the seller s. On relational frames, $\mathbb{C}_iC \sqcap \mathbb{C}_iD \sqsubseteq \mathbb{C}_i(C \sqcap D)$ is a valid formula, for any concepts C, D, known as the **C**-*principle* (or *agglomeration*). Therefore, by the **C**-principle, under relational semantics we would be forced to conclude that $\mathsf{SubmitOrd} \sqsubseteq \mathbb{C}_s(\mathsf{Confirm} \sqcap \mathsf{PartConf} \sqcap \mathsf{Reject})$, meaning that any submitted order is such that the seller s has the ability to make it confirmed, partially confirmed, and rejected, all *at once*, which is unreasonable.

Finally, consider the formula $\top \sqsubseteq \mathsf{Confirm} \sqcup \neg\mathsf{Confirm}$, i.e., the truism stating that anything is either confirmed or not confirmed. By the so called **N**-*principle* (or *necessitation*) of relational semantics, we have that if $\top \sqsubseteq C$ is valid on relational frames, then $\top \sqsubseteq \mathbb{D}_iC$ holds as well, for any concept C. Thus, from the **N**-principle it would follow on relational semantics that $\top \sqsubseteq \mathbb{D}_c(\mathsf{Confirm} \sqcup \neg\mathsf{Confirm})$, thereby forcing us to the consequence that every object is made by customer c to be either confirmed or not confirmed, hence leading again to an unreasonable connection between customer's actions and confirmation of orders.

In fact, since customer c plays no role in confirmation actions, it is sensible to assume that, for any object of the domain, it is not the case that c makes it confirmed or not confirmed. This can be achieved by the formula $\top \sqsubseteq \neg\mathbb{D}_c(\mathsf{Confirm} \sqcup \neg\mathsf{Confirm})$, which is equivalent to what is sometimes known as the **Q**-*principle* ($\top \sqsubseteq \neg\mathbb{D}_i\top$), asserting a form of *irrelevance of actions with respect to tautologies*, in accordance with the idea that agents cannot be responsible of something that holds independently from their action. This principle is *unsatisfiable* in relational frames, while admissible over neighbourhood ones.

The $\mathbb{D}_i$ and $\mathbb{C}_i$ modalities are axiomatised similarly to [16], by means of additional principles as well. The operator $\mathbb{D}_i$ obeys the **C**- (seen above) and the **T**-*principle* ($\mathbb{D}_iC \sqsubseteq C$, for any concept C), the latter stating a *factivity of actions* principle, which is well-known also in epistemic logic. In turn, the **T**-principle entails the **D**-*principle* ($\mathbb{D}_iC \sqsubseteq \neg\mathbb{D}_i\neg C$, for any concept C), asserting a form of *compatibility of actions*: this principle plays a role also in doxastic logic, where beliefs are typically considered to be compatible with each other (despite not necessarily entailing the truth of what is believed, as in epistemic logic under the **T**-principle). Moreover, both $\mathbb{D}_i$ and $\mathbb{C}_i$ satisfy the **Q**- (seen above) and the **E**-*principle* (or *congruence*: $C \equiv D$ entails $\mathbb{D}_iC \equiv \mathbb{D}_iD$ and $\mathbb{C}_iC \equiv \mathbb{C}_iD$, for any concepts C, D), where the latter is valid both on relational and neighbourhood frames.

In this paper, which is an extension of [13,14], we investigate reasoning in a family of non-normal modal description logics, providing terminating, sound, and complete tableau algorithms for checking formula satisfiability on neighbourhood models based on *varying domains* of objects. Moreover, we study the complexity of reasoning in a restricted fragment that disallows modalities on description logic concepts. For instance, such fragment allows us to state, in addition to the non-modal axiom $\mathsf{Confirm} \sqsubseteq \neg\mathsf{Reject}$ expressing that anything confirmed is not rejected, that the seller has no power in transforming confirmed objects into rejected ones, by means of the formula $\neg\mathbb{C}_s(\mathsf{Confirm} \sqsubseteq \mathsf{Reject})$. Finally, for two modal description logics interpreted on *constant domain* neighbourhood models, we adjust a reduction (known from the propositional case) to satisfiability with respect to standard relational semantics.

The paper is structured as follows. Section 2 provides the necessary definitions and the preliminary results on non-normal modal description logics. In Sect. 3 we present the tableau algorithms for the family of logics here considered. The case of fragments without modalised concepts is then studied in Sect. 4. Section 5 contains the results for the constant domain case. Finally, Sect. 6 concludes the paper, discussing related work and possible future research directions. Additional details and full proofs are available in an extended version of this paper [15].

2 Preliminaries

Here we introduce modal description logics, first presenting their syntax, and then their semantics based on neighbourhood and relational models, respectively. Finally, we introduce the family of frame conditions here considered.

2.1 Syntax

Let $\mathsf{N_C}$, $\mathsf{N_R}$ and $\mathsf{N_I}$ be countably infinite and pairwise disjoint sets of *concept*, *role*, and *individual names*, respectively. An $\mathcal{ML}^n_{\mathcal{ALC}}$ *concept* is an expression of the form $C ::= A \mid \neg C \mid C \sqcap C \mid \exists r.C \mid \Box_i C$, where $A \in \mathsf{N_C}$, $r \in \mathsf{N_R}$, and $\Box_i$ such that $i \in J = \{1, \ldots, n\}$. An $\mathcal{ML}^n_{\mathcal{ALC}}$ *atom* is a *concept inclusion* (*CI*) of the form $(C \sqsubseteq D)$, or an *assertion* of the form $C(a)$ or $r(a,b)$, with C, D $\mathcal{ML}^n_{\mathcal{ALC}}$ concepts, $r \in \mathsf{N_R}$, and $a, b \in \mathsf{N_I}$. An $\mathcal{ML}^n_{\mathcal{ALC}}$ *formula* has the form $\varphi ::= \pi \mid \neg\varphi \mid \varphi \wedge \varphi \mid \Box_i \varphi$, where π is an $\mathcal{ML}^n_{\mathcal{ALC}}$ atom and $i \in J$. We use the following standard definitions for concepts: $\forall r.C := \neg \exists r.\neg C$; $(C \sqcup D) := \neg(\neg C \sqcap \neg D)$; $\bot := A \sqcap \neg A$, $\top := A \sqcup \neg A$ (for an arbitrarily fixed $A \in \mathsf{N_C}$); $\Diamond_i C := \neg \Box_i \neg C$. Concepts of the form $\Box_i C$, $\Diamond_i C$ are *modalised concepts*. Analogous conventions hold for formulas, writing $C \equiv D$ for $(C \sqsubseteq D) \wedge (D \sqsubseteq C)$ and setting false $:= (\top \sqsubseteq \bot)$, true $:= (\bot \sqsubseteq \top)$.

2.2 Semantics

We now define neighbourhood semantics, which (as already mentioned) can be seen as a generalisation of the relational semantics, introduced immediately after.

Neighbourhood Semantics. A *neighbourhood frame*, or simply *frame*, is a pair $\mathcal{F} = (\mathcal{W}, \{\mathcal{N}_i\}_{i \in J})$, where $\mathcal{W}$ is a non-empty set of *worlds* and $\mathcal{N}_i \colon \mathcal{W} \to 2^{2^{\mathcal{W}}}$ is a *neighbourhood function*, for each *agent* $i \in J = \{1, \ldots, n\}$. An $\mathcal{ML}^n_{\mathcal{ALC}}$ *varying domain neighbourhood model*, or simply *model*, based on a neighbourhood frame $\mathcal{F}$ is a pair $\mathcal{M} = (\mathcal{F}, \mathcal{I})$, where $\mathcal{F} = (\mathcal{W}, \{\mathcal{N}_i\}_{i \in J})$ is a neighbourhood frame and $\mathcal{I}$ is a function associating with every $w \in \mathcal{W}$ an $\mathcal{ALC}$ *interpretation* $\mathcal{I}_w = (\Delta_w, \cdot^{\mathcal{I}_w})$, with non-empty *domain* Δ_w, and where $\cdot^{\mathcal{I}_w}$ is a function such that: for all $A \in \mathsf{N_C}$, $A^{\mathcal{I}_w} \subseteq \Delta_w$; for all $r \in \mathsf{N_R}$, $r^{\mathcal{I}_w} \subseteq \Delta_w \times \Delta_w$; for all $a \in \mathsf{N_I}$, $a^{\mathcal{I}_w} \in \Delta_w$. An $\mathcal{ML}^n_{\mathcal{ALC}}$ *constant domain neighbourhood model* is defined in the same way, except that, for all $w, w' \in \mathcal{W}$, we have that $\Delta_w = \Delta_{w'}$ and, for all

$u, v \in \mathcal{W}$, we require $a^{\mathcal{I}_u} = a^{\mathcal{I}_v}$ (denoted by $a^{\mathcal{I}}$), that is, individual names are *rigid designators*. We often write $\mathcal{M} = (\mathcal{F}, \Delta, \mathcal{I})$ to denote a constant domain neighbourhood model $\mathcal{M} = (\mathcal{F}, \mathcal{I})$ with domain $\Delta = \Delta_w$, for every $w \in \mathcal{W}$. Given a model $\mathcal{M} = (\mathcal{F}, \mathcal{I})$ and a world $w \in \mathcal{W}$ of $\mathcal{F}$ (or simply w in $\mathcal{F}$), the *interpretation* $C^{\mathcal{I}_w}$ of a concept C in w is defined as: $(\neg D)^{\mathcal{I}_w} = \Delta_w \setminus D^{\mathcal{I}_w}$, $(D \sqcap E)^{\mathcal{I}_w} = D^{\mathcal{I}_w} \cap E^{\mathcal{I}_w}$, $(\exists r.D)^{\mathcal{I}_w} = \{d \in \Delta_w \mid \exists e \in D^{\mathcal{I}_w} : (d, e) \in r^{\mathcal{I}_w}\}$, $(\Box_i D)^{\mathcal{I}_w} = \{d \in \Delta_w \mid [\![D]\!]_d^{\mathcal{M}} \in \mathcal{N}_i(w)\}$, where, for all $d \in \bigcup_{w \in \mathcal{W}} \Delta_w$, the set $[\![D]\!]_d^{\mathcal{M}} = \{v \in \mathcal{W} \mid d \in D^{\mathcal{I}_v}\}$ is called the *truth set of D with respect to $\mathcal{M}$ and d*. We say that a concept C is *satisfied in* $\mathcal{M}$ if there is w in $\mathcal{F}$ such that $C^{\mathcal{I}_w} \neq \emptyset$, and that C is *satisfiable* (over varying or constant neighbourhood models, respectively) if there is a (varying or constant domain, respectively) neighbourhood model in which it is satisfied. The *satisfaction of an* $\mathcal{ML}^n_{\mathcal{ALC}}$ *formula* φ *in* w *of* $\mathcal{M}$, written $\mathcal{M}, w \models \varphi$, is defined as follows:

$$\mathcal{M}, w \models C \sqsubseteq D \text{ iff } C^{\mathcal{I}_w} \subseteq D^{\mathcal{I}_w}, \qquad \mathcal{M}, w \models C(a) \text{ iff } a^{\mathcal{I}_w} \in C^{\mathcal{I}_w},$$

$$\mathcal{M}, w \models r(a, b) \text{ iff } (a^{\mathcal{I}_w}, b^{\mathcal{I}_w}) \in r^{\mathcal{I}_w}, \qquad \mathcal{M}, w \models \neg\psi \text{ iff } \mathcal{M}, w \not\models \psi,$$

$$\mathcal{M}, w \models \psi \wedge \chi \text{ iff } \mathcal{M}, w \models \psi \text{ and } \mathcal{M}, w \models \chi, \quad \mathcal{M}, w \models \Box_i\psi \text{ iff } [\![\psi]\!]^{\mathcal{M}} \in \mathcal{N}_i(w),$$

where $[\![\psi]\!]^{\mathcal{M}} = \{v \in \mathcal{W} \mid \mathcal{M}, v \models \psi\}$ is the *truth set of* ψ. As a consequence of the above definition, we obtain the following condition for $\Diamond_i$ formulas: $\mathcal{M}, w \models \Diamond_i\psi$ iff $[\![\neg\psi]\!]^{\mathcal{M}} \notin \mathcal{N}_i(w)$. Given a neighbourhood frame $\mathcal{F} = (\mathcal{W}, \{\mathcal{N}_i\}_{i \in J})$ and a neighbourhood model $\mathcal{M} = (\mathcal{F}, \mathcal{I})$, we say that φ is *satisfied in* $\mathcal{M}$ if there is $w \in \mathcal{W}$ such that $\mathcal{M}, w \models \varphi$, and that φ is *satisfiable* (over varying or constant domain neighbourhood models, respectively) if it is satisfied in some (varying or constant domain, respectively) neighbourhood model. Also, φ is *valid in* $\mathcal{M}$, $\mathcal{M} \models \varphi$, if it is satisfied in all w of $\mathcal{M}$, and it is *valid on* $\mathcal{F}$ if, for all $\mathcal{M}$ based on $\mathcal{F}$, φ is valid in $\mathcal{M}$, writing $\mathcal{F} \models \varphi$.

Relational Semantics. A *relational frame* is a pair $F = (W, \{R_i\}_{i \in J})$, with W non-empty set and R_i binary relation on W, for $i \in J = \{1, \ldots, n\}$. An $\mathcal{ML}^n_{\mathcal{ALC}}$ *(constant domain) relational model* based on a relational frame $F = (W, \{R_i\}_{i \in J})$ is a pair $M = (F, I)$, where I is a function associating with every $w \in W$ an $\mathcal{ALC}$ interpretation $I_w = (\Delta, \cdot^{I_w})$, having non-empty *constant domain* Δ, and where $\cdot^{I_w}$ is a function such that: for all $A \in \mathsf{N_C}$, $A^{I_w} \subseteq \Delta$; for all $r \in \mathsf{N_R}$, $r^{I_w} \subseteq \Delta \times \Delta$; for all $a \in \mathsf{N_I}$, $a^{I_w} \in \Delta$, and for all $u, v \in W$, $a^{I_u} = a^{I_v}$ (denoted by a^I). Given a relational model $M = (F, I)$ and a world $w \in W$ of F (or simply w in F), the *interpretation of a concept C in w*, written C^{I_w}, is defined by taking: $(\neg C)^{I_w} = \Delta \setminus C^{I_w}$, $(C \sqcap D)^{I_w} = C^{I_w} \cap D^{I_w}$, $(\exists r.C)^{I_w} = \{d \in \Delta \mid \exists e \in C^{I_w} : (d, e) \in r^{I_w}\}$, $(\Box_i C)^{I_w} = \{d \in \Delta \mid \forall v \in W : wR_iv \Rightarrow d \in C^{I_v}\}$.

A concept C is *satisfied in* M if there is w in F such that $C^{I_w} \neq \emptyset$, and that C is *satisfiable on relational models* if there is a relational model in which it is satisfied. The *satisfaction of a* $\mathcal{ML}_{\mathcal{ALC}}$ *formula* φ *in* w *of* M, written $M, w \models \varphi$, is defined, for atoms, negation and conjunction, similarly to the previous case, and as follows for the $\Box_i$ case: $M, w \models \Box_i\varphi$ iff $\forall v \in W : wR_iv \Rightarrow M, v \models \varphi$. Given a relational frame $F = (W, \{R_i\}_{i \in J})$ and a relational model $M = (F, \Delta, I)$, we say that φ is *satisfied in* M if there is $w \in W$ such that $M, w \models \varphi$, and that

φ is *satisfiable on relational models* if it is satisfied in some relational model. Also, φ is said to be *valid in M*, $M \models \varphi$, if it is satisfied in all w of M, and it is *valid on F* if, for all M based on F, φ is valid in M, writing $F \models \varphi$.

2.3 Frame Conditions and Formula Satisfiability

We consider the following conditions on neighbourhood frames $\mathcal{F} = (\mathcal{W}, \{\mathcal{N}_i\}_{i \in J})$. We say that $\mathcal{F}$ *satisfies the*:

> **E**-*condition* iff $\mathcal{N}_i$ is a neighbourhood function;
> **M**-*condition* iff $\alpha \in \mathcal{N}_i(w)$ and $\alpha \subseteq \beta$ implies $\beta \in \mathcal{N}_i(w)$;
> **C**-*condition* iff $\alpha \in \mathcal{N}_i(w)$ and $\beta \in \mathcal{N}_i(w)$ implies $\alpha \cap \beta \in \mathcal{N}_i(w)$;
> **N**-*condition* iff $\mathcal{W} \in \mathcal{N}_i(w)$;
> **T**-*condition* iff $\alpha \in \mathcal{N}_i(w)$ implics $w \in \alpha$;
> **D**-*condition* iff $\alpha \in \mathcal{N}_i(w)$ implies $\mathcal{W} \setminus \alpha \notin \mathcal{N}_i(w)$;
> **P**-*condition* iff $\emptyset \notin \mathcal{N}_i(w)$;
> **Q**-*condition* iff $\mathcal{W} \notin \mathcal{N}_i(w)$;

for every $w \in \mathcal{W}$, $\alpha, \beta \subseteq \mathcal{W}$. Combinations of conditions, such as the **EMCN**-condition, are obtained by suitably joining the ones above. Moreover, since the **E**-condition is always satisfied by any neighbourhood frame, we often omit the letter **E** from this naming scheme, writing for instance '**MCN**' in place of '**EMCN**'.

On the relationships among (combinations of) neighbourhood frame conditions, we make the following observations.

Theorem 1. *Given a neighbourhood frame $\mathcal{F} = (\mathcal{W}, \{\mathcal{N}_i\}_{i \in J})$, the following statements hold, for $i \in J$.*

1. *If $\mathcal{N}_i$ satisfies the **MQ**-condition then, for every $w \in \mathcal{W}$, $\mathcal{N}_i(w) = \emptyset$. Hence, $\mathcal{N}_i$ satisfies all but the **N**-condition.*
2. *$\mathcal{N}_i$ satisfies the **P**-condition, if $\mathcal{N}_i$ satisfies one of the following: (i) **MD**-condition; (ii) **ND**-condition; or (iii) **T**-condition.*
3. *$\mathcal{N}_i$ satisfies the **D**-condition, if $\mathcal{N}_i$ satisfies one of the following: (i) **CP**-condition; or (ii) **T**-condition.*
4. *$\mathcal{N}_i$ does not satisfy the **NQ**-condition.*

Based on these results, Fig. 1 depicts the relations between combinations of frame conditions: nodes are (groups of equivalent) conditions (with the canonical representative underlined), and arrows represent logical implications. Any combination containing the **NQ**-condition has been omitted, as it leads to inconsistency (Theorem 1, Point 4). Moreover, due to Theorem 1, Point 1, any combination that includes the **MQ**-condition is not considered, since for any neighbourhood frame $\mathcal{F}$ satisfying such condition and any $\mathcal{ML}^n_{\mathcal{ALC}}$ concept C, we have $\mathcal{F} \models \Box_i C \equiv \bot$, and similarly for formulas, hence trivialising the modal operators. Thus, we consider in the remainder the set Pantheon of 39 non-equivalent combinations shown (as nodes or canonical representatives) in Fig. 1.

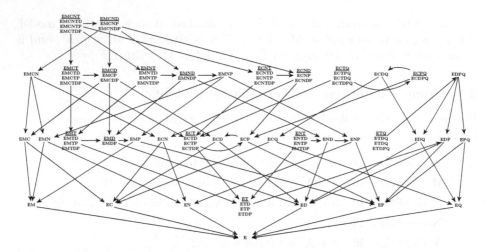

Fig. 1. Implications among L-conditions in Pantheon (equivalent ones are listed in the same nodes, with underlined representatives).

For $L \in$ Pantheon, we say that a neighbourhood frame $\mathcal{F} = (\mathcal{W}, \{\mathcal{N}_i\}_{i \in J})$, with $J = \{1, \ldots, n\}$, is an L^n *frame* iff its neighbourhood functions $\mathcal{N}_i$, for $i \in J$, satisfy the L-*condition*, obtained by combining the conditions associated with letters in L. For a class of neighbourhood frames $\mathcal{C}$, the *satisfiability in* $\mathcal{ML}^n_{\mathcal{ALC}}$ *on* (*varying* or *constant domain*, resp.) *neighbourhood models based on a frame in* $\mathcal{C}$ is the problem of deciding whether an $\mathcal{ML}^n_{\mathcal{ALC}}$ formula is satisfied in a (varying or constant domain, resp.) neighbourhood model based on a frame in $\mathcal{C}$. Satisfiability in $L^n_{\mathcal{ALC}}$ *on* (*varying* or *constant domain*, respectively) *neighbourhood models* is satisfiability in $\mathcal{ML}^n_{\mathcal{ALC}}$ on (varying or constant domain, resp.) neighbourhood models based on a frame in the class of L^n frames. Finally, *satisfiability in* $\mathbf{K}^n_{\mathcal{ALC}}$ *on* (*constant domain*) *relational models* is satisfiability in $\mathcal{ML}^n_{\mathcal{ALC}}$ on relational models based on any relational frame.

Table 1. Principles over neighbourhood or relational frames and models S.

E-*principle*	$S \models C \equiv D$ implies $S \models \Box_i C \equiv \Box_i D$. $\quad$ $S \models \varphi \leftrightarrow \psi$ implies $S \models \Box_i \varphi \leftrightarrow \Box_i \psi$.	**T**-*principle*	$S \models \Box_i C \sqsubseteq C$. $\quad$ $S \models \Box_i \varphi \rightarrow \varphi$.
M-*principle*	$S \models C \sqsubseteq D$ implies $S \models \Box_i C \sqsubseteq \Box_i D$. $\quad$ $S \models \varphi \rightarrow \psi$ implies $S \models \Box_i \varphi \rightarrow \Box_i \psi$.	**D**-*principle*	$S \models \Box_i C \sqsubseteq \Diamond_i C$. $\quad$ $S \models \Box_i \varphi \rightarrow \Diamond_i \varphi$.
C-*principle*	$S \models \Box_i C \sqcap \Box_i D \sqsubseteq \Box_i (C \sqcap D)$. $\quad$ $S \models \Box_i \varphi \wedge \Box_i \psi \rightarrow \Box_i (\varphi \wedge \psi)$.	**P**-*principle*	$S \models \top \sqsubseteq \neg \Box_i \bot$. $\quad$ $S \models \neg \Box_i \mathsf{false}$.
N-*principle*	$S \models \top \sqsubseteq C$ implies $S \models \top \sqsubseteq \Box_i C$. $\quad$ $S \models \varphi$ implies $S \models \Box_i \varphi$.	**Q**-*principle*	$S \models \top \sqsubseteq \neg \Box_i \top$. $\quad$ $S \models \neg \Box_i \mathsf{true}$.

We now study the correspondence between conditions presented in Sect. 2.2 and the principles in Table 1, where S is either a (neighbourhood or relational) frame or a (neighbourhood or relational) model and the L-principle is obtained by suitably combining the basic principles. We say that the L-principle holds in S if the corresponding expressions in Table 1 are satisfied. On the correspondence between the principles in Table 1 and conditions over frames and models, we have the following results (see e.g. [29] for the propositional case).

Proposition 1. *Given a neighbourhood frame $\mathcal{F}$, the L-principle holds in $\mathcal{F}$ iff $\mathcal{F}$ satisfies the L-condition.*

Proposition 2. *The following statements hold.*

1. *For a (varying or constant domain) neighbourhood model $\mathcal{M}$, we have that if $\mathcal{M}$ satisfies the L-condition, then the L-principle holds in $\mathcal{M}$. However, in general, the converse is not true.*
2. *For a relational frame F and a relational model M based on F, the* **EMCN**-*principle holds in M, hence in F. Moreover, in M, hence in F, the* **D**-*principle holds iff the* **P**-*principle holds, and the* **Q**-*principle does not hold.*

3 Tableaux for Formula Satisfiability

We provide terminating, sound, and complete tableau algorithms to check satisfiability of formulas in varying domain neighbourhood models. The notation partly adheres to that of [18], while the model construction in the soundness proof is based on the strategy of [12]. In this section, we use concepts and formulas in *negation normal form (NNF)* and, for this reason, we consider all the logical connectives $\sqcup, \vee, \forall, \Diamond$ as primitive, rather than defined. For a concept or formula γ, we denote by $\dot{\neg}\gamma$ the negation of γ put in NNF, defined as follows: a concept is in *NNF* if negation occurs in it only in front of concept names; a formula is in *NNF* if all concepts in it are in NNF and negation occurs in the formula only in front of CIs or assertions of the form $r(a, b)$ (regarding assertions of the form $A(a)$, we recall that a formula $\neg\psi$, with $\psi = C(a)$, is equivalent to the assertion $D(a)$, with $D = \neg C$). Given an $\mathcal{ML}^n_{\mathcal{ALC}}$ formula φ, we assume without loss of generality that φ is in NNF (using De Morgan laws) and it contains CIs only of the form $\top \sqsubseteq C$, since $C \sqsubseteq D$ is equivalent to $\top \sqsubseteq \neg C \sqcup D$). We denote by $\mathsf{con}(\varphi)$ and $\mathsf{for}(\varphi)$ the set of subconcepts and subformulas of φ, respectively, and then we set $\mathsf{con}_{\dot{\neg}}(\varphi) = \mathsf{con}(\varphi) \cup \{\dot{\neg}C \mid C \in \mathsf{con}(\varphi)\} \cup \{\top\}$ and $\mathsf{for}_{\dot{\neg}}(\varphi) = \mathsf{for}(\varphi) \cup \{\dot{\neg}\psi \mid \psi \in \mathsf{for}(\varphi)\}$. The sets $\mathsf{rol}(\varphi)$ and $\mathsf{ind}(\varphi)$ are, respectively, the sets of role names and of individual names occurring in φ. Let $\mathsf{Fg}(\varphi) = \mathsf{for}_{\dot{\neg}}(\varphi) \cup \mathsf{con}_{\dot{\neg}}(\varphi) \cup \mathsf{rol}(\varphi) \cup \mathsf{ind}(\varphi)$ be the *fragment induced by* φ.

Moreover, let $\mathsf{N_V}$ be a countable set of *variables*, denoted by the letters u, v. The *terms for* φ, denoted by the letters x, y, are either individual names in $\mathsf{ind}(\varphi)$ or variables in $\mathsf{N_V}$. We assume that the set of terms for φ is strictly well-ordered by the relation $<$. In addition, let $\mathsf{N_L}$ be a countable set of *labels*. Given an $\mathcal{ML}^n_{\mathcal{ALC}}$ formula φ and a label $n \in \mathsf{N_L}$, an *n-labelled constraint for* φ takes the form $n : \psi$, or $n : C(x)$, or $n : r(x,y)$, where $\psi \in \text{for}_{\dot{\neg}}(\varphi)$, x,y are terms for φ, $C \in \text{con}_{\dot{\neg}}(\varphi)$, and $r \in \text{rol}(\varphi)$. For every $n \in N_L$, an n-*labelled constraint system for* φ is a set S_n of n-labelled constraints for φ. A *labelled constraint for* φ is an n-labelled constraint for φ, for some $n \in N_L$, and similarly for a *labelled constraint system for* φ. A *completion set* T *for* φ is a non-empty union of labelled constraint systems for φ, and we set $L_T = \{n \in N_L \mid S_n \subseteq T\}$.

About terms, we adopt the following terminology. A term x *occurs in* S_n if S_n contains n-labelled constraints of the form $n : C(x)$ or $n : r(\tau, \tau')$, where $\tau = x$, or $\tau' = x$, and $n \in N_L$. In addition, a variable u is said to be *fresh for* S_n if u does not occur in S_n. (These notions can be used with respect to T, whenever $S_n \subseteq T$). Finally, given variables u, v in an n-labelled constraint system S_n, we say that u is *blocked by* v in S_n if $u > v$ and $\{C \mid n : C(u) \in S_n\} \subseteq \{C \mid n : C(v) \in S_n\}$.

A completion set T contains a *clash* if, for some $m \in N_L$, concept C, role r, and terms x,y, one of the following holds: $\{m : (\top \sqsubseteq C), m : \neg(\top \sqsubseteq C)\} \subseteq T$; or $\{m : A(x), m : \neg A(x)\} \subseteq T$; or $\{m : r(x,y), m : \neg r(x,y)\} \subseteq T$. A completion set that does not contain a clash is *clash-free*.

For every $L \in \text{Pantheon}$, we associate to L the set of $L^n_{\mathcal{ALC}}$-*rules* from Fig. 2 (bottom part) containing $R_\wedge$, $R_\sqcap$, $R_\vee$, $R_\sqcup$, $R_\exists$, $R_\forall$, $R_\sqsubseteq$, $R_{\not\sqsubseteq}$, R_L, and $R_{L\mathbf{X}}$, for every $\mathbf{X} \in \{\mathbf{N}, \mathbf{T}, \mathbf{P}, \mathbf{Q}, \mathbf{D}\}$ such that $\mathbf{X} \in L$. Given $L \in \text{Pantheon}$, a completion set T is $L^n_{\mathcal{ALC}}$-*complete* if no $L^n_{\mathcal{ALC}}$-rule is applicable to T, where γ_j is either $\psi_j \in \text{for}_{\dot{\neg}}(\varphi)$ or $C_j(x_j)$, with $C_j \in \text{con}_{\dot{\neg}}(\varphi)$, for $j = 1, \ldots, k$, and δ is either $\chi \in \text{for}_{\dot{\neg}}(\varphi)$ or $D(y)$, with $D \in \text{con}_{\dot{\neg}}(\varphi)$, with respect to the *application conditions* associated to each $L^n_{\mathcal{ALC}}$-rule from Fig. 2 (top part). The $L^n_{\mathcal{ALC}}$-rules essentially state how to extend a completion set on the basis of the information contained in it. Branching rules entail a *non-deterministic choice* in the completion set expansion.

For each $L \in \text{Pantheon}$, we now present a tableau-based non-deterministic decision procedure for the $L^n_{\mathcal{ALC}}$ formula satisfiability problem on varying domain neighbourhood models, based on Algorithm 1 (simply referred to as $L^n_{\mathcal{ALC}}$ *tableau algorithm*). We have that a formula φ is $L^n_{\mathcal{ALC}}$ satisfiable if and only if there exists at least one execution of the $L^n_{\mathcal{ALC}}$ tableau algorithm that constructs an $L^n_{\mathcal{ALC}}$-complete and clash-free completion set for φ. This non-deterministic algorithm gives priority to non-generating $L^n_{\mathcal{ALC}}$-rules, i.e., those that do not introduce new variables or labels, with respect to generating ones, so to minimise the size of the completion set constructed by its application, and terminates in exponential time for every formula φ. Thus, we obtain the following.

Theorem 2. *Satisfiability in $L^n_{\mathcal{ALC}}$ on varying domain neighbourhood models is decidable in* NExpTime.

As an immediate consequence of the correctness of the tableau we also obtain a (constructive) proof of the following kind of *exponential model property*.

Corollary 1. *Every $L^n_{\mathcal{ALC}}$ satisfiable formula φ has a model with at most $p(|\text{Fg}(\varphi)|)$ worlds, if $\mathbf{C} \notin L$, and at most $2^{q(|\text{Fg}(\varphi)|)})$ worlds, if $\mathbf{C} \in L$, each of them having a domain with at most $2^{r(|\text{Fg}(\varphi)|)}$ elements, with p, q, r polynomial functions.*

Application conditions

$(R_\wedge)$ $\{n : \psi, n : \chi\} \not\subseteq \mathcal{T}$;

$(R_\sqcap)$ $\{n : C(x), n : D(x)\} \not\subseteq \mathcal{T}$;

$(R_\vee)$ $\{n : \psi, n : \chi\} \cap \mathcal{T} = \emptyset$;

$(R_\sqcup)$ $\{n : C(x), n : D(x)\} \cap \mathcal{T} = \emptyset$;

$(R_\exists)$ x is not blocked by any variable in S_n, there is no y such that $\{n : r(x, y), n : C(y)\} \subseteq \mathcal{T}$, and v is the $<$-minimal variable fresh for S_n;

$(R_\forall)$ $n : C(y) \notin \mathcal{T}$;

$(R_\sqsubseteq)$ either x occurs in S_n and $n : C(x) \notin \mathcal{T}$; or no term occurs in S_n and x is the $<$-minimal variable fresh for S_n;

$(R_{\not\sqsubseteq})$ there is no x such that $n : \dot{\neg}C(x) \in \mathcal{T}$ and v is the $<$-minimal variable fresh for S_n;

(R_L) m is fresh for $\mathcal{T}$, and there is no $o \in N_L$ such that $\{o : \gamma_1, \dots, o : \gamma_k, o : \delta\} \subseteq \mathcal{T}$, or $\{o : \dot{\neg}\gamma_j, o : \dot{\neg}\delta\} \subseteq \mathcal{T}$, for some $j \leq k$;

(R_{LN}) m is fresh for $\mathcal{T}$, and there is no $o \in N_L$ such that $o : \gamma \in \mathcal{T}$;

(R_{LT}) $n : \gamma \notin \mathcal{T}$;

(R_{LP}) m is fresh for $\mathcal{T}$, and there is no $o \in N_L$ such that $\{o : \gamma_1, \dots, o : \gamma_k\} \subseteq \mathcal{T}$;

(R_{LQ}) m is fresh for $\mathcal{T}$, and there is no $o \in N_L$ such that $o : \dot{\neg}\gamma_j \in \mathcal{T}$, for some $j \leq k$;

(R_{LD}) m is fresh for $\mathcal{T}$, and there is no $o \in N_L$ such that $\{o : \gamma_1, \dots, o : \gamma_k, o : \delta_1, \dots, o : \delta_k\} \subseteq \mathcal{T}$, or $\{o : \dot{\neg}\gamma_j, o : \dot{\neg}\delta_\ell\} \subseteq \mathcal{T}$, for some $j \leq k$, $\ell \leq h$.

Rules

$$(R_\wedge) \ \frac{n : \psi \wedge \chi}{n : \psi \, , \, n : \chi} \qquad (R_\vee) \ \frac{n : \psi \vee \chi}{n : \psi \,|\, n : \chi} \qquad (R_\sqcap) \ \frac{n : C \sqcap D(x)}{n : C(x), \, n : D(x)} \qquad (R_\sqcup) \ \frac{n : C \sqcup D(x)}{n : C(x) \,|\, n : D(x)}$$

$$(R_\exists) \ \frac{n : \exists r.C(x)}{n : r(x, v), \, n : C(v)} \qquad (R_\forall) \ \frac{n : \forall r.C(x), \, n : r(x, y)}{n : C(y)}$$

$$(R_\sqsubseteq) \ \frac{n : \top \sqsubseteq C}{n : C(x)} \qquad (R_{\not\sqsubseteq}) \ \frac{n : \neg(\top \sqsubseteq C)}{n : \dot{\neg}C(v)}$$

$$(R_L) \ \frac{n : \Box_i \gamma_1, \dots, n : \Box_i \gamma_k, n : \Diamond_i \delta}{m : \gamma_1, \dots, m : \gamma_k \, , \, m : \delta \underbrace{\mid m : \dot{\neg}\gamma_1, m : \dot{\neg}\delta \mid \dots \mid m : \dot{\neg}\gamma_k, m : \dot{\neg}\delta}_{\text{if } M \notin L}}$$

$$(R_{LN}) \ \frac{n : \Diamond_i \gamma}{m : \gamma}$$

$$(R_{LT}) \ \frac{n : \Box_i \gamma}{n : \gamma} \qquad (R_{LP}) \ \frac{n : \Box_i \gamma_1, \dots, n : \Box_i \gamma_k}{m : \gamma_1, \dots, m : \gamma_k} \qquad (R_{LQ}) \ \frac{n : \Box_i \gamma_1, \dots, n : \Box_i \gamma_k}{m : \dot{\neg}\gamma_1 \mid \dots \mid m : \dot{\neg}\gamma_k}$$

$$(R_{LD}) \ \frac{n : \Box_i \gamma_1 \, , \, \dots , \, n : \Box_i \gamma_k \, , \, n : \Box_i \delta_1 \, , \, \dots , \, n : \Box_i \delta_h}{\begin{array}{c} m : \gamma_1, \dots, m : \gamma_k, \\ m : \delta_1, \dots, m : \delta_h \end{array} \underbrace{\left| \begin{array}{c} m : \dot{\neg}\gamma_1, \\ m : \dot{\neg}\delta_1 \end{array} \right| \dots \left| \begin{array}{c} m : \dot{\neg}\gamma_k, \\ m : \dot{\neg}\delta_1 \end{array} \right| \dots \left| \begin{array}{c} m : \dot{\neg}\gamma_1, \\ m : \dot{\neg}\delta_h \end{array} \right| \dots \left| \begin{array}{c} m : \dot{\neg}\gamma_k, \\ m : \dot{\neg}\delta_h \end{array} \right.}_{\text{if } M \notin L}}$$

Fig. 2. $L^n_{\mathcal{ALC}}$-rules, where $k, h \geq 1$ if $\mathbf{C} \in L$ and $k = h = 1$ if $\mathbf{C} \notin L$. In the rules R_L and R_{LD}, the number of possible expansions depend on whether $\mathbf{M} \in L$: if $\mathbf{M} \in L$ only the first expansion is possible, if $\mathbf{M} \notin L$ all other expansions are also possible.

Algorithm 1: $L_{\mathcal{ALC}}^n$ tableau algorithm on varying domain neighbourhood models for φ

Input: the initial completion set $\mathcal{T} := \{0 : \varphi\}$ of an $\mathcal{ML}_{\mathcal{ALC}}^n$ formula φ in NNF.

Output: a completion set for φ, extending the initial one, that either contains a clash, or is complete and clash-free.

1 **while** $\mathcal{T}$ *is clash-free and not* $L_{\mathcal{ALC}}^n$-*complete* **do**
2   **if** *a rule* $\mathsf{R} \in \{\mathsf{R}_\wedge, \mathsf{R}_\vee, \mathsf{R}_\sqcap, \mathsf{R}_\sqcup, \mathsf{R}_\forall, \mathsf{R}_\sqsubseteq, \mathsf{R}_{LT}\}$ *is applicable to* $\mathcal{T}$ **then**
3   apply R to $\mathcal{T}$;
4   **else if** *a rule* $\mathsf{R} \in \{\mathsf{R}_\exists, \mathsf{R}_L, \mathsf{R}_{LN}, \mathsf{R}_{LP}, \mathsf{R}_{LQ}, \mathsf{R}_{LD}\}$ *is applicable to* $\mathcal{T}$ **then**
5   apply R to $\mathcal{T}$;
6 **end**

---

4   Fragments Without Modalised Concepts

Here we study fragments of $\mathcal{ML}_{\mathcal{ALC}}^n$ without modalised concepts. An $\mathcal{ALC}\text{-}\mathcal{ML}^n$ *formula* is defined similarly to the $\mathcal{ML}_{\mathcal{ALC}}^n$ case, by disallowing modalised concepts. Given $L \in$ Pantheon, *satisfiability in* $\mathcal{ALC}\text{-}L^n$ *on varying domain neighbourhood models* is $\mathcal{ALC}\text{-}\mathcal{ML}^n$ satisfiability on varying domain neighbourhood models based on neighbourhood frames in the respective class for L. An $\mathcal{ML}^n$ *formula*, instead, is defined analogously to $\mathcal{ALC}\text{-}\mathcal{ML}^n$, except that we build it from the standard propositional (rather than $\mathcal{ALC}$) language over a countable set of *propositional letters* $\mathsf{N_P}$, disjoint from $\mathsf{N_C}$, $\mathsf{N_R}$, and $\mathsf{N_I}$. The semantics of $\mathcal{ML}^n$ formulas is given in terms of *propositional neighbourhood models* (or simply *models*) $\mathcal{M}^P = (\mathcal{W}, \{\mathcal{N}_i\}_{i \in J}, \mathcal{V})$, where $(\mathcal{W}, \{\mathcal{N}_i\}_{i \in J})$ is a neighbourhood frame, with $J = \{1, \dots, n\}$ in the following, and $\mathcal{V} : \mathsf{N_P} \to 2^{\mathcal{W}}$ is a function mapping propositional letters to sets of worlds (see [11,41]). *Satisfiability in* L^n is satisfiability in $\mathcal{ML}^n$ on propositional neighbourhood models based on neighbourhood frames in the respective class for L. A propositional neighbourhood model based on a neighbourhood frame in the respective class for L is called L^n *model*.

We prove tight complexity results for $\mathcal{ALC}\text{-}L^n$ satisfiability on varying domain neighbourhood models, where $L \in$ Pantheon, using the notion of a propositional abstraction of a formula (as in, e.g., [6]). Here, one can separate the satisfiability test into two parts, one for the description logic dimension and one for the neighbourhood frame dimension. For an $\mathcal{ALC}\text{-}\mathcal{ML}^n$ formula φ, the *propositional abstraction* φ_{prop} is the result of replacing each $\mathcal{ALC}$ atom π in φ by a propositional variable $p_\pi \in \mathsf{N_P}$. Define the set $\Sigma_\varphi = \{p_\pi \in \mathsf{N_P} \mid \pi \text{ is an } \mathcal{ALC} \text{ atom in } \varphi\}$. A (propositional neighbourhood) L^n model $\mathcal{M}^P = (\mathcal{W}, \{\mathcal{N}_i\}_{i \in J}, \mathcal{V})$ is Σ_φ-*consistent* if, for all $w \in \mathcal{W}$, the following $\mathcal{ALC}$ formula is satisfiable: $\hat{\varphi}_{\mathcal{V},w} = \bigwedge_{p_\pi \in f_\varphi^{\mathcal{V},w}} \pi \,\wedge\, \bigwedge_{p_\pi \in \Sigma_\varphi \setminus f_\varphi^{\mathcal{V},w}} \neg\pi$, where $f_\varphi^{\mathcal{V},w} = \{p_\pi \in \Sigma_\varphi \mid w \in \mathcal{V}(p_\pi)\}$. We formalise the connection between $\mathcal{ALC}\text{-}L^n$ satisfiable formulas and their propositional abstractions with the following lemma.

Lemma 1. *A formula φ is $\mathcal{ALC}\text{-}L^n$ satisfiable on varying domain neighbourhood models iff φ_{prop} is satisfied in a Σ_φ-consistent L^n model.*

We now introduce definitions and notation used to prove our complexity result on fragments without modalised concepts. Let $\Sigma = \{p_\pi \in \mathsf{N_P} \mid \pi$ is an $\mathcal{ALC}$ atom in $\varphi\}$, for a fixed but arbitrary $\mathcal{ALC}\text{-}\mathcal{ML}^n$ formula φ, and let ϕ be an $\mathcal{ML}^n$ formula built from symbols in Σ. We denote by $\mathsf{sub}(\phi)$ the set of subformulas of ϕ closed under single negation. A *valuation* for ϕ is a function $\nu : \mathsf{sub}(\phi) \to \{0,1\}$ that satisfies the conditions: (1) for all $\neg\psi \in \mathsf{sub}(\phi)$, $\nu(\psi) = 1$ iff $\nu(\neg\psi) = 0$; (2) for all $\psi_1 \wedge \psi_2 \in \mathsf{sub}(\phi)$, $\nu(\psi_1 \wedge \psi_2) = 1$ iff $\nu(\psi_1) = 1$ and $\nu(\psi_2) = 1$; and (3) $\nu(\phi) = 1$. A valuation ν for ϕ is Σ-*consistent* if the following $\mathcal{ALC}$ formula is satisfiable: $\bigwedge_{\nu(p_\pi)=1} \pi \wedge \bigwedge_{\nu(p_\pi)=0} \neg\pi$, where $p_\pi \in \Sigma$. Lemma 2 establishes that satisfiability of ϕ in a Σ-consistent model is characterised by the existence of a Σ-consistent valuation satisfying suitable properties. In the following, we use ff as an abbreviation for $p \wedge \neg p$, for a fixed but arbitrary $p \in \mathsf{N_P}$.

Lemma 2. *Given L and an $\mathcal{ML}^n$ formula ϕ built from symbols in Σ (defined as above), let:*

$$\kappa = \begin{cases} |\mathsf{sub}(\phi)|, & \text{if } \mathbf{C} \in L \\ 1, & \text{if } \mathbf{C} \notin L \end{cases}.$$

A formula ϕ is satisfied in a Σ-consistent L^n model iff there is a Σ-consistent valuation ν for ϕ such that, for every $1 \leq k \leq \kappa$, if $\Box_i\psi_1, \ldots, \Box_i\psi_k, \Box_i\chi \in \mathsf{sub}(\phi)$, $\nu(\Box_i\psi_j) = 1$ for all $1 \leq j \leq k$, and $\nu(\Box_i\chi) = 0$, then

1. $(\bigwedge_{j=1}^{k} \psi_j \wedge \neg\chi) \vee \vartheta$ *is satisfied in a Σ-consistent L^n model, where:*

$$\vartheta = \begin{cases} \mathsf{ff}, & \text{if } \mathbf{M} \in L \\ \bigvee_{j=1}^{k}(\neg\psi_j \wedge \chi), & \text{if } \mathbf{M} \notin L \end{cases};$$

   and

2. *for $\mathbf{X} \in \{\mathbf{N}, \mathbf{T}, \mathbf{P}, \mathbf{Q}, \mathbf{D}\}$, if $\mathbf{X} \in L$, then ν satisfies the condition $(\mathbf{X})$ below, for every $1 \leq k, h \leq \kappa$:*

   $(\mathbf{N})$ *if $\Box_i\psi \in \mathsf{sub}(\phi)$ and $\nu(\Box_i\psi) = 0$, then $\neg\psi$ is satisfied in a Σ-consistent L^n model;*

   $(\mathbf{T})$ *if $\Box_i\psi \in \mathsf{sub}(\phi)$ and $\nu(\Box_i\psi) = 1$ then $\nu(\psi) = 1$;*

   $(\mathbf{P})$ *if $\Box_i\psi_1, \ldots, \Box_i\psi_k \in \mathsf{sub}(\phi)$ and $\nu(\Box_i\psi_j) = 1$ for all $1 \leq j \leq k$, then $\bigwedge_{j=1}^{k} \psi_j$ is satisfied in a Σ-consistent L^n model;*

   $(\mathbf{Q})$ *if $\Box_i\psi_1, \ldots, \Box_i\psi_k \in \mathsf{sub}(\phi)$ and $\nu(\Box_i\psi_j) = 1$ for all $1 \leq j \leq k$, then $\bigvee_{j=1}^{k} \neg\psi_j$ is satisfied in a Σ-consistent L^n model;*

   $(\mathbf{D})$ *if $\Box_i\psi_1, \ldots, \Box_i\psi_k, \Box_i\chi_1, \ldots, \Box_i\chi_h \in \mathsf{sub}(\phi)$, $\nu(\Box_i\psi_j) = 1$ for all $1 \leq j \leq k$, and $\nu(\Box_i\chi_\ell) = 1$ for all $1 \leq \ell \leq h$, then $(\bigwedge_{j=1}^{k} \psi_j \wedge \bigwedge_{\ell=1}^{h} \chi_\ell) \vee \eta$ is satisfied in a Σ-consistent L^n model, where:*

$$\eta = \begin{cases} \mathsf{ff}, & \text{if } \mathbf{M} \in L \\ \neg(\bigwedge_{j=1}^{k} \psi_j) \wedge \neg(\bigwedge_{\ell=1}^{h} \chi_\ell), & \text{if } \mathbf{M} \notin L \end{cases}.$$

By using Lemmas 1–2, the following theorem provides a procedure that runs in exponential time to check $\mathcal{ALC}\text{-}L^n$ satisfiability on varying domains. Since $\mathcal{ALC}$ formula satisfiability is already ExpTime-hard, our upper bound is tight.

Theorem 3. *Satisfiability in $\mathcal{ALC}\text{-}L^n$ on varying domain neighbourhood models is ExpTime-complete.*

5   Reasoning on Constant Domain

We now study the complexity of the formula satisfiability problem in $\mathbf{E}^n_{\mathcal{ALC}}$ and $\mathbf{EM}^n_{\mathcal{ALC}}$ on constant domain neighbourhood models. We provide a NExpTime upper bound for satisfiability in $\mathbf{E}^n_{\mathcal{ALC}}$ and $\mathbf{EM}^n_{\mathcal{ALC}}$ by using a reduction, lifted from the propositional case, to multi-modal $\mathbf{K}^m_{\mathcal{ALC}}$. The translation $\cdot^\dagger$ from $\mathcal{ML}^n_{\mathcal{ALC}}$ to $\mathcal{ML}^{3n}_{\mathcal{ALC}}$ is defined as [19,22]: $A^\dagger = A$, $(\neg C)^\dagger = \neg C^\dagger$, $(C \sqcap D)^\dagger = C^\dagger \sqcap D^\dagger$, $(\exists r.C)^\dagger = \exists r.C^\dagger$; $(C(a))^\dagger = C^\dagger(a)$, $(r(a,b))^\dagger = r(a,b)$, $(C \sqsubseteq D)^\dagger = C^\dagger \sqsubseteq D^\dagger$, $(\neg \psi)^\dagger = \neg \psi^\dagger$, $(\psi \wedge \chi)^\dagger = \psi^\dagger \wedge \chi^\dagger$; $(\Box_i \gamma)^\dagger = \Diamond_{i_1}(\Box_{i_2} \gamma^\dagger \circ \Box_{i_3} \neg \gamma^\dagger)$; where $A \in \mathsf{N_C}$, $r \in \mathsf{N_R}$, γ is either an $\mathcal{ML}^n_{\mathcal{ALC}}$ concept or formula, and $\circ \in \{\sqcap, \wedge\}$ accordingly. Using this translation, one can show that satisfiability on neighbourhood models is reducible to satisfiability on the relational models [19,22]. Since satisfiability in $\mathbf{K}^{3n}_{\mathcal{ALC}}$ constant domain relational models is NExpTime-complete [18, Theorem 15.15], we obtain the following complexity result.

Theorem 4. *Satisfiability in $\mathbf{E}^n_{\mathcal{ALC}}$ on constant domain neighbourhood models is decidable in NExpTime.*

The translation $\cdot^\ddagger$ from $\mathcal{ML}^n_{\mathcal{ALC}}$ to $\mathcal{ML}^{2n}_{\mathcal{ALC}}$ is defined as $\cdot^\dagger$ on all concepts and formulas, except for the modalised concepts or formulas γ: $(\Box_i \gamma)^\ddagger = \Diamond_{i_1} \Box_{i_2} \gamma^\ddagger$. We obtain an upper bound analogous to the one for $\mathbf{E}^n_{\mathcal{ALC}}$ by a reduction of the formula satisfiability problem for $\mathbf{EM}^n_{\mathcal{ALC}}$ to the $\mathbf{K}^{2n}_{\mathcal{ALC}}$ one [18,19,22].

Theorem 5. *Satisfiability in $\mathbf{EM}^n_{\mathcal{ALC}}$ on constant domain neighbourhood models is decidable in NExpTime.*

6   Discussion

We investigated reasoning in non-normal modal description logics, focussing on: (*i*) tableaux algorithms to check satisfiability of multi-modal description logics formulas in varying domain neighbourhood models based on classes of frames for 39 different non-normal systems; (*ii*) complexity of satisfiability restricted to fragments with modal operators applied only over formulas, and interpreted on varying domain models; (*iii*) preliminary reduction of formula satisfiability for two non-normal modal description logics to satisfiability in the standard relational semantics on a constant domain. We now discuss possible future work.

First, we intend to devise tableaux for formula satisfiability on neighbourhood models with constant domain, by solving the problem of newly introduced variables that do not occur in other previously expanded labelled constraints systems. For instance, by applying the $\mathbf{M}^n_{\mathcal{ALC}}$-rules to the n-labelled constraint system $S_n = \{n : \Diamond_i \exists r.A(x), \Box_i \neg A(x)\}$, we get the m-labelled constraint system $S_m = \{m : \exists r.A(x), m : \neg A(x), m : r(x,y), m : A(y)\}$. The fresh variable y in S_m does not allow for the direct extraction of a constant domain model, as no object in the domain of the world associated with S_n would be capable of representing y correctly. An alternative approach involves *quasimodels* [18], to characterise satisfiability on constant domain models in terms of structures representing "abstractions" of the actual models of a formula. Objects across worlds can be represented by means of *runs*, i.e., functions to guarantee their modal properties and the constant domain assumption. A similar strategy is presented in [36–38], where the definition of runs (which is not carried out in detail) involves the introduction of suitable world "copies". We conjecture that a quasimodel-based approach with *marked variables*, as illustrated in [18], can also be adopted to solve the constant domain model extraction issue.

Moreover, we aim at tight complexities for $L^n_{\mathcal{ALC}}$ satisfiability, both in varying and in constant domain models. While $\mathcal{ALC}$ formula satisfiability is ExpTime-complete, it is unclear whether the upper bound for $L^n_{\mathcal{ALC}}$ on varying or constant domain neighbourhood models can be improved to ExpTime-membership, for any $L \in$ Pantheon. At the propositional level, the formula satisfiability problem for the systems based on the L-condition, with $\mathbf{C} \notin L$, is NP-complete, rising to PSpace if the $\mathbf{C}$-condition is included [41]. For normal modal description logics, instead, the (tight) NExpTime-hardness results are based on complexity proofs of *product logics* over relational product frames [18], and cannot be immediately adapted to neighbourhood semantics, where an analogous notion of product is not yet well understood. Nonetheless, we conjecture that the NExpTime-hardness known for, e.g., $\mathbf{K}_{\mathcal{ALC}}$ on constant domain relational models, also holds in the neighbourhood case, at least in presence of the $\mathbf{C}$-condition.

Finally, we plan to study: non-normal modal description logics in *coalitional* and *strategic* settings [31,38,39], with an interplay between abilities and powers of *groups* of agents, rather than single ones; additional description logics constructs (e.g. *nominals*, *inverse roles*, or *number restrictions* [7]); and *interactions between modalities*, with axioms expressing e.g. that an agent *can do* anything they *actually do*, by means of formulas of the form $\mathbb{D}_i C \sqsubseteq \mathbb{C}_i C$ or $\mathbb{D}_i \varphi \rightarrow \mathbb{C}_i \varphi$.

Acknowledgements. This research has been partially supported by the Province of Bolzano and DFG through the project D2G2 (DFG grant n. 500249124). Andrea Mazzullo acknowledges the support of the MUR PNRR project FAIR - Future AI Research (PE00000013) funded by the NextGenerationEU. Ana Ozaki is supported by the Research Council of Norway, project number 316022.

References

1. Ågotnes, T., Wáng, Y.N.: Somebody knows. In: KR, pp. 2–11 (2021)
2. Anglberger, A.J., Gratzl, N., Roy, O.: Obligation, free choice, and the logic of weakest permissions. Rev. Symb. Log. 8(4), 807–827 (2015)

3. Åqvist, L.: Good samaritans, contrary-to-duty imperatives, and epistemic obligations. Noûs **1**(4), 361–379 (1967)
4. Arló-Costa, H.L.: First order extensions of classical systems of modal logic; the role of the Barcan schemas. Stud. Log. **71**(1), 87–118 (2002)
5. Arló-Costa, H.L., Pacuit, E.: First-order classical modal logic. Stud. Log. **84**(2), 171–210 (2006)
6. Baader, F., Ghilardi, S., Lutz, C.: LTL over description logic axioms. ACM Trans. Comput. Log. **13**(3), 21:1–21:32 (2012)
7. Baader, F., Horrocks, I., Lutz, C., Sattler, U.: An Introduction to Description Logic. Cambridge University Press, Cambridge (2017)
8. Balbiani, P., Fernández-Duque, D., Lorini, E.: The dynamics of epistemic attitudes in resource-bounded agents. Stud. Log. **107**(3), 457–488 (2019)
9. Bozzato, L., Ferrari, M., Fiorentini, C., Fiorino, G.: A constructive semantics for ALC. In: DL, vol. 250. CEUR-WS.org (2007)
10. Brown, M.A.: On the logic of ability. J. Philos. Log. 1–26 (1988)
11. Chellas, B.F.: Modal Logic: An Introduction. Cambridge University Press, Cambridge (1980)
12. Dalmonte, T., Lellmann, B., Olivetti, N., Pimentel, E.: Hypersequent calculi for non-normal modal and deontic logics: countermodels and optimal complexity. J. Log. Comput. **31**(1), 67–111 (2021)
13. Dalmonte, T., Mazzullo, A., Ozaki, A.: On non-normal modal description logics. In: DL, vol. 2373. CEUR-WS.org (2019)
14. Dalmonte, T., Mazzullo, A., Ozaki, A.: Reasoning in non-normal modal description logics. In: ARQNL@IJCAR, vol. 2095, pp. 28–45 (2022)
15. Dalmonte, T., Mazzullo, A., Ozaki, A., Troquard, N.: Non-normal modal description logics (extended version). CoRR abs/2307.12265 (2023). https://arxiv.org/abs/2307.12265
16. Elgesem, D.: The modal logic of agency. Nord. J. Philos. Log. **2**, 1–46 (1997)
17. Forrester, J.W.: Gentle murder, or the adverbial Samaritan. J. Philos. **81**(4), 193–197 (1984)
18. Gabbay, D.M., Kurucz, A., Wolter, F., Zakharyaschev, M.: Many-dimensional Modal Logics: Theory and Applications. Elsevier, Amsterdam (2003)
19. Gasquet, O., Herzig, A.: From classical to normal modal logics. In: Wansing, H. (eds.) Proof Theory of Modal Logic. Applied Logic Series, vol. 2, pp. 293–311. Springer, Dordrecht (1996). https://doi.org/10.1007/978-94-017-2798-3_15
20. Goble, L.: Prima facie norms, normative conflicts, and dilemmas. In: Handbook of Deontic Logic and Normative Systems, vol. 1, pp. 241–351. College Publications, London (2013)
21. Governatori, G., Rotolo, A.: On the axiomatisation of elgesem's logic of agency and ability. J. Philos. Log. **34**(4), 403–431 (2005). https://doi.org/10.1007/s10992-004-6368-1
22. Kracht, M., Wolter, F.: Normal monomodal logics can simulate all others. J. Symb. Log. **64**(1), 99–138 (1999)
23. Kripke, S.A.: Semantical analysis of modal logic II: non-normal modal propositional calculi. In: The Theory of Models, pp. 206–220. Elsevier (2014)
24. Lemmon, E.J., Scott, D.: An Introduction to Modal Logic. Blackwell, Hoboken (1977)
25. Lewis, C.I., Langford, C.H., Lamprecht, P.: Symbolic Logic, vol. 170. Dover Publications, New York (1959)

26. Lismont, L., Mongin, P.: A non-minimal but very weak axiomatization of common belief. Artif. Intell. **70**(1–2), 363–374 (1994). https://doi.org/10.1016/0004-3702(94)90111-2
27. Montague, R.: Universal grammar. Theoria **36**(3), 373–398 (1970)
28. Montali, M., Pesic, M., van der Aalst, W.M.P., Chesani, F., Mello, P., Storari, S.: Declarative specification and verification of service choreographiess. ACM Trans. Web **4**(1), 3:1–3:62 (2010)
29. Pacuit, E.: Neighborhood Semantics for Modal Logic. Springer, Cham (2017). https://doi.org/10.1007/978-3-319-67149-9
30. de Paiva, V.: Constructive description logics: what, why and how. In: Context Representation and Reasoning, Riva del Garda (2006)
31. Pauly, M.: A modal logic for coalitional power in games. J. Log. Comput. **12**(1), 149–166 (2002)
32. Ross, A.: Imperatives and logic. Philos. Sci. **11**(1), 30–46 (1944)
33. Scheele, S.: Model and proof theory of constructive ALC: constructive description logics. Ph.D. thesis, University of Bamberg (2015)
34. Scott, D.: Advice on modal logic. In: Lambert, K. (eds.) Philosophical Problems in Logic. Synthese Library, vol. 29, pp. 143–173. Springer, Dordrecht (1970). https://doi.org/10.1007/978-94-010-3272-8_7
35. Segerberg, K.: An essay in classical modal logic. Ph.D. thesis, Stanford University (1971)
36. Seylan, I., Erdur, R.C.: A tableau decision procedure for $\mathcal{ALC}$ with monotonic modal operators and constant domains. ENTCS **231**, 113–130 (2009)
37. Seylan, I., Jamroga, W.: Coalition description logic with individuals. ENTCS **262**, 231–248 (2010)
38. Seylan, I., Jamroga, W.: Description logic for coalitions. In: AAMAS, pp. 425–432 (2009)
39. Troquard, N.: Reasoning about coalitional agency and ability in the logics of "bringing-it-about". Auton. Agents Multi-Agent Syst. **28**(3), 381–407 (2014)
40. Vardi, M.Y.: On epistemic logic and logical omniscience. In: TARK, pp. 293–305 (1986)
41. Vardi, M.Y.: On the complexity of epistemic reasoning. In: LICS, pp. 243–252 (1989)
42. Von Wright, G.H.: Deontic logic. Mind **60**(237), 1–15 (1951)
43. Wolter, F., Zakharyaschev, M.: On the decidability of description logics with modal operators. In: KR, pp. 512–523 (1998)

First Steps Towards Taming Description Logics with Strings

Stéphane Demri[1]($\boxtimes$) and Karin Quaas[2]($\boxtimes$)

[1] Université Paris-Saclay, CNRS, ENS Paris-Saclay, Laboratoire Méthodes Formelles,
91190 Gif-Sur-Yvette, France
demri@lsv.ens-cachan.fr
[2] Fakultät für Mathematik und Informatik, Universität Leipzig, Leipzig, Germany
quaas@informatik.uni-leipzig.de

Abstract. We consider the description logic $\mathcal{ALCF}^{\mathcal{P}}(\mathcal{D}_\Sigma)$ over the concrete domain $\mathcal{D}_\Sigma = (\Sigma^*, \prec, =, (=_{\mathfrak{w}})_{\mathfrak{w} \in \Sigma^*})$, where $\prec$ is the strict prefix order over finite strings in Σ^*. Using an automata-based approach, we show that the concept satisfiability problem w.r.t. general TBoxes for $\mathcal{ALCF}^{\mathcal{P}}(\mathcal{D}_\Sigma)$ is ExpTime-complete for all finite alphabets Σ. As far as we know, this is the first complexity result for an expressive description logic with a nontrivial concrete domain on strings.

1 Introduction

Description Logics with Concrete Domains. A concrete domain is a relational structure with a fixed nonempty domain and a family of relations. In this paper, we are most and for all interested in the concrete domain $(\Sigma^*, \prec, =, (=_{\mathfrak{w}})_{\mathfrak{w} \in \Sigma^*})$, where Σ is a finite alphabet, $\prec$ is the strict prefix relation over Σ^*, $=$ is the usual equality relation, and $=_{\mathfrak{w}}$ stands for equality with $\mathfrak{w}$. Other typical examples of concrete domains (also playing a role herein) are $(\mathbb{N}, <, =, (=_z)_{z \in \mathbb{N}})$ and $(\mathbb{Z}, <, =, (=_z)_{z \in \mathbb{Z}})$, that are the (nonnegative) integers with the usual order relation $<$, equality, and equality with z.

We aim to reason about concrete domains using description logics. A standard way to do so is to enrich the semantical structures with values from a concrete domain (see e.g. [5,14,22]); then, specific atomic concepts are used to express constraints between these values. In description logics with concrete domains, the domain elements are enriched with tuples of values coming from the concrete domain, see e.g. [5,7,30–33]. Constraints on concrete domains embedded in concepts from description logics may quickly be expressive enough to encode counting mechanisms, leading to the undecidability of the main reasoning tasks, see e.g. [30]. However, nontrivial properties of concrete domains have been identified to get decidability, see e.g. [9,11,33] and also [14].

The second author is supported by the Deutsche Forschungsgemeinschaft (DFG), project 504343613.

S. Gaggl et al. (Eds.): JELIA 2023, LNAI 14281, pp. 322–337, 2023.
https://doi.org/10.1007/978-3-031-43619-2_23

String Theories. Description logics with concrete domains on strings are often evoked in the literature, see e.g. [4,5,10,24], but such logics are seldom studied. There are a few exceptions, see e.g. [23] handling strings with equality and inequality relations (only). In a way, string domains remain only a potentiality for description logics with concrete domains, although it is believed that concrete domains on strings could be useful in ontologies. Reasoning about strings is often required in program verification, and much effort has been dedicated towards designing solvers that handle string theories, see e.g. [1,2,28]. An explanation for the lack of works on description logics may be the complexity inherent to string theories. For instance, first-order theory on strings with concatenation is undecidable [37]. On the other hand, satisfiability of word equations is in PSPACE [20,34,36]. Herein, we are interested in the challenging question of deciding reasoning tasks for description logics with a non-trivial string domain.

Our Motivations. What is particularly interesting about concrete domains on strings is to observe that these domains are absolutely not captured by the recent and sophisticated methods for determining decidability of description logics with concrete domains, see e.g. [8,9,33,39]. Moreover, the string domain $(\Sigma^*, <, =, (=_{\mathfrak{w}})_{\mathfrak{w} \in \Sigma^*})$, in the following denoted by $\mathcal{D}_\Sigma$, is known to be difficult to handle, see e.g. [13, Theorem 1]. This applies also to the concrete domain $\mathbb{N}$ (which can be understood as the string domain $\mathcal{D}_\Sigma$ with a singleton alphabet), but for this one, the remarkable works [15,26,27] lead to the ExpTime-completeness of reasoning tasks for the description logic $\mathcal{ALCF}^P(\mathbb{Z})$. The concrete domain $\mathbb{N}$ still requires complex developments, but at least it is known today how to manage it, see e.g. [14,18,40]. Our motivation in this work is to investigate the decidability/complexity status of $\mathcal{ALCF}^P(\mathcal{D}_\Sigma)$, that is, for the nontrivial string domain with the prefix order. To do so, we take advantage of recent results on tree constraint automata on $\mathbb{Z}$ from [19] combined with an encoding of string constraints by numerical constraints from [17]. These are only some first steps to tame reasoning tasks for description logics with string domains, and of course, other string domains are possibly interesting, see e.g. [35].

Our Contributions. In Sect. 2, we introduce the description logic $\mathcal{ALCF}^P(\mathcal{D}_\Sigma)$, similarly to the definition of $\mathcal{ALCF}^P(\mathbb{Z})$ in [26,27]. In Sect. 3, we introduce the class of tree constraint automata (TCA) accepting infinite finite-branching trees with nodes labelled by letters from a finite alphabet and finite tuples of values in Σ^*. Our definition for TCA naturally extends the constraint automata for words (see e.g. [16,21,25,38,40,43]) as well as a similar one for trees on $(\mathbb{Z}, <, =)$ from [19, Section 3.1]. In Sect. 4, the nonemptiness problem for TCA is shown ExpTime-complete. Though ExpTime-hardness is a consequence of [19, Section 3.1], the ExpTime-membership is by reduction to the nonemptiness problem for TCA on $\mathbb{N}$ by lifting arguments from [17, Section 3] to the automata-based setting.

In Sect. 5, we show how to reduce the concept satisfiability problem w.r.t. general TBoxes for $\mathcal{ALCF}^P(\mathcal{D}_\Sigma)$ (written TSAT($\mathcal{ALCF}^P(\mathcal{D}_\Sigma)$)) to the nonemptiness problem for TCA, following the automata-based approach developed in [42] (see also [3,44]). To do so, in Sect. 2, we establish a simple form for $\mathcal{ALCF}^P(\mathcal{D}_\Sigma)$

concepts from which TCA are defined, adapting the developments from [15, Lemma 15] and [27, Lemma 5]. Though we use a standard approach in Sect. 5, we need to carefully handle the constraints in the TCA in order to provide a complexity analysis that leads to the optimal upper bound. The complexity of $\mathcal{ALCF}^{\mathcal{P}}(\mathcal{D}_\Sigma)$ concepts requires sophisticated TCA constructions and involved developments. As a result, we establish that $\mathrm{TSAT}(\mathcal{ALCF}^{\mathcal{P}}(\mathcal{D}_\Sigma))$ is ExpTime-complete for all finite alphabets Σ. As far as we know, this is the first complexity characterisation for a reasoning task related to a description logic with a non-trivial string domain. As explained above, we reuse or adapt several results from the literature (not always related to description logics), and we provide several new insights to combine them adequately.

2   Description Logics with String Domains

Given a finite alphabet Σ, we consider the concrete domain $\mathcal{D}_\Sigma \overset{\text{def}}{=} (\Sigma^*, \prec, =, (=_\mathfrak{w})_{\mathfrak{w}\in\Sigma^*})$, where $\prec$ is the strict prefix relation on Σ^*, $=$ is the equality on Σ^*, and $=_\mathfrak{w}$ is a unary predicate stating the equality with the string $\mathfrak{w}$. In the following, we use $\mathrm{card}(\Sigma)$ to denote the cardinality of Σ.

Let $\mathrm{VAR} = \{x, y, \ldots\}$ be a countably infinite set of variables (also called *registers* in [27] and *concrete features* in the description logic literature). A *term* t *over* VAR is an expression of the form $S^i x$, where $x \in \mathrm{VAR}$ and S^i is a (possibly empty) sequence of i symbols 'S'. A term $S^i x$ should be understood as a variable (that needs to be interpreted) but, later on, we will see that the prefix S^i will have a relational interpretation. We write $\mathrm{T}_{\mathrm{VAR}}$ to denote the set of all terms over VAR. For all $i \in \mathbb{N}$, we write $\mathrm{T}_{\mathrm{VAR}}^{\leqslant i}$ to denote the subset of terms of the form $S^j x$, where $j \leqslant i$. For instance, $\mathrm{T}_{\mathrm{VAR}}^{\leqslant 0} = \mathrm{VAR}$. An *atomic constraint* θ over $\mathrm{T}_{\mathrm{VAR}}$ is an expression of one of the forms below:

$$t \prec t' \quad t = t' \quad =_\mathfrak{w}(t) \text{ (also written } t = \mathfrak{w}),$$

where $\mathfrak{w} \in \Sigma^*$ and $t, t' \in \mathrm{T}_{\mathrm{VAR}}$. A *constraint* Θ is defined as a Boolean combination of atomic constraints. Constraints are interpreted on valuations $\mathfrak{v} : \mathrm{T}_{\mathrm{VAR}} \to \Sigma^*$ that assign elements from Σ^* to the terms in $\mathrm{T}_{\mathrm{VAR}}$, so that $\mathfrak{v}$ *satisfies* θ, written $\mathfrak{v} \models \theta$ iff the interpretation of the terms in θ makes θ true in Σ^* in the usual way. Boolean connectives are interpreted as usual. A constraint Θ is *satisfiable* $\overset{\text{def}}{\Leftrightarrow}$ there is a valuation $\mathfrak{v} : \mathrm{T}_{\mathrm{VAR}} \to \Sigma^*$ such that $\mathfrak{v} \models \Theta$.

Below, we define the description logic $\mathcal{ALCF}^{\mathcal{P}}(\mathcal{D}_\Sigma)$ (over the concrete domain $\mathcal{D}_\Sigma$) defined exactly as the description logic $\mathcal{ALCF}^{\mathcal{P}}(\mathcal{Z}_c)$ from [27] except that $\mathcal{Z}_c$ is replaced by $\mathcal{D}_\Sigma$. We deliberately use the notations from [27] whenever possible and we provide a formal definition for $\mathcal{ALCF}^{\mathcal{P}}(\mathcal{D}_\Sigma)$ to be self-contained. Let $\mathsf{N_C} = \{A, B, \ldots\}$ and $\mathsf{N_R} = \{r, s, \ldots\}$, respectively, be countably infinite sets of *concept names* and *role names*. We further assume that $\mathsf{N_R}$ contains a sub-family $\mathsf{N_F} \subseteq \mathsf{N_R}$ of *functional role names* (a.k.a abstract features). A *role path* $P = r_1 \cdots r_n$ is a (possibly empty) word in $\mathsf{N_R^*}$. We use $|P|$ to denote the length of P (possibly zero). The set of $\mathcal{ALCF}^{\mathcal{P}}(\mathcal{D}_\Sigma)$-*concepts* is defined as follows.

$$C ::= \top \mid \bot \mid A \mid \neg C \mid C \sqcap C \mid C \sqcup C \mid \exists r.C \mid \forall r.C \mid \exists P.[\![\Theta]\!] \mid \forall P.[\![\Theta]\!],$$

where $A \in N_C$, $r \in N_R$, P is a role path, Θ is a Boolean constraint in Σ^* built over terms of the form $S^j x$. Moreover, if $S^j x$ occurs in Θ, then we require $j \leqslant |P|$. An *axiom* is an expression of the form $C \sqsubseteq D$, where C, D are $\mathcal{ALCF}^P(\mathcal{D}_\Sigma)$ concepts. A *terminological box* $\mathcal{T}$ *(TBox, for short)* is a finite set of axioms.

An *interpretation* is a tuple $\mathcal{I} = (\Delta^{\mathcal{I}}, \cdot^{\mathcal{I}}, \mathfrak{v})$, where $\Delta^{\mathcal{I}}$ is a nonempty set (the *domain*), $\mathfrak{v} \colon \Delta^{\mathcal{I}} \times \mathrm{VAR} \to \Sigma^*$ (the *valuation function*), and $\cdot^{\mathcal{I}}$ is an interpretation function that assigns $A^{\mathcal{I}} \subseteq \Delta^{\mathcal{I}}$ to every concept name $A \in N_C$, and $r^{\mathcal{I}} \subseteq \Delta^{\mathcal{I}} \times \Delta^{\mathcal{I}}$ to every role name $r \in N_R$. For all $f \in N_F$, we require $\{(\mathfrak{a}, \mathfrak{a}'), (\mathfrak{a}, \mathfrak{a}'')\} \subseteq f^{\mathcal{I}}$ implies $\mathfrak{a}' = \mathfrak{a}''$, that is, $f^{\mathcal{I}}$ is a partial function. Given a role path $P = r_1 r_2 \ldots r_n$, we define $P^{\mathcal{I}}$ to be the set of all tuples $(\mathfrak{a}_0, \ldots, \mathfrak{a}_n) \in \Delta^{n+1}$ such that $(\mathfrak{a}_{i-1}, \mathfrak{a}_i) \in r_i^{\mathcal{I}}$ for all $i \in [1, n]$. Given an interpretation $\mathcal{I}$ and a tuple $\pi = (\mathfrak{a}_0, \mathfrak{a}_1, \ldots, \mathfrak{a}_n)$ of elements in $\Delta^{\mathcal{I}}$, constraints Θ_1, Θ_2, and $\mathfrak{w} \in \Sigma^*$, we define

- $\mathcal{I}, \pi \models S^i x < S^j y \overset{\mathrm{def}}{\Leftrightarrow} \mathfrak{v}(\mathfrak{a}_i, x) < \mathfrak{v}(\mathfrak{a}_j, y)$,
- $\mathcal{I}, \pi \models S^i x = S^j y \overset{\mathrm{def}}{\Leftrightarrow} \mathfrak{v}(\mathfrak{a}_i, x) = \mathfrak{v}(\mathfrak{a}_j, y)$; $\mathcal{I}, \pi \models S^i x = \mathfrak{w} \overset{\mathrm{def}}{\Leftrightarrow} \mathfrak{v}(\mathfrak{a}_i, x) = \mathfrak{w}$,
- $\mathcal{I}, \pi \models \neg \Theta_1 \overset{\mathrm{def}}{\Leftrightarrow} \mathrm{not}\, \mathcal{I}, \pi \models \Theta_1$; $\mathcal{I}, \pi \models \Theta_1 \wedge \Theta_2 \overset{\mathrm{def}}{\Leftrightarrow} \mathcal{I}, \pi \models \Theta_1$ and $\mathcal{I}, \pi \models \Theta_2$,
- $\mathcal{I}, \pi \models \Theta_1 \vee \Theta_2 \overset{\mathrm{def}}{\Leftrightarrow} \mathcal{I}, \pi \models \Theta_1$ or $\mathcal{I}, \pi \models \Theta_2$.

We extend the interpretation function $\cdot^{\mathcal{I}}$ to complex concepts as follows:

- $\top^{\mathcal{I}} \overset{\mathrm{def}}{=} \Delta^{\mathcal{I}}$, $\bot^{\mathcal{I}} \overset{\mathrm{def}}{=} \varnothing$, $(\neg C)^{\mathcal{I}} \overset{\mathrm{def}}{=} \Delta^{\mathcal{I}} \backslash C^{\mathcal{I}}$,
- $(C \sqcap D)^{\mathcal{I}} \overset{\mathrm{def}}{=} C^{\mathcal{I}} \cap D^{\mathcal{I}}$; $(C \sqcup D)^{\mathcal{I}} \overset{\mathrm{def}}{=} C^{\mathcal{I}} \cup D^{\mathcal{I}}$,
- $(\exists r.C)^{\mathcal{I}} \overset{\mathrm{def}}{=} \{\mathfrak{a} \in \Delta^{\mathcal{I}} \mid \text{there is } \mathfrak{a}' \in \Delta^{\mathcal{I}} \text{ such that } \mathfrak{a}' \in C^{\mathcal{I}} \text{ and } (\mathfrak{a}, \mathfrak{a}') \in r^{\mathcal{I}}\}$,
- $(\forall r.C)^{\mathcal{I}} \overset{\mathrm{def}}{=} \{\mathfrak{a} \in \Delta^{\mathcal{I}} \mid \text{for all } \mathfrak{a}' \in \Delta^{\mathcal{I}}, (\mathfrak{a}, \mathfrak{a}') \in r^{\mathcal{I}} \text{ implies } \mathfrak{a}' \in C^{\mathcal{I}}\}$,
- $(\exists P.[\![\Theta]\!])^{\mathcal{I}} \overset{\mathrm{def}}{=} \{\mathfrak{a}_0 \in \Delta^{\mathcal{I}} \mid \text{there exist } \mathfrak{a}_1, \ldots, \mathfrak{a}_n \in \Delta^{\mathcal{I}} \text{ s.t. } \pi = (\mathfrak{a}_0, \mathfrak{a}_1, \ldots, \mathfrak{a}_n) \in P^{\mathcal{I}} \text{ and } \mathcal{I}, \pi \models \Theta\}$,
- $(\forall P.[\![\Theta]\!])^{\mathcal{I}} \overset{\mathrm{def}}{=} \{\mathfrak{a}_0 \in \Delta^{\mathcal{I}} \mid \text{for all } \mathfrak{a}_1, \ldots, \mathfrak{a}_n \in \Delta^{\mathcal{I}}, \pi = (\mathfrak{a}_0, \mathfrak{a}_1, \ldots, \mathfrak{a}_n) \in P^{\mathcal{I}} \text{ implies } \mathcal{I}, \pi \models \Theta\}$.

An interpretation $\mathcal{I}$ is a *model* of a TBox $\mathcal{T}$, written $\mathcal{I} \models \mathcal{T}$, if $C^{\mathcal{I}} \subseteq D^{\mathcal{I}}$ for all axioms $C \sqsubseteq D$ in $\mathcal{T}$. The *concept satisfiability problem with respect to general TBoxes*, written $\mathrm{TSAT}(\mathcal{ALCF}^P(\mathcal{D}_\Sigma))$, is defined as follows:

Input: An $\mathcal{ALCF}^P(\mathcal{D}_\Sigma)$ concept C_0, and a TBox $\mathcal{T}$.
Question: Is there an interpretation $\mathcal{I}$ of $\mathcal{T}$ such that $\mathcal{I} \models \mathcal{T}$ and $C_0^{\mathcal{I}} \neq \varnothing$?

For instance, $\exists rr'.[\![S^2 x < x]\!]$, $\{\top \sqsubseteq \exists rr'.[\![S^2 y < x]\!], \top \sqsubseteq \exists rr'.[\![x < S^2 x]\!], \top \sqsubseteq \exists r.\top, \top \sqsubseteq \exists r'.\top\}$ is a positive instance of $\mathrm{TSAT}(\mathcal{ALCF}^P(\mathcal{D}_\Sigma))$.

Given an $\mathcal{ALCF}^P(\mathcal{D}_\Sigma)$ concept C_0 and a TBox $\mathcal{T}$, we write $\mathrm{sub}(C_0, \mathcal{T})$ to denote the set of subconcepts obtained from the concepts in C_0 and $\mathcal{T}$. A concept C is in *simple form* iff it is in negation normal form (negation occurs only in constraints) and terms are only from $\mathrm{T}^{\leqslant 1}_{\mathrm{VAR}}$. For instance, $\exists rr'.[\![S^2 y < x]\!]$ is not in simple form but all the concepts in $\exists r.\exists r'.\exists \varepsilon.[\![y < x^{\dagger\dagger}]\!]$, $\top \sqsubseteq \forall r.[\![x = Sx^{\dagger}]\!]$ and $\top \sqsubseteq \forall r'.[\![x^{\dagger} = Sx^{\dagger\dagger}]\!]$ are. Negation normal form is easy to get by standard means as each concept constructor has its dual and the constraints Θ are closed under negations. In Sect. 5, we reduce $\mathrm{TSAT}(\mathcal{ALCF}^P(\mathcal{D}_\Sigma))$ to the nonemptiness problem for *tree constraint automata* (defined in Sect. 3). For this, we assume that the input concept and the concepts occurring in the TBox are in simple form. In Proposition 1 we state that this assumption is without loss of generality and does not cause any computational harm.

Proposition 1. *Let C_0 be an $\mathcal{ALCF}^{\mathcal{P}}(\mathcal{D}_\Sigma)$ concept and $\mathcal{T}$ be a TBox. One can construct in polynomial-time in the size of $C_0, \mathcal{T}$ a concept C_0' and a finite TBox $\mathcal{T}'$ in simple form such that $C_0, \mathcal{T}$ is a positive instance of $\mathrm{TSAT}(\mathcal{ALCF}^{\mathcal{P}}(\mathcal{D}_\Sigma))$ iff $C_0', \mathcal{T}'$ is a positive instance of $\mathrm{TSAT}(\mathcal{ALCF}^{\mathcal{P}}(\mathcal{D}_\Sigma))$.*

Proposition 1 is analogous to [15, Lemma 15] and [27, Lemma 5]. Though based on similar principles, our proof is slightly simpler than the ones cited above, because we demand less from concepts in simple form, as the forthcoming tree constraint automata can handle such concepts (see Sect. 5).

Before defining tree constraint automata, we give a formal definition of *trees*. Given $d \geqslant 1$, a *labeled tree of degree d* is a map $\mathbf{t} : dom(\mathbf{t}) \to \Sigma$ where Σ is some (potentially infinite) alphabet and $dom(\mathbf{t})$ is an infinite subset of $[0, d-1]^*$, that is, if $\mathbf{n} \cdot j \in dom(\mathbf{t})$ for some $\mathbf{n} \in [0, d-1]^*$ and $j \in [0, d-1]$, then $\mathbf{n} \in dom(\mathbf{t})$ and $\mathbf{n} \cdot i \in dom(\mathbf{t})$ for all $0 \leqslant i < j$, too. The elements of $dom(\mathbf{t})$ are called *nodes*. The empty word ε is the *root node* of $\mathbf{t}$. For every $\mathbf{n} \in dom(\mathbf{t})$, the elements $\mathbf{n} \cdot i$ (with $i \in [0, d-1]$) are called the *children nodes of* $\mathbf{n}$, and $\mathbf{n}$ is called the *parent node of* $\mathbf{n} \cdot i$. We say that the tree $\mathbf{t}$ is a *full d-ary tree* if every node $\mathbf{n}$ has exactly d children $\mathbf{n} \cdot 0, \ldots, \mathbf{n} \cdot (d-1)$. Given a tree $\mathbf{t}$ and a node $\mathbf{n}$ in $dom(\mathbf{t})$, an infinite *path* in $\mathbf{t}$ starting from $\mathbf{n}$ is an infinite sequence $\mathbf{n} \cdot j_1 \cdot j_2 \cdot j_3 \ldots$, where $j_i \in [0, d-1]$ and $\mathbf{n} \cdot j_1 \ldots j_i \in dom(\mathbf{t})$ for all $i \geqslant 1$.

3   Tree Constraint Automata Manipulating Strings

In this section, we introduce the class of tree constraint automata that accept sets of trees of the form $\mathbf{t} : [0, d-1]^* \to (\Sigma \times (\Sigma^*)^\beta)$ for some finite alphabet Σ and some $\beta \geqslant 1$. Note that two alphabets are involved here: Σ is a finite alphabet as usually in automata, Σ is inherited from $\mathcal{D}_\Sigma$ and used to interpret β variables at each position of the trees. The transition relation of such automata states constraints between the β string values at a node and the string values at its children nodes. To do so, we write $\mathrm{TreeCons}(\beta)$ to denote the Boolean constraints built over the terms $\mathbf{x}_1, \ldots, \mathbf{x}_\beta, S\mathbf{x}_1, \ldots, S\mathbf{x}_\beta$. These constraints are used to define the transition relation of such automata. We also write $\mathbf{x}_i'$ to denote the term $S\mathbf{x}_i$, and we shall use valuations $\mathfrak{v}$ with profile $\{\mathbf{x}_i, \mathbf{x}_i' \mid i \in [1, \beta]\} \to \Sigma^*$. In the forthcoming definition, the acceptance condition on infinite branches is a Büchi condition, but this can be easily extended to more general conditions. Moreover, the definition is specific to the concrete domain Σ^* but it can be easily adapted to other concrete domains. A *tree constraint automaton* (TCA) on $\mathcal{D}_\Sigma$ is a tuple $\mathbb{A} = (Q, \Sigma, d, \beta, Q_{\mathrm{in}}, \delta, F)$, where

- Q is a finite set of locations; Σ is a finite alphabet,
- $d \geqslant 1$ is the (branching) degree of (the trees accepted by) $\mathbb{A}$,
- $\beta \geqslant 1$ is the number of variables (a.k.a. registers) interpreted in Σ^*,
- $Q_{\mathrm{in}} \subseteq Q$ is the set of initial locations,

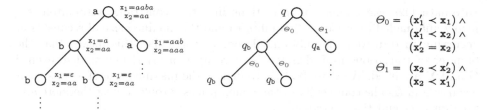

Fig. 1. On the left, the prefix of an infinite tree **t** with two string variables x_1 and x_2. In the middle, the beginning of a run of $\mathbb{A}$ from Example 1 on **t**.

- δ is a finite subset of $Q \times \Sigma \times (\mathrm{TreeCons}(\beta) \times Q)^d$, the transition relation. That is, δ consists of tuples of the form $(q, \mathtt{a}, (\Theta_0, q_0), \ldots, (\Theta_{d-1}, q_{d-1}))$, where $q, q_0, \ldots, q_{d-1} \in Q$, $\mathtt{a} \in \Sigma$, and $\Theta_0, \ldots, \Theta_{d-1}$ are constraints built over $x_1, \ldots, x_\beta, x_1', \ldots, x_\beta'$ for the concrete domain $\mathcal{D}_\Sigma$.
- $F \subseteq Q$ encodes the Büchi acceptance condition.

Let $\mathbf{t} : [0, d-1]^* \to (\Sigma \times (\Sigma^*)^\beta)$ be an infinite full d-ary tree over $\Sigma \times (\Sigma^*)^\beta$. A *run* of $\mathbb{A}$ on **t** is a mapping $\rho : [0, d-1]^* \to Q$ satisfying the following conditions:

- $\rho(\varepsilon) \in Q_{\mathrm{in}}$;
- for every $\mathbf{n} \in [0, d-1]^*$ with $\mathbf{t}(\mathbf{n}) = (\mathbf{a}, \boldsymbol{v})$ and $\rho(\mathbf{n}) = q$, $\mathbf{t}(\mathbf{n} \cdot i) = (\mathbf{a}_i, \boldsymbol{v}_i)$ and $\rho(\mathbf{n} \cdot i) = q_i$ for all $0 \leqslant i < d$, there exists $(q, \mathtt{a}, (\Theta_0, q_0), \ldots, (\Theta_{d-1}, q_{d-1})) \in \delta$ and $\Sigma^* \models \Theta_i(\boldsymbol{v}, \boldsymbol{v}_i)$ for all $0 \leqslant i < d$. Here, $\Sigma^* \models \Theta_i(\boldsymbol{v}, \boldsymbol{v}_i)$ is short for $[\mathbf{x} \leftarrow \boldsymbol{v}, \mathbf{x}' \leftarrow \boldsymbol{v}_i] \models \Theta_i$, where $[\mathbf{x} \leftarrow \boldsymbol{v}, \mathbf{x}' \leftarrow \boldsymbol{v}_i]$ is a valuation $\mathfrak{v}$ on $\{x_j, x_j' \mid j \in [1, \beta]\}$ with $\mathfrak{v}(x_j) = \boldsymbol{v}(j)$ and $\mathfrak{v}(x_j') = \boldsymbol{v}_i(j)$ for all $j \in [1, \beta]$.

Note that string expressions labelling the transitions may state constraints between string values at a node and its children nodes.

Suppose ρ is a run of $\mathbb{A}$ on **t**. Given an infinite path $\pi = j_1 \cdot j_2 \cdot j_3 \ldots$ in ρ starting from the root, we define $\inf(\rho, \pi)$ to be the set of control states that appear infinitely often in $\rho(\varepsilon)\rho(j_1)\rho(j_1 \cdot j_2)\rho(j_1 \cdot j_2 \cdot j_3) \ldots$. A run ρ is *accepting* if for all paths π in ρ starting from ε, we have $\inf(\rho, \pi) \cap F \neq \varnothing$. We write $L(\mathbb{A})$ to denote the set of trees **t** that admit an accepting run.

Example 1. Let $\mathbb{A} = (\{q, q_\mathtt{a}, q_\mathtt{b}\}, \{\mathtt{a}, \mathtt{b}\}, 2, 2, \{q\}, \delta, \{q_\mathtt{a}, q_\mathtt{b}\})$, and δ containing precisely $(q, \mathtt{a}, (\Theta_0, q_\mathtt{b}), (\Theta_1, q_\mathtt{a}))$, $(q_\mathtt{a}, \mathtt{a}, (\top, q_\mathtt{a}), (\top, q_\mathtt{a}))$, and $(q_\mathtt{b}, \mathtt{b}, (\Theta_0, q_\mathtt{b}), (\Theta_0, q_\mathtt{b}))$, where $\Theta_0 = (x_1' < x_1) \wedge (x_1' < x_2) \wedge (x_2' = x_2)$ and $\Theta_1 = (x_2 < x_2') \wedge (x_2 < x_1')$. In Fig. 1, we show the beginning of a run on the tree **t** on the left. Note that this run cannot be extended to an infinite run of $\mathbb{A}$ on **t**: on the leftmost branch, there is no value for x_1' that satisfies the constraint $x_1' < x_1$ for the value of x_1 being ε, hence no transition from $\mathbb{A}$ can be taken. In fact, there cannot be any infinite tree for which there exists some accepting run, and hence $L(\mathbb{A}) = \varnothing$.

As usual, the *nonemptiness problem for TCA*, written NE(TCA), takes as input a TCA $\mathbb{A} = (Q, \Sigma, d, \beta, Q_{\mathrm{in}}, \delta, F)$ and asks whether $L(\mathbb{A})$ is nonempty. We aim to prove that this problem is ExpTime-complete. Unlike (plain) Büchi tree automata [42], the number of transitions in a tree constraint automaton is *a priori* unbounded (TreeCons(β) is infinite) and the maximal size of a constraint occurring in transitions is unbounded too. In particular, this means that the number of transitions in δ, denoted by card(δ), is a priori unbounded, even if Q and Σ are fixed. We write MCS($\mathbb{A}$) to denote the maximal size of a constraint occurring in $\mathbb{A}$. The complexity of the nonemptiness problem must therefore also take into account these parameters.

Below, we use TCA on the concrete domain $(\mathbb{N}, <, =, (=_n)_{n\in\mathbb{N}})$. These are defined as for $\mathcal{D}_\Sigma$, but with Σ being a singleton alphabet. Moreover, we assume that the natural numbers are encoded in binary. As a consequence of [19, Section 4], the nonemptiness problem for TCA on $\mathbb{N}$ is EXPTIME-complete and the purpose of the next section is to show how to generalise this result for any concrete domain $\mathcal{D}_\Sigma$ (with a non-singleton alphabet Σ).

Our tree constraint automata differ from Presburger Büchi tree automata defined in [12,41] for which, in the runs, arithmetical expressions are constraints between the numbers of children labelled by different locations. Herein, the string expressions state constraints between string values (possibly at different nodes).

4   Nonemptiness Problem for TCA on $\mathcal{D}_\Sigma$

To reduce the nonemptiness problem for TCA on $\mathcal{D}_\Sigma$ to the nonemptiness problem for TCA on the concrete domain $(\mathbb{N}, <, =, (=_n)_{n\in\mathbb{N}})$, we show how to take advantage of [17, Lemma 6] dedicated to the transformation of prefix constraints into Boolean combinations of atomic constraints on $\mathbb{N}$. For the sake of being self-contained, we recall below a few definitions useful in Sect. 4.2.

4.1   From String Constraints to Natural Number Constraints

Given a string $\mathfrak{w} \in \Sigma^*$, we write $|\mathfrak{w}|$ to denote its *length*. Given $\mathfrak{w}, \mathfrak{w}' \in \Sigma^*$, we write $clen(\mathfrak{w}, \mathfrak{w}')$ to denote the *length of the longest common prefix* between $\mathfrak{w}$ and $\mathfrak{w}'$. We view the arguments of $clen(\cdot)$ as a set, so that $clen(\mathfrak{w}, \mathfrak{w}')$ and $clen(\mathfrak{w}', \mathfrak{w})$ are identical. More precisely, there are $\mathfrak{w}_0$, $\mathfrak{w}_1$, and $\mathfrak{w}'_1$ such that $\mathfrak{w} = \mathfrak{w}_0 \cdot \mathfrak{w}_1$, $\mathfrak{w}' = \mathfrak{w}_0 \cdot \mathfrak{w}'_1$ and, $\mathfrak{w}_1$ and $\mathfrak{w}'_1$ cannot start by the same first letter, if any. We set $clen(\mathfrak{w}, \mathfrak{w}') \stackrel{\text{def}}{=} |\mathfrak{w}_0|$. For example, $clen(aba, abbbab) = 2$. So, $clen(\mathfrak{w}, \mathfrak{w}) = |\mathfrak{w}|$, and $\mathfrak{w}$ is a strict prefix of $\mathfrak{w}'$ iff $clen(\mathfrak{w}, \mathfrak{w}) = clen(\mathfrak{w}, \mathfrak{w}')$ and $clen(\mathfrak{w}, \mathfrak{w}) < clen(\mathfrak{w}', \mathfrak{w}')$. Here are simple properties, see e.g. [17, Proposition 2], that play a special role in the sequel (assuming card(Σ) = k).

(I) For all $\mathfrak{w}, \mathfrak{w}' \in \Sigma^*$, $|\mathfrak{w}| \geqslant clen(\mathfrak{w}, \mathfrak{w}')$.

(II) For all $\mathfrak{w}_0, \mathfrak{w}_1, \ldots, \mathfrak{w}_k \in \Sigma^*$ such that $clen(\mathfrak{w}_0, \mathfrak{w}_1) = \cdots = clen(\mathfrak{w}_0, \mathfrak{w}_k)$ and for all $i \in [0, k]$, $clen(\mathfrak{w}_0, \mathfrak{w}_1) < |\mathfrak{w}_i|$, there are $i \neq j \in [1, k]$ such that $clen(\mathfrak{w}_0, \mathfrak{w}_1) < clen(\mathfrak{w}_i, \mathfrak{w}_j)$.

(III) For all $\mathfrak{w}_0, \mathfrak{w}_1, \mathfrak{w}_2 \in \Sigma^*$, $clen(\mathfrak{w}_0, \mathfrak{w}_1) < clen(\mathfrak{w}_1, \mathfrak{w}_2)$ implies $clen(\mathfrak{w}_0, \mathfrak{w}_1) = clen(\mathfrak{w}_0, \mathfrak{w}_2)$.

Let VAR' be a finite subset of VAR. A string valuation $\mathfrak{s}$ with respect to VAR' is a map $\mathfrak{s} : \text{VAR}' \to \Sigma^*$. A *counter valuation* $\mathfrak{c}$ with respect to VAR' is defined as a map $\mathfrak{c} : \{\texttt{clen}(\mathtt{x}, \mathtt{x}') : \mathtt{x}, \mathtt{x}' \in \text{VAR}'\} \to \mathbb{N}$, where expressions of the form $\texttt{clen}(\mathtt{x}, \mathtt{x}')$ are understood as "variables" interpreted on $\mathbb{N}$ (we also adopt a set-theoretical reading: $\texttt{clen}(\mathtt{x}, \mathtt{x}')$ and $\texttt{clen}(\mathtt{x}', \mathtt{x})$ are considered as identical). In forthcoming Sect. 4.2, we adopt a similar notation. We say that a counter valuation $\mathfrak{c}$ is *string-compatible* (with respect to VAR') if $\mathfrak{c}$ satisfies the conjunction of the three constraints below in the concrete domain $(\mathbb{N}, <, =, (=_n)_{n \in \mathbb{N}})$.

- Formula $\psi_{\mathrm{I}}(\text{VAR}')$ is related to (I): $\bigwedge_{\mathtt{x}, \mathtt{x}' \in \text{VAR}'}(\texttt{clen}(\mathtt{x}, \mathtt{x}) \geqslant \texttt{clen}(\mathtt{x}, \mathtt{x}'))$.
- Formula $\psi_{\mathrm{II}}(\text{VAR}')$ is related to (II):

$$\bigwedge_{\mathtt{x}_0, \ldots, \mathtt{x}_k \in \text{VAR}'} \left(\left(\bigwedge_{i \in [0,k]} (\texttt{clen}(\mathtt{x}_0, \mathtt{x}_1) < \texttt{clen}(\mathtt{x}_i, \mathtt{x}_i)) \right) \wedge \texttt{clen}(\mathtt{x}_0, \mathtt{x}_1) = \right.$$
$$\left. \cdots = \texttt{clen}(\mathtt{x}_0, \mathtt{x}_k) \right) \Rightarrow \left(\bigvee_{i \neq j \in [1,k]} (\texttt{clen}(\mathtt{x}_0, \mathtt{x}_1) < \texttt{clen}(\mathtt{x}_i, \mathtt{x}_j)) \right).$$

- Formula $\psi_{\mathrm{III}}(\text{VAR}')$ is related to (III):

$$\bigwedge_{\mathtt{x}, \mathtt{x}', \mathtt{x}'' \in \text{VAR}'} (\texttt{clen}(\mathtt{x}, \mathtt{x}') < \texttt{clen}(\mathtt{x}', \mathtt{x}'')) \Rightarrow (\texttt{clen}(\mathtt{x}, \mathtt{x}') = \texttt{clen}(\mathtt{x}, \mathtt{x}'')).$$

The size of the above conjunction is in $\mathcal{O}(\text{card}(\text{VAR}')^{k+2})$, i.e. polynomial in $\text{card}(\text{VAR}')$, assuming Σ is fixed. If $X \subseteq \text{VAR}'$ and $\mathfrak{c}$ is string-compatible w.r.t. VAR', the restriction of $\mathfrak{c}$ to X is also string-compatible with respect to X.

Let X be a nonempty subset of VAR', $\mathfrak{s}$ be a string valuation and $\mathfrak{c}$ be a counter valuation, both with respect to VAR'. We say that $\mathfrak{c}$ *agrees with* $\mathfrak{s}$ on X (written $\mathfrak{c} \approx_X \mathfrak{s}$) $\overset{\text{def}}{\Leftrightarrow}$ $\mathfrak{c}(\texttt{clen}(\mathtt{x}, \mathtt{x}')) = clen(\mathfrak{s}(\mathtt{x}), \mathfrak{s}(\mathtt{x}'))$ for all $\mathtt{x}, \mathtt{x}' \in X$ ('clen' is overloaded here, used to define natural number variables and a function on pairs of strings but we hope this does not lead to confusions). So, if $X' \subseteq X$ and $\mathfrak{c} \approx_X \mathfrak{s}$, then $\mathfrak{c} \approx_{X'} \mathfrak{s}$ too. Given a string valuation $\mathfrak{s}$, there is a counter valuation $\mathfrak{c}$ such that $\mathfrak{c} \approx_X \mathfrak{s}$ [17, Lemma 5] and $\mathfrak{c}$ can be defined obviously by: $\mathfrak{c}(\texttt{clen}(\mathtt{x}, \mathtt{x}')) \overset{\text{def}}{=} clen(\mathfrak{s}(\mathtt{x}), \mathfrak{s}(\mathtt{x}'))$ for all $\mathtt{x}, \mathtt{x}' \in X$.

However, there are counter valuations $\mathfrak{c}$ for which there exists no string valuation $\mathfrak{s}$ with $\mathfrak{c} \approx_X \mathfrak{s}$ (*cf.* Example 2 below). We state below the main property relating string constraints on $\mathcal{D}_\Sigma$ and constraints on $(\mathbb{N}, <, =, (=_n)_{n \in \mathbb{N}})$. Namely, for every string-compatible counter valuation $\mathfrak{c}$ for which the restriction to a subset of variables agrees with some string valuation $\mathfrak{s}$, it is possible to extend $\mathfrak{s}$ to all the variables so that $\mathfrak{c}$ agrees with it.

Proposition 2 [17, Lemma 6]. *Let $X \neq \varnothing$ and Y be finite and disjoint sets of string variables, $\mathfrak{c}$ be a string-compatible counter valuation with respect to $X \uplus Y$ and $\mathfrak{s} : Y \to \Sigma^*$ be such that $\mathfrak{c} \approx_Y \mathfrak{s}$. Then, there is a string valuation $\mathfrak{s}'$ that is a conservative extension of $\mathfrak{s}$, such that $\mathfrak{c} \approx_{X \uplus Y} \mathfrak{s}'$.*

Example 2. Let $\text{VAR}' = \{\mathtt{x}_1, \mathtt{x}_2, \mathtt{x}'_1, \mathtt{x}'_2\}$ and let $\mathfrak{s}(\mathtt{x}_1) = aaba$, $\mathfrak{s}(\mathtt{x}_2) = aa$, $\mathfrak{s}(\mathtt{x}'_1) = aab$, and $\mathfrak{s}(\mathtt{x}'_2) = aaa$. This string valuation satisfies the constraint $\mathtt{x}_2 < \mathtt{x}'_2 \wedge \mathtt{x}_2 <$

clen	x_1	x_2	x_1'	x_2'
x_1	4	2	3	2
x_2		2	2	2
x_1'			3	2
x_2'				3

c

clen	x_1	x_2	x_1'	x_2'
x_1	4	2	3	4
x_2		2	2	2
x_1'			3	2
x_2'				3

c_I

clen	x_1	x_2	x_1'	x_2'
x_1	4	2	2	2
x_2		2	2	2
x_1'			3	2
x_2'				3

c_{II}

clen	x_1	x_2	x_1'	x_2'
x_1	4	1	3	2
x_2		2	2	2
x_1'			3	2
x_2'				3

c_{III}

Fig. 2. Counter valuations. (Color figure online)

x_1'. In Fig. 2, we show the counter valuation c with respect to VAR$'$ induced by s; for instance, $c(\mathtt{clen}(x_1, x_2')) = 2$. Note that c satisfies the constraint over $\mathbb{N}$ corresponding to the above string constraint; for instance, $\mathtt{clen}(x_2, x_2) < \mathtt{clen}(x_2', x_2') \wedge \mathtt{clen}(x_2, x_2) = \mathtt{clen}(x_2, x_2')$ holds true (the yellow cells). The other three tables show three counter valuations that are not string-compatible:

- $< c_I(\mathtt{clen}(x_2', x_2')) < c_I(\mathtt{clen}(x_1, x_2'))$ violates constraint $\psi_I(\text{VAR}')$;
- $c_{II}(\mathtt{clen}(x_2', x_1')) = c_{II}(\mathtt{clen}(x_2', x_1)) = 2$, $c_{II}(\mathtt{clen}(x_2', x_2')) > 2$, $c_{II}(\mathtt{clen}(x_1, x_1)) > 2$, $c_{II}(\mathtt{clen}(x_1', x_1')) > 2$, $c_{II}(\mathtt{clen}(x_1', x_2')) = c_{II}(\mathtt{clen}(x_1, x_1'))$ violate the constraint $\psi_{II}(\text{VAR}')$, assuming card$(\Sigma) = 2$.
- $c_{III}(\mathtt{clen}(x_1, x_2)) < c_{III}(\mathtt{clen}(x_2, x_2'))$ and $c_{III}(\mathtt{clen}(x_1, x_2)) < c_{III}(\mathtt{clen}(x_1, x_2'))$ violate constraint $\psi_{III}(\text{VAR}')$.

Even though each of these counter valuations satisfies the constraint corresponding to the string constraint Θ_1, there does not exist any agreeing string valuation. Proposition 2 shows that if a counter valuation is string-compatible, then an agreeing string valuation exists.

4.2 Reducing TCA on Strings to TCA on Natural Numbers

Let $\mathbb{A} = (Q, \Sigma, d, \beta, Q_{in}, \delta, F)$ be a TCA on the concrete domain $\mathcal{D}_\Sigma$ for which we wish to check the nonemptiness of $L(\mathbb{A})$. Below, we define a TCA $\mathbb{A}' = (Q, \Sigma, d, \beta', Q_{in}, \delta', F)$ on the concrete domain $(\mathbb{N}, <, =, (=_n)_{n\in\mathbb{N}})$ such that $L(\mathbb{A})$ is nonempty iff $L(\mathbb{A}')$ is nonempty. It is worth noting that $\mathbb{A}$ and $\mathbb{A}'$ share the same set of locations, initial locations and the same acceptance condition. Moreover, the finite alphabet Σ and the degree d are identical too. The differences are related to the number of variables β' as well as the definition of the transition relation δ'. Since the two TCA are built over distinct concrete domains ($\mathcal{D}_\Sigma$ versus $\mathbb{N}$), the transition relations necessarily differ. As far as the number of variables is concerned, we lift what is done in Sect. 4.1 to all the string values occurring in trees accepted by the input TCA $\mathbb{A}$.

- Assume that the constant strings occurring in constraints in δ are $w_1, \ldots, w_\alpha$ for some $\alpha \geqslant 0$. We write VAR$_{\mathbb{A}'}$ to denote the expressions in $\{x_i \mid i \in [1, \beta + \alpha]\} \cup \{S^{-1}x_i \mid i \in [1, \beta + \alpha]\}$ (not yet variables in $\mathbb{A}'$). Here, $S^{-1}x$ refers to a value for the parent node, if any. The variables in $\mathbb{A}'$ are of the form $\mathtt{clen}(t_1, t_2)$ where $t_1, t_2 \in$ VAR$_{\mathbb{A}'}$ (ad-hoc notation). Consequently,

$\beta' = 4(\beta + \alpha)^2$ (polynomial in the size of $\mathbb{A}$). Each string $\mathfrak{w}_i$ from $\mathbb{A}$ is implicitly associated to an expression $x_{\beta+i}$ in $\mathrm{VAR}_{\mathbb{A}'}$. The variables $\mathtt{clen}(\mathtt{t}_1, \mathtt{t}_2)$'s with $\{\mathtt{t}_1, \mathtt{t}_2\} \cap \{x_{\beta+i}\} \neq \varnothing$ are intended to specify the length of the longest common prefix between $\mathfrak{w}_i$ and another value.

- The definition of δ' reflects that string-compatible counter valuations satisfy (I)–(III) above, as well as the way we manage the values between the parent node and its children nodes. Given $(q, \mathtt{a}, (\Theta_0, q_0), \ldots, (\Theta_{d-1}, q_{d-1}))$ in δ, there is a corresponding transition $(q, \mathtt{a}, (\Theta'_0, q_0), \ldots, (\Theta'_{d-1}, q_{d-1}))$ in δ' (leading to $\mathrm{card}(\delta') = \mathrm{card}(\delta)$ by construction). What remains to be done is to define each Θ'_ℓ from Θ_ℓ. Θ'_ℓ is a conjunction made of three conjuncts:

  - The 1st conjunct (independent of Θ_ℓ) stating that the counter valuations are string-compatible is equal to $\psi_{\mathrm{I}}(\mathrm{VAR}_{\mathbb{A}'}) \wedge \psi_{\mathrm{II}}(\mathrm{VAR}_{\mathbb{A}'}) \wedge \psi_{\mathrm{III}}(\mathrm{VAR}_{\mathbb{A}'})$, see Sect. 4.1. Its size is in $\mathcal{O}((\beta + \alpha)^{k+2})$ with $\mathrm{card}(\Sigma) = k$.
  - The 2nd conjunct has a double purpose: to define constraints between a node and its parent node (if any), and to guarantee that the expressions of the form $S^{-1}x_{\beta+i}$ and $x_{\beta+i}$ can be interpreted as the string $\mathfrak{w}_i$. Here is the 2nd conjunct (also independent of Θ_ℓ):

$$\left(\bigwedge_{i,j \in [1, \beta+\alpha]} \mathtt{clen}(S^{-1}x_i, S^{-1}x_j)' = \mathtt{clen}(x_i, x_j) \right) \wedge$$

$$\left(\bigwedge_{i,j \in [1, \alpha]} \mathtt{clen}(x_{\beta+i}, x_{\beta+j}) = clen(\mathfrak{w}_i, \mathfrak{w}_j) \right).$$

Observe that in the equalities in the second conjunct above, the left-hand side is a variable in $\mathbb{A}'$ (using our ad-hoc notation) whereas the right-hand side is a value in $\mathbb{N}$ (clearly bounded by the length of the longest string in $\mathbb{A}$). The size of this conjunct is in $\mathcal{O}((\beta + \alpha)^2 + \alpha^2 \times \max|\mathfrak{w}_i|)$.

  - The 3rd conjunct is equal to $\mathtt{t}(\Theta_\ell)$ where $\mathtt{t}$ is a translation map that is homomorphic for Boolean connectives. The translation of the atomic constraints is defined in Fig. 3, and it takes into account how the values are constrained between a parent node and its child node. For instance, if in some accepted tree $\mathtt{t}$ of $\mathbb{A}$, $\mathtt{t}(\mathbf{n}) = (\mathtt{a}, \mathbf{z})$ and $\mathtt{t}(\mathbf{n} \cdot \ell) = (\mathtt{a}_\ell, \mathbf{z}_\ell)$, the variable $\mathtt{clen}(x_i, S^{-1}x_j)'$ occuring in Θ'_ℓ refers to the length of the longest common prefix between the value of x_i at $\mathbf{n} \cdot \ell$ (i.e. $\mathbf{z}_\ell(i)$) and the value of x_j at the parent node of $\mathbf{n} \cdot \ell$ (i.e. $\mathbf{z}(j)$). The size of the 3rd conjunct $\mathtt{t}(\Theta_\ell)$ is linear in the size of Θ_ℓ.

Example 3. Consider $\mathbb{A}$ from Example 1. The automaton $\mathbb{A}'$ obtained from the above construction is of the form $(\{q, q_{\mathtt{a}}, q_{\mathtt{b}}\}, \{\mathtt{a}, \mathtt{b}\}, 2, 16, \{q\}, \delta', \{q_{\mathtt{a}}, q_{\mathtt{b}}\})$, where δ' contains the transitions $(q, \mathtt{a}, (\Theta'_0, q_{\mathtt{b}}), (\Theta'_1, q_{\mathtt{a}}))$, $(q_{\mathtt{a}}, \mathtt{a}, (\Theta', q_{\mathtt{a}}), (\Theta', q_{\mathtt{a}}))$, and $(q_{\mathtt{b}}, \mathtt{b}, (\Theta'_0, q_{\mathtt{b}}), (\Theta'_0, q_{\mathtt{b}}))$, with Θ'_0, Θ'_1, and Θ' obtained from the corresponding string constraints in $\mathbb{A}$ as described above. Θ'_1 consists (amongst others) of the constraints $\mathtt{clen}(S^{-1}x_2, S^{-1}x_2)' = \mathtt{clen}(S^{-1}x_2, x_1)' \wedge \mathtt{clen}(S^{-1}x_2, S^{-1}x_2)' < \mathtt{clen}(x_1, x_1)'$ (the translation of the string constraint $x_2 < x'_1$). By the 2nd conjunct in the definition of δ', we have $\mathtt{clen}(x_2, x_2) = \mathtt{clen}(S^{-1}x_2, S^{-1}x_2)'$.

Atomic θ	Translation $t(\theta)$
$x_i < x_j$	$\texttt{clen}(x_i, x_i) = \texttt{clen}(x_i, x_j) \wedge \texttt{clen}(x_i, x_i) < \texttt{clen}(x_j, x_j)$
$x_i = x_j$	$\texttt{clen}(x_i, x_i) = \texttt{clen}(x_i, x_j) = \texttt{clen}(x_j, x_j)$
$x_i = w_j$	$\texttt{clen}(x_i, x_i) = \texttt{clen}(x_i, x_{\beta+j}) = \texttt{clen}(x_{\beta+j}, x_{\beta+j})$
$x_i' < x_j$	$\texttt{clen}(x_i, x_i)' = \texttt{clen}(x_i, S^{-1}x_j)' \wedge$ $\texttt{clen}(x_i, x_i)' < \texttt{clen}(S^{-1}x_j, S^{-1}x_j)'$
$x_i' = x_j$	$\texttt{clen}(x_i, x_i)' = \texttt{clen}(x_i, S^{-1}x_j)' = \texttt{clen}(S^{-1}x_j, S^{-1}x_j)'$
$x_i' = w_j$	$\texttt{clen}(x_i, x_i)' = \texttt{clen}(x_i, x_{\beta+j})' = \texttt{clen}(x_{\beta+j}, x_{\beta+j})'$
$x_i < x_j'$	$\texttt{clen}(S^{-1}x_i, S^{-1}x_i)' = \texttt{clen}(S^{-1}x_i, x_j)' \wedge$ $\texttt{clen}(S^{-1}x_i, S^{-1}x_i)' < \texttt{clen}(x_j, x_j)'$
$x_i' < x_j'$	$\texttt{clen}(x_i, x_i)' = \texttt{clen}(x_i, x_j)' \wedge \texttt{clen}(x_i, x_i)' < \texttt{clen}(x_j, x_j)'$
$x_i' = x_j'$	$\texttt{clen}(x_i, x_i)' = \texttt{clen}(x_i, x_j)' = \texttt{clen}(x_j, x_j)'$

Fig. 3. Translation of atomic constraints.

The correctness of the construction of $\mathbb{A}'$ is best illustrated by the statement below, which can be viewed as an automata-based counterpart of [17, Lemma 10] and requires a lengthy proof. It relies on Proposition 2 when new string values need to be considered.

Lemma 1. $L(\mathbb{A}) \neq \varnothing$ iff $L(\mathbb{A}') \neq \varnothing$.

We are ready to present our main result about the complexity of $\text{NE}(\text{TCA}(\mathcal{D}_\Sigma))$.

Theorem 1. *For every finite alphabet* Σ, $\text{NE}(\text{TCA}(\mathcal{D}_\Sigma))$ *is* ExpTime-*complete.*

ExpTime-hardness of $\text{NE}(\text{TCA}(\mathcal{D}_\Sigma))$ is due to ExpTime-hardness of the problem $\text{NE}(\text{TCA}(\mathbb{N}))$ established in [19, Section 4.1]. To prove ExpTime-membership, given $\mathbb{A}'$ (on the concrete domain $\mathbb{N}$) built from $\mathbb{A}$ (on the concrete domain $\mathcal{D}_\Sigma$), we know from [19, Lemma 10] that, the nonemptiness of $L(\mathbb{A}')$ can be solved in time

$$\mathcal{O}\left(R_1\big(\text{card}(Q) \times \text{card}(\delta') \times \texttt{MCS}(\mathbb{A}') \times \text{card}(\Sigma) \times R_2(\beta')\big)^{R_2(\beta') \times R_3(d)} \right)$$

for some polynomials R_1, R_2 and R_3, where $\texttt{MCS}(\mathbb{A}')$ denotes the maximal size of a constraint occurring in $\mathbb{A}'$. Note that the result is stated for the concrete domain $\mathbb{Z}$ in [19, Lemma 10], but it applies to $\mathbb{N}$ too (there is a simple way to enforce $x_i \geq 0$ everywhere). We adopt a similar notation for $\mathbb{A}$ and from the above developments, $\texttt{MCS}(\mathbb{A}')$ is in $\mathcal{O}((\beta + \texttt{MCS}(\mathbb{A}) \times \text{card}(\delta) \times d)^{k+3})$ as α can be shown to be bounded above by $\texttt{MCS}(\mathbb{A}) \times \text{card}(\delta) \times d$. Since $\text{card}(\delta') = \text{card}(\delta)$, $\beta' = 4(\beta + \alpha)^2$, nonemptiness of $L(\mathbb{A})$ can be solved in time $\mathcal{O}\Big(R_1\big(\text{card}(Q) \times$ $\text{card}(\delta) \times (\beta + \texttt{MCS}(\mathbb{A}) \times \text{card}(\delta) \times d)^{k+3} \times \text{card}(\Sigma) \times R_2(\beta^\dagger)\big)^{R_2(\beta^\dagger) \times R_3(d)} \Big)$ with $\beta^\dagger = 4(\beta + \texttt{MCS}(\mathbb{A}) \times \text{card}(\delta) \times d)^2$. Hence, $\text{NE}(\text{TCA}(\mathcal{D}_\Sigma))$ is in ExpTime; this holds even if Σ is part of the input.

5 Automata-Based Approach for $\mathcal{ALCF}^{\mathcal{P}}(\mathcal{D}_\Sigma)$

Below, we reduce $\text{TSAT}(\mathcal{ALCF}^{\mathcal{P}}(\mathcal{D}_\Sigma))$ to $\text{NE}(\text{TCA})$: given an $\mathcal{ALCF}^{\mathcal{P}}(\mathcal{D}_\Sigma)$ concept C_0 and a TBox $\mathcal{T}$, we construct a TCA $\mathbb{A}$ on $\mathcal{D}_\Sigma$ such that $C_0, \mathcal{T}$ is a positive instance of $\text{TSAT}(\mathcal{ALCF}^{\mathcal{P}}(\mathcal{D}_\Sigma))$ iff $L(\mathbb{A}) \neq \varnothing$. The material below follows the arguments from [19, Section 5.2] but for $\mathcal{D}_\Sigma$. Obviously, the *tree interpretation property* of $\mathcal{ALCF}^{\mathcal{P}}(\mathcal{D}_\Sigma)$ (cf. the proof of Proposition 1) is of use in the reduction. Thanks to Proposition 1, we can assume that all input concepts are in negation normal form and terms are restricted to those in $\text{T}_{\text{VAR}}^{\leqslant 1}$, that is, the role paths are restricted to single role names r and to ε. This simplifies the reduction; for instance, $\forall \varepsilon.[\![\Theta]\!]$ is logically equivalent to $\exists \varepsilon.[\![\Theta]\!]$, and Θ contains solely variables that state constraints only for the current individual. At this point, it is worth noting that atomic concepts of the form $\exists P.[\![\Theta]\!]$ or $\forall P.[\![\Theta]\!]$ can be expressed by constraints in TCA, unlike the automata-based approach used in [18, 26, 27] that involves abstractions and finite alphabets only.

Since interpretations for $\mathcal{ALCF}^{\mathcal{P}}(\mathcal{D}_\Sigma)$ concepts provide a semantics for several role names, we use a standard trick and reserve directions in $[0, d-1]$ for each role name r occurring in the instance of $\text{TSAT}(\mathcal{ALCF}^{\mathcal{P}}(\mathcal{D}_\Sigma))$. This is needed because in the trees $\mathbf{t} : [0, d-1]^* \to \Sigma \times (\Sigma^*)^\beta$, the (implicit) edges are not labelled. Another way to proceed would be to add a role name to each location of the TCA in order to remember how the node in the tree $[0, d-1]^*$ is accessed to, which is a technique used in [3, Section 3.2]. We also have to handle the determinism of the binary relations $r^{\mathcal{I}}$ with $r \in \mathbf{N_F}$.

So let C_0 be an $\mathcal{ALCF}^{\mathcal{P}}(\mathcal{D}_\Sigma)$ concept and let $\mathcal{T}$ be $\{C_1 \sqsubseteq D_1, \ldots, C_\ell \sqsubseteq D_\ell\}$, with the above-mentioned syntactic restrictions. Given $X \subseteq \text{sub}(C_0, \mathcal{T})$, we say that X is *propositionally $\mathcal{T}$-consistent* iff the conditions below hold.

- There is no concept name A such that $\{A, \neg A\} \subseteq X$.
- X does not contain $\bot$ and if $\top \in \text{sub}(C_0, \mathcal{T})$, then $\top \in X$.
- If $E_1 \sqcup E_2 \in X$, then $\{E_1, E_2\} \cap X \neq \varnothing$. if $E_1 \sqcap E_2 \subset X$, then $\{E_1, E_2\} \subseteq X$.
- For all $k \in [1, \ell]$, if $C_k \in X$, then $D_k \in X$.

Propositionally $\mathcal{T}$-consistent sets correspond to Hintikka sets from [3, Section 3.2] and their introduction is common for developing an automata-based approach for (description) logics. There is no clause for the concept constructor negation because the concepts are in simple form and negation occurs only in front of concept names or within constraints Θ.

Given $r \in \mathbf{N_R}$, we define $\text{sub}_{\exists r}(C_0, \mathcal{T}) \stackrel{\text{def}}{=} \{\exists r.D \mid \exists r.D \in \text{sub}(C_0, \mathcal{T})\}$ and $\text{sub}_{\exists^{cst} r}(C_0, \mathcal{T}) \stackrel{\text{def}}{=} \{\exists r.[\![\Theta]\!] \mid \exists r.[\![\Theta]\!] \in \text{sub}(C_0, \mathcal{T})\}$. The superscript '$cst$' in $\exists^{cst}$ is intended to remind us that the respective sets are made of atomic concepts involving constraints in the string domain (a.k.a. predicate restrictions). We similarly define $\text{sub}_{\forall r}(C_0, \mathcal{T})$ and $\text{sub}_{\forall^{cst} r}(C_0, \mathcal{T})$. We further define $\mathbf{N_F}(C_0, \mathcal{T}) \stackrel{\text{def}}{=} \{r \in \mathbf{N_F} \mid \text{sub}_{\exists r}(C_0, \mathcal{T}) \cup \text{sub}_{\exists^{cst} r}(C_0, \mathcal{T}) \neq \varnothing\}$ and $\exists_{\overline{\mathbf{F}}}(C_0, \mathcal{T}) \stackrel{\text{def}}{=} \{\exists r.[\![\Theta]\!] \in \text{sub}(C_0, \mathcal{T}) \mid r \notin \mathbf{N_F}(C_0, \mathcal{T})\} \cup \{\exists r.D \in \text{sub}(C_0, \mathcal{T}) \mid r \notin \mathbf{N_F}(C_0, \mathcal{T})\}$. So $\mathbf{N_F}(C_0, \mathcal{T})$ contains functional role names r related to predicate or existential restrictions from $\text{sub}(C_0, \mathcal{T})$ involving r, $\exists_{\overline{\mathbf{F}}}(C_0, \mathcal{T})$ contains predicate or existential restrictions from $\text{sub}(C_0, \mathcal{T})$ involving non-functional role names. This difference of treatment is handy to define the value d below though we need to distinguish in several definitions functional role names from the other ones.

Set $d = \text{card}(\mathsf{N_F}(C_0, \mathcal{T})) + \text{card}(\exists_{\overline{\mathsf{F}}}(C_0, \mathcal{T}))$ and ι be a bijection $\iota :$ $(\mathsf{N_F}(C_0, \mathcal{T}) \cup \exists_{\overline{\mathsf{F}}}(C_0, \mathcal{T})) \to [1, d]$. We write $r \rhd j$ whenever $\iota^{-1}(j) = r$ or $\iota^{-1}(j)$ is of the form either $\exists r.D$ or $\exists r.[\![\Theta]\!]$ (direction j contributes to witnesses for r).

We build a TCA $\mathbb{A} = (Q, \Sigma, d+1, \beta, Q_{\text{in}}, \delta, F)$ such that $C_0, \mathcal{T}$ is a positive instance iff $L(\mathbb{A}) \neq \varnothing$. The automaton $\mathbb{A}$ accepts infinite trees of the form $\mathbf{t} : [0, d]^* \to \Sigma \times (\Sigma^*)^\beta$ where $\Sigma = \mathcal{P}(\{A_1, \ldots, A_M\})$, $\{A_1, \ldots, A_M\}$ being the set of concept names occurring in $C_0, \mathcal{T}$. Let us define $\mathbb{A}$ formally.

- Q is the set of propositionally $\mathcal{T}$-consistent subsets of $\text{sub}(C_0, \mathcal{T})$ plus the distinguished "dead-end" location $\bot$ (and never $D \in \bot$, for all concepts D). $\bot$ is useful as seriality is not required for the interpretation of role names.
- $Q_{\text{in}} \stackrel{\text{def}}{=} \{Y \in Q \mid C_0 \in Y\}$, $F \stackrel{\text{def}}{=} Q$ (all the locations are accepting similarly to looping automata, see e.g. [6, Section 3.2]).
- The transition relation δ is made of tuples $(Y, X, (\Theta_0, Y_0), \ldots, (\Theta_d, Y_d))$ s.t.:
  1. For all $A \in Y$, we have $A \in X$ and for all $\neg A \in Y$, we have $A \notin X$.
  2. If $Y = \bot$, then $Y_0 = \cdots = Y_d = \bot$.
  3. For all $j \in [1, d]$ such that $Y_j = \bot$, (a) if $\iota^{-1}(j) = r$ for some $r \in \mathsf{N_F}$, then Y has no concepts of the form either $\exists r.D$ or $\exists r.[\![\Theta]\!]$ and (b) if $\iota^{-1}(j) \notin \mathsf{N_F}$ then $\iota^{-1}(j) \notin Y$.
  4. For all $\exists r.D \in Y$, we have either $(r \in \mathsf{N_F}$ and $D \in Y_{\iota(r)})$ or $(r \notin \mathsf{N_F}$ and $D \in Y_{\iota(\exists r.D)})$. The direction to satisfy $\exists r.D$ is either $\iota(r)$ or $\iota(\exists r.D)$.
  5. For all $\forall r.D \in Y$ and $j \in [1, d]$ such that $Y_j \neq \bot$ and $r \rhd j$, we have $D \in Y_j$. In this case, the direction j is reserved for the role name r and for obligations related to the satisfaction of $\forall r.D$. The satisfaction of $\forall r.D$ implies the satisfaction of D for all the $r^\mathcal{I}$-successors, if any.
  6. For all $j \in [0, d]$, the constraint Θ_j is defined as follows.
     (a) If $Y = \bot$, then $\Theta_j \stackrel{\text{def}}{=} \top$.
     (b) Otherwise, if $j = 0$ or $Y_j = \bot$, then $\Theta_j \stackrel{\text{def}}{=} (\bigwedge_{\exists \varepsilon.[\![\Theta']\!], \forall \varepsilon.[\![\Theta']\!] \in Y} \Theta')$. This conjunction needs actually to be satisfied whenever $Y_j \neq \bot$.
     (c) Otherwise, if $((\exists r.[\![\Theta]\!] \notin Y$ and $\iota(\exists r.[\![\Theta]\!]) = j)$ or $\iota(\exists r.D) = j$ for some $\exists r.[\![\Theta]\!], \exists r.D \in \exists_{\overline{\mathsf{F}}}(C_0, \mathcal{T}))$ and $Y_j \neq \bot$ (necessarily $r \notin \mathsf{N_F}$), then
     $$\Theta_j \stackrel{\text{def}}{=} (\bigwedge_{\exists \varepsilon.[\![\Theta']\!], \forall \varepsilon.[\![\Theta']\!] \in Y} \Theta') \wedge (\bigwedge_{\forall r.[\![\Theta']\!] \in Y} \Theta').$$
     (d) Otherwise, if there is $\exists r.[\![\Theta]\!] \in Y$ s.t. $\iota(\exists r.[\![\Theta]\!]) = j$ (necessarily $r \notin \mathsf{N_F}$), $\Theta_j \stackrel{\text{def}}{=} (\bigwedge_{\exists \varepsilon.[\![\Theta']\!], \forall \varepsilon.[\![\Theta']\!] \in Y} \Theta') \wedge (\bigwedge_{\forall r.[\![\Theta']\!] \in Y} \Theta') \wedge \Theta$. By (3.) above, $\exists r.[\![\Theta]\!] \in Y$, $\iota(\exists r.[\![\Theta]\!]) = j$ and $r \notin \mathsf{N_F}$ imply $Y_j \neq \bot$. So, the direction j is reserved for the role name r and for obligations related to the satisfaction of $\exists r.[\![\Theta]\!]$. This case occurs if there are obligations to satisfy $\exists r.[\![\Theta]\!]$ whereas the case 6(b) gives more freedom because the satisfaction of $\exists r.[\![\Theta]\!]$ is not imposed from Y.
     (e) Otherwise, i.e. $r = \iota^{-1}(j) \in \mathsf{N_F}$ and $Y_j \neq \bot$,
     $$\Theta_j \stackrel{\text{def}}{=} (\bigwedge_{\exists \varepsilon.[\![\Theta']\!], \forall \varepsilon.[\![\Theta']\!] \in Y} \Theta') \wedge (\bigwedge_{\forall r.[\![\Theta']\!], \exists r.[\![\Theta']\!] \in Y} \Theta').$$

Unlike the previous cases, if $r \in \mathsf{N_F}$, then $\forall r.[\![\Theta']\!]$ and $\exists r.[\![\Theta']\!]$ are logically equivalent, assuming that there is one $r^{\mathcal{I}}$-successor.

We can show that our construction is correct.

Lemma 2. $C_0, \mathcal{T}$ *is a positive instance of* $\mathrm{TSAT}(\mathcal{ALCF}^{\mathcal{P}}(\mathcal{D}_\Sigma))$ *iff* $\mathrm{L}(\mathbb{A}) \neq \varnothing$.

Despite the involved construction of $\mathbb{A}$ due to the expressiveness of the logic $\mathcal{ALCF}^{\mathcal{P}}(\mathcal{D}_\Sigma)$, the proof follows a standard pattern. If $C_0, \mathcal{T}$ is a positive instance, then we can extract a tree interpretation that can be associated to a tree accepted by $\mathbb{A}$. Conversely, any tree accepted by $\mathbb{A}$ can be turned into a tree interpretation witnessing the satisfaction of $C_0, \mathcal{T}$. The result below is the main technical result in this paper, whose proof combines the previous key lemmas.

Theorem 2. *For every finite* Σ, $\mathrm{TSAT}(\mathcal{ALCF}^{\mathcal{P}}(\mathcal{D}_\Sigma))$ *is* ExpTime-*complete.*

Due to our complexity analysis, the ExpTime-membership is preserved if the alphabet Σ is part of the input (and not a parameter as in $\mathrm{TSAT}(\mathcal{ALCF}^{\mathcal{P}}(\mathcal{D}_\Sigma))$).

Concluding Remarks. We have shown that the nonemptiness problem for tree constraint automata on $\mathcal{D}_\Sigma$ is ExpTime-complete (Theorem 1) and the concept satisfiability problem w.r.t. general TBoxes for $\mathcal{ALCF}^{\mathcal{P}}(\mathcal{D}_\Sigma)$ is ExpTime-complete too (Theorem 2). The suite of key steps is schematised below.

$$\mathrm{TSAT}(\mathcal{ALCF}^{\mathcal{P}}(\mathcal{D}_\Sigma)) \xrightarrow{\text{Prop. 1}} \underset{\text{in simple form}}{\mathrm{TSAT}(\mathcal{ALCF}^{\mathcal{P}}(\mathcal{D}_\Sigma))} \xrightarrow{\text{Lemma 2}} \mathrm{NE}(\mathrm{TCA}(\mathcal{D}_\Sigma)) \xrightarrow{\text{Lemma 1}} \mathrm{NE}(\mathrm{TCA}(\mathbb{N}))$$

These are only first steps to handle more concrete domains based on strings and on richer description logics. Typically, though we believe we could generalise the developments herein to mix numerical constraints and prefix constraints or to admit an infinite alphabet (based on developments in [17]), it is unclear how to handle $\mathcal{D}_\Sigma$ within logics from [29] (see also [27, Section 4.1]). Similarly, it is open how to handle the string domain $\mathcal{D}_\Sigma$ with regularity constraints, to name another possibility for future work.

References

1. Abdulla, P.A., et al.: String constraints for verification. In: Biere, A., Bloem, R. (eds.) CAV 2014. LNCS, vol. 8559, pp. 150–166. Springer, Cham (2014). https://doi.org/10.1007/978-3-319-08867-9_10
2. Abdulla, P., et al.: Efficient handling of string-number conversion. In: PLDI 2020, pp. 943–957. ACM (2020)
3. Baader, F.: Description logics. In: Tessaris, S., et al. (eds.) Reasoning Web 2009. LNCS, vol. 5689, pp. 1–39. Springer, Heidelberg (2009). https://doi.org/10.1007/978-3-642-03754-2_1
4. Baader, F., Calvanese, D., Guinness, D.M., Nardi, D., Patel-Schneider, P. (eds.): The Description Logic Handbook: Theory, Implementation, and Applications. Cambridge University Press, Cambridge (2003)

5. Baader, F., Hanschke, P.: A scheme for integrating concrete domains into concept languages. In: IJCAI 1991, pp. 452–457 (1991)
6. Baader, F., Hladik, J., Lutz, C., Wolter, F.: From tableaux to automata for description logics. Fund. Inform. **57**(2–4), 247–279 (2003)
7. Baader, F., Horrocks, I., Lutz, C., Sattler, U.: An Introduction to Description Logic. Cambridge University Press, Cambridge (2017)
8. Baader, F., Rydval, J.: An algebraic view on p-admissible concrete domains for lightweight description logics. In: Faber, W., Friedrich, G., Gebser, M., Morak, M. (eds.) JELIA 2021. LNCS (LNAI), vol. 12678, pp. 194–209. Springer, Cham (2021). https://doi.org/10.1007/978-3-030-75775-5_14
9. Baader, F., Rydval, J.: Using model theory to find decidable and tractable description logics with concrete domains. JAR **66**(3), 357–407 (2022)
10. Baader, F., Sattler, U.: Description logics with concrete domains and aggregation. In: ECAI 1998, pp. 336–340. Wiley (1998)
11. Balbiani, P., Jean-François, C.: Computational complexity of propositional linear temporal logics based on qualitative spatial or temporal reasoning. In: Armando, A. (ed.) FroCoS 2002. LNCS (LNAI), vol. 2309, pp. 162–176. Springer, Heidelberg (2002). https://doi.org/10.1007/3-540-45988-X_13
12. Bednarczyk, B., Fiuk, O.: Presburger Büchi tree automata with applications to logics with expressive counting. In: Ciabattoni, A., Pimentel, E., de Queiroz, R.J.G.B. (eds.) WoLLIC 2022. LNCS, vol. 13468, pp. 295–308. Springer, Cham (2022). https://doi.org/10.1007/978-3-031-15298-6_19
13. Carapelle, C., Feng, S., Kartzow, A., Lohrey, M.: Satisfiability of ECTL* with local tree constraints. Theory Comput. Syst. **61**(2), 689–720 (2017)
14. Carapelle, C., Kartzow, A., Lohrey, M.: Satisfiability of ECTL* with constraints. J. Comput. Syst. Sci. **82**(5), 826–855 (2016)
15. Carapelle, C., Turhan, A.: Description logics reasoning w.r.t. general TBoxes is decidable for concrete domains with the EHD-property. In: ECAI 2016, vol. 285, pp. 1440–1448. IOS Press (2016)
16. Čerāns, K.: Deciding properties of integral relational automata. In: Abiteboul, S., Shamir, E. (eds.) ICALP 1994. LNCS, vol. 820, pp. 35–46. Springer, Heidelberg (1994). https://doi.org/10.1007/3-540-58201-0_56
17. Demri, S., Deters, M.: Temporal logics on strings with prefix relation. JLC **26**, 989–1017 (2016)
18. Demri, S., D'Souza, D.: An automata-theoretic approach to constraint LTL. I & C **205**(3), 380–415 (2007)
19. Demri, S., Quaas, K.: Constraint automata on infinite data trees: from CTL(Z)/CTL*(Z) to decision procedures. CoRR, abs/2302.05327 (2023)
20. Diekert, V., Gutierrez, C., Hagenah, C.: The existential theory of equations with rational constraints in free groups is PSPACE-complete. I & C **202**, 105–140 (2005)
21. Gascon, R.: An automata-based approach for CTL* with constraints. Electron. Notes Theor. Comput. Sci. **239**, 193–211 (2009)
22. Geatti, L., Gianola, A., Gigante, N.: Linear temporal logic modulo theories over finite traces. In: IJCAI 2022, pp. 2641–2647. ijcai.org (2022)
23. Haarslev, V., Möller, R.: Description logic systems with concrete domains: applications for the semantic web. In: KRDB 2003. CEUR Workshop Proceedings, vol. 79. CEUR-WS.org (2003)
24. Hustadt, U., Motik, B., Sattler, U.: Reasoning in description logics with a concrete domain in the framework of resolution. In: ECAI 2004, pp. 353–357. IOS Press (2004)

25. Kartzow, A., Weidner, T.: Model checking constraint LTL over trees. CoRR, abs/1504.06105 (2015)
26. Labai, N.: Automata-based reasoning for decidable logics with data values. Ph.D. thesis, TU Wien (2021)
27. Labai, N., Ortiz, M., Simkus, M.: An Exptime Upper Bound for $\mathcal{ALC}$ with integers. In: KR 2020, pp. 425–436. Morgan Kaufman (2020)
28. Liang, T., Reynolds, A., Tinelli, C., Barrett, C., Deters, M.: A DPLL(T) theory solver for a theory of strings and regular expressions. In: Biere, A., Bloem, R. (eds.) CAV 2014. LNCS, vol. 8559, pp. 646–662. Springer, Cham (2014). https://doi.org/10.1007/978-3-319-08867-9_43
29. Lutz, C.: NExpTime-complete description logics with concrete domains. In: Goré, R., Leitsch, A., Nipkow, T. (eds.) IJCAR 2001. LNCS, vol. 2083, pp. 45–60. Springer, Heidelberg (2001). https://doi.org/10.1007/3-540-45744-5_5
30. Lutz, C.: The complexity of description logics with concrete domains. Ph.D. thesis, RWTH, Aachen (2002)
31. Lutz, C.: Description logics with concrete domains–a survey. In: Advances in Modal Logics, vol. 4, pp. 265–296. King's College Publications (2003)
32. Lutz, C.: NEXPTIME-complete description logics with concrete domains. ACM ToCL 5(4), 669–705 (2004)
33. Lutz, C., Milicić, M.: A tableau algorithm for description logics with concrete domains and general Tboxes. JAR 38(1–3), 227–259 (2007)
34. Makanin, G.: The problem of solvability of equations in a free semigroup (English translation). Math. USSR-Sbornik 32(2), 129–198 (1977)
35. Peteler, D., Quaas, K.: Deciding emptiness for constraint automata on strings with the prefix and suffix order. In: MFCS 2022. LIPIcs, vol. 241, pp. 76:1–76:15. Schloss Dagstuhl - Leibniz-Zentrum für Informatik (2022)
36. Plandowski, W.: Satisfiability of word equations with constants is in PSPACE. J. Assoc. Comput. Mach. 51(3), 483–496 (2004)
37. Quine, W.: Concatenation as a basis for arithmetic. J. Symb. Log. 11(4), 105–114 (1946)
38. Revesz, P.: Introduction to Constraint Databases. Springer, New York (2002). https://doi.org/10.1007/b97430
39. Rydval, J.: Using model theory to find decidable and tractable description logics with concrete domains. Ph.D. thesis, Dresden University (2022)
40. Segoufin, L., Toruńczyk, S.: Automata based verification over linearly ordered data domains. In: STACS 2011, pp. 81–92 (2011)
41. Seidl, H., Schwentick, T., Muscholl, A.: Counting in trees. In: Logic and Automata: History and Perspectives. Texts in Logic and Games, vol. 2, pp. 575–612. Amsterdam University Press (2008)
42. Vardi, M., Wolper, P.: Automata-theoretic techniques for modal logics of programs. J. Comput. Syst. Sci. 32, 183–221 (1986)
43. Weidner, T.: Probabilistic logic, probabilistic regular expressions, and constraint temporal logic. Ph.D. thesis, University of Leipzig (2016)
44. Wolper, P.: On the relation of programs and computations to models of temporal logic. In: Banieqbal, B., Barringer, H., Pnueli, A. (eds.) Temporal Logic in Specification. LNCS, vol. 398, pp. 75–123. Springer, Heidelberg (1989). https://doi.org/10.1007/3-540-51803-7_23

Merge, Explain, Iterate: A Combination of MHS and MXP in an ABox Abduction Solver

Martin Homola[(✉)] ⓘ, Júlia Pukancová, Janka Boborová, and Iveta Balintová

Comenius University in Bratislava, Mlynská dolina, 842 48 Bratislava, Slovakia
{homola,pukancova}@fmph.uniba.sk, boborova3@uniba.sk

Abstract. Minimal Hitting Set (MHS) is a well-known and complete method to compute all minimal explanations of an ABox abduction problem in Description Logics (DL). MHS is NP-complete and generally recognized as inefficient. We leverage on MergeXplain (MXP) which is fast but incomplete – by combining it with MHS in a hybrid algorithm MHS-MXP to regain completeness. In this paper, we describe: (a) the underlying theory to establish the completeness of MHS-MXP and show its relevant properties; (b) a class of inputs on which MHS-MXP has the greatest advantage; (c) an experimental implementation; (d) an empirical evaluation on both favourable and unfavourable inputs.

Keywords: Abduction · Description logics · Ontologies

1 Introduction

ABox abduction [7] assumes a DL knowledge base (KB) $\mathcal{K}$ and an extensional observation O (in form of an ABox assertion). Explanations (also extensional) are sets of ABox assertions $\mathcal{E}$ such that $\mathcal{K}$ together with $\mathcal{E}$ entails O.

The MHS algorithm [15] is the classic method to find all minimal explanations of an ABox abduction problem. MHS systematically searches through all possible explanations, from the smallest (in terms of cardinality) towards the largest – thus it ensures *completeness*. It has a good chance to discover smaller explanations quite quickly, however if explanations of interest are larger, it is rather inefficient. Notably, the MHS problem itself is NP-complete [11] and consistency checking of DL KBs repeatedly called by MHS depends on the particular DL, but for many DLs it may be exponential or worse.

Alternatively QuickXplain (QXP) [10] and more recently its extension Merge-Xplain [17] employ a *divide and conquer* strategy to find one (QXP) or even multiple explanations (MXP) efficiently. But they are incomplete, i.e., there is no warranty that all explanations will be found. However, when MXP is run repeatedly, on slightly modified inputs, it divides the search space differently and it may return a different set of explanations. In fact, it is possible to regain completeness by using MHS on the background to track the search space exploration. We formally develop such a combined algorithm, that we call *MHS-MXP*.

ⓒ The Author(s), under exclusive license to Springer Nature Switzerland AG 2023
S. Gaggl et al. (Eds.): JELIA 2023, LNAI 14281, pp. 338–352, 2023.
https://doi.org/10.1007/978-3-031-43619-2_24

We study its relevant properties that allow us not only to establish its correctness but also to characterize inputs on which it may have an advantage over MHS: inputs with smaller explanations or with smaller number of explanations.

Our experimental implementation allows to switch between both algorithms. It integrates the JFact reasoner as a black box. MHS (and thus also MHS-MXP) requires not only to verify KB consistency but also to extract relevant information about the model. Not all DL reasoners can be used for this, but tableau reasoners such as JFact internally construct a sufficient part of the model – albeit it is not usual to output it. We were able to employ experimental features of OWL API to extract relevant model information from JFact. We then conducted an empirical evaluation on a favourable but also on an unfavourable class of inputs. MHS-MXP did not perform as well as MHS on the unfavourable class, however on the favourable class it outperformed MHS to a much larger extent.

Compared to other promising approaches in ABox abduction [4–6,13], the main advantage of our work is that as a black-box approach and thus it may be paired with any DL reasoner (if it allows for model extraction). Tableau-based reasoners such as Pellet and JFact can handle DL expressivity up to $\mathcal{SROIQ}$ [9], i.e. up to OWL 2 [3]. Indeed, the other approaches may be more tractable, but they are limited in DL expressivity. Du et al. [5] rely on a translation to Prolog and is complete up to Horn-$\mathcal{SHIQ}$; Du et al. [6] focus on strong tractability for very large ABoxes with a limitation to first-order rewritable TBoxes. Both Del-Pinto and Schmidt [4] and Koopmann et al. [13] support DL expressivity up to $\mathcal{ALC}$. In theory, MHS-MXP is not limited to the DL setting. It can be applied in any case in which MHS is applicable.

2   Preliminaries

We assume familiarity with the basics of DL [1,2], including vocabulary consisting of individuals $N_I = \{a, b, \ldots\}$, roles $N_R = \{P, Q, R, \ldots\}$, and atomic concepts $N_C = \{A, B, \ldots\}$; complex concepts $C, D, \ldots$ built by constructors (e.g. $\neg$, $\sqcap$, $\sqcup$, $\exists$, $\forall$, in case of $\mathcal{ALC}$ [16]); a KB $\mathcal{K} = \mathcal{T} \cup \mathcal{A}$ composed of a TBox $\mathcal{T}$ (with subsumption axioms of the form $C \sqsubseteq D$) and an ABox $\mathcal{A}$ (with concept assertions of the form $C(a)$ and (possibly negated [9]) role assertions of the form $R(a, b)$ and $\neg R(a, b)$). We also remind about the semantics that relies on models M of a KB $\mathcal{K}$, that satisfy all axioms or assertions ϕ in $\mathcal{K}$ ($M \models \phi$); and the reasoning tasks of checking the consistency of $\mathcal{K}$ (if it has a model) and entailment ($\mathcal{K} \models \phi$ if $M \models \phi$ for all its models M).

In *ABox abduction* [7], we are given a KB $\mathcal{K}$ and an observation O consisting of an ABox assertion. The task is to find an *explanation* $\mathcal{E}$, again, consisting of ABox assertions, such that $\mathcal{K} \cup \mathcal{E} \models O$. Explanations are drawn from some set of *abducibles* Abd.

Definition 1 (ABox Abduction Problem). *Let* Abd *be a finite set of ABox assertions. An ABox abduction problem is a pair* $\mathcal{P} = (\mathcal{K}, O)$ *such that* $\mathcal{K}$ *is a knowledge base in DL and* O *is an ABox assertion. An explanation of* $\mathcal{P}$ *(on* Abd*) is any finite set of ABox assertions* $\mathcal{E} \subseteq$ Abd *such that* $\mathcal{K} \cup \mathcal{E} \models O$.

We limit the explanations to atomic and negated atomic concept and role assertions; hence $\mathrm{Abd} \subseteq \{A(a), \neg A(a) \mid A \in N_C,\ a \in N_I\} \cup \{R(a, b), \neg R(a, b) \mid R \in N_R,\ a, b \in N_I\}$. Note that we do not limit the observations, apart from allowing only one (possibly complex) ABox assertion.

According to Elsenbroich et al. [7] it is reasonable to require from each explanation $\mathcal{E}$ of $\mathcal{P} = (\mathcal{K}, O)$ to be: (a) *consistent* ($\mathcal{K} \cup \mathcal{E}$ is consistent); (b) *relevant* ($\mathcal{E} \not\models O$); and (c) *explanatory* ($\mathcal{K} \not\models O$). Explanations that satisfy these three conditions will be called *desired*. In addition, in order to avoid excess hypothesizing, minimality is required.

Definition 2 (Minimality). *Assume an ABox abduction problem $\mathcal{P} = (\mathcal{K}, O)$. Given explanations $\mathcal{E}$ and $\mathcal{E}'$ of $\mathcal{P}$, $\mathcal{E}$ is (syntactically) smaller than $\mathcal{E}'$ if $\mathcal{E} \subseteq \mathcal{E}'$. An explanation $\mathcal{E}$ of $\mathcal{P}$ is (syntactically) minimal if there is no other explanation $\mathcal{E}'$ of $\mathcal{P}$ that is smaller than $\mathcal{E}$.*

3 Computing Explanations

We first review the complete MHS algorithm and then the faster but approximative MXP algorithm. The hybrid approach that tries to combine "the best of both worlds" is then introduced in Sect. 4.

3.1 Minimal Hitting Set

Adopting the well-known result of Reiter [15], computing all minimal explanations of $(\mathcal{K}, O)$ reduces to finding all minimal hitting sets of the set of models of $\mathcal{K} \cup \{\neg O\}$ in the following sense. Also, if some of the models contain no abducibles then there are no explanations.

Observation 1. *The minimal explanations of $(\mathcal{K}, O)$ on Abd directly correspond to the minimal hitting sets of $\{\mathrm{Abd}(M) \mid M \models \mathcal{K} \cup \{\neg O\}\}$ where $\mathrm{Abd}(M) = \{\phi \in \mathrm{Abd} \mid M \not\models \phi\}$.*

Observation 2. *If $\mathrm{Abd}(M) = \emptyset$ for some $M \models \mathcal{K} \cup \{\neg O\}$, then $(\mathcal{K}, O)$ has no explanations on Abd.*

In a labelled tree $T = (V, E, L)$ with root $r \in V$, let $H(n)$ denote the union of edge-labels on the path from r to n, for any node $n \in V$. If a node $n_1 \in V$ has a successor $n_2 \in V$ such that $L(\langle n_1, n_2 \rangle) = \sigma$ then n_2 is a σ-successor of n_1.

MHS (Algorithm 1) works by constructing an HS-tree. An HS-tree for $\mathcal{P} = (\mathcal{K}, O)$ is a labelled tree $T = (V, E, L)$ where (a) each node $n \in V$ is labelled by $L(n) = \mathrm{Abd}(M)$ for a model M of $\mathcal{K} \cup \{\neg O\}$ s.t. $L(n) \cap H(n) = \emptyset$ or by $L(n) = \emptyset$ if such a model does not exist; (b) and for any $n \in V$ there is a σ-successor of n for every $\sigma \in L(n)$.

Each label $L(n)$ can be found as $\mathrm{Abd}(M)$ of some model of $\mathcal{K} \cup \{\neg O\} \cup H(n)$, by one call to an external DL reasoner. If no such model M exists then $H(n)$ corresponds to a hitting set. Note that if M exists but $\mathrm{Abd}(M) = \emptyset$, then in accord with Observation 2 $H(n)$ cannot be extended to a hitting set.

Algorithm 1. MHS($\mathcal{K}$,O,Abd)

Input: Knowledge base $\mathcal{K}$, observation O, abducibles Abd
Output: $\mathcal{S}_{\mathcal{E}}$ all explanations of $\mathcal{P} = (\mathcal{K}, O)$ w.r.t. Abd

1: $M \leftarrow$ a model M of $\mathcal{K} \cup \{\neg O\}$
2: **if** $M =$ null **then**
3:     **return** "nothing to explain"
4: **end if**
5: $T \leftarrow (V = \{r\}, E = \emptyset, L = \{r \mapsto \text{Abd}(M)\})$

6: **for each** $\sigma \in L(r)$ create new σ-successor n_σ of r
7: $\mathcal{S}_{\mathcal{E}} \leftarrow \{\}$

8: **while** exists next node n in T w.r.t. BFS **do**
9:     **if** n can be pruned **then**
10:        prune n
11:     **else if** exists model M of $\mathcal{K} \cup \{\neg O\} \cup H(n)$ **then**
12:        label n by $L(n) \leftarrow \text{Abd}(M)$
13:     **else if** $H(n)$ is desired **then**
14:        $\mathcal{S}_{\mathcal{E}} \leftarrow \mathcal{S}_{\mathcal{E}} \cup \{H(n)\}$
15:     **end if**
16:     **for each** $\sigma \in L(n)$ create new σ-successor n_σ of n
17: **end while**
18: **return** $\mathcal{S}_{\mathcal{E}}$

We apply first two of Reiter's pruning conditions: (1) *subset pruning* eliminates non-minimal hitting sets: given a hitting set $H(n)$, nodes n' with $H(n) \subseteq H(n')$ are pruned; (2) *equal-paths pruning* prunes also nodes n' with $H(n) = H(n')$, even if $H(n)$ is not a hitting set. Once completed, a pruned HS-tree contains all minimal hitting sets [15]. MHS is sound and complete [14,15].

Theorem 1. *The MHS algorithm is sound and complete (i.e., it returns the set $\mathcal{S}_{\mathcal{E}}$ of all minimal desired explanations of $\mathcal{K}$ and O on* Abd*).*

The fact that MHS explores the search space using breadth-first search (BFS) allows to limit the search for explanations by maximum size. The algorithm is still complete w.r.t. any given target size [14].

3.2 MergeXplain

Both QXP [10] and MXP [17] were originally designed to find minimal inconsistent subsets (dubbed *conflicts*) of an over-constrained knowledge base $\mathcal{K} = \mathcal{B} \cup \mathcal{C}$, where $\mathcal{B}$ is the consistent background theory and $\mathcal{C}$ is the "suspicious" part from which the conflicts are drawn. The algorithm is listed in Algorithm 2.

The essence of QXP is captured in the function GETCONFLICT($\mathcal{B}, D, \mathcal{C}$), where the inputs $\mathcal{B}$ and $\mathcal{C}$ are as explained above, and D is an auxiliary control parameter. GETCONFLICT cleverly decomposes $\mathcal{C}$ by splitting it into smaller and smaller subsets such that it is always able to reconstruct one minimal conflict, if it only exists. The auxiliary function ISCONSISTENT($\mathcal{K}$) encapsulates calls to an external reasoner; it returns true if $\mathcal{K}$ is consistent and false otherwise. Thus, if we just need to find one minimal explanation of an ABox abduction problem, adopting a result of Junker [10] we may use GETCONFLICT in the following way.

Theorem 2. *Assume an ABox abduction problem $\mathcal{P} = (\mathcal{K}, O)$ and a set of abducibles* Abd*. If there is at least one explanation $\gamma \subseteq$ Abd of $\mathcal{P}$ then calling* GETCONFLICT($\mathcal{K} \cup \{\neg O\}, \mathcal{K} \cup \{\neg O\}$, Abd) *returns some minimal explanation $\delta \subseteq$ Abd of $\mathcal{P}$.*

Algorithm 2. MXP($\mathcal{B},\mathcal{C}$)

Input: background theory $\mathcal{B}$, set of possibly faulty constraints $\mathcal{C}$
Output: a set of minimal conflicts Γ
1: **if** $\neg$ISCONSISTENT($\mathcal{B}$) **then**
2:     return "no explanation"
3: **else if** ISCONSISTENT($\mathcal{B} \cup \mathcal{C}$) **then**
4:     return $\emptyset$
5: **end if**
6: $\langle \_, \Gamma \rangle \leftarrow$ FINDCONFLICTS($\mathcal{B},\mathcal{C}$)
7: **return** Γ

8: **function** FINDCONFLICTS($\mathcal{B},\mathcal{C}$)
9:     **if** ISCONSISTENT($\mathcal{B} \cup \mathcal{C}$) **then**
10:        **return** $\langle \mathcal{C}, \emptyset \rangle$
11:     **else if** $|\mathcal{C}| = 1$ **then**
12:        **return** $\langle \emptyset, \{\mathcal{C}\} \rangle$
13:     **end if**
14:     Split $\mathcal{C}$ into disjoint, non-empty sets $\mathcal{C}_1$ and $\mathcal{C}_2$
15:     $\langle \mathcal{C}_1', \Gamma_1 \rangle \leftarrow$ FINDCONFLICTS($\mathcal{B},\mathcal{C}_1$)
16:     $\langle \mathcal{C}_2', \Gamma_2 \rangle \leftarrow$ FINDCONFLICTS($\mathcal{B},\mathcal{C}_2$)
17:     $\Gamma \leftarrow \Gamma_1 \cup \Gamma_2$

18:     **while** $\neg$ISCONSISTENT($\mathcal{C}_1' \cup \mathcal{C}_2' \cup \mathcal{B}$) **do**
19:        $X \leftarrow$ GETCONFLICT($\mathcal{B} \cup \mathcal{C}_2', \mathcal{C}_2', \mathcal{C}_1'$)
20:        $\gamma \leftarrow X \cup$ GETCONFLICT($\mathcal{B} \cup X, X, \mathcal{C}_2'$)
21:        $\mathcal{C}_1' \leftarrow \mathcal{C}_1' \setminus \{\sigma\}$ where $\sigma \in X$
22:        $\Gamma \leftarrow \Gamma \cup \{\gamma\}$
23:     **end while**
24:     **return** $\langle \mathcal{C}_1' \cup \mathcal{C}_2', \Gamma \rangle$
25: **end function**

26: **function** GETCONFLICT($\mathcal{B}, D, \mathcal{C}$)
27:     **if** $D \neq \emptyset \wedge \neg$ISCONSISTENT($\mathcal{B}$) **then**
28:        **return** $\emptyset$
29:     **else if** $|\mathcal{C}| = 1$ **then**
30:        **return** $\mathcal{C}$
31:     **end if**
32:     Split $\mathcal{C}$ into disjoint, non-empty sets $\mathcal{C}_1$ and $\mathcal{C}_2$
33:     $D_2 \leftarrow$ GETCONFLICT($\mathcal{B} \cup \mathcal{C}_1, \mathcal{C}_1, \mathcal{C}_2$)
34:     $D_1 \leftarrow$ GETCONFLICT($\mathcal{B} \cup D_2, D_2, \mathcal{C}_1$)
35:     **return** $D_1 \cup D_2$
36: **end function**

The MXP algorithm is captured in the function FINDCONFLICTS($\mathcal{B},\mathcal{C}$), where again $\mathcal{B}$ is the consistent background theory and $\mathcal{C}$ is the set of conflicts inconsistent with it. It returns a pair $\langle \mathcal{C}', \Gamma \rangle$, where Γ contains as many conflicts $\gamma \subseteq \mathcal{C}$ as it is possible to reconstruct from one way in which $\mathcal{C}$ can be split, and $\mathcal{C}' \subseteq \mathcal{C}$ is maximal set consistent with $\mathcal{B}$ that can be reconstructed from this split. MXP relies on GETCONFLICT to recover some of the conflicts that would be lost due to splitting. This ensures that it keeps the important property of QXP that at least one minimal is found in each run, if it exists.

This approach can be immediately adopted for ABox abduction: in order to find explanations for an abduction problem $\mathcal{P} = (\mathcal{K}, O)$ on Abd one needs to call MXP($\mathcal{K} \cup \{\neg O\}$, Abd). This observation allows us to adopt the following result from Shchekotykhin et al. [17]:

Theorem 3. *Assume an ABox abduction problem* $\mathcal{P} = (\mathcal{K}, O)$ *and a set of abducibles* Abd. *If there is at least one explanation* $\gamma \subseteq$ Abd *of* $\mathcal{P}$ *then calling* MXP($\mathcal{K} \cup \{\neg O\}$, Abd) *returns a nonempty set* Γ *of minimal explanations of* $\mathcal{P}$.

In fact, MXP is thorough in its decomposition of $\mathcal{C}$, which is broken to smaller and smaller subsets until they are consistent with $\mathcal{B}$ or until only sets of size 1 remain. This directly implies that all conflicts of size 1 will always be found and returned by a single run of MXP. This observation will prove to be useful for our hybrid algorithm.

Observation 3. *Given an ABox abduction problem* $\mathcal{P} = (\mathcal{K}, O)$, *a set of abducibles* Abd, *and any* $\gamma \subseteq$ Abd *s.t.* $|\gamma| = 1$, *if* $\mathcal{K} \cup \gamma \models O$ *then* $\gamma \in$ MXP($\mathcal{K} \cup \{\neg O\}$, Abd).

Thus MXP is sound and it always finds at least one minimal explanation (Theorem 3), and it finds all explanations of size one (Observation 3). Still,

MXP is not complete. Some explanations may be lost, especially in cases with multiple partially overlapping explanations.

Example 1. Let $\mathcal{K} = \{A \sqcap B \sqsubseteq D, A \sqcap C \sqsubseteq D\}$ and let $O = D(a)$. Let us ignore negated ABox expressions and start with Abd $= \{A(a), B(a), C(a)\}$. There are two minimal explanations of $\mathcal{P} = (\mathcal{K}, O)$: $\{A(a), B(a)\}$, and $\{A(a), C(a)\}$. Calling MXP$(\mathcal{K} \cup \{\neg O\}, \text{Abd})$, it passes the initial tests and calls FINDCON-FLICTS$(\mathcal{K} \cup \{\neg O\}, \text{Abd})$.

FINDCONFLICTS needs to decide how to split $\mathcal{C} = \text{Abd}$ into $\mathcal{C}_1$ and $\mathcal{C}_2$. Let us assume the split was $\mathcal{C}_1 = \{A(a)\}$ and $\mathcal{C}_2 = \{B(a), C(a)\}$. Since both $\mathcal{C}_1$ and $\mathcal{C}_2$ are now conflict-free w.r.t. $\mathcal{K} \cup \{\neg O\}$, the two consecutive recursive calls return $\langle \mathcal{C}_1', \emptyset \rangle$ and $\langle \mathcal{C}_2', \emptyset \rangle$ where $\mathcal{C}_1' = \{A(a)\}$ and $\mathcal{C}_2' = \{B(a), C(a)\}$.

In the while loop, GETCONFLICT$(\mathcal{K} \cup \{\neg O\} \cup \{B(a), C(a)\}, \{B(a), C(a)\}, \{A(a)\})$ returns $X = \{A(a)\}$ while GETCONFLICT$(\mathcal{K} \cup \{\neg O\} \cup \{A(a)\}, \{A(a)\}, \{B(a), C(a)\})$ returns $B(a)$, and hence the first conflict $\gamma = \{A(a), B(a)\}$ is found and added into Γ.

However, consecutively $A(a)$ is removed from $\mathcal{C}_1'$ leaving it empty, and thus the other conflict is not found and $\Gamma = \{\{A(a), B(a)\}\}$ is returned.

Finally, not only MXP finds all explanations of size 1; it also has the property that if no larger explanations are returned in a given run then in fact this is because there are none. In such a case we are sure that we have found all explanations in a single run and we do not have to search any further.

Lemma 1. *Given an ABox abduction problem $\mathcal{P} = (\mathcal{K}, O)$, a set of abducibles Abd, let $\Gamma = \text{MXP}(\mathcal{K} \cup \{\neg O\}, \text{Abd})$. If there is no $\gamma \in \Gamma$ s.t. $|\gamma| > 1$, then for all minimal $\delta \subseteq \text{Abd}$ s.t. $\mathcal{K} \cup \delta \models O$ we have that $\delta \in \Gamma$.*

4 Combined MHS-MXP Algorithm

The idea to use MXP to find all explanations is based on the observation that running it multiple times in a row may result in a consecutive extension of the overall set of conflicts found so far. A naïve, and possibly to a large extent successful idea, would be to randomize the set splits MXP does in each recursive call. We would likely find different conflicts each time, however it would not be clear when to stop.

We will instead explore a hybrid approach, and we will show that by modifying MXP's inputs in its consecutive iterations, the search space exploration can be guided by the construction of an HS-tree from the obtained outputs, and thus completeness will be achieved.

The combined MHS-MXP algorithm, listed as Algorithm 3, therefore constructs the HS-tree T as usual, but in each node n, instead of simply retrieving one model of $\mathcal{K} \cup \{\neg O\} \cup H(n)$, it launches MXP by calling FINDCONFLICTS.

It starts by checking the consistency of $\mathcal{K} \cup \{\neg O\}$. We use a modified ISCON-SISTENT function which stores all previously found models in the model cache

Algorithm 3. MHS-MXP($\mathcal{K}$,O,Abd)

Input: knowledge base $\mathcal{K}$, observation O, set of abducibles Abd
Output: set $\mathcal{S}_\mathcal{E}$ of all explanations of $\mathcal{P} = (\mathcal{K}, O)$ of the class Abd

1: Con ← {}   ▷ Set of conflicts
2: Mod ← {}   ▷ Set of cached models
3: **if** ¬ISCONSISTENT($\mathcal{K} \cup \{\neg O\}$) **then**
4:     **return** "nothing to explain"
5: **else if** Abd(M) = ∅ where Mod = {M} **then**
6:     **return** $\mathcal{S}_\mathcal{E} = \emptyset$
7: **end if**
8: $T \leftarrow (V = \{r\}, E = \emptyset, L = \emptyset)$ ▷ Init. HS-Tree
9: **while** there is next node n in T w.r.t. BFS **do**
10:     **if** n can be pruned **then**
11:         prune n
12:     **else**
13:         $\langle \_, \Gamma \rangle \leftarrow$ FINDCONFLICTS($\mathcal{K} \cup \{\neg O\} \cup H(n)$, Abd $\setminus H(n)$)
14:         Con ← Con $\cup \{H(n) \cup \gamma \mid \gamma \in \Gamma\}$
15:         **if** $\exists \gamma \in \Gamma : |\gamma| > 1$ **then**   ▷ Extend HS-tree under n
16:             $L(n) \leftarrow$ Abd(M) $\setminus H(n)$ for some $M \in$ Mod s.t. $M \models H(n)$
17:             for each $\sigma \in L(n)$ create new σ-successor n_σ of n
18:         **end if**
19:     **end if**
20: **end while**
21: **return** $\mathcal{S}_\mathcal{E} \leftarrow \{\gamma \in$ Con $\mid \gamma$ is desired$\}$
22: **function** ISCONSISTENT($\mathcal{K}$)
23:     **if** there is $M \models \mathcal{K}$ **then**
24:         Mod ← Mod $\cup \{M\}$
25:         **return** true
26:     **else**
27:         **return** false
28:     **end if**
29: **end function**

Mod. The stored models are later used to construct the HS-tree and label its nodes. Also FINDCONFLICTS will use this modified ISCONSISTENT function.

Then the main loop is initiated. For the root node r, pruning is never applied. Then FINDCONFLICTS is simply called passing $\mathcal{K} \cup \{\neg O\}$ as the background theory and Abd as the set of conflicts (as $H(n) = \emptyset$ at this point). The obtained conflicts Γ are stored in Con. We then verify if all conflicts were already found or if the search needs to go on (line 15). From Theorem 3 we know that if no conflicts were returned in Γ, it means there are no conflicts whatsoever. Also from Observation 3 we know that all conflicts of size 1 are always found and returned in Γ. Finally, by Lemma 1 we have that if any larger conflicts remain, at least one is also present in Γ. Hence, if there is no $\gamma \in \Gamma$ with $|\gamma| > 1$ there are no other explanations to be found and the search can be terminated.

If however at least one such γ was returned in Γ then the HS-tree is extended under r using the model M that was previously found and stored in Mod.

When consecutively any other node $n \neq r$ is visited by the main loop, we first check if it can be pruned (line 10): n is pruned (1) either if there is a previously stored conflict $\gamma \in$ Con s.t. $\gamma \subseteq H(n)$, (2) or if there is another $n' \in V$ (that is not pruned) with $H(n') = H(n)$. This corresponds to Reiter's first two pruning conditions with condition (1) being modified to make use of conflicts cached in Con. If n is not pruned, we now want to use MXP with the goal to explore as much as possible of that part of the space of explanations that extends $H(n)$.

Therefore we call FINDCONFLICTS passing $\mathcal{K} \cup \{\neg O\} \cup H(n)$ as the background theory and Abd\$H(n)$ as the set of conflicts.

If we are lucky, we might cut off this branch completely in line 15, that is, if no extension of $H(n)$ of size greater than 1 is found (by Lemma 1). Otherwise we extend the HS-tree below n.

To be able to do that, we need a model of $\mathcal{K} \cup \{\neg O\} \cup H(n)$. However, we do not need to run another consistency check here, as by design of our algorithm at this point such a model is already cached in Mod.

Lemma 2. *For each node n of the HS-tree visited by the main loop of* MHS-MXP *($\mathcal{K}, O,$ Abd) either $H(n) \in$ Con or $\mathcal{K} \cup \{\neg O\} \cup H(n)$ is consistent and at least for one $M \in$ Mod, $M \models \mathcal{K} \cup \{\neg O\} \cup H(n)$.*

Finally, by the time a complete HS-tree is constructed, all explanations are accumulated in Con. However, due to calls to FINDCONFLICTS where (nonempty) $H(n)$ was passed together with $\mathcal{K}$ as the consistent background theory, some of these conflicts in Con may be non-minimal and they have to be filtered out. At this point we also filter out any other undesired explanations. Then the remaining minimal and desired explanations are returned as $\mathcal{S}_{\mathcal{E}}$.

Theorem 4. *The MHS-MXP algorithm is sound and complete (i.e., it returns the set $\mathcal{S}_{\mathcal{E}}$ of all minimal desired explanations of $\mathcal{K}$ and O on* Abd*).*

This follows from the fact that the algorithm correctly reconstructs the HS-tree to a sufficient extent. The parts which are cut off in comparison to a complete HS-tree (line 15) can be omitted thanks to Observation 3 and Lemma 1.

5   Advantages and Limitations

Apparently MHS-MXP absolutely crushes MHS in cases when all explanations are of size one. By Observation 3 and Lemma 1, the search may immediately stop after one call to MXP in the root node of the HS-tree. Without this "look ahead" capability provided to the hybrid algorithm by MXP, pure MHS has no way of knowing it could stop and has to generate the HS-tree completely. Let us now consider some cases when bigger explanations come into play.

Example 2. Let $\mathcal{K} = \{A \sqcap B \sqsubseteq F, D \sqcap \neg C(a), E(b)\}$, let $O = F(a)$, and let Abd $= \{A(a), B(a), C(a), D(a)\}$. There is exactly one explanation $\mathcal{E}_1 = \{A(a), B(a)\}$.

If we run MHS-MXP, it first checks $\mathcal{K} \cup \{\neg F(a)\}$ for consistency and it obtains a model M thereof, say one with Abd$(M) = \{A(a), C(a)\}$.

The call to FINDCONFLICTS in the root does not allow to terminate the search, since $\mathcal{E}_1$ was returned and $|\mathcal{E}_1| > 1$. Therefore n_1 and n_2 are added to the HS-tree with $H(n_1) = \{A(a)\}$ and $H(n_2) = \{C(a)\}$.

Calling FINDCONFLICTS n_1 returns one conflict $\{B(a)\}$ which together with $H(n_1)$ makes up for the explanation $\mathcal{E}_1$. This branch is consecutively cut off, as no greater conflicts were found. Notably, further exploration of branches extending $H(n_1)$ with $C(a)$ and $D(a)$ is avoided (in comparison with MHS).

Then FINDCONFLICTS is called in n_2 returning one conflict $\{A(a), B(a)\}$, corresponding to the non-minimal explanation $\{C(a), A(a), B(a)\}$. However, since there was a conflict extending $H(n_1)$ by a size greater than one, we may not terminate yet and must explore this branch in the HS-tree further, until only extensions of size one are returned by MXP in each path.

Cases similar to Example 2 with a small overall number of explanations can be handled rather efficiently, compared to MHS, as significant part of the search space is cut off. However consider the following modification of the inputs.

Example 3. Given $\mathcal{K}$ and O as in Example 2, let Abd $= \{A(a), B(a), C(a), D(a),$ $E(a), \neg E(a)\}$. The abduction problem $(\mathcal{K}, O)$ has two explanations $\mathcal{E}_1 = \{A(a),$ $B(a)\}$ and $\mathcal{E}_2 = \{E(a), \neg E(a)\}$, the second undesired (inconsistent). FINDCON-FLICTS called in the root r now returns conflicts $\{\{A(a), B(a)\}, \{E(a), \neg E(a)\}\}$. W.l.o.g. we may assume that the same model M was used to label r and that $M \not\models E(a)$. This time Abd$(M) = \{A(a), C(a), E(a)\}$ and in addition to n_1 and n_2 as above also n_3 is generated with $H(n_3) = \{E(a)\}$.

Now the search cannot be immediately cut off after MXP is called in any of the three nodes n_1, n_2, or n_3. E.g., in n_1 FINDCONFLICTS returns $\{\{B(a)\}, \{E(a), \neg E(a)\}\}$. Only branches where all but one element from each explanation is already present can be cut off safely.

Example 3 shows that the larger the overall amount of explanations and the greater their size, the less advantage MHS-MXP is likely to retain. While adding complementary assertions to abducibles does not make a difference for MHS, it does for MHS-MXP (for the worse), as it generates more explanations (even if they are inconsistent and thus undesired). Similarly for mutually inconsistent abducibles (due to the background ontology) yielding irrelevant explanations.

Thus while MHS-MXP provides an advantage on certain inputs we have no reason to suppose it is substantially better in the worst case. It is difficult to estimate to which extent the problem of conflicting abducibles demonstrated in Example 3 would affect real world use, especially if users (knowledgeable about the domain) would be able to specify abducibles suitable enough to contain all explanations they are interested in. There are no known real-world use cases to evaluate abductive reasoning with ontologies that would specify inputs with observations and respective sets of abducibles. Even works that conducted extensive empirical evaluations used artificially generated inputs [4,6,13].

To understand how MHS-MXP compares to MHS on unfavourable inputs with large amounts of conflicting abducibles, and jointly to which extent it is faster than MHS on favourable inputs without conflicting abducibles, we conducted an evaluation on which we report in the following.

6   Implementation

An implementation[1] of MHS-MXP was developed in Java. The *black box* implementation calls an external DL reasoner for consistency checks and extracts model information necessary to steer the HS-tree construction by both MHS and MHS-MXP. The latter is nontrivial as it is fairly nonstandard for any DL reasoner to make model data accessible to the user. In fact, some DL reasoners (e.g. consequence-based [12]) may not even construct any model-related structures, but tableau-based reasoners do construct a *completion graph* which is a finite representation of a model.

We are concerned with exploring all possible explanations that one can construct as (sets of) atomic and negated atomic concept and role assertions involving the named individuals from the ABox and from the input observation. Note that the corresponding part of the completion graph is always fully constructed by tableau-based DL reasoners and is not affected by blocking [1,2,9].

We rely on the `reasoner.knowledgeexploration` package[2] – an experimental package of OWL API – and its interface `OWLKnowledgeExplorerReasoner`. The interface is not commonly implemented by reasoners, however it is implemented by JFact[3], which we were hence able to use in our implementation.

It allows to read out information about the completion graph: nodes are accessed via the `getRoot(e)` method where e is the `OWLClassExpression` (nominal) corresponding to a given ABox individual. The `getObjectLabel()` method is then used to extract all atomic and negated atomic concepts to which the individual belongs (the latter is obtained as the complement of the former). The neighbouring nodes and the respective role assertions are then obtained using the `getObjectNeighbors()` method.

7   Evaluation

The experiments were executed on a virtual machine with 8 cores (16 threads) of Intel Xeon CPU E5-2695 v4, 2.10 GHz, with 32 GB RAM, running Ubuntu 20.04 and Oracle Java SE Runtime Environment v1.8.0_201. Execution times were measured using `ThreadMXBean` from the `java.lang.management` package. We measured user time – the actual time without system overhead. The maximum Java heap size to 4 GB.

Using the implementation, we ran tests in order to understand how MHS-MXP compares to plain MHS (a) in the general case, and (b) in case of inputs that we identified as favourable. We have used the LUBM ontology [8] and the solver's abducibles settings to generate suitable inputs to verify both cases.

---

[1] The implementation and the evaluation datasets are available at https://github.com/boborova3/MHS-MXP-algorithm.

[2] http://owlcs.github.io/owlapi/apidocs_5/org/semanticweb/owlapi/reasoner/knowledgeexploration/package-summary.html.

[3] https://github.com/owlcs/jfact.

Table 1. Statistics for input groups: #: number of inputs; C_m, C_a, C_M: min, average, and max count of explanations; S_m, S_a, S_M: min, average, and max size of the largest explanation

Set	#	C_m	C_a	C_M	S_m	S_a	S_M	Set	#	C_m	C_a	C_M	S_m	S_a	S_M
S1	10	1	7	20	1	1	1	C1	9	1	4.8	9	1	1.11	2
S2	10	8	69.5	159	2	2	2	C2	11	14	51	99	1	2	3
S3	10	47	212.4	479	3	3	3	C3	13	111	212.92	299	2	3.15	4
S4	10	251	417.8	839	4	4	4	C4	8	359	524.75	839	3	4	5
S5	10	503	2627	6719	5	5	5	C5	9	1175	2863	6719	5	5	5

In order to generate inputs with explanations of size up to n, we used a fresh individual a and composed observations in the form $A_1 \sqcap \cdots \sqcap A_n(a)$ where $A_1, \ldots, A_n$ were randomly drawn from LUBM concept names. If all $A_1, \ldots, A_n$ have mutually independent proper subconcepts then there is at least one explanation of size n. If some of them have more subconcepts then the input will have more explanations. If some A_i, A_j have shared subconcepts then (some of) the explanations will be shorter.

Targeting explanations of size up to 5, we generated inputs for $n \in [1..5]$ – 50 inputs altogether. We have aggregated the inputs into five groups S1–S5 based on the size of the largest explanation. The inputs were generated randomly (however LUBM concepts with subconcepts were drawn twice as often to ensure higher number of explanations). The number of generated samples was consecutively reduced in order to obtain balanced groups S1–S5, each with 10 inputs.

To verify the second part of our conjecture, i.e. that MHS-MXP may perform better on inputs with smaller number of explanations, we also aggregated the same 50 inputs differently, into groups C1–C5 accordingly. Basic characteristics of groups S1–S5 and C1–C5 are given in Table 1.

Our implementation supports atomic and negated atomic concept assertions as abducibles, where the latter may be suppressed by a switch. In accordance with our observations from Sect. 5, we have used this feature to obtain an unfavourable case for MHS-MXP (both atomic and negated atomic concepts allowed) and a favourable case (negated atomic concepts suppressed). Notably, all generated inputs only have explanations involving atomic concept assertions, hence each input has exactly the same number of explanations in either case (favourable and unfavourable) – only the search space in the unfavourable case (and the inherent difficulty for MHS-MXP to handle it) is larger.

Each individual input was run five times and the results were averaged. The timeout was set to 4 h (= 14,440 s).

The results for the unfavourable and favourable case are shown in Figs. 1 and 2, respectively. For each case the charts analogously plot the average time per group (y-axis) in which all explanations of a given size (x-axis) are guaranteed to be found. Input groups S1–S5 are shown on the left (a), and input groups C1–C5 in the right (b). Note that for MHS this equates to the time by which it fully explores the HS-tree down to depth x, however, by Observation 3, for

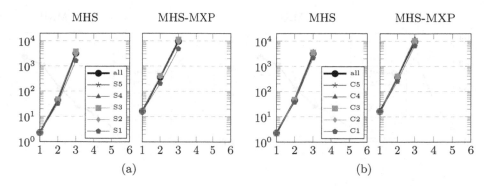

Fig. 1. Unfavourable inputs: Average time in seconds (y-axis) for fully exploring the search space up to the particular explanation size (x-axis) for input groups (a) S1–S5, (b) C1–C5

MHS-MXP this is the time by which it fully explores the HS-tree down to depth $x - 1$. Also note that once the respective group terminated it has fully explored the search space up to any size, hence the line is constantly extended towards the right; in contrast, if more than one third of inputs in the group reached the timeout before reaching the x-value, the y-value was omitted from the plot.

Looking first at the unfavourable inputs (Fig. 1) we observe that both algorithms exhibit steep exponential growth. Both managed to compute all explanations of size 3 within the timeout, but MHS reached this point faster. Notably, there is little difference among the groups S1–S5 and C1–C5. This case is strongly unfavourable for MSH-MXP, attacking its main weakness by swamping the search space with the highest possible amount of mutually inconsistent abducibles. The observed result is consistent with this setting.

In the favourable case (Fig. 2) the advantage of MHS-MXP over MHS is way more significant; e.g. while MHS again did only fully explore the search space up to the size 3 within the 4 h timeout, MHS-MXP managed to reach this point with the average time of 26 s. Also our conjecture of MHS-MXP having the greatest advantage on inputs with smaller count and/or smaller maximal size of explanations verified very clearly. We observe a clear correlation in the increase of computation time and the greatest size of an explanation (groups S) and likewise for the count of explanations (groups C). All groups except for S5 and C5 terminated within the timeout, while in S5 and C5 approx. half of the inputs reached the timeout. (Note that even in such cases, MHS-MXP found all explanations, the search continued and the timeout was reached due to the presence of irrelevant explanations of size greater than 5).

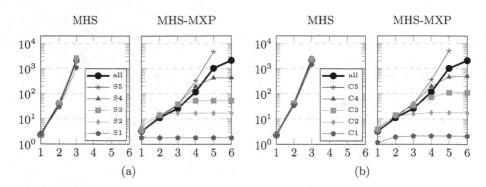

Fig. 2. Favourable inputs: Average time in seconds (y-axis) for fully exploring the search space up to the particular explanation size (x-axis) for input groups (a) S1–S5, (b) C1–C5

8   Conclusions

We have designed and implemented a hybrid combination of MHS and MXP algorithms and formally proved its correctness. One of the main disadvantages of MHS is that it always needs to tediously inspect each candidate solution in the whole search space – even in cases when there is just small number of solutions, and even after all of them have been already found. In such cases the advantage of the combination with MXP shows to be the most promising.

The empirical evaluation supports this conjecture. While on favourable inputs MHS-MXP significantly outperformed MHS, we have also found unfavourable cases on which MHS-MXP performs somewhat worse than MHS. Improving such cases is part of our ongoing work: for instance, we did not yet modify the inner working of the MXP called in each HS-tree node. This offers space for optimization, e.g. to exploit the cached conflicts Con from the previous runs when MXP splits the set of conflicts $\mathcal{C}$. We also want to characterize the performance on a wider scale of input classes to better understand the trade-off.

While there are currently approaches in ABox abduction [4–6,13] which are more tractable, they are also limited in supported DL expressivity, in our solver we were able to achieve black-box integration with JFact which supports DL expressivity up to $\mathcal{SROIQ}$ (i.e. OWL 2).

Even for tableau-based reasoners, model extraction is not a standard. So far, we were able to plug-in JFact exploiting the OWLKnowledgeExplorerReasoner extension of OWL API. In the future, we would like to integrate more tableau reasoners into our solver and allow for modular switching.

In the future, we would also like to look into a possible upgrade of the MHS part of the algorithm by some of its known more effective versions, e.g. by Wotawa [18].

While in this work we have studies and applied the MHS-MXP algorithm on the problem of ABox abduction in DL, it is worth noting that it is also applicable in other cases, more precisely in any case in which MHS is applicable. It can be applied in other languages (e.g. in propositional abduction, in which models can be extracted from a SAT solver) and even on other problems (e.g. computing justifications and maximally consistent subsets).

Acknowledgments. We would like to express our thanks to anonymous reviewers for their valuable feedback on this and also on the previous version of this report. This research was sponsored by the Slovak Republic under the grant APVV-19-0220 (ORBIS) and by the EU under the H2020 grant no. 952215 (TAILOR) and under Horizon Europe grant no. 101079338 (TERAIS).

References

1. Baader, F., Calvanese, D., McGuinness, D.L., Nardi, D., Patel-Schneider, P.F. (eds.): The Description Logic Handbook: Theory, Implementation, and Applications. Cambridge University Press, Cambridge (2003)
2. Baader, F., Horrocks, I., Lutz, C., Sattler, U.: An Introduction to Description Logic. Cambridge University Press, Cambridge (2017)
3. Cuenca Grau, B., Horrocks, I., Motik, B., Parsia, B., Patel-Schneider, P., Sattler, U.: OWL 2: the next step for OWL. J. Web Semant. **6**(4), 309–322 (2008)
4. Del-Pinto, W., Schmidt, R.A.: ABox abduction via forgetting in ALC. In: The Thirty-Third AAAI Conference on Artificial Intelligence, AAAI 2019, Honolulu, Hawaii, USA, pp. 2768–2775. AAAI Press (2019)
5. Du, J., Qi, G., Shen, Y., Pan, J.Z.: Towards practical ABox abduction in large description logic ontologies. Int. J. Semant. Web Inf. Syst. **8**(2), 1–33 (2012)
6. Du, J., Wang, K., Shen, Y.: A tractable approach to ABox abduction over description logic ontologies. In: Proceedings of the Twenty-Eighth AAAI Conference on Artificial Intelligence, Québec City, Québec, Canada, 27–31 July 2014, pp. 1034–1040 (2014)
7. Elsenbroich, C., Kutz, O., Sattler, U.: A case for abductive reasoning over ontologies. In: Proceedings of the OWLED*2006 Workshop on OWL: Experiences and Directions, Athens, GA, US, vol. 216. CEUR-WS (2006)
8. Guo, Y., Pan, Z., Heflin, J.: LUBM: a benchmark for OWL knowledge base systems. J. Web Semant. **3**(2–3), 158–182 (2005)
9. Horrocks, I., Kutz, O., Sattler, U.: The even more irresistible $\mathcal{SROIQ}$. In: Proceedings of Tenth International Conference on Principles of Knowledge Representation and Reasoning, Lake District of the United Kingdom, pp. 57–67. AAAI (2006)
10. Junker, U.: QuickXplain: preferred explanations and relaxations for over-constrained problems. In: Proceedings of the Nineteenth National Conference on Artificial Intelligence, Sixteenth Conference on Innovative Applications of Artificial Intelligence, San Jose, California, US, pp. 167–172. AAAI Press (2004)
11. Karp, R.M.: Reducibility among combinatorial problems. In: Proceedings of a Symposium on the Complexity of Computer Computations, 20–22 March 1972, at the IBM Thomas J. Watson Research Center, Yorktown Heights, New York, pp. 85–103 (1972)
12. Kazakov, Y., Krötzsch, M., Simančík, F.: The incredible ELK. J. Autom. Reason. **53**(1), 1–61 (2014). https://doi.org/10.1007/s10817-013-9296-3
13. Koopmann, P., Del-Pinto, W., Tourret, S., Schmidt, R.A.: Signature-based abduction for expressive description logics. In: Proceedings of the 17th International Conference on Principles of Knowledge Representation and Reasoning, KR 2020, Rhodes, Greece, pp. 592–602 (2020)

14. Pukancová, J., Homola, M.: ABox abduction for description logics: the case of multiple observations. In: Proceedings of the 31st International Workshop on Description Logics, Tempe, Arizona, US, vol. 2211. CEUR-WS (2018)
15. Reiter, R.: A theory of diagnosis from first principles. Artif. Intell. **32**(1), 57–95 (1987)
16. Schmidt-Schauß, M., Smolka, G.: Attributive concept descriptions with complements. Artif. Intell. **48**(1), 1–26 (1991)
17. Shchekotykhin, K.M., Jannach, D., Schmitz, T.: MergeXplain: fast computation of multiple conflicts for diagnosis. In: Proceedings of the Twenty-Fourth International Joint Conference on Artificial Intelligence, IJCAI 2015, Buenos Aires, Argentina. AAAI Press (2015)
18. Wotawa, F.: A variant of Reiter's hitting-set algorithm. Inf. Process. Lett. **79**(1), 45–51 (2001)

Tractable Closure-Based Possibilistic Repair for Partially Ordered DL-Lite Ontologies

Ahmed Laouar[1(✉)], Sihem Belabbes[2], and Salem Benferhat[1]

[1] CRIL, Univ. Artois & CNRS, Lens, France
{laouar,benferhat}@cril.fr
[2] LIASD, IUT de Montreuil, Univ. Paris 8, Saint-Denis, France
belabbes@iut.univ-paris8.fr

Abstract. Inconsistency in formal ontologies is usually addressed by computing repairs for the dataset. There are several strategies for selecting the repairs used to evaluate queries, with various levels of cautiousness and classes of computational complexity. This paper deals with inconsistent partially ordered lightweight ontologies. It introduces a new method that goes beyond the cautious strategies and that is tractable in the possibilistic setting, where uncertainty concerns only the data pieces. The proposed method, called Cπ-repair, proceeds as follows. It first interprets the partially ordered dataset as a family of totally ordered datasets. Then, it computes a single data repair for every totally ordered possibilistic ontology induced from the partially ordered possibilistic ontology. Next, it deductively closes each of these repairs in order to increase their productivity, without introducing conflicts or arbitrary data pieces. Finally, it intersects the closed repairs to obtain a single data repair for the initial ontology. The main contribution of this paper is an equivalent characterization that does not enumerate all the total orders, but also does not suffer from the additional computational cost naturally incurred by the deductive closure. We establish the tractability of our method by reformulating the problem using the notions of dominance and support. Intuitively, the valid conclusions are supported against conflicts by consistent inclusion-minimal subsets of the dataset that dominate all the conflicts. We also study the rationality properties of our method in terms of unconditional and conditional query-answering.

1 Introduction

The Ontology-Based Data Access (OBDA) paradigm relies on an ontology to provide a unified conceptual representation of some domain of interest, in order to improve access to data [27]. Lightweight fragments of description logics such as the DL-Lite family [1,15] are commonly used to encode ontologies, since they allow for efficient query-answering. The conceptual knowledge of an ontology (i.e., the TBox) is usually assumed to be consistent. However, the dataset (i.e., the ABox) may potentially be inconsistent with respect to the TBox. In this case, reasoning with an inconsistent ontology amounts to evaluating queries over one

© The Author(s), under exclusive license to Springer Nature Switzerland AG 2023
S. Gaggl et al. (Eds.): JELIA 2023, LNAI 14281, pp. 353–368, 2023.
https://doi.org/10.1007/978-3-031-43619-2_25

or several of its data repairs (i.e., inclusion-maximal subsets of the ABox that are consistent with respect to the TBox). A variety of inconsistency-tolerant semantics have been proposed, with different levels of cautiousness and classes of computational complexity. These strategies select one or several repairs of an ABox in order to evaluate queries, with tractability achieved mostly for DL-Lite ontologies (see [3,10] for a survey).

For instance, the well-known Intersection of ABox Repair (IAR) semantics [25] is a cautious strategy. Indeed, it avoids a random selection of the repairs since it evaluates queries over the intersection of all the repairs. It discards all the elements of the ABox that are involved in conflicts (i.e., inclusion-minimal subsets of the ABox that are inconsistent with respect to the TBox). Most notably, it is tractable in DL-Lite.

The Intersection of Closed ABox Repair (ICAR) semantics [25] applies the IAR semantics to the deductive closure of the ABox. This allows to derive more facts from the ABox, so ICAR is more productive[1] than IAR, while it is likewise tractable in DL-Lite. However, ICAR may return undesirable conclusions. Consider a TBox with the concept inclusion axiom Whale $\sqsubseteq$ Mammal, and the concept disjointness axiom Whale $\sqsubseteq \neg$ Shark. Say the ABox contains two facts Whale(Humphrey) and Shark(Humphrey), which are in conflict according to the disjointness axiom. ICAR returns Mammal(Humphrey) as a valid conclusion, although it follows from Whale(Humphrey), which is involved in a conflict.

For prioritized (or totally ordered) ontologies, computing repairs for the ABox is a challenging task. For instance, the Preferred Repair semantics [12] (based on the notion of preferred subtheories [13]) is coNP-complete in data complexity. The grounded repair [11] obtained from a Dung-style argumentation framework is tractable. However, the order relation only applies to the conflicts, so the ABox is assumed to be locally stratified (a similar order defined in propositional logic can be found in [8]). In contrast, three main tractable methods have been identified in [7] for totally ordered ABoxes. The non-defeated repair iteratively applies the IAR semantics to a cumulative sequence of strata of the ABox. The linear-based repair iteratively accumulates a sequence of strata of the ABox, by discarding any stratum that is inconsistent with respect to the TBox or that contradicts the preceding sequence of strata. The possibilistic repair leverages possibility theory, which supports inconsistent reasoning with incomplete, uncertain, qualitative and prioritized information [20,23]. It infers all the facts that are strictly more certain than some inconsistency degree of the ABox, computed from the uncertainty degrees assigned to the elements of the ABox.

A few tractable methods have also been proposed for partially ordered ontologies. There is the Elect method [6] which generalizes both the IAR semantics and the non-defeated repair. There is also the possibilistic repair method defined for partially ordered ontologies [5]. Both Elect and the possibilistic repair method extend the partial order over the ABox into a family of total orders. This yields as many totally ordered ABoxes, for which repairs can be computed then intersected to obtain a single repair for the initial ABox. Such methods are interesting

---

[1] Given two inconsistency-tolerant semantics s_1 and s_2. Then s_1 is more productive than s_2 if any conclusion derived with s_2 can also be derived with s_1.

since they derive the conclusions that follow from all the totally ordered repairs. However, their productivity is hampered by their cautiousness.

A natural way for increasing productivity is to compute the deductive closure of the totally ordered repairs before intersecting them, in the spirit of the Intersection of Closed Repairs (ICR) semantics [9].[2] However, it is well-known that closing the repairs increases time complexity. For instance, for flat ontologies, inference with the IAR semantics and the ICAR semantics is tractable, but it is coNP-complete with the ICR semantics in data complexity [3,9].

In this work, we undertake the difficult task of proposing a more productive, yet efficient method, in the case of partially ordered ontologies. We call the new method $C\pi$-repair and establish its tractability in the DL-Lite$_\mathcal{R}$ fragment, using an interpretation of possibility theory as a strategy for computing the repair. We characterize $C\pi$-repair equivalently based on the notions of dominance and support. Intuitively, the valid conclusions are supported against conflicts by consistent inclusion-minimal subsets of the ABox that dominate all the conflicts.

We also study the rationality properties of $C\pi$-repair in terms of unconditional and conditional query-answering mechanisms. In particular, we show that the deductive closure preserves the satisfied properties of possibilistic query-answering from the intersection of the (unclosed) possibilistic repairs.

This paper is organised as follows. Section 2 recalls the basics of DL-Lite$_\mathcal{R}$ and the possibilistic repair method. Section 3 defines the closure-based repair method $C\pi$-repair. Section 4 gives its tractable characterization. Section 5 studies its rationality properties, before concluding.

2   Preliminaries

We recall the underpinnings of the possibilistic repair for partially preordered ontologies [5] that are specified in the DL-Lite$_\mathcal{R}$ fragment [15].

Flat (or Non-prioritized) Ontology: A DL-Lite$_\mathcal{R}$ ontology is a knowledge base (KB) $\mathcal{K} = \langle \mathcal{T}, \mathcal{A} \rangle$, where $\mathcal{T}$ is a TBox composed of axioms encoding domain knowledge, and $\mathcal{A}$ is an ABox composed of assertions (i.e., ground facts or data pieces). The axioms may be positive inclusions of concepts (e.g. $B_1 \sqsubseteq B_2$) or of roles (e.g. $R_1 \sqsubseteq R_2$), and they allow to derive new assertions from the ABox. The axioms may also be negative inclusions of concepts (e.g. $B_1 \sqsubseteq \neg B_2$) or of roles (e.g. $R_1 \sqsubseteq \neg R_2$), and they serve to exhibit the conflicts in the ABox.

Definition 1. *(Conflict) Let $\mathcal{K} = \langle \mathcal{T}, \mathcal{A} \rangle$ be a KB. A conflict is a subset $\mathcal{C} \subseteq \mathcal{A}$ such that $\langle \mathcal{T}, \mathcal{C} \rangle$ is inconsistent, and for all $\varphi \in \mathcal{C}$, $\langle \mathcal{T}, \mathcal{C} \setminus \{\varphi\} \rangle$ is consistent. We denote by $\mathsf{Cf}(\mathcal{A})$ the set of all the conflicts of $\mathcal{A}$, a.k.a. the conflict set.*

Here, inconsistency means the absence of a model for the KB (we omit the semantics for space reasons). The conflict set $\mathsf{Cf}(\mathcal{A})$ can be computed in polynomial time in the size of the ABox in DL-Lite$_\mathcal{R}$ ontologies [15].

---

[2] Note the difference between the ICR semantics which deductively closes the repairs of an ABox, and the ICAR semantics which computes the repairs for a closed ABox.

Totally Preordered Possibilistic Ontology: Possibilistic logic and possibility theory [4,18,19] are long-standing approaches for reasoning with uncertain information, and are closely related to ordinal conditional functions [29] and consonant belief functions [17,22,28]. Uncertainty can be represented either in extension using possibility distributions, or in a compact way using weighted logics or graphical models. Here, we opt for a qualitative representation of the preference relation induced over the ABox, where only the plausibility ordering between the assertions matters (see [5] for details and an overview of possibility theory).

Let $\mathcal{K} = \langle \mathcal{T}, \mathcal{A} \rangle$ be a KB, where the axioms in $\mathcal{T}$ are fully certain and free of conflicts, while the elements of $\mathcal{A}$ may be uncertain and conflicting w.r.t. the axioms of $\mathcal{T}$. Consider a total preorder $\geq$ over $\mathcal{A}^3$, and let $>$ be the associated strict order, and let $\equiv$ denote the associated equivalence relation. We denote the resulting ABox by $\mathcal{A}_\geq$, and it can be represented as a well-ordered partition $(\mathcal{S}_1, \ldots, \mathcal{S}_n)$ such that:

- $\mathcal{S}_1 \cup \ldots \cup \mathcal{S}_n = \mathcal{A}$.
- $\mathcal{S}_1 = \{\varphi_j \in \mathcal{A} : \text{for all } \varphi_k \in \mathcal{A}, \varphi_j \geq \varphi_k\}$.
- $\mathcal{S}_i = \{\varphi_j \in \mathcal{A} \setminus (\mathcal{S}_1 \cup \cdots \cup \mathcal{S}_{i-1}) : \text{for all } \varphi_k \in \mathcal{A} \setminus (\mathcal{S}_1 \cup \cdots \cup \mathcal{S}_{i-1}), \varphi_j \geq \varphi_k\}$, for $i = 2, \ldots, n$.

The assertions in $\mathcal{S}_1$ (resp. $\mathcal{S}_n$) are the most (resp. least) certain. Those in any $\mathcal{S}_i$ $(i = 1, \ldots, n)$ are equally certain.

The totally preordered possibilistic repair [7], denoted $\mathcal{R}(\mathcal{A}_\geq)$, can be computed tractably like so:

- If $\mathcal{K}$ is consistent, then $\mathcal{R}(\mathcal{A}_\geq) = \mathcal{A}$.
- Otherwise, if $\langle \mathcal{T}, \mathcal{S}_1 \rangle$ is inconsistent, then $\mathcal{R}(\mathcal{A}_\geq) = \emptyset$.
- Otherwise, if for some i, $1 \leq i < n$, $\langle \mathcal{T}, \mathcal{S}_1 \cup \ldots \cup \mathcal{S}_i \rangle$ is consistent, and $\langle \mathcal{T}, \mathcal{S}_1 \cup \ldots \cup \mathcal{S}_{i+1} \rangle$ is inconsistent, then $\mathcal{R}(\mathcal{A}_\geq) = \mathcal{S}_1 \cup \ldots \cup \mathcal{S}_i$.

Partially Preordered Possibilistic Ontology: Consider a partial preorder $\unrhd$ over $\mathcal{A}^4$. Let $\rhd$ be the associated strict order, and let $\bowtie^5$ denote incomparability. We denote the resulting ABox by $\mathcal{A}_\unrhd$.

The partially preordered possibilistic repair [5], denoted $\pi(\mathcal{A}_\unrhd)$, relies on the notion of compatible bases. These are all the totally preordered ABoxes induced from $\mathcal{A}_\unrhd$ that preserve the ordering between its assertions. A totally preordered ABox $\mathcal{A}_\geq$ is compatible with $\mathcal{A}_\unrhd$ means that for all $\varphi_j \in \mathcal{A}_\unrhd$, for all $\varphi_k \in \mathcal{A}_\unrhd$, if $\varphi_j \unrhd \varphi_k$, then $\varphi_j \geq \varphi_k$. This entails that $\varphi_j \bowtie \varphi_k$ extends to three distinct cases: (i) $\varphi_j > \varphi_k$, (ii) $\varphi_k > \varphi_j$ or (iii) $\varphi_j \equiv \varphi_k$. Thus, $\pi(\mathcal{A}_\unrhd)$ is obtained like so:

1. First, extend the partial preorder $\unrhd$ into a family of total preorders, each of which is denoted by $\geq_i$, with $1 \leq i \leq m$ and m is the number of extensions of $\unrhd$. Each extension $\geq_i$ defines an ABox $\mathcal{A}_{\geq_i}$ that is compatible with $\mathcal{A}_\unrhd$.

---

[3] A binary relation $\geq$ over $\mathcal{A}$ is a total preorder if it is reflexive and transitive, and for all $\varphi_j \in \mathcal{A}$, for all $\varphi_k \in \mathcal{A}$, either $\varphi_j \geq \varphi_k$ or $\varphi_k \geq \varphi_j$.

[4] A binary relation $\unrhd$ over $\mathcal{A}$ is a partial preorder if it is reflexive and transitive. Thus somes elements of $\mathcal{A}$ may be incomparable according to $\unrhd$.

[5] Consider φ_j and φ_k in $\mathcal{A}$. $\varphi_j \bowtie \varphi_k$ means that neither $\varphi_j \unrhd \varphi_k$ nor $\varphi_k \unrhd \varphi_j$ holds.

2. Then for each compatible base $\mathcal{A}_{\geq_i}$, compute its totally preordered possibilistic repair $\mathcal{R}(\mathcal{A}_{\geq_i})$ as defined above.
3. Finally, intersect all the repairs $\mathcal{R}(\mathcal{A}_{\geq_i})$ to obtain $\pi(\mathcal{A}_{\trianglerighteq}) = \bigcap_{i=1}^{m} \mathcal{R}(\mathcal{A}_{\geq_i})$.

The repair $\pi(\mathcal{A}_{\trianglerighteq})$ has been characterized tractably [5], without exhibiting all the extensions $\geq_i$ of $\trianglerighteq$, using the notion of π-accepted assertions.

Definition 2. *(π-accepted assertion) Let $\mathcal{K}_{\trianglerighteq} = \langle \mathcal{T}, \mathcal{A}_{\trianglerighteq} \rangle$ be a partially preordered KB, and $\mathsf{Cf}(\mathcal{A}_{\trianglerighteq})$ its conflict set. An assertion $\varphi_j \in \mathcal{A}_{\trianglerighteq}$ is π-accepted if for all $\mathcal{C} \in \mathsf{Cf}(\mathcal{A}_{\trianglerighteq})$, there is $\varphi_k \in \mathcal{C}, \varphi_j \neq \varphi_k$, s.t. $\varphi_j \triangleright \varphi_k$.*

The repair $\pi(\mathcal{A}_{\trianglerighteq})$ is the set of all the π-accepted assertions, and it can be computed in polynomial time in the size of $\mathcal{A}_{\trianglerighteq}$ in DL-Lite$_{\mathcal{R}}$ ontologies [5].

We introduce a toy example of a sales company's information security policy.

Example 1. We build a KB from the following mutually disjoint sets $\mathsf{N_C}$, $\mathsf{N_R}$ and $\mathsf{N_I}$, containing respectively concept names, role names and individuals:

- $\mathsf{N_C} = \{\mathsf{Reports}, \mathsf{HRfiles}, \mathsf{Manager}, \mathsf{Sales}, \mathsf{Staff}, \mathsf{HR}\}$, where $\mathsf{Reports}, \mathsf{HRfiles}$ are file categories and $\mathsf{Manager}, \mathsf{Sales}, \mathsf{Staff}$ and HR are employee positions.
- $\mathsf{N_R} = \{\mathsf{Edit}, \mathsf{Sign}, \mathsf{Read}\}$, represent the privileges of an employee on a file.
- $\mathsf{N_I} = \{\mathsf{Bob}, \mathsf{Alice}, \mathsf{F17}, \mathsf{F78}\}$, where $\mathsf{Bob}, \mathsf{Alice}$ are employees and $\mathsf{F17}, \mathsf{F78}$ represent shared files.

Consider a partially preordered KB $\mathcal{K}_{\trianglerighteq} = \langle \mathcal{T}, \mathcal{A}_{\trianglerighteq} \rangle$ depicted in Fig. 1.

$$\mathcal{T} = \left\{ \begin{array}{l} \mathsf{Manager} \sqsubseteq \mathsf{Staff} \\ \mathsf{Sales} \sqsubseteq \mathsf{Staff} \\ \mathsf{Manager} \sqsubseteq \neg \exists \mathsf{Edit} \\ \mathsf{Sales} \sqsubseteq \neg \exists \mathsf{Sign} \end{array} \right\} \quad \mathcal{A}_{\trianglerighteq} = \left\{ \begin{array}{l} \mathsf{Manager(Bob)}, \\ \mathsf{Sales(Bob)}, \\ \mathsf{Reports(F78)}, \\ \mathsf{Edit(Bob, F78)}, \\ \mathsf{Sign(Bob, F78)} \end{array} \right\}$$

Fig. 1. Left: The TBox $\mathcal{T}$ ($\exists$ indicates the existential restriction on roles). Middle: The ABox $\mathcal{A}_{\trianglerighteq}$. Right: The conflicts of $\mathcal{A}_{\trianglerighteq}$ (dashed lines) and the relation $\trianglerighteq$ (solid arrows) represent the strict preference $\triangleright$, the other elements are incomparable).

According to $\mathcal{T}$, a manager and a sales person are staff members. A manager (resp. a sales person) does not have editing (resp. signing) rights on files.

Applying Definition 2 to Fig. 1 (right), since $\mathsf{Reports(F78)}$ is strictly preferred to at least one member of each conflict, we get $\pi(\mathcal{A}_{\trianglerighteq}) = \{\mathsf{Reports(F78)}\}$.

$\square$

3   The Cπ-Repair Method

In the literature, the notion of positive deductive closure is a natural way for obtaining more productive repairs. The idea is to apply the positive inclusion axioms of the TBox to the ABox in order to derive new assertions. However, this typically increases the computational cost. In this section, we propose a

new method, called Cπ-repair, which produces a larger partially preordered possibilistic repair, while maintaining tractability in DL-Lite$_\mathcal{R}$ and the satisfiability
of the rationality properties. Moreover, the tractability of the proposed method
is also applicable in fragments that are more expressive than DL-Lite$_\mathcal{R}$.

Let us first recall the definition of the closure operator in the case of a flat
KB [7,15], which can be applied in the partially preordered case (we assume
that the individuals included in the closure are limited to those present in the
ABox):

Definition 3. *(Closed ABox) Let $\mathcal{K} = \langle \mathcal{T}, \mathcal{A} \rangle$ be a DL-Lite$_\mathcal{R}$ KB. Let $\mathcal{T}_p$ denote
the set of all the positive inclusion axioms of $\mathcal{T}$. The deductive closure of $\mathcal{A}$
w.r.t. $\mathcal{T}$ is defined as:*
*$cl(\mathcal{A}) = \{B(a) | \langle \mathcal{T}_p, \mathcal{A} \rangle \vDash B(a)$ s.t. B is a concept name in $\mathcal{T}$, a is an individual
in $\mathcal{A}\} \bigcup \{R(a,b) | \langle \mathcal{T}_p, \mathcal{A} \rangle \vDash R(a,b)$ s.t. R is a role name in $\mathcal{T}$, a and b are
individuals in $\mathcal{A}\}$, where $\vDash$ is the standard DL-Lite$_\mathcal{R}$ inference relation.*

For partially preordered ABoxes, the deductive closure can be applied at two different levels to obtain a larger repair. The first option closes the initial ABox $\mathcal{A}_\unrhd$
(in the spirit of the ICAR semantics for flat ABoxes [25]). The second option
closes each one of the possibilistic repairs $\mathcal{R}(\mathcal{A}_{\geq_i})$ associated with the compatible
ABoxes $\mathcal{A}_{\geq_i}$ (in the spirit of the ICR semantics for flat ABoxes [9]).

In the first option, closing the ABox $\mathcal{A}_\unrhd$ before computing the repair may
lead to undesirable conclusions. For instance, assume a DL-Lite$_\mathcal{R}$ KB where $\mathcal{T} =
\{B \sqsubseteq E, A \sqsubseteq \neg B\}$ and $\mathcal{A}_\unrhd = \{A(a), B(a)\}$. Then $cl(\mathcal{A}_\unrhd) = \{A(a), B(a), E(a)\}$
and $Cf(cl(\mathcal{A}_\unrhd)) = \{\{A(a), B(a)\}\}$. Assume that $E(a) \rhd A(a) \rhd B(a)$. Using Definition 2, both $E(a)$ and $A(a)$ are π-accepted in $cl(\mathcal{A}_\unrhd)$. However, including $E(a)$
in the repair is questionable, since it is supported by $B(a)$ which conflicts with
the π-accepted assertion $A(a)$. Another issue with this approach concerns the
reliability of the assertions that are inferred from incomparable elements. For
instance, assume a DL-Lite$_\mathcal{R}$ KB where $\mathcal{T} = \{A \sqsubseteq E, B \sqsubseteq E\}$ and $\mathcal{A}_\unrhd = \{A(b),
B(b)\}$, where $A(b) \bowtie B(b)$. Then $cl(\mathcal{A}_\unrhd) = \{A(b), B(b), E(b)\}$ and all the asser-
tions are π-accepted (since the KB is consistent). The question is which certainty
level should be assigned to $E(b)$. The intuition is to consider $E(b)$ to be at least
as certain as $A(b)$ and $B(b)$, but this cannot be easily defined in a general way.

In the second option, closing the possibilistic repairs $\mathcal{R}(\mathcal{A}_{\geq_i})$ of the compatible ABoxes $\mathcal{A}_{\geq_i}$ is more appropriate, such that a more productive repair for $\mathcal{A}_\unrhd$
can be computed from the intersection of $cl(\mathcal{R}(\mathcal{A}_{\geq_i}))$.

Definition 4. *(Cπ-repair) Let $\mathcal{A}_\unrhd$ be a partially preordered ABox. Let $\mathcal{A}_{\geq_i}$, with
$1 \leq i \leq m$, denote all its compatible bases and let $\mathcal{R}(\mathcal{A}_{\geq_i})$ be the associated possibilistic repair. The closure-based partially preordered possibilistic repair of $\mathcal{A}_\unrhd$,
denoted $c\pi(\mathcal{A}_\unrhd)$, is obtained as follows:*

$$c\pi(\mathcal{A}_\unrhd) = \bigcap_{i=1}^{m} \{cl(\mathcal{R}(\mathcal{A}_{\geq_i})) \mid \mathcal{A}_{\geq_i} \text{ is compatible with } \mathcal{A}_\unrhd\}.$$

The closure-based repair $c\pi(\mathcal{A}_\unrhd)$ computed with this method is more productive than both the repair $\pi(\mathcal{A}_\unrhd)$ and its closure $cl(\pi(\mathcal{A}_\unrhd))$. Namely:

$$\pi(\mathcal{A}_\unrhd) \subseteq cl(\pi(\mathcal{A}_\unrhd)) \subseteq c\pi(\mathcal{A}_\unrhd).$$

Figure 2 shows the Cπ-repair process of Definition 4.

- First, extend the partially preordered ABox $\mathcal{A}_{\unrhd}$ into a family of totally preordered ABoxes, denoted $A_{\geq_1}, \ldots, A_{\geq_m}$ ("Extend" arc).
- Then, compute the repair $\mathcal{R}(A_{\geq_i})$ of each compatible base ("Repair" arc), and its deductive closure ("Close" arc).
- Finally, intersect all the closed repairs $cl(\mathcal{R}(A_{\geq_i}))$ ("Intersect" arc) to obtain a single closure-based repair for the initial ABox $c\pi(\mathcal{A}_{\unrhd})$.

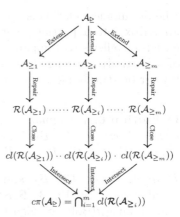

Fig. 2. The Cπ-repair process

Obviously, this method is naive and computationally expensive since enumerating all the compatible ABoxes may be exponential in the worst case.

Example 2. From Example 1, we have: $\pi(\mathcal{A}_{\unrhd}) = cl(\pi(\mathcal{A}_{\unrhd})) = \{\mathsf{Reports(F78)}\}$. Figure 1 illustrates $\mathcal{A}_{\unrhd}$, its two conflicts and the relation $\unrhd$. Recall that any compatible base $A_{\geq_i}$ preserves the ordering between the assertions of $\mathcal{A}_{\unrhd}$. Since $\mathsf{Reports(F78)}$ is the most certain assertion in $\mathcal{A}_{\unrhd}$, it belongs to every $\mathcal{R}(A_{\geq_i})$. Moreover, it is easy to check that each $\mathcal{R}(A_{\geq_i})$ contains either $\mathsf{Manager(Bob)}$ or $\mathsf{Sales(Bob)}$. Using the axioms $\mathsf{Manager} \sqsubseteq \mathsf{Staff}$ and $\mathsf{Sales} \sqsubseteq \mathsf{Staff}$ of $\mathcal{T}$, one can infer $\mathsf{Staff(Bob)}$ from each closed repair $cl(\mathcal{R}(A_{\geq_i}))$. Therefore, $c\pi(\mathcal{A}_{\unrhd}) = \{\mathsf{Reports(F78)}, \mathsf{Staff(Bob)}\}$. So, $c\pi(\mathcal{A}_{\unrhd})$ is larger than both $\pi(\mathcal{A}_{\unrhd})$ and $cl(\pi(\mathcal{A}_{\unrhd}))$. □

4   Characterization of Cπ-Repair

In this section, we propose an equivalent characterization of the closure-based repair introduced in Definition 4 without enumerating all the compatible bases. We first introduce two notions called support and dominance. The support (or an argument) of an assertion is an inclusion-minimal consistent subset of the ABox that allows to derive it. Formally:

Definition 5. *(Support) Let $\mathcal{K} = \langle \mathcal{T}, \mathcal{A} \rangle$ be a DL-Lite$_\mathcal{R}$ KB. Let B be a concept name and R be a role name in $\mathcal{T}$. Let a and b be individuals in $\mathcal{A}$. The subset $\mathcal{B} \subseteq \mathcal{A}$ is a support for $B(a)$ (resp. $R(a,b)$) in $\mathcal{A}$ if:*

- $\langle \mathcal{T}, \mathcal{B} \rangle$ *is consistent, and*
- $\langle \mathcal{T}, \mathcal{B} \rangle \vDash B(a)$, *(resp. $\langle \mathcal{T}, \mathcal{B} \rangle \vDash R(a,b)$), and*
- *for all $\mathcal{B}' \subsetneq \mathcal{B}$, $\langle \mathcal{T}, \mathcal{B}' \rangle \nvDash B(a)$, (resp. $\langle \mathcal{T}, \mathcal{B}' \rangle \nvDash R(a,b)$).*

Where $\vDash$ is the standard DL-Lite$_\mathcal{R}$ inference relation.

Example 3. We continue Example 1. We have $\{\mathsf{Manager(Bob)}\}$ supports $\mathsf{Staff(Bob)}$ since $\langle \mathcal{T}, \{\mathsf{Manager(Bob)}\} \rangle \vDash \mathsf{Staff(Bob)}$, and it is minimal and consistent.   □

The dominance relation is a way for extending the partial preorder defined over an ABox into a partial preorder defined over the subsets of the ABox. Such extension allows to compare supports and conflicts. Intuitively, the dominance of a partially preordered subset over another requires that each element of the former be strictly more certain than at least one element of the latter. Formally:

Definition 6. *(Dominance) Let $\mathcal{K}_{\unrhd} = \langle \mathcal{T}, \mathcal{A}_{\unrhd} \rangle$ be a partially preordered KB equipped with $\unrhd$. Let $\mathcal{B}_1 \subseteq \mathcal{A}_{\unrhd}$ and $\mathcal{B}_2 \subseteq \mathcal{A}_{\unrhd}$. We say that $\mathcal{B}_1$ dominates $\mathcal{B}_2$, denoted $\mathcal{B}_1 \rhd^{dom} \mathcal{B}_2$, if: for all $\varphi_j \in \mathcal{B}_1$, there is $\varphi_k \in \mathcal{B}_2$ s.t. $\varphi_j \rhd \varphi_k$.*

Example 4. Let $\mathcal{B}_1$, $\mathcal{B}_2$ and $\mathcal{B}_3$ be three subsets of $\mathcal{A}_{\unrhd}$ of Example 1, as illustrated by Fig. 3. $\mathcal{B}_1 \rhd^{dom} \mathcal{B}_2$ holds because Reports(F78) $\rhd$ Sales(Bob) and Manager(Bob) $\rhd$ Sign(Bob, F78). $\mathcal{B}_1 \rhd^{dom} \mathcal{B}_3$ does not hold because Manager(Bob) $\not\rhd$ Sales(Bob) and Manager(Bob) $\not\rhd$ Edit(Bob, F78).

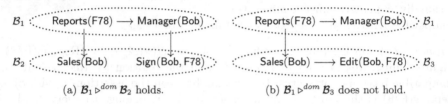

(a) $\mathcal{B}_1 \rhd^{dom} \mathcal{B}_2$ holds.   (b) $\mathcal{B}_1 \rhd^{dom} \mathcal{B}_3$ does not hold.

Fig. 3. Solid arrows represent the strict preference.

□

Before characterizing $C\pi$-repair in general, we first discuss the special case where the ABox is consistent w.r.t. the TBox, i.e., the conflict set is empty. Hence, $C\pi$-repair simply amounts to applying standard DL-Lite$_\mathcal{R}$ inference. Formally:

Lemma 1. *Let $\mathcal{K}_{\unrhd} = \langle \mathcal{T}, \mathcal{A}_{\unrhd} \rangle$ be a consistent, partially preordered KB, i.e., $\mathsf{Cf}(\mathcal{A}_{\unrhd}) = \emptyset$. Consider $cl(\cdot)$ given by Definition 3. Let φ be an assertion. Then: $c\pi(\mathcal{A}_{\unrhd}) = cl(\mathcal{A}_{\unrhd})$. Equivalently: $\varphi \in c\pi(\mathcal{A}_{\unrhd})$ iff there is $\mathcal{B} \subseteq \mathcal{A}_{\unrhd}$ s.t. $\langle \mathcal{T}, \mathcal{B} \rangle \models \varphi$.*

In the rest of this paper, we focus on the case where the ABox is inconsistent w.r.t. the TBox. Our goal is to use the notions of dominance and support (see Definitions 5 and 6) to characterize equivalently the assertions in the $C\pi$-repair. This allows to avoid enumerating all the totally preordered extensions of $\mathcal{A}_{\unrhd}$. The idea is that an assertion φ belongs to $C\pi$-repair if and only if for every conflict $\mathcal{C}$ in the ABox, there is a support $\mathcal{B}$ of φ that dominates $\mathcal{C}$. We provide two propositions to confirm this intuitive characterization.

Proposition 1. *Let $\mathcal{K}_{\unrhd} = \langle \mathcal{T}, \mathcal{A}_{\unrhd} \rangle$ be an inconsistent, partially preordered KB. Let $\mathsf{Cf}(\mathcal{A}_{\unrhd})$ be its conflict set and let φ be an assertion. If for all $\mathcal{C} \in \mathsf{Cf}(\mathcal{A}_{\unrhd})$, there is $\mathcal{B} \subseteq \mathcal{A}_{\unrhd}$ s.t.:*

1. $\mathcal{B}$ supports φ (as per Definition 5), and
2. $\mathcal{B} \rhd^{dom} \mathcal{C}$ (as per Definition 6),

then $\varphi \in c\pi(\mathcal{A}_{\unrhd})$.

We illustrate this result with our running example.

Example 5. Consider again Example 2. Let us use Proposition 1 to check that the assertion Staff(Bob) is indeed in $c\pi(\mathcal{A}_\unrhd)$. For each conflict in $\mathsf{Cf}(\mathcal{A}_\unrhd) = \{\{\mathsf{Manager(Bob)}, \mathsf{Edit(Bob, F78)}\}, \{\mathsf{Sales(Bob)}, \mathsf{Sign(Bob, F78)}\}\}$, it suffices to exhibit a dominating support for Staff(Bob), like so:

- For the conflict $\mathcal{C}_1 = \{\mathsf{Manager(Bob)}, \mathsf{Edit(Bob, F78)}\}$, $\mathcal{B}_1 = \{\mathsf{Sales(Bob)}\}$ supports Staff(Bob) and $\mathcal{B}_1 \rhd^{dom} \mathcal{C}_1$ (since Sales(Bob) $\rhd$ Edit(Bob, F78)).
- For the conflict $\mathcal{C}_2 = \{\mathsf{Sales(Bob)}, \mathsf{Sign(Bob, F78)}\}$, $\mathcal{B}_2 = \{\mathsf{Manager(Bob)}\}$ supports Staff(Bob) and $\mathcal{B}_2 \rhd^{dom} \mathcal{C}_2$ (since Manager(Bob) $\rhd$ Sign(Bob, F78)).

□

The other direction of Proposition 1, given in Proposition 2, is also true. In particular, if the characterization "for every conflict $\mathcal{C}$ in $\mathsf{Cf}(\mathcal{A}_\unrhd)$, there is a support $\mathcal{B}$ of φ in $\mathcal{A}_\unrhd$ that dominates $\mathcal{C}$" is not true, then φ cannot belong to $C\pi$-repair. The proposition also covers the particular case of an assertion without a support, which cannot belong to $C\pi$-repair.

Proposition 2. *Let $\mathcal{K}_\unrhd = \langle \mathcal{T}, \mathcal{A}_\unrhd \rangle$ be an inconsistent, partially preordered KB. Let $\mathsf{Cf}(\mathcal{A}_\unrhd)$ be its conflict set and φ be an assertion. If $\varphi \in c\pi(\mathcal{A}_\unrhd)$, then for all $\mathcal{C} \in \mathsf{Cf}(\mathcal{A}_\unrhd)$, there is $\mathcal{B} \subseteq \mathcal{A}_\unrhd$ s.t.:*

1. *$\mathcal{B}$ supports φ (as per Definition 5), and*
2. *$\mathcal{B} \rhd^{dom} \mathcal{C}$ (as per Definition 6).*

We illustrate this result with our running example.

Example 6. Let $\mathcal{K}'_\rhd = \langle \mathcal{T}', \mathcal{A}_\unrhd \rangle$, where the TBox $\mathcal{T}'$ is:

$$\mathcal{T}' = \{\mathsf{Manager} \sqsubseteq \neg \exists \mathsf{Edit}, \mathsf{Sales} \sqsubseteq \neg \exists \mathsf{Sign}, \mathsf{Sales} \sqsubseteq \mathsf{Staff}, \exists \mathsf{Edit} \sqsubseteq \mathsf{Staff}\}.$$

Thus, a manager (resp. a sales person) does not have editing (resp. signing) rights, and a sales person and a person with editing rights are staff members. The ABox $\mathcal{A}_\unrhd$ is the one of Example 1.

Consider $\mathcal{A}_{\geq_1}$ and $\mathcal{A}_{\geq_2}$ two ABoxes compatible with $\mathcal{A}_\unrhd$, and their well-ordered partitions, $\mathcal{A}_{\geq_1} = (\mathcal{S}_1 \cup \mathcal{S}_2 \cup \mathcal{S}_3 \cup \mathcal{S}_4)$ and $\mathcal{A}_{\geq_2} = (\mathcal{S}_1 \cup \mathcal{S}_2 \cup \mathcal{S}'_3 \cup \mathcal{S}'_4)$ such that: $\mathcal{S}_1 = \{\mathsf{Reports(F78)}\}$, $\mathcal{S}_2 = \{\mathsf{Manager(Bob)}\}$, $\mathcal{S}_3 = \{\mathsf{Sales(Bob)}\}$, $\mathcal{S}'_3 = \{\mathsf{Sales(Bob)}, \mathsf{Sign(Bob, F78)}\}$, $\mathcal{S}_4 = \{\mathsf{Sign(Bob, F78)}, \mathsf{Edit(Bob, F78)}\}$, and $\mathcal{S}'_4 = \{\mathsf{Edit(Bob, F78)}\}$.

Figure 4 illustrates $\mathcal{A}_\unrhd$, $\mathcal{A}_{\geq_1}$ and $\mathcal{A}_{\geq_2}$ (recall that $\equiv$ denotes equal certainty). It is easy to check that $\mathcal{A}_{\geq_1}$ and $\mathcal{A}_{\geq_2}$ are compatible with $\mathcal{A}_\unrhd$. Their associated repairs are: $\mathcal{R}(\mathcal{A}_{\geq_1}) = \{\mathsf{Reports(F78)}, \mathsf{Manager(Bob)}, \mathsf{Sales(Bob)}\}$ and $\mathcal{R}(\mathcal{A}_{\geq_2}) = \{\mathsf{Reports(F78)}, \mathsf{Manager(Bob)}\}$.

Consider the assertion Staff(Bob) and its two supports, $\mathcal{B}_1 = \{\mathsf{Sales(Bob)}\}$ and $\mathcal{B}_2 = \{\mathsf{Edit(Bob, F78)}\}$. Notice that $\mathcal{R}(\mathcal{A}_{\geq_1}) \models \mathsf{Staff(Bob)}$ but $\mathcal{R}(\mathcal{A}_{\geq_2}) \not\models \mathsf{Staff(Bob)}$. Hence, Staff(Bob) $\notin c\pi(\mathcal{A}_\unrhd)$. Proposition 2 confirms this result, since neither $\mathcal{B}_1$ nor $\mathcal{B}_2$ dominates the conflict $\{\mathsf{Sales(Bob)}, \mathsf{Sign(Bob, F78)}\}$.

□

Fig. 4. Solid arrows depict strict preference. Dashed lines show the conflicts.

Propositions 1 and 2 provide a full characterization for membership in $c\pi(\mathcal{A}_\trianglerighteq)$ based on the notions of support and dominance. The next proposition states (as expected) that $c\pi(\mathcal{A}_\trianglerighteq)$ is consistent and more productive than $\pi(\mathcal{A}_\trianglerighteq)$. Formally:

Proposition 3.

1. $\langle \mathcal{T}, c\pi(\mathcal{A}_\trianglerighteq) \rangle$ is consistent.
2. $\pi(\mathcal{A}_\trianglerighteq) \subseteq c\pi(\mathcal{A}_\trianglerighteq)$. The converse is false (i.e., $c\pi(\mathcal{A}_\trianglerighteq) \not\subseteq \pi(\mathcal{A}_\trianglerighteq)$).

Example 2 confirms that $c\pi(\mathcal{A}_\trianglerighteq) \not\subseteq \pi(\mathcal{A}_\trianglerighteq)$.

The next proposition establishes the tractability of $c\pi(\mathcal{A}_\trianglerighteq)$. This follows from the characterization given in Propositions 1 and 2, i.e., using the notions of dominance and support. Indeed, computing the conflicts and the supports can be achieved in polynomial time [10]. Besides, it can be shown that the number of conflicts and supports is bounded by $|cln(\mathcal{T})| * |\mathcal{A}_\trianglerighteq|$ (where $cln(\mathcal{T})$ denotes the negative closure of the TBox $\mathcal{T}$, i.e., all the negative axioms that can be inferred from it). Moreover, in the context of OBDA, the size of the TBox is often considered negligible compared to the size of the ABox, thus the main focus is on data complexity. Lastly, it is important to note that retrieving all the conflicts beforehand is not required. Instead, checking whether an assertion is in Cπ-repair can be performed by progressively examining the conflicts (an implementation is available at https://github.com/ahmedlaouar/py_reasoner). This incremental feature is particularly beneficial for evolving ABoxes.

Proposition 4. Let $\mathcal{K}_\trianglerighteq = \langle \mathcal{T}, \mathcal{A}_\trianglerighteq \rangle$ be a partially preordered KB and φ be an assertion. Checking if $\varphi \in c\pi(\mathcal{A}_\trianglerighteq)$ is done in polynomial time in DL-Lite$_\mathcal{R}$.

5   Rationality Properties of π-Acceptance and Cπ-Repair

In this section, we study the rationality properties of query-answering using the possibilistic repair method and its closure-based version.

Let $\mathcal{K}_\trianglerighteq = \langle \mathcal{T}, \mathcal{A}_\trianglerighteq \rangle$ be a partially preordered KB which may be inconsistent and let q be a query. Consider the KB's possibilistic repairs $\pi(\mathcal{A}_\trianglerighteq)$ (Definition 2) and $c\pi(\mathcal{A}_\trianglerighteq)$ (Definition 4).

Let us start with unconditional query-answering, which amounts to checking whether the query q follows from the repair $\pi(\mathcal{A}_{\unrhd})$ (resp. $c\pi(\mathcal{A}_{\unrhd})$), denoted with the symbol $\vDash^{\pi}$ (resp. $\vDash^{c\pi}$), and $\vDash$ denotes standard DL-Lite$_{\mathcal{R}}$ inference. Formally:

$$\mathcal{K}_{\unrhd} \vDash^{\pi} q \text{ (resp. } \mathcal{K}_{\unrhd} \vDash^{c\pi} q) \text{ iff } \langle \mathcal{T}, \pi(\mathcal{A}_{\unrhd}) \rangle \vDash q \text{ (resp. } \langle \mathcal{T}, c\pi(\mathcal{A}_{\unrhd}) \rangle \vDash q) \qquad (1)$$

The following result states that the unconditional inferences $\vDash^{\pi}$ and $\vDash^{c\pi}$ meet the rationality properties of unconditional inconsistency-tolerant semantics defined in [2]. Namely:

Proposition 5. *The unconditional possibilistic inference relation $\vDash^{s}$ (with $s \in \{\pi, c\pi\}$) satisfies the following properties:*

- **QCE** *(Query Conjunction Elimination) If $\mathcal{K}_{\unrhd} \vDash^{s} q_1 \wedge q_2$ then $\mathcal{K}_{\unrhd} \vDash^{s} q_1$ and $\mathcal{K}_{\unrhd} \vDash^{s} q_2$.*
- **QCI** *(Query Conjunction Introduction) If $\mathcal{K}_{\unrhd} \vDash^{s} q_1$ and $\mathcal{K}_{\unrhd} \vDash^{s} q_2$ then $\mathcal{K}_{\unrhd} \vDash^{s} q_1 \wedge q_2$.*
- **Cons** *(Consistency) For any set of assertions $\mathcal{B}$, if $\mathcal{K}_{\unrhd} \vDash^{s} \mathcal{B}$ then $\langle \mathcal{T}, \mathcal{B} \rangle$ is consistent.*
- **ConsC** *(Consistency of Conjunction) For any set of assertions $\mathcal{B}$, if for all $\varphi \in \mathcal{B}$, $\mathcal{K}_{\unrhd} \vDash^{s} \varphi$, then $\langle \mathcal{T}, \mathcal{B} \rangle$ is consistent.*
- **ConsS** *(Consistency of Support) For any set of assertions $\mathcal{B}$, if $\mathcal{K}_{\unrhd} \vDash^{s} \mathcal{B}$ then there is a maximally consistent subset $\mathcal{A}'$ of $\mathcal{A}_{\unrhd}$ s.t. $\langle \mathcal{T}, \mathcal{A}' \rangle \vDash \mathcal{B}$.*

The proof of Proposition 5 is immediate since it is based on a direct application of standard DL-Lite entailment to the repairs $\pi(\mathcal{A}_{\unrhd})$ (resp. $c\pi(\mathcal{A}_{\unrhd})$).

We now focus on conditional query-answering, which amounts to querying a partially preordered KB under a given set of assertions considered fully reliable and consistent with respect to the TBox, called an observation or a fully observable set and denoted by $\mathcal{O}$. We write $\mathcal{O} \mathrel{\vdash^{s}_{\mathcal{K}_{\unrhd}}} q$ to indicate that q follows from the KB $\mathcal{K}_{\unrhd}$, under the observation $\mathcal{O}$, using the inconsistency-tolerant semantics s (here $s = \pi$ for the possibilistic repair and $s = c\pi$ for its closure-based version). A standard way to proceed is to first add $\mathcal{O}$ to the ABox with the highest priority, then apply the possibilistic repair method (and its closure-based version) using Eq. 1 to unconditionally answer queries from the augmented KB.

Let us denote by $\mathcal{K}_{\mathcal{O}} = \langle \mathcal{T}, \mathcal{A}_{\unrhd_{\mathcal{O}}} \rangle$ the augmented KB where $\mathcal{A}_{\unrhd_{\mathcal{O}}} = (\mathcal{A}_{\unrhd} \cup \mathcal{O})$ results from adding $\mathcal{O}$ to $\mathcal{A}_{\unrhd}$ with the highest priority. Moreover, the partial preorder $\unrhd_{\mathcal{O}}$ over $(\mathcal{A}_{\unrhd} \cup \mathcal{O})$ is obtained from $\unrhd$ as follows:

(i) For all $\varphi_1 \in \mathcal{O}$, for all $\varphi_2 \in \mathcal{O}$: $\varphi_1 \unrhd_{\mathcal{O}} \varphi_2$ and $\varphi_2 \unrhd_{\mathcal{O}} \varphi_1$ (i.e., φ_1 and φ_2 are equally reliable).
(ii) For all $\varphi_1 \in \mathcal{O}$, for all $\varphi_2 \in \mathcal{A}_{\unrhd} \setminus \mathcal{O}$: $\varphi_1 \rhd_{\mathcal{O}} \varphi_2$ (i.e., every $\varphi_1 \in \mathcal{O}$ is strictly more preferred than any $\varphi_2 \in \mathcal{A}_{\unrhd} \setminus \mathcal{O}$. This serves to give priority to $\mathcal{O}$).
(iii) For all $\varphi_1 \in \mathcal{A}_{\unrhd} \setminus \mathcal{O}$, for all $\varphi_2 \in \mathcal{A}_{\unrhd} \setminus \mathcal{O}$: $\varphi_1 \unrhd_{\mathcal{O}} \varphi_2$ iff $\varphi_1 \unrhd \varphi_2$ (i.e., the relative ordering between the elements of $\mathcal{A}_{\unrhd}$ that are not in $\mathcal{O}$ is preserved).

Next, we define the partially preordered conditional query-answering relation.

Definition 7. *(Conditional inference) Let* $\mathcal{K}_{\trianglerighteq} = \langle \mathcal{T}, \mathcal{A}_{\trianglerighteq} \rangle$ *be a partially pre-ordered KB,* $\mathcal{O}$ *an observation and* q *a query. Then* q *follows from* $\mathcal{K}_{\trianglerighteq}$ *and* $\mathcal{O}$, *denoted* $\mathcal{O} \vdash_{\mathcal{K}_{\trianglerighteq}}^{s} q$, *if* $\mathcal{K}_{\mathcal{O}} \models^{s} q$ *(with* $s \in \{\pi, c\pi\}$), *where* $\mathcal{K}_{\mathcal{O}} = \langle \mathcal{T}, \mathcal{A}_{\trianglerighteq_{\mathcal{O}}} \rangle$ *is the augmented KB and* $\trianglerighteq_{\mathcal{O}}$ *its associated partial preorder (described in (i), (ii), (iii)), and* $\models^{s}$ *is the unconditional query-answering relation given by Eq. 1.*

One can check that $\mathcal{O} \vdash_{\mathcal{K}_{\trianglerighteq}}^{s} q$ is non-monotonic for both semantics (the possibilistic repair and its closure-based version). The well-known System P [24], originally defined in the context of propositional logic, has been adapted to DL-Lite$_{\mathcal{R}}$ in [3] (see also [14,21] for an adaptation to richer description logics).

The adaptation of System P's rules is given below, where $\mathcal{K}_{\trianglerighteq} = \langle \mathcal{T}, \mathcal{A}_{\trianglerighteq} \rangle$ is a KB, $\mathcal{O}_1$, $\mathcal{O}_2$, $\mathcal{O}_3$ are observations, s is an inconsistency-tolerant semantics with $s \in \{\pi, c\pi\}$, $\models$ and $\equiv$ denote standard DL-Lite$_{\mathcal{R}}$ inference and equivalence:

- **R** (Reflexivity) $\mathcal{O}_1 \vdash_{\mathcal{K}_{\trianglerighteq}}^{s} \mathcal{O}_1$.
- **LLE** (Left Logical Equivalence) If $\langle \mathcal{T}, \mathcal{O}_1 \rangle \equiv \langle \mathcal{T}, \mathcal{O}_2 \rangle$ and $\mathcal{O}_1 \vdash_{\mathcal{K}_{\trianglerighteq}}^{s} \mathcal{O}_3$ then $\mathcal{O}_2 \vdash_{\mathcal{K}_{\trianglerighteq}}^{s} \mathcal{O}_3$.
- **RW** (Right Weakening) If $\langle \mathcal{T}, \mathcal{O}_1 \rangle \models \langle \mathcal{T}, \mathcal{O}_2 \rangle$ and $\mathcal{O}_3 \vdash_{\mathcal{K}_{\trianglerighteq}}^{s} \mathcal{O}_1$, then $\mathcal{O}_3 \vdash_{\mathcal{K}_{\trianglerighteq}}^{s} \mathcal{O}_2$.
- **Cut** If $\mathcal{O}_1 \vdash_{\mathcal{K}_{\trianglerighteq}}^{s} \mathcal{O}_2$ and $\mathcal{O}_1 \cup \mathcal{O}_2 \vdash_{\mathcal{K}_{\trianglerighteq}}^{s} \mathcal{O}_3$, then $\mathcal{O}_1 \vdash_{\mathcal{K}_{\trianglerighteq}}^{s} \mathcal{O}_3$.
- **CM** (Cautious Monotony) If $\mathcal{O}_1 \vdash_{\mathcal{K}_{\trianglerighteq}}^{s} \mathcal{O}_2$ and $\mathcal{O}_1 \vdash_{\mathcal{K}_{\trianglerighteq}}^{s} \mathcal{O}_3$, then $\mathcal{O}_1 \cup \mathcal{O}_2 \vdash_{\mathcal{K}_{\trianglerighteq}}^{s} \mathcal{O}_3$.
- **And** If $\mathcal{O}_1 \vdash_{\mathcal{K}_{\trianglerighteq}}^{s} \mathcal{O}_2$ and $\mathcal{O}_1 \vdash_{\mathcal{K}_{\trianglerighteq}}^{s} \mathcal{O}_3$, then $\mathcal{O}_1 \vdash_{\mathcal{K}_{\trianglerighteq}}^{s} \mathcal{O}_2 \cup \mathcal{O}_3$.

In this paper, we propose to also consider two additional properties, originally defined in propositional logic, and which go beyond cautious monotony:

- **RM** (Rational Monotony) If $\mathcal{O}_1 \vdash_{\mathcal{K}_{\trianglerighteq}}^{s} \mathcal{O}_3$, then $\mathcal{O}_1 \cup \mathcal{O}_2 \vdash_{\mathcal{K}_{\trianglerighteq}}^{s} \mathcal{O}_3$ or $\langle \mathcal{T}, (\mathcal{O}_1 \cup \mathcal{O}_2 \cup \mathcal{A}_{\trianglerighteq}) \rangle$ is inconsistent.
- **Comp** (Completeness) If $\mathcal{O}_1 \vdash_{\mathcal{K}_{\trianglerighteq}}^{s} \mathcal{O}_3$, then either $\mathcal{O}_1 \cup \mathcal{O}_2 \vdash_{\mathcal{K}_{\trianglerighteq}}^{s} \mathcal{O}_3$ or $\langle \mathcal{T}, (\mathcal{O}_1 \cup \mathcal{O}_2 \cup \mathcal{O}_3 \cup \mathcal{A}_{\trianglerighteq}) \rangle$ is inconsistent.

Note that the adaptation of the last two properties that we propose uses the notion of inconsistency instead of negation in the original definition of rational monotony, and uses a disjunctive interpretation of **RM**[6]. Here, **RM** states that given a new observation, we can continue to believe in the previous plausible consequences of the KB, or the new observation conflicts with the KB. The **Comp** rule[7] is stronger than **RM**, and states that given a new observation $\mathcal{O}_2$, then either $\mathcal{O}_3$ continues to be derived from both $\mathcal{O}_1$ and $\mathcal{O}_2$, or $\mathcal{O}_2$ contradicts the whole KB (plus itself). Intuitively, this means that either we continue to believe in $\mathcal{O}_3$, or we should believe in its negation (there is no room for ignoring $\mathcal{O}_3$).

The next proposition summarizes the results of the conditional properties:

---

[6] In propositional logic (PL), **RM** is defined as: if $\alpha \vdash_{\mathcal{K}} \gamma$ and $\alpha \not\vdash_{\mathcal{K}} \neg\beta$, then $\alpha \wedge \beta \vdash_{\mathcal{K}} \gamma$, where α, β and γ are PL formulas. Our adaptation consists first in rewriting **RM** equivalently in a disjunctive way: if $\alpha \vdash_{\mathcal{K}} \gamma$, then $\alpha \wedge \beta \vdash_{\mathcal{K}} \gamma$ or $\alpha \vdash_{\mathcal{K}} \neg\beta$. Lastly, we replace $\alpha \vdash_{\mathcal{K}} \neg\beta$ with $\alpha \wedge \beta$ is inconsistent with the KB.

[7] In PL, **Comp** is defined as: if $\alpha \vdash_{\mathcal{K}} \gamma$, then either $\alpha \wedge \beta \vdash_{\mathcal{K}} \gamma$ or $\alpha \wedge \beta \vdash_{\mathcal{K}} \neg\gamma$. Here, we simply replace $\alpha \wedge \beta \vdash_{\mathcal{K}} \neg\gamma$ with $\alpha \wedge \beta \wedge \gamma$ is inconsistent with the KB.

Proposition 6. *Let* $\mathcal{K}_{\unrhd} = \langle \mathcal{T}, \mathcal{A}_{\unrhd} \rangle$ *be a partially preordered KB,* $\mathcal{O}$ *be an observation and* q *be a query. The query-answering relations* $\vdash^{\pi}_{\mathcal{K}_{\unrhd}}$ *and* $\vdash^{c\pi}_{\mathcal{K}_{\unrhd}}$ *satisfy the properties* ***R, LLE, RW, Cut, CM*** *and* ***And.*** *However, they fail to satisfy* ***RM*** *and* ***Comp.***

6 Concluding Discussions

Developing tractable and safe methods for inconsistency management is a challenge and is crucial for dealing with inconsistent large-scale knowledge bases. This paper follows this research line where we tackled the issue of computing a productive repair for possibilistic partially preordered ontologies. We defined the $C\pi$-repair method which interprets a partial preorder into a family of compatible ABoxes, computes their possibilistic repairs, closes those repairs and intersects them to yield a more productive repair.

An important result of this paper is that we characterized this method equivalently using the notions of dominance and support, which ensures the tractable calculation of the repair. This characterization can be generalized easily to more expressive description languages (it suffices to replace the DL-Lite$_{\mathcal{R}}$ inference relation in the support definition by that of a more expressive language). However, tractability is guaranteed only if the computation of the conflicts and supports is performed in polynomial time and their size remains polynomial in the ABoxe's size (a detailed discussion is given below). A future work is to characterize the linear repair [26] and the Elect [6] methods to partially preordered ABoxes.

We conclude this paper with a few discussion points on the rational properties as well as on the possibility of generalizing our method to richer languages or other inconsistency-tolerant semantics.

On the Rational Properties: The two possibilistic semantics studied in this paper satisfy the unconditional properties (Proposition 5) and the rules of System P (Proposition 6). If these propositions seem natural, even minimal, they are not always satisfied by some inconsistency-tolerant semantics. For example, the so-called majority semantics (a query is valid if it is obtained from the majority of the repairs of an inconsistent ABox) does not satisfy these minimal properties. More precisely, in [3] it has been shown that majority-based inference does not satisfy Cut, Cautious Monotony, and And properties, even in DL-Lite$_{\mathcal{R}}$. Another example where System P is not satisfied is existential inference, where a query is valid if it follows from one repair.

On the non-satisfaction of the rational monotony (RM) property, the result is expected if we draw a parallel with standard possibilistic propositional logic (LP) and with the properties of non-monotonic relations. Indeed, there is a representation theorem (KLM [24]) which shows that any non-monotonic relation which satisfies System P and RM is necessarily representable by a total order on the set of interpretations of propositional logic.

On the Extension to Richer Languages: From a semantic point of view, the definitions of $C\pi$-repair given in Sect. 3, that have been established within the framework of DL-Lite$_\mathcal{R}$, remain valid for richer languages (provided that the notion of deductive closure of an ABox with respect to a TBox can be defined). Indeed, the general process given in Fig. 2 is not proper to DL-Lite$_\mathcal{R}$ and easily applies to richer languages (e.g. Existential Rules). The challenge here is at the computational level, since we need first to find an equivalent characterization (like we did in this paper using support/dominance) and then show that it is tractable. For instance, in many description logics where conflicts may be composed of any number of assertions (unlike DL-Lite where conflicts consist of at most two assertions [16]), the extension of the support/dominance characterization is possible. However, even if the conflict set is computed in polynomial time, the size of this set itself can be exponential w.r.t. the size of the ABox. In this case, tractability cannot be preserved.

Furthermore, the main idea behind query-answering from inconsistent partially ordered knowledge bases is to extend the partial order into the set of its compatible total orders, then to apply a repair semantics to each one of them. The strategy we used in our approach (based on the possibilistic version of DL-Lite$_\mathcal{R}$) yields a single repair for each total order. However, in the general case, using a different strategy, each total order may return multiple repairs. Hence, a query needs to follow from all the repairs for all the compatible total orders.

On the Extension to Non-repair Based Semantics: We end this paper with a brief discussion on the applicability of inconsistency-tolerant semantics that are not directly based on repairs, such as paraconsistent multi-valued description logics, on partially ordered ABoxes. Let us first specify that an advantage of our approach is that once the possibilistic repair $C\pi$-repair is calculated, query-answering is done in a standard way. Within multi-valued semantics, the ABox remains unchanged, but the query-answering mechanisms need to be adapted and this can potentially generate an additional computational cost. Besides, from a semantic point of view, it is possible to redefine this work with multi-valued semantics. This can be done by first selecting a multi-valued semantics of DL-Lite$_\mathcal{R}$ (for example the 4-valued semantics given in [30]). The next step consists in extending it to the possibilistic framework with a totally ordered ABox. This requires an adaptation of the existing work (for flat ABox) to define preferred 4-valued canonical models. The last step consists in taking all the extensions of the total orders and defining the 4-valued canonical models of the partial ABox as the union of the preferred 4-valued canonical model of each total ABox extension. However, having an equivalent characterization (without generating all the extensions of the partial order) to the one given in this paper (Propositions 1 and 2), is not obvious to achieve.

Acknowledgements. This research has received support from the European Union's Horizon research and innovation programme under the MSCA-SE (Marie Skłodowska-Curie Actions Staff Exchange) grant agreement 101086252; Call: HORIZON-MSCA-2021-SE-01; Project title: STARWARS (STormwAteR and WastewAteR networkS heterogeneous data AI-driven management).

This research has also received support from the French national project ANR (Agence Nationale de la Recherche) EXPIDA (EXplainable and parsimonious Preference models to get the most out of Inconsistent DAtabases), grant number ANR-22-CE23-0017 and from the ANR project Vivah (Vers une intelligence artificielle à visage humain), grant number ANR-20-THIA-0004.

References

1. Artale, A., Calvanese, D., Kontchakov, R., Zakharyaschev, M.: The DL-Lite family and relations. J. Artif. Intell. Res. (JAIR) **36**, 1–69 (2009). https://doi.org/10.1613/jair.2820
2. Baget, J., et al.: A general modifier-based framework for inconsistency-tolerant query answering. In: Principles of Knowledge Representation and Reasoning (KR), Cape Town, South Africa, pp. 513–516 (2016)
3. Baget, J.F., et al.: Inconsistency-tolerant query answering: rationality properties and computational complexity analysis. In: Michael, L., Kakas, A. (eds.) JELIA 2016. LNCS (LNAI), vol. 10021, pp. 64–80. Springer, Cham (2016). https://doi.org/10.1007/978-3-319-48758-8_5
4. Banerjee, M., Dubois, D., Godo, L., Prade, H.: On the relation between possibilistic logic and modal logics of belief and knowledge. J. Appl. Non-Classical Logics **27**(3–4), 206–224 (2017)
5. Belabbes, S., Benferhat, S.: Computing a possibility theory repair for partially preordered inconsistent ontologies. IEEE Trans. Fuzzy Syst. **30**, 3237–3246 (2021)
6. Belabbes, S., Benferhat, S., Chomicki, J.: Handling inconsistency in partially preordered ontologies: the Elect method. J. Log. Comput. **31**(5), 1356–1388 (2021)
7. Benferhat, S., Bouraoui, Z., Tabia, K.: How to select one preferred assertional-based repair from inconsistent and prioritized DL-Lite knowledge bases? In: International Joint Conference on Artificial Intelligence (IJCAI), Buenos Aires, Argentina, pp. 1450–1456 (2015)
8. Benferhat, S., Garcia, L.: Handling locally stratified inconsistent knowledge bases. Stud. Logica. **70**(1), 77–104 (2002)
9. Bienvenu, M.: On the complexity of consistent query answering in the presence of simple ontologies. In: Proceedings of the Twenty-Sixth AAAI Conference on Artificial Intelligence, Toronto, Ontario, Canada (2012)
10. Bienvenu, M., Bourgaux, C.: Inconsistency-tolerant querying of description logic knowledge bases. In: Pan, J.Z., et al. (eds.) Reasoning Web 2016. LNCS, vol. 9885, pp. 156–202. Springer, Cham (2017). https://doi.org/10.1007/978-3-319-49493-7_5
11. Bienvenu, M., Bourgaux, C.: Querying and repairing inconsistent prioritized knowledge bases: complexity analysis and links with abstract argumentation. In: Principles of Knowledge Representation and Reasoning (KR), Virtual Event, pp. 141–151 (2020)
12. Bienvenu, M., Bourgaux, C., Goasdoué, F.: Querying inconsistent description logic knowledge bases under preferred repair semantics. In: AAAI, pp. 996–1002 (2014)
13. Brewka, G.: Preferred subtheories: an extended logical framework for default reasoning. In: IJCAI, Detroit, USA, pp. 1043–1048 (1989)
14. Britz, K., Casini, G., Meyer, T., Moodley, K., Sattler, U., Varzinczak, I.: Principles of KLM-style defeasible description logics. ACM Trans. Comput. Log. **22**(1), 1:1–1:46 (2021)
15. Calvanese, D., De Giacomo, G., Lembo, D., Lenzerini, M., Rosati, R.: Tractable reasoning and efficient query answering in description logics: the DL-Lite family. J. Autom. Reason. **39**(3), 385–429 (2007)

16. Calvanese, D., Kharlamov, E., Nutt, W., Zheleznyakov, D.: Evolution of *DL-Lite* knowledge bases. In: Patel-Schneider, P.F., et al. (eds.) ISWC 2010. LNCS, vol. 6496, pp. 112–128. Springer, Heidelberg (2010). https://doi.org/10.1007/978-3-642-17746-0_8

17. Dempster, A.P.: Upper and lower probabilities induced by a multivalued mapping. Ann. Math. Stat. **38**, 325–339 (1967)

18. Dubois, D., Prade, H.: Possibilistic logic - an overview. Comput. Logic **9**, 197–255 (2014)

19. Dubois, D., Prade, H.: A crash course on generalized possibilistic logic. In: Ciucci, D., Pasi, G., Vantaggi, B. (eds.) SUM 2018. LNCS (LNAI), vol. 11142, pp. 3–17. Springer, Cham (2018). https://doi.org/10.1007/978-3-030-00461-3_1

20. Dubois, D., Prade, H., Schockaert, S.: Generalized possibilistic logic: foundations and applications to qualitative reasoning about uncertainty. Artif. Intell. J. **252**, 139–174 (2017)

21. Everett, L., Morris, E., Meyer, T.: Explanation for KLM-style defeasible reasoning. In: Jembere, E., Gerber, A.J., Viriri, S., Pillay, A. (eds.) SACAIR 2021. CCIS, vol. 1551, pp. 192–207. Springer, Cham (2022). https://doi.org/10.1007/978-3-030-95070-5_13

22. Fagin, R., Halpern, J.Y., Moses, Y., Vardi, M.Y.: Reasoning About Knowledge. MIT Press, Cambridge (2003)

23. Finger, M., Godo, L., Prade, H., Qi, G.: Advances in weighted logics for artificial intelligence. Int. J. Approximate Reasoning **88**, 385–386 (2017)

24. Kraus, S., Lehmann, D., Magidor, M.: Nonmonotonic reasoning, preferential models and cumulative logics. Artif. Intell. J. **44**(1–2), 167–207 (1990)

25. Lembo, D., Lenzerini, M., Rosati, R., Ruzzi, M., Savo, D.F.: Inconsistency-tolerant semantics for description logics. In: Hitzler, P., Lukasiewicz, T. (eds.) RR 2010. LNCS, vol. 6333, pp. 103–117. Springer, Heidelberg (2010). https://doi.org/10.1007/978-3-642-15918-3_9

26. Nebel, B.: Base revision operations and schemes: semantics, representation and complexity. In: European Conference on Artificial Intelligence, pp. 341–345 (1994)

27. Poggi, A., Lembo, D., Calvanese, D., Giacomo, G.D., Lenzerini, M., Rosati, R.: Linking data to ontologies. J. Data Semant. **10**, 133–173 (2008)

28. Shafer, G.: A Mathematical Theory of Evidence. Princeton University Press, Princeton (1976)

29. Spohn, W.: The Laws of Belief - Ranking Theory and Its Philosophical Applications. Oxford University Press, Oxford (2014)

30. Zhou, L., Huang, H., Qi, G., Ma, Y., Huang, Z., Qu, Y.: Paraconsistent query answering over DL-Lite ontologies. Web Intell. Agent Syst. Int. J. **10**(1), 19–31 (2012)

Derivation-Graph-Based Characterizations of Decidable Existential Rule Sets*

Tim S. Lyon$^{(\boxtimes)}$ and Sebastian Rudolph

Computational Logic Group, TU Dresden, Dresden, Germany
{timothy_stephen.lyon,sebastian.rudolph}@tu-dresden.de

Abstract. This paper establishes alternative characterizations of very expressive classes of existential rule sets with decidable query entailment. We consider the notable class of greedy bounded-treewidth sets (**gbts**) and a new, generalized variant, called weakly gbts (**wgbts**). Revisiting and building on the notion of derivation graphs, we define (weakly) cycle-free derivation graph sets ((**w**)**cdgs**) and employ elaborate proof-theoretic arguments to obtain that **gbts** and **cdgs** coincide, as do **wgbts** and **wcdgs**. These novel characterizations advance our analytic proof-theoretic understanding of existential rules and will likely be instrumental in practice.

Keywords: TGDs · query entailment · bounded treewidth · proof-theory

1 Introduction

The formalism of existential rules has come to prominence as an effective approach for both specifying and querying knowledge. Within this context, a knowledge base takes the form $\mathcal{K} = (\mathcal{D}, \mathcal{R})$, where $\mathcal{D}$ is a finite collection of atomic facts (called a *database*) and $\mathcal{R}$ is a finite set of *existential rules* (called a *rule set*), which are first-order formulae of the form $\forall \mathbf{xy}(\varphi(\mathbf{x}, \mathbf{y}) \rightarrow \exists \mathbf{z} \psi(\mathbf{y}, \mathbf{z}))$. Although existential rules are written in a relatively simple language, they are expressive enough to generalize many important languages used in knowledge representation, including rule-based formalisms as well as such based on description logics. Moreover, existential rules have meaningful applications within the domain of ontology-based query answering [2], data exchange and integration [9], and have proven beneficial in the study of general decidability criteria [10].

The *Boolean conjunctive query entailment problem* consists of taking a knowledge base $\mathcal{K}$, a Boolean conjunctive query (BCQ) q, and determining if $\mathcal{K} \models q$. As this problem is known to be undecidable for arbitrary rule sets [7], much work has gone into identifying existential rule fragments for which decidability can be reclaimed. Typically, such classes of rule sets are described in one of two ways: either, a rule set's membership in said class can be established through easily verifiable *syntactic properties* (such classes are called *concrete classes*), or the property is more *abstract* (which is often defined on the basis of semantic

---

* Work supported by the ERC through Consolidator Grant 771779 (DeciGUT).

S. Gaggl et al. (Eds.): JELIA 2023, LNAI 14281, pp. 369–384, 2023.
https://doi.org/10.1007/978-3-031-43619-2_26

notions) and may be hard or even impossible to algorithmically determine (such classes are called *abstract classes*). Examples of concrete classes include functional/inclusion dependencies [11], datalog, and guarded rules [6]. Examples of abstract classes include finite expansion sets [4], finite unification sets [3], and bounded-treewidth sets (**bts**) [6].

Yet, there is another means of establishing the decidability of query entailment: only limited work has gone into identifying classes of rule sets with decidable query entailment based on their *proof-theoretic characteristics*, in particular, based on specifics of the derivations such rules produce. To the best of our knowledge, only the class of *greedy bounded treewidth sets* (**gbts**) has been identified in such a manner (see [14]). A rule set qualifies as **gbts** when every derivation it produces is *greedy*, in a sense that it is possible to construct a tree decomposition of finite width in a "greedy" fashion alongside the derivation, ensuring the existence of a model with finite treewidth for the knowledge base under consideration, thus warranting the decidability of query entailment [6].

In this paper, we investigate the **gbts** class and three new classes of rule sets where decidability is determined proof-theoretically. First, we define a weakened version of **gbts**, dubbed **wgbts**, where the rule set need only produce *at least one greedy derivation* relative to any given database. Second, we investigate two new classes of rule sets, dubbed *cycle-free derivation graph sets* (**cdgs**) and *weakly cycle-free derivation graph sets* (**wcdgs**), which are defined relative to the notion of a *derivation graph*. Derivation graphs were introduced by Baget et al. [5] and are directed acyclic graphs encoding *how* certain facts are derived in the course of a derivation. Notably, via the application of *reduction operations*, a derivation graph may be reduced to a tree, which serves as a tree decomposition of a model of the considered knowledge base. Such objects helped establish that (weakly) frontier-guarded rule sets are **bts** [5]. In short, our key contributions are (Fig. 1):

1. We investigate how proof-theoretic structures gives rise to decidable query entailment and propose three new classes of rule sets.
2. We show that **gbts** = **cdgs** and **wgbts** = **wcdgs**, establishing a correspondence between greedy derivations and reducible derivation graphs.
3. We show that **wgbts** *properly subsumes* **gbts** via a novel proof transformation argument. Therefore, by the former point, we also find that **wcdgs** properly subsumes **cdgs**.

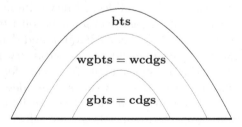

Fig. 1. A graphic depicting the containment relations between the classes of rule sets considered. The solid edges represent strict containment relations.

The paper is organized accordingly: In Section 2, we define preliminary notions. We study **gbts** and **wgbts** in Section 3, and show that the latter class properly subsumes the former via an intricate proof transformation argument. In Section 4, we define **cdgs** and **wcdgs** as well as show that **gbts** = **cdgs** and **wgbts** = **wcdgs**. In Section 5, we conclude and discuss future work. Last, we note that full proofs can be found in the appended version [12].

2 Preliminaries

Syntax and formulae. We let **Ter** be a set of *terms*, which is the the union of three countably infinite, pairwise disjoint sets, namely, the set of *constants* **Con**, the set of *variables* **Var**, and the set of *nulls* **Nul**. We use a, b, c, ... (occasionally annotated) to denote constants, and x, y, z, ... (occasionally annotated) to denote both variables and nulls. A *signature* Σ is a set of *predicates* p, q, r, ... (which may be annotated) such that for each $p \in \Sigma$, $ar(p) \in \mathbb{N}$ is the *arity* of p. For simplicity, we assume a fixed signature Σ throughout the paper.

An *atom* over Σ is defined to be a formula of the form $p(t_1, \ldots, t_n)$, where $p \in \Sigma$, $ar(p) = n$, and $t_i \in$ **Ter** for each $i \in \{1, \ldots, n\}$. A *ground atom* over Σ is an atom $p(a_1, \ldots, a_n)$ such that $a_i \in$ **Con** for each $i \in \{1, \ldots, n\}$. We will often use $\mathbf{t}$ to denote a tuple $(t_1, \ldots, t_n)$ of terms and $p(\mathbf{t})$ to denote a (ground) atom $p(t_1, \ldots, t_n)$. An *instance* over Σ is defined to be a (potentially infinite) set $\mathcal{I}$ of atoms over constants and nulls, and a *database* $\mathcal{D}$ is a finite set of ground atoms. We let $\mathcal{X}$, $\mathcal{Y}$, ... (occasionally annotated) denote (potentially infinite) sets of atoms with **Ter**$(\mathcal{X})$, **Con**$(\mathcal{X})$, **Var**$(\mathcal{X})$, and **Nul**$(\mathcal{X})$ denoting the set of terms, constants, variables, and nulls occurring in the atoms of $\mathcal{X}$, respectively.

Substitutions and homomorphisms. A *substitution* is a partial function over the set of terms **Ter**. A *homomorphism* h from a set $\mathcal{X}$ of atoms to a set $\mathcal{Y}$ of atoms, is a substitution $h :$ **Ter**$(\mathcal{X}) \rightarrow$ **Ter**$(\mathcal{Y})$ such that (i) $p(h(t_1), \ldots, h(t_n)) \in \mathcal{Y}$, if $p(t_1, \ldots, t_n) \in \mathcal{X}$, and (ii) $h(a) = a$ for each $a \in$ **Con**. If h is a homomorphism from $\mathcal{X}$ to $\mathcal{Y}$, we say that h *homomorphically maps* $\mathcal{X}$ to $\mathcal{Y}$. Atom sets $\mathcal{X}, \mathcal{Y}$ are *homomorphically equivalent*, written $\mathcal{X} \equiv \mathcal{Y}$, iff $\mathcal{X}$ homomorphically maps to $\mathcal{Y}$, and vice versa. An *isomorphism* is a bijective homomorphism h where h^{-1} is a homomorphism.

Existential rules. Whereas databases encode assertional knowledge, ontologies consist in the current setting of *existential rules*, which we will frequently refer to as *rules* more simply. An existential rule is a first-order sentence of the form:

$$\rho = \forall \mathbf{xy}(\varphi(\mathbf{x}, \mathbf{y}) \rightarrow \exists \mathbf{z} \psi(\mathbf{y}, \mathbf{z}))$$

where $\mathbf{x}$, $\mathbf{y}$, and $\mathbf{z}$ are pairwise disjoint collections of variables, $\varphi(\mathbf{x}, \mathbf{y})$ is a conjunction of atoms over constants and the variables $\mathbf{x}, \mathbf{y}$, and $\psi(\mathbf{y}, \mathbf{z})$ is a conjunction of atoms over constants and the variables $\mathbf{y}, \mathbf{z}$. We define $body(\rho) = \varphi(\mathbf{x}, \mathbf{y})$ to be the *body* of ρ, and $head(\rho) = \psi(\mathbf{y}, \mathbf{z})$ to be the *head* of ρ. For convenience, we will often interpret a conjunction $p_1(\mathbf{t}_1) \wedge \cdots \wedge p_n(\mathbf{t}_n)$ of atoms (such as the body or head of a rule) as a set $\{p_1(\mathbf{t}_1), \cdots, p_n(\mathbf{t}_n)\}$ of atoms; if h is a homomorphism, then $h(p_1(\mathbf{t}_1) \wedge \cdots \wedge p_n(\mathbf{t}_n)) := \{p_1(h(\mathbf{t}_1)), \cdots, p_n(h(\mathbf{t}_n))\}$ with h applied componentwise to each tuple $\mathbf{t}_i$ of terms. The *frontier* of ρ, written $fr(\rho)$, is the set of variables $\mathbf{y}$ that the body and head of ρ have in common, that is, $fr(\rho) = \mathbf{Var}(body(\rho)) \cap \mathbf{Var}(head(\rho))$. We define a *frontier atom* in a rule ρ to be an atom containing at least one frontier variable. We use ρ and annotated versions thereof to denote rules, as well as $\mathcal{R}$ and annotated versions thereof to denote finite sets of rules (simply called *rule sets*).

Models. We note that sets of atoms (which include instances and databases) may be seen as first-order interpretations, and so, we may use $\models$ to represent the satisfaction of formulae on such structures. A set of atoms $\mathcal{X}$ satisfies a set of atoms $\mathcal{Y}$ (or, equivalently, $\mathcal{X}$ is a model of $\mathcal{Y}$), written $\mathcal{X} \models \mathcal{Y}$, *iff* there exists a homomorphic mapping from $\mathcal{Y}$ to $\mathcal{X}$. A set of atoms $\mathcal{X}$ satisfies a rule ρ (or, equivalently, $\mathcal{X}$ is a model of ρ), written $\mathcal{X} \models \rho$, *iff* for any homomorphism h, if h is a homomorphism from $body(\rho)$ to $\mathcal{X}$, then it can be extended to a homomorphism $\overline{h}$ that also maps $head(\rho)$ to $\mathcal{X}$. A set of atoms $\mathcal{X}$ satisfies a rule set $\mathcal{R}$ (or, equivalently, $\mathcal{X}$ is a model of $\mathcal{R}$), written $\mathcal{X} \models \mathcal{R}$, *iff* $\mathcal{X} \models \rho$ for every rule $\rho \in \mathcal{R}$. If a model $\mathcal{X}$ of a set of atoms, a rule, or a rule set homomorphically maps into *every* model of that very set of atoms, rule, or rule set, then we refer to $\mathcal{X}$ as a *universal model* of that set of atoms, rule, or rule set [8].

Knowledge bases and querying. A *knowledge base (KB)* $\mathcal{K}$ is defined to be a pair $(\mathcal{D}, \mathcal{R})$, where $\mathcal{D}$ is a database and $\mathcal{R}$ is a rule set. An instance $\mathcal{I}$ is a *model* of $\mathcal{K} = (\mathcal{D}, \mathcal{R})$ *iff* $\mathcal{D} \subseteq \mathcal{I}$ and $\mathcal{I} \models \mathcal{R}$. We consider querying knowledge bases with *conjunctive queries (CQs)*, that is, with formulae of the form $q(\mathbf{y}) = \exists\mathbf{x}\varphi(\mathbf{x}, \mathbf{y})$, where $\varphi(\mathbf{x}, \mathbf{y})$ is a non-empty conjunction of atoms over the variables $\mathbf{x}, \mathbf{y}$ and constants. We refer to the variables $\mathbf{y}$ in $q(\mathbf{y})$ as *free* and define a *Boolean conjunctive query (BCQ)* to be a CQ without free variables, i.e. a BCQ is a CQ of the form $q = \exists\mathbf{x}\varphi(\mathbf{x})$. A knowledge base $\mathcal{K} = (\mathcal{D}, \mathcal{R})$ *entails* a CQ $q(\mathbf{y}) = \exists\mathbf{x}\varphi(\mathbf{x}, \mathbf{y})$, written $\mathcal{K} \models q(\mathbf{y})$, *iff* $\varphi(\mathbf{x}, \mathbf{y})$ homomorphically maps into every model $\mathcal{I}$ of $\mathcal{K}$; we note that this is equivalent to $\varphi(\mathbf{x}, \mathbf{y})$ homomorphically mapping into a universal model of $\mathcal{D}$ and $\mathcal{R}$.

As we are interested in extracting implicit knowledge from the explicit knowledge presented in a knowledge base $\mathcal{K} = (\mathcal{D}, \mathcal{R})$, we are interested in deciding the *BCQ entailment problem*:[1]

(BCQ Entailment) Given a KB $\mathcal{K}$ and a BCQ q, is it the case that $\mathcal{K} \models q$?

While it is well-known that the BCQ entailment problem is undecidable in general [7], restricting oneself to certain classes of rule sets (e.g. datalog or finite unification sets [5]) may recover decidability. We refer to classes of rule sets for which BCQ entailment is decidable as *query-decidable classes*.

Derivations. One means by which we can extract implicit knowledge from a given KB is through the use of *derivations*, that is, sequences of instances

---

[1] We recall that entailment of non-Boolean CQs or even query answering can all be reduced to BCQ entailment in logarithmic space.

obtained by sequentially applying rules to given data. We say that a rule $\rho = \forall \mathbf{xy}(\varphi(\mathbf{x}, \mathbf{y}) \rightarrow \exists \mathbf{z} \psi(\mathbf{y}, \mathbf{z}))$ is *triggered* in an instance $\mathcal{I}$ via a homomorphism h, written succinctly as $\tau(\rho, \mathcal{I}, h)$, iff h homomorphically maps $\varphi(\mathbf{x}, \mathbf{y})$ to $\mathcal{I}$. In this case, we define

$$\mathbf{Ch}(\mathcal{I}, \rho, h) = \mathcal{I} \cup \overline{h}(\psi(\mathbf{y}, \mathbf{z})),$$

where $\overline{h}$ is an extension of h mapping every variable z in $\mathbf{z}$ to a fresh null. Consequently, we define an $\mathcal{R}$-*derivation* to be a sequence $\mathcal{I}_0, (\rho_1, h_1, \mathcal{I}_1), \ldots, (\rho_n, h_n, \mathcal{I}_n)$ such that (i) $\rho_i \in \mathcal{R}$ for each $i \in \{1, \ldots, n\}$, (ii) $\tau(\rho_i, \mathcal{I}_{i-1}, h_i)$ holds for $i \in \{1, \ldots, n\}$, and (iii) $\mathcal{I}_i = \mathbf{Ch}(\mathcal{I}_{i-1}, \rho, h_i)$ for $i \in \{1, \ldots, n\}$. We will use δ and annotations thereof to denote $\mathcal{R}$-derivations, and we define the length of an $\mathcal{R}$-derivation $\delta = \mathcal{I}_0, (\rho_1, h_1, \mathcal{I}_1), \ldots, (\rho_n, h_n, \mathcal{I}_n)$, denoted $|\delta|$, to be n. Furthermore, for instances $\mathcal{I}$ and $\mathcal{I}'$, we write $\mathcal{I} \xrightarrow{\delta}_{\mathcal{R}} \mathcal{I}'$ to mean that there exists an $\mathcal{R}$-derivation δ of $\mathcal{I}'$ from $\mathcal{I}$. Also, if $\mathcal{I}''$ can be derived from $\mathcal{I}'$ by means of a rule $\rho \in \mathcal{R}$ and homomorphism h, we abuse notation and write $\mathcal{I} \xrightarrow{\delta}_{\mathcal{R}} \mathcal{I}', (\rho, h, \mathcal{I}'')$ to indicate that $\mathcal{I} \xrightarrow{\delta}_{\mathcal{R}} \mathcal{I}'$ and $\mathcal{I}' \xrightarrow{\delta'}_{\mathcal{R}} \mathcal{I}''$ with $\delta' = \mathcal{I}', (\rho, h, \mathcal{I}'')$. Derivations play a fundamental role in this paper as we aim to identify (and analyze the relationships between) query-decidable classes of rule sets based on *how* such rule sets derive information, i.e. we are interested in classes of rule sets that may be *proof-theoretically characterized*.

Chase. A tool that will prove useful in the current work is the *chase*, which in our setting is a procedure that (in essence) simultaneously constructs all $\mathcal{K}$-derivations in a breadth-first manner. Although many variants of the chase exist [5,9,13], we utilize the chase procedure (also called the k-*Saturation*) from Baget et al. [5]. We use the chase in the current work as a purely technical tool for obtaining universal models of knowledge bases, proving useful in separating certain query-decidable classes of rule sets.

We define the *one-step application* of all triggered rules from some $\mathcal{R}$ in $\mathcal{I}$ by

$$\mathbf{Ch}_1(\mathcal{I}, \mathcal{R}) = \bigcup_{\rho \in \mathcal{R}, \tau(\rho, \mathcal{I}, h)} \mathbf{Ch}(\mathcal{I}, \rho, h),$$

assuming all nulls introduced in the "parallel" applications of $\mathbf{Ch}$ to $\mathcal{I}$ are distinct. We let $\mathbf{Ch}_0(\mathcal{I}, \mathcal{R}) = \mathcal{I}$, as well as let $\mathbf{Ch}_{i+1}(\mathcal{I}, \mathcal{R}) = \mathbf{Ch}_1(\mathbf{Ch}_i(\mathcal{I}, \mathcal{R}), \mathcal{R})$, and define the *chase* to be

$$\mathbf{Ch}_\infty(\mathcal{I}, \mathcal{R}) = \bigcup_{i \in \mathbb{N}} \mathbf{Ch}_i(\mathcal{I}, \mathcal{R}).$$

For any KB $\mathcal{K} = (\mathcal{D}, \mathcal{R})$, the chase $\mathbf{Ch}_\infty(\mathcal{D}, \mathcal{R})$ is a universal model of $\mathcal{K}$, that is, $\mathcal{D} \subseteq \mathbf{Ch}_\infty(\mathcal{D}, \mathcal{R})$, $\mathbf{Ch}_\infty(\mathcal{D}, \mathcal{R}) \models \mathcal{R}$, and $\mathbf{Ch}_\infty(\mathcal{D}, \mathcal{R})$ homomorphically maps into every model of $\mathcal{D}$ and $\mathcal{R}$.

Rule dependence. Let ρ and ρ' be rules. We say that ρ' *depends* on ρ iff there exists an instance $\mathcal{I}$ such that (i) ρ' is not triggered in $\mathcal{I}$ via any homomorphism, (ii) ρ is triggered in $\mathcal{I}$ via a homomorphism h, and (iii) ρ' is triggered in $\mathbf{Ch}(\mathcal{I}, \rho, h)$ via a homomorphism h'. We define the *graph of rule dependencies* [1] of a set $\mathcal{R}$ of rules to be $G(\mathcal{R}) = (V, E)$ such that (i) $V = \mathcal{R}$ and (ii) $(\rho, \rho') \in E$ iff ρ' depends on ρ.

Treewidth. A *tree decomposition* of an instance $\mathcal{I}$ is defined to be a tree $T = (V, E)$ such that $V \subseteq 2^{\mathbf{Ter}(\mathcal{I})}$ (where each element of V is called a *bag*) and $E \subseteq V \times V$, satisfying the following three conditions: (i) $\bigcup_{X \in V} X = \mathbf{Ter}(\mathcal{I})$, (ii) for each $p(t_1, \ldots, t_n) \in \mathcal{I}$, there is an $X \in V$ such that $\{t_1, \ldots, t_n\} \subseteq X$, and (iii) for each $t \in \mathbf{Ter}(\mathcal{I})$, the subgraph of T induced by the bags $X \in V$ with $t \in X$ is connected (this condition is referred to as the *connectedness condition*). We define the *width* of a tree decomposition $T = (V, E)$ of an instance $\mathcal{I}$ as follows:

$$w(T) := \max\{|X| : X \in V\} - 1$$

i.e. the width is equal to the cardinality of the largest node in T minus 1. We let $w(T) = \infty$ *iff* for all $n \in \mathbb{N}$, $n \leq \max\{|X| : X \in V\}$. We define the *treewidth* of an instance $\mathcal{I}$, written $tw(\mathcal{I})$, as follows:

$$tw(\mathcal{I}) := \min\{w(T) : T \text{ is a tree decomposition of } \mathcal{I}\}$$

i.e. the treewidth of an instance equals the minimal width among all its tree decompositions. If no tree decomposition of $\mathcal{I}$ has finite width, we set $tw(\mathcal{I}) = \infty$.

3 Greediness

We now discuss a property of derivations referred to as *greediness*. In essence, a derivation is greedy when the image of the frontier of any applied rule consists solely of constants from a given KB and/or nulls introduced by a *single* previous rule application. Such derivations were defined by Thomazo et al. [14] and were used to identify the (query-decidable) class of *greedy bounded-treewidth sets* (**gbts**), that is, the class of rule sets that produce only *greedy derivations* (defined below) when applied to a database.

In this section, we also identify a new query-decidable class of rule sets, referred to as *weakly greedy bounded-treewidth sets* (**wgbts**). The **wgbts** class serves as a more liberal version of **gbts**, and contains rule sets that admit at least one greedy derivation of any derivable instance. It is straightforward to confirm that **wgbts** generalizes **gbts** since if a rule set is **gbts**, then every derivation of a derivable instance is greedy, implying that every derivable instance has *some* greedy derivation. Yet, what is non-trivial to show is that **wgbts** *properly subsumes* **gbts**. We are going to prove this fact by means of a proof-theoretic argument and counter-example along the following lines: first, we show under what conditions we can permute rule applications in a given derivation (see Lemma 1 below), and second, we provide a rule set which exhibits non-greedy derivations (witnessing that the rule set is not **gbts**), but for which every derivation can be transformed into a greedy derivation by means of rule permutations and replacements (witnessing **wgbts** membership).

Let us now formally define greedy derivations and provide examples to demonstrate the concept of (non-)greediness. Based on this, we then proceed to define the **gbts** and **wgbts** classes.

Definition 1 (Greedy Derivation [14]**).** *We define an $\mathcal{R}$-derivation*

$$\delta = \mathcal{I}_0, (\rho_1, h_1, \mathcal{I}_1), \ldots, (\rho_n, h_n, \mathcal{I}_n)$$

to be greedy *iff for each i such that $0 < i \leq n$, there exists a $j < i$ such that* $h_i(fr(\rho_i)) \subseteq \mathbf{Nul}(\overline{h}_j(head(\rho_j))) \cup \mathbf{Con}(\mathcal{I}_0, \mathcal{R}) \cup \mathbf{Nul}(\mathcal{I}_0)$.

To give examples of non-greedy and greedy derivations, let us define the database $\mathcal{D}_\dagger := \{p(a), r(b)\}$ and the rule set $\mathcal{R}_2 := \{\rho_1, \rho_2, \rho_3, \rho_4\}$, with

$$\rho_1 = p(x) \to \exists yz.q(x, y, z) \qquad \rho_3 = p(x) \land r(y) \to \exists zwuv.q(x, z, w) \land s(y, u, v)$$
$$\rho_2 = r(x) \to \exists yz.s(x, y, z) \qquad \rho_4 = q(x, y, z) \land s(w, u, v) \to \exists o.t(x, y, w, u, o)$$

An example of a non-greedy derivation is the following:

$$\delta_1 = \mathcal{D}_\dagger, (\rho_1, h_1, \mathcal{I}_1), (\rho_1, h_2, \mathcal{I}_2), (\rho_2, h_3, \mathcal{I}_3), (\rho_4, h_4, \mathcal{I}_4), \quad \text{with}$$

$$\mathcal{I}_4 = \{\underbrace{p(a), r(b)}_{\mathcal{D}_\dagger}, \underbrace{q(a, y_0, z_0)}_{\mathcal{I}_1 \backslash \mathcal{D}_\dagger}, \underbrace{q(a, y_1, z_1)}_{\mathcal{I}_2 \backslash \mathcal{I}_1}, \underbrace{s(b, y_2, z_2)}_{\mathcal{I}_3 \backslash \mathcal{I}_2}, \underbrace{t(a, y_0, b, y_2, o)}_{\mathcal{I}_4 \backslash \mathcal{I}_3}\} \quad \text{and}$$

$h_1 = h_2 = \{x \mapsto a\}$, $h_3 = \{x \mapsto b\}$, $h_4 = \{x \mapsto a, y \mapsto y_0, z \mapsto z_0, w \mapsto b, u \mapsto y_2, v \mapsto z_2\}$. Note that this derivation is not greedy because

$$h_4(fr(\rho_4)) = h_4(\{x, y, w, u\}) = \{a, \overbrace{y_0}^{\in \mathbf{Nul}(\overline{h}_1(head(\rho_1)))}, b, \underbrace{y_2}_{\in \mathbf{Nul}(\overline{h}_3(head(\rho_2)))}\}$$

That is to say, the image of the frontier from the last rule application (i.e. the application of ρ_4) contains nulls introduced by *two* previous rule applications (as opposed to containing nulls from just a single previous rule application), namely, the first application of ρ_1 and the application of ρ_2. In contrast, the following is an example of a greedy derivation

$$\delta_2 = \mathcal{D}_\dagger, (\rho_3, h'_1, \mathcal{I}'_1), (\rho_1, h'_2, \mathcal{I}'_2), (\rho_4, h'_3, \mathcal{I}'_3), \quad \text{with}$$

$$\mathcal{I}'_3 = \{\underbrace{p(a), r(b)}_{\mathcal{D}_\dagger}, \underbrace{q(a, y_0, z_0), s(b, y_2, z_2)}_{\mathcal{I}'_1 \backslash \mathcal{D}_\dagger}, \underbrace{q(a, y_1, z_1)}_{\mathcal{I}'_2 \backslash \mathcal{I}'_1}, \underbrace{t(a, y_0, b, y_2, o)}_{\mathcal{I}'_3 \backslash \mathcal{I}'_2}\} \quad \text{and}$$

$h'_1 = \{x \mapsto a, y \mapsto b\}$, $h'_2 = \{x \mapsto a\}$, $h'_3 = \{x \mapsto a, y \mapsto y_0, z \mapsto z_0, w \mapsto b, u \mapsto y_2, v \mapsto z_2\}$.

Greediness of δ_2 follows from the frontier of any applied rule being mapped to nothing but constants and/or nulls introduced by a sole previous rule application.

Definition 2 ((Weakly) Greedy Bounded-Treewidth Set). *A rule set $\mathcal{R}$ is a* greedy bounded-treewidth set (gbts) *iff if $\mathcal{D} \xrightarrow{\delta}_{\mathcal{R}} \mathcal{I}$, then δ is greedy. $\mathcal{R}$ is a* weakly greedy bounded-treewidth set (wgbts) *iff if $\mathcal{D} \xrightarrow{\delta}_{\mathcal{R}} \mathcal{I}$, then there exists some greedy $\mathcal{R}$-derivation δ' such that $\mathcal{D} \xrightarrow{\delta'}_{\mathcal{R}} \mathcal{I}$.*

Remark 1. Observe that **gbts** and **wgbts** are characterized on the basis of derivations starting from given *databases* only, that is, derivations of the form $\mathcal{I}_0, (\rho_1, h_1, \mathcal{I}_1), \ldots, (\rho_n, h_n, \mathcal{I}_n)$ where $\mathcal{I}_0 = \mathcal{D}$ is a database. In such a case, a derivation of the above form is greedy *iff* for each i with $0 < i \leq n$, there exists a $j < i$ such that $h_i(fr(\rho_i)) \subseteq \mathbf{Nul}(\overline{h}_j(head(\rho_j))) \cup \mathbf{Con}(\mathcal{D}, \mathcal{R})$ as databases only contain constants (and not nulls) by definition.

As noted above, it is straightforward to show that **wgbts** subsumes **gbts**. Still, establishing that **wgbts** strictly subsumes **gbts**, i.e. there are rule sets within **wgbts** that are outside **gbts**, requires more effort. As it so happens, the rule set $\mathcal{R}_2$ (defined above) serves as such a rule set, admitting non-greedy $\mathcal{R}_2$-derivations, but where it can be shown that every instance derivable using the rule set admits a greedy $\mathcal{R}_2$-derivation. As a case in point, observe that the $\mathcal{R}_2$-derivations δ_1 and δ_2 both derive the same instance $\mathcal{I}_4 = \mathcal{I}_3'$, however, δ_1 is a non-greedy $\mathcal{R}_2$-derivation of the instance and δ_2 is a greedy $\mathcal{R}_2$-derivation of the instance. Clearly, the existence of the non-greedy $\mathcal{R}_2$-derivation δ_1 witnesses that $\mathcal{R}_2$ is not **gbts**. To establish that $\mathcal{R}_2$ still falls within the **wgbts** class, we show that every non-greedy $\mathcal{R}_2$-derivation can be transformed into a greedy $\mathcal{R}_2$-derivation using two operations: (i) rule permutations and (ii) rule replacements.

Regarding rule permutations, we consider under what conditions we may swap consecutive applications of rules in a derivation to yield a new derivation of the same instance. For example, in the $\mathcal{R}_2$-derivation δ_1 above, we may swap the consecutive applications of ρ_1 and ρ_2 to obtain the following derivation:

$$\delta_1' = \mathcal{D}_\dagger, (\rho_1, h_1, \mathcal{I}_1), (\rho_2, h_3, \mathcal{I}_1 \cup (\mathcal{I}_3 \setminus \mathcal{I}_2)), (\rho_1, h_2, \mathcal{I}_3), (\rho_4, h_4, \mathcal{I}_4).$$

$\mathcal{I}_1 \cup (\mathcal{I}_3 \setminus \mathcal{I}_2) = \{p(a), r(b), q(a, y_0, z_0), s(b, y_2, z_2)\}$ is derived by applying ρ_2 and the subsequent application of ρ_1 reclaims the instance $\mathcal{I}_3$. Therefore, the same instance $\mathcal{I}_4$ remains the conclusion. Although one can confirm that δ_1' is indeed an $\mathcal{R}_2$-derivation, thus serving as a successful example of a rule permutation (meaning, the rule permutation yields another $\mathcal{R}_2$-derivation), the following question still remains: for a rule set $\mathcal{R}$, under what conditions will permuting rules within a given $\mathcal{R}$-derivation always yield another $\mathcal{R}$-derivation?

We pose an answer to this question, formulated as the *permutation lemma* below, which states that an application of a rule ρ may be permuted before an application of a rule ρ' so long as the former rule does not depend on the latter (in the sense formally defined in Section 2 based on the work of Baget [1]). Furthermore, it should be noted that such rule permutations preserve the greediness of derivations. In the context of the above example, ρ_2 may be permuted before ρ_1 in δ_1 because the former does not depend on the latter.

Lemma 1 (Permutation Lemma). *Let $\mathcal{R}$ be a rule set with $\mathcal{I}_0$ an instance. Suppose we have a (greedy) $\mathcal{R}$-derivation of the following form:*

$$\mathcal{I}_0, \ldots, (\rho_i, h_i, \mathcal{I}_i), (\rho_{i+1}, h_{i+1}, \mathcal{I}_{i+1}), \ldots, (\rho_n, h_n, \mathcal{I}_n)$$

If ρ_{i+1} does not depend on ρ_i, then the following is a (greedy) $\mathcal{R}$-derivation too:

$$\mathcal{I}_0, \ldots, (\rho_{i+1}, h_{i+1}, \mathcal{I}_{i-1} \cup (\mathcal{I}_{i+1} \setminus \mathcal{I}_i)), (\rho_i, h_i, \mathcal{I}_{i+1}), \ldots, (\rho_n, h_n, \mathcal{I}_n).$$

As a consequence of the above lemma, rules may always be permuted in a given $\mathcal{R}$-derivation so that its structure mirrors the graph of rule dependencies $G(\mathcal{R})$ (defined in Section 2). That is, given a rule set $\mathcal{R}$ and an $\mathcal{R}$-derivation δ, we may permute all applications of rules serving as sources in $G(\mathcal{R})$ (which do not depend on any rules in $\mathcal{R}$) to the beginning of δ, followed by all rule applications that depend only on sources, and so forth, with any applications of rules serving as sinks in $G(\mathcal{R})$ concluding the derivation. For example, in the graph of rule dependencies of $\mathcal{R}_2$, the rules ρ_1, ρ_2, and ρ_3 serve as source nodes (they do not depend on any rules in $\mathcal{R}_2$) and the rule ρ_4 is a sink node depending on each of the aforementioned three rules, i.e. $G(\mathcal{R}_2) = (V, E)$ with $V = \{\rho_1, \rho_2, \rho_3, \rho_4\}$ and $E = \{(\rho_i, \rho_4) \mid 1 \leq i \leq 3\}$. Hence, in any given $\mathcal{R}_2$-derivation δ, any application of ρ_1, ρ_2, or ρ_3 can be permuted backward (toward the beginning of δ) and any application of ρ_4 can be permuted forward (toward the end of δ).

Beyond the use of rule permutations, we also transform $\mathcal{R}_2$-derivations by making use of rule replacements. In particular, observe that $head(\rho_3)$ and $body(\rho_3)$ correspond to conjunctions of $head(\rho_1)$ and $head(\rho_2)$, and $body(\rho_1)$ and $body(\rho_2)$, respectively. Thus, we can replace the first application of ρ_1 and the succeeding application of ρ_2 in δ_1' above by a single application of ρ_3, thus yielding the $\mathcal{R}_2$-derivation $\delta_1'' = \mathcal{D}_\dagger, (\rho_3, h, \mathcal{I}_1 \cup (\mathcal{I}_3 \setminus \mathcal{I}_2)), (\rho_1, h_2, \mathcal{I}_3), (\rho_4, h_4, \mathcal{I}_4)$, where $h(x) = a$ and $h(y) = b$. Interestingly, inspecting the above $\mathcal{R}_2$-derivation, one will find that it is identical to the greedy $\mathcal{R}_2$-derivation δ_2 defined earlier in the section, and so, we have shown how to take a non-greedy $\mathcal{R}_2$-derivation (viz. δ_1) and transform it into a greedy $\mathcal{R}_2$-derivation (viz. δ_2) by means of rule permutations and replacements. In the same way, one can prove in general that any non-greedy $\mathcal{R}_2$-derivation can be transformed into a greedy $\mathcal{R}_2$-derivation, thus giving rise to the following theorem, and demonstrating that $\mathcal{R}_2$ is indeed **wgbts**.

Theorem 1. *$\mathcal{R}_2$ is* **wgbts,** *but not* **gbts.** *Thus,* **wgbts** *properly subsumes* **gbts.**

4   Derivation Graphs

We now discuss *derivation graphs* – a concept introduced by Baget et al. [5] and used to establish that certain classes of rule sets (e.g. weakly frontier guarded rule sets [6]) exhibit universal models of bounded treewidth. A derivation graph has the structure of a directed acyclic graph and encodes *how* atoms are derived throughout the course of an $\mathcal{R}$-derivation. By applying so-called *reduction operations*, a derivation graph may (under certain conditions) be transformed into a treelike graph that serves as a tree decomposition of an $\mathcal{R}$-derivable instance.

Below, we define derivation graphs and discuss how such graphs are transformed into tree decompositions by means of reduction operations. To increase comprehensibility, we provide an example of a derivation graph (shown in Figure 2) and give an example of applying each reduction operation (shown in Figure 3). After, we identify two (query-decidable) classes of rule sets on the basis of derivation graphs, namely, *cycle-free derivation graph sets* (**cdgs**) and *weakly cycle-free derivation graph sets* (**wcdgs**). Despite their prima facie distinctness, the **cdgs** and **wcdgs** classes coincide with **gbts** and **wgbts** classes, respectively, thus showing how the latter classes can be characterized in terms of derivation graphs. Let us now formally define derivation graphs, and after, we will demonstrate the concept by means of an example.

Definition 3 (Derivation Graph). *Let $\mathcal{D}$ be a database, $\mathcal{R}$ be a rule set, $C = \mathbf{Con}(\mathcal{D}, \mathcal{R})$, and δ be some $\mathcal{R}$-derivation $\mathcal{D}, (\rho_1, h_1, \mathcal{I}_1), \ldots, (\rho_n, h_n, \mathcal{I}_n)$. The derivation graph of δ is the tuple $G_\delta := (V, E, At, L)$, where $V := \{X_0, \ldots, X_n\}$ is a finite set of* nodes, *$E \subseteq V \times V$ is a set of* arcs, *and the functions $At : V \to 2^{\mathcal{I}_n}$ and $L : E \to 2^{\mathbf{Ter}(\mathcal{I}_n)}$ decorate nodes and arcs, respectively, such that:*

1. $At(X_0) := \mathcal{D}$ *and* $At(X_i) = \mathcal{I}_i \setminus \mathcal{I}_{i-1}$;
2. $(X_i, X_j) \in E$ *iff there is a $p(\mathbf{t}) \in At(X_i)$ and a frontier atom $p(\mathbf{t}')$ in ρ_j such that $h_j(p(\mathbf{t}')) = p(\mathbf{t})$. We then set $L(X_i, X_j) = \left(h_j\big(\mathbf{Var}(p(\mathbf{t}')) \cap fr(\rho_j)\big) \right) \setminus C$.*

We refer to X_0 as the initial node *and define the set of* non-constant terms *associated with a node to be $\overline{C}(X) = \mathbf{Ter}(X) \setminus C$ where $\mathbf{Ter}(X_i) := \mathbf{Ter}(At(X_i)) \cup C$.*

Toward an example, assume $\mathcal{D}_\ddagger = \{p(a, b)\}$ and $\mathcal{R}_3 = \{\rho_1, \rho_2, \rho_3, \rho_4\}$ where

$$\rho_1 = p(x, y) \to \exists z.q(y, z) \qquad\qquad \rho_3 = r(x, y) \wedge q(z, x) \to s(x, y)$$
$$\rho_2 = q(x, y) \to \exists z.(r(x, y) \wedge r(y, z)) \qquad \rho_4 = r(x, y) \wedge s(z, w) \to t(y, w)$$

Let us consider the following derivation:

$$\delta = \mathcal{D}_\ddagger, (\rho_1, h_1, \mathcal{I}_1), (\rho_2, h_2, \mathcal{I}_2), (\rho_3, h_3, \mathcal{I}_3), (\rho_4, h_4, \mathcal{I}_4) \quad \text{with}$$

$$\mathcal{I}_4 = \{\underbrace{p(a, b)}_{\mathcal{D}_\ddagger}, \underbrace{q(b, z_0)}_{\mathcal{I}_1 \setminus \mathcal{D}_\ddagger}, \underbrace{r(b, z_0), r(z_0, z_1)}_{\mathcal{I}_2 \setminus \mathcal{I}_1}, \underbrace{s(z_0, z_1)}_{\mathcal{I}_3 \setminus \mathcal{I}_2}, \underbrace{t(z_0, z_1)}_{\mathcal{I}_4 \setminus \mathcal{I}_3}\} \quad \text{and}$$

$h_1 = \{x \mapsto a, y \mapsto b\}$, $h_2 = \{x \mapsto b, y \mapsto z_0\}$, $h_3 = \{x \mapsto z_0, y \mapsto z_1, z \mapsto b\}$, as well as $h_4 = \{x \mapsto b, y \mapsto z_0, z \mapsto z_0, w \mapsto z_1\}$. The derivation graph $G_\delta = (V, E, At, L)$ corresponding to δ is shown in Figure 2 and has fives nodes, $V = \{X_0, X_1, X_2, X_3, X_4\}$. Each node $X_i \in V$ is associated with a set $At(X_i)$ of atoms depicted in the associated circle (e.g. $At(X_2) = \{r(b, z_0), r(z_0, z_1)\}$), and each arc $(X_i, X_j) \in E$ is represented as a directed arrow with $L(X_i, X_j)$ shown as the associated set of terms (e.g. $L(X_3, X_4) = \{z_1\}$). For each node $X_i \in V$, the set $\mathbf{Ter}(X_i)$ of terms associated with the node is equal to $\mathbf{Ter}(At(X_i)) \cup \{a, b\}$ (e.g. $\mathbf{Ter}(X_3) = \{z_0, z_1, a, b\}$) since $C = \mathbf{Con}(\mathcal{D}_\ddagger, \mathcal{R}_3) = \{a, b\}$.

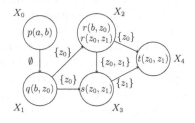

Fig. 2. The derivation graph G_δ.

As can be witnessed via the above example, derivation graphs satisfy a set of properties akin to those characterizing tree decompositions [5, Proposition 12].

Lemma 2 (Decomposition Properties). *Let $\mathcal{D}$ be a database, $\mathcal{R}$ be a rule set, and $C = \mathbf{Con}(\mathcal{D}, \mathcal{R})$. If $\mathcal{D} \xrightarrow{\delta}_{\mathcal{R}} \mathcal{I}$, then G_δ satisfies the following properties:*

1. $\bigcup_{X_n \in V} \mathbf{Ter}(X_n) = \mathbf{Ter}(\mathcal{I})$;
2. *For each $p(\mathbf{t}) \in \mathcal{I}$, there is an $X_n \in V$ such that $p(\mathbf{t}) \in \mathrm{At}(X_n)$;*
3. *For each term $x \in \overline{C}(\mathcal{I})$, the subgraph of G_δ induced by the nodes X_n such that $x \in \overline{C}(X_n)$ is connected;*
4. *For each $X_n \in V$ the size of $\mathbf{Ter}(X_n)$ is bounded by an integer that only depends on the size of $(\mathcal{D}, \mathcal{R})$, viz. $\max\{|\mathbf{Ter}(\mathcal{D})|, |\mathbf{Ter}(head(\rho_i))|_{\rho_i \in \mathcal{R}}\} + |C|$.*

Let us now introduce our set of *reduction operations*. As remarked above, in certain circumstances such operations can be used to transform derivation graphs into tree decompositions of an instance.

We make use of three reduction operations, namely, (i) *arc removal*, denoted $(\mathsf{ar})^{[i,j]}$, (ii) *term removal*, denoted $(\mathsf{tr})^{[i,j,k,t]}$, and (iii) *cycle removal*, denoted $(\mathsf{cr})^{[i,j,k,\ell]}$. The first two reduction operations were already proposed by Baget et al. [5] (they presented (tr) and (ar) as a single operation called *redundant arc removal*), whereas cycle removal is introduced by us as a new operation that will assist in characterizing **gbts** and **wgbts** in terms of derivation graphs.[2]

Definition 4 (Reduction Operations). *Let $\mathcal{D}$ be a database, $\mathcal{R}$ be a rule set, $\mathcal{D} \xrightarrow{\delta}_{\mathcal{R}} \mathcal{I}_n$, and G_δ be the derivation graph of δ. We define the set RO of reduction operations as $\{(\mathsf{ar})^{[i,j]}, (\mathsf{tr})^{[i,j,k,t]}, (\mathsf{cr})^{[i,j,k,\ell]} \mid i, j, k, \ell \leq n, t \in \mathbf{Ter}(\mathcal{I}_n)\}$, whose effect is further specified below. We let $(\mathsf{r})\Sigma(G_\delta)$ denote the output of applying the operation (r) to the (potentially reduced) derivation graph $\Sigma(G_\delta) = (V, E, \mathrm{At}, L)$, where $\Sigma \in \mathsf{RO}^*$ is a reduction sequence, that is, Σ is a (potentially empty) sequence of reduction operations.*

1. *Arc Removal $(\mathsf{ar})^{[i,j]}$: Whenever $(X_i, X_j) \in E$ and $L(X_i, X_j) = \emptyset$, then $(\mathsf{ar})^{[i,j]}\Sigma(G_\delta) := (V, E', \mathrm{At}, L')$ where $E' := E \setminus \{(X_i, X_j)\}$ and $L' = L \restriction E'$.*
2. *Term Removal $(\mathsf{tr})^{[i,j,k,t]}$: If $(X_i, X_k), (X_j, X_k) \in E$ with $X_i \neq X_j$ and $t \in L(X_i, X_k) \cap L(X_j, X_k)$, then $(\mathsf{tr})^{[i,j,k,t]}\Sigma(G_\delta) := (V, E, \mathrm{At}, L')$ where L' is obtained from L by removing t from $L(X_j, X_k)$.*
3. *Cycle Removal $(\mathsf{cr})^{[i,j,k,\ell]}$: If $(X_i, X_k), (X_j, X_k) \in E$ and there exists a node $X_\ell \in V$ with $\ell < k$ such that $L(X_i, X_k) \cup L(X_j, X_k) \subseteq \mathbf{Ter}(X_\ell)$ then, $(\mathsf{cr})^{[i,j,k,\ell]}\Sigma(G_\delta) := (V, E', \mathrm{At}, L')$ where*

$$E' := \big(E \setminus \{(X_i, X_k), (X_j, X_k)\}\big) \cup \{(X_\ell, X_k)\}$$

and L' is obtained from $L \restriction E'$ by setting $L(X_\ell, X_k)$ to $L(X_i, X_k) \cup L(X_j, X_k)$.

---

[2] Beyond (tr) and (ar), we note that Baget et al. [5] introduced an additional reduction operation, referred to as *arc contraction*. We do not consider this rule here however as it is unnecessary to characterize **gbts** and **wgbts** in terms of derivation graphs and prima facie obstructs the proof of Theorem 2.

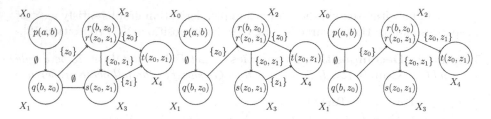

Fig. 3. Left to right: reduced derivation graphs $(\mathsf{tr})(G_\delta)$, $(\mathsf{ar})(\mathsf{tr})(G_\delta)$, and $(\mathsf{cr})(\mathsf{ar})(\mathsf{tr})(G_\delta)$.

Last, we say that a reduction sequence $\Sigma \in \mathsf{RO}^*$ is a complete reduction sequence relative to a derivation graph G_δ iff $\Sigma(G_\delta)$ is cycle-free.

Remark 2. When there is no danger of confusion, we will take the liberty to write (tr), (ar), and (cr) without superscript parameters. That is, given a derivation graph G_δ, the (reduced) derivation graph $(\mathsf{cr})(\mathsf{tr})(G_\delta)$ is obtained by applying an instance of (tr) followed by an instance of (cr) to G_δ. When applying a reduction operation we always explain *how* it is applied, so the exact operation is known.

We now describe the functionality of each reduction operation and illustrate each by means of an example. We will apply each to transform the derivation graph G_δ (shown in Figure 2) into a tree decomposition of $\mathcal{I}_4$ (which was defined above). The (tr) operation deletes a term t within the intersection of the sets labeling two converging arcs. For example, we may apply (tr) to the derivation graph G_δ from Figure 2, deleting the term z_0 from the label of the arc (X_1, X_3), and yielding the reduced derivation graph $(\mathsf{tr})(G_\delta)$, which is shown first in Figure 3. We may then apply (ar) to $(\mathsf{tr})(G_\delta)$, deleting the arc (X_1, X_3), which is labeled with the empty set, to obtain the reduced derivation graph $(\mathsf{ar})(\mathsf{tr})(G_\delta)$ shown middle in Figure 3.

The (cr) operation is more complex and works by considering two converging arcs (X_i, X_k) and (X_j, X_k) in a (reduced) derivation graph. If there exists a node X_ℓ whose index ℓ is less than the index k of the child node X_k and $\mathrm{L}(X_i, X_k) \cup \mathrm{L}(X_j, X_k) \subseteq \mathbf{Ter}(X_\ell)$, then the converging arcs (X_i, X_k) and (X_j, X_k) may be deleted and the arc (X_ℓ, X_k) introduced and labeled with $\mathrm{L}(X_i, X_k) \cup \mathrm{L}(X_j, X_k)$. As an example, the reduced derivation graph $(\mathsf{cr})(\mathsf{ar})(\mathsf{tr})(G_\delta)$ (shown third in Figure 3) is obtained from $(\mathsf{ar})(\mathsf{tr})(G_\delta)$ (shown middle in Figure 3) by applying (cr) in the following manner to the convergent arcs (X_2, X_4) and (X_3, X_4): since for X_2 (whose index 2 is less than the index 4 of X_4) $\mathrm{L}(X_2, X_4) \cup \mathrm{L}(X_3, X_4) \subseteq \mathbf{Ter}(X_2)$, we may delete the arcs (X_2, X_4) and (X_3, X_4) and introduce the arc (X_2, X_4) labeled with $\mathrm{L}(X_2, X_4) \cup \mathrm{L}(X_3, X_4) = \{z_0\} \cup \{z_1\} = \{z_0, z_1\}$. Observe that the reduced derivation graph $(\mathsf{cr})(\mathsf{ar})(\mathsf{tr})(G_\delta)$ is free of cycles, witnessing that $\Sigma = (\mathsf{cr})(\mathsf{ar})(\mathsf{tr})$ is a complete reduction sequence relative to G_δ. Moreover, if we replace each node by the set of its terms and disregard the labels on arcs, then $\Sigma(G_\delta)$ can be read as a tree decomposition of $\mathcal{I}_4$. In fact, one can show that every reduced derivation graph satisfies the decomposition properties mentioned in Lemma 2 above.

Lemma 3. *Let $\mathcal{D}$ be a database and $\mathcal{R}$ be a rule set. If $\mathcal{D} \xrightarrow{\mathcal{R}}_\delta \mathcal{I}$, then for any reduction sequence Σ, $\Sigma(G_\delta) = (\mathrm{V}, \mathrm{E}, \mathrm{At}, \mathrm{L})$ satisfies the decomposition properties 1-4 in Lemma 2.*

As illustrated above, derivation graphs can be used to derive tree decompositions of $\mathcal{R}$-derivable instances. By the fourth decomposition property (see Lemma 2 above), the width of such a tree decomposition is bounded by a constant that depends only on the given knowledge base. Thus, if a rule set $\mathcal{R}$ always yields derivation graphs that are reducible to *cycle-free* graphs – meaning that (un)directed cycles do not occur within the graph – then all $\mathcal{R}$-derivable instances have tree decompositions that are uniformly bounded by a constant. This establishes that the rule set $\mathcal{R}$ falls within the **bts** class, confirming that query entailment is decidable with $\mathcal{R}$. We define two classes of rule sets by means of reducible derivation graphs:

Definition 5 ((Weakly) Cycle-free Derivation Graph Set). *A rule set $\mathcal{R}$ is a cycle-free derivation graph set (**cdgs**) iff if $\mathcal{D} \xrightarrow{\delta}_\mathcal{R} \mathcal{I}$, then G_δ can be reduced to a cycle-free graph by the reduction operations. $\mathcal{R}$ is a weakly cycle-free derivation graph set (**wcdgs**) iff if $\mathcal{D} \xrightarrow{\delta}_\mathcal{R} \mathcal{I}$, then there is a derivation δ' where $\mathcal{D} \xrightarrow{\delta'}_\mathcal{R} \mathcal{I}$ and $G_{\delta'}$ can be reduced to a cycle-free graph by the reduction operations.*

It is straightforward to confirm that **wcdgs** subsumes **cdgs**, and that both classes are subsumed by **bts**.

Proposition 1. *Every **cdgs** rule set is **wcdgs** and every **wcdgs** rule set is **bts**.*

Furthermore, as mentioned above, **gbts** and **wgbts** coincide with **cdgs** and **wcdgs**, respectively. By making use of the (cr) operation, one can show that the derivation graph of any greedy derivation is reducible to a cycle-free graph, thus establishing that **gbts** $\subseteq$ **cdgs** and **wgbts** $\subseteq$ **wcdgs**. To show the converse (i.e. that **cdgs** $\subseteq$ **gbts** and **wcdgs** $\subseteq$ **wgbts**) however, requires more work. In essence, one shows that for every (non-source) node X_i in a cycle-free (reduced) derivation graph there exists another node X_j such that $j < i$ and the frontier of the atoms in $\mathrm{At}(X_i)$ only consist of constants and/or nulls introduced by the atoms in $\mathrm{At}(X_j)$. This property is preserved under *reverse* applications of the reduction operations, and thus, one can show that if a derivation graph is reducible to a cycle-free graph, then the above property holds for the original derivation graph, implying that the derivation graph encodes a greedy derivation. Based on such arguments, one can prove the following:

Theorem 2. **gbts** *coincides with* **cdgs** *and* **wgbts** *coincides with* **wcdgs**. *Membership in* **cdgs**, **gbts**, **wcdgs**, *or* **wgbts** *warrants decidable BCQ entailment.*

Note that by Theorem 1, this also implies that **wcdgs** properly contains **cdgs**.

An interesting consequence of the above theorem concerns the redundancy of (ar) and (tr) in the presence of (cr). In particular, since we know that (i) if a derivation graph can be reduced to a cycle-free graph, then the derivation graph encodes a greedy derivation, and (ii) the derivation graph of any greedy derivation can be reduced to an cycle-free graph by means of applying the (cr) operation only, it follows that if a derivation graph can be reduced to a cycle-free graph, then it can be reduced by only applying the (cr) operation. We refer to this phenomenon as *reduction-admissibility*, which is defined below.

Definition 6 (Reduction-admissible). *Suppose* $S_1 = \{(r_i) \mid 1 \le i \le n\}$ *and* $S_2 = \{(r_j) \mid n + 1 \le j \le k\}$ *are two sets of reduction operations. We say that* S_1 *is* reduction-admissible *relative to* S_2 *iff for any rule set* $\mathcal{R}$ *and* $\mathcal{R}$-*derivation* δ, *if* G_δ *is reducible to a cycle-free graph with* $S_1 \cup S_2$, *then* G_δ *is reducible to a cycle-free graph with just* S_2.

Corollary 1. $\{(tr), (ar)\}$ *is reduction-admissible relative to* (cr).

5   Conclusion

In this paper, we revisited the concept of a *greedy* derivation, which immediately gives rise to a bounded-width tree decomposition of the constructed instance. This well-established notion allows us to categorize rule sets as being *(weakly) greedy bounded treewidth sets* ((**w**)**gbts**), if all (some) derivations of a derivable instance are guaranteed to be greedy, irrespective of the underlying database. By virtue of being subsumed by **bts**, these classes warrant decidability of BCQ entailment, while at the same time subsuming various popular rule languages, in particular from the guarded family.

By means of an example together with a proof-theoretic argument, we exposed that **wgbts** strictly generalizes **gbts**. In pursuit of a better understanding and more workable methods to detect and analyze (**w**)**gbts** rule sets, we resorted to the previously proposed notion of *derivation graphs*. Through a refinement of the set of reduction methods for derivation graphs, we were able to make more advanced use of this tool, leading to the definition of *(weakly) cycle-free derivation graph sets* ((**w**)**cdgs**) of rules, of which we were then able to show the respective coincidences with (**w**)**gbts**. This way, we were able to establish alternative characterizations of **gbts** and **wgbts** by means of derivation graphs. En passant, we found that the newly introduced *cycle removal* reduction operation over derivation graphs is sufficient by itself and makes the other operations redundant.

For future work, we plan to put our newly found characterizations to use. In particular, we aim to investigate if a rule set's membership in **gbts** or **wgbts** is decidable. For **gbts**, this has been widely conjectured, but never formally established. In the positive case, derivation graphs might also be leveraged to pinpoint the precise complexity of the membership problem. We are also confident that the tools and insights in this paper – partially revived, partially upgraded, partially newly developed – will prove useful in the greater area of static analysis of existential rule sets. On a general note, we feel that the field of proof theory has a lot to offer for knowledge representation, whereas the cross-fertilization between these disciplines still appears to be underdeveloped.

References

1. Baget, J.F.: Improving the forward chaining algorithm for conceptual graphs rules. In: Proceedings of the Ninth International Conference on Principles of Knowledge Representation and Reasoning. p. 407–414. KR'04, AAAI Press (2004)
2. Baget, J.F., Leclère, M., Mugnier, M.L., Salvat, E.: Extending decidable cases for rules with existential variables. In: Proceedings of the 21st International Jont Conference on Artifical Intelligence. p. 677–682. IJCAI'09, Morgan Kaufmann Publishers Inc., San Francisco, CA, USA (2009)
3. Baget, J.F., Leclère, M., Mugnier, M.L., Salvat, E.: Extending decidable cases for rules with existential variables. In: Proceedings of the 21st International Joint Conference on Artificial Intelligence. p. 677–682. IJCAI'09, Morgan Kaufmann Publishers Inc., San Francisco, CA, USA (2009)
4. Baget, J.F., Mugnier, M.L.: Extensions of simple conceptual graphs: the complexity of rules and constraints. Journal of Artificial Intelligence Research **16**, 425–465 (2002)
5. Baget, J.F., Leclère, M., Mugnier, M.L., Salvat, E.: On rules with existential variables: Walking the decidability line. Artificial Intelligence **175**(9), 1620–1654 (2011). https://doi.org/10.1016/j.artint.2011.03.002
6. Calì, A., Gottlob, G., Kifer, M.: Taming the infinite chase: Query answering under expressive relational constraints. Journal of Artificial Intelligence Research **48**, 115–174 (2013). https://doi.org/10.1613/jair.3873
7. Chandra, A.K., Lewis, H.R., Makowsky, J.A.: Embedded implicational dependencies and their inference problem. In: Proceedings of the 13th Annual ACM Symposium on Theory of Computing (STOC'81). pp. 342–354. ACM (1981). https://doi.org/10.1145/800076.802488
8. Deutsch, A., Nash, A., Remmel, J.B.: The chase revisited. In: Lenzerini, M., Lembo, D. (eds.) Proceedings of the 27th ACM SIGMOD-SIGACT-SIGART Symposium on Principles of Database Systems (PODS'08). pp. 149–158. ACM (2008). https://doi.org/10.1145/1376916.1376938
9. Fagin, R., Kolaitis, P.G., Miller, R.J., Popa, L.: Data exchange: semantics and query answering. Theoretical Computer Science **336**(1), 89–124 (2005). https://doi.org/10.1016/j.tcs.2004.10.033, database Theory
10. Feller, T., Lyon, T.S., Ostropolski-Nalewaja, P., Rudolph, S.: Finite-Cliquewidth Sets of Existential Rules: Toward a General Criterion for Decidable yet Highly Expressive Querying. In: Geerts, F., Vandevoort, B. (eds.) 26th International Conference on Database Theory (ICDT 2023). Leibniz International Proceedings in Informatics (LIPIcs), vol. 255, pp. 18:1–18:18. Schloss Dagstuhl – Leibniz-Zentrum für Informatik, Dagstuhl, Germany (2023). https://doi.org/10.4230/LIPIcs.ICDT.2023.18
11. Johnson, D.S., Klug, A.: Testing containment of conjunctive queries under functional and inclusion dependencies. In: Proceedings of the 1st ACM SIGACT-SIGMOD Symposium on Principles of Database Systems. p. 164–169. PODS '82, Association for Computing Machinery, New York, NY, USA (1982). https://doi.org/10.1145/588111.588138
12. Lyon, T.S., Rudolph, S.: Derivation-graph-based characterizations of decidable existential rule sets. CoRR (2023). https://doi.org/10.48550/arXiv.2307.08481
13. Maier, D., Mendelzon, A.O., Sagiv, Y.: Testing implications of data dependencies. ACM Trans. Database Syst. **4**(4), 455–469 (December 1979). https://doi.org/10.1145/320107.320115

14. Thomazo, M., Baget, J.F., Mugnier, M.L., Rudolph, S.: A generic querying algorithm for greedy sets of existential rules. In: Brewka, G., Eiter, T., McIlraith, S.A. (eds.) Proceedings of the 13th International Conference on Principles of Knowledge Representation and Reasoning (KR'12). AAAI (2012), http://www.aaai.org/ocs/index.php/KR/KR12/paper/view/4542

Concept Combination in Weighted DL

Guendalina Righetti[1] , Pietro Galliani[2]([⊠]) , and Claudio Masolo[3]

[1] Free University of Bozen-Bolzano, Bolzano, Italy
guendalina.righetti@unibz.it
[2] Università degli studi dell'Insubria, Varese, Italy
pietro.galliani@uninsubria.it
[3] Laboratory for Applied Ontology, ISTC-CNR, Trento, Italy
masolo@loa.istc.cnr.it

Abstract. Building on previous work on Weighted Description Logic (WDL), we present and assess an algorithm for concept combination grounded in the experimental research in cognitive psychology. Starting from two WDL formulas representing concepts in a way similar to Prototype Theory and a knowledge base (KB) modelling background knowledge, the algorithm outputs a new WDL formula which represent the combination of the input concepts. First, we study the logical properties of the operator defined by our algorithm. Second, we collect data on the prototypical representation of concepts and their combinations and learn WDL formulas from them. Third, we evaluate our algorithm and the role of the KB by comparing the algorithm's outputs with the learned WDL formulas.

Keywords: Weighted DL · Concept Combination · Prototype Theory

1 Introduction

In knowledge representation, concepts are often assumed as purely extensional, and their combination is reduced to set-theoretic operations. This view has the undoubted advantage of offering formal *compositional* semantics where the meaning of the composed concept is a function of the one of the combining concepts. Experimental psychology has, however, shown that concept combination has more subtle (*intensional*) semantics than what is expressible through Boolean operations such as classical logical conjunction [23]. First, human concept combination is not commutative: an Apartment Dog is substantially different from a Dog Apartment [31]. In these cases, the *role* of the combining concepts in the composition seems to impact the resulting combination. Namely, the *Head* concept provides the category of the combination while the *Modifier* modifies some aspects of the Head. Second, and maybe more importantly, concept combination is subject to *typicality effects*: some instances of a concept are more representative (and then easier to be categorised) than others, which hardly reconcile with a purely set-theoretical view on concepts.

S. Gaggl et al. (Eds.): JELIA 2023, LNAI 14281, pp. 385–401, 2023.
https://doi.org/10.1007/978-3-031-43619-2_27

Different cognitive theories of concepts have been proposed to account for these phenomena. Among them, *Prototype Theory* is one of the most formally developed [20,40]. In this theory, concepts are represented through prototypes, i.e., lists of features (or attributes) associated with weights representing their importance (in terms of cognitive salience or frequency distribution) for the concepts. Typicality is considered as a function of the weights of the features in the prototype matched by an individual: the most typical members, the best exemplars, are the individuals with the highest score.

The capability of Prototype Theory to capture concept combination has been however sharply objected, see e.g. [12,33]. As advocated in a famous counterexample, a goldfish is an atypical example of both *Fish* and *Pet* but a very typical example of *PetFish*. Two phenomena are particularly challenging here: (*i*) feature *inheritance failure*, e.g., prototypical Pets are furry, prototypical Fishes are grey, but prototypical PetFishes are neither furry nor grey; and (*ii*) *emergence* of new features, e.g., prototypical PetFishes are small and colourful but both features are hardly associated with prototypical Fishes or Pets.

To resist this criticism several attempts to model the composition of prototypes have been considered in experimental cognitive psychology. The *attribute inheritance model* proposed by Hampton [20] is arguably one of the most clearly developed, able to account for inheritance failure and attribute emergence in the case of *conjunctive noun-noun combinations* with form *X which are also Y*.

This paper has three main goals: (*i*) to provide a formal account of Hampton's attribute inheritance model; (*ii*) to study the formal properties of concept combination; and (*iii*) to systematically test the attribute inheritance model on empirical data. To this end, we exploit previous work on Weighted Description Logic (WDL) [14,34,35,37], an extension of standard Description Logic (DL) languages [2] with prototype-inspired concept constructors, namely the Weighted Threshold Operators (called also Tooth operators and noted $\mathbb{W}$). Section 2 introduces the Tooth operators, i.e., m-ary connectives that compute a weighted sum of their constituent concepts (playing the role of the *features* or *attributes* considered in a prototype) and verify whether a given instance reaches a certain threshold. Starting from two $\mathbb{W}$-expressions and a knowledge base modelling background knowledge, the algorithm presented in Sect. 3 computes a new $\mathbb{W}$-expression representing the combination of the input concepts.[1] Sect. 4 analyses several formal properties of concept combination wrt logical conjunction. The algorithm is tested in Sect. 5 on different kinds of empirical data. Section 6 concludes the paper.

2   Weighted Description Logic

WDL extends standard DL languages with a class of m-ary tooth-operators denoted by the symbol $\mathbb{W}$.[2] Each $\mathbb{W}$ operator works as follows: (*i*) it takes a list of concepts, (*ii*) it associates a weight to each of them, and (*iii*) it returns a complex concept that applies to those instances for which, by summing up the weights of the satisfied concepts, a certain threshold is met.

---

[1] This algorithm revises the original one [35].

[2] Similar weighted accounts can be introduced in languages other than DL [29].

More precisely, the new logic extends $\mathcal{ALC}$ and is denoted by $\mathcal{ALC}_{\mathbb{W}}$: given weights $w_i \in \mathbb{R}^m$, a threshold value $t \in \mathbb{R}$, and concepts $C_1, \ldots, C_m \in \mathcal{ALC}$, then $\mathbb{W}^t(C_1{:}w_1, \ldots, C_m{:}w_m) \in \mathcal{ALC}_{\mathbb{W}}$, i.e., for $C_i \in \mathcal{ALC}$, the set of $\mathcal{ALC}_{\mathbb{W}}$ concepts is described by the grammar:

$$C ::= A \mid \neg C \mid C \sqcap C \mid C \sqcup C \mid \forall R.C \mid \exists R.C \mid \mathbb{W}^t(C_1{:}w_1, \ldots, C_m{:}w_m)$$

A *knowledge base* is a finite set of concept inclusions of the form $C \sqsubseteq D$, for C, D concept expressions. We write $C \equiv D$ to signify that $C \sqsubseteq D$ and $D \sqsubseteq C$.

Given finite, disjoint sets N_C and N_R of concept and role names, respectively, an interpretation I consists of a non-empty set Δ^I and a mapping $\cdot^I$ that maps every concept name C to a subset $C^I \subseteq \Delta^I$ and every role name $R \in N_R$ to a binary relation $R^I \subseteq \Delta^I \times \Delta^I$. The semantics of the operators is obtained by extending the standard semantics of $\mathcal{ALC}$ as follows. Let I be an interpretation of $\mathcal{ALC}$. The interpretation of a $\mathbb{W}$-concept $C = \mathbb{W}^t(C_1{:}w_1, \ldots, C_m{:}w_m)$ is:

$$C^I = \{d \in \Delta^I \mid v_C^I(d) \geq t\} \tag{1}$$

where $v_C^I(d) = \sum_{i \in \{1, \ldots, m\}} \{w_i \mid d \in C_i^I\}$ is the *value* of $d \in \Delta^I$ under C.

Consider, e.g., $C = \mathbb{W}^8(C_1{:}4, C_2{:}3, C_3{:}2, C_4{:}1)$. If $d \in C_1^I \cap C_3^I$ but $d \notin C_2^I$, then $d \notin C^I$ because even when $d \in C_4^I$ we have that $v_C^I(d) = 4 + 2 + 1 = 7 < 8$.

The notion of *model* of a knowledge base $\mathbb{K}$ as well as *entailment* and *satisfiability* are as usual. Adding tooth-expressions in $\mathcal{ALC}$ is thus done without modifying the standard notion of interpretation in DL.

The representation of concepts in WDL is inspired by Prototype Theory [40]. By exploiting the function v_C^I, individuals can be ordered in terms of typicality wrt to a concept C. WDL can thus be used to capture variations in terms of instances typicalities - and more generally effects [37]. Moreover, Tooth-operators do not increase the expressive power of any language that contains the standard Boolean operators [34], but offer a more *interpretable* representation of concepts [36]. Adding tooth-operators to such DL languages does not increase the complexity of the corresponding inference problem [15]. Tooth-operators behave like *perceptrons* [13,15]: a (non-nested) tooth expression is a linear classification model, which enables to *learn* weights and thresholds from real data exploiting standard linear classification algorithms (see Sect. 5.2).

3 An Algorithm to Combine $\mathbb{W}$-Concepts

In this section we present an algorithm for concept combination which is grounded on the work of Hampton [20]. It focuses on conjunctive noun-noun combinations with form X *which are also* Y. Hampton represents concepts as sets of features weighted by their importance for defining the concept. Starting from two concepts X and Y, Hampton determines the representation of X *which are also* Y as follows: (*i*) the union of the features of X and Y is collected; (*ii*) the importance of the features of the combination is a rising monotonic function of the constituent importance values, where for the features in both X and Y the average is considered; (*iii*) the features that are necessary for either constituent are also necessary for the combination; (*iv*) the features that are impossible for either constituent are impossible also for the combination.

This model predicts forms of *inheritance failure*, which occur when, because of (*iv*), one of the features of the combining concepts is not inherited by the combination. The dual effect is the *emergence* of new features. Hampton explains the effect by considering additional *background knowledge* entering into the combination [30, 32] or by *extensional feedbacks*, i.e., the influence of specific exemplars experienced by the subject on the features of the combination.

In the following we will embed the proposal of Hampton into the WDL framework where concepts are defined by $\mathbb{W}$-expression and where the background knowledge is explicitly represented by a *knowledge base*.

To conform with Prototype Theory some restrictions on the $\mathbb{W}$-expressions provided as input to the algorithm are in place:[3] (*i*) features have positive weights, i.e., they positively impact the categorisation of exemplars [43]; (*ii*) features are atomic (e.g., conjunctions or negations of concepts are discarded), i.e., features within a prototype are independent [22]; (*iii*) input $\mathbb{W}$-expressions are uniformly determined allowing the comparison of the weights of the features they share (this is crucial for the averaging process considered by Hampton).

Given a knowledge base $\mathbb{K}$ representing background knowledge, we consider only $\mathbb{W}$-concepts satisfiable in $\mathbb{K}$, i.e. no concept is necessarily empty. Given $C = \mathbb{W}^t(F_1 : w_1, ..., F_m : w_m)$, a concept D, and a knowledge base $\mathbb{K}$, we define:

- $\mathbf{ft}(C) = \{F_1, \ldots, F_m\}$ *(features of* C*)*
- $\mathbf{snc}(C) = \{F_i \in \mathbf{ft}(C) \mid \sum_{j \neq i} w_j < t\}$ *(strongly necessary features of* C*)*
- $\mathbf{nc}(C, \mathbb{K}) = \{F_i \in \mathbf{ft}(C) \mid \mathbb{K} \vDash C \sqsubseteq F_i\}$ *(necessary features of* C *wrt* $\mathbb{K}$*)*
- $\mathbf{im}(C, D, \mathbb{K}) = \{F_i \in \mathbf{ft}(C) \mid \mathbb{K} \vDash D \sqsubseteq \neg F_i\}$ *(impossible feat. of* C *wrt* D*,* $\mathbb{K}$*)*

Individuals lacking a feature in $\mathbf{snc}(C)$ cannot reach the threshold; $\mathbf{snc}(C)$ is defined in a purely syntactic way while $\mathbf{nc}(C, \mathbb{K})$ extends $\mathbf{snc}(C)$ by exploiting $\mathbb{K}$ and logical inference. We have that $\mathbf{snc}(C) \subseteq \mathbf{nc}(C, \emptyset)$; indeed when $\vDash F_i \sqsubseteq F_j$ (with $i \neq j$) we have that $\mathbf{snc}(C) \subset \mathbf{nc}(C, \mathbb{K})$ independently of the assumed $\mathbb{K}$. $\mathbf{im}(C, D, \mathbb{K})$ individuates the features of C that are inconsistent, in $\mathbb{K}$, with D.

The Algorithm. The algorithm considers as input a (possibly empty) $\mathbb{K}$ and the $\mathbb{W}$-definitions of two concepts, one (H) playing the role of *Head* and one (M) playing the role of *Modifier*. This distinction is based on linguistic evidences on noun-noun compounds [26], here is considered as given. Under certain conditions, see Phase 3, the algorithm outputs the $\mathbb{W}$-definition of the combined concept noted $\mathbb{K}$:M∘H ($\emptyset$:M∘H is simply noted M∘H), i.e., it encodes a partial function.

The algorithm consists of three phases: phase 1 selects the features of $\mathbb{K}$:M∘H by assuming that H dominates M; phase 2 assigns the weights to the features in $\mathbb{K}$:M∘H; and phase 3 determines the threshold for $\mathbb{K}$:M∘H when certain conditions are met. Logical inference is exploited (when $\mathbb{K} \neq \emptyset$) only in phase 1 to determine incompatibilities between the features of H and M. Phases 2 and 3 use only the information made available by the (intensional) $\mathbb{W}$-definitions.

---

[3] The algorithm can however accept more general inputs.

Phase 1: features. $\mathbf{ft}(\mathbb{K}\text{:}M\circ H)$ is built in two steps (where $\lceil \mathcal{S} \rceil$ is the conjunction of all the concepts in a given set $\mathcal{S}$):

1. $\bar{\mathbf{ft}}(\mathbb{K}\text{:}M\circ H) = \mathbf{nc}(H, \mathbb{K}) \cup (\mathbf{nc}(M, \mathbb{K}) \backslash \mathbf{im}(M, H, \mathbb{K}))$
2. $\mathbf{ft}(\mathbb{K}\text{:}M\circ H) = \mathbf{ft}(H) \backslash \mathbf{im}(H, H \sqcap \lceil \bar{\mathbf{ft}}(\mathbb{K}\text{:}M\circ H) \rceil, \mathbb{K}) \cup$
   $\mathbf{ft}(M) \backslash \mathbf{im}(M, M \sqcap \lceil \bar{\mathbf{ft}}(\mathbb{K}\text{:}M\circ H) \rceil, \mathbb{K})$

Step 1 collects all the necessary features of H together with the ones of M which are not impossible for H. This shows how H dominates M: in case of incompatibilities we discard necessary features of M, not of H. It follows that $\mathbf{ft}(\mathbb{K}\text{:}M\circ H)$ and $\mathbf{ft}(\mathbb{K}\text{:}H\circ M)$ can differ. Step 2 builds on the previous step, examining all the non-necessary features of both H and M. Specifically, it aims at excluding all the features of H (resp. M), which are impossible for H (resp. M) itself, once all the necessary features of M (resp. H) in $\bar{\mathbf{ft}}(\mathbb{K}\text{:}H\circ M)$ are added.

Example PetFish. Consider the following $\mathbb{W}$-definitions:

Fish $= \mathbb{W}^6$(LivesInWater : 3, BreathesThroughGill : 3, Grey : 1, HasFin : 1)
Pet $= \mathbb{W}^6$(Pretty : 3, LivesInHouse : 3, Furry : 0.9);

and the knowledge base $\mathbb{K} = \{(2a), (2b), (2c)\}$

$$\text{LivesInWater} \sqcap \text{LivesInHouse} \sqsubseteq \text{LivesInAquarium} \tag{2a}$$

$$\text{Furry} \sqsubseteq \neg\text{BreathesThroughGill} \tag{2b}$$

$$\text{Pretty} \sqcap \text{BreathesThroughGill} \sqsubseteq \neg\text{Grey} \tag{2c}$$

We have that $\bar{\mathbf{ft}}(\mathbb{K}\text{:}Pet\circ Fish) = \{$LivesInWater, BreathesThroughGill, LivesInHouse, Pretty$\}$. Given that BreathesThroughGill, Pretty $\in \bar{\mathbf{ft}}(\mathbb{K}\text{:}Pet\circ Fish)$, by (2b), we have that Furry $\notin \mathbf{ft}(\mathbb{K}\text{:}Pet\circ Fish)$ and, by (2c), that Grey $\notin \mathbf{ft}(\mathbb{K}\text{:}Pet\circ Fish)$, i.e., $\mathbf{ft}(\mathbb{K}\text{:}Pet\circ Fish)=\{$LivesInWater,BreathesThroughGill,LivesInHouse,Pretty,HasFin$\}$. Since LivesInWater, LivesInHouse $\in \bar{\mathbf{ft}}(\mathbb{K}\text{:}Pet\circ Fish)$, by (2a), LivesInAcquarium can be seen as an *emergent feature* of $\mathbb{K}\text{:}Pet\circ Fish$ even if it is not in $\mathbf{ft}(\mathbb{K}\text{:}Pet\circ Fish)$.

Phase 2: weights. The weights of the features in $\mathbf{ft}(\mathbb{K}\text{:}M\circ H)$ are assigned in the following way:

1. for all the features in $\mathbf{sft}(\mathbb{K}\text{:}M\circ H) = \bar{\mathbf{ft}}(\mathbb{K}\text{:}M\circ H) \cap (\mathbf{snc}(M) \cup \mathbf{snc}(H))$ we consider the original weights except for the ones in $\bar{\mathbf{sft}}(\mathbb{K}\text{:}M\circ H) \cap \mathbf{ft}(H) \cap \mathbf{ft}(M)$ for which we consider the maximal weight;
2. for all the features in $\mathbf{ft}(\mathbb{K}\text{:}M\circ H) \backslash \bar{\mathbf{sft}}(\mathbb{K}\text{:}M\circ H)$ we consider the original weights except for the ones in $(\mathbf{ft}(\mathbb{K}\text{:}M\circ H) \backslash \bar{\mathbf{sft}}(\mathbb{K}\text{:}M\circ H)) \cap \mathbf{ft}(H) \cap \mathbf{ft}(M)$ for which we consider the average weight (of the original weights).

Phase 2 preserves as much as possible the original weights. Exceptions are the features shared by the two concepts, i.e., features in $\mathbf{ft}(H) \cap \mathbf{ft}(M)$. In these cases, following Hampton [20], we consider the maximal weight for the strongly necessary features of H and M, i.e., the features in $\bar{\mathbf{sft}}(\mathbb{K}\text{:}M\circ H)$,[4] and the average weight for the other features. The assumption about the comparability of weights across different tooth-expressions is crucial here.

---

[4] The algorithm guarantees that $\bar{\mathbf{sft}}(\mathbb{K}\text{:}M\circ H) = \mathbf{snc}(\mathbb{K}\text{:}M\circ H)$, see Phase 3.

Example PetFish (*cont.*). We have that $\bar{\mathbf{ft}}(\mathbb{K}:\mathsf{Pet}\circ\mathsf{Fish}) = \bar{\mathbf{sft}}(\mathbb{K}:\mathsf{Pet}\circ\mathsf{Fish})$, and $\mathbf{ft}(\mathsf{Fish}) \cap \mathbf{ft}(\mathsf{Pet}) = \emptyset$. Therefore we simply obtain:

$\mathbb{K}:\mathsf{P}\circ\mathsf{F} = \mathbb{W}^t(\mathsf{LivesInWater}:3, \mathsf{Pretty}:3, \mathsf{BreathesThroughGill}:3, \mathsf{LivesInHouse}:3, \mathsf{HasFin}:1)$.

Phase 3: threshold. Our main requirement to set the threshold for $\mathbb{K}:\mathsf{M}\circ\mathsf{H}$ is to assure that $\bar{\mathbf{sft}}(\mathbb{K}:\mathsf{M}\circ\mathsf{H}) = \mathbf{snc}(\mathbb{K}:\mathsf{M}\circ\mathsf{H})$, i.e., the strongly necessary features of both H and M (that are compatible with the necessary features of H) are also strongly necessary features of $\mathbb{K}:\mathsf{M}\circ\mathsf{H}$. Assume that

- w is the sum of the weights of the features in $\mathbf{ft}(\mathbb{K}:\mathsf{M}\circ\mathsf{H})$;
- if $\bar{\mathbf{sft}}(\mathbb{K}:\mathsf{M}\circ\mathsf{H}) \neq \emptyset$, w^- is the minimal weight of the features in $\bar{\mathbf{sft}}(\mathbb{K}:\mathsf{M}\circ\mathsf{H})$ otherwise $w^- = w$;
- if $\bar{\mathbf{sft}}(\mathbb{K}:\mathsf{M}\circ\mathsf{H}) \subset \mathbf{ft}(\mathbb{K}:\mathsf{M}\circ\mathsf{H})$, w^+ is the maximal weight of the features in $\mathbf{ft}(\mathbb{K}:\mathsf{M}\circ\mathsf{H})\backslash\bar{\mathbf{sft}}(\mathbb{K}:\mathsf{M}\circ\mathsf{H})$ otherwise $w^+ = 0$.

When $w-w^- < w-w^+$, the algorithm sets the threshold in the open interval $(w-w^-, w-w^+)$ otherwise it returns no tooth-expression. For instance, if $\mathbb{K} = \emptyset$, $\mathsf{C} = \mathbb{W}^1(\mathsf{A}:1)$, $\mathsf{D} = \mathbb{W}^1(\mathsf{B}:1, \mathsf{C}:1)$ then $w-w^- = w-w^+ = 2$ and no tooth expression for $\mathsf{C}\circ\mathsf{D}$ is returned. Exploring if the condition $w-w^- < w-w^+$ is a good index of the uniformity of the input $\mathbb{W}$-expressions is left for future work.

In general, a threshold towards $w-w^-$ tends to widen the extension of $\mathbb{K}:\mathsf{M}\circ\mathsf{H}$ while a threshold towards $w-w^+$ tends to narrow it. Hampton talks, respectively, of *under-extension* and *over-extension* phenomena [21]. A neutral strategy would set the threshold at $[(w-w^+)-(w-w^-)]/2$. Here, we aim at a general evaluation of our algorithm abstracting from the strategy chosen to exactly set the threshold, our analysis just assumes that the threshold is in $(w-w^-, w-w^+)$.

Notice that, the features in $\mathbf{ft}(\mathbb{K}:\mathsf{M}\circ\mathsf{H})\backslash\bar{\mathbf{sft}}(\mathbb{K}:\mathsf{M}\circ\mathsf{H})$ (eventually) implied by $\lceil\bar{\mathbf{sft}}(\mathbb{K}:\mathsf{M}\circ\mathsf{H})\rceil$ become necessary without being strongly necessary. Moreover, it is possible that some features in $\bar{\mathbf{ft}}(\mathbb{K}:\mathsf{M}\circ\mathsf{H})\backslash\bar{\mathbf{sft}}(\mathbb{K}:\mathsf{M}\circ\mathsf{H})$ are not necessary for $\mathbb{K}:\mathsf{M}\circ\mathsf{H}$, i.e., the algorithm preserves the strong necessity but not the necessity.

Example PetFish (*cont.*). We have that $w = 13$, $w^- = 3$, $w^+ = 1$, i.e., $t \in (10, 12)$.

4   Logical Properties of Concept Combination

The combination '$\circ$' does not define a logical *connective* as the usual Boolean connectives or as the $\mathbb{W}$-operators. The algorithm is defined only for specific kinds of $\mathbb{W}$-expressions (see Sect. 3) and its output is not always guaranteed. Still, when the algorithm sets a threshold range, one may examine the logical properties of $\mathbb{K}:\mathsf{M}\circ\mathsf{H}$ (regardless of an exact threshold) and compare them with those of ordinary connectives. In particular, one may verify whether our formalisation matches Hampton's insight that concept combination is not reducible to logical conjunction.

1. Concept combination **is not idempotent**.
   Consider $\mathbb{K} = \emptyset$ and $X = \mathbb{W}^1(A\!:\!1, B\!:\!1, C\!:\!1, D\!:\!1)$. We obtain that $X \circ X = \mathbb{W}^t(A\!:\!1, B\!:\!1, C\!:\!1, D\!:\!1)$ with $t \in (0,3)$. $X \circ X$ is not necessarily equivalent to X: e.g., when $t > 1$, A is sufficient to reach the threshold of X but not of $X \circ X$.
2. Concept combination **is not entailed by conjunction**.
   For X as before, we also have that $X \sqcap X \equiv X$ is satisfied by individuals that satisfy only A but none of B, C and D, whereas $X \circ X$ may not be.
3. Concept combination **does not entail conjunction**.
   Let $\mathbb{K} = \emptyset$, $X = \mathbb{W}^1(A\!:\!1, B\!:\!1)$, and $Y = \mathbb{W}^1(C\!:\!1, D\!:\!1)$. Then $X \equiv A \sqcup B$ and $Y \equiv C \sqcup D$; but since $nc(X, \mathbb{K}) = nc(Y, \mathbb{K}) = \emptyset$, $X \circ Y = \mathbb{W}^t(A\!:\!1, B\!:\!1, C\!:\!1, D\!:\!1)$ with $t \in (0,3)$. When $t = 2$, we obtain an expression that is satisfied if at least two of $\{A, B, C, D\}$ are satisfied; and of course this does not entail $(A \sqcup B) \sqcap (C \sqcup D)$.
4. For non-empty knowledge bases, concept combination **is not associative**.
   Let $X = \mathbb{W}^1(A\!:\!1)$, $Y = \mathbb{W}^1(B\!:\!1)$, $Z = \mathbb{W}^1(C\!:\!1)$, and $\mathbb{K} = \{(1)\ A \sqcap B \sqsubseteq \bot$, $(2)\ B \sqcap C \sqsubseteq \bot\}$. Then (i) $\mathbb{K}\!:\!(\mathbb{K}\!:\!X \circ Y) \circ Z = \mathbb{W}^t(C\!:\!1)$ with $t \in (0,1)$: because of (1), A is removed from $\mathbb{K}\!:\!X \circ Y$, and because of (2), B is removed from $\mathbb{K}\!:\!(\mathbb{K}\!:\!X \circ Y) \circ Z$; but (ii) $\mathbb{K}\!:\!X \circ (\mathbb{K}\!:\!Y \circ Z) = \mathbb{W}^t(A\!:\!1, C\!:\!1)$ with $t \in (1,2)$ since $\mathbb{K}$ does not remove A from $\mathbb{K}\!:\!X \circ (\mathbb{K}\!:\!Y \circ Z)$ because $B \notin ft(\mathbb{K}\!:\!Y \circ Z)$.
5. Concept combination **is not truth-functional**: it is not necessarily true that if $X \equiv X'$ then $X \circ Y \equiv X' \circ Y$.
   Let $\mathbb{K} = \emptyset$, $X' = \mathbb{W}^3(A\!:\!2, B\!:\!1, C\!:\!1, D\!:\!0.02, E\!:\!0.02)$, $X = \mathbb{W}^3(A\!:\!2, B\!:\!1, C\!:\!1)$, $Y = \mathbb{W}^3(A\!:\!2, D\!:\!1, E\!:\!1)$. Then $X \equiv X' \equiv (A \sqcap B) \sqcup (A \sqcap C)$, $X \circ Y = \mathbb{W}^t(A\!:\!2, B\!:\!1, C\!:\!1, D\!:\!1, E\!:\!1)$ with $t \in (4,5)$, and $X' \circ Y = \mathbb{W}^t(A\!:\!2, B\!:\!1, C\!:\!1, D\!:\!0.51, E\!:\!0.51)$ with $t \in (3.02, 4.02)$ and these two sets of expressions are not equivalent: for example, no matter the choice of $t \in (4,5)$, $X \circ Y$ cannot be satisfied by A, B, and C alone, whereas these suffice to satisfy $X' \circ Y$ whenever $t \le 4$.

The failure of truth-functionality shows that concept combinations are not determined merely by the extensions of the input concepts. In the example, even though X and X' are extensionally equivalent, i.e. they apply to the same individuals, the presence of D and E in X' (but not in X) affects the combination even though such features are irrelevant to determine the extension of X'. This shows how $\mathbb{W}$-expressions may capture some intensional aspects of concepts.

5   Empirical Evaluation of the Algorithm

In what follows, we test our algorithm on *PetBird*, a classical example of noun-noun combination analysed by Hampton [20]. Different variations of the Prototype Theory interpret the nature of the features' weights dissimilarly. *Intensional* accounts (e.g., Hampton'one [20]), assess the weight of the features in terms of their relevance or salience in the definition of a concept. *Extensional* approaches (e.g., Rosch's one [40]), establish them in terms of their frequency distribution across the exemplars of the concepts. To study how these variations impact our algorithm, we conduct two kinds of tests: the first based on the data gathered by Hampton [20], where weights have an *intensional* meaning; the second based on data we collected, meant to explore an *extensional* view on the weights.

Our tests have the following design. First, we extract the $\mathbb{W}$-expressions for *Pet*, *Bird* and *PetBird* from both Hampton's (intensional) data and our (extensional) data, for a total of 6 tooth-expressions. Second, we run our algorithm (with and without a $\mathbb{K}$) on the $\mathbb{W}$-expressions for *Pet* (M) and *Bird* (H) extracted from uniform data. Third, we compare the $\mathbb{W}$-expressions for *PetBird* returned by our algorithm with the corresponding ones extracted from the data.

5.1   Evaluation on Intensional Data

Hampton [20] represents concepts as sets of intensionally weighted features. The features of a concept are individuated through a standard *feature generation task* where subjects are asked to list as many features as possible of a given concept [9]. Subjects are then asked to rate the *importance* of the features for the concept on a scale ranging from -2 to $+4$ (0 excluded): -2 stands for "necessarily false of all possible examples of the concept", and $+4$ for "necessarily true of all possible examples of the concept" (see [20, p.59]). The weights of the features are determined by averaging these ratings. The results for the concepts *Pet*, *Bird*, and *PetBird* (*Birds which are also Pets*) are reported in [20, Table 3, p.69].

To test his model, Hampton asked to evaluate the importance of a given feature across different concepts, e.g., to rate the importance of *Is cuddly* for *Bird* even though such feature was generated for *Pet*. Assuming this information in the context of our combination algorithm sounds artificial and *ad hoc*. The set of features for, e.g., *Bird* would depend on the features generated for the other concepts involved in the combination (*Pet* and *PetBird*) making their prototypes (and the tooth-expressions) task-dependent. To maximise the applicability of our approach, for *Pet* and *Bird*, we select only the features explicitly generated for these concepts, i.e., the ones with non-null production frequency (PF).[5] However, according to Hampton's model, all the features of the combining concepts may contribute to the combined concept.[6] Following Hampton, for *PetBird* we consider the union of the features produced for *Pet*, *Bird*, and *PetBird*.

Columns Bird/H, Pet/H, and PetBird/H of Table 1 report the mean rating MR of the importance of the features found by Hampton. In Bird/H and Pet/H, an "-" indicates a PF = 0. We include in the $\mathbb{W}$-definitions of the concepts Bird$_H$ and Pet$_H$ all the features not marked with "-" in Bird/H and Pet/H, respectively, which are weighted with the corresponding MRs.

Hampton discusses the idea of having a threshold, but he does not set one. However, the MRs offers an index of the features' necessity (the value $+4$ means "necessarily true of all possible examples of the concept"). We assumed as strongly necessary the features with MR>3 (underlined in Table 1). This makes

---

[5] We also dropped the feature *Are of different sizes* that applies to the whole concept and would have been tricky in the extensional evaluation of the weights, see below.

[6] "The model first proposes that the intension of a conjunction is formed as the union of the constituent attribute sets" [20, p.56].

Table 1. Comparison of attribute weights. H = Hampton, NB = Naive Bayes. The columns for "Bird", "Pet" and "Pet Bird" report the weights found in Hampton and extracted by our data via our modified Naive Bayes algorithm. Negative weights are also shown, even though they are removed before applying the concept combination algorithm. The columns for "Pet∘Bird" report the result of our concept combination algorithm under various scenarios: using Hampton's weights or using the weights extracted via the Naive Bayes algorithm, using no knowledge base $(-KB)$ or using a knowledge base (+KB). Underlined features are necessary for the threshold expression to be satisfied (that is, are in **s͞ft**).

Feature	Bird		Pet		PetBird		Pet∘Bird			
							-KB		+KB	
	H	NB	H	NB	H	NB	H	NB	H	NB
sings	1.62	0.52	-	-	1.12	0.79	1.62	0.52	1.62	0.52
flies	2.62	2.9	-	-	2.25	3.62	2.62	2.9	2.62	2.9
has feathers	3.62	4.03	-	-	3.25	3.62	3.62	4.03	3.62	4.03
has a beak	3.12	4.03	-	-	3.25	3.62	3.12	4.03	3.12	4.03
has wings	3.5	4.03	-	-	3.37	3.62	3.5	4.03	3.5	4.03
chirps	2.62	-0.02	-	-	2.12	-0.62	2.62	-	2.62	-
is small	0.87	0.55	-	-	2.12	0.34	0.87	0.55	0.87	0.55
is pretty	1.25	1.82	0.75	2.47	1.5	2.02	1	2.14	1	2.14
is colourful	1.62	0.12	-	-	1.37	1.9	1.62	0.12	1.62	0.12
is cared for, dependent	-	-	2.5	2.47	2.62	3.21	2.5	2.47	2.5	2.47
lives in a domestic home	-	-	2.75	2.59	1.87	2.47	2.75	2.59	2.75	2.59
is enjoyed	0.75	2.06	1.75	1.9	1.87	2.47	1.25	1.98	1.25	1.98
is kept by an owner	-	-	3.12	2.74	3.25	3.21	3.12	2.74	3.12	2.74
is playful	-	-	1.87	1.33	0.87	0.56	1.87	1.33	1.87	1.33
has claws	1	0.95	-	-	1.25	2.02	1	0.95	1	0.95
eats birdseed	1.62	0.48	-	-	1.62	3.62	1.62	0.48	1.62	0.48
is tame	-	-	2.12	1	1.87	0.62	2.12	1	2.12	1
is trained	-	-	1.75	0.12	1.62	0.34	1.75	0.12	1.75	0.12
is kept in a cage	-	-	-	-	2	1.26	-	-	-	-
talks	-	-	-	-	-0.5	-0.5	-	-	-	-
lays eggs	3.12	3.32	-	-	1.12	4.33	3.12	3.32	3.12	3.32
is an animal	3	4.03	3.25	4.74	2.5	4.33	3.25	4.74	3.25	4.74
builds nests	3.75	1.9	-	-	0	0.79	3.75	1.9	3.75	1.9
is carnivorous	0	-0.16	-	-	-0.5	-0.56	-	-	-	-
eats worms	2.25	0.23	-	-	0.87	-0.67	2.25	0.23	2.25	0.23
has two legs	2.87	4.03	-	-	3.25	3.62	2.87	4.03	2.87	4.03
lives in trees	2.75	0.55	-	-	0.25	-1.69	2.75	0.55	2.75	0.55
migrates	2.25	-1.13	-	-	-1.12	-2.67	2.25	-	2.25	-
is lightweight	1.62	0.44	-	-	2.25	1.69	1.62	0.44	1.62	0.44
is free	1.75	2.74	-	-	-0.62	-1.79	1.75	2.74	-	-
is common	1.87	0.02	-	-	0.5	-0.62	1.87	0.02	1.87	0.02
provides companionship	-	-	2.75	1.75	1.75	1.42	2.75	1.75	2.75	1.75
is friendly	-	-	1.87	1.68	1.12	1.05	1.87	1.68	1.87	1.68
provides security	-	-	1.75	-0.75	-0.87	-4.33	1.75	-	1.75	-
is loved	-	-	2	2.06	1.5	2.67	2	2.06	2	2.06
is cuddly	-	-	1	1.5	-0.5	-0.45	1	1.5	1	1.5
is alive	-	-	2.87	4.74	3.37	4.33	2.87	4.74	2.87	4.74
Threshold: >	46.32	35.09	28.98	27.69	54.42	60.15	73.17	57.66	71.42	54.92
Threshold: <	46.44	35.45	29.23	28.34	55.05	60.35	73.42	58.37	71.67	55.63

the choice of a precise threshold irrelevant for the output of our algorithm (which uses the threshold only to determine the strongly necessary features). Still, to assure that Hampton's data can be represented via $\overline{\mathbb{W}}$-expressions, one needs to check if a threshold can be set. To this end we follow Phase 3 of our algorithm with $\overline{\mathsf{sft}}$ containing the features with MR>3. As reported in the last two rows of Table 1, $\mathrm{Bird_H}$, $\mathrm{Pet_H}$ and $\mathrm{PetBird_H}$ have a non empty range of thresholds.

Columns Pet∘Bird/-KB/H and Pet∘Bird/+KB/H of Table 1 report the weights and the features of $\mathrm{Pet_H \circ Bird_H}$ and $\mathbb{K}:\mathrm{Pet_H \circ Bird_H}$ calculated by our algorithm. The weights of the features in $\overline{\mathsf{sft}}$ are underlined and the last two rows report the threshold ranges. Here and after, $\mathbb{K}$ is the following knowledge base which, as we will see, is enough to show feature inheritance failure and emergence:

$$\text{Animal} \sqcap \text{KeptInCage} \sqsubseteq \neg\text{Free} \tag{3a}$$

$$\text{Animal} \sqcap \text{KeptByOwner} \sqcap \text{HasWings} \sqsubseteq \text{KeptInCage} \tag{3b}$$

$$\text{Animal} \sqcap \text{CaredFor} \sqcap \text{LivesInDomesticHome} \sqsubseteq \text{KeptByOwner} \tag{3c}$$

Although the axioms in $\mathbb{K}$ represent plausible common-sense knowledge, one may wonder about their experimental validity. How the data provided by Hampton can be used to evaluate $\mathbb{K}$ is not straightforward, but Sect. 5.2 sketches a strategy to do this evaluation using the data we collected. The $\mathbb{K}$ is used here to introduce constraints between the features of the tooth expressions.

We evaluated the *linear correlation* ([41], §2.6) between the original weights of the features of *PetBird* as observed by Hampton [21] (column PetBird/H of Table 1) and, respectively, the ones computed by the algorithm with (column Pet∘Bird/+KB/H) and without (column Pet∘Bird/-KB/H) the knowledge base $\mathbb{K}$ (calculated by assuming a 0 weight for the features marked with "-"). We can observe a moderate but effective correlation: 0.45 without $\mathbb{K}$, 0.50 in the presence of the $\mathbb{K}$. Adding $\mathbb{K}$ slightly improves the correlation, however notice that in our example, $\mathbb{K}$ rules out only *Is free* which has a 1.75 weight in column Pet∘Bird/-KB/H (quite different from the original -0.62 weight in column PetBird/H). The reason is that *Is an animal*, *Has wings*, and *Is kept by an owner* are all necessary features of $\mathbb{K}:\mathrm{Pet_H \circ Bird_H}$. By axiom (3b), *Is kept in cage* becomes necessary and, by (3a), *Is free* is ruled out. This shows the role of $\mathbb{K}$ to capture inheritance failure, (*Is free* is discarded), and emergence (*Is kept in cage* becomes necessary for $\mathbb{K}:\mathrm{Pet_H \circ Bird_H}$). Note, however, that the necessity of *Is kept in cage* is only implicitly represented by the tooth-expression together with $\mathbb{K}$.

5.2   Evaluation on Extensional Data

We tested our algorithm on the weights' extensional interpretation as follows.

First, for *Pet*, *Bird* and *PetBird* we considered the features discussed in Sect. 5.1. Second, we collected 341 images of different exemplars (113 for *Bird*, 120 for *Pet*, and 108 for *PetBird*) with a simple Google search, where the images with the highest scores were considered representative for the concept at hand. We distributed the three sets of images to 8 judges (ranging between willing students and colleagues), asking them to (*i*) confirm, for each exemplar in an image, the categorisation under the concept under study; and (ii) select the features, among the ones of the category of the exemplar, exhibited by the exemplars in the images (only yes/no answers). Judges confirmed 113/113 exemplars of *Bird*, 113/120 exemplars of *Pet*, and only 75/108 exemplars of *PetBird*. The results of this process are three exemplar by feature applicability matrices [9].

Third, we calculated the weights of the features via the Naive Bayes model, a simple probabilistic classifier ([3], §8.2.2.) which we adapted to extract additive weights from positive examples of a concept only. Given a collection X of exemplars and features F_j for $j \in 1 \dots n$, we write Count_j^+ and Count_j^- for the numbers of exemplars in which F_j respectively does and does not occurs. We set then the weight w_j of F_j as[7]

$$w_j = \log \frac{\text{Count}_j^+(X) + 1}{\text{Count}_j^-(X) + 1}. \tag{4}$$

According to this rule, weights can be zero or negative if $\text{Count}_j^+ \leq \text{Count}_j^-$. Following Sect. 3, for *Pet* and *Bird* only features with $w_j > 0$ are considered.

Fourth, following Hampton, we set as strongly necessary the features of a concept that apply to the totality of the exemplars of such concept, with the tolerance of a single exception (to take into account potentially noisy data). Again, exact thresholds are irrelevant for the combination algorithm. Fifth, we considered the $\mathbb{K}$ introduced in Sect. 5.1.

Columns Bird/NB, Pet/NB, and PetBird/NB of Table 1 report the weights calculated from our data via the adapted Naive Bayes algorithm. Columns Pet∘Bird/-KB/NB and Pet∘Bird/+KB/NB report the weights of the features of, respectively, $\text{Pet}_{NB} \circ \text{Bird}_{NB}$ and $\mathbb{K}:\text{Pet}_{NB} \circ \text{Bird}_{NB}$ calculated by our algorithm. Table 1 also shows that all these concepts have a non-empty threshold range.

Before evaluating our algorithm, we can study the correlation between the intensional vs. extensional views about the weights of features (between, e.g., the weights of Bird/H and Bird/NB in Table 1). The correlation between the weights is 0.58 in the case of *Bird*, 0.55 in the case of *Pet* and 0.81 in the case of *PetBird*, which suggests that the two views are relatively close, especially in the case of *PetBird*. The correlation is higher for *PetBird*: this may plausibly be due to the greater number of involved features (23 for *Bird*, 15 for *Pet*, 37 for *PetBird*), as a smaller number naturally makes the corresponding comparisons more noise-sensitive. It is worth noticing that *Flies*, *Eats birdseeds*, *Lays eggs*, and *Is an animal* are all necessary features of PetBird_{NB} but not of PetBird_H. Moreover, *Flies* and *Eats birdseeds* are necessary features of PetBird_{NB} which are not necessary for either Bird_{NB} or Pet_{NB}: the combination's necessary features do not simply correspond to the union of the two constituents' necessary features. This mismatch could be explained by the set of exemplars we obtained from the google search (e.g., almost all the exemplars of PetBirds the subjects had to evaluate were flying birds, etc.). Interestingly, Hampton explains the emergence or strengthening of features also in terms of *extensional feedbacks*, i.e., feedbacks

---

[7] We add 1 to both counts to avoid potential infinities.

from the known exemplars of a given concept. The emergence observed here may thus have been strengthened by the way we collected our data, namely by the our extensional evaluation. The necessary features of $Pet_H \circ Bird_H$ and $Pet_{NB} \circ Bird_{NB}$ are much closer. This reflects the similarity between $Bird_H$ and $Bird_{NB}$ (resp. Pet) in terms of necessary features (which are preserved by our algorithm).

We also studied the *linear correlation* between the weights of the features we extracted from the data and the ones produced by our algorithm (with and without $\mathbb{K}$). The correlation between the weights of columns PetBird/NB and Pet∘Bird/-KB/NB of Table 1 is 0.73, and it reaches 0.79 in the case of Pet∘Bird/+KB/NB. This is significantly higher than the correlation found in the case of Hampton data. This is an intriguing phenomenon that we wish to verify via further experiments, and which, if confirmed, might highlight a crucial difference between how concept combination operates over intensional and extensional data. Again, in $\mathbb{K}:Pet_{NB} \circ Bird_{NB}$, *Is free* is discarded and *Is kept in cage* is an (implicitly) emergent necessary feature. However, note that now *Is kept by an owner* is not strongly necessary, it becomes necessary by (3c).

As anticipated, we can use our data to empirically assess the adequacy of an axiom with the collected data. For instance, we can evaluate axiom (3a) on the exemplar of *PetBird*, by checking if every time subjects selected both the features *Is an animal* and *Is kept in cage*, they did not select the feature *Is free*. A simple measure of the plausibility of an axiom is the percentage of the exceptions present in the data. All the axioms can be tested on the 75 exemplars of *PetBird* while (3c) can also be tested on the 113 exemplars of *Pet*. We found 3/75 exceptions for (3a), 14/75 for (3b), and 0/75-0/113 for (3c).

6   Related Work

Several systems have been proposed in the literature to introduce and model typicality in DL [1,4,6,7,18,44], however, fewer approaches have analysed the case of noun-noun combination in the same settings. Noticeable exceptions are the works proposed by Britz et al. [5] and Lieto and Pozzato [28].

Britz et al. build over their preferential semantics [6] to address the problem of derived typicality in combined concepts [5]. They distinguish between *defining features*, providing necessary and sufficient conditions for class membership, and *characteristic features*, inducing typicality within that class. However, strongly differing from our approach, the authors suggest that the selection of the features of the compound concept depends on a modelling choice, instead of on an algorithmic and automatic process.

Lieto and Pozzato exploit a non-monotonic preferential semantics [17] to distinguish between *rigid* properties, which define the concepts, and *typical*, defeasible, properties, associated with a number representing the degree of belief of some agent. They propose a combination algorithm which distinguishes between Head H and Modifier M concepts, and which outputs the typical properties of the combination subject to three constraint. The output must: (i) be consistent; (ii) not include all the typical properties of H; (iii) always favour H in case of couples of (jointly) inconsistent typical properties. Nevertheless, first, condition (*ii*) is established *a priori*. Our algorithm ensures this property only when some non-necessary features of H are inconsistent with the necessary features of M. Always discard some feature of H sounds, in contrast, quite artificial. Second, in our case, condition (*iii*) holds only in the case of necessary features , thus the effect is more conservative in our case. Third, in [28] the possibility to rule out a feature depends not only on the degree of belief about that feature, but also on the number of other typical properties with a lower degree of belief. Our approach is more robust. Finally, the authors do not provide any applications of the algorithm in the case of empirical data.

Related is also the work presented by Righetti et al. [38,39], which proposes a dialogic approach to combine concepts that are represented as small domain ontologies. The algorithm consists of a turn-based procedure, where two agents/ontologies try to iteratively build a combined ontology by adding their favourite axiom to the procedure, and where the procedure of axiom weakening [8] is used to solve possible inconsistencies. The algorithm distinguishes between Head and Modifier, but the technical apparatus is substantially different, in primis because here we rely on a representation of concepts motivated by Prototype Theory.

In a formal context, noun-noun combinations have also been analysed by Lewis and Lawry [27]. By exploiting the idea of a *hierarchy* of conceptual spaces [16], Lewis and Lawry's approach can combine different spaces (namely, concepts) to account for some of the phenomena observed in [20]. However, by building on the conceptual spaces framework, any appeal to a logical inference mechanism is lacking in their model. It is thus unclear how the model may apply to more complex scenarios, e.g., the modelling of real data proposed here.

Conceptual combination is also analysed in the literature on Computational Conceptual Blending [10,19,24,25,42,45] which is however motivated by a completely different literature [11]. The focus is then on the formal strategies to model creative *blends*, not on noun-noun combinations or typicality effects .

7   Conclusions

This paper builds on previous work on WDL and addresses the problem of the combination of tooth expressions from a cognitive perspective. We proposed an algorithm for combining tooth expressions designed upon Hampton's model of attribute inheritance [21], studied the logical properties of the operator it gives rise to, and offered a first empirical evaluation of the algorithm.

Studying the logical properties of combination sheds light on the existing disparity between concept combination and concept conjunction. This, in turn, raises the question of when and how concept combination should be favoured over simple conjunction. The distinction between conjunctive concepts and logical conjunctions has been extensively explored in cognitive literature, particularly regarding typicality and vagueness effects in the representation of natural concepts [20,23]. There exist contexts where these effects are limited or absent (e.g. in Biological domains) and conjunction is enough; and contexts (e.g. for common-sense concepts) where it is not. The different use of noun-noun combination and conjunction is thus a matter of context and user choice.

The primary focus of this paper lies in the attribute inheritance model introduced by Hampton, restricting the analysis to conjunctive combinations. However, we aspire to extend our research beyond Hampton's framework in the future: a possible line of work is to analyse conceptual combinations of different types [46].

Wrt the algorithm design, while Hampton does not discuss the choice of the threshold for prototypes, we need a threshold for the combined tooth, and phase 3 of the algorithm is guided only by the need of preserving necessary features. Additional, cognitively relevant criteria and further experiments are required to set a precise threshold.

Our evaluation sheds light on the complexity of extracting tooth-expressions from real data. On the one hand, the way data are collected can impact the tooth-definitions (see, e.g., the contrast between $Bird_H$ with $Bird_{NB}$). On the other hand, the chosen methodology can impact the uniformity of the weight assignment for the tooth-definitions extracted from a single dataset, complicating the comparison of the weights of the Head and Modifier. A more flexible approach would require a normalisation strategy for weights and thresholds, which is left for future work. Relatedly, and quite unexpectedly, the algorithm is slightly less performing, in terms of linear correlation, with Hampton's data than with the extensional ones. A possible explanation is that Hampton [20], unlike us, collects the totality of features produced for both the combining concepts and the combined concept: thus the number of features shared by the combining concepts increases, as well as the possibilities of weights averagings.

As argued in Sect. 5.1, we prefer to model feature incompatibilities at the level of $\mathbb{K}$, which can be seen as a step towards the Knowledge View on concepts [32]. We showed that even a simple $\mathbb{K}$ brings out the phenomena of inheritance failure and attribute emergence and contextually increases linear correlations. One may easily imagine more complex $\mathbb{K}$s, which would further improve such correlations. However, as discussed in Sect. 5.1, a $\mathbb{K}$ can impact the correlations only by ruling out some features. A direction for future work is to study how a $\mathbb{K}$ may be used to decrease (or increase) the weight of a feature without necessarily discarding it. A strategy might be to examine the (in-)compatibility with the $\mathbb{K}$ of *combinations* of features that satisfy the tooth-expression and update weights accordingly, rewarding the compatible ones and penalising the others. This is, however, a matter for future work.

References

1. Baader, F., Ecke, A.: Reasoning with prototypes in the description logic $\mathcal{ALC}$ using weighted tree automata. In: Dediu, A.-H., Janoušek, J., Martín-Vide, C., Truthe, B. (eds.) LATA 2016. LNCS, vol. 9618, pp. 63–75. Springer, Cham (2016). https://doi.org/10.1007/978-3-319-30000-9_5

2. Baader, F., Horrocks, I., Lutz, C., Sattler, U.: An Introduction to Description Logic. Cambridge University Press, Cambridge (2017). https://doi.org/10.1017/9781139025355

3. Bishop, C.M., Nasrabadi, N.M.: Pattern Recognition and Machine Learning, vol. 4. Springer, New York (2006)

4. Bonatti, P.A., Sauro, L.: On the logical properties of the nonmonotonic description logic DLN. Artif. Intell. **248**, 85–111 (2017)

5. Britz, K., Heidema, J., Meyer, T.A.: Modelling object typicality in description logics. In: Description Logics. CEUR Workshop Proceedings, vol. 477. CEUR-WS.org (2009)

6. Britz, K., Heidema, J., Meyer, T.A.: Semantic preferential subsumption. In: Brewka, G., Lang, J. (eds.) Principles of Knowledge Representation and Reasoning: Proceedings of the Eleventh International Conference, KR 2008, Sydney, Australia, September 16–19, 2008, pp. 476–484. AAAI Press (2008), http://www.aaai.org/Library/KR/2008/kr08-046.php

7. Casini, G., Straccia, U.: Rational closure for defeasible description logics. In: Janhunen, T., Niemelä, I. (eds.) JELIA 2010. LNCS (LNAI), vol. 6341, pp. 77–90. Springer, Heidelberg (2010). https://doi.org/10.1007/978-3-642-15675-5_9

8. Confalonieri, R., Galliani, P., Kutz, O., Porello, D., Righetti, G., Troquard, N.: Almost certain termination for $\mathcal{ALC}$ weakening. In: Marreiros, G., Martins, B., Paiva, A., Ribeiro, B., Sardinha, A. (eds.) EPIA 2022. LNCS, vol. 13566, pp. 663–675. Springer, Cham (2022). https://doi.org/10.1007/978-3-031-16474-3_54

9. De Deyne, S., et al.: Exemplar by feature applicability matrices and other Dutch normative data for semantic concepts. Behav. Res. Methods **40**(4), 1030–1048 (2008)

10. Eppe, M., et al.: A computational framework for conceptual blending. Artif. Intell. **256**, 105–129 (2018)

11. Fauconnier, G., Turner, M.: The Way We Think: Conceptual Blending and the Mind's Hidden Complexities. Basic Books, New York (2003)

12. Fodor, J., Lepore, E.: The red herring and the pet fish: why concepts still can't be prototypes. Cognition **58**(2), 253–270 (1996)

13. Galliani, P., Kutz, O., Porello, D., Righetti, G., Troquard, N.: On knowledge dependence in weighted description logic. In: Calvanese, D., Iocchi, L. (eds.) GCAI 2019. Proceedings of the 5th Global Conference on Artificial Intelligence, Bozen/Bolzano, Italy, 17–19 September 2019. EPiC Series in Computing, vol. 65, pp. 68–80. EasyChair (2019). https://doi.org/10.29007/hjt1, https://doi.org/10.29007/hjt1

14. Galliani, P., Kutz, O., Troquard, N.: Succinctness and complexity of $\mathcal{ALC}$ with counting perceptrons. In: Principles of Knowledge Representation and Reasoning: Proceedings of the 20th International Conference (KR 2023). Rhodes, Greece, September 2–8, 2023 (2023)

15. Galliani, P., Righetti, G., Kutz, O., Porello, D., Troquard, N.: Perceptron connectives in knowledge representation. In: Keet, C.M., Dumontier, M. (eds.) EKAW 2020. LNCS (LNAI), vol. 12387, pp. 183–193. Springer, Cham (2020). https://doi.org/10.1007/978-3-030-61244-3_13

16. Gärdenfors, P.: Conceptual Spaces - The Geometry of Thought. MIT Press, Cambridge (2000)

17. Giordano, L., Gliozzi, V., Olivetti, N., Pozzato, G.L.: Preferential description logics. In: Dershowitz, N., Voronkov, A. (eds.) LPAR 2007. LNCS (LNAI), vol. 4790, pp. 257–272. Springer, Heidelberg (2007). https://doi.org/10.1007/978-3-540-75560-9_20

18. Giordano, L., Gliozzi, V., Olivetti, N., Pozzato, G.L.: A non-monotonic description logic for reasoning about typicality. Artif. Intell. **195**, 165–202 (2013)

19. Goguen, J.A., Harrell, D.F.: Style: a computational and conceptual blending-based approach. In: Argamon, S., Burns, K., Dubnov, S. (eds.) The structure of style, pp. 291–316. Springer, Heidelberg (2010). https://doi.org/10.1007/978-3-642-12337-5_12

20. Hampton, J.A.: Inheritance of attributes in natural concept conjunctions. Memory Cogn. **15**(1), 55–71 (1987)

21. Hampton, J.A.: Overextension of conjunctive concepts: evidence for a unitary model of concept typicality and class inclusion. J. Exp. Psychol. Learn. Mem. Cogn. **14**(1), 12–32 (1988)

22. Hampton, J.A.: Testing the prototype theory of concepts. J. Mem. Lang. **34**(5), 686–708 (1995)

23. Hampton, J.A.: Compositionality and concepts. In: Hampton, J.A., Winter, Y. (eds.) Compositionality and Concepts in Linguistics and Psychology, pp. 95–121. Springer, Cham (2017). https://doi.org/10.1007/978-3-319-45977-6

24. Hedblom, M.M., Kutz, O., Neuhaus, F.: Image schemas in computational conceptual blending. Cogn. Syst. Res. **39**, 42–57 (2016)

25. Hedblom, M.M., Righetti, G., Kutz, O.: Deciphering the cookie monster: a case study in impossible combinations. In: ICCC, pp. 222–225 (2021)

26. Jackendoff, R.: English Noun-noun Compounds in Conceptual Semantics. The Semantics of Compounding, pp. 15–37 (2016)

27. Lewis, M., Lawry, J.: Hierarchical conceptual spaces for concept combination. Artif. Intell. **237**, 204–227 (2016). https://doi.org/10.1016/j.artint.2016.04.008

28. Lieto, A., Pozzato, G.L.: A description logic framework for commonsense conceptual combination integrating typicality, probabilities and cognitive heuristics. J. Exp. Theor. Artif. Intell. **32**(5), 769–804 (2020). https://doi.org/10.1080/0952813X.2019.1672799

29. Masolo, C., Porello, D.: Representing concepts by weighted formulas. In: Formal Ontology in Information Systems - Proceedings of the 10th International Conference, FOIS 2018, Cape Town, South Africa, 19–21 September 2018, pp. 55–68 (2018)

30. Murphy, G.L.: Noun phrase interpretation and conceptual combination. J. Mem. Lang. **29**(3), 259–288 (1990)

31. Murphy, G.L.: The Big Book of Concepts. MIT press, Cambridge (2002)

32. Murphy, G.L., Medin, D.: The role of theories in conceptual coherence. Psychol. Rev. **92**, 289–316 (1985)

33. Osherson, D.N., Smith, E.E.: On the adequacy of prototype theory as a theory of concepts. Cognition **9**(1), 35–58 (1981)

34. Porello, D., Kutz, O., Righetti, G., Troquard, N., Galliani, P., Masolo, C.: A toothful of concepts: Towards a theory of weighted concept combination. In: Proceedings of DL Workshop, vol. 2373. CEUR-WS.org (2019)

35. Righetti, G., Masolo, C., Troquard, N., Kutz, O., Porello, D.: Concept combination in weighted description logics. In: JOWO 2021. Proceedings of the Joint Ontology Workshops, Bozen/Bolzano, Italy, 13–17 September 2021. CEUR Workshop Proceedings (2021)

36. Righetti, G., Porello, D., Confalonieri, R.: Evaluating the interpretability of threshold operators. In: Corcho, Ó., Hollink, L., Kutz, O., Troquard, N., Ekaputra, F.J. (eds.) EKAW 2022. LNCS, vol. 13514, pp. 136–151. Springer, Cham (2022). https://doi.org/10.1007/978-3-031-17105-5_10

37. Righetti, G., Porello, D., Kutz, O., Troquard, N., Masolo, C.: Pink panthers and toothless tigers: three problems in classification. In: Proceedings of the 7th International Workshop on Artificial Intelligence and Cognition (AIC 2019), pp. 39–53 (2019)
38. Righetti, G., Porello, D., Troquard, N., Kutz, O., Hedblom, M., Galliani, P.: Asymmetric hybrids: dialogues for computational concept combination. In: Formal Ontology in Information Systems: Proceedings of the 12th International Conference (FOIS 2021). IOS Press (2021)
39. Righetti, G., Porello, D., Troquard, N., Kutz, O., Hedblom, M.M., Galliani, P.: Asymmetric hybrids: dialogues for computational concept combination (extended abstract). In: Raedt, L.D. (ed.) Proceedings of the Thirty-First International Joint Conference on Artificial Intelligence, IJCAI 2022, Vienna, Austria, 23–29 July 2022, pp. 5329–5333. ijcai.org (2022). https://doi.org/10.24963/ijcai.2022/745
40. Rosch, E.: Cognitive representations of semantic categories. J. Exp. Psychol. Gen. **104**, 192–233 (1975)
41. Ross, S.M.: Introduction to Probability and Statistics for Engineers and Scientists. Academic press, Cambridge (2020)
42. Schorlemmer, M., Plaza, E.: A uniform model of computational conceptual blending. Cogn. Syst. Res. **65**, 118–137 (2021)
43. Smith, E.E., Medin, D.L.: Categories and concepts, vol. 9. Harvard University Press, Cambridge (1981)
44. Varzinczak, I.: A note on a description logic of concept and role typicality for defeasible reasoning over ontologies. Log. Univers. **12**, 297–325 (2018)
45. Veale, T.: From conceptual mash-ups to badass blends: a robust computational model of conceptual blending. In: Veale, T., Cardoso, F. (eds.) Computational Creativity. CSCS, pp. 71–89. Springer, Cham (2019). https://doi.org/10.1007/978-3-319-43610-4_4
46. Wisniewski, E.J.: When concepts combine. Psychon. Bull. Rev. **4**(2), 167–183 (1997)

Logics of Knowledge and Belief

How Easy it is to Know How: An Upper Bound for the Satisfiability Problem

Carlos Areces[1,2], Valentin Cassano[1,2,3], Pablo F. Castro[1,3],
Raul Fervari[1,2,4(✉)], and Andrés R. Saravia[1,2]

[1] Consejo Nacional de Investigaciones Científicas y Técnicas (CONICET),
Buenos Aires, Argentina
rfervari@unc.edu.ar
[2] Universidad Nacional de Córdoba (UNC), Córdoba, Argentina
[3] Universidad Nacional de Río Cuarto (UNRC), Río Cuarto, Argentina
[4] Guangdong Technion - Israel Institute of Technology (GTIIT), Shantou, China

Abstract. We investigate the complexity of the satisfiability problem for a modal logic expressing 'knowing how' assertions, related to an agent's abilities to achieve a certain goal. We take one of the most standard semantics for this kind of logics based on linear plans. Our main result is a proof that checking satisfiability of a 'knowing how' formula can be done in Σ_2^P. The algorithm we present relies on eliminating nested modalities in a formula, and then performing multiple calls to a satisfiability checking oracle for propositional logic.

Keywords: Knowing How · Complexity · Satisfiability

1 Introduction

The term 'Epistemic Logic' [15] encompasses a family of logical formalisms aimed at reasoning about the knowledge of autonomous agents about a given scenario. Originally, epistemic logics restricted their attention to so-called *knowing that*, i.e., the capability of agents to know about certain facts. More recently, several logics have been proposed to reason about alternative forms of knowledge (see [32] for a discussion). For instance, *knowing whether* is looked into in [7]; *knowing why* in [34]; and *knowing the value* in [3,12], just to mention a few. Finally, a novel approach focuses on *knowing how* –related to an agent's ability to achieve a goal [8]. This concept is particularly interesting, as it has been argued to provide a fresh way to reason about scenarios involving strategies in AI, such as those found in automated planning (see, e.g., [6]).

The first attempts to capture knowing how were through a combination of 'knowing that' and actions (see, e.g., [14,18,25,26]). However, it has been discussed, e.g., in [13,16], that this idea does not lead to an accurate representation of knowing how. In response, a new logic is presented in [31,33] featuring an original modality specifically tailored to model the concept of 'knowing how'. In a nutshell, an agent knows how to a achieve a goal φ under some initial

S. Gaggl et al. (Eds.): JELIA 2023, LNAI 14281, pp. 405–419, 2023.
https://doi.org/10.1007/978-3-031-43619-2_28

condition ψ, written $\mathsf{Kh}(\psi, \varphi)$, if and only if there exists a 'proper' plan π, i.e., a finite sequence of actions, that unerringly leads the agent from situations in which ψ holds only to situations in which φ holds. A 'proper' plan is taken as one whose execution never aborts, an idea that takes inspiration from the notion of *strong executability* from contingent planning [29]. As discussed in, e.g., [13,17], the quantification pattern we just described cannot be captured using logics with 'knowing that' modalities and actions. For this reason, the new Kh modality from [31,33] has reached a certain consensus in the community as an accurate way of modelling 'knowing how'. Moreover, it has paved the way to a deep study of knowing how, and to a rich family of logics capturing variants of the initial reading. Some examples of which are a ternary modality of knowing how with intermediate constraints [21]; a knowing how modality with weak plans [19]; a local modality for strategically knowing how [9] (and some relatives, see [27,28]); and, finally, a knowing how modality which considers an epistemic indistinguishability relation among plans [1].

As witnessed by all the ideas it triggered, the foundational work in [31,33] greatly improved the understanding of 'knowing how' from a logical standpoint. The literature on logics of 'knowing how' explores a wide variety of results, such as axiom systems (in most of the works cited above), proof methods [20,23], and expressivity [10], just to name a few. Yet, if we consider 'knowing how' logics as suitable candidates for modelling problems in strategic reasoning, it is important to consider how difficult (or how easy) it is to use these logics for reasoning tasks. There have been some recent developments on the complexity of logics with 'knowing how' modalities. For instance, model-checking for the Kh modality above, and some of its variants, is investigated in [5]. The complexity of model-checking and the decidability status of satisfiability for the local 'knowing how' modality from [9], and some of its generalizations, is explored in [24]. These two problems are also explored for 'knowing how' with epistemic indistinguishability in [1]. Notwithstanding, the complexity of the satisfiability problem for the original Kh modality from [31,33] is still unknown ([22] presents only a decidability statement). In this work, we shed some light into this matter.

Our contribution is to provide an upper for the satisfiability problem of the knowing how logic from [31,33], called here $\mathsf{L_{Kh}}$. More precisely, we introduce an algorithm for deciding satisfiability that is in Σ_2^P, the second level of the polynomial hierarchy (PH) [30]. In short, this complexity class can be though as those problems invoking an NP oracle a polynomial number of times, and whose underlying problem is also in NP (see e.g. [2]). Currently, it is unknown whether PH collapses, or it is strictly contained in PSpace. This being said, having an algorithm in a lower level of PH is generally understood as a good indication that the problem is close to, e.g., NP or Co-NP. It is easy to see that NP is a lower bound for checking satisfiability in $\mathsf{L_{Kh}}$, as it extends propositional logic. For an upper bound, a natural candidate is PSpace, as for instance the model-checking problem for $\mathsf{L_{Kh}}$ is PSpace-complete [5], a potentially higher complexity of what is proved here for satisfiability. We argue that this is due to the fact that in model-checking the full expressivity of the semantics is exploited (specially related to properties of regular languages), whereas for satisfiability, all this expressivity is completely hidden. Although our procedure does not lead to a tight complexity characterization, it gives us an interesting upper bound towards filling this gap.

We put forth that our result is not obvious. To obtain it, we combine techniques such as defining a normal form to eliminate nested modalities, calling an NP oracle to guess propositional valuations and computing a closure over a matrix of formulas to combine them, adapting the Floyd-Warshall algorithm [4].

The article is organized as follows. In Sect. 2 we introduce some notation and the basic definitions of the logic L_{Kh}. Section 3 is devoted to incrementally show our result. Finally, in Sect. 4 we provide some remarks and future lines of research.

2   Knowing How Logic

From here onwards, we assume Prop is a denumerable set of *proposition symbols*, and Act is a denumerable set of *action symbols*. We refer to $\pi \in Act^*$ as a *plan*.

Definition 1. *The* language L_{Kh} *is determined by the grammar:*

$$\varphi, \psi ::= p \mid \neg\varphi \mid \varphi \vee \psi \mid Kh(\varphi, \psi),$$

where $p \in$ Prop. *We use* $\bot$, $\top$, $\varphi \wedge \psi$, $\varphi \rightarrow \psi$, *and* $\varphi \leftrightarrow \psi$ *as the usual abbreviations;* $A\varphi$ *is defined as* $Kh(\neg\varphi, \bot)$ *(see e.g. [31, 33]), while* $E\varphi$ *abbreviates* $\neg A \neg \varphi$. *The elements of* L_{Kh} *are formulas.*

We read $Kh(\varphi, \psi)$ as: "*the agent knows how to achieve ψ given φ*". We call φ and ψ, the precondition and the postcondition of $Kh(\varphi, \psi)$, respectively. We read $A\varphi$ as: "*φ holds anywhere*"; and its dual $E\varphi$ as: "*φ holds somewhere*". As it is usually done, we refer to A and E as the *universal* and *existential* modalities [11].

Formulas of L_{Kh} are interpreted with respect to *labelled transition systems* over so-called *strongly executable plans*. Sometimes, we refer to LTS as *models*. We introduce their definitions below.

Definition 2. *A labelled transition system (LTS) is a tuple* $\mathfrak{M} = \langle S, R, V \rangle$ *s.t.:*

(1) S *is a non-empty set of* states;
(2) $R = \{R_a \mid a \in Act\}$ *is a collection of binary relations on* S; *and*
(3) $V : Prop \rightarrow 2^S$ *is a valuation function.*

Definition 3. *Let* $\{R_a \mid a \in Act\}$ *be a collection of binary relations on* S. *Let* $\varepsilon \in Act^*$ *be the empty plan. We define:* $R_\varepsilon = \{(s,s) \mid s \in S\}$, *and for every* $\pi \in Act^*$, *and* $a \in Act$, $R_{\pi a} = R_\pi R_a$ *(i.e., their composition). For every relation* R_π, *and* $T \subseteq S$, *define* $R_\pi(T) = \{(s,t) \mid s \in T \text{ and } (s,t) \in R_\pi\}$, *and* $R_\pi(t) = R_\pi(\{t\})$.

The notion of *strong executability* determines the "adequacy" of a plan. Strong executability takes inspiration from conformant planning [29], and its jusification is discussed at length in [31].

Definition 4. *Let* $\pi = a_1 \ldots a_n \in \mathsf{Act}^*$, *and* $1 \le i \le j \le n$, *we denote:* $\pi_i = a_i$; $\pi[i,j] = a_i \ldots a_j$; *and* $|\pi| = n$. *Moreover, let* $\mathfrak{M} = \langle S, R, V \rangle$ *be an LTS; we say that* π *is strongly executable (SE) at* $s \in S$, *iff for all* $i \in [1, |\pi| - 1]$ *and all* $t \in R_{(\pi[1,i])}(s)$, *it follows that* $R_{\pi_{(i+1)}}(t) \ne \emptyset$. *The set of all states at which* π *is strongly executable is defined as* $\mathrm{SE}(\pi) = \{s \mid \pi \text{ is SE at } s\}$. *Note:* $\mathrm{SE}(\varepsilon) = S$.

We illustrate the notions we just introduced with a simple example.

Example 1. Let $\mathfrak{M} = \langle S, R, V \rangle$ be the LTS depicted below and $\pi = ab$. We have, $R_\pi(s) = \{u\}$, and $R_{\pi[1,1]}(s) = R_a(s) = \{t, v\}$. It can be seen that $s \in \mathrm{SE}(a)$; while $s \notin \mathrm{SE}(\pi)$ –since $v \in R_{\pi[1,1]}(s)$ and $R_{\pi_{(2)}}(v) = R_b(v) = \emptyset$. Finally, we have that $\mathrm{SE}(\varepsilon) = S$, $\mathrm{SE}(a) = \{s\}$ and $\mathrm{SE}(ab) = \emptyset$.

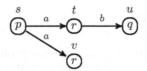

We are now ready to introduce the semantics of $\mathsf{L_{Kh}}$, based on [31,33].

Definition 5. *Let* $\mathfrak{M} = \langle S, R, V \rangle$ *be an LTS, we define* $[\![\varphi]\!]^{\mathfrak{M}}$ *inductively as:*

$$[\![p]\!]^{\mathfrak{M}} = V(p) \qquad [\![\neg\varphi]\!]^{\mathfrak{M}} = S \setminus [\![\varphi]\!]^{\mathfrak{M}} \qquad [\![\varphi \vee \psi]\!]^{\mathfrak{M}} = [\![\varphi]\!]^{\mathfrak{M}} \cup [\![\varphi]\!]^{\mathfrak{M}}$$

$$[\![\mathsf{Kh}(\varphi, \psi)]\!]^{\mathfrak{M}} = \begin{cases} S & \text{if exists } \pi \in \mathsf{Act}^* \text{s.t. } [\![\varphi]\!]^{\mathfrak{M}} \subseteq \mathrm{SE}(\pi) \text{ and } R_\pi([\![\varphi]\!]^{\mathfrak{M}}) \subseteq [\![\psi]\!]^{\mathfrak{M}} \\ \emptyset & \text{otherwise.} \end{cases}$$

We say that a plan $\pi \in \mathsf{Act}^*$ *is a* witness *for* $\mathsf{Kh}(\varphi, \psi)$ *iff* $[\![\varphi]\!]^{\mathfrak{M}} \subseteq \mathrm{SE}(\pi)$ *and* $R_\pi([\![\varphi]\!]^{\mathfrak{M}}) \subseteq [\![\psi]\!]^{\mathfrak{M}}$. *We use* $([\![\varphi]\!]^{\mathfrak{M}})^{\complement}$ *instead of* $S \setminus [\![\varphi]\!]^{\mathfrak{M}}$. *We write* $\mathfrak{M} \Vdash \varphi$ *as an alternative to* $[\![\varphi]\!]^{\mathfrak{M}} = S$; *and* $\mathfrak{M}, s \Vdash \varphi$ *as an alternative to* $s \in [\![\varphi]\!]^{\mathfrak{M}}$.

Example 2. Let $\mathfrak{M}$ be the LTS from Example 1. From Definition 5, we have $[\![\mathsf{Kh}(p, r)]\!]^{\mathfrak{M}} = S$ (using a as a witness), while $[\![\mathsf{Kh}(p, q)]\!]^{\mathfrak{M}} = \emptyset$ (there is no witness for the formula).

We included the universal modality A as abbreviation since formulas of the form $\mathsf{A}\varphi$ play a special role in our treatment of the complexity of the satisfiability problem for $\mathsf{L_{Kh}}$. It is proven in, e.g., [31,33], that $\mathsf{A}\varphi$ and $\mathsf{E}\varphi$ behave as the universal and existential modalities ([11]), respectively. Recall that $\mathsf{A}\varphi$ is defined as $\mathsf{Kh}(\neg\varphi, \bot)$, which semantically states that φ holds everywhere in a model iff $\neg\varphi$ leads always to impossible situations. Formulas of this kind are called here 'global'. Below, we formally restate the results just discussed.

Proposition 1. *Let* $\mathfrak{M} = \langle S, R, V \rangle$ *and* ψ *and* χ *be formulas s.t.* $[\![\chi]\!]^{\mathfrak{M}} = \emptyset$; *then* $[\![\mathsf{Kh}(\psi, \chi)]\!]^{\mathfrak{M}} = S$ *iff* $[\![\neg\psi]\!]^{\mathfrak{M}} = S$.

Corollary 1. *Let* $\mathfrak{M} = \langle S, R, V \rangle$ *and a formula* φ, $\mathfrak{M}, s \Vdash \mathsf{A}\varphi$ *iff* $[\![\varphi]\!]^{\mathfrak{M}} = S$.

We introduce now Proposition 2, which is of use in the rest of the paper.

Proposition 2. *Let ψ, ψ', χ, χ' and φ be formulas, and $\mathfrak{M}$ an LTS; then:*

(1) $[\![\psi']\!]^{\mathfrak{M}} \subseteq [\![\psi]\!]^{\mathfrak{M}}$ and $[\![\chi]\!]^{\mathfrak{M}} \subseteq [\![\chi']\!]^{\mathfrak{M}}$ implies $[\![\mathsf{Kh}(\psi, \chi)]\!]^{\mathfrak{M}} \subseteq [\![\mathsf{Kh}(\psi', \chi')]\!]^{\mathfrak{M}}$;
(2) $[\![\psi]\!]^{\mathfrak{M}} \subseteq [\![\psi']\!]^{\mathfrak{M}}$ implies $([\![\mathsf{Kh}(\varphi, \psi)]\!]^{\mathfrak{M}} \cap [\![\mathsf{Kh}(\psi', \chi)]\!]^{\mathfrak{M}}) \subseteq [\![\mathsf{Kh}(\varphi, \chi)]\!]^{\mathfrak{M}}$.

We conclude this section with some useful definitions.

Definition 6. *A formula φ is* satisfiable, *written* $\mathsf{Sat}(\varphi)$, *iff there is $\mathfrak{M}$ s.t. $[\![\varphi]\!]^{\mathfrak{M}} \neq \emptyset$. A finite set $\Phi = \{\varphi_1, \ldots, \varphi_n\}$ of formulas is* satisfiable, *written* $\mathsf{Sat}(\Phi)$, *iff $\mathsf{Sat}(\varphi_1 \wedge \cdots \wedge \varphi_n)$. For convenience, we define $\mathsf{Sat}(\emptyset)$ as true. We use $\mathsf{Unsat}(\varphi)$ iff $\mathsf{Sat}(\varphi)$ is false; similarly, $\mathsf{Unsat}(\Phi)$ iff $\mathsf{Sat}(\Phi)$ is false. Finally, whenever $\mathsf{Sat}(\varphi)$ iff $\mathsf{Sat}(\varphi')$, we call φ and φ'* equisatisfiable, *and write $\varphi \equiv_{\mathsf{Sat}} \varphi'$.*

Definition 7. *The* modal depth *of a formula φ, written $\mathsf{md}(\varphi)$, is defined as:*

$$\mathsf{md}(\varphi) = \begin{cases} 0 & \text{if } \varphi \in \mathsf{Prop} \\ \mathsf{md}(\psi) & \text{if } \varphi = \neg\psi \\ \max(\mathsf{md}(\psi), \mathsf{md}(\chi)) & \text{if } \varphi = \psi \vee \chi \\ 1 + \max(\mathsf{md}(\psi), \mathsf{md}(\chi)) & \text{if } \varphi = \mathsf{Kh}(\psi, \chi). \end{cases}$$

We use $\mathsf{sf}(\varphi)$ to indicate the set of subformulas *of φ. We say that $\mathsf{Kh}(\psi, \chi)$ is a leaf of φ iff $\mathsf{Kh}(\psi, \chi) \in \mathsf{sf}(\varphi)$ and $\mathsf{md}(\psi) = \mathsf{md}(\chi) = 0$ (i.e., $\mathsf{md}(\mathsf{Kh}(\psi, \chi)) = 1$).*

In words, the modal depth of a formula is the length of the longest sequence of nested modalities in the formula; whereas a leaf is a subformula of depth one. Notice that, since $\mathsf{A}\varphi$ is a shortcut for $\mathsf{Kh}(\neg\varphi, \bot)$, we have $\mathsf{md}(\mathsf{A}\varphi) = 1 + \mathsf{md}(\varphi)$.

Example 3. Let $\varphi = \mathsf{Kh}(p, \mathsf{Kh}(\neg q, p \rightarrow q)) \vee \mathsf{Kh}(r, t)$; it can easily be checked that $\mathsf{md}(\varphi) = 2$ and that $\mathsf{Kh}(\neg q, p \rightarrow q)$ and $\mathsf{Kh}(r, t)$ are its modal leaves.

3 An Upper Bound for the Satisfiability Problem of $\mathsf{L_{Kh}}$

In this section we establish an upper bound on the complexity of the satisfiability problem for $\mathsf{L_{Kh}}$, which is the main result of our paper. We start with some preliminary definitions and results.

Proposition 3. *Let φ' be the result of replacing all occurrences of a leaf θ in φ by a proposition symbol $k \notin \mathsf{sf}(\varphi)$; it follows that $\varphi \equiv_{\mathsf{Sat}} (\varphi' \wedge (\mathsf{A}k \leftrightarrow \theta))$.*

We say that φ is in *leaf normal form* iff $\mathsf{md}(\varphi) \leq 1$. Proposition 4 tells us that we can put any formula into an equisatisfiable formula in leaf normal form. The function FLATTEN in Algorithm 1 tells us how to do this in polynomial time.

Proposition 4. *Algorithm 1 is in P; on input φ, it outputs φ_0 and φ_1 such that $\mathsf{md}(\varphi_0) = 0$, $\mathsf{md}(\varphi_1) = 1$, and $\varphi \equiv_{\mathsf{Sat}} (\varphi_0 \wedge \varphi_1)$.*

The result in Proposition 4 allows us to think of the complexity of the satisfiability problem for $\mathsf{L_{Kh}}$ by restricting our attention to formulas in leaf normal form. In turn, this enables us to work towards a solution in terms of subproblems. More precisely, given φ_0 and φ_1 in the leaf normal form that results from FLATTEN, the subproblems are (i) determining the satisfiability of φ_0; and (ii) determining the satisfiability of φ_1 based on a solution to (i). The solution to (i) is well-known, φ_0 is a propositional formula. We split the solution of (ii) into (a) determining when formulas of the form $\mathsf{Kh}(\psi_1, \chi_1) \wedge \cdots \wedge \mathsf{Kh}(\psi_n, \chi_n)$ are satisfiable, see Proposition 5; (b) determining when formulas of the form $\neg\mathsf{Kh}(\psi_1', \chi_1') \wedge \cdots \wedge \neg\mathsf{Kh}(\psi_m', \chi_m')$ are satisfiable, see Proposition 7; and (c) combining (a) and (b), see Proposition 11. We present (a), (b), and (c), in a way such that they incrementally lead to a solution to the satisfiability problem for $\mathsf{L_{Kh}}$. Finally, in Proposition 12, we show how to combine (i) and (ii) to obtain an upper bound on the complexity of this problem.

Let us start by solving the first problem: checking whether a conjunction φ of positive formulas in leaf normal form are satisfiable altogether. In a nutshell, we show that solving this problem boils down to building a set I of the preconditions of those subformulas whose postconditions are falsified in the context of φ, and checking whether the formulas in I are satisfiable or not. Intuitively, the formulas in I correspond to 'global' formulas. We made precise these ideas in Proposition 5.

Proposition 5. *Let* $\varphi = \mathsf{Kh}(\psi_1, \chi_1) \wedge \cdots \wedge \mathsf{Kh}(\psi_n, \chi_n)$ *be such that* $\mathsf{md}(\varphi) = 1$; *and let the sets* $I_0, \ldots, I_n$ *be defined as follows:*

$$I_i = \begin{cases} \{k \in [1, n] \mid \mathsf{Unsat}(\chi_k)\} & \text{if } i = 0, \\ I_{(i-1)} \cup \{k \in [1, n] \mid \mathsf{Unsat}(\{\neg\psi_{k'} \mid k' \in I_{(i-1)}\} \cup \{\chi_k\})\} & \text{if } i > 0, \end{cases}$$

where $i \in [0, n]$; *further, let* $I = I_n$. *Then: (1)* $\mathsf{Sat}(\varphi)$ *iff (2)* $\mathsf{Sat}(\bigwedge_{i \in I} \neg\psi_i)$.

Proof. ($\Rightarrow$) Suppose that $\mathsf{Sat}(\varphi)$ holds, i.e., exists $\mathfrak{M}$ s.t. $[\![\varphi]\!]^{\mathfrak{M}} = \mathsf{S}$. From this assumption, we know that, for every $j \in [1, n]$, $[\![\mathsf{Kh}(\psi_i, \chi_i)]\!]^{\mathfrak{M}} = \mathsf{S}$. The proof is concluded if $[\![\bigwedge_{i \in I} \neg\psi_i]\!]^{\mathfrak{M}} \neq \emptyset$. We obtain this last result with the help of the following auxiliary lemma:

$$(*) \text{ for all } k \in I_i, [\![\chi_k]\!]^{\mathfrak{M}} = \emptyset \text{ and } [\![\neg\psi_k]\!]^{\mathfrak{M}} = \mathsf{S}$$

The lemma is obtained by induction on the construction of I_i. The base case is direct. Let $k \in I_0$; from the definition of I_0, we get $\mathsf{Unsat}(\chi_k)$; this implies $[\![\chi_k]\!]^{\mathfrak{M}} = \emptyset$; which implies $\mathsf{S} = [\![\mathsf{Kh}(\psi_k, \chi_k)]\!]^{\mathfrak{M}} = [\![\mathsf{A}\neg\psi_k]\!]^{\mathfrak{M}} = [\![\neg\psi_k]\!]^{\mathfrak{M}}$. For the inductive step, let $k \in I_{(i+1)} \setminus I_i$. From the Inductive Hypothesis, for all $k' \in I_i$, $[\![\chi_{k'}]\!]^{\mathfrak{M}} = \emptyset$ and $[\![\neg\psi_{k'}]\!]^{\mathfrak{M}} = \mathsf{S}$. This implies (†) $[\![\bigwedge_{k' \in I_i} \neg\psi_{k'}]\!]^{\mathfrak{M}} = \mathsf{S}$. From the definition of $I_{(i+1)}$, $\mathsf{Unsat}(\{\neg\psi_{k'} \mid k' \in I_i\} \cup \{\chi_k\})$. This is equivalent to $[\![\bigwedge_{k' \in I_i} \neg\psi_{k'}]\!]^{\mathfrak{M}} \subseteq [\![\neg\chi_k]\!]^{\mathfrak{M}}$. From (†), $\mathsf{S} \subseteq [\![\neg\chi_k]\!]^{\mathfrak{M}} = \mathsf{S}$. Thus, $[\![\chi_k]\!]^{\mathfrak{M}} = \emptyset$ and $[\![\neg\psi_k]\!]^{\mathfrak{M}} = \mathsf{S}$. Since $I = I_n$; using (*) we get $[\![\bigwedge_{i \in I} \neg\psi_i]\!]^{\mathfrak{M}} = \mathsf{S} \neq \emptyset$. This proves (2).

($\Leftarrow$) The proof is by contradiction. Suppose (2) and $\mathsf{Unsat}(\varphi)$. Then, for all $\mathfrak{M}$, (†) $[\![\varphi]\!]^{\mathfrak{M}} = \emptyset$. Let $J = \{j \in [1,n] \mid \mathsf{Unsat}(\{(\bigwedge_{i \in I} \neg \psi_i), \psi_j\})\}$. Moreover, let $\mathfrak{M} = \langle \mathrm{S}, \mathrm{R}, \mathrm{V} \rangle$ be s.t. S is the smallest set containing all valuations that make $(\bigwedge_{i \in I} \neg \psi_i)$ true. From (2), we know that $\mathrm{S} \neq \emptyset$ and $[\![\neg \psi_k]\!]^{\mathfrak{M}} = \mathrm{S}$ for all $k \in I$. By induction on the construction of $I = I_n$, we get that $[\![\chi_k]\!]^{\mathfrak{M}} = \emptyset$ for all $k \in I = \bigcup_{i=0}^{n} I_i$. The case for $k \in I_0$ is direct since $\mathsf{Unsat}(\chi_k)$, thus $[\![\chi_k]\!]^{\mathfrak{M}} = \emptyset$. For the inductive case, let $k \in I_i \setminus I_{i-1}$, then $\mathsf{Unsat}(\{\neg \psi_{k'} \mid k' \in I_{(i-1)}\} \cup \{\chi_k\})$. This is equivalent to say that the implication $((\bigwedge_{k' \in I_{(i-1)}} \neg \psi_{k'}) \rightarrow \neg \chi_k)$ is valid. Thus, $[\![\bigwedge_{k' \in I_{(i-1)}} \neg \psi_{k'}]\!]^{\mathfrak{M}} \subseteq [\![\neg \chi_k]\!]^{\mathfrak{M}}$. By hypothesis, $[\![\bigwedge_{k' \in I} \neg \psi_{k'}]\!]^{\mathfrak{M}} = \mathrm{S}$. Thus, $[\![\bigwedge_{k' \in I_{(i-1)}} \neg \psi_{k'}]\!]^{\mathfrak{M}} = \mathrm{S}$, and we get $[\![\neg \chi_k]\!]^{\mathfrak{M}} = \mathrm{S}$ and $[\![\chi_k]\!]^{\mathfrak{M}} = \emptyset$. In turn, for all $k \in J$, since $\mathsf{Unsat}(\{(\bigwedge_{i \in I} \neg \psi_i), \psi_k\})$ and $[\![\bigwedge_{i \in I} \neg \psi_i]\!]^{\mathfrak{M}} = \mathrm{S}$ we can conclude that $[\![\psi_k]\!]^{\mathfrak{M}} = \emptyset$. Thus, we have that $[\![\mathsf{Kh}(\psi_k, \chi_k)]\!]^{\mathfrak{M}} = [\![\mathsf{A} \neg \psi_k]\!]^{\mathfrak{M}} = \mathrm{S}$, for all $k \in I \cup J$. Then, from (†), exists $K = \{k \mid [\![\mathsf{Kh}(\psi_k, \chi_k)]\!]^{\mathfrak{M}} = \emptyset\}$ s.t. $\emptyset \subset K \subseteq [1,n] \setminus (I \cup J)$. For all $k \in K$, $[\![\psi_k]\!]^{\mathfrak{M}} \neq \emptyset$ since $\mathsf{Sat}(\{(\bigwedge_{i \in I} \neg \psi_i), \psi_k\})$; and $[\![\chi_k]\!]^{\mathfrak{M}} \neq \emptyset$ since $\mathsf{Sat}(\{\neg \psi_{k'} \mid k' \in I_{(i-1)}\} \cup \{\chi_k\})$ for all $i \geq 0$, even $I_{(i-1)} = I_n = I$. Without loss of generality, let $K = [1,m]$ and $\mathfrak{M}' = \langle \mathrm{S}, \mathrm{R}', \mathrm{V} \rangle$ be s.t. $\mathrm{R}' = \{\mathrm{R}'_{a_j} \mid a_j \in \mathsf{Act}\}$, where:

$$
\mathrm{R}'_{a_j} = \begin{cases} [\![\psi_j]\!]^{\mathfrak{M}'} \times [\![\chi_j]\!]^{\mathfrak{M}'} & \text{if } j \in K \\ \mathrm{R}_{a_{(j-m)}} & \text{if } j \notin K. \end{cases}
$$

In the definition of R', it is worth noticing that since $j \notin K$, $\mathrm{R}_{a_{(j-m)}}$ is defined, i.e., $\mathrm{R}_{a_{(j-m)}} \in \mathrm{R}$. Then clearly, for all $k \in K$, $[\![\mathsf{Kh}(\psi_k, \chi_k)]\!]^{\mathfrak{M}'} = \mathrm{S}$. The claim is that for all $k' \in I \cup J$, $[\![\mathsf{Kh}(\psi_{k'}, \chi_{k'})]\!]^{\mathfrak{M}'} = \mathrm{S}$. To prove this claim, consider a function $\sigma : \mathsf{Act}^* \rightarrow \mathsf{Act}^*$ s.t. $\sigma(\varepsilon) = \varepsilon$, and $\sigma(a_k \alpha) = a_{(k+m)} \sigma(\alpha)$. For all $\pi \in \mathsf{Act}^*$, if $[\![\psi_{k'}]\!]^{\mathfrak{M}} \subseteq \mathsf{SE}(\pi)$ and $\mathrm{R}_\pi([\![\psi_{k'}]\!]^{\mathfrak{M}}) \subseteq [\![\chi_{k'}]\!]^{\mathfrak{M}}$, then $[\![\psi_{k'}]\!]^{\mathfrak{M}'} \subseteq \mathsf{SE}(\sigma(\pi))$ and $\mathrm{R}_{\sigma(\pi)}([\![\psi_{k'}]\!]^{\mathfrak{M}'}) \subseteq [\![\chi_{k'}]\!]^{\mathfrak{M}'}$ —since the valuation functions for $\mathfrak{M}$ and $\mathfrak{M}'$ coincide, the truth sets in $\mathfrak{M}$ and $\mathfrak{M}'$ coincide for formulas with no modalities. Then, $[\![\mathsf{Kh}(\psi_{k'}, \chi_{k'})]\!]^{\mathfrak{M}'} = \mathrm{S}$. But we had assumed $\mathsf{Unsat}(\varphi)$. Thus, (1) follows.

The following example illustrates the result in Proposition 5.

Example 4. Let $\varphi = \mathsf{Kh}(p, \bot) \wedge \mathsf{Kh}(q, p)$, i.e., $\psi_1 = p$, $\psi_2 = q$, $\chi_1 = \bot$ and $\chi_2 = p$. It is clear that $\mathsf{Sat}(\varphi)$. Let us build the sets I_0, I_1 and I_2:

- $I_0 = \{1\}$, as $\mathsf{Unsat}(\chi_1)$ and $\mathsf{Sat}(\chi_2)$ hold;
- $I_1 = \{1, 2\}$, since it holds $\mathsf{Unsat}(\{\neg \psi_1, \chi_2\})$;
- $I_2 = \{1, 2\} = I$, as I_1 already contains all the indices in $[1, 2]$.

Thus (as it can be easily checked) we get $\mathsf{Sat}(\{\neg \psi_1, \neg \psi_2\})$ (i.e., $\mathsf{Sat}(\{\neg p, \neg q\})$).

Interestingly, the result in Proposition 5 tells us that the satisfiability of a formula $\mathsf{Kh}(\psi_1, \chi_1) \wedge \cdots \wedge \mathsf{Kh}(\psi_n, \chi_n)$ depends solely on the joint satisfiability of its 'global' subformulas (cf. Proposition 1); i.e., subformulas $\mathsf{Kh}(\psi_i, \chi_i)$ whose postconditions χ_i are falsified in the context of φ. The satisfiability of the 'global' subformulas provides us with the universe, i.e., set of states, on which to build the plans that witness those formulas that are not in I, and that are not 'trivially' true as a result of their preconditions being falsified in this universe.

Building on Proposition 5, the function Sat^+_{Kh} in Algorithm 2 gives us a way of checking whether a formula $\varphi = \text{Kh}(\psi_1, \chi_1) \wedge \cdots \wedge \text{Kh}(\psi_n, \chi_n)$ is satisfiable. The algorithm behind this function makes use of a (propositional) Sat oracle, and the function GLOBAL. The Sat oracle tests for pre and postconditions of Kh formulas, as these are propositional formulas. Intuitively, GLOBAL iteratively computes the indices in the sets I_i in Proposition 5, each of them corresponding to the 'global' subformulas of the input. Once this is done, Sat^+_{Kh} checks the joint satisfiability of the negation of the preconditions of 'global' subformulas.

Proposition 6. *Let φ be as in Proposition 5; Algorithm 2 solves $\text{Sat}(\varphi)$.*

Let us now move to determining the satisfiability conditions of a formula $\neg\text{Kh}(\psi_1, \chi_1) \wedge \cdots \wedge \neg\text{Kh}(\psi_n, \chi_n)$ in leaf normal form. Proposition 7 establishes that, for any such a formula, it is enough to check whether each conjunct $\psi_i \wedge \neg\chi_i$ is individually satisfiable. Note that this satisfiability check is purely propositional.

Proposition 7. *Let $\varphi = \neg\text{Kh}(\psi_1, \chi_1) \wedge \cdots \wedge \neg\text{Kh}(\psi_n, \chi_n)$ be s.t. $\text{md}(\varphi) = 1$; it follows that $\text{Sat}(\varphi)$ iff for all $i \in [1, n]$, $\text{Sat}(\psi_i \wedge \neg\chi_i)$.*

Proof. ($\Rightarrow$) The proof is by contradiction. Suppose that (†) $\text{Sat}(\varphi)$ and for some $i \in [1, n]$ we have (‡) $\text{Unsat}(\psi_i \wedge \neg\chi_i)$. Let $\mathfrak{M}$ be a model such that $[\![\varphi]\!]^{\mathfrak{M}} \neq \emptyset$, which exists by (†). Then, $[\![\text{Kh}(\psi_i, \chi_i)]\!]^{\mathfrak{M}} = \emptyset$. From this, we get $[\![\psi_i]\!]^{\mathfrak{M}} \neq \emptyset$; otherwise $[\![\text{Kh}(\psi_i, \chi_i)]\!]^{\mathfrak{M}} = S$. From (‡), we know that $[\![\psi_i]\!]^{\mathfrak{M}} \subseteq [\![\chi_i]\!]^{\mathfrak{M}}$. Since $\varepsilon \in \text{Act}^*$, we have $[\![\psi_i]\!]^{\mathfrak{M}} \subseteq \text{SE}(\varepsilon) = S$ and $[\![\psi_i]\!]^{\mathfrak{M}} = R_\varepsilon([\![\psi_i]\!]^{\mathfrak{M}}) \subseteq [\![\chi_i]\!]^{\mathfrak{M}}$. But this means $[\![\text{Kh}(\psi_i, \chi_i)]\!]^{\mathfrak{M}} = S$; which is a contradiction. Thus, $R_\varepsilon[\![\psi_i]\!]^{\mathfrak{M}} \not\subseteq [\![\chi_i]\!]^{\mathfrak{M}}$; i.e., $[\![\psi_i]\!]^{\mathfrak{M}} \not\subseteq [\![\chi_i]\!]^{\mathfrak{M}}$. This means $[\![\psi_i \wedge \neg\chi_i]\!]^{\mathfrak{M}} \neq \emptyset$. This establishes $\text{Sat}(\psi_i \wedge \neg\chi_i)$.

($\Leftarrow$) Suppose that (†) for all $i \in [1, n]$, $\text{Sat}(\psi_i \wedge \neg\chi_i)$. Let $\mathfrak{M} = \langle S, R, V \rangle$ where: (‡) S is s.t. for all i, $[\![\psi_i \wedge \neg\chi_i]\!]^{\mathfrak{M}} \neq \emptyset$; and (§) for all $R_a \in R$, $R_a = \emptyset$. From (†), we know that at least one S exists, as every ψ_i and χ_i are propositional; thus, each satisfiable conjunction can be sent to a different $s \in S$. From (§), we know for all $\pi \in \text{Act}^*$, $\text{SE}(\pi) \neq \emptyset$ iff $\pi = \varepsilon$. From (‡) and (§), we know that $[\![\psi_i]\!]^{\mathfrak{M}} = R_\varepsilon[\![\psi_i]\!]^{\mathfrak{M}} \not\subseteq [\![\chi_i]\!]^{\mathfrak{M}}$. This means that $[\![\text{Kh}(\psi_i, \chi_i)]\!]^{\mathfrak{M}} = \emptyset$, for all $i \in [1, n]$. Hence $[\![\varphi]\!]^{\mathfrak{M}} = S$ which implies $\text{Sat}(\varphi)$.

The key idea behind Proposition 7 is to build a discrete universe to force the only possible witness of a formula of the form $\text{Kh}(\psi_i, \chi_i)$ to be the empty plan. If in this discrete universe we always have at hand a state which satisfies $\psi_i \wedge \neg\chi_i$, then, the empty plan cannot be a witness for $\text{Kh}(\psi_i, \chi_i)$. If the latter is the case, then the satisfiability of $\neg\text{Kh}(\psi_i, \chi_i)$ is ensured. Building on this result, we define, in Algorithm 3, a function Sat^-_{Kh} to check the satisfiability of a formula $\neg\text{Kh}(\psi_1, \chi_1) \wedge \cdots \wedge \neg\text{Kh}(\psi_n, \chi_n)$ in leaf normal form. The function proceeds by traversing each subformula $\text{Kh}(\psi_i, \chi_i)$ and checking the satisfiability of $\psi_i \wedge \neg\chi_i$.

Proposition 8. *Let φ be as in Proposition 7; Algorithm 3 solves* Sat(φ).

We are now ready to extend the results in Propositions 5 and 7 to work out the joint satisfiability of a formula of the form $\varphi^+ = \text{Kh}(\psi_1, \chi_1) \wedge \cdots \wedge \text{Kh}(\psi_n, \chi_n)$, and a formula of the form $\varphi^- = \neg\text{Kh}(\psi'_1, \chi'_1) \wedge \cdots \wedge \neg\text{Kh}(\psi'_m, \chi'_m)$, both in leaf normal form. The main difficulty is how to "build" witnesses for the subformulas $\text{Kh}(\psi_i, \chi_i)$ of φ^+ in a way such that they do not yield witnesses for the subformulas $\neg\text{Kh}(\psi'_j, \chi'_j)$ of φ^-. We show that the key to the solution hinges on "composition". We start with a preliminary definition.

Definition 8. *Let $\varphi = \text{Kh}(\psi_1, \chi_1) \wedge \cdots \wedge \text{Kh}(\psi_n, \chi_n)$ and ψ be a formula; we define $\Pi(\varphi, \psi) = \bigcup_{i \geq 0} \Pi_i$ where:*

$$\Pi_0 = \{(x, x) \mid x \in [1, n]\}$$
$$\Pi_{(i+1)} = \Pi_i \cup \{(x, z) \mid (x, y) \subset \Pi_i, \; z \in [1, n], \; and \; \text{Unsat}(\{\psi, \chi_y, \neg\psi_z\})\}.$$

In words, $\Pi(\varphi, \psi)$ captures the notion of composition of formulas $\text{Kh}(\psi, \chi)$ and $\text{Kh}(\psi', \chi')$ into a formula $\text{Kh}(\psi, \chi')$. This composition is best explained by recalling the validity of $(\text{Kh}(\psi, \chi) \wedge \text{A}(\chi \rightarrow \psi') \wedge \text{Kh}(\psi', \chi')) \rightarrow \text{Kh}(\psi, \chi')$ (see, e.g. [31,33]). The definition of $\Pi(\varphi, \psi)$ records the conjuncts of φ which can be composed in this sense. Below, we list some properties of $\Pi(\varphi, \psi)$.

Proposition 9. *Let φ and ψ be as in Definition 8; if $(x, y) \in \Pi(\varphi, \psi)$, then, for any model $\mathfrak{M}$, it holds $[\![\varphi \wedge \text{A}\psi]\!]^{\mathfrak{M}} \subseteq [\![\text{Kh}(\psi_x, \chi_y)]\!]^{\mathfrak{M}}$.*

Proof. We start by stating and proving an auxiliary lemma: (∗) $(x, y) \in \Pi_i$ iff there is a non-empty sequence π of indices in $[1, n]$ s.t.:

(†) $x = \pi_1$ and $y = \pi_{|\pi|}$; and
(‡) for all $j \in [1, |\pi| - 1]$, $\text{Unsat}(\{\psi, \chi_{\pi_j}, \neg\psi_{\pi_{(j+1)}}\})$.

The proof of this lemma is by induction on i. The base case for (∗) is $i = 0$. We know that $(x, x) \in \Pi_0$, the sequence containing just x satisfies (†) and (‡). Conversely, we know that any sequence π of indices in $[1, n]$ s.t. $|\pi| = 1$ satisfies (†) and (‡); it is immediate that $(\pi_1, \pi_1) \in \Pi_0$. This proves the base case. For the inductive step, let $(x, z) \in \Pi_{(i+1)}$, $(x, y) \in \Pi_i$, $z \in [1, n]$, and $\text{Unsat}(\{\psi, \chi_y, \neg\psi_z\})$. From the Inductive Hypothesis, there is π that satisfies (†) and (‡). Immediately, $\pi' = \pi z$ also satisfies (†) and (‡).

It is easy to see that, if there is π satisfying (†) and (‡), then, (§) for every model $\mathfrak{M}$ and $j \in [1, |\pi| - 1]$, $[\![\text{A}\psi]\!]^{\mathfrak{M}} = \text{S}$ implies $[\![\chi_{\pi_j}]\!]^{\mathfrak{M}} \subseteq [\![\psi_{\pi_{(j+1)}}]\!]^{\mathfrak{M}}$.

Let us now resume with the main proof. Let $(x, y) \in \Pi(\varphi, \psi)$ and $\mathfrak{M}$ be any model. The result is direct if $[\![\varphi \wedge \text{A}\psi]\!]^{\mathfrak{M}} = \emptyset$. Thus, consider $[\![\varphi \wedge \text{A}\psi]\!]^{\mathfrak{M}} \neq \emptyset$; i.e., s.t. $[\![\varphi \wedge \text{A}\psi]\!]^{\mathfrak{M}} = \text{S}$. From (∗), we know that exists a sequence π of indices in $[1, n]$ that satisfies (†) and (‡). Then, for all $j \in [1, |\pi| - 1]$, $[\![\chi_{\pi_j}]\!]^{\mathfrak{M}} \subseteq [\![\psi_{\pi_{(j+1)}}]\!]^{\mathfrak{M}}$. Using Proposition 3, $[\![\varphi \wedge \text{A}\psi]\!]^{\mathfrak{M}} \subseteq \bigcap_{j=1}^{|\pi|} [\![\text{Kh}(\psi_{\pi_j}, \chi_{\pi_j})]\!]^{\mathfrak{M}} \subseteq [\![\text{Kh}(\psi_x, \chi_y)]\!]^{\mathfrak{M}}$.

Proposition 10. *Let* $\varphi = \mathsf{Kh}(\psi_1, \chi_1) \wedge \cdots \wedge \mathsf{Kh}(\psi_n, \chi_n)$ *and* ψ *be a formula;* $\Pi(\varphi, \psi)$ *is the smallest set s.t.: (1) for all* $x \in [1, n]$, $(x, x) \in \Pi(\varphi, \psi)$; *and (2) if* $\{(x, y_0), (y_1, z)\} \subseteq \Pi(\varphi, \psi)$ *and* $\mathsf{Unsat}(\{\psi, \chi_{y_0}, \neg\psi_{y_1}\})$, *then,* $(x, z) \in \Pi(\varphi, \psi)$.

The function PLANS in Algorithm 4 can be used to compute the set $\Pi(\varphi, \psi)$ in Definition 8. This function looks into whether a pair of indices belongs to this set using the result in Proposition 10.

	χ_1	χ_2	χ_3
ψ_1	$\top$	$\bot$	$\bot$
ψ_2	$\bot$	$\top$	$\bot$
ψ_3	$\bot$	$\bot$	$\top$

initial step

	χ_1	χ_2	χ_3
ψ_1	$\top$	$\top$	$\bot$
ψ_2	$\bot$	$\top$	$\bot$
ψ_3	$\bot$	$\bot$	$\top$

$x = 1, y_0 = 1$
$z = 2, y_1 = 2$

	χ_1	χ_2	χ_3
ψ_1	$\top$	$\top$	$\top$
ψ_2	$\bot$	$\top$	$\bot$
ψ_3	$\bot$	$\bot$	$\top$

$x = 1, y_0 = 2$
$z = 3, y_1 = 3$

	χ_1	χ_2	χ_3
ψ_1	$\top$	$\top$	$\top$
ψ_2	$\bot$	$\top$	$\top$
ψ_3	$\bot$	$\bot$	$\top$

$x = 2, y_0 = 2$
$z = 3, y_1 = 3$

Fig. 1. A Run of PLANS for $\varphi = \mathsf{Kh}(p, p \wedge q) \wedge \mathsf{Kh}(q, r) \wedge \mathsf{Kh}(r \vee s, t)$ and $\psi = \top$.

Example 5. Let $\varphi = \mathsf{Kh}(p, p \wedge q) \wedge \mathsf{Kh}(q, r) \wedge \mathsf{Kh}(r \vee s, t)$ and $\psi = \top$; in this case we have: $\psi_1 = p$, $\chi_1 = p \wedge q$, $\psi_2 = q$, $\chi_2 = r$, $\psi_3 = r \vee s$, and $\chi_3 = t$. We can easily verify that $\Pi(\varphi, \psi) = \{(1,1)(1,2)(1,3)(2,2)(2,3)(3,3)\}$. Indeed, in the initial step we get $\Pi_0 = \{(1,1)(2,2)(3,3)\}$. The pairs of indices correspond to those of the pre/post conditions of the subformulas $\mathsf{Kh}(\psi_i, \chi_i) \in \mathsf{sf}(\varphi)$. Then, since we have $\{(1,1)(2,2)\} \subseteq \Pi_0$, $\mathsf{Unsat}(\{\chi_1, \neg\psi_2\})$, and $\mathsf{Unsat}(\{\chi_2, \neg\psi_3\})$, it follows that $\Pi_1 = \Pi_0 \cup \{(1,2)(2,3)\}$. The new pairs of indices can intuitively be taken as the formulas $\mathsf{Kh}(\psi_1, \chi_2)$ and $\mathsf{Kh}(\psi_2, \chi_3)$. In this case, note the connection between $\mathsf{Kh}(\psi_1, \chi_2)$ and $(\mathsf{Kh}(\psi_1, \chi_1) \wedge \mathsf{A}(\chi_1 \to \psi_2) \wedge \mathsf{Kh}(\psi_2, \chi_2)) \to \mathsf{Kh}(\psi_1, \chi_2)$, and $\mathsf{Kh}(\psi_2, \chi_3)$ and $(\mathsf{Kh}(\psi_2, \chi_2) \wedge \mathsf{A}(\chi_2 \to \psi_3) \wedge \mathsf{Kh}(\psi_3, \chi_3)) \to \mathsf{Kh}(\psi_2, \chi_3)$. Finally, since we have $(1, 2) \in \Pi_2$ and $\mathsf{Unsat}(\{\chi_2, \neg\psi_3\})$, then $\Pi_2 = \Pi_1 \cup \{(1, 3)\}$. The justification for the pair $(1, 3)$ is similar to the one just offered. In Fig. 1 we illustrate a run of PLANS which computes this set (only the steps in which the matrix is updated are shown).

The composition of formulas $\mathsf{Kh}(\psi, \chi)$ and $\mathsf{Kh}(\psi', \chi')$ has an impact if we wish to add a formula $\neg\mathsf{Kh}(\psi'', \chi'')$ into the mix. The reason for this is that witness plans π and π' for $\mathsf{Kh}(\psi, \chi)$ and $\mathsf{Kh}(\psi', \chi')$, respectively, yield a witness plan $\pi'' = \pi\pi'$ for $\mathsf{Kh}(\psi, \chi')$. In adding $\neg\mathsf{Kh}(\psi'', \chi'')$ we need to ensure π'' is not a witness for $\mathsf{Kh}(\psi'', \chi'')$, as such a plan renders $\neg\mathsf{Kh}(\psi'', \chi'')$ unsatisfiable. We make these ideas precise in the definition of *compatible* below.

Definition 9. *Let* φ^+ *and* φ^- *be formulas s.t.:* $\mathsf{md}(\varphi^+) = 1$ *and* $\mathsf{md}(\varphi^-) = 1$; $\varphi^+ = \mathsf{Kh}(\psi_1, \chi_1) \wedge \cdots \wedge \mathsf{Kh}(\psi_n, \chi_n)$; *and* $\varphi^- = \neg\mathsf{Kh}(\psi'_1, \chi'_1) \wedge \cdots \wedge \neg\mathsf{Kh}(\psi'_m, \chi'_m)$. *Moreover, let* $I, J \subseteq [1, n]$ *be as in Proposition 5 and* $\psi = \bigwedge_{i \in I} \neg\psi_i$. *We say that* φ^+ *and* φ^- *are compatible iff the following conditions are met:*

(1) $\mathsf{Sat}(\psi)$;

(2) for all $\mathsf{Kh}(\psi'_{k'}, \chi'_{k'}) \in \mathsf{sf}(\varphi^-)$,
  (a) $\mathsf{Sat}(\{\psi, \psi'_{k'}, \neg\chi'_{k'}\})$; *and*
  (b) for all $(x, y) \in \Pi(\varphi^+, \psi)$,
      if $x \notin J$ *and* $\mathsf{Unsat}(\{\psi, \psi'_{k'}, \neg\psi_x\})$, *then,* $\mathsf{Sat}(\{\psi, \chi_y, \neg\chi'_{k'}\})$.

Definition 9 aims to single out the conditions under which the formulas φ^+ and φ^- can be jointly satisfied. Intuitively, (1) tells us φ^+ must be individually satisfied (cf. Proposition 5). In turn, (2.a) tells us φ^- must be individually satisfied (cf. Proposition 7), while (2.b) tells us φ^+ and φ^- can be satisfied together if no composition of subformulas in φ^+ contradicts a subformula in φ^-. Such a contradiction would originate only as a result of strengthening the precondition and/or weakening the postcondition of a composition of subformulas in φ^+, in a way such that they would result in the opposite of a subformula in φ^-. Proposition 11 states that the conditions in Definition 9 guarantee the satisfiability of a combination of φ^+ and φ^-.

Proposition 11. *It follows that* φ^+ *and* φ^- *are compatible iff* $\mathsf{Sat}(\varphi^+ \wedge \varphi^-)$.

Proof. ($\Rightarrow$) Suppose that φ^+ and φ^- are compatible. Let $\mathfrak{M} = \langle \mathrm{S}, \mathrm{R}, \mathrm{V} \rangle$ be s.t. S contains all valuations that make ψ true; and $\mathrm{R} = \{\mathrm{R}_{a_k} \mid a_k \in \mathsf{Act}\}$ where

$$\mathrm{R}_{a_k} = \begin{cases} [\![\psi_k]\!]^{\mathfrak{M}} \times [\![\chi_k]\!]^{\mathfrak{M}} & \text{if } k \in K \\ \emptyset & \text{otherwise,} \end{cases}$$

for $K = [1, n] \setminus (I \cup J)$. From (1), we know $\mathrm{S} \neq \emptyset$. It is not difficult to see that $[\![\varphi^+]\!]^{\mathfrak{M}} = \mathrm{S}$ (cf. Proposition 5). The proof is concluded if $[\![\varphi^-]\!]^{\mathfrak{M}} = \mathrm{S}$. We proceed by contradiction. Let $k' \in [1, m]$ be s.t. $[\![\mathsf{Kh}(\psi'_{k'}, \chi'_{k'})]\!]^{\mathfrak{M}} = \mathrm{S}$; i.e., (*) exists $\pi \in \mathsf{Act}^*$ s.t. $[\![\psi'_j]\!]^{\mathfrak{M}} \subseteq \mathrm{SE}(\pi)$ and $\mathrm{R}_\pi([\![\psi'_j]\!]^{\mathfrak{M}}) \subseteq [\![\chi'_j]\!]^{\mathfrak{M}}$. We consider the following cases.

($\pi = \varepsilon$) From (2.a), we know $[\![\psi'_{k'} \wedge \neg\chi'_{k'}]\!]^{\mathfrak{M}} \neq \emptyset$; i.e., $[\![\psi'_{k'}]\!]^{\mathfrak{M}} \not\subseteq [\![\chi'_{k'}]\!]^{\mathfrak{M}}$. This implies $[\![\psi'_{k'}]\!]^{\mathfrak{M}} = \mathrm{R}_\varepsilon([\![\psi'_{k'}]\!]^{\mathfrak{M}}) \not\subseteq [\![\chi'_{k'}]\!]^{\mathfrak{M}}$.
($\pi \neq \varepsilon$ and $\pi = a_{k_1}, \ldots, a_{k_{|\pi|}}$ with $k_j \in K$ and $j \in [1, |\pi|]$) In this case we have:
  (a) $\emptyset \neq [\![\psi'_{k'}]\!]^{\mathfrak{M}} \subseteq \mathrm{SE}(\pi) \subseteq \mathrm{SE}(a_{k_1}) = [\![\psi_{k_1}]\!]^{\mathfrak{M}}$;
  (b) $[\![\chi_{k_j}]\!]^{\mathfrak{M}} = \mathrm{R}_{a_{k_j}}([\![\psi_{k_j}]\!]^{\mathfrak{M}}) \subseteq [\![\psi_{k_{(j+1)}}]\!]^{\mathfrak{M}}$; and
  (c) $[\![\chi_{k_{|\pi|}}]\!]^{\mathfrak{M}} = \mathrm{R}_\pi([\![\psi'_{k'}]\!]^{\mathfrak{M}}) \subseteq [\![\chi'_{k'}]\!]^{\mathfrak{M}}$.
  Since S contains all valuations that make ψ true; from (a)–(d) we get:
  (d) $\mathsf{Unsat}(\{\psi, \psi'_{k'}, \neg\psi_{k_1}\})$ –from (a);
  (e) $\mathsf{Unsat}(\{\psi, \chi_{k_j}, \neg\psi_{k_{(j+1)}}\})$ –from (b);
  (f) $\mathsf{Unsat}(\{\psi, \chi_{k_{|\pi|}}, \neg\chi'_{k'}\})$ –from (c).
  From (e) and π, we obtain a sequence $k_1 \ldots k_{|\pi|}$ that satisfies the conditions (†) and (‡) in the proof of Proposition 9. Then, $(k_1, k_{|\pi|}) \in \Pi(\varphi^+, \psi)$. From (a) and (2.a), $k_1 \notin J$. We are in an impossible situation: $(k_1, k_{|\pi|}) \in \Pi(\varphi^+, \psi)$; $k_1 \notin J$; and $\mathsf{Unsat}(\{\psi, \chi_{k_{|\pi|}}, \neg\chi'_{k'}\})$. This contradicts (2.b); meaning that φ^+ and φ^- are not compatible.
(π is none of the above) It is clear that $[\![\psi'_{k'}]\!]^{\mathfrak{M}} \not\subseteq \mathrm{SE}(\pi)$.

In all the cases above we have: $[\![\psi'_{k'}]\!]^{\mathfrak{M}} \nsubseteq \mathsf{SE}(\pi)$ or $\mathsf{R}_\pi([\![\psi'_{k'}]\!]^{\mathfrak{M}}) \nsubseteq [\![\chi'_{k'}]\!]^{\mathfrak{M}}$; i.e., $[\![\mathsf{Kh}(\psi'_{k'}, \chi'_{k'})]\!]^{\mathfrak{M}} = \emptyset$, a contradiction. Then, $[\![\varphi^-]\!]^{\mathfrak{M}} = \mathsf{S}$; and so $\mathsf{Sat}(\varphi^+ \wedge \varphi^-)$.

($\Leftarrow$) Suppose $\mathsf{Sat}(\varphi^+ \wedge \varphi^-)$; i.e., exists (†) $\mathfrak{M}$ s.t. $[\![\varphi^+ \wedge \varphi^-]\!]^{\mathfrak{M}} = \mathsf{S}$. From (†) we get $[\![\varphi^+]\!]^{\mathfrak{M}} = \mathsf{S}$. Using Cor. 1, we get $[\![\mathsf{A}\psi]\!]^{\mathfrak{M}} = \mathsf{S}$. This establishes (1). The proof of (2.a) is by contradiction. Let $\mathsf{Kh}(\psi'_{k'}, \chi'_{k'}) \in \mathsf{sf}(\varphi^-)$ be s.t. $\mathsf{Unsat}(\{\psi, \psi'_{k'}, \neg\chi'_{k'}\})$. Then, $[\![\psi'_{k'}]\!]^{\mathfrak{M}} \subseteq [\![\chi'_{k'}]\!]^{\mathfrak{M}}$. Choosing $\pi = \epsilon$, we obtain $[\![\mathsf{Kh}(\psi'_{k'}, \chi'_{k'})]\!]^{\mathfrak{M}} = \mathsf{S}$. This contradicts $[\![\varphi^-]\!]^{\mathfrak{M}} = \mathsf{S}$. The proof of (2.b) is also by contradiction. Let $\mathsf{Kh}(\psi'_{k'}, \chi'_{k'}) \in \mathsf{sf}(\varphi^-)$, (∗) $(x, y) \in \Pi(\varphi^+, \psi)$, (†) $\mathsf{Unsat}(\{\psi, \psi'_{k'}, \neg\psi_x\})$, and (‡) $\mathsf{Unsat}(\{\psi, \chi_y, \neg\chi'_{k'}\})$. From (†) and (‡), $[\![\psi'_{k'}]\!]^{\mathfrak{M}} \subseteq [\![\psi_x]\!]^{\mathfrak{M}}$ and $[\![\chi_y]\!]^{\mathfrak{M}} \subseteq [\![\chi'_{k'}]\!]^{\mathfrak{M}}$. At the same time, from (∗) and Proposition 9, $\mathsf{S} = [\![\varphi^+]\!]^{\mathfrak{M}} \subseteq [\![\mathsf{Kh}(\psi_x, \chi_y)]\!]^{\mathfrak{M}}$. Then, using Proposition 3, $[\![\mathsf{Kh}(\psi'_j, \chi'_j)]\!]^{\mathfrak{M}} = \mathsf{S}$. This also contradicts $[\![\varphi^-]\!]^{\mathfrak{M}} = \mathsf{S}$. Thus, φ^+ and φ^- are compatible.

Having at hand the result in Proposition 11, we proceed to define an algorithm for checking the satisfiability of compatible formulas φ^+ and φ^-. This is done in two stages. In the first stage, we build the set $\Pi(\varphi^+, \psi)$, where ψ is the conjunction of the negation of the precondition of the 'global' subformulas in φ^+. This task is encapsulated in the function PLANS in Algorithm 4. Notice that the set $\Pi(\varphi^+, \psi)$ corresponds to a matrix which is computed using the result in Proposition 10. The second stage is encapsulated in the function COMPATIBLE in Algorithm 5. In this function, lines 2 and 3 check condition (1) in Definition 9, i.e., whether φ^+ is individually satisfiable, by verifying the joint satisfiability of the 'global' subformulas in φ^+ (cf. Algorithm 2). In turn, lines 4 to 6 in COMPATIBLE check condition (2.a) of Definition 9, i.e., whether φ^- is individually satisfiable, by verifying the individual satisfiability of the subformulas in φ^+ (cf. Algorithm 3). Lastly, in lines 7 to 18 in COMPATIBLE, we check whether the result of composing subformulas in φ^+ contradicts any of the subformulas in φ^-. We carry out this task by making use of the result of the function PLANS which computes such compositions.

Notice that the function COMPATIBLE in Algorithm 5 makes a polynomial number of calls to a propositional Sat solver. From this fact, we get the following result.

Proposition 12. *Let φ^+, φ^- be as in Definition 9; it follows that Algorithm 5 solves $\mathsf{Sat}(\varphi^+ \wedge \varphi^-)$ and is in P^{NP} (i.e., Δ_2^P in PH).*

Proof. By Proposition 11 we get that the function COMPATIBLE in Algorithm 5 solves $\mathsf{Sat}(\varphi^+ \wedge \varphi^-)$. Moreover, it makes a polynomial number of calls to a Sat solver for formulas of modal depth 0. Thus, it runs in polynomial time with access to a Sat oracle. Therefore, $\mathsf{Sat}(\varphi^+ \wedge \varphi^-)$ is in P^{NP}, i.e., in Δ_2^P.

Proposition 12 is the final step we need to reach the main result of our work.

Theorem 1. *The satisfiability problem for L_{Kh} is in NP^{NP} (i.e., Σ_2^P in PH).*

Proof. Let φ be a L_{Kh}-formula. By Algorithm 1, we can obtain, in polynomial time, a formula $\varphi' = \varphi_0 \wedge (\mathsf{Ap}_1 \leftrightarrow \mathsf{Kh}(\psi_1, \chi_1)) \wedge \cdots \wedge (\mathsf{Ap}_n \leftrightarrow \mathsf{Kh}(\psi_n, \chi_n))$ in leaf normal form such that $\varphi \equiv_{\mathsf{Sat}} \varphi'$. We know $\mathsf{md}(\varphi_0) = 0$ and $\mathsf{md}(\mathsf{Kh}(\psi_i, \chi_i)) = 1$. Let $Q = \{q_1 \ldots q_m\} \subseteq \mathsf{Prop}$ be the set of proposition symbols in φ'. To check $\mathsf{Sat}(\varphi')$, we start by guessing a propositional assignment $v : Q \to \{0, 1\}$ that makes φ_0 true. Then, we define sets $P^+ = \{i \mid v(p_i) = 1\}$ and $P^- = \{i \mid v(p_i) = 0\}$, from which we build formulas

$$\varphi^+ = \bigwedge_{i \in P^+} \mathsf{Kh}(\psi_i, \chi_i) \qquad \varphi^- = \left(\bigwedge_{i \in P^-} \neg\mathsf{Kh}(\psi_i, \chi_i)\right) \wedge \neg\mathsf{Kh}(\varphi_0, \bot)$$

(recall that $\neg\mathsf{Kh}(\varphi_0, \bot) = \neg\mathsf{A}\neg\varphi_0 = \mathsf{E}\varphi_0$.) Finally, we use Algorithm 5 to check $\mathsf{Sat}(\varphi^+ \wedge \varphi^-)$. Since Algorithm 5 is in P^{NP} (Proposition 12), the whole process is in $\mathsf{NP}^{\mathsf{NP}}$.

We conclude this section with an example of how to check the satisfiability of a formula using the procedure in the proof of Theorem 1.

Example 6. Let $\psi = \mathsf{Kh}(p \wedge q, r \wedge t) \vee \mathsf{Kh}(p, r)$. By applying Algorithm 1, we get $(k_1 \vee k_2) \wedge (\mathsf{A}k_1 \leftrightarrow \mathsf{Kh}(p \wedge q, r \wedge t)) \wedge (\mathsf{A}k_2 \leftrightarrow \mathsf{Kh}(p, r))$. Suppose that we set k_1 to true and k_2 to false. Based on this assignment, we build formulas $\varphi^+ = \mathsf{Kh}(p \wedge q, r \wedge t)$ and $\varphi^- = \neg\mathsf{Kh}(p, r) \wedge \neg\mathsf{Kh}(k_1 \wedge \neg k_2, \bot)$. Using Algorithm 5, we can check that they are not compatible (and hence not satisfiable; we have $\mathsf{Sat}(p \wedge q)$ and $\mathsf{Unsat}(\{(p \wedge q), \neg p\})$ but not $\mathsf{Sat}(\{r \wedge t, \neg r\})$). However, if we set both k_1 and k_2 to true, then, $\varphi^+ = \mathsf{Kh}(p \wedge q, r \wedge t) \wedge \mathsf{Kh}(p, r)$ and $\varphi^- = \neg\mathsf{Kh}(k_1 \wedge k_2, \bot)$. In this case, Algorithm 5 returns they are compatible, and thus satisfiable.

4   Final Remarks

We provided a satisfiability-checking procedure for $\mathsf{L_{Kh}}$, the 'knowing how' logic with linear plans from [31, 33], obtaining a Σ_2^P upper bound. Although not a tight bound (as the best lower bound known is NP), we argue this is an interesting result, as our bound is (unless PH collapses) below the PSpace-complete complexity of model-checking [5]. We argue that, this unusual situation is a consequence of that in model-checking the full expressive power is exploited, while here we showed that plans are almost irrelevant for the satisfiability of a formula.

Interestingly also, our procedure uses a polynomial transformation into a normal form without nested modalities, and calls to an NP oracle (i.e., to a propositional Sat solver). It is well-known that modern Sat solvers are able to efficiently deal with large formulas (having millions of variables), and usually support the exploration of the solution state space. Thus, the ideas presented in this paper can be used to implement a Sat solver for knowing-how logics relying on modern propositional Sat solving tools. We consider this as part of the future work to undertake. Also, we would like to obtain a tight bound for the satisfiability problem. In this regard, we will explore the possibility of providing a reduction from the problem of checking the truth of Quantified Boolean Formula (TQBF) with a single $\exists \forall$ quantification pattern (called $\Sigma_2 \mathsf{Sat}$ in [2]), which is known to be Σ_2^P-complete.

Acknowledgments. We thank the reviewers for their valuable comments. Our work is supported by the Laboratoire International Associé SINFIN, the EU Grant Agreement 101008233 (MISSION), the ANPCyT projects PICT-2019-03134, PICT-2020-3780, PICT-2021-00400, PICT-2021-00675, and PICTO-2022-CBA-00088, and the CONICET projects PIBAA-28720210100428CO, PIBAA-28720210100165CO, and PIP-11220200100812CO.

References

1. Areces, C., Fervari, R., Saravia, A.R., Velázquez-Quesada, F.R.: Uncertainty-based semantics for multi-agent knowing how logics. In: 18th Conference on Theoretical Aspects of Rationality and Knowledge (TARK 2021). EPTCS, vol. 335, pp. 23–37. Open Publishing Association (2021)
2. Arora, S., Barak, B.: Computational Complexity: A Modern Approach, 1st edn. Cambridge University Press, Cambridge (2009)
3. Baltag, A.: To know is to know the value of a variable. In: Advances in Modal Logic (AiML 2016), vol. 11, pp. 135–155. College Publications (2016)
4. Cormen, T., Leiserson, C., Rivest, R.L., Stein, C.: Introduction to Algorithms, 4th edn. MIT Press, Cambridge (2022)
5. Demri, S., Fervari, R.: Model-checking for ability-based logics with constrained plans. In: 37th AAAI Conference on Artificial Intelligence (AAAI 2023), pp. 6305–6312. AAAI Press (2023)
6. van Ditmarsch, H., Halpern, J.Y., van der Hoek, W., Kooi, B. (eds.): Handbook of Epistemic Logic. College Publications, Georgia (2015)
7. Fan, J., Wang, Y., van Ditmarsch, H.: Contingency and knowing whether. Rev. Symbolic Logic **8**, 75–107 (2015)
8. Fantl, J.: Knowledge how. In: The Stanford Encyclopedia of Philosophy. Metaphysics Research Lab, Stanford University, spring 2021 edn. (2021)
9. Fervari, R., Herzig, A., Li, Y., Wang, Y.: Strategically knowing how. In: 26th International Joint Conference on Artificial Intelligence (IJCAI 2017), pp. 1031–1038. International Joint Conferences on Artificial Intelligence (2017)
10. Fervari, R., Velázquez-Quesada, F.R., Wang, Y.: Bisimulations for knowing how logics. Rev. Symbolic Logic **15**(2), 450–486 (2022)
11. Goranko, V., Passy, S.: Using the universal modality: gains and questions. J. Log. Comput. **2**(1), 5–30 (1992)
12. Gu, T., Wang, Y.: "Knowing value" logic as a normal modal logic. In: Advances in Modal Logic (AiML 2016), vol. 11, pp. 362–381. College Publications (2016)
13. Herzig, A.: Logics of knowledge and action: critical analysis and challenges. Auton. Agent. Multi-Agent Syst. **29**(5), 719–753 (2015)
14. Herzig, A., Troquard, N.: Knowing how to play: uniform choices in logics of agency. In: 5th International Joint Conference on Autonomous Agents and Multiagent Systems (AAMAS 2006), pp. 209–216. ACM (2006)
15. Hintikka, J.: Knowledge and Belief. Cornell University Press, Ithaca (1962)
16. van der Hoek, W., Lomuscio, A.: Ignore at your peril - towards a logic for ignorance. In: 2nd International Conference on Autonomous Agents and MultiAgent Systems (AAMAS 2003), pp. 1148–1149. ACM (2003)
17. Jamroga, W., Ågotnes, T.: Constructive knowledge: what agents can achieve under imperfect information. J. Appl. Non Class. Logics **17**(4), 423–475 (2007)
18. Lespérance, Y., Levesque, H.J., Lin, F., Scherl, R.B.: Ability and knowing how in the situation calculus. Stud. Logica. **66**(1), 165–186 (2000)

19. Li, Y.: Stopping means achieving: a weaker logic of knowing how. Stud. Logic **9**(4), 34–54 (2017)
20. Li, Y.: Tableaux for the logic of strategically knowing how. In: 19th Conference on Theoretical Aspects of Rationality and Knowledge (TARK 2023). EPTCS, vol. 379, pp. 379–391. Open Publishing Association (2023)
21. Li, Y., Wang, Y.: Achieving while maintaining. In: Ghosh, S., Prasad, S. (eds.) ICLA 2017. LNCS, vol. 10119, pp. 154–167. Springer, Heidelberg (2017). https://doi.org/10.1007/978-3-662-54069-5_12
22. Li, Y.: Knowing what to do: a logical approach to planning and knowing how. Ph.D. thesis, University of Groningen (2017)
23. Li, Y.: Tableau-based decision procedure for logic of knowing-how via simple plans. In: Baroni, P., Benzmüller, C., Wáng, Y.N. (eds.) CLAR 2021. LNCS (LNAI), vol. 13040, pp. 266–283. Springer, Cham (2021). https://doi.org/10.1007/978-3-030-89391-0_15
24. Li, Y., Wang, Y.: Planning-based knowing how: a unified approach. Artif. Intell. **296**, 103487 (2021)
25. McCarthy, J., Hayes, P.J.: Some philosophical problems from the standpoint of artificial intelligence. In: Machine Intelligence, pp. 463–502. Edinburgh University Press (1969)
26. Moore, R.: A formal theory of knowledge and action. In: Formal Theories of the Commonsense World. Ablex Publishing Corporation (1985)
27. Naumov, P., Tao, J.: Second-order know-how strategies. In: 17th International Conference on Autonomous Agents and MultiAgent Systems (AAMAS 2018), pp. 390–398. ACM (2018)
28. Naumov, P., Tao, J.: Together we know how to achieve: an epistemic logic of know-how. Artif. Intell. **262**, 279–300 (2018)
29. Smith, D.E., Weld, D.S.: Conformant Graphplan. In: 15th National Conference on Artificial Intelligence and 10th Innovative Applications of Artificial Intelligence Conference (AAAI/IAAI 1998), pp. 889–896. AAAI Press/The MIT Press (1998)
30. Stockmeyer, L.J.: The polynomial-time hierarchy. Theoret. Comput. Sci. **3**(1), 1–22 (1976)
31. Wang, Y.: A logic of knowing how. In: van der Hoek, W., Holliday, W.H., Wang, W. (eds.) LORI 2015. LNCS, vol. 9394, pp. 392–405. Springer, Heidelberg (2015). https://doi.org/10.1007/978-3-662-48561-3_32
32. Wang, Y.: Beyond knowing that: a new generation of epistemic logics. In: van Ditmarsch, H., Sandu, G. (eds.) Jaakko Hintikka on Knowledge and Game-Theoretical Semantics. OCL, vol. 12, pp. 499–533. Springer, Cham (2018). https://doi.org/10.1007/978-3-319-62864-6_21
33. Wang, Y.: A logic of goal-directed knowing how. Synthese **195**(10), 4419–4439 (2018)
34. Xu, C., Wang, Y., Studer, T.: A logic of knowing why. Synthese **198**(2), 1259–1285 (2021)

Non-standard Modalities
in Paraconsistent Gödel Logic

Marta Bílková[1] , Sabine Frittella[2] , and Daniil Kozhemiachenko[2(✉)]

[1] The Czech Academy of Sciences, Institute of Philosophy, Prague, Czech Republic
bilkova@cs.cas.cz
[2] INSA Centre Val de Loire, Univ. Orléans, LIFO EA 4022, Bourges, France
{sabine.frittella,daniil.kozhemiachenko}@insa-cvl.fr

Abstract. We introduce a paraconsistent expansion of the Gödel logic with a De Morgan negation $\neg$ and modalities ■ and ♦. We dub the logic $\mathsf{G}^{2\pm}_{■,♦}$ and equip it with Kripke semantics on frames with two (possibly fuzzy) relations: R^+ and R^- (interpreted as the degree of trust in affirmations and denials by a given source) and valuations v_1 and v_2 (positive and negative support) ranging over $[0,1]$ and connected via $\neg$.

We motivate the semantics of ■ϕ (resp., ♦ϕ) as infima (suprema) of both positive and negative supports of ϕ in R^+- and R^--accessible states, respectively. We then prove several instructive semantical properties of $\mathsf{G}^{2\pm}_{■,♦}$. Finally, we devise a tableaux system for $\mathsf{G}^{2\pm}_{■,♦}$ over finitely branching frames and establish the complexity of satisfiability and validity.

Keywords: Gödel logic · modal logic · non-standard modalities · constraint tableaux

1 Introduction

When aggregating information from different sources, two of the simplest strategies are as follows: either one is sceptical regarding the information they provide thus requiring that they agree, or one is credulous and trusts their sources. In the classical setting, these two strategies could be modelled with □ and ◇ modalities defined on Kripke frames where states are sources, the accessibility relation represents references between them, and $w \vDash \phi$ is construed as 'w says that ϕ is true'. However, the sources could contradict themselves or be silent regarding a given question (as opposed to providing a clear denial). Furthermore, a source could be able to provide a degree to their confirmation or denial. In all of these cases, classical logic struggles to formalise reasoning with such information.

The research of Marta Bílková was supported by the project Logical Structure of Information Channels, no. 21-23610M of the Czech Science Foundation. The research of Sabine Frittella and Daniil Kozhemiachenko was funded by the grant ANR JCJC 2019, project PRELAP (ANR-19-CE48-0006). This research is part of the MOSAIC project financed by the European Union's Marie Skłodowska-Curie grant No. 101007627.

S. Gaggl et al. (Eds.): JELIA 2023, LNAI 14281, pp. 420–436, 2023.
https://doi.org/10.1007/978-3-031-43619-2_29

Paraconsistent Reasoning about Imperfect Data. In the setting described above, one can use the following setting. A source w gives a statement ϕ two valuations over $[0,1]$: v_1 standing for the degree with which w *asserts* ϕ (positive support or support of truth) and v_2 for the degree of *denial* (negative support or support of falsity). *Classically,* $v_1(\phi, w) + v_2(\phi, w) = 1$; if a source provides *contradictory information*, then $v_1(\phi, w) + v_2(\phi, w) > 1$; if the source provides *insufficient information*, then $v_1(\phi, w) + v_2(\phi, w) < 1$.

Now, if we account for the nonclassical information provided by the sources, the two aggregations described above can be formalised as follows. For the *sceptical* case, the agent considers *infima of positive and negative supports*. For the *credulous aggregation*, one takes *suprema of positive and negative supports*.

These two aggregation strategies were initially proposed and analysed in [8]. There, however, they were described in a two-layered framework[1] which prohibits the nesting of modalities. Furthermore, the Belnap–Dunn logic [4] (BD) that lacks implication was chosen as the propositional fragment. In this paper, we extend that approach to the Kripke semantics to incorporate possible references between the sources and the sources' ability to give modalised statements. Furthermore, we use a paraconsistent expansion G^2 from [5] of Gödel logic G as the propositional fragment.

Formalising Beliefs in Modal Expansions of G**.** When information is aggregated, the agent can further reason with it. For example, if the degrees of certainty of two given statements are represented as real numbers and one knows them, one can add them up, subtract them from one another, or compare them. In many contexts, however, an ordinary person does not represent their certainty in a given statement numerically and thus cannot conduct arithmetical operations with them. What they can do instead, is to *compare* their certainty in one statement vs the other.

Thus, since Gödel logic expresses order and comparisons but not arithmetic operations, it can be used as a propositional fragment of a modal logic formalising beliefs. For example, **K45** and **KD45** Gödel logics can be used to formalise possibilistic reasoning since they are complete w.r.t. normalised and, respectively, non-normalised possibilistic frames [35].

Furthermore, adding coimplication $\prec$ or, equivalently, Baaz' Delta operator $\triangle$ (cf. [2] for details), results in bi-Gödel ('symmetric Gödel' in the terminology of [20]) logic that can additionally express strict order.

Modal expansions of G are well-studied. In particular, the Hilbert [15] and Gentzen [27,28] formalisations of both $\square$ and $\lozenge$ fragments of the modal logic $\mathfrak{G}\mathfrak{K}^2$ are known. There are also complete axiomatisations for both fuzzy [16] and crisp [36] bi-modal Gödel logics. It is known that they and some of their extensions are both decidable and PSpace complete [13,14,17] even though they lack finite model property.

Furthermore, it is known that the addition of $\prec$ or $\triangle$ as well as of a paraconsistent negation $\neg$ that swaps the supports of truth and falsity does not increase

---

[1] We refer our readers to [3] and [7] for an exposition of two-layered modal logics.
[2] $\square$ and $\lozenge$ are not interdefinable in $\mathfrak{G}\mathfrak{K}$.

the complexity. Namely, satisfiability of **KbiG** and **GTL** (modal and temporal bi-Gödel logics, respectively) (cf. [6,9] for the former and [1] for the latter) as well as that of $\mathbf{KG}^2$ (expansion of crisp $\mathfrak{G}\mathfrak{K}$ with $\neg^3$) are in **PSpace**.

This paper. In this paper, we consider an expansion of G^2 with modalities ■ and ♦ that stand for the cautious and credulous aggregation strategies. We equip it with Kripke semantics, construct a sound and complete tableaux calculus, and explore its semantical and computational properties. Our inspiration comes from two sources: modal expansions of Gödel logics that we discussed above and modal expansions of Belnap–Dunn logic with Kripke semantics on bi-valued frames as studied by Priest [33,34], Odintsov and Wansing [31,32], and others (cf. [18] and references therein to related work in the field). In a sense, $\mathsf{G}^{2\pm}_{\blacksquare,\blacklozenge}$ can be thought of as a hybrid between modal logics over **BD**.

The remaining text is organised as follows. In Sect. 2, we define the language and semantics of $\mathsf{G}^{2\pm}_{\blacksquare,\blacklozenge}$. Then, in Sect. 3 we show how to define several important frame classes, in particular, finitely branching frames. We also argue for the use of $\mathsf{G}^{2\pm}_{\blacksquare,\blacklozenge_{fb}}$ ($\mathsf{G}^{2\pm}_{\blacksquare,\blacklozenge}$ over finitely branching frames) for the representation of agents' beliefs. In Sect. 4 we present a sound and complete tableaux calculus for $\mathsf{G}^{2\pm}_{\blacksquare,\blacklozenge_{fb}}$ and in Sect. 5, we use it to show that $\mathsf{G}^{2\pm}_{\blacksquare,\blacklozenge_{fb}}$ validity and satisfiability are **PSpace** complete. Finally, in Sect. 6, we wrap up the paper and provide a roadmap to future work.

2   Logical Preliminaries

Throughout the paper, we will be comparing $\mathsf{G}^{2\pm}_{\blacksquare,\blacklozenge}$ and **KbiG**. Hence, to make the text self-contained, we recall the language and semantics of the latter from [9].

Definition 1 (Frames).

- *A fuzzy frame is a tuple* $\mathfrak{F} = \langle W, R \rangle$ *with* $W \neq \varnothing$ *and* $R : W \times W \to [0,1]$ *(i.e., R is a fuzzy relation).*
- *A crisp frame is a tuple* $\mathfrak{F} = \langle W, R \rangle$ *with* $W \neq \varnothing$ *and* $R : W \times W \to \{0,1\}$ *(i.e., R is a crisp relation).*

Definition 2 (KbiG). *We fix a countable set* **Prop** *and define the language* $\mathrm{bi}\mathcal{L}_{\square,\lozenge}$ *as follows.*

$$\mathrm{bi}\mathcal{L}_{\square,\lozenge} \ni \phi := p \in \mathsf{Prop} \mid (\phi \wedge \phi) \mid (\phi \vee \phi) \mid (\phi \to \phi) \mid (\phi \prec \phi) \mid \square\phi \mid \lozenge\phi$$

A **KbiG** *model is a tuple* $\mathfrak{M} = \langle W, R, v \rangle$ *with* $\langle W, R \rangle$ *being a (crisp or fuzzy) frame, and* $v : \mathsf{Prop} \times W \to [0,1]$. *$v$ (a* **KbiG** *valuation) is extended on* $\mathrm{bi}\mathcal{L}_{\square,\lozenge}$-*formulas as follows.*

---

[3] Note that in the presence of $\neg$, $\phi \prec \phi'$ is definable as $\neg(\neg\phi' \to \neg\phi)$.

$$v(\phi \wedge \chi, w) = \min(v(\phi, w), v(\chi, w)) \qquad v(\phi \vee \chi, w) = \max(v(\phi, w), v(\chi, w))$$

$$v(\phi \rightarrow \chi, w) = \begin{cases} 1 \ if \ v(\phi, w) \le v(\chi, w) \\ v(\chi, w) \ else \end{cases} \qquad v(\phi \prec \chi, w) = \begin{cases} 0 \ if \ v(\phi, w) \le v(\chi, w) \\ v(\phi, w) \ else \end{cases}$$

$$v(\Box \phi, w) = \inf_{w' \in W} \{wRw' \rightarrow v(\phi, w')\} \qquad v(\Diamond \phi, w) = \sup_{w' \in W} \{wRw' \wedge v(\phi, w')\}$$

We say that $\phi \in \mathrm{bi}\mathcal{L}_{\Box, \Diamond}$ is KbiG *valid on frame $\mathfrak{F}$ (denote, $\mathfrak{F} \models_{\mathsf{KbiG}} \phi$) iff for any $w \in \mathfrak{F}$, it holds that $v(\phi, w) = 1$ for any model $\mathfrak{M}$ on $\mathfrak{F}$.*

Definition 3 ($\mathsf{G}^{2\pm}_{\blacksquare, \blacklozenge}$)**.** *We define the language $\mathcal{L}^{\neg}_{\blacksquare, \blacklozenge}$ via the following grammar.*

$$\mathcal{L}^{\neg}_{\blacksquare, \blacklozenge} \ni \phi := p \in \mathsf{Prop} \mid \neg \phi \mid (\phi \wedge \phi) \mid (\phi \rightarrow \phi) \mid \blacksquare \phi \mid \blacklozenge \phi$$

Constants $\mathbf{0}$ and $\mathbf{1}$, disjunction $\vee$, and coimplication $\prec$ as well as Gödel negation $\sim$ and Baaz' Delta $\triangle$ can be defined as expected:

$$\mathbf{1} := p \rightarrow p \qquad\qquad \mathbf{0} := \neg \mathbf{1} \qquad\qquad \sim \phi := \phi \rightarrow \mathbf{0}$$

$$\triangle \phi := \mathbf{1} \prec (\mathbf{1} \prec \phi) \qquad \phi \vee \phi' := \neg(\neg \phi \wedge \neg \phi') \qquad \phi \prec \phi' := \neg(\neg \phi' \rightarrow \neg \phi)$$

A bi-relational frame is a tuple $\mathfrak{F} = \langle W, R^+, R^- \rangle$ with $W \neq \varnothing$ and R^+, R^- being fuzzy or crisp relations. A model is a tuple $\mathfrak{M} = \langle W, R^+, R^-, v_1, v_2 \rangle$ with $\langle W, R^+, R^- \rangle$ being a frame and $v_1, v_2 : \mathsf{Prop} \rightarrow [0, 1]$ that are extended to the complex formulas as follows.

$$v_1(\neg \phi, w) = v_2(\phi, w) \qquad\qquad v_2(\neg \phi, w) = v_1(\phi, w)$$

$$v_1(\phi \wedge \chi, w) = \min(v_1(\phi, w), v_1(\chi, w)) \quad v_2(\phi \wedge \chi, w) = \max(v_2(\phi, w), v_2(\chi, w))$$

$$v_1(\phi \rightarrow \chi, w) = \begin{cases} 1 \ if \ v_1(\phi, w) \le v_1(\chi, w) \\ v_1(\chi, w) \ else \end{cases} \qquad v_2(\phi \rightarrow \chi, w) = \begin{cases} 0 \ if \ v_2(\chi, w) \le v_2(\phi, w) \\ v_2(\chi, w) \ else \end{cases}$$

$$v_1(\blacksquare \phi, w) = \inf_{w' \in W} \{wR^+ w' \rightarrow v_1(\phi, w')\} \quad v_2(\blacksquare \phi, w) = \inf_{w' \in W} \{wR^- w' \rightarrow v_2(\phi, w')\}$$

$$v_1(\blacklozenge \phi, w) = \sup_{w' \in W} \{wR^+ w' \wedge v_1(\phi, w')\} \quad v_2(\blacklozenge \phi, w) = \sup_{w' \in W} \{wR^- w' \wedge v_2(\phi, w')\}$$

We will further write $v(\phi, w) = (x, y)$ to designate that $v_1(\phi, w) = x$ and $v_2(\phi, w) = y$. Moreover, we set $S(w) = \{w' : wSw' > 0\}$.

We say that ϕ is v_1-valid on $\mathfrak{F}$ ($\mathfrak{F} \models^+ \phi$) iff for every model $\mathfrak{M}$ on $\mathfrak{F}$ and every $w \in \mathfrak{M}$, it holds that $v_1(\phi, w) = 1$. ϕ is v_2-valid on $\mathfrak{F}$ ($\mathfrak{F} \models^- \phi$) iff for every model $\mathfrak{M}$ on $\mathfrak{F}$ and every $w \in \mathfrak{M}$, it holds that $v_2(\phi, w) = 0$. ϕ is strongly valid on $\mathfrak{F}$ ($\mathfrak{F} \models \phi$) iff it is v_1 and v_2-valid.

ϕ is v_1 (resp., v_2, strongly) $\mathsf{G}^{2\pm}_{\blacksquare, \blacklozenge}$ valid iff it is v_1 (resp., v_2, strongly) valid on every frame. We will further use $\mathsf{G}^{2\pm}_{\blacksquare, \blacklozenge}$ to designate the set of all $\mathcal{L}^{\neg}_{\blacksquare, \blacklozenge}$ formulas strongly valid on every frame.

Observe in the definitions above that the semantical conditions governing the support of the truth of $\mathsf{G}^{2\pm}_{\blacksquare,\blacklozenge}$ connectives (except for $\neg$) coincide with the semantics of **KbiG** and thus Gödel modal logic $\mathfrak{G}\mathfrak{K}$. Note, however, that the semantics of $\mathsf{G}^{2\pm}_{\blacksquare,\blacklozenge}$ *does not generalise* that of **KbiG**. Indeed, in the paraconsistent setting, if one is sceptical (or credulous) w.r.t. their sources, then they are unlikely to trust both confirmations and denials (or, respectively, likely to trust both confirmations and denials) since they can be considered independently. On the other hand, if we generalised the semantics of modalities to the paraconsistent case in a usual way, $\square$ would stand for a *pessimistic* aggregation (when the infimum of the positive and the supremum of the negative support are taken), not the sceptical one; and $\lozenge$ would stand for an *optimistic* aggregation[4] (dually), not the credulous one. Note, moreover, that without separating the support of truth from the support of falsity via $\neg$, pessimistic (optimistic) aggregation is the same as sceptical (credulous).

The following example illustrates the semantics of $\blacksquare$ and $\blacklozenge$.

Example 1. A tourist (t) wants to go to a restaurant and asks their two friends (f_1 and f_2) to describe their impressions regarding the politeness of the staff (s) and the quality of the desserts (d). Of course, the friends' opinions are not always internally consistent, nor is it always the case that one or the other even noticed whether the staff was polite or was eating desserts. Furthermore, t trusts their friends to different degrees when it comes to their positive and negative opinions. The situation is depicted in Fig. 1.

The first friend says that half of the staff was really nice but the other half is unwelcoming and rude and that the desserts (except for the tiramisu and soufflé) are tasty. The second friend, unfortunately, did not have the desserts at all. Furthermore, even though, they praised the staff, they also said that the manager was quite obnoxious.

The tourist now makes up their mind. If they are sceptical w.r.t. s and d, they look for *trusted rejections*[5] of both positive and negative supports of s and d. Thus t uses the values of R^+ and R^- as thresholds above which the information provided by the source does not count as a trusted enough rejection. I.e., to accept rejection from a friend, it should be stronger than the degree of trust the tourist gives to the friend. E.g., $tR^+f_1 > v_1(s, f_1)$ but $tR^+f_2 \leq v(s, f_2)$ (Fig. 1). Thus, only the account of the first friend counts as a rejection. In our case, we have $v(\blacksquare s, t) = (0.5, 0.5)$ and $v(\blacksquare d, t) = (0, 0)$.

On the other hand, if t is credulous, they look for *trusted confirmations* of both positive and negative supports and use R^+ and R^- as thresholds up to which they accept the information provided by the source. In particular Thus, we have $v(\blacklozenge s, t) = (0.7, 0.4)$ and $v(\blacklozenge d, t) = (0.7, 0.3)$.

---

[4] We refer readers to [9] for a detailed discussion of pessimistic and optimistic aggregations.

[5] We differentiate between a *rejection* which we treat as *lack of support* and a *denial, disproof, refutation, counterexample*, etc. which we interpret as the *negative support*. Note that there may be a lack of both positive and negative support if there is not enough information.

$$f_1 : \begin{matrix} s = (0.5, 0.5) \\ d = (0.7, 0.3) \end{matrix} \xleftarrow{\;\;(0.8, 0.9)\;\;} t \xrightarrow{\;\;(0.7, 0.2)\;\;} f_2 : \begin{matrix} s = (1, 0.4) \\ d = (0, 0) \end{matrix}$$

Fig. 1. (x, y) stands for $wR^+ w' = x$, $wR^- w' = y$. R^+ (resp., R^-) is interpreted as the tourist's threshold of trust in positive (negative) statements by the friends.

More formally, note that we can combine v_1 and v_2 into a single valuation (denoted with •) on the following *bi-lattice* on the right. Now, if we let ⊓ and ⊔ be meet and join w.r.t. the rightward (informational) order, it is clear that ■ can be interpreted as an infinitary ⊓ and ◆ as an infinitary ⊔ across the accessible states, respectively.

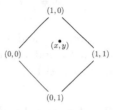

From here, it is expected that ■ and ◆ do not distribute over ∧ and ∨: ■$(p \wedge q) \leftrightarrow (\blacksquare p \wedge \blacksquare q)$, ■$1$, ◆$(p \vee q) \leftrightarrow (\blacklozenge p \vee \blacklozenge q)$, and ◆$0 \leftrightarrow 0$ are not valid.

Finally, we have called $\mathsf{G}^{2\pm}_{\blacksquare, \blacklozenge}$ 'paraconsistent'. In this paper, we consider the logic to be a set of valid formulas. It is clear that the explosion principle for →—$(p \wedge \neg p) \to q$—is not valid. Furthermore, in contrast to **K**, it is possible to believe in a contradiction without *believing in every statement*: ◆$(p \wedge \neg p) \to$ ◆q and ■$(p \wedge \neg p) \to$ ■q are not valid.

We end the section by proving that ◆ and ■ *are not interdefinable*.

Theorem 1. ■ *and* ◆ *are not interdefinable.*

Proof. Denote with $\mathcal{L}_\blacksquare$ and $\mathcal{L}_\blacklozenge$ the ◆- and ■-free fragments of $\mathcal{L}^\neg_{\blacksquare, \blacklozenge}$. We build a pointed model $\langle \mathfrak{M}, w_0 \rangle$ s.t. there is no ◆-free formula that has the same value at w_0 as ■p (and vice versa). Consider Fig. 2.

$$w_1 : p = \left(\tfrac{2}{3}, \tfrac{1}{2}\right) \longleftarrow w_0 : p = (1, 0) \longrightarrow w_2 : p = \left(\tfrac{1}{3}, \tfrac{1}{4}\right)$$

Fig. 2. All variables have the same values in all states exemplified by p. $R^+ = R^-$ is crisp, $v(\blacksquare p, w_0) = \left(\tfrac{1}{3}, \tfrac{1}{4}\right)$, $v(\blacklozenge p, w_0) = \left(\tfrac{2}{3}, \tfrac{1}{2}\right)$.

One can check by induction that if $\phi \in \mathcal{L}^\neg_{\blacksquare, \blacklozenge}$, then

$$v(\phi, w_1) \in \left\{ (0; 1), \left(\tfrac{1}{2}; \tfrac{2}{3}\right), \left(\tfrac{2}{3}; \tfrac{1}{2}\right), (0; 0), (1; 1), (1; 0) \right\}$$

$$v(\phi, w_2) \in \left\{ (0; 1), \left(\tfrac{1}{4}; \tfrac{1}{3}\right), \left(\tfrac{1}{3}; \tfrac{1}{4}\right), (0; 0), (1; 1), (1; 0) \right\}$$

Moreover, on the single-point irreflexive frame whose only state is u, it holds for every $\phi(p) \in \mathcal{L}^\neg_{\blacksquare, \blacklozenge}$, $v(\phi, u) \in \{v(p, u), v(\neg p, u), (1, 0), (1, 1), (0, 0), (0, 1)\}$.

Thus, for every $\blacklozenge$-free χ and every $\blacksquare$-free ψ it holds that

$$v(\blacksquare\chi, w_0) \in \left\{ (0;1), \left(\frac{1}{3};\frac{1}{4}\right), \left(\frac{1}{4};\frac{1}{3}\right), (0;0), (1;1), (1;0) \right\} = X$$

$$v(\blacklozenge\psi, w_0) \in \left\{ (0;1), \left(\frac{1}{2};\frac{2}{3}\right), \left(\frac{2}{3};\frac{1}{2}\right), (0;0), (1;1), (1;0) \right\} = Y$$

Since X and Y are closed w.r.t. propositional operations, it is now easy to check by induction that for every $\chi' \in \mathcal{L}_{\blacksquare}$ and $\psi' \in \mathcal{L}_{\blacklozenge}$, $v(\chi', w_0) \in X$ and $v(\psi', w_0) \in Y$.

3 Frame Definability

In this section, we explore some classes of frames that can be defined in $\mathcal{L}^{\neg}_{\blacksquare,\blacklozenge}$. However, since $\blacksquare$ and $\blacklozenge$ are non-normal and since we have two independent relations on frames, we expand the traditional notion of modal definability.

Definition 4.

1. ϕ positively defines *a class of frames* $\mathbb{F}$ *iff for every* $\mathfrak{F}$, *it holds that* $\mathfrak{F} \models^+ \phi$ *iff* $\mathfrak{F} \in \mathbb{F}$.
2. ϕ negatively defines *a class of frames* $\mathbb{F}$ *iff for every* $\mathfrak{F}$, *it holds that* $\mathfrak{F} \models^- \phi$ *iff* $\mathfrak{F} \in \mathbb{F}$.
3. ϕ (strongly) defines *a class of frames* $\mathbb{F}$ *iff for every* $\mathfrak{F}$, *it holds that* $\mathfrak{F} \in \mathbb{F}$ *iff* $\mathfrak{F} \models \phi$.

With the help of the above definition, we can show that every class of frames definable in **KbiG** is *positively definable* in $\mathsf{G}^{2\pm}_{\blacksquare,\blacklozenge}$.

Definition 5. *Let* $\mathfrak{F} = \langle W, S \rangle$ *be a (fuzzy or crisp) frame.*

1. *An* R^+-*counterpart of* $\mathfrak{F}$ *is any bi-relational frame* $\mathfrak{F}^+ = \langle W, S, R^- \rangle$.
2. *An* R^--*counterpart of* $\mathfrak{F}$ *is any bi-relational frame* $\mathfrak{F}^+ = \langle W, R^+, S \rangle$.

Convention 1 *Let* $\phi \in \mathsf{bi}\mathcal{L}_{\square,\lozenge}$.

1. *We denote with* $\phi^{+\bullet}$ *the* $\mathcal{L}^{\neg}_{\blacksquare,\blacklozenge}$-*formula obtained from* ϕ *by replacing all* $\square$'s *and* $\lozenge$'s *with* $\blacksquare$'s *and* $\blacklozenge$'s.
2. *We denote with* $\phi^{-\bullet}$ *the* $\mathcal{L}^{\neg}_{\blacksquare,\blacklozenge}$-*formula obtained from* ϕ *by replacing all* $\square$'s *and* $\lozenge$'s *with* $\neg\blacksquare\neg$'s *and* $\neg\blacklozenge\neg$'s.

Theorem 2. *Let* $\mathfrak{F} = \langle W, S \rangle$ *and let* $\mathfrak{F}^+$ *and* $\mathfrak{F}^-$ *be its* R^+ *and* R^- *counterparts. Then, for any* $\phi \in \mathsf{bi}\mathcal{L}_{\square,\lozenge}$, *it holds that*

$$\mathfrak{F} \models_{\mathsf{KbiG}} \phi \quad \text{iff} \quad \mathfrak{F}^+ \models^+ \phi^{+\bullet} \quad \text{iff} \quad \mathfrak{F}^- \models^+ \phi^{-\bullet}$$

Proof. Since the semantics of **KbiG** connectives is identical to v_1 conditions of Definition 3, we only prove that $\mathfrak{F} \models \phi$ iff $\mathfrak{F}^- \models^+ \phi^{-\bullet}$. It suffices to prove by induction the following statement.

Let **v** *be a* **KbiG** *valuation on* $\mathfrak{F}$, $\mathbf{v}(p, w) = v_1(p, w)$ *for every* $w \in \mathfrak{F}$, *and* v_2 *be arbitrary. Then* $\mathbf{v}(\phi, w) = v_1(\phi^{-\bullet}, w)$ *for every* ϕ.

The case of $\phi = p$ holds by Convention 1, the cases of propositional connectives are straightforward. Consider $\phi = \Box\chi$. We have that $\phi^{-\bullet} = \neg\blacksquare\neg(\chi^{-\bullet})$ and thus

$$
\begin{aligned}
v_1(\neg\blacksquare\neg(\chi^{-\bullet}), w) &= v_2(\blacksquare\neg(\chi^{-\bullet}), w) \\
&= \inf_{w' \in W}\{wSw' \rightarrow v_2(\neg(\chi^{-\bullet}))\} \\
&= \inf_{w' \in W}\{wSw' \rightarrow v_1(\chi^{-\bullet})\} \\
&= \inf_{w' \in W}\{wSw' \rightarrow \mathbf{v}(\chi)\} \quad\quad \text{(by IH)} \\
&= \mathbf{v}(\Box\chi, w)
\end{aligned}
$$

The above theorem allows us to *positively* define in $\mathsf{G}^{2\pm}_{\blacksquare,\blacklozenge}$ all classes of frames that are definable in **KbiG**. In particular, all **K**-definable frames are positively definable. Moreover, it follows that $\mathsf{G}^{2\pm}_{\blacksquare,\blacklozenge}$ (as $\mathfrak{G}\mathfrak{K}$ and **KbiG**) lacks the finite model property: $\sim\Box(p \vee \sim p)$ is false on every finite frame, and thus, $\sim\blacksquare(p \vee \sim p)$ is too. On the other hand, there are infinite models satisfying this formula as shown below (R^+ and R^- are crisp).

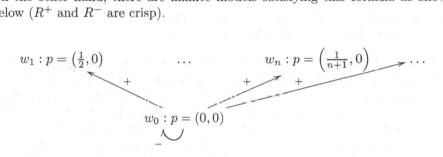

Furthermore, Theorem 2 gives us a degree of flexibility. For example, one can check that $\neg\blacksquare\neg(p \vee q) \rightarrow (\neg\blacksquare\neg p \vee \neg\blacklozenge\neg q)$ positively defines frames with crisp R^- but not necessarily crisp R^+. This models a situation when an agent *completely (dis)believes* in denials given by their sources while may have some degree of trust between 0 and 1 when the sources assert something. Let us return to Example 1.

Example 2. Assume that the tourist *completely trusts* the negative (but not positive) opinions of their friends. Thus, instead of Fig. 1, we have the following model.

$$
f_1 : \begin{aligned} s &= (0.5, 0.5) \\ d &= (0.7, 0.3) \end{aligned} \quad \xleftarrow{\;(0.8,1)\;} \quad t \quad \xrightarrow{\;(0.7,1)\;} \quad f_2 : \begin{aligned} s &= (1, 0.4) \\ d &= (0, 0) \end{aligned}
$$

The new values for the cautious and credulous aggregation are as follows: $v(\blacksquare s, t) = (0.5, 0.4)$, $v(\blacksquare d, t) = (0, 0)$, $v(\blacklozenge s, t) = (0.7, 0.5)$, and $v(\blacklozenge d, t) = (0.7, 0.3)$.

Furthermore, the agent can trust the sources to the same degree no matter whether they confirm or deny statements. This can be modelled with *mono-relational* frames where $R^+ = R^-$. We show that they are *strongly definable*.

Theorem 3. $\mathfrak{F}$ *is mono-relational iff* $\mathfrak{F} \models \blacksquare\neg p \leftrightarrow \neg\blacksquare p$ *and* $\mathfrak{F} \models \blacklozenge\neg p \leftrightarrow \neg\blacklozenge p$.

Proof. Let $\mathfrak{F}$ be mono-relational and $R^+ = R^- = R$. Now observe that

$$
\begin{aligned}
v_i(\blacksquare\neg p, w) &= \inf_{w' \in W} \{wRw' \to v_i(\neg p, w')\} && (i \in \{1, 2\}) \\
&= \inf_{w' \in W} \{wRw' \to v_j(p, w')\} && (i \neq j) \\
&= v_j(\blacksquare p, w) \\
&= v_i(\neg\blacksquare p, w)
\end{aligned}
$$

For the converse, let $R^+ \neq R^-$ and, in particular, $wR^+w' = x$ and $wR^-w' = y$. Assume w.l.o.g. that $x > y$. We set the valuation of p: $v(p, w') = (x, y)$ and for every $w'' \neq w'$, we have $v(p, w'') = (1, 1)$. It is clear that $v(\neg\blacksquare p, w) = (1, 1)$. On the other hand, $v(\neg p, w') = (y, x)$, whence $v_1(\blacksquare\neg p) \neq 1$.

The case of $\blacklozenge$ can be tackled in a dual manner.

In the remainder of the paper, we will be concerned with $\mathsf{G}^{2\pm}_{\blacksquare, \blacklozenge\, \mathsf{fb}} - \mathsf{G}^{2\pm}_{\blacksquare, \blacklozenge}$ over finitely branching (both fuzzy and crisp) frames. This is for several reasons. First, in the context of formalising beliefs and reasoning with data acquired from sources, it is reasonable to assume that every source refers to only a finite number of other sources and that agents have access to a finite number of sources as well. This assumption is implicit in many classical epistemic and doxastic logics since they are often complete w.r.t. finitely branching models [19], although cannot *define* them. Second, in the finitely branching models, the values of modal formulas are *witnessed*: if $v_i(\blacksquare\phi, w) = x < 1$, then, $v_i(\phi, w') = x$ for some w', and if $v_i(\blacklozenge\phi, w) = x$, then $wRw' = x$ or $v_i(\phi, w') = x$ for some w'. Intuitively, this means that the degree of w's certainty in ϕ is purely based on the information acquired from sources and from its degree of trust in those. Finally, the restriction to finitely branching frames allows for the construction of a simple constraint tableaux calculus that can be used in establishing the complexity valuation.

Note, finally, that both fuzzy and crisp finitely branching frames can be defined in $\mathfrak{GK}$ with $\sim\sim\square(p \vee \sim p)$ (cf. [9, Remark 3] and [6, Proposition 4.3]). Thus, by Theorem 2, frames with finitely R^+ are positively definable via $\sim\sim\blacksquare(p \vee \sim p)$ and those with finitely branching R^- via $\sim\sim\neg\blacksquare\neg(p \vee \sim p)$.

4 Tableaux Calculus

In this section, we construct a sound and complete constraint tableaux system $\mathcal{T}\left(\mathsf{G}^{2\pm}_{\blacksquare,\blacklozenge\mathsf{fb}}\right)$ for $\mathsf{G}^{2\pm}_{\blacksquare,\blacklozenge\mathsf{fb}}$. The first constraint tableaux were proposed in [21–23] as a decision procedure for the Łukasiewicz logic Ł. A similar approach for the Rational Pawełka logic was proposed in [24]. In [5], we constructed constraint tableaux for $\mathsf{Ł}^2$ and G^2 — the paraconsistent expansions of Ł and G, and in [9] for modal expansions of the bi-Gödel logic and G^2.

Constraint tableaux are *analytic* in the sense that their rules have the subformula property. Moreover, they provide an easy way to extract a countermodel from complete open branches. Furthermore, while the propositional connectives of G^2 allow for the construction of an analytic proof system, e.g., a display calculus extending that of $\mathsf{I}_4\mathsf{C}_4{}^6$ [38], the modal ones are not dual to one another w.r.t. $\neg$ nor the Gödel negation $\sim$. Thus, it is unlikely that an elegant (hyper-)sequent or display calculus for $\mathsf{G}^{2\pm}_{\blacksquare,\blacklozenge}$ or $\mathsf{G}^{2\pm}_{\blacksquare,\blacklozenge\mathsf{fb}}$ can be constructed.

The next definitions are adapted from [9].

Definition 6. *We fix a set of state-labels* W *and let* $\precsim\,\in\{<,\leqslant\}$ *and* $\succsim\,\in\{>,\geqslant\}$. *Let further* $w\in\mathsf{W}$, $\mathbf{x}\in\{1,2\}$, $\phi\in\mathcal{L}^{\neg}_{\blacksquare,\blacklozenge}$, *and* $c\in\{0,1\}$. *A* structure *is either* $w\!:\!\mathbf{x}\!:\!\phi$, c, $w\mathsf{R}^+w'$, *or* $w\mathsf{R}^+w'$. *We denote the set of structures with* Str. *Structures of the form* $w\!:\!\mathbf{x}\!:\!p$, $w\mathsf{R}^+w'$, *and* $w\mathsf{R}^-w'$ *are called* atomic *(denoted* AStr).

We define a constraint tableau *as a downward branching tree whose branches are sets containing constraints* $\mathfrak{X}\precsim\mathfrak{X}'$ $(\mathfrak{X},\mathfrak{X}'\in\mathsf{Str})$. *Each branch can be extended by an application of a rule*[7] *below (bars denote branching,* $i,j\in\{1,2\}$, $i\neq j$).

$$\neg_i{\precsim}\,\frac{w\!:\!i\!:\!\neg\phi\precsim\mathfrak{X}}{w\!:\!j\!:\!\phi\precsim\mathfrak{X}}\qquad \neg_i{\succsim}\,\frac{w\!:\!i\!:\!\neg\phi\succsim\mathfrak{X}}{w\!:\!j\!:\!\phi\succsim\mathfrak{X}}\qquad \rightarrow_1{\precsim}\,\frac{w\!:\!1\!:\!\phi\rightarrow\phi'\precsim\mathfrak{X}}{\mathfrak{X}\geqslant 1\,\left|\,\begin{matrix}w\!:\!1\!:\!\phi'\precsim\mathfrak{X}\\ w\!:\!1\!:\!\phi>w\!:\!1\!:\!\phi'\end{matrix}\right.}\qquad \rightarrow_2{\succsim}\,\frac{w\!:\!2\!:\!\phi\rightarrow\phi'\succsim\mathfrak{X}}{\mathfrak{X}\leqslant 0\,\left|\,\begin{matrix}w\!:\!2\!:\!\phi'\succsim\mathfrak{X}\\ w\!:\!2\!:\!\phi'>w\!:\!2\!:\!\phi\end{matrix}\right.}$$

$$\wedge_1{\succsim}\,\frac{w\!:\!1\!:\!\phi\wedge\phi'\succsim\mathfrak{X}}{\begin{matrix}w\!:\!1\!:\!\phi\succsim\mathfrak{X}\\ w\!:\!1\!:\!\phi'\succsim\mathfrak{X}\end{matrix}}\qquad \wedge_2{\precsim}\,\frac{w\!:\!2\!:\!\phi\wedge\phi'\precsim\mathfrak{X}}{\begin{matrix}w\!:\!2\!:\!\phi\precsim\mathfrak{X}\\ w\!:\!2\!:\!\phi'\precsim\mathfrak{X}\end{matrix}}\qquad \rightarrow_1{<}\,\frac{w\!:\!1\!:\!\phi\rightarrow\phi'<\mathfrak{X}}{\begin{matrix}w\!:\!1\!:\!\phi'<\mathfrak{X}\\ w\!:\!1\!:\!\phi>w\!:\!1\!:\!\phi'\end{matrix}}\qquad \rightarrow_2{>}\,\frac{w\!:\!2\!:\!\phi\rightarrow\phi'>\mathfrak{X}}{\begin{matrix}w\!:\!2\!:\!\phi'>\mathfrak{X}\\ w\!:\!2\!:\!\phi'>w\!:\!2\!:\!\phi\end{matrix}}$$

$$\wedge_1{\precsim}\,\frac{w\!:\!1\!:\!\phi\wedge\phi'\precsim\mathfrak{X}}{w\!:\!1\!:\!\phi\precsim\mathfrak{X}\,|\,w\!:\!1\!:\!\phi'\precsim\mathfrak{X}}\qquad\qquad \wedge_2{\succsim}\,\frac{w\!:\!2\!:\!\phi\wedge\phi'\succsim\mathfrak{X}}{w\!:\!2\!:\!\phi\succsim\mathfrak{X}\,|\,w\!:\!2\!:\!\phi'\succsim\mathfrak{X}}$$

$$\rightarrow_1{\succsim}\,\frac{w\!:\!1\!:\!\phi\rightarrow\phi'\succsim\mathfrak{X}}{\begin{matrix}w\!:\!1\!:\!\phi\leqslant w\!:\!1\!:\!\phi'\\ 1\succsim\mathfrak{X}\end{matrix}\,\left|\,w\!:\!1\!:\!\phi'\succsim\mathfrak{X}\right.}\qquad\qquad \rightarrow_2{\precsim}\,\frac{w\!:\!2\!:\!\phi\rightarrow\phi'\precsim\mathfrak{X}}{\begin{matrix}w\!:\!2\!:\!\phi'\leqslant w\!:\!2\!:\!\phi\\ 0\precsim\mathfrak{X}\end{matrix}\,\left|\,w\!:\!2\!:\!\phi'\precsim\mathfrak{X}\right.}$$

$$\blacksquare_i{\succsim}\,\frac{w\!:\!i\!:\!\blacksquare\phi\succsim\mathfrak{X}}{w'\!:\!i\!:\!\phi\succsim\mathfrak{X}\,|\,w\mathsf{S}w'\leqslant w'\!:\!i\!:\!\phi}\qquad \blacksquare_i{\leqslant}\,\frac{w\!:\!i\!:\!\blacksquare\phi\leqslant\mathfrak{X}}{\mathfrak{X}\geqslant 1\,\left|\begin{matrix}w\mathsf{S}w''>w''\!:\!i\!:\!\phi\\ w''\!:\!i\!:\!\phi\leqslant\mathfrak{X}\end{matrix}\right.}\qquad \blacksquare_i{<}\,\frac{w\!:\!i\!:\!\blacksquare\phi<\mathfrak{X}}{\begin{matrix}w\mathsf{S}w''>w''\!:\!i\!:\!\phi\\ w''\!:\!i\!:\!\phi<\mathfrak{X}\end{matrix}}$$

---

[6] This logic was introduced several times: in [38], then in [25], and further studied in [30]. It is, in fact, the propositional fragment of Moisil's modal logic [29]. We are grateful to Heinrich Wansing who pointed this out to us.

[7] If $\mathfrak{X}<1,\mathfrak{X}<\mathfrak{X}'\in\mathcal{B}$ or $0<\mathfrak{X}',\mathfrak{X}<\mathfrak{X}'\in\mathcal{B}$, the rules are applied only to $\mathfrak{X}<\mathfrak{X}'$.

$$\blacklozenge_i{\gtrsim}\ \dfrac{w:i:\blacklozenge\phi\gtrsim\mathfrak{x}}{\substack{wSw''\gtrsim\mathfrak{x}\\ w'':i:\phi\gtrsim\mathfrak{x}}}\qquad \blacklozenge_i{\lesssim}\ \dfrac{w:i:\blacklozenge\phi\lesssim\mathfrak{x}}{w':i:\phi\lesssim\mathfrak{x}\mid wSw'\lesssim\mathfrak{x}}\qquad \left[\begin{array}{c} w''\ \textit{is fresh on the branch}\\ \textit{if } i{=}1,\ \textit{then } \mathsf{S}{=}\mathsf{R}^+\\ \textit{if } i{=}2,\ \textit{then } \mathsf{S}{=}\mathsf{R}^-\\ \textit{in } \blacksquare_i{\gtrsim},\blacklozenge_i{\lesssim}\ wSw'\ \textit{occurs on the branch} \end{array}\right]$$

A tableau's branch $\mathcal{B}$ is closed *iff one of the following conditions applies:*

- *the transitive closure of $\mathcal{B}$ under $\lesssim$ contains $\mathfrak{x}<\mathfrak{x}$;*
- $0\geqslant 1\in\mathcal{B}$, *or* $\mathfrak{x}>1\in\mathcal{B}$, *or* $\mathfrak{x}<0\in\mathcal{B}$.

A tableau is closed *iff all its branches are closed. We say that there is a tableau proof of ϕ iff there are closed tableaux starting from $w\!:\!1\!:\!\phi<1$ and $w\!:\!2\!:\!\phi>0$. An open branch $\mathcal{B}$ is* complete *iff the following condition is met.*

∗ If all premises of a rule occur on $\mathcal{B}$, then one of its conclusions[8] occurs on $\mathcal{B}$.

As one can see, the propositional rules remain the same but we have to account for the fuzzy relation. Thus, we introduce not only constraints that compare the values of the formulas but also constraints comparing the values of relations between two states.

Convention 2. *The table below summarises the interpretations of entries.*

entry	interpretation
$w\!:\!1\!:\!\phi\leqslant w'\!:\!2\!:\!\phi'$	$v_1(\phi,w)\le v_2(\phi',w')$
$w\!:\!2\!:\!\phi\leqslant c$	$v_2(\phi,w)\le c$ with $c\in\{0,1\}$
$wR^-w'\leqslant w'\!:\!2\!:\!\phi$	$wR^-w'\le v_2(\phi,w')$

Definition 7 (Branch realisation). *A model $\mathfrak{M}=\langle W,R^+,R^-,v_1,v_2\rangle$ with $W=\{w:w \text{ occurs on } \mathcal{B}\}$ realises a branch $\mathcal{B}$ of a tableau iff there is a function $\mathsf{rl}:\mathsf{Str}\to[0,1]$ s.t. for every $\mathfrak{x},\mathfrak{Y},\mathfrak{Y}',\mathfrak{z},\mathfrak{z}'\in\mathsf{Str}$ with $\mathfrak{x}=w:\mathbf{x}:\phi$, $\mathfrak{Y}=w_iR^+w_j$, and $\mathfrak{Y}'=w'_iR^-w'_j$ the following holds ($\mathbf{x}\in\{1,2\}$, $c\in\{0,1\}$).*

- *If $\mathfrak{z}\lesssim\mathfrak{z}'\in\mathcal{B}$, then $\mathsf{rl}(\mathfrak{z})\lesssim\mathsf{rl}(\mathfrak{z}')$.*
- $\mathsf{rl}(\mathfrak{x})=v_{\mathbf{x}}(\phi,w)$, $\mathsf{rl}(c)=c$, $\mathsf{rl}(\mathfrak{Y})=w_iR^+w_j$, $\mathsf{rl}(\mathfrak{Y}')=w'_iR^-w'_j$

To facilitate the understanding of the rules, we give an example of a failed tableau proof and extract a counter-model. The proof goes as follows: first, we apply all the possible propositional rules, then the modal rules that introduce new states, and then those that use the states already on the branch. We repeat the process until all structures are decomposed into atomic ones.

$$w_0:2:\neg\blacksquare p\to\blacksquare\neg p>0$$
$$w_0:2:\neg\blacksquare p<w_0:2:\blacksquare\neg p$$
$$0<w_0:2:\blacksquare\neg p$$
$$w_0:1:\blacksquare p<w_0:2:\blacksquare\neg p$$
$$w_0R^+w_1>w_1:1:p$$
$$w_1:1:p<w_0:2:\blacksquare\neg p$$

$w_1:2:\neg p>w_1:1:p$ $w_0R^-w_1\leqslant w_1:2:\neg p$
$w_1:1:p>w_1:1:p$ $w_0R^-w_1\leqslant w_1:1:p$
          ×   ☺

$w_0 \quad \overset{R^+=1}{\longrightarrow} \quad w_1:p=\left(\tfrac{1}{2},0\right)$, $\quad \underset{R^-=\frac{1}{2}}{\longrightarrow}$

---

[8] Note that branching rules have *two* conclusions.

We can now extract a model from the complete open branch marked with $\odot$ s.t. $v_2(\neg\blacksquare p \to \blacksquare\neg p, w_0) > 0$. We use w's that occur thereon as the carrier and assign the values of variables and relations so that they correspond to $\lesssim$.

Theorem 4 $\left(\mathcal{T}\left(\mathsf{G}^{2\pm}_{\blacksquare,\blacklozenge\,\mathsf{fb}}\right)\right.$ **completeness**$\left.\right)$. ϕ is v_1-valid $(v_2$-valid$)$ in $\mathsf{G}^{2\pm}_{\blacksquare,\blacklozenge}$, iff there is a closed tableau beginning with $w\!:\!1\!:\!\phi < 1$ $(w\!:\!2\!:\!\phi > 0)$.

Proof. The proof is an easy adaptation of [9, Theorem 3], whence we provide only a sketch. To prove soundness, we need to show that if the premise of the rule is realised, then so is at least one of its conclusions. This can be done by a routine check of the rules. Note that since we work with finitely branching frames, infima and suprema from Definition 3 become maxima and minima. We consider the case of $\blacksquare_1\gtrsim$ and show that, if $\mathfrak{M} = \langle W, R^+, R^-, v_1, v_2\rangle$ realises the premise of the rule, it also realises one of its conclusions.

Assume w.l.o.g. that $\mathfrak{X} = w''\!:\!2\!:\!\psi$, and let $\mathfrak{M}$ realise $w\!:\!1\!:\!\blacksquare\phi \geqslant w''\!:\!2\!:\!\psi$. Now, since R^+ and R^- are finitely branching, we have that $\min_{w'\in W}\{wR^+w' \to v_1(\phi, w')\} \geq v_2(\psi, w)$, i.e., at each $w' \in W$ s.t. $wR^+w' > 0^9$, either $v_1(\phi, w') \geq v_2(\psi, w'')$ or $wR^+w' \geq v_2(\psi, w'')$. Thus, at least one conclusion of the rule is satisfied. Since closed branches are not realisable, the result follows.

To prove completeness, we show that every complete open branch $\mathcal{B}$ is realisable. We show how to construct a realising model from the branch. First, we set $W = \{w : w \text{ occurs in } \mathcal{B}\}$. Denote the set of atomic structures appearing on $\mathcal{B}$ with $\mathsf{AStr}(\mathcal{B})$ and let $\mathcal{B}^+$ be the transitive closure of $\mathcal{B}$ under $\lesssim$. Now, we assign values to them. For $i \in \{1,2\}$, if $w\!:\!i\!:\!p \geqslant 1 \in \mathcal{B}$, we set $v_i(p, w) = 1$. If $w\!:\!i\!:\!p \leqslant 0 \in \mathcal{B}$, we set $v_i(p, w) = 0$. If $wSw' < \mathfrak{X} \notin \mathcal{B}^+$, we set $wSw' = 1$. If $w\!:\!i\!:\!p$ or wSw' with $S \in \{R^+, R^-\}$ does not occur on $\mathcal{B}$, we set $v_i(p, w) = 0$ and $wSw' = 0$.

For each $\mathsf{str} \in \mathsf{AStr}$, we now set

$$[\mathsf{str}] = \left\{\mathsf{str}' \;\middle|\; \begin{array}{c} \mathsf{str} \leqslant \mathsf{str}' \in \mathcal{B}^+ \text{ and } \mathsf{str} < \mathsf{str}' \notin \mathcal{B}^+ \\ \text{or} \\ \mathsf{str} \geqslant \mathsf{str}' \in \mathcal{B}^+ \text{ and } \mathsf{str} > \mathsf{str}' \notin \mathcal{B}^+ \end{array}\right\}$$

Denote the number of $[\mathsf{str}]$'s with $\#^{\mathsf{str}}$. Since the only possible loop in $\mathcal{B}^+$ is $\mathsf{str} \leqslant \mathsf{str}' \leqslant \ldots \leqslant \mathsf{str}$ where all elements belong to $[\mathsf{str}]$, it is clear that $\#^{\mathsf{str}} \leq 2 \cdot |\mathsf{AStr}(\mathcal{B})| \cdot |W|$. Put $[\mathsf{str}] \prec [\mathsf{str}']$ iff there are $\mathsf{str}_i \in [\mathsf{str}]$ and $\mathsf{str}_j \in [\mathsf{str}']$ s.t. $\mathsf{str}_i < \mathsf{str}_j \in \mathcal{B}^+$. We now set the valuation of these structures as follows:

$$\mathsf{str} = \frac{|\{[\mathsf{str}'] \mid [\mathsf{str}'] \prec [\mathsf{str}]\}|}{\#^{\mathsf{str}}}$$

It is clear that constraints containing only atomic structures and constants are now satisfied. To show that all other constraints are satisfied, we prove that if at least one conclusion of the rule is satisfied, then so is the premise. Again, the proof is a slight modification of [9, Theorem 3] and can be done by considering the cases of rules.

---

^{9} Recall that if $uSu' \notin \mathcal{B}$, we set $uSu' = 0$.

5 Complexity

In this section, we use the tableaux to provide the upper bound on the size of falsifying (satisfying) models and prove that satisfiability and validity[10] of $G^{2\pm}_{\blacksquare,\blacklozenge fb}$ are PSpace complete.

The following statement follows immediately from Theorem 4.

Corollary 1. *Let $\phi \in \mathcal{L}^{\neg}_{\blacksquare,\blacklozenge}$ be not $G^{2\pm}_{\blacksquare,\blacklozenge fb}$ valid, and let k be the number of modalities in it. Then there is a model $\mathfrak{M}$ of the size $\leq k^{k+1}$ and depth $\leq k$ and $w \in \mathfrak{M}$ s.t. $v_1(\phi,w) \neq 1$ or $v_2(\phi,w) \neq 0$.*

To tackle the PSpace-hardness of *strong validity*, we introduce an additional constant $\mathbf{B}$ to $\mathcal{L}^{\neg}_{\blacksquare,\blacklozenge}$. The semantics is as expected: $v(\mathbf{B},w) = (1,1)$. Note that the dual constant $\mathbf{N}$ s.t. $v(\mathbf{N},w) = (0,0)$ is definable via $\mathbf{B}$ as $\mathbf{N} := \sim\mathbf{B}$.

Let us now use $G^{2\pm}_{\blacksquare,\blacklozenge}(\mathbf{B})$ to denote the expansion of $G^{2\pm}_{\blacksquare,\blacklozenge}$ with $\mathbf{B}$. The following statement is immediate.

Proposition 1.

1. *$\phi \in \mathcal{L}^{\neg}_{\blacksquare,\blacklozenge}$ is v_1-valid on $\mathfrak{F}$ iff $\mathbf{B} \to \phi$ is strongly valid on $\mathfrak{F}$.*
2. *$\phi \in \mathcal{L}^{\neg}_{\blacksquare,\blacklozenge}$ is v_2-valid on $\mathfrak{F}$ iff $\mathbf{N} \to \phi$ is strongly valid on $\mathfrak{F}$.*

It is also clear that adding the following rules to the tableaux calculus in Definition 6 will make it complete w.r.t. $G^{2\pm}_{\blacksquare,\blacklozenge fb}(\mathbf{B})$.

$$\frac{w\!:\!i\!:\!\mathbf{B}\lesssim\mathfrak{X}}{w\!:\!i\!:\!1\lesssim\mathfrak{X}} \qquad\qquad \frac{w\!:\!i\!:\!\mathbf{B}\gtrsim\mathfrak{X}}{w\!:\!i\!:\!1\gtrsim\mathfrak{X}} \qquad (i \in \{1,2\})$$

The proof of PSpace membership adapts the method from [9] and is inspired by the proof of the PSpace membership of $\mathbf{K}$ from [10]. For the hardness, we prove separately that v_1- and v_2-validities are PSpace-hard and that strong validity is PSpace-hard as well. The main difference between this proof and the one in [9] is that now we have to account for relational terms of the form wSw' having different values.

Theorem 5.

1. *$G^{2\pm}_{\blacksquare,\blacklozenge fb}(\mathbf{B})$ validity and satisfiability are PSpace complete.*
2. *v_1- and v_2-validities in $G^{2\pm}_{\blacksquare,\blacklozenge fb}$ are PSpace-complete*

Proof. We provide a sketch of the proof. For the membership, we tackle both parts at once since if $G^{2\pm}_{\blacksquare,\blacklozenge fb}(\mathbf{B})$ is in PSpace, then so is $G^{2\pm}_{\blacksquare,\blacklozenge fb}$. Now observe from the proof of Theorem 4 that ϕ is satisfiable (falsifiable) on $\mathfrak{M} = \langle W, R^+, R^-, v_1, v_2 \rangle$ iff all variables, wR^+w''s, and wR^-w''s have values from $\mathsf{V} = \left\{0, \frac{1}{\#^{\mathrm{str}}}, \dots, \frac{\#^{\mathrm{str}}-1}{\#^{\mathrm{str}}}, 1\right\}$ under which ϕ is satisfied (falsified).

---

[10] Satisfiability and falsifiability (non-validity) are reducible to each other: ϕ is satisfiable iff $\sim\sim(\phi \prec \mathbf{0})$ is falsifiable; ϕ is falsifiable iff $\sim\sim(\mathbf{1} \prec \phi)$ is satisfiable.

Since $\#^{\text{str}}$ is bounded from above, we can now replace constraints with labelled formulas and relational structures of the form $w:i:\phi=\mathsf{v}$ or $wSw'=\mathsf{v}$ ($\mathsf{v}\in V$) avoiding comparisons of values of formulas in different states. We close the branch if it contains $w:i:\psi=\mathsf{v}$ and $w:i:\psi=\mathsf{v}'$ or $wSw'=\mathsf{v}$ and $wSw'=\mathsf{v}'$ for $\mathsf{v}\neq\mathsf{v}'$.

Now we replace the rules from Definition 6 with new ones that work with labelled structures. Below, we give as an example the rules[11] that replace $\blacklozenge_i\lesssim$.

$$\frac{w:i:\blacklozenge\phi=\frac{r}{\#^{\text{str}}}}{\left.\frac{wSw'=1}{w:i:\phi=\frac{r}{\#^{\text{str}}}}\right|\left.\frac{wSw'=\frac{r}{\#^{\text{str}}}}{w:i:\phi=1}\right|\cdots\left|\frac{wSw'=\frac{r}{\#^{\text{str}}}}{w:i:\phi=\frac{r}{\#^{\text{str}}}}\right.} \qquad \frac{w:i:\blacklozenge\phi=\frac{r}{\#^{\text{str}}};\left(\begin{array}{c}wSw'=\mathsf{v}\text{ for }\mathsf{v}\geq\frac{r}{\#^{\text{str}}}\\ \text{is on the branch}\end{array}\right)}{w':i:\phi=\frac{r}{\#^{\text{str}}}\mid\ldots\mid w':i:\phi=0}$$

Observe that once all rules are rewritten in this manner, we will not need to compare values of formulas *in different states*.

We then proceed as follows: first, we apply the propositional rules, then *one* modal rule requiring a new state (e.g., $w_0:i:\blacklozenge\phi=\frac{r}{\#^{\text{str}}}$), then the rules that use that state guessing the tableau branch when needed. By repeating this process, we are building *the model branch by branch*. The model has the depth bounded by the length of ϕ and we work with modal formulas one by one, whence we need to store subformulas of ϕ and wSw'''s with their values $O(|\phi|)$ times, so, we need only $O(|\phi|^2)$ space. Once the branch is constructed, we can delete the entries of the tableau and repeat the process with the next formula at w_0 that would introduce a new state.

For hardness, we reduce the $\mathfrak{GK}$ validity of $\{0,\wedge,\vee,\rightarrow,\Diamond\}$ formulas to strong validity as well as to v_1- and v_2-validities. Recall that the $\Diamond$ fragment of $\mathfrak{GK}$ has the finite model property [15, Theorem 7.1] and is PSpace-complete [28, Theorem 5.9].

Since the semantics of $\mathfrak{GK}$ is the same as KbiG (cf. Definition 2) and coincides with the v_1-conditions of $\mathsf{G}^{2\pm}_{\blacksquare,\blacklozenge}$ (recall Definition 3), it is immediate by Theorem 2 that ϕ over $\{0,\wedge,\vee,\rightarrow,\Diamond\}$ $\mathfrak{GK}$-valid iff $\phi^{+\bullet}$ is v_1-valid. This also gives us the reduction to $\mathsf{G}^{2\pm}_{\blacksquare,\blacklozenge\text{fb}}(\mathbf{B})$ strong validity using Proposition 1: ϕ is $\mathfrak{GK}$-valid iff $\mathbf{B}\rightarrow\phi^{+\bullet}$ is strongly $\mathsf{G}^{2\pm}_{\blacksquare,\blacklozenge\text{fb}}$-valid.

For v_2-validity, we proceed as follows. We let ϕ be over $\{0,\wedge,\vee,\rightarrow,\Diamond\}$ and inductively define ϕ^∂:

$$\mathbf{0}^\partial=1 \qquad\qquad p^\partial=p \qquad\qquad (\chi\wedge\psi)^\partial=\chi^\partial\vee\psi^\partial$$
$$(\chi\vee\psi)^\partial=\chi^\partial\wedge\psi^\partial \qquad (\chi\rightarrow\psi)^\partial=\psi^\partial\prec\chi^\partial \qquad (\Diamond\chi)^\partial=\blacklozenge(\chi^\partial)$$

It is clear that ϕ is $\mathfrak{GK}$-valid on a given frame $\mathfrak{F}=\langle W,S\rangle$ iff $v_2(\phi^\partial,w)=1$ for every valuation v_2 and every state w in the R^--counterpart $\mathfrak{F}^-$ of $\mathfrak{F}$. Hence, ϕ is $\mathfrak{GK}$-valid iff $\mathbf{1}\prec\phi^\partial$ is v_2-valid.

---

[11] For a value $\mathsf{v}>0$ of $\blacklozenge\phi$ at w, we add a new state that witnesses v, and for a state on the branch, we guess a value not greater than v. Other modal rules can be rewritten similarly.

6   Conclusions and Future Work

We presented a modal expansion $G^{2\pm}_{\blacksquare,\blacklozenge}$ of G^2 with non-standard modalities and provided it with Kripke semantics on bi-relational frames with two valuations. We established its connection with the bi-Gödel modal logic KbiG presented in [6,9] and obtained decidability and complexity results considering $G^{2\pm}_{\blacksquare,\blacklozenge}$ over finitely branching frames.

The next steps are as follows. First of all, we plan to explore the decidability of the full $G^{2\pm}_{\blacksquare,\blacklozenge}$ logic. We conjecture that it is also PSpace complete. However, the standard way of proving PSpace completeness of Gödel modal logics described in [13,14] and used in [6] to establish PSpace completeness of KbiG may not be straightforwardly applicable here as the reduction from $G^{2\pm}_{\blacksquare,\blacklozenge}$ validity to KbiG validity can be hard to obtain for it follows immediately from Theorem 3 that $G^{2\pm}_{\blacksquare,\blacklozenge}$ lacks negation normal forms.

Second, it is interesting to design a complete Hilbert-style axiomatisation of $G^{2\pm}_{\blacksquare,\blacklozenge}$ and study its correspondence theory w.r.t. *strong validity*. This can be non-trivial since $\blacksquare(p \to q) \to (\blacksquare p \to \blacksquare q)$ and $\blacklozenge(p \lor q) \to \blacklozenge p \lor \blacklozenge q$ are not $G^{2\pm}_{\blacksquare,\blacklozenge}$ valid, even though, it is easy to check that the following rules are sound.

$$\frac{\phi \to \chi}{\blacksquare \phi \to \blacksquare \chi} \qquad\qquad \frac{\phi \to \chi}{\blacklozenge \phi \to \blacklozenge \chi}$$

The other direction of future research is to study global versions of $\blacksquare$ and $\blacklozenge$ as well as description logics based on them. Description Gödel logics are well-known and studied [11,12] and allow for the representation of uncertain data that cannot be represented in the classical ontologies. Furthermore, they are the only decidable family of fuzzy description logics which contrasts them to e.g., Łukasiewicz description (and global) logics which are not even axiomatisable [37]. On the other hand, there are known description logics over BD (cf., e.g. [26]), and thus it makes sense to combine the two approaches.

References

1. Aguilera, J., Diéguez, M., Fernández-Duque, D., McLean, B.: Time and Gödel: fuzzy temporal reasoning in PSPACE. In: Ciabattoni, A., Pimentel, E., de Queiroz, R.J.G.B. (eds.) Logic, Language, Information, and Computation. LNCS, vol. 13368, pp. 18–35. Springer, Cham (2022). https://doi.org/10.1007/978-3-031-15298-6_2

2. Baaz, M.: Infinite-valued Gödel logics with 0-1-projections and relativizations. In: Logical foundations of mathematics, computer science and physics–Kurt Gödel's legacy, Gödel 1996, Brno, Czech Republic, Proceedings, pp. 23–33. Association for Symbolic Logic (1996)

3. Baldi, P., Cintula, P., Noguera, C.: Classical and fuzzy two-layered modal logics for uncertainty: translations and proof-theory. Int. J. Comput. Intell. Syst. **13**, 988–1001 (2020). https://doi.org/10.2991/ijcis.d.200703.001

4. Belnap, N.D.: How a computer should think. In: New Essays on Belnap-Dunn Logic. SL, vol. 418, pp. 35–53. Springer, Cham (2019). https://doi.org/10.1007/978-3-030-31136-0_4

5. Bílková, M., Frittella, S., Kozhemiachenko, D.: Constraint tableaux for two-dimensional fuzzy logics. In: Das, A., Negri, S. (eds.) TABLEAUX 2021. LNCS (LNAI), vol. 12842, pp. 20–37. Springer, Cham (2021). https://doi.org/10.1007/978-3-030-86059-2_2
6. Bílková, M., Frittella, S., Kozhemiachenko, D.: Crisp bi-Gödel modal logic and its paraconsistent expansion. https://arxiv.org/abs/2211.01882 (2022)
7. Bílková, M., Frittella, S., Kozhemiachenko, D., Majer, O.: Qualitative reasoning in a two-layered framework. Int. J. Approximate Reason. **154**, 84–108 (2023)
8. Bílková, M., Frittella, S., Majer, O., Nazari, S.: Belief based on inconsistent information. In: Martins, M.A., Sedlár, I. (eds.) DaLi 2020. LNCS, vol. 12569, pp. 68–86. Springer, Cham (2020). https://doi.org/10.1007/978-3-030-65840-3_5
9. Bílková, M., Frittella, S., Kozhemiachenko, D.: Paraconsistent Gödel modal logic. In: Blanchette, J., Kovacs, L., Pattinson, D. (eds.) IJCAR 2022. LNCS, vol. 13385, pp. 429–448. Springer International Publishing, Cham (2022). https://doi.org/10.1007/978-3-031-10769-6_26
10. Blackburn, P., Rijke, M.D., Venema, Y.: Modal logic. Cambridge tracts in theoretical computer science, vol. 53, Cambridge University Press (2010)
11. Bobillo, F., Delgado, M., Gómez-Romero, J., Straccia, U.: Fuzzy description logics under gödel semantics. Int. J. Approximate Reason. **50**(3), 494–514 (2009)
12. Bobillo, F., Delgado, M., Gómez-Romero, J., Straccia, U.: Joining Gödel and Zadeh fuzzy logics in fuzzy description logics. Int. J. Uncertainty Fuzziness Knowl.-Based Syst. **20**(04), 475–508 (2012)
13. Caicedo, X., Metcalfe, G., Rodríguez, R., Rogger, J.: A finite model property for Gödel modal logics. In: Libkin, L., Kohlenbach, U., de Queiroz, R. (eds.) WoLLIC 2013. LNCS, vol. 8071, pp. 226–237. Springer, Heidelberg (2013). https://doi.org/10.1007/978-3-642-39992-3_20
14. Caicedo, X., Metcalfe, G., Rodríguez, R., Rogger, J.: Decidability of order-based modal logics. J. Comput. Syst. Sci. **88**, 53–74 (2017)
15. Caicedo, X., Rodriguez, R.: Standard Gödel modal logics. Stud. Logica. **94**(2), 189–214 (2010)
16. Caicedo, X., Rodríguez, R.: Bi-modal Gödel logic over [0,1]-valued Kripke frames. J. Logic and Comput. **25**(1), 37–55 (2015)
17. Diéguez, M., Fernández-Duque, D.: Decidability for **S4** Gödel modal logics. In: Cornejo, M.E., Harmati, I.A., Koczy, L.T., Medina-Moreno, J. (eds.) Computational Intelligence and Mathematics for Tackling Complex Problems, Studies in computational intelligence, vol. 4, pp. 1–7. Springer, Cham (2023). https://doi.org/10.1007/978-3-031-07707-4_1
18. Drobyshevich, S.: A general framework for FDE-based modal logics. Stud. Logica. **108**(6), 1281–1306 (2020)
19. Fagin, R., Halpern, J., Moses, Y., Vardi, M.: Reasoning About Knowledge. MIT Press, Cambridge, MA, USA (2003)
20. Grigolia, R., Kiseliova, T., Odisharia, V.: Free and projective bimodal symmetric Gödel algebras. Stud. Logica. **104**(1), 115–143 (2016)
21. Hähnle, R.: A new translation from deduction into integer programming. In: Calmet, J., Campbell, J.A. (eds.) AISMC 1992. LNCS, vol. 737, pp. 262–275. Springer, Heidelberg (1993). https://doi.org/10.1007/3-540-57322-4_18
22. Hähnle, R.: Many-valued logic and mixed integer programming. Ann. Math. Artif. Intell. **12**(3-4), 231–263 (1994)
23. Hähnle, R.: Tableaux for many-valued logics. In: D'Agostino, M., Gabbay, D., Hähnle, R., Posegga, J. (eds.) Handbook of Tableaux Methods, pp. 529–580. Springer, Dordrecht (1999)

24. Lascio, L.D., Gisolfi, A.: Graded tableaux for rational Pavelka logic. Int. J. Intell. Syst. **20**(12), 1273–1285 (2005)
25. Leitgeb, H.: Hype: a system of hyperintensional logic (with an application to semantic paradoxes). J. Philos. Logic **48**(2), 305–405 (2019)
26. Ma, Y., Hitzler, P., Lin, Z.: Algorithms for paraconsistent reasoning with OWL. In: Franconi, E., Kifer, M., May, W. (eds.) ESWC 2007. LNCS, vol. 4519, pp. 399–413. Springer, Heidelberg (2007). https://doi.org/10.1007/978-3-540-72667-8_29
27. Metcalfe, G., Olivetti, N.: Proof systems for a Gödel modal logic. In: Giese, M., Waaler, A. (eds.) TABLEAUX 2009. LNCS (LNAI), vol. 5607, pp. 265–279. Springer, Heidelberg (2009). https://doi.org/10.1007/978-3-642-02716-1_20
28. Metcalfe, G., Olivetti, N.: Towards a Proof Theory of Gödel Modal Logics. Logical Methods Comput. Sci. **7** (2011)
29. Moisil, G.: Logique modale. Disquisitiones mathematicae physicae **2**, 3–98 (1942)
30. Odintsov, S., Wansing, H.: Routley star and hyperintensionality. J. Philos. Logic **50**, 33–56 (2021)
31. Odintsov, S., Wansing, H.: Modal logics with Belnapian truth values. J. Appl. Non-Class. Logics **20**(3), 279–301 (2010). https://doi.org/10.3166/jancl.20.279-301
32. Odintsov, S.P., Wansing, H.: Disentangling FDE-based paraconsistent modal logics. Stud. Logica. **105**(6), 1221–1254 (2017). https://doi.org/10.1007/s11225-017-9753-9
33. Priest, G.: An Introduction to Non-Classical Logic: From If to Is, 2nd edn. Cambridge University Press, Cambridge (2008)
34. Priest, G.: Many-valued modal logics: a simple approach. Rev. Symbol. Logic **1**(2), 190–203 (2008)
35. Rodriguez, R., Tuyt, O., Esteva, F., Godo, L.: Simplified Kripke semantics for K45-like Gödel modal logics and its axiomatic extensions. Stud. Logica. **110**(4), 1081–1114 (2022)
36. Rodriguez, R., Vidal, A.: Axiomatization of crisp Gödel modal logic. Stud. Logica. **109**, 367–395 (2021)
37. Vidal, A.: Undecidability and non-axiomatizability of modal many-valued logics. J. Symbol. Logic **87**(4), 1576–1605 (2022)
38. Wansing, H.: Constructive negation, implication, and co-implication. J. Appl. Non-Class. Logics **18**(2–3), 341–364 (2008). https://doi.org/10.3166/jancl.18.341-364

Base-Based Model Checking
for Multi-agent only Believing

Tiago de Lima[1]([⊠]), Emiliano Lorini[2], and François Schwarzentruber[3]

[1] CRIL, Univ Artois and CNRS, Lens, France
delima@cril.fr
[2] IRIT, CNRS, Toulouse University, Toulouse, France
lorini@irit.fr
[3] ENS Rennes, Bruz, France
francois.schwarzentruber@ens-rennes.fr

Abstract. We present a novel semantics for the language of multi-agent only believing exploiting belief bases, and show how to use it for automatically checking formulas of this language. We provide a PSPACE algorithm for model checking relying on a reduction to QBF, an implementation and some experimental results on computation time in a concrete example.

1 Introduction

Using belief bases for building a semantics for epistemic logic was initially proposed by Lorini [17,19]. In [18] it was shown that such a semantics allows to represent the concept of universal epistemic model which is tightly connected with the concept of universal type space studied by game theorists [20]. A qualitative version of the universal type space with no probabilities involved is defined by Fagin et al. [6] (see also [7]). Broadly speaking, a universal epistemic model for a given situation is the most general model which is compatible with that situation. It is the model which only contains information about the situation and makes no further assumption. From an epistemic point view, it can be seen as the model with maximal ignorance with respect to the description of the situation at stake.

Such a universal epistemic model has been shown to be crucial for defining a proper semantics for the concept of multi-agent only knowing (or believing) [12,14], as a generalization of the concept of single-agent only knowing (or believing) [15].[1] However, the construction of this semantics is far from

---

[1] As usual, the difference between knowledge and belief lies in the fact that the former is always correct while the latter can be incorrect.

This work is partially supported by the project epiRL ("Epistemic Reinforcement Learning") ANR-22-CE23-0029, the project CoPains ("Cognitive Planning in Persuasive Multimodal Communication") ANR-18-CE33-0012 and the AI Chair project Responsible AI (ANR-19-CHIA-0008) both from the French National Agency of Research. Support from the Natural Intelligence Toulouse Institute (ANITI) is also gratefully acknowledged.

S. Gaggl et al. (Eds.): JELIA 2023, LNAI 14281, pp. 437–445, 2023.
https://doi.org/10.1007/978-3-031-43619-2_30

being straightforward. Halpern & Lakemeyer [13] use the proof-theoretic notion of canonical model for defining it. The limitation of the canonical model is its being infinite thereby not being exploitable in practice. In a more recent work, Belle & Lakemeyer [2] provided an inductive proof-independent definition of the semantics for multi-agent only knowing which departs from the standard semantics of multi-agent epistemic logic based on multi-relational Kripke structures. Finally, Aucher & Belle [1] have shown how to interpret the language of multi-agent only knowing on standard Kripke structures. Although being independent from the proof theory, these last two accounts are fairly non-standard or quite involved. They rely either on an inductive definition (Belle & Lakemeyer) or on a complex syntactic representation up to certain modal depth (Aucher & Belle) of the multi-agent epistemic structure used for interpreting the multi-agent only knowing language.

In this paper, we concentrate on the logic of multi-agent only believing based on the logic K for beliefs. We show how to use the belief base semantics and its construction of the universal model to automatically check formulas of the corresponding language. The novel contribution of the paper is twofold:

– Although the idea of using belief bases as a semantics for epistemic logic has been proposed in previous work, this is the first attempt to use them in the context of the logic of multi-agent only believing.
– Moreover, we are the first to provide a model checking algorithm for the logic of multi-agent only believing, to implement it and to test it experimentally on a concrete example. The belief base semantics helped us to accomplish this task given its compactness and manageability.

Outline. In Sect. 2, we first recall the belief base semantics introduced in our previous work [17,19]. We show how to interpret the language of multi-agent only believing and how to define the universal model in it. In Sect. 3, we move to model checking formulated in the belief base semantics. In Sect. 4, we present an implementation of the QBF-based algorithm and some experimental results on computation time in the example. Section 5 concludes.[2]

2   Language and Semantics

The multi-agent epistemic language introduced in [19] has two basic epistemic modalities: one for explicit belief, and another one for implicit belief. An agent's explicit belief corresponds to a piece of information in the agent's belief base. An agent's implicit belief corresponds to a piece of information that is derivable from the agent's explicit beliefs. In other words, if an agent can derive φ from its explicit beliefs, it implicitly believes *at least* that φ is true. We consider the extension of this epistemic language by complementary modalities for implicitly believing *at most*. The *at least* and *at most* modalities can be combined to represent the concept of *only* believing.

---

[2] The extended version of this paper, including proofs and examples, is available at ArXiv: https://arxiv.org/abs/2307.14893.

The semantics over which the language is interpreted exploits belief bases. Unlike the standard multi-relational Kripke semantics for epistemic logic in which the agents' epistemic accessibility relations over possible worlds are given as primitive, in this semantics they are computed from the agents' belief bases. Specifically, in this semantics it is assumed that at state S an agent considers a state S' possible (or state S' is epistemically accessible to the agent at state S) if and only if S' satisfies all formulas included in the agent's belief base at S. This idea of computing the agents' accessibility relations from the state description is shared with the semantics of epistemic logic based on interpreted systems [8,16]. However, there is an important difference. While the interpreted system semantics relies on the abstract notion of an agent's local state, in the belief base semantics an agent's local state is identified with its concrete belief base.

2.1 Semantics

Assume a countably infinite set of atomic propositions $Atm = \{p, q, \dots\}$ and a finite set of agents $Agt = \{1, \dots, n\}$. We define the language $\mathcal{L}_0$ for explicit belief by the following grammar in Backus-Naur Form (BNF):

$$\mathcal{L}_0 \overset{\text{def}}{=} \alpha ::= p \mid \neg\alpha \mid \alpha \wedge \alpha \mid \triangle_i\alpha,$$

where p ranges over Atm and i ranges over Agt. $\mathcal{L}_0$ is the language used to represent explicit beliefs. The formula $\triangle_i\alpha$ reads "agent i has the explicit belief that α". In our semantics, a state is not a primitive notion but it is decomposed into different elements: one belief base per agent and an interpretation of propositional atoms.

Definition 1 (State). *A state is a tuple $S = \big((B_i)_{i \in Agt}, V\big)$ where $B_i \subseteq \mathcal{L}_0$ is agent i's belief base, and $V \subseteq Atm$ is the actual environment. The set of all states is noted $\mathbf{S}$.*

The following definition specifies truth conditions for formulas in $\mathcal{L}_0$.

Definition 2 (Satisfaction relation). *Let $S = \big((B_i)_{i \in Agt}, V\big) \in \mathbf{S}$. Then,*

$$S \models p \Longleftrightarrow p \in V,$$
$$S \models \neg\alpha \Longleftrightarrow S \not\models \alpha,$$
$$S \models \alpha_1 \wedge \alpha_2 \Longleftrightarrow S \models \alpha_1 \text{ and } S \models \alpha_2,$$
$$S \models \triangle_i\alpha \Longleftrightarrow \alpha \in B_i.$$

Observe in particular the set-theoretic interpretation of the explicit belief operator in the previous definition: agent i has the explicit belief that α if and only if α is included in its belief base.

The following definition introduces the agents' epistemic relations. They are computed from the agents' belief bases.

Definition 3 (Epistemic relation). *Let $i \in Agt$. Then, $\mathcal{R}_i$ is the binary relation on $\mathbf{S}$ such that, for all $S = \big((B_i)_{i \in Agt}, V\big), S' = \big((B'_i)_{i \in Agt}, V'\big) \in \mathbf{S}$, we have $S\mathcal{R}_iS'$ if and only if $\forall\alpha \in B_i : S' \models \alpha$.*

$S\mathcal{R}_i S'$ means that S' is an epistemic alternative for agent i at S, that is to say, S' is a state that at S agent i considers possible. The idea of the previous definition is that S' is an epistemic alternative for agent i at S if and only if, S' satisfies all facts that agent i explicitly believes at S.

The following definition introduces the concept of model, namely a state supplemented with a set of states, called *context*. The latter includes all states that are compatible with the agents' common ground, i.e., the body of information that the agents commonly believe to be the case [21].

Definition 4 (Model). *A model is a pair (S, Cxt) with $S \in \mathbf{S}$ and $Cxt \subseteq \mathbf{S}$. The class of models is noted $\mathbf{M}$.*

Note that in a model (S, Cxt), the state S is not necessarily an element of the context Cxt due to the fact that we model belief instead of knowledge. Therefore, the agents' common ground represented by the context Cxt may be incorrect and not include the actual state. If we modeled knowledge instead of belief, we would have to suppose that $S \in Cxt$.

Let $\Gamma = (\Gamma_i)_{i \in Agt}$ where, for every $i \in Agt$, Γ_i represents agent i's vocabulary. A Γ-universal model is a model containing all states at which an agent i's explicit beliefs are built from its vocabulary Γ_i. In other words, an agent's vocabulary plays a role analogous to that of the notion of awareness in the formal semantics of awareness [9]. The notion of Γ-universal model is defined as follows.

Definition 5 (Universal model). *The model (S, Cxt) in $\mathbf{M}$ is said to be Γ-universal if $S \in Cxt = \mathbf{S}_\Gamma$, with $\mathbf{S}_\Gamma = \left\{ ((B_i')_{i \in Agt}, V') \in \mathbf{S} \mid \forall i \in Agt, B_i' \subseteq \Gamma_i \right\}$. The class of Γ-universal models is noted $\mathbf{M}_{univ}(\Gamma)$.*

$\Gamma = (\Gamma_i)_{i \in Agt}$ is also called agent vocabulary profile. Clearly, when $\Gamma = \mathcal{L}_0^n$, we have $\mathbf{S}_\Gamma = \mathbf{S}$. A model $(S, \mathbf{S})$ in $\mathbf{M}_{univ}(\mathcal{L}_0^n)$ is a model with maximal ignorance: it only contains the information provided by the actual state S. For simplicity, we write $\mathbf{M}_{univ}$ instead of $\mathbf{M}_{univ}(\mathcal{L}_0^n)$.

2.2   Language

In this section, we introduce a language for implicitly believing *at most* and implicitly believing *at least* on the top of the language $\mathcal{L}_0$ defined above. It is noted $\mathcal{L}$ and defined by:

$$\mathcal{L} \stackrel{\text{def}}{=} \phi ::= \alpha \mid \neg\phi \mid \phi \wedge \phi \mid \Box_i \phi \mid \Box_i^{\mathsf{C}} \phi,$$

where α ranges over $\mathcal{L}_0$ and i ranges over Agt. The other Boolean constructions $\top$, $\bot$, $\vee$, $\rightarrow$, $\oplus$, and $\leftrightarrow$ are defined from α, $\neg$ and $\wedge$ in the standard way.

The formula $\Box_i \phi$ is read "agent i *at least* implicitly believes that φ", while $\Box_i^{\mathsf{C}} \phi$ is read "agent i *at most* implicitly believes that $\neg\varphi$". Alternative readings of formulas $\Box_i \phi$ and $\Box_i^{\mathsf{C}} \phi$ are, respectively, "ϕ is true at all states that agent i considers possible" and "ϕ is true at all states that agent i does not consider possible". The latter is in line with the reading of the normal modality and the corresponding "window" modality in the context of Boolean modal logics [10]. The duals of the operators $\Box_i$ and $\Box_i^C$ are defined in the usual way, as follows: $\Diamond_i\phi \overset{\text{def}}{=} \neg\Box_i\neg\phi$ and $\Diamond_i^C\phi \overset{\text{def}}{=} \neg\Box_i^C\neg\phi$. Formulas in the language $\mathcal{L}$ are interpreted relative to a model (S, Cxt). (Boolean cases are omitted since they are defined as usual.)

Definition 6 (Satisfaction relation (cont.)). *Let $(S, Cxt) \in \mathbf{M}$. Then:*

$$(S, Cxt) \models \alpha \Longleftrightarrow S \models \alpha,$$
$$(S, Cxt) \models \Box_i\phi \Longleftrightarrow \forall S' \in Cxt : \text{if } S\mathcal{R}_iS' \text{ then } (S', Cxt) \models \phi,$$
$$(S, Cxt) \models \Box_i^C\phi \Longleftrightarrow \forall S' \in Cxt : \text{if } S\mathcal{R}_i^C S' \text{ then } (S', Cxt) \models \phi,$$

with $\mathcal{R}_i^C = (\mathbf{S} \times \mathbf{S}) \setminus \mathcal{R}_i$.

Note that $S\mathcal{R}_i^C S'$ just means that at state S agent i does not consider state S' possible. Moreover, interpretations of the two modalities $\Box_i$ and $\Box_i^C$ are restricted to the actual context Cxt. The only believing modality ($\Box_i^o$) is defined as follows:

$$\Box_i^o\varphi \overset{\text{def}}{=} \Box_i\phi \wedge \Box_i^C\neg\phi.$$

Notions of satisfiability and validity of $\mathcal{L}$-formulas for the class of models $\mathbf{M}$ are defined in the usual way: ϕ is satisfiable if there exists $(S, Cxt) \in \mathbf{M}$ such that $(S, Cxt) \models \phi$, and φ is valid if $\neg\phi$ is not satisfiable.

3   Model Checking

The model checking problem is defined in our framework as follows:

input: an agent vocabulary profile $\Gamma = (\Gamma_i)_{i \in Agt}$ with Γ_i finite for every $i \in Agt$,
    a finite state S_0 in $\mathbf{S}_\Gamma$, and a formula $\phi_0 \in \mathcal{L}$;
output: yes if $(S_0, \mathbf{S}_\Gamma) \models \phi_0$; no otherwise.

Remark 1. We suppose w.l.o.g. that outer most subformulas of φ_0 of the form $\triangle_i\alpha$ are such that $\alpha \in \Gamma_i$. If this is not the case for some subformulas $\triangle_i\alpha$, then the subformula $\triangle_i\alpha$ will be false anyway and can be replaced by $\bot$.

We propose a reduction to TQBF (true quantified binary formulas). We introduce TQBF propositional variables $x_{\alpha,k}$ for all $\alpha \in \mathcal{L}_0$ and for all integers k. The variables indexed by k are said to be of level k. For instance, $x_{\alpha,k}$ is true if α is true at some state at depth k. Let X_k be the set of formulas of level k. More precisely, X_k contains exactly formulas $x_{\triangle_i\alpha,k}$ with $\alpha \in \Gamma_i$ for any agent i, and $x_{p,k}$ with p appearing in Γ or φ_0.

Definition 7. *We define the function tr that maps any formula of $\mathcal{L}$ to a QBF-formula by $tr(\varphi_0) := tr_0(\varphi_0)$ with:*

- $tr_k(p) = x_{p,k}$
- $tr_k(\neg\phi) = \neg tr_k(\phi)$
- $tr_k(\phi \wedge \psi) = tr_k(\phi) \wedge tr_k(\psi)$
- $tr_k(\triangle_i\alpha) = x_{\triangle_i\alpha,k}$
- $tr_k(\square_i\phi) = \forall X_{k+1}(R_{i,k} \rightarrow tr_{k+1}(\phi))$
- $tr_k(\square_i^C\phi) = \forall X_{k+1}(\neg R_{i,k} \rightarrow tr_{k+1}(\phi))$

where:

$$R_{i,k} := \bigwedge_{\alpha\in\Gamma_i} x_{\triangle_i\alpha,k} \rightarrow tr_{k+1}(\alpha).$$

State S (resp. S') is represented by the truth values of variables in X_k (resp. X_{k+1}). Formula $R_{i,k}$ reformulates $S\mathcal{R}_i S'$.

Proposition 1. *Let $\varphi_0 \in \mathcal{L}$ and $S_0 = ((B_i)_{i\in Agt}, V)$. The following two statements are equivalent:*

- $(S_0, \mathbf{S}_\Gamma) \models \phi_0$
- $\exists X_0(\text{desc}_{S_0}(X_0) \wedge tr_0(\phi_0))$ *is QBF-true,*

where:

$$\text{desc}_{S_0}(X_0) := \bigwedge_{i\in Agt} \left(\bigwedge_{\alpha\in B_i} x_{\triangle_i\alpha,0} \wedge \bigwedge_{\alpha\in\Gamma_i\backslash B_i} \neg x_{\triangle_i\alpha,0} \right) \wedge \bigwedge_{p\in V} x_{p,0} \wedge \bigwedge_{p\notin V} \neg x_{p,0}.$$

Theorem 1. *Model checking $\mathcal{L}$-formulas is PSPACE-complete.*

4   Implementation and Experimental Results

We implemented a symbolic model checker,[3] which uses the translation to TQBF. The resulting TQBF is then translated into a binary decision diagram (BDD), in the same way as done in [3]. The program is implemented in Haskell and the BDD library used is HasCacBDD [11]. It was compiled with GHC 9.2.7 in a MacBook Air with a 1.6 GHz Dual-Core Intel Core i5 processor and 16 GB of RAM, running macOS Ventura 13.3.1.

Table 1 shows the performance of the model checker on the two variants of the example. It shows execution times for different instances. For both examples, the size of the model (*states*) is given by the number of possible valuations times the number of possible multi-agent belief bases: $2^{|Atm|} \times (2^{ratoms})^{|Agt|}$. The value of *ratoms* is the number of "relevant atoms". There is one such atom for each formula in Γ, each propositional variable appearing in Γ and in the input formula, each formula α that is a sub-formula of the input formula, plus one atom for each formula $\triangle_i\alpha$ such that $\alpha \in \Gamma$. The number of states gives an idea of the size of the search space for modal formulas. In principle, to check a formula of the form $\square^\circ\phi$, one must check ϕ in every state of the model. Because

---

[3] Available at https://src.koda.cnrs.fr/tiago.de.lima/lda/.

Table 1. Symbolic model checker performance on two examples.

$cands = voters = \|Agt\|$	3	4	5	6	7	8	9	10
$\|Atm\|$	9	16	25	36	49	64	81	100
$ratoms$	100	164	244	340	452	580	724	884
$states$	2^{309}	2^{672}	2^{1245}	2^{2076}	2^{3213}	2^{4704}	2^{6597}	2^{8940}
Execution time (sec.)	0.076	0.015	0.026	0.047	0.066	0.101	0.157	0.248
$cands = voters = \|Agt\|$	3	4	5	6	7	8	9	10
$\|Atm\|$	9	16	25	36	49	64	81	100
$ratoms$	133	210	305	418	549	698	865	1050
$states$	2^{408}	2^{856}	2^{1550}	2^{2544}	2^{3892}	2^{5648}	2^{7866}	2^{10600}
Execution time (sec.)	0.081	0.063	0.334	3.066	17.588	90.809	KO	KO

of that, a naive implementation cannot be used. Indeed, in our tests with such a solution, no instance could be solved under the timeout of 10 min.

One can notice that the model checker is slower in the case of 3 candidates than in the case of 4 candidates (and in the first example the latter is true even up to 7 candidates). The reason is that the input formula is true for 3 candidates, whereas it is false on all the other cases. Checking that a box formula is false is easier, because the checker needs to find only one state where the formula in the scope of the box operator is false. Also note that instances of the first example are solved much faster than those of the second. This is due to two factors. First, the second example has larger belief bases, which imply a larger number of states. Second, the input formula of the second example has a larger modal depth, which obliges the checker to generate a larger search tree.

5 Conclusion

This paper describes optimal procedures for model checking multi-agent only believing formulas. As far as we know, we are the first to tackle the problem of automating model checking for the logic of multi-agent only believing or knowing. We implemented these procedures and presented some experimental results on computation time. We intend to apply our semantics for multi-agent only believing and model checking approach to epistemic planning. We believe that the compactness of our semantics can offer an advantage in terms of ease of implementation compared to the multi-relational Kripke semantics traditionally used in the context of epistemic planning [4,5].

References

1. Aucher, G., Belle, V.: Multi-agent only knowing on planet kripke. In: Yang, Q., Wooldridge, M.J. (eds.) Proceedings of the Twenty-Fourth International Joint Conference on Artificial Intelligence, IJCAI 2015, Buenos Aires, Argentina, 25-31 July 2015, pp. 2713–2719. AAAI Press (2015). http://ijcai.org/Abstract/15/384
2. Belle, V., Lakemeyer, G.: Multi-agent only-knowing revisited. In: Lin, F., Sattler, U., Truszczynski, M. (eds.) Principles of Knowledge Representation and Reasoning: Proceedings of the Twelfth International Conference, KR 2010, Toronto, Ontario, Canada, 9-13 May 2010. AAAI Press (2010). http://aaai.org/ocs/index.php/KR/KR2010/paper/view/1361
3. van Benthem, J., van Eijck, J., Gattinger, M., Su, K.: Symbolic model checking for dynamic epistemic logic - S5 and beyond. J. Log. Comput. **28**(2), 367–402 (2018)
4. Bolander, T., Andersen, M.B.: Epistemic planning for single- and multi-agent systems. J. Appl. Non-Classical Logics **21**(1), 656–680 (2011)
5. Bolander, T., Jensen, M.H., Schwarzentruber, F.: Complexity results in epistemic planning. In: Yang, Q., Wooldridge, M.J. (eds.) Proceedings of the Twenty-Fourth International Joint Conference on Artificial Intelligence, IJCAI 2015, Buenos Aires, Argentina, 25-31 July 2015, pp. 2791–2797. AAAI Press (2015). http://ijcai.org/Abstract/15/395
6. Fagin, R., Halpern, J.Y., Vardi, M.Y.: A model-theoretic analysis of knowledge. J. ACM **38**(2), 382–428 (1991). https://doi.org/10.1145/103516.128680
7. Fagin, R., Geanakoplos, J., Halpern, J.Y., Vardi, M.Y.: The hierarchical approach to modeling knowledge and common knowledge. Internat. J. Game Theory **28**(3), 331–365 (1999)
8. Fagin, R., Halpern, J., Moses, Y., Vardi, M.: Reasoning about Knowledge. MIT Press, Cambridge (1995)
9. Fagin, R., Halpern, J.Y.: Belief, awareness, and limited reasoning. Artif. Intell. **34**(1), 39–76 (1987)
10. Gargov, G., Passy, S.: A note on Boolean modal logic. In: Petkov, P.P. (ed.) Mathematical Logic, pp. 299–309. Springer, Boston (1990). https://doi.org/10.1007/978-1-4613-0609-2_21
11. Gattinger, M.: HasCacBDD (2023). https://github.com/m4lvin/HasCacBDD. version 0.1.0.4
12. Halpern, J.Y.: Reasoning about only knowing with many agents. In: Fikes, R., Lehnert, W.G. (eds.) Proceedings of the 11th National Conference on Artificial Intelligence. Washington, DC, USA, 11-15 July 1993, pp. 655–661. AAAI Press / The MIT Press (1993). http://www.aaai.org/Library/AAAI/1993/aaai93-098.php
13. Halpern, J.Y., Lakemeyer, G.: Multi-agent only knowing. J. Log. Comput. **11**(1), 41–70 (2001). https://doi.org/10.1093/logcom/11.1.41
14. Lakemeyer, G.: All they know: a study in multi-agent autoepistemic reasoning. In: Bajcsy, R. (ed.) Proceedings of the 13th International Joint Conference on Artificial Intelligence. Chambéry, France, August 28 - September 3, 1993, pp. 376–381. Morgan Kaufmann (1993). http://ijcai.org/Proceedings/93-1/Papers/053.pdf
15. Levesque, H.J.: All I know: a study in autoepistemic logic. Artif. Intell. **42**(2–3), 263–309 (1990). https://doi.org/10.1016/0004-3702(90)90056-6
16. Lomuscio, A., Qu, H., Raimondi, F.: MCMAS: an open-source model checker for the verification of multi-agent systems. Int. J. Softw. Tools Technol. Transfer **19**, 9–30 (2017)

17. Lorini, E.: In praise of belief bases: Doing epistemic logic without possible worlds. In: Proceedings of the Thirty-Second AAAI Conference on Artificial Intelligence (AAAI 2018), pp. 1915–1922. AAAI Press (2018)
18. Lorini, E.: Exploiting belief bases for building rich epistemic structures. In: Moss, L.S. (ed.) Proceedings of the Seventeenth Conference on Theoretical Aspects of Rationality and Knowledge (TARK 2019). EPTCS, vol. 297, pp. 332–353 (2019)
19. Lorini, E.: Rethinking epistemic logic with belief bases. Arti. Intell. **282**, 103233 (2020). https://doi.org/10.1016/j.artint.2020.103233
20. Mertens, J.F., Zamir, S.: Formulation of Bayesian analysis for games with incomplete information. Internat. J. Game Theory **14**, 1–29 (1985). https://doi.org/10.1007/BF01770224
21. Stalnaker, R.: Common ground. Linguist. Philos. **25**(5–6), 701–721 (2002)

Belief Reconfiguration

Sébastien Konieczny[✉][ID], Elise Perrotin[ID], and Ramón Pino Pérez[ID]

CRIL, CNRS, Université d'Artois, Arras, France
konieczny@cril.fr

Abstract. We study a generalisation of iterated belief revision in a setting where we keep track not only of the received information (in the form of messages) but also of the source of each message. We suppose that we have a special source, the oracle, which never fails. That is, all of the information provided by the oracle is assumed to be correct. We then evaluate the reliability of each source by confronting its messages with the facts given by the oracle. In this case it is natural to give higher priority to messages coming from more reliable sources. We therefore re-order (reconfigurate) the messages with respect to the reliability of the sources before performing iterated belief revision. We study how to compute this reliability, and the properties of the corresponding reconfiguration operators.

1 Introduction

In this work our aim is to provide a more realistic account of iterated belief revision [2,5,13]. A requirement in standard iterated belief revision is that every new evidence acquired by the agent is more plausible than the previous one. This assumption is usually not explicitly stated, but it is enforced by the postulates characterizing these operators. This is usually called "Primacy of Update".

However, if this assumption is plausible in some scenarios, for instance when one wants to model the evolution of scientific theories, it makes relatively little sense in everyday-life scenarios: we usually obtain pieces of information at different points in time, which we consider sufficiently reliable to be taken into account, but they are not magically ordered from least to most plausible over the course of our life. We therefore need to adapt this "ideal" framework of iterated belief revision so that we can represent real, practical applications.

One way of doing this is to weaken the postulates in order to remove primacy of update altogether. This leads for instance to improvement operators [14,15], which make 'softer' changes than revision operators. With improvement operators it is possible to completely get rid of primacy of update [19]. Another way to do this is by considering credibility limited revision operators [3,4,8,9,11].

Rather than weakening all of the revision steps, in this work we wish to base priority given to the information on the reliability of the source behind it, while remaining as close as possible to the standard iterated revision framework. To this end, we need to explicitly introduce a way of measuring reliability of these

S. Gaggl et al. (Eds.): JELIA 2023, LNAI 14281, pp. 446–461, 2023.
https://doi.org/10.1007/978-3-031-43619-2_31

sources of information. In order to do this, we define a more general framework in which we attach to each received piece of evidence the source that provides this information. We suppose that we have a special source, the oracle, which never fails (i.e. it only provides truthful information). Then, by comparing the claims of the different sources with the truth that we obtain from the oracle, we can have an estimation of their reliability. Once we have this reliability estimation, in order to work with the iterated revision operators, we reconsider the sequence of received information with respect to this reliability by reordering the messages, putting the messages of the more reliable sources after those of the less reliable ones. Hence the name of "reconfiguration" for these operators.

This reordering does not affect the relative order of messages of individual sources (or of sources of the same reliability). This is also expected, as we can expect more recent messages of a given source to be more reliable: this source may learn new things, and correct some of her initial mistakes.

The proposed setting is very natural in numerous scenarios. Suppose for instance that you receive information from different friends, whom you consider reliable enough to be listened to. Here the oracle is directly observed evidence, i.e. what you can experiment about the world. Your direct observations of the world will sometimes contradict previous information you have received from friends; in this case you can reevaluate the reliability of those friends.

In the next section we give the definitions of our reconfiguration operators, as well as their associated iterated belief revision operators and reliability functions. In Sect. 3 we focus on the reliability functions, propose expected properties for these functions, enumerate several possible instantiations, and check which properties they satisfy. Then in Sect. 4 we study the properties of the corresponding reconfiguration operators. In Sect. 5 we provide an example illustrating the behavior of these operators. We then conclude in Sect. 6 with a discussion of related and future work.

2   Reconfiguration

In this section we formally describe the reconfiguration process. We consider a propositional language $\mathcal{L}_P$ built from a finite set of propositional variables P and the usual connectives. Lowercase letters of the Greek alphabet denote formulas. An interpretation ω is a total function from P to $\{0, 1\}$. The set of all interpretations is denoted by $\mathcal{W}$. An interpretation ω is a model of a formula $\varphi \in \mathcal{L}_P$ if and only if it makes it true in the usual truth functional way. The set of models of a formula φ is denoted by $[\![\varphi]\!]$. The set of consistent formulae is denoted by $\mathcal{L}_P^c$. $\bot$ (resp. $\top$) is the Boolean constant always false (resp. true).

2.1   The Ingredients

We consider an *epistemic space* $\mathcal{E} = \langle E, B \rangle$, where E is a set of epistemic states and B is a mapping $B : E \to \mathcal{L}_P$ characterizing beliefs in each epistemic state. We suppose the existence of an epistemic state $\Psi_\top$ such that $B(\Psi_\top) = \top$ (for a systematic treatment of these structures and revision operators defined on them see [20]).

We also consider a DP revision operator (i.e. an operator satisfying all postulates of [5]) $\circ : E \times \mathcal{L}_P^c \to E$. If $\varphi_1 \ldots \varphi_k$ is a sequence of formulas we define $\circledast(\varphi_1 \ldots \varphi_k)$ as $\circledast(\varphi_1 \ldots \varphi_k) = (\cdots((\Psi_\top \circ \varphi_1) \circ \varphi_2) \cdots) \circ \varphi_n$.

In our framework we consider sequences of messages sent by a variety of sources. To formalize this, let $\mathcal{S}$ be a finite set of sources of information, and o be an additional special source, called the oracle, which only provides correct information. We define $\mathcal{S}^* = \mathcal{S} \cup \{o\}$.

A *message* m is a couple (s, φ) where $s \in \mathcal{S}^*$ is the source of the message and $\varphi \in \mathcal{L}_P$ is the information given by the message. We denote by $\mathcal{M}$ the set of messages. For a message $m_i = (s_i, \varphi_i)$, we denote by m_i^s the source of the message, that is s_i, and we denote by m_i^φ the information of m, that is φ_i. We consider that individual messages are always consistent, i.e. for any message m, $m^\varphi \not\vdash \bot$.

Given a finite sequence of messages $\sigma = m_1 \ldots m_n$, we define $src(\sigma)$, the set of sources of σ, as $src(\sigma) = \{m_k^s : k = 1, \ldots, n\}$. For any source $s \in \mathcal{S}^*$, we denote by σ_s the sequence of formulas in the messages from source s in σ. For example, if $\sigma = (s_1, p)(s_2, q)(s_1, r)$ then $\sigma_{s_1} = \langle p, r \rangle$. We furthermore define $\varphi_s^\sigma = \bigwedge_{\varphi \in \sigma_s} \varphi$ the conjunction of all information given by s in σ. In particular, if σ_s is the empty sequence (i.e. there are no messages from s in the sequence σ) then $\varphi_s^\sigma = \top$. As the messages of s in σ may be inconsistent with each other, resulting in $\varphi_s^\sigma \equiv \bot$, we also define the *opinion* of s as $\mathcal{O}_s^\sigma = B(\circledast \sigma_s)$.

As the oracle never fails, we suppose that $\varphi_o^\sigma \not\vdash \bot$ in all considered sequences σ. We call *Seq* the set of finite sequences σ of messages such that $\varphi_o^\sigma \not\vdash \bot$. We use $\cdot$ as a concatenation symbol: if $\sigma = m_1 \ldots m_n$ then $\sigma \cdot m = m_1 \ldots m_n m$.

We assume that we have a function δ assigning a degree of reliability to a source in $\mathcal{S}$ appearing in a finite sequence of messages as well as to the oracle. The mapping δ is a partial function having domain *Seq* $\times \mathcal{S}^*$ and co-domain $\mathbb{R}^+$. If $(\sigma, s) \in Seq \times \mathcal{S}$ and $s \in src(\sigma)$ then $\delta(\sigma, s)$ is defined. The value $\delta(\sigma, s)$ represents the reliability degree of the source s given the sequence σ. $\delta(\sigma, o)$ is always defined, and required to be maximal, that is, $\delta(\sigma, o) > \delta(\sigma, s)$ for any source $s \in \mathcal{S}$. We adopt the notation $\delta_\sigma(s)$ instead of $\delta(\sigma, s)$.

2.2 The Framework

In order to reorganize messages of a sequence $\sigma = m_1 \ldots m_n$ from least to most reliable, we define a permutation function r which is a bijection from $\{1, \ldots, n\}$ to $\{1, \ldots, n\}$ as follows:

$$r(i) < r(j) \text{ iff } \begin{cases} \delta_\sigma(m_i^s) < \delta_\sigma(m_j^s), \text{ or} \\ \delta_\sigma(m_i^s) = \delta_\sigma(m_j^s) \text{ and } i < j \end{cases}$$

Intuitively, $r(i)$ is the relative reliability of the message m_i in σ. That is, a message m_i is considered less reliable than a message m_j if either the source of m_i is less reliable than that of m_j, or the sources of both messages have the same reliability and m_i was announced before m_j.

Finally, a sequence of messages $\sigma \in Seq$ induces an epistemic state $\Psi_\sigma \in E$ in which all messages have been taken into account relative to their respective reliability. Let $\sigma = m_1 \ldots m_n$ be a sequence of messages. We define $r_i = r^{-1}(i)$ for $i \leqslant n$. Because we assume the oracle to be the (strictly) most reliable source, we know that if at least one message in σ is not from the oracle then there is a $k \leqslant n$ such that $m_{r_k}^s \neq o$ and $m_{r_j}^s = o$ for all $j > k$. We define Ψ_σ as follows:

$$\Psi_\sigma = (\circledast(m_{r_1}^\varphi \ldots m_{r_k}^\varphi)) \circ \varphi_o^\sigma.$$

In order to study the mechanisms of this revision process when receiving new messages, we define a new epistemic space as follows.

Definition 1. *The epistemic space of sequences $\mathcal{E}_{Seq}$ associated to a DP operator $\circ$ and a reliability function δ is defined by putting $\mathcal{E}_{Seq} = \langle Seq, B_{Seq} \rangle$, where the epistemic states are sequences of messages and B_{Seq} is the mapping $B_{Seq} : Seq \to \mathcal{L}_P$ defined by $B_{Seq}(\sigma) = B(\Psi_\sigma)$.*

3 Reliability Functions

A key element of the reconfiguration framework is the function δ, which evaluates the reliability of sources by comparing their messages with those of the oracle. There are many possible definitions for this function. In this section we give a few general properties that such a function should satisfy. We then give some natural examples of δ functions, and check these functions against the stated properties.

3.1 Desirable Properties

We give some natural properties which we expect any "good" reliability function δ to satisfy. We call these properties "general properties". We then provide some additional optional properties which make sense in some contexts, and can be satisfied depending on the desired behavior of δ.

General Properties

1. **(Source independence)** If $\sigma_s = \sigma'_{s'}$ and $\sigma_o = \sigma'_o$ then $\delta_\sigma(s) = \delta_{\sigma'}(s')$.
   i.e.: A source's evaluation is independent of other sources. It depends solely on what the source and the oracle have announced.
2. **(Syntax independence)** If $\sigma = m_1 \ldots m_n$ and $m_i^\varphi \equiv \psi$ for some i then $\delta_{\sigma[(m_i^s, \psi)/m_i]} = \delta_\sigma$, where $\sigma[(m_i^s, \psi)/m_i]$ is the sequence σ in which m_i has been replaced by the message (m_i^s, ψ).
   i.e.: Two logically equivalent messages have exactly the same effect.
3. **(Oracle)** For any $s \in src(\sigma) \setminus \{o\}$, we have $\delta_\sigma(s) < \delta_\sigma(o)$.
   i.e.: The oracle is the (strictly) most reliable source.

4. **(Maximality)** For any $s, s' \in src(\sigma) \setminus \{o\}$, if $\varphi_s^\sigma \wedge \varphi_o^\sigma \nvdash \bot$ then $\delta_\sigma(s') \leqslant \delta_\sigma(s)$.

   i.e.: All consistent sources which have never contradicted the oracle have the same reliability, which is the maximal reliability among sources other than the oracle.

5. **(Non-maximality)** For any $s, s' \in src(\sigma) \setminus \{o\}$ if $\varphi_s^\sigma \wedge \varphi_o^\sigma \nvdash \bot$, $\varphi_{s'}^\sigma \nvdash \bot$ and $\varphi_{s'}^\sigma \wedge \varphi_o^\sigma \vdash \bot$ then $\delta_\sigma(s') < \delta_\sigma(s)$.

   i.e.: A source who has contradicted the oracle will always be strictly less reliable than one who has made no mistakes.

Optional Properties

6. If $\varphi_s^\sigma \equiv \varphi_s^{\sigma'}$ and $\varphi_s^\sigma \nvdash \bot$ then $\delta_\sigma(s) = \delta_{\sigma'}(s)$.

   i.e.: The reliability function does not depend on the exact messages provided by the agent, but only on their conjunction. In other words, providing any number of messages or just one message with their conjunction leads to the same reliability.

7. If $s \in src(\sigma) \setminus \{o\}$ and $\psi \wedge \varphi_o^\sigma \nvdash \bot$ then $\delta_{\sigma \cdot (s, \psi)}(s) \geqslant \delta_\sigma(s)$.

   i.e.: Not contradicting the oracle cannot decrease reliability of a source.

8. If $s \in src(\sigma) \setminus \{o\}$ and $\psi \wedge \varphi_o^\sigma \vdash \bot$ then $\delta_{\sigma \cdot (s, \psi)}(s) \leqslant \delta_\sigma(s)$.

   i.e.: Contradicting the oracle cannot increase reliability of a source.

9. If $s, s' \in src(\sigma) \setminus \{o\}$, $\delta_\sigma(s) \leqslant \delta_\sigma(s')$, $\psi \wedge \varphi_o^\sigma \vdash \bot$ and $\psi' \wedge \varphi_o^\sigma \nvdash \bot$ then $\delta_{\sigma \cdot (s, \psi)}(s) < \delta_{\sigma \cdot (s', \psi')}(s')$.

   i.e.: A message directly contradicting the oracle is strictly worse (for reliability) than a message that does not contradict it.

10. If $\delta_\sigma(s) \leqslant \delta_\sigma(s')$ then $\delta_{\sigma \cdot (s, \psi) \cdot (s', \psi)}(s) \leqslant \delta_{\sigma \cdot (s, \psi) \cdot (s', \psi)}(s')$.

    i.e.: If two sources give the same information then their relative reliability remains unchanged.

11. If $\sigma = m_1 \ldots m_n$ and m is a message, call $\sigma^{+i, m}$ the sequence σ in which m is inserted after m_i: $\sigma^{+i, m} = m_1 \ldots m_i m m_{i+1} \ldots m_n$. Consider ψ such that $\psi \wedge \varphi_o^\sigma \vdash \bot$, and suppose that $\psi \wedge \varphi_s^\sigma \nvdash \bot$ and for any α in σ_s, $\alpha \wedge \varphi_o^\sigma \nvdash \bot$. Then $\delta_{\sigma^{+i, (s, \psi)}}(s) \leqslant \delta_{\sigma^{+j, (s, \psi)}}(s)$ if $i \geqslant j$.

    i.e.: This is a temporality property. Contradicting the oracle is more problematic the more recently it has been done. This implies that we consider as more reliable a source has made a mistake a long time ago (and has had the time to correct it) than one that has made a mistake more recently.

12. if $\psi \wedge \varphi_s^\sigma \vdash \bot$, $\psi' \wedge \varphi_s^\sigma \nvdash \bot$, $\psi \wedge \varphi_o^\sigma \nvdash \bot$ and $\psi' \wedge \varphi_o^\sigma \nvdash \bot$ then $\delta_{\sigma \cdot (s, \psi)}(s) < \delta_{\sigma \cdot (s, \psi')}(s)$.

    i.e.: All the other properties focus on comparing messages from a given source to the messages of the oracle. Here we add a more local estimation of reliability, only confronting messages from a same source, and "punishing" sources that contradict themselves.

3.2   Some Options for δ

We now give some examples of definitions for the reliability function δ. For all the considered functions we put $\delta_\sigma(o) = \infty$, and only give definitions of $\delta_\sigma(s)$ for $s \neq o$.

We wish to assess sources' reliability based on the consistency of their messages with the information from the oracle. We do this by using some inconsistency measure, that is, a function $d : \mathcal{L}_P^c \times \mathcal{L}_P^c \to \mathbb{R}^+$ which is intended to measure the disagreement between two consistent formulas [1,10,12,23,24]. We suppose that d is congruent with respect to logical equivalence and symmetric. We also suppose that for any formulas φ and ψ, if $\varphi \wedge \psi \nvdash \bot$ then $d(\varphi, \psi) = 0$, and if $\varphi \wedge \psi \vdash \bot$ then $d(\varphi, \psi) > 0$. One example of such a function is the drastic measure d_D, defined by $d_D(\varphi, \psi) = 0$ if $\varphi \wedge \psi$ is consistent, otherwise $d_D(\varphi, \psi) = 1$.

We define $M_d = max\{d(\varphi, \psi) : \varphi, \psi \in \mathcal{L}_P^c\}$. We extend d to $\mathcal{L}_P \times \mathcal{L}_P$ by putting $d(\varphi, \psi) = M_d + 1$ if φ or ψ is inconsistent.

A first naive definition for a reliability function is as follows:

$$\delta_\sigma^1(s) = M_d - d(\varphi_s^\sigma, \varphi_o^\sigma).$$

Note that if a source s is contradictory, that is, if $\varphi_s^\sigma \equiv \bot$, then $\delta_\sigma^1(s) = -1$. More generally, the messages from one source may become inconsistent with each other over time, and we wish to give sources the opportunity to correct past mistakes. We consider that when a source contradicts its past messages, its current opinion is that conveyed by its later messages, and that is what its reliability should be assessed from. There are several ways to implement this. The first is to consider the source's opinion as defined in Sect. 2.1:

$$\delta_\sigma^2(s) = M_d - d(\mathcal{O}_s^\sigma, \varphi_o^\sigma).$$

However, as the properties of a source's opinion $\mathcal{O}_s^\sigma$ are difficult to characterize, we might want a simpler way to take into account the combination of its messages even when it contradicts itself. One way to achieve this is, when $\sigma_s = \alpha_1 \ldots \alpha_k$, to define $c_s^\sigma = \alpha_{j_{cons}(\sigma_s)} \wedge \cdots \wedge \alpha_k$, where $j_{cons}(\sigma_s) = \min\{j \mid \alpha_j \wedge \cdots \wedge \alpha_k \nvdash \bot\}$. For example, if $\sigma_s = \langle p, q, r, \neg q \rangle$ then $j_{cons}(\sigma_s) = 3$ and $c_s^\sigma = r \wedge \neg q$. We then define

$$\delta_\sigma^3(s) = M_d - d(c_s^\sigma, \varphi_o^\sigma).$$

Rather than considering a 'global opinion' for each source, we might want to take into account separately each individual message. This allows us, in particular to put weights on the evaluation of messages, so that older messages 'count less' when assessing a source's reliability. We may then also consider not only how much the source contradicts the oracle, but also how much the source contradicts itself from message to message. A general formula for computing the reliability of a source $s \neq o$ after a sequence σ in which $\sigma_s = \alpha_1 \ldots \alpha_k$ could be:

$$\delta_\sigma^*(s) = \frac{1}{W_k} \sum_{i=1}^k w_{i,k}(A \cdot \mathsf{OC}(\alpha_i, \varphi_o^\sigma) + B \cdot \mathsf{SC}(\alpha_i, \alpha_1 \ldots \alpha_{i-1}))$$

where W_k is a normalization factor, $w_{i,k}$ is a weight function favoring more recent messages, $\mathsf{OC}(\alpha_i, \varphi_o^\sigma)$ is a measure of how much the oracle is contradicted by α_i, $\mathsf{SC}(\alpha_i, \alpha_1 \ldots \alpha_{i-1})$ is a measure of how much α_i contradicts its own previous messages, and A and B are weights representing the importance given to consistency with the oracle and with own previous messages respectively.

We put the following constraints on the elements of this definition: first, $A > 0$ and $B \geqslant 0$. For weights, we require for all k and i:

$$W_k, w_{i,k} > 0; \qquad w_{k,k} = 1; \qquad w_{i,k} \leqslant w_{i+1,k}; \qquad w_{i,k} \leqslant w_{i,k+1}; \qquad W_k \leqslant W_{k+1}.$$

As for the contradiction factors $\mathsf{OC}(\alpha_i, \varphi_o^\sigma)$ and $\mathsf{SC}(\alpha_i, \alpha_1 \ldots \alpha_{i-1})$, we suppose that both $\mathsf{OC}(\alpha_i, \varphi_o^\sigma)$ and $\mathsf{SC}(\alpha_i, \alpha_1 \ldots \alpha_{i-1})$ have a maximum and a minimum possible value, denoted maxOC, minOC, maxSC and minSC respectively. We then require $\mathsf{minOC}, \mathsf{minSC} \leqslant 0 \leqslant \mathsf{maxOC}, \mathsf{maxSC}$ and:

$$\mathsf{OC}(\alpha_i, \varphi_o^\sigma) = \mathsf{maxOC} \text{ iff } \alpha_i \wedge \varphi_o^\sigma \nvdash \bot;$$

$$\text{if } \alpha_1 \wedge \cdots \wedge \alpha_i \nvdash \bot \text{ then } \mathsf{SC}(\alpha_i, \alpha_1 \ldots \alpha_{i-1}) = \mathsf{maxSC};$$

$$\text{if } \alpha_{i-1} \wedge \alpha_i \vdash \bot \text{ then } \mathsf{SC}(\alpha_i, \alpha_1 \ldots \alpha_{i-1}) < \mathsf{maxSC};$$

$$\text{if } \alpha_1 \wedge \cdots \wedge \alpha_{i-1} \nvdash \bot \text{ and } \alpha_1 \wedge \cdots \wedge \alpha_i \vdash \bot \text{ then } \mathsf{SC}(\alpha_i, \alpha_1 \ldots \alpha_{i-1}) < \mathsf{maxSC}.$$

Here are some examples of instantiations of these elements:

- $W_k = 1$ (no normalization) or $W_k = \sum_{i=1}^k w_{i,k}$;
- $w_{i,k} = 1$ (no weighting) or $w_{i,k} = (1 - \varepsilon)^{k-i}$ for some $\varepsilon < 1$;
- $\mathsf{OC}(\alpha_i, \varphi_o^\sigma) = M_d - d(\alpha_i, \varphi_o^\sigma)$ (here $\mathsf{maxOC} = M_d$) or $\mathsf{OC}(\alpha_i, \varphi_o^\sigma) = -d(\alpha_i, \varphi_o^\sigma)$ (here $\mathsf{maxOC} = 0$);
- for $i > 1$, $\mathsf{SC}(\alpha_i, \alpha_1 \ldots \alpha_{i-1}) = -\frac{j_{cons}(\alpha_1 \ldots \alpha_i) - 1}{i - 1}$.

We now give a few instantiations of this definition:

$$\delta_\sigma^4(s) = \tfrac{1}{k} \sum_{i=1}^k (M_d - d(\alpha_i, \varphi_o^\sigma));$$

$$\delta_\sigma^5(s) = \tfrac{1}{W_k} \sum_{i=1}^k w_{i,k} (M_d - d(\alpha_i, \varphi_o^\sigma));$$

$$\delta_\sigma^6(s) = \sum_{i=1}^k w_{i,k} (M_d - d(\alpha_i, \varphi_o^\sigma));$$

$$\delta_\sigma^7(s) = \tfrac{1}{W_k} \sum_{i=1}^k w_{i,k} (-d(\alpha_i, \varphi_o^\sigma) + ctr(\alpha_i));$$

$$\delta_\sigma^8(s) = -\sum_{i=1}^k w_{i,k} d(\alpha_i, \varphi_o^\sigma);$$

where $w_{i,k}$ follow the non-trivial definition given above, $W_k = \sum_{i=1}^k w_{i,k}$, and $ctr(\alpha_i)$ follows the definition for $\mathsf{SC}(\alpha_i, \alpha_1 \ldots \alpha_{i-1})$ given above. The function δ^4 is normalized, but all messages have the same weight. It is a special case of δ^5 (for $\varepsilon = 0$), which features normalization and increasing weights for each message. The function δ^6 has increasing weights, but no normalization. Finally, the functions δ^7 and δ^8 consider negative reliability evaluations, with δ^7 also taking into account whether the source contradicts itself, and δ^8 not being normalized.

Here we have proposed two approaches to computing a source's reliability: either aggregating its messages into a 'global opinion' to compare to the oracle's announcements, or considering each of its messages separately. A core difference in these two approaches can be seen as follows: suppose that the oracle has announced $\neg(p \wedge q)$, and that a source announces p, then q. With the first approach we consider this to be equivalent to the source announcing $p \wedge q$, and being completely incorrect. With the second approach, we allow an interpretation in which the announcement of q is a correction of previous statements, that is, the source might have updated its opinion from $p \wedge \neg q$ to $q \wedge \neg p$.

3.3   Discussion of the Proposed Functions and Properties

We now evaluate the properties and δ functions proposed above against each other, to confirm whether they indeed make sense[1].

General Properties. We first check whether the proposed functions satisfy the required general properties.

Proposition 1. *The functions δ^1, δ^2, δ^3, and δ^* satisfy properties 1, 2, and 3, that is, source and syntax independence and oracle maximality.*

Proof. This follows from the definition of the functions and the fact that the inconsistency measure d is syntax-independent.

Proposition 2. *The function δ^1 satisfies properties 4 (Maximality) and 5 (Non-maximality). The functions δ^2 and δ^3 satisfy property 4 but not property 5. The function δ^* satisfies properties 4 and 5 if either $\frac{\sum_{i=1}^{k} w_{i,k}}{W_k}$ is constant or $\mathsf{maxOC} = B\mathsf{maxSC} = 0$; otherwise it satisfies neither property.*

The function δ^1 therefore satisfies all general properties, whereas δ^2 and δ^3 fail to satisfy property 5, so they should not be considered as satisfying reliability functions. For the general δ^* function, properties 1, 2 and 3 are always satisfied, and we need some mild additional condition to satisfy also properties 4 and 5.

Optional Properties. We now turn to the optional properties and check which of them are satisfied by the different proposed reliability functions.

Following Proposition 2, from now on we consider for δ^* only the cases where either $\frac{\sum_{i=1}^{k} w_{i,k}}{W_k}$ is constant in k (we can consider w.l.o.g. that this constant is 1), or $\mathsf{maxOC} = B\mathsf{maxSC} = 0$. This, in particular, rules out the function δ^6.

Proposition 3. *The functions δ^1, δ^2 and δ^3 satisfy property 6; the function δ^* does not.*

The intuition here is that with δ^* a source can increase its reliability by repeating tautologies. We now study properties 7, 8 and 9.

Proposition 4. *The functions δ^1, δ^2 and δ^3 do not satisfy property 7 or property 9; they satisfy property 8 when the inconsistency measure d is the drastic measure d_D.*

Intuitively, these functions compute 'how wrong' the combination of a source's messages is; a message might be correct but result in a mistake when combined with previous messages, or it might be incorrect but result in a lesser

---

[1] Because of space constraints we do not put the proofs in the paper and only give some intuitions behind the results. The full proofs can be found in the supplementary material.

mistake when combined with previous messages. In particular, even if a source only makes mistakes, their evaluation can evolve from being 'very wrong in general' to being 'almost correct in general'. Requiring d to be a $0/1$ function removes this possibility of being 'almost correct'.

The interplay between the different elements of δ^* are more complex, and we give some cases in which δ^* satisfies the different properties rather than giving a general criteria. We consider three additional properties in particular. The first is $B = 0$, so that not contradicting oneself cannot compensate for contradicting the oracle, or the other way around. The second is for there to be an $\varepsilon < 1$ such that $w_{i,k+1} = (1 - \varepsilon)w_{i,k}$ for all k and $i \leqslant k$, so that we can better characterize the evolution of a source's reliability when it provides a new message. The third is for OC to be a $0/1$ function. This means that for all formulas φ and ψ either $\mathsf{OC}(\psi, \varphi) = \mathsf{minOC}$ or $\mathsf{OC}(\psi, \varphi) = \mathsf{maxOC}$. As noted above, this prevents sources' reliability from increasing when making a mistake by removing the possibility of being 'almost correct'.

We start by considering the case where $\sum_{i=1}^{k} w_{i,k} = W_k$.

Proposition 5. δ^* *satisfies property 7 when* $\frac{\sum_{i=1}^{k} w_{i,k}}{W_k} = 1$, $B = 0$ *and there exists some* $\varepsilon \leqslant 1$ *such that* $w_{i,k+1} = (1 - \varepsilon)w_{i,k}$ *for all i and k. In this case we have* $\delta^*_{\sigma \cdot (s,\psi)}(s) = \delta^*_{\sigma}(s)$ *iff* $\delta^*_{\sigma}(s) = \mathsf{AmaxOC}$ *and* $\psi \wedge \varphi^{\sigma}_o \not\vdash \bot$.

Proposition 6. *When* $\frac{\sum_{i=1}^{k} w_{i,k}}{W_k} = 1$ *for all k, $B = 0$, the function δ^* satisfies property 8 iff OC is a $0/1$ function. In this case we have* $\delta^*_{\sigma \cdot (s,\psi)}(s) = \delta^*_{\sigma}(s)$ *iff* $\delta^*_{\sigma}(s) = \mathsf{AminOC}$ *and* $\psi \wedge \varphi^{\sigma}_o \vdash \bot$.

Proposition 7. *The function δ^* satisfies property 9 when* $\frac{\sum_{i=1}^{k} w_{i,k}}{W_k} = 1$ *for all k, there exists some* $\varepsilon \leqslant 1$ *such that* $w_{i,k+1} = (1 - \varepsilon)w_{i,k}$ *for all i and k, $B = 0$, and OC is a $0/1$ function.*

In particular the functions δ^4 and δ^5 satisfy property 7, and they satisfy properties 8 and 9 when d is the drastic measure d_D.

We now consider the case where $\frac{\sum_{i=1}^{k} w_{i,k}}{W_k}$ is not constant in k. Then in particular $\mathsf{maxOC} = \mathsf{BmaxSC} = 0$.

Recall that W_k is a normalization factor. There are essentially two meaningful options in terms of normalization: either having $\frac{\sum_{i=1}^{k} w_{i,k}}{W_k}$ be constant, or having no normalization. We now focus on the latter case and require W_k to be constant in k. We once again consider the particular case where $\frac{w_{i,k+1}}{w_{i,k}}$ is constant in i and k.

Proposition 8. *Suppose that* $\mathsf{maxOC} = \mathsf{BmaxSC} = 0$ *and that there exist some W and ε such that* $W_k = W$ *and* $w_{i,k+1} = (1 - \varepsilon)w_{i,k}$ *for all k and $i \leqslant k$. Then the function δ^* satisfies property 7 iff $B = 0$; it satisfies property 8 iff either $\varepsilon = 0$ or $B = 0$ and OC is a $0/1$ function; it satisfies property 9 iff for all ψ and φ such that $\psi \wedge \varphi \vdash \bot$ we have* $\mathsf{OC}(\psi, \varphi) \leqslant \frac{B}{A}\mathsf{minSC}$.

Table 1. Properties satisfied by the proposed reliability functions. Conditions that are both necessary and sufficient are in dark blue; merely sufficient conditions are in cyan.

	1	2	3	4	5	6	7	8	9	10	11	12
δ^1	✓	✓	✓	✓	✓	✓	×	0/1	×	×	✓	✓
δ^2	✓	✓	✓	✓	×	✓	×	0/1	×	×	×	×
δ^3	✓	✓	✓	✓	×	✓	×	0/1	×	×	×	×
δ^4	✓	✓	✓	✓	✓	×	✓	0/1	0/1	×	✓	×
δ^5	✓	✓	✓	✓	✓	×	✓	0/1	0/1	×	✓	×
δ^6	✓	✓	✓	×	×							
δ^7	✓	✓	✓	✓	✓	×	×	$\varepsilon=0$ and 0/1	$\psi\wedge\varphi\vdash\bot\Rightarrow OC(\psi,\varphi)\leqslant-1$	×	✓	✓
δ^8	✓	✓	✓	✓	✓	×	✓	0/1	✓	✓	✓	×

In particular δ^7 does not satisfy property 7; it satisfies property 8 iff $\varepsilon = 0$ and d is the drastic measure d_D; and it satisfies 9 iff $d(\psi,\varphi) \geqslant 1$ for any φ and ψ such that $\varphi \wedge \psi \vdash \bot$. On the other hand, δ^8 satisfies properties 7 and 9, and it satisfies property 8 when d is the drastic measure d_D.

Proposition 9. *The functions δ^1, δ^2 and δ^3 do not satisfy property 10. The function δ^* does not satisfy it if W_k is not constant in k for $k > 1$ or $B \neq 0$. The function δ^* does satisfy property 10 when W_k is constant in k, $B = 0$ and $\frac{w_{i,k+1}}{w_{i,k}}$ is constant in i and k.*

Intuitively, property 10 requires the impact of announcing a formula on a source's reliability not to depend on the rest of the source's messages. In particular, the function δ^8 satisfies this property, while the functions δ^4, δ^5 and δ^7 do not.

Proposition 10. *The functions δ^1 and δ^* satisfy property 11; δ^2 and δ^3 do not.*

Proposition 11. *The function δ^1 satisfies property 12; the functions δ^2 and δ^3 do not. The function δ^* satisfies it iff $B \neq 0$.*

Table 1 sums up the properties satisfied by the reliability functions δ^1–δ^8. The 0/1 symbol represents the condition that d is the drastic measure d_D.

4   Reconfiguration Operators

Let us now study the properties of the corresponding reconfiguration operators, i.e. the operators that we obtain when we use the reliability function to re-order (reconfigurate) the sequence of messages.

Recall that using a DP operator $\circ$ defined on an epistemic space $\mathcal{E} = \langle E, B \rangle$ and a reliability function δ, we build a new epistemic space $\mathcal{E}_{Seq} = \langle Seq, B_{Seq} \rangle$ where the elements of Seq (the new epistemic states) are sequences of messages and B_{Seq} is as in Definition 1. In this epistemic space we define a new operator • as follows:

Definition 2. *The function* • : $Seq \times \mathcal{M} \to Seq$, *called a* reconfiguration operator, *is defined in the following way: if* $\sigma = m_1 \ldots m_n$, *then* $\sigma \bullet m = m_1 \ldots m_n m$.

Let us give the translation[2] of the standard DP postulates [5] in this framework:

(r-R*1) $B_{Seq}(\sigma \bullet m) \vdash m^\varphi$
(r-R*2) If $B_{Seq}(\sigma) \wedge m^\varphi \not\vdash \bot$ then $B_{Seq}(\sigma \bullet m) \equiv B_{Seq}(\sigma) \wedge m^\varphi$
(r-R*3) $B_{Seq}(\sigma \bullet m) \not\vdash \bot$
(r-R*4) If $m^\varphi \equiv m'^\varphi$ and $m^s = m'^s$ then $B_{Seq}(\sigma \bullet m) \equiv B_{Seq}(\sigma \bullet m')$
(r-R*5) Let μ be a formula and m_1, m_2 messages such that $m_1^s = m_2^s$ and
$m_2^\varphi = m_1^\varphi \wedge \mu$; then $B_{Seq}(\sigma \bullet m_1) \wedge \mu \vdash B_{Seq}(\sigma \bullet m_2)$
(r-R*6) Let μ be a formula and m_1, m_2 messages such that $m_1^s = m_2^s$ and
$m_2^\varphi = m_1^\varphi \wedge \mu$; then, if $B_{Seq}(\sigma \bullet m_1) \wedge \mu \not\vdash \bot$ then $\vdash B_{Seq}(\sigma \bullet m_2) \vdash B_{Seq}(\sigma \bullet m_1) \wedge \mu$
(r-C1) If $m_2^\varphi \vdash m_1^\varphi$ then $B_{Seq}((\sigma \bullet m_1) \bullet m_2) \equiv B_{Seq}(\sigma \bullet m_2)$
(r-C2) If $m_2^\varphi \vdash \neg m_1^\varphi$ then $B_{Seq}((\sigma \bullet m_1) \bullet m_2) \equiv B_{Seq}(\sigma \bullet m_2)$
(r-C3) If $B_{Seq}(\sigma \bullet m_2) \vdash m_1^\varphi$ then $B_{Seq}((\sigma \bullet m_1) \bullet m_2) \vdash m_1^\varphi$
(r-C4) If $B_{Seq}(\sigma \bullet m_2) \not\vdash \neg m_1^\varphi$ then $B_{Seq}((\sigma \bullet m_1) \bullet m_2) \not\vdash \neg m_1^\varphi$

Please see [5] for a more complete description of these postulates. Briefly,
(r-R*1) means that the last information of the sequence should be believed
after the change. **(r-R*2)** means that when the new piece of information is
consistent with the current beliefs of the agent, then the result should be the
conjunction. **(r-R*3)** is a bit stronger than the original DP postulate, requiring
coherence unconditionally (since we suppose that each message is consistent).
(r-R*4) is the Independence of syntax postulate. **(r-R*5)** and **(r-R*6)** relates
the change by a conjunction with the change by an element of the conjunction.
(r-C1) says that if a message m_2^φ is logically stronger than m_1^φ (and provided
by the same source), then we obtain the same result if we make the change my
m_1^φ and then by m_2^φ and if we make the change directly by m_2^φ. **(r-C2)** says
that if m_2^φ contradicts m_1^φ (and if they are provided by the same source), then
we obtain the same result if we make the change my m_1^φ and then by m_2^φ and if
we make the change directly by m_2^φ. **(r-C3)** says that if a change by m_2^φ implies
m_1^φ, then making the change by m_1^φ before the one by m_2^φ should not hurt m_1^φ
(so the result still implies m_1^φ). **(r-C4)** says that if a change by m_2^φ does not
implies $\neg m_1^\varphi$, then making the change by m_1^φ before the one by m_2^φ should not
helps $\neg m_1^\varphi$ (so the result still not implies $\neg m_1^\varphi$).

It is easy to see that these postulates do not hold in general for reconfiguration, due to the reordering during the process, but they hold under certain
restrictions on the reliability of the new information, showing that we keep the
DP behavior when possible:

Definition 3. *We say that the operator* • *has a DP behavior with respect to the
triple* σ, m_1, m_2 *(a sequence of messages and two messages respectively) if the
postulates (r-R*1–r-R*6) and (r-C1–r-C4) are satisfied.*

---

[2] We put the prefix r- (for reconfiguration) before the translated postulate.

Proposition 12. *Let σ, m_1, m_2 be a sequence of messages and two messages respectively. Then*

1. *If m_1^s and m_2^s are two sources with highest reliability in the sequences $\sigma \cdot m_1$ and $\sigma \cdot m_2$, then $\bullet$ has a DP behavior with respect to the triple σ, m_1, m_2.*
2. *If $m_1^s, m_2^s \neq o$ and m_1^s (resp. m_2^s) is the source with highest reliability among the sources different from the oracle in the sequence $\sigma \cdot m_1$ (resp. $\sigma \cdot m_2$) and $\varphi_o^\sigma \equiv \top$, then $\bullet$ has a DP behavior with respect to the triple σ, m_1, m_2.*

Despite the fact that reconfiguration operators are not designed to be DP iterated belief revision operators, as the reconfiguration (re-ordering) has an important impact on how the last message is treated, these results illustrate the fact that we keep the DP iteration flavor, and maintain the DP iteration behavior in particular when receiving messages from a most reliable source.

5 Example

We now provide an example illustrating the impact of recomputing reliability following announcements from the oracle. For simplicity we use the epistemic space of total preorders over interpretations, where for a total preorder $\preccurlyeq$, $[\![B(\preccurlyeq)]\!] = min(\preccurlyeq)$ and the underlying belief revision operator is Nayak's lexicographic revision operator $\circ_N$ [18] defined as follows: $\preccurlyeq \circ_N \alpha = \preccurlyeq'$ where $\omega \preccurlyeq' \omega'$ iff $\omega \in [\![\alpha]\!]$ or $\omega' \notin [\![\alpha]\!]$. We consider the reliability function $\delta^{4_{d_D}}$, which uses the drastic measure d_D and computes the proportion of messages from a given source which contradicts the oracle. We denote by $\bullet_N^{d_D}$ the reconfiguration operator defined from $\circ_N$ and the reliability function $\delta^{4_{d_D}}$.

Example 1. We consider three sources, and the following sequence of messages: $(s_1, a \wedge \neg c) \bullet_N^{d_D} (s_2, a \wedge c) \bullet_N^{d_D} (s_1, b) \bullet_N^{d_D} (s_3, \neg a \wedge \neg c) \bullet_N^{d_D} (o, a) \bullet_N^{d_D} (s_3, a \wedge b) \bullet_N^{d_D} (s_2, c \wedge \neg b) \bullet_N^{d_D} (o, \neg c)$. Let us see and comment what happens at each iteration. In order to simplify the notations, we will write $\Psi \equiv \alpha$ instead of $B_{Seq}(\Psi) \equiv \alpha$.

1. $(s_1, a \wedge \neg c) \equiv a \wedge \neg c$. There is only one message for the moment, so there is no reason to reject it.

2. $(s_1, a \wedge \neg c) \bullet_N^{d_D} (s_2, a \wedge c) \equiv a \wedge c$. Source s_2 contradicts source s_1, but as the oracle has not yet given any information we keep the messages in order of reception, and accept the message from s_2. Taking this temporal order into account (instead of finding some kind of consensus or compromise with operators such as belief merging [16]) can be justified by the fact that s_2 has potentially benefited from more time than s_1 to check this piece of information.

3. $(s_1, a \wedge \neg c) \bullet_N^{d_D} (s_2, a \wedge c) \bullet_N^{d_D} (s_1, b) \equiv a \wedge b \wedge c$. Source s_1 sends a new message about b. As b had not been mentioned up to this point we can accept it in addition to the previous message of s_2.

4. $(s_1, a \wedge \neg c) \bullet_N^{d_P} (s_2, a \wedge c) \bullet_N^{d_P} (s_1, b) \bullet_N^{d_P} (s_3, \neg a \wedge \neg c) \equiv \neg a \wedge b \wedge \neg c$. Source s_3 sends a message that contradicts both s_1 and s_2, but as it is the most recent message we accept it.

5. $(s_1, a \wedge \neg c) \bullet_N^{d_P} (s_2, a \wedge c) \bullet_N^{d_P} (s_1, b) \bullet_N^{d_P} (s_3, \neg a \wedge \neg c) \bullet_N^{d_P} (o, a) \equiv a \wedge b \wedge c$. We receive our first message from the oracle, which makes us realize that s_3 is the least reliable source; we still cannot distinguish between s_1 and s_2. The reconfiguration gives the following sequence: ($\Psi_\top \circ_N \neg a \wedge \neg c \circ_N a \wedge \neg c \circ_N a \wedge c \circ_N b \circ_N a$).

6. $(s_1, a \wedge \neg c) \bullet_N^{d_P} (s_2, a \wedge c) \bullet_N^{d_P} (s_1, b) \bullet_N^{d_P} (s_3, \neg a \wedge \neg c) \bullet_N^{d_P} (o, a) \bullet_N^{d_P} (s_3, a \wedge b) \equiv a \wedge b \wedge c$. We receive a new message from s_3, which does not contradict the oracle, but contradicts the previous message from s_3. This can mean that source s_3 has realized that it was wrong, revised its beliefs, and now sends a message it believes to be correct. Depending on the reliability function used, this can increase or decrease its reliability (since on the one hand this last message was consistent with the oracle, but on the other hand s_3 has contradicted itself). With the reliability function we have chosen, s_3 remains less reliable than the other sources. The corresponding reconfiguration gives the sequence ($\top \circ_N \neg a \wedge \neg c \circ_N a \wedge b \circ_N a \wedge \neg c \circ_N a \wedge c \circ_N b \circ_N a$).

7. $(s_1, a \wedge \neg c) \bullet_N^{d_P} (s_2, a \wedge c) \bullet_N^{d_P} (s_1, b) \bullet_N^{d_P} (s_3, \neg a \wedge \neg c) \bullet_N^{d_P} (o, a) \bullet_N^{d_P} (s_3, a \wedge b) \bullet_N^{d_P}$ $(s_2, c \wedge \neg b) \equiv a \wedge \neg b \wedge c$. We receive a new message from s_2, which is one of the most trustworthy sources. We therefore accept this message. The corresponding reconfiguration sequence is ($\top \circ_N \neg a \wedge \neg c \circ_N a \wedge b \circ_N a \wedge \neg c \circ_N a \wedge c \circ_N b \circ_N c \wedge \neg b \circ_N a$).

8. $(s_1, a \wedge \neg c) \bullet_N^{d_P} (s_2, a \wedge c) \bullet_N^{d_P} (s_1, b) \bullet_N^{d_P} (s_3, \neg a \wedge \neg c) \bullet_N^{d_P} (o, a) \bullet_N^{d_P} (s_3, a \wedge b) \bullet_N^{d_P}$ $(s_2, c \wedge \neg b) \bullet_N^{d_P} (o, \neg c) \equiv a \wedge b \wedge \neg c$. We receive a new message from the oracle, which contradicts the two messages of s_2. Hence s_2 become less reliable than s_3, as only half of s_3's two messages contradict the oracle. The source s_1 which has never contradicted the oracle is now the single most reliable source. The corresponding reconfiguration sequence is ($\Psi_\top \circ_N a \wedge c \circ_N c \wedge \neg b \circ_N \neg a \wedge \neg c \circ_N a \wedge b \circ_N a \wedge \neg c \circ_N b \circ_N a \wedge \neg c$).

6   Discussion and Conclusion

Reconfiguration operators are a very large family of operators as they have many parameters. It could be interesting to focus on particular subclasses, or to consider variations in the definitions we have given in this paper.

For instance, we have defined the epitemic state Ψ_σ as $(\circledast(m_{r_1}^\varphi \ldots m_{r_k}^\varphi)) \circ \varphi_o^\sigma$, i.e. we place the conjunction of all the messages of the oracle at the end of the sequence. Some interesting variations could be for instance $\Psi_\sigma^1 = (\circledast(m_{r_1}^\varphi \ldots m_{r_k}^\varphi)) \circ (\circledast \sigma_o)$, in which the sequence of the oracle's messages is considered rather than merely their conjunction; or $\Psi_\sigma^2 = \circledast((m_{r_1}^\varphi \wedge \varphi_o^\sigma) \ldots (m_{r_k}^\varphi \wedge \varphi_o^\sigma))$, in which every message from the sources is filtered by the information from the oracle. The latter approach would lead to ignoring all messages that contradict the oracle, as we know those messages to be incorrect. It could however be argued that this is too strong: for instance, if the message of a source is $a \wedge b \wedge c \wedge \ldots \wedge z$ and the message of the oracle is $\neg a$, should the entire conjunction be ignored because of the conflict on a? Studying the properties of these (and other) alternative definitions seems interesting.

With most of the reliability functions we have given, a source is more reliable the more correct messages it provides. This can be justified, since this evaluates how many "proofs" of reliability have been provided. However all of these correct messages can be of very little use if they are not very informative (if a source sends the message "the sky is blue" 50 times, does this make it a reliable source?). Moreover, this feature makes the evaluation weak to certain strategies: a manipulative source could provide many correct, but not very informative, messages, in order to raise its reliability, before sending a deliberately false (but not yet proven incorrect by oracle's messages) piece of information which it wants you to believe. Note that the importance of this issue must be balanced by the fact that such a strategy could be very difficult to carry out, as the malicious agent cannot predict the messages of the oracle, which could, at any moment before or after the planned false message of the source, provide a message that contradicts it. Nevertheless, taking into account the quantity of information a message carries could help avoid this problem.

Another choice we have made, once the reliability function is computed, is to use a standard iterated revision operator. One could instead use some weighted merging operator [6,7,17] to aggregate all messages. We claim that, even if reliability should be the most important point, between equally reliable agents, it still makes sense to take recency into account: agents can evolve and correct their beliefs, so we can still expect that, for a single agent or for several agents of the same reliability, more recent information is more correct: sources may learn new things, and correct some of their initial mistakes. Note that this recency could be encoded by adding a second step, after the reliability computation, in order to modify the obtained weights to add information about recency, and then use a weighted merging operator. But this is more naturally taken into account by iterated belief revision operators. Another advantage of iterated revision over merging is that, even though the reliability of the sources is computed numerically, what matters when it comes to the revision process in our framework is only the order between the sources, in contrast with the more arbitrary numerical weights used in weighted merging.

There are two other closely related works. The first one is [22], which starts from a very similar motivation to ours, but presents several important differences: in [22] the credibility relation is a partial pre-order that is given as input, while we compute our (total) relation from the sequences of messages in a dynamic way. Moreover, in [22] they use the framework of multiple (belief base) revision to take into account messages of same credibility, whereas, as explained previously, iterated revision allows us to also take into account recency of the messages. Similarly to our framework, in [21] reliability of different sources is evaluated based on their announcements and on a special source which is known to be reliable. However their setting is different from ours: they consider a 0/1 notion of expertise of agents on formulas (e.g. "having disease X"), which is evaluated through the agents' reports across different cases (e.g. patients).

In the future we plan to extend this work in two directions. The first is to consider that the oracle is not perfect, but almost perfect (it makes mistakes much less often that standard sources), and/or that we have several oracles, which may contradict each other. The second direction is to consider this reconfiguration framework, but with no oracle at all. The reliability of each source will then be computed by confronting its messages not with those of the oracle, but with those of the other sources.

Acknowledgements. This work has benefited from the support of the AI Chair BE4musIA of the French National Research Agency (ANR-20-CHIA-0028).

References

1. Besnard, P.: Revisiting postulates for inconsistency measures. In: Fermé, E., Leite, J. (eds.) JELIA 2014. LNCS (LNAI), vol. 8761, pp. 383–396. Springer, Cham (2014). https://doi.org/10.1007/978-3-319-11558-0_27
2. Booth, R., Meyer, T.A.: Admissible and restrained revision. J. Artif. Intell. Res. **26**, 127–151 (2006)
3. Booth, R., Fermé, E., Konieczny, S., Pino Pérez, R.: Credibility-limited revision operators in propositional logic. In: Proceedings of the 13th International Conference on the Principles of Knowledge Representation and Reasoning (2012)
4. Booth, R., Fermé, E.L., Konieczny, S., Pino Pérez, R.: Credibility-limited improvement operators. In: Proceedings of the 21st European Conference on Artificial Intelligence (ECAI 2014), vol. 263, pp. 123–128 (2014)
5. Darwiche, A., Pearl, J.: On the logic of iterated belief revision. Artif. Intell. **89**(1–2), 1–29 (1997)
6. Delgrande, J.P., Dubois, D., Lang, J.: Iterated revision as prioritized merging. In: Proceedings of the 10th International Conference on Principles of Knowledge Representation and Reasoning (KR 2006), pp. 210–220 (2006)
7. Everaere, P., Fellah, C., Konieczny, S., Pérez, R.P.: Weighted merging of propositional belief bases. In: Proceedings of the International Conference on Principles of Knowledge Representation and Reasoning (KR 2023) (2023)
8. Fermé, E.L., Mikalef, J., Taboada, J.: Credibility-limited functions for belief bases. J. Log. Comput. **13**(1), 99–110 (2003)
9. Garapa, M., Fermé, E., Reis, M.D.L.: Credibility-limited base revision: new classes and their characterizations. J. Artif. Intell. Res. **69**, 1023–1075 (2020)
10. Grant, J., Martinez, M.V.: Measuring Inconsistency in Information. College Publications, London (2018)
11. Hansson, S.O., Fermé, E.L., Cantwell, J., Falappa, M.A.: Credibility limited revision. J. Symb. Log. **66**(4), 1581–1596 (2001)
12. Hunter, A., Konieczny, S.: Approaches to measuring inconsistent information. In: Bertossi, L., Hunter, A., Schaub, T. (eds.) Inconsistency Tolerance. LNCS, vol. 3300, pp. 191–236. Springer, Heidelberg (2005). https://doi.org/10.1007/978-3-540-30597-2_7
13. Jin, Y., Thielscher, M.: Iterated belief revision, revised. Artif. Intell. **171**(1), 1–18 (2007)

14. Konieczny, S., Medina Grespan, M., Pino Pérez, R.: Taxonomy of improvement operators and the problem of minimal change. In: Proceedings of the 12th International Conference on Principles of Knowledge Representation and Reasoning (KR 2010), pp. 161–170 (2010)
15. Konieczny, S., Pino Pérez, R.: Improvement operators. In: Proceedings of the 11th International Conference on Principles of Knowledge Representation and Reasoning (KR 2008), pp. 177–187 (2008)
16. Konieczny, S., Pino Pérez, R.: Merging information under constraints: a logical framework. J. Log. Comput. **12**(5), 773–808 (2002)
17. Lin, J.: Integration of weighted knowledge bases. Artif. Intell. **83**(2), 363–378 (1996)
18. Nayak, A.: Iterated belief change based on epistemic entrenchment. Erkenntnis **41**, 353–390 (1994)
19. Schwind, N., Konieczny, S.: Non-prioritized iterated revision: improvement via incremental belief merging. In: Proceedings of the 17th International Conference on Principles of Knowledge Representation and Reasoning (KR 2020), pp. 738–747 (2020)
20. Schwind, N., Konieczny, S., Pino Pérez, R.: On the representation of Darwiche and Pearl's epistemic states for iterated belief revision. In: Proceedings of the 19th International Conference on Principles of Knowledge Representation and Reasoning (KR 2022) (2022)
21. Singleton, J., Booth, R.: Who's the expert? On multi-source belief change. In: Proceedings of the 19th International Conference on Principles of Knowledge Representation and Reasoning (KR 2022) (2022)
22. Tamargo, L.H., Deagustini, C.A., García, A.J., Falappa, M.A., Simari, G.R.: Multi-source multiple change on belief bases. Int. J. Approx. Reason. **110**, 145–163 (2019)
23. Thimm, M.: Inconsistency measurement. In: Ben Amor, N., Quost, B., Theobald, M. (eds.) SUM 2019. LNCS (LNAI), vol. 11940, pp. 9–23. Springer, Cham (2019). https://doi.org/10.1007/978-3-030-35514-2_2
24. Thimm, M., Wallner, J.P.: On the complexity of inconsistency measurement. Artif. Intell. **275**, 411–456 (2019)

Splitting Techniques for Conditional Belief Bases in the Context of c-Representations

Marco Wilhelm[1]([⊠]) [ID], Meliha Sezgin[1] [ID], Gabriele Kern-Isberner[1] [ID], Jonas Haldimann[2] [ID], Christoph Beierle[2] [ID], and Jesse Heyninck[3] [ID]

[1] Department of Computer Science, TU Dortmund University, Dortmund, Germany
{marco.wilhelm,meliha.sezgin}@tu-dortmund.de,
gabriele.kern-isberner@cs.tu-dortmund.de
[2] Department of Mathematics and Computer Science, FernUniversität in Hagen, Hagen, Germany
{jonas.haldimann,christoph.beierle}@fernuni-hagen.de
[3] Open Universiteit, Heerlen, The Netherlands
jesse.heyninck@ou.nl

Abstract. Splitting belief bases is fundamental for efficient reasoning and for better understanding interrelationships among the knowledge entities. In this paper, we survey the most important splitting techniques for conditional belief bases in the context of c-representations which constitute a specific class of ranking models with outstanding behavior not only with respect to belief base splitting, as shown in recent papers. We provide a splitting hierarchy, in particular by proving that safe conditional syntax splittings and case splittings are so-called CSP-constraint splittings. We advance the level of knowledge about CSP-constraint splittings and present an algorithm for computing CSP-constraint splittings.

1 Introduction

In logic-based knowledge representation, *conditionals* $(B|A)$ are used to express defeasible statements of the form "if A holds, then usually B holds, too" [16]. In qualitative settings, the formal semantics of such conditionals is usually given by *preference relations* over *possible worlds* [14]. Here, we express preferences by *ranking functions* κ [20] which assign a degree of implausibility to possible worlds and accept a conditional if its *verification* is more plausible than its *falsification*, i.e., iff $\kappa(A \wedge B) < \kappa(A \wedge \neg B)$. Such semantic approaches are typically computationally expensive because the number of possible worlds is exponential in the size of the underlying signature. Further, the influences of the conditionals in a belief base on the ranking functions usually interfere in an unapparent manner. Resolving spurious dependencies between the conditionals can lead to a *splitting* of the belief base with a beneficial influence on the performance of reasoning methods thanks to decomposition as local computations on the sub-bases reduce complexity in a natural way by restricting calculations to the relevant sub-signature. Consequently, investigating splitting techniques

S. Gaggl et al. (Eds.): JELIA 2023, LNAI 14281, pp. 462–477, 2023.
https://doi.org/10.1007/978-3-031-43619-2_32

for conditional belief bases both has a long tradition [17,18] and is still highly relevant [2,7,9,12,13].

In this paper, we survey the most important splitting techniques for conditional belief bases and provide a splitting hierarchy that helps unifying different approaches. In general, we say that a belief base Δ *splits* into a set of sub-bases $\mathcal{D} = \{\Delta_1, \ldots, \Delta_m\}$ iff $\mathcal{D}$ is a partition of Δ which satisfies additional properties specified by the respective splitting formalism. The most popular splitting formalism is *syntax splitting* [12,17] which forces the sub-bases Δ_i to be defined over disjoint sub-languages. Beyond syntax splitting there are further meaningful splitting techniques like *(safe) conditional syntax splitting* [9], *case splitting* [19], and *semantic splitting* [1]. (Safe) conditional syntax splitting generalizes syntax splitting by allowing the sub-bases to share parts of their syntax. Conditional syntax splitting is particularly interesting because it provides a general formalization of and solution to the well-known *drowning problem* [6,9] in nonmonotonic reasoning. *Case splitting* is somehow orthogonal to syntax splitting and splits belief bases into sub-bases that make statements about exclusive cases. The common goal of these splittings is to localize computations such that the ranking models of the sub-bases Δ_i can be assembled to a ranking model of the whole belief base Δ and, ideally, every model of Δ can be achieved in this way.

Here, we analyze and show relations between splitting techniques for conditional belief bases in the context of *c-representations* [10,11]. c-Representations constitute a specific class of ranking models which penalize possible worlds ω if they *falsify* a conditional $(B|A)$ from Δ, i.e., iff $\omega \models A \wedge \neg B$. The κ-rank of a possible world then is the sum of its penalty points. While c-representations have proved to provide most advanced methods for reasoning with conditionals, their basically semantic definition seems to necessarily imply a high computational complexity. Fortunately, c-representations are particularly amicable with regard to belief base splitting because they are given as solutions of a constraint satisfaction problem $\mathsf{CSP}_\Sigma(\Delta)$ which exploits the conditional logical structure of the belief base. In [1], the concept of *constraint splitting* of a belief base Δ is introduced, along with rewriting rules for simplifying $\mathsf{CSP}_\Sigma(\Delta)$. When the constraints in $\mathsf{CSP}_\Sigma(\Delta)$ split, this transfers to a splitting of Δ. Constraint splittings bring together syntactic and semantic aspects of splitting.

The main contributions of this paper are:

(a) We propose additional rewriting rules to further simplify the constraint satisfaction problem $\mathsf{CSP}_\Sigma(\Delta)$. This leads to more fine-grained CSP-*constraint splittings*. In addition, we provide an algorithm for computing CSP-constraint splittings.

(b) We provide a hierarchy of splitting techniques where CSP-constraint splittings have a central position. In particular, we prove that case splittings and safe conditional syntax splittings form a sub-class of CSP-constraint splittings. This allows for applying different splitting techniques to a belief base in a coherent setting.

The rest of the paper is organized as follows. First, we recall some foundations on conditional belief bases and c-representations. After that, we give a brief overview of basic splitting techniques (syntax splitting, CSP-solution splitting, and c-semantic splitting) before we discuss CSP-constraint splittings in detail. Eventually, we show that case splittings and safe conditional syntax splittings constitute sub-classes of (strong) CSP-constraint splittings and conclude.

2   Preliminaries

Let $\mathcal{L}(\Sigma)$ be a *propositional language* which is defined over a finite *signature* Σ by using the connectives $\neg$, $\wedge$, and $\vee$ as usual. We call elements in Σ *atoms* and use the abbreviations $\overline{A}$ for $\neg A$, AB for $A \wedge B$, $\top$ for $A \vee \overline{A}$, and $\bot$ for $A \wedge \overline{A}$.

We extend $\mathcal{L}(\Sigma)$ by *conditionals* $(B|A)$ where $A, B \in \mathcal{L}(\Sigma)$, stating that "if A holds, then usually B holds, too." With $\mathcal{CL}(\Sigma)$ we denote the set of all conditionals over Σ. A finite set of conditionals Δ is called *belief base*. Throughout the paper, we enumerate the conditionals in belief bases and write $\Delta = \{\delta_1, \ldots, \delta_n\}$. We refer to the *premise* and the *conclusion* of $\delta_i = (B_i|A_i)$ with A_i resp. B_i. With $\Sigma(\Delta)$ we denote the *signature* of Δ, i.e., the set of atoms which occur in Δ.

A common way of giving conditionals a formal semantics is by introducing *ranking functions* over *possible worlds* [5]. We represent possible worlds as complete conjunctions of *literals*, i.e., conjunctions in which every atom from Σ occurs once, either negated or positive. We denote the set of all possible worlds with $\Omega(\Sigma)$. If Σ' is a sub-signature of Σ, then $\omega \in \Omega(\Sigma)$ can be *marginalized* on Σ' via $\omega_{|\Sigma'} = \bigwedge_{a \in \Sigma'} \sigma_\omega(a)$ where $\sigma_\omega(a) = a$ if $\omega \models a$ and $\sigma_\omega(a) = \bar{a}$ otherwise.

Ranking functions $\kappa: \Omega(\Sigma) \to \mathbb{N}_0^\infty$ introduced by Spohn [20] map possible worlds to a degree of implausibility such that $\kappa^{-1}(0) \neq \emptyset$. The lower the rank of a possible world, the more plausible it is. Ranking functions are extended to formulas $A \in \mathcal{L}(\Sigma)$ by $\kappa(A) = \min\{\kappa(\omega) \mid \omega \models A\}$ and *model* a conditional $(B|A)$ if $\kappa(AB) < \kappa(A\overline{B})$. A ranking function κ is a *ranking model* of a belief base Δ iff κ models every conditional in Δ. If a belief base has a ranking model, then it is called *consistent*.

c-Representations constitute a specific class of ranking models [11]. Let

$$v_\Delta(\omega) = \{i \mid \delta_i \in \Delta, \ \omega \models A_i B_i\} \quad \text{and} \quad f_\Delta(\omega) = \{i \mid \delta_i \in \Delta, \ \omega \models A_i \overline{B_i}\}$$

record the conditionals from the belief base Δ which are *verified* resp. *falsified* in the possible world ω. Then, a ranking function is a *c-representation* of Δ if it is a ranking model of Δ and of the form

$$\kappa_\eta(\omega) = \sum_{i \in f_\Delta(\omega)} \eta_i, \qquad \boldsymbol{\eta} = (\eta_1, \ldots, \eta_n) \in \mathbb{N}_0^n,$$

where η_i is a *penalty point* for falsifying the i-th conditional in Δ and $\boldsymbol{\eta}$ satisfies

$$\eta_i > \min\{ \sum_{j \neq i: \ j \in f_\Delta(\omega)} \eta_j \mid \omega \in \Omega(\Sigma) : i \in v_\Delta(\omega)\}$$

$$- \min\{ \sum_{j \neq i: \ j \in f_\Delta(\omega)} \eta_j \mid \omega \in \Omega(\Sigma) : i \in f_\Delta(\omega)\}. \quad (1)$$

With $\mathsf{Mod}^c_\Sigma(\Delta)$ we denote the set of all c-representations of Δ over Σ. For a more in-depth discussion of c-representations, we refer to [11]. Here, we focus on c-representations particularly because of their outstanding compatibility with splitting techniques [12,13].

3 Syntax Splitting, CSP-Solution Splitting, and c-Semantic Splitting

We propose to split consistent belief bases Δ into partitions $\{\Delta_1, \ldots, \Delta_m\}$ with the goal to localize computations and, therewith, reduce the complexity of reasoning with c-representations and gain insights into (non-)dependencies between the conditionals in Δ. In terms of ranking models this means that the (local) ranking models of the sub-bases Δ_i can be assembled to a (global) ranking model of Δ and that, ideally, each model of Δ can be achieved in this way. The following definition transfers the concept of *semantic splittings* [1] to the context of c-representations.

Definition 1 (c-Semantic Splitting [1]). *Let Δ be a consistent belief base. A partition $\{\Delta_1, \ldots, \Delta_m\}$ of Δ is a c-semantic splitting if, for $i = 1, \ldots, m$, there is $\Sigma_i \subseteq \Sigma$ with $\Sigma(\Delta_i) \subseteq \Sigma_i$ such that $\mathsf{Mod}^c_\Sigma(\Delta) = \bigoplus_{i=1}^m \mathsf{Mod}^c_{\Sigma_i}(\Delta_i)$, where*

$$\bigoplus_{i=1}^m \mathsf{Mod}^c_{\Sigma_i}(\Delta_i) = \{\kappa \mid \kappa(\omega) = \sum_{i=1}^m \kappa_i(\omega_{|\Sigma_i}), \quad \omega \in \Omega(\Sigma), \kappa_i \in \mathsf{Mod}^c_{\Sigma_i}(\Delta_i)\}.$$

Because the c-representations of a consistent belief base Δ are calculated by solving the *constraint satisfaction problem* $\mathsf{CSP}_\Sigma(\Delta)$ given by (1), c-semantic splittings can be equivalently formulated on the basis of the solutions of $\mathsf{CSP}_\Sigma(\Delta)$. For this, we exploit that a vector $\boldsymbol{\eta} \in \mathbb{N}_0^n$ is a solution of $\mathsf{CSP}_\Sigma(\Delta)$ iff $\kappa_{\boldsymbol{\eta}}$ is a c-representation of Δ [11]. We denote the solution set of $\mathsf{CSP}_\Sigma(\Delta)$ with $\mathsf{Sol}(\mathsf{CSP}_\Sigma(\Delta))$.

Definition 2 (CSP-Solution Splitting [1]). *Let Δ be a consistent belief base. A partition $\{\Delta_1, \ldots, \Delta_m\}$ of Δ is a CSP-solution splitting if, for $i = 1, \ldots, m$, there is $\Sigma_i \subseteq \Sigma$ with $\Sigma(\Delta_i) \subseteq \Sigma_i$ such that*

$$\mathsf{Sol}(\mathsf{CSP}_\Sigma(\Delta)) = \bigotimes_{i=1}^m \mathsf{Sol}(\mathsf{CSP}_{\Sigma_i}(\Delta_i)),$$

where $\bigotimes$ is the concatenation of each combination of the solution vectors.[1]

One of the most intensively studied classes of splittings in the context of conditional belief bases is *syntax splitting* [2,7,9,12,13,17]. A belief base syntactically splits into sub-bases if the sub-bases have pairwise disjoint signatures.

---

[1] The entries of the concatenated solution vectors have to be reordered such that they fit the ordering of the conditionals in Δ.

Definition 3 (Syntax Splitting [12]). *Let Δ be a consistent belief base. A partition $\{\Delta_1, \ldots, \Delta_m\}$ of Δ is a syntax splitting if, for $i = 1, \ldots, m$, there is $\Sigma_i \subseteq \Sigma$ with $\Sigma(\Delta_i) \subseteq \Sigma_i$ such that*

$$\Sigma_i \cap \Sigma_j = \emptyset \text{ for } i, j \in \{1, \ldots, m\} \text{ with } i \neq j.$$

Syntax splittings constitute a proper sub-class of c-semantic splittings [1] and are easy to compute based on a syntactic comparison of the conditionals in Δ. However, only few belief bases syntactically split into fine-grained partitions as conditional statements about the same topic naturally share syntax elements.

In order to find further meaningful classes of c-semantic splittings, in [1] the constraint satisfaction problem $\mathsf{CSP}_\Sigma(\Delta)$ is investigated more closely following the idea that if sets of the constraints in $\mathsf{CSP}_\Sigma(\Delta)$ can be solved independently, then this leads to a CSP-solution splitting. In the following, we continue this line of research, identify CSP-*constraint splittings* as the central class of conditional belief base splittings in the context of c-representations, propose an algorithm for computing CSP-constraint splittings, and discuss important sub-classes of CSP-constraint splittings.

4   (Strong) CSP-Constraint Splitting

The constraint satisfaction problem $\mathsf{CSP}_\Sigma(\Delta)$ mentions for each conditional $\delta_i \in \Delta$ a distinct penalty point η_i and, likewise, a distinct constraint of the form (1). We denote the constraint that is associated with δ_i with C_i and the set of the conditionals whose associated penalty points are mentioned in C_i with $\mathsf{scope}(C_i)$. We say that a sub-base $\Delta' \subseteq \Delta$ is *constraint-wise independent* if the corresponding set of constraints, $\mathcal{C}(\Delta') = \{C_i \mid \delta_i \in \Delta'\}$, mentions penalty points that are associated with conditionals in Δ' only, i.e., if $\bigcup_{\delta_i \in \Delta'} \mathsf{scope}(C_i) \subseteq \Delta'$.

Definition 4 (Strong CSP-Constraint Splitting). *Let Δ be a consistent belief base. A partition $\{\Delta_1, \ldots, \Delta_m\}$ of Δ is a strong CSP-constraint splitting if, for $i = 1, \ldots, m$, the sub-base Δ_i is constraint-wise independent.*

Because the constraint sets $\mathcal{C}(\Delta_1), \ldots, \mathcal{C}(\Delta_m)$ of strong CSP-constraint splittings $\{\Delta_1, \ldots, \Delta_m\}$ can be solved independently, strong CSP-constraint splittings are CSP-solution splittings.

Example 1. Let $\Sigma_{e1} = \{a, b, c\}$ and $\Delta_{e1} = \{\delta_1, \delta_2, \delta_3\}$ with

$$\delta_1 = (b|a), \quad \delta_2 = (\bar{b}|\bar{a}), \quad \delta_3 = (b|\bar{a}c).$$

The constraint satisfaction problem $\mathsf{CSP}_{\Sigma_{e1}}(\Delta_{e1})$ consists of the constraints (cf. (1) and Table 1)

$$
\begin{aligned}
C_1: \quad & \eta_1 > \min\{0\} - \min\{0\}, \\
C_2: \quad & \eta_2 > \min\{0, \eta_3\} - \min\{0\}, \\
C_3: \quad & \eta_3 > \min\{\eta_2\} - \min\{0\}.
\end{aligned}
$$

Table 1. For each possible world $\omega \in \Omega(\Sigma_{e1})$, the verified and falsified conditionals from Δ_{e1} are shown (cf. Example 1).

ω	$v_{\Delta_{e1}}(\omega)$	$f_{\Delta_{e1}}(\omega)$	ω	$v_{\Delta_{e1}}(\omega)$	$f_{\Delta_{e1}}(\omega)$
abc	$\{1\}$	$\emptyset$	$\bar{a}bc$	$\{3\}$	$\{2\}$
$ab\bar{c}$	$\{1\}$	$\emptyset$	$\bar{a}b\bar{c}$	$\emptyset$	$\{2\}$
$a\bar{b}c$	$\emptyset$	$\{1\}$	$\bar{a}\bar{b}c$	$\{2\}$	$\{3\}$
$a\bar{b}\bar{c}$	$\emptyset$	$\{1\}$	$\bar{a}\bar{b}\bar{c}$	$\{2\}$	$\emptyset$

The constraint C_1 does not mention a penalty point other than η_1 and the two remaining constraints, C_2 and C_3, do not mention η_1. Hence, we have $\mathsf{scope}(C_1) = \{\delta_1\}$ and $\mathsf{scope}(C_2) \cup \mathsf{scope}(C_3) = \{\delta_2, \delta_3\}$ so that $\{\{\delta_1\}, \{\delta_2, \delta_3\}\}$ is a strong CSP-constraint splitting of Δ_{e1}.

Note that in the example above no syntax splitting is applicable to Δ because δ_3 mentions all three atoms. Nevertheless, on the level of CSP-constraint splittings, a semantic decomposition along conditional dependencies is possible.

It can happen that in constraints $C_i \in \mathsf{CSP}_\Sigma(\Delta)$ penalty points η_j with $j \neq i$ occur which do not affect the satisfaction of C_i. This particularly happens when the sums in the min-terms in (1) which mention η_j cannot change the minimum (like η_3 in C_2 in Example 1). In this case, the penalty point η_j may prevent the constraints in $\mathsf{CSP}_\Sigma(\Delta)$ from splitting "for no good reason." To counteract this, in [1] some generic strategies for simplifying the constraints in $\mathsf{CSP}_\Sigma(\Delta)$ are proposed which lead to more fine-grained splittings of the constraints by removing unnecessary dependencies between the penalty points. We continue this line of research and suggest further strategies for removing expressions from the min-terms in (1) which are redundant for the minima. Beforehand, $\mathsf{CSP}_\Sigma(\Delta)$ is transformed into a set representation first proposed in [3,4] that is a more convenient form for applying these simplifications.

Characterization 1 (Constraint Satisfaction Problem in Set Notation). *Let Δ be a consistent belief base. For $i = 1, \ldots, n$, let*

$$\breve{f}_\Delta^i(\omega) = \{j \mid \delta_j \in \Delta : j \neq i, \omega \models A_j \overline{B}_j\} = f_\Delta(\omega) \setminus \{i\}$$

be the index set of the conditionals in $\Delta \setminus \{\delta_i\}$ which are falsified in $\omega \in \Omega(\Sigma)$. Then, the limits of the sums in (1) can be rewritten from $\sum_{j \neq i: \, j \in f_\Delta(\omega)}$ to $\sum_{j \in \breve{f}_\Delta^i(\omega)}$ and we define

$$V_i = V_i(\Delta) = \{\breve{f}_\Delta^i(\omega) \mid \omega \in \Omega(\Sigma) : i \in v_\Delta(\omega)\}, \\ F_i = F_i(\Delta) = \{\breve{f}_\Delta^i(\omega) \mid \omega \in \Omega(\Sigma) : i \in f_\Delta(\omega)\}. \quad (2)$$

We obtain, for $i = 1, \ldots, n$, the following equivalent reformulation of (1):

$$\eta_i > \min\{\sum_{j \in S} \eta_j \mid S \in V_i\} - \min\{\sum_{j \in S} \eta_j \mid S \in F_i\}. \quad (3)$$

The only difference between the constraints (1) and (3) is that the conditions which restrict the sums in the min-terms are transferred to the definitions of the sets V_i and F_i. The benefit of this set-based representation of $\mathsf{CSP}_\Sigma(\Delta)$ is that we can modify $\mathsf{CSP}_\Sigma(\Delta)$ easily by set manipulation now. The goal of such a modification is to find representations of $\mathsf{CSP}_\Sigma(\Delta)$ which preserve the solutions in $\mathsf{Sol}(\mathsf{CSP}_\Sigma(\Delta))$ while yielding more fine-grained splittings of the constraints. We formalize the modifications by mappings called *constraint reductions*.

Definition 5 ((Solution Preserving) Constraint Reduction). *Let Δ be a consistent belief base. We call $\phi: (V_i, F_i)_{i=1,\ldots,n} \mapsto (\phi(V_i), \phi(F_i))_{i=1,\ldots,n}$ a constraint reduction if, for $i = 1,\ldots,n$, it holds that $\phi(V_i) \sqsubseteq V_i$ and $\phi(F_i) \sqsubseteq F_i$, where $X' \sqsubseteq X$ means that (a) for all $x' \in X'$, there is $x \in X$ such that $x' \subseteq x$, and (b) for all $x \in X$, there is $x' \in X'$ such that $x' \subseteq x$.*

A constraint reduction ϕ is solution preserving if, for all consistent belief bases Δ, it holds that $\mathsf{Sol}(\mathsf{CSP}_\Sigma^\phi(\Delta)) = \mathsf{Sol}(\mathsf{CSP}_\Sigma(\Delta))$, where $\mathsf{CSP}_\Sigma^\phi(\Delta)$ is the constraint satisfaction problem $\mathsf{CSP}_\Sigma(\Delta)$ after applying ϕ, i.e., $\mathsf{CSP}_\Sigma^\phi(\Delta)$ is given by, for $i = 1,\ldots,n$,

$$C_i^\phi: \quad \eta_i > \min\{\sum_{j \in S} \eta_j \mid S \in \phi(V_i)\} - \min\{\sum_{j \in S} \eta_j \mid S \in \phi(F_i)\}. \tag{4}$$

We abbreviate "solution preserving constraint reduction" with spcr.

Constraint reductions remove sets from V_i resp. F_i or elements from sets in V_i resp. F_i. The most radical constraint reduction maps both V_i and F_i to $\{\emptyset\}$ which satisfies the conditions (a) and (b) in Definition 5 but perhaps affects the solutions of the constraint satisfaction problem and, hence, is not always solution preserving. In [1], it is shown that a constraint reduction ϕ is solution preserving if it is specified by the (repeated) application of the following rewriting rules.

R1 If $S, S' \in V_i$ with $S \subset S'$, then $V_i \leftarrow V_i \setminus \{S'\}$.
R2 If $S, S' \in F_i$ with $S \subset S'$, then $F_i \leftarrow F_i \setminus \{S'\}$.
R3 If $V_i \neq \{\emptyset\} \neq F_i$ and $j \in S$ for all $S \in V_i \cup F_i$, then

$$V_i \leftarrow \{S \setminus \{j\} \mid S \in V_i\} \text{ and } F_i \leftarrow \{S \setminus \{j\} \mid S \in F_i\}.$$

Here we propose three further rewriting rules, **R4-R6**.

R4 If $V_i = F_i$, then $V_i \leftarrow \{\emptyset\}$ and $F_i \leftarrow \{\emptyset\}$.
R5 If there are $\mathcal{D} \subseteq 2^{\{1,\ldots,n\}}$ and $T, T' \subseteq \{1,\ldots,n\}$ such that

$$V_i = \{S \,\dot\cup\, T \mid S \in \mathcal{D}\} \text{ and } F_i = \{S \,\dot\cup\, T' \mid S \in \mathcal{D}\},$$

then $V_i \leftarrow \{T\}$ and $F_i \leftarrow \{T'\}$.
R6 If $F_i = F_j = \{\emptyset\}$ for $i \neq j$ and there is $\mathcal{D} \subseteq 2^{\{1,\ldots,n\}}$ such that $V_i = \mathcal{D} \cup \{\{j\}\}$ and $V_j = \mathcal{D} \cup \{\{i\}\}$, then $V_i \leftarrow \mathcal{D}$ and $V_j \leftarrow \mathcal{D}$.

Beyond **R1-R6**, further rewriting rules are imaginable. Nevertheless, **R1-R6** implement major and straightforward ideas for eliminating structural redundancies in (1). We give examples for the application of **R1-R6** below.

Proposition 1. *Let Δ be a consistent belief base. If a constraint reduction ϕ is specified by exhaustively applying any subset of the rewriting rules **R1-R6**, then ϕ is solution preserving. $\mathsf{CSP}^\phi_\Sigma(\Delta)$ is independent of the order in which the rules are applied if ϕ is specified by any superset of **R1+R2**.*

Proof. We show that the application of **R6** is solution preserving. The rest of the proof is omitted due to space restrictions.

For $i, j \in \{1, \ldots, n\}$ with $i \neq j$, let $F_i = F_j = \{\emptyset\}$, and let $\mathcal{D} \subseteq 2^{\{1,\ldots,n\}}$ such that $V_i = \mathcal{D} \cup \{\{j\}\}$ and $V_j = \mathcal{D} \cup \{\{i\}\}$. Then, for i and j, (3) becomes

$$\eta_i > \min(\{\sum_{k \in S} \eta_k \mid S \in \mathcal{D}\} \cup \{\eta_j\}) =: \min \mathcal{H}_i,$$

$$\eta_j > \min(\{\sum_{k \in S} \eta_k \mid S \in \mathcal{D}\} \cup \{\eta_i\}) =: \min \mathcal{H}_j.$$

Assume that $\eta_j = \min \mathcal{H}_i$ and $\eta_i = \min \mathcal{H}_j$. Then, for i and j, (3) reduces to $\eta_i > \eta_j$ resp. $\eta_j > \eta_i$ which is obviously contradictory. Now, assume that $\eta_j = \min \mathcal{H}_i$ and $H = \min \mathcal{H}_j$ for some $H \in \{\sum_{k \in S} \eta_k \mid S \in \mathcal{D}\}$ with $H < \eta_i$. Then, (3) becomes $\eta_j > H$ which contradicts the assumption that η_j minimizes $\mathcal{H}_i$ (note that $H \in \mathcal{H}_i$).

Putting both cases together, we have that η_j cannot be minimal in $\mathcal{H}_i$. Analogously, we can show that η_i is not minimal in $\mathcal{H}_j$, and (3) simplifies to

$$\eta_i > \min\{\sum_{k \in S} \eta_k \mid S \in \mathcal{D}\}, \quad \eta_j > \min\{\sum_{k \in S} \eta_k \mid S \in \mathcal{D}\},$$

which proves the statement. $\qquad\qquad\qquad\qquad\qquad\qquad\qquad\qquad\qquad\qquad\quad\square$

Based on solution preserving constraint reductions, we have the following advanced notion of CSP-*constraint splitting*.

Definition 6 (CSP-constraint splitting (cf. [1])). *Let Δ be a consistent belief base. A partition $\{\Delta_1, \ldots, \Delta_m\}$ of Δ is a CSP-constraint splitting if there is a solution preserving constraint reduction ϕ such that, for $i = 1, \ldots, m$, it holds that $\bigcup_{\delta_j \in \Delta_i} \mathsf{scope}(C^\phi_j) \subseteq \Delta_i$.*

The essence of CSP-constraint splittings is that the sub-bases Δ_i are constraint-wise independent *after applying an* spcr *to the constraints in* $\mathsf{CSP}_\Sigma(\Delta)$ and, therewith, generalize strong CSP-constraint splittings.

Example 2. Let $\Sigma_{e2} = \{a, b, c, d\}$ and $\Delta_{e2} = \{\delta_1, \ldots, \delta_4\}$ with

$$\delta_1 = (b|a), \quad \delta_2 = (c|a), \quad \delta_3 = (d|a), \quad \delta_4 = (\bar{c}|b).$$

Table 2 shows for each possible world $\omega \in \Omega(\Sigma_{e2})$ the verified and falsified conditionals. Based on that, we compute the sets V_i and F_i for $i = 1, \ldots, 4$ (Table 3) and apply the spcr ϕ specified by the rewriting rules **R1-R3** (Table 4). Now, $\phi(V_3) = \phi(F_3)$ holds such that rule **R4** applies. In addition, $\phi(F_1) = \phi(F_2) = \{\emptyset\}$

Table 2. For each possible world $\omega \in \Omega(\Sigma_{e2})$, the verified and falsified conditionals from Δ_{e2} are shown (cf. Example 2).

ω	$v_{\Delta_{e2}}(\omega)$	$f_{\Delta_{e2}}(\omega)$	ω	$v_{\Delta_{e2}}(\omega)$	$f_{\Delta_{e2}}(\omega)$
$abcd$	$\{1,2,3\}$	$\{4\}$	$\bar{a}bcd$	$\emptyset$	$\{4\}$
$abc\bar{d}$	$\{1,2\}$	$\{3,4\}$	$\bar{a}bc\bar{d}$	$\emptyset$	$\{4\}$
$ab\bar{c}d$	$\{1,3,4\}$	$\{2\}$	$\bar{a}b\bar{c}d$	$\{4\}$	$\emptyset$
$ab\bar{c}\bar{d}$	$\{1,4\}$	$\{2,3\}$	$\bar{a}b\bar{c}\bar{d}$	$\{4\}$	$\emptyset$
$a\bar{b}cd$	$\{2,3\}$	$\{1\}$	$\bar{a}\bar{b}cd$	$\emptyset$	$\emptyset$
$a\bar{b}c\bar{d}$	$\{2\}$	$\{1,3\}$	$\bar{a}\bar{b}c\bar{d}$	$\emptyset$	$\emptyset$
$a\bar{b}\bar{c}d$	$\{3\}$	$\{1,2\}$	$\bar{a}\bar{b}\bar{c}d$	$\emptyset$	$\emptyset$
$a\bar{b}\bar{c}\bar{d}$	$\emptyset$	$\{1,2,3\}$	$\bar{a}\bar{b}\bar{c}\bar{d}$	$\emptyset$	$\emptyset$

Table 3. For each conditional $\delta_i \in \Delta_{e2}$, the sets V_i and F_i are shown (cf. Example 2).

δ_i	V_i	F_i
$(b\|a)$	$\{\{2\},\{2,3\},\{3,4\},\{4\}\}$	$\{\emptyset,\{2\},\{2,3\},\{3\}\}$
$(c\|a)$	$\{\{1\},\{1,3\},\{3,4\},\{4\}\}$	$\{\emptyset,\{1\},\{1,3\},\{3\}\}$
$(d\|a)$	$\{\{1\},\{2\},\{1,2\},\{4\}\}$	$\{\{1\},\{1,2\},\{2\},\{4\}\}$
$(\bar{c}\|b)$	$\{\emptyset,\{2\},\{2,3\}\}$	$\{\emptyset,\{3\}\}$

and there is $\mathcal{D} = \{\{4\}\}$ such that $\phi(V_1) = \mathcal{D} \cup \{\{2\}\}$ and $\phi(V_2) = \mathcal{D} \cup \{\{1\}\}$, i.e., rule **R6** applies, too. Thus, we consider a second spcr ϕ' which is specified by **R1-R6**. The results of applying ϕ' are also shown in Table 4. We realize that $\{\{\delta_1, \delta_2, \delta_4\}, \{\delta_3\}\}$ is a constraint splitting of Δ_{e2}: In the simplified constraint $C_1^{\phi'}$, the penalty points η_1 and η_4 are mentioned (cf. Table 3), i.e., $\mathsf{scope}(C_1^{\phi'}) = \{\delta_1, \delta_4\}$. In addition, $\mathsf{scope}(C_2^{\phi'}) = \{\delta_2, \delta_4\}$ and $\mathsf{scope}(C_4^{\phi'}) = \{\delta_4\}$ and, consequently, δ_1, δ_2 and δ_4 have to be in the same partitioning set. In contrast, the simplified constraint $C_3^{\phi'}$ mentions η_3 only, i.e., $\mathsf{scope}(C_3^{\phi'}) = \{\delta_3\}$, and δ_3 builds its own partitioning set. Note that this is not reachable on the basis of ϕ. In the end, the constraint satisfaction problem of Δ_{e2} has been simplified to

$$\mathsf{CSP}_{\Sigma}^{\phi'}(\Delta_{e2}) = \{\ \eta_1 > \eta_4,\quad \eta_2 > \eta_4,\quad \eta_3 > 0,\quad \eta_4 > 0\ \},$$

and a (minimal) c-representation κ_{η} of Δ_{e2} is given by $\boldsymbol{\eta} = (2,2,1,1)$. Note that this example illustrates the quality of c-representations well because κ_{η} does not suffer from the *drowning problem* (cf. [9]) as it still accepts both conditionals $(d|a\bar{b})$ and $(d|a\bar{c})$, which cannot be ensured by System Z [6], for instance.

Example 3. Let $\Sigma_{e3} = \{a, b, c, d\}$ and $\Delta_{e3} = \{\delta_1, \ldots, \delta_5\}$ with

$$\delta_1 = (c|a), \quad \delta_2 = (\bar{c}|b), \quad \delta_3 = (c|ab), \quad \delta_4 = (d|a), \quad \delta_5 = (\bar{d}|b).$$

Table 4. For each conditional $\delta_i \in \Delta_{e2}$, the sets V_i and F_i are shown after applying one of the spcrs ϕ and ϕ' (cf. Example 2).

δ_i	$\phi(V_i)$	$\phi(F_i)$	$\phi'(V_i)$	$\phi'(F_i)$
$(b\|a)$	$\{\{2\},\{4\}\}$	$\{\emptyset\}$	$\{\{4\}\}$	$\{\emptyset\}$
$(c\|a)$	$\{\{1\},\{4\}\}$	$\{\emptyset\}$	$\{\{4\}\}$	$\{\emptyset\}$
$(d\|a)$	$\{\{1\},\{2\},\{4\}\}$	$\{\{1\},\{2\},\{4\}\}$	$\{\emptyset\}$	$\{\emptyset\}$
$(\bar{c}\|b)$	$\{\emptyset\}$	$\{\emptyset\}$	$\{\emptyset\}$	$\{\emptyset\}$

Algorithm 1. (Computation of CSP-Constraint Splittings)

Input: Consistent belief base Δ, solution preserving constraint reduction ϕ
Output: CSP-Constraint splitting $\{\Delta_1,\ldots,\Delta_m\}$ of Δ

```
1    for i = 1,...,n:
2        calculate Vᵢ and Fᵢ and reduce to Vᵢ ← φ(Vᵢ) and Fᵢ ← φ(Fᵢ)
3        Iᵢ = {i} ∪ ⋃_{S∈Vᵢ} S ∪ ⋃_{S∈Fᵢ} S
4    I = {I₁,...,Iₙ}
5    while I, J ∈ I with I ≠ J and I ∩ J ≠ ∅:
6        I ← (I ∪ {I ∪ J}) \ {I, J}
7    m = 1
8    while I ≠ ∅:
9        select I from I and set Δₘ = {δⱼ | j ∈ I}
10       I ← I \ {I} and m ← m + 1
11   return {Δ₁,...,Δₘ}
```

One has $V_3 = \{\{2,4\},\{2,5\}\}$ and $F_3 = \{\{1,4\},\{1,5\}\}$. From this, we deduce that the only strong CSP-constraint splitting of Δ_{e3} is the trivial splitting $\{\Delta_{e3}\}$. Applying the rewriting rules **R1-R3** do not change V_3 and F_3. Applying an spcr ϕ which uses rule **R5**, in addition, yields $\phi(V_3) - \{\{2\}\}$ and $\phi(F_3) = \{\{1\}\}$, however, because $\{\{4\},\{5\}\}$ takes the role of $\mathcal{D}$ in **R5**. Further, one can show that $\phi(V_i) = \phi(F_i) = \{\emptyset\}$ holds for $i = 1, 2, 4, 5$ such that $\{\{\delta_1, \delta_2, \delta_3\}, \{\delta_4, \delta_5\}\}$ is a CSP-constraint splitting of Δ_{e3}.

Of course, each strong CSP-constraint splitting is also a CSP-constraint splitting as the identity mapping is solution preserving. In [1], it is shown that syntax splittings are CSP-constraint splittings and CSP-constraint splittings are CSP-solution splittings. But, typically, syntax splittings are not strong CSP-constraint splittings. For example, $\{(b|a), (d|c)\}$ syntactically splits into $\mathcal{D} = \{\{(b|a)\}, \{(d|c)\}\}$ but the possible world $\omega = a\bar{b}c\bar{d}$ falsifies both conditionals which already shows that $\mathcal{D}$ is not a strong CSP-constraint splitting.

Next, we discuss how to algorithmically compute CSP-constraint splittings. The definition of CSP-constraint splittings is constructive in the sense that a CSP-constraint splitting of a consistent belief base Δ can be obtained just by comparing the sets $V_i(\Delta)$ and $F_i(\Delta)$ for $i = 1,\ldots,n$ which, if desired, were simplified by a solution preserving constrained transformation (spcr) beforehand. The general procedure is shown in Algorithm 1. First, for all conditionals $\delta_i \in \Delta$,

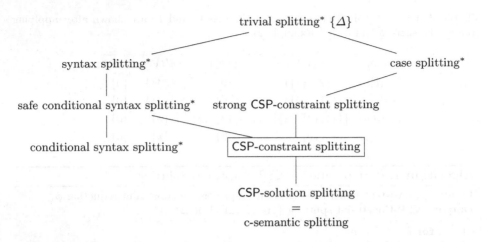

Fig. 1. Hierarchy of splitting techniques for conditional belief bases Δ in the context of c-representations. Splitting techniques marked with * are independent of the semantics of c-representations. Implications are to be read from top to bottom along the lines.

the sets V_i and F_i are calculated and reduced by an spcr ϕ (lines 1+2). Then, the indices of the involved conditionals are extracted (lines 3+4). As long as these sets of indices are not pairwise disjoint, intersecting sets are consolidated (lines 5+6). This procedure results in a partition $\mathcal{I}$ of $\{1, \ldots, n\}$. Each partitioning set $I_i \in \mathcal{I}$ corresponds to a set of conditionals Δ_i which is calculated and returned as part of the CSP-constraint splitting of Δ (lines 7–11).

Example 4. We illustrate how Algorithm 1 works for the input (Δ_{e2}, ϕ') from Example 2. The sets calculated in lines 1+2 of Algorithm 1 are already shown in the Tables 3 and 4. From these, we calculate the sets of indices I_i for $i = 1, \ldots, 4$ and obtain $\mathcal{I} = \{\{1,4\}, \{2,4\}, \{3\}, \{4\}\}$ (lines 3+4). Because the first two sets in $\mathcal{I}$ are not disjoint, we update $\mathcal{I}$ according to lines 7–10: $\mathcal{I} \leftarrow \{\{1,2,4\}, \{3\}, \{4\}\}$. Now, joining the first and the last set from $\mathcal{I}$ yields $\mathcal{I} \leftarrow \{\{1,2,4\}, \{3\}\}$ which corresponds to the CSP-constraint splitting $\{\{\delta_1, \delta_2, \delta_4\}, \{\delta_3\}\}$ that we already calculated in Example 2.

Syntax splittings do not constitute the only important sub-class of CSP-constraint splittings. In the next two sections, we consider two kinds of splittings where the sub-signatures of the belief bases are not disjoint but can nevertheless be captured by CSP-constraint splitting. More precisely, we show that so-called *case splittings* are strong CSP-constraint splittings and *safe conditional syntax splittings* are CSP-constraint splittings. Figure 1 shows interrelationships among these splittings, identifying CSP-constraint splitting as a central splitting technique which combines ideas from both syntax and case splittings.

5   Case Splitting

Case splittings are splittings of belief bases which were initially discussed in the context of belief change (cf. [19], here named as *premise splittings*). The idea of case splittings is to split a consistent belief base Δ into sub-bases that deal with different, exclusive cases.

Definition 7 (Case Splitting [19]). *Let Δ be a consistent belief base. A partition $\{\Delta_1, \ldots, \Delta_m\}$ of Δ is a* case splitting *if there is a set of exhaustive and exclusive formulas $\{E_1, \ldots, E_m\} \subseteq \mathcal{L}(\Sigma)$, i.e., $E_i \wedge E_j \equiv \bot$ for $i \neq j$ and $\bigvee_{i=1}^m E_i \equiv \top$, such that, for $i = 1, \ldots, m$ and for all conditionals $(B|A) \in \Delta_i$, it holds that $A \models E_i$.*

In plain words, the sub-base Δ_i of a case splitting $\{\Delta_1, \ldots, \Delta_m\}$ deals with beliefs about what happens in case of E_i.

Example 5. Let $\Sigma_{e4} = \{a, b, c, d\}$ and $\Delta_{e4} = \{\delta_1, \delta_2, \delta_3\}$ with $\delta_1 = (b|a)$, $\delta_2 = (\bar{b}|\bar{a}c)$, and $\delta_3 = (d|a \vee \bar{c})$. Then, $\{\{\delta_1, \delta_3\}, \{\delta_2\}\}$ is a case splitting of Δ_{e4} because the set $\{a \vee \bar{c}, \bar{a}c\}$ is a set of exhaustive and exclusive formulas with $a \models a \vee \bar{c}$ and $a \vee \bar{c} \models a \vee \bar{c}$ as well as $\bar{a}c \models \bar{a}c$.

Note that the strong CSP-constraint splitting from Example 1 is also a case splitting.

Proposition 2. *Let Δ be a consistent belief base. Every case splitting of Δ is a strong CSP-constraint splitting of Δ.*

Proof. Let $\mathcal{D} = \{\Delta_1, \ldots, \Delta_m\}$ be a case splitting of Δ wrt. the set of exhaustive and exclusive formulas $\{E_1, \ldots, E_m\}$, let $i \in \{1, \ldots, m\}$, and let $\delta_j \in \Delta_i$. We have to show that there is no $\delta_k \in \Delta \setminus \Delta_i$ such that there is $S \in V_j \cup F_j$ with $k \in S$. That is, because $V_j \cup F_j = \{f^j \Delta(\omega) \mid \omega \in \Omega(\Sigma) \colon \omega \models A_j\}$, we have to show that there is no $\omega \in \Omega(\Sigma)$ with $\omega \models A_j$ and $\omega \models A_k \overline{B_k}$. This, however, cannot happen as $\omega \models A_j$ implies $\omega \models E_i$ (because $\delta_j \in \Delta_i$) and $\omega \models A_k \overline{B_k}$ implies $\omega \models E_l$ for some $l \in \{1, \ldots, m\} \setminus \{i\}$ (because $\delta_k \in \Delta \setminus \Delta_i$). This would imply that $\omega \models E_i \wedge E_l \equiv \bot$ which is a contradiction. $\square$

While syntax splittings split belief bases on a syntactic level, case splittings take on a semantic perspective. Actually, the exclusiveness of the cases $E_1, \ldots, E_m$ leads to an inherent syntactic linkage between the conditionals in Δ. Thus, both splitting mechanisms can be seen as orthogonal counterparts. In particular, case splittings form a distinct sub-class of CSP-constraint splittings and both case splittings and syntax splittings constitute strict sub-classes of CSP-constraints splittings. Note that the two splitting techniques can be applied consecutively to obtain even more fine-grained splittings.

6   (Safe) Conditional Syntax Splitting

In [8] a conditional version of syntax splitting is introduced.

Definition 8 (Conditional Syntax Splitting [8]). *Let Δ be a consistent belief base. A partition $\{\Delta_1, \ldots, \Delta_m\}$ of Δ is a conditional syntax splitting if there are $\Sigma_0, \Sigma_1, \ldots, \Sigma_m \subseteq \Sigma$ such that $\Sigma(\Delta_i) \subseteq \Sigma_i \cup \Sigma_0$ for $i = 1, \ldots, m$, and $\Sigma_i \cap \Sigma_j = \emptyset$ for $i, j = 0, 1, \ldots, m$ with $i \neq j$.*

The sub-bases of a conditional syntax splitting syntactically split except for some atoms from Σ_0. With $\Sigma_0 = \emptyset$, every syntax splitting is also a conditional syntax splitting. But, in general, not all conditional syntax splittings are CSP-constraint splittings as the following example shows.

Example 6. We consider Σ_{e2} and Δ_{e2} from Example 2. The partition

$$\mathcal{D} = \{ \quad \{(b|a), (\bar{c}|b)\}, \quad \{(c|a), (d|a)\} \quad \}$$

of Δ_{e2} is a conditional syntax splitting. To see this, let $\Sigma_0 = \{a, c\}$, $\Sigma_1 = \{b\}$, and $\Sigma_2 = \{d\}$. Then, $(b|a), (\bar{c}|b) \in \mathcal{CL}(\Sigma_1 \cup \Sigma_0)$ and $(c|a), (d|a) \in \mathcal{CL}(\Sigma_2 \cup \Sigma_0)$. However, $\mathcal{D}$ is not a CSP-constraint splitting of Δ_{e2}. Table 3 shows that the penalty point η_4 is mentioned in the constraint $C_2^{\phi'}$, and there is no solution preserving constraint reduction which can remove η_4 from $C_2^{\phi'}$ (obviously, there cannot be a more effective reduction than ϕ' from Example 2 because η_4 is relevant for the minimum of the first min-term in $C_2^{\phi'}$).

Under specific conditions, however, it can be guaranteed that conditional syntax splittings are CSP-constraint splittings (cf. [8]).

Definition 9 (Safe Conditional Syntax Splitting [8]). *Let Δ be a consistent belief base. A partition $\{\Delta_1, \ldots, \Delta_m\}$ of Δ is a safe conditional syntax splitting if it is a conditional syntax splitting wrt. the sub-signatures $\Sigma_0, \Sigma_1, \ldots, \Sigma_m$ and, in addition, for $i = 1, \ldots, m$ and every $\omega \in \Omega(\Sigma_i \cup \Sigma_0)$, there is $\omega' \in \Omega(\Sigma \setminus (\Sigma_i \cup \Sigma_0))$ such that $\omega \wedge \omega' \in \Omega(\Sigma)$ falsifies no conditional from $\Delta \setminus \Delta_i$.*

Safe conditional syntax splitting ensures locality for falsification which is also the basic idea of constraint-wise independence.

Proposition 3. *Let Δ be a consistent belief base. Every safe conditional syntax splitting of Δ is a CSP-constraint splitting of Δ.*

Proof. Let $\mathcal{D} = \{\Delta_1, \ldots, \Delta_m\}$ be a safe conditional syntax splitting of Δ, let $i \in \{1, \ldots, m\}$, and let $\delta_j \in \Delta_i$. We have to show that there is an spcr ϕ such that no $\delta_k \in \Delta \setminus \Delta_i$ exists such that there is $S \in \phi(V_j) \cup \phi(F_j)$ with $k \in S$. By assumption, $\Delta_i \subseteq \mathcal{CL}(\Sigma_i \cup \Sigma_0)$ and, hence, $\delta_j \in \mathcal{CL}(\Sigma_i \cup \Sigma_0)$. Thus, for all $\omega \in \Omega(\Sigma)$ with $\omega \models A_j B_j$ it holds that $\omega_{|(\Sigma_i \cup \Sigma_0)} \models A_j B_j$. Each of these (partial) possible worlds $\omega_{|(\Sigma_i \cup \Sigma_0)}$ can be completed to a possible world $\hat{\omega} \in \Omega(\Sigma)$ such that $\hat{\omega}$ does not falsify any conditional from $\Delta \setminus \Delta_i$ (because $\mathcal{D}$ is safe). As a consequence, for each set $S \in V_j$, there is a set $S' \in V_j$ with $S' \subseteq S$ and $S' \subseteq T_i$ where $T_i = \{l \mid \delta_l \in \Delta_i\}$. Eventually, let ϕ be an spcr which applies **R1**. Then, $\phi(V_j) \subseteq 2^{T_i}$. Analogously, one can show that $\phi(F_j) \subseteq 2^{T_i}$ if ϕ also applies **R2**. Together, one has $\phi(V_j) \cup \phi(F_j) \subseteq 2^{T_i}$ and it is impossible to find a conditional $\delta_k \in \Delta \setminus \Delta_i$ such that k is an element of any set $S \in \phi(V_j) \cup \phi(F_j)$ (because $k \notin T_i$). □

We eventually give an example which illustrates the concept of safeness for conditional syntax splittings.

Example 7. We consider Σ_{e2} and Δ_{e2} from Example 2 but now split Δ_{e2} into

$$\mathcal{D}' = \{ \quad \{(b|a),(c|a),(c|\bar{b})\}, \quad \{(d|a)\} \quad \}.$$

$\mathcal{D}'$ is a conditional syntax splitting of Δ_{e2} with $\Sigma_0 = \{a\}$, $\Sigma_1 = \{b,c\}$, and $\Sigma_2 = \{d\}$. In contrast to $\mathcal{D}$ from Example 6, $\mathcal{D}'$ is safe:

$\mathcal{D}$ is not safe because the possible world $ab\bar{c} \in \Omega(\{a,b,c\})$ (cf. Example 6 for the sub-signatures used for the splitting $\mathcal{D}$) can not be completed to a possible world $\omega \in \Omega(\{a,b,c,d\})$ such that both $\omega \models ab\bar{c}$ and there is no conditional from $\{(c|a),(d|a)\}$ which is falsified because $(c|a)$ is already falsified by $ab\bar{c}$. $\mathcal{D}'$, however, is safe as every possible world $\omega_1 \in \Omega(\{a,b,c\})$ can be completed to $\omega_1 \wedge d$ which does not falsify $(d|a)$, independent of the specification of ω_1. In addition, every possible world $\omega_2 \in \Omega(\{a,d\})$ can be completed to $\omega_2 \wedge bc$ which does not falsify any conditional from $\{(b|a),(c|a),(c|\bar{b})\}$. Note that $\mathcal{D}'$ is the CSP-constraint splitting of Δ_{e2} calculated in Example 2.

7   Conclusions and Future Work

Splitting techniques are fundamental for organizing conditional belief bases both in order to better understand interdependencies between the conditionals and to reduce computational costs when performing model-based reasoning like reasoning with c-representations. In this paper, we gave an overview of the most common splitting techniques for conditional belief bases in the context of c-representations and provided a hierarchy of these splitting techniques. In particular, we identified CSP-constraint splittings as a central class of splittings that combines ideas from both syntax and case splitting by proving that every case splitting is a strong CSP-constraint splitting and that every safe conditional syntax splitting is a CSP-constraint splitting. The impact of our findings goes beyond c-representations. For example, it has been shown in [9] that lexicographic inference [15] can be represented as a c-representation, and thus, all splitting techniques studied in this paper also apply to lexicographic inference.

In future work, we want to elaborate further rewriting rules in order to minimize the gap between CSP-constraint splittings and CSP-solution splittings and study how the splitting techniques can be applied to other inductive inference formalisms. Our main focus, however, will be on the extension of CSP-constraint splittings to a notion of CSP-constraint networks in the case where the belief bases do not split satisfactorily.

Acknowledgments. This work was supported by grants of the German Research Foundation (DFG) awarded to Gabriele Kern-Isberner (KE 1413/14-1) and to Christoph Beierle (BE 1700/10-1).

References

1. Beierle, C., Haldimann, J., Kern-Isberner, G.: Semantic splitting of conditional belief bases. In: Raschke, A., Riccobene, E., Schewe, K.-D. (eds.) Logic, Computation and Rigorous Methods. LNCS, vol. 12750, pp. 82–95. Springer, Cham (2021). https://doi.org/10.1007/978-3-030-76020-5_5
2. Beierle, C., Kern-Isberner, G.: Selection strategies for inductive reasoning from conditional belief bases and for belief change respecting the principle of conditional preservation. In: Bell, E., Keshtkar, F. (eds.) Proceedings of the Thirty-Fourth International Florida Artificial Intelligence Research Society Conference, North Miami Beach, Florida, USA, 17–19 May 2021 (2021)
3. Beierle, C., Kutsch, S., Sauerwald, K.: Compilation of conditional knowledge bases for computing C-inference relations. In: Ferrarotti, F., Woltran, S. (eds.) FoIKS 2018. LNCS, vol. 10833, pp. 34–54. Springer, Cham (2018). https://doi.org/10.1007/978-3-319-90050-6_3
4. Beierle, C., Kutsch, S., Sauerwald, K.: Compilation of static and evolving conditional knowledge bases for computing induced nonmonotonic inference relations. Ann. Math. Artif. Intell. **87**(1–2), 5–41 (2019)
5. Carnap, R.: Meaning and Necessity: A Study in Semantics and Modal Logic. University of Chicago Press, Chicago (1947)
6. Goldszmidt, M., Pearl, J.: Qualitative probabilities for default reasoning, belief revision, and causal modeling. Artif. Intell. **84**, 57–112 (1996)
7. Haldimann, J., Beierle, C.: Inference with system W satisfies syntax splitting. In: Kern-Isberner, G., Lakemeyer, G., Meyer, T. (eds.) Proceedings of the 19th International Conference on Principles of Knowledge Representation and Reasoning, KR 2022, Haifa, Israel, 31 July–5 August 2022 (2022)
8. Heyninck, J., Kern-Isberner, G., Meyer, T., Haldimann, J.P., Beierle, C.: Conditional syntax splitting for non-monotonic inference operators. In: Proceedings of the AAAI Conference on Artificial Intelligence, vol. 37, pp. 6416–6424 (2023)
9. Heyninck, J., Kern-Isberner, G., Meyer, T.A.: Lexicographic entailment, syntax splitting and the drowning problem. In: Raedt, L.D. (ed.) Proceedings of the Thirty-First International Joint Conference on Artificial Intelligence, IJCAI 2022, Vienna, Austria, 23–29 July 2022, pp. 2662–2668. ijcai.org (2022)
10. Kern-Isberner, G.: Conditionals in Nonmonotonic Reasoning and Belief Revision, vol. 2087. Springer, Heidelberg (2001). https://doi.org/10.1007/3-540-44600-1
11. Kern-Isberner, G.: A thorough axiomatization of a principle of conditional preservation in belief revision. Ann. Math. Artif. Intell. **40**(1–2), 127–164 (2004)
12. Kern-Isberner, G., Beierle, C., Brewka, G.: Syntax splitting = relevance + independence: new postulates for nonmonotonic reasoning from conditional belief bases. In: Calvanese, D., Erdem, E., Thielscher, M. (eds.) Proceedings of the 17th International Conference on Principles of Knowledge Representation and Reasoning, KR 2020, Rhodes, Greece, 12–18 September 2020, pp. 560–571 (2020)
13. Kern-Isberner, G., Brewka, G.: Strong syntax splitting for iterated belief revision. In: Sierra, C. (ed.) Proceedings of the Twenty-Sixth International Joint Conference on Artificial Intelligence, IJCAI 2017, Melbourne, Australia, 19–25 August 2017, pp. 1131–1137. ijcai.org (2017)

14. Kraus, S., Lehmann, D., Magidor, M.: Nonmonotonic reasoning, preferential models and cumulative logics. Artif. Intell. **44**(1–2), 167–207 (1990)
15. Lehmann, D.: Another perspective on default reasoning. Ann. Math. Artif. Intell. **15**(1), 61–82 (1995)
16. Nute, D.: Conditional Logic. In: Gabbay, D., Guenthner, F. (eds.) Handbook of Philosophical Logic, pp. 387–439. Springer, Dordrecht (1984). https://doi.org/10.1007/978-94-009-6259-0_8
17. Parikh, R.: Beliefs, belief revision, and splitting languages, pp. 266–278. Center for the Study of Language and Information (1999)
18. Pearl, J.: System Z: A natural ordering of defaults with tractable applications to nonmonotonic reasoning. In: Parikh, R. (ed.) Proceedings of the 3rd Conference on Theoretical Aspects of Reasoning about Knowledge, Pacific Grove, CA, USA, March 1990, pp. 121–135. Morgan Kaufmann (1990)
19. Sezgin, M., Kern-Isberner, G., Beierle, C.: Ranking kinematics for revising by contextual information. Ann. Math. Artif. Intell. **89**(10–11), 1101–1131 (2021)
20. Spohn, W.: The Laws of Belief - Ranking Theory and Its Philosophical Applications. Oxford University Press, Oxford (2014)

Non-monotonic Reasoning

Complexity and Scalability of Defeasible Reasoning with Typicality in Many-Valued Weighted Knowledge Bases

Mario Alviano[1] , Laura Giordano[2] , and Daniele Theseider Dupré[2(✉)]

[1] DEMACS, University of Calabria, Via Bucci 30/B, 87036 Rende, CS, Italy
mario.alviano@unical.it
[2] DISIT, University of Piemonte Orientale, Viale Michel 11, 15121 Alessandria, Italy
{laura.giordano,dtd}@uniupo.it

Abstract. Weighted knowledge bases for description logics with typicality under a "concept-wise" multi-preferential semantics provide a logical interpretation of MultiLayer Perceptrons. In this context, Answer Set Programming (ASP) has been shown to be suitable for addressing defeasible reasoning in the finitely many-valued case, providing a Π_2^p upper bound on the complexity of the problem, nonetheless leaving unknown the exact complexity and only providing a proof-of-concept implementation. This paper fulfils the lack by providing a $P^{NP[log]}$-completeness result and new ASP encodings that deal with weighted knowledge bases with large search spaces.

Keywords: Typicality Logics · Multi-valued Logics · Answer Set Programming

1 Introduction

Description logics (DLs) are widely used for knowledge representation (KR), often to verify and discover properties of individuals in a concept by means of DLs inference services [5,33]. Many properties of real world concepts, however, are *defeasible*, that is, they are not universally true, but have exceptions, and actually hold only for some *typical* individuals in the concept. For example, horses are usually tall, but *atypical* horses not being tall exist. This has led to a line of research which deals with *defeasible DLs* [14,18,26]. Specifically, to represent the defeasible properties of a concept, DLs can be extended with a *typicality operator* **T** that is applied to concepts to obtain *typicality inclusions* of the form $\mathbf{T}(C) \sqsubseteq D$ [26]. Intuitively, $\mathbf{T}(C) \sqsubseteq D$ means that the typical individuals in the concept C also belong to concept D (that, *normally* C's are D's), and corresponds to a *conditional implication* $C \mathrel{|\!\sim} D$ in KLM preferential logics [35,36]. A (conditional) knowledge base (KB) comprising typicality inclusions enables *defeasible reasoning*, as in fact the *prototypical properties* of concept C are not necessarily enforced on all individuals in C.

S. Gaggl et al. (Eds.): JELIA 2023, LNAI 14281, pp. 481–497, 2023.
https://doi.org/10.1007/978-3-031-43619-2_33

Some control on the strength of the applicability of typicality inclusions (which, otherwise, depends on specificity) is obtained by assigning them a rank, that is, a natural number as large as strong is the expressed property. The resulting *ranked DL KBs*—reminiscent of ranked KBs by Brewka [11]—are interpreted according to a concept-wise *multi-preferential* semantics, that is, by associating a preference relation to single concepts to identify *the most typical* individuals in a concept [27]. A more fine-grained control is obtained by assigning weights to typicality inclusions, hence obtaining *weighted DL KBs* [29]. In fact, weighing typicality inclusions with positive and negative real numbers allow for representing their plausibility or implausibility. A concrete application of the extended concept-wise multi-preferential semantics is represented by the *fuzzy interpretation of MultiLayer Perceptrons* (MLPs) [32] obtained by encoding synaptic connections as weighted typicality inclusions [29]. Then, the widespread interest in neural networks strongly motivates the development of proof methods for reasoning with weighted DL KBs.

Entailment for fuzzy DLs is in general undecidable [7,20], and this motivates the investigation of many-valued approximations of fuzzy multi-preferential entailment. In particular, the finitely many-valued case is widely studied in the DL literature [6,8,24], and has been recently considered also in the context of weighted DL KBs [30] by means of the notions of *coherent, faithful* and φ *-coherent* models of such KBs, previously considered in the fuzzy case [25,29,30]. A proof-of-concept implementation in Answer Set Programming (ASP) and *asprin* [12] has been provided for the $\mathcal{LC}$ fragment of $\mathcal{ALC}$, which is obtained by disabling roles, and universal and existential restrictions. The approach adopts Gödel connectives (alternatively, Łukasiewicz connectives) and addresses φ-coherent entailment, a form of defeasible reasoning based on canonical φ-coherent models. As concerns the complexity of the problem, a Π_2^p upper bound was given [30].

This paper contributes to the understanding of the problem both from a theoretical point of view and on the practical side. In fact, after introducing the required background (Sect. 2), the upper bound is improved to $P^{NP[log]}$ by showing an algorithm running in polynomial time and performing *parallel* queries to an NP oracle ($P^{||NP}$; Sect. 3). As $P^{||NP}$ is known to coincide with $P^{NP[log]}$ [16], while $\Pi_2^p = P^{NP[log]}$ is unlikely to hold (unless the polynomial hierarchy collapses to $P^{NP[log]}$), there must be space for improving the proof-of-concept implementation. A contribution in this respect is given by the ASP encodings reported in Sect. 4, obtaining the desired multi-preferential semantics by taking advantage of weak constraints, possibly without the need for weights. Further improvements at an asymptotic level are unlikely, as the problem can be shown to be actually $P^{NP[log]}$-complete by giving a polynomial-time reduction of the MAX SAT ODD problem [45], which amounts to determining whether the maximum number of jointly satisfiable clauses among a given set is an odd number. Finally, the scalability of the different ASP encodings powering the implemented system is evaluated empirically on defeasible entailment queries over synthetic weighted DL KBs, reporting results on KBs (Sect. 5) with large search spaces, while the earlier proof-of-concept implementation can only deal with small KBs and search spaces.

2 Weighted Finitely-Valued $\mathcal{LC}_n$ with Typicality

Let $\mathcal{C}_n = \{0, \frac{1}{n}, \ldots, \frac{n-1}{n}, \frac{n}{n}\}$, for an integer $n \geq 1$, denote the finitely-valued set of truth degrees, also called *truth space*. The *truth degree functions* $\otimes$, $\oplus$, $\ominus$ and $\rhd$ associated with the connectives $\wedge$, $\vee$, $\neg$ and $\rightarrow$, respectively, are the following: $a \otimes b = min\{a,b\}$, $a \oplus b = max\{a,b\}$, $\ominus a = 1 - a$, and $a \rhd b = 1$ *if* $a \leq b$ *and* b *otherwise* (as in Gödel logic with involutive negation). Let N_C be a set of concept names and N_I be a set of individual names. The set of $\mathcal{LC}_n$ *concepts* is defined inductively as follows: (i) $A \in N_C$, $\top$ and $\bot$ are concepts; (ii) if C and D are concepts, then $C \sqcap D$, $C \sqcup D$, $\neg C$ are concepts. An $\mathcal{LC}_n$ KB K is a pair $(\mathcal{T}, \mathcal{A})$, where $\mathcal{T}$ (the TBox) is a set of *concept inclusions* of the form $C \sqsubseteq D \; \theta\alpha$, and $\mathcal{A}$ (the ABox) is a set of *assertions* of the form $C(a) \; \theta \; \alpha$, with C and D being concepts, $a \in N_I$, $\theta \in \{\geq, \leq, >, <\}$ and $\alpha \in [0,1]$. Concept inclusions and assertions are collectively called *axioms*.

A *finitely many-valued interpretation* (short. interpretation) is a pair $I = \langle \Delta^I, \cdot^I \rangle$, where Δ^I is a non-empty domain and $\cdot^I$ is an *interpretation function* that assigns to each $a \in N_I$ a value $a^I \in \Delta^I$, and to each $A \in N_C$ a function $A^I : \Delta^I \rightarrow \mathcal{C}_n$. Hence, a domain element $x \in \Delta^I$ belongs to the extension of a concept name $A \in N_C$ to some degree $A^I(x)$ in $\mathcal{C}_n$, and to a composed concept according to the following inductive definition:

$$\top^I(x) = 1 \qquad (C \sqcap D)^I(x) = C^I(x) \otimes D^I(x) \qquad (\neg C)^I(x) = \ominus C^I(x)$$
$$\bot^I(x) = 0 \qquad (C \sqcup D)^I(x) = C^I(x) \oplus D^I(x)$$

The interpretation function $\cdot^I$ is also extended to axioms as follows:

$$(C \sqsubseteq D)^I = inf_{x \in \Delta^I} C^I(x) \rhd D^I(x) \quad (C(a))^I = C^I(a^I)$$

(note that in our setting the *infimum truth degree* in $\mathcal{C}_n$ in the above expression coincides with the *minimum truth degree* in $\mathcal{C}_n$).

Definition 1 (Satisfiability and entailment for $\mathcal{LC}_n$ knowledge bases).
Let $K = (\mathcal{T}, \mathcal{A})$ be a weighted $\mathcal{LC}_n$ KB, and I be an interpretation. Relation $\models$ is defined as follows: $I \models C \sqsubseteq D \; \theta \; \alpha$ if $(C \sqsubseteq D)^I \; \theta \; \alpha$; $I \models C(a) \; \theta \; \alpha$ if $C^I(a^I) \; \theta \; \alpha$; for a set S of axioms, $I \models S$ if $I \models E$ for all $E \in S$; $I \models K$ if $I \models \mathcal{T}$ and $I \models \mathcal{A}$. If $I \models \Gamma$, we say that I satisfies Γ or that I is a model of Γ (for Γ being an axiom, a set of axioms, or a KB). An axiom E is entailed by K, written $K \models E$, if $I \models E$ holds for all models I of K.

$\mathcal{LC}_n$ is extended with typicality concepts of the form $\mathbf{T}(C)$ so that the degree of membership of domain individuals in C defines the typical elements of C. For an interpretation $I = \langle \Delta^I, \cdot^I \rangle$, a preference relation $\prec_C$ on Δ^I (where $x \prec_C y$ means that x *is preferred to* y) is obtained as follows: for all $x, y \in \Delta^I$, $x \prec_C y$ if and only if $C^I(x) > C^I(y)$. The typical elements of C are the ones belonging to C with the greatest positive truth degree. Formally, the interpretation of a typicality concept $\mathbf{T}(C)$ is as follows: for all $x \in \Delta^I$, $(\mathbf{T}(C))^I(x) = 0$ if there is $y \in \Delta^I$ such that $y \prec_C x$, and $C^I(x)$ otherwise. When $(\mathbf{T}(C))^I(x) > 0$, x is said to be a *typical C-element* in I. Note that each relation $\prec_C$ has the properties of a preference relation in KLM-style ranked interpretations by [36], that is, $\prec_C$ is a modular and well-founded strict partial order.

Although non-nested typicality concepts may be allowed to freely occur in the KB and in the queries, typicality inclusions of the form $\mathbf{T}(C) \sqsubseteq D$ have a special interest, as they correspond to conditional implications $C \mathrel{|\!\sim} D$ in KLM conditional knowledge bases [36]. Here, we restrict to such typicality inclusions, further considering assigning weights to typicality inclusions to describe saliency of properties for the individuals belonging to a given concept (category).

Weighted typicality inclusions for a concept C have the form $(\mathbf{T}(C) \sqsubseteq D_i, w_i)$, and describe the *prototypical properties of C-elements* (where D_i is a concept, and the weight w_i is a real number); concept C is also said to be a *distinguished concept*. A *weighted $\mathcal{LC}_n\mathbf{T}$ KB* is a a tuple $\langle \mathcal{T}, \mathcal{D}, \mathcal{A} \rangle$, where the TBox $\mathcal{T}$ is a set of concept inclusions, $\mathcal{D}$ (defeasible TBox) is a set of weighted typicality inclusions for ther distinguished concepts C, and $\mathcal{A}$ is a set of assertions. For an interpretation $I = \langle \Delta^I, \cdot^I \rangle$, the *weight of $x \in \Delta^I$ with respect to a distinguished concept C* is given by $weight_C(x) = \sum_{(\mathbf{T}(C) \sqsubseteq D, w) \in \mathcal{T}} w \cdot D^I(x)$. Intuitively, the higher the value of $weight_C(x)$, the more typical is x relative to the defeasible properties of C. The weight of an individual is then mapped to a truth degree by means of a monotonically non-decreasing function $\varphi : \mathbb{R} \to \mathcal{C}_n$, so that the notion of model can be naturally extended to weighted $\mathcal{LC}_n\mathbf{T}$ KBs. For example, the weighted $\mathcal{LC}_n\mathbf{T}$ KB $\langle\{Tall \sqcap Small \sqsubseteq \perp \geq 1\}, \{(\mathbf{T}(Horse) \sqsubseteq Has\_Tail, +50), (\mathbf{T}(Horse) \sqsubseteq Tall, +40), (\mathbf{T}(Horse) \sqsubseteq Has\_Stripes, -50)\}, \emptyset\rangle$ encodes that a horse normally has a tail and is tall, but usually does not have stripes. Accordingly, a tall horse with tail and without stripes is more typical than a tall horse with tail and stripes. Moreover, as usual in preferential semantics, we restrict to *canonical models*, which are large enough to contain a domain element for any possible valuation of concepts.

Definition 2 (Canonical φ-coherent model and φ-coherent entailment). *Let $K = \langle \mathcal{T}, \mathcal{D}, \mathcal{A} \rangle$ be a weighted $\mathcal{LC}_n\mathbf{T}$ KB, and $\varphi : \mathbb{R} \to \mathcal{C}_n$ be a monotonically non-decreasing function. An interpretation $I = \langle \Delta^I, \cdot^I \rangle$ is φ-coherent if $C^I(x) = \varphi(weight_C(x))$ holds for each distinguished concept C in $\mathcal{D}$ and for all $x \in \Delta^I$. I is a φ-coherent model of K if it is a φ-coherent interpretation satisfying $\mathcal{T}$ and $\mathcal{A}$. I is a canonical φ-coherent model of K if (i) I is a φ-coherent model of K, and (ii) for each φ-coherent model $J = (\Delta^J, \cdot^J)$ of K and each $x \in \Delta^J$, there is an element $y \in \Delta^I$ such that, for all concept names A occurring in K, $A^I(y) = A^J(x)$.[1] An axiom E is φ-coherently entailed by K (written $K \models E$) if $I \models E$ holds for all canonical φ-coherent models I of K.*

---

[1]   Note that the semantics adopted here slightly differs from the original definition given by [30] in the interpretation of typicality concepts, which is not crisp in Definition 2. Anyway, the existence of canonical φ-coherent models, for weighted KBs having at least a φ-coherent model, can be proved as with the crisp interpretation of typicality concepts (see the supplementary material for paper [30], Appendix A).

According to the above definition, for every distinguished concept C, the degree of membership of typical C-elements is the same in all canonical φ-coherent models; it is the highest degree of membership among all φ-coherent models. Without loss of generality, we can as well restrict to a unique canonical model, as in defeasible $\mathcal{ALC}$ [13]. In the next sections, we take advantage of such a property to study φ-coherent entailment. We prove that deciding φ-entailment of a query $\mathbf{T}(C) \sqsubseteq D \; \theta \; \alpha$ is a $P^{NP[log]}$-complete problem, we introduce several ASP encodings addressing the computational problem and investigate their scalability. (We refer to [17] for background on ASP.)

The interest for the entailment of queries of the form $\mathbf{T}(C) \sqsubseteq D \; \theta \; \alpha$ lies again in the fact that they are the many-valued correspondent of conditionals $C \vdash D$. Moreover, weighted typicality inclusions can be associated [29,30] to trained MultiLayer Perceptrons, with φ corresponding to the neuron activation function; in this case, φ-coherent entailment of formulae $\mathbf{T}(C) \sqsubseteq D \; \theta \; \alpha$ may be used to verify what has been learned by the neural network, in particular if C is the concept associated to an output unit and D is a boolean combination of concepts associated with input units. Using $\mathbf{T}(C)$ restricts the attention to the inputs that are classified by the network as Cs with highest degree.

3   Computing φ-Coherent Entailment in ASP is in $P^{NP[log]}$

In this section we elaborate on the encoding by [30] to obtain an upper bound on the complexity of deciding φ-coherent entailment of a typicality inclusion of the form $\mathbf{T}(C_q) \sqsubseteq D_q \; \theta\alpha$ from a weighted $\mathcal{LC}_n\mathbf{T}$ knowledge base $K = \langle \mathcal{T}, \mathcal{D}, \mathcal{A} \rangle$. Specifically, we first introduce a P^{NP} algorithm, and then refine it to obtain a $P^{NP[log]}$ upper bound.

We associate with K an ASP program Π_K with the following main features:

(i) Names in N_C and in N_I occurring in K, as well as an *anonymous* individual name, are encoded by constant terms (i.e., strings starting by lowercase), composed concepts such as $C \sqcap D$ are encoded by composed terms such as $and(c,d)$, and any $C \sqsubseteq D$ is encoded by $impl(c,d)$. Predicates $concept/1$ and $ind/1$ are used to mark concepts and individual names in K, and each weighted typicality inclusion $(\mathbf{T}(C) \sqsubseteq D, w)$ is encoded by the fact $wti(c,d,w)$.

(ii) $\mathcal{C}_n$ is encoded by $val(0..n)$, and an interpretation I is guessed by rules

$$\{eval(c, X, V) : val(V)\} = 1 \leftarrow ind(X). \qquad (1)$$

for each $C \in N_C$, so that an atom of the form $eval(c, x, v)$ means that $C^I(x) = \frac{v}{n} \in \mathcal{C}_n$. Relation $eval/3$ is extended to complex concepts naturally. Additionally, for any $C \sqsubseteq D$, the valuation $C^I(x) \rhd D^I(x)$ is obtained by the following rules:

$$eval(impl(c,d), X, 1) \leftarrow eval(c, X, V), eval(d, X, V'), V \leq V'.$$
$$eval(impl(c,d), X, V') \leftarrow eval(c, X, V), eval(d, X, V'), V > V'.$$

(*iii*) For instance, each concept inclusion $C \sqsubseteq D \geq \alpha$ in $\mathcal{T}$, each assertion $C(a) \geq \alpha$ in the ABox $\mathcal{A}$, each $C \sqsubseteq D < \alpha$ in $\mathcal{T}$, and each typicality inclusion for a distinguished concept C in $\mathcal{D}$ are enforced by the following constraints:

$$\bot \leftarrow eval(impl(c,d), X, V), V < \alpha. \qquad \bot \leftarrow eval(c, a, V), V < \alpha.$$
$$\bot \leftarrow eval(impl(c,d), ci(c, d, < \alpha), V), V \geq \alpha.$$
$$\bot \leftarrow ind(X), W = \#sum\{W_D * V_D, D : wti(c, D, W_D), eval(D, X, V_D)\},$$
$$eval(c, X, V), \; valphi(n, W, V'), V \neq V'.$$

the last one imposing φ-coherence, where $valphi/3$ is defined so that $\varphi(W) = \frac{V'}{n}$; the term $ci(c, d, < \alpha)$ is introduced to represent a domain element satisfying $C \sqsubseteq D < \alpha$.

From the next proposition (which extends Lemma 1 in [30]), there is a duality relation between domain individuals in a φ-coherent model $I = \langle \Delta^I, \cdot^I \rangle$ of K and the answer sets of Π_K.

Proposition 1. *Let $C \in N_C$ and $\frac{v}{n} \in \mathcal{C}_n$. If there is a φ-coherent model $I = \langle \Delta^I, \cdot^I \rangle$ of a knowledge base K and $x \in \Delta^I$ such that $C^I(x) = \frac{v}{n}$, then there is an answer set S of Π_K such that $eval(c, anonymous, v) \in S$, and vice-versa.*

For the query $\mathbf{T}(C_q) \sqsubseteq D_q \geq \alpha$, entailment can be decided by the following algorithm:

(a) find the highest value $\frac{v}{n} \in \mathcal{C}_n$ such that there is a φ-coherent model I of K with $C_q^I(x) = \frac{v}{n}$ for some $x \in \Delta^I$;
(b) verify that for all φ-coherent models I of K and all $x \in \Delta^I$, if $C_q^I(x) = \frac{v}{n}$ then $C_q^I(x) \rhd D_q^I(x) \geq \alpha$ holds (note that the implication trivially holds when $v = 0$).

Step (a) identifies the degree of membership of typical C_q-elements (if any) by invoking multiple times an ASP solver for Π_K extended with

$$\bot \leftarrow \#count\{X : ind(X), \; eval(c_q, X, v)\} = 0$$

in order to verify the existence of an answer set containing $eval(c_q, x, v)$, for some x. Specifically, the ASP solver can be called no more than n times, for decreasing $v = n, \ldots, 1$ and stopping at the first successful call; if none is successful, there are no typical C-elements, and the query is trivially true.

Step (b) checks that, for the selected $\frac{v}{n}$, there is no answer set of Π_K containing both $eval(c_q, x, v)$ and $eval(d_q, x, v')$ whenever $\frac{v}{n} \rhd \frac{v'}{n} < \alpha$, for any x. It requires one additional solver call to check that there is an answer set for Π_K extended with

$$counterexample \leftarrow eval(c_q, X, v), \; eval(d_q, X, V'), \; V' > v, \; V' < \alpha.$$
$$\bot \leftarrow not \; counterexample.$$

i.e., a counterexample exists. As the size of Π_K and its extensions is polynomial in the size of K and of the query, and no disjunctive head or recursive aggregate is used, each call to the ASP solver can be answered by a call to an NP oracle. In the worst case, $n + 1$ calls to the NP oracle are performed, which provides a P^{NP} upper bound on the complexity of the decision problem.

The upper bound can be refined by observing that step (a) can be executed in parallel for each $v = 1, \ldots, n$, and similarly step (b) can be speculatively checked for each value $\frac{v}{n}$, regardless from $\frac{v}{n}$ being the degree of membership of typical C_q-elements (if any). Once the answers to such $2n$ calls are obtained, the decision problem can be answered by selecting the highest value $\frac{v}{n}$ for which calls of type (a) returned *yes*, and flipping the answer obtained for the corresponding call of type (b)—all other answers to calls of type (b) are simply ignored.

For the query $\mathbf{T}(C_q) \sqsubseteq D_q < \alpha$, note that $K \models \mathbf{T}(C_q) \sqsubseteq D_q < \alpha$, iff $K \not\models \mathbf{T}(C_q) \sqsubseteq D_q \geq \alpha$ (as we can restrict to a unique canonical model).

The next result follows from Proposition 1 and algorithm above:

Theorem 1 (Complexity upper bound for φ-coherent entailment). *Deciding φ-coherent entailment of inclusion $\mathbf{T}(C) \sqsubseteq D \; \theta \; \alpha$ from a weighted $\mathcal{LC}_n\mathbf{T}$ KB K can be achieved using a polynomial number of parallel queries to an NP-oracle.*

It follows that the decision algorithm is in $P^{NP[log]}$ [16]. The upper bound is actually strict, as the problem can be shown to be $P^{NP[log]}$-hard by means of a reduction from the $P^{NP[log]}$-complete problem MAX SAT ODD [45], asking to verify whether the maximum number of jointly satisfiable clauses in a given set is odd.

Theorem 2 (Strict complexity lower bound for φ-coherent entailment). *Determining if a typicality inclusion $\mathbf{T}(C) \sqsubseteq D \; \theta \; \alpha$ is φ-coherently entailed by a weighted $\mathcal{LC}_n\mathbf{T}$ KB $K = \langle \mathcal{T}, \mathcal{D}, \mathcal{A} \rangle$ is $P^{NP[log]}$-hard, even if $\mathcal{T}$ and $\mathcal{A}$ are empty, C and D are concept names, and $\theta\alpha$ is fixed to ≥ 1.*

4   Comparing Different ASP Encodings of φ-Coherent Entailment

We present four ASP encodings improving the one in Sect. 3 both in terms of generality and of scalability. The encodings adopt a combination of several ASP constructs, among them @-terms, custom propagators, weak constraints and weight constraints. First of all, the input is encoded by the following facts (with weights represented as integers):

- `valphi(v, LB, UB)` whenever $\varphi(w) = \frac{v}{n}$ if and only if $LB < w \leq UB$ holds;
- `concept(C)` for each relevant concept C, where named concepts are represented as constant terms, and complex terms by means of the uninterpreted functions `and`, `or`, `neg` and `impl`;
- `ind(a)` for each individual name a, among them the `anonymous` one;

- concept_inclusion(C,D,θ,α) for each concept inclusion $C \sqsubseteq D\ \theta\frac{\alpha}{n}$;
- assertion(C,a,θ,α) for each assertion $C(a)\ \theta\frac{\alpha}{n}$;
- wti(C,D,w) for each weighted typicality inclusion $(\mathbf{T}(C) \sqsubseteq D, w)$;
- query(C_q,D_q,θ,α) for the typicality inclusion $\mathbf{T}(C_q) \sqsubseteq D_q\ \theta\frac{\alpha}{n}$;
- crisp(C) as an optimization for $(\mathbf{T}(C) \sqsubseteq C, \infty)$, to enforce a crisp evaluation of concept C (where ∞ is a sufficiently large integer to obtain $\varphi(\infty \cdot \frac{1}{n}) = 1$; see equation (1) for an example);
- exactly_one(ID) and exactly_one_element(ID,C_i) $(i = 1..k)$ to optimize $\top \sqsubseteq C_1 \sqcup \cdots \sqcup C_k \geq 1$ (at least one) and $C_i \sqcap C_j \sqsubseteq \perp \geq 1$ with $j = i + 1..k$ (at most one)

The *latter* two predicates are useful to express membership of individuals in mutually exclusive concepts. Moreover, the following interpreted functions are implemented via @-terms: @is_named_concept(C), returning 1 if C is a named concept, and 0 otherwise; @min(v,v), @max(v,v), @neg(v), and @impl(v,v,n), for the truth degree functions $\otimes$, $\oplus$, $\ominus$ and $\triangleright$ in Gödel logic (other truth degree functions can be considered, see Sect. 2).

```
1  val(0..n). concept(bot). eval(bot,X,0) :- ind(X). concept(top). eval(top,X,n) :- ind(X).
2  {eval(C,X,V) : val(V)} = 1 :- concept(C), ind(X), @is_named_concept(C) = 1, not crisp(C).
3  {eval(C,X,0); eval(C,X,n)} = 1 :- concept(C), ind(X), @is_named_concept(C) = 1, crisp(C).
4  eval(and(A,B),X,@min(V,V')) :- concept(and(A,B)), eval(A,X,V), eval(B,X,V').
5  eval( or(A,B),X,@max(V,V')) :- concept( or(A,B)), eval(A,X,V), eval(B,X,V').
6  eval(neg(A),X,@neg(V)) :- concept(neg(A)), eval(A,X,V).
7  eval(impl(A,B),X,@impl(V,V',n)) :- concept(impl(A,B)), eval(A,X,V), eval(B,X,V').
8  :- concept(C), @is_named_concept(C)!=1, crisp(C); ind(X), not eval(C,X,0), not eval(C,X,n).
9  :- concept_inclusion(C,D,θ>,α), eval(impl(C,D),X,V), not V θ> α.
10 ind(ci(C,D,θ<,α)) :- concept_inclusion(C,D,θ<,α).
11 :- concept_inclusion(C,D,θ<,α), eval(impl(C,D),ci(C,D,θ<,α),V), not V θ< α.
12 :- assertion(C,X,θ,α); eval(C,X,V), not V θ α.
13 :- exactly_one(ID), ind(X), #count{C : exactly_one_element(ID,C), eval(C,X,n)} != 1.
14 % find the largest truth degree for the left-hand-side concept of query
15 :~ query(C,_,_,_), eval(C,X,V), V > 0. [-1@V+1]
16 % verify if there is a counterexample to the truth of query (θ>) or to its falsity (θ<)
17 typical(C,X) :- query(C,_,_,_), eval(C,X,V), V = #max{V' : eval(C,X',V')}.
18 witness :- query(C,D,θ>,α); typical(C,X), eval(impl(C,D),X,V), not V θ> α.
19 witness :- query(C,D,θ<,α); typical(C,X), eval(impl(C,D),X,V),      V θ< α.
20 :~ witness. [-1@1]
21 #show witness : witness.
22 #show eval(C,X,V) : witness, eval(C,X,V), concept(C), @is_named_concept(C) = 1.
```

Fig. 1. Base encoding, with $\theta \in \{\geq, \leq, >, <\}$, $\theta_> \in \{>, \geq\}$, and $\theta_< \in \{<, \leq\}$

The *base encoding* is shown in Fig. 1. Line 1 introduces the truth degrees from $\mathcal{C}_n$ and fixes the interpretation of $\perp$ and $\top$. Lines 2–3 guess a truth degree for named concept, using only crisp truth degrees for crisp concepts. Lines 4–8 evaluate composed concepts, and impose crisp truth degrees for crisp concepts. Lines 9–12 enforce concept inclusions and assertions; note that, by the semantic definition given in Sect. 2, concept inclusions with $\geq$ and $>$ define properties holding for all individuals, while concept inclusions with $\leq$ and $<$ define properties holding for at least one individual; such an individual is introduced by line 10. Line 13 enforces *exactly one* constraints. Line 15 expresses a preference for assigning a large truth degree to C_q. Lines 17–20 define typical C_q-elements and express a weaker preference for the existence of a witness: if the query uses $\theta_> \in \{>, \geq\}$, a witness is a φ-coherent model I and an element $x \in \Delta^I$ such that $(\mathbf{T}(C_q))^I(x) \rhd D_q^I(x)\ \theta_> \frac{\alpha}{n}$ does not hold (i.e., x makes the query false), and the query is true if such a witness does not exist; if the query uses $\theta_< \in \{<, \leq\}$, a witness is a φ-coherent model I and an element $x \in \Delta^I$ such that $(\mathbf{T}(C_q))^I(x) \rhd D_q^I(x)\ \theta_< \frac{\alpha}{n}$ holds (i.e., x makes the query true), and the query is false if such a witness does not exist. Lines 21–22 report in output whether a witness was found (and the truth degrees it assigns to named concepts).

The encoding must be enriched with the enforcement of φ-coherence. A first solution is the addition, for each distinguished concept C, of a *custom propagator* that infers eval(C,x,v) whenever $\varphi(weight_C(x)) = \frac{v}{n}$. In case of conflict, the propagator provides

$$:- \text{ eval}(D_1,x,v_1), \ \ldots, \ \text{eval}(D_k,x,v_k), \ \text{not eval}(C,x,v).$$

as the reason of inference, where $(\mathbf{T}(C) \sqsubseteq D_i, w_i)$, for $i = 1..k$, are all the weighted typicality inclusions for C in $\mathcal{T}$ and eval(D_i,x,v_i) is true in the current assignment.

```
23  :∼ query(C,_,_,_), eval_ge(C,X,V). [-1@2]
24  {eval_ge(C,X,V) : val(V), V > 0} :- concept(C), ind(X).
25  :- eval_ge(C,X,V), V > 1, not eval_ge(C,X,V-1). % C^I(x) ≥ v/n ⟹ C^I(x) ≥ (v-1)/n

26  % C^I(x) = v/n ⟺ C^I(x) ≥ v/n and C^I(x) < (v+1)/n
27  :- concept(C), ind(X); eval(C,X,V), V > 0; not eval_ge(C,X,V).
28  :- concept(C), ind(X); eval(C,X,V); eval_ge(C,X,V+1).
29  :- concept(C), ind(X); eval_ge(C,X,V), not eval_ge(C,X,V+1); not eval(C,X,V).

30  % (A ⊓ B)^I(x) ≥ v/n ⟺ A^I(x) ≥ v/n and B^I(x) ≥ v/n
31  :- concept(and(A,B)), ind(X), eval_ge(and(A,B),X,V); not eval_ge(A,X,V).
32  :- concept(and(A,B)), ind(X); eval_ge(and(A,B),X,V); not eval_ge(B,X,V).
33  :- concept(and(A,B)), ind(X); eval_ge(A,X,V), eval_ge(B,X,V); not eval_ge(and(A,B),X,V).

34  % (A ⊔ B)^I(x) ≥ v/n ⟺ A^I(x) ≥ v/n or B^I(x) ≥ v/n
35  :- concept(or(A,B)), ind(X); eval_ge(or(A,B),X,V); not eval_ge(A,X,V), not eval_ge(B,X,V).
36  :- concept(or(A,B)), ind(X); eval_ge(A,X,V); not eval_ge(or(A,B),X,V).
37  :- concept(or(A,B)), ind(X); eval_ge(B,X,V); not eval_ge(or(A,B),X,V).

38  % (¬A)^I(x) ≥ v/n ⟺ A^I(x) ≤ 1 - v/n
39  :- concept(neg(A)), ind(X); eval_ge(neg(A),X,V); eval_ge(A,X,n-V+1).
40  :- concept(neg(A)), ind(X), val(V), V > 0; not eval_ge(A,X,n-V+1); not eval_ge(neg(A),X,V).

41  % (A ⊑ B)^I(x) ≥ v/n ⟺ A^I(x) ≤ B^I(x) or B^I(x) ≥ v/n
42  l_gt_r(A,B,X) :- concept(impl(A,B)), ind(X); eval_ge(A,X,V); not eval_ge(B,X,V).
43  :- concept(impl(A,B)), ind(X); eval_ge(impl(A,B),X,V); l_gt_r(A,B,X); not eval_ge(B,X,V).
44  :- concept(impl(A,B)), ind(X), val(V), V>0; not l_gt_r(A,B,X); not eval_ge(impl(A,B),X,V).
45  :- concept(impl(A,B)), ind(X); eval_ge(B,X,V); not eval_ge(impl(A,B),X,V).
```

Fig. 2. Rules replacing line 15 of the base encoding to obtain the order encoding

The base encoding is not suitable to obtain a strict upper bound for our problem, due to the weak constraint in line 15 using a linear number of levels with respect to the size of $\mathcal{C}_n$. Such levels can be removed by replacing [-1@V+1] with [-2^V@1] [2], which however results into a weighted preference relation giving a P^{NP} upper bound [15]. Removing such weights is less trivial, nonetheless can be achieved by introducing atoms representing $C^I(x) \geq \frac{v}{n}$, that is, an *order encoding* [44] for finitely many-valued interpretations as shown in Fig. 2. Note that the level in line 23 can be removed by replacing [-1@2] with [-2@1], and in turn the weight -2 can be removed by introducing two copies of the weak constraint using [-1@1, 1] and [-1@1, 2]. As for the other rules, lines 24–25 define the search space for predicate eval_ge/2, lines 27–29 match the assignment of eval/2 and eval_ge/2, and lines 31–45 implement inferences of eval_ge/2 over composed concepts. We therefore have an alternative proof of Theorem 1: Deciding φ-coherent entailment of a typicality inclusion $\mathbf{T}(C) \sqsubseteq D \; \theta\alpha$ from a weighted $\mathcal{LC}_n\mathbf{T}$ KB K is in $P^{NP[log]}$.

```
46 % C^I(x) = v/n ⟺ LB < weight_C(x) ≤ UB
47 :- val(V), val_phi(V,LB,UB); wti(C,_,_), ind(X); eval(C,X,V);
48    not LB < #sum{W*VD, D,VD : wti(C,D,W), eval(D,X,VD)} <= UB.
49 :- val(V), val_phi(V,LB,UB); wti(C,_,_), ind(X); not eval(C,X,V);
50    LB < #sum{W*VD, D,VD : wti(C,D,W), eval(D,X,VD)} <= UB.

51 % C^I(x) ≥ v/n ⟺ weight_C(x) > LB
52 :- val(V), V > 0, val_phi(V,LB,UB); wti(C,_,_), ind(X); eval(C,X,V);
53    #sum{W ,D,VD : wti(C,D,W), eval_ge(D,X,VD)} > LB.
54 :- val(V), V > 0, val_phi(V,LB,UB); wti(C,_,_), ind(X); not eval(C,X,V);
55    #sum{W, D,VD : wti(C,D,W), eval_ge(D,X,VD)} > LB.
```

Fig. 3. Rules added to the base encoding (lines 46–50) and to the order encoding (lines 51–55) to enforce φ-coherence via weight constraints.

Even if the custom propagators provide a sensible performance gain with respect to the previously implemented encoding, indeed settling the grounding bottleneck, they miss the opportunity for several deterministic and inexpensive inferences. An alternative way to enforce φ-coherence is given by the weight constraints reported in Fig. 3, for both the base and order encodings, leading to the results in Sect. 5. The idea is to just check membership of $weight_C(x)$ in the intervals of interest, without materializing its actual value so to avoid the reintroduction of the grounding bottleneck.

5 Experiment

The encoding in [30] was shown to work as a proof-of-concept for small instances, and the variation described in Sect. 3 is already challenged by KBs corresponding to fully-connected neural networks with 20 *binary* inputs and 150 weighted typicality inclusions. Such KBs are acyclic, considering the graph with an edge from C to D for $(\mathbf{T}(C) \sqsubseteq D, w)$—where C and D are concept names. The size of the search space is around 10^6, since, for such KBs, it is given by the combination of values for concepts corresponding to input nodes, as in fact the values of the other nodes is implied. We observed that the number of weighted typicality inclusions has a significant impact on the size of the grounding of these encodings.

We therefore focus on the encodings presented in Sect. 4, and consider synthetic KBs encoding fully-connected multi-layer perceptrons with one input layer, two hidden layers and one output node; nodes are encoded by concept names, edges are encoded by weighted typicality inclusions, and there are edges from any node in a layer to any node in the next layer. We consider KBs of four different sizes, comprising 50/100/200/400 nodes, including 10/20/40/80 input nodes. For each size, we generated 10 instances by randomizing edge weights. As for the query, we fix it to $\mathbf{T}(O) \sqsubseteq I_1 \sqcup I_2 \geq 0.5$; that is, we check whether instances classified as Os with highest degree belong to I_1 or I_2 with at least degree 0.5. We use as φ the approximation in $\mathcal{C}_n$ of the logistic function $S(x) = 1/(1 + e^{-x})$, widely used as activation function in multi-layer perceptrons.

The experiment was run on an Intel Xeon 5520 2.26 GHz, with runtime limited to 30 min. Figure 4 and Table 1 report data on running times for answering the queries using the truth spaces $\mathcal{C}_4$ and $\mathcal{C}_9$, that is, 5 and 10 truth degrees; the resulting search spaces have sizes ranging from 5^{10} (around 10^7) to 10^{80}. Data is reported for the base and order encodings relying on the use of weight constraints; the results using the custom propagator are worse. The percentage of 10 cases solved within a timeout of 30 min is shown, as well as the minimum, average and maximum time for the solved instances. The two scatter plots highlight that, with a few exceptions, the order encoding provides a performance gain to the system. Finally, there is an impact of the number of truth degrees on performance, but there could be space for a compromise between the level of approximation of reasoning and the consumed computational resources.

Table 1. Runtime of the base and order encodings relying on weight constraints to answer queries over weighted KBs encoding fully-connected neural networks of different sizes (10 for each size). The KBs have a concept for each node, and a weighted typicality inclusion for each edge. Best performance in terms of solved instances is highlighted in bold, and ties are broken by smallest average execution time.

	Size (number of)			$|\mathcal{C}_n| = 5$				$|\mathcal{C}_n| = 10$			
				Solved	Runtime (seconds)			Solved	Runtime (seconds)		
	inputs	nodes	edges		min	avg	max		min	avg	max
ORDER	10	50	580	**90%**	4	139	798	**40%**	6	393	1534
	20	100	2360	**60%**	15	30	70	**50%**	21	**24**	30
	40	200	9520	**70%**	67	**79**	118	50%	94	242	766
	80	400	38240	**60%**	298	**309**	339	**50%**	400	412	433
BASE	10	50	580	40%	4	465	1639	20%	6	7	8
	20	100	2360	50%	16	21	34	**50%**	22	89	150
	40	200	9520	**70%**	69	96	187	**60%**	95	180	444
	80	400	38240	**60%**	415	608	1125	40%	500	813	1330

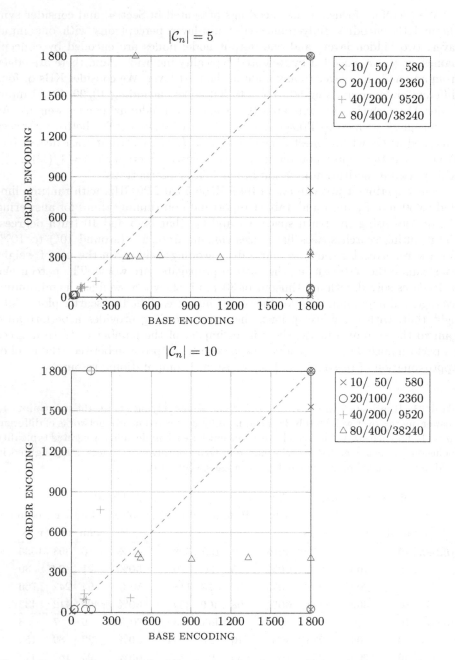

Fig. 4. Runtime (in seconds) of the base and order encodings relying on weight constraints to answer queries over weighted KBs encoding fully-connected neural networks of different sizes (input nodes/total nodes/total edges). Timeouts are normalized to 1800 s.

6   Related Work

Fuzzy description logics (DLs) have been widely studied in the literature for representing vagueness in DLs, e.g., by [7,39,43], based on the idea that concepts and roles can be interpreted as fuzzy sets and fuzzy relations. In fuzzy DLs, formulas have a truth degree from a truth space $\mathcal{S}$, usually either the interval $[0,1]$, as in Mathematical Fuzzy Logic [21], or the finitely-valued set $\mathcal{C}_n$. Moreover, the *truth degree functions* $\otimes$, $\oplus$, $\ominus$ and $\triangleright$, used to define the semantics of operators $\sqcap$, $\sqcup$, $\neg$ and inclusion axioms, are chosen as t-norm, s-norm, negation function and implication function in some well known system of many-valued logic [31]. The finitely-valued case is also well studied for DLs [6,8,24], and in this paper we have considered a variant of the boolean fragment $\mathcal{LC}_n$ of the finitely-valued $\mathcal{ALC}$ with typicality considered by [30], by considering a *many-valued interpretation of typicality concepts* rather than a crisp one. We have taken $\mathcal{C}_n$ as the truth degree set and restricted our consideration to Gödel many-valued logic with involutive negation.

$\mathcal{LC}_n$ is extended with typicality concepts of the form $\mathbf{T}(C)$, in the spirit of the extension of $\mathcal{ALC}$ with typicality in the two-valued case [26], but in the many-valued case we use the degree of membership of domain individuals in a concept C to identify the typical elements of C. While the semantics has strong relations with KLM logics by [35] and with other preferential semantics, such as *c-representations* [34] which also consider weights, we have adopted a *concept-wise* multi-preferential semantics, in which different preferences $\prec_C$ are associated with different concepts C. This also makes our formalism different form the one considered by Casini and Straccia [19], in their rational closure construction for fuzzy logic. The choice of a finitely-valued interpretation of the typicality operator has been first considered in [1] to develop a conditional semantics for gradual argumentation.

The notion of typicality we have considered is clearly reminiscent of *prototype theory* [42] and it also relates to Freund's ordered models for concept representation [22]. Under some respects, our approach can be regarded as a simplification of the ordered model approach (in the many-valued case), as we regard features as concepts and we consider a single (rather then two) preference relation $<_C$ for a concept C. On the other hand, the idea of associating weights/ranks to the properties of concepts in weighted KBs, as a measure of their saliency, was also inspired by Brewka's framework for basic preference descriptions [10,11], and to Lehmann's lexicographic closure [37]. Among the recent work on preference combination, let us mention the algebraic framework for preference combination in multi-relational contextual hierarchies proposed by Bozzato et al. [9], and the work by Lieto and Pozzato on concept combination based on typicality [38]. Weighted DL KBs also relate to *threshold concepts* [4] and to *weighted threshold operators* [23,41] which, however, lead to monotonic DLs for weighted concept combination.

7 Conclusions

Defeasible reasoning over weighted $\mathcal{LC}_n$ KBs is a computationally intensive task, previously addressed in the finitely many-valued case by adopting solving techniques suitable for problems in the complexity class Π_2^p [30]. As shown in Sect. 3, the ASP encoding powering the available solution in the literature can be the basis for defining an algorithm asking all required queries to the NP oracle in parallel, and then inspecting the obtained answers to decide if the entailment holds. We therefore refined the upper bound on the complexity of the problem to $P^{||NP} = P^{NP[log]}$, which is optimal as the problem is also $P^{NP[log]}$-hard.

On a more practical side, in Sect. 4 we revised the previously proposed ASP encoding by taking advantage of several linguistic extensions and coding techniques for ASP, among them @-terms, custom propagators, weak constraints, weight constraints and order encoding. While all such constructs improve readability of the code, it turns out that the implementation and maintenance of the custom propagator has a higher cost than the others. In fact, the implemented custom propagator was very helpful to settle the grounding bottleneck, but it was also clear that capturing all deterministic and inexpensive inferences was non-trivial. A pondered use of weight constraints showed to be more rewarding, performing better on the verification of typicality properties of the test cases considered in Sect. 5. Source code is available at https://github.com/alviano/valphi.

Among acyclic KBs, we have considered KBs corresponding to Multilayer Perceptrons which represent a specific case of interest for applications. A natural direction to extend this work is allowing different φ_i functions for different concepts C_i, to address the verification of typicality properties of MultiLayer Perceptrons (MLPs) with different activation functions for different layers, as considered in [40].

This work is also a step towards the definition of proof methods for reasoning from weighted KBs under a finitely many-valued preferential semantics in lightweight DLs, in the spirit of the weighted KBs with typicality for $\mathcal{EL}$ [3] (in the two valued case [28] and in the fuzzy case [29]), as well as for more expressive DLs, starting from a many-valued $\mathcal{ALC}$ with typicality [25].

The co-existence of strict and defeasible inclusions in weighted KBs allows for combining empirical knowledge with elicited knowledge for reasoning and, specifically for verification.

Acknowledgements. We thank the anonymous referees for their helpful suggestions. This research was partially supported by INDAM-GNCS. Mario Alviano was partially supported by Italian Ministry of Research (MUR) under PNRR project FAIR "Future AI Research", CUP H23C22000860006 and by LAIA lab (part of the SILA labs).

References

1. Alviano, M., Giordano, L., Theseider Dupré, D.: Many-valued argumentation, conditionals and a probabilistic semantics for gradual argumentation. CoRR abs/2212.07523 (2022)

2. Alviano, M.: Algorithms for solving optimization problems in answer set programming. Intell. Artif. **12**(1), 1–14 (2018)
3. Baader, F., Brandt, S., Lutz, C.: Pushing the $\mathcal{EL}$ envelope. In: Kaelbling, L., Saffiotti, A. (eds.) Proceedings of the 19th International Joint Conference on Artificial Intelligence (IJCAI 2005), pp. 364–369. Professional Book Center, Edinburgh (2005)
4. Baader, F., Brewka, G., Gil, O.F.: Adding threshold concepts to the description Logic $\mathcal{EL}$. In: Lutz, C., Ranise, S. (eds.) FroCoS 2015. LNCS (LNAI), vol. 9322, pp. 33–48. Springer, Cham (2015). https://doi.org/10.1007/978-3-319-24246-0_3
5. Baader, F., Calvanese, D., McGuinness, D., Nardi, D., Patel-Schneider, P.: The Description Logic Handbook - Theory, Implementation, and Applications. Cambridge (2007)
6. Bobillo, F., Delgado, M., Gómez-Romero, J., Straccia, U.: Joining Gödel and Zadeh fuzzy logics in fuzzy description logics. Int. J. Uncertain. Fuzziness Knowl. Based Syst. **20**(4), 475–508 (2012)
7. Borgwardt, S., Peñaloza, R.: Undecidability of fuzzy description logics. In: Brewka, G., Eiter, T., McIlraith, S.A. (eds.) Proceedings of the KR 2012, 10–14 June 2012, Rome, Italy (2012)
8. Borgwardt, S., Peñaloza, R.: The complexity of lattice-based fuzzy description logics. J. Data Semant. **2**(1), 1–19 (2013)
9. Bozzato, L., Eiter, T., Kiesel, R.: Reasoning on multirelational contextual hierarchies via answer set programming with algebraic measures. Theory Pract. Log. Program. **21**(5), 593–609 (2021). https://doi.org/10.1017/S1471068421000284
10. Brewka, G.: Preferred subtheories: an extended logical framework for default reasoning. In: Proceedings of the 11th International Joint Conference on Artificial Intelligence. Detroit, MI, USA, August 1989, pp. 1043–1048 (1989)
11. Brewka, G.: A rank based description language for qualitative preferences. In: 6th European Conference on Artificial Intelligence, ECAI 2004, Valencia, Spain, 22–27 August 2004. pp. 303–307 (2004)
12. Brewka, G., Delgrande, J.P., Romero, J., Schaub, T.: Asprin: customizing answer set preferences without a headache. In: Proceedings of the AAAI 2015, pp. 1467–1474 (2015)
13. Britz, K., Casini, G., Meyer, T., Moodley, K., Sattler, U., Varzinczak, I.: Principles of KLM-style defeasible description logics. ACM Trans. Comput. Log. **22**(1), 1:1–1:46 (2021)
14. Britz, K., Heidema, J., Meyer, T.: Semantic preferential subsumption. In: Brewka, G., Lang, J. (eds.) KR 2008, pp. 476–484. AAAI Press, Sydney (2008)
15. Buccafurri, F., Leone, N., Rullo, P.: Strong and weak constraints in disjunctive datalog. In: Dix, J., Furbach, U., Nerode, A. (eds.) LPNMR 1997. LNCS, vol. 1265, pp. 2–17. Springer, Heidelberg (1997). https://doi.org/10.1007/3-540-63255-7_2
16. Buss, S.R., Hay, L.: On truth-table reducibility to SAT. Inf. Comput. **91**(1), 86–102 (1991)
17. Calimeri, F., et al.: ASP-core-2 input language format. Theory Pract. Log. Program. **20**(2), 294–309 (2020)
18. Casini, G., Straccia, U.: Rational closure for defeasible description logics. In: Janhunen, T., Niemelä, I. (eds.) JELIA 2010. LNCS (LNAI), vol. 6341, pp. 77–90. Springer, Heidelberg (2010). https://doi.org/10.1007/978-3-642-15675-5_9
19. Casini, G., Straccia, U.: Towards rational closure for fuzzy logic: the case of propositional Gödel logic. In: McMillan, K., Middeldorp, A., Voronkov, A. (eds.) LPAR 2013. LNCS, vol. 8312, pp. 213–227. Springer, Heidelberg (2013). https://doi.org/10.1007/978-3-642-45221-5_16

20. Cerami, M., Straccia, U.: On the undecidability of fuzzy description logics with GCIs with Lukasiewicz t-norm. CoRR abs/1107.4212 (2011)
21. Cintula, P., Hájek, P., Noguera, C. (eds.): Handbook of Mathematical Fuzzy Logic, vol. 37–38. College Publications (2011)
22. Freund, M.: Ordered models for concept representation. J. Log. Comput. **30**(6), 1143–1181 (2020)
23. Galliani, P., Righetti, G., Kutz, O., Porello, D., Troquard, N.: Perceptron connectives in knowledge representation. In: Keet, C.M., Dumontier, M. (eds.) EKAW 2020. LNCS (LNAI), vol. 12387, pp. 183–193. Springer, Cham (2020). https://doi.org/10.1007/978-3-030-61244-3_13
24. García-Cerdaña, A., Armengol, E., Esteva, F.: Fuzzy description logics and t-norm based fuzzy logics. Int. J. Approx. Reason. **51**(6), 632–655 (2010)
25. Giordano, L.: On the KLM properties of a Fuzzy DL with typicality. In: Vejnarová, J., Wilson, N. (eds.) ECSQARU 2021. LNCS (LNAI), vol. 12897, pp. 557–571. Springer, Cham (2021). https://doi.org/10.1007/978-3-030-86772-0_40
26. Giordano, L., Gliozzi, V., Olivetti, N., Pozzato, G.L.: ALC+T: a preferential extension of Description Logics. Fund. Inform. **96**, 1–32 (2009)
27. Giordano, L., Theseider Dupré, D.: An ASP approach for reasoning in a concept-aware multipreferential lightweight DL. TPLP **10**(5), 751–766 (2020)
28. Giordano, L., Theseider Dupré, D.: Weighted conditional $EL^{\perp}$ knowledge bases with integer weights: an ASP approach. In: Proceedings of the 37th International Conference on Logic Programming, ICLP 2021 (Technical Communications), Porto, 20–27 September 2021. EPTCS, vol. 345, pp. 70–76 (2021)
29. Giordano, L., Theseider Dupré, D.: Weighted defeasible knowledge bases and a multipreference semantics for a deep neural network model. In: Faber, W., Friedrich, G., Gebser, M., Morak, M. (eds.) JELIA 2021. LNCS (LNAI), vol. 12678, pp. 225–242. Springer, Cham (2021). https://doi.org/10.1007/978-3-030-75775-5_16
30. Giordano, L., Theseider Dupré, D.: An ASP approach for reasoning on neural networks under a finitely many-valued semantics for weighted conditional knowledge bases. Theory Pract. Log. Program. **22**(4), 589–605 (2022). https://doi.org/10.1017/S1471068422000163
31. Gottwald, S.: A Treatise on Many-Valued Logics. Research Studies Press (2001)
32. Haykin, S.: Neural Networks - A Comprehensive Foundation. Pearson (1999)
33. Hitzler, P., Krötzsch, M., Rudolph, S.: Foundations of Semantic Web Technologies. Chapman and Hall/CRC Press (2010). http://www.semantic-web-book.org/
34. Kern-Isberner, G.: Conditionals in Nonmonotonic Reasoning and Belief Revision - Considering Conditionals as Agents. LNCS, vol. 2087. Springer, Heidelberg (2001). https://doi.org/10.1007/3-540-44600-1_3
35. Kraus, S., Lehmann, D., Magidor, M.: Nonmonotonic reasoning, preferential models and cumulative logics. Artif. Intell. **44**(1–2), 167–207 (1990)
36. Lehmann, D., Magidor, M.: What does a conditional knowledge base entail? Artif. Intell. **55**(1), 1–60 (1992)
37. Lehmann, D.J.: Another perspective on default reasoning. Ann. Math. Artif. Intell. **15**(1), 61–82 (1995)
38. Lieto, A., Pozzato, G.L.: A description logic of typicality for conceptual combination. In: Ceci, M., Japkowicz, N., Liu, J., Papadopoulos, G.A., Raś, Z.W. (eds.) ISMIS 2018. LNCS (LNAI), vol. 11177, pp. 189–199. Springer, Cham (2018). https://doi.org/10.1007/978-3-030-01851-1_19
39. Lukasiewicz, T., Straccia, U.: Description logic programs under probabilistic uncertainty and fuzzy vagueness. Int. J. Approx. Reason. **50**(6), 837–853 (2009)

40. Alviano, M., et al.: A preferential interpretation of multilayer perceptrons in a conditional logic with typicality. CoRR (2023)
41. Porello, D., Kutz, O., Righetti, G., Troquard, N., Galliani, P., Masolo, C.: A toothful of concepts: towards a theory of weighted concept combination. In: Proceedings of the 32nd International Workshop on Description Logics, Oslo, Norway, 18–21 June 2019. CEUR Workshop Proceedings, vol. 2373. CEUR-WS.org (2019)
42. Rosch, E.: Natural categories. Cogn. Psychol. 4(3), 328–350 (1973)
43. Stoilos, G., Stamou, G.B., Tzouvaras, V., Pan, J.Z., Horrocks, I.: Fuzzy OWL: uncertainty and the semantic web. In: OWLED*05 Workshop. CEUR Workshop Proceedings, vol. 188 (2005)
44. Tamura, N., Taga, A., Kitagawa, S., Banbara, M.: Compiling finite linear CSP into SAT. Constraints Int. J. 14(2), 254–272 (2009)
45. Wagner, K.W.: Bounded query classes. SIAM J. Comput. 19(5), 833–846 (1990)

Deontic Equilibrium Logic with eXplicit Negation

Pedro Cabalar[1]([✉])[iD], Agata Ciabattoni[2][iD], and Leendert van der Torre[3][iD]

[1] University of A Coruña, A Coruña, Spain
cabalar@udc.es
[2] TU Wien, Vienna, Austria
agata@logic.at
[3] University of Luxembourg, Luxembourg City, Luxembourg
leon.vandertorre@uni.lu

Abstract. Equilibrium logic is a logical characterization of Answer Set Programming (ASP). We introduce *Deontic Equilibrium Logic with eXplicit negation* (DELX), its extension for normative reasoning. In contrast to modal approaches, DELX utilizes a normal form that restricts deontic operators solely to atoms. We establish that any theories in DELX can be reduced to ASP, and demonstrate the efficacy of this minimalist approach in addressing key challenges from the defeasible deontic logic literature.

1 Introduction

Before deploying AI systems in real-world settings, it is imperative that they satisfy legal and ethical requirements. Regulators, researchers and practitioners from various disciplines are providing such requirements, which are typically expressed as norms involving obligations and related concepts. To assess whether AI systems comply with them, we need formal languages to represent norms, and automated reasoning tools to derive conclusions from their representation.

Normative reasoning is the realm of deontic logic, which formalizes obligation and related concepts. While there is consensus on the importance of defeasibility in dealing with norms or on the fact that obligations cannot be defeated by their violations, the specific properties of deontic operators vary depending on the application. This has resulted in the emergence of numerous deontic systems (refer to the handbooks [15,16]) as advancements over the "standard" deontic logic KD [45], which proved inadequate in tackling various scenarios commonly referred to as deontic 'paradoxes'; in particular the necessity operator $\mathbf{O}\varphi$ in KD (read as "φ is obligatory") could not deal with secondary obligations (aka *contrary-to-duty*) or defeasible reasoning, as in the following well-known scenario

Example 1 (Cottage Fence [41]). The scenario consists of the norms

(i) There must be no fence (f).
(ii) If there is a fence, it must be a white (w) fence.
(iii) If the cottage is by the sea (s), there must be a fence.

If we build a fence f, we violate the norm $\mathbf{O}\neg f$ from (i) but then we are subject to the secondary obligation of a white fence $\mathbf{O}w$, that implies $\mathbf{O}f$ since a white fence is a fence. Thus, we may have to accept situations in which both $\mathbf{O}\neg f$ and $\mathbf{O}f$ coexist, something impossible in KD whose main axiom D: $\neg(\mathbf{O}f \wedge \mathbf{O}\neg f)$ states that this is inconsistent. Furthermore a cottage by the sea (iii) is usually read as an exception to the prohibition (i) when we understand the latter as a default, something that cannot be represented using (a monotonic logic like) KD.

To represent and reason about norms, deontic logic is commonly used in combination with techniques from nonmonotonic reasoning (e.g. [29,34]). Few tools exist e.g. [5,21,24], but flexible computational techniques and standardization are still lacking. Standardization and flexibility are among the key features of Answer Set Programming (ASP)—one of the most prominent paradigms of knowledge representation and reasoning for problem solving [6]. ASP's success can be attributed to its wide range of applications [14], efficient tools like clingo [17] and DLV [32], and others used in ASP competitions [18], but also to its solid theoretical foundations. The logical characterization of ASP based on *Equilibrium Logic* [39] allows the treatment of the ASP connectives, including both default and explicit negation [2]. It has been extended to deal with quantifiers [40], functions, sets and aggregates [9] and has also facilitated the homogeneous extension of ASP with temporal [1] and epistemic [8] modalities. A hybrid combination with the logic KD has been introduced in [3], and called Deontic Equilibrium Logic (DEL). Syntactically, DEL builds upon Equilibrium Logic and replaces the role of atoms by KD modal formulas that use a distinct set of Boolean connectives. This orientation is less integrated than other modal extensions of equilibrium logic, e.g. [1,8], in the sense that modal and non-modal operators cannot be freely combined. Besides, instead of collapsing to regular ASP, the non-modal fragment of DEL can capture Reiter's Default Logic [42]. More importantly, being based on KD, DEL considers the simultaneous obligation and prohibition of the same fact as inconsistent, which may need to be relaxed to deal with contrary-to-duties.

In this paper we present a novel deontic extension of Equilibrium Logic that, instead of dealing with a modal language, focuses on reasoning about literals built with *explicit negation*, originally known in ASP as "classical" negation [19]. To this aim, in Sect. 3, we introduce *deontic logic programs* that minimally extend ASP with two new propositions representing obligation and prohibition of atoms. This framework can be straightforwardly encoded in ASP, maintaining the same computational complexity. To overcome the syntactic limitations of logic programs, we propose *Deontic Equilibrium Logic with eXplicit negation* (DELX) in Sect. 4. DELX is a full logical language that extends equilibrium logic (with explicit negation) by incorporating obligations and prohibitions as new connectives. We demonstrate that any DELX theory can be reduced to a deontic logic program, enabling the use of ASP to compute its (deontic) equilibrium models. To assess the adequacy of the proposed formalism, we use our framework to tackle the most salient challenges of normative reasoning, which we formalize and discuss in Sect. 5 as variations of Example 1. Through various DELX expressions, we capture nuanced interpretations of norms in a formal manner, showcasing a high degree of elaboration tolerance [33].

2   ASP in a Nutshell

We recall the definition of answer sets for propositional logic programs with explicit negation; we extend here the original definition in [19] by allowing default negation in the head, something familiar in modern ASP. We start from a propositional *signature*, a set of atoms At, and define an *explicit literal* as any $p \in At$ or its explicit negation $\neg p$. A *default literal* is any explicit literal L or its default negation $not\ L$. A *rule* is an implication of the form:

$$H_1 \vee \cdots \vee H_n \leftarrow B_1 \wedge \cdots \wedge B_m \tag{1}$$

where $n, m \geq 0$ and all H_i and B_j are default literals. The disjunction $H_1 \vee \cdots \vee H_n$ in (1) is called the rule *head*. When $n = 0$, the head is the empty disjunction $\bot$, and the rule is said to be a *constraint*. The conjunction $B_1 \wedge \cdots \wedge B_m$ in (1) is called the rule *body*. When $m = 0$, it corresponds to the empty conjunction $\top$ and, when this happens, we normally omit both the body $\top$ and the $\leftarrow$ symbol. Moreover, if $m = 0$, $n = 1$, and the head consists of a unique explicit literal H_1 (no default negation), we say that the rule is a *fact*. A *logic program* is a set of rules. For simplicity, in this paper we deal with finite programs and we sometimes represent them as the conjunction of their rules. Logic programs may contain variables, but they are understood as an abbreviation of all their possible ground instances (for simplicity, we do not allow function symbols).

A *propositional interpretation* T for a signature At is any set of explicit literals that is *consistent*, i.e., it contains no pair of literals p and $\neg p$ for a same atom $p \in At$. Given any rule r like (1) containing no default negation, we say that an interpretation *satisfies* r if there is some head explicit literal $H_i \in T$ whenever all body literals $B_j \in T$. The *reduct* of a logic program Π with respect to an interpretation T, written Π^T, is the result of: (1) removing all rules with a default literal $not\ L$ in the body such that $L \in T$; (2) removing all rules with a default literal $not\ L$ in the head such that $L \notin T$; and (3) removing the rest of default literals. An interpretation T is an *answer set* of a logic program Π if it is $\subseteq$-minimal among all the interpretations satisfying all rules of Π^T.

3   Deontic Logic Programs

Following a minimalist approach, we extend ASP with two new types of propositions that talk about atomic *obligations* $\mathbf{O}p$ (read as "p is obligatory") and atomic *prohibitions* $\mathbf{F}p$ ("p is forbidden"), for any atom $p \in At$. In many deontic logics (e.g. KD [45]) the prohibition $\mathbf{F}p$ can be defined as the obligation $\mathbf{O}\neg p$. However, at this point, we refrain from reading $\mathbf{O}$ and $\mathbf{F}$ as real operators, and see them as prefixes for new ASP atoms called "$\mathbf{O}p$" and "$\mathbf{F}p$" in the signature.

Keeping p, $\mathbf{O}p$ and $\mathbf{F}p$ separated as three independent propositions makes sense since, for instance, there is no established connection between $\mathbf{O}p$ and p, as one may have the obligation of p but yet, p may not hold (i.e., the obligation is not fulfilled), and similarly for prohibitions. In addition, under certain conditions we will allow $\mathbf{O}p$ and $\mathbf{F}p$ to hold together, as discussed in the introduction.

A *deontic atom* is either $p \in At$ or any of the expressions $\mathbf{O}p$ or $\mathbf{F}p$. The *deontic signature At'* is defined as $At' := At \cup \{\mathbf{O}p \mid p \in At\} \cup \{\mathbf{F}p \mid p \in At\}$. We may now form explicit literals for At'. Intuitively, p (and $\neg p$) means that p is true (false, resp.) in a factual sense, so that when none of the two hold, there is no evidence that p or $\neg p$ hold or have happened. E.g., if p means "pay taxes", when p holds we can read it as "the payment can be checked", and when $\neg p$ holds as "we can prove that the payment was not done". The explicit literals $\mathbf{O}p$ and $\neg\mathbf{O}p$ stand for "the obligation of p is true" and "is explicitly false", or "$\neg p$ is explicitly permitted" (we will see below that permissions can also be expressed in a weaker way by using default negation). Again, we may also have that none of the two hold. We permit having at the same time both the literal $\neg p$ in the real world and an obligation $\mathbf{O}p$, meaning that the latter is violated. Finally, the prohibition $\mathbf{F}p$ is dual to the obligation. Its explicit negation $\neg\mathbf{F}p$ can be read as "p is explicitly permitted" whereas a violation happens when both $\mathbf{F}p$ and p hold simultaneously. By introducing default negation, for any atom $p \in At$ we can form 12 default literals corresponding to (atomic) *normative positions* (cf. [43]):

$$p, \neg p, \mathbf{O}p, \neg\mathbf{O}p, \mathbf{F}p, \neg\mathbf{F}p, not\ p, not\ \neg p, not\ \mathbf{O}p, not\ \neg\mathbf{O}p, not\ \mathbf{F}p, not\ \neg\mathbf{F}p$$

For instance, the reading of *not* $\mathbf{O}p$ is "there is no evidence about $\mathbf{O}p$" as opposed to $\neg\mathbf{O}p$ that provides evidence for $\mathbf{O}p$ to be explicitly false. In fact, we can also see *not* $\mathbf{O}p$ as an implicit permission for $\neg p$, and something similar happens with *not* $\mathbf{F}p$, that becomes an implicit permission for p (see C1 in Sect. 5). A literal like *not* $\neg\mathbf{F}p$ reads as "there is no reason to conclude the explicit permission of p".

An interpretation containing both the obligation $\mathbf{O}p$ and the prohibition $\mathbf{F}p$ is a dilemma and should be inconsistent. This corresponds to the Deontic axiom D, present in most deontic logics. Let us encode (i)–(iii) from Example 1 as:

$$\mathbf{F}f \qquad\qquad \mathbf{O}w \leftarrow f \wedge \mathbf{F}f \qquad\qquad \mathbf{O}f \leftarrow s \qquad\qquad (2)$$

and assume we add the fact s ("the cottage is by the sea"). The only answer set is $\{\mathbf{F}f, \mathbf{O}f, s\}$ and so, we have a specification demanding both the presence and absence of a fence simultaneously. This specification should be considered inconsistent because, somehow, we have *contradicting indications on how to proceed*. To achieve the inconsistency of the program $(2) \cup \{s\}$ we could define the *deontic answer sets* as those in which for no atom p, $\mathbf{O}p, \mathbf{F}p$ occurs. However, to deal with secondary obligations, we may require that both $\mathbf{O}p$ and $\mathbf{F}p$ hold, if one of them has been violated. As a white fence is also a fence, we add:

$$f \leftarrow w \qquad\qquad \mathbf{O}f \leftarrow \mathbf{O}w \qquad\qquad (3)$$

and if we take the extended program $(2) \cup (3) \cup \{f\}$ we obtain the answer set $\{f, \mathbf{F}f, \mathbf{O}w, \mathbf{O}f\}$ so, we conclude both $\mathbf{F}f$ and $\mathbf{O}f$. These two deontic atoms however *do not provide indications on how to proceed*, as the decision to put a fence has been already taken, forcing the violation of $\mathbf{F}f$ and the fulfillment of $\mathbf{O}f$, derived from $\mathbf{O}w$. The conclusion is that $\mathbf{O}f$ and $\mathbf{F}f$ may coexist, provided that one of the two has been violated. This leads us to the following definition.

Definition 1. *A* deontic interpretation *T is a propositional interpretation for At' satisfying: $\{\mathbf{O}p, \mathbf{F}p\} \subseteq T$ implies $\{p, \neg p\} \cap T \neq \emptyset$, for any $p \in At$.*

T is consistent by definition, that is, T cannot contain literals A and $\neg A$ for a same deontic atom A. To be a deontic interpretation, we additionally require that the atoms $\mathbf{O}p$ and $\mathbf{F}p$ can only hold together when T contains information about p, i.e., either p or its explicit negation $\neg p$ are in T. Note that the mere presence of $\mathbf{O}p$ and $\mathbf{F}p$ together will not permit to derive p or $\neg p$, as the derivation can only be achieved by application of rules in the logic program. We call *deontic answer sets* to the answer sets of a deontic logic program that are also deontic interpretations. To obtain them, we can use the axiom schema (for any $p \in At$):

$$\bot \leftarrow \mathbf{O}p \wedge \mathbf{F}p \wedge not\ p \wedge not\ \neg p \qquad \text{(wD)}$$

that is a weaker version of the Deontic axiom D, and states that the conjunction of $\mathbf{O}p$ and $\mathbf{F}p$ is inconsistent only if none of the two has been violated.

Proposition 1. *T is a deontic answer set of a deontic logic program Π iff T is an answer set of $\Pi \cup (\mathbf{wD})$.*

To see the effect of $(\mathbf{wD})$, consider again the program $\Pi = (2) \cup \{s\}$. As mentioned before, the only answer set of this program would be $T = \{\mathbf{F}f, \mathbf{O}f, s\}$ but this is ruled out by constraint $(\mathbf{wD})$. In fact, T is not a deontic answer set since we have both the obligation and the prohibition of f but we did not provide any information about f or $\neg f$. This means we face a dilemma, because we have two contradictory norms and none of them has been violated. If we take program $\Pi' = \Pi \cup \{f\}$ (that is, we decide to put a fence) then $\mathbf{F}f$ is violated and consistency is restored, obtaining the answer set $T' = \{\mathbf{F}f, \mathbf{O}f, s, f, \mathbf{O}w\}$. Note how we derive the obligation of a white fence $\mathbf{O}w$, and that the prohibition of $\mathbf{F}f$ *has not been retracted*, but is being violated instead. If, instead of f, we are said that no fence will be built $\neg f$ (i.e. we have evidence that there is no fence), then program $\Pi'' = \Pi \cup \{\neg f\}$ also becomes consistent, leading this time to answer set $T'' = \{\mathbf{F}f, \mathbf{O}f, s, \neg f\}$ where $\mathbf{O}f$ is violated.

Proposition 1 allows a direct encoding of any deontic logic program Π into a regular ASP program Π'. To do so, a compact representation can be achieved by reifying all atoms in Π to become arguments of three predicates in Π', say h, ob and fb respectively standing for *holds* (in a factual sense), *obligatory* and *forbidden*. As an illustration, (2)–(3) can be represented as the ASP program[1] below where the constraint in the last line is an encoding of $(\mathbf{wD})$.

---

[1] In the ASP-core-2 input language, $\leftarrow$, $\neg$ and $\wedge$ are represented as ':-', '-' and commas.

```
fb(f).                              % The fence is forbidden
ob(w) :- h(f), fb(f).              % CTD: if fence, it must be white
ob(f) :- h(s).                      % Obligatory fence if by the sea
h(f).                               % We have a fence
h(f) :- h(w).                       % White fence means fence
ob(f) :- ob(w).                     % The same for obligation
:- ob(P), fb(P), not h(P), not -h(P). % Axiom (wD)
```

This encoding can be easily automated in linear time, so the complexity results of deontic logic programs are as in the regular (disjunctive) ASP case [13]. In particular we have the following:

Proposition 2. *Deciding whether a deontic logic program Π has a deontic answer set is Σ_2^P-complete. If every head in Π is free from disjunction, deciding the existence of a deontic answer set is NP-complete.*

4   Extension to Equilibrium Logic

Introducing deontic atoms in logic programs provides a simple and practical approach for formalizing deontic scenarios, but falls short if we need a proper logical formalism. Note that, so far, **O** and **F** are not proper operators but just a kind of prefix for atoms: in fact, all program operators in ASP are also treated under a very restricted syntax, and their semantics relies on a syntactic transformation (the program reduct). If we are interested in arbitrary nesting of operators, defining new constructs or extensions to incorporate temporal or epistemic reasoning, we need a logical formalisation that overcomes the syntax limitations and the program reduct operation. An excellent starting point for our purposes is the logical characterization of ASP based on *Equilibrium Logic* [39] which has also been extended to deal with strong [36] or explicit negation [2]. As happens in ASP, when explicit negation is used, equilibrium models become three-valued (an atom can be true p, false $\neg p$ or none of the two). To introduce **O** and **F** in this setting, we adopt a practical approach, so that, although they will be applicable now on other operators, their expressive power is still limited to a kind of three-valued semantics. The advantage of this approach is to reduce arbitrary formulas to theories where deontic operators are only used in *explicit literals*, something that can be easily translated into ASP logic programs. Yet, when compared to a modal interpretation of **O** and **F**, the price to pay is a loss in expressiveness when dealing with obligations on compound formulas: for example, $\mathbf{O}(\varphi \lor \psi)$ will simply be $\mathbf{O}\varphi \lor \mathbf{O}\psi$. This coincides with the ASP reading of disjunction, and in fact to the natural language reading of disjunction in the free choice permission scenario [30].

Equilibrium models are defined by a selection among models from the intermediate logic called *Here-and-There* [28] (HT), or 3-valued Gödel logic. We now incorporate deontic operators in the extension $\mathcal{X}_5$ of HT with explicit negation [2], thus defining the logic of *Deontic Here-and-There with Explicit Negation*

(DHTX for short). A *formula* φ of DHTX follows the grammar:

$$\varphi ::= p \in At \mid \bot \mid \varphi \wedge \varphi \mid \varphi \vee \varphi \mid \varphi \to \varphi \mid \neg\varphi \mid \mathbf{O}\varphi \mid \mathbf{F}\varphi$$

We define the derived operators $\varphi \leftrightarrow \psi \stackrel{\text{def}}{=} (\varphi \to \psi) \wedge (\psi \to \varphi)$, $not\ \varphi \stackrel{\text{def}}{=} (\varphi \to \bot)$ and the constant $\top$ as $not\ \bot$. We assume that the conditional rule $\varphi \leftarrow \psi$ in logic programs is nothing but the reversed implication $\psi \to \varphi$. We also define the following derived deontic operators:

$$\mathbf{O}^{\mathbf{v}}\,\varphi \stackrel{\text{def}}{=} \mathbf{O}\varphi \wedge \neg\varphi \qquad\qquad \mathbf{O}^{\mathbf{f}}\,\varphi \stackrel{\text{def}}{=} \mathbf{O}\varphi \wedge \varphi$$

$$\mathbf{O}^{\mathbf{nf}}\,\varphi \stackrel{\text{def}}{=} \mathbf{O}\varphi \wedge not\ \varphi \qquad\qquad \mathbf{O}^{\mathbf{nv}}\,\varphi \stackrel{\text{def}}{=} \mathbf{O}\varphi \wedge not\ \neg\varphi$$

$$\mathbf{O}^{\mathbf{u}}\,\varphi \stackrel{\text{def}}{=} \mathbf{O}\varphi \wedge not\ (\varphi \vee \neg\varphi) \qquad\qquad \mathbf{P}\varphi \stackrel{\text{def}}{=} \neg\mathbf{F}\varphi$$

$$\mathbf{O}^{\mathbf{d}}\,\varphi \stackrel{\text{def}}{=} (not\ \mathbf{P}\neg\varphi \to \mathbf{O}\varphi) \qquad\qquad \mathbf{P}^{\mathbf{d}}\,\varphi \stackrel{\text{def}}{=} (not\ \mathbf{F}\varphi \to \mathbf{P}\varphi)$$

$$\mathbf{O}(\varphi \mid \psi) \stackrel{\text{def}}{=} (\psi \vee \mathbf{O}^{\mathbf{nv}}\,\psi \to \mathbf{O}\varphi) \qquad\qquad \mathbf{F}^{x}\,\varphi \stackrel{\text{def}}{=} \mathbf{O}^{x}\,\neg\varphi$$

$\mathbf{P}\varphi$ stands for the explicit permission for φ whereas $\mathbf{P}^{\mathbf{d}}\,\varphi$ is its default version. The superindexed variants of $\mathbf{O}$ stand for: $\mathbf{d}$=*default*, $\mathbf{f}$=*fulfilled*, $\mathbf{v}$=*violated*, $\mathbf{nv}$=*non-violated*, $\mathbf{nf}$=*non-fulfilled* and $\mathbf{u}$=*undetermined*. We define the same variants $\mathbf{F}^x$ in terms of $\mathbf{O}^x$ for all $x \in \{\mathbf{d}, \mathbf{f}, \mathbf{v}, \mathbf{nv}, \mathbf{nf}, \mathbf{u}\}$ having in mind that we can now replace $\mathbf{F}\varphi$ by $\mathbf{O}\neg\varphi$. The conditional obligation $\mathbf{O}(\varphi \mid \psi)$ ("φ is obligatory, given ψ") is explained in Sect. 5 (challenge C6).

A formula is said to be *deontic* if it contains deontic operators, and *non-deontic* otherwise. A *theory* is a set of formulas. Finite theories (or subtheories) are understood as the conjunction of their formulas. Notice that deontic logic programs are theories.

Definition 2. *A Deontic HT-interpretation is a pair $\langle H, T \rangle$ of sets of explicit literals s.t. T is a deontic interpretation and $H \subseteq T$. $\langle H, T \rangle$ is total when $H = T$.*

Intuitively, literals in H ("here") can be considered founded or proved, literals in $T \setminus H$ are assumed but unfounded and literals not in T ("there") are not assumed and they directly do not hold. For instance, the pair $H = \{\mathbf{O}p, \mathbf{F}p\}$ and $T = \{\neg p, \mathbf{O}p, \mathbf{F}p, \neg\mathbf{F}q\}$ is a deontic HT-interpretation where $\mathbf{O}p$ and $\mathbf{F}p$ are founded whereas $\neg p$ and $\neg\mathbf{F}q$ are assumed but unfounded. The interpretation just considers the rest of literals as not assumed. Note that the potential inconsistency between $\mathbf{O}p$ and $\mathbf{F}p$ is only checked at the component T. The same effect is obtained if $(\mathbf{wD})$ is added as an axiom instead of requiring T to be a deontic interpretation in Definition 2. In this case, the two literals can occur together because $\neg p \in T$, so we assume that $\mathbf{O}p$ is violated. On the other hand, $\neg p$ is not justified at H but we still allow $\mathbf{O}p$ and $\mathbf{F}p$ in H, since $\neg p$ is assumed at T.

We define the set of "deontic worlds" as $\{r, o, f\}$ respectively standing for *real*, *obligation* and *forbidden*. Given a world $w \in \{r, o, f\}$, its complementary world $\overline{w}$ is defined as $\overline{r} \stackrel{\text{def}}{=} r$, $\overline{o} \stackrel{\text{def}}{=} f$ and $\overline{f} \stackrel{\text{def}}{=} o$.

Definition 3. $M = \langle H, T \rangle$ satisfies *(resp. falsifies) a formula φ at a deontic world $w \in \{r, o, f\}$, written $M, w \models \varphi$ ($M, w =\!\mid \varphi$), if the conditions below hold:*

φ	$M, w \models \varphi$ when	$M, w =\!\mid \varphi$ when
$\top$ ($\bot$)	always (never)	never (always)
$\alpha \wedge \beta$	$M, w \models \alpha$ and $M, w \models \beta$	$M, w =\!\mid \alpha$ or $M, w =\!\mid \beta$
$\alpha \vee \beta$	$M, w \models \alpha$ or $M, w \models \beta$	$M, w =\!\mid \alpha$ and $M, w =\!\mid \beta$
$\alpha \to \beta$	$M', w \not\models \alpha$ or $M', w \models \beta$ for $M' \in \{M, \langle T, T \rangle\}$	$\langle T, T \rangle, w \models \alpha$ and $M, w =\!\mid \beta$
$\neg \alpha$	$M, \overline{w} =\!\mid \alpha$	$M, \overline{w} \models \alpha$
p	$p \in H$ if $w = r$ $\mathbf{O}p \in H$ if $w = o$ $\neg \mathbf{F}p \in H$ if $w = f$	$\neg p \in H$ if $w = r$ $\neg \mathbf{O}p \in H$ if $w = o$ $\mathbf{F}p \in H$ if $w = f$
$\mathbf{O}\alpha$	$M, o \models \alpha$	$M, o =\!\mid \alpha$
$\mathbf{F}\alpha$	$M, f =\!\mid \alpha$	$M, f \models \alpha$

In the definition above, if we just take the syntactic fragment for $\wedge$, $\vee$, $\neg$, $\bot$, $\top$ and atoms (we can fix $w = r$), we obtain *classical logic with strong negation* [44]. If we further extend it with the evaluation of $\to$ (still fixing $w = r$) we get *Equilibrium Logic with explicit negation* $\mathcal{X}_5$ [2]. So, the new features are the three deontic worlds and their interplay with the operators $\mathbf{O}$, $\mathbf{F}$ and $\neg$. As we can see, the interpretation of an atom $p \in At$ depends on each specific world. The real world $w = r$ works as expected whereas, in world $w = o$, satisfying (resp. falsifying) an atom p actually corresponds to requiring that the literal $\mathbf{O}p$ (resp. $\neg \mathbf{O}p$) holds in the interpretation. In the world $w = f$ the roles of literals are swapped, so satisfaction of an atom p corresponds to including the literal $\neg \mathbf{F}p$ whereas falsifying p corresponds to the literal $\mathbf{F}p$. The reason for this swapping is that a prohibition $\mathbf{F}\alpha$ is a kind of negation (we will see later that it is actually equivalent to $\mathbf{O}\neg\alpha$). The operators that permit moving to a different deontic world are $\neg$, $\mathbf{O}$ and $\mathbf{F}$. To satisfy $\mathbf{O}\alpha$ we simply check the satisfaction of α after "jumping" to world o, regardless of the world we started from, and the same happens for the falsification of $\mathbf{O}\alpha$. With $\mathbf{F}\alpha$ a similar effect is obtained for the world f, but again, it additionally swaps satisfaction to falsification and vice versa. In the case of explicit negation, satisfaction of $\neg\alpha$ becomes falsification of α but, additionally, if we are not in the real world $w \neq r$, we switch from w to $\overline{w}$. An example on how these three operators work: $M, r \models \mathbf{O}\neg p$ becomes $M, o \models \neg p$ that is interpreted as $M, f =\!\mid p$ and, finally, it amounts to $\mathbf{F}p \in H$.

An HT-interpretation $\langle H, T \rangle$ is a *model* of a theory Γ, written $\langle H, T \rangle \models \Gamma$, if $\langle H, T \rangle, r \models \varphi$ for all $\varphi \in \Gamma$. A formula φ is a DHTX-*tautology* (or DHTX-*valid*), $\models \varphi$ in symbols, if any DHTX-interpretation is a model of φ. DHTX is the logic induced by all DHTX-tautologies.

The properties below are fundamental in any extension of HT.

Theorem 1 (Persistence). *For any DHTX-interpretation* $\langle H, T \rangle$, *any world* $w \in \{r, o, f\}$ *and any formula* φ: (i) $\langle H, T \rangle, w \models \varphi$ *implies* $\langle T, T \rangle, w \models \varphi$ *for any world* w, *and* (ii) $\langle H, T \rangle, w =\!\mid \varphi$ *implies* $\langle T, T \rangle, w =\!\mid \varphi$ *for any world* w. □

Proposition 3. *For any* $\langle H, T \rangle$, *world* w *and formula* φ: (i) $\langle H, T \rangle, w \models$ *not* φ *iff* $\langle T, T \rangle, w \not\models \varphi$; (ii) $\langle H, T \rangle, w =\!\mid$ *not* φ *iff* $\langle T, T \rangle, w \models \varphi$. □

DHTX is an extension of $\mathcal{X}_5$ in the following sense:

Proposition 4. *If* φ *is* $\mathcal{X}_5$-*valid then* φ *is DHTX-valid.*

For instance, the following $\mathcal{X}_5$ tautologies are also DHTX-valid:

$$\neg(\varphi \to \psi) \leftrightarrow \text{not not } \varphi \wedge \neg\psi \qquad \neg\text{not } \varphi \leftrightarrow \text{not not } \varphi \qquad (4)$$

As happens in $\mathcal{X}_5$ the validity of $\varphi \leftrightarrow \psi$ does not guarantee that we can always substitute φ by ψ. To this aim, we introduce the following stronger relation (taken from [2]). Two formulas φ and ψ are DHTX-*equivalent*, written $\varphi \equiv \psi$, if for any DHTX-interpretation $M = \langle H, T \rangle$ and any world $w \in \{r, o, f\}$, we have both: (1) $M, w \models \varphi$ iff $M, w \models \psi$; and (2) $M, w =\!\mid \varphi$ iff $M, w =\!\mid \psi$.

Proposition 5. *For any pair of formulas* φ *and* ψ, *if* $\varphi \equiv \psi$ *then* $\models \varphi \leftrightarrow \psi$.

In general, the other direction does not hold. As a counterexample (already used in [2]) take the DHTX-tautology $p \wedge \text{not } p \leftrightarrow \bot$ (which is also an $\mathcal{X}_5$-tautology). It is not difficult to see, however, that $p \wedge \text{not } p \not\equiv \bot$. In fact, we cannot replace $p \wedge \text{not } p$ inside $\neg(p \wedge \text{not } p)$ to get $\neg\bot$. Indeed, the former amounts to a rule $\neg p \leftarrow \text{not } p$ while the latter to $\top$.

   Yet, we can still use $\models \varphi \leftrightarrow \psi$ to perform substitutions in some contexts:

Theorem 2. $\models \varphi \leftrightarrow \psi$ *iff* φ *and* ψ *have the same DHTX-models.*

Corollary 1. *Let* $\Gamma[\varphi]$ *be a theory containing a subformula* φ *not in the scope of* $\neg$, **F** *or* **O** *and let* $\models \varphi \leftrightarrow \psi$. *Then,* $\Gamma[\varphi]$ *and* $\Gamma[\psi]$ *have the same DHTX-models.*

Definition 4. *A total DHTX-interpretation* $\langle T, T \rangle$ *is an* equilibrium model *of a theory* Γ *if* $\langle T, T \rangle \models \Gamma$ *and there is no* $H \subset T$ *such that* $\langle H, T \rangle \models \Gamma$.

Deontic Equilibrium logic is the non-monotonic logic induced by equilibrium models. For deontic logic programs, answer sets and equilibrium models coincide:

Theorem 3. *Let* Π *be a deontic logic program. A deontic interpretation* T *is a deontic answer set of* Π *iff* $\langle T, T \rangle$ *is an equilibrium model of* Π. □

   We show below that any deontic theory can be reduced to a deontic logic program, and so, its equilibrium models can be eventually computed via regular ASP. We start observing a group of DHTX-equivalences that also hold in $\mathcal{X}_5$:

$$\neg(\varphi \vee \psi) \equiv \neg\varphi \wedge \neg\psi \quad \neg(\varphi \wedge \psi) \equiv \neg\varphi \vee \neg\psi \quad \neg\neg\varphi \equiv \varphi \quad \neg\bot \equiv \top \quad \neg\top \equiv \bot \quad (5)$$

We can use (4)–(5) from the outermost occurrences of $\neg$ to push this operator inside non-deontic connectives. As a result we get an *Explicit-negation Normal*

Form (XNF), where all outermost occurrences of ¬ are applied to atoms, to **O** or to **F**. To unfold expressions inside **O** or **F** we can further apply the equivalences:

$$\mathbf{O}(\varphi \vee \psi) \equiv \mathbf{O}\varphi \vee \mathbf{O}\psi \qquad \mathbf{F}(\varphi \vee \psi) \equiv \mathbf{F}\varphi \wedge \mathbf{F}\psi \qquad (6)$$

$$\mathbf{O}(\varphi \wedge \psi) \equiv \mathbf{O}\varphi \wedge \mathbf{O}\psi \qquad \mathbf{F}(\varphi \wedge \psi) \equiv \mathbf{F}\varphi \vee \mathbf{F}\psi \qquad (7)$$

$$\mathbf{O}\bot \equiv \bot; \quad \mathbf{F}\bot \equiv \top \qquad \mathbf{O}\top \equiv \top; \quad \mathbf{F}\top \equiv \bot \qquad (8)$$

$$\mathbf{O}(\varphi \to \psi) \equiv \mathbf{O}\varphi \to \mathbf{O}\psi \qquad (9)$$

$$\mathbf{O}\,not\,\varphi \equiv not\,\mathbf{O}\varphi \qquad \mathbf{F}\,not\,\varphi \equiv not\,not\,\neg\mathbf{F}\varphi \qquad (10)$$

$$\mathbf{O}\neg\varphi \equiv \mathbf{F}\varphi \qquad \mathbf{F}\neg\varphi \equiv \mathbf{O}\varphi \qquad (11)$$

$$\mathbf{O}\mathbf{O}\varphi \equiv \mathbf{O}\varphi \qquad \mathbf{F}\mathbf{O}\varphi \equiv \neg\mathbf{O}\varphi \qquad (12)$$

$$\mathbf{O}\mathbf{F}\varphi \equiv \mathbf{F}\varphi \qquad \mathbf{F}\mathbf{F}\varphi \equiv \neg\mathbf{F}\varphi \qquad (13)$$

By (11), we may choose either **O** or **F** as a primitive connective, and hence the primitive DELX connectives can be reduced to five $\wedge, \vee, \to, \neg, \mathbf{O}$, together with the constant $\bot$. Equivalences (6)–(13) do not cover the case when **F** is applied to an implication: if so, we can only proceed from the outermost occurrences of this operator (as happened with explicit negation) using the valid double implications:

$$\mathbf{F}(\varphi \to \psi) \leftrightarrow not\,not\,\neg\mathbf{F}\varphi \wedge \mathbf{F}\psi \qquad \neg\mathbf{F}(\varphi \to \psi) \leftrightarrow \neg\mathbf{F}\varphi \to \neg\mathbf{F}\psi \qquad (14)$$

Using these properties we can reach the syntactic form we call *Deontic-Atom Normal Form* (DANF), in which all deontic operators are applied to atoms. Once in DANF, we can then resort to $\mathcal{X}_5$ reduction to logic programs.

Theorem 4. *Any deontic theory can be reduced to a deontic logic program having the same DHTX models.*

It is not hard to see that the reduction to DANF is polynomial whereas the step from arbitrary combinations of $\wedge, \vee, not, \to$ into a logic program may be exponential due to distributivity laws. Yet, [11] proposes an alternative polynomial reduction that avoids the combinatorial blowup by introducing auxiliary atoms.

5 DELX at Work on Challenging Normative Problems

We discuss the nuances of defeasible deontic reasoning that we aimed to capture, using variants of the cottage regulation (Example 1). We consider below the starting program $\Pi = (2) \cup (3)$ and analyze the challenges from [7] we refer to as C1–C6.

C1 (Explicit versus Negative permission). We want to distinguish between the existence of permission vs absence of prohibition. Suppose that a new neighbor ignores the local regulations and has in mind the practical reasoning rule:

(iv) *If it is permitted, I build a fence around my cottage*

A cautious behavior is to wait for an *explicit permission* to build the fence. A more adventurous behavior is to build it if there is no explicit prohibition (*negative or implicit permission*): without more information, she concludes to build the fence, but retracts that conclusion once she becomes aware of norm (i). Explicit and implicit permissions can be respectively captured by the rules:

$$f \leftarrow \neg \mathbf{F} f \qquad (15) \qquad\qquad f \leftarrow not \; \mathbf{F} f \qquad (16)$$

The program (16) alone permits to conclude f (the adventurous neighbor builds the fence), but with $\Pi \cup (16)$ this is not possible anymore, as we have $\mathbf{F}f$. On the other hand, the cautious neighbor cannot conclude f from $\Pi \cup (15)$ or even from (15) alone, since it requires the permission $\neg \mathbf{F} f$. We could get it with a cottage by the sea, but then (i) should be formalized as a default (see C4).

We may be sometimes interested in generalizing this distinction into a Closed World Assumption for a given set Γ of formulas. For instance, a *Closed Explicit Permission Assumption* (CEPA) stands for "anything not explicitly forbidden is permitted" and can be simply formalized as $\mathbf{P^d} \varphi$ for every $\varphi \in \Gamma$. Similarly, a *Closed Negative Permission Assumption* (CNPA) rather means "anything not explicitly permitted is forbidden" and just corresponds to $\mathbf{F^d} \varphi$, for all $\varphi \in \Gamma$.

C2 (Contrary-to-Duty (CTD) and Compliance). A *CTD* or *secondary* obligation comes into force only when another (the primary) obligation is violated. For instance, the two sentences (i) and (ii) from Example 1 are primary obligation and CTD. A different, though related concept is that of compensatory obligation, as:

(v) *If you put a fence when forbidden, you should pay a fine.*

If we combine the prohibition (i) with the existence of a fence we want to derive from (v) that fences are forbidden and that a fine must be paid. This is known as *monitoring*, *compliance*, or *conformance checking*. Likewise, if obligations are fulfilled, rewards may be given. Encoding compliance in DELX is straightforward: we may just use the derived operators for violation $\mathbf{F^v}$ or fulfillment $\mathbf{F^f}$. E.g., (v) is formalized as $(\mathbf{F^v} f \rightarrow \mathbf{O} pay)$ that amounts to the logic program rule:

$$\mathbf{O} pay \leftarrow \mathbf{F} f \wedge f \qquad (17)$$

C3 (CTD and Dilemmas). A *dilemma* is a situation where we deal with the simultaneous obligation and prohibition of a same fact. For instance having (i) together with $\mathbf{O}w$ leads to a dilemma. There is consensus in the literature that such dilemmas should be inconsistent. This is, in fact, what happens with the program $\Pi \cup \{\mathbf{O}w\}$ that has no answer set, since axiom ($\mathbf{wD}$) does not accept $\mathbf{O}f \wedge \mathbf{F}f$ without information about f. However, when a dilemma follows from a CTD, consistency should be restored. E.g., suppose we have the premises (i)–(iii) plus (v) and, additionally, there exists a fence f. By (ii), we must have a white fence, but this is in conflict with (i), that says we must have *no fence at all*. This scenario is consistent in DELX: the program $\Pi \cup (17) \cup \{f\}$ has a unique answer set $\{f, \mathbf{F}f, \mathbf{O}w, \mathbf{O}f, \mathbf{O}pay\}$ where $\mathbf{O}f \wedge \mathbf{F}f$ is now consistent because $\mathbf{F}f$ has been violated. Notice that some deontic approaches remove the CTD dilemma by retracting the primary prohibition (i) to have a fence. This leads to the so-called *drowning problem* [38]: we would no longer have a violation of $\mathbf{F}f$ so we cannot derive the payment of the fine $\mathbf{O}pay$. Note that the combination of compliance and dilemmas has become problematic for some deontic approaches (most notably Dyadic Deontic Logic [27,37]), requiring *ad hoc* representations like the introduction of so-called *violation constants*.

C4 (CTD and Defeasible Obligations). Some obligations should be read as defaults in the presence of exceptions. Let us rephrase (iii) as the permission:

(vi) *If the cottage is by the sea (s), there **may** be a fence.*

This was the original wording for the Cottage scenario in [41], introduced to illustrate the distinction between CTD reasoning ((i) and (ii)) and exceptions ((i) and (vi)); the two types of reasoning should be treated differently. Indeed, if we consider (i) and (ii) as instances of defeasible reasoning, we would let the primary obligation (i) be defeated by the secondary obligation (ii), which is not desirable. Premise (vi) leads to a new reading of the normative scenario: on the one hand, being by the sea provides now an *explicit permission* to build the fence; on the other hand, (i) is read now as *"There must be no fence, unless a permission is granted"* becoming a *default prohibition*. In our DELX formalization we may simply replace the first and third formulas in (2) respectively by $\mathbf{F}^{\mathbf{d}}f$ (default prohibition) and $\mathbf{P}f \leftarrow s$ (explicit permission) leading to:

$$\mathbf{F}f \leftarrow not\ \neg\mathbf{F}f \qquad \mathbf{O}w \leftarrow f \wedge \mathbf{F}f \qquad \neg\mathbf{F}f \leftarrow s \qquad (18)$$

If we have no information about the location, we consider the program $(18) \cup (3)$ alone, and the only answer set is $\{\mathbf{F}f\}$, we cannot put a fence by default. If we add the fact s we obtain $\{s, \neg\mathbf{F}f\}$, that is, we have the permission to put a fence, and $\mathbf{F}f$ is no longer derived. If we further know there is a fence, the program $(18) \cup (3) \cup \{s, f\}$ produces the answer set $\{s, f, \neg\mathbf{F}f\}$ so there is no CTD obligation of a white fence, because there is no violated prohibition.

C5 (Constitutive Norms). We now deal with the derivation of obligations in presence of an "is a" or a "count as" relation. Though there exist various kinds of constitutive norms of increasing complexity, in this paper we only consider simple factual rules. In the example we assume that a white fence *is a* fence. Does this also imply that the obligation for white fences implies the obligation for fences? And does the prohibition for fences imply the prohibition for white fences? In general yes, but as we see next, it is useful to allow for exceptions.

Our previous formalization was already considering a constitutive norm (3), namely, since a white fence w is a fence f, we also want to derive $\mathbf{O}f$ from $\mathbf{O}w$. In fact, contraposition for explicit negation could also be added:

$$\neg w \leftarrow \neg f \qquad\qquad \mathbf{F}w \leftarrow \mathbf{F}f \qquad (19)$$

where the former means that not having a fence implies not having a white fence, and the latter, that a prohibition to put a fence is also a prohibition to put a white fence. The program $\Pi \cup (19) \cup \{f\}$, however, has no answer set. This is because we derive $\mathbf{O}w$ and $\mathbf{F}w$, whereas no evidence about the fence color is given: once w or $\neg w$ is added to the program, consistency is restored. A less rigid formalization of these implicit derived obligations is to replace (3) by:

$$f \leftarrow w \qquad \neg w \leftarrow \neg f \qquad \mathbf{O}f \leftarrow \mathbf{O}^{nv} w \qquad \mathbf{F}w \leftarrow \mathbf{F}^{nv} f \qquad (20)$$

where the rules for obligations become now default rules. The condition $\mathbf{O}^{nv} w$ stands for $\mathbf{O}w \wedge not\ \neg w$, i.e., we derive the obligation of a fence if we have a non-violated obligation of a white fence. In the example, this is the case. Similarly, the condition $\mathbf{F}^{nv} f$ stands for $\mathbf{F}f \wedge not\ f$ meaning that the prohibition of a white fence is derived when we had a non-violated prohibition of a fence. In our example, we do have the prohibition of a fence, but it has been violated, so the default does not apply, and we do not obtain a prohibition to put a white fence. As a result, the only equilibrium model of $(2) \cup (20) \cup \{f\}$ is again $\{f, \mathbf{F}f, \mathbf{O}w, \mathbf{O}f\}$.

C6 (Defeasible Deontic Detachment). This requirement is related to the distinction between *factual* versus *deontic detachment*, that is, when a conditional obligation should sometimes be triggered by facts and sometimes by other obligations. This is typically illustrated by the notorious scenario in [12] adapted below to our running example. Assume we add the norms:

(vii) *If we put a fence, we must put a street mailbox (m).*
(viii) *If we do not put a fence, we must not put a street mailbox.*

If we have information about the presence or absence of a fence, we will respectively derive the obligation or prohibition to have a mailbox by factual detachment. However, when no information is given, by default, we still want to derive the prohibition of a mailbox from the prohibition to have a fence in (i). This corresponds to a (defeasible) deontic detachment.

A direct reading of the premises (vii) and (viii) could be formalized as:

$$\mathbf{O}m \leftarrow f \qquad\qquad \mathbf{F}m \leftarrow \neg f \qquad (21)$$

The program $\Pi \cup (21) \cup \{f \vee \neg f\}$ as the two answer sets $\{\neg f, \mathbf{F}f, \mathbf{F}m\}$ and $\{f, \mathbf{F}f, \mathbf{O}w, \mathbf{O}f, \mathbf{O}m\}$ so the obligation about the mailbox is derived from the facts f or $\neg f$ respectively (factual detachment). The problem with (21) arises in presence of $\Pi \cup (21)$ without further evidence about f or $\neg f$. In that case, no obligation is derived, whereas given $\mathbf{F}f$, the mailbox would be also forbidden (deontic detachment). To strengthen our representation, we replace (21) by the conditional obligations:

$$\mathbf{O}(m \mid f) \qquad\qquad \mathbf{O}(\neg m \mid \neg f) \qquad (22)$$

The derived operator $\mathbf{O}(m \mid f)$ is an abbreviation of $(\mathbf{O}m \leftarrow f \vee \mathbf{O}^{nv} f)$ and the disjunction in the antecedent can be unfolded into the two rules $(\mathbf{O}m \leftarrow f)$ and $(\mathbf{O}m \leftarrow \mathbf{O}^{nv} f)$. Note that $\mathbf{O}^{nv} f$, in turn, stands for $\mathbf{O}f \wedge not\ \neg f$. A similar unfolding can be done for $\mathbf{O}(\neg m \mid \neg f)$ to find out that (22) amounts to the two rules (21) we had before plus the following account for deontic detachment:

$$\mathbf{O}m \leftarrow \mathbf{O}f \wedge not\ \neg f \qquad \mathbf{F}m \leftarrow \mathbf{F}f \wedge not\ f$$

As a result, for $\Pi \cup (22) \cup \{f \vee \neg f\}$ we get the same answer sets as before, but when we just consider $\Pi \cup (22)$, the only answer set is $\{\mathbf{F}f, \mathbf{F}m\}$ and we cannot put a mailbox because we have a (non-violated) prohibition to put a fence.

6   Related and Future Work

Related deontic extensions of ASP are *Deontic Logic Programs* (DLP) [22,23] and *Deontic Temporal ASP* (DTASP) [21]. Both make use of the KD modality [45] (in DTASP, also temporal operators) and define answer sets in terms of the (syntactic) reduct operation on logic programs. DLP was later extended to Deontic Equilibrium Logic (DEL) [3] that avoids the reduct but, as already discussed, maintains a strict syntactic separation between logic program connectives and deontic formulas. In contrast, DELX relies on logical semantics, applicable to arbitrary combinations of operators and free from syntactic restrictions or transformations. The modal logic KD allows DLP and DTASP to deal with obligations on compound formulas, while DELX is specifically designed for obligations on literals. One final important difference is that DELX makes an homogeneous integration of explicit negation, a feature *already existing* in ASP and commonly used in its applications. This permits to deal with factual situations where no information, e.g., about *fence* nor $\neg fence$, is available. Representing incomplete information about the real world in DLP or DTASP, requires instead epistemic modalities or the use of ASP explicit negation, whose semantic treatment is *different* from negation inside a modality.

A computationally oriented approach for deontic logic extended with features from nonmonotonic reasoning is *Defeasible Deontic Logic* (DDL) [24] (extending *Defeasible Logic* [35]) whose syntax is similar to logic programming without the default negation. To express defeasibility, DDL relies on different types of implications in rules (strict, defeasible and defeaters) additionally subscripted with deontic modalities. This contrasts with the five primitive DELX connectives. DDL also has a more complex semantics w.r.t. DELX, that employs neighbourhood models [25] or argumentation [26], and uses a dedicated theorem prover [31].

As immediate future work, we plan to develop a deontic ASP tool that accepts both deontic logic programs and DELX expressions as input, enabling the integration of deontic knowledge into existing ASP domains or encodings. Also, we will explore the extrapolation to DELX of other ASP features, such as the temporal extension [1], the generation of explanations [10] or ASP-based policies such as [20]. As a long term goal, we plan to obtain a translation of (temporal) DELX into monitors and use them in combination with Reinforcement Learning (cf. [4]) to design autonomous agents sensitive to legal, social and ethical norms.

512   P. Cabalar et al.

Acknowledgments. Work partially supported by the WWTF project ICT22-023, by the Spanish Ministry of Science and Innovation, Spain, MCIN/AEI/10.13039/5011 00011033 (grant PID2020-116201GB-I00), by Xunta de Galicia, Spain and the European Union (grant GPC ED431B 2022/33) and by project LIANDA - BBVA Foundation Grants for Scientific Research Projects, Spain.

References

1. Aguado, F., et al.: Linear-time temporal answer set programming. Theory Pract. Logic Program. **23**(1), 2–56 (2023). https://doi.org/10.1017/S1471068421000557
2. Aguado, F., Cabalar, P., Fandinno, J., Pearce, D., Pérez, G., Vidal, C.: Revisiting explicit negation in answer set programming. Theory Pract. Logic Program. **19**(5–6), 908–924 (2019). https://doi.org/10.1017/S1471068419000267
3. Alferes, J.J., Gonçalves, R., Leite, J.: Equivalence of defeasible normative systems. J. Appl. Non Class. Logics **23**(1–2), 25–48 (2013)
4. Alshiekh, M., Bloem, R., Ehlers, R., Könighofer, B., Niekum, S., Topcu, U.: Safe reinforcement learning via shielding. In: Proceedings of the AAAI, pp. 2669–2678 (2018)
5. Benzmüller, C., Parent, X., van der Torre, L.: A deontic logic reasoning infrastructure. In: Manea, F., Miller, R.G., Nowotka, D. (eds.) CiE 2018. LNCS, vol. 10936, pp. 60–69. Springer, Cham (2018). https://doi.org/10.1007/978-3-319-94418-0_6
6. Brewka, G., Eiter, T., Truszczyński, M.: Answer set programming at a glance. Commun. ACM **54**(12), 92–103 (2011)
7. Broersen, J., van der Torre, L.: Ten problems of deontic logic and normative reasoning in computer science. In: Bezhanishvili, N., Goranko, V. (eds.) ESSLLI 2010-2011. LNCS, vol. 7388, pp. 55–88. Springer, Heidelberg (2012). https://doi.org/10.1007/978-3-642-31485-8_2
8. Cabalar, P., Fandinno, J., Fariñas del Cerro, L.: Autoepistemic answer set programming. Artif. Intell. **289**, 103382 (2020). https://doi.org/10.1016/j.artint.2020.103382
9. Cabalar, P., Fandinno, J., Fariñas del Cerro, L., Pearce, D.: Functional ASP with intensional sets: application to Gelfond-Zhang aggregates. Theory Pract. Logic Program. **18**(3–4), 390–405 (2018). https://doi.org/10.1017/S1471068418000169
10. Cabalar, P., Fandinno, J., Muñiz, B.: A system for explainable answer set programming. In: Ricca, F., et al. (eds.) Proceedings of the 36th International Conference on Logic Programming (Technical Communications). EPTCS, vol. 325, pp. 124–136 (2020). https://doi.org/10.4204/EPTCS.325.19
11. Cabalar, P., Pearce, D., Valverde, A.: Reducing propositional theories in equilibrium logic to logic programs. In: Bento, C., Cardoso, A., Dias, G. (eds.) EPIA 2005. LNCS (LNAI), vol. 3808, pp. 4–17. Springer, Heidelberg (2005). https://doi.org/10.1007/11595014_2
12. Chisholm, R.M.: Contrary-to-duty imperatives and deontic logic. Analysis **24**(2), 33–36 (1963)
13. Eiter, T., Gottlob, G.: Complexity results for disjunctive logic programming and application to nonmonotonic logics. In: Miller, D. (ed.) Logic Programming, Proceedings of the 1993 International Symposium, pp. 266–278. MIT Press (1993)
14. Erdem, E., Gelfond, M., Leone, N.: Applications of answer set programming. AI Mag. **37**(3), 53–68 (2016). https://doi.org/10.1609/aimag.v37i3.2678

15. Gabbay, D., Horty, J., Parent, X., van der Mayden, R., van der Torre, L. (eds.): Handbook of Deontic Logic and Normative Systems, vol. 2. College Publications (2021)
16. Gabbay, D., Horty, J., Parent, X., van der Meyden, R., van der Torre, L. (eds.): Handbook of Deontic Logic and Normative Systems. College Publications (2013)
17. Gebser, M., Kaminski, R., Kaufmann, B., Ostrowski, M., Schaub, T., Wanko, P.: Theory solving made easy with clingo 5. In: Carro, M., King, A., Saeedloei, N., Vos, M.D. (eds.) Technical Communications of the 32nd International Conference on Logic Programming, ICLP 2016 TCs. OASIcs, vol. 52, pp. 2:1–2:15. Schloss Dagstuhl - Leibniz-Zentrum für Informatik (2016). https://doi.org/10.4230/OASIcs.ICLP.2016.2
18. Gebser, M., Maratea, M., Ricca, F.: The seventh answer set programming competition: design and results. Theory Pract. Logic Program. **20**(2), 176–204 (2020). https://doi.org/10.1017/S1471068419000061
19. Gelfond, M., Lifschitz, V.: Classical negation in logic programs and disjunctive databases. N. Gener. Comput. **9**(3/4), 365–386 (1991). https://doi.org/10.1007/BF03037169
20. Gelfond, M., Lobo, J.: Authorization and obligation policies in dynamic systems. In: Garcia de la Banda, M., Pontelli, E. (eds.) ICLP 2008. LNCS, vol. 5366, pp. 22–36. Springer, Heidelberg (2008). https://doi.org/10.1007/978-3-540-89982-2_7
21. Giordano, L., Martelli, A., Dupré, D.T.: Temporal deontic action logic for the verification of compliance to norms in ASP. In: Francesconi, E., Verheij, B. (eds.) International Conference on Artificial Intelligence and Law, ICAIL 2013, pp. 53–62. ACM (2013)
22. Gonçalves, R., Alferes, J.J.: An embedding of input-output logic in deontic logic programs. In: Ågotnes, T., Broersen, J., Elgesem, D. (eds.) DEON 2012. LNCS (LNAI), vol. 7393, pp. 61–75. Springer, Heidelberg (2012). https://doi.org/10.1007/978-3-642-31570-1_5
23. Gonçalves, R., Alferes, J.J.: Deontic logic programs. In: Gini, M.L., Shehory, O., Ito, T., Jonker, C.M. (eds.) International Conference on Autonomous Agents and Multi-agent Systems, pp. 1333–1334. IFAAMAS (2013)
24. Governatori, G., Olivieri, F., Rotolo, A., Scannapieco, S.: Computing strong and weak permissions in defeasible logic. J. Philos. Log. **42**(6), 799–829 (2013). https://doi.org/10.1007/s10992-013-9295-1
25. Governatori, G., Rotolo, A., Calardo, E.: Possible world semantics for defeasible deontic logic. In: Ågotnes, T., Broersen, J., Elgesem, D. (eds.) DEON 2012. LNCS (LNAI), vol. 7393, pp. 46–60. Springer, Heidelberg (2012). https://doi.org/10.1007/978-3-642-31570-1_4
26. Governatori, G., Rotolo, A., Riveret, R.: A deontic argumentation framework based on deontic defeasible logic. In: Miller, T., Oren, N., Sakurai, Y., Noda, I., Savarimuthu, B.T.R., Cao Son, T. (eds.) PRIMA 2018. LNCS (LNAI), vol. 11224, pp. 484–492. Springer, Cham (2018). https://doi.org/10.1007/978-3-030-03098-8_33
27. Hansson, B.: An analysis of some deontic logics. Nôus **3**, 373–398 (1969)
28. Heyting, A.: Die formalen Regeln der intuitionistischen Logik. Sitzungsberichte der Preussischen Akademie der Wissenschaften, Physikalisch-mathematische Klasse, pp. 42–56 (1930)
29. Horty, J.F.: Deontic logic as founded on nonmonotonic logic. Ann. Math. Artif. Intell. **9**(1–2), 69–91 (1993). https://doi.org/10.1007/BF01531262
30. Kamp, H.: Free choice permission. In: Proceedings of the Aristotelian Society, vol. 74, pp. 57–74 (1973)

31. Lam, H.-P., Governatori, G.: The making of SPINdle. In: Governatori, G., Hall, J., Paschke, A. (eds.) RuleML 2009. LNCS, vol. 5858, pp. 315–322. Springer, Heidelberg (2009). https://doi.org/10.1007/978-3-642-04985-9_29

32. Leone, N., et al.: The DLV system for knowledge representation and reasoning. ACM Trans. Comput. Log. **7**(3), 499–562 (2006). https://doi.org/10.1145/1149114.1149117

33. McCarthy, J.: Elaboration tolerance (1998). http://www-formal.stanford.edu/jmc/elaboration.html

34. Nute, D. (ed.): Defeasible Deontic Logic. Kluwer, Dordrecht (1997)

35. Nute, D.: Defeasible logic. In: Handbook of Logic in Artificial Intelligence and Logic Programming. Oxford University Press (1993)

36. Odintsov, S., Pearce, D.: Routley semantics for answer sets. In: Baral, C., Greco, G., Leone, N., Terracina, G. (eds.) LPNMR 2005. LNCS (LNAI), vol. 3662, pp. 343–355. Springer, Heidelberg (2005). https://doi.org/10.1007/11546207_27

37. Parent, X.: Preference-based semantics for Hansson-type dyadic deontic logics: a survey of results. In: Gabbay, D., Horty, J., Parent, X., van der Meyden, R., van der Torre, L. (eds.) Handbook of Deontic Logic and Normative Systems, vol. 2, pp. 7–70 (2021)

38. Parent, X., van der Torre, L.: I/O logics with a consistency check. In: Broersen, J.M., Condoravdi, C., Shyam, N., Pigozzi, G. (eds.) Deontic Logic and Normative Systems - 14th International Conference, DEON 2018, pp. 285–299. College Publications (2018)

39. Pearce, D.: A new logical characterisation of stable models and answer sets. In: Dix, J., Pereira, L.M., Przymusinski, T.C. (eds.) NMELP 1996. LNCS, vol. 1216, pp. 57–70. Springer, Heidelberg (1997). https://doi.org/10.1007/BFb0023801

40. Pearce, D., Valverde, A.: Quantified equilibrium logic and foundations for answer set programs. In: Garcia de la Banda, M., Pontelli, E. (eds.) ICLP 2008. LNCS, vol. 5366, pp. 546–560. Springer, Heidelberg (2008). https://doi.org/10.1007/978-3-540-89982-2_46

41. Prakken, H., Sergot, M.: Dyadic deontic logic and contrary-to-duty obligations. In: Nute, D. (ed.) Defeasible Deontic Logic, pp. 223–262. Springer, Dordrecht (1997). https://doi.org/10.1007/978-94-015-8851-5_10

42. Reiter, R.: A logic for default reasoning. Artif. Intell. **13**(1–2), 81–132 (1980)

43. Sergot, M.: Normative positions. In: Gabbay, D., Horty, J., Parent, X., van der Meyden, R., van der Torre, L. (eds.) Handbook of Deontic Logic and Normative Systems, vol. 1, pp. 353–406 (2013)

44. Vakarelov, D.: Notes on N-lattices and constructive logic with strong negation. Stud. Logica. **36**(1–2), 109–125 (1977)

45. von Wright, G.H.: Deontic logic. Mind **60**(237), 1–15 (1951)

Categorical Approximation Fixpoint Theory

Angelos Charalambidis[1](✉) and Panos Rondogiannis[2]

[1] Department of Informatics and Telematics, Harokopio University, Athens, Greece
acharal@hua.gr
[2] Department of Informatics and Telecommunications, National and Kapodistrian
University of Athens, Athens, Greece
prondo@di.uoa.gr

Abstract. *Approximation fixpoint theory (AFT)* is a powerful framework that has been widely used for defining the semantics of non-monotonic formalisms in artificial intelligence and logic programming. In particular, AFT is used to derive the fixed points of (potentially non-monotonic) operators over complete lattices. However, in certain application domains, there arise operators defined over structures that are not necessarily complete lattices. Therefore, the quest for a more general version of AFT has been lingering as an interesting research direction. We develop an extension of AFT, namely *Categorical AFT*, that allows us to study the fixed points of (potentially non-functorial) operators defined over categories. Since categories are more general structures than complete lattices, we argue that our approach provides a more general and unified framework for the study of non-monotonicity. The versatility of category theory creates the potential of new insights and applications.

Keywords: Approximation Fixpoint Theory · Category Theory · Non-Monotonicity · Domain Theory

1 Introduction

Approximation fixpoint theory (AFT) [14,15] has been developed to provide semantics for non-monotonic formalisms that arise in artificial intelligence and logic programming. Associated with every such formalism, there usually exists a non-monotonic operator defined over an appropriate structure of semantic objects. AFT provides a means for finding the fixed points of such operators: given an arbitrary operator $O : L \rightarrow L$, where L is a complete lattice, AFT *approximates* O using a monotonic operator A_O, called the *approximator of O*. The fixed points of A_O can be shown to approximate those of O (and in many cases to actually coincide with those of O). An alternative view of AFT is that it represents an extension of the Knaster-Tarski fixed point theorem of monotone lattice operators [30], to arbitrary ones. It has been used in several application domains, such as extensions of logic programming [7,11,22], non-monotonic logics [32], argumentation theory [29], description logics [20], and so on.

There often arise applications that require deviations from the standard framework of AFT [11,12,19]. Therefore, the quest for more general versions of AFT has been lingering as an interesting research direction. We develop an extension of AFT, namely *Categorical AFT*, that allows us to study the fixed points of (potentially non-functorial) operators over arbitrary categories. Since categories are much more general mathematical structures than complete lattices, Categorical AFT provides a genuine extension of classical AFT. In a more specific view, the two main contributions of the present paper, are the following:

- We generalize classical AFT [14,15] and make it applicable to a much broader, categorical, setting. AFT is currently applicable to operators that are defined over complete lattices. Our development extends AFT to handle operators that are defined over arbitrary categories that possess both an initial and a terminal object. We generalize (almost all) the results of classical AFT [14] to corresponding results in our categorical framework.
- We argue that all the standard applications of AFT can be retrieved in our framework by specializing our results to categories that are complete lattices. Moreover, we argue that there exist novel categorical applications that can not be handled by classical AFT. In particular, we identify the connections of our approach with fundamental domain-theoretic constructions that have been developed in the semantics of programming languages. Linking domain theory with the techniques that have arisen in the area of non-monotonic logics, creates the potential of new insights and applications. In particular, we argue that such applications can lead to the development of novel higher-order non-monotonic formalisms for artificial intelligence.

As a brief preview of the analogies between AFT and Categorical AFT, the reader can consult the following table. All these analogies will be explained in detail in the forthcoming sections of the paper. We assume familiarity with the basic notions of category theory (see, for example, [3]) and AFT (see [14,15]). Moreover, the proofs of all the results of the paper have been omitted; they will be provided in an extended version of the paper that will appear online.

AFT	Categorical AFT
Complete lattice L	Category $\mathbf{K}$ with initial and terminal objects
Elements of L	Objects in $\mathbf{K}$
Partial order $\sqsubseteq$ of L	Arrows in $\mathbf{K}$
Equality in L	Object isomorphism in $\mathbf{K}$
Monotonic function	Functor
Least fixed point of a function	Initial fixed point of a functor
Operator $O : L \rightarrow L$	Partial Functor $O : \mathbf{K} \rightarrow \mathbf{K}$
Approximator $A : L^2 \rightarrow L^2$	Functor $A : \mathbf{K} \times \mathbf{K}^{\mathrm{op}} \rightarrow \mathbf{K} \times \mathbf{K}^{\mathrm{op}}$

The paper is organized as follows. Section 2 presents preliminary concepts regarding fixed points of functors in categories. Section 3 initiates our development of a categorical version of AFT. In particular, it introduces the notion of a *(categorical) approximator*, defines its *Kripke-Kleene fixed point* and investigates its properties. Section 4 introduces the *well-founded fixed point of a (categorical) approximator* and studies its properties. Section 5 examines conditions under which the initial fixed point of an approximator corresponds to an initial fixed point of an operator. Section 6 discusses applications of Categorical AFT. Finally, Sect. 7 gives pointers for future work.

2   Fixed Points in Categories

The notion of "functor" in category theory is a conceptual generalization of the familiar mathematical notion of "monotonic function". This section contains background material on the key notions that arise when studying the fixed points of functors. In our presentation we follow the notation and definitions of [27].

Definition 1. *Let* $\mathbf{K}$ *be a category and let* $F : \mathbf{K} \to \mathbf{K}$ *be a functor. A pair* (x, v) *will be called a* fixed point *of* F *if* x *is an object of* $\mathbf{K}$ *and* $v : F(x) \to x$ *is an isomorphism of* $\mathbf{K}$. *A* prefixed point *(respectively,* postfixed point*) of* F *is a pair* (x, v) *where* x *is an object of* $\mathbf{K}$ *and* $v : F(x) \to x$ *(respectively,* $v : x \to F(x)$*) is a morphism of* $\mathbf{K}$.

Prefixed points (respectively, postfixed points) of a functor F are usually called *algebras* (respectively, *coalgebras*) of F. For compatibility with the glossary of AFT, we find it more convenient to use the terms "prefixed point" and "postfixed point" instead of "algebra" and "coalgebra" (although the latter are clearly more standard in categorical contexts).

In some cases, when the actual isomorphism in the above definition is not needed in our discussion, instead of writing "(x, v) is a fixed point of F", we will write $F(x) \cong x$ (where $\cong$ denotes isomorphism between objects). The following lemma is easy to establish.

Lemma 1. *Let* $\mathbf{K}$ *be a category, let* $F : \mathbf{K} \to \mathbf{K}$ *be a functor, and let* (x, v) *be a fixed point of* F. *Let* y *be an object in* $\mathbf{K}$ *such that* $y \cong x$. *Then, there exists an isomorphism* $u : F(y) \to y$, *i.e.,* (y, u) *is a fixed point of* F.

The notions of *initial prefixed point* and *initial fixed point* of a functor F, are defined through the categories $PFP(F)$ and $FP(F)$ of the prefixed points and fixed points of F, respectively. The following definition introduces $PFP(F)$ and $FP(F)$; for a proof that these are indeed categories, see for example [9].

Definition 2. *Let* $\mathbf{K}$ *be a category and let* $F : \mathbf{K} \to \mathbf{K}$ *be a functor. The category of prefixed points of* F, *denoted by* $PFP(F)$, *is defined as follows:*

- *The objects of* $PFP(F)$ *are the prefixed points of* F.
- *For all objects* (x, v), (x', v') *in* $PFP(F)$, *the arrows from* (x, v) *to* (x', v') *in* $PFP(F)$ *are those arrows* f *in* $\mathbf{K}$ *for which the following diagram commutes:*

$$F(x) \xrightarrow{\quad v \quad} x$$
$$\downarrow{\scriptstyle F(f)} \qquad \downarrow{\scriptstyle f}$$
$$F(x') \xrightarrow{\quad v' \quad} x'$$

The category $FP(F)$ of fixed points of F, is defined analogously as above.

Definition 3. *Let $\mathbf{K}$ be a category and let $F : \mathbf{K} \to \mathbf{K}$ be a functor. The initial prefixed point (respectively, initial fixed point) of F, is the initial object, if it exists, of the category $PFP(F)$ (respectively, $FP(F)$).*

The notions of *terminal postfixed point* and *terminal fixed point* are dual to the above ones and can be defined in an analogous way (see, for example, [2]). A functor may have many fixed points; however, the initial (respectively, terminal) fixed point is unique up to a natural isomorphism. Not every functor has an initial (respectively, terminal) fixed point. However, many "reasonable" functors over appropriate categories can be shown to have initial (respectively, terminal) fixed points.

3 Extending AFT to Categories

In some applications of category theory, there arise mappings which are not functors. Moreover, we are often interested in the fixed points of such mappings, and the standard categorical fixed point constructions [6,27] can not (directly) be used in such cases since they only apply to functors (for a classical such example, see Sect. 6). We extend AFT to a categorical setting so as to capture such mappings. We start by defining the notion of an *operator* over a category $\mathbf{K}$. Intuitively, an operator is a partial functor that is defined for all the objects but not necessarily for all the arrows of $\mathbf{K}$.

Definition 4. *Let $\mathbf{K}$ be a category. We say that a mapping $O : \mathbf{K} \to \mathbf{K}$ is an operator if for every object x in $\mathbf{K}$ there is an object $O(x)$ in $\mathbf{K}$ and for every morphism $f : x \to y$ in $\mathbf{K}$ either there is an arrow $O(f) : O(x) \to O(y)$ in $\mathbf{K}$, or $O(f)$ is undefined. Moreover:*

- *for every object x of $\mathbf{K}$, $O(\mathrm{id}_x)$ is defined and $O(\mathrm{id}_x) = \mathrm{id}_{O(x)}$; and*
- *for all arrows f, g of $\mathbf{K}$, if both $O(f)$ and $O(g)$ are defined and composable, then $O(f \cdot g) = O(f) \cdot O(g)$.*

Fixed points of operators can be defined analogously to fixed points of functors.

Definition 5. *Let $\mathbf{K}$ be a category and let $O : \mathbf{K} \to \mathbf{K}$ be an operator. A pair (x, v) will be called a fixed point of O if x is an object and $v : O(x) \to x$ is an isomorphism in $\mathbf{K}$.*

We will also need the notion of the *opposite* of an operator.

Definition 6. *Let* **K** *be a category and let* $O : \mathbf{K} \to \mathbf{K}$ *be an operator. The opposite operator* $O^{\mathrm{op}} : \mathbf{K}^{\mathrm{op}} \to \mathbf{K}^{\mathrm{op}}$ *of* O *is an operator such that:*

- *for every object* x, $O^{\mathrm{op}}(x) = O(x)$; *and,*
- *for every arrow* f, *if* $O(f)$ *is undefined then* $O^{\mathrm{op}}(f^{\mathrm{op}})$ *is undefined and if* $O(f)$ *is defined then* $O(f) = O^{\mathrm{op}}(f^{\mathrm{op}})^{\mathrm{op}}$.

Since operators are not necessarily (total) functors, the well-known techniques [2,4,27] for finding fixed points of functors, are not always applicable in this more general setting. We revise and extend the principles of AFT in order to derive fixed points of categorical operators. A key notion in our development is that of an *approximation category*. More specifically, given a category **K**, we define its approximation category to be the category $\mathbf{K} \times \mathbf{K}^{\mathrm{op}}$. This allows us to define approximators as functors in $\mathbf{K} \times \mathbf{K}^{\mathrm{op}} \to \mathbf{K} \times \mathbf{K}^{\mathrm{op}}$. We require that our category **K** has both an initial and a terminal object, and by duality, the same is true of $\mathbf{K}^{\mathrm{op}}$. The initial fixed point of an approximator $A : \mathbf{K} \times \mathbf{K}^{\mathrm{op}} \to \mathbf{K} \times \mathbf{K}^{\mathrm{op}}$, if it exists, will be called the *Kripke-Kleene fixed point of* A.

Definition 7. *Let* **K** *be a category. Then,* $\mathbf{K} \times \mathbf{K}^{\mathrm{op}}$ *is the* approximation category *of* **K** *and is denoted by* $\mathbf{K}^{\approx}$.

In the rest of the paper we fix **K** to denote a category which has both an initial and a terminal object, and we will use **K** free in definitions and results.

Let $A : \mathbf{K}^{\approx} \to \mathbf{K}^{\approx}$ be an endofunctor. Then, it is easy to verify that there exist functors $A^1 : \mathbf{K} \times \mathbf{K}^{\mathrm{op}} \to \mathbf{K}$ and $A^2 : \mathbf{K} \times \mathbf{K}^{\mathrm{op}} \to \mathbf{K}^{\mathrm{op}}$ such that for all objects x in **K** and y in $\mathbf{K}^{\mathrm{op}}$ it is $A(x,y) = (A^1(x,y), A^2(x,y))$, and for all arrows f in **K** and g in $\mathbf{K}^{\mathrm{op}}$ it is $A(f,g) = (A^1(f,g), A^2(f,g))$.

Given an operator $O : \mathbf{K} \to \mathbf{K}$, we will define an endofunctor $A : \mathbf{K}^{\approx} \to \mathbf{K}^{\approx}$ which will be closely related to O. The fixed points of A will give insights on the fixed points of O. Of special interest will be the fixed points of A that are *exact*.

Definition 8. *A pair* (x,y) *in* $\mathbf{K}^{\approx}$ *is called* exact *if* $x \cong y$. *A fixed point* $((x,y),v)$ *of a functor* $F : \mathbf{K}^{\approx} \to \mathbf{K}^{\approx}$ *is called* exact *if* (x,y) *is an exact pair.*

Definition 9. *Let* $O : \mathbf{K} \to \mathbf{K}$ *be an operator and let* $A : \mathbf{K}^{\approx} \to \mathbf{K}^{\approx}$ *be a functor. We will say that* A approximates O *(or,* A *is an approximator of* O*), if for all* (x,y) *in* $\mathbf{K}^{\approx}$ *with* $x \cong y$, *it holds* $A(x,y) \cong (O(x), O(y))$.

Many of the approximators that arise in practice are symmetric:

Definition 10. *An approximator* $A : \mathbf{K}^{\approx} \to \mathbf{K}^{\approx}$ *is* symmetric *iff*

- *for all objects* x *in* **K** *and* y *in* $\mathbf{K}^{\mathrm{op}}$, $A^1(x,y) = A^2(y,x)$; *and,*
- *for all arrows* f *in* **K** *and* g *in* $\mathbf{K}^{\mathrm{op}}$, $A^1(f,g) = A^2(g^{\mathrm{op}}, f^{\mathrm{op}})^{\mathrm{op}}$.

The following lemma demonstrates that when we seek the exact fixed points of a functor A that approximates O, it suffices to look at pairs of the form (x,x).

Lemma 2. *Let $O : \mathbf{K} \to \mathbf{K}$ be an operator and let $A : \mathbf{K}^{\approx} \to \mathbf{K}^{\approx}$ be an approximator of O. Let x, y be objects in $\mathbf{K}$ such that $x \cong y$. If $A(x, y) \cong (x, y)$, then $A(x, x) \cong (x, x)$ and $A(y, y) \cong (y, y)$.*

The following proposition indicates that we can study the fixed points of an operator O by examining the exact fixed points (if they exist) of its approximators.

Proposition 1. *Let $O : \mathbf{K} \to \mathbf{K}$ be an operator and let $A : \mathbf{K}^{\approx} \to \mathbf{K}^{\approx}$ be an approximator of O. Then, for all x in $\mathbf{K}$, $O(x) \cong x$ if and only if $A(x, x) \cong (x, x)$.*

The following corollary is a direct consequence of Lemma 2 and Proposition 1.

Corollary 1. *Let $O : \mathbf{K} \to \mathbf{K}$ be an operator and let $A : \mathbf{K}^{\approx} \to \mathbf{K}^{\approx}$ be a functor that approximates O. Assume that A has an initial fixed point $((x, y), v)$ that is exact. Then $O(x) \cong x$ and $O(y) \cong y$.*

As in classical AFT, we will refer to the initial fixed point of A as the *Kripke-Kleene fixed point of A*. For many applications, the Kripke-Kleene fixed point suffices (see Subsect. 6.3 for one such case). However, in certain application domains a different fixed point seems more appropriate. This is the main topic of the next section.

4　The Stable Operator and the Well-Founded Fixed Point

Given an operator $O : \mathbf{K} \to \mathbf{K}$ and an approximator $A : \mathbf{K}^{\approx} \to \mathbf{K}^{\approx}$ of O, we define the *stable operator* $C_A : \mathbf{K}^{\approx} \to \mathbf{K}^{\approx}$ of A. As it turns out, every fixed point of C_A induces a corresponding fixed point of A. In particular, the initial fixed point of C_A (if it exists) is a distinguished one, which, in general, is different from the initial fixed point of A. We will call the initial fixed point of C_A the *well-founded fixed point of A*. In many applications (such as for example, in logic programming), the well-founded fixed point can give more insight than the Kripke-Kleene one.

In order to define C_A, we will use the initial (respectively, terminal) fixed points of two auxiliary operators, namely $S_A^1 : \mathbf{K}^{\mathrm{op}} \to \mathbf{K}$ and $S_A^2 : \mathbf{K} \to \mathbf{K}^{\mathrm{op}}$. We start with some preliminary definitions and propositions.

Definition 11. *Let $\mathbf{K}$ be a category and let $A : \mathbf{K}^{\approx} \to \mathbf{K}^{\approx}$ be a functor. Then:*

- *For every y in $\mathbf{K}^{\mathrm{op}}$, we introduce the mapping $A^1(\cdot, y) : \mathbf{K} \to \mathbf{K}$, which for every object x and arrow f in $\mathbf{K}$ is defined as $A^1(\cdot, y)(x) = A^1(x, y)$ and $A^1(\cdot, y)(f) = A^1(f, \mathrm{id}_y)$.*
- *For every x in $\mathbf{K}$, we introduce the mapping $A^2(x, \cdot) : \mathbf{K}^{\mathrm{op}} \to \mathbf{K}^{\mathrm{op}}$, which for every object y and arrow g in $\mathbf{K}^{\mathrm{op}}$ is defined as $A^2(x, \cdot)(y) = A^2(x, y)$ and $A^2(x, \cdot)(g) = A^2(\mathrm{id}_x, g)$.*

The following proposition generalizes [14, Proposition 5].

Proposition 2. *Let* **K** *be a category and let* $A : \mathbf{K}^{\approx} \to \mathbf{K}^{\approx}$ *be a functor. Then, for all objects x in* **K** *and y in* $\mathbf{K}^{\text{op}}$, *the mappings* $A^1(\cdot, y) : \mathbf{K} \to \mathbf{K}$ *and* $A^2(x, \cdot) : \mathbf{K}^{\text{op}} \to \mathbf{K}^{\text{op}}$, *are functors.*

In order for an approximator to have a well-founded fixed point, we will require that it is *sensible*:

Definition 12. *A functor $A : \mathbf{K}^{\approx} \to \mathbf{K}^{\approx}$ will be called* sensible *iff for all objects x in* **K** *and y in* $\mathbf{K}^{\text{op}}$, *the functor $A^1(\cdot, y)$ has an initial fixed point, denoted by $\mu A^1(\cdot, y)$, and the functor $A^2(x, \cdot)$ has a terminal fixed point, denoted by $\nu A^2(x, \cdot)$.*

By abuse of notation, we will also use $\mu A^1(\cdot, y)$ and $\nu A^2(x, \cdot)$ to denote the underlying objects of these fixed points.

Given a sensible functor $A : \mathbf{K}^{\approx} \to \mathbf{K}^{\approx}$, we define the mappings $S_A^1 : \mathbf{K}^{\text{op}} \to$ **K** and $S_A^2 : \mathbf{K} \to \mathbf{K}^{\text{op}}$ which operate on objects as follows: for all x in **K** and y in $\mathbf{K}^{\text{op}}$, $S_A^1(y) = \mu A^1(\cdot, y)$ and $S_A^2(x) = \nu A^2(x, \cdot)$. The definitions of S_A^1 and S_A^2 on arrows, are more involved (see [5, Notation 7.1] for the case of S_A^1 and [5, Notation 7.5] for S_A^2). We can now define the *stable operator* of a sensible functor:

Definition 13. *Let $A : \mathbf{K}^{\approx} \to \mathbf{K}^{\approx}$ be a sensible functor. The* stable operator $\mathcal{C}_A : \mathbf{K}^{\approx} \to \mathbf{K}^{\approx}$ *of A is defined as follows: for every pair of objects (x, y) in $\mathbf{K}^{\approx}$, $\mathcal{C}_A(x, y) = (S_A^1(y), S_A^2(x))$, and for every pair of arrows (f, g) in $\mathbf{K}^{\approx}$, $\mathcal{C}_A(f, g) = (S_A^1(g), S_A^2(f))$.*

The following proposition is a direct consequence of the definitions of S_A^1, S_A^2, and $\mathcal{C}_A$.

Proposition 3. *Let $A : \mathbf{K}^{\approx} \to \mathbf{K}^{\approx}$ be a sensible functor. Then, $\mathcal{C}_A : \mathbf{K}^{\approx} \to \mathbf{K}^{\approx}$ is a functor.*

As it turns out, the fixed points of a sensible functor are closely related to those of its stable operator.

Lemma 3. *Let $A : \mathbf{K}^{\approx} \to \mathbf{K}^{\approx}$ be a sensible functor. Let (x, y) in $\mathbf{K}^{\approx}$ such that $\mathcal{C}_A(x, y) \cong (x, y)$. Then, $A(x, y) \cong (x, y)$.*

Remark 1. Notice that in the above lemma the fixed point of $\mathcal{C}_A$ is not necessarily identical to that of A. More specifically, the lemma suggests that if $((x, y), v)$ is a fixed point of $\mathcal{C}_A$, then there exists an isomorphism v' such that $((x, y), v')$ is a fixed point of A. The object parts of the two fixed points are identical, however the isomorphisms may differ. In the following, in situations where the above lemma is used, we will talk about the *fixed point of A induced by the given fixed point of $\mathcal{C}_A$.*

If O is an operator and A is an approximator of O, then every exact fixed point of $\mathcal{C}_A$ gives rise to a closely related fixed point of O. Formally:

Corollary 2. *Let $O : \mathbf{K} \to \mathbf{K}$ be an operator and let $A : \mathbf{K}^{\approx} \to \mathbf{K}^{\approx}$ be a sensible functor that approximates O. Let (x, y) in $\mathbf{K}^{\approx}$, such that $x \cong y$. If $\mathcal{C}_A(x, y) \cong (x, y)$ then $O(x) \cong x$ and $O(y) \cong y$.*

Of special interest is the initial fixed point of $\mathcal{C}_A$, if it exists. Notice that if this fixed point is exact, then, by Corollary 2, it gives rise to corresponding fixed points of O. We have the following definition.

Definition 14. *Let $O : \mathbf{K} \to \mathbf{K}$ be an operator and let $A : \mathbf{K}^\approx \to \mathbf{K}^\approx$ be a sensible functor that approximates O. Assume that $\mathcal{C}_A$ has an initial fixed point. Then, the fixed point of A induced by the initial fixed point of $\mathcal{C}_A$ is called the well-founded fixed point of A.*

We now demonstrate that the proposed approach is compatible with the categorical approaches for deriving initial fixed points of functors (such as, for example, [2,4,27]). In particular, we show that if O is a (total) functor, then there exists an obvious approximator A_O of O whose well-founded fixed point is the initial fixed point of O.

Proposition 4. *Let $O : \mathbf{K} \to \mathbf{K}$ be a functor that has an initial fixed point. Then, there exists a sensible functor A_O that approximates O, such that $\mathcal{C}_{A_O}$ has the initial fixed point $((\mu O, \mu O), v)$, where $v = \mathrm{id}_{(\mu O, \mu O)}$.*

Therefore, when O is a functor, then the well-founded fixed point of the obvious approximator of O, leads us to the initial fixed point of O.

5   Initiality of Fixed Points

The approach followed in this paper in order to construct the Kripke-Kleene fixed point of an operator O, is to define an approximator A_O and compute its initial fixed point. If this fixed point is of the form $((x, y), v)$, with $x \cong y$, then we know that there exist isomorphisms u_1, u_2 such that (x, u_1) and (y, u_2) are fixed points of O. However, we do not know whether (x, u_1) or (y, u_2) are initial fixed points of O; actually, we don't even know if O has an initial fixed point, because we know nothing about the "ordering" of the fixed points of O.

In order to get an initiality result like the one described above, we need some more insight into the way that O behaves on arrows – recall that, at present, we have no assumptions regarding the way that O operates on arrows. Below, we define the notion of *smooth operator*, which intuitively means that O is a (total) functor when restricted to the fixed points of O.

Definition 15. *Let $O : \mathbf{K} \to \mathbf{K}$ be an operator. Then, O is a smooth operator if for all fixed points (x, u) and (y, v) of O, and for every arrow $f : x \to y$ in $\mathbf{K}$, $O(f) : O(x) \to O(y)$ is an arrow in $\mathbf{K}$.*

It is straightforward to verify that the fixed points of a smooth operator, form a category.

Definition 16. *Let $O : \mathbf{K} \to \mathbf{K}$ be a smooth operator. The fixed points of O define a category $FP(O)$, as follows:*

– *The objects of $FP(O)$ are the fixed points of O.*

– *For all objects (x,v), (x',v') in $FP(O)$, the arrows from (x,v) to (x',v') in $FP(O)$ are those arrows f in $\mathbf{K}$ for which the following diagram commutes:*

$$
\begin{array}{ccc}
O(x) & \xrightarrow{\ v\ } & x \\
\downarrow{\scriptstyle O(f)} & & \downarrow{\scriptstyle f} \\
O(x') & \xrightarrow{\ v'\ } & x'
\end{array}
$$

We now show that when O is a smooth operator and we are given an exact initial fixed point of A, then there exists a corresponding initial fixed point of O. Before proceeding to the statement of this result, we need to strengthen our definition of approximator. This requires a notion of isomorphism for arrows.

Definition 17. *Let $f_1 : x \to x'$ and $f_2 : y \to y'$ be arrows in $\mathbf{K}$ such that $x \cong y$ and $x' \cong y'$. We will say that f_1 is strongly isomorphic to f_2, written $f_1 \stackrel{\sim}{=} f_2$, if for all isomorphisms $v : x \to y$ and $u : x' \to y'$, the following diagram commutes:*

$$
\begin{array}{ccc}
x & \xrightarrow{\ v\ } & y \\
\downarrow{\scriptstyle f_1} & & \downarrow{\scriptstyle f_2} \\
x' & \xrightarrow{\ u\ } & y'
\end{array}
$$

It can be verified that the above notion is a stronger version of arrow isomorphism than the one that can be defined through the arrow category $Arr(\mathbf{K})$ of $\mathbf{K}$ (see [3] for a formal definition of the arrow category).

Definition 18. *Let $O : \mathbf{K} \to \mathbf{K}$ be an operator and let $A : \mathbf{K}^{\approx} \to \mathbf{K}^{\approx}$ be a functor. We will say that A strongly approximates O, if the following two conditions are satisfied:*

– *for all x,y in $\mathbf{K}$ with $x \cong y$, it holds $A(x,y) \cong (O(x), O(y))$; and,*
– *for all arrows $f : x \to x'$ in $\mathbf{K}$ and $g : y \to y'$ in $\mathbf{K}^{op}$ such that $O(f)$ and $O^{op}(g)$ are both defined and $x \cong y$ and $x' \cong y'$, it holds $A(f,g) \cong (O(f), O^{op}(g))$.*

Lemma 4. *Let $O : \mathbf{K} \to \mathbf{K}$ be a smooth operator and let $A : \mathbf{K}^{\approx} \to \mathbf{K}^{\approx}$ be a functor that strongly approximates O. If $((x,y),(v_1,v_2))$ is an exact initial fixed point of A, then there exist isomorphisms w_1, w_2 such that (x, w_1) is an initial fixed point of O and (y, w_2) is an initial fixed point of O^{op}.*

In the case where our category $\mathbf{K}$ is a partial order, we get the following proposition.

Proposition 5. *Let $\mathbf{K}$ be a category that corresponds to a partial order. Let $O : \mathbf{K} \to \mathbf{K}$ be a smooth operator and let $A : \mathbf{K}^{\approx} \to \mathbf{K}^{\approx}$ be a functor that approximates O. Then, A strongly approximates O.*

The above proposition implies that if $\mathbf{K}$ is a partial order and A is an approximator of a smooth operator O, then, by Lemma 4, if the least fixed of A is exact, then it is also the least fixed point of O. This result generalizes the discussion just after [14, Corollary 15].

6   Comparison with AFT and a Novel Application Area

In this section, we compare Categorical AFT with classical AFT and discuss how
the former can be used to handle common AFT applications. However, the most
important contribution of this section is the development of a novel application
in the area of domain theory. Since domain theory is the main semantic tool for
capturing most features of modern programming languages, we believe that Categorical AFT paves the way for the development of powerful new non-monotonic
formalisms for artificial intelligence and logic programming.

6.1   A Comparison with Classical AFT

As we have already discussed, classical AFT can be used for operators $O : L \to L$,
where L is a complete lattice. This guarantees that if $A_O : L^2 \to L^2$ is an
approximator of O, then A_O has a least fixed point. Moreover, as shown in [14],
the stable operator C_{A_O} of A_O also has a least fixed point. On the other hand,
Categorical AFT considers operators $O : \mathbf{K} \to \mathbf{K}$, where $\mathbf{K}$ is an arbitrary
category that has both an initial and a terminal object. However, in our case,
if $A_O : \mathbf{K}^\approx \to \mathbf{K}^\approx$ is an approximator of O, then it is not always guaranteed
to have an initial fixed point (because, functors over arbitrary categories do not
always have initial fixed points). Similarly, the stable operator C_{A_O} of A_O in
our framework, does not always have an initial fixed point (we require A_O to
be sensible in order for C_{A_O} to have a fixed point). Recapitulating, in classical
AFT the fixed points of A_O and C_{A_O} are always guaranteed to exist, while in
Categorical AFT, due to its generality, the existence of the specific fixed points
(especially in the case of demanding applications, see Subsect. 6.3 below) must
be established as a separate task.

Despite the above difference, Categorical AFT is clearly a proper extension
of classical AFT: it is well-known that every preordered set defines a category,
and therefore every complete lattice L defines a corresponding category $\mathbf{K}$ that
has an initial and terminal object (namely, the least and greatest element of L).
In this special case, all the results of Sects. 3 and 4 collapse to corresponding
results in [14]. However, categories are much more general structures than preordered sets and therefore they have a much broader applicability (see also the
forthcoming discussion in Subsect. 6.3). Of course, it is important to note that
since complete lattices have more specific properties than arbitrary categories,
there exist certain results of [14], such as for example the minimality property of
the well-founded fixed point (see [14, Theorem 19]), which do not seem to hold
for arbitrary categories. Notice also that, due to the more abstract nature of
categories, certain results are harder to establish in the categorial setting (such
as, for example, the minimality result of Sect. 5).

6.2   Classical Applications Through the Prism of Categorical AFT

In this subsection we give an example of how Categorical AFT can be used
in classical applications of AFT. We consider the case of logic programming,

which is one of the most well-known application domains of AFT. We assume some familiarity with the basic concepts that arise in the semantics of logic programming (see for example [16, 21]). Let P be a normal logic program, namely a program consisting of rules that may use negation-as-failure in their bodies. The semantics of such programs is developed based on the notion of *Herbrand interpretation*. Given a program P, let us denote by B_P the so-called *Herbrand Base* of P, namely the set of atoms that appear in P. A Herbrand interpretation of P is a subset of the Herbrand Base of P. The semantics of logic programs is based on the so-called *immediate consequence operator* T_P of P, which maps Herbrand interpretations to Herbrand interpretations, i.e., $T_P : 2^{B_P} \rightarrow 2^{B_P}$. For logic programs that do not use negation, it can be easily demonstrated that T_P is monotonic [21]. Moreover, 2^{B_P} is a complete lattice under set inclusion, and therefore the least fixed point of T_P exists and can be computed using the Knaster-Tarski fixed point theorem. This least fixed point of T_P is taken as the meaning of program P. However, for general logic programs the function T_P is not monotonic in general, and it does not always have a least fixed point. The fixed points of T_P however, are of paramount importance even in the non-monotonic case and the semantics of such programs is centered around these fixed points.

We can model the above state of affairs in category theoretic terms. Given program P, we define the category $\mathbf{H}_P$ of the Herbrand interpretations of P. The objects of $\mathbf{H}_P$ are the Herbrand interpretations of P. Given interpretations I, J in $\mathbf{H}_P$, an arrow $f : I \rightarrow J$ exists if and only if $I \subseteq J$. Given an arrow $f : I \rightarrow J$, $T_P(f)$ is defined if and only if $T_P(I) \subseteq T_P(J)$; in this case, $T_P(f)$ is the unique arrow from $T_P(I)$ to $T_P(J)$. It is straightforward to establish that, under the above definition, T_P is an operator in the sense of Definition 4.

It has been shown [13, pages 181–182] that there exists a simple approximator for T_P in the classical AFT sense, namely a $\leq_i$-monotonic function on $2^{B_P} \times 2^{B_P} \rightarrow 2^{B_P} \times 2^{B_P}$. A reformulation of this approximator in our categorical setting is straightforward and gives a functor $A_{T_P} : \mathbf{H}_P^{\approx} \rightarrow \mathbf{H}_P^{\approx}$. Since A_{T_P} is essentially a monotonic function over the complete lattice of Herbrand interpretations, it has a least fixed point. Notice that we can obtain the same result by easily verifying that A_{T_P} is a smooth operator that strongly approximates T_P in the sense of Definition 18; therefore Lemma 4 applies to it and it has a least fixed point. Moreover, A_{T_P} is a sensible functor (in the sense of our Definition 12) and therefore $\mathcal{C}_{A_{T_P}}$ also has a least fixed point.

6.3 A Novel Application: Non-monotonicity in Domain Theory

As it turns out, non-monotonicity emerges in unexpected contexts that are not directly related to traditional application areas of AFT. As we are going to discuss in this subsection, non-monotonicity is a key concept in the area of *domain theory* [1]. Categorical AFT gives an elegant approach for finding the fixed points of domain equations that involve non-monotonic operators. Since domain theory is the theoretical cornerstone for developing the semantics of modern programming languages, we believe that the connections established in this subsection will form the basis for developing the semantics of novel formalisms for knowledge representation and logic programming. In particular, since the semantics of higher-order languages are heavily based on domain theory, the material in this subsection may form the basis for the development of non-monotonic higher-order knowledge representation systems (possibly unifying and extending existing approaches such as [10, 11, 24, 25]).

The solution of recursive domain equations is one of the fundamental issues in the area of the denotational semantics of programming languages. For example, the solution of $D \cong At + [D \to D]$ specifies the semantics of the untyped lambda calculus over a domain At of atoms. The early tools for the solution of such equations were provided by the pioneering work of Dana Scott, based on his *inverse limit construction* (see, for example, [26, 28] for accessible introductions).

The possibility of solving domain equations using a categorical approach, was advocated by Wand [33], Smyth and Plotkin [27], Adámek and Koubek [2, 4], and others. Motivated introductions to the categorical approach can be found in many standard texts, such as [1, 18, 23, 31]. The key idea is that, under certain conditions, a recursive domain equation gives rise to a functor. The initial fixed point of this functor can be taken as the solution of the domain equation. There exist some well-known constructions for obtaining the initial fixed point of a functor (see for example *Adámek's theorem* [6] and the closely related *Smyth-Plotkin Basic Lemma* [27]). Despite their fundamental nature, these constructions can not be used *directly* to solve certain involved domain equations such as the $D \cong At + [D \to D]$ one mentioned above. The problem with this equation is that the aforementioned categorical fixed point constructions can only be applied directly to covariant functors, while the arrow functor $[- \to -]$ has mixed variance: it is contravariant in its left argument and covariant in its right one (see [23, page 68] or [18, page 327] for a thorough discussion of this issue). To paraphrase the problem using AFT terminology, *the arrow functor is non-monotonic and therefore we can not find the least fixed point of the corresponding domain equation using standard categorical techniques.* To bypass this problem, Smyth and Plotkin in [27] take an indirect route in order to make the Basic Lemma applicable to such domain equations. This state of affairs has been noted and discussed in the literature [1]: "*While it may seem harmless to restrict a covariant functor to embeddings in order to solve a recursive domain equation, it is nevertheless not clear what the philosophical justification for this step is. For mixed variant functors this question becomes even more pressing since we explicitly change the functor*".

In the following, we describe a solution to the above problem in the context of Categorical AFT. We assume familiarity with some background material that, due to space limitations, we can not include here. An accessible source for this material is [5], from which we will cite the needed results.

Let $\mathbf{K}$ be a *strict* **DCPO**-*enriched* category (see [5, Section 4, page 50]). As discussed in Sect. 3, we also require that $\mathbf{K}$ has both an initial and a terminal object. Such categories are common: by Lemma 4.4 of [5] (which is attributed to Barr [8, Proposition 4.7]), every strict **DCPO**-enriched category with ω-colimits, has an initial object that is also a terminal object. A well-known example of a strict **DCPO**-enriched category is $\mathbf{DCPO}_\perp$, the category of directed complete partial orders with least element and continuous functions that preserve the least element. Notice that $\mathbf{DCPO}_\perp$ has the dcpo $\{\perp\}$ as both an initial and terminal object. The following lemma, mentioned in [5] and attributed to Smyth and Plotkin [27], will play an important role in our discussion. The notion of *local continuity* is a fundamental one, initially introduced in [27, Definition 10].

Lemma 5 (Smyth and Plotkin [27]). *Every locally continuous endofunctor on a strict **DCPO**-enriched category, has an initial fixed point which is also a terminal fixed point.*

We can use the above result to give a solution to the domain equation $D \cong At + [D \to D]$. Assume that $\mathbf{K} = \mathbf{DCPO}_\perp$. Moreover, consider the operator $O : \mathbf{K} \to \mathbf{K}$ defined as $O(D) = At + [D \to D]$, $O(\mathrm{id}_D) = \mathrm{id}_{O(D)}$, and $O(f)$ is undefined for all other arrows in $\mathbf{K}$. Before defining the approximator $A_O : \mathbf{K}^\approx \to \mathbf{K}^\approx$ for O, we define, as an intermediate step, a mixed variant functor $F : \mathbf{K}^{\mathrm{op}} \times \mathbf{K} \to \mathbf{K}$ as follows: for objects D in $\mathbf{K}$ and E in $\mathbf{K}^{\mathrm{op}}$, $F(E, D) = At + [E \to D]$, and for arrows f in $\mathbf{K}$ and g in $\mathbf{K}^{\mathrm{op}}$, $F(g, f) = \mathrm{id}_{At} + [g \to f]$. It is straightforward to verify that F is locally continuous (see the discussion in [27, pages 774–775]). Let $F^{\mathrm{op}} : \mathbf{K} \times \mathbf{K}^{\mathrm{op}} \to \mathbf{K}^{\mathrm{op}}$ be the opposite functor of F. Then, we define $A_O(D, E) = (F(E, D), F^{\mathrm{op}}(D, E))$ and $A_O(f, g) = (F(g, f), F^{\mathrm{op}}(f, g))$. Again, it is straightforward to verify that A_O is locally continuous (see the discussion just after [27, Definition 10]). The proof of the following lemma follows as a special case of the more general Lemma 7 that will be stated shortly.

Lemma 6. $A_O : \mathbf{K}^\approx \to \mathbf{K}^\approx$ *is a symmetric approximator of O and it has an initial fixed point that is exact.*

The above example for the given domain equation, can be extended to a wider context, namely to all operators O that can be defined using a locally continuous mixed variant functor F. Let $\mathbf{K}$ be a strict **DCPO**-enriched category that has both an initial and a terminal object. Consider the operator $O : \mathbf{K} \to \mathbf{K}$ defined on objects through a locally continuous mixed variant functor $F : \mathbf{K}^{\mathrm{op}} \times \mathbf{K} \to \mathbf{K}$. For any object x in $\mathbf{K}$, $O(x) = F(x, x)$ and $O(f)$ is defined only for identity arrows. Let $F^{\mathrm{op}} : \mathbf{K} \times \mathbf{K}^{\mathrm{op}} \to \mathbf{K}^{\mathrm{op}}$ be the opposite functor of F. We define $A_O : \mathbf{K}^\approx \to \mathbf{K}^\approx$ as follows: for all x in $\mathbf{K}$ and y in $\mathbf{K}^{\mathrm{op}}$, $A_O(x, y) = (F(y, x), F^{\mathrm{op}}(x, y))$, and for all f in $\mathbf{K}$ and g in $\mathbf{K}^{\mathrm{op}}$, $A_O(f, g) = (F(g, f), F^{\mathrm{op}}(f, g))$. The following lemma holds (which generalizes Lemma 6):

Lemma 7. $A_O : \mathbf{K}^\approx \to \mathbf{K}^\approx$ *is a symmetric approximator of O and it has an initial fixed point that is exact.*

7   Future Work

An aspect of this work that we believe is important to further investigate, is the construction of approximators. One of the shortcomings of AFT (which is also shared by Categorical AFT), is that there is no "automatic" way to find the correct approximator of a given operator. This problem has been alleviated with the development of the theory of *ultimate approximators* [15]. More specifically, as it is demonstrated in [15], the set of approximators of a given operator O, forms a complete lattice, and therefore it has a greatest element denoted by U_O; this is the *ultimate approximator* of O. Then, given an operator O, we can use unambiguously U_O to study the fixed points of O. Although the details of the results in [15] are not straightforward, it is conceivable that a similar theory can be developed for Categorical AFT.

Another promising topic for future work, has to do with new applications of the proposed approach. We believe that Categorical AFT can be used to investigate the semantics of novel non-monotonic (and, possibly, higher-order and typed) formalisms for knowledge representation and logic programming. Moreover, we believe that there exist applications in domain theory that might require the introduction of non-exact fixed points. One possible such application is that of *negation types* [17], for which, to our knowledge, there does not exist at present a domain-theoretic semantics.

References

1. Abramsky, S., Jung, A.: Domain Theory, pp. 1–168. Oxford University Press Inc. (1995)
2. Adámek, J.: Recursive data types in algebraically omega-complete categories. Inf. Comput. **118**(2), 181–190 (1995). https://doi.org/10.1006/inco.1995.1061
3. Adámek, J., Herrlich, H., Strecker, G.E.: Abstract and Concrete Categories - The Joy of Cats. Dover Publications (2009)
4. Adámek, J., Koubek, V.: Least fixed point of a functor. J. Comput. Syst. Sci. **19**(2), 163–178 (1979). https://doi.org/10.1016/0022-0000(79)90026-6
5. Adámek, J., Milius, S., Moss, L.S.: Fixed points of functors. J. Log. Algebraic Methods Program. **95**, 41–81 (2018). https://doi.org/10.1016/j.jlamp.2017.11.003
6. Adámek, J.: Free algebras and automata realizations in the language of categories. Comment. Math. Univ. Carol. **015**(4), 589–602 (1974)
7. Antić, C., Eiter, T., Fink, M.: Hᴇx semantics via approximation fixpoint theory. In: Cabalar, P., Son, T.C. (eds.) LPNMR 2013. LNCS (LNAI), vol. 8148, pp. 102–115. Springer, Heidelberg (2013). https://doi.org/10.1007/978-3-642-40564-8_11
8. Barr, M.: Algebraically compact functors. J. Pure Appl. Algebra **82**(3), 211–231 (1992). https://doi.org/10.1016/0022-4049(92)90169-G
9. Bos, R., Hemerik, C.: An Introduction to the Category-Theoretic Solution of Recursive Domain Equations. Computing Science Notes. Technische Universiteit Eindhoven (1988)
10. Charalambidis, A., Ésik, Z., Rondogiannis, P.: Minimum model semantics for extensional higher-order logic programming with negation. Theory Pract. Log. Program. **14**(4–5), 725–737 (2014). https://doi.org/10.1017/S1471068414000313
11. Charalambidis, A., Rondogiannis, P., Symeonidou, I.: Approximation fixpoint theory and the well-founded semantics of higher-order logic programs. Theory Pract. Log. Program. **18**(3–4), 421–437 (2018). https://doi.org/10.1017/S1471068418000108

12. Dasseville, I., van der Hallen, M., Bogaerts, B., Janssens, G., Denecker, M.: A compositional typed higher-order logic with definitions. In: Carro, M., King, A., Saeedloei, N., Vos, M.D. (eds.) Technical Communications of the 32nd International Conference on Logic Programming, ICLP 2016 TCs, New York City, USA, 16–21 October 2016. OASIcs, vol. 52, pp. 14:1–14:13. Schloss Dagstuhl - Leibniz-Zentrum für Informatik (2016). https://doi.org/10.4230/OASIcs.ICLP.2016.14

13. Denecker, M., Bruynooghe, M., Vennekens, J.: Approximation fixpoint theory and the semantics of logic and answers set programs. In: Erdem, E., Lee, J., Lierler, Y., Pearce, D. (eds.) Correct Reasoning. LNCS, vol. 7265, pp. 178–194. Springer, Heidelberg (2012). https://doi.org/10.1007/978-3-642-30743-0_13

14. Denecker, M., Marek, V., Truszczyński, M.: Approximations, stable operators, well-founded fixpoints and applications in nonmonotonic reasoning. In: Minker, J. (ed.) Logic-Based Artificial Intelligence, pp. 127–144. Kluwer Academic Publishers, Dordrecht (2000)

15. Denecker, M., Marek, V.W., Truszczynski, M.: Ultimate approximation and its application in nonmonotonic knowledge representation systems. Inf. Comput. 192(1), 84–121 (2004). https://doi.org/10.1016/j.ic.2004.02.004

16. Fitting, M.: Fixpoint semantics for logic programming: a survey. Theor. Comput. Sci. 278(1–2), 25–51 (2002). https://doi.org/10.1016/S0304-3975(00)00330-3

17. Frisch, A., Castagna, G., Benzaken, V.: Semantic subtyping: dealing set-theoretically with function, union, intersection, and negation types. J. ACM 55(4), 19:1–19:64 (2008). https://doi.org/10.1145/1391289.1391293

18. Gunter, C.A.: Semantics of Programming Languages - Structures and Techniques. Foundations of Computing. MIT Press (1993)

19. Liu, F., Bi, Y., Chowdhury, M.S., You, J.-H., Feng, Z.: Flexible approximators for approximating fixpoint theory. In: Khoury, R., Drummond, C. (eds.) AI 2016. LNCS (LNAI), vol. 9673, pp. 224–236. Springer, Cham (2016). https://doi.org/10.1007/978-3-319-34111-8_28

20. Liu, F., You, J.: Alternating fixpoint operator for hybrid MKNF knowledge bases as an approximator of AFT. Theory Pract. Log. Program. 22(2), 305–334 (2022). https://doi.org/10.1017/S1471068421000168

21. Lloyd, J.W.: Foundations of Logic Programming, 2nd edn. Springer, Heidelberg (1987). https://doi.org/10.1007/978-3-642-83189-8

22. Pelov, N., Denecker, M., Bruynooghe, M.: Well-founded and stable semantics of logic programs with aggregates. Theory Pract. Log. Program. 7(3), 301–353 (2007). https://doi.org/10.1017/S1471068406002973

23. Pierce, B.C.: Basic Category Theory for Computer Scientists. Foundations of Computing. MIT Press (1991)

24. Rondogiannis, P., Symeonidou, I.: The intricacies of three-valued extensional semantics for higher-order logic programs. Theory Pract. Log. Program. 17(5–6), 974–991 (2017). https://doi.org/10.1017/S1471068417000357

25. Rondogiannis, P., Symeonidou, I.: Extensional semantics for higher-order logic programs with negation. Log. Methods Comput. Sci. 14(2) (2018). https://doi.org/10.23638/LMCS-14(2:19)2018

26. Schmidt, D.A.: Denotational Semantics: A Methodology for Language Development. William C. Brown Publishers (1986)

27. Smyth, M.B., Plotkin, G.D.: The category-theoretic solution of recursive domain equations. SIAM J. Comput. 11(4), 761–783 (1982). https://doi.org/10.1137/0211062

28. Stoy, J.E.: Denotational Semantics: The Scott-Strachey Approach to Programming Language Theory. MIT Press, Cambridge (1977)

29. Strass, H., Wallner, J.P.: Analyzing the computational complexity of abstract dialectical frameworks via approximation fixpoint theory. Artif. Intell. **226**, 34–74 (2015). https://doi.org/10.1016/j.artint.2015.05.003
30. Tarski, A.: A lattice-theoretical fixpoint theorem and its applications. Pac. J. Math. **5**(2), 285–309 (1955)
31. Tennent, R.D.: Semantics of Programming Languages. Prentice Hall International Series in Computer Science. Prentice Hall (1991)
32. Vennekens, J., Gilis, D., Denecker, M.: Splitting an operator: algebraic modularity results for logics with fixpoint semantics. ACM Trans. Comput. Log. **7**(4), 765–797 (2006). https://doi.org/10.1145/1183278.1183284
33. Wand, M.: Fixed-point constructions in order-enriched categories. Theor. Comput. Sci. **8**, 13–30 (1979). https://doi.org/10.1016/0304-3975(79)90053-7

Deciding Subsumption in Defeasible $\mathcal{ELI}_\perp$ with Typicality Models

Igor de Camargo e Souza Câmara[1]($\boxtimes$)(iD) and Anni-Yasmin Turhan[2,3](iD)

[1] University of São Paulo, São Paulo, Brazil
igor.camara@alumni.usp.br
[2] Technische Universität Dresden, Dresden, Germany
anni-yasmin.turhan@tu-dresden.de
[3] Center for Scalable Data Analytics and Artificial Intelligence (ScaDS.AI)
Dresden/Leipzig, Dresden, Germany

Abstract. Some reasoning methods for Defeasible Description Logics (DDLs) suffer from quantification neglect (QN) as they omit un-defeated information for quantified objects. Reasoning in defeasible $\mathcal{EL}_\perp$ based on so-called typicality models (TMs), which extend canonical models of classical $\mathcal{EL}_\perp$, can alleviate QN. The DDL $\mathcal{ELI}_\perp$ extends $\mathcal{EL}_\perp$ by inverse roles, i.e., a limited form of value restriction. Extending TMs to inverse roles is challenging due to their interaction with existential restrictions. In this paper, we develop TMs for $\mathcal{ELI}_\perp$ for 4 different semantics reliant on rational and relevant closure. Our computation methods for those TMs are effective decision procedures for subsumption in defeasible $\mathcal{ELI}_\perp$ and the stronger forms of TMs can mitigate QN.

Keywords: Description Logics · Defeasible Logics · Nonmonotonic Reasoning

1 Introduction

Defeasible Description Logics (DDLs) are nonmonotonic extension of Description Logics. DDL knowledge bases extend those for DLs by a DBox in which *defeasible* concept inclusions (DCIs) are stated. Intuitively, DCIs state sub-concept relationships that hold unless contradictory information overrides them. There are different semantics defined for DDLs [4,6,9,12,13,16,17,22]. A well-investigated approach to terminological reasoning in DDLs is to use materialization to answer (defeasible) subsumption queries, say $C \mathrel{\underset{\sim}{\sqsubseteq}} D$, by enriching C with DBox information [7,12–15]. As observed in [5,19], materialization-based methods often suffer from *quantification neglect* (QN), i.e., they omit un-defeated information from the DBox for quantified objects in relational neighborhood leading to weaker, essentially propositional consequences of DCIs.

To solve QN for the DDL $\mathcal{EL}_\perp$ so-called typicality models were introduced in [19,20]. Typicality models extend the canonical models of classical $\mathcal{EL}_\perp$. Canonical models have interpretation domains that contain an element for each concept

© The Author(s), under exclusive license to Springer Nature Switzerland AG 2023
S. Gaggl et al. (Eds.): JELIA 2023, LNAI 14281, pp. 531–546, 2023.
https://doi.org/10.1007/978-3-031-43619-2_36

occurring in the ontology, the concept representative. Since classical entailments, e.g. subsumption, can be read-off directly from canonical models [1,3], reasoning in $\mathcal{EL}_\perp$ amounts to computing the canonical model of an ontology. This can be done in polynomial time [1,3]. Typicality models for defeasible $\mathcal{EL}_\perp$ are also canonical in that sense for (skeptical) defeasible consequences.

In typicality interpretations, domain elements are pairs of a concept representative and a set of DCIs that is a subset of the DBox. Intuitively, an element $A_\mathcal{V}$ represents members of concept A satisfying all DCIs in $\mathcal{V}$. The varying sets of DCIs admit reasoning w.r.t. differing "degrees" of typicality. Typicality models can be parameterized to achieve different semantics [18,21]. The collection of subsets of the DBox used for domain elements determines the *strength of reasoning*, e.g. rational or relevant strength. Another parameter for the semantics is *coverage of reasoning*. Propositional coverage admits as role successors only atypical elements, i.e. elements of the form $A_\emptyset$. Reasoning w.r.t. such *minimal typicality models* can reproduce materialization-based reasoning. Nested coverage is achieved by *maximal typicality models*, which use role successors that are "fully saturated" with defeasible information, i.e., adding one more DCI from the DBox would render them inconsistent. These models are faithful to the idea of defeasible logics, as they discard typicality information only, if overriding does necessitate it.

In this paper we investigate defeasible subsumption under different semantics for the DL $\mathcal{ELI}_\perp$, which extends $\mathcal{EL}_\perp$ by inverse roles. Initial results of this investigation were published in [11]. Classical $\mathcal{ELI}$ also enjoys the canonical model property. Inverse roles can express a limited form of value restriction that interact with existential restrictions. Due to this interaction, the domain of canonical models contains representatives for each set of named concepts from the signature of the KB, making reasoning ExpTime-hard [2,3]. We develop typicality models for the DDL $\mathcal{ELI}_\perp$ where domain elements now combine representatives for *concept sets* with sets of DCIs. The minimal typicality models are then used to define semantics of propositional coverage. We show that minimal typicality models for rational and for relevant strength can attain classical subsumption and materialization-based defeasible subsumption.

A main contribution of this paper is the computation method for maximal typicality models for $\mathcal{ELI}_\perp$. The approach to compute these models that are saturated with defeasible information, is a fix-point construction, where each iteration strengthens the typicality of some successor element in the interpretation domain by increasing its set of DCIs, and then "restores" the resulting interpretation s.t. that becomes a model. Our algorithm extends the method for $\mathcal{EL}_\perp$ substantially. For instance, we need to introduce a labeling function for the edges to be able to track which endpoint is to be updated. We show termination of our computation method and define semantics for nested coverage based on maximal typicality models and for rational and relevant strength. Finally, we show that nested coverage yields more consequences than propositional coverage for both of the considered strengths. By the virtue of each domain element being fully saturated with defeasible information, reasoning under nested coverage alleviates quantification neglect. The full proofs can be found in [10].

2   Preliminaries

We assume that the reader is familiar with basic notions of DLs and the computation of canonical models for monotone $\mathcal{ELI}$, as described in [3], Ch. 6. We use the following countable, disjoint name sets: N_C for concept names and N_R for role names. We also use $N_R^- := \{r^- \mid r \in N_R\}$ and $R := N_R \cup N_R^-$.

$\mathcal{ELI}_\perp$ concepts are defined inductively by: $C, D := A \mid \perp \mid \top \mid C \sqcap D \mid \exists r.C$ where $A \in N_C$ and $r \in R$. $\mathcal{EL}_\perp$ is the fragment of $\mathcal{ELI}_\perp$, where $R = N_R$. We also use value restrictions $\forall r.C$. The semantics of concepts in the DL $\mathcal{ELI}_\perp$ is the usual one. *General concept inclusions* (GCIs) are axioms of the form $C \sqsubseteq D$. A TBox $\mathcal{T}$ is a finite set of GCIs. An interpretation $\mathcal{I}$ *satisfies* a GCI ($\mathcal{I} \models C \sqsubseteq D$) iff $C^\mathcal{I} \subseteq D^\mathcal{I}$ holds. $\mathcal{I}$ is a *model* of a TBox $\mathcal{T}$ iff it satisfies every GCI in $\mathcal{T}$. Concept C is *subsumed* by D w.r.t. $\mathcal{T}$ iff $C^\mathcal{I} \subseteq D^\mathcal{I}$ in every model $\mathcal{I}$ of $\mathcal{T}$. The *signature* of X ($\mathsf{sig}(X)$) contains all names occurring in X and $\mathsf{sig}_C(X) := \mathsf{sig}(X) \cap N_C$ and $\mathsf{sig}_R(X) := \mathsf{sig}(X) \cap N_R$.

Note, that $(\exists r.A \sqsubseteq B) \equiv (A \sqsubseteq \forall r^-.B)$ holds. A TBox $\mathcal{T}$ is in *TBox normal form* (T-NF($\mathcal{T}$)), iff all of its GCIs are either of type: $A_1 \sqsubseteq B$, $A_1 \sqcap A_2 \sqsubseteq B$, $A \sqsubseteq \exists r.B$, or $A \sqsubseteq \forall r^-.B$, where $r \in R$. $\mathcal{ELI}_\perp$ has the *canonical model property* that admits to read-off subsumption relationships from concept memberships of domain elements directly. In canonical models for $\mathcal{ELI}_\perp$, the domain elements are conjunctions of concept names. Let $M = \{A_1, \ldots, A_n\}$ be a set of concept names, then $\lceil M \rceil := \bigsqcap_{i=1}^n A_i$. Construction of canonical models relies on prime role successors. A set N is an *r-prime successor* of M in $\mathcal{I}$ iff (i) $\mathcal{K} \models \lceil M \rceil \sqsubseteq \exists r.\lceil N \rceil$ and (ii) $\nexists N' \supset N$ s.t. $\mathcal{K} \models \lceil M \rceil \sqsubseteq \exists r.\lceil N' \rceil$. A canonical model for the DL $\mathcal{ELI}_\perp$ has only role edges between elements and their prime successors. Deciding subsumption between conjunctions of concept names, e.g. $\lceil M \rceil \sqsubseteq \lceil N \rceil$, is to check whether the element M is an instance of $\lceil N \rceil$ in the canonical model $\mathcal{I}_C$, i.e. $\mathcal{K} \models \lceil M \rceil \sqsubseteq \lceil N \rceil$ iff $M \in \lceil N \rceil^{\mathcal{I}_C}$.

Defeasible Description Logics (DDLs) extend DLs by *defeasible concept inclusions* (DCIs), which are axioms of the form $C \mathbin{\sqsubset\mkern-10mu\sim} D$. A finite set of DCIs is a DBox $\mathcal{D}$ and a *defeasible knowledge base* (DKB) is a pair $\mathcal{K} = (\mathcal{T}, \mathcal{D})$. Materialization-based semantics are nonmonotonic entailment relations using reductions to classical DL reasoning by transforming DCIs into material implications. For $\mathcal{ELI}_\perp$, we use materialization by TBox extension from [21]. Then, define *DCI materialization* as $\overline{E \mathbin{\sqsubset\mkern-10mu\sim} F} := A_{E \mathbin{\sqsubset\mkern-10mu\sim} F}$, where $A_{E \mathbin{\sqsubset\mkern-10mu\sim} F}$ is a fresh concept name, *DBox materialization* as $\overline{\mathcal{D}} := \bigsqcap_{(E \mathbin{\sqsubset\mkern-10mu\sim} F) \in \mathcal{D}} \overline{E \mathbin{\sqsubset\mkern-10mu\sim} F}$, and *DKB materialization* as $\overline{\mathcal{K}} := (\mathcal{T} \cup \{(\overline{E \mathbin{\sqsubset\mkern-10mu\sim} F} \sqcap E) \sqsubseteq F \mid E \mathbin{\sqsubset\mkern-10mu\sim} F \in \mathcal{D}\}, \emptyset)$. Note, that each new GCI in the TBox of $\overline{\mathcal{K}}$ represents a DCI and describes the typical members of E and that the DBox in $\overline{\mathcal{K}}$ is always empty.

Materialization-based defeasible subsumption selects some set of DCIs $\mathcal{U} \subseteq \mathcal{D}$ to materialize in conjunction with the concept C from a subsumption query $C \mathbin{\sqsubset\mkern-10mu\sim} D$. Different selection criteria produce distinct kinds of materialization-based reasoning, called *strengths*. This is formalized by a *consistent-selection function* $\mathsf{sel_s}$, which is a function that gets an $\mathcal{ELI}_\perp$ concept C and a DKB $\mathcal{K}$ as input and returns a set where each element $\mathcal{U}$ is a subset of the DBox $\mathcal{D}$ s.t.

$C \sqcap \overline{U}$ is satisfiable w.r.t. $\overline{K}$. Formally, $K \models_{\mathsf{mat,s}} C \mathrel{\vcenter{\hbox{$\sqsubset$}}\kern-0.4em\raise0.3ex\hbox{$\sim$}} D$ iff $\overline{K} \models C \sqcap \overline{U} \sqsubseteq D$, for every $U \in \mathsf{sel_s}(C, K)$.

Both rational and relevant closures rely on the *exceptionality chain* of K, originally defined in [13]. The exceptionality chain is a sequence of sets $\mathcal{E}_0, \mathcal{E}_1, \ldots, \mathcal{E}_n$ s.t. $\mathcal{D} = \mathcal{E}_0$, $\mathcal{E}_{i+1} \subset \mathcal{E}_i$ and $C \mathrel{\vcenter{\hbox{$\sqsubset$}}\kern-0.4em\raise0.3ex\hbox{$\sim$}} D \in \mathcal{E}_{i+i}$ iff $\overline{K} \models C \sqcap \overline{\mathcal{E}_i} \sqsubseteq \bot$. The set $\mathcal{E}_n$ is either a fixpoint or $\emptyset$. If it is $\emptyset$, $\mathcal{D}$ is *well-separated*. For every DKB there is an equivalent well-separated DKB [8], thus we can assume w.l.o.g. that all DKBs are well-separated. The *rank of a concept* C, denoted by $r_K(C)$, is the least i s.t. $\overline{K} \not\models C \sqcap \overline{\mathcal{E}_i} \sqsubseteq \bot$. The *rank of a DCI* $C \mathrel{\vcenter{\hbox{$\sqsubset$}}\kern-0.4em\raise0.3ex\hbox{$\sim$}} D$ is given by the rank of the concept on its left-hand side, i.e. $r_K(C \mathrel{\vcenter{\hbox{$\sqsubset$}}\kern-0.4em\raise0.3ex\hbox{$\sim$}} D) := r_K(C)$.

The consistent selection function for the rational closure uses the exceptionality chain directly by setting $\mathsf{sel_{rat}}(C, K) := \{\mathcal{E}_i \mid r_K(C) = i\}$. The relevant closure [12] uses *justifications*, i.e., subset minimal sets of axioms from K causing an inconsistency. A C-justification is a set $\mathcal{J} \subseteq \mathcal{D}$ s.t. $\overline{K} \models C \sqcap \overline{\mathcal{J}} \sqsubseteq \bot$ and for every $\mathcal{J}' \subset \mathcal{J}$, it holds that $\overline{K} \not\models C \sqcap \overline{\mathcal{J}'} \sqsubseteq \bot$. The relevant closure is then defined by excluding minimally ranked axioms from all C-justifications, i.e. $\mathsf{sel_{rel}}(C, K) := \mathcal{D} \setminus \{E \mathrel{\vcenter{\hbox{$\sqsubset$}}\kern-0.4em\raise0.3ex\hbox{$\sim$}} F \in \mathcal{D} \mid E$ is minimally ranked for a C-justification $\mathcal{J}\}$.

3   Typicality Models for Defeasible $\mathcal{ELI}_\bot$

We give a general definition of minimal typicality models of a DKB parameterized with strength **s**. To do so, we require the input DKB to be in a normal form that moves complex concepts from the DBox to the TBox, but keeps their semantics by introducing new concept names. For a DKB $K = (\mathcal{T}, \mathcal{D})$, define $\mathsf{NF}(\mathcal{D}) := \{A_C \mathrel{\vcenter{\hbox{$\sqsubset$}}\kern-0.4em\raise0.3ex\hbox{$\sim$}} A_D \mid C \mathrel{\vcenter{\hbox{$\sqsubset$}}\kern-0.4em\raise0.3ex\hbox{$\sim$}} D \in \mathcal{D}\}$, where $A_C, A_D \in \mathsf{N_C} \setminus \mathsf{sig_C}(K)$ and define $\mathcal{T}_{\mathsf{aux}} := \{C \sqsubseteq A_C, A_D \sqsubseteq D \mid A_C \mathrel{\vcenter{\hbox{$\sqsubset$}}\kern-0.4em\raise0.3ex\hbox{$\sim$}} A_D \in \mathsf{NF}(\mathcal{D})\}$, then finally $\mathsf{NF}(K) := (\mathsf{T\text{-}NF}(\mathcal{T} \cup \mathcal{T}_{\mathsf{aux}}), \mathsf{NF}(\mathcal{D}))$ is the *normal form* of K. It is straightforward to show that the normalization does not affect the computation of the rank. *We assume* in the following that we want to decide for $K = (\mathcal{T}, \mathcal{D})$ already in normal form whether $K \models C \mathrel{\vcenter{\hbox{$\sqsubset$}}\kern-0.4em\raise0.3ex\hbox{$\sim$}} D$ holds.

Typicality interpretations are built on the representative domain of a DKB, which collects concept names possibly occurring in the scope of quantifiers. The *set of quantified concepts* of an axiom is $Qc(C \mathrel{\vcenter{\hbox{$\sqsubset$}}\kern-0.4em\raise0.3ex\hbox{$\sim$}} D) := Qc(C \sqsubseteq D) := \{A \in \mathsf{sig_C}(C \sqsubseteq D) \mid \exists r \in \mathsf{N_R}.\exists r.A$ or $\forall r.A$ occurs in C or $D\}$. The *representative domain* of $K = (\mathcal{T}, \mathcal{D})$ is $\Delta^K := \{\{A\} \mid A \in \mathsf{sig_C}(\mathcal{T} \cup \mathcal{D})\} \cup \mathcal{P}(Qc(\mathcal{T} \cup \mathcal{D}))$. The combination of existential and value restrictions, say $\exists r.E$ and $\forall r.F$, necessitates representatives for $E \sqcap F$. For a domain element $M \in \Delta^K$, the *corresponding concept* is $\lceil M \rceil := \bigsqcap_{A \in M} A$, if $M \neq \emptyset$ and $\top$, otherwise. Each domain element is the representative of its corresponding concept. Typicality interpretations have 2-dimensional domains and their elements M_U are pairs, where $M \in \Delta^K$ is the *concept set* and $U \subseteq \mathcal{D}$ is the *typicality set*. Intuitively, M_U represents instances of concept $\lceil M \rceil$ that conform with the DCIs in U.

Definition 1. *Let Δ^K be the representative domain of $K = (\mathcal{T}, \mathcal{D})$. A typicality domain of K is $\Delta^{T(K)} \subseteq \Delta^K \times \mathcal{P}(\mathcal{D})$ s.t. if $M \in \Delta^K$, then $M_\emptyset \in \Delta^{T(K)}$. $\mathcal{I} = (\Delta^{\mathcal{I}}, \cdot^{\mathcal{I}})$ is a typicality interpretation iff $\Delta^{\mathcal{I}}$ is a typicality domain.*

The *maximally typical instances of* a concept set M in a typicality interpretation domain in $\mathcal{I} = (\Delta^{\mathcal{I}}, \cdot^{\mathcal{I}})$ are those $M_{\mathcal{U}} \in \Delta^{\mathcal{I}}$ s.t. there is no $M_{\mathcal{V}} \in \Delta^{\mathcal{I}}$ with $\mathcal{U} \subset \mathcal{V}$. Intuitively, satisfaction of $\lceil M \rceil \sqsubsetsim A$ holds in $\mathcal{I}$, if it is satisfied by the "most typical" instances of M.

Definition 2. *Let C, D be concepts, $A \in \mathsf{N_C}$, $M \in \mathcal{P}(\mathsf{N_C})$, and $\mathcal{I} = (\Delta^{\mathcal{I}}, \cdot^{\mathcal{I}})$ a typicality interpretation. Then satisfaction of DKB axioms is defined as follows:*

- *$\mathcal{I}$ satisfies a GCI $C \sqsubseteq D$ (denoted $\mathcal{I} \models C \sqsubseteq D$) iff $C^{\mathcal{I}} \subseteq D^{\mathcal{I}}$,*
- *$\mathcal{I}$ satisfies a DCI $\lceil M \rceil \sqsubsetsim A$ (denoted $\mathcal{I} \models \lceil M \rceil \sqsubsetsim A$) iff $M_{\mathcal{U}} \in A^{\mathcal{I}}$ for every maximally typical instance $M_{\mathcal{U}}$ of M in $\Delta^{\mathcal{I}}$.*

$\mathcal{I}$ is a model of a (normalized) DKB $\mathcal{K} = (\mathcal{T}, \mathcal{D})$ iff $\mathcal{I} \models \alpha$ holds for all $\alpha \in \mathcal{T} \cup \mathcal{D}$.

4 Minimal Typicality Models for Propositional Coverage

We define general minimal typicality models that can be parameterized with a strength **s**. We show that these structures are models of the given $\mathcal{K}$ and that they are canonical, so that (defeasible) subsumption relations can be read-off from the elements. Finally, we define kinds of typicality domains tailored to **s** that realize this strength of reasoning.

In canonical models for monotone $\mathcal{ELI}$, an element is connected to those elements that are $\subseteq$-maximal r-successors. Limiting connections to these "strongest" successors guarantees that concept membership to existential restrictions can be read-off. We want to achieve this property for typicality models as well. Now, in defeasible $\mathcal{ELI}_{\perp}$, the "strongest" successors need to be selected according to the concept set and the typicality set. We use the $\mathsf{N_C}$-type of an element to identify its maximally typical r-successors.

Definition 3. *Let $\mathcal{K} = (\mathcal{T}, \mathcal{D})$ be a DKB, $\mathcal{I} = (\Delta^{\mathcal{I}}, \cdot^{\mathcal{I}})$ be an interpretation, and $d \in \Delta^{\mathcal{I}}$ be an element. The $\mathsf{N_C}$-type of d w.r.t. $\mathcal{K}$ and $\mathcal{I}$ is $\mathsf{N_C}\text{-type}_{\mathcal{K}}(d, \mathcal{I}) := \{A \in \mathsf{sig_C}(\mathcal{K}) \mid d \in A^{\mathcal{I}}\}$.*

Let $\mathcal{I} = (\Delta^{T(\mathcal{K})}, \cdot^{\mathcal{I}})$ be a typicality interpretation, and $r \in \{s, s^-\}$ with $s \in \mathsf{sig_R}(\mathcal{K})$. Then, $N_{\mathcal{V}} \in \Delta^{T(\mathcal{K})}$ with $N \in \Delta^{\mathcal{K}}$ is a prime r-successor of $M_{\mathcal{U}}$ in $\mathcal{I}$ iff:

1. *$\overline{\mathcal{K}} \models \lceil \mathsf{N_C}\text{-type}_{\mathcal{K}}(M_{\mathcal{U}}, \mathcal{I}) \rceil \sqcap \overline{\mathcal{U}} \sqsubseteq \exists r.\lceil N \rceil$, and*
2. *there is no $N' \in \Delta^{\mathcal{K}}$ s.t. it fulfills Property 1 and $N \subset N'$.*

In minimal typicality models all role-successors are atypical elements, i.e., elements with $\emptyset$ as their typicality set.

Definition 4. *Let $\mathcal{K} = (\mathcal{T}, \mathcal{D})$ be a DKB and $\Delta^{T(\mathcal{K})}$ its typicality domain. The minimal typicality model is $\mathcal{I}_{\min}^{\mathcal{K}} := (\Delta^{T(\mathcal{K})}, \cdot^{\mathcal{I}_{\min}^{\mathcal{K}}})$, where:*

$$A^{\mathcal{I}_{\min}^{\mathcal{K}}} := \{M_{\mathcal{U}} \mid \overline{\mathcal{K}} \models \lceil M \rceil \sqcap \overline{\mathcal{U}} \sqsubseteq A\} \text{ for all } A \in \mathsf{sig_C}(\mathcal{K})$$

$$r^{\mathcal{I}_{\min}^{\mathcal{K}}} := \{(N_{\emptyset}, M_{\mathcal{U}}) \mid N \text{ is a prime } r^-\text{-successor for } M_{\mathcal{U}} \text{ in } \mathcal{I}_{\min}^{\mathcal{K}}\} \cup$$
$$\{(M_{\mathcal{U}}, N_{\emptyset}) \mid N \text{ is a prime } r\text{-successor for } M_{\mathcal{U}} \text{ in } \mathcal{I}_{\min}^{\mathcal{K}}\} \text{ for all } r \in \mathsf{sig_R}(\mathcal{K})$$

It still needs to be shown that $\mathcal{I}_{\min}^{\mathcal{K}}$ is a model of $\mathcal{K}$, i.e. it satisfies GCIs in $\overline{\mathcal{K}}$ and that every element $M_{\mathcal{U}}$ satisfies all DCIs in its typicality set $\mathcal{U}$.

Lemma 1. *Let* $\mathcal{K} = (\mathcal{T}, \mathcal{D})$ *be a DKB,* $\Delta^{T(\mathcal{K})}$ *be a typicality domain over* $\mathcal{K}$, *and* $\mathcal{I}_{\min}^{\mathcal{K}} = (\Delta^{T(\mathcal{K})}, \cdot^{\mathcal{I}_{\min}^{\mathcal{K}}})$ *its minimal typicality model. Then,*

1. $C^{\mathcal{I}_{\min}^{\mathcal{K}}} \subseteq D^{\mathcal{I}_{\min}^{\mathcal{K}}}$ *for every* $C \sqsubseteq D \in \overline{\mathcal{K}}$, *i.e.* $\mathcal{I}_{\min}^{\mathcal{K}}$ *is a model of* $\overline{\mathcal{K}}$.
2. *for all* $M_{\mathcal{U}} \in \Delta^{T(\mathcal{K})}$ *and all* $A \subsetsim B \in \mathcal{U}$ *holds:* $M_{\mathcal{U}} \in A^{\mathcal{I}_{\min}^{\mathcal{K}}} \Rightarrow M_{\mathcal{U}} \in B^{\mathcal{I}_{\min}^{\mathcal{K}}}$.

This lemma implies that minimal typicality models of a DKB $\mathcal{K}$ are models of $\mathcal{K}$, i.e. that $\mathcal{I}_{\min}^{\mathcal{K}} \models \mathcal{K}$ holds. The main argument is that every GCI $C \sqsubseteq D$ is satisfied by construction, since the following sequence of implications holds: $M_{\mathcal{U}} \in C^{\mathcal{I}_{\min}^{\mathcal{K}}} \Rightarrow \overline{\mathcal{K}} \models \lceil M \rceil \sqcap \overline{\mathcal{U}} \sqsubseteq C \Rightarrow \overline{\mathcal{K}} \models \lceil M \rceil \sqcap \overline{\mathcal{U}} \sqsubseteq D \Rightarrow M_{\mathcal{U}} \in D^{\mathcal{I}_{\min}^{\mathcal{K}}}$. For the DCIs, the entailment relation that defines membership for $M_{\mathcal{U}}$ is defined over $\lceil M \rceil \sqcap \overline{\mathcal{U}}$, ensuring that it satisfies the DCIs in $\mathcal{U}$.

Recall, that DCIs are satisfied in $\mathcal{I}_{\min}^{\mathcal{K}}$ if all most typical instances of the concept from the left-hand side satisfy it. In order to be canonical for a selected strength **s**, the maximally typical instances of the concepts in the representative domain must be exactly those selected by the consistent selection function for **s**. More formally, the typicality domain must

1. contain all the elements $M_{\mathcal{U}}$, where $\mathcal{U}$ is the set of DCIs to be materialized with $\lceil M \rceil$ in **s**, and
2. *not* contain any maximally typical instance of M, $M_{\mathcal{U}'}$, s.t. $\mathcal{U}'$ is not selected by $\mathsf{sel_s}$.

Theorem 1. *Let* $\mathsf{sel_s}$ *be a consistent-selection function for some strength* **s**, $\mathcal{K}$ *a DKB, and* $A \in \mathsf{sig_C}(\mathcal{K})$. *Let* $\mathcal{I}_{\min}^{\mathcal{K}} = (\Delta^{T(\mathcal{K})}, \cdot^{\mathcal{I}_{\min}^{\mathcal{K}}})$ *be a minimal typicality model of* $\mathcal{K}$ *s.t. for every* $M \in \Delta^{\mathcal{K}}$ *holds that* $M_{\mathcal{U}}$ *is maximally typical in* $\Delta^{T(\mathcal{K})}$ *iff* $\mathcal{U} \in \mathsf{sel_s}(\lceil M \rceil, \mathcal{K})$. *Then, for every* $M \in \Delta^{\mathcal{K}}$ *it holds that:*

1. $\mathcal{K} \models \lceil M \rceil \sqsubseteq A$ *iff* $M_{\emptyset} \in A^{\mathcal{I}_{\min}^{\mathcal{K}}}$, *and*
2. $\mathcal{K} \models_{\mathsf{mat,s}} \lceil M \rceil \subsetsim A$ *iff* $M_{\mathcal{U}} \in A^{\mathcal{I}_{\min}^{\mathcal{K}}}$, *for all maximally typical instances* $M_{\mathcal{U}}$ *of* M *in* $\Delta^{T(\mathcal{K})}$.

Proof. Claim 1. follows directly from the definition of minimal typicality models. *Claim 2.* $\mathcal{K} \models_{\mathsf{mat,s}} \lceil M \rceil \subsetsim A$ holds iff $M_{\mathcal{U}} \in A^{\mathcal{I}_{\min}^{\mathcal{K}}}$ for every maximally typical instance of A, where $A \in \Delta^{T(\mathcal{K})}$. By the requirement on the maximally typical instances in the theorem, every maximally typical instance of $M_{\mathcal{U}} \in \Delta^{T(\mathcal{K})}$ of M is such that $\mathcal{U} \in \mathsf{sel_s}(\lceil M \rceil, \mathcal{K})$. Then, notice that $\mathcal{K} \models_{\mathsf{mat,s}} \lceil M \rceil \subsetsim A$ iff $\overline{\mathcal{K}} \models \lceil M \rceil \sqcap \overline{\mathcal{U}} \sqsubseteq A$ iff $M_{\mathcal{U}} \in A^{\mathcal{I}_{\min}^{\mathcal{K}}}$.

Theorem 1 guarantees canonicity of $\mathcal{I}_{\min}^{\mathcal{K}}$, provided that the domain $\Delta^{T(\mathcal{K})}$ selected by strength **s** does not omit consistent elements. This condition holds for rational and relevant strength and their typicality domain, which extends the definition for the DDL $\mathcal{EL}_\perp$ [18,21]. Intuitively, for rational strength, the second dimension of $\Delta^{T(\mathcal{K})}$ is the exceptionality chain of the DKB returned by $\mathsf{sel_{rat}}$, and in case of relevant strength it is the part of the $\subset$-lattice over $\mathcal{P}(\mathcal{D})$ returned by $\mathsf{sel_{rel}}$.

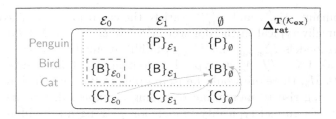

Fig. 1. Fragment of the minimal typicality domain built over $\Delta_{\mathbf{rat}}^{T(\mathcal{K}_{ex})}$ from Example 1, depicting only singleton concept sets. Arrows represent the role eats; the dotted area, the extension of Bird; and the dashed area, the extension of Flying.

Definition 5. *Let $\mathcal{E}_0, \ldots, \mathcal{E}_n$ be the exceptionality chain of $\mathcal{K} = (\mathcal{T}, \mathcal{D})$. Then*

- $\Delta_{\mathbf{rat}}^{T(\mathcal{K})} := \{M_{\mathcal{E}_i} \in \Delta^{\mathcal{K}} \times \{\mathcal{E}_0, \ldots, \mathcal{E}_n\} \mid 0 \le i \le n \text{ and } \overline{\mathcal{K}} \not\models \lceil M \rceil \sqcap \overline{\mathcal{E}_i} \sqsubseteq \perp\}.$
  is the rational typicality domain *of $\mathcal{K}$ and*
- $\Delta_{\mathbf{rel}}^{T(\mathcal{K})} := \{M_{\mathcal{U}} \in \Delta^{\mathcal{K}} \times \mathcal{P}(\mathcal{D}) \mid \mathcal{U} \subseteq \mathcal{V} \in \mathsf{sel}_{\mathbf{rel}}(\lceil M \rceil, \mathcal{K})\}$
  is the relevant typicality domain *of $\mathcal{K}$.*

Using the rational and relevant typicality domain and the mapping function $\cdot^{\mathcal{I}_{\min}^{\mathcal{K}}}$ for minimal typicality models, we can define the corresponding minimal typicality models for s and based on these the resulting semantics.

Definition 6. *A* minimal typicality model *of a DKB $\mathcal{K}$*

- $\mathcal{I}_{\min,\mathbf{rat}}^{\mathcal{K}} := (\Delta_{\mathbf{rat}}^{T(\mathcal{K})}, \cdot^{\mathcal{I}_{\min}^{\mathcal{K}}})$ *is a* rational minimal typicality model *of $\mathcal{K}$.*
- $\mathcal{I}_{\min,\mathbf{rel}}^{\mathcal{K}} := (\Delta_{\mathbf{rel}}^{T(\mathcal{K})}, \cdot^{\mathcal{I}_{\min}^{\mathcal{K}}})$ *is a* relevant minimal typicality model *of $\mathcal{K}$.*

Let $\alpha \in \{\lceil M \rceil \sqsubseteq A, \lceil M \rceil \mathrel{\underset{\sim}{\sqsubseteq}} A\}$ be an axiom. The semantics of

- *rational strength and propositional coverage (denoted $\models_{\mathsf{prop,rat}}$) is defined as $\mathcal{K} \models_{\mathsf{prop,rat}} \alpha$ iff $\mathcal{I}_{\min,\mathbf{rat}}^{\mathcal{K}} \models \alpha$.*
- *relevant strength and propositional coverage (denoted $\models_{\mathsf{prop,rel}}$) is defined as $\mathcal{K} \models_{\mathsf{prop,rel}} \alpha$ iff $\mathcal{I}_{\min,\mathbf{rel}}^{\mathcal{K}} \models \alpha$.*

We illustrate rational minimal typicality models by an example.

Example 1. Let $\mathcal{K}_{ex} = (\mathcal{T}_{ex}, \mathcal{D}_{ex})$, with

$$\mathcal{T}_{ex} = \{\mathsf{Cat} \sqsubseteq \exists\mathsf{eats}.\mathsf{Bird}, \mathsf{Penguin} \sqsubseteq \mathsf{Bird}\} \quad \text{and}$$
$$\mathcal{D}_{ex} = \{\mathsf{Bird} \mathrel{\underset{\sim}{\sqsubseteq}} \mathsf{Flying}, \mathsf{Bird} \mathrel{\underset{\sim}{\sqsubseteq}} \mathsf{Feathered}, \mathsf{Penguin} \sqcap \mathsf{Flying} \mathrel{\underset{\sim}{\sqsubseteq}} \perp\}.$$

The exceptionality chain for $\mathcal{K}_{ex}$ is: $\mathcal{E}_0 = \mathcal{D}_{ex}, \mathcal{E}_1 = \{\mathsf{Penguin} \sqcap \mathsf{Flying} \mathrel{\underset{\sim}{\sqsubseteq}} \perp\}$ and $\mathcal{E}_2 = \emptyset$. Figure 1 depicts a fragment of the rational minimal typicality model $\mathcal{I}_{\min,\mathbf{rat}}^{\mathcal{K}_{ex}}$. The rational domain for $\mathcal{K}_{ex}$ is a matrix of $\Delta^{\mathcal{K}_{ex}}$ and the exceptionality chain. The element $\mathsf{Penguin}_{\mathcal{E}_0}$ is omitted in $\Delta_{\mathbf{rat}}^{T(\mathcal{K}_{ex})}$ as $\overline{\mathcal{K}} \models \mathsf{Penguin} \sqcap \overline{\mathcal{E}_0} \sqsubseteq \perp$.

Both domains $\Delta_{\mathbf{rat}}^{T(\mathcal{K})}$ and $\Delta_{\mathbf{rel}}^{T(\mathcal{K})}$ satisfy the condition from Theorem 1, i.e. $M_{\mathcal{U}}$ is maximally typical in the domain $\Delta^{T(\mathcal{K})}$ iff $\mathcal{U} \in \mathsf{sels}(\lceil M \rceil, \mathcal{K})$. Therefore, the resulting models $\mathcal{I}_{\min,\mathbf{rat}}^{\mathcal{K}}$ and $\mathcal{I}_{\min,\mathbf{rel}}^{\mathcal{K}}$ fulfill canonicity.

In general, if $\mathcal{K} = (\mathcal{T}, \emptyset)$, its typicality domain would only contain the atypical elements $M_{\emptyset}$, therefore would be isomorphic to the canonical model for the DL $\mathcal{ELI}_{\perp}$ giving rise to monotonic reasoning as expected. On the whole, the computation of minimal typicality models for a strength s fulfilling the condition from Theorem 1 is an effective reasoning method for deciding defeasible subsumption for propositional coverage and strength s.

5   Computing Maximal Typicality Models

In maximal typicality models successors of elements are fully saturated with defeasible information from $\mathcal{D}$. The computation of a maximal typicality model of a given DKB $\mathcal{K}$ and a strength s starts from a minimal typicality model $\mathcal{I}_{\min}^{\mathcal{K}}$ on which model upgrades are performed exhaustively. Each *model upgrade* of a model $\mathcal{I}$ consists of two phases:

1. *model update*: for an edge in $\mathcal{I}$, introduce a new edge to an element with the same concept set, but an extended typicality set, i.e. increase the set of DCIs that the (inverse) role successor must satisfy.
2. *model recovery*: preserving the edge introduced by the upgrade, add and replace a minimal amount of information in $\mathcal{I}'$ necessary to transform it into a canonical model again (if possible).

This general computation method was introduced for $\mathcal{EL}_{\perp}$ in [18,20]. Extending it to inverse roles is non-trivial and requires overcoming challenges in both phases of an upgrade.

5.1   Updates of Typicality Models

An effect caused by inverse roles is that edges in typicality models need not be "initiated" by the predecessor, but can be "initiated" by the successor (or even by both). Thus an edge, say $(M_{\mathcal{U}}, N_{\mathcal{V}}) \in r^{\mathcal{I}}$, does not indicate whether $\overline{\mathcal{K}}$ entails $\lceil M \rceil \sqcap \overline{\mathcal{U}} \sqsubseteq \exists r.\lceil N \rceil$ or $\lceil N \rceil \sqcap \overline{\mathcal{V}} \sqsubseteq \exists r^{-}.\lceil M \rceil$ and thus the information present in $\mathcal{I}$ does not suffice to decide whether to update $M_{\mathcal{U}}$ or $N_{\mathcal{V}}$. To address this problem, we extend typicality interpretation by an edge labeling function that indicates which of the end-points of the edge initiates the edge.

Definition 7. *Let $\mathcal{I}$ be a typicality interpretation and $\mathcal{K}$ be a DKB. For $r \in \mathsf{N_R}$ an edge $(M_{\mathcal{U}}, N_{\mathcal{V}}) \in r^{\mathcal{I}}$ is*

– p-initiated *if $\overline{\mathcal{K}} \models \lceil \mathsf{N_C}\text{-type}_{\mathcal{K}}(M_{\mathcal{U}}, \mathcal{I}) \rceil \sqsubseteq \exists r.\lceil N \rceil$ and N is a prime r-successor for $\mathsf{N_C}\text{-type}_{\mathcal{K}}(M_{\mathcal{U}}, \mathcal{I})$ in $\mathcal{I}$.*
– s-initiated *if $\overline{\mathcal{K}} \models \lceil \mathsf{N_C}\text{-type}_{\mathcal{K}}(N_{\mathcal{V}}, \mathcal{I}) \rceil \sqsubseteq \exists r^{-}.\lceil M \rceil$ and M is a prime r^{-}-successor for $\mathsf{N_C}\text{-type}_{\mathcal{K}}(N_{\mathcal{V}}, \mathcal{I})$ in $\mathcal{I}$.*

A function $\text{Init}_\mathcal{I} : \Delta^\mathcal{I} \times \text{sig}_R(\mathcal{K}) \times \Delta^\mathcal{I} \to \mathcal{P}(\{\mathsf{s}, \mathsf{p}\})$ *is an* initiator labeling *for* $\mathcal{I}$ *w.r.t.* $\mathcal{K}$, *if it fulfills the following conditions:*

1. *If* $\mathsf{p} \in \text{Init}_\mathcal{I}(d, r, e)$, *then* $(d, e) \in r^\mathcal{I}$ *is* p-*initiated,*
2. *If* $\mathsf{s} \in \text{Init}_\mathcal{I}(d, r, e)$, *then* $(d, e) \in r^\mathcal{I}$ *is* s-*initiated, and*
3. $\text{Init}_\mathcal{I}(d, r, e) = \emptyset$ *iff* $(d, e) \notin r^\mathcal{I}$.

A pair $(\mathcal{I}, \text{Init}_\mathcal{I})$ *is a* labeled interpretation. *We abbreviate* $\mathsf{p} \in \text{Init}_\mathcal{I}(e, r, d)$ *by* $(d, e) \in r_\mathsf{p}^\mathcal{I}$ *and* $\mathsf{s} \in \text{Init}_\mathcal{I}(e, r, d)$ *by* $(d, e) \in r_\mathsf{s}^\mathcal{I}$.

The input to the first model update is $\mathcal{I}_{\text{min}}^\mathcal{K}$ with a labeling $\text{Init}_{\mathcal{I}_{\text{min}}^\mathcal{K}}$ determined by $\mathcal{K}$ and the fact that all successors are atypical elements. The *initiator labeling for* $\mathcal{I}_{\text{min}}^\mathcal{K}$ maps each $(M_\mathcal{U}, r, N_\mathcal{V})$ to the set containing p, if $(M_\mathcal{U}, N_\mathcal{V}) \in r^{\mathcal{I}_{\text{min}}^\mathcal{K}}$ is p-initiated and $\mathcal{V} = \emptyset$ and to a set containing s, if $(M_\mathcal{U}, N_\mathcal{V}) \in r^{\mathcal{I}_{\text{min}}^\mathcal{K}}$ is s-initiated and $\mathcal{U} = \emptyset$. One can show that this mapping is an initiator labeling.

An *update candidate* for a typicality model $\mathcal{I}$ is a pair of a domain element d and an edge from or to d that is initiated by d. Adding this edge to $\mathcal{I}$ would increase the typicality of a successor of d. We define a function that returns a set of update candidates for a labeled interpretation. Let $d, M_\mathcal{U}, M_\mathcal{V} \in \Delta^\mathcal{I}$ and $r \in \mathsf{N_R}$. The *set of r-update candidates* for $(\mathcal{I}, \text{Init}_\mathcal{I})$ is:

$$\text{UpCan}_r(\mathcal{I}, \text{Init}_\mathcal{I}) := \{((d, M_\mathcal{U}), d) \mid (d, M_\mathcal{V}) \in r_\mathsf{p}^\mathcal{I} \text{ and } \mathcal{V} \subset \mathcal{U}\} \cup$$
$$\{((M_\mathcal{U}, d), d) \mid (M_\mathcal{V}, d) \in r_\mathsf{s}^\mathcal{I} \text{ and } \mathcal{V} \subset \mathcal{U}\}.$$

We call element d the *update root* and the other element $M_\mathcal{U}$ the *update target*. Update candidates preserve the concept set M of the successor so that the update target becomes a prime successor if the successor that it supersedes was already a prime successor. A model update augments a given labeled typicality interpretation by realizing an update candidate, i.e., it adds the edge connecting the update root with the target, and it updates the initiator labeling accordingly.

Definition 8. *Let* $(\mathcal{I}, \text{Init}_\mathcal{I})$ *be a labeled typicality model, with the interpretation* $\mathcal{I} = (\Delta^\mathcal{I}, \cdot^\mathcal{I})$. *Furthermore, let* $((d_1, d_2), d_i) \in \text{UpCan}_r(\mathcal{I}, \text{Init}_\mathcal{I})$ *an update candidate for some root* $d_i \in \{d_1, d_2\}$ *and* $r \in \mathsf{N_R}$. *A typicality model r-update is* $\text{Upd}_r(\mathcal{I}, \text{Init}_\mathcal{J}, ((d_1, d_2), d_i)) := (\mathcal{J}, \text{Init}_\mathcal{J}, d_i)$, *where* $\mathcal{J} = (\Delta^\mathcal{I}, \cdot^\mathcal{J})$ *with*

$$A^\mathcal{J} := A^\mathcal{I}, \qquad r^\mathcal{J} := r^\mathcal{I} \cup \{(d_1, d_2)\}, \qquad s^\mathcal{J} := s^\mathcal{I}, \text{ for all } s \in \mathsf{N_R}, s \neq r,$$

$\text{init} := \mathsf{p}$ *if* $d_i = d_1$ *and* $\text{init} := \mathsf{s}$ *if* $d_i = d_2$ *and* $\text{Init}_\mathcal{J}$ *is the following mapping:*

$$\text{Init}_\mathcal{J}(d_1, r, d_2) := \text{Init}_\mathcal{I}(d_1, r, d_2) \cup \{\text{init}\}$$
$$\text{Init}_\mathcal{J}(e_1, r', e_2) := \text{Init}_\mathcal{I}(e_1, r', e_2) \text{ if } e_1 \neq d_1 \text{ or } e_2 \neq d_2 \text{ or } r' \neq r$$

Obviously, $\text{Init}_\mathcal{J}$ is an initiator labeling of $\mathcal{J}$. Note that $\text{Init}_\mathcal{J}$ differs from $\text{Init}_\mathcal{I}$ only in the label for the edge from the update candidate. Since realizing some update candidates can block the realization of others, it is necessary to consider all candidates in parallel by using sets of updates. Let $(\mathcal{I}, \text{Init}_\mathcal{I})$ be a labeled typicality interpretation for $\mathcal{K}$. The *set of all labeled typicality interpretation updates* of $(\mathcal{I}, \mathsf{Init}_{\mathcal{I}})$ w.r.t. $\mathcal{K}$ is

$$\mathsf{Upd}_{\mathcal{K}}(\mathcal{I}, \mathsf{Init}_{\mathcal{I}}) := \bigcup_{r \in \mathsf{sig}_R(\mathcal{K})} \big\{ \mathsf{Upd}_r(\mathcal{I}, \mathsf{Init}_{\mathcal{I}}, ((d_1, d_2), d_i)) \mid$$
$$((d_1, d_2), d_i) \in \mathsf{UpCan}_r(\mathcal{I}, \mathsf{Init}_{\mathcal{I}}) \big\}.$$

After an update, a model need no longer be a canonical model of $\mathcal{K}$, but some can be recovered into one in the second phase of an upgrade.

5.2   Model Recovery of Typicality Interpretations

A model recovery aims to transform elements from $\mathsf{Upd}_{\mathcal{K}}(\mathcal{I}, \mathsf{Init}_{\mathcal{I}})$ into models of $\mathcal{K}$. More precisely, it mends violations of GCIs from $\overline{\mathcal{K}}$ caused (in)directly by the last update, but without revoking the update. Our model recovery procedure only changes elements affected by the last update and preserves the property that an element can be a successor only if its concept set is prime. Under these conditions, not all updates can be transformed into a model, due to clashes.

Definition 9. *Let* $(\mathcal{I}, \mathsf{Init}_{\mathcal{I}})$ *be a labeled typicality interpretation for* $\mathcal{K}$, *where* $\mathcal{I} = (\Delta^{T(\mathcal{K})}, \cdot^{\mathcal{I}})$, $r \in \mathsf{R}$, *and* $M_{\mathcal{U}}, N_{\mathcal{V}} \in \Delta^{\mathcal{I}}$. $(\mathcal{I}, \mathsf{Init}_{\mathcal{I}})$ *contains a*

- *direct clash, if* $\{C \sqsubseteq \bot, C \sqsubseteq \exists r.\bot\} \cap \overline{\mathcal{K}} \neq \emptyset$ *and* $M_{\mathcal{U}} \in C^{\mathcal{I}}$.
- *successor clash, if* $A \sqsubseteq \forall r.\bot \in \overline{\mathcal{K}}$, $M_{\mathcal{U}} \in A^{\mathcal{I}}$, *and* $A \in (\exists r.\top)^{\mathcal{I}}$.
- *successor domain clash, if* $A \sqsubseteq \forall r.B \in \overline{\mathcal{K}}$, $(M_{\mathcal{U}}, N_{\mathcal{V}}) \in r_{\mathsf{p}}^{\mathcal{I}}$, $B \notin N$, *and* $N \cup \{B\}_{\mathcal{V}} \notin \Delta^{T(\mathcal{K})}$.
- *predecessor domain clash, if* $A \sqsubseteq \forall r^-.B \in \overline{\mathcal{K}}$, $(N_{\mathcal{V}}, M_{\mathcal{U}}) \in r_{\mathsf{s}}^{\mathcal{I}}$, $B \notin N$, *and* $N \cup \{B\}_{\mathcal{V}} \notin \Delta^{T(\mathcal{K})}$.

A domain clash is encountered, if the typicality domain $\Delta^{T(\mathcal{K})}$ lacks an element that the selection function $\mathsf{sel}_{\mathsf{s}}$ omitted. For $\mathsf{sel}_{\mathsf{rat}}$ and $\mathsf{sel}_{\mathsf{rel}}$ such an omission is due to an inconsistency between $N \cup \{B\}$ and the DCIs in $\mathcal{V}$.

As fixing one violation of a GCI can cause another, *model recovery* results from exhaustively applying a set of fix rules which are similar to completion rules for monotone $\mathcal{EL}$. Now, to replace information in a labeled typicality interpretation $(\mathcal{I}, \mathsf{Init}_{\mathcal{I}})$ it is necessary to align the resulting $\mathcal{I}'$ and $\mathsf{Init}_{\mathcal{I}'}$. While addition of information is simply set union, removal is more complex. Let $M_{\mathcal{U}}, N_{\mathcal{V}} \in \Delta^{\mathcal{I}}$, and let $\ell \in \{\mathsf{p}, \mathsf{s}\}$. To *remove* $(M_{\mathcal{U}}, N_{\mathcal{U}'})$ from $r_{\ell}^{\mathcal{I}}$ in $(\mathcal{I}, \mathsf{Init}_{\mathcal{I}})$ results in a labeled typicality interpretation $(\mathcal{J}, \mathsf{Init}_{\mathcal{J}})$ differs from $(\mathcal{I}, \mathsf{Init}_{\mathcal{I}})$ only in:

1. $\mathsf{Init}_{\mathcal{J}}(M_{\mathcal{U}}, r, N_{\mathcal{V}}) := \mathsf{Init}_{\mathcal{I}}(M_{\mathcal{U}}, r, N_{\mathcal{V}}) \setminus \{\ell\}$ and
2. if $\mathsf{Init}_{\mathcal{J}}(M_{\mathcal{U}}, r, N_{\mathcal{V}}) = \emptyset$, then $r^{\mathcal{J}} := r^{\mathcal{I}} \setminus \{(M_{\mathcal{U}}, N_{\mathcal{V}})\}$.

The *fix rules* for model recovery in defeasible $\mathcal{ELI}$ are listed in Fig. 2. The rules $\mathbf{R}\sqsubseteq$, $\mathbf{R}\sqcap$, $\mathbf{R}\exists$, $\mathbf{R}\exists^-$, $\mathbf{R}\forall\mathsf{C}$, and $\mathbf{R}\forall^-\mathsf{C}$ ensure for each type of GCI from a normalized DKB, that violations of this type of GCI are fixed. The rules $\mathbf{R}\forall\mathsf{prime}$ and $\mathbf{R}\forall^-\mathsf{prime}$ serve the purpose to strengthen successors into prime successors (possibly successively). Observe that each fix rule can only be applied once to a particular set of domain elements.

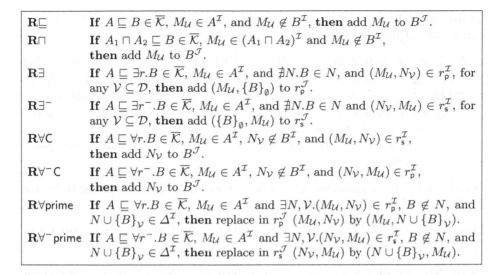

R⊑	If $A \sqsubseteq B \in \overline{\mathcal{K}}$, $M_\mathcal{U} \in A^\mathcal{I}$, and $M_\mathcal{U} \notin B^\mathcal{I}$, **then** add $M_\mathcal{U}$ to $B^\mathcal{J}$.
R⊓	If $A_1 \sqcap A_2 \sqsubseteq B \in \overline{\mathcal{K}}$, $M_\mathcal{U} \in (A_1 \sqcap A_2)^\mathcal{I}$ and $M_\mathcal{U} \notin B^\mathcal{I}$, **then** add $M_\mathcal{U}$ to $B^\mathcal{J}$.
R∃	If $A \sqsubseteq \exists r.B \in \overline{\mathcal{K}}$, $M_\mathcal{U} \in A^\mathcal{I}$, and $\nexists N.B \in N$, and $(M_\mathcal{U}, N_\mathcal{V}) \in r_\mathsf{p}^\mathcal{I}$, for any $\mathcal{V} \subseteq \mathcal{D}$, **then** add $(M_\mathcal{U}, \{B\}_\emptyset)$ to $r_\mathsf{p}^\mathcal{J}$.
R∃⁻	If $A \sqsubseteq \exists r^-.B \in \overline{\mathcal{K}}$, $M_\mathcal{U} \in A^\mathcal{I}$, and $\nexists N.B \in N$ and $(N_\mathcal{V}, M_\mathcal{U}) \in r_\mathsf{s}^\mathcal{I}$, for any $\mathcal{V} \subseteq \mathcal{D}$, **then** add $(\{B\}_\emptyset, M_\mathcal{U})$ to $r_\mathsf{s}^\mathcal{J}$.
R∀C	If $A \sqsubseteq \forall r.B \in \overline{\mathcal{K}}$, $M_\mathcal{U} \in A^\mathcal{I}$, $N_\mathcal{V} \notin B^\mathcal{I}$, and $(M_\mathcal{U}, N_\mathcal{V}) \in r_\mathsf{s}^\mathcal{I}$, **then** add $N_\mathcal{V}$ to $B^\mathcal{J}$.
R∀⁻C	If $A \sqsubseteq \forall r^-.B \in \overline{\mathcal{K}}$, $M_\mathcal{U} \in A^\mathcal{I}$, $N_\mathcal{V} \notin B^\mathcal{I}$, and $(N_\mathcal{V}, M_\mathcal{U}) \in r_\mathsf{p}^\mathcal{I}$, **then** add $N_\mathcal{V}$ to $B^\mathcal{J}$.
R∀prime	If $A \sqsubseteq \forall r.B \in \overline{\mathcal{K}}$, $M_\mathcal{U} \in A^\mathcal{I}$ and $\exists N, \mathcal{V}.(M_\mathcal{U}, N_\mathcal{V}) \in r_\mathsf{p}^\mathcal{I}$, $B \notin N$, and $N \cup \{B\}_\mathcal{V} \in \Delta^\mathcal{I}$, **then** replace in $r_\mathsf{p}^\mathcal{J}$ $(M_\mathcal{U}, N_\mathcal{V})$ by $(M_\mathcal{U}, N \cup \{B\}_\mathcal{V})$.
R∀⁻prime	If $A \sqsubseteq \forall r^-.B \in \overline{\mathcal{K}}$, $M_\mathcal{U} \in A^\mathcal{I}$ and $\exists N, \mathcal{V}.(N_\mathcal{V}, M_\mathcal{U}) \in r_\mathsf{s}^\mathcal{I}$, $B \notin N$, and $N \cup \{B\}_\mathcal{V} \in \Delta^\mathcal{I}$, **then** replace in $r_\mathsf{s}^\mathcal{J}$ $(N_\mathcal{V}, M_\mathcal{U})$ by $(N \cup \{B\}_\mathcal{V}, M_\mathcal{U})$.

Fig. 2. The fix rules for model recovery.

Definition 10. *Let $(\mathcal{I}', \mathsf{Init}'_\mathcal{I})$ be a labeled typicality model of $\mathcal{K}$ and $(\mathcal{I}, \mathsf{Init}_\mathcal{I}) \in \mathsf{Upd}_\mathcal{K}(\mathcal{I}', \mathsf{Init}_{\mathcal{I}'})$ with $\mathcal{I} = (\Delta^\mathcal{I}, \cdot^\mathcal{I})$.*

The labeled typicality interpretation $(\mathcal{J}, \mathsf{Init}_\mathcal{J})$ is a model recovery of $(\mathcal{I}, \mathsf{Init}_\mathcal{I})$ iff it is a result of applying the fix rules to $(\mathcal{I}, \mathsf{Init}_\mathcal{I})$ exhaustively and it does not contain a clash. The set of all model recoveries for $(\mathcal{I}, \mathsf{Init}_\mathcal{I})$ w.r.t. $\mathcal{K}$ is $\mathsf{ModRec}_\mathcal{K}(\mathcal{I}, \mathsf{Init}_\mathcal{I}) := \{(\mathcal{J}, \mathsf{Init}_\mathcal{J}) \mid \mathcal{J} \text{ is a model recovery of } (\mathcal{I}, \mathsf{Init}_\mathcal{I}) \text{ w.r.t. } \mathcal{K}\}$.

There can be several model recoveries for an interpretation or even none, if all sequences of fix rule applications lead to a clash. In this case, the corresponding update is unsuccessful and is discarded. For successful updates and model recoveries, we show that they result indeed in models of $\mathcal{K}$.

Lemma 2. *Let $(\mathcal{I}', \mathsf{Init}'_\mathcal{I})$ be a labeled typicality model of $\mathcal{K}$ and $(\mathcal{I}, \mathsf{Init}_\mathcal{I}) \in \mathsf{Upd}_\mathcal{K}(\mathcal{I}', \mathsf{Init}_{\mathcal{I}'})$. Then, for all $(\mathcal{J}, \mathsf{Init}_\mathcal{J}) \in \mathsf{ModRec}_\mathcal{K}(\mathcal{I}, \mathsf{Init}_\mathcal{I})$ holds $\mathcal{J} \models \mathcal{K}$.*

Proof (sketch). Since $\mathcal{K} \subseteq \overline{\mathcal{K}}$, any violated GCI in $\mathcal{K}$ appears in $\overline{\mathcal{K}}$. We make a case distinction on the GCI types in a normalized $\mathcal{K}$. For GCI type $A \sqsubseteq \forall r.B$ and every $(M_\mathcal{U}, N_\mathcal{V}) \in r^\mathcal{J}$, the labeling $\mathsf{Init}_\mathcal{J}(M_\mathcal{U}, r, N_\mathcal{V}) \neq \emptyset$ by definition. If $(M_\mathcal{U}, N_\mathcal{V}) \in r_\mathsf{p}^\mathcal{J}$ and $M_\mathcal{U} \in A^\mathcal{J}$, the violation can trigger **R∀prime** if $N \cup \{B\}_\mathcal{V} \in \Delta^\mathcal{J}$. If $N \cup \{B\}_\mathcal{V} \notin \Delta^\mathcal{J}$, then $\mathcal{J}$ contains a successor domain clash and $\mathcal{J}$ is not a model recovery. If $(M_\mathcal{U}, N_\mathcal{V}) \in r_\mathsf{s}^\mathcal{J}$ and $M_\mathcal{U} \in A^\mathcal{J}$, then $N_\mathcal{V}$ is added to $B^\mathcal{J}$ by rule **R∀C**. Note, for the dual case with $r \in \mathsf{N_R}^-$, the same argument holds, with applications of **R∀⁻prime** and **R∀⁻C** or $\mathcal{J}$ contains a predecessor domain clash. The proofs for the other 3 GCI types are easier and thus omitted here due to space constraints.

Model recoveries yield canonical models, i.e. subsumption is indicated by concept membership and role edges to prime successors indicate existential restrictions.

Definition 11. *Let $(\mathcal{I}, \mathsf{Init}_{\mathcal{I}})$ be a labeled typicality interpretation for $\mathcal{K}$. The pair $(\mathcal{I}, \mathsf{Init}_{\mathcal{I}})$ is quasi-canonical w.r.t. $\mathcal{K}$ iff the following conditions hold:*

1. *If $\overline{\mathcal{K}} \models \lceil \mathsf{N_C}\text{-type}_{\mathcal{K}}(M_{\mathcal{U}}, \mathcal{I}) \rceil \sqcap \overline{\mathcal{U}} \sqsubseteq \exists r.\lceil N \rceil$ for a prime r-successor N, then $\exists N_{\mathcal{V}} \in \Delta^{\mathcal{I}}$ s.t. $(M_{\mathcal{U}}, N_{\mathcal{V}}) \in r_{\mathsf{p}}^{\mathcal{I}}$, if $r \in \mathsf{N_R}$ and $(N_{\mathcal{V}}, M_{\mathcal{U}}) \in r_{\mathsf{s}}^{-\mathcal{I}}$, if $r \in \mathsf{N_R}^-$.*
2. *If $(M_{\mathcal{U}}, N_{\mathcal{V}}) \in r_{\ell}^{\mathcal{I}}$, for some non-empty $\ell \subseteq \{\mathsf{p}, \mathsf{s}\}$, then it must hold that*
   - *if $\mathsf{p} \in \ell$, then $\overline{\mathcal{K}} \models \lceil \mathsf{N_C}\text{-type}_{\mathcal{K}}(M_{\mathcal{U}}, \mathcal{I}) \rceil \sqcap \overline{\mathcal{U}} \sqsubseteq \exists r.\lceil N \rceil$ and N is a prime r-successor of $M_{\mathcal{U}}$ and*
   - *if $\mathsf{s} \in \ell$, then $\overline{\mathcal{K}} \models \lceil \mathsf{N_C}\text{-type}_{\mathcal{K}}(N_{\mathcal{V}}, \mathcal{I}) \rceil \sqcap \overline{\mathcal{V}} \sqsubseteq \exists r^-.\lceil M \rceil$ and M is a prime r^--successor of $N_{\mathcal{V}}$.*

Quasi-canonicity is preserved by model recoveries, but not necessarily by the application of a single fix rule.

Lemma 3. *Let $(\mathcal{J}, \mathsf{Init}_{\mathcal{J}}) \in \mathsf{ModRec}_{\mathcal{K}}(\mathcal{I}, \mathsf{Init}_{\mathcal{I}})$. If $(\mathcal{I}, \mathsf{Init}_{\mathcal{I}})$ is quasi-canonical, then $(\mathcal{J}, \mathsf{Init}_{\mathcal{J}})$ is quasi-canonical.*

Proof (sketch). We consider w.l.o.g. only the case $r \in \mathsf{N_R}$. The proof is symmetric for $r \in \mathsf{N_R}^-$. For Property (1), let $\overline{\mathcal{K}} \models \lceil \mathsf{N_C}\text{-type}_{\mathcal{K}}(M_{\mathcal{U}}, \mathcal{J}) \rceil \sqcap \overline{\mathcal{U}} \sqsubseteq \exists r.\lceil N \rceil$, for a prime r-successor N of some $M_{\mathcal{U}} \in \Delta^{\mathcal{I}}$. The edge $(M_{\mathcal{U}}, N_{\mathcal{V}}) \in r_{\mathsf{p}}^{\mathcal{J}}$ is guaranteed by either $(M_{\mathcal{U}}, \{B\}_{\emptyset}) \in r_{\mathsf{p}}^{\mathcal{I}_k}$ in some intermediate interpretation $\mathcal{I}_k$ generated from the **R∃** rule during the transformation of $\mathcal{I}$ into $\mathcal{J}$ or by $(M_{\mathcal{U}}, N'_{\mathcal{V}}) \in r_{\mathsf{p}}^{\mathcal{I}}$, where in both cases the successor is not prime and thereby making **R∀prime** applicable (multiple times).

For Property (2): If $(M_{\mathcal{U}}, N_{\mathcal{V}}) \in r_{\mathsf{p}}^{\mathcal{J}}$ for which N is a prime r-successor, then either $(M_{\mathcal{U}}, N_{\mathcal{V}}) \in r_{\mathsf{p}}^{\mathcal{I}}$, or $(M_{\mathcal{U}}, N_{\mathcal{V}}) \in r_{\mathsf{p}}^{\mathcal{J}} \setminus r_{\mathsf{p}}^{\mathcal{I}}$. If $(M_{\mathcal{U}}, N_{\mathcal{V}}) \in r_{\mathsf{p}}^{\mathcal{I}}$, then $N_{\mathcal{V}}$ is prime, since $\mathcal{I}$ is quasi-canonical. If $(M_{\mathcal{U}}, N_{\mathcal{V}}) \in r_{\mathsf{p}}^{\mathcal{J}} \setminus r_{\mathsf{p}}^{\mathcal{I}}$, then one can show that the edge was generated either by **R∃** (and $\mathcal{V} = \emptyset$) or from an edge that made **R∀prime** applicable (more than once).

With model update and recovery being shown to be well-behaved, we can define an upgrade step. Generally, an upgrade step gets a labeled typicality model as input, starting with $(\mathcal{I}_{\min}^{\mathcal{K}}, \mathsf{Init}_{\mathcal{I}_{\min}^{\mathcal{K}}})$ as the initial input. An upgrade computes all update candidates and the corresponding set of updates, then model recovery is applied to each of the updates in that set. Upgrades are performed exhaustively.

Definition 12. *Let $(\mathcal{I}, \mathsf{Init}_{\mathcal{I}})$ be a labeled typicality model for $\mathcal{K}$. An upgrade step over $(\mathcal{I}, \mathsf{Init}_{\mathcal{I}})$ and $\mathcal{K}$ is defined as:*

$$\mathsf{UpGr}((\mathcal{I}, \mathsf{Init}_{\mathcal{I}}), \mathcal{K}) := \bigcup\nolimits_{(\mathcal{J}, \mathsf{Init}_{\mathcal{J}}, d) \in \mathsf{Upd}_{\mathcal{K}}(\mathcal{I}, \mathsf{Init}_{\mathcal{I}})} \mathsf{ModRec}_{\mathcal{K}}(\mathcal{J}, \mathsf{Init}_{\mathcal{J}})$$

A full upgrade applies upgrade steps exhaustively and is defined as the sequence:

$$S_0 := \mathsf{UpGr}((\mathcal{I}_{\min}^{\mathcal{K}}, \mathsf{Init}_{\mathcal{I}_{\min}^{\mathcal{K}}}), \mathcal{K}) \qquad S_{i+1} := \bigcup\nolimits_{(\mathcal{I}, \mathsf{Init}_{\mathcal{I}}) \in S_i} \mathsf{UpGr}((\mathcal{I}, \mathsf{Init}_{\mathcal{I}}), \mathcal{K})$$

We show that iterating the upgrade steps always terminates, if the initial input is a labeled minimal typicality model.

Theorem 2. *Let $(\mathcal{I}^\mathcal{K}_{\min}, \mathsf{Init}_{\mathcal{I}^\mathcal{K}_{\min}})$ be a labeled minimal typicality model for $\mathcal{K}$. Computation of a full upgrade of $(\mathcal{I}^\mathcal{K}_{\min}, \mathsf{Init}_{\mathcal{I}^\mathcal{K}_{\min}})$ always reaches a fixpoint that is denoted by $\mathsf{UpGr}_{\max}((\mathcal{I}^\mathcal{K}_{\min}, \mathsf{Init}_{\mathcal{I}^\mathcal{K}_{\min}}), \mathcal{K})$.*

Proof. Clearly, for one (labeled) typicality model there are only finitely many updates and for one (labeled) typicality interpretation, there are only finitely many model recoveries. While termination of an update is trivial, termination of model recovery can be shown by inspection of the fix rules. W.l.o.g. let $\mathcal{I}^\mathcal{K}_{\min} = (\Delta^{\mathcal{I}^\mathcal{K}_{\min}}, \cdot^{\mathcal{I}^\mathcal{K}_{\min}})$, $|\Delta^{\mathcal{I}^\mathcal{K}_{\min}}| = n$, $|\mathsf{sig}_\mathsf{C}(\mathcal{K})| = m$, and $|\mathsf{sig}_\mathsf{R}(\mathcal{K})| = k$. The rules $\mathbf{R}\sqsubseteq$, $\mathbf{R}\sqcap$, $\mathbf{R}\forall\mathsf{C}$, and $\mathbf{R}\forall^- \mathsf{C}$ add a concept membership and thus can each be applied at most $n * m$ times. Rule $\mathbf{R}\exists^-$ adds a new role edge, thus $\mathbf{R}\exists^-$ can be applied up to $k * n^2$ times. The rules $\mathbf{R}\forall\mathsf{prime}$ and $\mathbf{R}\forall^-\mathsf{prime}$ replace an edge between elements $M_\mathcal{U}$ and $N_\mathcal{V}$ with a corresponding one between $M_\mathcal{U}$ and $N \cup \{B\}_\mathcal{V}$. There are only up to m many candidates for such B and thus there are only up to $k * n^2 * m$ rule applications of $\mathbf{R}\forall\mathsf{prime}$ and $\mathbf{R}\forall^-\mathsf{prime}$ each.

6 Maximal Typicality Models for Nested Coverage

Nested reasoning is reasoning under preferred model semantics, where the preferred models are maximal typicality models. Recall, that in those models all (successor) elements are fully saturated with defeasible information. To define semantics based on maximal typicality models, alleviates quantification neglect immediately.

Definition 13. *Let $\mathcal{K}$ be a DKB, $A \in \mathsf{sig}_\mathsf{C}(\mathcal{K})$, and $M \in \Delta^\mathcal{K}$ be an element. Let $\mathbf{s}$ be a strength and $(\mathcal{I}^\mathcal{K}_{\min}, \mathsf{Init}_{\mathcal{I}^\mathcal{K}_{\min}})$ the minimal labeled typicality model with the domain selected by $\mathsf{sel}_\mathbf{s}$. We define $\mathbf{s}$ nested entailment by:*

- $\mathcal{K} \models_{\mathsf{nest},\mathbf{s}} \lceil M \rceil \sqsubseteq A$ *iff* $\lceil M \rceil^\mathcal{I} \sqsubseteq A^\mathcal{I}$.
- $\mathcal{K} \models_{\mathsf{nest},\mathbf{s}} \lceil M \rceil \mathrel{\rlap{\sqsubseteq}{\;\sim}} A$ *iff* $M_\mathcal{U} \in A^\mathcal{I}$ *for every maximally typical instance of M in the domain..*

For every $\mathcal{I} \in \mathsf{UpGr}_{\max}((\mathcal{I}^\mathcal{K}_{\min}, \mathsf{Init}_{\mathcal{I}^\mathcal{K}_{\min}}), \mathcal{K})$. For nested coverage, again the domain and thus ultimately the consistent selection function determines the strength of reasoning.

Definition 14. *Let $\alpha \in \{\lceil M \rceil \sqsubseteq A, \lceil M \rceil \mathrel{\rlap{\sqsubseteq}{\;\sim}} A\}$, $\mathcal{I}^\mathcal{K}_{\min,\mathbf{rat}}$ be the minimal rational and $\mathcal{I}^\mathcal{K}_{\min,\mathbf{rel}}$ the minimal relevant typicality model of some $\mathcal{K}$. The semantics of*

- *rational strength and nested coverage (denoted $\models_{\mathsf{nest},\mathbf{rat}}$) is defined as*
  $\mathcal{K} \models_{\mathsf{nest},\mathbf{rat}} \alpha$ *iff* $\mathcal{I} \models \alpha$, $\forall\mathcal{I} \in \mathsf{UpGr}_{\max}((\mathcal{I}^\mathcal{K}_{\min,\mathbf{rat}}, \mathsf{Init}_{\mathcal{I}^\mathcal{K}_{\min,\mathbf{rat}}}), \mathcal{K})$.
- *relevant strength and nested coverage (denoted $\models_{\mathsf{nest},\mathbf{rel}}$) is defined as*
  $\mathcal{K} \models_{\mathsf{nest},\mathbf{rel}} \alpha$ *iff* $\mathcal{I} \models \alpha$, $\forall\mathcal{I} \in \mathsf{UpGr}_{\max}((\mathcal{I}^\mathcal{K}_{\min,\mathbf{rel}}, \mathsf{Init}_{\mathcal{I}^\mathcal{K}_{\min,\mathbf{rel}}}), \mathcal{K})$.

Theorem 3. *Let $\mathcal{K}$ be a DKB, $\mathbf{s}$ be a strength, $A \in \mathsf{sig}_\mathsf{C}(\mathcal{K})$, and $M \in \Delta^\mathcal{K}$ be a set of concept names in the representative domain. Then the following holds:*

1. $\mathcal{K} \models \lceil M \rceil \sqsubseteq A \Leftrightarrow \mathcal{K} \models_{\mathsf{prop},s} \lceil M \rceil \sqsubseteq A \Leftrightarrow \mathcal{K} \models_{\mathsf{nest},s} \lceil M \rceil \sqsubseteq A$.

2. $\mathcal{K} \models_{\mathsf{prop},s} \lceil M \rceil \sqsubsetneq A \Rightarrow \mathcal{K} \models_{\mathsf{nest},s} \lceil M \rceil \sqsubsetneq A$.

3. If $s \in \{\mathbf{rat},\mathbf{rel}\}$, then $\mathcal{K} \models_{\mathsf{prop},s} \lceil M \rceil \sqsubsetneq A \not\Leftarrow \mathcal{K} \models_{\mathsf{nest},s} \lceil M \rceil \sqsubsetneq A$.

Proof (Sketch).   *Claim 1.* follows from the following facts (i) the atypical instance $M_\emptyset$ does not change during the full upgrade, and (ii) it is canonical for $\lceil M \rceil$. Therefore, any element d added to $\lceil M \rceil^{\mathcal{I}}$ during the full upgrade must also be added to $A^{\mathcal{I}}$.

   Claim 2. can be shown as follows: the maximally typical instances of any element M stay the same during the upgrade, as the domain does not change. The upgrade procedure only increases the $\mathsf{N_C}$-type of the elements. Hence, if $M_\mathcal{U} \in A^{\mathcal{I}_{\min}^{\mathcal{K}}}$, $M_\mathcal{U} \in A^{\mathcal{I}}$, for any $\mathcal{I} \in \mathsf{UpGr}_{\max}((\mathcal{I}_{\min}^{\mathcal{K}}, \mathsf{Init}_{\mathcal{I}_{\min}^{\mathcal{K}}}), \mathcal{K})$.

   Claim 3. is shown by a counter-example. Let $\mathcal{K}_{ex}$ be as in Example 1. The most typical instance of Cat is $\mathsf{Cat}_{\mathcal{E}_0}$ for both domains, $\Delta_{\mathbf{rat}}^{T(\mathcal{K}_{ex})}$ and $\Delta_{\mathbf{rel}}^{T(\mathcal{K}_{ex})}$. For both $(\mathcal{J}, \mathsf{Init}_{\mathcal{J}}) \in \{(\mathcal{I}_{\min,\mathbf{rat}}^{\mathcal{K}}, \mathsf{Init}_{\mathcal{I}_{\min,\mathbf{rat}}^{\mathcal{K}}}), (\mathcal{I}_{\min,\mathbf{rel}}^{\mathcal{K}}, \mathsf{Init}_{\mathcal{I}_{\min,\mathbf{rel}}^{\mathcal{K}}})\}$ it holds that $(\mathsf{Cat}_{\mathcal{E}_0}, \mathsf{Bird}_\emptyset) \in \mathsf{eats}_{\mathsf{p}}^{\mathcal{J}}$ and thus $((\mathsf{Cat}_{\mathcal{E}_0}, \mathsf{Bird}_\mathcal{U}), \mathsf{Cat}_{\mathcal{E}_0})$ is an eats-upgrade candidate. The set $\mathcal{U}$ differs for $\mathbf{rat}$ and $\mathbf{rel}$, but each contains $\mathsf{Bird} \sqsubsetneq \mathsf{Flying}$. This upgrade step leads to a full upgrade for which $\mathcal{K}_{ex} \models_{\mathsf{nest},s} \mathsf{Cat} \sqsubsetneq \exists\mathsf{eats}.\mathsf{Flying}$ with $s \in \{\mathbf{rat},\mathbf{rel}\}$. Clearly, this inference is not obtained in propositional coverage.

7   Conclusion

We have proposed four semantics for defeasible subsumption in $\mathcal{ELI}_\perp$ that are defined by typicality models. Typicality models can simply be parameterized with strength and coverage for reasoning making these models a versatile approach for nonmonotonic reasoning. We have investigated rational and relevant strength and have shown that for both strengths, propositional coverage is equivalent to materialization-based semantics, while nested coverage is stronger than materialization-based semantics and alleviates quantification neglect. Our decision procedure for defeasible inference is simply to compute the appropriate typicality model. This can be done by a reduction to classical reasoning—facilitating implementations by the use of optimized DL reasoners.

   As future work, we plan to compare the different semantics and to provide a complexity analysis of reasoning by computing typicality models. We conjecture a single exponential upper bound even for the $\models_{\mathsf{nest},\mathbf{rel}}$ semantics. Furthermore, we plan to investigate ABox reasoning problems, such as instance checking.

Acknowledgements. This work was partially supported by the Coordenação de Aperfeiçoamento de Pessoal de Nível Superior - Brasil (CAPES) - Finance Code 001, by the Conselho Nacional de Desenvolvimento Científico e Tecnológico (CNPq), the INCT of the Future Internet for Smart Cities funded by CNPq proc. 465446/2014-0, Coordenação de Aperfeiçoamento de Pessoal de Nível Superior - Brasil (CAPES) - Finance Code 001, FAPESP proc. 14/50937-1, and FAPESP proc. 15/24485-9, and by the AI competence center ScaDS.AI Dresden/Leipzig.

References

1. Baader, F., Brandt, S., Lutz, C.: Pushing the $\mathcal{EL}$ envelope. In: Kaelbling, L.P., Saffiotti, A. (eds.) IJCAI 2005, Proceedings of the Nineteenth International Joint Conference on Artificial Intelligence, pp. 364–369. Professional Book Center (2005)
2. Baader, F., Brandt, S., Lutz, C.: Pushing the $\mathcal{EL}$ envelope further. In: Clark, K., Patel-Schneider, P.F. (eds.) Proceedings of the OWLED 2008 DC Workshop on OWL: Experiences and Directions (2008)
3. Baader, F., Horrocks, I., Lutz, C., Sattler, U.: An Introduction to Description Logic. Cambridge University Press, Cambridge (2017)
4. Bonatti, P.A.: Rational closure for all description logics. Artif. Intell. **274**, 197–223 (2019)
5. Bonatti, P.A., Faella, M., Petrova, I.M., Sauro, L.: A new semantics for overriding in description logics. Artif. Intell. **222**, 1–48 (2015)
6. Bonatti, P.A., Faella, M., Sauro, L.: $\mathcal{EL}$ with default attributes and overriding. In: Patel-Schneider, P.F., et al. (eds.) ISWC 2010. LNCS, vol. 6496, pp. 64–79. Springer, Heidelberg (2010). https://doi.org/10.1007/978-3-642-17746-0_5
7. Britz, K., Casini, G., Meyer, T., Moodley, K., Sattler, U., Varzinczak, I.: Principles of KLM-style defeasible description logics. ACM Trans. Comput. Log. **22**(1), 1–46 (2021)
8. Britz, K., Casini, G., Meyer, T., Moodley, K., Varzinczak, I.: Ordered interpretations and entailment for defeasible description logics. Technical report, CAIR, CSIR Meraka and UKZN, South Africa (2013)
9. Britz, K., Meyer, T., Varzinczak, I.: Semantic foundation for preferential description logics. In: Wang, D., Reynolds, M. (eds.) AI 2011. LNCS (LNAI), vol. 7106, pp. 491–500. Springer, Heidelberg (2011). https://doi.org/10.1007/978-3-642-25832-9_50
10. Câmara, I.: Quantification in description logics of typicality. Ph.D. thesis, University of São Paulo (2023, to appear)
11. Câmara, I., Turhan, A.Y.: Rational defeasible subsumption in DLS with nested quantifiers: the case of $\mathcal{ELI}_\perp$. In: Arieli, O., Casini, G., Giordano, L. (eds.) Proceedings of the 20th International Workshop on Non-Monotonic Reasoning, NMR 2022, Part of FLoC 2022. CEUR Workshop Proceedings, vol. 3197, pp. 159–162. CEUR-WS.org (2022)
12. Casini, G., Meyer, T., Moodley, K., Nortjé, R.: Relevant closure: a new form of defeasible reasoning for description logics. In: Fermé, E., Leite, J. (eds.) JELIA 2014. LNCS (LNAI), vol. 8761, pp. 92–106. Springer, Cham (2014). https://doi.org/10.1007/978-3-319-11558-0_7
13. Casini, G., Straccia, U.: Rational closure for defeasible description logics. In: Janhunen, T., Niemelä, I. (eds.) JELIA 2010. LNCS (LNAI), vol. 6341, pp. 77–90. Springer, Heidelberg (2010). https://doi.org/10.1007/978-3-642-15675-5_9
14. Casini, G., Straccia, U.: Lexicographic closure for defeasible description logics. In: Proceedings of Australasian Ontology Workshop, vol. 969, pp. 28–39 (2012)
15. Giordano, L., Dupré, D.T.: A framework for a modular multi-concept lexicographic closure semantics. CoRR abs/2009.00964 (2020)
16. Giordano, L., Gliozzi, V., Olivetti, N., Pozzato, G.L.: A non-monotonic description logic for reasoning about typicality. Artif. Intell. **195**, 165–202 (2013)
17. Giordano, L., Olivetti, N., Gliozzi, V., Pozzato, G.L.: $\mathcal{ALC} + \mathbf{T}$: a preferential extension of description logics. Fund. Inform. **96**(3), 341–372 (2009)

18. Pensel, M.: A lightweight defeasible description logic in depth-quantification in rational reasoning and beyond. Ph.D. thesis, TU Dresden, Germany (2019)
19. Pensel, M., Turhan, A.-Y.: Including quantification in defeasible reasoning for the description logic $\mathcal{EL}_\perp$. In: Balduccini, M., Janhunen, T. (eds.) LPNMR 2017. LNCS (LNAI), vol. 10377, pp. 78–84. Springer, Cham (2017). https://doi.org/10.1007/978-3-319-61660-5_9
20. Pensel, M., Turhan, A.Y.: Computing standard inferences under rational and relevant semantics in defeasible $\mathcal{EL}_\perp$. In: Proceedings of the 31st International Workshop on Description Logics (2018)
21. Pensel, M., Turhan, A.Y.: Reasoning in the defeasible description logic $\mathcal{EL}_\perp$– computing standard inferences under rational and relevant semantics. Int. J. Approximate Reasoning (IJAR) **103**, 28–70 (2018). https://doi.org/10.1016/j.ijar.2018.08.005
22. Varzinczak, I.: A note on a description logic of concept and role typicality for defeasible reasoning over ontologies. Log. Univers. **12**(3–4), 297–325 (2018)

Truth and Preferences - A Game Approach for Qualitative Choice Logic

Robert Freiman$^{(\boxtimes)}$ and Michael Bernreiter

Institute of Logic and Computation, TU Wien, Vienna, Austria
`robert@logic.at`, `mbernrei@dbai.tuwien.ac.at`

Abstract. In this paper, we introduce game-theoretic semantics (GTS) for Qualitative Choice Logic (QCL), which, in order to express preferences, extends classical propositional logic with an additional connective called ordered disjunction. In particular, we present a new semantics that makes use of GTS negation and, by doing so, avoids contentious behavior of negation in existing QCL-semantics.

1 Introduction

Preferences are a key research area in artificial intelligence, and thus a multitude of preference formalisms have been described in the literature [12]. An interesting example is Qualitative Choice Logic (QCL) [6], which extends classical propositional logic by the connective $\vec{\times}$ called ordered disjunction. $F\vec{\times}G$ states that F or G should be satisfied, but satisfying F is more preferable than satisfying only G. This allows to express soft constraints (preferences) and hard constraints (truth) in a single language.

For example, say we want to formalize our choice of pizza toppings: we definitely want tomato-sauce (t); Moreover, we want either mushrooms (m) or artichokes (a), but preferably mushrooms. This can easily be expressed in QCL via the formula $t \wedge (m \vec{\times} a)$. This formula has three models in QCL, namely $M_1 = \{t, m, a\}$, $M_2 = \{t, m\}$, and $M_3 = \{t, a\}$. QCL-semantics then ranks these models via so-called satisfaction degrees. The lower this degree, the more preferable the model. In this case, M_1 and M_2 would be assigned a degree of 1 and M_3 would be assigned a degree of 2, i.e., M_1 and M_2 are the preferred models of this formula.

In the literature, QCL has been studied with regards to possible applications [13], computational properties [4], and proof systems [3]. However, not all aspects of QCL-semantics are uncontroversial. For example, a QCL-formula F is not logically equivalent to its double negation $\neg\neg F$, as all information about preferences is erased by $\neg$. This issue has been addressed by Prioritized QCL (PQCL) [1], which defines ordered disjunction in the same way as QCL but changes the meaning of the classical connectives, including negation. While PQCL solves QCL's problem with double negation, it in turn introduces other controversial behavior, e.g., a formula F and its negation $\neg F$ can be satisfied by the same interpretation. No alternative semantics for QCL is known to us that addresses both of these issues at the same time.

In order to tackle these issues, we develop game-theoretic semantics (GTS) for QCL, embedding choice logics in the rich intersection of the fields of

© The Author(s), under exclusive license to Springer Nature Switzerland AG 2023
S. Gaggl et al. (Eds.): JELIA 2023, LNAI 14281, pp. 547–560, 2023.
https://doi.org/10.1007/978-3-031-43619-2_37

game-theory and logics [2,11,15]. Building on the concepts of rational behavior and strategic thinking, GTS offer a natural dynamic viewpoint of dealing with truth and preferences. Originally, GTS go back to Jaakko Hintikka [10], who designed a win/lose game for two players, called *Me* (or *I*) and *You*, both of which can act in the role of Proponent or Opponent of a formula F over an interpretation $\mathcal{I}$. The game proceeds by rules for step-wise reducing F to an atomic formula. It turns out that I have a winning strategy for this game if and only if F is classically true over $\mathcal{I}$. Most importantly, negation in GTS is interpreted as *dual negation*, [14]: at formulas $\neg G$, the game continues with G and a role switch.

To capture not only truth but also preferences, we extend the two-valued game of Hintikka with more fine-grained outcomes and introduce a game-theoretic interpretation of ordered disjunction. Moreover, we reinterpret negation in QCL using game-theoretic methods. From our GTS we extract a new logic we call Game-induced Choice Logics (GCL), where negation behaves as in classical logic.

2   Qualitative Choice Logic (QCL)

We now recall QCL [6]. $\mathcal{U}$ denotes an infinite set of propositional variables. An interpretation $\mathcal{I} \subseteq \mathcal{U}$ is a set of variables, with $a \in \mathcal{U}$ true under $\mathcal{I}$ iff $a \in \mathcal{I}$.

Definition 1 (QCL-formula). *The set $\mathcal{F}$ of QCL-formulas is built inductively: if $a \in \mathcal{U}$, then $a \in \mathcal{F}$; if $F \in \mathcal{F}$, then $(\neg F) \in \mathcal{F}$; if $F, G \in \mathcal{F}$, then $(F \circ G) \in \mathcal{F}$ for $\circ \in \{\wedge, \vee, \vec{\times}\}$.*

The semantics of QCL is based on two functions: optionality and satisfaction degree. The satisfaction degree of a formula can be a natural number or ∞ and is used to rank interpretations (lower degrees are better). The optionality of a formula represents the maximum finite satisfaction degree the formula can obtain and is used to penalize interpretations that do not satisfy F in $F \vec{\times} G$.

Definition 2 (Optionality in QCL). *The optionality of QCL-formulas is defined inductively as follows: (i) $\mathrm{opt}(a) = 1$ for $a \in \mathcal{U}$, (ii) $\mathrm{opt}(\neg F) = 1$, (iii) $\mathrm{opt}(F \wedge G) = \mathrm{opt}(F \vee G) = \max(\mathrm{opt}(F), \mathrm{opt}(G))$, and (iv) $\mathrm{opt}(F \vec{\times} G) = \mathrm{opt}(F) + \mathrm{opt}(G)$.*

Definition 3 (Satisfaction Degree in QCL). *The satisfaction degree of QCL-formulas under an interpretation $\mathcal{I}$ is defined inductively as follows:*

$$\deg_{\mathcal{I}}(a) = 1 \text{ if } a \in \mathcal{I}, \infty \text{ otherwise}$$
$$\deg_{\mathcal{I}}(\neg F) = 1 \text{ if } \deg_{\mathcal{I}}(F) = \infty, \infty \text{ otherwise}$$
$$\deg_{\mathcal{I}}(F \wedge G) = \max(\deg_{\mathcal{I}}(F), \deg_{\mathcal{I}}(G))$$
$$\deg_{\mathcal{I}}(F \vee G) = \min(\deg_{\mathcal{I}}(F), \deg_{\mathcal{I}}(G))$$
$$\deg_{\mathcal{I}}(F \vec{\times} G) = \begin{cases} \deg_{\mathcal{I}}(F) & \text{if } \deg_{\mathcal{I}}(F) < \infty \\ \mathrm{opt}(F) + \deg_{\mathcal{I}}(G) & \text{if } \deg_{\mathcal{I}}(F) = \infty, \deg_{\mathcal{I}}(G) < \infty \\ \infty & \text{otherwise} \end{cases}$$

If $\deg_{\mathcal{I}}(F) = k$ we say that $\mathcal{I}$ satisfies F to a degree of k. If $\deg_{\mathcal{I}}(F) < \infty$ we say that $\mathcal{I}$ (classically) satisfies F, or that $\mathcal{I}$ is a model of F. A crucial notion in QCL is that of *preferred models*, i.e., models with minimal degree.

Definition 4 (Preferred Model under QCL-semantics). *Let F be a QCL-formula. An interpretation $\mathcal{I}$ is a preferred model of F iff $\deg_{\mathcal{I}}(F) < \infty$ and, for all interpretations $\mathcal{J}$, $\deg_{\mathcal{I}}(F) \le \deg_{\mathcal{J}}(F)$.*

Satisfaction degrees are bounded by optionality, i.e., either $\deg_{\mathcal{I}}(F) \le \mathrm{opt}(F)$ or $\deg_{\mathcal{I}}(F) = \infty$ must hold. As stated earlier, optionality is used to penalize non-satisfaction: given $F \vec{\times} G$, if $\deg_{\mathcal{I}}(F) < \infty$ we get $\deg_{\mathcal{I}}(F \vec{\times} G) = \deg_{\mathcal{I}}(F) \le \mathrm{opt}(F)$; if $\deg_{\mathcal{I}}(F) = \infty$ we get $\deg_{\mathcal{I}}(F \vec{\times} G) = \mathrm{opt}(F) + \deg_{\mathcal{I}}(G) > \mathrm{opt}(F)$.

Moreover, ordered disjunction is associative under QCL-semantics, which means that we can simply write $A_1 \vec{\times} A_2 \vec{\times} \ldots \vec{\times} A_n$ to express that we must satisfy at least one of $A_1, \ldots, A_n$, and that we prefer A_i to A_j for $i < j$.

Example 1. Consider $F = (a \wedge b) \vec{\times} a \vec{\times} b$. Then $\mathrm{opt}(F) = 3$, $\deg_{\emptyset}(F) = \infty$, $\deg_{\{b\}}(F) = 3$, $\deg_{\{a\}}(F) = 2$, and $\deg_{\{a,b\}}(F) = 1$. Thus, $\{a\}, \{b\}, \{a, b\}$ are models of F while $\{a, b\}$ is also a preferred model of F.

Now consider $F' = F \wedge \neg(a \wedge b)$. Again, $\deg_{\emptyset}(F') = \infty$, $\deg_{\{b\}}(F') = 3$, and $\deg_{\{a\}}(F') = 2$. However, $\deg_{\{a,b\}}(F') = \infty$. Since it is not possible to satisfy F' to a degree of 1, $\{a\}$ is a preferred model of F'.

An alternative semantics for QCL has been proposed in the form of PQCL [1]. Specifically, PQCL changes the semantics for the classical connectives ($\neg, \vee, \wedge$), but defines ordered disjunction ($\vec{\times}$) in the same way as QCL. For our purposes it suffices to note that negation in PQCL propagates to the atom level, meaning that $\neg(F \wedge G)$ is assigned the satisfaction degree of $\neg F \vee \neg G$, $\neg(F \vee G)$ is assigned the degree of $\neg F \wedge \neg G$, and $\neg(F \vec{\times} G)$ is assigned the degree of $\neg F \vec{\times} \neg G$.

3   Comments on Negation

While choice logics are a useful formalism to express both soft constraints (preferences) and hard constraints (truth) in a single language, existing semantics (such as QCL and PQCL) are not entirely uncontroversial. Table 1 shows how negation acts on ordered disjunction in both systems: negation in QCL erases preferences, while in PQCL it is possible to satisfy a formula and its negation at the same time ($\{a\}$ and $\{b\}$ classically satisfy both $a \vec{\times} b$ and $\neg a \vec{\times} \neg b$). Moreover, in PQCL, the satisfaction degree of $\neg F$ does not only depend on the degree and optionality of F ($\{a\}$ and $\{a, b\}$ satisfy $a \vec{\times} b$ to degree 1, but $\{a\}$ satisfies $\neg a \vec{\times} \neg b$ to degree 2 while $\{a, b\}$ does not satisfy $\neg a \vec{\times} \neg b$ at all).

We will make use of game-theoretic negation to define an alternative semantics for the language of QCL. Our main goal is to define a negation that acts both on hard constraints as in QCL and soft constraints as in PQCL. Specifically, we will ensure that (i) the satisfaction degree of $\neg F$ depends only on the degree of F, (ii) formulas and their negation can not be classically satisfied by the same interpretation, (iii) formulas are equivalent to their double negation.

Table 1. Truth table showing the satisfaction degrees of $\neg(a\vec{\times}b)$ in QCL (equivalent to $\neg a \wedge \neg b$) and PQCL (equivalent to $\neg a \vec{\times} \neg b$).

$\mathcal{I}$	$a\vec{\times}b$	$\neg a \wedge \neg b$	$\neg a \vec{\times} \neg b$
$\emptyset$	∞	1	1
$\{b\}$	2	∞	1
$\{a\}$	1	∞	2
$\{a,b\}$	1	∞	∞

4   A Game for Ordered Disjunction

In this section, we introduce GTS for the language of QCL. As a first step, let us briefly recall Hintikka's game [10] over a classical propositional formula F and an interpretation $\mathcal{I}$. There are two players, *Me* and *You*, both of which can act in the role of Proponent (**P**) or Opponent (**O**). The game starts with *Me* as **P** of the formula F and *You* as **O**. At formulas of the form $G_1 \vee G_2$, **P** chooses a formula G_i that the game continues with. At formulas of the form $G_1 \wedge G_2$ it is **O**'s choice. At negations $\neg G$, the game continues with G and a role switch. The outcome of the game is a propositional variable a. The player currently in the role of **P** wins the game (and **O** loses) iff $a \in \mathcal{I}$. Otherwise, **P** wins and **O** loses. It turns out that I have a winning strategy for the game iff $\mathcal{I} \models F$.

The first question we must answer in order to introduce our GTS for QCL is how ordered disjunction should be handled in a game-theoretic setting. We propose the following solution: at $G_1 \vec{\times} G_2$ it is **P**'s choice whether to continue with G_1 or with G_2, *but this player prefers G_1*. My aim in the game is now not only to win the game but to do so with as little compromise to *My* preferences as possible. Thus, it is natural to express *My* preference of G_1-outcomes O_1 over G_2-outcomes O_2 via the relation $O_2 \ll O_1$.

The second question to answer is how the classical connectives should interact with the newly introduced preferences $\ll$ between outcomes. For $G_1 \wedge G_2$ and $G_1 \vee G_2$ it suffices to simply combine the preferences of G_1 and G_2, as we will see. For $\neg G$, the preferences associated with G will be inverted in order to ensure that negation not only acts on hard constraints but also on soft constraints.

Formally, game states will be either of the form **P** : F or **O** : F, where F is a QCL-formula and "**P**" and "**O**" signify that I currently act in the role of Proponent and Opponent respectively. Each game state appears in the game tree defined below. Every node is labeled with either "I" (when it is *My* turn) or "Y" (when it is *Your* turn). If the game reaches a game state g, then the player whose turn it is chooses a child of g in the game tree where the game continues. The relation $\ll$ captures *My* preferences on outcomes, as motivated above.

Definition 5 (Game Tree). *We inductively define the game tree $T(\mathbf{P} : F) = (V, E, l)$ with (game) states V and edges E. Leafs of T are called* outcomes *and are denoted $\mathcal{O}(T)$. The labeling function l maps nodes of T to the set $\{I, Y\}$. Moreover, we define a partial order $\ll$ over outcomes.*

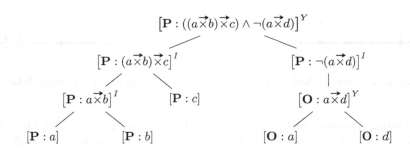

Fig. 1. The game tree from Example 2

(R_a) $T(\mathbf{P} : a)$ consists of the single leaf and $\ll_{\mathbf{P}:a} = \emptyset$.

$(R_\neg)$ $T(\mathbf{P} : \neg G)$ consists of a root labeled "I", the immediate subtree $T(\mathbf{O} : G)$, and $\ll_{\mathbf{P}:\neg G}$ equal to $\ll_{\mathbf{O}:G}$.

$(R_\wedge)$ $T(\mathbf{P} : G_1 \wedge G_2)$ consists of a root labeled "Y" and immediate subtrees $T(\mathbf{P} : G_1), T(\mathbf{P} : G_2)$. The preference is given by $\ll_{\mathbf{P}:G_1 \wedge G_2} = \ll_{\mathbf{P}:G_1} \cup \ll_{\mathbf{P}:G_2}$.

$(R_\vee)$ $T(\mathbf{P} : G_1 \vee G_2)$ consists of a root labeled "I" and immediate subtrees $T(\mathbf{P} : G_1), T(\mathbf{P} : G_2)$. The preference is given by $\ll_{\mathbf{P}:G_1 \wedge G_2} = \ll_{\mathbf{P}:G_1} \cup \ll_{\mathbf{P}:G_2}$.

$(R_{\vec{\times}})$ $T(\mathbf{P} : G_1 \vec{\times} G_2)$ consists of a root labeled "I" and the immediate subtrees $T(\mathbf{P} : G_1), T(\mathbf{P} : G_2)$. Moreover, $O_2 \ll_{\mathbf{P}:G_1 \vec{\times} G_2} O_1$ iff $O_1 \in \mathcal{O}(T(\mathbf{P} : G_1))$ and $O_2 \in \mathcal{O}(T(\mathbf{P} : G_2))$, or $O_2 \ll_{\mathbf{P}:G_j} O_1$ for $j \in \{1,2\}$.

The tree $T(\mathbf{O} : F)$ is defined analogously to $T(\mathbf{P} : F)$, except that labels are swapped and preferences are switched, i.e., $O_1 \ll_{\mathbf{O}:F} O_2$ iff $O_2 \ll_{\mathbf{P}:F} O_1$.

Example 2. Figure 1 depicts the game tree for $F = ((a\vec{\times}b)\vec{\times}c) \wedge \neg(a\vec{\times}d)$. Note that $\mathbf{O} : a\vec{\times}d$ is labeled "Y" since roles are switched in $\mathbf{P} : \neg(a\vec{\times}d)$. The order on outcomes is given by $\mathbf{P} : c \ll \mathbf{P} : b \ll \mathbf{P} : a$ and $\mathbf{O} : a \ll \mathbf{O} : d$.

An outcome $\mathbf{P} : a$ is true in $\mathcal{I}$ iff $a \in \mathcal{I}$. Conversely, $\mathbf{O} : a$ is true iff $a \notin \mathcal{I}$. An outcome O is a winning outcome w.r.t an interpretation $\mathcal{I}$ iff O is true in $\mathcal{I}$.

To evaluate an interpretation via a game tree, we introduce the payoff function $\delta_\mathcal{I}$ which will respect *My* preferences $\ll$ on *My* winning outcomes. Given outcome O, let $\pi_\ll(O) = O_1, ..., O_n$ be the longest $\ll$-chain starting in O, i.e. $O_1 = O$, all O_i are pairwise different, and $O_i \ll O_{i+1}$ for $1 \le i < n$. The length of $\pi_\ll(O)$ is $|\pi_\ll(O)| = n$.

Definition 6 (Payoff). $\delta_\mathcal{I}$ maps outcomes of a game tree T into $Z := (\mathbb{Z} \setminus \{0\}, \trianglelefteq)$. The ordering $\trianglelefteq$ is the inverse of the natural ordering on $\mathbb{Z}^-$ and on $\mathbb{Z}^+$ and for $k \in \mathbb{Z}^-, \ell \in \mathbb{Z}^+$ we set $k \triangleleft \ell$, i.e. $-1 \triangleleft -2 \triangleleft \ldots \triangleleft 2 \triangleleft 1$. For an outcome $O \in \mathcal{O}(T)$, we set[1]

$$\delta_\mathcal{I}(O) = \begin{cases} |\pi_\ll(O)|, & \text{if } O \text{ is true,} \\ -|\pi_\gg(O)|, & \text{if } O \text{ is false.} \end{cases}$$

We write δ instead of $\delta_\mathcal{I}$ if $\mathcal{I}$ is clear from context.

Fig. 2. Preferences and winning payoffs of the two players in the game **NG**.

Winning outcomes are ascribed a payoff in $\mathbb{Z}^+$ and losing outcomes have a payoff in $\mathbb{Z}^-$. Intuitively, it is better for *Me* to have a higher payoff with respect to $\trianglelefteq$. If both O_1 and O_2 are winning outcomes (or if they both are losing outcomes), then $\delta_{\mathcal{I}}(O_1) \triangleleft \delta_{\mathcal{I}}(O_2)$ iff $O_1 \ll O_2$. If O_1 is a losing outcome and O_2 is a winning outcome, then $\delta_{\mathcal{I}}(O_1) \triangleleft \delta_{\mathcal{I}}(O_2)$. See Fig. 2 for a graphical representation of winning ranges and preferences.

Example 3 (Example 2 cont.). The winning outcomes for $\mathcal{I} = \{a\}$ are **P** : a, **O** : d with $\delta(\mathbf{P} : a) = 1$, $\delta(\mathbf{P} : b) = -2$, $\delta(\mathbf{P} : c) = -1$, $\delta(\mathbf{O} : a) = -1$, $\delta(\mathbf{O} : d) = 1$.

We are now ready to formally define the notion of a game.

Definition 7 (Game). *A game* **NG** $= (T(\mathbf{Q} : F), \delta_{\mathcal{I}})$, *also written* **NG**(**Q** : $F, \mathcal{I}$), *is a pair, where* $T(\mathbf{Q} : F)$ *is a game tree and* $\delta_{\mathcal{I}}$ *is a payoff-function with respect to some interpretation* $\mathcal{I}$.

The goal of both players is to win the game with as little compromise as possible, and thus force the opponent in as much compromise as possible. To this end, we must consider the optimal strategies that both players have at their disposal. A strategy σ for *Me* in a game can be understood as *My* complete game plan. For every node of the game tree labeled "I", σ tells *Me* to which node I have to move.

Definition 8 (Strategy). *A strategy* σ *for* Me *for the game* **NG** *is a subset of the nodes of the underlying tree such that (i) the root of T is in σ and for all $v \in \sigma$, (ii) if $l(v) = I$, then at least one successor of v is in σ and (iii) if $l(v) = Y$, then all successors of v are in σ. A strategy for* You *is defined symmetrically. We denote by* Σ_I *and* Σ_Y *the set of all strategies for* Me *and* You, *respectively.*

Conditions (i) and (iii) make sure that all possible moves by the other player are taken care of by the game plan. Note that each pair of strategies $\sigma_I \in \Sigma_I$, $\sigma_Y \in \Sigma_Y$ defines a *unique* outcome of **NG**, which we will denote by $O(\sigma_I, \sigma_Y)$. We abbreviate $\delta(O(\sigma_I, \sigma_Y))$ by $\delta(\sigma_I, \sigma_Y)$. A strategy σ_I^* for *Me* is called *winning* if, playing according to this strategy, I win the game, no matter how *You* move, i.e. for all $\sigma_Y \in \Sigma_Y$, $\delta(\sigma_I^*, \sigma_Y) \in \mathbb{Z}^+$. An outcome O that maximizes *My* pay-off in light of *Your* best strategy is called *maxmin-outcome*. Formally, O is a maxmin-outcome iff $\delta(O) = \max_{\sigma_I}^{\trianglelefteq} \min_{\sigma_Y}^{\trianglelefteq} \delta(\sigma_I, \sigma_Y)$ and $\delta(O)$ is called the *maxmin-value* of the game. A strategy σ_I^* for *Me* is a *maxmin-strategy* for **NG** if $\sigma_I^* \in \arg\max_{\sigma_I}^{\trianglelefteq} \min_{\sigma_Y}^{\trianglelefteq} \delta(\sigma_I, \sigma_Y)$, i.e. the maximum is reached at σ_I^*. *Minmax* values and strategies for *You* are defined symmetrically.

---

[1] Notice the flipped $\ll$-sign in the second case.

The class of games that we have defined falls into the category of *zero-sum perfect information games* in game theory. They are characterized by the fact that the players have strictly opposing interests. In these games, the minmax and maxmin value always coincide and is referred to as the *value of the game*.

Example 4 (Example 2 cont.). I have a winning strategy for $\mathcal{I} = \{a, d\}$: if you move to the left at the root, I will reach $\mathbf{P} : a$ with optimal payoff 1. If *You* go to the right instead, *You* still cannot win the game but *You* can minimize *My* payoff by reaching $\mathbf{O} : a$ with $\delta(\mathbf{O} : a) = 2$ instead of $\mathbf{O} : d$ with $\delta(\mathbf{O} : d) = 1$. Thus, the value of the game is 2.

Now let $\mathcal{I} = \{d\}$ with payoffs $\delta_{\mathcal{I}}(\mathbf{P} : c) = -1$, $\delta(\mathbf{P} : b) = -2$, $\delta(\mathbf{P} : a) = -3$, $\delta(\mathbf{O} : a) = 2$, $\delta(\mathbf{O} : d) = -2$. In this game, I have no winning strategy: if *You* move to the left at the root, it is best for *Me* to reach $\mathbf{P} : a$ with payoff -3. If *You* move to the right, *You* can force $\mathbf{O} : d$ with payoff -2. Thus, it is better for *You* to move to the right at the root note, giving us the game value -2.

5   Game-Induced Choice Logic (GCL)

To examine the properties of our GTS and compare it with QCL, we extract a novel degree-based semantics for the language of QCL from our game **NG**. The resulting logic will be called Game-induced Choice Logic (GCL). Syntactically, GCL is defined in the same way as QCL (cf. Definition 1), i.e., F is a GCL-formula iff F is a QCL-formula. The optionality function of GCL is denoted by $\text{opt}^{\mathcal{G}}$ and defined in the same way as opt (cf. Definition 2), except for negation.

Definition 9 (Optionality in GCL). *The optionality of GCL-formulas is defined inductively as follows: (i)* $\text{opt}^{\mathcal{G}}(a) = 1$ *for* $a \in \mathcal{U}$, *(ii)* $\text{opt}^{\mathcal{G}}(\neg F) = \text{opt}^{\mathcal{G}}(F)$, *(iii)* $\text{opt}^{\mathcal{G}}(F \wedge G) = \text{opt}^{\mathcal{G}}(F \vee G) = \max(\text{opt}^{\mathcal{G}}(F), \text{opt}^{\mathcal{G}}(G))$, *(iv)* $\text{opt}^{\mathcal{G}}(F \vec{\times} G) = \text{opt}^{\mathcal{G}}(F) + \text{opt}^{\mathcal{G}}(G)$.

The degree-function of GCL is denoted by $\text{deg}_{\mathcal{I}}^{\mathcal{G}}$, and maps pairs of formulas and interpretations to values in the domain $(Z, \trianglelefteq)$ (cf. Definition 6).

Definition 10 (Satisfaction Degree in GCL). *The satisfaction degree of GCL-formulas under an interpretation* $\mathcal{I}$ *is defined inductively as follows:*

$$\text{deg}_{\mathcal{I}}^{\mathcal{G}}(a) = 1 \text{ if } a \in \mathcal{I}, -1 \text{ otherwise}$$

$$\text{deg}_{\mathcal{I}}^{\mathcal{G}}(\neg F) = -\text{deg}_{\mathcal{I}}^{\mathcal{G}}(F)$$

$$\text{deg}_{\mathcal{I}}^{\mathcal{G}}(F \wedge G) = \min_{\trianglelefteq}(\text{deg}_{\mathcal{I}}^{\mathcal{G}}(F), \text{deg}_{\mathcal{I}}^{\mathcal{G}}(G))$$

$$\text{deg}_{\mathcal{I}}^{\mathcal{G}}(F \vee G) = \max_{\trianglelefteq}(\text{deg}_{\mathcal{I}}^{\mathcal{G}}(F), \text{deg}_{\mathcal{I}}^{\mathcal{G}}(G))$$

$$\text{deg}_{\mathcal{I}}^{\mathcal{G}}(F \vec{\times} G) = \begin{cases} \text{deg}_{\mathcal{I}}^{\mathcal{G}}(F) & \text{if } \text{deg}_{\mathcal{I}}^{\mathcal{G}}(F) \in \mathbb{Z}^{+} \\ \text{opt}^{\mathcal{G}}(F) + \text{deg}_{\mathcal{I}}^{\mathcal{G}}(G) & \text{if } \text{deg}_{\mathcal{I}}^{\mathcal{G}}(F) \in \mathbb{Z}^{-}, \text{deg}_{\mathcal{I}}^{\mathcal{G}}(G) \in \mathbb{Z}^{+} \\ \text{deg}_{\mathcal{I}}^{\mathcal{G}}(F) - \text{opt}^{\mathcal{G}}(G) & \text{otherwise} \end{cases}$$

If $\deg_{\mathcal{I}}^{\mathcal{G}}(F) \in \mathbb{Z}^+$, then $\mathcal{I}$ classically satisfies F ($\mathcal{I}$ is a model of F). In contrast to QCL, those interpretations that result in a higher degree relative to the ordering $\trianglelefteq$ are more preferable, which is why we take the maximum degree for disjunction and the minimum degree for conjunction. However, since $\trianglelefteq$ inverts the order on $\mathbb{Z}^+$, a degree of 1 is considered to be higher than a degree of 2. Preferred models are defined analogously to QCL (cf. Definition 4).

Definition 11 (Preferred Model under GCL-semantics). *Let F be a GCL-formula. An interpretation $\mathcal{I}$ is a preferred model of F iff $\deg_{\mathcal{I}}^{\mathcal{G}}(F) \in \mathbb{Z}^+$ and, for all interpretations $\mathcal{J}$, $\deg_{\mathcal{J}}^{\mathcal{G}}(F) \trianglelefteq \deg_{\mathcal{I}}^{\mathcal{G}}(F)$.*

We are now ready to show that **NG** and GCL are semantically equivalent, which will allow us to examine properties of **NG** via GCL. As a first step, we show that the the notion of optionality, which must be defined a-priori in degree-based semantics, arises naturally in our game.

Proposition 1. *The longest $\ll$-chain in $\mathcal{O}(\mathbf{Q} : F)$ has length $\mathrm{opt}^{\mathcal{G}}(F)$, where $\mathbf{Q} \in \{\mathbf{P}, \mathbf{O}\}$.*

Proof. By structural induction. For the base case $F = a$, where $a \in \mathcal{U}$, this clearly holds, as $\mathrm{opt}^{\mathcal{G}}(a) = 1$.

Induction step: for the inductive hypothesis we assume that for two GCL-formulas A, B the longest $\ll$-chain $O_1, \ldots, O_k$ in $\mathcal{O}(\mathbf{Q} : A)$ has length $k = \mathrm{opt}^{\mathcal{G}}(A)$ and the longest $\ll$-chain $O'_1, \ldots, O'_\ell$ in $\mathcal{O}(\mathbf{Q} : B)$ has length $\ell = \mathrm{opt}^{\mathcal{G}}(B)$.

$F = \neg A$: since negation results in a role switch with inverted preferences, the longest $\ll$-chain in $\mathcal{O}(\mathbf{Q}' : \neg A)$, where $\mathbf{Q}' \in \{\mathbf{P}, \mathbf{O}\} \setminus \{\mathbf{Q}\}$, is $O_k, \ldots, O_1$ with length $k = \mathrm{opt}^{\mathcal{G}}(A) = \mathrm{opt}^{\mathcal{G}}(\neg A)$.

$F = (A \wedge B)$: Note that $\ll_{\mathbf{Q}:A \wedge B} = \ll_{\mathbf{Q}:A} \cup \ll_{\mathbf{Q}:B}$. Moreover, $\mathcal{O}(\mathbf{Q} : A)$ and $\mathcal{O}(\mathbf{Q} : B)$ are disjoint, i.e., the longest $\ll$-chain in $\mathcal{O}(\mathbf{Q} : A \wedge B)$ has length $\max(k, \ell) = \max(\mathrm{opt}^{\mathcal{G}}(A), \mathrm{opt}^{\mathcal{G}}(B)) = \mathrm{opt}^{\mathcal{G}}(A \wedge B)$.

$F = (A \vee B)$ is analogous to $F = (A \wedge B)$.

$F = (A \vec{\times} B)$: by construction of $\ll_{\mathbf{Q}:A\vec{\times}B}$ (cf. Definition 5), the longest $\ll$-chain in $\mathcal{O}(\mathbf{Q} : A\vec{\times}B)$ is $O_1, \ldots, O_k, O'_1, \ldots, O'_\ell$ with a length of $k + \ell = \mathrm{opt}^{\mathcal{G}}(A) + \mathrm{opt}^{\mathcal{G}}(B) = \mathrm{opt}^{\mathcal{G}}(A\vec{\times}B)$. $\qquad\square$

The following results express semantic equivalence between **NG** and GCL. The key is to show that the degree-based semantics captures *My* preferences in the game as induced by the choice connective $\vec{\times}$.

Theorem 1. *The value of* $\mathbf{NG}(\mathbf{P} : F, \mathcal{I})$ *is* $\deg_{\mathcal{I}}^{\mathcal{G}}(F)$. *The value of* $\mathbf{NG}(\mathbf{O} : F, \mathcal{I})$ *is* $-\deg_{\mathcal{I}}^{\mathcal{G}}(F)$.

Proof. We fix an interpretation $\mathcal{I}$. For this proof, we introduce some handy notation: for a game state $\mathbf{Q} : F$, let $d(\mathbf{Q} : F)$ denote the maxmin-value and $O(\mathbf{Q} : F)$ the maxmin-outcome of the game $\mathbf{NG}(\mathbf{Q} : F, \mathcal{I})$, and $W(\mathbf{Q} : F)$ and $L(\mathbf{Q} : F)$ the set of its winning and losing outcomes, respectively. Let $\delta_{\mathcal{I}}^{\mathbf{Q}:F}$

denote the payoff function for the game $\mathbf{NG}(\mathbf{Q} : F, \mathcal{I})$. We proceed by structural induction on F, starting with the cases where $\mathbf{Q} = \mathbf{P}$.

$F = a$: This game consists of a single node v. The longest $\ll$-chain starting at v has length 1. Therefore, $d(\mathbf{P} : a) = 1$ iff $a \in \mathcal{I}$ iff $\deg_{\mathcal{I}}^{\mathcal{G}}(a) = 1$, and $d(\mathbf{P} : a) = -1$ iff $a \notin \mathcal{I}$ iff $\deg_{\mathcal{I}}^{\mathcal{G}}(a) = -1$.

$F = G_1 \vee G_2$: In the first round, I choose between $\mathbf{P} : G_1$ and $\mathbf{P} : G_2$. By the inductive hypothesis, the values of these games are $\deg_{\mathcal{I}}^{\mathcal{G}}(\mathbf{P} : G_1)$ and $\deg_{\mathcal{I}}^{\mathcal{G}}(\mathbf{P} : G_2)$, respectively. Since I am looking to maximize My payoff, I move to the subgame with maximal payoff:

$$d(\mathbf{P} : G_1 \vee G_2) = \max_{\trianglelefteq}\{d(\mathbf{P} : G_1), d(\mathbf{P} : G_2)\}$$
$$= \max_{\trianglelefteq}\{\deg_{\mathcal{I}}^{\mathcal{G}}(G_1), \deg_{\mathcal{I}}^{\mathcal{G}}(G_2)\} = \deg_{\mathcal{I}}^{\mathcal{G}}(G_1 \wedge G_2)$$

$F = G_1 \wedge G_2$ is analogous to $F = G_1 \vee G_2$.

$F = G_1 \overrightarrow{\times} G_2$: From the fact that $\delta_{\mathcal{I}}$ respects $\ll$ for the winning outcomes of both players and the game rule of $\overrightarrow{\times}$, we observe the following facts: First, if the G_1-game is winning for Me, I go to G_1 in the first round. Secondly, if G_1 is losing and G_2 is winning, I go to G_2. And thirdly, if both games are losing, I go to G_1. Since all outcomes of the G_2-games are in $\ll$-relation to all outcomes of the G_1-game, we have by Proposition 1 for all outcomes O:

$$\delta_{\mathcal{I}}^{\mathbf{P}:F}(O) = \begin{cases} \delta_{\mathcal{I}}^{\mathbf{P}:G_1}(O), & \text{if } O \in W(\mathbf{P} : G_1), \\ \delta_{\mathcal{I}}^{\mathbf{P}:G_2}(O) + \mathrm{opt}(G_1), & \text{if } O \in W(\mathbf{P} : G_2), \\ \delta_{\mathcal{I}}^{\mathbf{P}:G_1}(O) - \mathrm{opt}(G_2), & \text{if } O \in L(\mathbf{P} : G_1). \end{cases}$$

The last case comes from the fact that $O \gg O'$ for all $O' \in \mathcal{O}(\mathbf{P} : G_2)$, Proposition 1 and the definition of $\delta_{\mathcal{I}}$. We now use the inductive hypothesis: in the first case from above, $O(\mathbf{P} : F) \in W(\mathbf{P} : G_1)$ and therefore $d(\mathbf{P} : F) = d(\mathbf{P} : G_1) - \deg_{\mathcal{I}}^{\mathcal{G}}(G_1)$. In the second case, $O(\mathbf{P} : F) \in W(\mathbf{P} : G_2)$ and therefore $d(\mathbf{P} : F) = d(\mathbf{P} : G_2) + \mathrm{opt}(G_1) = \deg_{\mathcal{I}}^{\mathcal{G}}(G_2) + \mathrm{opt}(G_1)$. Finally, in the third case, $O(\mathbf{P} : F) \in L(\mathbf{P} : G_1)$ and therefore $d(\mathbf{P} : F) = d(\mathbf{P} : G_1) - \mathrm{opt}(G_2) = \deg_{\mathcal{I}}^{\mathcal{G}}(G_2) - \mathrm{opt}(G_2)$.

$F = \neg G$: The game continues at $\mathbf{O} : G$. Therefore, using the inductive hypothesis, $d(\mathbf{P} : F) = d(\mathbf{O} : G) = -\deg_{\mathcal{I}}^{\mathcal{G}}(G) = \deg_{\mathcal{I}}^{\mathcal{G}}(F)$.

Cases where I am in the role of Opponent are similar. For example, let us consider $\mathbf{O} : G_1 \wedge G_2$. In the first move I choose between the two subgames $\mathbf{O} : G_1$ and $\mathbf{O} : G_2$. I seek to maximize My payoff, so I go to the subgame with maximal value. Therefore, using the inductive hypothesis,

$$d(\mathbf{O} : G_1 \wedge G_2) = \max_{\trianglelefteq}\{d(\mathbf{O} : G_1), d(\mathbf{O} : G_2)\}$$
$$= \max_{\trianglelefteq}\{-\deg_{\mathcal{I}}^{\mathcal{G}}(G_1), -\deg_{\mathcal{I}}^{\mathcal{G}}(G_2)\}$$
$$= -\min_{\trianglelefteq}\{\deg_{\mathcal{I}}^{\mathcal{G}}(G_1), \deg_{\mathcal{I}}^{\mathcal{G}}(G_2)\} = -\deg_{\mathcal{I}}^{\mathcal{G}}(G_1 \wedge G_2).$$

The argument can be adapted analogously for the other logical connectives. $\square$

Negation in our new semantics behaves as desired. To see this, compare the discussion in Sect. 3 to statements (i–iii) in Proposition 2 below. Intuitively, negation in GCL preserves information on preferences by allowing for *degrees of dissatisfaction*. For example, the formula $\neg(a \vec{\times} b)$ can only be satisfied by $\emptyset$. However, we must also inspect the interpretations that do not satisfy the formula: $\{b\}$ results in a degree of -2 while $\{a\}$ and $\{a, b\}$ result in a degree of -1, meaning that $\{b\}$ is more preferable than $\{a\}$ and $\{a, b\}$.

Moreover, De Morgan's laws still hold in GCL, and ordered disjunction is still associative (see statements (iv–vi) in Proposition 2).

Definition 12 (Equivalence). *Two GCL-formulas F and G are equivalent, written $F \equiv G$, iff $\text{opt}^{\mathcal{G}}(F) = \text{opt}^{\mathcal{G}}(G)$ and $\deg_{\mathcal{I}}^{\mathcal{G}}(F) = \deg_{\mathcal{I}}^{\mathcal{G}}(G)$ for all $\mathcal{I} \subseteq \mathcal{U}$.*

Proposition 2. *The following holds:*

(i) $\deg_{\mathcal{I}}^{\mathcal{G}}(F) = \deg_{\mathcal{J}}^{\mathcal{G}}(F) \iff \deg_{\mathcal{I}}^{\mathcal{G}}(\neg F) = \deg_{\mathcal{J}}^{\mathcal{G}}(\neg F)$

(ii) $\deg_{\mathcal{I}}^{\mathcal{G}}(F) \in \mathbb{Z}^{+} \iff \deg_{\mathcal{I}}^{\mathcal{G}}(\neg F) \in \mathbb{Z}^{-}$

(iii) $F \equiv \neg\neg F$

(iv) $\neg(F \wedge G) \equiv \neg F \vee \neg G$

(v) $\neg(F \vee G) \equiv \neg F \wedge \neg G$

(vi) $((F \circ G) \circ H) \equiv (F \circ (G \circ H))$ *for* $\circ \in \{\wedge, \vee, \vec{\times}\}$

Proof. Statements (i–iii) follow by definition of negation in GCL, i.e., $\deg_{\mathcal{I}}^{\mathcal{G}}(\neg F) = -\deg_{\mathcal{I}}^{\mathcal{G}}(F)$. Let us consider statements (iv–vi):

(iv) First, note that $\text{opt}^{\mathcal{G}}(\neg(F \wedge G)) = \text{opt}^{\mathcal{G}}(F \wedge G) = \max\{\text{opt}(F), \text{opt}(G)\} = \max\{\text{opt}(\neg F), \text{opt}(\neg G)\} = \text{opt}^{\mathcal{G}}(\neg F \vee \neg G)$. Moreover, for any $\mathcal{I} \subseteq \mathcal{U}$, we have $\deg_{\mathcal{I}}(\neg(F \wedge G)) = -\min_{\lhd}\{\deg_{\mathcal{I}}(F), \deg_{\mathcal{I}}(G)\} = \max_{\lhd}\{-\deg_{\mathcal{I}}(F), -\deg_{\mathcal{I}}(G)\} = \deg_{\mathcal{I}}(\neg F \vee \neg G)$.

(v) Analogous to (iv).

(vi) Associativity of $\wedge, \vee$ follows from associativity of $\min/\max$ over any total order like Z (cf. Definition 6). For example: $\min_{\lhd}\{a, \min_{\lhd}\{b, c\}\} = \min_{\lhd}\{a, b, c\} = \min_{\lhd}\{\min_{\lhd}\{a, b\}, \min_{\lhd}\{c\}\}$.

We now show associativity of $\vec{\times}$. Let $F_1 = ((A \vec{\times} B) \vec{\times} C)$, $F_2 = (A \vec{\times} (B \vec{\times} C))$. $\text{opt}^{\mathcal{G}}(F_1) = \text{opt}^{\mathcal{G}}(F_2)$ is immediate. Let $\mathcal{I}$ be an arbitrary interpretation. We can show $\deg_{\mathcal{I}}^{\mathcal{G}}(F_1) = \deg_{\mathcal{I}}^{\mathcal{G}}(F_2)$ by distinguishing all cases for $\deg_{\mathcal{I}}^{\mathcal{G}}(A), \deg_{\mathcal{I}}^{\mathcal{G}}(B), \deg_{\mathcal{I}}^{\mathcal{G}}(C) \in \{\mathbb{Z}^{-}, \mathbb{Z}^{+}\}$.

– $\deg_{\mathcal{I}}^{\mathcal{G}}(A) \in \mathbb{Z}^{+}$. Then $\deg_{\mathcal{I}}^{\mathcal{G}}(F_2) = \deg_{\mathcal{I}}^{\mathcal{G}}(A)$. Moreover, $\deg_{\mathcal{I}}^{\mathcal{G}}(A \vec{\times} B) = \deg_{\mathcal{I}}^{\mathcal{G}}(A)$ and therefore $\deg_{\mathcal{I}}^{\mathcal{G}}(F_1) = \deg_{\mathcal{I}}^{\mathcal{G}}(A)$.

– $\deg_{\mathcal{I}}^{\mathcal{G}}(A) \in \mathbb{Z}^{-}$ and $\deg_{\mathcal{I}}^{\mathcal{G}}(B) \in \mathbb{Z}^{+}$. Then $\deg_{\mathcal{I}}^{\mathcal{G}}(A \vec{\times} B) = \text{opt}^{\mathcal{G}}(A) + \deg_{\mathcal{I}}^{\mathcal{G}}(B)$ and $\deg_{\mathcal{I}}^{\mathcal{G}}(B \vec{\times} C) = \deg_{\mathcal{I}}^{\mathcal{G}}(B)$. Thus, $\deg_{\mathcal{I}}^{\mathcal{G}}(F_1) = \deg_{\mathcal{I}}^{\mathcal{G}}(F_2) = \text{opt}^{\mathcal{G}}(A) + \deg_{\mathcal{I}}^{\mathcal{G}}(B)$.

– $\deg_{\mathcal{I}}^{\mathcal{G}}(A) \in \mathbb{Z}^{-}$, $\deg_{\mathcal{I}}^{\mathcal{G}}(B) \in \mathbb{Z}^{-}$, and $\deg_{\mathcal{I}}^{\mathcal{G}}(C) \in \mathbb{Z}^{+}$. Then $\deg_{\mathcal{I}}^{\mathcal{G}}(A \vec{\times} B) = \deg_{\mathcal{I}}^{\mathcal{G}}(A) - \text{opt}^{\mathcal{G}}(B)$ and $\deg_{\mathcal{I}}^{\mathcal{G}}(B \vec{\times} C) = \text{opt}^{\mathcal{G}}(B) + \deg_{\mathcal{I}}^{\mathcal{G}}(C)$. Observe that $\deg_{\mathcal{I}}^{\mathcal{G}}(A \vec{\times} B) \in \mathbb{Z}^{-}$ and thus $\deg_{\mathcal{I}}^{\mathcal{G}}(F_1) = \text{opt}^{\mathcal{G}}(A \vec{\times} B) + \deg_{\mathcal{I}}^{\mathcal{G}}(C) = \text{opt}^{\mathcal{G}}(A) + \text{opt}^{\mathcal{G}}(B) + \deg_{\mathcal{I}}^{\mathcal{G}}(C) = \text{opt}^{\mathcal{G}}(A) + \deg_{\mathcal{I}}^{\mathcal{G}}(B \vec{\times} C) = \deg_{\mathcal{I}}^{\mathcal{G}}(F_2)$.

- $\deg_{\mathcal{I}}^{\mathcal{G}}(A) \in \mathbb{Z}^-$, $\deg_{\mathcal{I}}^{\mathcal{G}}(B) \in \mathbb{Z}^-$, and $\deg_{\mathcal{I}}^{\mathcal{G}}(C) \in \mathbb{Z}^-$. Then $\deg_{\mathcal{I}}^{\mathcal{G}}(A \vec{\times} B) = \deg_{\mathcal{I}}^{\mathcal{G}}(A) - \mathrm{opt}^{\mathcal{G}}(B)$ and $\deg_{\mathcal{I}}^{\mathcal{G}}(B \vec{\times} C) = \deg_{\mathcal{I}}^{\mathcal{G}}(B) - \mathrm{opt}^{\mathcal{G}}(C)$. Thus, $\deg_{\mathcal{I}}^{\mathcal{G}}(F_1) = \deg_{\mathcal{I}}^{\mathcal{G}}(A \vec{\times} B) - \mathrm{opt}^{\mathcal{G}}(C) = \deg_{\mathcal{I}}^{\mathcal{G}}(A) - \mathrm{opt}^{\mathcal{G}}(B) - \mathrm{opt}^{\mathcal{G}}(C) = \deg_{\mathcal{I}}^{\mathcal{G}}(A) - \mathrm{opt}^{\mathcal{G}}(B \vec{\times} C) = \deg_{\mathcal{I}}^{\mathcal{G}}(F_2)$q.   □

While GCL deviates from QCL, the two logics agree when it comes to classical satisfaction, as expressed by the following result.

Proposition 3. $\deg_{\mathcal{I}}^{\mathcal{G}}(F) \in \mathbb{Z}^+$ iff $\deg_{\mathcal{I}}(F) < \infty$.

Proof. By structural induction. Let $\mathcal{I} \subseteq \mathcal{U}$. For the base case $F = a$, where $a \in \mathcal{U}$, we distinguish two cases: If $a \in \mathcal{I}$, then $\deg_{\mathcal{I}}(a) = \deg_{\mathcal{I}}^{\mathcal{G}}(a) = 1$. If $a \notin \mathcal{I}$, then $\deg_{\mathcal{I}}(a) = \infty$ and $\deg_{\mathcal{I}}^{\mathcal{G}}(a) = -1$.

Induction step: the I.H. is that $\deg_{\mathcal{I}}^{\mathcal{G}}(A) \in \mathbb{Z}^+$ iff $\deg_{\mathcal{I}}(A) < \infty$, and that $\deg_{\mathcal{I}}^{\mathcal{G}}(B) \in \mathbb{Z}^+$ iff $\deg_{\mathcal{I}}(B) < \infty$.

$F = \neg A$: $\deg_{\mathcal{I}}^{\mathcal{G}}(\neg A) \in \mathbb{Z}^+$ iff $\deg_{\mathcal{I}}^{\mathcal{G}}(A) \in \mathbb{Z}^-$ iff $\deg_{\mathcal{I}}(A) = \infty$ iff $\deg_{\mathcal{I}}(\neg A) < \infty$.

$F = (A \wedge B)$: $\deg_{\mathcal{I}}^{\mathcal{G}}(A \wedge B) \in \mathbb{Z}^+$ iff $\deg_{\mathcal{I}}^{\mathcal{G}}(A) \in \mathbb{Z}^+$ and $\deg_{\mathcal{I}}^{\mathcal{G}}(B) \in \mathbb{Z}^+$ iff $\deg_{\mathcal{I}}(A) < \infty$ and $\deg_{\mathcal{I}}(B) < \infty$ iff $\deg_{\mathcal{I}}(A \wedge B) < \infty$.

$F = (A \vee B)$: $\deg_{\mathcal{I}}^{\mathcal{G}}(A \vee B) \in \mathbb{Z}^+$ iff $\deg_{\mathcal{I}}^{\mathcal{G}}(A) \in \mathbb{Z}^+$ or $\deg_{\mathcal{I}}^{\mathcal{G}}(B) \in \mathbb{Z}^+$ iff $\deg_{\mathcal{I}}(A) < \infty$ or $\deg_{\mathcal{I}}(B) < \infty$ iff $\deg_{\mathcal{I}}(A \vee B) < \infty$.

$F = (A \vec{\times} B)$: analogous to $F = (A \vee B)$.   □

Moreover, if we allow negation only in front of classical formulas, QCL and GCL agree even when it comes to (positive) satisfaction degrees.

Proposition 4. *If F is a QCL-formula in which negation is only applied to classical formulas, $\deg_{\mathcal{I}}^{\mathcal{G}}(F) \in \mathbb{Z}^+$ implies $\deg_{\mathcal{I}}^{\mathcal{G}}(F) = \deg_{\mathcal{I}}(F)$.*

Proof. By structural induction. Let $\mathcal{I} \subseteq \mathcal{U}$. In this proof, $\min_{\trianglelefteq}$ and $\max_{\trianglelefteq}$ are relative to $\trianglelefteq$ (cf. Definition 6) while $\min_{\leq}$ and $\max_{\leq}$ are relative to the regular order on integers.

Base case: let F be a classical formula. Assume $\deg_{\mathcal{I}}^{\mathcal{G}}(a) \in \mathbb{Z}^+$. By Proposition 3 this implies $\deg_{\mathcal{I}}^{\mathcal{G}}(F) < \infty$. Thus, $\deg_{\mathcal{I}}(F) = \deg_{\mathcal{I}}^{\mathcal{G}}(F) = 1$.

Induction step: let A and B be formulas such that negation only appears in front of classical formulas, i.e., if $\neg G$ is a subformula of A or B then G is a classical formula. The I.H. is that $\deg_{\mathcal{I}}^{\mathcal{G}}(A) \in \mathbb{Z}^+$ implies $\deg_{\mathcal{I}}^{\mathcal{G}}(A) = \deg_{\mathcal{I}}(A)$ and $\deg_{\mathcal{I}}^{\mathcal{G}}(B) \in \mathbb{Z}^+$ implies $\deg_{\mathcal{I}}^{\mathcal{G}}(B) = \deg_{\mathcal{I}}(B)$.

$F = (A \wedge B)$: assume $\deg_{\mathcal{I}}^{\mathcal{G}}(A \wedge B) \in \mathbb{Z}^+$. Then we have $\deg_{\mathcal{I}}^{\mathcal{G}}(A) \in \mathbb{Z}^+$ and $\deg_{\mathcal{I}}^{\mathcal{G}}(B) \in \mathbb{Z}^+$. This means that, $\deg_{\mathcal{I}}^{\mathcal{G}}(A \wedge B) = \min_{\trianglelefteq}(\deg_{\mathcal{I}}^{\mathcal{G}}(A), \deg_{\mathcal{I}}^{\mathcal{G}}(B)) = \max_{\leq}(\deg_{\mathcal{I}}^{\mathcal{G}}(A), \deg_{\mathcal{I}}^{\mathcal{G}}(B)) = \max_{\leq}(\deg_{\mathcal{I}}(A), \deg_{\mathcal{I}}(B)) = \deg_{\mathcal{I}}(A \wedge B)$.

$F = (A \vee B)$: assume $\deg_{\mathcal{I}}^{\mathcal{G}}(A \vee B) \in \mathbb{Z}^+$. Then either $\deg_{\mathcal{I}}^{\mathcal{G}}(A) \in \mathbb{Z}^+$ or $\deg_{\mathcal{I}}^{\mathcal{G}}(B) \in \mathbb{Z}^+$. If both $\deg_{\mathcal{I}}^{\mathcal{G}}(A) \in \mathbb{Z}^+$ and $\deg_{\mathcal{I}}^{\mathcal{G}}(B) \in \mathbb{Z}^+$ the proof is analogous to $F = (A \wedge B)$. Suppose $\deg_{\mathcal{I}}^{\mathcal{G}}(A) \in \mathbb{Z}^+$ and $\deg_{\mathcal{I}}^{\mathcal{G}}(B) \in \mathbb{Z}^-$ (the other case is symmetric). By Proposition 3, $\deg_{\mathcal{I}}(B) = \infty$. Thus, $\deg_{\mathcal{I}}^{\mathcal{G}}(A \vee B) = \max_{\trianglelefteq}(\deg_{\mathcal{I}}^{\mathcal{G}}(A), \deg_{\mathcal{I}}^{\mathcal{G}}(B)) = \deg_{\mathcal{I}}^{\mathcal{G}}(A) = \deg_{\mathcal{I}}(A) = \min_{\leq}(\deg_{\mathcal{I}}(A), \deg_{\mathcal{I}}(B)) = \deg_{\mathcal{I}}(A \vee B)$.

$F = (A \vec{\times} B)$: assume $\deg_{\mathcal{I}}^{\mathcal{G}}(A \vec{\times} B) \in \mathbb{Z}^+$. If $\deg_{\mathcal{I}}^{\mathcal{G}}(A) \in \mathbb{Z}^+$, then $\deg_{\mathcal{I}}^{\mathcal{G}}(A \vec{\times} B) = \deg_{\mathcal{I}}^{\mathcal{G}}(A) = \deg_{\mathcal{I}}(A) = \deg_{\mathcal{I}}(A \vec{\times} B)$. If $\deg_{\mathcal{I}}^{\mathcal{G}}(A) \in \mathbb{Z}^-$, then

$\deg_{\mathcal{I}}^{\mathcal{G}}(B) \in \mathbb{Z}^+$. By Proposition 3, $\deg_{\mathcal{I}}(A) = \infty$. Then $\deg_{\mathcal{I}}^{\mathcal{G}}(A \vec{\times} B) = \mathrm{opt}^{\mathcal{G}}(A) +$ $\deg_{\mathcal{I}}^{\mathcal{G}}(B) = \mathrm{opt}(A) + \deg_{\mathcal{I}}(B) = \deg_{\mathcal{I}}(A \vec{\times} B)$. Note that $\mathrm{opt}^{\mathcal{G}}(A) = \mathrm{opt}(A)$ holds because negation is only applied to classical formulas in A, and, except for negation, optionality is defined equivalently in QCL and GCL. $\qquad\square$

Note that Propositions 3 and 4 do not hold if we substitute QCL for PQCL. Regarding Proposition 3, recall that, in PQCL, an interpretation may classically satisfy a formula F and its negation $\neg F$ (see Sect. 3), which is not possible in GCL. As for Proposition 4, classical conjunction and disjunction are defined differently in PQCL compared to QCL and GCL.

Lastly, we investigate the computational complexity of GCL (and therefore our game **NG**). Familiarity with complexity classes P, NP, and coNP is assumed. Moreover, the complexity class Θ_2^P contains the problems solvable in polynomial time with access to $O(\log(n))$-many NP-oracle calls [16]. We consider decision problems pertaining to the preferred models of a formula.

Definition 13. *We define the following two decision problems:*

- PMCHECKING: *given a GCL-formula F and an interpretation $\mathcal{I}$, is $\mathcal{I}$ a preferred model of F?*
- PMCONTAINMENT: *given a GCL-formula F and a variable $x \in \mathcal{U}$, is there a preferred model $\mathcal{I}$ of F such that $x \in \mathcal{I}$?*

For QCL, PMCHECKING is coNP-complete while PMCONTAINMENT is Θ_2^P-complete [4]. Intuitively, PMCHECKING is coNP-complete for QCL since we must go through all other interpretations to check that our given interpretation $\mathcal{I}$ results in an optimal degree. The same is true in the case of GCL.

Proposition 5. PMCHECKING *is* coNP-*complete for GCL.*

Proof. NP-membership of the complementary problem: given a GCL-formula F and an interpretation $\mathcal{I}$, compute $k = \deg_{\mathcal{I}}^{\mathcal{G}}(F)$ (this can be done in polynomial time) and check whether $k \in \mathbb{Z}^+$. If no, then $\mathcal{I}$ is not a preferred model and we are done. If yes, non-deterministically guess an interpretation $\mathcal{J}$ and check whether $k \lhd \deg_{\mathcal{J}}^{\mathcal{G}}(F)$. If yes, then $\mathcal{I}$ is not a preferred model, i.e. $(F, \mathcal{I})$ is a yes-instance for the complementary problem of PMCHECKING.

coNP-hardness by reduction from UNSAT[2]: given a classical formula F, we construct the GCL-formula

$$F' = (F \vee ((a \wedge \neg a) \vec{\times} a)) \wedge \neg(F \wedge a)$$

where a is a fresh variable that does not occur in F. It holds that F is unsatisfiable iff $\{a\}$ is a preferred model of F':

Assume F is unsatisfiable. Note that $\{a\}$ satisfies F' to a degree of 2. Moreover, $((a \wedge \neg a) \vec{\times} a)$ can not be satisfied to a degree more preferable than 2. Thus, to satisfy F' to a degree of 1 we must satisfy F, which is not possible.

---

[2] In the coNP-complete UNSAT problem we are given a classical formula F and ask whether $\mathcal{I} \not\models F$ for all interpretations $\mathcal{I}$.

Assume F is satisfiable, i.e., there is some interpretation $\mathcal{I}$ that satisfies F. Note that we can assume $a \notin \mathcal{I}$, since a is a fresh variable. Then $\mathcal{I}$ satisfies F' to a degree of 1. But $\{a\}$ satisfies F' to a degree of 2.   □

As for PMCONTAINMENT, Θ_2^P-completeness in the case of QCL can intuitively be explained by the fact that we must first find the optimal degree m for the given formula F. This can be done via binary search, using $O(\log(\mathrm{opt}(F)))$ NP-oracle calls. Then, a last oracle call suffices to guess an interpretation $\mathcal{I}$ and check whether $\deg_{\mathcal{I}}(F) = m$ and $a \in \mathcal{I}$. This algorithm can be adapted for GCL.

Proposition 6. PMCONTAINMENT *is Θ_2^P-complete for GCL.*

Proof. Θ_2^P-membership: let F be a GCL-formula and $a \in \mathcal{U}$. First, using an NP-oracle call, check whether there is some interpretation $\mathcal{I}$ such that $\deg_{\mathcal{I}}^{\mathcal{G}}(F) \in \mathbb{Z}^+$. If no, then F has no preferred models and we have a no-instance. If yes, we continue. We conduct a binary search over $(1, \dots, \mathrm{opt}^{\mathcal{G}}(F))$. At each step of the binary search we use an NP-oracle call to check whether there is some interpretation $\mathcal{I}$ such that $k \trianglelefteq \deg_{\mathcal{I}}^{\mathcal{G}}(F)$, where k is the current mid-point of the binary search. If yes, we continue the binary search over $(1, \dots, k-1)$, otherwise we continue with $(k+1, \dots, \mathrm{opt}^{\mathcal{G}}(F))$. In this way, we find the optimal degree m with which F can be satisfied, i.e., every preferred model of F must satisfy F to a degree of m. The binary search requires $O(\log(\mathrm{opt}^{\mathcal{G}}(F)))$ NP-oracle calls. Note that $\mathrm{opt}^{\mathcal{G}}(F)$ is linear in the size of F, since $\mathrm{opt}^{\mathcal{G}}(A \vec{\times} B) = \mathrm{opt}^{\mathcal{G}}(A) + \mathrm{opt}^{\mathcal{G}}(B)$. Finally, we make one last NP-oracle call to guess an interpretation $\mathcal{I}$ and check whether $\deg_{\mathcal{I}}^{\mathcal{G}}(F) = m$ and $a \in \mathcal{I}$.

Θ_2^P-hardness: in the Θ_2^P-hardness proof of PMCONTAINMENT for QCL (see Proposition 19 in [4]), a formula F' is constructed in which negation is only applied to atoms, i.e., if $\neg G$ is a subformula of F' then G is a propositional variable. By our Proposition 4, this means that an interpretation $\mathcal{I}$ is a preferred model of F' in QCL if and only if $\mathcal{I}$ is a preferred model of F' in GCL. Thus, the same construction used in the hardness proof of QCL works for GCL.   □

We have shown that the complexity of GCL with respect to preferred models is the same as that of QCL. Note that the complexity of PQCL has not been formally investigated yet (to the best of our knowledge).

6   Conclusion

We propose a game-theoretic semantics (GTS) for the language of Qualitative Choice Logic (QCL), and thereby show that GTS are well-suited for languages in which soft and hard constraints are expressed in a single language.

We extract the degree-based Game-induced Choice Logic (GCL) from our GTS and show equivalence between the two formalisms. By leveraging game-theoretic negation, our new semantics avoids the contentious behavior of negation in QCL and Prioritized QCL (PQCL) while retaining desirable properties such as associativity of ordered disjunction. Moreover, we show that the complexity of GCL is the same as that of QCL when it comes to preferred models.

Regarding future work, our game semantics can be lifted to a provability game [8,9] by which a cut-free sequent calculus can be obtained. We also plan to investigate how our approach can be adapted to formalisms related to QCL such as other choice logics [4,5] or the recently introduced lexicographic logic [7].

Acknowledgements. We thank the anonymous reviewers for their feedback. This work was funded by the Austrian Science Fund (FWF) under grants P32830 and P32684, the Vienna Science and Technology Fund (WWTF) under grant ICT19-065, and partially funded by the EU (Marie Skłodowska-Curie RISE) project MOSAIC, grant 101007624.

References

1. Benferhat, S., Sedki, K.: Two alternatives for handling preferences in qualitative choice logic. Fuzzy Sets Syst. **159**(15), 1889–1912 (2008)
2. van Benthem, J.: Logic in Games. MIT Press, Cambridge (2014)
3. Bernreiter, M., Lolic, A., Maly, J., Woltran, S.: Sequent calculi for choice logics. In: Blanchette, J., Kovács, L., Pattinson, D. (eds.) IJCAR 2022. LNCS, vol. 13385, pp. 331–349. Springer, Cham (2022). https://doi.org/10.1007/978-3-031-10769-6_20
4. Bernreiter, M., Maly, J., Woltran, S.: Choice logics and their computational properties. Artif. Intell. **311**, 103755 (2022)
5. Boudjelida, A., Benferhat, S.: Conjunctive choice logic. In: ISAIM 2016, Fort Lauderdale, Florida, USA, 4–6 January 2016 (2016)
6. Brewka, G., Benferhat, S., Berre, D.L.: Qualitative choice logic. Artif. Intell. **157**(1–2), 203–237 (2004)
7. Charalambidis, A., Papadimitriou, G., Rondogiannis, P., Troumpoukis, A.: A many-valued logic for lexicographic preference representation. In: KR 2021, Online event, 3–12 November 2021, pp. 646–650 (2021)
8. Fermüller, C.G., Metcalfe, G.: Giles's game and the proof theory of Łukasiewicz logic. Stud. Logica **92**(1), 27–61 (2009)
9. Freiman, R.: Games for hybrid logic. In: Silva, A., Wassermann, R., de Queiroz, R. (eds.) WoLLIC 2021. LNCS, vol. 13038, pp. 133–149. Springer, Cham (2021). https://doi.org/10.1007/978-3-030-88853-4_9
10. Hintikka, J.: Logic, Language-Games and Information: Kantian Themes in the Philosophy of Logic. Clarendon Press, Oxford (1973)
11. Hodges, W., Väänänen, J.: Logic and games. In: Zalta, E.N. (ed.) The Stanford Encyclopedia of Philosophy. Metaphysics Research Lab, Stanford University, fall 2019 edn. (2019)
12. Pigozzi, G., Tsoukiàs, A., Viappiani, P.: Preferences in artificial intelligence. Ann. Math. Artif. Intell. **77**(3–4), 361–401 (2016)
13. Sedki, K., Lamy, J., Tsopra, R.: Qualitative choice logic for modeling experts recommendations of antibiotics. In: Proceedings of the Thirty-Fifth International Florida Artificial Intelligence Research Society Conference, FLAIRS 2022, Hutchinson Island, Jensen Beach, Florida, USA, 15–18 May 2022 (2022)
14. Tulenheimo, T.: Classical negation and game-theoretical semantics. Notre Dame J. Form. Logic **55**(4), 469–498 (2014)
15. Väänänen, J.: Models and Games. Cambridge Studies in Advanced Mathematics. Cambridge University Press, Cambridge (2011)
16. Wagner, K.W.: Bounded query classes. SIAM J. Comput. **19**(5), 833–846 (1990)

Rational Closure Extension in SPO-Representable Inductive Inference Operators

Jonas Haldimann[1]([✉])[ID], Thomas Meyer[2][ID], Gabriele Kern-Isberner[3][ID], and Christoph Beierle[1][ID]

[1] FernUniversität in Hagen, Hagen, Germany
{jonas.haldimann,christoph.beierle}@fernuni-hagen.de
[2] University of Cape Town and CAIR, Cape Town, South Africa
tmeyer@cs.uct.ac.za
[3] University of Dortmund, Dortmund, Germany
gabriele.kern-isberner@cs.tu-dortmund.de

Abstract. The class of inductive inference operators that extend rational closure, as introduced by Lehmann or via Pearl's system Z, exhibits desirable inference characteristics. The property that formalizes this, known as (RC Extension), has recently been investigated for basic defeasible entailment relations. In this paper, we explore (RC Extension) for more general classes of inference relations. First, we semantically characterize (RC Extension) for preferential inference relations in general. Then we focus on operators that can be represented with strict partial orders (SPOs) on possible worlds and characterize SPO-representable inductive inference operators. Furthermore, we show that for SPO-representable inference operators, (RC Extension) is semantically characterized as a refinement of the Z-rank relation on possible worlds.

1 Introduction

Inductive reasoning from (conditional) belief bases is one of the major tasks in knowledge representation. Especially in the field of non-monotonic reasoning, research often deals with inferences that can be drawn from a set of given defeasible rules, and the resulting inference relations are assessed in terms of broadly accepted axiomatic properties, like system P [25]. Beyond the inference relations, the seminal papers [27,30] put the role of the belief base into the focus of reasoning methods, proposing closure operations for reasoning from defeasible rule bases that have inspired many other works on non-monotonic reasoning since then. In particular, *Rational Closure, (RC)* [27] (or equivalently *system Z* [30]) are inductive inference operators that can be characterized by a certain closure of a belief base under *rational monotony* (RM) [25,29] and exhibit desirable properties. Every inference relation satisfying system P and (RM) is induced by a ranked model (or equivalently a total preorder (TPO) on worlds) [26]. An inference relation satisfying system P is called *preferential* and is induced by a *preferential model* [25]. Both system P and (RM) have benefits and drawbacks:

© The Author(s), under exclusive license to Springer Nature Switzerland AG 2023
S. Gaggl et al. (Eds.): JELIA 2023, LNAI 14281, pp. 561–576, 2023.
https://doi.org/10.1007/978-3-031-43619-2_38

- System P is generally seen as a kind of gold standard which a non-monotonic inference relation should fulfil. However, inference only with the axioms of system P (p-entailment) is very skeptical because it takes *all* preferential models of a belief base Δ into account. Therefore, system P on its own is often perceived to be too weak for drawing informative inferences.
- If $A \mathrel{|\!\sim} C$, the postulate (RM) licences the entailment $A \wedge B \mathrel{|\!\sim} C$ for *every* B as long as from A we cannot defeasibly entail the negation of B. Therefore, because no other condition on B is required, (RM) is often perceived to be too strong.

Thus, one would expect inference operators to comply with system P while possibly licensing additional conditional entailments. The postulate (Classic Preservation) [7] requires that the inductive inference operator licenses an entailment of the form $A \mathrel{|\!\sim}_\Delta \bot$ only if $A \mathrel{|\!\sim}^p_\Delta \bot$, i.e., if it is a p-entailment. Note that $A \mathrel{|\!\sim}_\Delta \bot$ causes all models of A to be completely infeasible, thus expressing that $\neg A$ is a strict belief.

The postulate (RC Extension) [7] restricts the closure under (RM) to the belief base Δ and thus makes a difference between beliefs explicitly given in Δ and implicit beliefs derived from Δ by non-monotonic entailment. This distinction between explicit and implicit beliefs perfectly fits the basic idea of inductive inference operators [22], which map a belief base Δ to a complete inference relation induced by Δ. Inference relations satisfying (RM), *Classic Preservation* (CP), and (RC Extension) can be semantically characterized by ranked models that are *rank preserving* with respect to the Z-ranking [7].

In this paper, we explore the field of inference relations involving system P respectively (RM) as limiting characterizations, and extend the work started in [7] by dropping the rather strong requirement of (RM). Instead, we consider more general classes of so-called RCP inductive inference operators, i.e., inductive inference operators satisfying (RC Extension) and (Classic Preservation). For RCP inductive inference operators that satisfy system P (RCP preferential inductive inference operators) we show that these are characterized by *Z-rank refining* preferential models, where *Z-rank refining* is a newly introduced adaption of *rank preserving* to preferential models. The intuition of Z-rank refining is that the preferential model respects and possibly refines the structure on worlds that is induced by Z-ranking functions κ^z_Δ.

While preferential models are more general than TPOs, they are also more complex. Between the class of preferential inference relations and the class of inference relations induced by TPOs there is the class of inductive inference operators induced by strict partial orders (SPOs) on worlds. SPOs on worlds are more expressive than TPOs but less complex than preferential models: e.g., for signatures of size $|\Sigma| = 2$ there are 75 TPOs, 219 SPOs, and 485 (non-equivalent) preferential models on the four Σ-worlds [3–5]. Thus, to fill the gap between TPOs and preferential models we also consider the class of RCP inductive inference operators induced by SPOs on worlds, called RCP *SPO-representable* inductive inference operators. We show that RCP SPO-representable inductive inference operators are characterized by *Z-rank refining* SPOs on worlds. Furthermore, we investigate inference relations induced by SPOs on formulas and show that such inductive inference operators satisfy RCP if they are based on Z-rank refining SPOs on formulas. Thus, our work extends [7] in different directions, in particular by providing characterization theorems for different classes of RCP inductive inference operators. To summarize, the main contributions of this paper are:

- A characterization theorem showing that *RCP* preferential inductive inference operators can be characterized by *Z-rank refining* preferential models.
- Introduction of the class of *SPO-representable* inductive inference operators, which prove to be central within a map of inductive inference operators.
- A characterization theorem showing that *RCP* SPO-representable inductive inference operators can be characterized by *Z-rank refining* SPOs on formulas.

After recalling preliminaries of conditional logic (Sect. 2) and non-monotonic reasoning (Sect. 3), we introduce RCP preferential and SPO representable inductive inference operators (Sect. 4 and 5) and prove corresponding characterizations in Sect. 6. In Sect. 7, we conclude and point out future work.

2 Conditional Logic

A *(propositional) signature* is a finite set Σ of propositional variables. Assuming an underlying signature Σ, we denote the resulting propositional language by $\mathcal{L}$. Usually, we denote elements of signatures with lowercase letters $a, b, c, \ldots$ and formulas with uppercase letters $A, B, C, \ldots$. We may denote a conjunction $A \wedge B$ by AB and a negation $\neg A$ by $\overline{A}$ for brevity of notation. The set of interpretations over the underlying signature is denoted as Ω. Interpretations are also called *worlds* and Ω is called the *universe*. An interpretation $\omega \in \Omega$ is a *model* of a formula $A \in \mathcal{L}$ if A holds in ω, denoted as $\omega \models A$. The set of models of a formula (over a signature Σ) is denoted as $Mod(A) = \{\omega \in \Omega \mid \omega \vdash A\}$ or short as Ω_A. A formula A *entails* a formula B if $\Omega_A \subseteq \Omega_B$. By slight abuse of notation we sometimes interpret worlds as the corresponding complete conjunction of all elements in the signature in either positive or negated form.

A *conditional* $(B|A)$ connects two formulas A, B and represents the rule "If A then usually B", where A is called the *antecedent* and B the *consequent* of the conditional. The conditional language is denoted as $(\mathcal{L}|\mathcal{L}) = \{(B|A) \mid A, B \in \mathcal{L}\}$. A finite set Δ of conditionals is called a *belief base*.

We use a three-valued semantics of conditionals in this paper [9]: for a world ω a conditional $(B|A)$ is either *verified* by ω if $\omega \models AB$, *falsified* by ω if $\omega \models A\overline{B}$, or *not applicable* to ω if $\omega \models \overline{A}$. Popular models for belief bases are ranking functions (also called ordinal conditional functions, OCFs) [31] and total preorders (TPOs) on Ω [8]. An OCF $\kappa : \Omega \to \mathbb{N}_0 \cup \{\infty\}$ maps worlds to a *rank* such that at least one world has rank 0, i.e., $\kappa^{-1}(0) \neq \emptyset$. The intuition is that worlds with lower ranks are more plausible than worlds with higher ranks; worlds with rank ∞ are considered infeasible. OCFs are lifted to formulas by mapping a formula A to the smallest rank of a model of A, or to ∞ if A has no models. An OCF κ is a model of a conditional $(B|A)$, denoted as $\kappa \models (B|A)$, if $\kappa(AB) < \kappa(A\overline{B})$;

κ is a model of a belief base Δ, denoted as $\kappa \models \Delta$, if it is a model of every conditional in Δ. A belief base Δ is called *consistent* if there exists at least one ranking function κ with $\kappa \models \Delta$ and $\kappa^{-1}(\infty) = \emptyset$, i.e., if there is at least one ranking function modelling Δ that considers all worlds feasible. This notion of consistency is used in many approaches, e.g., in [14] while in, e.g., [7,13] a more relaxed notion of consistency is used. The latter is characterized precisely by the notion of weak consistency introduced in [20] which is obtained by dropping the condition $\kappa^{-1}(\infty) = \emptyset$, i.e., a belief base Δ is *weakly consistent* if there exists at least one ranking function κ with $\kappa \models \Delta$.

3   Defeasible Entailment

Having the ability to answer conditional questions of the form *does A entail B?* enables an agent to draw appropriate conclusions in different situations. The set of conditional beliefs the agent can draw is formally captured by a binary relation $\mid\!\sim$ on propositional formulas with $A \mid\!\sim B$ representing that A (defeasibly) entails B; this relation is called *inference* or *entailment relation*. As we consider defeasible or non-monotonic entailment, it is possible that there are formulas A, B, C with both $A \mid\!\sim B$ and $AC \not\!\mid\!\sim B$: given more specific information the agent might revoke a conclusion that she drew based on more general information.

There are different sets of properties for inference relations suggested in the literature. A *preferential inference relation* is an inference relation satisfying the following set of postulates called system P [1,25], which is often considered as minimal requirement for inference relations:

(REF)	*Reflexivity*	for all $A \in \mathcal{L}$ it holds that $A \mid\!\sim A$
(LLE)	*Left Logical Equivalence*	$A \equiv B$ and $B \mid\!\sim C$ imply $A \mid\!\sim C$
(RW)	*Right Weakening*	$B \models C$ and $A \mid\!\sim B$ imply $A \mid\!\sim C$
(CM)	*Cautious Monotony*	$A \mid\!\sim B$ and $A \mid\!\sim C$ imply $AB \mid\!\sim C$
(CUT)		$A \mid\!\sim B$ and $AB \mid\!\sim C$ imply $A \mid\!\sim C$
(OR)		$A \mid\!\sim C$ and $B \mid\!\sim C$ imply $(A \vee B) \mid\!\sim C$

Beyond system P, another axiom has been proposed that seems to be desirable in general, and is also satisfied by Rational Closure (or system Z [30]):

(RM)	*Rational Monotony*	$A \mid\!\sim C$ and $A \not\!\mid\!\sim \overline{B}$ imply $(A \wedge B) \mid\!\sim C$

Besides ranking functions, preferential models are another kind of models for conditionals that are useful to represent preferential inference relations.

Definition 1 (preferential model [25]). *Let $\mathcal{M} = (S, l, \prec)$ be a triple consisting of a set S of states, a function $l : S \to \Omega$ mapping states to interpretations, and a strict partial order $\prec$ on S. For $A \in \mathcal{L}$ and $s \in S$ we denote $l(s) \models A$ by $s \models A$; and we define $[\![A]\!]_{\mathcal{M}} = \{s \in S \mid s \models A\}$. We say $\mathcal{M}$ is a preferential model if for any $A \in \mathcal{L}$ and $s \in [\![A]\!]_{\mathcal{M}}$ either s is minimal in $[\![A]\!]_{\mathcal{M}}$ or there is a $t \in [\![A]\!]_{\mathcal{M}}$ such that t is minimal in $[\![A]\!]_{\mathcal{M}}$ and $t \prec s$ (smoothness condition).*

Note that the smoothness condition is automatically satisfied for finite sets of interpretations. As this paper only considers propositional logic with finite signatures, we can ignore this condition. A preferential model $\mathcal{M} = (S, l, \prec)$ induces an inference relation $\vdash_{\mathcal{M}}$ by $A \vdash_{\mathcal{M}} B$ iff $\min(\llbracket A \rrbracket_{\mathcal{M}}, \prec) \subseteq \llbracket B \rrbracket_{\mathcal{M}}$.

One result from [25] states that preferential models characterize preferential entailment relations: ever inference relation $\vdash_{\mathcal{M}}$ induced by a preferential model $\mathcal{M}$ is preferential, and for every preferential inference relation $\vdash$ there is a preferential model $\mathcal{M}$ with $\vdash_{\mathcal{M}} = \vdash$. Two preferential models $\mathcal{M}, \mathcal{N}$ are called *equivalent* if they induce the same inference relation, i.e., if $\vdash_{\mathcal{M}} = \vdash_{\mathcal{N}}$.

Inductive inference is the process of completing a given belief base to an inference relation, formally defined by the concept of inductive inference operators.

Definition 2 (inductive inference operator [22]). *An* inductive inference operator *is a mapping* $C : \Delta \mapsto \vdash_{\Delta}$ *that maps each belief base to an inference relation such that direct inference (DI) and trivial vacuity (TV) are fulfilled, i.e.,*

(DI) if $(B|A) \in \Delta$ *then* $A \vdash_{\Delta} B$, *and*
(TV) if $\Delta = \emptyset$ *and* $A \vdash_{\Delta} B$ *then* $\models B$.

We can define p-entailment [25] as an inductive inference operator.

Definition 3 (p-entailment). *Let* Δ *be a belief base and* A, B *be formulas. A p-entails B with respect to* Δ, *denoted as* $A \vdash_{\Delta}^{p} B$, *if* $A \vdash_{\mathcal{M}} B$ *for every preferential model* $\mathcal{M}$ *of* Δ. *P-entailment is the inductive inference operator mapping each* Δ *to* $\vdash_{\Delta}^{p}$.

In the context of conditional beliefs, a conditional of the form $(\bot|A)$ or an entailment $A \vdash \bot$ expresses a strict belief in the sense that every A-world is considered to be impossible. The following postulate (Classic Preservation) formalizes that an inference relation treats strict beliefs in the same way as p-entailment.

Postulate (Classic Preservation). *An inference relation* $\vdash$ *satisfies (Classic Preservation) [7] w.r.t. a belief base* Δ *if for all* $A \in \mathcal{L}$, $A \vdash \bot$ *iff* $A \vdash_{\Delta}^{p} \bot$.

An inductive inference operator satisfies (Classic Preservation) if every Δ *is mapped to an inference relation satisfying (Classic Preservation) w.r.t.* Δ.

We are now ready to formally define the first two subclasses of inductive inference operators that we will use in this paper (for an overview over all classes of inductive inference operators considered here, see Fig. 1 on page 11).

Definition 4 (preferential inductive inference operator, basic defeasible inductive inference operator). *An inductive inference operator C is called a*

- preferential inductive inference operator *if every inference relation* $\vdash_{\Delta}$ *in the image of C satisfies system P;*
- basic defeasible inductive inference operator, *for short* BD-inductive inference operator, *if every inference relation* $\vdash_{\Delta}$ *in the image of C satisfies system P, rational monotony (RM), and (Classic Preservation).*

The original definition of BD-inductive inference operator is based on the notion of basic defeasible entailment relations [7] (short BD-entailment relations) which satisfy system P and rational monotony (RM) and, additionally, direct inference (DI) and (Classic Preservation) with respect to a belief base Δ.

BD-entailment relations can be characterized in many different ways. For instance, an inference relation $\mathrel{\vdash}_{\Delta}$ is a BD-entailment relation with respect to a belief base Δ iff there is a ranked model of Δ inducing $\mathrel{\vdash}_{\Delta}$, or equivalently iff there is a rank function that is a model of Δ and induces $\mathrel{\vdash}_{\Delta}$ [7, Theorem 1]. BD-entailment relations can also be characterized by ranking functions. The *inference relation* $\mathrel{\vdash}_{\kappa}$ *induced by a ranking function* κ is defined by

$$A \mathrel{\vdash}_{\kappa} B \quad \text{iff} \quad \kappa(A) = \infty \text{ or } \kappa(AB) < \kappa(A\overline{B}). \tag{1}$$

Note that the condition $\kappa(A) = \infty$ in (1) ensures that system P's axiom (REF) is satisfied for $A \equiv \bot$. Exploiting the relationship between ranked models and ranking functions, it is easy to show that $\mathrel{\vdash}_{\Delta}$ is a BD-entailment relation with respect to Δ iff there is a ranking function κ with $\kappa \models \Delta$ that induces $\mathrel{\vdash}_{\Delta}$.

System Z is a BD-inductive inference operator that is defined based on the Z-partition of a belief base [30]. Here we use an extended version of system Z that also covers belief bases that are only weakly consistent and that was shown to be equivalent to *rational closure* [27] in [15].

Definition 5 ((extended) Z-partition). *A conditional $(B|A)$ is tolerated by* $\Delta = \{(B_i|A_i) \mid i = 1, \ldots, n\}$ *if there exists a world* $\omega \in \Omega$ *such that* ω *verifies* $(B|A)$ *and* ω *does not falsify any conditional in* Δ, *i.e.,* $\omega \models AB$ *and* $\omega \models \bigwedge_{i=1}^{n}(\overline{A_i} \vee B_i)$. *The (extended) Z-partition* $EZP(\Delta) = (\Delta^0, \ldots, \Delta^k, \Delta^\infty)$ *of a belief base* Δ *is the ordered partition of* Δ *that is constructed by letting* Δ^i *be the inclusion maximal subset of* $\bigcup_{j=i}^{n} \Delta^j$ *that is tolerated by* $\bigcup_{j=i}^{n} \Delta^j$ *until* $\Delta^{k+1} = \emptyset$. *The set* Δ^∞ *is the remaining set of conditionals that contains no conditional which is tolerated by* Δ^∞.

It is well-known that the construction of $EZP(\Delta)$ is successful with $\Delta^\infty = \emptyset$ iff Δ is consistent, and because the Δ^i are chosen inclusion-maximal, the Z-partition is unique [30]. Also, it holds that $EZP(\Delta)$ has $\Delta^0 \neq \emptyset$ iff $\top \mathrel{\not\vdash}_{\Delta}^{p} \bot$.

Definition 6 ((extended) system Z). *Let* Δ *be a belief base with* $EZP(\Delta) = (\Delta^0, \ldots, \Delta^k, \Delta^\infty)$. *If* Δ *satisfies* $\top \mathrel{\vdash}_{\Delta}^{p} \bot$, *then let* $A \mathrel{\vdash}_{\Delta}^{z} B$ *for any* $A, B \in \mathcal{L}$.

Otherwise, the (extended) Z-ranking function κ_{Δ}^{z} *is defined as follows. For a world* $\omega \in \Omega$, *if one of the conditionals in* Δ^∞ *is applicable to* ω *define* $\kappa_{\Delta}^{z}(\omega) = \infty$. *Otherwise, let* Δ^j *be the last partition in* $EZP(\Delta)$ *that contains a conditional falsified by* ω. *Then let* $\kappa_{\Delta}^{z}(\omega) = j + 1$. *If* ω *does not falsify any conditional in* Δ, *then let* $\kappa_{\Delta}^{z}(\omega) = 0$. *(Extended) system Z maps* Δ *to the inference relation* $\mathrel{\vdash}_{\Delta}^{z}$ *induced by* κ_{Δ}^{z}.

For consistent belief bases the extended system Z coincides with system Z as defined in [14, 30].

4   Extending Rational Closure

In [7], the authors explored BD-inductive inference relations that extend the rational closure (i.e., the system Z inference relation) of a belief base. This property of a belief base is formally defined by (RC Extension).

Postulate (RC Extension). *An inference relation $\mathrel{\vdash\mkern-9mu\sim}$ satisfies (RC Extension) [7] with respect to a belief base Δ if for all $A, B \in \mathcal{L}$, $A \mathrel{\vdash\mkern-9mu\sim}^z_\Delta B$ implies $A \mathrel{\vdash\mkern-9mu\sim} B$.*

An inductive inference operator satisfies (RC Extension) if every Δ is mapped to an inference relation satisfying (RC Extension) with respect to Δ.

This formulation of (RC Extension) uses the fact that rational closure and system Z coincide. In [7] the BD-inductive inference relations satisfying (RC Extension) are called *rational defeasible entailment relations* and are characterized in different ways, among them the following: an inference relation is a rational defeasible entailment relation (with respect to a belief base Δ) iff it is induced by some base rank preserving ranked model of Δ, or equivalently iff it is induced by some base rank preserving rank function that is a model of Δ. In this paper we apply (RC Extension) to inductive inference operators in general.

Definition 7 (RCP inductive inference operator). *An RCP inductive inference operator is an inductive inference operator satisfying (RC Extension) and (Classic Preservation).*

As BD-inductive inference operators satisfy (Classic Preservation) by definition, BD-inductive inference operators satisfying (RC Extension) are RCP.

Similar to the results in [7] we can provide model-based characterizations of RCP inductive inference operators. For preferential inference operators we identify the following property which we will show to characterize RCP preferential inductive inference operators.

Definition 8 (Z-rank refining). *A preferential model $\mathcal{M} = (S, l, \prec)$ is called Z-rank refining (with respect to a belief base Δ) if $l(S) = \{\omega \in \Omega \mid \kappa^z_\Delta(\omega) < \infty\}$ and additionally $\kappa^z_\Delta(\omega) < \kappa^z_\Delta(\omega')$ implies that for every $s' \in l^{-1}(\omega')$ there is an $s \in l^{-1}(\omega)$ s.t. $s \prec s'$ for any $\omega, \omega' \in \Omega$. A preferential model for Δ with $\top \mathrel{\vdash\mkern-9mu\sim}^p_\Delta \bot$ is said to be Z-rank refining if and only if $S = \emptyset$.*

Building on the result from [25] that preferential inference relations are characterized by preferential models, we can show that RCP preferential inductive inference operators are characterized by Z-rank refining preferential models. For every inference relation satisfying (Classic Preservation) and (RC Extension) there is a Z-rank refining preferential model inducing this inference relation. In the other direction, every Z-rank refining preferential model induces an inference relation satisfying (Classic Preservation) and (RC Extension).

Theorem 1. (1.) *If $\mathrel{\vdash\mkern-9mu\sim}$ is a preferential inference relation satisfying (Classic Preservation) and (RC Extension) w.r.t. a belief base Δ, then every preferential model inducing $\mathrel{\vdash\mkern-9mu\sim}$ is Z-rank refining with respect to Δ.*

(2.) If a preferential model $\mathcal{M} = (S, l, \prec)$ is Z-rank refining with respect to a belief base Δ, then the inference relation $\mathrel{\vert\!\sim}_{\mathcal{M}}$ induced by it satisfies (Classic Preservation) and (RC Extension) with respect to Δ.

Proof (sketch). **Ad (1.):** Let $\mathcal{M} = (S, l, \prec)$ be a preferential model inducing $\mathrel{\vert\!\sim}$. First use (Classic Preservation) to show that $\kappa_{\Delta}^{z}(\omega) = \infty$ iff $\omega \mathrel{\vert\!\sim} \bot$. Therefore, $l(S) = \{\omega \in \Omega \mid \kappa_{\Delta}^{z}(\omega) < \infty\}$. Then use (RC Extension) to show that $\kappa_{\Delta}^{z}(\omega) < \kappa_{\Delta}^{z}(\omega')$ implies that for every $s' \in l^{-1}(\omega')$ there is an $s \in l^{-1}(\omega)$ with $s \prec s'$.

Ad (2.): For $F \in \mathcal{L}$, we show that $F \mathrel{\vert\!\sim}_{\Delta}^{p} \bot$ iff $[\![F]\!]_{\mathcal{M}} = \emptyset$ which is equivalent to $F \mathrel{\vert\!\sim}_{\mathcal{M}} \bot$. Therefore, $\mathrel{\vert\!\sim}_{\mathcal{M}}$ satisfies (Classic Preservation). For $A, B \in \mathcal{L}$ with $A \mathrel{\vert\!\sim}_{\Delta}^{z} B$, let $s_A \in \min([\![A]\!]_{\mathcal{M}}, \prec)$. We show that every $\omega_A \in l^{-1}(s_A)$ satisfies $\omega_A \models B$ by contradiction. Hence, $\mathrel{\vert\!\sim}_{\mathcal{M}}$ satisfies (RC Extension).   □

Theorem 2 (RCP preferential). *An inductive inference operator is RCP iff it maps each belief base Δ to an inference relation that is induced by a preferential model that is Z-rank refining with respect to Δ.*

The proof of Theorem 2 is a direct consequence of Theorem 1.

5   Entailment Based on SPOs

Preferential models are not the only structures that can model belief bases and entail an inference relation. Sometimes it is sufficient to consider a strict partial order (SPO), i.e., a transitive, antisymmetric, and irreflexive binary relation, on the possible worlds to induce an inference relation. For example system W [24] is an inductive inference operator defined based on SPOs on worlds.

Note that we allow an SPO $\prec$ to order only a subset Ω^{feas} of all worlds in Ω. This supports expressing beliefs of the form $\overline{A} \mathrel{\vert\!\sim} \bot$, i.e., A strictly holds, by choosing $\Omega^{feas} \subseteq Mod(A)$. The worlds in Ω^{feas} are called *feasible*.

Definition 9 (SPO on worlds). *An SPO on worlds (over Σ) is an SPO $\prec$ on a set $\Omega^{feas} \subseteq \Omega$ of feasible worlds, denoted as $feas(\prec) = \Omega^{feas}$. A full SPO on worlds $\prec$ is an SPO on worlds s.t. $feas(\prec) = \Omega$, i.e., if all possible worlds are feasible. An SPO on worlds $\prec$ on Ω models a conditional $(B|A)$, denoted as $\prec \models (B|A)$, if for any feasible $\omega' \in \Omega_{A\overline{B}}$ there is a feasible $\omega \in \Omega_{AB}$ with $\omega \prec \omega'$. We say $\prec$ models a belief base Δ if $\prec$ models every conditional in Δ, in this case $\prec$ is also called an SPO model of Δ.*

The *inference relation* $\mathrel{\vert\!\sim}_{\prec}$ induced by an SPO on worlds $\prec$ is defined by

$$A \mathrel{\vert\!\sim}_{\prec} B \quad \text{iff} \quad \prec \models (B|A). \tag{2}$$

The SPOs on worlds are defined on a subset of Ω to allow modelling belief bases that force some worlds to be completely implausible. If we consider only consistent belief bases we only need full SPOs on worlds.

Example 1. Let $\Sigma = \{a, b\}$ and let $\prec$ be the full SPO on worlds defined by $\prec = \{(\overline{a}b, a\overline{b}), (a\overline{b}, ab), (\overline{a}b, \overline{a}b), (\overline{a}b, ab), (\overline{a}b, ab)\}$. Then we have, e.g., $\top \mathrel{\vert\!\sim}_{\prec} \overline{a}$ and $a \vee b \mathrel{\vert\!\sim}_{\prec} \overline{a} \vee \overline{b}$.

Equation (2) enables us to introduce a new class of inductive inference operators.

Definition 10 (SPO-representable inductive inference operator). *An inference relation $\vdash$ is SPO-representable if there is an SPO on worlds inducing $\vdash$. An SPO-representable inductive inference operator is an inductive inference operator $C : \Delta \mapsto \vdash_\Delta$ s.t. every $\vdash_\Delta$ in the image of C is an SPO-representable inference relation.*

An SPO-representable inductive inference operator can alternatively be written as a mapping $C^{spo} : \Delta \mapsto \prec_\Delta$ that maps each belief base to an SPO on worlds $\prec_\Delta$. The induced inference relation $\vdash_\Delta$ is obtained from $\prec_\Delta$ as in (2). Then (DI) and (TV) amount to $\prec_\Delta \models \Delta$ and $\prec_\emptyset = \emptyset$. For every SPO on worlds, there is an equivalent preferential model on the respective subset of worlds.

Proposition 1. *Let $\prec$ be an SPO on worlds with $\Omega^{feas} = feas(\prec)$. The preferential model $\mathcal{M} = (\Omega^{feas}, \mathrm{id}, \prec)$ induces the inference relation $\vdash_\prec$.*

Therefore, every SPO-representable inference relation is a preferential inference relation and every SPO-representable inductive inference operator is a preferential inductive inference operator. This implies that every SPO-representable inductive inference operator C extends p-entailment, i.e., for a belief base Δ, and formulas A, B we have that $A \vdash^p_\Delta B$ implies $A \vdash^C_\Delta B$. Because not every preferential inference relation is induced by an SPO on worlds, the inference relations induced by SPOs on worlds form a proper subclass of all preferential inference relations. BD-inference relations are a subclass of SPO-representable inference relations. The reverse is not true in general because there are SPO-representable inference relations that are not BD-inference relations.

Proposition 2. *Every basic defeasible inference relation is an SPO-representable inference relation.*

Now we present a property that characterizes SPO-representable inference relations. The following Proposition 3 is based on the representation result for *injective preferential models* in [10, Theorem 4.13] and the observation that injective preferential models are equivalent to strict partial orders on worlds for our setting of a finite logical language. An injective preferential model is a preferential model $\mathcal{M} = (S, l, \prec)$ such that l is injective.

Proposition 3. *An inference relation $\vdash$ is SPO-representable iff it is preferential and satisfies that, for any $A, B, D \in \mathcal{L}$ and $C_\vdash (X) := \{Y \in \mathcal{L} \mid X \vdash Y\}$,*

$$A \vee B \vdash D \quad implies \quad (C_\vdash (A) \cup C_\vdash (B)) \models D. \tag{3}$$

Proof (sketch). First we show that $\vdash$ is SPO-representable iff it is representable by an injective model. Then we use that $\vdash$ is representable by an injective model iff it is a preferential inference relation satisfying (3) [10, Theorem 4.13]. □

Requiring the function l in a preferential model $(S, l, \prec)$ to be injective means that for any world there is at most one state mapping to it. This allows to identify each state $s \in S$ with the world $l(s) \in l(S)$. By considering the set of feasible worlds $\Omega^{feas} = l(S)$ we can see that an injective preferential model is equivalent to an SPO on the set $\Omega^{feas} \subseteq \Omega$.

To obtain a model of a belief base, instead of considering an SPO on worlds we could also consider an SPO on formulas. To support expression of strict beliefs, the SPO may order only a subset $\mathcal{L}^{feas}$ of all formulas in $\mathcal{L}$; the formulas in $\mathcal{L}^{feas}$ are called feasible. If $\neg A \notin \mathcal{L}^{feas}$ then it is strictly believed that A holds.

Definition 11 (SPO on formulas). *An SPO on formulas is an SPO $<$ on a set $\mathcal{L}^{feas}$ of feasible formulas that satisfies*

- *syntax independence, i.e., for $A, B, C, D \in \mathcal{L}$ with $A \equiv C$ and $B \equiv D$ it holds that $A < B$ iff $C < D$ and $A \in \mathcal{L}^{feas}$ iff $C \in \mathcal{L}^{feas}$*
- *plausibility preservation, i.e., for $E, F \in \mathcal{L}$ with $E \models F$ it holds that $E \not< F$ and $E \in \mathcal{L}^{feas}$ implies $F \in \mathcal{L}^{feas}$.*

The set of feasible formulas of an SPO on formulas is denoted as $feas(<) = \mathcal{L}^{feas}$. An SPO on formulas $<$ is a full SPO on formulas if $feas(<) = \mathcal{L} \setminus \{\bot\}$, i.e., if all consistent formulas are feasible. An SPO on formulas $<$ models a conditional $(B|A)$, denoted as $< \models (B|A)$, if $A\overline{B}$ is not feasible or if $AB < A\overline{B}$. We say $<$ models a belief base Δ if $<$ models every conditional in Δ.

Thus, to rule out models that are too obscure, an SPO on formulas requires that equivalent formulas have the same position in the SPO and that the logical entailments of a formula F may not be considered less plausible than F itself.

Analogously to $\vDash_{\prec}$ in Eq. (2), the inference relation $\vDash_{<}$ induced by a SPO on formulas $<$ is defined by

$$A \vDash_{<} B \quad \text{iff} \quad < \models (B|A). \tag{4}$$

Example 2. Let $<$ be the full SPO on formulas defined by $A < B$ if $A \equiv a\overline{b} \vee \overline{a}b$ and $B \equiv ab$. We have $a \vee b \vDash_{<} \overline{a} \vee \overline{b}$.

An SPO on worlds induces an equivalent SPO on formulas.

Definition 12 (SPO on formulas induced by an SPO on worlds). *Let $\prec$ be an SPO on worlds. The SPO on formulas $\prec_{\mathcal{L}}$ over $\mathcal{L}^{feas} = \{A \in \mathcal{L} \mid \Omega_A \cap \Omega^{feas} \neq \emptyset\}$ induced by $\prec$ is defined by, for any formulas $A, B \in \mathcal{L}^{feas}$,*

$$A \prec_{\mathcal{L}} B \quad \text{iff} \quad \text{for every feasible } \omega' \in \Omega_B \tag{5}$$
$$\text{there is a feasible } \omega \in \Omega_A \text{ such that } \omega \prec \omega'.$$

Proposition 4. *Let $\prec$ be an SPO on worlds and $\prec_{\mathcal{L}}$ the SPO on formulas induced by $\prec$. For $A, B \in \mathcal{L}$ we have that $\prec \models (B|A)$ iff $\prec_{\mathcal{L}} \models (B|A)$.*

With Proposition 4 and (2) and (4) we can see that $A \vDash_{\prec} B$ iff $A \vDash_{\prec_{\mathcal{L}}} B$. This entails that for every SPO on worlds $\prec$ there is an SPO on formulas $<$ that induces the same inference relation. Lemma 1 states that the reverse is not true.

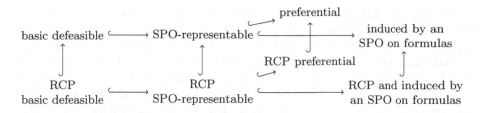

Fig. 1. Relationships among the classes of inductive inference operators. $C_1 \hookrightarrow C_2$ indicates that C_1 is a proper subclass of C_2.

Lemma 1. *There are SPOs on formulas $<$ that induce an inference relation that is not SPO-representable.*

To summarize the relations between the class of SPO-representable inductive inference operators and other classes of inference operators: every BD-inductive inference operator is SPO-representable. Every SPO-representable inductive inference operator is preferential and can be induced by an SPO on formulas. The reverse of none of these statements is true. An overview over these classes of inference operators is given in Fig. 1.

6   RCP SPO-Representable Inference

After introducing SPO-representable inductive inference operators in the previous section, in this section we consider RCP SPO-representable inductive inference operators, i.e. SPO-representable inductive inference operators that satisfy (RC Extension) and (Classic Preservation).

Just as Z-rank refining preferential models characterize RCP preferential inductive inference operators, we can characterize RCP SPO representable inductive inference operators with Z-rank refining SPOs on worlds.

Definition 13 (Z-rank refining). *An SPO on worlds $\prec$ with $\Omega^{feas} = feas(\prec)$ is called Z-rank refining (with respect to a belief base Δ) if $\Omega^{feas} = \{\omega \in \Omega \mid \kappa_\Delta^z(\omega) < \infty\}$ and additionally $\kappa_\Delta^z(\omega) < \kappa_\Delta^z(\omega')$ implies $\omega \prec \omega'$ for any $\omega, \omega' \in \Omega^{feas}$. For Δ with $\top \hspace{0.3em}\vdash\!\!\!\!\!\sim_\Delta^p \bot$ the only Z-rank refining SPO on worlds is defined to be $\prec$ with $feas(\prec) = \emptyset$.*

While Definition 13 for Z-rank refining SPOs on worlds deviates from Definition 8 for Z-rank refining preferential models, they both formulate the same idea that the structure on worlds induced by the Z-ranking function κ_Δ^z is preserved and possibly refined.

Theorem 3. *(1.) Let $\hspace{0.3em}\vdash\!\!\!\!\!\sim$ be an inference relation. If $\hspace{0.3em}\vdash\!\!\!\!\!\sim$ satisfies (Classic Preservation) and (RC Extension) w.r.t. Δ then every SPO on worlds inducing $\hspace{0.3em}\vdash\!\!\!\!\!\sim$ is Z-rank refining w.r.t. Δ.   (2.) Let $\prec$ be an SPO on worlds and $\hspace{0.3em}\vdash\!\!\!\!\!\sim_\prec$ be the inference relation induced by it. If $\prec$ is Z-rank refining then $\hspace{0.3em}\vdash\!\!\!\!\!\sim_\prec$ satisfies (Classic Preservation) and (RC Extension).*

Proof (sketch). **Ad (1.):** Let $\prec$ be an SPO on worlds inducing $\mathrel{\vert\!\sim}$. Use (Classic Preservation) to show that $\kappa_\Delta^z(\omega) = \infty$ iff $\omega \notin feas(\prec)$, i.e., $\Omega^{feas} = \{\omega \in \Omega \mid \kappa_\Delta^z(\omega) < \infty\}$. Use (RC Extension) to show that $\kappa^z(\omega) < \kappa^z(\omega)$ entails $\omega \prec \omega'$.

Ad (2.): Let $\prec$ be Z-rank refining. First we show that for $F \in \mathcal{L}$ we have $F \mathrel{\vert\!\sim}_\Delta^p \bot$ iff $\Omega_F \cap feas(\prec) = \emptyset$ which is equivalent to $F \mathrel{\vert\!\sim}_\prec \bot$. Therefore, $\mathrel{\vert\!\sim}_\prec$ satisfies (Classic Preservation). Then, for any $A, B \in \mathcal{L}$ with $A \mathrel{\vert\!\sim}_\Delta^z B$ let $\omega \in \arg\min_{\omega \in \Omega_{AB}} \kappa_\Delta^z(\omega)$. Then we show that $\omega \prec \omega'$ for any feasible $\omega' \in \Omega_{A\overline{B}}$. Therefore, $A \mathrel{\vert\!\sim}_\prec B$. Hence, $\mathrel{\vert\!\sim}_\prec$ satisfies (RC Extension). $\qquad\square$

From Theorem 3 we obtain the following characterization of RCP SPO-representable inductive inference operators.

Theorem 4 (RCP SPO-representable). *Let $C : \Delta \mapsto \mathrel{\vert\!\sim}_\Delta^C$ be an SPO-representable inductive inference operator. C is RCP iff for each belief base Δ the inference relation $C(\Delta)$ is induced by a SPO on worlds that is Z-rank refining.*

As every SPO-representable inductive inference operator is preferential we have that every RCP SPO-representable inductive inference operator is an RCP preferential inductive inference operator. Similarly, every RCP BD-inductive inference operator is an RCP SPO-representable inductive inference operator. The reverse of these statements is not true, as observed by the Lemmas 2 and 3.

Lemma 2. *There are RCP preferential inductive inference operators that are not RCP SPO-representable inductive inference operators.*

Lemma 3. *There are RCP SPO-representable inductive inference operators that are not RCP basic defeasible inductive inference operators.*

Finally, we can extend the notion of Z-rank refining to SPOs on formulas, and we can show its connection to RCP inductive inference operators that map each belief base to an inference relation induced by some SPO on formulas.

Definition 14 (Z-rank refining). *An SPO on formulas $<$ with $\mathcal{L}^{feas} = feas(<)$ is called Z-rank refining (with respect to a belief base Δ) if $\mathcal{L}^{feas} = \{A \in \mathcal{L} \mid \kappa_\Delta^z(A) < \infty\}$ and additionally $\kappa_\Delta^z(A) < \kappa_\Delta^z(B)$ implies $A < B$ for any $A, B \in \mathcal{L}^{feas}$. For Δ with $\top \mathrel{\vert\!\sim}_\Delta^p \bot$ the only Z-rank refining SPO on formulas is defined to be $<$ with $feas(<) = \emptyset$.*

While Definition 13 describes preserving the structure on worlds induced by Z-ranking functions, Definition 14 describes preserving the structure on formulas that is induced by Z-ranking functions. Note that Z-rank refining SPOs on worlds always induce Z-rank refining SPOs on formulas.

Theorem 5. *Let $\prec$ be an SPO on worlds, $\prec_\mathcal{L}$ be the SPO on formulas induced by $\prec$, and Δ a belief base. Then $\prec$ is Z-rank refining iff $\prec_\mathcal{L}$ is Z-rank refining (each with respect to Δ).*

Theorem 5 implies that every RCP SPO-representable inference operator maps belief bases to inference relations that can be obtained from Z-rank refining SPOs on formulas. The reverse is not true in general: not every Z-rank refining SPO on formulas induces an SPO-representable inference relation.

Lemma 4. *Let $C : \Delta \mapsto \mathop{\vdash}\limits^{C}_{\Delta}$ be an RCP SPO-representable inductive inference operator. For every Δ there is a Z-rank refining SPO on formulas inducing $\mathop{\vdash}\limits^{C}_{\Delta}$.*

We can show that Z-rank refining SPOs on formulas induce inference relations satisfying (Classic Preservation) and (RC Extension). In the other direction we have that if an SPOs on formulas induces an inference relation that satisfies (Classic Preservation) and (RC Extension) then it must be Z-rank refining, provided that $E \not\equiv F$, $E \models F$ implies $F \prec E$. This additional assumption is necessary as information about entailments, as provided by (RC Extension), can only be translated to information about formulas with disjoint sets of models. The additional assumption allows connecting formulas that share models.

Theorem 6. *Let $\prec$ be an SPO on formulas, $\mathop{\vdash}\limits_{\prec}$ be the inference relation induced by $\prec$, and let Δ be a belief base.*

1. *If $\prec$ is Z-rank refining with respect to Δ then $\mathop{\vdash}\limits_{\prec}$ satisfies (Classic Preservation) and (RC Extension) with respect to Δ.*
2. *If additionally $\prec$ satisfies that for $E, F \in \mathcal{L}$, $E \not\equiv F$ it holds that $E \models F$ implies $F \prec E$, then $\mathop{\vdash}\limits_{\prec}$ satisfying (Classic Preservation) and (RC Extension) with respect to Δ implies that $\prec$ is Z-rank refining with respect to Δ.*

Proof (sketch). Ad (1.): For $F \in \mathcal{L}$ we have $F \mathop{\vdash}\limits_{\prec} \bot$ iff $\kappa^{z}_{\Delta}(F) = \infty$ because $\prec$ is Z-rank refining. This yields (Classic Preservation). For $A, B \in \mathcal{L}$ with $A \mathop{\vdash}\limits^{z}_{\Delta} B$ we have $AB \prec A\overline{B}$ because $\prec$ is Z-rank refining. Therefore, (RC Extension) holds.

Ad (2.): For $F \in \mathcal{L}$ we can show that $\kappa^{z}_{\Delta}(F) = \infty$ iff $F \notin feas(\prec)$ using (Classic Preservation). For $A, B \in feas(\prec)$ with $\kappa^{z}_{\Delta}(A) < \kappa^{z}_{\Delta}(B)$ we get $A \vee B \mathop{\vdash}\limits_{\prec} \overline{B}$ with (RC Extension). This yields $A\overline{B} \prec B$ and thus $A \prec B$. $\square$

Theorem 6 shows that an inductive inference operator mapping a belief base to an inference relation induced by a Z-rank refining SPO on formulas is RCP.

Rational BD-inductive inference operators like lexicographic inference [28] are examples of RCP SPO-representable inductive inference operators because they are based on TPOs and every TPO is also an SPO. System W [23,24] is an example of an RCP SPO-representable inductive inference operator that is not a BD-inductive inference operator. In addition to the Z-partition of a belief base Δ, system W also takes into account the structural information which conditionals are falsified. The definition of system W is based on a binary relation called a *preferred structure on worlds* $<^{w}_{\Delta}$ over Ω that is assigned to every belief base Δ. Here, we use an extended version of system W introduced in [20] that also covers weakly consistent belief bases.

Definition 15 (ξ^{j}, ξ, **preferred structure** $<^{w}_{\Delta}$ **on worlds** [20,24]). *Let Δ be a belief base with the Z-partition $EZP(\Delta) = (\Delta^{0}, \dots, \Delta^{k}, \Delta^{\infty})$. For $j = 0, \dots, k, \infty$ the functions ξ^{j} and ξ are the functions mapping worlds to the set of falsified conditionals in Δ^{j} given by $\xi^{j}(\omega) = \{(B_{i}|A_{i}) \in \Delta^{j} \mid \omega \models A_{i}\overline{B_{i}}\}$. Let $\Omega^{feas} = \Omega \setminus \{\omega \mid \xi^{\infty}(\omega) \neq \emptyset\}$. The preferred structure on worlds is the relation $<^{w}_{\Delta} \subseteq \Omega^{feas} \times \Omega^{feas}$ defined by*

$$\omega <^w_\Delta \omega' \ \textit{iff there exists an } m \in \{0,\dots,k\} \ \textit{such that}$$
$$\xi^i(\omega) = \xi^i(\omega') \quad \forall i \in \{m+1,\dots,k\} \ \textit{and}$$
$$\xi^m(\omega) \subsetneq \xi^m(\omega').$$

Thus, $\omega <^w_\Delta \omega'$ iff ω falsifies strictly fewer conditionals than ω' in the partition with the biggest index m where the conditionals falsified by ω and ω' differ.

Definition 16 (system W, $\mathrel|\!\sim^w_\Delta$ [20,24]). *Let Δ be a belief base and A, B be formulas. Then B is a system W inference from A, denoted $A \mathrel|\!\sim^w_\Delta B$, if for every $\omega' \in \Omega_{A\overline{B}}$ there is a feasible $\omega \in \Omega_{AB}$ such that $\omega <^w_\Delta \omega'$.*

Multipreference-closure (short *MP-closure*) is an inference method developed for the description logic with typicality $\mathcal{ALC} + \mathbf{T_R}$ introduced in [11]. MP-closure was adapted for reasoning with conditionals based on propositional logic in [12]. While system W and MP-closure were developed independently in different contexts and defined using distinct approaches, it is interesting that it has been shown that MP-closure for propositional conditionals and system W coincide both for consistent belief bases [16] and weakly consistent belief bases [20].

Since $<^w_\Delta$ is a strict partial order [24, Lemma 3], system W, and thus also MP-closure, is an SPO representable inductive inference operator $C^w : \Delta \mapsto \mathrel|\!\sim_{<^w_\Delta}$. System W fulfils the postulates of system P, strictly extends both system Z [30] and also c-inference [2], and enjoys further desirable properties like avoiding the drowning problem, [6,24] fully complying with syntax splitting [17,18,20, 22], and also with conditional syntax splitting [21]; a map of approximations of system W by other inductive inference operators is given in [19]. Because system W satisfies (RC Extension) and (Classic Preservation), it is an RCP SPO-representable inductive inference operator.

7 Conclusions and Future Work

In this paper we investigated RCP inductive inference operators, i.e., inductive inference operators satisfying (RC Extension) and (Classic Preservation). Doing this we focused on SPO-representable inference relations, i.e., inference relations that can be obtained from SPOs on worlds. We showed that this class of inductive inference operators is a subclass of preferential inductive inference operators and a superclass of basic defeasible inductive inference operators. We provided characterization theorems for RCP preferential and RCP SPO-representable inductive inference operators using the newly introduced property 'Z-rank refining' for preferential models and SPOs on worlds. Future work includes to further investigate instances of rational inductive inference operators; especially the characterization of such inference operators by their properties will be of interest.

Acknowledgements. This work was supported by the Deutsche Forschungsgemeinschaft (DFG, German Research Foundation), grant BE 1700/10-1 awarded to Christoph Beierle as part of the priority program "Intentional Forgetting in Organizations" (SPP 1921). Jonas Haldimann was supported by this grant.

References

1. Adams, E.W.: The Logic of Conditionals: An Application of Probability to Deductive Logic. SYLI, Springer, Dordrecht (1975). https://doi.org/10.1007/978-94-015-7622-2
2. Beierle, C., Eichhorn, C., Kern-Isberner, G., Kutsch, S.: Properties and interrelationships of skeptical, weakly skeptical, and credulous inference induced by classes of minimal models. Artif. Intell. **297**, 103489 (2021)
3. Beierle, C., Haldimann, J.: Normal forms of conditional belief bases respecting inductive inference. In: Keshtkar, F., Franklin, M. (eds.) Proceedings of the Thirty-Fifth International Florida Artificial Intelligence Research Society Conference (FLAIRS), Hutchinson Island, Florida, USA, 15–18 May 2022 (2022)
4. Beierle, C., Haldimann, J., Kutsch, S.: A complete map of conditional knowledge bases in different normal forms and their induced system P inference relations over small signatures. In: Bell, E., Keshtkar, F. (eds.) Proceedings of the Thirty-Fourth International Florida Artificial Intelligence Research Society Conference, North Miami Beach, Florida, USA, 17–19 May 2021 (2021). https://doi.org/10.32473/flairs.v34i1.128467
5. Beierle, C., Haldimann, J., Schwarzer, L.: Observational equivalence of conditional belief bases. In: Chun, S.A., Franklin, M. (eds.) Proceedings of the Thirty-Sixth International Florida Artificial Intelligence Research Society Conference (2023)
6. Benferhat, S., Cayrol, C., Dubois, D., Lang, J., Prade, H.: Inconsistency management and prioritized syntax-based entailment. In: Proceedings of the IJCAI 1993, San Francisco, CA, USA, vol. 1, pp. 640–647. Morgan Kaufmann Publishers (1993)
7. Casini, G., Meyer, T., Varzinczak, I.: Taking defeasible entailment beyond rational closure. In: Calimeri, F., Leone, N., Manna, M. (eds.) JELIA 2019. LNCS (LNAI), vol. 11468, pp. 182–197. Springer, Cham (2019). https://doi.org/10.1007/978-3-030-19570-0_12
8. Darwiche, A., Pearl, J.: On the logic of iterated belief revision. Artif. Intell. **89**(1–2), 1–29 (1997)
9. de Finetti, B.: La prévision, ses lois logiques et ses sources subjectives. Ann. Inst. H. Poincaré **7**(1), 1–68 (1937). Engl. transl. Theory of Probability (1974)
10. Freund, M.: Injective models and disjunctive relations. J. Log. Comput. **3**(3), 231–247 (1993). https://doi.org/10.1093/logcom/3.3.231
11. Giordano, L., Gliozzi, V.: Reasoning about multiple aspects in DLs: semantics and closure construction. CoRR abs/1801.07161 (2018). http://arxiv.org/abs/1801.07161
12. Giordano, L., Gliozzi, V.: A reconstruction of multipreference closure. Artif. Intell. **290**, 103398 (2021). https://doi.org/10.1016/j.artint.2020.103398
13. Giordano, L., Gliozzi, V., Olivetti, N., Pozzato, G.L.: Semantic characterization of rational closure: from propositional logic to description logics. Artif. Intell. **226**, 1–33 (2015). https://doi.org/10.1016/j.artint.2015.05.001
14. Goldszmidt, M., Pearl, J.: Qualitative probabilities for default reasoning, belief revision, and causal modeling. Artif. Intell. **84**, 57–112 (1996)
15. Goldszmidt, M., Pearl, J.: On the relation between rational closure and system-Z. In: Proceedings of the Third International Workshop on Nonmonotonic Reasoning, 31 May–3 June, pp. 130–140 (1990)
16. Haldimann, J., Beierle, C.: Characterizing multipreference closure with system W. In: de Saint-Cyr, F.D., Öztürk-Escoffier, M., Potyka, N. (eds.) SUM 2022. LNCS, vol. 13562, pp. 79–91. Springer, Cham (2022). https://doi.org/10.1007/978-3-031-18843-5_6

17. Haldimann, J., Beierle, C.: Inference with system W satisfies syntax splitting. In: Kern-Isberner, G., Lakemeyer, G., Meyer, T. (eds.) Proceedings of the 19th International Conference on Principles of Knowledge Representation and Reasoning, KR 2022, Haifa, Israel, 31 July–5 August 2022, pp. 405–409 (2022)
18. Haldimann, J., Beierle, C.: Properties of system W and its relationships to other inductive inference operators. In: Varzinczak, I. (ed.) FoIKS 2022. LNCS, vol. 13388, pp. 206–225. Springer, Cham (2022). https://doi.org/10.1007/978-3-031-11321-5_12
19. Haldimann, J., Beierle, C.: Approximations of system W between C-inference, system Z, and lexicographic inference. In: Bouraoui, Z., Jabbour, S., Vesic, S. (eds.) ECSQARU 2023. LNCS, Springer, Cham (2023)
20. Haldimann, J., Beierle, C., Kern-Isberner, G., Meyer, T.: Conditionals, infeasible worlds, and reasoning with system W. In: The International FLAIRS Conference Proceedings, vol. 36, no. 1 (2023)
21. Heyninck, J., Kern-Isberner, G., Meyer, T., Haldimann, J.P., Beierle, C.: Conditional syntax splitting for non-monotonic inference operators. In: Williams, B., Chen, Y., Neville, J. (eds.) Proceedings of the 37th AAAI Conference on Artificial Intelligence, vol. 37, pp. 6416–6424 (2023). https://doi.org/10.1609/aaai.v37i5.25789
22. Kern-Isberner, G., Beierle, C., Brewka, G.: Syntax splitting = relevance + independence: new postulates for nonmonotonic reasoning from conditional belief bases. In: Calvanese, D., Erdem, E., Thielscher, M. (eds.) Principles of Knowledge Representation and Reasoning: Proceedings of the 17th International Conference, KR 2020, pp. 560–571. IJCAI Organization (2020)
23. Komo, C., Beierle, C.: Nonmonotonic inferences with qualitative conditionals based on preferred structures on worlds. In: Schmid, U., Klügl, F., Wolter, D. (eds.) KI 2020. LNCS (LNAI), vol. 12325, pp. 102–115. Springer, Cham (2020). https://doi.org/10.1007/978-3-030-58285-2_8
24. Komo, C., Beierle, C.: Nonmonotonic reasoning from conditional knowledge bases with system W. Ann. Math. Artif. Intell. **90**(1), 107–144 (2022)
25. Kraus, S., Lehmann, D., Magidor, M.: Nonmonotonic reasoning, preferential models and cumulative logics. Artif. Intell. **44**(1–2), 167–207 (1990)
26. Lehmann, D., Magidor, M.: What does a conditional knowledge base entail? Artif. Intell. **55**, 1–60 (1992)
27. Lehmann, D.: What does a conditional knowledge base entail? In: Brachman, R.J., Levesque, H.J., Reiter, R. (eds.) Proceedings of the 1st International Conference on Principles of Knowledge Representation and Reasoning (KR 1989), Toronto, Canada, 15–18 May 1989, pp. 212–222. Morgan Kaufmann (1989)
28. Lehmann, D.: Another perspective on default reasoning. Ann. Math. Artif. Intell. **15**(1), 61–82 (1995). https://doi.org/10.1007/BF01535841
29. Makinson, D., Gärdenfors, P.: Relations between the logic of theory change and nonmonotonic logic. In: Fuhrmann, A., Morreau, M. (eds.) The Logic of Theory Change. LNCS, vol. 465, pp. 183–205. Springer, Heidelberg (1991). https://doi.org/10.1007/BFb0018421
30. Pearl, J.: System Z: a natural ordering of defaults with tractable applications to nonmonotonic reasoning. In: Parikh, R. (ed.) Proceedings of the 3rd Conference on Theoretical Aspects of Reasoning About Knowledge (TARK 1990), San Francisco, CA, USA, pp. 121–135. Morgan Kaufmann Publishers Inc. (1990)
31. Spohn, W.: Ordinal conditional functions: a dynamic theory of epistemic states. In: Harper, W., Skyrms, B. (eds.) Causation in Decision, Belief Change, and Statistics, II, pp. 105–134. Kluwer Academic Publishers (1988)

Planning

Planning

DELPHIC: Practical DEL Planning via Possibilities

Alessandro Burigana[1]([✉])(iD), Paolo Felli[2](iD), and Marco Montali[1](iD)

[1] Free University of Bozen-Bolzano, Bolzano, Italy
{burigana,montali}@inf.unibz.it
[2] University of Bologna, Bologna, Italy
paolo.felli@unibo.it

Abstract. Dynamic Epistemic Logic (DEL) provides a framework for epistemic planning that is capable of representing non-deterministic actions, partial observability, higher-order knowledge and both factual and epistemic change. The high expressivity of DEL challenges existing epistemic planners, which typically can handle only restricted fragments of the whole framework. The goal of this work is to push the envelop of practical DEL planning, ultimately aiming for epistemic planners to be able to deal with the full range of features offered by DEL. Towards this goal, we question the traditional semantics of DEL, defined in terms on Kripke models. In particular, we propose an equivalent semantics defined using, as main building block, so-called *possibilities*: non well-founded objects representing both factual properties of the world, and what agents consider to be possible. We call the resulting framework DELPHIC. We argue that DELPHIC indeed provides a more compact representation of epistemic states. To substantiate this claim, we implement both approaches in ASP and we set up an experimental evaluation to compare DELPHIC with the traditional, Kripke-based approach. The evaluation confirms that DELPHIC outperforms the traditional approach in space and time.

1 Introduction

Multiagent Systems are employed in a wide range of settings, where autonomous agents are expected to face dynamic situations and to be able to adapt in order to reach a given goal. In these contexts, it is crucial for agents to be able to reason on their physical environment as well as on the *knowledge* that they have about other agents and the knowledge those possess.

Bolander and Andersen [5] introduced *epistemic planning* as a planning framework based on Dynamic Epistemic Logic (DEL), where *epistemic states* are represented as Kripke models, *event models* are used for representing epistemic actions, and *product updates* define the application of said actions on states. On the one hand, the resulting framework is very expressive, and it allows one to naturally represent non-deterministic actions, partial observability of agents, higher-order knowledge and both factual and epistemic changes. On the other

S. Gaggl et al. (Eds.): JELIA 2023, LNAI 14281, pp. 579–594, 2023.
https://doi.org/10.1007/978-3-031-43619-2_39

hand, decidability of epistemic planning is not guaranteed in general [5]. This has led to a considerable body of research adopting the DEL framework to obtain (un)decidability results for fragments of the epistemic planning problem (see [6] for a detailed exposition), typically by constraining the event models of actions. Nonetheless, even when such restriction are in place, epistemic planners directly employing the Kripke-based semantics of possible worlds face high complexities, hence considerable efforts have been put in studying action languages that are more amenable computationally [4,10,14].

In contrast with the traditional approach in the literature, in this paper we depart from the Kripke-based semantics for DEL and adopt an alternative representation called *possibilities*, first introduced by Gerbrandy and Groeneveld [12]. As we are going to show experimentally, this choice is motivated primarily by practical considerations. In fact, as we expand in Sect. 3, possibilities support a concise representation of factual and epistemic information and yield a light update operator that promises to achieve better performances compared to the traditional Kripke-based semantics. This is due to the fact that possibilities are *non-well-founded objects*, namely objects that have a *circular* representation (see Aczel [1] for an exhaustive introduction on non-well-founded set theory). In fact, due to their non-well-founded nature, possibilities naturally reuse previously calculated information, thus drastically reducing the computational overhead deriving from redundant information. Conceptually, whenever an agent does not update his knowledge upon an action, then the possibilities representing its knowledge are directly reused (see Examples 3 and 6).

This paper presents a novel formalization of epistemic planning based on possibilities. Although these objects have been previously used in place of Kripke models to represent epistemic states [10], previous semantics lacked a general characterization of actions. In this paper, we complement the possibility-based representation of states by formalizing two novel concepts: *eventualities*, representing epistemic actions, and *union update*, providing an update operator based on possibilities and eventualities. The resulting planning framework, called DELPHIC (*DEL-planning with a Possibility-based Homogeneous Information Characterisation*), benefits from the compactness of possibilities and promises to positively impact the performance of planning. This suggests that DELPHIC is a viable but also convenient alternative to Kripke-based representations. We support this claim by implementing both frameworks in ASP and by setting up an experimental evaluation of the two implementations aimed at comparing the traditional Kripke semantics for DEL and DELPHIC. The comparison confirms that DELPHIC outperforms the traditional approach in terms of both space and time. We point out that time and space gains are obtained in the *average case*, as there exist extreme (*worst*) cases where the two semantics produce epistemic states with the same structure. This follows by the fact that the DELPHIC framework is semantically equivalent to the Kripke-based one (Theorem 1). As a result, the plan existence problems of both frameworks have the same complexity.

Partial evidences of the advantages of adopting possibilities were already experimentally witnessed in [10]. However, the planning framework therein corresponds only to a fragment of the DEL framework. Indeed, as mentioned above, an actual possibility-based formalization of actions is there absent, in favour of a direct, ad-hoc encoding of the transition functions of three prototypical types of actions described in the action language $m\mathcal{A}^*$ [4], namely *ontic*, *sensing* and *announcements* actions. As already mentioned, we overcome this limitation by equipping DELPHIC with eventualities, which we relate to DEL event models.

In conclusion, we provide a threefold contribution: *(i)* we introduce DELPHIC as a general DEL planning framework based on possibilities; *(ii)* we formally show that DELPHIC constitutes an alternative but semantically equivalent framework for epistemic planning, compared to the Kripke-based framework; *(iii)* we experimentally show that the underlying model employed by DELPHIC indeed offers promising advantages in performance, in terms of both time and space.

The paper is organised as follows. In Sect. 2, we recall the necessary preliminaries on DEL; in Sect. 3, we formally define DELPHIC and we show its equivalence with the Kripke-based framework and in Sect. 4 we show our experimental evaluation.

2   Preliminaries

In this section we provide the required preliminaries on DEL [9] by illustrating its fundamental components: epistemic models in Sect. 2.1, event models in Sect. 2.2, and the product update in Sect. 2.3. Although the notion of possibility is part of the preliminaries [12], we defer these to Sect. 3, as this allows us to illustrate the components of DELPHIC by following a similar structure.

2.1   Epistemic Models

Let us fix a countable set $\mathcal{P}$ of propositional atoms and a finite set $\mathcal{AG} = \{1, \ldots, n\}$ of agents. The language $\mathcal{L}_{\mathcal{P},\mathcal{AG}}$ of *multi-agent epistemic logic on* $\mathcal{P}$ *and* $\mathcal{AG}$ *with common knowledge/belief* is defined by the following BNF:

$$\varphi ::= \top \mid p \mid \neg\varphi \mid \varphi \wedge \varphi \mid \Box_i\varphi,$$

where $p \in \mathcal{P}$, $i \in \mathcal{AG}$, and $G \subseteq \mathcal{AG}$. Formulae of the form $\Box_i\varphi$ are read as "agent i knows/believes that φ". We define the dual operators $\Diamond_i$ as usual. The semantics of DEL formulae is based on the concept of *possible worlds*. *Epistemic models* are defined as *Kripke models* [15] and they contain both factual information about possible worlds and epistemic information, i.e., which worlds are considered possible by each agent.

Definition 1 (Kripke Model). *A Kripke model for* $\mathcal{L}_{\mathcal{P},\mathcal{AG}}$ *is a triple* $M = (W, R, V)$ *where:*

- $W \neq \varnothing$ *is the set of possible worlds.*
- $R : \mathcal{AG} \to 2^{W \times W}$ *assigns to each agent i an accessibility relation $R(i)$.*
- $V : \mathcal{P} \to 2^W$ *assigns to each atom a set of worlds.*

We abbreviate the relations $R(i)$ with R_i and use the infix notation wR_iv in place of $(w,v) \in R_i$. An *epistemic state* in DEL is defined as a *multi-pointed Kripke model (MPKM)*, *i.e.*, as a pair (M, W_d), where $W_d \subseteq W$ is a non-empty set of designated worlds.

Example 1 (Coin in the Box). Agents a and b are in a room where a box is placed. Inside the box there is a coin. None of the agent knows whether the coin lies heads (h) or tails up $(\neg h)$. Both agents know the perspective of the other. This is represented by the following MPKM (where the circled bullet represent the designated world).

$$a,b \;\circlearrowright\; \overset{a,b}{\underset{w_1:h \;\bullet\!\!\longleftarrow\!\!\longrightarrow\!\!\bullet\; w_2:\neg h}{}} \;\circlearrowleft\; a,b$$

Definition 2 (Truth in Kripke Models). *Let $M = (W, R, V)$ be a Kripke model, $w \in W$, $i \in \mathcal{AG}$, $p \in \mathcal{P}$ and $\varphi, \psi \in \mathcal{L}^C_{\mathcal{P},\mathcal{AG}}$ be two formulae. Then,*

$$
\begin{aligned}
(M, w) &\models p & &\text{iff}\;\; w \in V(p) \\
(M, w) &\models \neg\varphi & &\text{iff}\;\; (M, w) \not\models \varphi \\
(M, w) &\models \varphi \wedge \psi & &\text{iff}\;\; (M, w) \models \varphi \text{ and } (M, w) \models \psi \\
(M, w) &\models \Box_i\varphi & &\text{iff}\;\; \forall v \text{ if } wR_iv \text{ then } (M, v) \models \varphi
\end{aligned}
$$

Moreover, $(M, W_d) \models \varphi$ iff $(M, v) \models \varphi$, for all $v \in W_d$.

We recall the notion of bisimulation for MPKMs [7].

Definition 3 (Bisimulation). *A bisimulation between MPKMs $((W, R, V), W_d)$ and $((W', R', V'), W'_d)$ is a binary relation $B \subseteq W \times W'$ satisfying:*

- *Atoms: if $(w, w') \in B$, then for all $p \in \mathcal{P}$, $w \in V(p)$ iff $w' \in V'(p)$.*
- *Forth: if $(w, w') \in B$ and wR_iv, then there exists $v' \in W'$ such that $w'R'_iv'$ and $(v, v') \in B$.*
- *Back: if $(w, w') \in B$ and $w'R'_iv'$, then there exists $v \in W$ such that wR_iv and $(v, v') \in B$.*
- *Designated: if $w \in W_d$, then there exists a $w' \in W'_d$ such that $(w, w') \in B$, and vice versa.*

We say that two MPKMs s and s' are *bisimilar* (denoted by $s \leftrightarrow s'$) when there exists a bisimulation between them. It is well known that bisimilar states satisfy the same formulae, hence encode the same information.

2.2 Event Models

In DEL, actions are modeled by *event models* [3,8], which capture action preconditions and effects from the perspectives of multiple agents at once. Intuitively, *events* represent possible outcomes of the action, accessibility relations describe which events are considered possible by agents, preconditions capture the applicability of events, and postconditions specify how events modify worlds.

Definition 4 (Event Model). *An* event model *for* $\mathcal{L}_{\mathcal{P},\mathcal{AG}}$ *is a quadruple* $\mathcal{E} = (E, Q, pre, post)$ *where:*

- $E \neq \varnothing$ *is a finite set of events.*
- $Q : \mathcal{AG} \to 2^{E \times E}$ *assigns to each agent* i *an accessibility relation* $Q(i)$.
- $pre : E \to \mathcal{L}_{\mathcal{P},\mathcal{AG}}$ *assigns to each event a precondition.*
- $post : E \to (\mathcal{P} \to \mathcal{L}_{\mathcal{P},\mathcal{AG}})$ *assigns to each event a postcondition for each atom.*

We abbreviate $Q(i)$ with Q_i and use the infix notation eQ_if in place of $(e, f) \in Q_i$. An *epistemic action*[1] in DEL is defined as a *multi-pointed event model (MPEM)*, i.e., as a pair $(\mathcal{E}, E_d)$, where $E_d \subseteq E$ is a non-empty set of designated events. An action is *purely epistemic* if, for each $e \in E$, $post(e)$ is the identity function *id*; otherwise it is *ontic*.

Example 2. Suppose that, in the scenario of Example 1, agent a peeks inside the box to learn how the coin has been placed while b is distracted. Two events are needed to represent this situation: e_1 (the designated event) represents the perspective of agent a, who is looking inside the box; e_2 represents the fact that agent b does not know what a is doing. In the figure below, a pair $\langle pre(e), post(e) \rangle$ represents the precondition and the postconditions of event e.

We give a notion of bisimulation for actions, which will be needed to show an important relationship with our model.

Definition 5 (Bisimulation for actions). *A bisimulation between MPEMs* $((E, Q, pre, post), E_d)$ *and* $((E', Q', pre', post'), E_d')$ *is a binary relation* $B \subseteq E \times E'$ *satisfying:*

- *Formulae: if* $(e, e') \in B$, *then* $pre(e) = pre'(e')$ *and, for all* $p \in \mathcal{P}$, $post(e)(p) = post'(e')(p)$.
- *Forth: if* $(e, e') \in B$ *and* eQ_if, *then there exists* $f' \in W'$ *such that* $e'Q_i'f'$ *and* $(f, f') \in B$.
- *Back: if* $(e, e') \in B$ *and* $e'Q_i'f'$, *then there exists* $f \in W$ *such that* eQ_if *and* $(f, f') \in B$.
- *Designated: if* $e \in E_d$, *then there exists a* $e' \in E_d'$ *such that* $(e, e') \in B$, *and vice versa.*

We say that two MPEMs α and α' are *bisimilar* (denoted by $\alpha \underline{\leftrightarrow} \alpha'$) when there exists a bisimulation between them.

2.3   Product Update

The product update of a MPKM with a MPEM results into a new MPKM that contains the updated information of agents. Here we adapt the definition of van Ditmarsch and Kooi [8] to deal with multi-pointed models. An MPEM $(\mathcal{E}, E_d)$

---

[1] We use "epistemic action" with a broad meaning, simply referring to actions in epistemic planning, irrespective of their effects.

is *applicable* in (M, W_d) if for each world $w \in W_d$ there exists an event $e \in E_d$ such that $(M, w) \models pre(e)$.

Definition 6 (Product Update). *The* product update *of a MPKM* (M, W_d) *with an applicable MPEM* $(\mathcal{E}, E_d)$*, with* $M = (W, R, V)$ *and* $\mathcal{E} = (E, Q, pre,$ $post)$*, is the MPKM* $(M, W_d) \otimes (\mathcal{E}, E_d) = ((W', R', V'), W'_d)$*, where:*

$$
\begin{aligned}
W' &= \{(w, e) \in W \times E \mid (M, w) \models pre(e)\} \\
R'_i &= \{((w, e), (v, f)) \in W' \times W' \mid wR_iv \text{ and } eQ_if\} \\
V'(p) &= \{(w, e) \in W' \mid (M, w) \models post(e)(p)\} \\
W'_d &= \{(w, e) \in W' \mid w \in W_d \text{ and } e \in E_d\}
\end{aligned}
$$

Example 3. The product update of the MPKM of Example 1 with the MPEM of Example 2 is the MPKM below, where $v_3 = (w_1, e_1)$, $v_1 = (w_1, e_2)$ and $v_2 = (w_2, e_2)$. Now, agent a knows that the coin lies heads up, while b did not change its perspective. Importantly, notice that w_1 (resp., w_2) and v_1 (resp., v_2) encode the same information, but they are *distinct* objects.

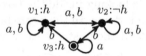

2.4 Plan Existence Problem

We recall the notions of planning task and plan existence problem in DEL [2].

Definition 7 (DEL-Planning Task). *A DEL-planning task is a triple* $T = (s_0, \mathcal{A}, \varphi_g)$*, where: (i)* s_0 *is the initial MPKM; (ii)* $\mathcal{A}$ *is a finite set of MPEMs; (iii)* $\varphi_g \in \mathcal{L}^C_{\mathcal{P}, \mathcal{AG}}$ *is a goal formula.*

Definition 8. *A* solution *(or* plan*) to a DEL-planning task* $(s_0, \mathcal{A}, \varphi_g)$ *is a finite sequence* $\alpha_1, \ldots, \alpha_\ell$ *of actions of* $\mathcal{A}$ *such that:*

1. $s_0 \otimes \alpha_1 \otimes \cdots \otimes \alpha_\ell \models \varphi_g$*, and*
2. *For each* $1 \leq k \leq \ell$*,* α_k *is applicable in* $s_0 \otimes \alpha_1 \otimes \cdots \otimes \alpha_{k-1}$*.*

Definition 9 (Plan Existence Problem). *Let* $n \geq 1$ *and* $\mathcal{T}$ *be a class of DEL-planning tasks.* PLANEX$(\mathcal{T}, n)$ *is the following decision problem: "Given a DEL-planning task* $T \in \mathcal{T}$*, where* $|\mathcal{AG}| = n$*, does* T *have a solution?"*

3 DELPHIC

We introduce the DELPHIC framework for epistemic planning. DELPHIC is built around the concept of *possibility* (Definition 10), first introduced by Gerbrandy and Groeneveld to represent epistemic states. We develop a novel representation for epistemic actions inspired by possibilities, which we term *eventualities* (Definition 15). Then, we present a novel characterisation of update, called *union update* (Definition 19), based on possibilities and eventualities.

3.1 Possibilities

Possibilities are tightly related to *non-well-founded sets*, *i.e.*, sets that may give rise to infinite *descents* $X_1 \in X_2 \in \ldots$ (*e.g.*, $\Omega = \{\Omega\}$ is a n.w.f. set). We refer the reader to Aczel [1] for a detailed account on non-well-founded set theory.

Definition 10 (Possibility). *A* possibility u *for* $\mathcal{L}_{\mathcal{P},\mathcal{AG}}$ *is a function that assigns to each atom* $p \in \mathcal{P}$ *a truth value* $u(p) \in \{0,1\}$ *and to each agent* $i \in \mathcal{AG}$ *a set of possibilities* $u(i)$, *called* information state.

Definition 11 (Possibility Spectrum). *A* possibility spectrum *is a finite set of possibilities* $U = \{u_1, \ldots u_k\}$ *that we call* designated possibilities.

Possibility spectrums represent epistemic states in DELPHIC and are able to represent the same information as MPKMs. Intuitively, each possibility u represent a possible world and the components $u(p)$ and $u(i)$ correspond to the valuation function and the accessibility relations of the world, respectively. Finally, the possibilities in a possibility spectrum represent the designated worlds. We formalize this intuition in Proposition 1.

Definition 12 (Truth in Possibilities). *Let* u *be a possibility,* $i \in \mathcal{AG}$, $p \in \mathcal{P}$ *and* $\varphi, \psi \in \mathcal{L}^C_{\mathcal{P},\mathcal{AG}}$ *be two formulae. Then,*

$$
\begin{aligned}
&u \models p &&\textit{iff } u(p) = 1 \\
&u \models \neg\varphi &&\textit{iff } u \not\models \varphi \\
&u \models \varphi \wedge \psi &&\textit{iff } u \models \varphi \textit{ and } u \models \psi \\
&u \models \Box_i\varphi &&\textit{iff } \forall v \textit{ if } v \in u(i) \textit{ then } v \models \varphi
\end{aligned}
$$

Moreover, $U \models \varphi$ *iff* $v \models \varphi$, *for all* $v \in U$.

Comparing Possibilities and Kripke Models. Gerbrandy and Groeneveld [12] show how possibilities and Kripke models correspond to each other. In what follows, we extend this result by analyzing the relation between possibility spectrums and MPKMs. First, following [12], we give some definitions.

Definition 13 (Decoration of Kripke Model). *The* decoration *of a Kripke model* $M = (W, R, V)$ *is a function* δ *that assigns to each world* $w \in W$ *a possibility* $w = \delta(w)$, *such that:*

- $w(p) = 1$ *iff* $w \in V(p)$, *for each* $p \in \mathcal{P}$;
- $w(i) = \{\delta(w') \mid wR_iw'\}$, *for each* $i \in \mathcal{AG}$.

Intuitively, decorations provide a link between Kripke-based representations and their equivalent possibility-based ones: given w in M, the decoration of M returns the possibility that encodes w (its valuation and accessibility relation).

Definition 14 (Picture and Solution). *If* δ *is the decoration of a Kripke model* $M = (W, R, V)$ *and* $W_d \subseteq W$, *then* (M, W_d) *is the* picture *of the possibility spectrum* $W = \{\delta(w) \mid w \in W_d\}$. W *is called* solution *of* (M, W_d).

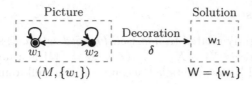

Fig. 1. Relation between picture, decoration and solution.

Namely, the solution of a MPKM (M, W_d) is the possibility spectrum W that contains the possibilities calculated by the decoration function, one for each designated world in W_d. Finally, (M, W_d) is the picture of W. Notice that, in general, *different* MPKMs may share the *same* solution. This observation will be formally stated in Proposition 1. We now give an example (see also Fig. 1).

Example 4. The decoration δ of the MPKM of Example 1 assigns the possibilities $w_1 = \delta(w_1)$, $w_2 = \delta(w_2)$. Since $W_d = \{w_1\}$, we have that $W = \{w_1\}$ is the solution of (M, W_d), where:

- $w_1(h) = 1$ and $w_1(a) = w_1(b) = \{w_1, w_2\}$;
- $w_2(h) = 0$ and $w_2(a) = w_2(b) = \{w_1, w_2\}$.

Notice that, in Example 4, although the possibility w_2 is not explicitly part of W, it is "stored" *within* w_1. That is, we do not lose the information about w_2.

Given the above definitions, we are now ready to formally compare possibility spectrums with MPKMs. The following result generalize the one by Gerbrandy and Groeneveld [12, Proposition 3.4]:

Proposition 1.

1. *Each MPKM has a unique decoration;*
2. *Each possibility spectrum has a MPKM as its picture;*
3. *Two MPKMs have the same solution iff they are bisimilar.*

From item 3 of the above Proposition, we obtain the following remark:

Remark 1. Let $s = (M, W_d)$ be a MPKM and let s' be its bisimulation contraction (*i.e.*, the smallest MPKM that is bisimilar to s). Since s and s' share the same solution W, it follows that possibility spectrums naturally provide a more compact representation w.r.t. MPKMs.

Finally, we show that the solution of a MPKM preserves the truth of formulae.

Proposition 2. *Let (M, W_d) be a MPKM and let W be its solution. Then, for every $\varphi \in \mathcal{L}_{\mathcal{P}, \mathcal{AG}}$, $(M, W_d) \models \varphi$ iff $W \models \varphi$.*

Proof. Let δ be the decoration of (M, W_d). We denote with $eq(\psi)$ the fact that $(M, w) \models \psi$ iff $\delta(w) \models \psi$, for all $w \in W$.

Consider now $w \in W$ and let $w = \delta(w)$. We only need to show that $eq(\varphi)$ holds for any $\varphi \in \mathcal{L}_{\mathcal{P}, \mathcal{AG}}$. The proof is by induction of the structure of φ. For the base case, let $\varphi = p$. By Definition 13, we immediately have that, for any $p \in \mathcal{P}$ and $w \in W$, $(M, w) \models p$ iff $w \models p$ (i.e., $eq(p)$). For the inductive step, we have:

- *Let $\varphi = \neg\psi$. From $eq(\psi)$ we get $eq(\neg\psi)$;*
- *Let $\varphi = \psi_1 \wedge \psi_2$. From $eq(\psi_1)$, $eq(\psi_2)$ we get $eq(\psi_1 \wedge \psi_2)$;*
- *Let $\varphi = \Box_i \psi$ and assume $eq(\psi)$. Then we have:*

$$(M,w) \models \Box_i \psi \overset{\text{Def. 2}}{\Leftrightarrow} \forall v \text{ if } w R_i v, \text{ then } (M,v) \models \psi$$

$$\overset{\text{Def. 13, } eq(\psi)}{\Leftrightarrow} \forall \mathsf{v} \text{ if } \mathsf{v} \in \mathsf{u}_i, \text{ then } \mathsf{v} \models \psi \overset{\text{Def. 12}}{\Leftrightarrow} \mathsf{w} \models \Box_i \psi$$

3.2   Eventualities

In DELPHIC, we introduce the novel concept of *eventuality* to model epistemic actions that is compatible with possibilities. In the remainder of the paper, we fix a fresh propositional atom $pre \notin \mathcal{P}$ and let $\mathcal{P}' = \mathcal{P} \cup \{pre\}$. In the following definition, pre encodes the precondition of an event, while the remaining atoms in $\mathcal{P}$ encode postconditions.

Definition 15 (Eventuality). *An eventuality e for $\mathcal{L}_{\mathcal{P},\mathcal{AG}}$ is a function that assigns to each atom $p' \in \mathcal{P}'$ a formula $\mathsf{e}(p') \in \mathcal{L}_{\mathcal{P},\mathcal{AG}}$ and to each agent $i \in \mathcal{AG}$ a set of eventualities $\mathsf{e}(i)$, called* information state.

Note that an eventuality is essentially a possibility that associates to each atom a formula (instead of a truth value).

Definition 16 (Eventuality Spectrum). *An* eventuality spectrum *is a finite set of eventualities $\mathsf{E} = \{\mathsf{e}_1, \ldots \mathsf{e}_k\}$ that we call* designated eventualities.

Eventuality spectrums represent epistemic actions in DELPHIC. Moreover, we can easily show that they are able to represent the same information as MPEMs. Intuitively, each eventuality e represents an event and the components $\mathsf{e}(pre)$ and $\mathsf{e}(p)$ represent the precondition and the postconditions of the event, respectively. Finally, the eventualities in an eventuality spectrum represent the designated events. We formalize this intuition in Proposition 3.

Comparing Eventualities and Event Models. We now analyze the relationship between eventuality spectrums and MPEMs. We introduce the notions of decoration, picture and solution for event models.

Definition 17 (Decoration of an Event Model). *The* decoration *of an event model $\mathcal{E} = (E, Q, pre, post)$ is a function δ that assigns to each $e \in E$ an eventuality $\mathsf{e} = \delta(e)$, where:*

- *$\mathsf{e}(pre) = pre(e)$ and $\mathsf{e}(p) = post(e)(p)$, for each $p \in \mathcal{P}$;*
- *$\mathsf{e}(i) = \{\delta(e') \mid eQ_i e'\}$, for each $i \in \mathcal{AG}$.*

Definition 18 (Picture and Solution). *If δ is the decoration of an event model $\mathcal{E} = (E, Q, pre, post)$ and $E_d \subseteq E$, then $(\mathcal{E}, E_d)$ is the* picture *of the eventuality spectrum $\mathsf{E} = \{\delta(e) \mid e \in E_d\}$ and E is the* solution *of $(\mathcal{E}, E_d)$.*

The above definitions are the counterparts of the notions of decoration and picture given in Definitions 13 and 14.

Example 5. The decoration δ of the MPEM of Example 2 assigns the eventualities $e_1 = \delta(e_1)$ and $e_2 = \delta(e_2)$. Since $E_d = \{e_1\}$, we have that $E = \{e_1\}$ is the solution of $(\mathcal{E}, E_d)$, where:

- $e_1(pre) = h$; $e_1(h) = h$; $e_1(a) = \{e_1\}$ and $w_1(b) = \{w_2\}$;
- $e_2(pre) = \top$; $e_2(h) = h$; $e_2(a) = w_2(b) = \{e_2\}$.

The following results formally compare eventuality spectrums with MPEMs.

Proposition 3.

- *Each MPEM has a unique decoration;*
- *Each eventuality spectrum has a MPEM as its picture;*
- *Two MPEMs have the same solution iff they are bisimilar.*

Thus, analogously to the case of possibility spectrums, we can see that eventuality spectrums provide us with a compact representation of epistemic actions.

3.3   Union Update

We are now ready to present the novel formulation of update of DELPHIC. We say that an eventuality e is *applicable* in a possibility u iff $u \models e(pre)$. Then, an eventuality spectrum E is *applicable* in a possibility spectrums U iff for each $u \in U$ there exists an applicable eventuality $e \in E$.

Definition 19 (Union Update). *The* union update *of a possibility* u *with an applicable eventuality* e *is the possibility* $u' = u \uplus e$, *where:*
$$u'(p) = 1 \text{ iff } u \models e(p)$$
$$u'(i) = \{v \uplus f \mid v \in u(i), f \in e(i) \text{ and } v \models f(pre)\}$$
The union update *of a possibility spectrum* U *with an applicable eventuality spectrum* E *is the possibility spectrum*
$$U \uplus E = \{u \uplus e \mid u \in U, e \in E \text{ and } u \models e(pre)\}.$$

Example 6. The union update of the possibility spectrum W of Example 4 with the eventuality spectrum of Example 5 is $W \uplus E = \{w_1 \uplus e_1\} = \{v_3\}$, where $v_3(h) = 1$, $v_3(a) = \{v_3\}$ and $v_3(b) = \{w_1 \uplus e_2, w_2 \uplus e_2\} = \{w_1, w_2\}$.

Notice that, since $w_1 \uplus e_2 = w_1$ and $w_2 \uplus e_2 = w_2$ the union update allows to reuse previously calculated information.

Comparing Union Update and Product Update. Intuitively, it is easy to see that the possibility spectrum of Example 6 represents the same information of the MPKM of Example 3. We formalize this intuition with the following lemma, witnessing the equivalence between product and union updates (full proof in the arXiv Appendix).

Lemma 1. *Let* $(\mathcal{E}, E_d)$ *be a MPEM applicable in a MPKM* (M, W_d), *with solutions* E *and* W, *respectively. Then the possibility spectrum* $W' = W \uplus E$ *is the solution of* $(M', W_d') = (M, W_d) \otimes (\mathcal{E}, E_d)$.

3.4   Plan Existence Problem in DELPHIC

We conclude this section by giving the definitions of planning task and plan existence problem in DELPHIC.

Definition 20 (DELPHIC-Planning Task). *A* DELPHIC-*planning task is a triple* $T = (W_0, \Sigma, \varphi_g)$, *where: (i)* W_0 *is an initial possibility spectrum; (ii)* Σ *is a finite set of eventuality spectrums; (iii)* $\varphi_g \in \mathcal{L}^C_{\mathcal{P}, \mathcal{AG}}$ *is a goal formula.*

Definition 21. *A* solution *(or* plan*) to a* DELPHIC-*planning task* (W_0, Σ, φ_g) *is a finite sequence* $E_1, \dots, E_\ell$ *of actions of* Σ *such that:*

1. $W_0 \uplus E_1 \uplus \dots \uplus E_\ell \models \varphi_g$, *and*
2. *For each* $1 \leq k \leq \ell$, E_k *is applicable in* $W_0 \uplus E_1 \uplus \dots \uplus E_{k-1}$.

Definition 22 (Plan Existence Problem). *Let* $n \geq 1$ *and* $\mathcal{T}$ *be a class of* DELPHIC-*planning tasks.* PLANEX$(\mathcal{T}, n)$ *is the following decision problem: "Given a* DELPHIC-*planning task* $T \in \mathcal{T}$, *where* $|\mathcal{AG}| = n$, *does* T *have a solution?"*

From Lemma 1, we immediately get the following result:

Theorem 1. *Let* $T = (s_0, \mathcal{A}, \varphi_g)$ *be a DEL-planning task and let* T $= (W_0, \Sigma, \varphi_g)$ *be a* DELPHIC-*planning task such that* W_0 *is the solution of* s_0 *and* Σ *is the set of solutions of* $\mathcal{A}$. *Then,* $\alpha_1, \dots, \alpha_\ell$ *is a plan for* PLANEX(T, n) *iff* $E_1, \dots, E_\ell$ *is a plan for* PLANEX(T, n), *where* E_i *is the solution of* α_i, *for each* $1 \leq i \leq \ell$.

4   Experimental Evaluation

In this section, we describe our experimental evaluation of the Answer Set Programming (ASP) encodings of DELPHIC and of the traditional Kripke semantics for DEL. Due to space constraints, we provide a brief overview of the encodings[2] (the full presentation can be found in the arXiv Appendix).

The aim of the evaluation is to compare the semantics of DELPHIC and the traditional Kripke-based one in terms of both time and space. We do so by testing the encodings on epistemic planning benchmarks collected from the literature[3] (*e.g., Collaboration and Communication, Grapevine* and *Selective Communication*). Time and space performances are respectively evaluated on the total solving time (given in seconds) and the grounding size (*i.e.,* the number of ground ASP atoms) provided by the ASP-solver *clingo* output statistics. We now describe the encodings (Sect. 4.1) and discuss the obtained results (Sect. 4.2).

---

[2] The full code and documentation of the ASP encodings are available at https://github.com/a-burigana/delphic_asp.

[3] Due to space limits, the description of the benchmarks is delegated to the arXiv Appendix. All benchmarks are available at https://github.com/a-burigana/delphic_asp.

4.1 ASP Encodings

Since our goal is to achieve a fair comparison the two semantics, we implemented a baseline ASP encoding for both of them. Although optimizations for both encoding are possible, the baseline implementations are sufficient to show our claim. Towards the goal of a fair and transparent comparison, we opted for a declarative language such as ASP (notice that, as our goal is simply to compare the two baselines, the choice of an alternative declarative language would make little difference). In fact, while imperative approaches would render the comparison less clear, as one would need to delve into opaque implementation details, ASP allows to write the code that is transparent and easy to analyze. In fact, the two ASP encodings are very similar, since the representation of DELPHIC objects (possibility/eventuality spectrums) and DEL objects (MPKMs/MPEMs) closely mirror each other. The only difference is in the two update operators (*i.e.*, union update and product update). This homogeneity is instrumental to obtain a fair experimental comparison of the two encodings.

We now briefly describe our encodings, assuming that the reader is familiar with the basics concepts of ASP. The two encodings were developed by following the formal definitions of DELPHIC and DEL objects (possibility/eventuality spectrums and MPKMs/MPEMs) and update operators (union and product update) introduced in the previous sections. To increase the efficiency of the solving and grounding phases, the two encodings make use of the *multi-shot* solving approach provided by the ASP-solver *clingo*, which allows for a fine-grained control over grounding and solving of ASP programs. Specifically, this approach allows one to divide an ASP encoding into sub-programs, then handling grounding and solving of these sub-programs separately. In particular, this technique is useful to implement *incremental solving*, which, at each time step, allows to extend the ASP program in order to look for solutions of increasing size. Intuitively, every step mimics a Breadth-First Search over the planning state space: at each time step t, if a solution is not found (*i.e.*, there is no plan of length t that satisfies the goal), the ASP program is expanded to look for a longer plan. For a detailed introduction on multi-shot ASP, we refer the reader to [11,13].

Finally, to visually witness the compactness that possibility spectrums provide w.r.t. MPKMs (see Remark 1), we exploited the Python API offered by *clingo* to implement a graphical representation of the epistemic states visited by the planner. This provides an immediate way of concretely compare the size of output of the two encodings on a given domain instance. Due to space reasons, we report an example of graphical comparison in the arXiv Appendix.

4.2 Results

We ran our test on a 1.4 GHz Quad-Core Intel Core i5 machine with 8 GB of memory and with a macOS 12.6 operating system and using *clingo* version 5.6.2 with timeout (t.o.) of 10 min. The results are shown in Fig. 2. Space and time results are expressed in number of ASP atoms and in seconds, respectively. The comparison clearly shows that the DELPHIC encoding outperforms the one based

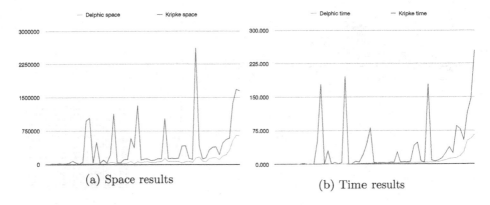

Fig. 2. Results of the evaluation of the DELPHIC and Kripke encodings.

on the traditional Kripke semantics both in terms of space and time. As shown in Fig. 2.a, the number of ASP atoms produced by the DELPHIC encoding is smaller than the ones produced by the Kripke-based ones. The "spikes" witnessed in the latter case are found in presence of instances with longer solutions. This indicates that DELPHIC scales much better in terms of plan length than the traditional Kripke-semantics. In turn, this is positively reflected by the time results graph. In fact, observing space and time results together, we can see how the growth of the size of the epistemic states negatively affects the planning process in terms of time performances. This concretely shows that possibilities can be exploited to achieve more efficient planning tools, thus allowing epistemic planners to be able to deal with the full range of features offered by DEL.

We now analyze the results in detail. The central factor that contributes to the performance gains of DELPHIC is the fact that possibilities allow for a more efficient use of space during the computation of a solution. Specifically, this efficiency results from two key aspects. First, as shown in Remark 1, possibility spectrums are able to represent epistemic information in a more compact way. Working with compact objects contributes significantly to reducing the size of epistemic states after sequences of updates. Second, as shown in Example 6, possibilities naturally allow to reuse previously calculated information (*i.e.,* other possibilities that were calculated in previous states). We give a more concrete example of this property in Fig. 3, that shows a sequence of epistemic states (surrounded by rectangles) from a generalization of the Coin in the Box domain of Example 1. We clearly see how the possibilities w_0 and w_1 are *reused* in the epistemic states s_1, s_2, s_3 and s_4. The space efficiency provided by DELPHIC is clearly witnessed in Fig. 2.a. In presence of instances with longer solutions, DELPHIC outperforms the Kripke-based representation, as the latter requires a considerable amount of space to compute a solution (*i.e.,* the spikes of the graph).

The space efficiency of DELPHIC is directly reflected on time performances. Indeed, in Fig. 2.b are shown the same peaks in correspondence of instances with longer solutions. As a result, we can conclude that the DELPHIC framework

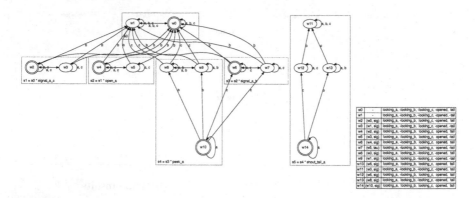

Fig. 3. Reuse of previously calculated information in DELPHIC. This figure was obtained by running the terminal command `python delphic.py -i exp/CB/instance__ pl_5.lp --print` (see https://github.com/a-burigana/delphic_asp for the complete documentation).

allows for a more scalable implementation both in terms of space and time performances. Finally, we point out that the analyzed performance gains are obtained in the *average case*, as there exist extreme (*worst*) cases where the two semantics produce epistemic states with the same structure. In fact, we recall that the DELPHIC framework is semantically equivalent to the Kripke-based one (Theorem 1). Thus, we can conclude that DELPHIC provides a practical and usable framework for DEL planning that can be exploited to tackle a wide range of concrete epistemic planning scenarios.

We close this section by noting that a similar, but less general result, was obtained by Fabiano et al. [10], where a possibility-based semantics is compared to the traditional Kripke-based one on a fragment of DEL called $m\mathcal{A}^*$ [4], that allows three kinds of actions, *i.e.*, *ontic*, *sensing* and *announcement* actions. Since DELPHIC is equivalent to the full DEL framework (see Theorem 1), our comparison indeed provides a generalization of the claim made by Fabiano et al.

5   Conclusions

We have introduced a novel epistemic planning framework, called DELPHIC, based on the formal notion of possibility, in place of the more traditional Kripke-based DEL representation. We have formally shown that these two frameworks are semantically equivalent. Possibilities provide a more compact representation of epistemic states, in particular by reusing common information across states. To show the benefits of possibilities, we have implemented DELPHIC and the Kripke-based approach in ASP, performing a comparative experimental evaluation with known benchmark domains. The results show that DELPHIC indeed outperforms the Kripke-based approach both in terms of space and time performances, and is thus a good candidate for practical DEL planning.

In the future, we plan to exploit the performance gains provided by the DELPHIC semantics in more competitive implementations based on C++. An interesting avenue of work is to deepen our analysis of possibility-based succinctness on fragments of DEL, where only a set of specific types of actions are allowed (*e.g.*, the language $m\mathcal{A}^*$ [4] and the framework by Kominis and Geffner [14]).

Acknowledgements. This research has been partially supported by the Italian Ministry of University and Research (MUR) under PRIN project PINPOINT Prot. 2020FNEB27, and by the Free University of Bozen-Bolzano with the ADAPTERS project.

References

1. Aczel, P.: Non-well-founded sets, CSLI lecture notes series, vol. 14. CSLI (1988)
2. Aucher, G., Bolander, T.: Undecidability in epistemic planning. In: Rossi, F. (ed.) IJCAI 2013, Proceedings of the 23rd International Joint Conference on Artificial Intelligence, Beijing, China, 3–9 August 2013, pp. 27–33. IJCAI/AAAI (2013)
3. Baltag, A., Moss, L.S., Solecki, S.: The logic of public announcements and common knowledge and private suspicions. In: Gilboa, I. (ed.) Proceedings of the 7th Conference on Theoretical Aspects of Rationality and Knowledge (TARK-98), Evanston, IL, USA, 22–24 July 1998, pp. 43–56. Morgan Kaufmann (1998)
4. Baral, C., Gelfond, G., Pontelli, E., Son, T.C.: An action language for multi-agent domains: foundations. CoRR abs/1511.01960 (2015)
5. Bolander, T., Andersen, M.B.: Epistemic planning for single and multi-agent systems. J. Appl. Non Class. Log. **21**(1), 9–34 (2011)
6. Bolander, T., Charrier, T., Pinchinat, S., Schwarzentruber, F.: Del-based epistemic planning: decidability and complexity. Artif. Intell. **287**, 103304 (2020)
7. Bolander, T., Dissing, L., Herrmann, N.: DEL-based epistemic planning for human-robot collaboration: theory and implementation. In: Proceedings of the 18th International Conference on Principles of Knowledge Representation and Reasoning, pp. 120–129 (11 2021)
8. van Ditmarsch, H., Kooi, B.: Semantic results for ontic and epistemic change, pp. 87–117. Texts in Logic and Games 3, Amsterdam University Press (2008)
9. van Ditmarsch, H.P., van der Hoek, W., Kooi, B.P.: Dynamic Epistemic Logic, vol. 337. Springer, Dordrecht, Netherlands (2007). https://doi.org/10.1007/978-1-4020-5839-4
10. Fabiano, F., Burigana, A., Dovier, A., Pontelli, E.: EFP 2.0: a multi-agent epistemic solver with multiple e-state representations. In: Beck, J.C., Buffet, O., Hoffmann, J., Karpas, E., Sohrabi, S. (eds.) Proceedings of the Thirtieth International Conference on Automated Planning and Scheduling, Nancy, France, 26–30 October 2020, pp. 101–109. AAAI Press (2020)
11. Gebser, M., Kaminski, R., Kaufmann, B., Schaub, T.: Multi-shot ASP solving with clingo. Theory Pract. Log. Program. **19**(1), 27–82 (2019)
12. Gerbrandy, J., Groeneveld, W.: Reasoning about information change. J. Log. Lang. Inf. **6**(2), 147–169 (1997)
13. Kaminski, R., Romero, J., Schaub, T., Wanko, P.: How to build your own asp-based system?! Theory Pract. Log. Program. **23**(1), 299–361 (2023)

14. Kominis, F., Geffner, H.: Beliefs in multiagent planning: from one agent to many. In: Brafman, R.I., Domshlak, C., Haslum, P., Zilberstein, S. (eds.) Proceedings of the Twenty-Fifth International Conference on Automated Planning and Scheduling, ICAPS 2015, Jerusalem, Israel, 7–11 June 2015, pp. 147–155. AAAI Press (2015)
15. Kripke, S.A.: Semantical considerations on modal logic. Acta Philos. Fenn. **16**(1963), 83–94 (1963)

Enhancing Temporal Planning
by Sequential Macro-Actions

Marco De Bortoli[1]([✉]), Lukáš Chrpa[2], Martin Gebser[1,3],
and Gerald Steinbauer-Wagner[1]

[1] Graz University of Technology, Graz, Austria
mbortoli@ist.tugraz.at
[2] Czech Technical University in Prague, Prague, Czechia
[3] University of Klagenfurt, Klagenfurt, Austria

Abstract. Temporal planning is an extension of classical planning
involving concurrent execution of actions and alignment with temporal constraints. Unfortunately, the performance of temporal planning
engines tends to sharply deteriorate when the number of agents and
objects in a domain gets large. A possible remedy is to use macro-actions
that are well-studied in the context of classical planning. In temporal planning settings, however, introducing macro-actions is significantly
more challenging when the concurrent execution of actions and shared
use of resources, provided the compliance to temporal constraints, should
not be suppressed entirely. Our work contributes a general concept of
sequential temporal macro-actions that guarantees the applicability of
obtained plans, i.e., the sequence of original actions encapsulated by a
macro-action is always executable. We apply our approach to several
temporal planners and domains, stemming from the International Planning Competition and RoboCup Logistics League. Our experiments yield
improvements in terms of obtained satisficing plans as well as plan quality for the majority of tested planners and domains.

1 Introduction

Temporal planning is a framework dealing with concurrent actions and timing
requirements, providing an intuitive syntax for representing planning domains,
such as PDDL 2.1 [15], together with off-the-shelf planners, e.g., Optic [2], to
generate plans. As an extension of classical planning, temporal planning offers
support for durative actions, their concurrent execution, and the management of
temporal constraints. Logistics domains are prominent examples in which such
timing information matters, e.g., for planning transport and delivery, cargo ship-
ment, shuttle services, or just-in-time production, to mention some application
areas. However, with larger numbers of tasks and/or resources to operate and
synchronize, the performance of (temporal) planning engines tends to sharply
deteriorate, which limits their usability for practical problem solving.

As a possible remedy for the scalability issue, in this paper, we provide a general concept of sequential temporal macro-actions (Sect. 2), i.e., macros encapsulating sequences of durative actions, where preconditions, invariants, and effects

S. Gaggl et al. (Eds.): JELIA 2023, LNAI 14281, pp. 595–604, 2023.
https://doi.org/10.1007/978-3-031-43619-2_40

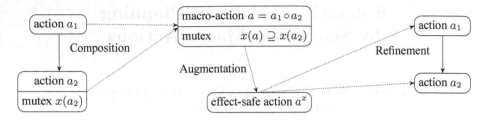

Fig. 1. Outline of the composition and refinement of macro-actions, augmented with mutex atoms for sound temporal planning.

are assembled in a fine-grained way to enable concurrent execution when it does not compromise the macro-action applicability. We evaluate our approach using state-of-the-art planners on domains from the International Planning Competition as well as the RoboCup Logistics League (Sect. 3), obtaining improvements in coverage and in some cases also plan quality. Finally, we discuss related work (Sect. 4) and provide conclusions along with directions for future work (Sect. 5). An extended version of this paper is available online [10].

2 Sequential Macro-Actions

In contrast to classical planning, where actions are viewed as instantaneous events and modeling their sequential execution by a macro-action boils down to accumulating preconditions and effects independently of other actions, concurrent actions must be taken into account for temporal planning, which makes it non-trivial to guarantee the applicability of plans with macro-actions. These considerations lead us to the question how a sequence of durative actions can be turned into a sequential macro to be used for temporal planning (in place of its constituent actions), so that the resulting plan guarantees the sequential applicability of the original actions but does not suppress other concurrent actions unnecessarily. Adhering to these design objectives, the principal steps of our construction of macro-actions are outlined in Fig. 1. In this paper, these steps are presented through a running example. Definitions of *Composition*, *Augmentation* and *Refinement*, together with the related theorems and proofs, can be found in the extended version of the paper [10].

We use the following notation: a durative *action* a is defined by a *duration* $dur(a) \in \mathbb{R}^+$, the sets $pre^{\vdash}(a)$, $pre^{\dashv}(a)$, and $pre^{\dashv}(a)$ of atoms specifying *preconditions* that must hold at the start, as invariants during, or at the end of the action a, respectively, as well as the sets $eff^{\vdash}(a)$ and $eff^{\dashv}(a)$ of literals determining *effects* that apply at the start or at the end of a. Let $add^{\vdash}(a)$ (or $add^{\dashv}(a)$) and $del^{\vdash}(a)$ (or $del^{\dashv}(a)$) denote the sets of atoms occurring as positive or negative literals, respectively, in $eff^{\vdash}(a)$ (or $eff^{\dashv}(a)$).

The three steps outlined in Fig. 1 are now briefly introduced. For a formal definition, the reader is referred to [10]. *Composition* specifies how the sequential execution of two actions, a_1 and a_2, is mapped to a macro-action $a = a_1 \circ a_2$,

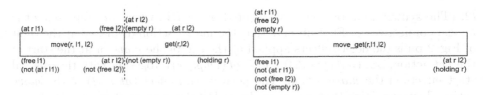

Fig. 2. Description of two actions and the resulting macro. Literals below each action represent effects, while the literals above them provide preconditions (at the start, end, or during an action, as indicated by their positions). The mutex atoms of the macro are omitted for better readability.

where the internal structure incorporating the ending event for a_1, the starting event for a_2, as well as the invariants $pre^{\vdash}(a_1)$ and $pre^{\vdash}(a_2)$ requires particular attention. In case some literal ℓ needs to be excluded from the effects of events taking place within the duration of the macro-action a, we introduce a mutex atom x_ℓ in the set $x(a)$ associated with a, which extends the corresponding set $x(a_2)$ for a_2. This inductive accumulation of mutex atoms accommodates the right-associative chaining of macro-action composition steps, starting from $x(a_2) = \emptyset$ for an ordinary action a_2.

After composing macro-actions a and gathering their associated mutex atoms $x(a)$, *Augmentation* incorporates mutex atoms into the preconditions and effects of effect-safe (macro-)actions a^x. The main idea is that the precondition of any event is augmented with x_ℓ for corresponding effects ℓ that must not apply during some macro-action a. Such an effect-safe macro-action a^x in turn falsifies x_ℓ at the start and re-enables it at the end, thus suppressing undesired effects of events and also ruling out interferences with (other) macro-actions whose associated mutex atoms include x_v or $x_{\neg v}$ for $\ell \in \{v, \neg v\}$. The latter restriction on the concurrent applicability of macro-actions guarantees that mutex atoms are neither manipulated in uncontrolled ways nor that unfolding macro-actions into their constituent actions risks the release of undesired effects.

Given a solution for a planning task built from effect-safe (macro-)actions, *Refinement* formalizes how a time-stamped macro-action (t, a) with $a = a_1 \circ a_2$ is unfolded into the sequence of (t_1, a_1) and (t_2, a_2) to obtain a refined plan. The introduced time stamps t_1 and t_2 are chosen such that $t_1 < t$, $t_1 + dur(a_1) < t_2$, and $t_2 + dur(a_2) < t + dur(a)$, where no other starting or ending event takes place in-between t_1 and t, $t_1 + dur(a_1)$ and t_2, or $t_2 + dur(a_2)$ and $t + dur(a)$, respectively.

Our macro-action concept combines preconditions and effects at the start and end of composed actions as well as their invariants in a fine-grained way, based on the idea of incorporating invariants if they do not spoil the applicability of a macro-action, or to gather mutex atoms on literals otherwise.

Example 1. Fig. 2 visualizes how two actions from a simple temporal domain are composed into a macro-action. The actions at the top involve an agent r capable of moving from a location $l1$ to $l2$ for picking up an object at location *l*2. (The syntax used for literals is inspired by PDDL, where *not* represents the logical connective ¬.) First observe that the macro-action displayed at the right of Fig. 2 pulls the delete effects applied at the end of the *move* or at the start of the *get* action, i.e., (*not* (*free l*2)) and (*not* (*empty r*)), together with the original start effects of the *move* action. The positive end effect (*at r l*2) of the *move* action, however, joins (*holding r*) at the end of the composed macro-action.

Preconditions at the start of the macro-action include the original (*at r l*1) atom from *move* together with (*free l*2) and (*empty r*) required at the end of *move* or at the start of *get*, respectively. The reason for not turning the latter two atoms into invariants required throughout the macro-action is that their negative literals occur as new start effects, so that invariants would render the macro-action inapplicable. Moreover, the precondition and invariant (*at r l*2) of *get* is not taken as a precondition or invariant of the macro-action since it is enabled by the end effect of *move*, which is now postponed to the end of the macro-action. Hence, it would be overcautious to insist on the truth of (*at r l*2) at the start or during the entire macro-action. In fact, considering that any other actions in the domain will hardly admit (*at r l*1), which is a precondition at the start, and (*at r l*2) to hold simultaneously, turning the latter into a precondition or invariant would most likely yield an (unnoticed) inapplicable macro-action.□

In general, the idea of *Composition* is to forward delete effects $del^{\dashv}(a_1) \cup del^{\vdash}(a_2)$ ((*not* (*free l*2)) and (*not* (*empty r*)) in Example 1) from the ending event for a_1 or the starting event for a_2 to the start of the composed macro-action $a = a_1 \circ a_2$. In this way, atoms getting falsified in the course of the macro-action become false, so that the preconditions of other actions are not met after the macro-action starts. Similarly, the add effects $add^{\dashv}(a_1) \cup add^{\vdash}(a_2)$ ((*at r l*2) in Example 1), which may enable preconditions of other actions, are postponed to the end of the macro-action (unless they get canceled by subsequently occurring delete effects $del^{\vdash}(a_2)$ and $del^{\dashv}(a_2)$). Taken together, the early application of delete effects and postponement of add effects prevent that other actions building on the volatile atoms are applied.

Concerning the preconditions of the macro-action a, $pre^{\dashv}(a)$ consists of the atoms in $pre^{\dashv}(a_2)$ that are not enabled by the add effects $add^{\dashv}(a_1) \cup add^{\vdash}(a_2)$ during the macro-action. Note that atoms in $add^{\vdash}(a_2)$ may also belong to the delete effects $del^{\dashv}(a_1)$, in which case they are included in $del^{\vdash}(a)$ at the start of a and listing them among the preconditions $pre^{\dashv}(a)$ at the end would render a inapplicable. For the same reason, atoms of the invariant $pre^{\mapsto}(a_2)$ that get enabled by $add^{\dashv}(a_1) \cup add^{\vdash}(a_2)$ during a are not required as invariants in $pre^{\mapsto}(a)$ for not (unnecessarily) compromising the applicability of a. Atoms of the invariant $pre^{\mapsto}(a_1)$ as well as the preconditions $pre^{\dashv}(a_1)$ and $pre^{\vdash}(a_2)$ during a are taken as invariants in $pre^{\mapsto}(a)$ only if they are not falsified by subsequent delete effects in $del^{\dashv}(a_1)$ or $del^{\vdash}(a_2)$. Otherwise, such atoms ((*free l*2) and (*empty r*) in Example 1) augment the original preconditions $pre^{\vdash}(a_1)$ at the start of a_1 in $pre^{\vdash}(a)$ (unless they get readily enabled by add effects $add^{\vdash}(a_1)$ and $add^{\dashv}(a_1)$, as with (*at r l*2) in Example 1). While the composition of a_1 and a_2 into $a = a_1 \circ a_2$ aims at restricting the preconditions $pre^{\vdash}(a)$, $pre^{\mapsto}(a)$, and $pre^{\dashv}(a)$ to necessary parts, it can happen that a_1 and a_2 are incompatible in the sense that delete effects undo required preconditions, and checking that $del^\vdash(a) \cap pre^\dashv(a) = \emptyset$ as well as $pre^\dashv(a_2) \cap (del^\dashv(a_1) \cup del^\vdash(a_2)) \setminus add^\vdash(a_2) = \emptyset$ excludes the composition of incompatible actions.

Although the specific delete effects in Example 1 do not permit taking atoms as invariants of the composed macro-action $a = a_1 \circ a_2$, it would be the first choice for, e.g., $(empty\ r)$ from $pre^\vdash(a_2)$ if it were not also included in $del^\vdash(a_2)$. If this choice cannot be made for an atom v of interest, as in Example 1, a mutex atom $x_{\neg v}$ is collected in $x(a)$ to express that any delete effects on v need to be rejected as long as the macro-action a is in progress. The respective cases in *Composition* cover all atoms from the preconditions $pre^\vdash(a_1)$, $pre^\dashv(a_1)$, and $pre^\vdash(a_2)$ subject to subsequent delete effects, atoms from $pre^\vdash(a_2)$ and $pre^\dashv(a_2)$ getting enabled in the course of the macro-action a, as well as postponed effects from $add^\dashv(a_1)$ and $add^\vdash(a_2)$ that are not to be removed before the ending event for a (unless any of these atoms belongs to the invariants of a). Additional mutex atoms of the form x_v are included in $x(a)$ for delete effects $del^\dashv(a_1) \cup del^\vdash(a_2)$ occurring during a. They signal that add effects on v must be rejected to prevent concurrent actions building on atoms that get falsified during a. Mutex atoms of macro-actions are then used to model mutex locks by *Augmentation*.

Example 2. Continuing Example 1, the mutex atoms (omitted in Fig. 2 for better readability) associated with the composed *move* and *get* macro-action are $x_{(not\ (free\ l2))}$, $x_{(not\ (empty\ r))}$, $x_{(not\ (at\ r\ l2))}$, $x_{(free\ l2)}$, and $x_{(empty\ r)}$. In the *not* cases, they result from preconditions at the end of *move* and at the start of or during *get* that are canceled by subsequent delete effects or enabled during the macro-action, respectively. On the other hand, $x_{(free\ l2)}$ and $x_{(empty\ r)}$ stem from the delete effects at the end of *move* and at the start of *get*. The effect-safe version of the macro-action includes the above mutex atoms as well as $x_{(at\ r\ l2)}$, $x_{(free\ l1)}$, and $x_{(not\ (at\ r\ l1))}$ as additional preconditions at the start (provided that the latter show up among the mutex atoms associated with other macro-actions composed for the domain) to rule out any interferences with other macro-actions on start effects or the original atoms v occurring as x_v or $x_{\neg v}$ among mutex atoms. When the macro-action composed from *move* and *get* is applied, its associated mutex atoms are set to false at the start in order to reject undesired effects of other actions, i.e., effects falsifying some required precondition or enabling an atom falsified during the macro-action (too early). These mutex locks get released again at the end of the macro-action, where $x_{(at\ r\ l2)}$ and $x_{(holding\ r)}$ for the end effects $(at\ r\ l2)$ and $(holding\ r)$ constitute preconditions (in case any other macro-actions have them as associated mutex atoms). Importantly, if either of these atoms were among the mutex atoms associated with the macro-action itself, it would not be taken as a precondition for the ending event; e.g., if $(not\ (holding\ r))$ were an effect at the start of the *get* action, $x_{(holding\ r)}$ would be included in the mutex atoms, so that $x_{(holding\ r)}$ is certainly false until the end of the macro-action due to the modeled mutex lock.   □

3   Evaluation

We evaluate the impact of sequential macro-actions on planning performance by applying three state-of-the-art planners to solve instances from four domains. The first domain consists of a PDDL encoding of the RoboCup Logistics League (RCLL) along with the instance collection used in [11] for assessing and comparing domain models with manually defined macros. In the RCLL domain, a team of three autonomous mobile robots cooperatively assembles products by interacting with production stations. The other three domains originate from the International Planning Competition (IPC) [23]: Road Traffic Accident Management (RTAM), Driverlog, and Satellite. Like RCLL, RTAM and Driverlog encode logistics domains. However, due to different characteristics, the number of defined macros is considerably lower (17 macros for RCLL and 2 macros only for both RTAM and Driverlog). The Satellite domain is rather simple, also featuring 2 macros only. For each domain, the original actions composing the introduced macros are replaced by the macro-actions in order to improve the solving process, at the potential cost of losing optimality in case applying the ordinary actions off sequence permits plans to finish earlier.

Our comparison includes three state-of-the-art planners: the popular Optic system [2], also serving as baseline planner at the IPC 2018 edition, as well as the Temporal Fast Downward (TFD) [12] and YAHSP3 [24] planners, which achieved the runner-up and winner positions at the IPC 2014 edition [23]. The benchmark set consists of 50 instances for RCLL, 20 instances for both RTAM and Satellite, and 44 instances for Driverlog, where we run each planner for up to 15 min per instance on a PC equipped with an Intel i5 10300 h CPU and 16 GB RAM under Ubuntu 18.04, using either the original or the macro-action domain. Notably, the composition of macro-actions described in Sect. 2 is automatically performed at the level of first-order PDDL domains by a Java tool we developed for this purpose. Table 1 indicates the original domain by "Nat." and the new one replacing some of the ordinary actions by "Macro". The displayed metrics are Coverage, i.e., the ratio of instances for which some satisficing plan is obtained to the number of all instances in a domain, and average Relative Makespan, comparing the finishing time of best plans found in 15 min between the original domain and the one with macro-actions. That is, the Relative Makespan considers instances such that a planner found at least one solution for either version of the domain, where values greater than 1 express better plan quality for the domain with macros, or worse plan quality otherwise. In addition, we quantify the Relative Makespan deviance as an indicator of the plan quality differences, and greater values mean that the plan quality per instance varies significantly w.r.t. the (non-)use of macros.

As can be seen by the results displayed in Table 1, equipping domains with macro-actions can change the landscape of heuristic features, having an impact on the quality of solutions and how fast planners can find them. The particularly positive effects on the RCLL domain show that replacing a large portion of ordinary actions by macros can significantly improve the planner performance and plan quality. However, when the majority of ordinary actions remain in com-

Table 1. For each combination of domain and planner, the table displays the Coverage (% of solved instances) and average Relative Makespan (ratio between makespans of native and macro) over the instance set, with corresponding deviance. Makespan results bigger than 1 are highlighted, meaning better makespan for the macro version.

	RCLL				RTAM			
planner	Cov. Nat	Cov. Macro	Rel. Mkspan	Dev	Cov. Nat	Cov. Macro	Rel. Mkspan	Dev
OPTIC	0.66	**1.00**	**1.08**	0.07	0.95	0.95	0.72	0.01
TFD	0.22	**1.00**	0.76	0.00	**0.16**	0.05	n/a	n/a
YAHSP	1.00	1.00	**1.38**	0.26	1.00	1.00	0.93	0.03
	SATELLITE				DRIVERLOG			
planner	Cov. Nat	Cov. Macro	Rel. Mkspan	Dev.	Cov. Nat.	Cov. Macro	Rel. Mkspan	Dev.
OPTIC	0.15	**0.45**	0.75	0.01	0.15	**0.27**	0.99	0.00
TFD	**0.85**	0.25	0.95	0.03	0.03	**0.15**	0.94	0.00
YAHSP	**1.00**	0.75	**1.37**	0.30	**0.91**	0.82	0.53	0.04

parison to those replaced by macros, the overhead induced by the mutex atoms associated with macro-actions can outweigh the performance gains, particularly when considering the makespan of the obtained plans.

4 Related Work

Macro-actions are well-known in classical planning, starting with the STRIPS [14] and REFLECT [9] systems in the 1970s. Classical planning systems may generate macro-actions in pre-processing [3–6,18,19,21,22] or on the fly during the planning process [7,8]. In contrast to classical planning, very few works consider macro-actions in the context of temporal planning. A technique to generate macro-actions out of partially overlapping temporal actions is presented in [25]. To our knowledge, the most recent approach to define temporal macro-actions stems from a master thesis [17], but the used model of durative actions deviates from PDDL 2.1 [15]. Macro-actions and abstractions also find application in languages and paradigms beyond PDDL, like Situation Calculus and other ad-hoc languages [1,13,16,20].

5 Conclusion and Future Work

Temporal planning allows for modeling and solving a variety of planning and scheduling tasks. However, the high computational complexity of temporal planning remains a notorious obstacle for its successful application to challenging target domains. A popular approach in classical planning to reduce combinatorics and boost the performance of the planning process is the introduction of macro-actions. In this paper, we propose a general concept of sequential macro-actions for temporal planning that guarantees the applicability of plans. Sequential macro-actions are particularly advantageous in logistics domains, where it is common that the activities of agents follow specific patterns.

Our experiments investigate the performance of three state-of-the-art planners on four domains (three of which are logistics-related). For the majority of tested planners and domains, more satisficing plans and in some cases also better plan quality are obtained when frequent sequences of ordinary actions are encapsulated and replaced by a macro. In fact, while native domains always admit solutions that are at least as good as a plan with macro-actions, enhancing temporal domains by macro-actions can sometimes help to guide planners to suitable solutions in shorter solving time. This is particularly the case when the macro-actions subsume and replace a large portion of ordinary actions, which is not unlikely for logistics domains. However, our macro-action concept is not exclusive to logistics domains and can be applied to any temporal planning task.

As future work, we want to develop methods to automatically detect suitable candidates for macro-actions in a given domain. Moreover, the formalization of further kinds of macros in temporal planning, like parallel or, more generally, overlapping macro-actions and support for numeric fluents, constitutes an interesting future work direction.

Acknowledgements. M. De Bortoli and M. Gebser were funded by Kärntner Wirtschaftsförderungs Fonds (project no. 28472), cms electronics GmbH, FunderMax GmbH, Hirsch Armbänder GmbH, incubed IT GmbH, Infineon Technologies Austria AG, Isovolta AG, Kostwein Holding GmbH, and Privatstiftung Kärntner Sparkasse. L. Chrpa was funded by the Czech Science Foundation (project no. 23-05575S). M. De Bortoli's and M. Gebser's visit to CTU in Prague was funded by the OP VVV project no. EF15_003/0000470 "Robotics 4 Industry 4.0" and by the Czech Ministry of Education, Youth and Sports under the Czech-Austrian Mobility programme (project no. 8J22AT003), respectively. L. Chrpa's visits to University of Klagenfurt were funded by OeAD, Austria's Agency for Education and Internationalisation (project no. CZ 15/2022).

References

1. Banihashemi, B., De Giacomo, G., Lespérance, Y.: Abstraction in situation calculus action theories. In: Proceedings of the AAAI Conference on Artificial Intelligence, pp. 1048–1055. AAAI Press (2017). https://doi.org/10.1609/aaai.v31i1.10693
2. Benton, J., Coles, A., Coles, A.: Temporal planning with preferences and time-dependent continuous costs. In: Proceedings of the International Conference on Automated Planning and Scheduling, pp. 2–10. AAAI Press (2012). https://doi.org/10.1609/icaps.v22i1.13509
3. Botea, A., Enzenberger, M., Müller, M., Schaeffer, J.: Macro-FF: improving AI planning with automatically learned macro-operators. J. Artif. Intell. Res. **24**, 581–621 (2005). https://doi.org/10.1613/jair.1696
4. Chrpa, L., Vallati, M.: Improving domain-independent planning via critical section macro-operators. In: Proceedings of the AAAI Conference on Artificial Intelligence, pp. 7546–7553. AAAI Press (2019). https://doi.org/10.1609/aaai.v33i01.33017546
5. Chrpa, L., Vallati, M.: Planning with critical section macros: theory and practice. J. Artif. Intell. Res. **74**, 691–732 (2022). https://doi.org/10.1613/jair.1.13269
6. Chrpa, L., Vallati, M., McCluskey, T.L.: MUM: a technique for maximising the utility of macro-operators by constrained generation and use. In: Proceedings of

the International Conference on Automated Planning and Scheduling, pp. 65–73. AAAI Press (2014). https://doi.org/10.1609/icaps.v24i1.13626

7. Coles, A., Smith, A.: On the inference and management of macro-actions in forward-chaining planning. In: Proceedings of the UK Planning and Scheduling SIG. University of Strathclyde (2005). www.strathprints.strath.ac.uk/2751/1/strathprints002751.pdf

8. Coles, A., Smith, A.: Marvin: a heuristic search planner with online macro-action learning. J. Artif. Intell. Res. **28**, 119–156 (2007). https://doi.org/10.1613/jair.2077

9. Dawson, C., Siklóssy, L.: The role of preprocessing in problem solving systems. In: Proceedings of the International Joint Conference on Artificial Intelligence, pp. 465–471. William Kaufmann (1977). www.ijcai.org/Proceedings/77-1/Papers/078.pdf

10. De Bortoli, M., Chrpa, L., Gebser, M., Steinbauer-Wagner, G.: Enhancing temporal planning domains by sequential macro-actions (extended version) (2023). https://doi.org/10.48550/arXiv.2307.12081

11. De Bortoli, M., Steinbauer-Wagner, G.: Evaluating action-based temporal planners performance in the RoboCup logistics league. In: Eguchi, A., Lau, N., Paetzel-Prüsmann, M., Wanichanon, T. (eds.) RoboCup 2022, RoboCup 2022. Lecture Notes in Computer Science, vol. 13561, pp. 87–99. Springer, Cham (2023). https://doi.org/10.1007/978-3-031-28469-4_8

12. Eyerich, P., Mattmüller, R., Röger, G.: Using the context-enhanced additive heuristic for temporal and numeric planning. In: Proceedings of the International Conference on Automated Planning and Scheduling, pp. 130–137. AAAI Press (2009). https://doi.org/10.1609/icaps.v19i1.13373

13. Fadel, R.: Planning with complex actions. Master's thesis, Stanford University (2002). www.ksl.stanford.edu/pub/KSL_Reports/KSL-02-03.pdf

14. Fikes, R., Nilsson, N.: STRIPS: a new approach to the application of theorem proving to problem solving. Artif. Intell. **2**(3/4), 189–208 (1971). https://doi.org/10.1016/0004-3702(71)90010-5

15. Fox, M., Long, D.: PDDL2.1: an extension to PDDL for expressing temporal planning domains. J. Artif. Intell. Res. **20**, 61–124 (2003). https://doi.org/10.1613/jair.1129

16. Gabaldon, A.: Programming hierarchical task networks in the situation calculus. In: Proceedings of the AIPS 2002 Workshop on On-line Planning and Scheduling (2002). www.cs.toronto.edu/~alfredo/Papers/Gabaldon-KRA11.pdf

17. Hansson, E.: Temporal task and motion plans: planning and plan repair–repairing temporal task and motion plans using replanning with temporal macro operators. Master's thesis, Linkoping University (2018). www.liu.diva-portal.org/smash/get/diva2:1263869/FULLTEXT01.pdf

18. Hofmann, T., Niemueller, T., Lakemeyer, G.: Initial results on generating macro actions from a plan database for planning on autonomous mobile robots. In: Proceedings of the International Conference on Automated Planning and Scheduling, pp. 498–503. AAAI Press (2017). https://doi.org/10.1609/icaps.v27i1.13868

19. Hofmann, T., Niemueller, T., Lakemeyer, G.: Macro operator synthesis for ADL domains. In: Proceedings of the European Conference on Artificial Intelligence, pp. 761–768. IOS Press (2020). https://doi.org/10.3233/FAIA200164

20. Lifschitz, V., Ren, W.: A modular action description language. In: Proceedings of the AAAI Conference on Artificial Intelligence, pp. 853–859. AAAI Press (2006). www.aaai.org/Papers/AAAI/2006/AAAI06-135.pdf

21. Miura, S., Fukunaga, A.: Automatic extraction of axioms for planning. In: Proceedings of the International Conference on Automated Planning and Scheduling, pp. 218–227. AAAI Press (2017). https://doi.org/10.1609/icaps.v27i1.13815
22. Newton, M., Levine, J., Fox, M., Long, D.: Learning macro-actions for arbitrary planners and domains. In: Proceedings of the International Conference on Automated Planning and Scheduling, pp. 256–263. AAAI Press (2007). https://aaai.org/papers/icaps-07-033-learning-macro-actions-for-arbitrary-planners-and-domains/
23. Vallati, M., Chrpa, L., McCluskey, T.: What you always wanted to know about the deterministic part of the international planning competition (IPC) 2014 (but were too afraid to ask). Knowl. Eng. Rev. **33**, e3 (2018). https://doi.org/10.1017/S0269888918000012
24. Vidal, V.: YAHSP3 and YAHSP3-MT in the 8th International Planning Competition. In: Proceedings of the International Planning Competition, pp. 64–65 (2014). www.v.vidal.free.fr/onera/publis/ipc14-yahsp3.pdf
25. Wullinger, P., Schmid, U., Scholz, U.: Spanning the middle ground between classical and temporal planning. In: Workshop Planen und Konfigurieren (2008). www.cogsys.wiai.uni-bamberg.de/publications/pw_us_us_puk_22.pdf

Planning with Partial Observability by SAT

Saurabh Fadnis[(✉)] and Jussi Rintanen

Department of Computer Science, Aalto University, Espoo, Finland
saurabh_fadnis@yahoo.co.in

Abstract. Geffner & Geffner (2018) have shown that finding plans by reduction to SAT is not limited to classical planning, but is competitive also for fully observable non-deterministic planning. This work extends these ideas to planning with partial observability. Specifically, we handle partial observability by requiring that during the execution of a plan, the same actions have to be taken in all indistinguishable circumstances. We demonstrate that encoding this condition directly leads to far better scalability than an explicit encoding of observations-to-actions mapping, for high numbers of observations.

1 Introduction

Geffner and Geffner [7] have shown how SAT yields an effective method for solving non-deterministic fully observable (conditional) planning problems. This is the first time SAT has been directly used for solving a broad class of problems outside deterministic planning, by only a polynomial number of SAT calls in the size of the plan being constructed. This approach is in strong contrast with earlier constraint-based approaches, which have required formalisms stronger than SAT, for example Σ_2^p-hard SSAT [11,12] or QBF [16], or separate calls to SAT solvers for plan generation and verification [6] (again going up to Σ_2^p) and using SAT as a sub procedure of an otherwise exponential search algorithm, even when restricting to plans of a polynomial size.

We view as the core idea in Geffner & Geffner's work that contingent planning is in NP whenever *all executions of a plan* have a representation that has polynomial size. Our work demonstrates that *the same applies also to the far harder problem of planning with partial observability*.

1.1 Background

Finding plans in classical planning, with one initial state and deterministic actions, can be represented as propositional formulas of a size that is linear in the number of actions in a plan. The formula with length parameter n is satisfiable if and only if there is a sequence of n actions that reaches a goal state from the given initial state. For plans with a polynomial length, the NP-complete problem of finding them can be done with a SAT solver [8,9].

When a plan can have multiple alternative executions, planning is harder. Conditional planning, with branching program-like plans, is in the complexity class Σ_2^p for poly-sized plans, and hence – in general – believed to be outside the reach of the NP-complete SAT problem, and to require the more powerful framework of quantified Boolean formulas (QBF) [15,16,21].

The idea that Σ_2^p complexity was somehow inherent to practically significant conditional planning was broken by Geffner & Geffner [7] who showed that – under full observability – the two separate NP computations for plan search and for plan verification collapse to a single NP computation, if execution graphs and plans have the same form. Plans are (possibly cyclic) graphs, with non-terminal nodes associated with actions, and executions are viewed as paths in the graph. The states in a node are represented by the literals that are true in it.

Given a problem instance of size m and an $n \geqslant 0$, Geffner & Geffner generate a propositional formula so that any satisfying assignment represents a graph that has n nodes and represents a conditional plan and all of its executions. The size of the formula is polynomial in n and m. The formula leaves the structure of the plan open, and it is the SAT solver that chooses the (positive) literals in each node, the action in each node, and the outgoing arcs for each node.

1.2   Contributions

Our contributions are as follows. We present the first *SAT-based* encodings of *succinctly* represented (state variable based) planning problems under *partial observability*. Earlier works either use more powerful (and less scalable) formalisms than SAT such as QBF or effectively simulate such [6,16], use a non-succinct enumerative representation [5], or cover full observability only [7,14].

We use 3-valued (partial) execution graphs to represent all possible executions of a plan. Earlier 3-valued representations [1] have low complexity and are scalable, but lead to incompleteness, as most state sets do not have a 3-valued representation. We will show how *case analysis* on state variables marked *unknown* makes the 3-valued approach *complete*, that is, being able to represent a plan whenever one exists, by selectively eliminating partiality.

Finally, we show how an *implicit* representation of *small memory* plans can make the approach better scalable. Instead of accurately keeping track of the belief state, only an abstraction of the belief state is maintained, as a state as in a finite automaton, in order to distinguish between different execution histories. Plans are mappings from memory states and observations to next actions and next memory states. As the number of observables increases, the sizes of these mappings increase exponentially, making an explicit representation impractical: a smaller and smaller fraction of all observation combinations actually occur in any execution of a plan. A main result is that replacing an explicit encoding of small memory plans (as in [5]) by an implicit encoding can lead to substantial scalability improvements. We can still guarantee *the existence* of these mappings, and they can be easily extracted from satisfying assignments.

2   Planning with Partial Observability

A key idea in Geffner & Geffner's representation of branching plans as graphs is that each path can represent multiple possible executions as the nodes correspond to *partial* states which determine the values of some state variables only. A partial state is essentially a representation of a *set* of states. For example, with state variables a, b, c and d, the partial state represented by the partial valuation $\{a = 1, b = 0\}$ corresponds to the set of those four states that match the partial valuation on a and b, and assign any value combination to c and d.

Example 1. In this navigation problem moving into a wall is not allowed, and hence it must be possible to detect which cells are next to a wall (observations $N = y_4$, $S = y_0$, $E = x_4$, $W = x_0$, indicating which wall(s) the robot is next to).

Considering the non-wall locations as possible starting locations, the plan that first moves to north until the north wall is encountered, and then moves west until the NW corner is encountered, is depicted on the right in Fig. 1.

One graph that represents all executions of this plan is partly given in Fig. 1. The rest of graph would be similar and repeats the "move west" action when north wall is observed until the NW corner location is reached.

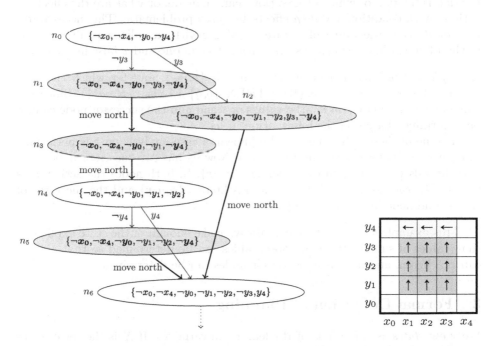

Fig. 1. Execution of a grid navigation problem (part)

In this example, the topmost branching (node n_0 in the graph) is on the variable y_3. We call such branching *Case Analysis* and it is discussed in the next subsection. The thing to note here is that y_3 is not observable, and in general the branching is not directly related to observations, but to the different execution paths of a given plan. Despite the branching being on an unobservable variable, the graph is still a faithful representation of all executions of the plan. The key property here is that if an action is taken, then it is the same action that is taken in all mutually indistinguishable states with respect to observations: move north in all (partial) states that are not next to any wall (nodes n_1,n_2,n_3 and n_5 in Fig. 1), and move west whenever next to the north wall.

In this example there is no need to remember any of the previous belief states. In cases where this memory is needed, the same action is taken in all mutually indistinguishable states with respect to observations and *memory*. If the plan includes memory, more fine-grained choice of actions is possible. We consider small-memory plans [5,10,13], which means that at execution time there are only a small number of possible "memories" in the execution mechanism, and they – together with the observations – determine the next action and memory. We represent the different memories as integers from 0 to some small $M_{\max}$.

2.1   Case Analysis

For 3-valued partial representations, if some state variable values are *unknown*, the determination of which observations can be made, or what are the effects of actions with conditional *if-then* effects becomes problematic. This necessitates *case analysis* on the values of a state variable x with an unknown value: a node in the plan will have two successors, with x true in one and x false in the other.

Example 2. Consider a node n_0 with literals $\{p, \neg q\}$, and for which the plan assigns the action $a_1 = (\neg q, \{\text{IF } r \text{ THEN } \{p, q\} \text{ ELSE } \{\neg p, \neg q\}\})$. Since the value of r is not known in n_0, the values of p and q in the successor node cannot be determined based on the information in n_0.

If some of these values need to be known, a case-analysis on r is performed in n_0 instead, before executing the action. Now n_0 has two successor nodes, one with literals $\{p, \neg q, r\}$ and the other $\{p, \neg q, \neg r\}$. In both nodes the action a_1 is taken. The successor of the first node has literals $\{p, q, r\}$ and the successor of the second node has $\{\neg p, \neg q, \neg r\}$.

This example shows that we can always make enough of the state explicit so that values of sufficiently many observables can be determined so that actions can be chosen, and literals in successor nodes can be determined.

3   Formal Definition of Planning

We view *states* as valuations of Boolean state variables. If X is the set of state variables, then a state $s : X \rightarrow \{0, 1\}$ assigns a value to every state variable in X. By identifying states and Boolean valuations, we can directly use definitions from the Propositional Logic to talk about states. For example, we can say that a formula ϕ is *true in a state s* if $s \models \phi$, that is, this formula ϕ is true in the valuation s. We denote the set of all states (over some fixed set X) by $\$$.

Next, problem instances are formally defined. *Atomic effects* are of the form $x := 0$ or $x := 1$, where x is a state variable. A *conditional effect* has the form IF ϕ THEN e, where ϕ is a formula over X, and e is a set of atomic effects. An action is associated with a set of atomic and conditional effects. For simplicity, we don't discuss non-deterministic actions in this work.

Definition 1 (Problem Instance). *A problem instance in planning is a tuple* $\Pi = \langle X, A, I, G, O \rangle$ *where*

- *X is a set of state variables,*
- *A is a set of actions (p, e), where*
  - *p is a formula over X, and*
  - *e is a set of effects,*
- *the initial states are represented by a formula I over X,*
- *the goal states are represented by a formula G over X, and*
- *the observations are a set O of formulas over X.*

4   Execution Graphs

Our introduction of *case analysis* nodes in the execution graphs allows to complete, on demand, the approximated information sufficiently that every problem instance has a solution as a 3-valued execution graph.

Below we show a basic formalization of (2-valued) execution graphs without partiality, and then provide a proof sketch of the *completeness* of our approach by showing that any execution graph can be represented in terms of a (sometimes much more compact) 3-valued execution graph. The key result maps every non-approximate 2-valued execution graph to a 3-valued execution graph that includes case analysis nodes so that all executions in the former are represented also in the latter. Additionally, the approach is *sound*, so the 3-valued representation only represents solutions that are representable in the 2-valued framework.

Definition 2 (Execution graphs). *Given an instance $\Pi = \langle X, A, I, G, O \rangle$, an execution graph is $G = \langle N, E, P, S, M, B \rangle$ where*

- *N is a finite set of nodes,*
- *$E \subseteq N \times N$ are the arcs of the graph,*
- *the (partial) function $P : N \to A$ maps non-terminal nodes to actions,*
- *the function $S : N \to \$$ assigns a state to every node.*
- *$M = \{0, \ldots, M_{max}\}$ is the set of memory states with $M_{max} \geq 1$, and*
- *the function $B : N \to M$ assigns a memory state to every node.*

The memory state with the highest index $M_{\max}$ is for indicating that a goal state has been reached.

Definition 3 (Solutions as execution graphs). *An execution graph $G = \langle N, E, P, S, M, B \rangle$ is a solution to $\Pi = \langle X, A, I, G, O \rangle$ if the following hold.*

1. *The graph $\langle N, E \rangle$ is acyclic (it has no directed cycles.)*
2. *$\{s \in \$ \mid s \models I\} = \{S(n) \mid n \in N, n$ has no parents$\}$*

3. $S(n) \models G$ for every $n \in N$ such that $B(n) = M_{max}$
4. $B(n) = 0$ for every node n with no parent
5. $B(n) = M_{max}$ for every node n that has no successors
6. $S(n) \models p$ if $P(n) = (p, e)$
7. For $x \in X$ and nodes n' with a parent, $S(n') \models x$ iff there is $n \in N$ such that $(n, n') \in E$ and $P(n) = (p, e)$, and either
   - $(x := 1) \in e$,
   - (IF ϕ THEN $x := 1$) $\in e$ and $S(n) \models \phi$, or
   - $S(n) \models x$ and $(x := 0) \notin e$ and $S(n) \not\models \phi$ for all (IF ϕ THEN $x := 0$) $\in e$.
8. $S(n') \models \neg x$ analogously
9. For all $n_1, n_2 \in N$, if $P(n_1) \neq P(n_2)$, then either $B(n_1) \neq B(n_2)$ or for some $\omega \in O$, $S(n_1) \models \omega$ iff $S(n_2) \not\models \omega$.
10. For all $(n_1, n_1'), (n_2, n_2') \in E$, if $B(n_1') \neq B(n_2')$, then either $B(n_1) \neq B(n_2)$ or for some $\omega \in O$, $S(n_1) \models \omega$ iff $S(n_2) \not\models \omega$.

Condition 7 guarantees that the changes in the values of state variables between a node and its successor exactly correspond to the changes caused by the action in that node.

Conditions 9 and 10 express the *distinguishability* between two situations during the execution of a plan: if two situations cannot be distinguished through the memory or the observations, then the same actions have to be taken in both, and the next memory states have to be the same.

An execution graph represents every possible execution $s_0, \ldots, s_n$ explicitly, and different executions (state sequences) are represented by different paths in the graph. Hence, for any problem instance for which an exponential number of different states has to be considered, the size of the execution graph is exponential. Next we define *partial execution graphs* that can represent large numbers of states and executions more compactly.

5   Partial Execution Graphs

Partial execution graphs can be exponentially smaller than execution graphs if many executions share the same structure. The nodes in partial execution graphs are labelled with *partial states* which only determine the values of a subset of state variables. One partial state represents all states that assign the same values to the represented state variables. This same idea has been used by Geffner & Geffner in their work on planning with full observability [7].

Definition 4. *A* partial state *is a partial function* $z : X \to \{0, 1\}$.

Toggle the table of contents We denote the set of all partial states by $\mathbb{S}_p$. Clearly, $\mathbb{S} \subset \mathbb{S}_p$. A partial state z represents all states that do not disagree on the value of any state variable. That is, z represents $\{s \in \mathbb{S} \mid s(x) = z(x) \text{ or } z(x) \text{ is not defined, for all } x \in X\}$.

Definition 5. *A partial execution graph* $G = \langle N, E, P, C, S, M, B \rangle$ *for a problem instance* $\Pi = \langle X, A, I, G, O \rangle$ *consists of*

- *a finite set N of nodes,*
- *a set $E \subseteq N \times N$ of arcs,*
- *a (partial) function $P : N \to A$ that assigns an action to some of the nodes,*
- *a (partial) function $C : N \to X$ that assigns a state variable to some of the nodes (for case analysis),*
- *a function $S : N \to \mathbb{S}_p$ that assigns a partial state to every node.*
- $M = \{0, \ldots, M_{max}\}$ *is the set of memory states with $M_{max} \geq 1$, and*
- *the function $B : N \to M$ assigns a memory state to every node.*

The function C indicates in which nodes a case analysis is performed. If $C(n) = x$, then node n has two successor states n_1 and n_2 so that $S(n_1) \vdash x$ and $S(n_2) \models \neg x$. From now on, we assume all formulas to be in Negation Normal Form (NNF)[1]. We define truth of a formula in a partial state as follows.

1. $s \models_3 x$ if $s(x) = 1$, and $s \models_3 \neg x$ if $s(x) = 0$
2. $s \models_3 \alpha \wedge \beta$ iff $s \models_3 \alpha$ and $s \models_3 \beta$
3. $s \models_3 \alpha \vee \beta$ iff $s \models_3 \alpha$ or $s \models_3 \beta$

Here it is critical that we do not define a formula $\neg\phi$ to be true if ϕ is not true (as in 2-valued logic), because the value of ϕ might be undetermined due to the partiality of the state.

Define cubeof(s) that maps a partial state s to a corresponding conjunction of literals cubeof(s) = $\bigwedge(\{x \in X \mid s(x) = 1\} \cup \{\neg x \mid x \in X, s(x) = 0\})$.

Definition 6. *A partial execution graph* $G = \langle N, E, P, C, S, M, B \rangle$ *is a solution to* $\Pi = \langle X, A, I, G, O \rangle$ *if the following hold.*

1. *The graph $\langle N, E \rangle$ is acyclic (it has no directed cycles.)*
2. $I \models_3 \delta_1 \vee \cdots \vee \delta_m$, *where $n_1, \ldots, n_m$ are the nodes with no parents, and $\delta_i = $ cubeof($S(n_i)$) for every $i \in \{1, \ldots, m\}$*
3. $S(n) \models_3 G$ *for every $n \in N$ such that $B(n) = M_{max}$*
4. $B(n) = 0$ *for every $n \in N$ with no parent*
5. $B(n) = M_{max}$ *for every $n \in N$ that has no successors*
6. $S(n) \models_3 p$ *if $P(n) = (p, e)$, for every $n \in N$*
7. *For every $n \in N$, exactly one of the following holds.*
   - *$C(n)$ is defined*
   - *$P(n)$ is defined*
   - $B(n) = M_{max}$
8. *If $C(n) = x$ for some $x \in X$, then n has exactly two successors, n_1 and n_2, and $S(n_1) \models_3 x$ and $S(n_2) \models_3 \neg x$.*
9. *If $C(n)$ is defined and $(n, n') \in E$, then $B(n) = B(n')$.*
10. *If $C(n) = x$ and $s = S(n)$, then $s(x)$ is not defined.*

---

[1] In NNF, a formula contains only connectives $\vee$, $\wedge$ and $\neg$, and all negations $\neg$ are directly in front of an atomic proposition.

11. If $S(n') \models_3 x$ for $n' \in N$ that has a parent $n \in N$, then either
    (a) $(n, n') \in E$ and $P(n) = (p, e)$ and
        - $(x := 1) \in e$,
        - (IF ϕ THEN $x := 1) \in e$ and $S(n) \models_3 \phi$, or
        - $S(n) \models_3 x$ and $(x := 0) \notin e$ and $S(n) \not\models_3 \phi$ for all (IF ϕ THEN $x := 0) \in e$.
    (b) or n is a case analysis node with $C(n) = x$,
    (c) or n is a case analysis node with $C(n) \neq x$ and $S(n) \models_3 x$.
12. $S(n') \models_3 \neg x$ analogously
13. For all $n_1, n_2 \in N$, if $P(n_1) \neq P(n_2)$, then either $B(n_1) \neq B(n_2)$ or for some $\omega \in O$, either $S(n_1) \models_3 \omega$ and $S(n_2) \models_3 \neg\omega$, or $S(n_1) \models_3 \neg\omega$ and $S(n_2) \models_3 \omega$.
14. For all $n_1, n_2 \in N$ and n_1', n_2' such that $(n_1, n_1'), (n_2, n_2') \in E$, if $B(n_1') \neq B(n_2')$, then either $B(n_1) \neq B(n_2)$ or for some $\omega \in O$ either $S(n_1) \models_3 \omega$ and $S(n_2) \models_3 \neg\omega$, or $S(n_1) \models_3 \neg\omega$ and $S(n_2) \models_3 \omega$.

A key feature of partial execution graphs, similarly to the work by Geffner & Geffner [7], is that some state variable values may be "forgotten" when going from a node to its successor. Increasing the partiality this way allows parts of a plan to be more general in being applicable for more states.

An important question about partial execution graphs is whether they can represent any solution, as expressible by an execution graph.

Proposition 1. *For every execution graph G, there is a partial execution graph G' that represents exactly the same solution.*

Proof. Sketch: The most trivial way to eliminate all partiality is to enumerate all states that satisfy the initial state formula I, and create an initial node for each of those states s. So the partial states in all initial states are (total) states. The partial execution graph in this case does not contain any case analysis nodes, and its structure is exactly the same as that of the execution graph. Stated differently, execution graphs are a special case partial execution graphs, only without case analysis nodes, and with (total) states instead of partial states.

6   Encodings of Partial Execution Graphs

Next we describe the encoding of partial execution graphs as propositional formulas. Table 1 lists the atomic propositions used in the encoding.

State variable x is true in node n if P_x^n holds and false if N_x^n holds. Otherwise its value is unknown (could be either true or false.) To refer to the truth of arbitrary formulas in a node, we define L_n^ϕ as the formula obtained from ϕ by transforming it to the Negation Normal Form (NNF) and then (for all $x \in X$) replacing subformulas $\neg x$ by N_x^n, and finally replacing subformulas x by P_x^n. Hence L_n^ϕ is true in a partial state z iff ϕ is true in all states represented by z.

In the rest of the section, the schema variables n, a, x (possibly with subscripts or other embellishments) are instantiated with all possible nodes, action names or state variable names, unless stated otherwise.

Table 1. Atomic propositions used in the encoding

P_x^n, N_x^n	State variable x is true or false in node n, respectively
$^oP_\omega^n, ^oN_\omega^n$	Observation ω or $\neg\omega$ is made in n, respectively, for $\omega \in O$
(n, a)	Action a is applied in node n
(n, a, n')	n' is the next node after action a is applied in node n
(n, n')	n' is a successor node of n
A_n	Node n is an action node
CA^n	n is a case analysis node
CA_x^n	Case analysis is done in node n on variable x
$CA_{n,n'}^1$	n' is the successor node with $P_x^{n'}$ when case analysis is done on x in n
$CA_{n,n'}^0$	n' is the successor node with $N_x^{n'}$ when case analysis is done on x in n
(n, m)	node n has the memory state m
$Z_{i,j}^m$	Nodes i and j have the same memory state m
$Z_{i,j}^\omega$	Nodes i and j are indistinguishable w.r.t. observation ω
$Z_{i,j}$	Nodes i and j are indistinguishable w.r.t. memory state and all observations

6.1 Nodes and Arcs

State variables are true, false or unknown (1). Preconditions are true (2).

$$\neg P_x^n \vee \neg N_x^n \quad (1) \qquad (n, a) \to L_n^\phi \text{ where } \phi \text{ is the precondition of } a \quad (2)$$

The acyclicity of the encoding is handled by instantiating all formulas referring to arcs from node n to a successor n' so that the index of n' is strictly higher than the index of n.

Node n has at least one action if and only if A_n is true (3), and A_n excludes case analysis in the same node (4). The variable (n, a) is defined by (5). Action nodes have exactly one successor node (6).[2]

$$A_n \leftrightarrow \bigvee_{a \in A} (n, a) \quad (3) \qquad\qquad \neg(A_n \wedge CA^n) \quad (4)$$

$$(n, a) \leftrightarrow \bigvee_{n' \in N \setminus \{n\}} (n, a, n') \quad (5)$$

$$A_n \to \text{exactly1}(\{(n, n') \mid n' \in N\}) \quad (6)$$

Anything true in a successor node of an action node is an effect of the action or something that was true already and not made false by the preceding action.

$$(n, n') \wedge A_n \wedge P_x^{n'} \to L_n^{\text{Ppc}_x \vee (x \wedge \neg \text{Npc}_x)} \quad (7)$$

$$(n, n') \wedge A_n \wedge N_x^{n'} \to L_n^{\text{Npc}_x \vee (\neg x \wedge \neg \text{Ppc}_x)} \quad (8)$$

where $\text{Ppc}_x = \chi_1 \vee \cdots \vee \chi_m$ and is the disjunction of the conditions χ_i under which action a_i makes x true, and Npc_x is the same for making x false. Each χ_i consists of the action variable (n, a_i) and additionally for conditional effects the condition under which x becomes *true* or *false*. This encodes Condition 11a.

---

[2] To encode the constraints *exactly-one* and *at-most-one* for $\phi_1, \ldots, \phi_k$, we use the quadratic encoding $\neg\phi_i \vee \neg\phi_j$ for all $1 \le i < j \le k$. Better encodings exist [18].

For the implicit encoding in Sect. 6.4 we have to enforce this explicitly by

$$\neg(n, a_1) \vee \neg(n, a_2) \text{ whenever } a_1 \neq a_2 \tag{9}$$

Note that (7) and (8) allow the effects of an action to be true in the successor node, but they do not have to be. This is because those values might not be needed, and the successor node is more *general* the fewer values are made explicit. This is as in the work by Geffner & Geffner [7].

6.2   Case Analysis

The following formulas encode how case analysis is done on some x so that a node has two successors, respectively with x true and false.

$$\mathrm{CA}^n \leftrightarrow \bigvee_{x \in X} \mathrm{CA}_x^n \tag{10}$$

For case analysis nodes, there is some variable to do the case analysis on, and there are two successor nodes (respectively for x and $\neg x$).

$$\bigvee_{n' \in N \setminus \{n\}} \mathrm{CA}_{n,n'}^1 \rightarrow \bigvee_{x \in X} \mathrm{CA}_x^n \tag{11} \qquad \bigvee_{n' \in N \setminus \{n\}} \mathrm{CA}_{n,n'}^0 \rightarrow \bigvee_{x \in X} \mathrm{CA}_x^n \tag{12}$$

$$\mathrm{CA}_x^n \rightarrow \text{exactly}1_{n' \in N \setminus \{n\}} \mathrm{CA}_{n,n'}^1 \tag{13} \qquad \mathrm{CA}_x^n \rightarrow \text{exactly}1_{n' \in N \setminus \{n\}} \mathrm{CA}_{n,n'}^0 \tag{14}$$

Case analysis is on at most one variable (15). Case analysis on x is only possible if its value is unknown (16). If node n does case analysis on x, then n has two successor nodes, and they respectively have x and $\neg x$ (17–18). The only new facts in the successor nodes of a case analysis node are x and $\neg x$ (19–22).

$$\text{atmost}1(\{\mathrm{CA}_x^n \mid x \in X\}) \tag{15} \qquad \mathrm{CA}_x^n \rightarrow \neg P_x^n \wedge \neg N_x^n \tag{16}$$

$$\mathrm{CA}_x^n \wedge \mathrm{CA}_{n,n'}^1 \rightarrow P_x^{n'} \tag{17} \qquad \mathrm{CA}_x^n \wedge \mathrm{CA}_{n,n'}^0 \rightarrow N_x^{n'} \tag{18}$$

$$\mathrm{CA}_{n,n'}^1 \wedge P_x^{n'} \rightarrow \mathrm{CA}_x^n \vee P_x^n \tag{19} \qquad \mathrm{CA}_{n,n'}^1 \wedge N_x^{n'} \rightarrow N_x^n \tag{20}$$

$$\mathrm{CA}_{n,n'}^0 \wedge N_x^{n'} \rightarrow \mathrm{CA}_x^n \vee N_x^n \tag{21} \qquad \mathrm{CA}_{n,n'}^0 \wedge P_x^{n'} \rightarrow P_x^n \tag{22}$$

The last six are for nodes n and n' such that $n \neq n'$.

Arcs are induced by case analysis or by actions only.

$$(n, n') \leftrightarrow \left(\mathrm{CA}_{n,n'}^1 \vee \mathrm{CA}_{n,n'}^0 \vee \bigvee_{a \in A} (n, a, n') \right) \tag{23}$$

6.3   Initial and Goal Nodes

We assume the initial state formula to be in DNF as $I = \phi_1 \vee \cdots \vee \phi_k$. Let $\Phi_I = \{\phi_1, \ldots, \phi_k\}$. We require that for each $\phi \in \Phi_I$, at least one of the nodes $n_0, \ldots, n_{k-1}$ does not falsify any of the literals in ϕ (and hence all initial states for ϕ are "included" in some initial node), and that node has memory 0. We have for every $\phi \in \Phi_I$ the following.

$$\bigvee_{i=0}^{k-1} ((n_i, m_0) \wedge \neg L_{n_i}^{\neg \phi} \wedge \bigwedge_{w \in O} (\neg^\circ P_w^{n_i} \wedge \neg^\circ N_w^{n_i})) \tag{24}$$

The unique goal node n_g has memory $m_{M_{\max}}$ and the formula G holds in n_g, and other node has memory $m_{M_{\max}}$.

$$(n_g, m_{M_{\max}}) \wedge L^G_{n_g} \qquad (25) \qquad\qquad \neg(n, m_{M_{\max}}) \text{ for all } n \neq n_g \qquad (26)$$

6.4   Encoding of Small-Memory Plans Implicitly

The implicit encoding, which does not make the plans explicit and only guarantees that one exists that matches the execution graph, is the one better scalable than the explicit encoding when there is a high number of observation combinations. It consists of the following.

$$\text{exactly1}((n, m_0), \dots, (n, m_{M_{\max}})) \qquad (27)$$

For case analysis nodes, the successor nodes have the same memory.

$$CA^1_{n,n'} \to ((n, m) \leftrightarrow (n', m)) \text{ for } m \in M \qquad (28)$$

$$CA^0_{n,n'} \to ((n, m) \leftrightarrow (n', m)) \text{ for } m \in M \qquad (29)$$

Formulas (30–32) define the indistinguishability of two nodes w.r.t. memory, observations, and both respectively as $Z^m_{i,j}$, $Z^\omega_{i,j}$ and $Z_{i,j}$.

$$(n_i, m) \wedge (n_j, m) \to Z^m_{i,j} \text{ for } i < j, m \in M \qquad (30)$$

$$\neg({}^oP^{n_i}_\omega \wedge {}^oN^{n_j}_\omega) \wedge \neg({}^oN^{n_i}_\omega \wedge {}^oP^{n_j}_\omega) \to Z^\omega_{i,j} \qquad (31)$$

$$Z^m_{i,j} \wedge \bigwedge_{\omega \in O} Z^\omega_{i,j} \to Z_{i,j} \qquad (32)$$

If a node has observation ω, then ω must hold in the preceding node.

$$(n, n') \wedge {}^oP^{n'}_\omega \to L^\omega_n \qquad (33) \qquad\qquad (n, n') \wedge {}^oN^{n'}_\omega \to L^{\neg\omega}_n \qquad (34)$$

If two action nodes are indistinguishable, same action must be taken in both, and successor nodes must have the same memory state.

$$Z_{i,j} \wedge A_{n_i} \wedge A_{n_j} \to ((n_i, a) \leftrightarrow (n_j, a)) \qquad (35)$$

$$Z_{i,j} \wedge (n_i, n') \wedge (n_j, n'') \wedge A_{n_i} \wedge A_{n_j} \to ((n', m) \leftrightarrow (n'', m)) \qquad (36)$$

6.5   Encodings of Small Memory Plans Explicitly

Here we briefly describe the encoding of explicitly represented small-memory plans. The standard way of representing small-memory plans is by explicitly encoding the whole mapping from all observation combinations and the memory state to the action to be taken and the new memory state [5]. A finite memory plan is an automaton with

- $k \geqslant 1$ memory states $M = \{m_1, \dots, m_k\}$,
- mapping $A_{M,O} : M \times O \to A$ from the current memory state and observation to an action,

- mapping $M_{M,O} : M \times O \to M$ from the current memory state and observation to the next memory state.

New atoms in the encoding:

- (n, ω): observation ω is observed in node n.
- $(n, \mathcal{O})$: $\mathcal{O}$ is the combination of observations observed in node n. To define the atoms, $\mathcal{O}$ is enumerated by valuation of all possible observations ω. For k observations and node n, there are 2^k different valuations and $(n, \mathcal{O})$ atoms.
- $(\mathcal{O}, m, a)$: action a is mapped to observation combination $\mathcal{O}$ and the current memory state is m.
- $(\mathcal{O}, m_i, m_j)$: the memory state m_j is mapped to observation combination $\mathcal{O}$ and the memory state is m_i.

Explicit encoding of the small-memory plans is as follows.

$$\text{valuation}((n, \omega_1), (n, \omega_2) \dots) \leftrightarrow (n, \mathcal{O}) \qquad (37)$$

Map each observation valuation to an observation combination $\mathcal{O}$ for all nodes.

$$\text{exactly1}((\mathcal{O}, m, a_1), (\mathcal{O}, m, a_2), \dots) \qquad (38)$$

$$\text{exactly1}((\mathcal{O}, m_i, m_1), (\mathcal{O}, m_i, m_2), \dots) \qquad (39)$$

Each pair of observation combination and memory state is mapped to exactly one action and to exactly one memory state.

$$(n_i, m_j) \wedge (n_i, \mathcal{O}) \wedge (\mathcal{O}, m_j, a) \wedge A_{n_i} \to (n_i, a) \qquad (40)$$

$$(n_i, m_j) \wedge (n_i, \mathcal{O}) \wedge (n_i, a) \to (\mathcal{O}, m_j, a) \qquad (41)$$

Only the action mapped to the memory and the observation combination can be applied in an action node with that memory and observation combination. Also if an action is taken in a node, then the memory and the observation combination must be mapped to that action in the plan.

$$(n_i, n_j) \wedge (n_i, \mathcal{O}) \wedge (n_i, m_k) \wedge (\mathcal{O}, m_k, m_l) \wedge A_{n_i} \to (n_j, m_l) \qquad (42)$$

$$(n_i, n_j) \wedge (n_i, \mathcal{O}) \wedge (n_i, m_k) \wedge (n_j, m_l) \to (\mathcal{O}, m_k, m_l) \qquad (43)$$

If memory state m_l is mapped to observation combination $\mathcal{O}$ and memory state m_k, then the successor of an action node with those observations and memory should have memory state m_l.

$$(n_i, n_j) \wedge (n_i, m_k) \wedge \text{CA}^{n_i} \to (n_j, m_k) \qquad (44)$$

The memory stays the same in the successor nodes after case analysis.

$$\text{exactly1}((n, m_1), (n, m_2), \dots) \qquad (45)$$

Each node can have only one memory state.

$$(n, n') \wedge \neg\text{CA}^n \wedge (n', \omega) \to L_n^\omega \quad (46) \qquad (n, n') \wedge \neg(n', \omega) \to \neg L_n^\omega \quad (47)$$

If a node has an observation for ω, the formula ω must hold in the predecessor. In case analysis nodes, the observations are copied forward.

$$(n, n') \wedge \text{CA}^n \to ((n', \omega) \leftrightarrow (n, \omega)) \qquad (48)$$

7   Sizes of the Encodings

In the implicit encoding, as given in Sect. 6.4, the largest component is formula (36) with size $|N|^4 \times |M|$. Other dominant formulas are only quadratic with sizes $|N|^2 \times |A|$ (35), $|N|^2 \times |M|$ (28–30) and $|N|^2 \times |O|$ (31, 33 , 34).

On the other hand, the dominant formulas in the explicit encoding of small memory plans have components of size $2^{|O|}$ simply because the mapping has an exponential size, making the encoding quickly impractical for higher numbers of observations.

There are a number of components quadratic in $|N|$ used by both the implicit and explicit encoding, addressing arcs between nodes, for example in Sect. 6.2.

8   Invariants

Invariants are formulas (over state variables) that hold in all reachable states. They reduce the search performed by a SAT solver. With our 3-valued partial states, invariants don't have an obvious representation as redundant constraints, unlike in classical planning, as their interaction with frame axioms becomes more complicated due to partiality. Our solution is to *compile* invariants to actions: if $l_1 \vee l_2$ is an invariant, and $\overline{l_1}$ is an effect, then include l_2 as an effect. This makes it unnecessary to handle invariants explicitly in (7) and (8). Additionally we add redundant constraints that help SAT solvers prune the search space: For an invariant $x \vee y$, we include $\neg N_x^n \vee \neg N_y^n$ in the encoding, to allow inferring $\neg N_y^n$ whenever N_x^n has been inferred. Note that inferring P_y^n would be too strong, as abstraction/generalization may call for not making the value of y explicit.

We use 2-literal invariants $l_1 \vee l_2$ that are found with invariant algorithms that apply to non-deterministic actions [17].

9   Experiments

We have a proof-of-concept implementation of our framework, and we have run computational experiments to demonstrate its potential. Table 2 shows statistics on solving a number of planning problems. All runs were with a 2400 s time limit and performed on Xeon E5 2680 2.50 GHz CPUs with a memory limit of 8 GB. We tested by increasing number of nodes by 5 and memory states by 2 until the instances became solvable. All experiments used the KisSAT solver [2].

The largest instances reported here have tens of thousands of states, which is outside the scalability of methods that represent all states explicitly [5]. While this shows good potential for this approach, it is currently not competitive with the state-of-the-art, specifically the DNF/CNF family of planners [19, 20] or reductions of partial observability to fully observable problems [3, 4].

Table 2. Comparison of the implicit and explicit encodings. V: *number of variables*; A: *number of actions*; O: *number of observations*; TO: *time-out*; OM: *out-of-memory*

				Implicit			Explicit		
INSTANCE	V	A	O	n	m	time	n	m	time
doors2	6	12	4	10	6	7.78	15	6	17.59
medical002	6	10	2	10	4	2.85	10	4	1.48
medical003	8	11	3	10	4	3.28	10	4	3.75
medical004	9	11	3	15	4	332.86	15	4	94.64
medical005	11	12	4	20	6	1364.99	35	10	TO
bombRB1	3	3	2	10	4	1.82	10	4	0.77
bombRB2	5	6	4	10	4	1.9	20	8	1501.97
bombRB3	7	9	6	15	4	74.64	35	8	TO
bombRB4	9	12	8	15	4	346.75	15	4	OM
bts010	11	20	10	15	2	93.27	5	4	OM
gridXY13	3	3	2	10	4	1.37	10	4	0.97
gridXY15	5	3	2	15	4	52.09	50	8	TO
gridXY33	6	5	4	15	4	60.31	25	8	OM
rovers2	10	17	2	15	10	1505.43	15	10	180.66
elogistics1	13	24	6	15	6	66.21	15	8	770.26
elogistics3	19	39	9	20	6	795.27	10	4	OM
egrid2	42	100	20	15	10	1815.77	5	2	OM
logistics1	13	24	6	10	6	7.94	15	8	OM
logistics3	19	39	9	15	8	137.99	5	4	OM
medpks2	6	6	2	10	4	2.64	10	4	1.68
grid2	42	100	20	15	10	1816.62	5	2	OM
blocks3	15	51	15	10	4	3.41	5	2	OM
erovers2	10	17	2	15	10	1485.55	15	8	100.47

10   Conclusion

We have shown how planning with a complex actions and partial observability, can be effectively reduced to propositional logic and solved with SAT solvers. This is the first time that planning with partial observability has been solved with single SAT solver calls that both find a plan and determine its correctness, showing significant potential in the ideas presented by Geffner & Geffner [7].

Our framework is effective when belief states can be represented as conjunctions of literals. Complex dependencies between state variables, representable e.g. as disjunctions $a \lor b$, require making plan executions more explicit, increasing the size of the graphs and the search cost. More expressive belief state representations should be investigated.

An obvious inefficiency in our encoding is that the use of case analysis is not restricted in any way, for example allowing forgetting immediately followed by case analysis on the same variable. Another inefficiency worth further research is symmetry reduction for the graphs.

References

1. Baral, C., Kreinovich, V., Trejo, R.: Computational complexity of planning and approximate planning in the presence of incompleteness. Artif. Intell. **122**(1), 241–267 (2000)
2. Biere, A., Fazekas, K., Fleury, M., Heisinger, M.: CaDiCaL, kissat, paracooba, plingeling and treengeling entering the SAT competition 2020. In: Proceedings of SAT Competition 2020 - Solver and Benchmark Descriptions, pp. 51 53. Department of Computer Science Report Series B, vol. B-2020-1, University of Helsinki (2020)
3. Bonet, B., Geffner, H.: Planning under partial observability by classical replanning: theory and experiments. In: Proceedings of the 22nd International Joint Conference on Artificial Intelligence, pp. 1936–1941 (2011)
4. Bonet, B., Geffner, H.: Flexible and scalable partially observable planning with linear translations. In: Proceedings of the 28th AAAI Conference on Artificial Intelligence (AAAI-14), pp. 2235–2241. Citeseer (2014)
5. Chatterjee, K., Chmelik, M., Davies, J.: A symbolic SAT-based algorithm for almost-sure reachability with small strategies in POMDPs. In: Proceedings of the 30th AAAI Conference on Artificial Intelligence (AAAI-16), pp. 3225–3232. AAAI Press (2016)
6. Ferraris, P., Giunchiglia, E.: Planning as satisfiability in nondeterministic domains. In: Proceedings of the 17th National Conference on Artificial Intelligence (AAAI-2000) and the 12th Conference on Innovative Applications of Artificial Intelligence (IAAI-2000), pp. 748–753. AAAI Press (2000)
7. Geffner, T., Geffner, H.: Compact policies for non-deterministic fully observable planning as SAT. In: Proceedings of the Twenty-Eighth International Conference on Automated Planning and Scheduling, ICAPS 2018, pp. 88–96. AAAI Press (2018)
8. Kautz, H., Selman, B.: Planning as satisfiability. In: Proceedings of the 10th European Conference on Artificial Intelligence, pp. 359–363. John Wiley & Sons (1992)
9. Kautz, H., Selman, B.: Pushing the envelope: planning, propositional logic, and stochastic search. In: Proceedings of the 13th National Conference on Artificial Intelligence and the 8th Innovative Applications of Artificial Intelligence Conference, pp. 1194–1201. AAAI Press (1996)
10. Lusena, C., Li, T., Sittinger, S., Wells, C., Goldsmith, J.: My brain is full: when more memory helps. In: Uncertainty in Artificial Intelligence, Proceedings of the Fifteenth Conference (UAI 1999), pp. 374–381. Morgan Kaufmann Publishers (1999)
11. Majercik, S.M., Littman, M.L.: MAXPLAN: a new approach to probabilistic planning. In: Proceedings of the Fourth International Conference on Artificial Intelligence Planning Systems, pp. 86–93. Pittsburgh, Pennsylvania (1998)
12. Majercik, S.M., Littman, M.L.: Contingent planning under uncertainty via stochastic satisfiability. Artif. Intell. **147**(1–2), 119–162 (2003)

13. Meuleau, N., Kim, K.E., Kaelbling, L.P., Cassandra, A.R.: Solving POMDPs by searching the space of finite policies. In: Uncertainty in Artificial Intelligence, Proceedings of the Fifteenth Conference (UAI 1999), pp. 417–426. Morgan Kaufmann Publishers (1999)
14. Pandey, B., Rintanen, J.: Planning for partial observability by SAT and graph constraints. In: ICAPS 2018. Proceedings of the Twenty-Eighth International Conference on Automated Planning and Scheduling, pp. 190–198. AAAI Press (2018)
15. Rintanen, J.: Constructing conditional plans by a theorem-prover. J. Artif. Intell. Res. **10**, 323–352 (1999)
16. Rintanen, J.: Asymptotically optimal encodings of conformant planning in QBF. In: Proceedings of the 22nd AAAI Conference on Artificial Intelligence (AAAI 2007), pp. 1045–1050. AAAI Press (2007)
17. Rintanen, J.: Regression for classical and nondeterministic planning. In: Proceedings of the 18th European Conference on Artificial Intelligence, ECAI 2008, pp. 568–571. IOS Press (2008)
18. Sinz, C.: Towards an optimal CNF encoding of Boolean cardinality constraints. In: van Beek, P. (ed.) CP 2005. LNCS, vol. 3709, pp. 827–831. Springer, Heidelberg (2005). https://doi.org/10.1007/11564751_73
19. To, S.T., Pontelli, E., Son, T.C.: On the effectiveness of CNF and DNF representations in contingent planning. In: Proceedings of the 22nd International Joint Conference on Artificial Intelligence, pp. 2033–2038. AAAI Press (2011)
20. To, S.T., Son, T.C., Pontelli, E.: A generic approach to planning in the presence of incomplete information: theory and implementation. Artif. Intell. **227**, 1–51 (2015)
21. Turner, H.: Polynomial-length planning spans the polynomial hierarchy. In: Flesca, S., Greco, S., Ianni, G., Leone, N. (eds.) JELIA 2002. LNCS (LNAI), vol. 2424, pp. 111–124. Springer, Heidelberg (2002). https://doi.org/10.1007/3-540-45757-7_10

Optimal Planning with Expressive Action Languages as Constraint Optimization

Enrico Giunchiglia and Armando Tacchella[(✉)]

DIBRIS - University of Genoa, V.le Causa 13, 16145 Genoa, Italy
{enrico.giunchiglia,armando.tacchella}@dibris.unige.it

Abstract. We consider the problem of optimal planning in deterministic domains specified with expressive action languages. We show how it is possible to reduce such problem to finding an optimal solution of a constraint optimization problem incorporating a bound n on the maximum length of the plan. By solving the latter, we can conclude whether (*i*) the plan found is optimal even for bounds greater than n; or (*ii*) we need to increase n; or (*iii*) it is useless to increase n since the planning problem has no solution.

1 Introduction

We consider the problem of optimal planning in deterministic domains (action descriptions) specified with expressive action languages. In particular, for each domain/action description D in the state variables $\mathcal{X}$ and action variables $\mathcal{A}$, we assume to be able to compute a quantifier free formula $T(\mathcal{X}, \mathcal{A}, \mathcal{X}')$ in the variables $\mathcal{X}$, $\mathcal{A}$ and $\mathcal{X}'$ whose models correspond to the valid transitions of D (as usual, $\mathcal{X}'$ is a copy of the set of state variables encoding their value in the state resulting from the execution of the action). Computing $T(\mathcal{X}, \mathcal{A}, \mathcal{X}')$ starting from D is already known for many action languages, like PDDL [9], or $\mathcal{C}+$ [11], the latter being the language we are particularly interested in, given its high expressive capabilities that enable the modelling of complex robotics scenarios with, e.g., constraints, concurring interacting actions and events. More in general, $\mathcal{C}+$ allows to specify any transition system with action variables (the ones under agents' control) and state variables (the ones changing because of actions and/or of external events), see [10]. Such generality comes at a price, since it is not possible to exploit the specific properties of the transition systems being captured (as it would be possible for systems specified, e.g., in STRIPS), and this is why we consider problems in which $T(\mathcal{X}, \mathcal{A}, \mathcal{X}')$ is an arbitrary conjunction of formulas. On the bright side, our contribution is applicable to all determistic planning problems in which the action description represents a transition system. Thus, we consider problems specified as a pair $\langle \Pi, C \rangle$ where Π is a deterministic planning problem specified with three formulas $T(\mathcal{X}, \mathcal{A}, \mathcal{X}')$,

The authors wish to thank Erika Ábrahám, Francesco Leofante and Marco Maratea for useful discussions about the research topic presented in this paper.

S. Gaggl et al. (Eds.): JELIA 2023, LNAI 14281, pp. 621–637, 2023.
https://doi.org/10.1007/978-3-031-43619-2_42

$I(\mathcal{X})$ and $G(\mathcal{X})$ in conjunctive normal form (CNF), where $I(\mathcal{X})$ represents the initial state and $G(\mathcal{X})$ the set of goal states, and C associates a non-negative cost to each transition. Our objective is to determine an optimal plan, i.e., a sequence of actions leading from the initial state to a goal state with minimum associated total cost, defined as the sum of the costs of the transitions induced by the actions in the plan.

With such objective, we extend the planning as satisfiability approach [18] and reduce the problem of finding an optimal plan for $\langle \Pi, C \rangle$ to the one of solving a corresponding constraint optimization problem incorporating a bound n on the maximum length of the plan. The basic idea is to construct an encoding Π_n^O of Π and C_n^O of C such that each valid plan π of Π with cost $C(\pi)$ bijectively corresponds to a model π_n^O of Π_n^O having cost $C_n^O(\pi_n^O) = C(\pi)$, if π is shorter than n, and corresponds to a model π_n^O of Π_n^O having cost $C_n^O(\pi_n^O) \leq C(\pi)$, if π is longer than n. Thus, if π_n^O is an optimal model of $\langle \Pi_n^O, C_n^O \rangle$ then if π_n^O corresponds to a plan π of Π with at most n actions, then π is an optimal plan of Π, and if π_n^O does not correspond to a plan of Π with at most n actions then we have to increase the bound n. Moreover, if Π_n^O is unsatisfiable then Π does not admit a valid plan and it is useless to increase the bound n. Our work substantially generalizes previous approaches for optimal symbolic deterministic planning, including [20] which considers numeric planning problems expressible in PDDL2.1 level 2 [9]. Despite being far more general than [20], (i) we provide non trivial lower bounds on the cost and length of the optimal plans, and (ii) we guarantee that our encoding is linear in the size of Π and the bound n (while the one in [20] is worst case exponential).

The paper is structured as follows. After the formal framework, we focus on how to encode plans shorter than or equal to the bound (Sect. 3), and then we consider plans longer than the bound (Sect. 4). We put all the pieces together in Sect. 5, ending the paper in Sect. 6 with some remarks, including related and future works. For the lack of space, most examples and all the proofs are moved to appendices.

2   Formal Framework

We consider deterministic planning problems (i) that can be described using finitely many state and action variables, and (ii) whose initial state, valid transitions and goal states are the models of corresponding quantifier free CNF formulas.

For the language signature, we assume to have

1. a non empty finite set $\mathcal{X}$ of *state variables*, each variable $x \in \mathcal{X}$ equipped with its *domain* $dom(x)$, with $|dom(x)| \geq 2$, representing the values x can assume,
2. a finite set $\mathcal{A}$ of Boolean *action variables*,
3. a copy $\mathcal{X}'$ of $\mathcal{X}$ of *next state variables* such that, for each state variable $x \in \mathcal{X}$, there is a corresponding variable $x' \in \mathcal{X}'$ with $dom(x') = dom(x)$.

An *assignment* to a set of variables $\mathcal{V}$ is a function mapping each variable in $\mathcal{V}$ to an element of its domain. In the case of Boolean variables, their domain is $\{\top, \bot\}$ for truth and falsity, and we use v in place of $v = \top$. A *state* (resp. *action*, resp. *next state*) is an assignment to the variables $\mathcal{X}$ (resp. $\mathcal{A}$, resp. $\mathcal{X}'$). States, actions and next states are denoted with $\sigma, \sigma_0, \ldots, \alpha, \alpha_0, \ldots$, and $\sigma', \sigma'_0, \ldots$, respectively. A *transition* is an assignment to all the state, action and next state variables at hand. Besides variables, we assume to have other, possibly theory dependent, symbols (like "0", "+", "≥") and auxiliary symbols (like "(" and ")") that are used to define atomic formulas, literals and well formed formulas. We take for granted standard logic notions like satisfiability, entailment, model, and the like. Unless explicitly noted, assignments are total. (Partial) actions are represented with the set of action literals they satisfy.

A *(deterministic) planning problem* Π is a 5 tuple $\langle \mathcal{X}, \mathcal{A}, I(\mathcal{X}), T(\mathcal{X}, \mathcal{A}, \mathcal{X}'), G(\mathcal{X}) \rangle$ where

1. $I(\mathcal{X})$ is the *initial state formula* in the state variables $\mathcal{X}$, assumed to be satisfied by exactly one state;
2. $T(\mathcal{X}, \mathcal{A}, \mathcal{X}')$ is the *transition relation*, i.e., a formula in the $\mathcal{X}, \mathcal{A}, \mathcal{X}'$ variables, whose models are the *valid* transitions. For each state σ and action α it is assumed that there is at most one valid transition σ, α, σ';
3. $G(\mathcal{X})$ is the *goal formula* in the state variables $\mathcal{X}$, whose models are the *goal states*.

In the following, $lx, lx_1, \ldots$ (resp. $la, la_1, \ldots$, resp. $lx', lx'_1, \ldots$) denote state (resp. action, resp. next state) literals, i.e., literals in the $\mathcal{X}$ (resp. $\mathcal{A}$, resp. $\mathcal{X}'$) variables. When convenient, we use also the symbol "→" for implication and write clauses in $T(\mathcal{X}, \mathcal{A}, \mathcal{X}')$ either as

$$\bigwedge_{i=1}^{p} la_i \rightarrow \bigvee_{i=1}^{q} lx_i \tag{1}$$

$(p, q \geq 0)$ to model that $(\bigvee_{i=1}^{q} lx_i)$ is an *explicit precondition* of the partial actions which satisfy $(\bigwedge_{i=1}^{p} la_i)$, or as

$$\bigwedge_{i=1}^{p} la_i \wedge \bigwedge_{i=1}^{q} lx_i \rightarrow \bigvee_{i=1}^{r} lx'_i \tag{2}$$

$(p, q \geq 0, r \geq 1)$, to model that $(\bigvee_{i=1}^{r} lx'_i)$ is an *explicit (conditional) effect* of the actions and states which satisfy $\bigwedge_{i=1}^{p} la_i \wedge \bigwedge_{i=1}^{q} lx_i$.

Example 1. Consider a domain SQUARE in which an integer variable *var* is initialized to a value V_I and should reach a value $V_G \geq 0$. The value of *var* can be changed only in states with *var* ≥ 0, and the value of *var* is automatically incremented by 1 in the next state, unless it is squared. This domain can be formalized as the planning problem $\Pi = \langle \mathcal{X}, \mathcal{A}, I(\mathcal{X}), T(\mathcal{X}, \mathcal{A}, \mathcal{X}'), G(\mathcal{X}) \rangle$ where

$\mathcal{X} = \{var\}$, $\mathcal{A} = \{square\}$, $I(\mathcal{X}) = (var = V_I)$, $G(\mathcal{X}) = (var \geq V_G)$, and $T(\mathcal{X}, \mathcal{A}, \mathcal{X}')$ is the formula

$$(\neg square \wedge var \geq 0 \rightarrow var' = var + 1)\wedge$$
$$(square \rightarrow var \geq 0) \wedge (square \rightarrow var' = var^2)\wedge \qquad (3)$$
$$(var < 0 \rightarrow var' = var).$$

In $\mathcal{C}+$ [11], the SQUARE domain can be formalized as the action description consisting, for each value V, of the following static and dynamic causal laws

> $\neg square$ **causes** $var = V + 1$ **if** $var = V \wedge V \geq 0$,
> **nonexecutable** $square$ **if** $var < 0$,
> $square$ **causes** $var = V^2$ **if** $var = V$,
> **caused** $var = V$ **after** $var = V \wedge V < 0$.

Analogous formalizations are possible in other languages for describing actions, like $\mathcal{BC}+$ [2]. □

The fact that the transition relation formula in the example corresponds to an action description in $\mathcal{C}+$ is not coincidental. It can be easily proved that for any transition relation $T(\mathcal{X}, \mathcal{A}, \mathcal{X}')$ there exists a definite action description D in $\mathcal{C}+$ whose transitions are the models of $T(\mathcal{X}, \mathcal{A}, \mathcal{X}')$.[1] On the converse, for any definite action description D in $\mathcal{C}+$ with state and action variables $\mathcal{X}$ and $\mathcal{A}$, respectively, there exists a CNF formula $T(\mathcal{X}, \mathcal{A}, \mathcal{X}')$ whose models are the transitions of D [11].

Let $\Pi = \langle \mathcal{X}, \mathcal{A}, I(\mathcal{X}), T(\mathcal{X}, \mathcal{A}, \mathcal{X}'), G(\mathcal{X}) \rangle$ be a planning problem. Our next step is to define the valid plans of Π — most of our terminology is from [9,15]. If $F(\mathcal{V})$ is a formula/function in the $\mathcal{V}$ variables and μ is a partial assignment to $\mathcal{V}$ defined on $\mathcal{U} \subseteq \mathcal{V}$, by $F(\mu)$ we mean the formula/function obtained by substituting each variable $v \in \mathcal{U}$ with $\mu(v)$ in $F(\mathcal{V})$.

An action α is *executable* in a state σ if there is a next state σ' satisfying $T(\sigma, \alpha, \mathcal{X}')$, in which case the *result of executing* α in σ is the state σ'' such that, for each state variable x, $\sigma''(x) = \sigma'(x')$. A plan (*of length k*) is a sequence of $k \geq 0$ actions.

Consider a plan $\pi = \alpha_0; \ldots; \alpha_{k-1}$. π is *executable* if for each $i \in [0, k-1]$, α_i is executable in σ_i, where σ_0 is the state satisfying the initial state formula, and σ_{i+1} is the result of executing α_i in σ_i. If π is executable, the state σ_i ($0 \leq i \leq k$) as above defined is the *i-th state induced by* π. The plan π is *valid* if it is executable and the k-th induced state σ_k satisfies $G(\mathcal{X})$.

For the definition of optimal plan, we introduce a cost associated to each valid transition. By C_{min} we denote a fixed positive constant. A pair $\langle \Pi, C \rangle$ is a *planning problem with costs* if C is a cost function such that for each valid transition σ, α, σ', (i) $C(\sigma, \alpha, \sigma') \geq C_{min}$ whenever $\sigma'(x') \neq \sigma(x)$ for some state variable x, and (ii) $C(\sigma, \alpha, \sigma') \geq 0$ otherwise. If π is a valid plan of length k, the *cost* $C(\pi)$ of π is the sum of the costs of each transition, i.e.,

---

[1] Formal statement and proof omitted for lack of space.

$$C(\pi) = \sum_{i=0}^{k-1} C(\sigma_i, \alpha_i, \sigma'_{i+1}) \tag{4}$$

where σ_i and σ_{i+1} are the i-th and $(i+1)$-th states induced by π and, for each $x \in \mathcal{X}$, $\sigma'_{i+1}(x') = \sigma_{i+1}(x)$. The plan π is *optimal* if it is valid and there is no valid plan with a smaller cost.

Example 2. In SQUARE, assume that the cost of each transition is the maximum between 1 and the difference between the new and old values of *var*. Formally,

$$C(\mathcal{X}, \mathcal{A}, \mathcal{X}') = max(var' - var, 1).$$

Then, if $V_I = 1$ and $V_G = 9$, the plans $\xi = \{square\}; \{\neg square\}; \{\neg square\}; \{square\}$, and $\pi = \{\neg square\}; \{\neg square\}; \{square\}$, are both valid, but only π is optimal (since $C(\xi) = 9$ and $C(\pi) = 8$). There are only two other optimal plans (a^i means action a repeated i times): $\omega = \{\neg square\}; \{square\}; \{\neg square\}^5$ and $\varrho = \{\neg square\}^8$ of length 7 and 8, respectively. If we assume that the cost of each transition is equal to the difference between the new and old values of *var*, i.e.,

$$C(\mathcal{X}, \mathcal{A}, \mathcal{X}') = var' - var$$

then also ξ is optimal, and indeed there are infinitely many optimal plans, simply obtained by adding at the beginning of π, ω, ϱ, finitely many times the action $\{square\}$.   □

As the example shows, a plan π can contain loops, but to compute optimal plans, we can focus on plans without loops.

Proposition 1. *Let* $\langle \Pi, C \rangle$ *be a planning problem with costs. Let* $\pi = \alpha_0; \ldots; \alpha_{k-1}$ $(k \geq 0)$ *be a valid plan such that for given* $0 \leq i < j \leq k$, *the i-th state σ_i and j-th state σ_j induced by π are the same. Then,* $\pi' = \alpha_0; \ldots; \alpha_{i-1}; \alpha_j; \ldots; \alpha_{k-1}$ *is a valid plan and*

1. $C(\pi) \geq C(\pi')$, *and*
2. $C(\pi) = C(\pi')$ *only if all the states induced by π in between σ_i and σ_j are equal to σ_i.*

As a consequence of the above proposition[2], if the plan π contains loops of length $j - i - 1 > 0$, i.e., if the i-th state σ_i and the j-th state induced by π are the same, but some state in between σ_i and σ_j is different from σ_i then π is not optimal. The presence of loops of length 0 may cause the existence of arbitrarily long optimal plans, as it happens in Example 2, and termination problems for approaches (like ours) imposing a bound on the maximum length of the plan. For this reason, we will restrict to the valid/optimal plans which are *0-loop free*, i.e., which do not contain loops of length 0. Determining the existence of a valid or optimal plan (and thus the existence of a bound n for which there exists a

---

[2] We omit the proof of proposition 1 as it is an easy consequence of the hypothesis and the definitions.

valid or optimal plan of length $\leq n$) in our framework is, in general, undecidable [16], but the existence of a valid plan implies the existence of an optimal plan with an upper bound on its length.

Proposition 2. *Let* $\langle \Pi, C \rangle$ *be a planning problem with costs. If* π *is a valid plan of* Π *with cost* $C(\pi)$ *then there exists an optimal plan of length less than or equal to* $\lfloor C(\pi)/C_{min} \rfloor$.

3   Plans Shorter Than or Equal to the Bound

Let $\Pi = \langle \mathcal{X}, \mathcal{A}, I(\mathcal{X}), T(\mathcal{X}, \mathcal{A}, \mathcal{X}'), G(\mathcal{X}) \rangle$ be a planning problem with costs given by $C(\mathcal{X}, \mathcal{A}, \mathcal{X}')$, and let $n \geq 0$ be a fixed integer called *bound* or *number of steps*.

Following the approach of [18], we make $n + 1$ disjoint copies $\mathcal{X}_0, \ldots, \mathcal{X}_n$ of the set $\mathcal{X}$ of state variables, and n copies $\mathcal{A}_0, \ldots, \mathcal{A}_{n-1}$ of the set $\mathcal{A}$ of action variables. Then, for each $i \in [0, n-1]$, $T(\mathcal{X}_i, \mathcal{A}_i, \mathcal{X}_{i+1})$ is the formula obtained substituting each variable $x \in \mathcal{X}$ (resp. $a \in \mathcal{A}$, $x' \in \mathcal{X}'$) with $x_i \in \mathcal{X}_i$ (resp. $a_i \in \mathcal{A}_i$, $x_{i+1} \in \mathcal{X}_{i+1}$) in $T(\mathcal{X}, \mathcal{A}, \mathcal{X}')$, and similarly for other formulas like $I(X_0)$, $G(\mathcal{X}_n)$ and $C(\mathcal{X}_i, \mathcal{A}_i, \mathcal{X}_{i+1})$.

Then, we define

$$\begin{aligned} \Pi_n^S &= I(\mathcal{X}_0) \wedge \bigwedge_{i=0}^{n-1} T(\mathcal{X}_i, \mathcal{A}_i, \mathcal{X}_{i+1}) \wedge G(\mathcal{X}_n), \\ C_n^S &= \textstyle\sum_{i=0}^{n-1} C(\mathcal{X}_i, \mathcal{A}_i, \mathcal{X}_{i+1}). \end{aligned}$$

Π_n^S and C_n^S define a constraint optimization problem, whose *optimal models* are the models of Π_n^S that have minimum associated cost C_n^S.

We now establish the correspondence between the plans of Π and the models of Π_n^S.

For a plan $\pi = \alpha_0; \ldots; \alpha_{n-1}$ with induced states $\sigma_0; \ldots; \sigma_n$, we define π_n^S to be the assignment to the variables in Π_n^S such that, for each state variable $x \in \mathcal{X}$, each action variable $a \in \mathcal{A}$ and each $i \in [0, n)$, $\pi_i^S(x_i) = \sigma_i(x)$, $\pi_n^S(a_i) = \alpha_i(a)$, $\pi_n^S(x_{i+1}) = \sigma_{i+1}(a)$. Notice that the above definition of π_n^S assumes π to be executable, otherwise the state sequence induced by π is not defined and thus also π_n^S is not defined. We state[3] the following:

Proposition 3. *Let* $\langle \Pi, C \rangle$ *be a planning problem with costs. Let* π *be a plan of length* $n \geq 0$. π *is a valid plan of* Π *iff* π_n^S *is a model of* Π_n^S, *and* $C(\pi) = C_n^S(\pi_n^S)$.

Notice that Π_n^S and $C_n^S(\pi_n^S)$ encode the validity and the cost of plans of length exactly n. Indeed, it is possible that valid plans shorter than n exist and do not correspond to models of Π_n^S with the same cost. This is because, in general, it is not the case that the transition relation $T(\mathcal{X}, \mathcal{A}, \mathcal{X}')$ and cost function $C(\mathcal{X}, \mathcal{A}, \mathcal{X}')$ are *inertial*, i.e., that for every state σ there exists an action α whose execution in σ results in the same state σ with cost 0. We thus,

1. extend the action signature with the variable *NoOp*, and

---

[3] The proof is an easy induction on the length of the plan.

2. define $T^I(\mathcal{X}, \mathcal{A} \cup \{NoOp\}, \mathcal{X}')$ as

$$(\neg NoOp \rightarrow T(\mathcal{X}, \mathcal{A}, \mathcal{X}')) \wedge (NoOp \equiv \bigwedge_{x \in \mathcal{X}} x' = x) \wedge \bigwedge_{a \in \mathcal{A}} (NoOp \rightarrow \neg a).$$

Imposing in the definition above

1. that $NoOp$ is true whenever the resulting state is equal to the state in which the action is executed, and
2. that all the action variables $a \in \mathcal{A}$ have to be false whenever $NoOp$ is true,

yields a one-to-one correspondence between the 0-loop free valid plans of Π of length $k \leq n$ and the models of

$$\Pi_n^I = I(\mathcal{X}_0) \wedge \bigwedge_{i=0}^{n-1} T^I(\mathcal{X}_i, \mathcal{A}_i \cup \{NoOp_i\}, \mathcal{X}_{i+1})$$
$$\wedge \bigwedge_{i=0}^{n-2} (NoOp_i \rightarrow NoOp_{i+1}) \wedge G(\mathcal{X}_n).$$

For a plan π of length $k \leq n$, we define the assignment π_n^I to the variables of Π_n^I to be the extension of π_k^S such that $\pi_n^I(NoOp_0) = \ldots = \pi_n^I(NoOp_{k-1}) = \bot$, $\pi_n^I(NoOp_k) = \ldots = \pi_n^I(NoOp_{n-1}) = \top$, and for each $i \in [k, n)$, for each state variable $x \in \mathcal{X}$ and for each action variable $a \in \mathcal{A}$, $\pi_n^I(x_i) = \pi_n^I(x_{i+1}) = \pi_k^S(x_k)$ and $\pi_n^I(a_i) = \bot$.

If we define $C^I(\mathcal{X}, \mathcal{A} \cup \{NoOp\}, \mathcal{X}')$ to be such that, for each assignment σ, α, σ' to $\mathcal{X}, \mathcal{A}, \mathcal{X}'$,

$$C^I(\sigma, \alpha \cup \{\neg NoOp\}, \sigma') = C(\sigma, \alpha, \sigma'),$$
$$C^I(\sigma, \alpha \cup \{NoOp\}, \sigma') = 0,$$

then we have also that the cost $C(\pi)$ of a plan π of length $k \leq n$ is equal to $C_n^I(\pi_n^I)$, defined as:

$$C_n^I = \sum_{i=0}^{n-1} C^I(\mathcal{X}_i, \mathcal{A}_i \cup \{NoOp_i\}, \mathcal{X}_{i+1}).$$

Proposition 4. *Let $\langle \Pi, C \rangle$ be a planning problem with costs. Let π be a plan of length $k \leq n$. π is a 0-loop free valid plan of Π iff π_n^I is a model of Π_n^I, and $C(\pi) = C_n^I(\pi_n^I)$.*

Owing to proposition 4, we know that if a model π_n^I of Π_n^I is optimal (i.e., all the other models ρ_n^I of Π_n^I are such that $C_n^I(\rho_n^I) \geq C_n^I(\pi_n^I)$), then there is no valid plan of Π with length $\leq n$ and cost smaller than $C(\pi)$.

Example 3. Assume that $V_I = 1$ and $V_G = 9$ in our $\langle \Pi, C \rangle$ formalization of the SQUARE domain. From the previous example, we know that the plans π, ω and ρ of length 3, 7 and 8, respectively, are optimal. Assuming $n = 8$, from the proposition we can conclude that π_n^I, ω_n^I and ρ_n^I are optimal models of $\langle \Pi_n^I, C_n^I \rangle$. On the other hand, from the fact that π_n^I, ω_n^I and ρ_n^I are optimal models of $\langle \Pi_n^I, C_n^I \rangle$, the proposition does not allow us to conclude that π, ω and ρ are optimal plans of $\langle \Pi, C \rangle$. $\square$

4   Plans Longer Than or Equal to the Bound

Let $\Pi = \langle \mathcal{X}, \mathcal{A}, I(\mathcal{X}), T(\mathcal{X}, \mathcal{A}, \mathcal{X}'), G(\mathcal{X}) \rangle$ be a planning problem with costs given by $C(\mathcal{X}, \mathcal{A}, \mathcal{X}')$, and let $n \geq 0$ be the selected bound. We build an abstract encoding Π_n^A of Π such that for each valid plan π of length $k \geq n$ there exists a corresponding model π_n^A of Π_n^A with cost $C_n^A(\pi_n^A) \leq C(\pi)$.

Consider a valid plan $\pi = \alpha_0; \ldots; \alpha_{k-1}$ of length $k \geq n$ and let σ_i, $i \in [0, k]$, be the i-th state induced by π.

The definition of Π_n^A is based

1. on the *abstract transition relation* $T^A(\mathcal{X}, \mathcal{LX}, \mathcal{LA}, \mathcal{VX})$ defined on the basis of $T(\mathcal{X}, \mathcal{A}, \mathcal{X}')$, and on
2. the *abstract goal* $G^A(\mathcal{X}, \mathcal{LX}, \mathcal{VX}, \{\lambda_G\})$ defined on the basis of $G(\mathcal{X})$.

Both formulas are over the sets of variables $\mathcal{X}, \mathcal{LX}, \mathcal{LA}, \mathcal{VX}, \{\lambda_G\}$, where

1. $\mathcal{LX}$ is a finite set of variables of the form λ_{lx}, each corresponding to a state literal lx.
2. $\mathcal{LA}$ contains a variable λ_{la} for each action literal la (thus, $|\mathcal{LA}| = 2 \times |\mathcal{A}|$).
3. $\mathcal{VX}$ contains a variable $\lambda_{x' \neq x}$ for each state variable $x \in \mathcal{X}$ (thus, $|\mathcal{VX}| = |\mathcal{X}|$).
4. λ_G is a variable associated to the goal formula $G(\mathcal{X})$.

For each variable $\lambda_v \in \mathcal{LX}, \mathcal{LA}, \mathcal{VX}, \{\lambda_G\}$, λ_v defines the *level of v* and provides a lower bound on the step at which v is true in π_k. More precisely,

1. for each state literal lx with $\lambda_{lx} \in \mathcal{LX}$, for each $i \in [n, k]$, if $\sigma_i(lx) = \top$ then $\pi_n^A(\lambda_{lx}) \leq min(i - n, |\mathcal{X}|)$,
2. for each action literal la, for each $i \in [n, k)$, if $\alpha_i(la) = \top$ then $\pi_n^A(\lambda_{la}) \leq min(i - n, |\mathcal{X}|)$,
3. for each state variable x, for each $i \in (n, k]$, if $\sigma_i(x) \neq \sigma_{i-1}(x)$ then $\pi_n^A(\lambda_{x' \neq x}) \leq min(i - n, |\mathcal{X}|)$, and
4. for each $i \in [n, k]$, if $\sigma_i(G(\mathcal{X})) = \top$ then $\pi_n^A(\lambda_G) \leq min(i - n, |\mathcal{X}|)$.

Notice that there can be infinitely many state literals lx, but we are going to introduce only finitely many variables $\lambda_{lx} \in \mathcal{LX}$. For each state literal lx in the state variables $x_1, \ldots, x_m$ with $\lambda_{lx} \in \mathcal{LX}$, the value of λ_{lx} is defined by the two formulas

$$lx \rightarrow \lambda_{lx} = 0$$
$$\neg lx \rightarrow \lambda_{lx} = min(\lambda_{x_1' \neq x_1}, \ldots, \lambda_{x_m' \neq x_m}). \tag{5}$$

In order to show how the values for the variables in $\mathcal{LA}$ are defined, consider an action literal la. The value of λ_{la} is defined on the basis of a given set $\mathcal{P}^{la}(\mathcal{X})$ of preconditions of la. A disjunction p of state literals is a *precondition* of la if $T(\mathcal{X}, \mathcal{A}, \mathcal{X}')$ entails $(la \rightarrow p)$. Since the set of the preconditions of la is equivalent to

$$\exists \mathcal{A} \exists \mathcal{X}'(la \land T(\mathcal{X}, \mathcal{A}, \mathcal{X}')), \tag{6}$$

each precondition is entailed by (6). Computing a set of preconditions starting from equation (6) requires the theory behind the planning problem to admit a quantifier elimination procedure, which, in general, cannot be guaranteed. However, there are cases in which such quantifier elimination is possible, though computationally expensive, e.g., using Fourier-Motzkin procedure, assuming variables are either Boolean or range over the reals, and that in $T(\mathcal{X}, \mathcal{A}, \mathcal{X}')$ there are only Boolean variables and linear inequalities. Furthermore, in many cases all preconditions are explicit in $T(\mathcal{X}, \mathcal{A}, \mathcal{X}')$, e.g., for PDDL encoded problems. Finally, in all cases — since we wish to compute a superset of the set of actions literals la which have their precondition satisfied — we do not need all the (infinitely many) preconditions of la, and we can just consider some of the preconditions of la, like the explicit ones of the partial actions $\{la\}$ in $T(\mathcal{X}, \mathcal{A}, \mathcal{X}')$ (we recall that each explicit precondition of $\{la\}$ corresponds to a formula of the form (1) with either $p = 0$ or $p = 1$ and $la_1 = la$). If $T(\mathcal{X}, \mathcal{A}, \mathcal{X}')$ contains a clause of the form (1) with either $p = 0$ or $p = 1$ and $la_1 = la$, then (6) is equivalent to $(\bigvee_{i=1}^{q} lx_i \wedge \exists \mathcal{A} \exists \mathcal{X}'(la \wedge T(\mathcal{X}, \mathcal{A}, \mathcal{X}')))$, and thus every explicit precondition of the partial action $\{la\}$ is entailed by (6).

Example 4. The preconditions of $square$ coincide with its explicit precondition $(var \geq 0)$, while $\neg square$ has no preconditions. Indeed, in this case, the explicit preconditions of $square$ and $\neg square$ are equivalent to the formula (6). However, in general, the preconditions of an action literal are not necessarily equivalent to its explicit preconditions, since there can be also other, implicit, preconditions. For instance, if we add the clause $(var' > var)$ to (3), the precondition of $square$ and $\neg square$ become respectively $(var > 1)$ and $(var \geq 0)$. □

Consider a finite subset $\mathcal{P}^{la}(\mathcal{X})$ of the preconditions of la, which, as mentioned above, it is reasonable to expect it includes the explicit preconditions of $\{la\}$. Then, the *abstract precondition formula* defining the value of λ_{la} is

$$\lambda_{la} \neq |\mathcal{X}| + 1 \to \lambda_{la} = max(\lambda_p : p \in \mathcal{P}^{la}(\mathcal{X}), 0), \tag{7}$$

where, for each precondition $p = \bigvee_{i=1}^{q} lx_i$ with $q \geq 0$,

$$\lambda_p = min(\lambda_{lx_1}, \ldots, \lambda_{lx_q}, |\mathcal{X}| + 1).$$

The above equation imposes that if the level λ_{la} of la is not $|\mathcal{X}| + 1$, then λ_{la} is equal to the maximum among the levels associated to all the preconditions in $\mathcal{P}^{la}(\mathcal{X})$ and 0.

Given a state variable x, we now consider how the value of λ_x is defined. Similarly to the previous case, the value of $\lambda_{x' \neq x}$ is defined on the basis of a given set $\mathcal{E}^x(\mathcal{X}, \mathcal{A})$ of conditions with (possible) effect $x' \neq x$. A conjunction e of state and action literals is a *condition with effect* $x' \neq x$ if $T(\mathcal{X}, \mathcal{A}, \mathcal{X}')$ entails $(e \to x' \neq x)$ and there exists a state σ and an action α executable in σ such that σ, α satisfies e. Computing conditions with effect $x' \neq x$ can be based on

$$\exists \mathcal{X}'(x' \neq x \wedge T(\mathcal{X}, \mathcal{A}, \mathcal{X}')). \tag{8}$$

As for the preconditions of an action literal, computing a quantifier free formula equivalent to Eq. (8) may not be possible. However, we need to find a superset of the set of next state variables x' which change value, and we can consider an overapproximation of the conditions with effect $x' \neq x$. Formally, let $\mathcal{E}^x(\mathcal{X}, \mathcal{A})$ be a finite set of state and action literals whose disjunction is entailed by (8). One such set can be determined by taking the set of the antecedents of the explicit effects (2) in $T(\mathcal{X}, \mathcal{A}, \mathcal{X}')$ such that

1. $r = 1$ and x' occurs in the next state literal lx_1', and
2. $(\bigwedge_{j=1}^q lx_j \wedge lx_1')$ does not entail $x' = x$.

The above conditions are generalized by the following proposition.

Proposition 5. *Let Π be a planning problem with transition relation $T(\mathcal{X}, \mathcal{A}, \mathcal{X}')$. Consider a subset S of the set of formulas (2) in $T(\mathcal{X}, \mathcal{A}, \mathcal{X}')$ with $(\bigwedge_{i=1}^q lx_i \wedge \bigvee_{i=1}^r lx_i')$ entailing $x' = x$. Let S' be the set of conjunctions $(\bigwedge_{i=1}^p la_i \wedge \bigwedge_{i=1}^q lx_i)$ for which there exists a formula (2) in $T(\mathcal{X}, \mathcal{A}, \mathcal{X}')$ and not in S and in which x' occurs. The disjunction of the formulas in S' is entailed by (8).*

Consider a finite set $\mathcal{E}^x(\mathcal{X}, \mathcal{A})$ of conjunctions whose disjunction is entailed by (8), which, given proposition (5) can be the antecedents of the explicit effects formulas in which $x' = x$ is not entailed by the conjunction of the antecedent and of the consequent. Then, the *abstract effect formula* defining the value of $\lambda_{x' \neq x}$ is

$$\lambda_{x' \neq x} = min(\lambda_e : e \in \mathcal{E}^x(\mathcal{X}, \mathcal{A}), |\mathcal{X}|) + 1. \tag{9}$$

where, for each conjunction $e = \bigwedge_{i=1}^p la_i \wedge \bigwedge_{i=1}^q lx_i \in \mathcal{E}^x(\mathcal{X}, \mathcal{A})$ $(p, q \geq 0)$, λ_e stands for

$$\lambda_e = max(\lambda_{la_1}, \ldots, \lambda_{la_p}, \lambda_{lx_1}, \ldots, \lambda_{lx_q}, 0).$$

The previous definitions (7) and (9) of λ_{la} and $\lambda_{x' \neq x}$ include the terms λ_{lx} (i) corresponding to the state literals positively occurring in $\mathcal{P}^{la}(\mathcal{X})$ and $\mathcal{E}^x(\mathcal{X}, \mathcal{A})$, and thus (ii) that we assume to be elements of $\mathcal{LX}$.

The *abstract transition relation* $T^A(\mathcal{X}, \mathcal{LX}, \mathcal{LA}, \mathcal{VX})$ is the conjunction of the formulas in (5), (7) and (9), for each state literal in $\mathcal{LX}$, for each action literal la and corresponding set $\mathcal{P}^{la}(\mathcal{X})$, and for each state variable x and corresponding set $\mathcal{E}^x(\mathcal{X}, \mathcal{A})$. Of course, for each set $\mathcal{P}^A(\mathcal{X})$ and each set $\mathcal{E}^X(\mathcal{X}, \mathcal{A})$ we have a corresponding abstract transition relation $T^A(\mathcal{X}, \mathcal{LX}, \mathcal{LA}, \mathcal{VX})$. For sake of readability, we do not stress in the notation the dependency of $T^A(\mathcal{X}, \mathcal{LX}, \mathcal{LA}, \mathcal{VX})$ on $\mathcal{P}^A(\mathcal{X})$ and $\mathcal{E}^X(\mathcal{X}, \mathcal{A})$. Example 5 shows how to construct the abstract transition relation in the SQUARE domain according to the following:

Proposition 6. *Let Π be a planning problem. Let $T^A(\mathcal{X}, \mathcal{LX}, \mathcal{LA}, \mathcal{VX})$ be the abstract transition relation corresponding to the chosen sets $\mathcal{P}^A(\mathcal{X})$ and $\mathcal{E}^X(\mathcal{X}, \mathcal{A})$.*

1. *For every model μ of $T^A(\mathcal{X}, \mathcal{LX}, \mathcal{LA}, \mathcal{VX})$, for every variable λ_z in $\mathcal{LX}, \mathcal{LA}, \mathcal{VX}$, $\mu(\lambda_z) \in [0, |\mathcal{X}| + 1]$.*
2. *For every state σ and pair of distinct models μ_1 and μ_2 of $T^A(\mathcal{X}, \mathcal{LX}, \mathcal{LA}, \mathcal{VX})$ extending σ, there exists a variable $\lambda_{la} \in \mathcal{LA}$ such that $\mu_1(\lambda_{la}) < \mu_2(\lambda_{la}) = |\mathcal{X}| + 1$ or $\mu_2(\lambda_{la}) < \mu_1(\lambda_{la}) = |\mathcal{X}| + 1$.*

3. For every state variable x and model μ of $T^A(\mathcal{X}, \mathcal{LX}, \mathcal{LA}, \mathcal{VX})$, if $\mu(\lambda_{x' \neq x}) = \mu(\lambda_e) + 1$ for some $e \in \mathcal{E}^X(\mathcal{X}, \mathcal{A})$ then $\mu(\lambda_{x' \neq x}) \leq |\mathcal{X}|$.

4. For every state σ there is a model μ of $T^A(\mathcal{X}, \mathcal{LX}, \mathcal{LA}, \mathcal{VX})$ extending σ and such that for each action literal la $\mu(\lambda_{la}) = |\mathcal{X}| + 1$.

Example 5. Let $\mathcal{P}^{square} = \{var \geq 0\}$ and $\mathcal{P}^{\neg square} = \emptyset$, corresponding to the explicit preconditions of $\{square\}$ and $\{\neg square\}$ respectively. Let $\mathcal{E}^{var} = \{(\neg square \wedge var \geq 0), square\}$, corresponding to the first and third clauses in (3). Then, $\mathcal{LX}$ includes $\lambda_{var \geq 0}$ and from $T^A(\mathcal{X}, \mathcal{LX}, \mathcal{LA}, \mathcal{VX})$, the following formulas follow

$$var \geq 0 \rightarrow \lambda_{var \geq 0} = 0, \neg var \geq 0 \rightarrow \lambda_{var \geq 0} = \lambda_{var' \neq var},$$
$$\lambda_{square} \neq 2 \rightarrow \lambda_{square} = max(\lambda_{var \geq 0}, 0), \lambda_{\neg square} \neq 2 \rightarrow \lambda_{\neg square} = 0,$$
$$\lambda_{var' \neq var} = min(max(\lambda_{\neg square}, |\lambda_{var \geq 0}, 0), max(\lambda_{square}, 0), 1) + 1.$$

1. If $(var \geq 0)$, then the equations above entail

$$\lambda_{var \geq 0} = 0, \lambda_{square} = 2 \vee \lambda_{square} = 0, \lambda_{\neg square} = 2 \vee \lambda_{\neg square} = 0,$$
$$\lambda_{var' \neq var} = min(\lambda_{\neg square}, \lambda_{square}, 1) + 1.$$

2. if $(var < 0)$, then the following formulas are entailed

$$\lambda_{var \geq 0} = \lambda_{var' \neq var}, \lambda_{square} = 2 \vee \lambda_{square} = \lambda_{var' \neq var},$$
$$\lambda_{\neg square} = 2 \vee \lambda_{\neg square} = 0,$$
$$\lambda_{var' \neq var} = min(max(\lambda_{\neg square}, \lambda_{var \geq 0}), \lambda_{square}, 1) + 1.$$

The equations above entail $\lambda_{var \geq 0} = \lambda_{var' \neq var} = 2$. In fact $max(\lambda_{\neg square}, \lambda_{var \geq 0}) \geq \lambda_{var' \neq var}$, and $\lambda_{square} \geq \lambda_{var' \neq var}$ and hence $\lambda_{var' \neq var} \geq min(\lambda_{var' \neq var}, 1) + 1$ which holds only if $\lambda_{var' \neq var} = 2$. Since $\lambda_{var' \neq var} = 2$, then $\lambda_{square} = 2$ while $\lambda_{\neg square}$ can take value either 0 or 2.

$\square$

Now we consider $G^A(\mathcal{X}, \mathcal{LX}, \mathcal{VX}, \{\lambda_G\})$, the abstract version of the goal formula $G(\mathcal{X})$. Consider the goal formula $G(\mathcal{X}) = \bigwedge_{i=1}^{s} \bigvee_{j=1}^{s_i} lx_{ij}$. Let $\lambda_{c_i}, i \in [1, s]$ stand for $min(\lambda_{lx_{i1}}, \ldots, \lambda_{lx_{is_i}}, |\mathcal{X}| + 1)$; then $G^A(\mathcal{X}, \mathcal{LX}, \mathcal{VX}, \{\lambda_G\})$ consists of the formula

$$\lambda_G = max(\lambda_{c_1}, \ldots, \lambda_{c_s}, 0), \qquad \lambda_G \leq |\mathcal{X}| \qquad (10)$$

and of the formulas (5) corresponding to the variables $\lambda_{lx_{i1}}, \ldots, \lambda_{lx_{is_i}}$ which are assumed to be included in $\mathcal{LX}$.

Proposition 7. Let Π be a planning problem with transition relation $T(\mathcal{X}, \mathcal{A}, \mathcal{X}')$ and goal $G(\mathcal{X})$. Let $T^A(\mathcal{X}, \mathcal{LX}, \mathcal{LA}, \mathcal{VX})$ and $G^A(\mathcal{X}, \mathcal{LX}, \mathcal{VX}, \{\lambda_G\})$ be an abstract transition relation and the abstract goal. For any model μ of $T^A(\mathcal{X}, \mathcal{LX}, \mathcal{LA}, \mathcal{VX})$ and $G^A(\mathcal{X}, \mathcal{LX}, \mathcal{VX}, \{\lambda_G\})$,

1. $\mu(\lambda_G) = 0$ iff $\mu(G) = \top$, and
2. $\mu(\lambda_G) \leq |\mathcal{X}|$ iff $\mu(G^A) = \top$.

Example 6. $G^A(\mathcal{X}, \mathcal{LX}, \mathcal{VX}, \{\lambda_G\})$ is equivalent to the conjunction of

$$\lambda_G = \lambda_{var \geq V_G}, \quad \lambda_G \leq 1, (var \geq V_G \to \lambda_{var \geq V_G} = 0),$$
$$(var < V_G \to \lambda_{var \geq V_G} = \lambda_{var' \neq var}).$$

Considering the conjunction $T^A(\mathcal{X}, \mathcal{LX}, \mathcal{LA}, \mathcal{VX}) \wedge G^A(\mathcal{X}, \mathcal{LX}, \mathcal{VX}, \{\lambda_G\})$ (see the running example 5) we have three cases:

1. if $(var < 0)$, then $\lambda_{var' \neq var} = 2$ and thus the conjunction is unsatisfiable.
2. if $(0 \leq var < V_G)$, then if $\lambda_{square} = 0$ or $\lambda_{\neg square} = 0$ then $\lambda_{var' \neq var} = 1$ and thus also $\lambda_G = 1$, and
3. if $(var \geq V_G)$, then $\lambda_G = 0$.

□

The definition of the level ordering λ_G associated to the goal formula allows us to define (i) a lower bound λ_G on the number of steps necessary, starting from the n-th induced state σ_n, to reach a goal state, and (ii) a lower bound

$$C_n^G = \lambda_G \times C_{min} \tag{11}$$

of the cost to reach a goal state starting from σ_n. The above cost C_n^G is a lower bound which makes no assumption whatsoever about the cost function other than that each transition to a different state has an associated cost $\geq C_{min}$. If the cost of each transition is equal to the sum of a constant cost $c_a > 0$ associated to each action variable a, then also

$$\sum_{a: a \in \mathcal{A}, \pi_n^A(\lambda_a) \leq |\mathcal{X}|} c_a \tag{12}$$

is a lower bound, possibly much stronger than $\lambda_G \times C_{min}$. Both ways to compute C_n^G are admissible. An *abstract cost function* $C_n^G(\mathcal{X}_n, \mathcal{LX}, \mathcal{LA}, \mathcal{VX}, \{\lambda_G\})$ is *admissible* if, for each valid plan π of Π of length $k \geq n$, we have $C_n^G(\pi_n^A) \leq \sum_{i=n}^{k-1} C(\sigma_i, \alpha_i, \sigma'_{i+1})$ where π_n^A is the model of Π_n^A corresponding to π — defined below in proposition 8 — and $C(\sigma_i, \alpha_i, \sigma'_{i+1})$ as in (4).

We can now state the correspondence between the plan π with cost $C(\pi)$ and the model π_n^A of Π_n^A with cost C_n^A, defined as

$$\Pi_n^A = I(\mathcal{X}_0) \wedge \bigwedge_{i=0}^{n-1} T(\mathcal{X}_i, \mathcal{A}_i, \mathcal{X}_{i+1}) \wedge T^A(\mathcal{X}_n, \mathcal{LX}, \mathcal{LA}, \mathcal{VX})$$
$$\wedge G^A(\mathcal{X}_n, \mathcal{LX}, \mathcal{VX}, \{\lambda_G\}). \tag{13}$$
$$C_n^A = C_n^S + C_n^G.$$

Proposition 8. *Let $\langle \Pi, C \rangle$ be a planning problem with costs. Let $n \geq 0$ be a bound. Let $\pi = \alpha_0; \ldots; \alpha_{k-1}$ be a valid plan of Π of length $k \geq n$. Let σ_i, $i \in [0, k]$, be the i-th state induced by π.*

There exists exactly one model π_n^A of Π_n^A such that

1. *for each $i \in [0, n]$ and for each state variable $x \in \mathcal{X}$, $\pi_n^A(x_i) = \sigma_i(x)$,*
2. *for each $i \in [0, n)$ and for each action variable $a \in \mathcal{A}$, $\pi_n^A(a_i) = \alpha_i(a)$, and*

3. *for each variable $\lambda_{la} \in \mathcal{LA}$, $\pi_n^A(\lambda_{la}) \leq |\mathcal{X}|$ iff there exists $i \in [n, k)$ such that $\alpha_i(la) = \top$.*

Further, π_n^A satisfies the following properties:

1. *for each $i \in [n, k)$, for each variable $\lambda_{la} \in \mathcal{LA}$, if $\alpha_i(la) = \top$ then $\pi_n^A(\lambda_{la}) \leq min(i - n, |\mathcal{X}|)$,*
2. *for each $i \in [n, k]$, for each variable $\lambda_{x' \neq x} \in \mathcal{VX}$, if $\sigma_n(x) \neq \sigma_i(x)$ then $\pi_n^A(\lambda_{x' \neq x}) \leq min(i - n, |\mathcal{X}|)$,*
3. *for each $i \in [n, k]$, for each variable $\lambda_{lx} \in \mathcal{LX}$, if $\sigma_i(lx) = \top$ then $\pi_n^A(\lambda_{lx}) \leq min(i - n, |\mathcal{X}|)$, and*
4. *$\pi_n^A(\lambda_G) \leq min(k - n, |\mathcal{X}|)$ and $C_n^A(\pi_n^A) \leq C(\pi)$.*

From statement 7 of the above proposition, if a model π_n^A of Π_n^A is optimal (i.e., all the other models ρ_n^A of Π_n^A have $C_n^A(\rho_n^A) \geq C_n^A(\pi_n^A)$) and satisfies $\lambda_G = 0$, then there is no valid plan of Π with length $\geq n$ and cost smaller than $C(\pi)$.

5   Optimal Planning as Constraint Optimization

Let $\Pi = \langle \mathcal{X}, \mathcal{A}, I(\mathcal{X}), T(\mathcal{X}, \mathcal{A}, \mathcal{X}'), G(\mathcal{X}) \rangle$ be a planning problem with costs given by $C(\mathcal{X}, \mathcal{A}, \mathcal{X}')$, and let $n \geq 0$ be a bound. We combine the results in Sects. 3, 4 and define a constraint optimization problem $\langle \Pi_n^O, C_n^O \rangle$ allowing to determine (i) an optimal plan of length $k \leq n$, or (ii) the non existence of a valid plan, or (iii) whether the bound n needs to be increased. These statements are consequences of the Theorem below, based on the following definition of $\langle \Pi_n^O, C_n^O \rangle$:

$$\Pi_n^O = I(\mathcal{X}_0) \wedge \bigwedge_{i=0}^{n-1} T^I(\mathcal{X}_i, \mathcal{A}_i \cup \{NoOp_i\}, \mathcal{X}_{i+1})$$
$$\wedge \bigwedge_{i=0}^{n-2} (NoOp_i \rightarrow NoOp_{i+1}) \wedge T^A(\mathcal{X}_n, \mathcal{LX}, \mathcal{LA}, \mathcal{VX})$$
$$\wedge (NoOp_{n-1} \rightarrow \lambda_G = 0) \wedge G^A(\mathcal{X}_n, \mathcal{LX}, \mathcal{VX}, \{\lambda_G\}),$$
$$C_n^O = C_n^I + C_n^G.$$

Proposition 9. *Let $\langle \Pi, C \rangle$ be a planning problem with costs. Let n be a bound. Let $\pi = \alpha_0; \ldots; \alpha_{k-1}$ be a 0-loop free valid plan of Π. There exists exactly one model π_n^O of Π_n^O such that, if $m = min(k, n)$, for every $i \in [0, m)$ and action variable a, $\pi_n^O(a_i) = \alpha_i(a)$ and $\pi_n^O(NoOp_m) = \ldots = \pi_n^O(NoOp_{n-1}) = \bot$, for every action literal la, $\pi_n^O(\lambda_{la}) \leq |\mathcal{X}|$ iff there exists an action α_i with $i \in [m, k-1]$ and $\alpha_i(la) = \top$, then $C_n^O(\pi_n^O) \leq C(\pi)$.*

Theorem 1. *Let $\langle \Pi, C \rangle$ be a planning problem with costs.*

1. *A plan π of length k is optimal and 0-loop free iff there exists a bound $n \geq k$ such that π_n^O is an optimal model of $\langle \Pi_n^O, C_n^O \rangle$ and $\pi_n^O(\lambda_G) = 0$.*
2. *For a bound $n \geq 0$, if π_n^O is an optimal model of $\langle \Pi_n^O, C_n^O \rangle$ and $\pi_n^O(\lambda_G) = 0$, then for every $m \geq n$, π_m^O is an optimal model of $\langle \Pi_m^O, C_m^O \rangle$ and $\pi_m^O(\lambda_G) = 0$.*

3. For a bound $n \geq 0$, if Π_n^O is unsatisfiable then for every $m \geq n$, Π_m^O is unsatisfiable and Π has no valid plans.
4. For a bound $n \geq 0$, if π_n^O is an optimal model of $\langle \Pi_n^O, C_n^O \rangle$ then any valid plan of Π has cost greater than or equal to $C_n^O(\pi_n^O)$.
5. For a bound $n \geq 0$, if π_n^O is an optimal model of $\langle \Pi_n^O, C_n^O \rangle$ and $\pi_n^O(\lambda_G) \neq 0$ then any valid plan of Π has length greater than or equal to $(n + \pi_n^O(\lambda_G))$.
6. Assuming the size of $T^A(\mathcal{X}_n, \mathcal{LX}, \mathcal{LA}, \mathcal{VX})$ is linear in the size $[\Pi]$ of Π, the size of Π_n^O is $\mathcal{O}([\Pi] \times n)$.

Given Proposition 2, the Theorem guarantees that, assuming the existence of a valid plan for Π, we are able to determine an optimal plan by repeatedly solving the constraint optimization problem $\langle \Pi_n^O, C_n^O \rangle$ for increasing n, till an optimal model π_n^O is found with $\pi_n^O(\lambda_G) = 0$. The second and third statements imply that we do not need to increment the bound in unitary steps: indeed, we can fix the new bound according to some policy (see, e.g., [25,26]). The fourth and fifth statements provide the lower bounds on the cost and length of valid plans. Notice that if π_n^O is an optimal model of $\langle \Pi_n^O, C_n^O \rangle$ and $\pi_n^O(\lambda_G) \neq 0$, we can conclude neither the existence of a valid plan nor that valid plans have length $\geq n + \pi_n^O(\lambda_G)$. Indeed, the latter holds (fifth statement) assuming that the cost function of the optimization problem is fixed to C_n^G (and not to $C_n^O = (C_n^I + C_n^G)$). Finally, the last statement ensures that our encoding is linear in the size of Π and n.

Example 7. If $V_I < 0$ and $V_G \neq V_I$ then, for any $n \geq 0$, Π_n^O is unsatisfiable and indeed Π does not have valid plans. If $V_I = 1$ and $V_G = 9$ there are three optimal plans of length 3, 7 and 8; and (i) for $n \leq 6$, Π_n^O has one optimal model with cost $(n-1)$ and satisfying $\lambda_G = 1$; (ii) for $n = 7$, Π_n^O has 3 optimal models with cost 8 but only two of them satisfy $\lambda_G = 0$; and (iii) for $n \geq 8$, there are 3 optimal models and all of them satisfy $\lambda_G = 0$. If we extend the transition relation (3) with the constraint $(var < 9)$ and $V_I = 1$ and $V_G = 10$, then Π_n^O admits one optimal model satisfying $\lambda_G = 1$ for $n \leq 8$, while for $n \geq 9$, Π_n^O is unsatisfiable, proving that Π has no valid plan. $\square$

The example shows that it is possible to have (i) a bound n greater than the length of an optimal plan π and π_n^O is not an optimal model of $\langle \Pi_n^O, C_n^O \rangle$; (ii) a bound n for which various optimal models of $\langle \Pi_n^O, C_n^O \rangle$ exist, but only some of them convey optimal plans; (iii) a bound n after which for every optimal plan π, π_n^O is an optimal model of $\langle \Pi_n^O, C_n^O \rangle$.

6   Conclusions

Our results are applicable to planning problems specified, e.g., in various versions of the PDDL language (in particular, in subsets of PDDL 2.1, 2.2, 3.1) and in the action language $\mathcal{C}$ when the domain is deterministic. We are not aware of comparable approaches as general as ours. Previous attempts to find solutions for optimal planning problems include [27], where partial weighted MaxSAT is proposed as a backend to solve specific kinds of optimal planning problems. More recently, in [4] a mixed-integer programming encoding of a perfect heuristic is developed, landing on an incremental Boolean satisfiability encoding, while our results can be applied to back-ends dealing with decidable first order theories, e.g., satisfiability modulo theories.

Work on additive fluents [19] provides an approach to check whether a plan found is also of minimal cost, but it does not generalize, e.g., to state-dependent costs. Also, previous work on computing the cumulative value of numeric fluents [7] considers only additive or measure fluents, whereas our approach is not restricted in this sense. The framework for extending Answer Set Programming with theories, called ASPMT by [3] is closely related to our work as it shows that the tight fragment of ASPMT programs can be turned into SMT instances, thereby allowing SMT solvers to compute stable models of ASPMT programs. Howver, the optimization part does not seem to be developed in this context. Finally, our approach is also closely related to delete relaxations as found in several works. For instance, in the case of lower bounds, some results related to ours can be found in [13] presenting incremental lower bounds, but limited to additive cost planning problems, and [14] discussing optimal planning with conditional effects using a mechanism of relaxation similar to ours. In [1] upper bounds on the length of cost optimal plans that are valid for problems with 0-cost actions are investigated.

More in general, there are many papers focusing on optimal planning and/or showing how to translate planning problems in logic-based formalisms — see, e.g., [10] for an overview. Literature considering action costs is available in the field of Answer Set Programming — see, e.g., [6] — as well as in the field of Constraint Logic Programming — see, e.g., [5]. As mentioned, our work generalizes [20] which considers numeric problems specified in PDDL 2.1 level 2. If we do not take into account the optimizations introduced by [20] enabled by the restricted language used, the substantial difference is in the encoding of plans longer than the bound. In particular, to eliminate the unwanted models caused by loops between preconditions and effects, we use level order formulas based on [8,12,17,23], while in [20] loop formulas based on [22] are considered. However, with loop formulas (i) the size of the encoding is worst-case exponential [21], and (ii) it is not possible to compute non trivial lower bounds of the length of valid plans and of their cost.

This work is still preliminary, a primary extension being to assess whether the proposed theory and/or a generalization/specialization scales in practice, also compared to other approaches. The results in [20], and also in [24] for numeric problems, are encouraging even for sequential planning problems in which, in every action, at most one variable is true. Indeed, in the non sequential case, planners based on search have to evaluate $2^{|A|}$ possible actions in every state, making symbolic approaches like ours very appealing.

References

1. Abdulaziz, M.: Cost optimal planning as satisfiability. CoRR abs/2103.02355 (2021). arxiv.org/abs/2103.02355
2. Babb, J., Lee, J.: Action language $\mathcal{BC}$+. J. Log. Comput. **30**(4), 899–922 (2020). https://doi.org/10.1093/logcom/exv062
3. Bartholomew, M., Lee, J.: System ASPMT2SMT: computing ASPMT theories by SMT solvers. In: Fermé, E., Leite, J. (eds.) JELIA 2014. LNCS (LNAI), vol. 8761, pp. 529–542. Springer, Cham (2014). https://doi.org/10.1007/978-3-319-11558-0_37
4. Davies, T.O., Pearce, A.R., Stuckey, P.J., Lipovetzky, N.: Sequencing operator counts. In: Kambhampati, S. (ed.) Proceedings of the Twenty-Fifth International Joint Conference on Artificial Intelligence, IJCAI 2016, New York, NY, USA, 9–15 July 2016, pp. 4140–4144. IJCAI/AAAI Press (2016)
5. Dovier, A., Formisano, A., Pontelli, E.: An investigation of multi-agent planning in CLP. Fundam. Inform. **105**(1–2), 79–103 (2010). https://doi.org/10.3233/FI-2010-359
6. Eiter, T., Faber, W., Leone, N., Pfeifer, G., Polleres, A.: Answer set planning under action costs. J. Artif. Intell. Res. **19**, 25–71 (2003). https://doi.org/10.1613/jair.1148
7. Erdem, E., Gabaldon, A.: Cumulative effects of concurrent actions on numeric-valued fluents. In: Veloso, M.M., Kambhampati, S. (eds.) Proceedings, The Twentieth National Conference on Artificial Intelligence and the Seventeenth Innovative Applications of Artificial Intelligence Conference, 9–13 July 2005, Pittsburgh, Pennsylvania, USA, pp. 627–632. AAAI Press/The MIT Press (2005). www.aaai.org/Library/AAAI/2005/aaai05-098.php
8. Erdem, E., Lifschitz, V.: Tight logic programs. Theory Pract. Log. Program. **3**(4–5), 499–518 (2003). https://doi.org/10.1017/S1471068403001765
9. Fox, M., Long, D.: PDDL2.1: an extension to PDDL for expressing temporal planning domains. J. Artif. Intell. Res. (JAIR) **20**, 61–124 (2003)
10. Ghallab, M., Nau, D.S., Traverso, P.: Automated Planning - Theory and Practice. Elsevier, Amsterdam (2004)
11. Giunchiglia, E., Lee, J., Lifschitz, V., McCain, N., Turner, H.: Nonmonotonic causal theories. Artif. Intell. **153**(1–2), 49–104 (2004). https://doi.org/10.1016/j.artint.2002.12.001
12. Giunchiglia, E., Maratea, M.: A simple characterization of Stable Models and corresponding reduction to Difference Logic (2022). submitted
13. Haslum, P.: Incremental lower bounds for additive cost planning problems. In: McCluskey, L., Williams, B.C., Silva, J.R., Bonet, B. (eds.) Proceedings of the Twenty-Second International Conference on Automated Planning and Scheduling, ICAPS 2012, Atibaia, São Paulo, Brazil, 25–19 June 2012. AAAI (2012)
14. Haslum, P.: Optimal delete-relaxed (and semi-relaxed) planning with conditional effects. In: Rossi, F. (ed.) IJCAI 2013, Proceedings of the 23rd International Joint Conference on Artificial Intelligence, Beijing, China, 3–9 August 2013, pp. 2291–2297. IJCAI/AAAI (2013)
15. Haslum, P., Lipovetzky, N., Magazzeni, D., Muise, C.: An Introduction to the Planning Domain Definition Language. Synthesis Lectures on Artificial Intelligence and Machine Learning. Morgan & Claypool Publishers, San Rafael (2019). https://doi.org/10.2200/S00900ED2V01Y201902AIM042

16. Helmert, M.: Decidability and undecidability results for planning with numerical state variables. In: Ghallab, M., Hertzberg, J., Traverso, P. (eds.) Proceedings of the Sixth International Conference on Artificial Intelligence Planning Systems, 23–27 April 2002, Toulouse, France, pp. 44–53. AAAI (2002). www.aaai.org/Library/AIPS/2002/aips02-005.php
17. Janhunen, T.: Representing normal programs with clauses. In: de Mántaras, R.L., Saitta, L. (eds.) Proceedings of the 16th Eureopean Conference on Artificial Intelligence, ECAI'2004, including Prestigious Applicants of Intelligent Systems, PAIS 2004, Valencia, Spain, 22–27 August 2004, pp. 358–362. IOS Press (2004)
18. Kautz, H.A., Selman, B.: Planning as satisfiability. In: ECAI, pp. 359–363 (1992)
19. Lee, J., Lifschitz, V.: Additive fluents. In: Provetti, A., Son, T.C. (eds.) Answer Set Programming, Towards Efficient and Scalable Knowledge Representation and Reasoning, Proceedings of the 1st Intl. ASP'01 Workshop, Stanford, CA, USA, 26–28 March 2001. www.cs.nmsu.edu/%7Etson/ASP2001/14.ps
20. Leofante, F., Giunchiglia, E., Ábrahám, E., Tacchella, A.: Optimal planning modulo theories. In: Bessierc, C. (ed.) Proceedings of the Twenty-Ninth International Joint Conference on Artificial Intelligence, IJCAI 2020, pp. 4128–4134. ijcai.org (2020). https://doi.org/10.24963/ijcai.2020/571
21. Lifschitz, V., Razborov, A.A.: Why are there so many loop formulas? ACM Trans. Comput. Log. 7(2), 261–268 (2006). https://doi.org/10.1145/1131313.1131316
22. Lin, F., Zhao, Y.: ASSAT: computing answer sets of a logic program by SAT solvers. In: AAAI, pp. 112–118 (2002)
23. Niemelä, I.: Stable models and difference logic. Ann. Math. Artif. Intell. 53(1–4), 313–329 (2008)
24. Piacentini, C., Castro, M.P., Ciré, A.A., Beck, J.C.: Compiling optimal numeric planning to mixed integer linear programming. In: ICAPS, pp. 383–387 (2018)
25. Rintanen, J.: Planning as satisfiability: heuristics. Artif. Intell. 193, 45–86 (2012). https://doi.org/10.1016/j.artint.2012.08.001
26. Rintanen, J., Heljanko, K., Niemelä, I.: Planning as satisfiability: parallel plans and algorithms for plan search. Artif. Intell. 170(12–13), 1031–1080 (2006)
27. Robinson, N., Gretton, C., Pham, D.N., Sattar, A.: Partial weighted MaxSAT for optimal planning. In: PRICAI, pp. 231–243 (2010)

Plan Selection Framework for Policy-Aware Autonomous Agents

Charles Harders and Daniela Inclezan$^{(\boxtimes)}$ (iD)

Miami University, Oxford, OH 45056, USA
{harderc2,inclezd}@miamioh.edu

Abstract. This paper proposes a framework for representing and reasoning about the plan selection process of an autonomous agent that is
expected to operate within the boundaries of a given policy. We assume
that the agent takes into consideration both policy compliance and plan
length, and may prioritize one of these aspects over the other, based on
circumstances. We consider authorization and obligation policies specified in the language $\mathcal{AOPL}$ by Gelfond and Lobo. Our framework builds
upon the AAA agent architecture and is implemented in ASP.

Keywords: Planning · ASP · Authorization and Obligation Policies

1 Introduction

In this work, we propose a framework for the controller of an autonomous agent
to specify the agent's intended behavior and plan selection strategy with respect
to policy compliance. Policies written by the controllers of autonomous agents
may specify actions that the autonomous agents are *required* to perform (or not
perform) in specific situations, and actions they are *allowed* (or not) to perform.
The former are referred to as *obligation policies*, while the latter are *authorization
policies*. An autonomous agent can decide whether to abide by these policies or
not, depending on the priorities set for it by its controller. In normal scenarios,
compliance with policies may take precedence over all other aspects, but there
are also situations in which it may be preferred to select a shorter and less
compliant plan than a longer but more compliant one, for instance if the agent
is performing a rescue operation. In our framework, the desired agent behavior
is defined by setting preferences and constraints for several metrics related to
policy compliance and plans. Reasoning about compliance and planning with
preferences is achieved using Answer Set Programming (ASP) [8–10,15].

A first policy-aware autonomous agent was implemented in the $\mathcal{APIA}$ architecture [16], based on the AAA [1] and AIA agent architectures [2]. The language
$\mathcal{AOPL}$ by Gelfond and Lobo [12] was used in $\mathcal{APIA}$ for policy specification,
as it allows for the description of complex policies, either strict or defeasible.
$\mathcal{APIA}$ agents operate with a coarse-grained characterization of plans borrowed
from Gelfond and Lobo's work that is only able to compare plans that consist of

S. Gaggl et al. (Eds.): JELIA 2023, LNAI 14281, pp. 638–646, 2023.
https://doi.org/10.1007/978-3-031-43619-2_43

actions with the same level of compliance (e.g., plans consisting of only explicitly compliant actions vs plans consisting of only non-compliant actions). In our
work, we consider: (1) plans that consist of a mix of actions at different levels of
compliance; (2) additional features of a plan, for instance the length of a plan;
and (3) ambiguities in policy specification not addressed in the original work by
Gelfond and Lobo, i.e., *modality conflicts* [4]. To illustrate the importance of a
finer-grained characterization of plans let's consider the following example:

Example 1. There are six rooms, labeled $r_1, \ldots, r_6$, laid out as shown in Fig. 1.
Our autonomous agent is currently in room r_1 and wants to move to r_3. The
agent a is able to enter a room r, $enter(a, r)$, from an *adjacent* room. Some
of the agent's possible actions are indicated by arrows in Fig. 1. All actions
are compliant w.r.t obligations. However, w.r.t. authorizations, some actions are
known to be compliant (called *strongly-compliant* and labeled "s" in the picture);
others are unknown to be compliant or non-compliant (*underspecified* actions
labeled "u"), and others are known to be non-compliant (labeled "n").

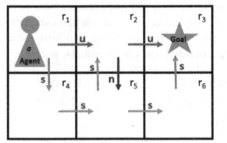

Fig. 1. Example Scenario: Moving between Rooms

Let's consider the following possible plans:
$\alpha_1 = \langle enter(a, r_4), enter(a, r_5), enter(a, r_6), enter(a, r_3)\rangle$,
$\alpha_2 = \langle enter(a, r_4), enter(a, r_5), enter(a, r_2), enter(a, r_3)\rangle$,
$\alpha_3 = \langle enter(a, r_2), enter(a, r_3)\rangle$, and
$\alpha_4 = \langle enter(a, r_2), enter(a, r_5), enter(a, r_6), enter(a, r_3)\rangle$.

According to Gelfond and Lobo [12], α_1 is strongly-compliant and also
weakly-compliant; α_2, α_3 are weakly-compliant. Nothing can be said about α_4
because its actions are not at the same level of compliance. Instead, we want
to create an ordering of plans, whenever possible, based on preferences set by
the agent's controller. A simple preference could be prioritizing compliance over
plan length. In that case α_1 would be the best plan, followed by α_2 and α_3.
Plan α_4 may not even be considered due to the inclusion of a non-compliant
action. If instead plan length is prioritized over compliance (as may be the case
in emergency rescue operations), then α_3 would be the best, followed by α_1 and
α_2. Here, note that α_1 and α_2 have the same length, but the compliance of all
actions of α_1 is guaranteed, whereas one action of α_2 is not explicitly stated to be

compliant (but it is not non-compliant either). Existing work does not currently address comparisons between plans and the setting of preferences described here.

2   Background: Policy Specification Language $\mathcal{AOPL}$

Gelfond and Lobo [12] introduced the Authorization and Obligation Policy Language $\mathcal{AOPL}$, which works in conjunction with a dynamic system description of the agent's environment written in an action language [11], such as $\mathcal{AL}_d$ [7,8]. The signature of the dynamic system description includes: *sorts* for the elements in the domain; *fluents*; and *(elementary) actions*.

Strict $\mathcal{AOPL}$ policies are specified using predicates *permitted* for authorizations and *obl* for obligations, and statements of the form:

$$permitted\,(e)\ \textbf{if}\ cond$$
$$\neg permitted\,(e)\ \textbf{if}\ cond \qquad\qquad (1)$$

where e is an elementary action and *cond* is a collection of atoms of the signature, except those obtained from a predicate *prefer*. In obligation rules, $permitted(e)$ is replaced by $obl(h)$ where h is a happening (i.e., an elementary action or its negation). $\mathcal{AOPL}$ also supports *defeasible* statements, shown here for authorizations, and priorities between them encoded via the predicate *prefer*:

$$d: \textbf{normally}\ permitted(e) \qquad\qquad \textbf{if}\ cond \qquad (2a)$$
$$d: \textbf{normally}\ \neg permitted(e) \qquad\qquad \textbf{if}\ cond \qquad (2b)$$
$$prefer(d_i, d_j) \qquad\qquad\qquad\qquad\qquad (2c)$$

Reasoning about the compliance of an agent to a policy is defined via a translation lp into ASP of the policy and dynamic system description, which is straightforward for atoms, literals, and strict rules. Below we indicate the lp translation for defeasible rule (2a) and preference rule (2c) respectively:

$$permitted(e) \leftarrow lp(cond),\ \text{not}\ ab(d),\ \text{not}\ \neg permitted(e)$$
$$ab(d_j) \quad\ \leftarrow lp(cond_i)$$

where $cond_i$ is the condition of defeasible rule with label d_i; "$\neg$" is strong negation; and "not" is default negation read as "there is no reason to believe."

Given a policy $\mathcal{P}$ and a state σ, $lp(\mathcal{P}, \sigma) =_{def} lp(\mathcal{P}) \cup lp(\sigma)$.

Gelfond and Lobo define a policy as *consistent* if, for every state σ, the logic program $lp(\mathcal{P}, \sigma)$ has an answer set, and *categorical* if it has exactly one answer set. Below, we include compliance definitions, where ca denotes a compound action and e refers to an elementary action.

Definition 1 (Compliance for Authorizations). *(Defs. 4 and 5 [12])*

- *An event $\langle \sigma, ca \rangle$ is* strongly-compliant *with authorization policy $\mathcal{P}$ if $lp(\mathcal{P}, \sigma)$ $\models permitted(e)$, $\forall e \in ca$. Similarly, $\langle \sigma, ca \rangle$ is weakly-compliant if $lp(\mathcal{P}, \sigma)$ $\not\models \neg permitted(e)$, and* non-compliant *if $lp(\mathcal{P}, \sigma) \models \neg permitted(e)$, $\forall e \in ca$.*

- A path $\langle \sigma_0, ca_0, \sigma_1, \ldots, \sigma_{n-1}, ca_{n-1}, \sigma_n \rangle$ is strongly (weakly) compliant with authorization policy $\mathcal{P}$ if, for every $0 \leq i < n$, the event $\langle \sigma_i, ca_i \rangle$ is strongly (weakly) compliant with $\mathcal{P}$.

Definition 2 (Compliance for Obligations). *(Def. 9 [12])*
An event $\langle \sigma, ca \rangle$ is compliant with obligation policy $\mathcal{P}$ if

- For every e such that $lp(\mathcal{P}, \sigma) \models obl(e)$ we have that $e \in ca$, and
- For every e such that $lp(\mathcal{P}, \sigma) \models obl(\neg e)$ we have that $e \notin ca$.

3 Policy-Driven Plan Selection Framework

In *Answer Set Planning* [14,18] (i.e., planning using ASP) a problem is defined as a triple $\langle \mathcal{D}, \Gamma, \Delta \rangle$ where $\mathcal{D}$ is the ASP encoding of the dynamic system in which the autonomous agent is acting; Γ is a collection of fluent literals that hold in the initial state; and Δ is the set of fluent literals representing the goal to be achieved by the agent. A solution to a planning problem is a sequence of actions to be performed by the agent to achieve the goal state; it is generated by the ASP program expanded with a planning module. In this work, we limit ourselves to *deterministic* dynamic system descriptions and *complete knowledge* about the initial state (to remove complexities [5,19,20] orthogonal to policy compliance). In this case, a solution to a planning problem is a sequence of agent actions $\alpha = \langle a_0, \ldots, a_{n-1} \rangle$ that *guarantees* to reach a desired state.

With respect to planning with $\mathcal{AOPL}$ policies, Inclezan [13] showed that a division of paths into strongly- and weakly-compliant is too coarse and the label "weakly-compliant" is not specific enough to create a relative priority order between plans, because all strongly-compliant events are also weakly-compliant. Instead Inclezan introduced the terminology of an "underspecified" event $\langle \sigma, ca \rangle$ if, for every $e \in ca$, the logic program $lp(\mathcal{P}, \sigma)$ entails both "not *permitted(e)*" and "not $\neg permitted(e)$". In categorical policies, an event $\langle \sigma, ca \rangle$ is either strongly-compliant, non-compliant, or underspecified with respect to $\mathcal{P}$ [13].

With respect to obligations, situations when $lp(\mathcal{P}, \sigma)$ entails $obl(\neg e)$ and e is not planned to be executed in state σ tend to abound. Thus, what needs to be tracked instead is the occurrence of non-compliant actions with respect to obligations. A final case that requires attention is when a plan contains an event $\langle \sigma, ca \rangle$ such that $e \in ca$ and $lp(\mathcal{P}, \sigma) \models \{obl(e), \neg permitted(e)\}$ or $lp(\mathcal{P}, \sigma) \models \{obl(\neg e), permitted(e)\}$. Such situations are not considered by Gelfond and Lobo, and thus a policy in which these situations occur can still be deemed categorical. However, policies that allow this have a certain level of ambiguity. We refer to such events as *modality ambiguous*, as they reflect an ambiguity that arises at the intersection between two modalities, obligation and authorization. Including a *modality ambiguous* event $\langle \sigma, ca \rangle$ in a plan should be avoided.

Based on these considerations, our framework qualifies a plan $\alpha = \langle a_0, \ldots, a_{n-1} \rangle$ based on the following metrics (i.e., functions): (1) the plan **length** ($l(\alpha) =_{def} n$) and (2) the **number** and **percentage** of:

- modality ambiguous events, $n\_ma(\alpha)$ and $p\_ma(\alpha) =_{def} (n\_ma(\alpha)*100)/l(\alpha)$ respectively;
- non-compliant events w.r.t. obligation; and
- strongly-compliant/underspecified/non-compliant events w.r.t. authorization.

To compute these metrics in ASP, we extend predicates *permitted* and *obl* with a new parameter representing the time step I, use predicate $occurs(A, I)$ to indicate that action A is planned to be executed at time step I, and introduce new predicates (e.g., *mod_ambg* for modality ambiguous actions). ASP rules like the ones below are added to calculate the metrics:

$$mod\_ambg(A, I) \leftarrow occurs(A, I),\ obl(A, I),\ \neg permitted(A, I).$$
$$mod\_ambg(A, I) \leftarrow occurs(A, I),\ obl(\neg A, I),\ permitted(A, I).$$
$$n\_ma(N) \qquad \leftarrow \#count\{A, I : mod\_ambg(A, I)\} = N.$$
$$p\_ma(N) \qquad \leftarrow n\_ma(N_1),\ l(N_2), N = (N_1 * 100)/N_2.$$

Here predicate l indicates the length of a plan and is calculated w.r.t. to the horizon h (maximum plan length considered) by adding a new *wait* action, similar to action *noop* introduced by Son and Pontelli [17], and rules:

$$n\_wait(N) \leftarrow \#count\{I : occurs(wait, I)\} = N.$$
$$l(N) \qquad \leftarrow n\_wait(N_1), N = h + 1 - N_1.$$

These metrics can be used to describe acceptable and "best" plans. Here, we show how they can be used to describe some predefined agent behavior modes:

- **Safe Behavior Mode:** Do not accept plans with non-compliant actions or modality ambiguous events; maximize the percentage of strictly-compliant actions, then prioritize plan length. A safe agent would select plan α_1 from Example 1 as it has the highest percentage of strongly-compliant events.
- **Normal Behavior Mode** Do not accept plans with non-compliant actions or modality ambiguous events; prioritize plan length first and then maximize the percentage of strongly-compliant actions. A normal agent would select plan α_3 from Example 1 as it prioritizes plans with a minimal length over plans with a higher percentage of strongly-compliant actions.
- **Risky Behavior Mode** Do not try to follow policy rules, but do not go out of your way to break rules either. A risky agent would also select plan α_3 from Example 1 as it is the shortest plan.

These behavior modes are encoded using the $\#maximize$ directive of the ASP solver CLINGO [3,6], as in:

$$\leftarrow n\_undes(N), \text{not } N = 0.$$
$$\#maximize\{N@2 : p\_sa(N); M@1 : n\_wait(M)\}.$$

for the Safe Behavior Mode, where n_undes is a predicate representing the sum of modality ambiguous and non-compliant actions and p_sa is the percentage of strongly-compliant actions.

4   Experimental Analysis and Discussion

We empirically evaluated our implementation on an elaborated scenario in which there is an agent that operates in a building with nine rooms, $r0$ to $r8$. Rooms may be connected by doors, some of which may be one-way doors. Doors can be locked and unlocked by the agent using either a key specific to a door or a badge that can open any door. The agent is located in one of the rooms initially and wants to get to another room. The agent has information about extreme situations such as an active fire or contamination in a room. The agent may have a special protective equipment. Our scenario contains both authorization and obligation policies, both strict and defeasible, some of which are listed below:

1. The agent is obligated to use the key before using the badge if it has both.
2. The agent is not permitted to use its badge more than 3 times.
3. The agent is not permitted to open a one-way door from the wrong side.
4. Normally, the agent is obligated not to enter a room where there is a fire.
5. However, the agent is allowed to enter (i.e., not obligated to not enter) a room in which there is an active fire if it has a special protective equipment.
6. Normally, the agent is not permitted to enter a contaminated room.

We tested the ASP implementation of our framework on fourteen planning scenarios.[1] For each scenario, we ran the planning agent in the three different modes listed in Sect. 3: *Safe*, *Normal*, and *Risky*. Table 1 shows average times over 10 runs and the length of the optimal plan for each category. All experiments were performed on a machine with an Intel(R) Core(TM) i5-1135G7 CPU 2.40 GHz RAM 8 GB.

Table 1. Experimental Results (*NU* - number of undesirable actions)

Scenario	Safe		Normal		Risky		
	Time (ms)	Plan Length	Time (ms)	Plan Length	Time (ms)	Plan Length	NU
1	4124.7	3	4104.4	3	4037.0	3	0
2	4189.3	5	4143.2	5	4109.7	4	1
3	4098.0	8	4032.4	6	3972.2	5	1
4	4349.0	10	4173.5	10	4078.3	3	1
5	4455.6	7	4064.9	7	4001.3	2	1
6	4249.4	3	4009.7	3	4004.9	3	0
7	4556.2	9	4176.3	5	4116.5	3	1
8	3894.6	10	4078.9	4	4014.7	4	0
9	5425.4	5	4121.9	3	4144.4	3	0
10	3550.3	0	3628.8	0	3503.4	0	0
11	4402.6	5	4186.4	4	4176.3	3	1
12	4532.2	3	4080.6	3	4000.0	3	0
13	4081.5	10	4117.3	6	4113.6	6	0
14	5749.3	6	4227.3	4	4105.1	4	0

---

[1] Available at https://tinyurl.com/4exs9ens.

Optimal plans in the *Risky* mode are generally the fastest to compute and the shortest, since policy compliance is not enforced in this mode. Overall though, there is not a big difference in terms of computational time between the three behavior modes. The plans matched the priorities set for their respective mode. We also compared the plans found for a scenario across behavior modes and deemed the *Normal Agent* mode as the most desirable and closest to the decision process of a human. The *Risky Agent* mode sometimes included non-compliant actions (see column *NU* in Table 1), as expected based on the specification. This is undesirable in general, as policies are set in order to be followed. The *Safe Agent* mode sometimes created longer-than-needed plans in which the agent went out of its way and performed unnecessary strongly-compliant actions just to maximize the percentage of strongly-compliant events, as illustrated below:

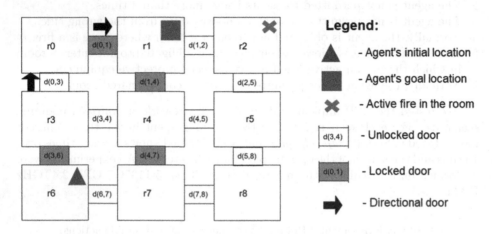

Fig. 2. Layout for Scenario 3

Scenario 3: The agent must move from room $r6$ to room $r1$ (see Fig. 2). It is equipped with the keys to the doors from room $r0$ to $r1$, $r0$ to $r3$, and $r1$ to $r4$. The directions in place are from room $r0$ to room $r1$ and from $r3$ to $r0$. Doors between the following rooms are locked: $r0$ and $r1$, $r1$ and $r4$, $r4$ and $r7$, $r3$ and $r6$. There is an active fire in room $r2$. The *Safe Agent* chooses the following 8-step plan: Move from $r6$ to $r7$. Move from $r7$ to $r8$. Move from $r8$ to $r5$. Move from $r5$ to $r4$. Move from $r4$ to $r3$. Move from $r3$ to $r0$. Unlock the door from 0 to 1. Move from $r0$ to $r1$. The *Normal Agent* takes a different approach – the following 6-step plan: Move from $r6$ to $r7$. Move from $r7$ to $r8$. Move from $r8$ to $r5$. Move from $r5$ to $r4$. Unlock the door from $r4$ to $r1$. Move from $r4$ to $r1$. The *Risky Agent* ignores the active fire in room $r2$ and policy rules associated with such situations, and executes a 5-step long plan: Move from $r6$ to $r7$, then $r7$ to $r8$, then $r8$ to $r5$, then $r5$ to $r2$, and finally $r2$ to $r1$. Notice that, when located in room $r4$, the *Safe Agent* chooses to move to room $r0$ so that it can maximize its strong-compliance by unlocking the door from $r0$ to $r1$ from the correct direction. The *Normal Agent* simply moves from room $r4$ to room $r1$, which is an underspecified action (neither permitted nor not permitted).

5   Conclusions

We introduced a framework that allows the specification of the desired behavior of an autonomous agent in terms of plan selection with respect to policy compliance. The framework defines various metrics that can be used to define different behavior modes, including the *Safe*, *Normal*, and *Risky* agent modes. We deemed the *Normal* mode to be the most suitable and reasonable one, as shown by the experimental results.

References

1. Balduccini, M., Gelfond, M.: The AAA architecture: an overview. In: Architectures for Intelligent Theory-Based Agents, Papers from the 2008 AAAI Spring Symposium, 2008, pp. 1–6. AAAI Press (2008)
2. Blount, J., Gelfond, M., Balduccini, M.: A theory of intentions for intelligent agents - (extended abstract). In: Calimeri, F., Ianni, G., Truszczynski, M. (eds.) Logic Programming and Nonmonotonic Reasoning. LPNMR 2015. LNCS, vol. 9345, pp. 134–142. Springer, Cham (2015). https://doi.org/10.1007/978-3-319-23264-5_12
3. Calimeri, F., et al.: ASP-Core-2 input language format. Theory Pract. Log. Program. **20**(2), 294–309 (2020)
4. Craven, R., Lobo, J., Ma, J., Russo, A., Lupu, E., Bandara, A.: Expressive policy analysis with enhanced system dynamicity. In: Proceedings of the 4th International Symposium on Information, Computer, and Communications Security, pp. 239–250. ASIACCS '09, Association for Computing Machinery, New York, NY, USA (2009)
5. Eiter, T., Faber, W., Leone, N., Pfeifer, G., Polleres, A.: A logic programming approach to knowledge-state planning, II: the DLV^k system. Artif. Intell. **144**(1–2), 157–211 (2003)
6. Gebser, M., et al.: Potassco user guide, 2 ed. University of Potsdam (2015)
7. Gelfond, M., Inclezan, D.: Some properties of system descriptions of $\mathcal{ALd}$. J. Appl. Non Class. Log. **23**(1–2), 105–120 (2013)
8. Gelfond, M., Kahl, Y.: Knowledge Representation, Reasoning, and the Design of Intelligent Agents. Cambridge University Press, Cambridge (2014)
9. Gelfond, M., Lifschitz, V.: The stable model semantics for logic programming. In: Proceedings of the International Conference on Logic Programming (ICLP88), pp. 1070–1080 (1988)
10. Gelfond, M., Lifschitz, V.: Classical negation in logic programs and disjunctive databases. N. Gener. Comput. **9**(3/4), 365–386 (1991)
11. Gelfond, M., Lifschitz, V.: Action languages. Electron. Trans. AI **3**(16), 193–210 (1998)
12. Gelfond, M., Lobo, J.: Authorization and obligation policies in dynamic systems. In: Garcia de la Banda, M., Pontelli, E. (eds.) ICLP 2008. LNCS, vol. 5366, pp. 22–36. Springer, Heidelberg (2008). https://doi.org/10.1007/978-3-540-89982-2_7
13. Inclezan, D.: An ASP framework for the refinement of authorization and obligation policies. Theory Pract. Log. Program. 1–16 (2023). https://doi.org/10.1017/S147106842300011X
14. Lifschitz, V.: Answer set planning. In: Schreye, D.D. (ed.) Logic Programming: The 1999 International Conference, Las Cruces, New Mexico, USA, November 29–4 December 1999, pp. 23–37. MIT Press (1999)

15. Marek, V.W., Truszczynski, M.: Stable models and an alternative logic programming paradigm. In: Apt, K.R., Marek, V.W., Truszczynski, M., Warren, D.S. (eds.) The Logic Programming Paradigm. Artificial Intelligence, pp. 375–398. Springer, Berlin, Heidelberg (1999). https://doi.org/10.1007/978-3-642-60085-2_17

16. Meyer, J., Inclezan, D.: APIA: an architecture for policy-aware intentional agents. In: Formisano, A., et al. (eds.) Proceedings 37th International Conference on Logic Programming (Technical Communications), ICLP Technical Communications 2021, Porto (virtual event), 20–27th September 2021. EPTCS, vol. 345, pp. 84–98 (2021)

17. Son, T.C., Pontelli, E.: Planning with preferences using logic programming. Theory Pract. Log. Program. **6**(5), 559–607 (2006)

18. Son, T.C., Pontelli, E., Balduccini, M., Schaub, T.: Answer set planning: a survey. Theory Pract. Log. Program. **23**(1), 226–298 (2023)

19. Son, T.C., Tu, P.H., Gelfond, M., Morales, A.R.: Conformant planning for domains with constraints-a new approach. In: Veloso, M.M., Kambhampati, S. (eds.) Proceedings, The Twentieth National Conference on Artificial Intelligence and the Seventeenth Innovative Applications of Artificial Intelligence Conference, 9–13 July 2005, Pittsburgh, Pennsylvania, USA, pp. 1211–1216. AAAI Press/The MIT Press (2005)

20. Tu, P.H., Son, T.C., Gelfond, M., Morales, A.R.: Approximation of action theories and its application to conformant planning. Artif. Intell. **175**(1), 79–119 (2011)

Reasoning About Causes
and Dependencies

Strongly Complete Axiomatization for a Logic with Probabilistic Interventionist Counterfactuals

Fausto Barbero[1](✉) [iD] and Jonni Virtema[2](✉) [iD]

[1] University of Helsinki, Helsinki, Finland
fausto.barbero@helsinki.fi
[2] University of Sheffield, Sheffield, UK
j.t.virtema@sheffield.ac.uk

Abstract. Causal multiteam semantics is a framework where probabilistic notions and causal inference can be studied in a unified setting. We study a logic ($\mathcal{PCO}$) that features marginal probabilities, observations and interventionist counterfactuals, and allows expressing conditional probability statements, *do* expressions and other mixtures of causal and probabilistic reasoning. Our main contribution is a strongly complete infinitary axiomatisation for $\mathcal{PCO}$.

1 Introduction

In the past few decades, the study of causation has transformed from being a topic of mere philosophical speculation to a discipline making use of rigorous mathematical tools. The main two strands of this new discipline, paralleling the division of roles between probability and statistics, are *causal inference* ([16,28,29]) and *causal discovery* ([33]). The former studies which causal effects can be inferred from data coupled with causal assumptions about the processes which generated the data. The latter studies which causal connections are compatible with given data (coming from observations or experiments). In both strands new languages, capable of expressing concepts that lie beyond the merely associational or probabilistic properties of data, are needed. A key novel concept that is required is the notion of an *intervention* (modifying a given system). One way of describing interventions is given by expressions called *interventionist counterfactuals*. In their simplest form, these are expressions such as:

If variables $X_1, \dots, X_n$ were fixed to values $x_1, \dots, x_n$, then variable Y would take value y

or their (causal-)probabilistic counterparts:

If variables $X_1, \dots, X_n$ were fixed to values $x_1, \dots, x_n$, then the probability that variable Y takes value y would be ϵ.

Typically, such expressions are given precise semantics by *causal models* (also known as *structural equation models*). Causal models and interventionist counterfactuals have been reabsorbed as mainstream ideas in the philosophical debate on causation [22,35]

S. Gaggl et al. (Eds.): JELIA 2023, LNAI 14281, pp. 649–664, 2023.
https://doi.org/10.1007/978-3-031-43619-2_44

but also became widespread tools for the study of causation in disparate applied fields such as epidemiology [21], econometrics [19], social sciences [25] and machine learning [31]. As a recent development, J. Pearl argued that the capability of AI systems to represent and reason about causal knowledge will be the next important leap in the field of artificial intelligence (see, e.g., [30]).

The simple interventionist counterfactuals exhibited above do not exhaust the wide variety of causal-probabilistic expressions that appear in the literature on causal inference (an extended discussion of this issue can be found in [10]). In [28], Pearl emphasizes two kinds of formal notations, the (conditional) *do expressions*, and what we may call, for lack of a better terminology, *Pearl counterfactuals*. These expressions concern probabilities in a post-intervention scenario, but differ in whether one conditions upon events of the pre-intervention or the post-intervention scenario. A conditional *do* expression discusses conditioning over a post-intervention event, as in the statement "The probability that a patient abandons treatment, if he does not quickly improve, is ϵ"; in symbols:

$$Pr(Abandon = 1 \mid do(Treated = 1), Improve = 0) = \epsilon$$

where *Abandon*, *Treated* and *Improve* are Boolean variables taking values 1 or 0 depending on whether a certain fact holds or not. On the other hand, a Pearl counterfactual conditions in the pre-intervention system, so that there might even be contradictions between the measured and the conditioning event. E.g., "The probability that a patient who died would have recovered if treated is ϵ":

$$Pr(Dies = 0 \mid do(Treated = 1), Dies = 1) = \epsilon.$$

In [4], Barbero and Sandu propose to tame this wild proliferation of notational devices by decomposing these kinds of expressions in terms of three simpler ingredients: marginal probabilities, interventionist counterfactuals ($\Box\!\!\rightarrow$), and selective implications ($\supset$). The selective implication describes the effect of acquiring new information, whereas the interventionist counterfactual describes the effect of an action. The complex expressions described above become, respectively,

$$Treated = 1 \ \Box\!\!\rightarrow (Improve = 0 \supset Pr(Abandon = 1) = \epsilon)$$

$$Dies = 1 \supset (Treated = 1 \ \Box\!\!\rightarrow Pr(Dies = 0) = \epsilon)$$

showing that qualitative difference between the two kinds of expressions amounts to an inversion in the order of application of two logical operators.

Interventionist counterfactuals, selective implications, and marginal probability statements can be studied in a shared semantic framework called *causal multiteam semantics*. The framework is meaningful already in a non-probabilistic context, where it generalizes causal models by providing a (qualitative) account of imperfect information,[1] and where it has been studied both from a semantic and a proof-theoretic perspective [3,5,9]. The proof-theoretic results rely on a body of earlier work ([12,14,17])

---

[1] The idea of modeling imperfect information via *team semantics* was developed by Hodges [23] and Väänänen [34].

on proof systems for (non-probabilistic) counterfactuals evaluated on causal models. In the probabilistic setting, some work in the semantic direction is forthcoming [6,7].

In this paper, we initiate the proof-theoretic study of logics involving probabilistic counterfactuals in the causal multiteam setting. To the best of our knowledge, there has been only one proposal in the literature of a deduction system for probabilistic interventionist counterfactuals ([24]). The language considered in [24] differs in many respects from those we are interested in. It is more expressive in allowing the use of arithmetical operations (sums and products of probabilities and scalars). In contrast, it is also less expressive, since it does not allow for nesting of counterfactuals (iterated interventions), and it has no obvious means for describing complex interactions of interventions and conditioning. For example, it has no obvious way to condition at the same time on *both* a pre-intervention and a post-intervention scenario, or condition on a state of affairs that holds at an intermediate stage between two interventions. Both of these scenarios can be dealt with in relative ease using the framework of Barbero and Sandu [6]: the former by expressions of the form $\alpha \supset (X = x \boxminus\rightarrow (\beta \supset \Pr(\gamma) = \epsilon))$ and the latter by $X = x \boxminus\rightarrow (\alpha \supset (Z = z \boxminus\rightarrow \Pr(\gamma) = \epsilon))$.

Axiomatizing probabilistic logics is a notoriously difficult problem. As soon as a language allows expressing inequalities of the form $\Pr(\alpha) \leq \epsilon$ (ϵ being a rational number), it is not compact, as for example the set of formulas of the form $\Pr(\alpha) \leq \frac{1}{n}$ (n natural number) entails that $\Pr(\alpha) = 0$, but no finite subset yields the same conclusion. Consequently, no usual, finitary deduction system can be strongly complete for such a language. A possible answer to this problem is to settle for a deductive system that is weakly complete, i.e. it captures all the correct inferences from *finite* sets of formulas. This has been achieved for a variety of probabilistic languages with arithmetic operations (e.g. [13]). The result for probabilistic interventionist counterfactuals mentioned above ([24]) is a weak completeness result in this tradition. Proving weak completeness for probabilistic languages *without* arithmetical operations seems to be a more difficult task, and we could find only one such result in the literature ([20])[2]. Unfortunately, the completeness proof of [20] relies on a model-building method that seems not to work for languages where *conditional* probabilities are expressible; thus, it is not adaptable in any straightforward way to our case.

Another path, on which we embark, is to respond to the failure of compactness by aiming for strong completeness using a deduction system with some kind of infinitary resources. The use of infinitary deduction rules (with countably many premises) has proved to be very fruitful and has led to strong completeness theorems for a plethora of probabilistic languages (cf. [27]). Of particular interest to us are [32], where strong completeness is obtained for a language with conditional probabilities, and [26], which obtains strong completeness for "qualitative probabilities" (i.e., for expressions such as $\Pr(\alpha) \leq \Pr(\beta)$, that do not involve numerical constants). We build on these works in order to obtain a strongly complete deduction system (with two infinitary rules) for the probabilistic-causal language $\mathcal{PCO}$ used in [6,7]. The proof proceeds via a canonical model construction, relying on a Lindenbaum lemma whose proof takes into account

---

[2] An axiomatization of this kind has also been found for a probabilistic *fuzzy* logic ([15]), which has been proved to be intertranslatable with (classical) probabilistic logic with arithmetical operators ([2]).

the role of infinitary rules. While the proof follows essentially the scheme of [32], it presents peculiar difficulties of its own due to the presence of additional operators (counterfactuals and comparison atoms).

2   Preliminaries

Capital letters such as $X, Y, \ldots$ denote **variables** (thought to stand for specific magnitudes such as "temperature", "volume", etc.) which take **values** denoted by small letters (e.g. the values of the variable X will be denoted by $x, x', \ldots$). Sets (and tuples, depending on the context) of variables and values are denoted by boldface letters such as $\mathbf{X}$ and $\mathbf{x}$. We consider probabilities that arise from the counting measures of finite (multi)sets. For finite sets $S \subseteq T$, we define $P_T(S) := \frac{|S|}{|T|}$.

A **signature** is a pair (Dom, Ran), where Dom is a nonempty, finite set of variables and Ran is a function that associates to each variable $X \in$ Dom a nonempty, finite set Ran(X) of values (the **range** of X). We consider throughout the paper a fixed ordering of Dom, and write $\mathbf{W}$ for the tuple of all variables of Dom listed in such order. Furthermore, we write $\mathbf{W}_X$ for the variables of Dom \ $\{X\}$ listed according to the fixed order. Given a tuple $\mathbf{X} = (X_1, \ldots, X_n)$ of variables, we denote as Ran($\mathbf{X}$) the Cartesian product Ran(X_1) $\times \cdots \times$ Ran(X_n). An **assignment** of signature σ is a mapping $s : \text{Dom} \to \bigcup_{X \in \text{Dom}} \text{Ran}(X)$ such that $s(X) \in \text{Ran}(X)$ for each $X \in$ Dom. The set of all assignments of signature σ is denoted by $\mathbb{B}_\sigma$. Given an assignment s that has the variables of $\mathbf{X}$ in its domain, $s(\mathbf{X})$ will denote the tuple $(s(X_1), \ldots, s(X_n))$. For $\mathbf{X} \subseteq$ Dom, $s_{\restriction \mathbf{X}}$ denotes the restriction of s to the variables in $\mathbf{X}$.

A **team** T of signature σ is a subset of $\mathbb{B}_\sigma$. Intuitively, a multiteam is just a multiset analogue of a team. We represent **multiteams** as (finite) sets of assignments with an extra variable Key (not belonging to the signature) ranging over $\mathbb{N}$, which takes different values over different assignments of the team, and which is never mentioned in the formal languages. A multiteam can be represented as a table, in which each row represents an assignment. For example, if $Dom = \{X, Y, Z\}$, a multiteam may look like this:

Key	X	Y	Z
0	x	y	z
1	x'	y'	z'
2	x'	y'	z'

The purpose of a multiteam is to encode a probability distribution (over the team obtained by removing the variable Key); in this case, that the assignment $s(X) = x, s(Y) = y, s(Z) = z$ has probability $\frac{1}{3}$ while the assignment $t(X) = x', t(Y) = y', t(Z) = z'$ has probability $\frac{2}{3}$. Multiteams by themselves do not encode any solid notion of causation; they do not tell us how a system would be affected by an intervention. We therefore need to enrich multiteams with additional structure.

Definition 1. *A **causal multiteam** T of signature* (Dom(T), Ran(T)) *with endogenous variables* $\mathbf{V} \subseteq$ Dom(T) *is a pair* $T = (T^-, \mathcal{F})$ *such that*

1. T^- is a multiteam of domain Dom(T),

2. $\mathcal{F}$ *is a function* $\{(V, \mathcal{F}_V) \mid V \in \mathbf{V}\}$ *that assigns to each endogenous variable* V *a non-constant* $|\mathbf{W}_V|$-*ary function* $\mathcal{F}_V : \mathrm{Ran}(\mathbf{W}_V) \to \mathrm{Ran}(V)$, *and*
3. *The* **compatibility constraint** *holds:* $\mathcal{F}_V(s(\mathbf{W}_V)) = s(V)$ *for all* $s \in T^-$ *and* $V \in \mathbf{V}$.

We will also write $\mathrm{End}(T)$ for the set of endogenous variables of T. Due to the compatibility constraint, not all instances for $\mathbf{V}$ and T^- give rise to causal multiteams.

The function $\mathcal{F}$ induces a system of structural equations; an equation

$$V := \mathcal{F}_V(\mathbf{W}_V)$$

for each variable $V \in \mathrm{End}(T)$. A structural equation tells how the value of V should be recomputed if the value of some variables in $\mathbf{W}_V$ is modified. Note that that some of the variables in $\mathbf{W}_V$ may not be necessary for evaluating V. For example, if V is given by the structural equation $V := X + 1$, all the variables in $\mathbf{W}_V \setminus \{X\}$ are irrelevant (we call them **dummy arguments** of $\mathcal{F}_V$). The set of non-dummy arguments of $\mathcal{F}_V$ is denoted as PA_V (the set of **parents** of V).

We associate to each causal multiteam T a **causal graph** G_T, whose vertices are the variables in Dom and where an arrow is drawn from each variable in PA_V to V, whenever $V \in \mathrm{End}(T)$. The variables in $\mathrm{Dom}(T) \setminus \mathrm{End}(T)$ are called **exogenous**. In this paper, we will always assume that causal graphs are acyclic; a causal multiteam with an acyclic causal graph is said to be **recursive**.

Definition 2. *A causal multiteam* $S = (S^-, \mathcal{F}_S)$ *is a* **causal sub-multiteam** *of* $T = (T^-, \mathcal{F}_T)$, *if they have same signature,* $S^- \subseteq T^-$, *and* $\mathcal{F}_S = \mathcal{F}_T$. *We then write* $S \leq T$.

We consider causal multiteams as dynamic models, that can be affected by various kinds of operations – specifically, by observations and interventions. Given a causal multiteam $T = (T^-, \mathcal{F})$ and a formula α of some formal language (evaluated over assignments according to some semantic relation $\models$), "observing α" produces the causal sub-multiteam $T^\alpha = ((T^\alpha)^-, \mathcal{F})$ of T, where[3]

$$(T^\alpha)^- := \{s \in T^- \mid (\{s\}, \mathcal{F}) \models \alpha\}.$$

An intervention on T will *not*, in general, produce a sub-multiteam of T. It will instead modify the values that appear in some of the columns of T. We consider interventions that are described by formulas of the form $X_1 = x_1 \wedge \cdots \wedge X_n = x_n$ (or, shortly, $\mathbf{X} = \mathbf{x}$). Such a formula is **inconsistent** if there are two indexes i, j such that X_i and X_j denote the same variable, while x_i and x_j denote distinct values; it is **consistent** otherwise.

Applying an intervention $do(\mathbf{X} = \mathbf{x})$, where $\mathbf{X} = \mathbf{x}$ is consistent, to a causal multiteam $T = (T^-, \mathcal{F})$ will produce a causal multiteam $T_{\mathbf{X}=\mathbf{x}} = (T^-_{\mathbf{X}=\mathbf{x}}, \mathcal{F}_{\mathbf{X}=\mathbf{x}})$, where the function component is $\mathcal{F}_{\mathbf{X}=\mathbf{x}} := \mathcal{F}_{\restriction(\mathbf{V}\setminus\mathbf{X})}$ (the restriction of $\mathcal{F}$ to the set of variables $\mathbf{V}\setminus\mathbf{X}$) and the multiteam component is $T^-_{\mathbf{X}=\mathbf{x}} := \{s^{\mathcal{F}}_{\mathbf{X}=\mathbf{x}} \mid s \in T^-\}$, where each $s^{\mathcal{F}}_{\mathbf{X}=\mathbf{x}}$ is the unique

---

[3] Throughout the paper, the semantic relation in terms of which T^α is defined will be the semantic relation for language CO, which will soon be defined.

assignment compatible with $\mathcal{F}_{\mathbf{X}=\mathbf{x}}$ defined (recursively) as

$$
s^{\mathcal{F}}_{\mathbf{X}=\mathbf{x}}(V) = \begin{cases} x_i & \text{if } V = X_i \in \mathbf{X} \\ s(V) & \text{if } V \in Exo(T) \setminus \mathbf{X} \\ \mathcal{F}_V(s^{\mathcal{F}}_{\mathbf{X}=\mathbf{x}}(\mathrm{PA}_V)) & \text{if } V \in End(T) \setminus \mathbf{X}. \end{cases}
$$

Example 3. Consider the following table:

T^{-}:

Key	X→Y→Z		
0	0	1	0
1	1	2	2
2	1	2	2
3	2	3	6

where each row represents an assignment (e.g., the fourth row represents an assignment s with $s(Key) = 3$, $s(X) = 2$, $s(Y) = 3$, $s(Z) = 6$). Assume further that the variable Z is generated by the function $\mathcal{F}_Z(X, Y) = X \times Y$, Y is generated by $\mathcal{F}_Y(X) = X + 1$, and X is exogenous. The rows of the table are compatible with these laws, so this is a causal multiteam (call it T). It encodes many probabilities; for example, $P_T(Z = 2) = \frac{1}{2}$. Suppose we have a way to enforce the variable Y to take the value 1. We represent the effect of such an intervention ($do(Y = 1)$) by recomputing the Y and then the Z column:

Key	X	Y→Z		
0	0	1	...	
1	1	1	...	
2	1	1	...	
3	2	1	...	

$\rightsquigarrow$ $T^{-}_{Y=1}$:

Key	X	Y→Z		
0	0	1	0	
1	1	1	1	
2	1	1	1	
3	2	1	2	

where the new value of Z is computed, in each row, as the product of the value for X and the (new) value for Y. The probability distribution has changed: now $P_{T_{Y=1}}(Z = 2)$ is $\frac{1}{4}$. Furthermore, the function $\mathcal{F}_Y$ is now omitted from $T_{Y=1}$ (otherwise the assignments would not be compatible anymore with the laws). Correspondingly, the arrow from X to Y has been omitted from the causal graph.

3   Languages for Events and Probabilities

The language CO ("causation and observations") is for the description of events; later we incorporate it in a language for the discussion of probabilities of CO formulas. For any fixed signature, the formulas of CO are defined by the following BNF grammar:

$$\alpha ::= Y = y \mid Y \neq y \mid \alpha \wedge \alpha \mid \alpha \supset \alpha \mid \mathbf{X} = \mathbf{x} \boxminus\!\!\rightarrow \alpha,$$

where $\mathbf{X} \cup \{Y\} \subseteq \mathrm{Dom}$, $y \in \mathrm{Ran}(Y)$, and $\mathbf{x} \in \mathrm{Ran}(\mathbf{X})$. Formulae of the forms $Y = y$ and $Y \neq y$ are called **literals**. The semantics for CO is given by the following clauses:

$T \models Y = y$	iff	$s(Y) = y$ for all $s \in T^-$.
$T \models Y \neq y$	iff	$s(Y) \neq y$ for all $s \in T^-$.
$T \models \alpha \wedge \beta$	iff	$T \models \alpha$ and $T \models \beta$.
$T \models \alpha \supset \beta$	iff	$T^\alpha \models \beta$.
$T \models \mathbf{X} = \mathbf{x} \,\square\!\!\rightarrow \psi$	iff	$T_{\mathbf{X}=\mathbf{x}} \models \psi$ or $\mathbf{X} = \mathbf{x}$ is inconsistent.

where T^α is defined simultaneously with the semantic clauses. We will reserve the letters α, β to denote CO formulas.

We can introduce more logical operators as useful abbreviations. $\top$ stands for $X = x \,\square\!\!\rightarrow X = x$, and $\bot$ stands for $X = x \,\square\!\!\rightarrow X \neq x$. $\neg\alpha$ (*dual negation*) stands for $\alpha \supset \bot$. This is not a classical (contradictory) negation; it is easy to see that its semantics is:

- $(T^-, \mathcal{F}) \models \neg\alpha$ iff, for every $s \in T^-$, $(\{s\}, \mathcal{F}) \not\models \alpha$.

Thus, it is not the case, in general, that $T \models \alpha$ or $T \models \neg\alpha$. Note that $X \neq x$ is semantically equivalent to $\neg(X = x)$, and $X = x$ is semantically equivalent to $\neg(X \neq x)$. In previous works $\vee$ (*tensor disjunction*) was taken as a primitive operator, but here we define $\alpha \vee \beta$ as $\neg(\neg\alpha \wedge \neg\beta)$. Its semantic clause can be described as follows:

- $T \models \alpha \vee \beta$ iff there are $T_1, T_2 \leq T$ s.t. $T_1^- \cup T_2^- = T^-$, $T_1 \models \alpha$ and $T_2 \models \beta$.

In contrast with the statement above, the formula $\alpha \vee \neg\alpha$ *is* valid. Furthermore, $\alpha \equiv \beta$ abbreviates $(\alpha \supset \beta) \wedge (\beta \supset \alpha)$. Notice that this formula does not state that α and β are logically equivalent, but only that they are satisfied by the same assignments in the specific causal multiteam at hand.

All the operators discussed here (primitive and defined) behave classically over causal multiteams containing exactly one assignment.

A causal multiteam $(T^-, \mathcal{F})$ is **empty** (resp. **nonempty**) if the multiteam T^- is. All the logics $\mathcal{L}$ considered in the paper have the **empty team property**: if T is empty, then $T \models \alpha$ for any $\alpha \in \mathcal{L}$ (and any $\mathcal{F}$ of the same signature).

Our main object of study is the probabilistic language $\mathcal{PCO}$. Besides literals, it allows for **probabilistic atoms**:

$$\mathrm{Pr}(\alpha) \geq \epsilon \mid \mathrm{Pr}(\alpha) > \epsilon \mid \mathrm{Pr}(\alpha) \geq \mathrm{Pr}(\beta) \mid \mathrm{Pr}(\alpha) > \mathrm{Pr}(\beta)$$

where $\alpha, \beta \in CO$ and $\epsilon \in [0, 1] \cap \mathbb{Q}$. The first two are called **evaluation atoms**, and the latter two **comparison atoms**. Probabilistic atoms together with literals of CO are called **atomic formulas**. The probabilistic language $\mathcal{PCO}$ is then given by the following grammar:

$$\varphi ::= \eta \mid \varphi \wedge \varphi \mid \varphi \sqcup \varphi \mid \alpha \supset \varphi \mid \mathbf{X} = \mathbf{x} \,\square\!\!\rightarrow \varphi,$$

where $\mathbf{X} \subseteq \mathrm{Dom}$, $\mathbf{x} \in \mathrm{Ran}(\mathbf{X})$, η is an atomic formula, and α is a CO formula. Note that the antecedents of $\supset$ and the arguments of probability operators are CO formulas.

Semantics for the additional operators are given below:

$$T \models \psi \sqcup \chi \qquad \text{iff} \qquad T \models \psi \text{ or } T \models \chi$$
$$T \models \Pr(\alpha) \triangleright \epsilon \qquad \text{iff} \qquad T^- = \emptyset \text{ or } P_T(\alpha) \triangleright \epsilon$$
$$T \models \Pr(\alpha) \triangleright \Pr(\beta) \qquad \text{iff} \qquad T^- = \emptyset \text{ or } P_T(\alpha) \triangleright P_T(\beta)$$

where $\triangleright \in \{\geq, >\}$ and $P_T(\alpha)$ is a shorthand for $P_{T^-}((T^\alpha)^-)$.

As usual, for a set of formulas Γ, we write $T \models \Gamma$ if T satisfies each of the formulas in Γ. For $\Gamma \cup \{\varphi\} \subseteq \mathcal{PCO}$, we write $\Gamma \models_\sigma \varphi$ if $T \models \Gamma$ implies $T \models \varphi$, for all causal teams T of signature σ. $\models_\sigma \varphi$ abbreviates $\emptyset \models_\sigma \varphi$. We will always assume that some signature is fixed, and omit the subscripts.

The abbreviations $\top, \bot$ can be used freely in $\mathcal{PCO}$, while $\neg, \vee$ and $\equiv$ can be applied only to $\mathcal{CO}$ arguments. The definability of the dual negation in $\mathcal{CO}$ allows us to introduce more useful abbreviations:

$$\Pr(\alpha) \leq \epsilon := \Pr(\neg\alpha) \geq 1 - \epsilon \qquad \Pr(\alpha) = \epsilon := \Pr(\alpha) \geq \epsilon \wedge \Pr(\alpha) \leq \epsilon$$
$$\Pr(\alpha) < \epsilon := \Pr(\neg\alpha) > 1 - \epsilon \qquad \Pr(\alpha) \neq \epsilon := \Pr(\alpha) > \epsilon \sqcup \Pr(\alpha) < \epsilon.$$

Furthermore, the $\supset$ operator enables us to express some statements involving conditional probabilities. Writing, as usual, $\Pr(\alpha \mid \gamma)$ for the probability of α conditional on γ, we can define corresponding atoms as follows (where $\triangleright \in \{\geq, >\}$):

$$T \models \Pr(\alpha \mid \gamma) \triangleright \epsilon \qquad \text{iff} \qquad (T^\gamma)^- = \emptyset \text{ or } P_{T^\gamma}(\alpha) \triangleright \epsilon.$$
$$T \models \Pr(\alpha \mid \gamma) \triangleright \Pr(\beta \mid \gamma) \qquad \text{iff} \qquad (T^\gamma)^- = \emptyset \text{ or } P_{T^\gamma}(\alpha) \triangleright P_{T^\gamma}(\beta).$$

It was observed in [6] that $\Pr(\alpha \mid \gamma) \triangleright \epsilon$ and $\Pr(\alpha \mid \gamma) \triangleright \Pr(\beta \mid \gamma)$ can be defined by $\gamma \supset \Pr(\alpha) \triangleright \epsilon$ and $\gamma \supset \Pr(\alpha) \triangleright \Pr(\beta)$, respectively.

The *weak contradictory negation* φ^C of a formula φ is inductively definable in $\mathcal{PCO}$; this is an operator that behaves exactly as a contradictory negation, except on empty causal multiteams. We list the definitory clauses together with the values produced by the negation of defined formulas.

- $(\Pr(\alpha) \geq \epsilon)^C$ is $\Pr(\alpha) < \epsilon$ (and vice versa)
- $(\Pr(\alpha) > \epsilon)^C$ is $\Pr(\alpha) \leq \epsilon$ (and vice versa)
- $(\Pr(\alpha) = \epsilon)^C$ is $\Pr(\alpha) \neq \epsilon$ (and vice versa)
- $(\mathbf{X} = \mathbf{x} \boxarrow \chi)^C$ is $\mathbf{X} = \mathbf{x} \boxarrow \chi^C$
- $(\alpha \supset \chi)^C$ is $\Pr(\alpha) > 0 \wedge \alpha \supset \chi^C$
- $(\Pr(\alpha) \geq \Pr(\beta))^C$ is $\Pr(\beta) > \Pr(\alpha)$ (and vice versa)
- $(\psi \wedge \chi)^C$ is $\psi^C \sqcup \chi^C$
- $(\psi \sqcup \chi)^C$ is $\psi^C \wedge \chi^C$
- $(\bot)^C$ is $\top$ (and vice versa)
- $(X = x)^C$ is $\Pr(X = x) < 1$
- $(X \neq x)^C$ is $\Pr(X \neq x) < 1$.

In the clause for $\supset$, the conjunct $\Pr(\alpha) > 0$ (whose intuitive interpretation is "if T is nonempty, then T^α is nonempty") is added to insure that $(\alpha \supset \chi)^C$ is not satisfied by T in case (T is nonempty and) T^α is empty.[4]

---

[4] Whereas $\Pr(\alpha) > 0$ could be replaced with $(\neg\alpha)^C$, and $(X = x)^C$ could be also expessed as $\bigvee_{x' \neq x} X = x'$, the use of probability atoms in $(X \neq x)^C$ seems essential.

We emphasise that, since CO formulas are $\mathcal{PCO}$ formulas, the weak contradictory negation can also be applied to them; however, the contradictory negation of a CO formula will typically *not* be itself a CO formula. The meaning of the weak contradictory negation is as follows.

Theorem 4. *For every $\varphi \in \mathcal{PCO}_\sigma$ and nonempty causal multiteam $T = (T^-, \mathcal{F})$ of signature σ, $T \models \varphi^C \Leftrightarrow T \not\models \varphi$.*

Proof. The proof proceeds by induction on the structure of formulas φ. We show the only non-trivial case of $\supset$.

Suppose $T \models \Pr(\alpha) > 0 \wedge \alpha \supset \chi^C$. Thus $T^\alpha \models \chi^C$. Since T is nonempty and $T \models \Pr(\alpha) > 0$, we conclude that T^α is nonempty as well. Now by applying the induction hypothesis on χ, we obtain $T^\alpha \not\models \chi$. Thus, $T \not\models \alpha \supset \chi$.

For the converse, assume $T \not\models \alpha \supset \chi$. Then $T^\alpha \not\models \chi$, which (by the empty team property) entails that T^α is nonempty, and thus $T \models \Pr(\alpha) > 0$. Moreover, applying the induction hypothesis to χ yields $T^\alpha \models \chi^C$, and thus $T \models \alpha \supset \chi^C$.   □

Using the weak contradictory negation, we can define an operator that behaves exactly as the material conditional:

- $\psi \rightarrow \chi$ stands for $\psi^C \sqcup \chi$.

Indeed, $T \models \psi \rightarrow \chi$ iff T is empty or $T \not\models \psi$ or $T \models \chi$. However, since $\mathcal{PCO}$ has the empty multiteam property, "T is empty" entails $T \models \chi$; thus, for $\mathcal{PCO}$, $\rightarrow$ really is the material conditional:

- $\psi \rightarrow \chi$ iff $T \not\models \psi$ or $T \models \chi$.

Similarly, we let $\psi \leftrightarrow \chi$ denote $(\psi \rightarrow \chi) \wedge (\chi \rightarrow \psi)$.

Note that $\alpha \rightarrow \beta$ and $\alpha \supset \beta$ are not in general equivalent even if α, β are CO formulas. Consider for example a causal multiteam T with two assignments $s = \{(X, 0), (Y, 0)\}$ and $t = \{(X, 1), (Y, 1)\}$. Clearly $T \models X = 0 \rightarrow Y = 1$ (since $T \not\models X = 0$), while $T \not\models X = 0 \supset Y = 1$ (since $T^{X=0} \not\models Y = 1$). However, the entailment from $\alpha \supset \psi$ to $\alpha \rightarrow \psi$ always holds, provided both formulas are in $\mathcal{PCO}$ (i.e., provided $\alpha \in CO$). Indeed, suppose $T \models \alpha \supset \psi$ and $T \models \alpha$. From the former we get $T^\alpha \models \psi$. From the latter we get $T = T^\alpha$. Thus, $T \models \psi$. The opposite direction does not preserve truth, but it does preserve validity: if $\models \alpha \rightarrow \psi$, then $\models \alpha \supset \psi$. Indeed, the former tells us that any causal multiteam that satisfies α also satisfies ψ. Thus, in particular, for any T, $T^\alpha \models \psi$, and thus $T \models \alpha \supset \psi$.

Similar considerations as above apply to the pair of operators $\equiv$ and $\leftrightarrow$. Futher differences in the proof-theoretical behaviour of these (and other) pairs of operators are illustrated by the axioms T1 and T2 presented in Sect. 4.2.

4   The Axiom System

We present a formal deduction system with infinitary rules for $\mathcal{PCO}$ and show it to be strongly complete over recursive causal multiteams. We follow the approach of [32], which proved a similar result for a language with probabilities and conditional probabilities. Our result adds to the picture comparison atoms, counterfactuals, and pre-intervention observations ("Pearl's counterfactuals").

4.1 Further Notation

The formulation of some of the axioms – in particular, those involving reasoning with counterfactuals – will involve some additional abbreviations. For example, we will write $\mathbf{X} \neq \mathbf{x}$ for a disjunction $X_1 \neq x_1 \sqcup \cdots \sqcup X_n \neq x_n$.

There will be an axiom (C11) that characterizes recursivity as done in [17]. For it, we need to define the atom $X \rightsquigarrow Y$ ("X causally affects Y") by the formula:

$$\bigvee_{\substack{\mathbf{Z} \subseteq Dom \\ x \neq x' \in Ran(X) \\ y \neq y' \in Ran(Y) \\ \mathbf{z} \in Ran(\mathbf{Z})}} [((\mathbf{Z} = \mathbf{z} \wedge X = x) \,\Box\!\!\rightarrow Y = y) \wedge ((\mathbf{Z} = \mathbf{z} \wedge X = x') \,\Box\!\!\rightarrow Y = y')].$$

This formula states that there is some intervention on X that makes a difference for Y; it is the weakest form of causation that is definable in terms of interventionist counterfactuals.

We will also need a formula (from [5]) characterizing the stricter notion of direct cause (X is a direct cause of Y iff $X \in PA_Y$), which is expressible by a $\mathcal{PCO}$ formula $\varphi_{DC(X,Y)}$ defined as:

$$\bigvee_{\substack{x \neq x' \in Ran(X) \\ y \neq y' \in Ran(Y) \\ \mathbf{w} \in Ran(\mathbf{W}_{XY})}} [((\mathbf{W}_{XY} = \mathbf{w} \wedge X = x) \,\Box\!\!\rightarrow Y = y) \wedge ((\mathbf{W}_{XY} = \mathbf{w} \wedge X = x') \,\Box\!\!\rightarrow Y = y')].$$

where $\mathbf{W}_{XY}$ stands for $Dom \setminus \{X, Y\}$. The formula asserts that modifying the value of X may alter the value of Y even when all other variables are held fixed (thus excluding causation via intermediate variables).

Now, some axioms describe specific properties of exogenous or endogenous variables, which can be again characterized in $\mathcal{PCO}$. We can express the fact that a variable Y is endogenous by the following formula (where, as before, $\mathbf{W}_V$ stands for $Dom \setminus \{V\}$):

$$\varphi_{End(Y)} : \bigsqcup_{X \in \mathbf{W}_Y} \varphi_{DC(X,Y)}$$

and its contradictory negation $(\varphi_{End(Y)})^C$ will express that Y is exogenous.

Finally, for each function component $\mathcal{F}$, $\Phi^{\mathcal{F}}$ is a formula that characterizes the fact that a causal team has function component $\mathcal{F}$. In detail,

$$\Phi^{\mathcal{F}} : \bigwedge_{V \in End(\mathcal{F})} \eta_\sigma(V) \wedge \bigwedge_{V \notin End(\mathcal{F})} \xi_\sigma(V)$$

where

$$\eta_\sigma(V) : \bigwedge_{\mathbf{w} \in Ran(\mathbf{W}_V)} (\mathbf{W}_V = \mathbf{w} \,\Box\!\!\rightarrow V = \mathcal{F}_V(\mathbf{w}))$$

and

$$\xi_\sigma(V) : \bigwedge_{\substack{\mathbf{w} \in Ran(\mathbf{W}_V) \\ v \in Ran(V)}} V = v \supset (\mathbf{W}_V = \mathbf{w} \,\Box\!\!\rightarrow V = v).$$

A nonempty causal multiteam $T = (T^-, \mathcal{G})$ satisfies $\Phi^{\mathcal{F}}$ iff $\mathcal{G} = \mathcal{F}$.[5]

---

[5] Save for some inessential differences, this is is the content of Theorem 3.4 from [9].

4.2 Axioms and Rules

We present a few axiom schemes and rules for $\mathcal{PCO}$, roughly divided in six groups. Each axiom and rule is restricted to formulas of a fixed signature σ, so that actually we have a distinct axiom system for each signature. As usual, α and β are restricted to be CO formulas.

Tautologies

T1. All instances of classical propositional tautologies in $\wedge, \sqcup, \rightarrow,{}^C, \top, \bot$.
T2. All CO instances of classical propositional tautologies in $\wedge, \vee, \supset, \neg, \top, \bot$.

Rule MP. $\dfrac{\psi \quad \psi \rightarrow \chi}{\chi}$

Rule Rep. $\dfrac{\vdash \varphi \quad \vdash \theta \leftrightarrow \theta'}{\vdash \varphi[\theta'/\theta]}$ (provided $\varphi[\theta'/\theta]$ is well-formed)

Probabilities

P1. $\alpha \leftrightarrow \Pr(\alpha) = 1$.
P2. $\Pr(\alpha) \geq 0$.
P3. $(\Pr(\alpha) = \delta \wedge \Pr(\beta) = \epsilon \wedge \Pr(\alpha \wedge \beta) = 0) \rightarrow \Pr(\alpha \vee \beta) = \delta + \epsilon$
(when $\delta + \epsilon \leq 1$).
P3b. $\Pr(\alpha) \geq \epsilon \wedge \Pr(\alpha \wedge \beta) = 0 \rightarrow \Pr(\beta) \leq 1 - \epsilon$.
P4. $\Pr(\alpha) \leq \epsilon \rightarrow \Pr(\alpha) < \delta$ (if $\delta > \epsilon$).
P5. $\Pr(\alpha) < \epsilon \rightarrow \Pr(\alpha) \leq \epsilon$.
P6. $(\alpha \equiv \beta) \rightarrow (\Pr(\alpha) = \epsilon \rightarrow \Pr(\beta) = \epsilon)$.
P6b. $(\alpha \supset \beta) \rightarrow (\Pr(\alpha) = \epsilon \rightarrow \Pr(\beta) \geq \epsilon)$.

Rule $\bot^\omega$. $\dfrac{\psi \rightarrow \Pr(\alpha) \neq \epsilon, \forall \epsilon \in [0,1] \cap \mathbb{Q}}{\psi \rightarrow \bot}$

Comparison

CP1. $(\Pr(\alpha) = \delta \wedge \Pr(\beta) - \epsilon) \rightarrow \Pr(\alpha) \geq \Pr(\beta)$.   (if $\delta \geq \epsilon$)
CP2. $(\Pr(\alpha) = \delta \wedge \Pr(\beta) = \epsilon) \rightarrow \Pr(\alpha) > \Pr(\beta)$.   (if $\delta > \epsilon$)

Observations

O1. $\Pr(\alpha) = 0 \rightarrow (\alpha \supset \psi)$.
O1b. $(\alpha \supset \bot) \rightarrow \Pr(\alpha) = 0$.
O2. $(\Pr(\alpha) = \delta \wedge \Pr(\alpha \wedge \beta) = \epsilon) \rightarrow (\alpha \supset \Pr(\beta) = \frac{\epsilon}{\delta})$.   (when $\delta \neq 0$)
O3. $(\alpha \supset \Pr(\beta) = \epsilon) \rightarrow (\Pr(\alpha) = \delta \leftrightarrow \Pr(\alpha \wedge \beta) = \epsilon \cdot \delta)$ (when $\epsilon \neq 0$).
O4. $(\alpha \supset \psi) \rightarrow (\alpha \rightarrow \psi)$.
O5$_\wedge$. $\alpha \supset (\psi \wedge \chi) \leftrightarrow (\alpha \supset \psi) \wedge (\alpha \supset \chi)$.
O5$_\sqcup$. $\alpha \supset (\psi \sqcup \chi) \leftrightarrow (\alpha \supset \psi) \sqcup (\alpha \supset \chi)$.
O5$_\supset$. $\alpha \supset (\beta \supset \chi) \leftrightarrow (\alpha \wedge \beta) \supset \chi$.

Rule Mon$_\supset$. $\dfrac{\vdash \psi \rightarrow \chi}{\vdash (\alpha \supset \psi) \rightarrow (\alpha \supset \chi)}$

Rule $\rightarrow$to$\supset$. $\dfrac{\vdash \alpha \rightarrow \psi}{\vdash \alpha \supset \psi}$

Rule $\supset^\omega$. $\dfrac{\psi \rightarrow (\Pr(\alpha \wedge \beta) = \delta \epsilon \leftrightarrow \Pr(\alpha) = \epsilon), \forall \epsilon \in (0,1] \cap \mathbb{Q}}{\psi \rightarrow (\alpha \supset \Pr(\beta) = \delta)}$

Literals

A1. $\mathbf{Y} = \mathbf{y} \to \mathbf{Y} \neq \mathbf{y}'$.   (when $\mathbf{y} \neq \mathbf{y}'$)

A2. $X \neq x \leftrightarrow (X = x \supset \bot)$.

A3. $\bigvee_{y \in \mathrm{Ran}(Y)} \mathbf{Y} = \mathbf{y}$.

Counterfactuals

C1. $(\mathbf{X} = \mathbf{x} \,\square\!\!\rightarrow (\psi \wedge \chi)) \leftrightarrow ((\mathbf{X} = \mathbf{x} \,\square\!\!\rightarrow \psi) \wedge (\mathbf{X} = \mathbf{x} \,\square\!\!\rightarrow \chi))$.

C2. $(\mathbf{X} = \mathbf{x} \,\square\!\!\rightarrow (\psi \sqcup \chi)) \leftrightarrow ((\mathbf{X} = \mathbf{x} \,\square\!\!\rightarrow \psi) \sqcup (\mathbf{X} = \mathbf{x} \,\square\!\!\rightarrow \chi))$.

C3. $(\mathbf{X} = \mathbf{x} \,\square\!\!\rightarrow (\alpha \supset \chi)) \leftrightarrow ((\mathbf{X} = \mathbf{x} \,\square\!\!\rightarrow \alpha) \supset (\mathbf{X} = \mathbf{x} \,\square\!\!\rightarrow \chi))$.

C4. $(\mathbf{X} = \mathbf{x}\,\square\!\!\rightarrow (\mathbf{Y} = \mathbf{y}\,\square\!\!\rightarrow \chi)) \to ((\mathbf{X}' = \mathbf{x}' \wedge \mathbf{Y} = \mathbf{y})\,\square\!\!\rightarrow \chi)$

(where $\mathbf{X}' = \mathbf{X} \setminus \mathbf{Y}$ and $\mathbf{x}' = \mathbf{x} \setminus \mathbf{y}$; and provided $\mathbf{X} = \mathbf{x}$ is consistent).

C4b. $((\mathbf{X} = \mathbf{x} \wedge \mathbf{Y} = \mathbf{y})\,\square\!\!\rightarrow \chi) \to (\mathbf{X} = \mathbf{x}\,\square\!\!\rightarrow (\mathbf{Y} = \mathbf{y}\,\square\!\!\rightarrow \chi))$.

C5. $(\mathbf{X} = \mathbf{x} \,\square\!\!\rightarrow \bot) \to \psi$.   (when $\mathbf{X} = \mathbf{x}$ is consistent)

C6. $(\mathbf{X} = \mathbf{x} \wedge Y = y) \,\square\!\!\rightarrow Y = y$.

C7. $(\mathbf{X} = \mathbf{x} \wedge \gamma) \to (\mathbf{X} = \mathbf{x} \,\square\!\!\rightarrow \gamma)$.   (where $\gamma \in \mathcal{PCO}$ without occurrences of $\square\!\!\rightarrow$)

C8. $(\mathbf{X} = \mathbf{x} \,\square\!\!\rightarrow \mathrm{Pr}(\alpha) \rhd \epsilon) \leftrightarrow \mathrm{Pr}(\mathbf{X} = \mathbf{x} \,\square\!\!\rightarrow \alpha) \rhd \epsilon$.   (where $\rhd = \geq$ or $>$)

C8b. $(\mathbf{X} = \mathbf{x} \,\square\!\!\rightarrow \mathrm{Pr}(\alpha) \rhd \mathrm{Pr}(\beta)) \leftrightarrow \mathrm{Pr}(\mathbf{X} = \mathbf{x} \,\square\!\!\rightarrow \alpha) \rhd \mathrm{Pr}(\mathbf{X} = \mathbf{x} \,\square\!\!\rightarrow \beta)$

(where $\rhd = \geq$ or $>$).

C9. $\varphi_{End(Y)} \to (\mathbf{W}_Y = \mathbf{w} \,\square\!\!\rightarrow \bigsqcup_{y \in \mathrm{Ran}(Y)} Y = y)$.

C10. $(\varphi_{End(Y)})^C \to (Y = y \supset (\mathbf{W}_V = \mathbf{w} \,\square\!\!\rightarrow Y = y))$.

C11. $(X_1 \rightsquigarrow X_2 \wedge \cdots \wedge X_{n-1} \rightsquigarrow X_n) \to (X_n \rightsquigarrow X_1)^C$.   (for $n > 1$).

Rule Mon$_{\square\!\!\rightarrow}$.
$$\frac{\vdash \psi \to \chi}{\vdash (\mathbf{X} = \mathbf{x} \square\!\!\rightarrow \psi) \to (\mathbf{X} = \mathbf{x} \square\!\!\rightarrow \chi)}$$

We will refer to this list of axioms and rules as the **deduction system**, and write $\Gamma \vdash \varphi$ if there is a countable sequence of $\mathcal{PCO}$ formulas $\varphi_1, \ldots, \varphi_\kappa = \varphi$ (enumerated by ordinals $\leq \kappa$) where each formula in the list is either an axiom, a formula from Γ, or it follows from earlier formulas in the list by one of the rules. The sequence itself is called a **proof**.

We write $\vdash \varphi$ for $\emptyset \vdash \varphi$; if it holds, we say that φ is a **theorem**. Notice that some of the rules (Rep, Mon$_\supset$, Mon$_{\square\!\!\rightarrow}$, $\to$to$\supset$) can only be applied to theorems, since they preserve validity but not truth.

5   Discussion of the Proof System

We have described a family of infinitary axiom systems, one for each finite signature σ. Our main result is that each such axiom system is sound and strongly complete for $\mathcal{PCO}_\sigma$ over the corresponding class of multiteams of signature σ. By saying that a deduction system is **sound** for $\mathcal{PCO}_\sigma$ we mean that, for all formulas $\Gamma \cup \{\varphi\} \subseteq \mathcal{PCO}_\sigma$, $\Gamma \vdash \varphi$ entails $\Gamma \models_\sigma \varphi$; and it is **strongly complete** for $\mathcal{PCO}_\sigma$ if $\Gamma \models_\sigma \varphi$ entails $\Gamma \vdash \varphi$. As discussed in the Introduction, a finitary axiom system could at most aspire to be (sound and) *weakly* complete for $\mathcal{PCO}_\sigma$, i.e. to satisfy the equivalence $\Gamma_0 \models \varphi$ iff $\Gamma_0 \vdash \varphi$, for *finite* sets Γ_0.

Theorem 5 (Soundness and strong completeness). *Let σ be a signature and $\Gamma \cup \{\varphi\} \subseteq \mathcal{PCO}_\sigma$. Then $\Gamma \models \varphi$ if and only if $\Gamma \vdash \varphi$.*

The proof of this result (which can be found in the full version of the paper, [8]) uses a Henkin-style canonical model construction, i.e. it proceeds by showing that each maximal consistent set Γ of formulas of $\mathcal{PCO}_\sigma$ provides sufficient information for constructing a *canonical causal multiteam* $\mathbb{T}$ that satisfies Γ. The proof essentially follows the lines of the completeness proof given in [32], but it presents some novel difficulties in dealing with the additional operators $\supset$ and $\Box\!\!\rightarrow$, especially towards obtaining a Truth Lemma, which takes the unusual form:

$$\text{For all } \alpha \in CO \text{ and } \varphi \in \mathcal{PCO}, \mathbb{T}^\alpha \models \varphi \iff \alpha \supset \varphi \in \Gamma.$$

The choice of axioms and rules is largely built on earlier axiomatizations of simpler languages for probabilistic or causal reasoning; let us briefly illustrate how our system adapts or differs from earlier sources. Rules MP, $\perp^\omega$, $\supset^\omega$ and axioms P1-2-3-4-5 and O1-2-3 are essentially adapted from the paper [32] (the rule $\perp^\omega$ comes from the earlier [1]). Keeping in mind that a formula of the form $\alpha \supset \text{Pr}(\beta) = \epsilon$ is semantically equivalent to a conditional probability statement $\text{Pr}(\beta \mid \alpha) = \epsilon$, axioms O2-3 encode the usual definition of conditional probability in terms of marginal probability. Our Rule Mon$_\supset$ allows omitting axioms 8, 11 and 12 from [32], which follow from it. Our restriction $\delta + \epsilon \leq 1$ in axiom P3 is imposed by the syntax (we do not allow numbers greater than 1 as symbols). The additional axiom P3b guarantees that, despite this restriction, axiom scheme P3 is always applicable, in the sense that, if an instance of it is not admitted as an axiom, then the premises of said instance are contradictory.[6] Axiom P6 derives from [32], but in our case the correct formulation requires the interaction of the two conditionals $\supset$ (used to define $\equiv$) and $\rightarrow$; notice that the analogous formulation $(\alpha \leftrightarrow \beta) \rightarrow (\text{Pr}(\alpha) = \epsilon \rightarrow \text{Pr}(\beta) = \epsilon)$ is *not* valid. The variant P6b is our addition. These adaptations are due both to differences in the syntax ([32] has an explicit conditional probability operator, while we talk of conditional probabilities only indirectly, by means of the selective implication; and we have distinct logical operators at the level of events vs. the level of probabilities) and in the semantics (in particular, we differ in the treatment of truth over empty models).

Regarding comparison atoms, analogues of CP1-2 appear, for example, in [26], and in earlier literature. An interesting difference from [26] is that in our system we do not need an additional infinitary rule to deal with the comparison atoms.

Axioms C6, C7 and C11 take the same roles as the principles of *Effectiveness, Composition* and *Recursivity* from [14]. The current, more intuitive form of axiom C7 was introduced in [9]; it captures the intuition that intervening by fixing some variables to values they already possess will not alter the value of any variable (although it may alter the set of causal laws, whence the restriction to γ without occurrences of $\Box\!\!\rightarrow$). Halpern [17] noticed that $\Box\!\!\rightarrow$ distributes over Boolean operators, and formulated analogues of C1 and C2. The validity of C3-4-4b was pointed out in [5] (although an earlier axiom for dealing with nested counterfactuals had already been devised in [12]), and the importance of C5 emerged in [9].

---

[6] It seems to us that an axiom analogous to P3b should be added also to the system in [32].

6   Conclusions

We produced a strongly complete axiom system for a language $\mathcal{PCO}$ for probabilistic counterfactual reasoning (without arithmetical operations). As for most analogous results in the literature on interventionist counterfactuals, we have assumed that the signatures are finite; it would be interesting to find out if the recently developed methods of [18] for axiomatizatizing infinite signatures may be extended to our case. Our system features infinitary rules, and it is therefore natural to wonder whether finitary axiomatizations could be obtained. Due to the failure of compactness, such axiomatizations can aspire at most at weak completeness.

There is another closely related axiomatization issue that would be important to settle. In [6], an extension $\mathcal{PCO}^{\omega}$ of $\mathcal{PCO}$ is considered that features a countably infinite version of the global disjunction ⊔. This uncountable language is much more expressive than $\mathcal{PCO}$ and it can be proved that, in a sense, it encompasses all the expressive resources that a probabilistic language for interventionist counterfactuals should have. Given the special semantic role of this language, it would be important to find out whether an (infinitary) strongly complete axiomatization can be obtained for it. The main obstacle is proving an appropriate Lindenbaum lemma; as shown e.g. in [11], for an uncountable language with an infinitary axiom system the Lindenbaum lemma can even be false.

Acknowledgments. Fausto Barbero was partially supported by the DFG grant VI 1045-1/1 and by the Academy of Finland grants 316460 and 349803. Jonni Virtema was partially supported by the DFG grant VI 1045-1/1 and by the Academy of Finland grant 338259.

References

1. Alechina, N.: Logic with probabilistic operators. Proc. ACCOLADE **1994**, 121–138 (1995)
2. Baldi, P., Cintula, P., Noguera, C.: Classical and fuzzy two-layered modal logics for uncertainty: translations and proof-theory. Int. J. Comput. Intell. Syst. **13**, 988–1001 (2020). https://doi.org/10.2991/ijcis.d.200703.001
3. Barbero, F., Galliani, P.: Embedding causal team languages into predicate logic. Ann. Pure Appl. Logic **173**, 103–159 (2022). https://doi.org/10.1016/j.apal.2022.103159
4. Barbero, F., Sandu, G.: Interventionist counterfactuals on causal teams. In: CREST 2018 Proceedings - Electronic Proceedings in Theoretical Computer Science, vol. 286, pp. 16–30. Open Publishing Association (2019). https://doi.org/10.4204/eptcs.286.2
5. Barbero, F., Sandu, G.: Team semantics for interventionist counterfactuals: observations vs. interventions. J. Philos. Logic **50**, 471–521 (2021)
6. Barbero, F., Sandu, G.: Multiteam semantics for interventionist counterfactuals: probabilities and causation (2023). pre-print, arxiv:2305.02613
7. Barbero, F., Virtema, J.: Expressivity landscape for logics with probabilistic interventionist counterfactuals. CoRR abs/2303.11993 (2023). https://doi.org/10.48550/arXiv.2303.11993
8. Barbero, F., Virtema, J.: Strongly complete axiomatization for a logic with probabilistic interventionist counterfactuals. arXiv preprint arXiv:2304.02964 (2023)

9. Barbero, F., Yang, F.: Characterizing counterfactuals and dependencies over (generalized) causal teams. Notre Dame J. Formal Logic **63**(3), 301–341 (2022). https://doi.org/10.1215/00294527-2022-0017
10. Bareinboim, E., Correa, J., Ibeling, D., Icard, T.: On pearl's hierarchy and the foundations of causal inference (1st edition). In: Geffner, H., Dechter, R., Halpern, J.Y. (eds.) Probabilistic and Causal Inference: the Works of Judea Pearl, pp. 507–556. ACM Books (2022)
11. Bílková, M., Cintula, P., Lávička, T.: Lindenbaum and Pair extension lemma in infinitary logics. In: Moss, L.S., de Queiroz, R., Martinez, M. (eds.) WoLLIC 2018. LNCS, vol. 10944, pp. 130–144. Springer, Heidelberg (2018). https://doi.org/10.1007/978-3-662-57669-4_7
12. Briggs, R.: Interventionist counterfactuals. Philos. Stud. Int. J. Philos. Anal. Trad. **160**(1), 139–166 (2012)
13. Fagin, R., Halpern, J.Y., Megiddo, N.: A logic for reasoning about probabilities. Inf. Comput. **87**(1–2), 78–128 (1990)
14. Galles, D., Pearl, J.: An axiomatic characterization of causal counterfactuals. Found. Sci. **3**(1), 151–182 (1998)
15. Hájek, P., Godo, L., Esteva, F.: Fuzzy logic and probability. In: Proceedings of the Uncertainty in Artificial Intelligence UAI, vol. 95, pp. 237–244 (1995)
16. Halpern, J.: Actual Causality. MIT Press, Cambridge (2016)
17. Halpern, J.Y.: Axiomatizing causal reasoning. J. Artif. Int. Res. **12**(1), 317–337 (2000)
18. Halpern, J.Y., Peters, S.: Reasoning about causal models with infinitely many variables. In: Proceedings of the AAAI Conference on Artificial Intelligence, vol. 36, pp. 5668–5675 (2022)
19. Heckman, J.J., Vytlacil, E.J.: Econometric evaluation of social programs, part i: causal models, structural models and econometric policy evaluation. Handb. Econ. **6**, 4779–4874 (2007)
20. Heifetz, A., Mongin, P.: Probability logic for type spaces. Games Econom. Behav. **35**(1), 31–53 (2001). https://doi.org/10.1006/game.1999.0788
21. Hernan, M., Robins, J.: Causal Inference: What if. Chapman & Hall/CRC, Boca Raton (forthcoming)
22. Hitchcock, C.: Causal models. In: Zalta, E.N., Nodelman, U. (eds.) The Stanford Encyclopedia of Philosophy. Metaphysics Research Lab, Stanford University, Spring 2023 edn. (2023)
23. Hodges, W.: Compositional semantics for a language of imperfect information. Logic J. IGPL **5**, 539–563 (1997)
24. Ibeling, D., Icard, T.: Probabilistic reasoning across the causal hierarchy. In: Proceedings of the AAAI Conference on Artificial Intelligence, vol. 34, pp. 10170–10177 (2020)
25. Morgan, S.L., Winship, C.: Counterfactuals and Causal Inference. Cambridge University Press, Cambridge (2015)
26. Ognjanović, Z., Perović, A., Rašković, M.: Logics with the qualitative probability operator. Logic J. IGPL **16**(2), 105–120 (2008). https://doi.org/10.1093/jigpal/jzm031
27. Ognjanović, Z., Rašković, M., Marković, Z.: Probability Logics: Probability-Based Formalization of Uncertain Reasoning. Springer, Berlin (2016)
28. Pearl, J.: Causality: Models, Reasoning, and Inference. Cambridge University Press, New York, NY, USA (2000)
29. Pearl, J., Glymour, M., Jewell, N.P.: Causal Inference in Statistics: A Primer. Wiley, Hoboken (2016)
30. Pearl, J., Mackenzie, D.: The Book of Why: The New Science Of Cause and Effect. Basic Books, New York City (2018)
31. Peters, J., Janzing, D., Schölkopf, B.: Elements of Causal Inference: Foundations and Learning Algorithms. MIT Press, Cambridge (2017)
32. Rašković, M., Ognjanović, Z., Marković, Z.: A logic with conditional probabilities. In: Alferes, J.J., Leite, J. (eds.) JELIA 2004. LNCS (LNAI), vol. 3229, pp. 226–238. Springer, Heidelberg (2004). https://doi.org/10.1007/978-3-540-30227-8_21

33. Spirtes, P., Glymour, C., Scheines, R.N.: Causation, Prediction, and Search. Lecture Notes in Statistics, vol. 81. Springer, New York (1993)
34. Väänänen, J.: Dependence Logic: A New Approach to Independence Friendly Logic, London Mathematical Society Student Texts, vol. 70. Cambridge University Press, Cambridge (2007)
35. Woodward, J.: Making Things Happen, Oxford Studies in the Philosophy of Science, vol. 114. Oxford University Press, Oxford (2003)

Logics with Probabilistic Team Semantics and the Boolean Negation

Miika Hannula[1] , Minna Hirvonen[1(✉)] , Juha Kontinen[1] ,
Yasir Mahmood[2] , Arne Meier[3] , and Jonni Virtema[4]

[1] Department of Mathematics and Statistics, University of Helsinki, Helsinki, Finland
{miika.hannula,minna.hirvonen,juha.kontinen}@helsinki.fi
[2] DICE Group, Department of Computer Science, Paderborn University,
Paderborn, Germany
yasir.mahmood@uni-paderborn.de
[3] Institut für Theoretische Informatik, Leibniz Universität Hannover,
Hannover, Germany
meier@thi.uni-hannover.de
[4] Department of Computer Science, University of Sheffield, Sheffield, UK
j.t.virtema@sheffield.ac.uk

Abstract. We study the expressivity and the complexity of various logics in probabilistic team semantics with the Boolean negation. In particular, we study the extension of probabilistic independence logic with the Boolean negation, and a recently introduced logic FOPT. We give a comprehensive picture of the relative expressivity of these logics together with the most studied logics in probabilistic team semantics setting, as well as relating their expressivity to a numerical variant of second-order logic. In addition, we introduce novel entropy atoms and show that the extension of first-order logic by entropy atoms subsumes probabilistic independence logic. Finally, we obtain some results on the complexity of model checking, validity, and satisfiability of our logics.

Keywords: Probabilistic Team Semantics · Model Checking · Satisfiability · Validity · Computational Complexity · Expressivity of Logics

1 Introduction

Probabilistic team semantics is a novel framework for the logical analysis of probabilistic and quantitative dependencies. Team semantics, as a semantic framework for logics involving qualitative dependencies and independencies, was introduced by Hodges [17] and popularised by Väänänen [25] via his dependence logic. Team semantics defines truth in reference to collections of assignments, called *teams*, and is particularly suitable for the formal analysis of properties, such as the functional dependence between variables, that arise only in the presence of multiple assignments. The idea of generalising team semantics to the probabilistic setting can be traced back to the works of Galliani [6] and Hyttinen et al. [18], however the beginning of a more systematic study of the topic dates back to works of Durand et al. [4].

S. Gaggl et al. (Eds.): JELIA 2023, LNAI 14281, pp. 665–680, 2023.
https://doi.org/10.1007/978-3-031-43619-2_45

Table 1. Overview of our results. Unless otherwise noted, the results are completeness results. Satisfiability and Validity are considered for finite structures.

Logic	MC for sentences	SAT	VAL
FOPT($\leq_c^\delta$)	PSPACE (Corollary 20)	RE [11, Theorem 5.2]	coRE [11, Theorem 5.2]
FO($\perp\!\!\!\perp_c$)	$\in$ EXPSPACE and NEXPTIME-hard (Theorem 24)	RE (Theorem 26)	coRE (Theorem 26)
FO($\sim$)	AEXPTIME[poly] [22, Proposition 5.16, Lemma 5.21]	RE [22, Theorem 5.6]	coRE [22, Theorem 5.6]
FO($\approx$)	$\in$ EXPTIME, PSPACE-hard (Theorem 22)	RE (Theorem 26)	coRE (Theorem 26)
FO($\sim, \perp\!\!\!\perp_c$)	$\in$ 3-EXPSPACE, AEXPTIME[poly]-hard (Theorem 25)	RE (Theorem 26)	coRE (Theorem 26)

In *probabilistic team semantics* the basic semantic units are probability distributions (i.e., *probabilistic teams*). This shift from set-based to distribution-based semantics allows probabilistic notions of dependency, such as conditional probabilistic independence, to be embedded in the framework[1]. The expressivity and complexity of non-probabilistic team-based logics can be related to fragments of (existential) second-order logic and have been studied extensively (see, e.g., [5,7,9]). Team-based logics, by definition, are usually not closed under Boolean negation, so adding it can greatly increase the complexity and expressivity of these logics [15,19]. Some expressivity and complexity results have also been obtained for logics in probabilistic team semantics (see below). However, richer semantic and computational frameworks are sometimes needed to characterise these logics.

Metafinite Model Theory, introduced by Grädel and Gurevich [8], generalises the approach of *Finite Model Theory* by shifting to two-sorted structures, which extend finite structures by another (often infinite) numerical domain and weight functions bridging the two sorts. A particularly important subclass of metafinite structures are the so-called $\mathbb{R}$-*structures*, which extend finite structures with the real arithmetic on the second sort. *Blum-Shub-Smale machines* (BSS machines for short) [1] are essentially register machines with registers that can store arbitrary real numbers and compute rational functions over reals in a single time step. Interestingly, Boolean languages which are decidable by a non-deterministic polynomial-time BSS machine coincide with those languages which are PTIME-reducible to the true existential sentences of real arithmetic (i.e., the complexity class $\exists\mathbb{R}$) [2,24].

Recent works have established fascinating connections between second-order logics over $\mathbb{R}$-structures, complexity classes using the BSS-model of computation, and logics using probabilistic team semantics. In [13], Hannula et al. establish that the expressivity and complexity of probabilistic independence logic coincide with a particular fragment of existential second-order logic over $\mathbb{R}$-structures and NP on BSS-machines. In [16], Hannula and Virtema focus on probabilistic inclusion logic, which is shown to be tractable (when restricted to Boolean inputs), and relate it to linear programming.

---

[1] In [21] Li recently introduced *first-order theory of random variables with probabilistic independence (FOTPI)* whose variables are interpreted by discrete distributions over the unit interval. The paper shows that true arithmetic is interpretable in FOTPI whereas probabilistic independence logic is by our results far less complex.

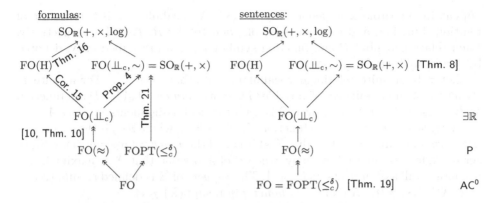

Fig. 1. Landscape of relevant logics as well as relation to some complexity classes. Note that for the complexity classes, finite ordered structures are required. Single arrows indicate inclusions and double arrows indicate strict inclusions.

In this paper, we focus on the expressivity and model checking complexity of probabilistic team-based logics that have access to Boolean negation. We also study the connections between probabilistic independence logic and a logic called $\text{FOPT}(\leq_c^\delta)$, which is defined via a computationally simpler probabilistic semantics [11]. The logic $\text{FOPT}(\leq_c^\delta)$ is the probabilistic variant of a certain team-based logic that can define exactly those dependencies that are first-order definable [20]. We also introduce novel entropy atoms and relate the extension of first-order logic with these atoms to probabilistic independence logic.

See Fig. 1 for our expressivity results and Table 1 for our complexity results.

2 Preliminaries

We assume the reader is familiar with the basics in complexity theory [23]. In this work, we will encounter complexity classes PSPACE, EXPTIME, NEXPTIME, EXPSPACE and the class AEXPTIME[poly] together with the notion of completeness under the usual polynomial time many to one reductions. A bit more formally for the latter complexity class which is more uncommon than the others, AEXPTIME[poly] consists of all languages that can be decided by alternating Turing machines within an exponential runtime of $O(2^{n^{O(1)}})$ and polynomially many alternations between universal and existential states. There exist problems in propositional team logic with generalized dependence atoms that are complete for this class [14]. It is also known that truth evaluation of alternating dependency quantified boolean formulae (ADQBF) is complete for this class [14].

2.1 Probabilistic Team Semantics

We denote first-order variables by x, y, z and tuples of first-order variables by $\mathbf{x}, \mathbf{y}, \mathbf{z}$. For the length of the tuple $\mathbf{x}$, we write $|\mathbf{x}|$. The set of variables that appear in the tuple $\mathbf{x}$ is denoted by $\mathrm{Var}(\mathbf{x})$. A vocabulary τ is a finite set of relation, function, and constant symbols, denoted by R, f, and c, respectively. Each relation symbol R and function symbol f has a prescribed arity, denoted by $\mathrm{Ar}(R)$ and $\mathrm{Ar}(f)$.

Let τ be a finite relational vocabulary such that $\{=\} \subseteq \tau$. For a finite τ-structure $\mathcal{A}$ and a finite set of variables D, an *assignment* of $\mathcal{A}$ for D is a function $s: D \to A$. A *team* X of $\mathcal{A}$ over D is a finite set of assignments $s: D \to A$.

A *probabilistic team* $\mathbb{X}$ is a function $\mathbb{X}: X \to \mathbb{R}_{\geq 0}$, where $\mathbb{R}_{\geq 0}$ is the set of non-negative real numbers. The value $\mathbb{X}(s)$ is called the *weight* of assignment s. Since zero-weights are allowed, we may, when useful, assume that X is maximal, i.e., it contains all assignments $s: D \to A$. The *support* of $\mathbb{X}$ is defined as $\mathrm{supp}(\mathbb{X}) := \{s \in X \mid \mathbb{X}(s) \neq 0\}$. A team $\mathbb{X}$ is *nonempty* if $\mathrm{supp}(\mathbb{X}) \neq \varnothing$.

These teams are called probabilistic because we usually consider teams that are probability distributions, i.e., functions $\mathbb{X}: X \to \mathbb{R}_{\geq 0}$ for which $\sum_{s \in X} \mathbb{X}(s) = 1$.[2] In this setting, the weight of an assignment can be thought of as the probability that the values of the variables are as in the assignment. If $\mathbb{X}$ is a probability distribution, we also write $\mathbb{X}: X \to [0, 1]$.

For a set of variables V, the restriction of the assignment s to V is denoted by $s \upharpoonright V$. The *restriction of a team* X to V is $X \upharpoonright V = \{s \upharpoonright V \mid s \in X\}$, and the *restriction of a probabilistic team* $\mathbb{X}$ to V is $\mathbb{X} \upharpoonright V: X \upharpoonright V \to \mathbb{R}_{\geq 0}$ where

$$(\mathbb{X} \upharpoonright V)(s) = \sum_{\substack{s' \upharpoonright V = s, \\ s' \in X}} \mathbb{X}(s').$$

If ϕ is a first-order formula, then $\mathbb{X}_\phi$ is the restriction of the team X to those assignments in X that satisfy the formula ϕ. The weight $|\mathbb{X}_\phi|$ is defined analogously as the sum of the weights of the assignments in X that satisfy ϕ, e.g.,

$$|\mathbb{X}_{\mathbf{x}=\mathbf{a}}| = \sum_{\substack{s \in X, \\ s(\mathbf{x})=\mathbf{a}}} \mathbb{X}(s).$$

For a variable x and $a \in A$, we denote by $s(a/x)$, the modified assignment $s(a/x): D \cup \{x\} \to A$ such that $s(a/x)(y) = a$ if $y = x$, and $s(a/x)(y) = s(y)$ otherwise. For a set $B \subseteq A$, the modified team $X(B/x)$ is defined as the set $X(B/x) := \{s(a/x) \mid a \in B, s \in X\}$.

Let $\mathbb{X}: X \to \mathbb{R}_{\geq 0}$ be any probabilistic team. Then the probabilistic team $\mathbb{X}(B/x)$ is a function $\mathbb{X}(B/x): X(B/x) \to \mathbb{R}_{\geq 0}$ defined as

$$\mathbb{X}(B/x)(s(a/x)) = \sum_{\substack{t \in X, \\ t(a/x)=s(a/x)}} \mathbb{X}(t) \cdot \frac{1}{|B|}.$$

---

[2] In some sources, the term probabilistic team only refers to teams that are distributions, and the functions $\mathbb{X}: X \to \mathbb{R}_{\geq 0}$ that are not distributions are called *weighted teams*.

If x is a fresh variable, the summation can be dropped and the right-hand side of the equation becomes $\mathbb{X}(s) \cdot \frac{1}{|B|}$. For singletons $B = \{a\}$, we write $X(a/x)$ and $\mathbb{X}(a/x)$ instead of $X(\{a\}/x)$ and $\mathbb{X}(\{a\}/x)$.

Let then $\mathbb{X}\colon X \to [0,1]$ be a distribution. Denote by p_B the set of all probability distributions $d\colon B \to [0,1]$, and let F be a function $F\colon X \to p_B$. Then the probabilistic team $\mathbb{X}(F/x)$ is a function $\mathbb{X}(F/x)\colon X(B/x) \to [0,1]$ defined as

$$\mathbb{X}(F/x)(s(a/x)) = \sum_{\substack{t \in X, \\ t(a/x)=s(a/x)}} \mathbb{X}(t) \cdot F(t)(a)$$

for all $a \in B$ and $s \in X$. If x is a fresh variable, the summation can again be dropped and the right-hand side of the equation becomes $\mathbb{X}(s) \cdot F(s)(a)$.

Let $\mathbb{X}\colon X \to [0,1]$ and $\mathbb{Y}\colon Y \to [0,1]$ be probabilistic teams with common variable and value domains, and let $k \in [0,1]$. The k-scaled union of $\mathbb{X}$ and $\mathbb{Y}$, denoted by $\mathbb{X} \sqcup_k \mathbb{Y}$, is the probabilistic team $\mathbb{X} \sqcup_k \mathbb{Y}\colon Y \to [0,1]$ defined as

$$\mathbb{X} \sqcup_k \mathbb{Y}(s) := \begin{cases} k \cdot \mathbb{X}(s) + (1-k) \cdot \mathbb{Y}(s) & \text{if } s \in X \cap Y, \\ k \cdot \mathbb{X}(s) & \text{if } s \in X \setminus Y, \\ (1-k) \cdot \mathbb{Y}(s) & \text{if } s \in Y \setminus X. \end{cases}$$

3 Probabilistic Independence Logic with Boolean Negation

In this section, we define probabilistic independence logic with Boolean negation, denoted by $\mathrm{FO}(\perp\!\!\!\perp_c, \sim)$. The logic extends first-order logic with *probabilistic independence atom* $\mathbf{y} \perp\!\!\!\perp_{\mathbf{x}} \mathbf{z}$ which states that the tuples $\mathbf{y}$ and $\mathbf{z}$ are independent given the tuple $\mathbf{x}$. The syntax for the logic $\mathrm{FO}(\perp\!\!\!\perp_c, \sim)$ over a vocabulary τ is as follows:

$$\phi ::= R(\mathbf{x}) \mid \neg R(\mathbf{x}) \mid \mathbf{y} \perp\!\!\!\perp_{\mathbf{x}} \mathbf{z} \mid \sim\phi \mid (\phi \wedge \phi) \mid (\phi \vee \phi) \mid \exists x \phi \mid \forall x \phi,$$

where x is a first-order variable, $\mathbf{x}$, $\mathbf{y}$, and $\mathbf{z}$ are tuples of first-order variables, and $R \in \tau$.

Let ψ be a first-order formula. We denote by $\psi^{\neg}$ the formula which is obtained from $\neg\psi$ by pushing the negation in front of atomic formulas. We also use the shorthand notations $\psi \to \phi := (\psi^{\neg} \vee (\psi \wedge \phi))$ and $\psi \leftrightarrow \phi := \psi \to \phi \wedge \phi \to \psi$.

Let $\mathbb{X}\colon X \to [0,1]$ be a probability distribution. The semantics for the logic is defined as follows:

- $\mathcal{A} \models_{\mathbb{X}} R(\mathbf{x})$ iff $\mathcal{A} \models_s R(\mathbf{x})$ for all $s \in \operatorname{supp}(\mathbb{X})$.
- $\mathcal{A} \models_{\mathbb{X}} \neg R(\mathbf{x})$ iff $\mathcal{A} \models_s \neg R(\mathbf{x})$ for all $s \in \operatorname{supp}(\mathbb{X})$.
- $\mathcal{A} \models_{\mathbb{X}} \mathbf{y} \perp\!\!\!\perp_{\mathbf{x}} \mathbf{z}$ iff $|\mathbb{X}_{\mathbf{xy}=s(\mathbf{xy})}| \cdot |\mathbb{X}_{\mathbf{xz}=s(\mathbf{xz})}| = |\mathbb{X}_{\mathbf{xyz}=s(\mathbf{xyz})}| \cdot |\mathbb{X}_{\mathbf{x}=s(\mathbf{x})}|$ for all $s\colon \operatorname{Var}(\mathbf{xyz}) \to A$.
- $\mathcal{A} \models_{\mathbb{X}} \sim\phi$ iff $\mathcal{A} \not\models_{\mathbb{X}} \phi$.
- $\mathcal{A} \models_{\mathbb{X}} \phi \wedge \psi$ iff $\mathcal{A} \models_{\mathbb{X}} \phi$ and $\mathcal{A} \models_{\mathbb{X}} \psi$.

- $\mathcal{A} \models_X \phi \vee \psi$ iff $\mathcal{A} \models_Y \phi$ and $\mathcal{A} \models_Z \psi$ for some Y, Z, k such that $Y \sqcup_k Z = X$.
- $\mathcal{A} \models_X \exists x\phi$ iff $\mathcal{A} \models_{X(F/x)} \phi$ for some $F \colon X \to p_A$.
- $\mathcal{A} \models_X \forall x\phi$ iff $\mathcal{A} \models_{X(A/x)} \phi$.

The satisfaction relation $\models_s$ above refers to the Tarski semantics of first-order logic. For a sentence ϕ, we write $\mathcal{A} \models \phi$ if $\mathcal{A} \models_{X_\emptyset} \phi$, where $X_\emptyset$ is the distribution that maps the empty assignment to 1.

The logic also has the following useful property called *locality*. Denote by $\mathrm{Fr}(\phi)$ the set of the free variables of a formula ϕ.

Proposition 1 (Locality, [4, Proposition 12]). *Let ϕ be any $\mathrm{FO}(\perp\!\!\!\perp_c, \sim)[\tau]$-formula. Then for any set of variables V, any τ-structure $\mathcal{A}$, and any probabilistic team $X \colon X \to [0,1]$ such that $\mathrm{Fr}(\phi) \subseteq V \subseteq D$,*

$$\mathcal{A} \models_X \phi \iff \mathcal{A} \models_{X \restriction V} \phi.$$

In addition to probabilistic conditional independence atoms, we may also consider other atoms. If $\mathbf{x}$ and $\mathbf{y}$ are tuples of variables, then $=(\mathbf{x}, \mathbf{y})$ is a *dependence atom*. If $\mathbf{x}$ and $\mathbf{y}$ are also of the same length, $\mathbf{x} \approx \mathbf{y}$ is a *marginal identity atom*. The semantics for these atoms are defined as follows:

- $\mathcal{A} \models_X =(\mathbf{x}, \mathbf{y})$ iff for all $s, s' \in \mathrm{supp}(X)$, $s(\mathbf{x}) = s'(\mathbf{x})$ implies $s(\mathbf{y}) = s'(\mathbf{y})$,
- $\mathcal{A} \models_X \mathbf{x} \approx \mathbf{y}$ iff $|X_{\mathbf{x}=\mathbf{a}}| = |X_{\mathbf{y}=\mathbf{a}}|$ for all $\mathbf{a} \in A^{|\mathbf{x}|}$.

We write $\mathrm{FO}(=(\cdot))$ and $\mathrm{FO}(\approx)$ for first-order logic with dependence atoms or marginal identity atoms, respectively. Analogously, for $C \subseteq \{=(\cdot), \approx, \perp\!\!\!\perp_c, \sim\}$, we write $\mathrm{FO}(C)$ for the logic with access to the atoms (or the Boolean negation) from C.

For two logics L and L' over probabilistic team semantics, we write $L \leq L'$ if for any formula $\phi \in L$, there is a formula $\psi \in L'$ such that $\mathcal{A} \models_X \phi \iff \mathcal{A} \models_X \psi$ for all $\mathcal{A}$ and X. The equality $\equiv$ and strict inequality $<$ are defined from the above relation in the usual way. The next two propositions follow from the fact that dependence atoms and marginal identity atoms can be expressed with probabilistic independence atoms.

Proposition 2 ([3, Proposition 24]) $\mathrm{FO}(=(\cdot)) \leq \mathrm{FO}(\perp\!\!\!\perp_c)$.

Proposition 3 ([10, Theorem 10]) $\mathrm{FO}(\approx) \leq \mathrm{FO}(\perp\!\!\!\perp_c)$.

On the other hand, omitting the Boolean negation strictly decreases the expressivity as witnessed by the next proposition.

Proposition 4. $\mathrm{FO}(\perp\!\!\!\perp_c) < \mathrm{FO}(\perp\!\!\!\perp_c, \sim)$.

Proof. By Theorems 4.1 and 6.5 of [13], over a fixed universe size, any open formula of $\mathrm{FO}(\perp\!\!\!\perp_c)$ defines a closed subset of $\mathbb{R}^n$ for a suitable n depending on the size of the universe and the number of free variables. Now, clearly, this cannot be true for all of the formulas of $\mathrm{FO}(\perp\!\!\!\perp_c, \sim)$ as it contains the Boolean negation, e.g., the formula $\sim x \perp\!\!\!\perp_y z$. $\qquad\square$

4   Metafinite Logics

In this section, we consider logics over $\mathbb{R}$-structures. These structures extend finite relational structures with real numbers $\mathbb{R}$ as a second domain and add functions that map tuples from the finite domain to $\mathbb{R}$.

Definition 5 ($\mathbb{R}$-structures). *Let τ and σ be finite vocabularies such that τ is relational and σ is functional. An $\mathbb{R}$-structure of vocabulary $\tau \cup \sigma$ is a tuple $\mathcal{A} = (A, \mathbb{R}, F)$ where the reduct of $\mathcal{A}$ to τ is a finite relational structure, and F is a set that contains functions $f^{\mathcal{A}} \colon A^{\mathrm{Ar}(f)} \to \mathbb{R}$ for each function symbol $f \in \sigma$. Additionally, (i) for any $S \subseteq \mathbb{R}$, if each $f^{\mathcal{A}}$ is a function from $A^{\mathrm{Ar}(f)}$ to S, $\mathcal{A}$ is called an S-structure, (ii) if each $f^{\mathcal{A}}$ is a distribution, $\mathcal{A}$ is called a $d[0,1]$-structure.*

Next, we will define certain metafinite logics which are variants of functional second-order logic with numerical terms. The numerical σ-terms i are defined as follows:

$$i ::= f(\mathbf{x}) \mid i \times i \mid i + i \mid \mathrm{SUM}_{\mathbf{y}} i \mid \log i,$$

where $f \in \sigma$ and $\mathbf{x}$ and $\mathbf{y}$ are first-order variables such that $|\mathbf{x}| = \mathrm{Ar}(f)$. The interpretation of a numerical term i in the structure $\mathcal{A}$ under an assignment s is denoted by $[i]_s^{\mathcal{A}}$. We define

$$[\mathrm{SUM}_{\mathbf{y}} i]_s^{\mathcal{A}} := \sum_{\mathbf{a} \in A^{|\mathbf{y}|}} [i]_{s(\mathbf{a}/\mathbf{y})}^{\mathcal{A}}.$$

The interpretations of the rest of the numerical terms are defined in the obvious way.

Suppose that $\{=\} \subseteq \tau$, and let $O \subseteq \{+, \times, \mathrm{SUM}, \log\}$. The syntax for the logic $\mathrm{SO}_{\mathbb{R}}(O)$ is defined as follows:

$$\phi ::= i = j \mid \neg i = j \mid R(\mathbf{x}) \mid \neg R(\mathbf{x}) \mid (\phi \wedge \phi) \mid (\phi \vee \phi) \mid \exists x \phi \mid \forall x \phi \mid \exists f \psi \mid \forall f \psi,$$

where i and j are numerical σ-terms constructed using operations from O, $R \in \tau$, $x, y,$ and $\mathbf{x}$ are first-order variables, f is a function variable, and ψ is a $\tau \cup \sigma \cup \{f\}$-formula of $\mathrm{SO}_{\mathbb{R}}(O)$.

The semantics of $\mathrm{SO}_{\mathbb{R}}(O)$ is defined via $\mathbb{R}$-structures and assignments analogous to first-order logic, except for the interpretations of function variables f, which range over functions $A^{\mathrm{Ar}(f)} \to \mathbb{R}$. For any $S \subseteq \mathbb{R}$, we define $\mathrm{SO}_S(O)$ as the variant of $\mathrm{SO}_{\mathbb{R}}(O)$, where the quantification of function variables ranges over $A^{\mathrm{Ar}(f)} \to S$. If the quantification of function variables is restricted to distributions, the resulting logic is denoted by $\mathrm{SO}_{d[0,1]}(O)$. The existential fragment, in which universal quantification over function variables is not allowed, is denoted by $\mathrm{ESO}_{\mathbb{R}}(O)$.

For metafinite logics L and L', we define expressivity comparison relations $L \leq L'$, $L \equiv L'$, and $L < L'$ in the usual way, see e.g. [13]. For the proofs of the following two propositions, see the full version [12] of this paper in ArXiv.

Proposition 6. $\mathrm{SO}_{\mathbb{R}}(\mathrm{SUM}, \times) \equiv \mathrm{SO}_{\mathbb{R}}(+, \times)$.

Proposition 7. $\mathrm{SO}_{d[0,1]}(\mathrm{SUM}, \times) \equiv \mathrm{SO}_{\mathbb{R}}(+, \times)$.

5   Equi-Expressivity of FO($\perp\!\!\!\perp_c$, $\sim$) and SO$_{\mathbb{R}}$(+, ×)

In this section, we show that the expressivity of probabilistic independence logic with the Boolean negation coincides with full second-order logic over $\mathbb{R}$-structures.

Theorem 8. FO($\perp\!\!\!\perp_c$, $\sim$) ≡ SO$_{\mathbb{R}}$(+, ×).

We first show that FO($\perp\!\!\!\perp_c$, $\sim$) ≤ SO$_{\mathbb{R}}$(+, ×). Note that by Proposition 7, we have SO$_{d[0,1]}$(SUM, ×) ≡ SO$_{\mathbb{R}}$(+, ×), so it suffices to show that FO($\perp\!\!\!\perp_c$, $\sim$) ≤ SO$_{d[0,1]}$(SUM, ×). We may assume that every independence atom is in the form $\mathbf{y} \perp\!\!\!\perp_{\mathbf{x}} \mathbf{z}$ or $\mathbf{y} \perp\!\!\!\perp_{\mathbf{x}} \mathbf{y}$ where $\mathbf{x}, \mathbf{y}$, and $\mathbf{z}$ are pairwise disjoint tuples. [4, Lemma 25]

Theorem 9. *Let formula $\phi(\mathbf{v}) \in$ FO($\perp\!\!\!\perp_c$, $\sim$) be such that its free-variables are from $\mathbf{v} = (v_1, \dots, v_k)$. Then there is a formula $\psi_\phi(f) \in$ SO$_{d[0,1]}$(SUM, ×) with exactly one free function variable such that for all structures $\mathcal{A}$ and all probabilistic teams $\mathbb{X}: X \to [0,1]$, $\mathcal{A} \models_{\mathbb{X}} \phi(\mathbf{v})$ if and only if $(\mathcal{A}, f_{\mathbb{X}}) \models \psi_\phi(f)$, where $f_{\mathbb{X}}: A^k \to [0,1]$ is a probability distribution such that $f_{\mathbb{X}}(s(\mathbf{v})) = \mathbb{X}(s)$ for all $s \in X$.*

Proof. Define the formula $\psi_\phi(f)$ as follows:

1. If $\phi(\mathbf{v}) = R(v_{i_1}, \dots, v_{i_l})$, where $1 \le i_1, \dots, i_l \le k$, then $\psi_\phi(f) := \forall \mathbf{v}(f(\mathbf{v}) = 0 \lor R(v_{i_1}, \dots, v_{i_l}))$.
2. If $\phi(\mathbf{v}) = \neg R(v_{i_1}, \dots, v_{i_l})$, where $1 \le i_1, \dots, i_l \le k$, then $\psi_\phi(f) := \forall \mathbf{v}(f(\mathbf{v}) = 0 \lor \neg R(v_{i_1}, \dots, v_{i_l}))$.
3. If $\phi(\mathbf{v}) = \mathbf{v}_1 \perp\!\!\!\perp_{\mathbf{v}_0} \mathbf{v}_2$, where $\mathbf{v}_0, \mathbf{v}_1, \mathbf{v}_2$ are disjoint, then

$$\psi_\phi(f) := \forall \mathbf{v}_0 \mathbf{v}_1 \mathbf{v}_2 (\text{SUM}_{\mathbf{v} \setminus (\mathbf{v}_0 \mathbf{v}_1)} f(\mathbf{v}) \times \text{SUM}_{\mathbf{v} \setminus (\mathbf{v}_0 \mathbf{v}_2)} f(\mathbf{v}) = $$
$$\text{SUM}_{\mathbf{v} \setminus (\mathbf{v}_0 \mathbf{v}_1)} f(\mathbf{v}) \times \text{SUM}_{\mathbf{v} \setminus \mathbf{v}_0} f(\mathbf{v})).$$

4. If $\phi(\mathbf{v}) = \mathbf{v}_1 \perp\!\!\!\perp_{\mathbf{v}_0} \mathbf{v}_1$, where $\mathbf{v}_0, \mathbf{v}_1$ are disjoint, then

$$\psi_\phi(f) := \forall \mathbf{v}_0 \mathbf{v}_1 (\text{SUM}_{\mathbf{v} \setminus (\mathbf{v}_0 \mathbf{v}_1)} f(\mathbf{v}) = 0 \lor \text{SUM}_{\mathbf{v} \setminus (\mathbf{v}_0 \mathbf{v}_1)} f(\mathbf{v}) = \text{SUM}_{\mathbf{v} \setminus \mathbf{v}_0} f(\mathbf{v})).$$

5. If $\phi(\mathbf{v}) = \sim \phi_0(\mathbf{v})$, then $\psi_\phi(f) := \psi_{\phi_0}^{\neg}(f)$, where $\psi_{\phi_0}^{\neg}$ is obtained from $\neg \psi_{\phi_0}$ by pushing the negation in front of atomic formulas.
6. If $\phi(\mathbf{v}) = \phi_0(\mathbf{v}) \wedge \phi_1(\mathbf{v})$, then $\psi_\phi(f) := \psi_{\phi_0}(f) \wedge \psi_{\phi_1}(f)$.
7. If $\phi(\mathbf{v}) = \phi_0(\mathbf{v}) \lor \phi_1(\mathbf{v})$, then

$$\psi_\phi(f) := \psi_{\phi_0}(f) \lor \psi_{\phi_1}(f)$$
$$\lor (\exists g_0 g_1 g_2 g_3 (\forall \mathbf{v} \forall x (x = l \lor x = r \lor (g_0(x) = 0 \wedge g_3(\mathbf{v}, x) = 0))$$
$$\wedge \forall \mathbf{v}(g_3(\mathbf{v}, l) = g_1(\mathbf{v}) \times g_0(l) \wedge g_3(\mathbf{v}, r) = g_2(\mathbf{v}) \times g_0(r))$$
$$\wedge \forall \mathbf{v}(\text{SUM}_x g_3(\mathbf{v}, x) = f(\mathbf{v})) \wedge \psi_{\phi_0}(g_1) \wedge \psi_{\phi_1}(g_2))).$$

8. If $\phi(\mathbf{v}) = \exists x \phi_0(\mathbf{v}, x)$, then $\psi_\phi(f) := \exists g(\forall \mathbf{v}(\text{SUM}_x g(\mathbf{v}, x) = f(\mathbf{v})) \wedge \psi_{\phi_0}(g))$.
9. If $\phi(\mathbf{v}) = \exists x \phi_0(\mathbf{v}, x)$, then

$$\psi_\phi(f) := \exists g(\forall \mathbf{v}(\forall x \forall y (g(\mathbf{v}, x) = g(\mathbf{v}, y)) \wedge \text{SUM}_x g(\mathbf{v}, x) = f(\mathbf{v})) \wedge \psi_{\phi_0}(g)).$$

Since the the above is essentially same as the translation in [4, Theorem 14], but extended with the Boolean negation (for which the claim follows directly from the semantical clauses), it is easy to show that $\psi_\phi(f)$ satisfies the claim.   □

We now show that $\mathrm{SO}_\mathbb{R}(+, \times) \leq \mathrm{FO}(\perp\!\!\!\perp_c, \sim,)$. By Propositions 3 and 7, $\mathrm{FO}(\perp\!\!\!\perp_c, \sim, \approx) \equiv \mathrm{FO}(\perp\!\!\!\perp_c, \sim)$ and $\mathrm{SO}_\mathbb{R}(+, \times) \equiv \mathrm{SO}_{d[0,1]}(\mathrm{SUM}, \times)$, so it suffices to show that $\mathrm{SO}_{d[0,1]}(\mathrm{SUM}, \times) \leq \mathrm{FO}(\perp\!\!\!\perp_c, \sim, \approx)$.

Note that even though we consider $\mathrm{SO}_{d[0,1]}(\mathrm{SUM}, \times)$, where only distributions can be quantified, it may still happen that the interpretation of a numerical term does not belong to the unit interval. This may happen if we have a term of the form $\mathrm{SUM}_\mathbf{x} i(\mathbf{y})$ where $\mathbf{x}$ contains a variable that does not appear in $\mathbf{y}$. Fortunately, for any formula containing such terms, there is an equivalent formula without them [16, Lemma 19]. Thus, it suffices to consider formulas without such terms.

To prove that $\mathrm{SO}_{d[0,1]}(\mathrm{SUM}, \times) \leq \mathrm{FO}(\perp\!\!\!\perp_c, \sim, \approx)$, we construct a useful normal form for $\mathrm{SO}_{d[0,1]}(\mathrm{SUM}, \times)$-sentences. The following lemma is based on similar lemmas from [4, Lemma, 16] and [16, Lemma, 20]. The proofs of the next two lemmas are in the full version [12] of this paper.

Lemma 10. *Every formula* $\phi \in \mathrm{SO}_{d[0,1]}(\mathrm{SUM}, \times)$ *can be written in the form* $\phi^* := Q_1 f_1 \ldots Q_n f_n \forall \mathbf{x} \theta$, *where* $Q \in \{\exists, \forall\}$, θ *is quantifier-free and such that all the numerical identity atoms are in the form* $f_i(\mathbf{uv}) = f_j(\mathbf{u}) \times f_k(\mathbf{v})$ *or* $f_i(\mathbf{u}) = \mathrm{SUM}_\mathbf{v} f_j(\mathbf{uv})$ *for distinct* f_i, f_j, f_k *such that at most one of them is not quantified.*

Lemma 11. *We use the abbreviations* $\forall^* x \phi$ *and* $\phi \rightarrow^* \psi$ *for the* $\mathrm{FO}(\perp\!\!\!\perp_c, \sim, \approx)$-*formulas* $\sim \exists x \sim \phi$ *and* $\sim(\phi \wedge \sim \psi)$, *respectively. Let* $\phi_\exists := \exists \mathbf{y}(\mathbf{x} \perp\!\!\!\perp \mathbf{y} \wedge \psi(\mathbf{x}, \mathbf{y}))$ *and* $\phi_\forall := \forall^* \mathbf{y}(\mathbf{x} \perp\!\!\!\perp \mathbf{y} \rightarrow^* \psi(\mathbf{x}, \mathbf{y}))$ *be* $\mathrm{FO}(\perp\!\!\!\perp_c, \sim)$-*formulas with free variables form* $\mathbf{x} = (x_1, \ldots, x_n)$. *Then for any structure* $\mathcal{A}$ *and probabilistic team* $\mathbb{X}$ *over* $\{x_1, \ldots, x_n\}$,

(i) $\mathcal{A} \models_\mathbb{X} \phi_\exists$ *iff* $\mathcal{A} \models_{\mathbb{X}(d/\mathbf{y})} \psi$ *for some distribution* $d: A^{|\mathbf{y}|} \rightarrow [0, 1]$,

(ii) $\mathcal{A} \models_\mathbb{X} \phi_\forall$ *iff* $\mathcal{A} \models_{\mathbb{X}(d/\mathbf{y})} \psi$ *for all distributions* $d: A^{|\mathbf{y}|} \rightarrow [0, 1]$.

Theorem 12. *Let* $\phi(p) \in \mathrm{SO}_{d[0,1]}(\mathrm{SUM}, \times)$ *be a formula in the form* $\phi^* := Q_1 f_1 \ldots Q_n f_n \forall \mathbf{x} \theta$, *where* $Q \in \{\exists, \forall\}$, θ *is quantifier-free and such that all the numerical identity atoms are in the form* $f_i(\mathbf{uv}) = f_j(\mathbf{u}) \times f_k(\mathbf{v})$ *or* $f_i(\mathbf{u}) = \mathrm{SUM}_\mathbf{v} f_j(\mathbf{uv})$ *for distinct* f_i, f_j, f_k *from* $\{f_1, \ldots, f_n, p\}$. *Then there is a formula* $\Phi \in \mathrm{FO}(\perp\!\!\!\perp_c, \sim, \approx)$ *such that for all structures* $\mathcal{A}$ *and probabilistic teams* $\mathbb{X} := p^\mathcal{A}$,

$$\mathcal{A} \models_\mathbb{X} \Phi \text{ if and only if } (\mathcal{A}, p) \models \phi.$$

Proof. Define

$$\Phi := \forall \mathbf{x} Q_1^* \mathbf{y}_1(\mathbf{x} \perp\!\!\!\perp \mathbf{y}_1 \circ_1 Q_2^* \mathbf{y}_2(\mathbf{xy}_1 \perp\!\!\!\perp \mathbf{y}_2 \circ_2 Q_3^* \mathbf{y}_3(\mathbf{xy}_1 \mathbf{y}_2 \perp\!\!\!\perp \mathbf{y}_3 \circ_3 \ldots$$
$$Q_n^* \mathbf{y}_n(\mathbf{xy}_1 \ldots \mathbf{y}_{n-1} \perp\!\!\!\perp \mathbf{y}_n \circ_n \Theta) \ldots))),$$

where $Q_i^* = \exists$ and $\circ_i = \wedge$, whenever $Q_i = \exists$ and $Q_i^* = \forall^*$ and $\circ_i =\rightarrow^*$, whenever $Q_i = \forall$. By Lemma 11, it suffices to show that for all distributions $f_1, \ldots, f_n$, subsets $M \subseteq A^{|\mathbf{x}|}$, and probabilistic teams $\mathbb{Y} := \mathbb{X}(M/\mathbf{x})(f_1/\mathbf{y}_1)\ldots(f_n/\mathbf{y}_n)$, we have

$$\mathcal{A} \models_{\mathbb{Y}} \Theta \iff (\mathcal{A}, p, f_1, \ldots, f_n) \models \theta(\mathbf{a}) \text{ for all } \mathbf{a} \in M.$$

The claim is shown by induction on the structure of the formula Θ. For the details, see the full ArXiv version [12] of the paper.

1. If θ is an atom or a negated atom (of the first sort), then we let $\Theta := \theta$.
2. Let $\theta = f_i(\mathbf{x}_i) = f_j(\mathbf{x}_j) \times f_k(\mathbf{x}_k)$. Then define

$$\Theta := \exists \alpha \beta((\alpha = 0 \leftrightarrow \mathbf{x}_i = \mathbf{y}_i) \wedge (\beta = 0 \leftrightarrow \mathbf{x}_j \mathbf{x}_k = \mathbf{y}_j \mathbf{y}_k) \wedge \mathbf{x}\alpha \approx \mathbf{x}\beta).$$

The negated case $\neg f_i(\mathbf{x}_i) = f_j(\mathbf{x}_j) \times f_k(\mathbf{x}_k)$ is analogous; just add $\sim$ in front of the existential quantification.
3. Let $\theta = f_i(\mathbf{x}_i) = \mathrm{SUM}_{\mathbf{x}_k} f_j(\mathbf{x}_k \mathbf{x}_j)$. Then define

$$\Theta := \exists \alpha \beta((\alpha = 0 \leftrightarrow \mathbf{x}_i = \mathbf{y}_i) \wedge (\beta = 0 \leftrightarrow \mathbf{x}_j = \mathbf{y}_j) \wedge \mathbf{x}\alpha \approx \mathbf{x}\beta).$$

The negated case $\neg f_i(\mathbf{x}_i) = \mathrm{SUM}_{\mathbf{x}_k} f_j(\mathbf{x}_k \mathbf{x}_j)$ is again analogous.
4. If $\theta = \theta_0 \wedge \theta_1$, then $\Theta = \Theta_0 \wedge \Theta_1$.
5. If $\theta = \theta_0 \vee \theta_1$, then $\Theta := \exists z(z \perp\!\!\!\perp_{\mathbf{x}} z \wedge ((\Theta_0 \wedge z = 0) \vee (\Theta_1 \wedge \neg z = 0)))$.   □

6   Probabilistic Logics and Entropy Atoms

In this section we consider extending probabilistic team semantics with novel entropy atoms. For a discrete random variable X, with possible outcomes $x_1, \ldots, x_n$ occuring with probabilities $\mathrm{P}(x_1), \ldots, \mathrm{P}(x_n)$, the Shannon entropy of X is given as:

$$\mathrm{H}(X) := -\sum_{i=1}^{n} \mathrm{P}(x_i) \log \mathrm{P}(x_i),$$

The base of the logarithm does not play a role in this definition (usually it is assumed to be 2). For a set of discrete random variables, the entropy is defined in terms of the vector-valued random variable it defines. Given three sets of discrete random variables X, Y, Z, it is known that X is conditionally independent of Y given Z (written $X \perp\!\!\!\perp Y \mid Z$) if and only if the conditional mutual information $\mathrm{I}(X; Y|Z)$ vanishes. Similarly, functional dependence of Y from X holds if and only if the conditional entropy $H(Y|X)$ of Y given X vanishes. Writing UV for the union of two sets U and V, we note that $\mathrm{I}(X; Y|Z)$ and $H(Y|X)$ can respectively be expressed as $H(ZX) + H(ZY) - H(Z) - H(ZXY)$ and $H(XY) - H(X)$. Thus many familiar dependency concepts over random variables translate into linear equations over Shannon entropies. In what follows, we shortly consider similar information-theoretic approach to dependence and independence in probabilistic team semantics.

Let $\mathbb{X}: X \rightarrow [0,1]$ be a probabilistic team over a finite structure $\mathcal{A}$ with universe A. Let $\mathbf{x}$ be a k-ary sequence of variables from the domain of $\mathbb{X}$. Let $P_{\mathbf{x}}$ be the vector-valued random variable, where $P_{\mathbf{x}}(\mathbf{a})$ is the probability that x takes value **a** in the probabilistic team $\mathbb{X}$. The *Shannon entropy* of **x** in $\mathbb{X}$ is defined as follows:

$$H_{\mathbb{X}}(\mathbf{x}) := -\sum_{\mathbf{a} \in A^k} P_{\mathbf{x}}(\mathbf{a}) \log P_{\mathbf{x}}(\mathbf{a}). \tag{1}$$

Using this definition we now define the concept of an entropy atom.

Definition 13 (Entropy atom). *Let* **x** *and* **y** *be two sequences of variables from the domain of* $\mathbb{X}$. *These sequences may be of different lengths. The* entropy atom *is an expression of the form* $H(\mathbf{x}) = H(\mathbf{y})$, *and it is given the following semantics:*

$$\mathcal{A} \models_{\mathbb{X}} H(\mathbf{x}) = H(\mathbf{y}) \iff H_{\mathbb{X}}(\mathbf{x}) = H_{\mathbb{X}}(\mathbf{y}).$$

We then define *entropy logic* FO(H) as the logic obtained by extending first-order logic with entropy atoms. The entropy atom is relatively powerful compared to our earlier atoms, since, as we will see next, it encapsulates many familiar dependency notions such as dependence and conditional independence. The proof of the theorem is in the full version [12] of this paper.

Theorem 14. *The following equivalences hold over probabilistic teams of finite structures with two distinct constants 0 and 1:*

1. $=(\mathbf{x}, \mathbf{y}) \equiv H(\mathbf{x}) = H(\mathbf{xy})$.
2. $\mathbf{x} \perp\!\!\!\perp \mathbf{y} \equiv \phi$, *where* ϕ *is defined as*

$$\forall z \exists \mathbf{uv} \Big([z = 0 \rightarrow (\ =(\mathbf{u}, \mathbf{x}) \wedge\ =(\mathbf{x}, \mathbf{u}) \wedge\ =(\mathbf{v}, \mathbf{xy}) \wedge\ =(\mathbf{xy}, \mathbf{v}))] \wedge$$
$$[z = 1 \rightarrow (\ =(\mathbf{u}, \mathbf{y}) \wedge\ =(\mathbf{y}, \mathbf{u}) \wedge \mathbf{v} = \mathbf{0})] \wedge$$
$$[(z = 0 \vee z = 1) \rightarrow H(\mathbf{u}z) = H(\mathbf{v}z)] \Big),$$

where $|\mathbf{u}| = \max\{|\mathbf{x}|, |\mathbf{y}|\}$ *and* $|\mathbf{v}| = |\mathbf{xy}|$.

Since conditional independence can be expressed with marginal independence, i.e., $FO(\perp\!\!\!\perp_c) \equiv FO(\perp\!\!\!\perp)$ [10, Theorem 11], we obtain the following corollary:

Corollary 15. $FO(\perp\!\!\!\perp_c) \leq FO(H)$.

It is easy to see at this point that entropy logic and its extension with negation are subsumed by second-order logic over the reals with exponentiation.

Theorem 16. $FO(H) \leq ESO_{\mathbb{R}}(+, \times, \log)$ *and* $FO(H, \sim) \leq SO_{\mathbb{R}}(+, \times, \log)$.

Proof. The translation is similar to the one in Theorem 9, so it suffices to notice that the entropy atom $H(\mathbf{x}) = H(\mathbf{y})$ can be expressed as

$$SUM_{\mathbf{z}} f(\mathbf{x}, \mathbf{z}) \log f(\mathbf{x}, \mathbf{z}) = SUM_{\mathbf{z}'} f(\mathbf{y}, \mathbf{z}') \log f(\mathbf{y}, \mathbf{z}').$$

Since SUM can be expressed in $ESO_{\mathbb{R}}(+, \times, \log)$ and $SO_{\mathbb{R}}(+, \times, \log)$, we are done. □

7   Logic for First-Order Probabilistic Dependecies

Here, we define the logic $\mathrm{FOPT}(\leq_c^\delta)$, which was introduced in [11].[3] Let δ be a quantifier- and disjunction-free first-order formula, i.e., $\delta ::= \lambda \mid \neg\delta \mid (\delta \wedge \delta)$ for a first-order atomic formula λ of the vocabulary τ. Let x be a first-order variable. The syntax for the logic $\mathrm{FOPT}(\leq_c^\delta)$ over a vocabulary τ is defined as follows:

$$\phi ::= \delta \mid (\delta|\delta) \leq (\delta|\delta) \mid {\sim}\phi \mid (\phi \wedge \phi) \mid (\phi \vee\!\!\!\vee \phi) \mid \exists^1 x\phi \mid \forall^1 x\phi.$$

Let $\mathbb{X}: X \to \mathbb{R}_{\geq 0}$ be any probabilistic team, not necessarily a probability distribution. The semantics for the logic is defined as follows:

- $\mathcal{A} \models_{\mathbb{X}} \delta$ iff $\mathcal{A} \models_s \delta$ for all $s \in \mathrm{supp}(\mathbb{X})$.
- $\mathcal{A} \models_{\mathbb{X}} (\delta_0|\delta_1) \leq (\delta_2|\delta_3)$ iff $|\mathbb{X}_{\delta_0 \wedge \delta_1}| \cdot |\mathbb{X}_{\delta_3}| \leq |\mathbb{X}_{\delta_2 \wedge \delta_3}| \cdot |\mathbb{X}_{\delta_1}|$.
- $\mathcal{A} \models_{\mathbb{X}} {\sim}\phi$ iff $\mathcal{A} \not\models_{\mathbb{X}} \phi$ or $\mathbb{X}$ is empty.
- $\mathcal{A} \models_{\mathbb{X}} \phi \wedge \psi$ iff $\mathcal{A} \models_{\mathbb{X}} \phi$ and $\mathcal{A} \models_{\mathbb{X}} \psi$.
- $\mathcal{A} \models_{\mathbb{X}} \phi \vee\!\!\!\vee \psi$ iff $\mathcal{A} \models_{\mathbb{X}} \phi$ or $\mathcal{A} \models_{\mathbb{X}} \psi$.
- $\mathcal{A} \models_{\mathbb{X}} \exists^1 x\phi$ iff $\mathcal{A} \models_{\mathbb{X}(a/x)} \phi$ for some $a \in A$.
- $\mathcal{A} \models_{\mathbb{X}} \forall^1 x\phi$ iff $\mathcal{A} \models_{\mathbb{X}(a/x)} \phi$ for all $a \in A$.

Next, we present some useful properties of $\mathrm{FOPT}(\leq_c^\delta)$.

Proposition 17. (Locality, [11, Proposition 3.2]). *Let ϕ be any $\mathrm{FOPT}(\leq_c^\delta)$ $[\tau]$-formula. Then for any set of variables V, any τ-structure $\mathcal{A}$, and any probabilistic team $\mathbb{X}: X \to \mathbb{R}_{\geq 0}$ such that $\mathrm{Fr}(\phi) \subseteq V \subseteq D$,*

$$\mathcal{A} \models_{\mathbb{X}} \phi \iff \mathcal{A} \models_{\mathbb{X}\restriction V} \phi.$$

Over singleton traces the expressivity of $\mathrm{FOPT}(\leq_c^\delta)$ coincides with that of FO. For $\phi \in \mathrm{FOPT}(\leq_c^\delta)$, let ϕ^* denote the FO-formula obtained by replacing the symbols ${\sim}, \vee\!\!\!\vee, \exists^1$, and $\forall^1$ by $\neg, \vee, \exists$, and $\forall$, respectively, and expressions of the form $(\delta_0 \mid \delta_1) \leq (\delta_2 \mid \delta_3)$ by the formula $\neg\delta_0 \vee \neg\delta_1 \vee \delta_2 \vee \neg\delta_3$.

Proposition 18. (Singleton equivalence). *Let ϕ be a $\mathrm{FOPT}(\leq_c^\delta)[\tau]$-formula, $\mathcal{A}$ a τ structure, and $\mathbb{X}$ a probabilistic team of $\mathcal{A}$ with support $\{s\}$. Then $\mathcal{A} \models_{\mathbb{X}} \phi$ iff $\mathcal{A} \models_s \phi^*$.*

Proof. The proof proceeds by induction on the structure of formulas. The cases for literals and Boolean connectives are trivial. The cases for quantifiers are immediate once one notices that interpreting the quantifiers $\exists^1$ and $\forall^1$ maintain singleton supportness. We show the case for $\leq$. Let $\|\delta\|_{\mathcal{A},s} = 1$ if $\mathcal{A} \models_s \delta$, and $\|\delta\|_{\mathcal{A},s} = 0$ otherwise. Then

$$\begin{aligned}
\mathcal{A} \models_{\mathbb{X}} (\delta_0 \mid \delta_1) \leq (\delta_2 \mid \delta_3) &\iff |\mathbb{X}_{\delta_0 \wedge \delta_1}| \cdot |\mathbb{X}_{\delta_3}| \leq |\mathbb{X}_{\delta_2 \wedge \delta_3}| \cdot |\mathbb{X}_{\delta_1}| \\
&\iff \|\delta_0 \wedge \delta_1\|_{\mathcal{A},s} \cdot \|\delta_3\|_{\mathcal{A},s} \leq \|\delta_2 \wedge \delta_3\|_{\mathcal{A},s} \cdot \|\delta_1\|_{\mathcal{A},s} \\
&\iff \mathcal{A} \models_s \neg\delta_0 \vee \neg\delta_1 \vee \delta_2 \vee \neg\delta_3.
\end{aligned}$$

---

[3] In [11], two sublogics of $\mathrm{FOPT}(\leq_c^\delta)$, called $\mathrm{FOPT}(\leq^\delta)$ and $\mathrm{FOPT}(\leq^\delta, \perp\!\!\!\perp_c^\delta)$, were also considered. Note that the results of this section also hold for these sublogics.

The first equivalence follows from the semantics of $\leq$ and the second follows from the induction hypotheses after observing that the support of $\mathbb{X}$ is $\{s\}$. The last equivalence follows via a simple arithmetic observation.

The following theorem follows directly from Propositions 17 and 18.

Theorem 19. *For sentences we have that* $\mathrm{FOPT}(\leq_c^\delta) \equiv \mathrm{FO}$.

For a logic L, we write $\mathsf{MC}(L)$ for the following variant of the model checking problem: given a *sentence* $\phi \in L$ and a structure $\mathcal{A}$, decide whether $\mathcal{A} \models \phi$. The above result immediately yields the following corollary.

Corollary 20. $\mathsf{MC}(\mathrm{FOPT}(\leq_c^\delta))$ *is* PSPACE-*complete.*

Proof. This follows directly from the linear translation of $\mathrm{FOPT}(\leq_c^\delta)$-sentences into equivalent FO -sentences of Theorem 19 and the well-known fact that the model-checking problem of FO is PSPACE-complete.

The first claim of the next theorem follows from the equi-expressivity of $\mathrm{FO}(\perp\!\!\!\perp_c, \sim)$ and $\mathrm{SO}_{\mathbb{R}}(+, \times)$, and the fact that every $\mathrm{FOPT}(\leq_c^\delta)$ formula can be translated to $\mathrm{ESO}_{\mathbb{R}}(\mathrm{SUM}, +, \times)$, a sublogic of $\mathrm{SO}_{\mathbb{R}}(+, \times)$. For the details and the proof of the second claim, see the full version [12] of this paper.

Theorem 21. $\mathrm{FOPT}(\leq_c^\delta) \leq \mathrm{FO}(\perp\!\!\!\perp_c, \sim)$ *and* $\mathrm{FOPT}(\leq_c^\delta)$ *is non-comparable to* $\mathrm{FO}(\perp\!\!\!\perp_c)$ *for open formulas.*

8   Complexity of Satisfiability, Validity and Model Checking

We now define satisfiability and validity in the context of probabilistic team semantics. Let $\phi \in \mathrm{FO}(\perp\!\!\!\perp_c, \sim, \approx)$. The formula ϕ *is satisfiable in a structure* $\mathcal{A}$ if $\mathcal{A} \models_{\mathbb{X}} \phi$ for some probabilistic team $\mathbb{X}$, and ϕ *is valid in a structure* $\mathcal{A}$ if $\mathcal{A} \models_{\mathbb{X}} \phi$ for all probabilistic teams $\mathbb{X}$ over $\mathrm{Fr}(\phi)$. The formula ϕ is *satisfiable* if there is a structure $\mathcal{A}$ such that ϕ is satisfiable in $\mathcal{A}$, and ϕ is *valid* if ϕ is valid in $\mathcal{A}$ for all structures $\mathcal{A}$.

For a logic L, the satisfiability problem $\mathsf{SAT}(L)$ and the validity problem $\mathsf{VAL}(L)$ are defined as follows: given a formula $\phi \in L$, decide whether ϕ is satisfiable (or valid, respectively).

Theorem 22. $\mathsf{MC}(\mathrm{FO}(\approx))$ *is in* EXPTIME *and* PSPACE-*hard.*

Proof. First note that $\mathrm{FO}(\approx)$ is clearly a conservative extension of FO, as it is easy to check that probabilistic semantics and Tarski semantics agree on first-order formulas over singleton traces. The hardness now follows from this and the fact that model checking problem for FO is PSPACE-complete.

For upper bound, notice first that any $\mathrm{FO}(\approx)$-formula ϕ can be reduced to an almost conjunctive formula ψ^* of $\mathrm{ESO}_R(+, \leq, \mathrm{SUM})$ [16, Lem, 17]. Then the desired bounds follow due to the reduction from Proposition 3 in [16]. The mentioned reduction yields families of systems of linear inequalities $\mathcal{S}$ from a structure $\mathcal{A}$ and assignment s such that a system $S \in \mathcal{S}$ has a solution if and only if $\mathcal{A} \models_s \phi$. For a $FO(\approx)$-formula ϕ, this transition requires exponential time and this yields membership in EXPTIME.

This lemma is used to prove the upper-bounds in the next three theorems. See the full version [12], for the proofs of the lemma and the theorems.

Lemma 23. *Let $\mathcal{A}$ be a finite structure and $\phi \in FO(\perp\!\!\!\perp_c, \sim)$. Then there is a first-order sentence $\psi_{\phi,\mathcal{A}}$ over vocabulary $\{+, \times, \leq, 0, 1\}$ such that ϕ is satisfiable in $\mathcal{A}$ if and only if $(\mathbb{R}, +, \times, \leq, 0, 1) \models \psi_{\phi,\mathcal{A}}$.*

Theorem 24. $MC(FO(\perp\!\!\!\perp_c))$ *is in* EXPSPACE *and* NEXPTIME-*hard.*

Theorem 25. $MC(FO(\sim, \perp\!\!\!\perp_c)) \in$ 3-EXPSPACE *and* AEXPTIME[poly]-*hard.*

Theorem 26. $SAT(FO(\perp\!\!\!\perp_c, \sim))$ *is* RE-, $VAL(FO(\perp\!\!\!\perp_c, \sim))$ *is* coRE-*complete.*

Corollary 27. $SAT(FO(\approx))$ *and* $SAT(FO(\perp\!\!\!\perp_c))$ *are* RE- *and* $VAL(FO(\approx))$ *and* $VAL(FO(\perp\!\!\!\perp_c))$ *are* coRE-*complete.*

Proof. The lower bound follows from the fact that $FO(\approx)$ and $FO(\perp\!\!\!\perp_c)$ are both conservative extensions of FO. We obtain the upper bound from the previous theorem, since $FO(\perp\!\!\!\perp_c, \sim)$ includes both $FO(\approx)$ and $FO(\perp\!\!\!\perp_c)$.

9   Conclusion

We have studied the expressivity and complexity of various logics in probabilistic team semantics with the Boolean negation. Our results give a quite comprehensive picture of the relative expressivity of these logics and their relations to numerical variants of (existential) second-order logic. An interesting question for further study is to determine the exact complexities of the decision problems studied in Sect. 8. Furthermore, dependence atoms based on various notions of entropy deserve further study, as do the connections of probabilistic team semantics to the field of information theory.

Acknowledgements. The first author is supported by the ERC grant 101020762. The second author is supported by Academy of Finland grant 345634. The third author is supported by Academy of Finland grants 338259 and 345634. The fourth author appreciates funding by the European Union's Horizon Europe research and innovation programme within project ENEXA (101070305). The fifth author appreciates funding by the German Research Foundation (DFG), project ME 4279/3-1. The sixth author is partially funded by the German Research Foundation (DFG), project VI 1045/1-1.

References

1. Blum, L., Shub, M., Smale, S.: On a theory of computation over the real numbers; NP completeness, recursive functions and universal machines. In: 29th Annual Symposium on Foundations of Computer Science, pp. 387–397 (1988)
2. Bürgisser, P., Cucker, F.: Counting complexity classes for numeric computations II: algebraic and semialgebraic sets. J. Complex. **22**(2), 147–191 (2006)
3. Durand, A., Hannula, M., Kontinen, J., Meier, A., Virtema, J.: Approximation and dependence via multiteam semantics. Ann. Math. Artif. Intell. **83**(3–4), 297–320 (2018)
4. Durand, A., Hannula, M., Kontinen, J., Meier, A., Virtema, J.: Probabilistic team semantics. In: Ferrarotti, F., Woltran, S. (eds.) FoIKS 2018. LNCS, vol. 10833, pp. 186–206. Springer, Cham (2018). https://doi.org/10.1007/978-3-319-90050-6_11
5. Durand, A., Kontinen, J., de Rugy-Altherre, N., Väänänen, J.: Tractability frontier of data complexity in team semantics. ACM Trans. Comput. Log. **23**(1), 3:1–3:21 (2022)
6. Galliani, P.: Game values and equilibria for undetermined sentences of dependence logic. MSc Thesis. ILLC Publications, MoL-2008-08 (2008)
7. Galliani, P., Hella, L.: Inclusion logic and fixed point logic. In: CSL. LIPIcs, vol. 23, pp. 281–295. Schloss Dagstuhl - Leibniz-Zentrum für Informatik (2013)
8. Grädel, E., Gurevich, Y.: Metafinite model theory. Inf. Comput. **140**(1), 26–81 (1998)
9. Hannula, M., Hella, L.: Complexity thresholds in inclusion logic. Inf. Comput. **287**, 104759 (2022)
10. Hannula, M., Hirvonen, Å., Kontinen, J., Kulikov, V., Virtema, J.: Facets of distribution identities in probabilistic team semantics. In: Calimeri, F., Leone, N., Manna, M. (eds.) JELIA 2019. LNCS (LNAI), vol. 11468, pp. 304–320. Springer, Cham (2019). https://doi.org/10.1007/978-3-030-19570-0_20
11. Hannula, M., Hirvonen, M., Kontinen, J.: On elementary logics for quantitative dependencies. Ann. Pure Appl. Log. **173**(10), 103104 (2022)
12. Hannula, M., Hirvonen, M., Kontinen, J., Mahmood, Y., Meier, A., Virtema, J.: Logics with probabilistic team semantics and the Boolean negation. arXiv arXiv:2306.00420 (2023)
13. Hannula, M., Kontinen, J., den Bussche, J.V., Virtema, J.: Descriptive complexity of real computation and probabilistic independence logic. In: LICS, pp. 550–563. ACM (2020)
14. Hannula, M., Kontinen, J., Lück, M., Virtema, J.: On quantified propositional logics and the exponential time hierarchy. In: GandALF. EPTCS, vol. 226, pp. 198–212 (2016)
15. Hannula, M., Kontinen, J., Virtema, J., Vollmer, H.: Complexity of propositional logics in team semantic. ACM Trans. Comput. Log. **19**(1), 2:1–2:14 (2018)
16. Hannula, M., Virtema, J.: Tractability frontiers in probabilistic team semantics and existential second-order logic over the reals. Ann. Pure Appl. Log. **173**(10), 103108 (2022)
17. Hodges, W.: Compositional semantics for a language of imperfect information. Log. J. IGPL **5**(4), 539–563 (1997)
18. Hyttinen, T., Paolini, G., Väänänen, J.: A logic for arguing about probabilities in measure teams. Arch. Math. Log. **56**(5–6), 475–489 (2017)
19. Kontinen, J., Nurmi, V.: Team logic and second-order logic. Fundam. Informaticae **106**(2–4), 259–272 (2011)

20. Kontinen, J., Yang, F.: Complete logics for elementary team properties. J. Symbolic Logic **88**, 579–619 (2022). https://doi.org/10.1017/jsl.2022.80
21. Li, C.T.: First-order theory of probabilistic independence and single-letter characterizations of capacity regions. In: ISIT, pp. 1536–1541. IEEE (2022)
22. Lück, M.: Team logic: axioms, expressiveness, complexity. Ph.D. thesis, University of Hanover, Hannover, Germany (2020). www.repo.uni-hannover.de/handle/123456789/9430
23. Papadimitriou, C.H.: Computational complexity. Academic Internet Publ. (2007)
24. Schaefer, M., Stefankovic, D.: Fixed points, Nash equilibria, and the existential theory of the reals. Theory Comput. Syst. **60**(2), 172–193 (2017)
25. Väänänen, J.A.: Dependence Logic - A New Approach to Independence Friendly Logic. London Mathematical Society Student Texts, vol. 70. Cambridge University Press, Cambridge (2007)

Formalizing Statistical Causality
via Modal Logic

Yusuke Kawamoto[1,2](✉) 🆔, Tetsuya Sato[3] 🆔, and Kohei Suenaga[4] 🆔

[1] AIST, Tokyo, Japan
yusuke.kawamoto@aist.go.jp
[2] PRESTO, JST, Tokyo, Japan
[3] Tokyo Institute of Technology, Tokyo, Japan
[4] Kyoto University, Kyoto, Japan

Abstract. We propose a formal language for describing and explaining statistical causality. Concretely, we define *Statistical Causality Language* (StaCL) for expressing causal effects and specifying the requirements for causal inference. StaCL incorporates modal operators for interventions to express causal properties between probability distributions in different possible worlds in a Kripke model. We formalize axioms for probability distributions, interventions, and causal predicates using StaCL formulas. These axioms are expressive enough to derive the rules of Pearl's do-calculus. Finally, we demonstrate by examples that StaCL can be used to specify and explain the correctness of statistical causal inference.

1 Introduction

Statistical causality has been gaining significant importance in a variety of research fields. In particular, in life sciences, more and more researchers have been using statistical techniques to discover *causal relationships* from experiments and observations. However, these statistical methods can easily be misused or misinterpreted. In fact, it is reported that many research articles have serious errors in the applications and interpretations of statistical methods [8,27].

A common mistake is to misinterpret statistical *correlation* as statistical *causality*. Notably, when we analyze observational data without experimental interventions, we may overlook some requirements for causal inference and make wrong calculations, leading to incorrect conclusions about the causality.

For this reason, the scientific community has developed guidelines on many requirements for statistical analyses [29,37]. However, since there is no formal language to describe the entire procedures and their requirements, we refer to guidelines manually and cannot formally guarantee the correctness of analyses.

To address these problems, we propose a logic-based approach to formalizing and explaining the correctness of statistical causal inference. Specifically, we introduce a formal language called *statistical causality language* (StaCL) to formally describe and check the requirements for statistical causal inference. We consider this work as the first step to building a framework for formally guaranteeing and explaining the reliability of scientific research.

S. Gaggl et al. (Eds.): JELIA 2023, LNAI 14281, pp. 681–696, 2023.
https://doi.org/10.1007/978-3-031-43619-2_46

Contributions. Our main contributions are as follows:

– We propose *statistical causality language* (StaCL) for formalizing and explaining statistical causality by using modal operators for interventions.
– We define a *Kripke model for statistical causality*. To formalize not only statistical correlation but also statistical causality, we introduce a *data generator* in a possible world to model a causal diagram in a Kripke model.
– We introduce the notion of *causal predicates* to express statistical causality and interpret them using a data generator instead of a valuation in a Kripke model. In contrast, *(classical) predicates* are interpreted using a valuation in a Kripke model to express only *statistical correlations*.
– We introduce a sound deductive system $\mathbf{AX^{CP}}$ for StaCL with axioms for probability distributions, interventions, and causal predicates. These axioms are expressive enough to reason about all causal effects identifiable by Pearl's *do-calculus* [30]. We show that $\mathbf{AX^{CP}}$ can reason about the correctness of causal inference methods (e.g., backdoor adjustment). Unlike prior work, $\mathbf{AX^{CP}}$ does not aim to conduct causal inference about a specific causal diagram; rather, it concerns the correctness of the inference methods for any diagram. To the best of our knowledge, ours appears to be the first modal logic that can specify and reason about the requirements for causal inference.

Related Work. Many studies on causal reasoning rely on causal diagrams [31]. Whereas they aim to reason about a specific diagram, our logic-based approach aims to specify and reason about the requirements for causal inference methods.

Logic-based approaches for formalizing causal reasoning have been proposed. To name a few, Halpern and Pearl provide logic-based definitions of actual causes where logical formulas with events formalize counterfactuals [11–13]. Probabilistic logical languages [19] are proposed to axiomatize causal reasoning with observation, intervention, and counterfactual inference. Unlike our logic, however, their framework does not aim to syntactically derive the correctness of statistical causal inference. The causal calculus [28] is used to provide a logical representation [3,4] of Pearl [31]'s structural causal model. The counterfactual-observational language [1] can reason about interventionist counterfactuals and has an axiomatization that is complete w.r.t. a causal team semantics. A modal logic in [2] integrates causal and epistemic reasoning. While these works deal with deterministic cases only, our StaCL can reason about statistical causality in probabilistic settings.

There have been studies on incorporating probabilities into team semantics [15]. For example, team semantics is used to deal with the dependence and independence among random variables [5,6]. A probabilistic team semantics is provided for a first-order logic that can deal with conditional independence [7]. A team semantics is also introduced for logic with exact/approximate dependence and independence atoms [14]. Unlike our StaCL, however, these works do not allow for deriving the do-calculus or the correctness of causal inference methods.

Concerning the axiomatic characterization of causality, Galles and Pearl [9] prove that the axioms of composition, effectiveness, and reversibility are sound and complete with respect to the structural causal models. They also show that the reversibility axiom can be derived from the composition axiom if the causal diagram is acyclic (i.e., has no feedback loop). Halpern [10] provides axiomatizations for more general classes of causal models with feedback and with equations that may have no solutions. In contrast, our deductive system $\mathbf{AX}^{\mathbf{CP}}$ has axioms for causal predicates and two forms of interventions that can derive the rules of Pearl's do-calculus [30], while being equipped with axioms corresponding to the composition and effectiveness axioms mentioned above only for acyclic diagrams.

For the efficient computation of causal reasoning, constraint solving is applied [17,18,35]. Probabilistic logic programming is used to encode and reason about a specific causal diagram [32]. These are orthogonal to the goal of our work.

Finally, a few studies propose modal logic for statistical methods. Statistical epistemic logic [20–22] specifies various properties of machine learning. Belief Hoare logic [24,26] can reason about statistical hypothesis testing programs. However, unlike our StaCL, these cannot reason about statistical causality.

2 Illustrating Example

We first present a simple example to explain our framework.

Example 1 (Drug's efficacy). We attempt to check a drug's efficacy for a disease by observing a situation where some patients take a drug and the others do not.

Table 1 shows the recovery rates and the numbers of patients treated with/without the drug. For both males and females, *more* patients recover by taking the drug. However, for the combined population, the recovery rate with the drug (0.73) is *less* than that without it (0.80). This inconsistency is called *Simpson's paradox* [34], showing the difficulty of identifying causality from observed data.

To model this, we define three variables: a *treatment* x (1 for drug, 0 for no-drug), an *outcome* y (1 for recovery, 0 for non-recovery), and a gender z. Figure 1a depicts their causal dependency; the arrow $x \rightarrow y$ denotes that y depends on x. The *causal effect* $p(y|do(x = c))$ of a treatment $x = c$ on an outcome y [31] is defined as the distribution of y in case y were generated from $x = c$ (Fig. 1b).

However, since the gender z influences the choice of the treatment x in reality (Fig. 1a), the causal effect $p(y|do(x = c))$ depends on the common cause z of x and y and differs from the correlation $p(y|x = c)$. Indeed, in Table 1, 80 % of females chose to take the drug ($x = 1$) while only 20 % of males did so; this dependency of x on the gender z leads to Simpson's paradox in Table 1. Thus, calculating the causal effect requires an "adjustment" for z, as explained below.

Overview of the Framework. We describe reasoning about the causal effect in Example 1 using logical formulas in our formal language StaCL (Sect. 5).

We define $\varphi_{\mathrm{RCT}} \stackrel{\mathrm{def}}{=} \lceil c/x \rceil (c_0 = y)$ to express a *randomized controlled trial (RCT)*, where we randomly divide the patients into two groups: one taking the drug ($x = 1$) and the other not ($x = 0$). This random choice of the treatment x is expressed by the intervention $\lceil c/x \rceil$ for $c = 0, 1$ in the diagram $G\lceil c/x \rceil$ (Fig. 1b). Since x is independent of z in $G\lceil c/x \rceil$, the causal effect $p(y|do(x = c))$ of x on the outcome y is given as y's distribution c_0 observed in the experiment in $G\lceil c/x \rceil$.

Table 1. Recovery rates of patients with/without taking a drug.

	Drug $x = 1$	No-drug $x = 0$
Male	**0.90** (18/20)	0.85 (68/80)
Female	**0.69** (55/80)	0.60 (12/20)
Total	0.73 (73/100)	**0.80** (80/100)

(a) The actual diagram G with a gender (confounder) z, a treatment x, and an outcome y.

(b) The diagram $G\lceil c/x \rceil$ with an intervention to x.

Fig. 1. Causal diagrams in Example 1.

In contrast, $\varphi_{\text{BDA}} \stackrel{\text{def}}{=} (f = y|_{z,x=c} \land c_1 = z \land c_0 = f(c_1) \downarrow_y)$ describes the inference about the causal effect from observation *without* intervention to x (Fig. 1a). This saves the cost of the experiment and avoids ethical issues in random treatments. Instead, to avoid Simpson's paradox, the inference φ_{BDA} conducts a *backdoor adjustment* (Sect. 7) to cope with the confounder z.

Concretely, the backdoor adjustment φ_{BDA} computes x's causal effect on y as follows. We first obtain the conditional distribution $f \stackrel{\text{def}}{=} y|_{z,x=c}$ and the prior $c_1 \stackrel{\text{def}}{=} z$. Then we conduct the adjustment by calculating the joint distribution $f(c_1)$ from f and c_1 and then taking the marginal distribution $c_0 \stackrel{\text{def}}{=} f(c_1) \downarrow_y$. The resulting c_0 is the same as the c_0 in the RCT experiment φ_{RCT}; that is, the backdoor adjustment φ_{BDA} can compute the causal effect obtained by φ_{RCT}.

For this adjustment, we need to check the requirement $pa(z, x) \land pos(x :: z)$, that is, z is x's parent in the diagram G and the joint distribution $x :: z$ satisfies the positivity (i.e., it takes each value with a non-zero probability).

Now we formalize the *correctness* of this causal inference method (for any diagram G) as the judgment expressing that under the above requirements, the backdoor adjustment computes the same causal effect as the RCT experiment:

$$pa(z, x) \land pos(x :: z) \vdash_g \varphi_{\text{RCT}} \leftrightarrow \varphi_{\text{BDA}}. \tag{1}$$

By deriving this judgment in a deductive system called **AX^{CP}** (Sect. 6), we show the correctness of this causal inference method for any diagram (Sect. 7). We show all proofs of the technical results in this paper's full version [25].

3   Language for Data Generation

In this section, we introduce a language for describing data generation.

Constants and Causal Variables. We introduce a set Const of *constants* to denote probability distributions of data values and a set dConst $\subseteq$ Const of *deterministic constants*, each denoting a single data value (strictly speaking, denoting a distribution having a single data value with probability 1).

We introduce a finite set CVar of *causal variables*. A tuple $\langle x_1, \ldots, x_k \rangle$ of causal variables represents the joint distribution of k variables $x_1, \ldots, x_k$. We denote the set of all non-empty (resp. possibly empty) tuples of variables by CVar^+ (resp. CVar^*). We use the bold font for a *tuple*; e.g., $\boldsymbol{x} = \langle x_1, \ldots, x_k \rangle$. We write $size(\boldsymbol{x})$ for the *dimension* k of a tuple $\boldsymbol{x}$. We assume that the variables in a tuple $\boldsymbol{x}$ are sorted lexicographically.

For disjoint tuples $\boldsymbol{x}$ and $\boldsymbol{y}$, $\boldsymbol{x} :: \boldsymbol{y}$ denotes the *joint distribution* of $\boldsymbol{x}$ and $\boldsymbol{y}$. Formally, '$::$' is *not* a function symbol, but a meta-operator on CVar^*; $\boldsymbol{x} :: \boldsymbol{y}$ is the tuple obtained by merging $\boldsymbol{x}$ and $\boldsymbol{y}$ and sorting the variables lexicographically.

We use *conditional causal variables* $\boldsymbol{y}|_{\boldsymbol{z}, \boldsymbol{x} = \boldsymbol{c}}$ to denote the conditional distribution of $\boldsymbol{y}$ given $\boldsymbol{z}$ and $\boldsymbol{x} = \boldsymbol{c}$. We write FVar for the set of all conditional causal variables. For a conditional distribution $\boldsymbol{y}|_{\boldsymbol{x}}$ and a prior distribution $\boldsymbol{x}$, we write $\boldsymbol{y}|_{\boldsymbol{x}}(\boldsymbol{x})$ for the joint distribution $\boldsymbol{x} :: \boldsymbol{y}$.

Terms. We define *terms* to express how data are generated. Let Fsym be a set of *function symbols* denoting algorithms. We define the set CTerm of *causal terms* as the terms of depth at most 1; i.e., $u ::= c \mid f(v, \ldots, v)$ where $c \in \mathsf{Const}$, $f \in \mathsf{Fsym}$, and $v \in \mathsf{CVar} \cup \mathsf{Const}$. For example, $f(c)$ denotes a data generated by an algorithm f with input c. We denote the set of variables (resp. the set of constants) occurring in a term u by $\mathsf{fv}(u)$ (resp. $\mathsf{fc}(u)$).

We also define the set Term of *terms* by the BNF: $u ::= \boldsymbol{x} \mid c \mid f(u, \ldots, u)$, where $\boldsymbol{x} \in \mathsf{CVar}^+$, $c \in \mathsf{Const}$, and $f \in \mathsf{Fsym} \cup \mathsf{FVar}$. Unlike CTerm, terms in Term may repeatedly apply functions to describe multiple steps of data generation.

We introduce the special function symbol $\downarrow_{\boldsymbol{x}}$ for marginalization. $\boldsymbol{y} \downarrow_{\boldsymbol{x}}$ denotes the *marginal distribution* of $\boldsymbol{x}$ given a joint distribution $\boldsymbol{y}$; e.g., for a joint distribution $\boldsymbol{x} = \langle x_0, x_1 \rangle$, $\boldsymbol{x} \downarrow_{x_0}$ expresses the marginal distribution x_0. We also introduce the special constant $\perp$ for *undefined values*.

Data Generators. To describe how data are generated, we introduce the notion of a *data generator* as a function $g : \mathsf{CVar} \to \mathsf{CTerm} \cup \{\perp\}$ that maps a causal variable x to a causal term representing how the data assigned to x is generated. If $g(y) = u$ for $u \in \mathsf{CTerm}$ and $y \in \mathsf{CVar}$, we write $u \to_g y$. For instance, the data generator g in Fig. 2 models the situation in Example 1. To express that a variable x's value is generated by an algorithm f_1 with an input z, the data generator g maps x to $f_1(z)$, i.e., $f_1(z) \to_g x$. Since the causal term $f_1(z)$'s depth is at most 1, z represents the *direct cause* of x. We denote the set of all variables x satisfying $g(x) \neq \perp$ by $dom(g)$, and the range of g by $range(g)$.

We assume the following *at-most-once* condition: Each function symbol and constant can be used at most once in a single data generator. This ensures that different sampling uses different randomness and is denoted by different symbols.

We say that a data generator g is *finite* if $dom(g)$ is a finite set. We say that a data generator g is *closed* if no undefined variable occurs in the terms that g assigns to variables, namely, $\mathsf{fv}(range(g)) \subseteq dom(g)$.

Data generator g	Causal diagram G given from g
$dom(g) = \{x, y, z\}$ $f_1(z) \to_g x$ $f_2(z, x) \to_g y$	

Fig. 2. The data generator and causal diagram for Example 1.

We write $x \prec_g y$ iff y's value depends on x's, i.e., there are variables $z_1, \ldots, z_i$ ($i \geq 2$) such that $z_1 = x$, $z_i = y$, and $z_j \in \mathsf{fv}(g(z_{j+1}))$ for $1 \leq j \leq i - 1$. A data generator g is *acyclic* if $\prec_g$ is a strict partial order over $dom(g)$. Then we can avoid the cyclic definitions of g. E.g., the data generator g_1 defined by $f(z) \twoheadrightarrow_{g_1} x$ and $f(c) \twoheadrightarrow_{g_1} z$ is acyclic, whereas g_2 by $f(z) \twoheadrightarrow_{g_2} x$ and $f(x) \twoheadrightarrow_{g_2} z$ is cyclic.

4   Kripke Model for Statistical Causality

In this section, we introduce a Kripke model for statistical causality.

We write $\mathcal{O}$ for the set of all data values we deal with, such as the Boolean values, integers, real numbers, and lists of data values. We write $\perp$ for the undefined value. For a set S, we denote the set of all probability distributions over S by $\mathbb{D}S$. For a probability distribution $m \in \mathbb{D}S$, we write $supp(m)$ for the set of m's non-zero probability elements.

Causal Diagrams. To model causal relations corresponding to a given data generator g, we consider a *causal diagram* $G = (U, V, E)$ [31] where $U \cup V$ is the set of all nodes and E is the set of all edges such that:

- $U \overset{\text{def}}{=} \mathsf{fc}(range(g)) \subseteq \mathsf{Const}$ is a set of symbols called *exogenous variables* that denote distributions of data;
- $V \overset{\text{def}}{=} dom(g) \subseteq \mathsf{CVar}$ is a set of symbols called *endogenous variables* that may depend on other variables;
- $E \overset{\text{def}}{=} \{x \to y \in V \times V \mid x \in \mathsf{fv}(g(\mathsf{y}))\} \cup \{\mathsf{c} \to \mathsf{y} \in U \times V \mid \mathsf{c} \in \mathsf{fc}(g(\mathsf{y}))\}$ is the set of all *structural equations*, i.e., directed edges (arrows) denoting the direct causal relations between variables defined by the data generator g.

For instance, in Fig. 2, Example 1 is modeled as the causal diagram G.

Since a causal term's depth is at most 1, g specifies all information for defining G. By g's acyclicity, G is a directed acyclic graph (DAG) (See Proposition 4 in the full version [25] for details).

Pre-/Post-intervention Distributions. For a causal diagram $G = (U, V, E)$ and a tuple $\boldsymbol{y} \subseteq V$, we write $P_G(\boldsymbol{y})$ for the joint distribution of $\boldsymbol{y}$ over $\mathcal{O}^{size(\boldsymbol{y})}$ generated according to G. As shown in the standard textbooks (e.g., [31]), $P_G(V)$ is factorized into conditional distributions according to G as follows:

$$P_G(V) \overset{\text{def}}{=} \prod_{y_i \in V} P_G(y_i \mid pa_G(y_i)), \tag{2}$$

where $pa_G(y_i)$ is the set of parent variables of y_i in G. For example, in Fig. 2, for $V = \{x, y, z\}$, $P_G(V) = P_G(y \mid x, z) P_G(x \mid z) P_G(z)$.

For tuples $\boldsymbol{x} \subseteq V$ and $\boldsymbol{o} \subseteq \mathcal{O}$ with $size(\boldsymbol{x}) = size(\boldsymbol{o})$, the *post-intervention distribution* $P_G(V \mid do(\boldsymbol{x}=\boldsymbol{o}))$ is the joint distribution of V after $\boldsymbol{x}$ is assigned $\boldsymbol{o}$ and all the variables dependent on $\boldsymbol{x}$ in G are updated by $\boldsymbol{x} := \boldsymbol{o}$ as follows:

$$P_G(V \mid do(\boldsymbol{x}=\boldsymbol{o})) \overset{\text{def}}{=} \begin{cases} \prod_{y_i \in V \setminus \boldsymbol{x}} P_G(y_i \mid pa_G(y_i)) \\ \qquad \text{for values of } V \text{ consistent with } \boldsymbol{x} = \boldsymbol{o} \\ 0 \qquad \text{otherwise.} \end{cases}$$

For instance, in Fig. 2, $P_G(y, z \mid do(x = o)) = P_G(y \mid x = o, z) P_G(z)$ for any $o \in \mathcal{O}$.

Possible Worlds. We introduce the notion of a *possible world* to define the probability distribution of causal variables from a data generator. Formally, a possible world is a tuple (g, ξ, m) of (i) a finite and acyclic data generator $g :$ CVar $\rightarrow$ CTerm $\cup \{\bot\}$, (ii) an interpretation ξ that maps a function symbol in Fsym with arity $k \geq 0$ to a function from $\mathcal{O}^k$ to $\mathbb{D}\mathcal{O}$, and (iii) a memory m that maps a tuple of variables to a joint distribution of data values, which is determined by g and ξ. We denote these components of a world w by g_w, ξ_w, and m_w, and the set of all defined variables in w by $\mathsf{Var(w)} = dom(\mathsf{m_w})$.

The interpretation ξ can be constructed using a probability distribution I over an index set $\mathcal{I}$ and a family $\{\xi^r\}_{r \in \mathcal{I}}$ of interpretations each mapping a function symbol f with arity $k \geq 0$ to a deterministic function $\xi^r(f)$ from $\mathcal{O}^k$ to $\mathcal{O}$. Then $\xi(f)$ maps data values o to the probability distribution over $\mathcal{O}$ obtained by randomly drawing an index r from I and then computing $\xi^r(f)(o)$.

If $k = 0$, f is a constant and $\xi^r(f) \in \mathcal{O}$, hence $\xi(f) \in \mathbb{D}\mathcal{O}$ is a distribution of data values. For the undefined constant, we assume $\xi^r(\bot) = \bot$.

Interpretation of Terms. Terms are interpreted in a possible world $w = (\xi, g, m)$ as follows. First, for each index $r \in \mathcal{I}$, we define the *interpretation* $[\![\_]\!]^r_{\xi,g}$ that maps a tuple of k terms to k data values in $\mathcal{O}$ or $\bot$ by:

$$[\![x]\!]^r_{\xi,g} = [\![g(x)]\!]^r_{\xi,g} \qquad [\![\langle u_1, \ldots, u_k \rangle]\!]^r_{\xi,g} = ([\![u_1]\!]^r_{\xi,g}, \ldots, [\![u_k]\!]^r_{\xi,g})$$
$$[\![c]\!]^r_{\xi,g} = \xi^r(c) \qquad [\![f(u_1, \ldots, u_k)]\!]^r_{\xi,g} = \xi^r(f)([\![\langle u_1, \ldots, u_k \rangle]\!]^r_{\xi,g}).$$

For instance, in Fig. 2, we have $[\![x]\!]^r_{\xi,g} = [\![g(x)]\!]^r_{\xi,g} = [\![f_1(z)]\!]^r_{\xi,g} = \xi^r(f_1)([\![z]\!]^r_{\xi,g})$, where the interpretation of z does not depend on that of x due to g's acyclicity. We define the probability distribution $[\![u]\!]_w$ over $\mathcal{O}$ by randomly drawing r and then computing $[\![u]\!]^r_{\xi,g}$. Similarly, we define $[\![\langle u_1, \ldots, u_k \rangle]\!]_w$ via $[\![\langle u_1, \ldots, u_k \rangle]\!]^r_{\xi,g}$.

We remark that the interpretation $[\![\_]\!]_w$ defines the joint distribution P_{G_w} of all variables in the causal diagram G_w; e.g., $[\![y|_z]\!]_w = P_{G_w}(y \mid z)$ (See Proposition 5 in the full version [25] for details). A function symbol f is interpreted as the function $\xi(f)$ that maps data values in $\mathcal{O}$ to the distribution over $\mathcal{O}$. We define the memory m by $m(x) = [\![x]\!]_w$ for all $x \in \mathsf{CVar}^+$. Notice that $[\![\_]\!]_w$ is defined using g and ξ without using m.

We expand the interpretation $[\![\_]\!]_w$ to a conditional causal variable $y|_{z,x=c} \in \mathsf{FVar}$ to interpret it as a function that maps a value c' of z to the distribution $[\![(x :: y :: z)|_{z=c', x=c}]\!]_w$. We then have $[\![y|_{z,x=c}(z|_{x=c})]\!]_w = [\![y|_{z,x=c}]\!]_w([\![z|_{x=c}]\!]_w)$.

For the sake of reasoning in Sect. 6, for each data generator g, $x \in \mathsf{CVar}^+$, and $y|_{z,x=c} \in \mathsf{FVar}$, we introduce a constant $c^{(g,x)}$ and a function symbol $f^{(g,y|_{z,x=c})}$. For brevity, we often omit the superscripts of these symbols.

Eager/Lazy Interventions. We introduce two forms of *interventions* and their corresponding *intervened worlds*. Intuitively, in a causal diagram, an *eager intervention* $\lceil c/x \rceil$ expresses the removal of all arrows pointing *to* a variable x by replacing x's value with c.

In contrast, a *lazy intervention* $\lfloor c/x \rfloor$ expresses the removal of all arrows emerging *from* x, which does not change the value of x itself but affects the values of the variables dependent on x, computed using $[\![c]\!]$ (instead of $[\![x]\!]$) as the value of x.

For instance, Fig. 3 shows how two interventions $\lceil c/x \rceil$ and $\lfloor c/x \rfloor$ change the data generator and the causal diagram in a world w that models Example 1.

World	Data generator	Causal diagram
w	$f_1(z) \to x;$ $f_2(z,x) \to y$	
$w\lceil c/x \rceil$	$c \to x;$ $f_2(z,x) \to y$	
$w\lfloor c/x \rfloor$	$f_1(z) \to x;$ $f_2(z,c) \to y$	

Fig. 3. Eager/lazy interventions.

For a world w and a $c \in$ dConst, we define an *eagerly intervened world* $w\lceil c/x \rceil$ as the world where $[\![c]\!]_w$ is assigned to x and is used to compute the other variables dependent on x. Formally, $w\lceil c/x \rceil$ is defined by $\xi_{w\lceil c/x \rceil} = \xi_w$, $g_{w\lceil c/x \rceil}(y) = c$ if $y = x$, and $g_{w\lceil c/x \rceil}(y) = g_w(y)$ if $y \neq x$. For instance, in Fig. 3, in the world $w\lceil c/x \rceil$, we use the value of c to compute $[\![x]\!]_{w\lceil c/x \rceil} = \xi_w(c)$ and $[\![y]\!]_{w\lceil c/x \rceil} = [\![f_2(z,x)]\!]_{w\lceil c/x \rceil} = [\![f_2(z,c)]\!]_w$.

Then the interpretation $[\![\_]\!]_{w\lceil c/x \rceil}$ defines the joint distribution of all variables in the causal diagram G_w after the intervention $\boldsymbol{x} := [\![c]\!]_w$; e.g., $[\![y|z]\!]_{w\lceil c/x \rceil} = P_{G_w}(\boldsymbol{y} \mid do(\boldsymbol{x} = [\![c]\!]_w), \boldsymbol{z})$ (See Proposition 5 in the full version [25] for details).

We next define a *lazily intervened world* $w\lfloor c/x \rfloor$ as the world where x's value is unchanged but the other variables dependent on x are computed using $[\![c]\!]_w$ instead of $[\![x]\!]_w$. Formally, $w\lfloor c/x \rfloor$ is defined by $\xi_{w\lfloor c/x \rfloor} = \xi_w$, $g_{w\lfloor c/x \rfloor}(y) = x$ if $y = x$, and $g_{w\lfloor c/x \rfloor}(y) = g_w(y)[x \mapsto c]$ if $y \neq x$. E.g., in Fig. 3, $[\![x]\!]_{w\lfloor c/x \rfloor} = [\![f_1(z)]\!]_w$.

For $\boldsymbol{x} = \langle x_1, \ldots, x_k \rangle$ and $\boldsymbol{c} = \langle c_1, \ldots, c_k \rangle$, we define $\lceil c/x \rceil$ from the simultaneous replacement $g_{w\lceil c_1/x_1, \ldots, c_k/x_k \rceil}$. We also define $\lfloor c/x \rfloor$ analogously.

Kripke Model. Let Psym be a set of predicate symbols. For a variable tuple $\boldsymbol{x}$ and a deterministic constant tuple $\boldsymbol{c}$, we introduce an *intervention relation* $w\mathcal{R}_{\lceil c/x \rceil}w'$ that expresses a transition from a world w to another w' by the intervention $\lceil c/x \rceil$; namely, $\mathcal{R}_{\lceil c/x \rceil} = \{(w, w') \in \mathcal{W} \times \mathcal{W} \mid w' = w\lceil c/x \rceil\}$.

Then we define a *Kripke model for statistical causality* as a tuple $\mathfrak{M} = (\mathcal{W}, (\mathcal{R}_{\lceil c/x \rceil})_{x \in \mathsf{CVar}^+, c \in \mathsf{dConst}^+}, \mathcal{V})$ consisting of: (1) a set $\mathcal{W}$ of all possible worlds over the set CVar of causal variables; (2) for each $\boldsymbol{x} \in \mathsf{CVar}^+$ and $\boldsymbol{c} \in \mathsf{dConst}^+$, an *intervention relation* $\mathcal{R}_{\lceil c/x \rceil}$; (3) a valuation $\mathcal{V}$ that maps a k-ary predicate symbol $\eta \in \mathsf{Psym}$ to a set $\mathcal{V}(\eta)$ of k-tuples of distributions.

Notice that different worlds w and w' in $\mathcal{W}$ may have different data generators g_w and $g_{w'}$ corresponding to different causal diagrams; that is, $\mathcal{W}$ specifies all possible causal diagrams. Furthermore, different worlds w and w' may also have different interpretations ξ_w and $\xi_{w'}$ of function symbols if we do not have the knowledge of functions [23].

5 Statistical Causality Language

Predicates and Causal Predicates. Classical predicates in Psym describe *statistical correlation* among the distributions of variables, and are interpreted using a valuation $\mathcal{V}$. For example, $pos(x)$ expresses that x takes each value in the domain $\mathcal{O}$ with a non-zero probability. However, predicates cannot express the *statistical causality* among variables, whose interpretation relies on a causal diagram. Thus, we introduce a set CPsym of *causal predicates* (e.g., *dsep*, *nanc*, *allnanc*) and interpret them using a data generator g instead of a valuation $\mathcal{V}$.

Syntax and Semantics of StaCL. We define the set Fml of *formulas*: For $\eta \in$ Psym, $\chi \in$ CPsym, $\boldsymbol{x} \in$ Var$^+$, $\boldsymbol{u} \in$ Term$^+$, $c \in$ Const$^+$, and $f \in$ Fsym $\cup$ FVar,

$$\varphi ::= \eta(\boldsymbol{x}, \ldots, \boldsymbol{x}) \mid \chi(\boldsymbol{x}, \ldots, \boldsymbol{x}) \mid \boldsymbol{u} = \boldsymbol{u} \mid f = f \mid \mathtt{true} \mid \neg\varphi \mid \varphi \wedge \varphi \mid \lceil c/\boldsymbol{x} \rceil \varphi \mid \lfloor c/\boldsymbol{x} \rfloor \varphi.$$

Intuitively, $\lceil c/\boldsymbol{x} \rceil \varphi$ (resp. $\lfloor c/\boldsymbol{x} \rfloor \varphi$) expresses that φ is satisfied in the eager (resp. lazy) intervened world. We assume that each variable appears at most once in $\boldsymbol{x}$ in $\lceil c/\boldsymbol{x} \rceil$ and $\lfloor c/\boldsymbol{x} \rfloor$. We use syntax sugar $\mathtt{false}$, $\vee$, $\rightarrow$, and $\leftrightarrow$ as usual. Note that the formulas have no quantifiers over variables.

We interpret a formula in a world w in a Kripke model $\mathfrak{M}$ by:

$$\mathfrak{M}, w \models \eta(x_1, \ldots, x_k) \text{ iff } (\llbracket x_1 \rrbracket_w, \ldots, \llbracket x_k \rrbracket_w) \in \mathcal{V}(\eta)$$

$$\mathfrak{M}, w \models \boldsymbol{u} = \boldsymbol{u}' \text{ iff } \llbracket \boldsymbol{u} \rrbracket_w = \llbracket \boldsymbol{u}' \rrbracket_w \qquad \mathfrak{M}, w \models f = f' \text{ iff } \llbracket f \rrbracket_w = \llbracket f' \rrbracket_w$$

$$\mathfrak{M}, w \models \neg\varphi \text{ iff } \mathfrak{M}, w \not\models \varphi \qquad \mathfrak{M}, w \models \varphi \wedge \varphi' \text{ iff } \mathfrak{M}, w \models \varphi \text{ and } \mathfrak{M}, w \models \varphi'$$

$$\mathfrak{M}, w \models \lceil c/\boldsymbol{x} \rceil \varphi \text{ iff } \mathfrak{M}, w\lceil c/\boldsymbol{x} \rceil \models \varphi \qquad \mathfrak{M}, w \models \lfloor c/\boldsymbol{x} \rfloor \varphi \text{ iff } \mathfrak{M}, w\lfloor c/\boldsymbol{x} \rfloor \models \varphi,$$

where $w\lceil c/\boldsymbol{x} \rceil$ and $w\lfloor \boldsymbol{u}/\boldsymbol{x} \rfloor$ are intervened worlds and the interpretation of atomic formulas with causal predicates χ is given below. For brevity, we often omit $\mathfrak{M}$.

Note that $\eta(x_1, \ldots, x_k)$ represents a property of k independent distributions $\llbracket x_1 \rrbracket_w, \ldots, \llbracket x_k \rrbracket_w$, where the randomness r_i in each $\llbracket x_i \rrbracket_w^{r_i}$ is chosen independently. In contrast, $\eta(\langle x_1, \ldots, x_k \rangle)$ expresses a property of a single joint distribution, since the same r is used in all of $\llbracket x_1 \rrbracket_w^r, \ldots, \llbracket x_k \rrbracket_w^r$.

Atomic formulas with causal predicates χ are interpreted using a causal diagram G_w corresponding to g_w. Let $\mathtt{ANC}(\boldsymbol{y})$ is the set of all ancestors of $\boldsymbol{y}$ in G_w, and $\mathtt{PA}(\boldsymbol{y})$ be the set of all parent variables of $\boldsymbol{y}$ in G_w. Then:

$$w \models dsep(\boldsymbol{x}, \boldsymbol{y}, \boldsymbol{z}) \text{ iff } \boldsymbol{x} \text{ and } \boldsymbol{y} \text{ are } d\text{-separated by } \boldsymbol{z} \text{ in } G_w$$

$$w \models nanc(\boldsymbol{x}, \boldsymbol{y}) \text{ iff } \boldsymbol{x} \cap \mathtt{ANC}(\boldsymbol{y}) = \emptyset \text{ and } \boldsymbol{x} \cap \boldsymbol{y} = \emptyset$$

$$w \models allnanc(\boldsymbol{x}, \boldsymbol{y}, \boldsymbol{z}) \text{ iff } \boldsymbol{x} = \boldsymbol{y} \setminus \mathtt{ANC}(\boldsymbol{z})$$

$$w \models pa(\boldsymbol{x}, \boldsymbol{y}) \text{ iff } \boldsymbol{x} = \mathtt{PA}(\boldsymbol{y}) \text{ and } \boldsymbol{x} \cap \boldsymbol{y} = \emptyset,$$

where the *d*-separation[1] of $\boldsymbol{x}$ and $\boldsymbol{y}$ by $\boldsymbol{z}$ [36] is a sufficient condition for the conditional independence of $\boldsymbol{x}$ and $\boldsymbol{y}$ given $\boldsymbol{z}$ (See Appendix A in the full version [25]).

Formalization of Causal Effect. Conventionally, the conditional probability of $\boldsymbol{y}$ given $\boldsymbol{z} = \boldsymbol{o_2}$ after an intervention $\boldsymbol{x} = \boldsymbol{o_1}$ is expressed using the *do*-operator by $P(\boldsymbol{y} \mid do(\boldsymbol{x} = \boldsymbol{o_1}), \boldsymbol{z} = \boldsymbol{o_2})$. This causal effect can be expressed using StaCL:

---

[1] An undirected path in a causal diagram G_w is said to be *d-separated* by $\boldsymbol{z}$ if it has either (a) a chain $v' \rightarrow v \rightarrow v''$ s.t. $v \in \boldsymbol{z}$, (b) a fork $v' \leftarrow v \rightarrow v''$ s.t. $v \in \boldsymbol{z}$, or (c) a collider $v' \rightarrow v \leftarrow v''$ s.t. $v \notin \boldsymbol{z} \cup \mathtt{ANC}(\boldsymbol{z})$. $\boldsymbol{x}$ and $\boldsymbol{y}$ are said to be *d-separated* by $\boldsymbol{z}$ if all undirected paths between variables in $\boldsymbol{x}$ and in $\boldsymbol{z}$ are *d*-separated by $\boldsymbol{z}$.

Axioms for probability distributions	
EQ_C	$\vdash_g c^{(g,\boldsymbol{x})} = \boldsymbol{x}$
EQ_F	$\vdash_g f^{(g,\boldsymbol{y}\vert_{\boldsymbol{x},\boldsymbol{x}=c})} = \boldsymbol{y}\vert_{\boldsymbol{z},\boldsymbol{x}=c}$
PD	$\vdash_g (pos(\boldsymbol{x}) \wedge c_0 = \boldsymbol{x} \wedge f = \boldsymbol{y}\vert_{\boldsymbol{x}} \wedge c_1 = \boldsymbol{x} :: \boldsymbol{y}) \rightarrow c_1 = f(c_0)$
MPD	$\vdash_g \boldsymbol{x}_1 \downarrow_{\boldsymbol{x}_2} = \boldsymbol{x}_2$ if $\boldsymbol{x}_2 \subseteq \boldsymbol{x}_1$

Fig. 4. The axioms of **AX** for probability distributions, where $\boldsymbol{x}, \boldsymbol{x}_1, \boldsymbol{x}_2, \boldsymbol{y} \in \mathsf{CVar}^+$ are disjoint, $c_0, c_1, c^{(g,\boldsymbol{x})} \in \mathsf{Const}$, $f, f^{(g,\boldsymbol{y}\vert_{\boldsymbol{x},x=c})} \in \mathsf{Fsym}$.

Axioms for eager interventions	
DG_{EI}	$\vdash_g \lceil c/\boldsymbol{x} \rceil \varphi$ iff $\vdash_{g\lceil c/\boldsymbol{x}\rceil} \varphi$
$EFFECT_{EI}$	$\vdash_g \lceil c/\boldsymbol{x} \rceil (\boldsymbol{x} = c)$
EQ_{EI}	$\vdash_g u_1 = u_2 \leftrightarrow \lceil c/\boldsymbol{x} \rceil (u_1 = u_2)$ if $\mathsf{fv}(u_1) = \mathsf{fv}(u_2) = \emptyset$
$SPLIT_{EI}$	$\vdash_g \lceil c_1/\boldsymbol{x}_1, c_2/\boldsymbol{x}_2 \rceil \varphi \rightarrow \lceil c_1/\boldsymbol{x}_1 \rceil \lceil c_2/\boldsymbol{x}_2 \rceil \varphi$
$SIMUL_{EI}$	$\vdash_g \lceil c_1/\boldsymbol{x}_1 \rceil \lceil c_2/\boldsymbol{x}_2 \rceil \varphi \rightarrow \lceil c'_1/\boldsymbol{x}'_1, c_2/\boldsymbol{x}_2 \rceil \varphi$ if $\boldsymbol{x}'_1 = \boldsymbol{x}_1 \backslash \boldsymbol{x}_2$, $c'_1 = c_1 \backslash c_2$
RPT_{EI}	$\vdash_g \lceil c/\boldsymbol{x} \rceil \varphi \rightarrow \lceil c/\boldsymbol{x} \rceil \lceil c/\boldsymbol{x} \rceil \varphi$
CMP_{EI}	$\vdash_g (\lceil c_1/\boldsymbol{x}_1 \rceil (\boldsymbol{x}_2 = c_2) \wedge \lceil c_1/\boldsymbol{x}_1 \rceil (\boldsymbol{x}_3 = u)) \rightarrow \lceil c_1/\boldsymbol{x}_1, c_2/\boldsymbol{x}_2 \rceil (\boldsymbol{x}_3 = u)$
$DISTR_{EI}^{\neg}$	$\vdash_g (\lceil c/\boldsymbol{x} \rceil \neg \varphi) \leftrightarrow (\neg \lceil c/\boldsymbol{x} \rceil \varphi)$
$DISTR_{EI}^{\wedge}$	$\vdash_g (\lceil c/\boldsymbol{x} \rceil (\varphi_1 \wedge \varphi_2)) \leftrightarrow (\lceil c/\boldsymbol{x} \rceil \varphi_1 \wedge \lceil c/\boldsymbol{x} \rceil \varphi_2)$

Axioms for lazy interventions	
$COND_{LI}$	$\vdash_g (f = \boldsymbol{y}\vert_{\boldsymbol{x}=c}) \leftrightarrow \lfloor c/\boldsymbol{x} \rfloor (f = \boldsymbol{y}\vert_{\boldsymbol{x}=c})$

Other axioms are analogous to eager interventions except for $EFFECT_{EI}$.

Axioms for the exchanges of eager and lazy interventions	
$EXPD_{EILI}$	$\vdash_g (\lceil c/\boldsymbol{x} \rceil c' = \boldsymbol{y}) \leftrightarrow (\lfloor c/\boldsymbol{x} \rfloor c' = \boldsymbol{y})$
$EXCD_{EILI}$	$\vdash_g pos(\boldsymbol{z}) \rightarrow ((\lceil c/\boldsymbol{x} \rceil f = \boldsymbol{y}\vert_{\boldsymbol{z}}) \leftrightarrow (\lfloor c/\boldsymbol{x} \rfloor f = \boldsymbol{y}\vert_{\boldsymbol{z}}))$

Fig. 5. The axioms of **AX**, where $\boldsymbol{x}, \boldsymbol{x}_1, \boldsymbol{x}_2, \boldsymbol{x}_3, \boldsymbol{y}, \boldsymbol{z} \in \mathsf{CVar}^+$ are disjoint, $f \in \mathsf{Fsym}$, $c, c_1, c_2 \in \mathsf{dConst}^+$, $c' \in \mathsf{Const}^+$, $u, u_1, u_2 \in \mathsf{Term}^+$, and $\varphi, \varphi_1, \varphi_2 \in \mathsf{Fml}$.

Proposition 1 (Causal effect). *Let w be a world, $\boldsymbol{x}, \boldsymbol{y}, \boldsymbol{z} \in \mathsf{Var}(w)^+$ be disjoint, $c \in \mathsf{dConst}^+$, $c' \in \mathsf{Const}^+$, and $f \in \mathsf{Fsym}$. Then:*

(i) $w \models \lceil c/\boldsymbol{x} \rceil (c' = \boldsymbol{y})$ *iff there is a distribution P_{G_w} that is factorized according to G_w and satisfies $P_{G_w}(\boldsymbol{y} \mid do(\boldsymbol{x} = c)) = [\![c']\!]_w$.*

(ii) $w \models \lceil c/\boldsymbol{x} \rceil (f = \boldsymbol{y}\vert_{\boldsymbol{z}})$ *iff there is a distribution P_{G_w} that is factorized according to G_w and satisfies $P_{G_w}(\boldsymbol{y} \mid do(\boldsymbol{x} = c), \boldsymbol{z}) = [\![f]\!]_w$.*

If $\boldsymbol{x}$ and $\boldsymbol{y}$ are d-separated by $\boldsymbol{z}$, they are conditionally independent given $\boldsymbol{z}$ [36] (but not vice versa). StaCL can express this by $\models_g (dsep(\boldsymbol{x}, \boldsymbol{y}, \boldsymbol{z}) \wedge pos(\boldsymbol{z}) \rightarrow \boldsymbol{y}\vert_{\boldsymbol{z}, \boldsymbol{x}=c} = \boldsymbol{y}\vert_{\boldsymbol{z}}$, where $pos(\boldsymbol{z})$ means that $\boldsymbol{z}$ takes each value with a positive probability, and $\models_g \varphi$ is defined as $w \models_g \varphi$ for all world w having the data generator g. Furthermore, if $[\![\boldsymbol{x}]\!]_w$ and $[\![\boldsymbol{y}]\!]_w$ are conditionally independent given $[\![\boldsymbol{z}]\!]_w$ for any world w with the data generator g_w, then they are d-separated by $\boldsymbol{z}$: $\models_g \boldsymbol{y}\vert_{\boldsymbol{z}, \boldsymbol{x}=c} = \boldsymbol{y}\vert_{\boldsymbol{z}} \wedge pos(\boldsymbol{z})$ implies $\models_g dsep(\boldsymbol{x}, \boldsymbol{y}, \boldsymbol{z})$ (See Proposition 15 in the full version [25] for details).

6   Axioms for StaCL

We present a sound deductive system for StaCL in the Hilbert style. Our system consists of axioms and rules for the judgments of the form $\Gamma \vdash_g \varphi$.

The deductive system is stratified into two groups. The system **AX**, determined by the axioms in Figs. 4 and 5, concerns the derivation of $\Gamma \vdash_g \varphi$ that does not involve causal predicates (e.g., *pa*, *nanc*, *dsep*). The system **AX$^{\mathbf{CP}}$**, determined by the axioms in Fig. 6, concerns the derivation of a formula φ possibly equipped with causal predicates in a judgment $\Gamma \vdash_g \varphi$.

In these systems, we deal only with the reasoning that is independent of a causal diagram. Indeed, in Sect. 7, we will present examples of reasoning using the deductive system **AX$^{\mathbf{CP}}$** that do not refer to a specific causal diagram.

Axioms of AX. Figure 4 shows the axioms of the deductive system **AX**, where we omitted the axioms for propositional logic and equations (PT for the propositional tautologies, MP for the modus ponens, EQ1 for the reflexivity, and EQ2 for the substitutions for formulas). EQ$_C$ and EQ$_F$ represent the definitions of constants and function symbols corresponding to causal variables. PD describes the relationships among the prior distribution x, the conditional distribution $y|_x$ of y given x, and the joint distribution $x :: y$. MPD represents the computation $\downarrow_{x_2}$ of the marginal distribution x_2 from a joint distribution x_1.

The axioms named with the subscript EI deal with eager intervention. Remarkably, DG$_{\mathrm{EI}}$ reduces the derivation of $\vdash_g \lceil c/x \rceil \varphi$, which involves an intervention modality $\lceil c/x \rceil$, to the derivation of $\vdash_{g \lceil c/x \rceil} \varphi$, which does not involve the modality under the modified data generator $g \lceil c/x \rceil$. The axioms DISTR$_{\mathrm{EI}}{}'$ and DISTR$_{\mathrm{EI}}{}^\wedge$ allow for pushing intervention operators outside logical connectives.

The axioms with the subscript LI deal with lazy intervention; they are analogous to the corresponding EI-rules. The axioms with the subscript EILI describe when an eager intervention can be exchanged with a lazy intervention.

Axioms of AX$^{\mathbf{CP}}$. Figure 6 shows the axioms for **AX$^{\mathbf{CP}}$**. DSEPCI represents that d-separation implies conditional independence. DSEPSM, DSEPDC, DSEPWU, and DSEPCN are the *semi-graphoid* axioms [36], characterizing the d-separation. However, these well-known axioms are not sufficient to derive the relationships between d-separation and interventions. Therefore, we introduce two axioms DSEP$_{\mathrm{EI}}$ and DSEP$_{\mathrm{LI}}$ in Fig. 6 for the d-separation before/after interventions, and four axioms to reason about the relationships between the causal predicate *nanc* and the interventions/d-separation (named NANC$_{\{1,2,3,4\}}$ in Fig. 6). By ALLNANC, PANANC, and PADSEP, we transform the formulas using *allnanc* and *pa* into those with *nanc* or *dsep*.

Properties of Axiomatization. For a data generator g, a set $\Gamma \overset{\mathrm{def}}{=} \{\psi_1, \ldots, \psi_n\}$ of formulas, and a formula φ, we write $\Gamma \vdash_g \varphi$ if there is a derivation of $\vdash_g (\psi_1 \wedge \cdots \wedge \psi_n) \to \varphi$ using axioms of **AX** or **AX$^{\mathbf{CP}}$**. We write $\Gamma \models_g \varphi$ if for all model $\mathfrak{M}$ and all world w having the data generator g, $\mathfrak{M}, w \models \varphi$. Then we obtain the *soundness* of **AX** and **AX$^{\mathbf{CP}}$**.

Axioms for d-separation

DSEPCI $\vdash_g (dsep(\boldsymbol{x},\boldsymbol{y},\boldsymbol{z}) \wedge pos(\boldsymbol{z})) \to \boldsymbol{y}|_{\boldsymbol{z},\boldsymbol{x}=c} = \boldsymbol{y}|_{\boldsymbol{z}}$

DSEPSM $\vdash_g dsep(\boldsymbol{x},\boldsymbol{y},\boldsymbol{z}) \leftrightarrow dsep(\boldsymbol{y},\boldsymbol{x},\boldsymbol{z})$

DSEPDC $\vdash_g dsep(\boldsymbol{x},\boldsymbol{y} \cup \boldsymbol{y}',\boldsymbol{z}) \to (dsep(\boldsymbol{x},\boldsymbol{y},\boldsymbol{z}) \wedge dsep(\boldsymbol{x},\boldsymbol{y}',\boldsymbol{z}))$

DSEPWU $\vdash_g dsep(\boldsymbol{x},\boldsymbol{y} \cup \boldsymbol{v},\boldsymbol{z}) \to dsep(\boldsymbol{x},\boldsymbol{y},\boldsymbol{z} \cup \boldsymbol{v})$

DSEPCN $\vdash_g (dsep(\boldsymbol{x},\boldsymbol{y},\boldsymbol{z}) \wedge dsep(\boldsymbol{x},\boldsymbol{v},\boldsymbol{z} \cup \boldsymbol{y})) \to dsep(\boldsymbol{x},\boldsymbol{y} \cup \boldsymbol{v},\boldsymbol{z})$

Axioms for d-separation with interventions

DSEP_{EI} $\vdash_g (\lceil c/\boldsymbol{z}\rceil dsep(\boldsymbol{x},\boldsymbol{y},\boldsymbol{z})) \leftrightarrow dsep(\boldsymbol{x},\boldsymbol{y},\boldsymbol{z})$

DSEP_{LI} $\vdash_g (\lfloor c/\boldsymbol{z}\rfloor dsep(\boldsymbol{x},\boldsymbol{y},\boldsymbol{z})) \leftrightarrow dsep(\boldsymbol{x},\boldsymbol{y},\boldsymbol{z})$

Axioms with other causal predicates

NANC1 $\vdash_g (nanc(\boldsymbol{x},\boldsymbol{y}) \wedge nanc(\boldsymbol{x},\boldsymbol{z})) \to (f = \boldsymbol{y}|_{\boldsymbol{z}} \leftrightarrow \lceil c/\boldsymbol{x}\rceil (f = \boldsymbol{y}|_{\boldsymbol{z}}))$

NANC2 $\vdash_g nanc(\boldsymbol{x},\boldsymbol{y}) \leftrightarrow \lceil c/\boldsymbol{x}\rceil nanc(\boldsymbol{x},\boldsymbol{y})$

NANC3 $\vdash_g nanc(\boldsymbol{x},\boldsymbol{y}) \to \lceil c/\boldsymbol{x}\rceil dsep(\boldsymbol{x},\boldsymbol{y},\emptyset)$

NANC4 $\vdash_g (nanc(\boldsymbol{x},\boldsymbol{z}) \wedge dsep(\boldsymbol{x},\boldsymbol{y},\boldsymbol{z})) \to nanc(\boldsymbol{x},\boldsymbol{y})$

ALLNANC $\vdash_g allnanc(\boldsymbol{x},\boldsymbol{y},\boldsymbol{z}) \to nanc(\boldsymbol{x},\boldsymbol{z})$

PANANC $\vdash_g pa(\boldsymbol{x},\boldsymbol{y}) \to nanc(\boldsymbol{y},\boldsymbol{x})$

PADSEP $\vdash_g pa(\boldsymbol{z},\boldsymbol{x}) \to \lfloor c/\boldsymbol{x}\rfloor dsep(\boldsymbol{x},\boldsymbol{y},\boldsymbol{z})$

Fig. 6. The additional axioms for $\mathbf{AX}^{\mathbf{CP}}$ where $x,y,y',z,v \in \mathsf{CVar}^+$ are disjoint, $c \in \mathsf{dConst}^+$, and $f \in \mathsf{Fsym}$.

Theorem 1 (Soundness). *Let g be a finite, closed, and acyclic data generator. $\Gamma \subseteq \mathsf{Fml}$, and $\varphi \in \mathsf{Fml}$. If $\Gamma \vdash_g \varphi$ then $\Gamma \models_g \varphi$.*

We show the proof in Appendices B and C in the full version [25]. As shown in Sect. 7, $\mathbf{AX}^{\mathbf{CP}}$ is expressive enough to derive the rules of Pearl's do-calculus [30]; it can reason about all causal effects identifiable by the do-calculus (without referring to a specific causal diagram). Furthermore, $\mathbf{AX}$ includes/derives the axioms used in the previous work [1] that are complete w.r.t. a different semantics without dealing with probability distributions. We leave investigating whether $\mathbf{AX}$ is complete w.r.t. our Kripke model for future work. We also remark that $\mathbf{AX}^{\mathbf{CP}}$ has axioms corresponding to the composition and effectiveness axioms introduced by Galles and Pearl [9].

7 Reasoning About Statistical Causality

Deriving the Rules of the Do-Calculus. Using StaCL, we express the *do-calculus*'s rules [30], which are sufficient to compute all identifiable causal effects from observable quantities [16,33]. Let $\mathsf{fv}(\varphi)$ be the set of all variables occurring in a formula φ, and $\mathsf{cdv}(\varphi)$ be the set of all *conditioning variables* in φ.

Proposition 2 (Do-calculus rules). *Let $v,x,y,z \in \mathsf{CVar}^+$ be disjoint, $x_1,x_2 \in \mathsf{CVar}^+$, and $c_0,c_1,c_2 \in \mathsf{dConst}^+$. Let $S = \mathsf{cdv}(\varphi_0) \cup \mathsf{cdv}(\varphi_1)$.*

$$\cfrac{\cfrac{\overline{\vdash_g \psi_{\mathrm{nanc}} \to (([\ulcorner c/x \urcorner]\psi_2) \leftrightarrow \psi_2)} \; \text{NANC3}}{\vdash_g \psi_{\mathrm{d2}} \to (([\ulcorner c/x \urcorner]\psi_2) \leftrightarrow \psi_2)} \; \text{Do3} \quad \cfrac{}{\vdash_g ([\ulcorner c/x \urcorner]\psi_3) \leftrightarrow \psi_3} \; \text{EQ}_{\mathrm{EI}}}{\psi_{\mathrm{pre}} \vdash_g ([\ulcorner c/x \urcorner]\psi_0 \wedge [\ulcorner c/x \urcorner]\psi_2 \wedge [\ulcorner c/x \urcorner]\psi_3) \leftrightarrow (\psi_1 \wedge \psi_2 \wedge \psi_3)}$$

where $\cfrac{\vdash_g \psi_{\mathrm{d1}} \to (([\ulcorner c/x \urcorner]\psi_0) \leftrightarrow \psi_1)}{} \; \text{Do2}$ sits at top left.

$$\cfrac{\cfrac{\cfrac{\cfrac{\psi_{\mathrm{pre}} \vdash_g ([\ulcorner c/x \urcorner]\psi_0 \wedge [\ulcorner c/x \urcorner]\psi_2 \wedge [\ulcorner c/x \urcorner]\psi_3) \leftrightarrow (\psi_1 \wedge \psi_2 \wedge \psi_3)}{\psi_{\mathrm{pre}} \vdash_g ([\ulcorner c/x \urcorner](\psi_0 \wedge \psi_2 \wedge \psi_3)) \leftrightarrow (\psi_1 \wedge \psi_2 \wedge \psi_3)} \; \text{DISTR}_{\mathrm{EI}} \wedge}{\psi_{\mathrm{pre}} \vdash_g ([\ulcorner c/x \urcorner]c_0 = (y|_z(z))\!\downarrow_y) \leftrightarrow (\psi_1 \wedge \psi_2 \wedge \psi_3)} \; \text{EQ}_{\mathrm{C}}, \text{EQ}_{\mathrm{F}}, \text{EQ2}}{\psi_{\mathrm{pre}} \vdash_g ([\ulcorner c/x \urcorner]c_0 = (y :: z)\!\downarrow_y) \leftrightarrow (\psi_1 \wedge \psi_2 \wedge \psi_3)} \; \text{PD}, \text{EQ2}}{\psi_{\mathrm{pre}} \vdash_g ([\ulcorner c/x \urcorner]c_0 = y) \leftrightarrow (\psi_1 \wedge \psi_2 \wedge \psi_3)} \; \text{MPD}, \text{EQ2}$$

Fig. 7. Sketch of a derivation tree for the correctness of the backdoor adjustment (Sect. 2) using $\mathbf{AX^{CP}}$ where $\psi_{\mathrm{pos}} \overset{\mathrm{def}}{=} pos(z :: x)$, $\psi_{\mathrm{d1}} \overset{\mathrm{def}}{=} \lfloor c/x \rfloor dsep(x, y, z) \wedge \psi_{\mathrm{pos}}$, $\psi_{\mathrm{d2}} \overset{\mathrm{def}}{=} \lceil c/x \rceil dsep(x, z, \emptyset) \wedge \psi_{\mathrm{pos}}$, $\psi_{\mathrm{nanc}} \overset{\mathrm{def}}{=} nanc(x, z) \wedge \psi_{\mathrm{pos}}$, $\psi_{\mathrm{pre}} \overset{\mathrm{def}}{=} \psi_{\mathrm{d1}} \wedge \psi_{\mathrm{nanc}}$, $\psi_0 \overset{\mathrm{def}}{=} (f = y|_z)$, $\psi_1 \overset{\mathrm{def}}{=} (f = y|_{z,x=c})$, $\psi_2 \overset{\mathrm{def}}{=} (c_1 = z)$, and $\psi_3 \overset{\mathrm{def}}{=} (c_0 = f(c_1)\!\downarrow_y)$.

1. Do1.   Introduction/elimination of conditioning:

$$\vdash_g \lceil c_0/v \rceil (dsep(x, y, z) \wedge \bigwedge_{s \in S} pos(s)) \to ((\lceil c_0/v \rceil \varphi_0) \leftrightarrow \lceil c_0/v \rceil \varphi_1)$$

where φ_1 is obtained by replacing some occurrences of $y|_z$ in φ_0 with $y|_{z,x=c_1}$;

2. Do2.   Exchange between intervention and conditioning:

$$\vdash_g \lceil c_0/v \rceil \lfloor c_1/x \rfloor (dsep(x, y, z) \wedge \bigwedge_{s \in S} pos(s)) \to ((\lceil c_0/v, c_1/x \rceil \varphi_0) \leftrightarrow \lceil c_0/v \rceil \varphi_1)$$

where φ_1 is obtained by replacing every occurrence of $y|_z$ in φ_0 with $y|_{z,x=c_1}$;

3. Do3

Introduction/elimination of intervention:

$$\vdash_g \lceil c_0/v \rceil (allnanc(x_1, x, y) \wedge \lceil c_1/x_1 \rceil (dsep(x, y, z) \wedge pos(z)))$$
$$\to ((\lceil c_0/v \rceil \varphi) \leftrightarrow \lceil c_0/v, c_1/x_1, c_2/x_2 \rceil \varphi)$$

where $\mathsf{fv}(\varphi) = \{y|_z\}$ and $x \overset{def}{=} x_1 :: x_2$.

By using the deductive system $\mathbf{AX^{CP}}$, we can derive those rules. Thanks to the modal operators for lazy interventions, our derivation of those rules is partly different from Pearl's [30] in that it does not use diagrams augmented with the intervention arc of the form $F_x \to x$ (See Appendix D in the full version [25]).

Reasoning About Statistical Adjustment. We present how $\mathbf{AX^{CP}}$ can be used to reason about the correctness of the backdoor adjustment discussed in Sect. 2 (See Appendix A.6 in the full version [25] for the details of the backdoor adjustment).

Figure 7 shows the derivation of the judgment:

$$\psi_{\mathrm{pre}} \vdash_g ([\ulcorner c/x \urcorner]c_0 = y) \leftrightarrow (\psi_1 \wedge \psi_2 \wedge \psi_3). \tag{3}$$

This judgment asserts the correctness of the backdoor adjustment in any causal diagram. Recall that $\varphi_{\mathrm{RCT}} \overset{\mathrm{def}}{=} ([\ulcorner c/x \urcorner]c_0 = y)$ expresses the RCT and $\varphi_{\mathrm{BDA}} \overset{\mathrm{def}}{=} (\psi_1 \wedge \psi_2 \wedge \psi_3)$ expresses the backdoor adjustment. The correctness of the backdoor adjustment ($\varphi_{\mathrm{RCT}} \leftrightarrow \varphi_{\mathrm{BDA}}$) depends on the precondition ψ_{pre}.

By reading the derivation tree in a bottom-up manner, we observe that the proof first converts ($\lceil c/x \rceil c_0 = y$) to a formula to which $\mathrm{EQ_C}$ and $\mathrm{EQ_F}$ are applicable. Then, the derived axioms Do2 and Do3 in Proposition 2 are used to complete the proof at the leaves of the derivation.

In Sect. 2, we stated the correctness of the backdoor adjustment in (1) using a simpler requirement $pa(z,x)$ instead of ψ_{d1} and ψ_{nanc}. We can derive the judgment (1) from (3), thanks to the axioms PaDsep and PaNanc.

The derivation does not mention the data generator g representing the causal diagram G. This exhibits that our logic successfully separates the reasoning about the properties of arbitrary causal diagrams from those depending on a specific causal diagram. Once we prove $\psi_{pre} \vdash_g \varphi_{RCT} \leftrightarrow \varphi_{BDA}$ using $\mathbf{AX^{CP}}$, one can claim the correctness of the causal inference ($\varphi_{RCT} \leftrightarrow \varphi_{BDA}$) by checking that the requirement ψ_{pre} indeed holds for a specific causal diagram G.

8   Conclusion

We proposed statistical causality language (StaCL) to formally describe and explain the correctness of statistical causal inference. We introduced the notion of causal predicates and Kripke models equipped with data generators. We defined a sound deductive system $\mathbf{AX^{CP}}$ that can deduce all causal effects derived using Pearl's do-calculus. In ongoing and future work, we study the completeness of $\mathbf{AX}$ and $\mathbf{AX^{CP}}$ and develop a decision procedure for $\mathbf{AX^{CP}}$ for automated reasoning.

Acknowledgements. We thank Kenji Fukumizu for providing helpful information on the literature on causal inference. The authors are supported by ERATO HASUO Meta-mathematics for Systems Design Project (No. JPMJER1603), JST. Yusuke Kawamoto is supported by JST, PRESTO Grant Number JPMJPR2022, Japan, and by JSPS KAKENHI Grant Number 21K12028, Japan. Tetsuya Sato is supported by JSPS KAK-ENHI Grant Number 20K19775, Japan. Kohei Suenaga is supported by JST CREST Grant Number JPMJCR2012, Japan.

References

1. Barbero, F., Sandu, G.: Team semantics for interventionist counterfactuals: observations vs. interventions. J. Philos. Log. **50**(3), 471–521 (2021). https://doi.org/10.1007/s10992-020-09573-6
2. Barbero, F., Schulz, K., Smets, S., Velázquez-Quesada, F.R., Xie, K.: Thinking about causation: a causal language with epistemic operators. In: Martins, M.A., Sedlár, I. (eds.) DaLi 2020. LNCS, vol. 12569, pp. 17–32. Springer, Cham (2020). https://doi.org/10.1007/978-3-030-65840-3_2
3. Bochman, A.: A Logical Theory of Causality. MIT Press, Cambridge (2021)
4. Bochman, A., Lifschitz, V.: Pearl's causality in a logical setting. In: Proceedings of the Twenty-Ninth AAAI Conference on Artificial Intelligence, pp. 1446–1452. AAAI Press (2015), http://www.aaai.org/ocs/index.php/AAAI/AAAI15/paper/view/9686

5. Corander, J., Hyttinen, A., Kontinen, J., Pensar, J., Väänänen, J.: A logical approach to context-specific independence. Ann. Pure Appl. Log. **170**(9), 975–992 (2019). https://doi.org/10.1016/j.apal.2019.04.004
6. Durand, A., Hannula, M., Kontinen, J., Meier, A., Virtema, J.: Approximation and dependence via multiteam semantics. In: Gyssens, M., Simari, G. (eds.) FoIKS 2016. LNCS, vol. 9616, pp. 271–291. Springer, Cham (2016). https://doi.org/10.1007/978-3-319-30024-5_15
7. Durand, A., Hannula, M., Kontinen, J., Meier, A., Virtema, J.: Probabilistic team semantics. In: Ferrarotti, F., Woltran, S. (eds.) FoIKS 2018. LNCS, vol. 10833, pp. 186–206. Springer, Cham (2018). https://doi.org/10.1007/978-3-319-90050-6_11
8. Fernandes-Taylor, S., Hyun, J.K., Reeder, R.N., Harris, A.H.: Common statistical and research design problems in manuscripts submitted to high-impact medical journals. BMC Res. Notes **4**(1), 304 (2011)
9. Galles, D., Pearl, J.: An axiomatic characterization of causal counterfactuals. Found. Sci. **3**, 151–182 (1998)
10. Halpern, J.Y.: Axiomatizing causal reasoning. J. Artif. Intell. Res. **12**, 317–337 (2000)
11. Halpern, J.Y.: A modification of the Halpern-Pearl definition of causality. In: Proceedings of the IJCAI 2015, pp. 3022–3033. AAAI Press (2015)
12. Halpern, J.Y., Pearl, J.: Causes and explanations: A structural-model approach - part II: explanations. In: Proceedings of the IJCAI 2001, pp. 27–34. Morgan Kaufmann (2001)
13. Halpern, J.Y., Pearl, J.: Causes and explanations: a structural-model approach: part 1: causes. In: Proceedings of the UAI 2001, pp. 194–202. Morgan Kaufmann (2001)
14. Hirvonen, Å., Kontinen, J., Pauly, A.: Continuous team semantics. In: Gopal, T.V., Watada, J. (eds.) TAMC 2019. LNCS, vol. 11436, pp. 262–278. Springer, Cham (2019). https://doi.org/10.1007/978-3-030-14812-6_16
15. Hodges, W.: Compositional semantics for a language of imperfect information. Log. J. IGPL **5**(4), 539–563 (1997). https://doi.org/10.1093/jigpal/5.4.539
16. Huang, Y., Valtorta, M.: Pearl's calculus of intervention is complete. In: Proceedings of the UAI 2006, pp. 217–224. AUAI Press (2006)
17. Hyttinen, A., Eberhardt, F., Järvisalo, M.: Constraint-based causal discovery: conflict resolution with answer set programming. In: Proceedings of the Thirtieth Conference on Uncertainty in Artificial Intelligence (UAI 2014), pp. 340–349. AUAI Press (2014)
18. Hyttinen, A., Eberhardt, F., Järvisalo, M.: Do-calculus when the true graph is unknown. In: Proceedings of the Thirty-First Conference on Uncertainty in Artificial Intelligence (UAI 2015), pp. 395–404. AUAI Press (2015)
19. Ibeling, D., Icard, T.: Probabilistic reasoning across the causal hierarchy. In: Proceedings of the Thirty-Fourth AAAI Conference on Artificial Intelligence (AAAI 2020), pp. 10170–10177. AAAI Press (2020). http://aaai.org/ojs/index.php/AAAI/article/view/6577
20. Kawamoto, Y.: Statistical epistemic logic. In: Alvim, M.S., Chatzikokolakis, K., Olarte, C., Valencia, F. (eds.) The Art of Modelling Computational Systems: A Journey from Logic and Concurrency to Security and Privacy. LNCS, vol. 11760, pp. 344–362. Springer, Cham (2019). https://doi.org/10.1007/978-3-030-31175-9_20
21. Kawamoto, Y.: Towards logical specification of statistical machine learning. In: Proceedings of the SEFM, pp. 293–311 (2019). https://doi.org/10.1007/978-3-030-30446-1_16

22. Kawamoto, Y.: An epistemic approach to the formal specification of statistical machine learning. Softw. Syst. Model. **20**(2), 293–310 (2020). https://doi.org/10.1007/s10270-020-00825-2
23. Kawamoto, Y., Mano, K., Sakurada, H., Hagiya, M.: Partial knowledge of functions and verification of anonymity. Trans. Jpn. Soc. Industr. Appl. Math. **17**(4), 559–576 (2007). https://doi.org/10.11540/jsiamt.17.4_559
24. Kawamoto, Y., Sato, T., Suenaga, K.: Formalizing statistical beliefs in hypothesis testing using program logic. In: Proceedings of the KR 2021, pp. 411–421 (2021). https://doi.org/10.24963/kr.2021/39
25. Kawamoto, Y., Sato, T., Suenaga, K.: Formalizing statistical causality via modal logic. CoRR abs/2210.16751 (2022). https://doi.org/10.48550/arXiv.2210.16751
26. Kawamoto, Y., Sato, T., Suenaga, K.: Sound and relatively complete belief Hoare logic for statistical hypothesis testing programs. CoRR abs/2208.07074 (2022)
27. Makin, T.R., de Xivry, J.J.O.: Science forum: Ten common statistical mistakes to watch out for when writing or reviewing a manuscript. Elife **8**, e48175 (2019)
28. McCain, N., Turner, H.: Causal theories of action and change. In: Proceedings of the Fourteenth National Conference on Artificial Intelligence and Ninth Innovative Applications of Artificial Intelligence Conference (AAAI 1997/IAAI 1997), pp. 460–465. AAAI Press/The MIT Press (1997)
29. Moher, D., et al.: Consort 2010 explanation and elaboration: updated guidelines for reporting parallel group randomised trials. Int. J. Surg. **10**(1), 28–55 (2012)
30. Pearl, J.: Causal diagrams for empirical research. Biometrika **82**(4), 669–688 (1995). http://www.jstor.org/stable/2337329
31. Pearl, J.: Causality. Cambridge University Press, Cambridge (2009)
32. Rückschloß, K., Weitkämper, F.: Exploiting the full power of Pearl's causality in probabilistic logic programming. In: Proceedings of the 9th Workshop on Probabilistic Logic Programming (PLP 2022). CEUR Workshop Proceedings, vol. 3193. CEUR-WS.org (2022). http://ceur-ws.org/Vol-3193/paper1PLP.pdf
33. Shpitser, I., Pearl, J.: Identification of conditional interventional distributions. In: Proceedings of the UAI 2006, pp. 437–444. AUAI Press (2006)
34. Simpson, E.H.: The interpretation of interaction in contingency tables. J. Roy. Stat. Soc. Ser. B (Methodol.) **13**(2), 238–241 (1951). http://www.jstor.org/stable/2984065
35. Triantafillou, S., Tsamardinos, I.: Constraint-based causal discovery from multiple interventions over overlapping variable sets. J. Mach. Learn. Res. **16**, 2147–2205 (2015)
36. Verma, T., Pearl, J.: Causal networks: semantics and expressiveness. In: Proceedings of the UAI 1988, pp. 69–78. North-Holland (1988)
37. Von Elm, E., Altman, D.G., Egger, M., Pocock, S.J., Götzsche, P.C., Vandenbroucke, J.P.: The strengthening the reporting of observational studies in epidemiology (strobe) statement: guidelines for reporting observational studies. Bull. World Health Organ. **85**, 867–872 (2007)

Boosting Definability Bipartition Computation Using SAT Witnesses

Jean-Marie Lagniez[1] and Pierre Marquis[1,2]($\boxtimes$)

[1] Univ. Artois, CNRS, CRIL, Lens, France
{lagniez,marquis}@cril.fr
[2] Institut Universitaire de France, Paris, France

Abstract. Bipartitioning the set of variables $Var(\Sigma)$ of a propositional formula Σ w.r.t. definability consists in pointing out a bipartition $\langle I, O \rangle$ of $Var(\Sigma)$ such that Σ defines the variables of O (outputs) in terms of the variables in I (inputs), i.e., for every $o \in O$, there exists a formula Φ_o over I such that $o \Leftrightarrow \Phi_o$ is a logical consequence of Σ. The existence of Φ_o given o, I, and Σ is a coNP-complete problem, and as such, it can be addressed in practice using a SAT solver. From a computational perspective, definability bipartitioning has been shown as a valuable preprocessing technique for model counting, a key task for a number of AI problems involving probabilities. To maximize the benefits offered by such a preprocessing, one is interested in deriving *subset-minimal bipartitions* in terms of input variables, i.e., definability bipartitions $\langle I, O \rangle$ such that for every $i \in I$, $\langle I \setminus \{i\}, O \cup \{i\} \rangle$ is not a definability bipartition. We show how the computation of subset-minimal bipartitions can be boosted by leveraging not only the decisions furnished by SAT solvers (as done in previous approaches), but also the SAT witnesses (models and cores) justifying those decisions.

Keywords: Automated reasoning including satisfiability checking and its extensions · definability · propositional logic

1 Introduction

In this paper, we are interested in identifying *definability relations* between variables occurring in a given propositional formula Σ. When I is a subset of the variables of Σ and o is a variable of Σ, Σ is said to define o in terms of I if and only if (1) there exists a formula Φ_o over I such that $o \Leftrightarrow \Phi_o$ is a logical consequence of Σ. o can be considered as an *output* variable provided that the variables in I are viewed as *input* variables, since Σ defines o in terms of I if and only if (2) under every assignment γ_I of variables from I that is consistent with Σ, either o or $\neg o$ is implied by Σ (i.e., the truth value of variable o is fixed). The two characterizations (1) and (2), namely explicit definability and implicit definability, are known to be equivalent in classical logic [2].

More precisely, in the following, our goal is to compute *definability bipartitions*: we want to split the set $Var(\Sigma)$ of variables occurring in Σ into disjoint

© The Author(s), under exclusive license to Springer Nature Switzerland AG 2023
S. Gaggl et al. (Eds.): JELIA 2023, LNAI 14281, pp. 697–711, 2023.
https://doi.org/10.1007/978-3-031-43619-2_47

subsets I and O such that Σ defines every variable of O in terms of the variables in I. The resulting pair $\langle I, O \rangle$ is referred to as a *definability bipartition*.

Deriving such bipartitions has been shown as a valuable preprocessing technique for model counting, a key task for a number of AI problems involving probabilities (see e.g., [4–7,14]). Indeed, whenever a variable o has been identified as an output variable from O, it can be *forgotten* from Σ without modifying the number of models. The forgetting of o from Σ [9,11] is the quantified formula $\exists o \cdot \Sigma$, i.e., Σ into which o is existentially quantified. This quantified formula is equivalent to the standard formula given by $(\Sigma|\neg o) \vee (\Sigma|o)$. Here, $\Sigma|\neg o$ (resp. $\Sigma|o$) is the formula Σ where every occurrence of variable o has been replaced by the Boolean constant $\bot$ (falsum) (resp. the Boolean constant $\top$ (verum)). Thus, when $\langle I, O \rangle$ is a definability bipartition of $Var(\Sigma)$, the number of models of Σ is precisely the number of models of Σ once projected onto I.

This observation led us to design and evaluate a preprocessing technique dedicated to model counting, which consists in deriving first a definability bipartition $\langle I, O \rangle$ of $Var(\Sigma)$ and then in eliminating in Σ the implicit existential quantifications over variables from O [6,7]. Accordingly, the corresponding preprocessing algorithm B + E consists of a pipeline of two algorithms B (for deriving a bipartition) and E for eliminating the output variables. Many experiments with various model counters considered upstream have shown that huge computational benefits can be achieved by taking advantage of B + E (see [7] for details). In order to avoid trivial bipartitions (e.g., $\langle Var(\Sigma), \emptyset \rangle$) to be considered and maximize the leverage of the approach, the focus was on deriving *subset-minimal bipartitions* in terms of input variables, i.e., definability bipartitions $\langle I, O \rangle$ such that for every $i \in I$, $\langle I \setminus \{i\}, O \cup \{i\} \rangle$ is not a definability bipartition.[1]

B mainly is a greedy algorithm, equipped with a definability oracle based on a SAT solver. The definability oracle used in B relies only on the *decision* returned by the SAT solver, i.e., whether the CNF formula considered as input is consistent or not. However, modern SAT solvers furnish more information that can be exploited for further treatments when used in an incremental way. Especially, when the input formula is consistent, a truth assignment forming a *model* of the formula is computed; when it is inconsistent, a subset of clauses that is conjunctively inconsistent (alias a *core*) can be extracted as well.

In the following, we show how the computation of subset-minimal bipartitions can be boosted by taking into account not only the decisions furnished by SAT solvers (as done in B), but also the SAT witnesses (models and cores) justifying those decisions. We present an improved bipartition algorithm, named B+, which takes advantage of extra-information reported by the SAT solver. We prove the correctness of the algorithm and present an empirical evaluation of it based on a large number of benchmarks (CNF instances) from various families. In order to figure out the benefits offered by the use of SAT witnesses of each type, we measure the number of instances for which B+ (using models, cores, both of them, or none of them) succeeds in computing a subset-minimal bipartition in

---

[1] In practice, computing smallest bipartitions in terms of input variables, i.e., bipartitions $\langle I, O \rangle$ such that $|I|$ is minimal, is in general too demanding for being useful.

a given amount of time. The experiments made show that taking advantage of both models and cores is useful in practice and that B+ outperforms B (which boils down to the variant of B+ where neither models nor cores are exploited). For space reasons, proofs are not provided in the paper, but they are available online at http://www.cril.univ-artois.fr/~marquis/BDBCSW.pdf.

2 Preliminaries

Let $\mathcal{L}$ be the (classical) propositional language defined inductively from a countable set $\mathcal{P}$ of propositional variables, the usual connectives ($\neg$, $\vee$, $\wedge$, $\leftrightarrow$, etc.) and including the Boolean constants $\top$ (verum) and $\bot$ (falsum). A *literal* ℓ is a variable $\ell = x$ from $\mathcal{P}$ or a negated one $\ell = \neg x$. When ℓ is a literal, $var(\ell)$ denotes the variable from $\mathcal{P}$ upon which ℓ is built. An *interpretation* ω is a mapping from $\mathcal{P}$ to $\{0,1\}$, represented as a set of literals. Formulae Σ are interpreted in the classical way. If $\Sigma(\omega) = 1$, then ω is called a *model* of Σ and Σ is *consistent*. In the case when Σ has no model, Σ is said to be *inconsistent*. $\models$ denotes logical entailment. For any formula Σ from $\mathcal{L}$, $Var(\Sigma)$ is the set of variables from $\mathcal{P}$ occurring in Σ. A *term* is a conjunction of literals or $\top$, and a *clause* is a disjunction of literals or $\bot$. A CNF formula Σ is a conjunction of clauses (also viewed as a set of clauses when convenient). Let X be any subset of $\mathcal{P}$. A *canonical term* γ_X over a subset X of $\mathcal{P}$ is a consistent term into which every variable from X appears (either as a positive literal or as a negative one, i.e., as a negated variable).

Let us now recall the concept of definability in propositional logic (the following definition is about implicit definability, i.e., it does not refer to any definition of y in Σ):

Definition 1 (definability). *Let $\Sigma \in \mathcal{L}$, $X \subseteq \mathcal{P}$ and $y \in \mathcal{P}$. Σ defines y in terms of X if and only if for every canonical term γ_X over X, we have $\gamma_X \wedge \Sigma \models y$ or $\gamma_X \wedge \Sigma \models \neg y$.*

Example 1. Let Σ be the CNF formula consisting of the following clauses:

$\neg a \vee b$	$\neg a \vee c$	$a \vee \neg b \vee \neg c$	$\neg e \vee c \vee d$	$\neg c \vee e$
$\neg d \vee e$	$b \vee \neg c \vee d$	$d \vee \neg a$		

a and e are defined in Σ in terms of $X = \{b, c, d\}$. For instance, the canonical term $\gamma_X = b \wedge c \wedge d$ over $\{b, c, d\}$ is such that $\Sigma \wedge \gamma_X \models a \wedge e$.

Clearly enough, Definition 1 shows that the concept of definability trivializes when Σ is inconsistent, in the sense that Σ defines each of its variables in terms of $\emptyset$ when Σ is inconsistent. Thus, in the rest of the paper, we suppose that Σ is consistent.

In the following, we state that a subset Y of variables from $\mathcal{P}$ is defined in terms of X in Σ (denoted by $X \sqsubseteq_\Sigma Y$) when every variable $y \in Y$ is defined in terms of X in Σ. It is known that deciding whether Σ defines y in terms of X is "only" coNP-complete [10]. Indeed, we can take advantage of the following result (Padoa's theorem [13]), restricted to propositional logic and recalled in [10], to decide whether Σ defines y in terms of X. This theorem gives an entailment-based characterization of definability:

Theorem 1. *For any $\Sigma \in \mathcal{L}$ and any $X \subseteq \mathcal{P}$, let Σ'_X be the formula obtained by replacing in Σ in a uniform way every propositional symbol z from $Var(\Sigma) \setminus X$ by a new propositional symbol z'. Let $y \in \mathcal{P}$. If $y \notin X$, then Σ (implicitly) defines y in terms of X if and only if $\Sigma \wedge \Sigma'_X \wedge y \wedge \neg y'$ is inconsistent.[2]*

In [6,7], the authors took advantage of Theorem 1 in order to design a greedy bipartition algorithm, called B. Given a CNF formula Σ, B makes intensive use of Theorem 1 to compute a subset-minimal bipartition $\langle I, O \rangle$ of $Var(\Sigma)$, where a definability bipartition $\langle I, O \rangle$ of $Var(\Sigma)$ is a subset-minimal bipartition of $Var(\Sigma)$ if $\nexists x \in I$ such that $I \setminus \{x\} \sqsubseteq_\Sigma O \cup \{x\}$. Algorithm 1 presents a version of B where some technicalities (the ordering under which the variables are processed and the possibility to limit the number of learned clauses) are abstracted away. At line 1, `backbone`(Σ) computes the backbone of Σ (i.e., the set of all literals implied by Σ), and initializes O with the corresponding variables (indeed, if a literal ℓ belongs to the backbone of Σ, then $var(\ell)$ is defined in Σ in terms of $\emptyset$). Still at line 1, I is initialized to the empty set. Then, variables that are not yet identified as inputs or outputs are considered iteratively (lines 2 – 4). At line 3, `defined?` takes advantage of Theorem 1 for determining whether x is defined in Σ in terms of $Var(\Sigma) \setminus (O \cup \{x\})$, i.e., all the variables but x and those in the current set of output variables. `defined?` uses a SAT solver `solve` based on CDCL architecture [12] for achieving the (in)consistency test required by Padoa's method. Note that `solve` allows SAT solving "under assumptions" [3], i.e., the input CNF formula consists of two parts, F a CNF formula and $\mathcal{A}$, a conjunction of unit clauses. Thanks to the use of assumptions, clauses that are learnt at each call to `solve` are kept for the subsequent calls to `solve` within B.

`defined?`$(x, \Sigma, Var(\Sigma) \setminus (O \cup \{x\}))$ returns true precisely when `solve` indicates that the CNF formula $F \wedge \mathcal{A}$ is inconsistent, where

$$F = Padoa(\Sigma) = \Sigma \wedge \Sigma'_\emptyset \wedge \bigwedge_{z \in Var(\Sigma)} ((\neg s_z \vee \neg z \vee z') \wedge (\neg s_z \vee z \vee \neg z'))$$

and $\mathcal{A} = (\bigwedge_{s_z | z \in Var(\Sigma) \setminus (O \cup \{x\})} s_z) \wedge x \wedge \neg x'$. Variables s_z are fresh variables, used as selectors: whenever s_z is set to 1, z and z' must take the same truth value in $Padoa(\Sigma)$. Depending on the result returned by `defined?`, x is added either to O (line 3) or to I (line 4). Finally, the bipartition that has been computed is returned at line 5.

---

[2] Obviously enough, in the remaining case when $y \in X$, Σ defines y in terms of X.

Algorithm 1: B

---

input : a CNF formula Σ

output : $\langle I, O \rangle$ a subset-minimal definability bipartition of $Var(\Sigma)$

1 $\langle \Sigma, O \rangle \leftarrow$ backbone(Σ); $I \leftarrow \emptyset$;

2 foreach $x \in Var(\Sigma) \setminus (I \cup O)$ **do**

3   **if** defined?$(x, \Sigma, Var(\Sigma) \setminus (O \cup \{x\}))$ **then** $O \leftarrow O \cup \{x\}$;

4   **else** $I \leftarrow I \cup \{x\}$;

5 return $\langle I, O \rangle$

Example 2 (Example 1 cont'ed). Let us consider the CNF formula given in Example 1, we have:

$$
\begin{array}{llll}
Padoa(\Sigma) = & \neg a \vee b & \neg a \vee c & a \vee \neg b \vee \neg c & \neg e \vee c \vee d \\
& \neg c \vee e & \neg d \vee e & d \vee \neg a & b \vee \neg c \vee d \\
& \neg a' \vee b' & \neg a' \vee c' & a' \vee \neg b' \vee \neg c' & \neg e' \vee c' \vee d' \\
& \neg c' \vee e' & \neg d' \vee e' & d' \vee \neg a' & b' \vee \neg c' \vee d' \\
& s_a \vee a \vee \neg a' & s_a \vee \neg a \vee a' & s_b \vee b \vee \neg b' & s_b \vee \neg b \vee b' \\
& s_c \vee c \vee \neg c' & s_c \vee \neg c \vee c' & s_d \vee d \vee \neg d' & s_d \vee \neg d \vee d' \\
& s_e \vee e \vee \neg e' & s_e \vee \neg e \vee e'
\end{array}
$$

To check whether e is defined in Σ in terms of $X = \{a, b, c\}$, it is enough to test the consistency of $Padoa(\Sigma)$ under the assumption $\mathcal{A} = \{s_a, s_b, s_c, e, \neg e'\}$. Since $\{\neg a, b, \neg c, d, e, \neg a', b', \neg c', \neg d', \neg e', s_a, s_b, s_c, \neg s_d, \neg s_e\}$ is a model of $Padoa(\Sigma)$ under the given assumption $\mathcal{A}$, we can conclude that e is not defined in Σ in terms of X. On the other hand, e is defined in Σ in terms of $X' = \{b, c, d\}$, since $Padoa(\Sigma)$ under the assumption $\mathcal{A}' = \{s_b, s_c, s_d, e, \neg e'\}$ is inconsistent.

3 Exploiting SAT Oracle Witnesses

Interestingly, modern SAT solvers "under assumptions" $\mathcal{A}$ may provide an output that does not consist only of the decision made about the consistency of its input, but may also contain a justification of the decision, alias a SAT witness. Thus, a triple $(s, \mathcal{V}, \mathcal{C})$ can be reported by the SAT solver when run on F and $\mathcal{A}$. In such a triple, s (the decision) is a Boolean value set to true when $F \wedge \mathcal{A}$ is consistent, $\mathcal{V}$ is a model of $F \wedge \mathcal{A}$ when s is true (the SAT witness), and $\mathcal{C} \subseteq \mathcal{A}$ is an inconsistent core of $F \wedge \mathcal{A}$, i.e., $\mathcal{C}$ is such that $F \wedge \mathcal{C}$ is inconsistent, when s is false (the UNSAT witness).

In order to understand how the witnesses offered by the SAT solver can be exploited in the context of a definability bipartition algorithm, it is necessary to enter into the details about the way B and **defined?** precisely work. At each iteration of the greedy algorithm B, the focus is on a variable x that has not been considered so far in previous iterations. When encountered, x is *undecided*, i.e., it has not been classified yet as input or as output. For every x, $Var(\Sigma)$ can be split into four pairwise-disjoint sets of variables: $\{x\}$, the set I_x of variables already encountered when x is processed, classified as input variables, and put in I, the set O_x of variables already encountered when x is processed, classified as output variables, and put in O, and finally the remaining set U_x of variables that will be considered next and are still undecided when x is processed. Each of the variables $u \in U_x$ will be classified either as input (noted $u \in U_x^I$) or as output (noted $u \in U_x^O$) in a subsequent iteration, thus when all the variables will be processed, we will have either $u \in I$ or $u \in O$. When $I_x \cup U_x \sqsubseteq_\Sigma \{x\}$, since $U_x = U_x^I \cup U_x^O$, $U_x^I \subseteq I$, $U_x^O \subseteq O$, and $I \sqsubseteq_\Sigma O$, we can conclude that $I \sqsubseteq_\Sigma \{x\}$, as expected. Thus, no backtracking is necessary: the classification of each variable x achieved by the greedy algorithm when x is processed never has to be questioned. This ensures the correctness of B for computing a definability bipartition of $Var(\Sigma)$ (see Proposition 3 in [7]).

At each step, `defined?` is called to determine whether or not Σ defines x in terms of $I_x \cup U_x$. Finally, deciding whether or not Σ defines x in terms of $I_x \cup U_x$ amounts to calling `solve` on $F = Padoa(\Sigma) = \Sigma \wedge \Sigma'_\emptyset \wedge \bigwedge_{z \in Var(\Sigma)}((\neg s_z \vee \neg z \vee z') \wedge (\neg s_z \vee z \vee \neg z'))$ and $\mathcal{A} = \{x, \neg x'\} \cup \{s_x \mid x \in I_x \cup U_x\}$.

In the definability bipartition algorithm B presented in [6,7], only the decision value s of the triple returned by `solve` has been considered. We now explain how the two other components of the triple, i.e., the two types of SAT witnesses, can be exploited to improve the performance of the algorithm. Basically, at each iteration, when `defined?` is called to decide whether or not Σ defines x in terms of $I_x \cup U_x$, the goal is to take advantage of the SAT witnesses furnished by `solve` when providing a decision about x to reduce the computational efforts to be made by the definability bipartition algorithm in subsequent iterations. The two types of witnesses will be leveraged in two different ways.

When the decision returned by `solve` is false, Σ defines x in terms of $I_x \cup U_x$ and an inconsistent core $\mathcal{C}$ will be exhibited. This core makes precise a subset of assumptions of $X_\mathcal{C} \subseteq I_x \cup U_x$ such that Σ defines x in terms of $X_\mathcal{C}$. The idea is to keep track of this definability relation by forming a clause (based on selectors) $(\bigvee_{v \in X_\mathcal{C}} \neg s_v) \vee s_x)$ that reflects that Σ defines x in terms of $X_\mathcal{C}$. This clause can be freely added to $Padoa(\Sigma)$ in subsequent iterations: adding it does not change the definability relationships that may exist among variables in Σ but enables to reducing the search space visited by `solve` in the next iterations. As a matter of example, suppose that $\mathcal{C}$ indicates that Σ defines x in terms of $X_\mathcal{C} \subseteq I_x \cup U_x$. For each variable y processed after x by the definability bipartition algorithm, if $X_\mathcal{C} \subseteq I_y \cup U_y$, then the part of the search space where x and x' do not take the same truth value does not have to be explored by `solve`. The clause $(\bigvee_{v \in X_\mathcal{C}} \neg s_v) \vee s_x$ that is recorded prevents such an exploration.

When the decision returned by `solve` is true, Σ does not define x in terms of $I_x \cup U_x$. A model $\mathcal{V}$ of $F \wedge \mathcal{A}$ is exhibited and by construction, the restriction of $\mathcal{V}$ to $Var(\Sigma)$ is a model of Σ. Let y be any variable from U_x. If the canonical term $\gamma_{I_x \cup \{x\} \cup U_x}^{flip(\mathcal{V},y)}$ that coincides with $\mathcal{V}$ on $I_x \cup \{x\}$ and on every variable from U_x but y is consistent with Σ, then Σ does not define y in terms of $I_x \cup \{x\} \cup U_x$. Since $I_x \cup \{x\} \cup U_x \subseteq I_y \cup U_y$ when y is processed after x and x has been put into I, this implies that Σ does not define y in terms of $I_y \cup U_y$. Therefore, y can be put in I as well (and removed from the current set of undecided variables) as soon as x is processed. That way, there is no need to process y later on (one iteration of the definability bipartition algorithm is saved). In order to avoid an expensive SAT call to determine whether $\gamma^{flip(\mathcal{V},y)}_{I_x \cup \{x\} \cup U_x}$ is consistent with Σ, an incomplete local search approach is used instead. The neighborhood of $\mathcal{V}$ constrained by $\gamma^{flip(\mathcal{V},y)}_{I_x \cup \{x\} \cup U_x}$ is explored in search for a partial assignment of the variables of O_x that extends $\gamma^{flip(\mathcal{V},y)}_{I_x \cup \{x\} \cup U_x}$ into a model of Σ.

In the following, before presenting our improved definability bipartition algorithm B+, we first point out a couple of formal results that will be useful to establish the correctness of B+.

3.1 Exploiting UNSAT Witnesses

First, let us consider the case when the decision s returned by solve when x is processed is false. In this case, x is defined in terms of X. Hence, $x \leftrightarrow x'$ is a logical consequence of $\Sigma \wedge \Sigma'_X$. As a consequence, assigning in $Padoa(\Sigma)$ the corresponding selector s_x to true or false does not matter when the selectors associated to the variables $v \in X$ have been set to true. Formally:

Proposition 1. *If Σ defines $x \in Var(\Sigma)$ in terms of $X \subseteq Var(\Sigma) \setminus \{x\}$, then $Padoa(\Sigma) \wedge \bigwedge_{v \in X} s_v$ does not depend on s_x, i.e., it can be rewritten into an equivalent formula into which s_x does not occur.*

As a consequence, *definability recording clauses* that keep track of previously identified definability relationships $X \sqsubseteq_\Sigma \{x\}$ can be freely added to $Padoa(\Sigma)$. Formally, $(\bigvee_{v \in X} \neg s_v) \vee s_x$ is a definability recording clause of Σ if $X \sqsubseteq_\Sigma \{x\}$ holds. The presence of such clauses does not modify the definability relationships between variables of Σ that can be found using $Padoa(\Sigma)$. This is made precise by the following proposition:

Proposition 2. *If R is a set of definability recording clauses of Σ, then for any set $X \subseteq Var(\Sigma)$ of variables and variable $x \in Var(\Sigma)$, we have that $Padoa(\Sigma) \wedge R \wedge \bigwedge_{v \in X} s_v \wedge x \wedge \neg x'$ is inconsistent if and only if $Padoa(\Sigma) \wedge \bigwedge_{v \in X} s_v \wedge x \wedge \neg x'$ is inconsistent.*

A last observation is that the inconsistent core $\mathcal{C}$ returned by solve can be exploited to derive a definability recording clause that is, in general, logically stronger than $(\bigvee_{v \in X} \neg s_v) \vee s_x$:

Proposition 3. *Let $(s, \mathcal{V}, \mathcal{C}) \leftarrow$ solve$(Padoa(\Sigma), \{x, \neg x'\} \cup \{s_v \mid v \in X\})$. If s is false, then Σ defines x in terms of $S = \{v \mid s_v \in \mathcal{C}\}$.*

The definability recording clause $(\bigvee_{v \in S} \neg s_v) \vee s_x$ found using the extracted core can then be added to $Padoa(\Sigma)$ for subsequent computations, as justified by Proposition 2.

Example 3 (Example 2 cont'ed). Suppose that the variables are considered in the following order by the definability bipartition algorithm: e, a, b, c, d. Thus, the first definability test that occurs aims to decide whether Σ defines e in terms of $\{a, b, c, d\}$. In this case, the assumption under consideration is $\mathcal{A} = \{s_a, s_b, s_c, s_d, e, \neg e'\}$. $(false, \emptyset, \{s_b, s_c, s_d, e, \neg e'\})$ could be an outcome returned by the SAT solver. This reflects the fact that $\{b, c, d\} \sqsubseteq_\Sigma \{e\}$ (there is no need to consider a as an input variable for defining e in Σ when b, c, d are already considered as input variables). Consequently, the clause added into F is $\neg s_b \vee \neg s_c \vee \neg s_d \vee s_e$. In the next iteration, when we will check whether Σ defines a in terms of $\{b, c, d\}$, the assumption $\mathcal{A} = \{s_b, s_c, s_d, a, \neg a'\}$ will enforce s_e to be assigned to true without any significant computational effort, thanks to the added clause. Consequently, the two clauses $\neg e \vee e'$ and $e \vee \neg e'$ will be activated, so that solve will not explore the part of the search space where e and e' take distinct truth values.

3.2   Exploiting SAT Witnesses

Now let us consider the case when s is true, so that the variable x tested at the current iteration of the definability bipartition algorithm must be added to I. As we will see, in this case, it is possible to take advantage of the model $\mathcal{V}$ returned by solve and to "dig around" it in order to classify as inputs variables y that are still undecided.

Proposition 4. *Let $X \subseteq Var(\Sigma)$ and $x \in Var(\Sigma)$. If there exists a canonical term γ_X over X such that $\gamma_X \wedge x$ is consistent with Σ and $\gamma_X \wedge \neg x$ is consistent with Σ, then Σ does not define x in terms of X.*

Since the restriction to $Var(\Sigma)$ of the SAT witness returned by solve is a model of Σ, Proposition 4 gives a sufficient condition based on $\mathcal{V}$ that ensures that a variable $y \in U_x$ can be put into I. Indeed, if the canonical term $\gamma_{I_x \cup \{x\} \cup U_x}^{flip(\mathcal{V},y)}$ that coincides with $\mathcal{V}$ on $I_x \cup \{x\}$ and on every variable from U_x but y is consistent with Σ, then Σ does not define y in terms of $I_x \cup \{x\} \cup U_x$. Hence, as explained previously, y can be put in I and removed from the current set of undecided variables.

Because deciding whether $\gamma_{I_x \cup \{x\} \cup U_x}^{flip(\mathcal{V},y)}$ is consistent with Σ is computationally expensive in general (it requires to call a SAT solver if a complete algorithm is expected), we turn to a much cheaper, though incomplete, greedy local search to do the job. One looks for a canonical term γ_{O_x} over O_x such that the interpretation that satisfies $\gamma_{I_x \cup \{x\} \cup U_x}^{flip(\mathcal{V},y)}$ and γ_{O_x} satisfies Σ. Since every variable of $Var(\Sigma)$ is assigned either in $\gamma_{I_x \cup \{x\} \cup U_x}^{flip(\mathcal{V},y)}$ or in γ_{O_x}, the latter model checking test can be achieved in linear time.

Thus, once solve has shown that x must be put in the set I of input variables and has returned a model $\mathcal{V}$ justifying this decision, the variables $y \in U_x$ are considered successively. For each y, starting from $\mathcal{V}$ where the truth value of y has been flipped, we iteratively flip the truth value of variables of O_x. Such flipping operations are made while they lead to an interpretation that decreases

---

Algorithm 2: greedyLS

> **input**   : a CNF formula Σ, (I, U, O) a partition of $Var(\Sigma)$ s.t. Σ defines O in terms of $I \cup U$ and $\mathcal{V}$ a model of Σ over $Var(\Sigma)$.
>
> **output** : $I_U \subseteq U$ such that Σ does not define any variable $y \in I_U$ in terms of $(I \cup U) \setminus \{y\}$.

1 $I_U \leftarrow \emptyset$;

2 foreach $y \in U$ **do**

3 $\quad \mathcal{V}' \leftarrow flip(\mathcal{V}, y)$;

4 $\quad$ **while** $\exists o \in O$ *and* #false$(\Sigma, \ \mathcal{V}') >$ #false$(\Sigma, \ flip(\mathcal{V}', o))$ **do**

5 $\quad \quad \lfloor \ \mathcal{V}' \leftarrow flip(\mathcal{V}', o)$;

6 $\quad$ **if** #false$(\Sigma, \ \mathcal{V}') = 0$ **then** $I_U \leftarrow I_U \cup \{y\}$;

7 return I_U

---

the number of falsified clauses in Σ. If at the end of the process, the number of falsified clauses is zero, then the current interpretation is a model of Σ and since it satisfies $\gamma_{I_x \cup \{x\} \cup U_x}^{flip(\mathcal{V}, y)}$ by construction, y can be definitely put in the set I of input variables that will be returned by the definability bipartition algorithm, so it is removed from the current set of undecided variables. In the remaining case when the number of falsified clauses is not null, no conclusion can be drawn. y is kept in the current set of undecided variables and it will be put in I or in O later on (at last, during the iteration when y will be processed).

Algorithm 2 implements the greedy local search process greedyLS. It takes as input the CNF formula Σ, a partition (I, U, O) of $Var(\Sigma)$ s.t. Σ defines O in terms of $I \cup U$, and a model $\mathcal{V}$ of Σ over $Var(\Sigma)$. The algorithm returns a subset of variables I_U of U such that Σ does not define any variable y of I_U in terms of $(I \cup U) \setminus \{y\}$. It starts by initializing I_U to the empty set (line 1). For each variable y in U, the algorithm tests whether y can be moved into I_U (lines 2–6). To do so, at line 3 the interpretation $\mathcal{V}'$ obtained by flipping the truth value of y in $\mathcal{V}$ is considered. Then, while it is possible to decrease the number of falsified clauses of Σ by flipping the truth value of some output variable $o \in O$, the truth value of o in $\mathcal{V}'$ is flipped (lines 4–5). If at line 6 the number of falsified clauses is zero, then y fulfills the expected requirement (the resulting interpretation $\mathcal{V}'$ is a model of Σ) and y can be added safely to the set I_U of variables (thus, its status changes from "undecided" to "input"). Finally, I_U is returned at line 7.

A last, yet useful observation, is that the SAT witness $\mathcal{V}$ returned by solve run on its input $F \wedge \mathcal{A}$ when variable x is processed can be exploited to derive not only one model of Σ but in general *two* models of Σ that can be used to classify as inputs variables that are still undecided when x is processed. As explained before, the restriction of $\mathcal{V}$ to $Var(\Sigma)$ is one of them, but there is a second interpretation that can be exploited, namely the interpretation over $Var(\Sigma)$ obtained from the restriction of $\mathcal{V}$ to $\{v' \mid v \in Var(\Sigma)\}$ by "renaming back" every variable v' into v.

Example 4 (Example 3 cont'ed). Suppose now that the variables have been considered in the following order by the definability bipartition algorithm: e, b, a,

---

Algorithm 3: B+

    input   : a CNF formula Σ
    output : $\langle I, O \rangle$ a subset-minimal definability bipartition of $Var(\Sigma)$
 1 $\langle \Sigma, O, \mathbb{M} \rangle \leftarrow$ backbone(Σ);
 2 $I \leftarrow \emptyset$;
 3 **foreach** $\mathcal{M} \in \mathbb{M}$ **do**
 4     $\lfloor$ $I \leftarrow I \cup$ greedyLS$(\Sigma, (I, Var(\Sigma) \setminus (I \cup O), O), \mathcal{M})$;
 5 $\Psi \leftarrow Padoa(\Sigma)$;
 6 $U \leftarrow Var(\Sigma) \setminus (I \cup O)$;
 7 **while** $U \neq \emptyset$ **do**
 8   Pick a variable x in U and remove it from U;
 9     $(s, \mathcal{V}, \mathcal{C}) \leftarrow$ solve$(\Psi, \{s_v | v \in I \cup U\} \cup \{x, \neg x'\})$;
10   **if** s *is false* **then**
11        $\mid$ $O \leftarrow O \cup \{x\}$;
12        $\mid$ $\Psi \leftarrow \Psi \wedge (s_x \vee \bigvee_{s_v \in \mathcal{C}} \neg v)$
13   **else**
14        $I \leftarrow I \cup \{x\}$;
15        $I \leftarrow I \cup$ greedyLS$(\Sigma, (I, U, O), \{\ell \in \mathcal{V} \mid var(\ell) \in Var(\Sigma)\})$;
16        $U \leftarrow U \setminus I$;
17        $I \leftarrow I \cup$ greedyLS$(\Sigma, (I, U, O), \{\ell \mid \ell' \in \mathcal{V}$ and $var(\ell') \in Var(\Sigma'_{\emptyset})\})$;
18        $\lfloor$ $U \leftarrow U \setminus I$;
19 **return** $\langle I, O \rangle$

---

c, d. And that e has already been processed and classified as an output variable. Then the next step is to determine whether Σ defines b in terms of $\{a, c, d\}$. In this case, the assumption under consideration is $\mathcal{A} = \{s_a, s_c, s_d, b, \neg b'\}$ and a possible outcome of solve is $(true, \mathcal{V} = \{\neg a, b, \neg c, d, e, \neg a', \neg b', \neg c', d', e', s_a, \neg s_b, s_c, s_d, s_e\}, \emptyset)$. Hence, b can be put into the set of input variables. Before considering the next iteration of the definability bipartition algorithm, it is possible to take advantage of two models of Σ to determine whether some variables that are currently undecided can be classified as inputs. The two models are $\{\neg a, b, \neg c, d, e\}$ (obtained by restricting $\mathcal{V}$ to $Var(\Sigma)$) and $\{\neg a, \neg b, \neg c, d, e\}$ (obtained from the restriction of $\mathcal{V}$ to $\{v' \mid v \in Var(\Sigma)\}$ by "renaming back" every variable v' into v). Digging around $\{\neg a, b, \neg c, d, e\}$, we can check that the interpretation $\{\neg a, b, \neg c, \neg d, \neg e\}$ is a model of Σ. As a consequence, variable d which is still undecided can be put into the set of input variables. Digging around $\{\neg a, \neg b, \neg c, d, e\}$, we can check that the interpretation $\{\neg a, \neg b, c, d, e\}$ also is a model of Σ. Therefore, the undecided variable c can be put as well into the set of input variables. Hence, only variable a remains undecided after two iterations provided that the order e, b, a, c, d has been used.

3.3 Improving B by Considering SAT Oracle Witnesses

Algorithm 3 gives the pseudo-code of B+, our implementation of the improved version of B that exploits the witnesses returned by the SAT oracle solve.

B+ starts by computing the backbone of Σ using the algorithm proposed in [8]. Starting from a model ω of Σ and considering each literal ℓ satisfied by ω in an iterative way, one tests the consistency of $\Sigma \wedge \neg\ell$. If $\Sigma \wedge \neg\ell$ is consistent, then a model of Σ different from ω is exhibited and we can conclude that neither ℓ nor its negation belongs to the backbone of Σ. Otherwise, ℓ belongs to the backbone of Σ. Contrary to what happens in B, where the models generated during the computation of the backbone are not used, they are exploited in B+. At line 1, Σ is simplified by its backbone, O is assigned to the set of variables belonging to the backbone and $\mathbb{M}$ is a set of models of Σ found as a by-product of the computation of the backbone. I is set to the empty set at line 2. Then, for each model $\mathcal{M}$ in $\mathbb{M}$, the greedy algorithm `greedyLS` is called in order to spot input variables (lines 3–4). More precisely, additional input variables are gathered into I in an iterative way by calling `greedyLS` on Σ and the given model $\mathcal{M}$. O is not modified during those iterations over $\mathbb{M}$, but as soon as input variables are detected, they are added into I (line 4), hence I usually changes (and as a consequence $Var(\Sigma) \setminus (I \cup O)$ changes as well) during the iterations.

Then, Padoa's theorem is leveraged. First, at line 5, Ψ is initialized with the CNF formula $Padoa(\Sigma)$. At line 6, the set of undecided variables U is set to the variables that have not been classified so far as inputs or outputs. Then, while some undecided variables remain, one variable is selected and a call to the SAT solver `solve` is performed (lines 7–18). More precisely, at line 8, a variable x belonging to U is selected and it is removed from U. `solve` is called at line 9 with the formula Ψ, and its output is stored in the triple $(s, \mathcal{V}, \mathcal{C})$. The set of assumption variables used for this call contains x, x' and the propositional variables that correspond to selectors s_v making equivalent the pairs of variables v, v' in $I \cup U$.

Depending on the value of s, two cases have to be considered (lines 10–18). If s is false, which means Ψ is inconsistent regarding the given assumptions, then x is added into the set of output variables (line 11) and a definability recording clause, as presented in Sect. 3.1, is added to Ψ (line 12). If s is true, which means Ψ is consistent under the considered assumptions, then the input set of variables I is updated with x (line 14). From the model $\mathcal{V}$ found by `solve`, two models of Σ can be extracted in general, as explained previously. Consequently, it is possible to call `greedyLS` twice in order to try and collect additional input variables (lines 15–18). The first call is made at line 15, where the function `greedyLS` is called with the CNF formula Σ, O the set of already identified output variables, U the set of undecided variables and the restriction of $\mathcal{V}$ to the variables of Σ. Then, the set of undecided variables U is updated to take into account the variables that have just been identified as inputs (line 16). The second call to `greedyLS` differs from the first one only as to the model of Σ used. For the second call, the restriction of $\mathcal{V}$ to $\{v' \mid v \in Var(\Sigma)\}$ obtained by "renaming back" its literals is considered. Again, at line 18, U is updated to take account for the update of I at line 17. Finally, the computed bipartition is returned at line 19.

The following proposition ensures that the bipartition computed by Algorithm 3, when considering Σ as an input, is a subset-minimal definability bipartition of Σ.

Proposition 5. *Algorithm 3 is correct and it terminates after a number of calls to a SAT oracle that does not exceed $2n + 1$ if n is the number of variables in $Var(\Sigma)$.*

4   Experimental Evaluation

Our objective was to evaluate empirically the benefits offered by the use of SAT witnesses of each type within B+. In our experiments, we have considered 1942 CNF instances from the *Compile!* project.[3] Those instances are gathered into 8 datasets, as follows: BN (Bayes nets) (1116), BMC (Bounded Model Checking) (18), Circuit (41), Configuration (35), Handmade (58), Planning (557), Random (104), Qif (7) (Quantitative Information Flow analysis - security) and Scheduling (6). We have also considered 1200 instances from the model counting and the projected model counting tracks of the last model counting competitions (see https://mccompetition.org (2020–2022)). The SAT solver (solve) used was Glucose [1]. Our experiments have been conducted on Intel Xeon E5-2643 (3.30 GHz) processors with 32 GiB RAM on Linux CentOS. A time-out of 100 s and a memory-out of 7.6 GiB have been considered for each instance.

For each instance, we measured the time needed by B+ to derive a subset-minimal definability bipartition. For each run, the opportunity of exploiting cores (core) or models (model) has been activated or not, rendering possible to compare four variants of B+ depending on the choices made for the two parameters. The version where cores and models are not used is noted (init) in the following. It merely boils down to B and is considered as a baseline approach in the comparison.

Table 1 presents the number of instances for which B+ terminated in due time and returned a subset-minimal definability bipartition. From this table, it is clear that exploiting SAT witnesses really helps in practice to reduce the time needed to compute a subset-minimal bipartition. Furthermore, whatever the benchmark category considered, the version of B+ equipped with both SAT and UNSAT witnesses solved systematically at least as many instances as B (init), and for several datasets, significantly more instances. A similar conclusion can be drawn for the versions of B+ equipped with either SAT or UNSAT witnesses. No significant degradation of performance in terms of the number of instances solved in due time can be observed (compared to B (init), only one instance from the Planning dataset is lost by B+ equipped with SAT witnesses). Thus, B+ equipped with both SAT and UNSAT solved 72 more instances than the baseline approach (2859 vs. 2787), 21 more instances than the version of B+ that only uses SAT witnesses (2859 vs. 2838), and 51 more instances than the version of B+ that only uses UNSAT witnesses (2859 vs. 2808). From this table, we also observe

---

[3] See http://www.cril.univ-artois.fr/kc/benchmarks.html for details.

Table 1. The table shows the number of instances solved by different versions of B+ within a time limit of 100 s and a memory limit of 7680 MB.

	Method			
	init	model	core	core+model
Competition	930	966	937	**973**
BN	1078	**1081**	1079	**1081**
Handmade	38	39	42	**43**
Circuit	**36**	**36**	**36**	**36**
Planning	548	547	**557**	**557**
Random	95	**104**	95	**104**
BMC	**18**	**18**	**18**	**18**
Configuration	**35**	**35**	**35**	**35**
Qif	**7**	**7**	**7**	**7**
Scheduling	2	5	2	5
Total	2787	2838	2808	**2859**

that the best improvement is obtained when considering the two types of SAT witnesses at the same time, which means that the benefits offered by each type of witness are complementary.

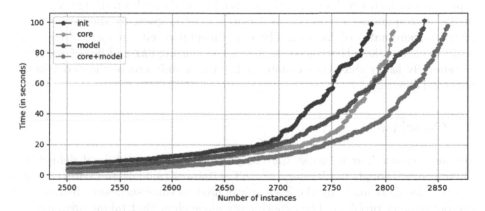

Fig. 1. Cactus plot used to compare different versions of B+. The number of instances solved is provided on the x-axis and the time needed to solve them on the y-axis.

The cactus plot in Fig. 1 compares the run times of the four different versions of B+. It shows that whatever the time limit between 10 and 100 s, the `init` configuration solves systematically less instances than the other configurations (this behavior still occurs when the time limit is set to a value less than 10 s, we do not report this part of the cactus here because the figure becomes hard to be

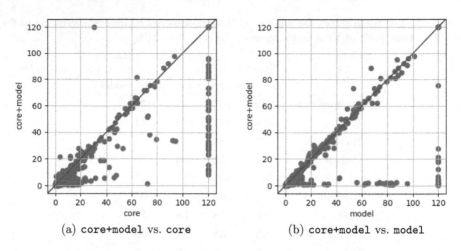

(a) core+model vs. core   (b) core+model vs. model

Fig. 2. Comparing the run times of different versions of B+.

read). Figure 1 also shows that when instances become harder, the performance gap between B+ and B increases with the time bound, which demonstrates that using SAT witnesses is all the more efficient when the instance under consideration appears as difficult.

Figure 2 shows a comparison between between B+ equipped with core+model and the versions of B+ where only one of core or model is used. Each dot represents an instance. The time (in seconds) needed to solve it using the version of B+ corresponding to the x-axis (resp. y-axis) is given by the x-coordinate (resp. y-coordinate) of the dot. The experimental results, reported in Figs. 2a and 2b, clearly show that the version of B+ exploiting SAT and UNSAT witnesses is generally faster than the versions of B+ where only one of the two types of witness is leveraged.

5   Conclusion

We have shown how to boost the computation of subset-minimal definability bipartitions through the leverage of SAT witnesses (models and cores) justifying the decisions made by the SAT solver used to solve successive instances of the definability problem. The experiments made show that taking advantage of both models and cores is useful in practice. Our new algorithm B+ for computing subset-minimal definability bipartitions clearly outperforms the previous algorithm, B, developed so far for the same purpose.

Acknowledgements. The authors would like to thank the anonymous reviewers for their comments and insights. This work has benefited from the support of the PING/ACK project (ANR-18-CE40-0011) of the French National Research Agency (ANR).

References

1. Audemard, G., Lagniez, J.-M., Simon, L.: Improving glucose for incremental SAT solving with assumptions: application to MUS extraction. In: Järvisalo, M., Van Gelder, A. (eds.) SAT 2013. LNCS, vol. 7962, pp. 309–317. Springer, Heidelberg (2013). https://doi.org/10.1007/978-3-642-39071-5_23
2. Beth, E.: On Padoa's method in the theory of definition. Indag. Math. **15**, 330–339 (1953)
3. Eén, N., Sörensson, N.: An extensible SAT-solver. In: Giunchiglia, E., Tacchella, A. (eds.) SAT 2003. LNCS, vol. 2919, pp. 502–518. Springer, Heidelberg (2004). https://doi.org/10.1007/978-3-540-24605-3_37
4. Ivrii, A., Malik, S., Meel, K.S., Vardi, M.Y.: On computing minimal independent support and its applications to sampling and counting. Constraints Int. J. **21**(1), 41–58 (2016). https://doi.org/10.1007/s10601-015-9204-z
5. Kiesel, R., Totis, P., Kimmig, A.: Efficient knowledge compilation beyond weighted model counting. Theory Pract. Log. Program. **22**(4), 505–522 (2022). https://doi.org/10.1017/S147106842200014X
6. Lagniez, J., Lonca, E., Marquis, P.: Improving model counting by leveraging definability. In: Kambhampati, S. (ed.) Proceedings of the Twenty-Fifth International Joint Conference on Artificial Intelligence, IJCAI 2016, New York, NY, USA, 9–15 July 2016, pp. 751–757. IJCAI/AAAI Press (2016). http://www.ijcai.org/Abstract/16/112
7. Lagniez, J., Lonca, E., Marquis, P.: Definability for model counting. Artif. Intell. **281**, 103229 (2020). https://doi.org/10.1016/j.artint.2019.103229
8. Lagniez, J., Marquis, P.: On preprocessing techniques and their impact on propositional model counting. J. Autom. Reason. **58**(4), 413–481 (2017). https://doi.org/10.1007/s10817-016-9370-8
9. Lang, J., Liberatore, P., Marquis, P.: Propositional independence: formula-variable independence and forgetting. J. Artif. Intell. Res. **18**, 391–443 (2003)
10. Lang, J., Marquis, P.: On propositional definability. Artif. Intell. **172**(8–9), 991–1017 (2008). https://doi.org/10.1016/j.artint.2007.12.003
11. Lin, F., Reiter, R.: Forget it! In: Proceedings of AAAI Fall Symposium on Relevance, pp. 154–159 (1994)
12. Marques-Silva, J., Lynce, I., Malik, S.: Conflict-driven clause learning SAT solvers. In: Biere, A., Heule, M., van Maaren, H., Walsh, T. (eds.) Handbook of Satisfiability - Second Edition. Frontiers in Artificial Intelligence and Applications, vol. 336, pp. 133–182. IOS Press (2021). https://doi.org/10.3233/FAIA200987
13. Padoa, A.: Essai d'une théorie algébrique des nombres entiers, précédé d'une introduction logique à une théorie déductive quelconque. In: Bibliothèque du Congrès International de Philosophie, Paris, pp. 309–365 (1903)
14. Soos, M., Meel, K.S.: Arjun: an efficient independent support computation technique and its applications to counting and sampling. In: Mitra, T., Young, E.F.Y., Xiong, J. (eds.) Proceedings of the 41st IEEE/ACM International Conference on Computer-Aided Design, ICCAD 2022, San Diego, California, USA, 30 October–3 November 2022, p. 71. ACM (2022). https://doi.org/10.1145/3508352.3549406

Hybrid Modal Operators for Definite Descriptions

Przemysław Andrzej Wałęga[1,2] and Michał Zawidzki[1,2(✉)]

[1] University of Łódź, Łódź, Poland
[2] University of Oxford, Oxford, UK
{przemyslaw.walega,michal.zawidzki}@cs.ox.ac.uk

Abstract. In this paper, we study computational complexity and expressive power of modal operators for definite descriptions, which correspond to statements 'the modal world which satisfies formula φ'. We show that adding such operators to the basic (propositional) modal language has a price of increasing complexity of the satisfiability problem from PSpace to ExpTime. However, if formulas corresponding to descriptions are Boolean only, there is no increase of complexity. Furthermore, we compare definite descriptions with the related operators from hybrid and counting logics. We prove that the operators for definite descriptions are strictly more expressive than hybrid operators, but strictly less expressive than counting operators. We show that over linear structures the same expressive power results hold as in the general case; in contrast, if the linear structures are isomorphic to integers, definite descriptions become as expressive as counting operators.

Keywords: Definite descriptions · Modal logics · Hybrid operators · Counting operators · Computational complexity · Expressive power

1 Introduction

Definite descriptions are term-forming expressions such as 'the x such that $\varphi(x)$', which are usually represented with Peano's ι-operator as $\iota x\varphi(x)$ [28]. Such expressions intend to denote a single object satisfying a property φ, but providing a complete formal theory for them turns out to be a complex task due to several non-intuitive cases, for example, when there exists no object satisfying φ, when there are multiple such objects, or when a formula with a definite description is in the scope of negation. As a result, a number of competing theories have been proposed [7,20,24,33,34], including Russell's famous approach according to which the underlying logical form of a sentence '$\iota x\varphi(x)$ satisfies ψ' is that 'there exists exactly one x which satisfies φ and moreover this x satisfies ψ' [29].

More recently it has been observed that definite descriptions, and referring expressions in general, provide a convenient way of identifying objects in information and knowledge base management systems [6,13]. Such expressions can be

S. Gaggl et al. (Eds.): JELIA 2023, LNAI 14281, pp. 712–726, 2023.
https://doi.org/10.1007/978-3-031-43619-2_48

used to replace obscure identifiers [13,14], enhance query answering [38], identify problems in conceptual modelling [12], and identity resolution in ontology-based data access [39,40]. For this reason referring expressions have been studied in the setting of description logics (DLs) [5,25,38]—well-known formalisms for ontologies and the Semantic Web. In particular, Neuhaus et al. [26] introduced free DLs (free of the presupposition that each term denotes) with three alternative dual-domain semantics: positive, negative, and gapping, where statements in ABoxes and TBoxes involving non-referring expressions can still be true, become automatically false, or lack a truth value, respectively. Artale et al. [6], in turn, proposed free DLs using single domain semantics; they introduced definite descriptions in DLs by allowing for expressions of the form $\{\iota C\}$, whose extension is a singleton containing the unique element of which a (potentially complex) concept C holds, or the empty set if there does not exist such a unique element. Definite descriptions can therefore be seen as a generalisation of nominals, which in DLs take the form $\{a\}$ with a being an individual name. Since Artale et al. do not assume that all individual names must refer, a nominal $\{a\}$ with a being a non-referring name, denotes the empty set. As shown by Artale et al. [6], definite descriptions can be simulated in DLs with nominals and the universal role. In particular, adding definite descriptions to $\mathcal{ALCO}_u$ (i.e., $\mathcal{ALC}$ with nominals and the universal role) does not increase the computational complexity of checking ontology satisfiability, which remains ExpTime-complete.

In modal logics nominals are treated as specific atoms which must hold in single modal worlds [9,15,19,32]. Satisfaction operators $@_i$, in turn, are indexed with nominals i and allow us to write formulas such as $@_i\varphi$, whose meaning is that φ holds in the unique modal world in which nominal i holds (but φ can also hold in other worlds). Nominals and satisfaction operators constitute the standard *hybrid machinery*, which added to the basic modal logic gives rise to the hybrid logic $\mathcal{H}(@)$ [3,8]. Such a machinery increases the expressiveness of the basic modal logic by making it possible, for example, to encode irreflexivity or atransitivity of the accessibility relation. At the same time the computational complexity of the satisfiability problem in $\mathcal{H}(@)$ remains PSpace-complete, so the same as in the basic modal logic [1]. On the other hand, introducing further hybrid operators or considering temporal hybrid logics oftentimes has a drastic impact on the computational complexity [1–3,18,36].

Closely related are also the *difference* D and the *universal* A modalities. Adding any of them to the basic modal language makes the satisfiability problem ExpTime-complete [10]. It is not hard to show that D allows us to express nominals and satisfaction operators; what is more interesting, however, is that the basic modal logic with D is equivalent to the hybrid modal logic with A [19]. Furthermore, one can observe that having access to both A and nominals enables to express definite descriptions by marking with a nominal the unique world in which the definite description holds, and using A to state that this description holds only it the world satisfying this nominal (as observed by Artale et al. [6]).

Uniqueness of a world can also be expressed in the *modal logic with counting* $\mathcal{MLC}$, which extends the basic modal language with counting operators of the form $\exists_{\geq n}$, where $n \in \mathbb{N}$, and $\exists_{\geq n}\varphi$ states that φ holds in at least n distinct worlds [4]. Using Boolean connectives and $\exists_{\geq n}$ enables to also express the counting operators of the forms $\exists_{\leq n}$ and $\exists_{=n}$. Such operators can be used to encode the hybrid machinery, as well as A and D, but this comes at a considerable complexity cost. In particular, the satisfiability problem in $\mathcal{MLC}$ is ExpTime-complete if numbers n in counting operators are encoded in unary [37] and it is NExpTime-complete if the numbers are encoded in binary [30,31,41].

In contrast to the extensive studies of hybrid and counting modal operators, as well as definite descriptions in first-order modal logics [17,21,22,27], definite descriptions have not been thoroughly analysed in propositional modal logics, which we address in this paper. To this end, we consider the basic modal language and extend it with a (hybrid) modal operator for definite descriptions $@_\varphi$ which can be indexed with an arbitrary modal formula φ. The intuitive meaning of $@_\varphi\psi$ is that ψ holds in the unique world in which φ holds. Our goal is to determine the computational cost of adding such definite descriptions to the language, and to investigate the expressive power of the obtained logic, denoted as $\mathcal{ML}(\mathsf{DD})$.

The main contributions of this paper are as follows:

1. We show that adding to the basic modal language definite descriptions $@_\varphi$ with Boolean φ (so φ does not mention modal operators) can be done with no extra computational cost. In other words, satisfiability of $\mathcal{ML}(\mathsf{DD})$-formulas with Boolean definite descriptions is PSpace-complete. The main part of the proof is to show the upper bound by reducing $\mathcal{ML}(\mathsf{DD})$-satisfiability to the existence of a winning strategy in a specific game played on Hintikka sets.

2. On the other hand, if we allow for arbitrary φ's in definite descriptions, the satisfiability problem becomes ExpTime-complete. Thus, the computational price of adding non-Boolean definite descriptions is the same as for adding the universal modal operator A or counting operators $\exists_{\geq n}$ with numbers n encoded in unary. The important ingredient of the proof is showing the lower bound by reducing satisfiability in the basic modal logic with the universal modality A to $\mathcal{ML}(\mathsf{DD})$-satisfiability.

3. We show that, over the class of all frames, $\mathcal{ML}(\mathsf{DD})$ is strictly more expressive than $\mathcal{H}(@)$, but strictly less expressive than $\mathcal{MLC}$. In particular, $\mathcal{MLC}$ can define frames with domains of cardinality n, for any $n \in \mathbb{N}$. On the other hand, the only frame cardinality $\mathcal{ML}(\mathsf{DD})$ can define is 1, and $\mathcal{H}(@)$ cannot define any frame properties related to cardinality.

4. We prove that over linear frames the same expressiveness results hold as for arbitrary frames, but over the integer frame $\mathcal{ML}(\mathsf{DD})$ becomes as expressive as $\mathcal{MLC}$. In particular, over such a frame the operators $\exists_{\geq n}$ become expressible in $\mathcal{ML}(\mathsf{DD})$, which is still not the case for $\mathcal{H}(@)$.

The rest of the paper is organised as follows. In Sect. 2 we present $\mathcal{ML}(\mathsf{DD})$ formally. We obtain its syntax by extending the basic modal logic with definite description operators $@_\varphi$ and we provide the semantics for these operators exploiting the standard Russellian theory of definite descriptions. We also present $\mathcal{H}(@)$ and $\mathcal{MLC}$, which are considered in the later parts of the paper. In Sect. 3 we prove both of our computational complexity results, namely tight PSpace and

ExpTime bounds. Then, in Sect. 4 we turn our attention to expressive power; we define notions used to compare the expressive power of the logics in question and present a variant of bisimulation which is adequate for $\mathcal{ML}(\mathsf{DD})$. We show results that hold over arbitrary and linear frames, and we finish with results that hold over integers. Finally, we briefly conclude the paper in Sect. 5.

2   Logic of Definite Descriptions and Related Formalisms

In what follows, we introduce formally the modal logic of definite descriptions $\mathcal{ML}(\mathsf{DD})$ and present closely related logics which were studied in the literature.

We let formulas of $\mathcal{ML}(\mathsf{DD})$ be defined as in the basic modal logic, but we additionally allow for using the operator @ to construct formulas of the form $@_\varphi\psi$ whose intended meaning is that formula ψ holds in the unique world in which formula φ holds.

Formally, $\mathcal{ML}(\mathsf{DD})$-formulas are generated by the grammar

$$\varphi ::= p \mid \neg\varphi \mid \varphi \vee \varphi \mid \Diamond\varphi \mid @_\varphi\varphi,$$

where p ranges over the set PROP of propositional variables. We refer to an expression $@_\varphi$ as a *definite description*—DD in short—and we call it *Boolean* if so is φ (i.e., φ does not mention $\Diamond$ or @). We will also use $\bot$, $\top$, $\wedge$, $\rightarrow$, and $\Box$, which stand for the usual abbreviations. We let $\mathsf{PROP}(\varphi)$ be the set of propositional variables occurring in φ and the *modal depth*, $\mathsf{md}(\varphi)$, of φ the deepest nesting of $\Diamond$ in φ.

We will consider the Kripke-style semantics of $\mathcal{ML}(\mathsf{DD})$, where a *frame* is a pair $\mathcal{F} = (W, R)$ consisting of a non-empty set W of worlds and an accessibility relation $R \subseteq W \times W$. A *model* based on a frame $\mathcal{F} = (W, R)$ is a tuple $\mathcal{M} = (W, R, V)$, where $V : \mathsf{PROP} \longrightarrow \mathcal{P}(W)$ is a valuation assigning a set of worlds to each propositional variable. The *satisfaction relation* $\models$ for $\mathcal{M} = (W, R, V)$ and $w \in W$ is defined inductively as follows:

$$
\begin{aligned}
\mathcal{M}, w \models p \qquad &\text{iff} \quad w \in V(p), \text{ for each } p \in \mathsf{PROP} \\
\mathcal{M}, w \models \neg\varphi \qquad &\text{iff} \quad \mathcal{M}, w \not\models \varphi \\
\mathcal{M}, w \models \varphi_1 \vee \varphi_2 \qquad &\text{iff} \quad \mathcal{M}, w \models \varphi_1 \text{ or } \mathcal{M}, w \models \varphi_2 \\
\mathcal{M}, w \models \Diamond\varphi \qquad &\text{iff} \quad \text{there exists } v \in W \text{ such that } (w, v) \in R \text{ and } \mathcal{M}, v \models \varphi \\
\mathcal{M}, w \models @_{\varphi_1}\varphi_2 \qquad &\text{iff} \quad \text{there exists } v \in W \text{ such that } \mathcal{M}, v \models \varphi_1, \mathcal{M}, v \models \varphi_2 \\
&\qquad\quad \text{and } \mathcal{M}, v' \not\models \varphi_1 \text{ for all } v' \neq v \text{ in } W
\end{aligned}
$$

We say that φ is *satisfiable* if there exist $\mathcal{M}$ and w such that $\mathcal{M}, w \models \varphi$; we will focus on checking satisfiability as the main reasoning task.

It is worth observing that $\mathcal{ML}(\mathsf{DD})$ allows us to naturally express definite descriptions with both the *external* and *internal* negation. The first type of negation corresponds to sentences of the form 'it is not the case that the x such that φ satisfies ψ' which can be written as $\neg@_\varphi\psi$. The internal negation occurs in sentences of the form 'the x such that φ does not satisfy ψ', which can be expressed in $\mathcal{ML}(\mathsf{DD})$ as $@_\varphi \neg \psi$.

Next, we present well-studied extensions of the basic modal language which are particularly relevant for investigating $\mathcal{ML}(\mathsf{DD})$, namely the logic $\mathcal{MLC}$ with counting operators $\exists_{\geq n}$, with any $n \in \mathbb{N}$ [2,4], and the logic $\mathcal{H}(@)$ with hybrid operators $@_i$, where i is a nominal (i.e., an atom which holds in exactly one world) [1,3]. The intended reading of $\exists_{\geq n}\varphi$ is that φ holds in at least n distinct worlds, whereas $@_i\varphi$ is that φ holds in the unique world labelled by i.

Formally, $\mathcal{MLC}$-formulas are generated by the grammar

$$\varphi ::= p \mid \neg\varphi \mid \varphi \vee \varphi \mid \Diamond\varphi \mid \exists_{\geq n}\varphi,$$

where $p \in \mathsf{PROP}$ and $n \in \mathbb{N}$. We will also use $\exists_{\leq n}\varphi$ as an abbreviation for $\neg\exists_{\geq n+1}\varphi$ and $\exists_{=n}\varphi$ as an abbreviation for $\exists_{\geq n}\varphi \wedge \exists_{\leq n}\varphi$. The semantics of $\mathcal{MLC}$ is obtained by extending the basic modal logic semantics with the condition

$$\mathcal{M}, w \models \exists_{\geq n}\varphi \quad \text{iff} \quad \text{there are at least } n \text{ worlds } v \in W \text{ such that } \mathcal{M}, v \models \varphi$$

Formulas of $\mathcal{H}(@)$, in turn, are generated by the grammar

$$\varphi ::= p \mid i \mid \neg\varphi \mid \varphi \vee \varphi \mid \Diamond\varphi \mid @_i\varphi,$$

for $p \in \mathsf{PROP}$ and i belonging to the set NOM of *nominals*. The semantics of $\mathcal{H}(@)$ exploits *hybrid models* $\mathcal{M} = (W, R, V)$ which are defined like standard modal models except that $V : \mathsf{PROP} \cup \mathsf{NOM} \longrightarrow \mathcal{P}(W)$ assigns not only sets of worlds to propositional variables, but also singleton sets to nominals. Then the conditions of the satisfaction relation are extended with

$$\mathcal{M}, w \models i \qquad \text{iff} \qquad V(i) = \{w\}, \text{ for each } i \in \mathsf{NOM}$$
$$\mathcal{M}, w \models @_i\varphi \qquad \text{iff} \qquad \mathcal{M}, v \models \varphi, \text{ for } v \text{ such that } V(i) = \{v\}$$

We can already observe some relations between definite descriptions $@_\varphi$, the counting operator $\exists_{=1}$, and satisfaction operators $@_i$. For example, $@_\varphi\psi$ can be expressed as $\exists_{=1}\varphi \wedge \exists_{=1}(\varphi \wedge \psi)$, which states that φ holds in a single world and that ψ also holds in this world. On the other hand we can simulate a nominal i with a propositional variable p_i by writing a formula $@_{p_i}\top$, which guarantees the existence of the unique world in which p_i holds. Then $@_i\varphi$ can be simulated as $@_{p_i}\varphi$; note that for the latter simulation we use only Boolean DDs. In the following sections we will study the relation between logics with these operators in detail. In particular, we will aim to determine how the complexity and expressiveness of $\mathcal{ML}(\mathsf{DD})$ compares to the ones of the related logics.

3   Computational Complexity

In this section, we investigate the computational complexity of the satisfiably problem in $\mathcal{ML}(\mathsf{DD})$. First, we show that if we allow for Boolean DDs only, the problem is PSpace-complete, that is, the same as in the language without DDs;

hence, extending the language in this way can be performed with no computational cost. However, in the second result we show that in the case of arbitrary DDs the problem becomes ExpTime-complete, and so, the computational price of adding DDs is the same as for adding counting quantifiers (with numbers encoded in unary) [2,37] or for adding the universal modality [10].

We start by showing PSpace-completeness of the satisfiability problem in the case of Boolean DDs. The lower bound follows trivially from PSpace-completeness of the same problem in basic modal logic [10,23]. For the upper bound, we show that the problem reduces to checking the existence of a winning strategy in a specific two-player game. States of this game can be represented in polynomial space, and so, we can check the existence of a winning strategy in PSpace. It is worth observing that a similar technique was used to show the PSpace upper bound for $\mathcal{H}(@)$ [1] and for modal logics of topological spaces with the universal modality [35].

Our game for checking if an input formula φ is satisfiable will be played using φ-Hintikka sets defined as follows.

Definition 1. *We let the* closure, $cl(\varphi)$, *of an $\mathcal{ML}(DD)$-formula φ be the minimal set of formulas which contains all subformulas of φ, and such that if $\psi \in cl(\varphi)$ but ψ is not of the form $\neg\chi$, then $\neg\psi \in cl(\varphi)$. A φ-Hintikka set H is any maximal subset of $cl(\varphi)$ which satisfies the following conditions, for all $\psi, \psi_1, \psi_2 \in H$:*

- *if $\neg\psi \in cl(\varphi)$, then $\neg\psi \in H$ if and only if $\psi \notin H$,*
- *if $\psi_1 \vee \psi_2 \in cl(\varphi)$, then $\psi_1 \vee \psi_2 \in H$ if and only if $\psi_1 \in H$ or $\psi_2 \in H$.*

For example, if φ is of the form $@_{\neg(p\vee\neg p)}$ then $\{p, (p\vee\neg p), @_{\neg(p\vee\neg p)}\}$ constitutes a φ-Hintikka set. Note that although φ-Hintikka sets are consistent with respect to Boolean connectives, they do not need to be consistent (i.e., satisfiable) in general; indeed, $@_{\neg(p\vee\neg p)}$ in the set above is unsatisfiable.

Given the definition of a φ-Hintikka set we are ready to present the game. To this end, we will use the symbol $DD(\varphi)$ to represent the set of all formulas ψ such that $@_\psi$ occurs in φ.

Definition 2. *For an $\mathcal{ML}(DD)$-formula φ we let the φ-game be played between Eloise and Abelard as follows. In the first turn Eloise needs to provide a set $\mathcal{H}$ of at most $|DD(\varphi)| + 1$ φ-Hintikka sets and a relation $R \subseteq \mathcal{H} \times \mathcal{H}$ such that:*

- *$\varphi \in H$, for some $H \in \mathcal{H}$,*
- *each $\psi \in DD(\varphi)$ can occur in at most one $H \in \mathcal{H}$,*
- *for all $@_\psi\chi \in cl(\varphi)$ and $H \in \mathcal{H}$ we have $@_\psi\chi \in H$ iff there is $H' \in \mathcal{H}$ such that $\{\psi, \chi\} \subseteq H'$,*
- *and for all $\Diamond\psi \in cl(\varphi)$, if $R(H, H')$ and $\psi \in H'$, then $\Diamond\psi \in H$.*

Then Abelard and Eloise play in turns. Abelard selects $H \in$ Current (initially Current $= \mathcal{H}$) and a formula $\Diamond\varphi' \in H$, which he wants to verify. This $\Diamond\varphi'$ needs to have the modal depth not larger than $md(\varphi)$ decreased by the number of turns Abelard already played. Then it is Eloise's turn in which she needs to provide a witnessing φ-Hintikka set H' such that

- $\varphi' \in H'$,
- if $H' \cap \mathsf{DD}(\varphi) \neq \emptyset$, then $H' \in \mathcal{H}$,
- for all $@_\psi \chi \in \mathsf{cl}(\varphi)$ we have $@_\psi \chi \in H'$ iff there is $H'' \in \mathcal{H}$ such that $\{\psi, \chi\} \subseteq H''$,
- and for all $\Diamond \psi \in \mathsf{cl}(\varphi)$, if $\psi \in H'$, then $\Diamond \psi \in H$.

If $H' \cap \mathsf{DD}(\varphi) \neq \emptyset$, then Eloise wins. Otherwise the game continues with Abelard's turn in which H' is added to $\mathcal{H}$ and the set Current becomes $\{H'\}$. When one of the players cannot make any move, the game ends and this player loses.

We observe that a φ-game needs to terminate, as Abelard can play at most $\mathsf{md}(\varphi) + 1$ turns. Moreover, we show next that verifying the satisfiability of φ reduces to checking the existence of Eloise's winning strategy in the φ-game.

Lemma 3. *For any $\mathcal{ML}(\mathsf{DD})$-formula φ with Boolean DDs, φ is satisfiable if and only if Eloise has a winning strategy in the φ-game.*

Proof. If φ is satisfiable, then Eloise can construct a winning strategy by reading the required φ-Hintikka sets from a model of φ. For the opposite direction, assume that Eloise has a winning strategy that starts by playing $\mathcal{H}_0 = \{H_0, \ldots, H_n\}$. We define $\mathcal{H}_1, \ldots, \mathcal{H}_{\mathsf{md}(\varphi)}$ such that each $\mathcal{H}_{k+1}$ is the set of all φ-Hintikka sets not belonging to $\mathcal{H}_0$ which Eloise would play (using the winning strategy) as a response to Abelard having played some set (and a formula) in $\mathcal{H}_k$. We exploit these $\mathcal{H}_0, \ldots, \mathcal{H}_{\mathsf{md}(\varphi)}$ to construct a model $\mathcal{M} = (W, R, V)$ such that

$$W = \{w_k^H \mid k \in \{0, \ldots, \mathsf{md}(\varphi)\} \text{ and } H \in \mathcal{H}_k\},$$
$$R = \{(w_k^H, w_{k'}^{H'}) \in W \times W \mid \psi \in H' \text{ implies } \Diamond \psi \in H, \text{ for all } \Diamond \psi \in \mathsf{cl}(\varphi)\},$$
$$V(p) = \{w_k^H \in W \mid p \in H\}, \quad \text{for each } p \in \mathsf{PROP}.$$

We can show by induction on the structure of formulas that for any $w_k^H \in W$ and any $\psi \in \mathsf{cl}(\varphi)$ with $\mathsf{md}(\psi) \leq \mathsf{md}(\varphi) - k$ it holds that $\mathcal{M}, w_k^H \models \psi$ if and only if $\psi \in H$. Thus, $\mathcal{M}, w_0^H \models \varphi$, for $H \in \mathcal{H}_0$ such that $\varphi \in H$ (which needs to exist by the definition of the φ-game). $\qquad\square$

We observe that each state of the φ-game can be represented in polynomial space with respect to the size of φ. In particular, in each state we need to specify a set of polynomially many φ-Hintikka sets played so far, each containing polynomially many formulas, which in total uses polynomial space. The existence of a winning strategy for Eloise can therefore be decided in PSpace (e.g., by exploiting the fact that PSpace coincides with the class of problems decided by alternating Turing machines in polynomial time [16]).

Theorem 4. *Checking satisfiability of $\mathcal{ML}(\mathsf{DD})$-formulas with Boolean DDs is PSpace-complete.*

Importantly, Theorem 4 does not hold if we allow for non-Boolean DDs, which disallows us to conduct the induction from the proof of Lemma 3. As we show next, this is not a coincidence, namely the satisfiability problem for $\mathcal{ML}(\mathsf{DD})$ with non-Boolean DDs is ExpTime-complete.

The ExpTime upper bound follows from an observation that DDs can be simulated with the counting operator $\exists_{=1}$; recall that we can simulate $@_\varphi\psi$ with $\exists_{=1}\varphi \wedge \exists_{=1}(\varphi \wedge \psi)$. As we use only one counting operator $\exists_{=1}$ and $\mathcal{MLC}$-satisfiability with numbers encoded in unary is ExpTime-complete [2,37], our upper bound follows. The proof of the matching lower bound is more complicated and is obtained by simulating the universal modal operator A with DDs, where $\mathsf{A}\varphi$ stands for 'φ holds in all worlds'. To simulate A we start by guaranteeing that there exists a unique 'trash' world in which a special propositional variable s holds and which is accessible with $\Diamond$ only from itself; this can be obtained by the formula $@_s\top \wedge @_{\Diamond s}s$. Now, we can use this world to simulate $\mathsf{A}\varphi$ with $@_{(s\vee\neg\varphi)}\top$, which states that φ holds in all worlds in which s does not hold, that is, in all worlds different from our 'trash' world. Although this does not allow us to express the exact meaning of $\mathsf{A}\varphi$, it turns out to be sufficient to reduce satisfiability of formulas of the logic $\mathcal{ML}(\mathsf{A})$ with the A operator to $\mathcal{ML}(\mathsf{DD})$-satisfiability. As the former problem is ExpTime-complete [10], we obtain the required lower bound.

Theorem 5. *Checking satisfiability of $\mathcal{ML}(\mathsf{DD})$-formulas (with arbitrarily complex DDs) is ExpTime-complete.*

Proof. As we have observed, the upper bound is trivial, so we focus on showing ExpTime-hardness. To this end, we reduce $\mathcal{ML}(\mathsf{A})$-satisfiability to $\mathcal{ML}(\mathsf{DD})$-satisfiability. First, given an $\mathcal{ML}(\mathsf{A})$-formula, we transform it into a formula φ in the negation normal form NNF, where negations occur only in front of propositional variables. This can be done in logarithmic space, but requires using additional operators, namely $\wedge$, $\sqcup$, and E. In particular, E stands for 'somewhere' and is dual to A similarly to $\Diamond$ being dual to $\square$. Then, we construct a translation of such formulas in NNF to $\mathcal{ML}(\mathsf{DD})$-formulas as follows:

$$\tau(p) = p, \qquad\qquad \tau(\Diamond\psi) = \Diamond\tau(\psi),$$
$$\tau(\neg p) = \neg p, \qquad\qquad \tau(\square\psi) = \square\tau(\psi),$$
$$\tau(\psi \vee \chi) = \tau(\psi) \vee \tau(\chi), \qquad \tau(\mathsf{E}\psi) = @_{p_\psi}(\tau(\psi) \wedge \neg s),$$
$$\tau(\psi \wedge \chi) = \tau(\psi) \wedge \tau(\chi), \qquad \tau(\mathsf{A}\psi) = @_{(s\vee\neg\tau(\psi))}\top,$$

where $p \in \mathsf{PROP}$, ψ and χ are subformulas of φ, s is a fresh variable marking a 'trash' world, and p_ψ is a fresh variable for each ψ. Our finally constructed formula φ' is defined as follows:

$$\varphi' = \tau(\varphi) \wedge \neg s \wedge @_s\top \wedge @_{\Diamond s}s.$$

Since φ' is constructed in logarithmic space from φ, it remains to show that φ and φ' are equisatisfiable.

If φ is satisfiable, then $\mathcal{M}, w \models \varphi$, for some $\mathcal{M} = (W, R, V)$ and $w \in W$. To show that φ' is satisfiable, we construct, in two steps, a model $\mathcal{M}' = (W', R', V')$ extending $\mathcal{M}$. First, for each subformula ψ of φ which is satisfied in some world in $\mathcal{M}$ we choose an arbitrary world $v \in W$ such that $\mathcal{M}, v \models \psi$ and we let $V'(p_\psi) = \{v\}$. Second, we add a single new world w_s to W' as well as we set $V'(s) = \{w_s\}$ and $(w_s, w_s) \in R'$. Then, we can show by induction on the structure of φ that for all $v \in W$, if $\mathcal{M}, v \models \varphi$ then $\mathcal{M}', v \models \tau(\varphi)$. This, in particular, implies that $\mathcal{M}', w \models \tau(\varphi)$. By the construction of $\mathcal{M}'$ we have also $\mathcal{M}', w \models \neg s \wedge @_s \top \wedge @_{\lozenge s} s$, so we can conclude that $\mathcal{M}', w \models \varphi'$.

For the opposite direction we assume that φ' is satisfiable, so $\mathcal{M}', w \models \varphi'$ for some $\mathcal{M}' = (W', R', V')$ and $w \in W'$. In particular $\mathcal{M}', w \models \neg s \wedge @_s \top \wedge @_{\lozenge s} s$, so there exists a unique world $w_s \in W'$ such that $\mathcal{M}', w_s \models s$, and $\mathcal{M}', w \models \neg s$ implies that $w_s \neq w$. Now, we construct $\mathcal{M} = (W, R, V)$ by deleting from $\mathcal{M}'$ the world w_s and restricting the accessibility relation and the valuation to this smaller set of worlds. Then, we can show by induction on the structure of φ that for any $v \in W$, if $\mathcal{M}', v \models \tau(\varphi)$, then $\mathcal{M}, v \models \varphi$. Since $\mathcal{M}', w \models \tau(\varphi)$ and $w \in W$, we obtain that $\mathcal{M}, w \models \varphi$.   □

Note that the reduction in the proof above provides us with a satisfiability preserving translation between languages. The existence of such a reduction does not mean, however, that there exists a translation preserving equivalence of formulas. In the next section we will study the existence of the second type of translations to compare the expressiveness of $\mathcal{ML}(\mathsf{DD})$ with that of $\mathcal{H}(@)$ and $\mathcal{MLC}$.

4   Expressive Power

In the previous section we have established the computational complexity of reasoning in $\mathcal{ML}(\mathsf{DD})$. Now, we will compare $\mathcal{ML}(\mathsf{DD})$ with $\mathcal{H}(@)$ and $\mathcal{MLC}$ from the point of view of expressiveness. We will study their relative expressive power over the class of all frames, as well as over linear frames L (where the accessibility relation is irreflexive, transitive, and trichotomous), and over the frames $\mathbb{Z}$ which are isomorphic to the standard (strict) order of integers.

To this end, for a class F of frames below we define the *greater-than expressiveness* relation $\preccurlyeq_\mathsf{F}$ (we drop the index F in the case of all frames). If logics $\mathcal{L}_1$ and $\mathcal{L}_2$ are non-hybrid, then we let $\mathcal{L}_1 \preccurlyeq_\mathsf{F} \mathcal{L}_2$, if, for any $\mathcal{L}_1$-formula φ, there is an $\mathcal{L}_2$-formula φ' such that $\mathcal{M}, w \models \varphi$ if and only if $\mathcal{M}, w \models \varphi'$, for any model $\mathcal{M}$ based on a frame from the class F and any world w in $\mathcal{M}$. If $\mathcal{L}_1$ is hybrid but $\mathcal{L}_2$ is not, we treat nominals as fresh propositional variables in $\mathcal{L}_2$, so we can still require that $\mathcal{M}, w \models \varphi$ implies $\mathcal{M}, w \models \varphi'$. For the opposite direction we require that if $\mathcal{M}, w \models \varphi'$, for a non-hybrid model $\mathcal{M} = (W, R, V)$, then $V(i)$ is a singleton for each $i \in \mathsf{NOM}(\varphi)$; thus we can treat $\mathcal{M}$ as a hybrid model and require now that $\mathcal{M}, w \models \varphi$. If $\mathcal{L}_1$ is non-hybrid but $\mathcal{L}_2$ is hybrid, we define $\mathcal{L}_1 \preccurlyeq \mathcal{L}_2$ analogously. Then, $\mathcal{L}_2$ has a *strictly higher expressiveness* than $\mathcal{L}_1$, in symbols $\mathcal{L}_1 \prec_\mathsf{F} \mathcal{L}_2$, if $\mathcal{L}_1 \preccurlyeq_\mathsf{F} \mathcal{L}_2$, but $\mathcal{L}_2 \not\preccurlyeq_\mathsf{F} \mathcal{L}_1$, whereas $\mathcal{L}_1$ have the *same expressiveness* as $\mathcal{L}_2$, in symbols $\mathcal{L}_1 \approx_\mathsf{F} \mathcal{L}_2$, if both $\mathcal{L}_1 \preccurlyeq_\mathsf{F} \mathcal{L}_2$ and $\mathcal{L}_2 \preccurlyeq_\mathsf{F} \mathcal{L}_1$.

For $\mathcal{L}_1 \preccurlyeq_F \mathcal{L}_2$ it suffices to construct a translation, but showing that $\mathcal{L}_1 \npreccurlyeq_F \mathcal{L}_2$ is usually more complicated. It can be obtained, for example, by using an adequate notion of bisimulation, which we present for $\mathcal{ML}(\mathsf{DD})$ below.

Definition 6. *A DD-bisimulation between* $\mathcal{M} = (W, R, V)$ *and* $\mathcal{M}' = (W', R', V')$ *is any total (i.e., serial and surjective) relation* $Z \subseteq W \times W'$ *such that whenever* $(w, w') \in Z$, *the following conditions hold:*

Atom: *w and w' satisfy the same propositional variables,*
Zig: *if there is $v \in W$ such that $(w, v) \in R$, then there is $v' \in W'$ such $(v, v') \in Z$ and $(w', v') \in R'$,*
Zag: *if there is $v' \in W'$ such that $(w', v') \in R'$, then there is $v \in W$ such $(v, v') \in Z$ and $(w, v) \in R$,*
Singular: *$Z(w) = \{w'\}$ if and only if $Z^{-1}(w') = \{w\}$*[1].

Note that by relaxing the definition of DD-bisimulation, namely not requiring the totality of Z and removing Condition (Singular), we obtain the standard notion of bisimulation, which is adequate for basic modal language [10, 11]. Additional restrictions imposed on the bisimulation give rise to bisimulations adequate for $\mathcal{MLC}$ and $\mathcal{H}(@)$. In particular, $\mathcal{MLC}$-bisimulation is defined by extending the standard bisimulation (for basic modal language) with the requirement that Z contains a bijection between W and W' [4]. In turn, an $\mathcal{H}$-bisimulation introduces to the standard bisimualtion an additional condition (Nom): for each $i \in \mathsf{NOM}$, if $V(i) = \{w\}$ and $V'(i) = \{w'\}$, then $Z(w, w')$ [3]. We write $\mathcal{M}, w \underline{\leftrightarrow}_{\mathsf{DD}} \mathcal{M}', w'$ if there is a DD-bisimulation Z between $\mathcal{M}$ and $\mathcal{M}'$ such that $(w, w') \in Z$. Similarly, in the cases of $\mathcal{MLC}$ and $\mathcal{H}(@)$ we write $\mathcal{M}, w \underline{\leftrightarrow}_{\mathcal{MLC}} \mathcal{M}', w'$ and $\mathcal{M}, w \underline{\leftrightarrow}_{\mathcal{H}} \mathcal{M}', w'$, respectively. These bisimulations satisfy invariance lemmas for the corresponding languages, namely if $\mathcal{M}, w \underline{\leftrightarrow}_{\mathcal{MLC}} \mathcal{M}', w'$ (resp. $\mathcal{M}, w \underline{\leftrightarrow}_{\mathcal{H}} \mathcal{M}', w'$), then, for any $\mathcal{MLC}$-formula (resp. $\mathcal{H}(@)$-formula) φ, it holds that $\mathcal{M}, w \models \varphi$ if and only if $\mathcal{M}', w' \models \varphi$ [3,4]. Next, we show an analogous result for DD-bisimulation.

Lemma 7. *If $\mathcal{M}, w \underline{\leftrightarrow}_{\mathsf{DD}} \mathcal{M}', w'$ then, for any $\mathcal{ML}(\mathsf{DD})$-formula φ, it holds that $\mathcal{M}, w \models \varphi$ if and only if $\mathcal{M}', w' \models \varphi$.*

Proof. Assume that Z is a DD-bisimulation between models $\mathcal{M} = (W, R, V)$ and $\mathcal{M}' = (W', R', V')$ satisfying $\mathcal{M}, w \underline{\leftrightarrow}_{\mathsf{DD}} \mathcal{M}', w'$. The proof is by induction on the structure of φ, where the non-standard part is for the inductive step for DDs, where φ is of the form $@_{\psi_1} \psi_2$. If $\mathcal{M}, w \models @_{\psi_1} \psi_2$, there is a unique world $v \in W$ such that $\mathcal{M}, v \models \psi_1$, and moreover $\mathcal{M}, v \models \psi_2$. As Z is serial, there is $v' \in Z(v)$, and so, by the inductive assumption, $\mathcal{M}', v' \models \psi_1 \wedge \psi_2$. Suppose towards a contradiction that $\mathcal{M}', w' \not\models @_{\psi_1} \psi_2$, so there is $u' \neq v'$ such that $\mathcal{M}', u' \models \psi_1$. Since Z is surjective, there is $u \in W$ such that $u' \in Z(u)$. Moreover, by the inductive assumption we obtain that $\mathcal{M}, u \models \psi_1$. However, v is the only world in W which satisfies ψ_1, so $u = v$ and consequently $u' \in Z(v)$. For the same reason there cannot be in W any world different than v which is

---

[1] We use here the functional notation where $Z(w) = \{v \mid (w, v) \in Z\}$.

mapped by Z to v'. Hence, $Z^{-1}(v') = \{v\}$ and thus $Z(v) = \{v'\}$. This, however, contradicts the fact that $u' \in Z(v)$ and $u' \neq v'$. The opposite implication is shown analogously. □

We will exploit bisimulations in our analysis. We start by considering arbitrary frames and we show that $\mathcal{H}(@) \prec \mathcal{ML}(\mathsf{DD})$ and $\mathcal{ML}(\mathsf{DD}) \prec \mathcal{MLC}$.

Theorem 8. *It holds that $\mathcal{H}(@) \prec \mathcal{ML}(\mathsf{DD})$; the result holds already over the class of finite frames.*

Proof. Given an $\mathcal{H}(@)$-formula φ we construct an $\mathcal{ML}(\mathsf{DD})$-formula φ' by setting $\varphi' = \varphi \wedge \bigwedge_{i \in \mathsf{NOM}(\varphi)} @_i \top$. The conjunction $\bigwedge_{i \in \mathsf{NOM}(\varphi)} @_i \top$ guarantees that each $i \in \mathsf{NOM}(\varphi)$ holds in exactly one world, so $\mathcal{H}(@) \preccurlyeq \mathcal{ML}(\mathsf{DD})$.

To prove that $\mathcal{ML}(\mathsf{DD}) \not\preccurlyeq \mathcal{H}(@)$, we show that the $\mathcal{ML}(\mathsf{DD})$-formula $@_\top \top$, defining the class of frames with exactly one world, cannot be expressed in $\mathcal{H}(@)$. For this, we construct models $\mathcal{M}$ and $\mathcal{M}'$ and an $\mathcal{H}$-bisimulation Z between them:

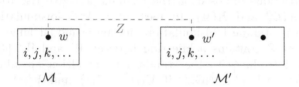

Clearly $\mathcal{M}, w \models @_\top \top$, but $\mathcal{M}', w' \not\models @_\top \top$. However, since Z is an $\mathcal{H}$-bisimulation, there exists no $\mathcal{H}(@)$-formula which holds in w, but not in w'. □

Next, we use DD-bisimulation to show that $\mathcal{ML}(\mathsf{DD}) \prec \mathcal{MLC}$.

Theorem 9. *It holds that $\mathcal{ML}(\mathsf{DD}) \prec \mathcal{MLC}$; the result holds already over the class of finite frames.*

Proof. To show that $\mathcal{ML}(\mathsf{DD}) \preccurlyeq \mathcal{MLC}$, we observe that $@_\varphi \psi$ can be expressed as $\mathsf{E}(\varphi \wedge \psi \wedge \neg \mathsf{D}\varphi)$, where E and D are the 'somewhere' and 'difference' operators. Both E and D can be expressed in $\mathcal{MLC}$, for example, $\mathsf{E}\varphi$ can be expressed as $\exists_{\geq 1}\varphi$ and $\mathsf{D}\varphi$ as $(\varphi \rightarrow \exists_{\geq 2}\varphi) \wedge (\neg\varphi \rightarrow \exists_{\geq 1}\varphi)$ [4]. Thus $\mathcal{ML}(\mathsf{DD}) \preccurlyeq \mathcal{MLC}$.

To prove that $\mathcal{MLC} \not\preccurlyeq \mathcal{ML}(\mathsf{DD})$, we show that $\mathcal{ML}(\mathsf{DD})$ cannot express the $\mathcal{MLC}$-formula $\exists_{=2}\top$ defining frames with exactly two worlds in the domain. Indeed, consider models $\mathcal{M}$ and $\mathcal{M}'$ and a DD-bisimulation between them as below:

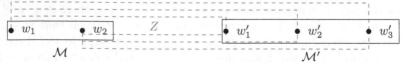

Clearly $\mathcal{M}, w_1 \models \exists_{=2}\top$, but $\mathcal{M}', w_1' \not\models \exists_{=2}\top$. Since Z is a DD-bisimulation mapping w_1 to w_1', these words satisfy the same $\mathcal{ML}(\mathsf{DD})$-formulas. □

We note that the argument from the proof above, showing that there is no $\mathcal{ML}(DD)$ formula which defines the class of frames with domains of cardinality 2, can be easily generalised to any cardinality larger than 1. In contrast, as we showed in the proof of Theorem 8, the frame property of having the domain of cardinality 1 can be captured by the $\mathcal{ML}(DD)$-formula $@_\top \top$. In other words, $\mathcal{ML}(DD)$ cannot define frames bigger than singletons.

Next, we focus on linear frames where the following result holds

Theorem 10. *The following relations hold:* $\mathcal{H}(@) \prec_L \mathcal{ML}(DD) \prec_L \mathcal{MLC}$.

Proof. Clearly, $\mathcal{H}(@) \preccurlyeq_L \mathcal{ML}(DD)$ and $\mathcal{ML}(DD) \preccurlyeq_L \mathcal{MLC}$ follow from Theorem 8 and 9, so it remains to show that $\mathcal{ML}(DD) \npreccurlyeq_L \mathcal{H}(@)$ and $\mathcal{MLC} \npreccurlyeq_L \mathcal{ML}(DD)$.

To show that $\mathcal{ML}(DD) \npreccurlyeq_L \mathcal{H}(@)$ we construct models $\mathcal{M}$ and $\mathcal{M}'$ over $\mathbb{Z}$ with an $\mathcal{H}$-bisimulation Z, as depicted below (note that the accessibility relation in the models is the transitive closure of the relation depicted by arrows):

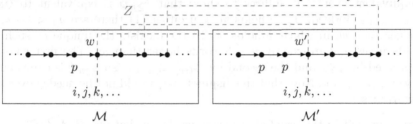

Clearly $\mathcal{M}, w \models @_p \top$, but $\mathcal{M}', w' \not\models @_p \top$. However, since Z is an $\mathcal{H}$-bisimulation mapping w to w', these worlds need to satisfy the same $\mathcal{H}(@)$-formulas.

To show that $\mathcal{MLC} \npreccurlyeq_L \mathcal{ML}(DD)$ we construct models $\mathcal{N}$ and $\mathcal{N}'$, each of them over a frame $\mathbb{Z} + \mathbb{Z}$ consisting of two copies of $\mathbb{Z}$, as depicted below:

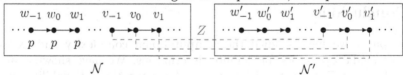

It holds that $\mathcal{N}, v_0 \models \exists_{\geq 1} p$, but $\mathcal{N}', v_0' \not\models \exists_{\geq 1} p$. However, we can show that v_0 and v_0' satisfy the same $\mathcal{ML}(DD)$-formulas. To this end, we observe that Z is a (standard) bisimulation, so v_0 and v_0' satisfy the same formulas from the basic modal language. The language of $\mathcal{ML}(DD)$ contains also formulas of the form $@_\varphi \psi$, but none of them is satisfied in any world of $\mathcal{N}$ or $\mathcal{N}'$. Indeed, in the case of $\mathcal{N}$ we can construct a DD-bisimulation $Z_\mathcal{N}$ between $\mathcal{N}$ and itself which consists of pairs (w_n, w_m) and (v_n, v_m) for all $n, m \in \mathbb{Z}$. Hence, all worlds of the form w_n satisfy the same $\mathcal{ML}(DD)$-formulas, and the same holds for all worlds v_n. Thus, no formula of the form $@_\varphi \psi$ can be satisfied in $\mathcal{N}$, as there are either no worlds satisfying φ or there are infinitely many of them. An analogous argument shows that no formula of the form $@_\varphi \psi$ can be satisfied in $\mathcal{N}'$.   □

Next we show that expressiveness results change when we consider frames $\mathbb{Z}$.

Theorem 11. *The following relations hold:* $\mathcal{H}(@) \prec_{\mathbb{Z}} \mathcal{ML}(\text{DD}) \approx_{\mathbb{Z}} \mathcal{MLC}$.

Proof. The fact that $\mathcal{H}(@) \prec_{\mathbb{Z}} \mathcal{ML}(\text{DD})$ follows from the proof of Theorem 10 as the $\mathcal{H}$-bisimulation constructed therein is over $\mathbb{Z}$. To show $\mathcal{ML}(\text{DD}) \approx_{\mathbb{Z}} \mathcal{MLC}$ it suffices to prove $\mathcal{MLC} \preccurlyeq_{\mathbb{Z}} \mathcal{ML}(\text{DD})$, as $\mathcal{ML}(\text{DD}) \preccurlyeq_{\mathbb{Z}} \mathcal{MLC}$ follows from Theorem 9.

To express $\mathcal{MLC}$-formulas in $\mathcal{ML}(\text{DD})$ it will be convenient to introduce, for any $n \in \mathbb{N}$, a formula ψ_n as the following abbreviation

$$\psi_n = \psi \wedge \Diamond(\psi \wedge \Diamond(\psi \wedge \ldots)), \qquad \text{where } \psi \text{ occurs } n \text{ times.}$$

We observe that by the irreflexivity of the accessibility relation over $\mathbb{Z}$ we obtain that ψ_n holds in all worlds w_1 of a model such that there exists a chain $w_1 < w_2 < \cdots < w_n$ of (not necesarily consecutive) distinct worlds satisfying ψ.

Given an $\mathcal{MLC}$-formula φ, we let φ' be an $\mathcal{ML}(\text{DD})$-formula obtained by replacing in φ each $\exists_{\geq n}\psi$ with $\Diamond\psi_n \vee @_{(\psi_n \wedge \neg\Diamond\psi_n)}\top$. To show that φ and φ' are equivalent over $\mathbb{Z}$ it suffices to show that $\exists_{\geq n}\psi$ is equivalent to $\Diamond\psi_n \vee @_{(\psi_n \wedge \neg\Diamond\psi_n)}\top$. Indeed, $\exists_{\geq n}\psi$ holds at w if either (1) there are $w_1 < \cdots < w_n$, all larger than w, in which ψ holds or (2) there exists the unique w' such that ψ holds in w' and in exactly $n - 1$ words larger than w'. The first condition is expressed by $\Diamond\psi_n$ and the second by $@_{(\psi_n \wedge \neg\Diamond\psi_n)}\top$, so $\exists_{\geq n}\psi$ is equivalent to $\Diamond\psi_n \vee @_{(\psi_n \wedge \neg\Diamond\psi_n)}\top$. Note that the disjunct $\Diamond\psi_n$ would not be needed over finite linear frames. □

Observe that in the proof above we have shown that over $\mathbb{Z}$ $\mathcal{ML}(\text{DD})$ allows us to count the number of occurrences of p in a model, which is impossible over arbitrary frames and over linear frames, as we showed in the proof of Theorem 10.

5   Conclusions

In this paper we have studied the computational complexity and expressive power of modal operators for definite descriptions. We have shown that after adding Boolean DDs to the basic modal language the satisfiability problem remains PSpace-complete, so such an extension can be obtained with no computational cost. However, if we allow for arbitrary DDs, the problem becomes ExpTime-complete, so the computational price is the same as for adding the universal modal operator or counting quantifiers with numbers encoded in unary. Moreover, we have shown that in this setting DDs provide strictly higher expressive power than the (basic) hybrid machinery, but strictly lower expressive power than counting operators. The same holds over linear structures, but over integers DDs become as expressive as counting operators.

Regarding the future research directions, it would be interesting to provide a complexity-wise optimal decision procedure for $\mathcal{ML}(\text{DD})$-satisfiability, for example, using a tableaux systems. We would also like to study the complexity and expressiveness of well-behaving fragments of modal logic, such as Horn fragments.

Acknowledgments. This research is funded by the European Union (ERC, ExtenDD, project number: 101054714). Views and opinions expressed are however those of the authors only and do not necessarily reflect those of the European Union or the European Research Council. Neither the European Union nor the granting authority can be held responsible for them.

References

1. Areces, C., Blackburn, P., Marx, M.: A road-map on complexity for hybrid logics. In: Flum, J., Rodriguez-Artalejo, M. (eds.) CSL 1999. LNCS, vol. 1683, pp. 307–321. Springer, Heidelberg (1999). https://doi.org/10.1007/3-540-48168-0_22
2. Areces, C., Blackburn, P., Marx, M.: The computational complexity of hybrid temporal logics. Log. J. IGPL 8(5), 653–679 (2000)
3. Areces, C., ten Cate, B.: Hybrid logics. In: Handbook of Modal Logic, vol. 3, chap. 14, pp. 821–868 (2007)
4. Areces, C., Hoffmann, G., Denis, A.: Modal logics with counting. In: Dawar, A., de Queiroz, R. (eds.) WoLLIC 2010. LNCS (LNAI), vol. 6188, pp. 98–109. Springer, Heidelberg (2010). https://doi.org/10.1007/978-3-642-13824-9_9
5. Areces, C., Koller, A., Striegnitz, K.: Referring expressions as formulas of description logic. In: Proceedings of INLG, pp. 42–49 (2008)
6. Artale, A., Mazzullo, A., Ozaki, A., Wolter, F.: On free description logics with definite descriptions. In: Proceedings of KR, pp. 63–73 (2021)
7. Bencivenga, E.: Free logics. In: Gabbay, D.M., Guenthner, F. (eds.) Handbook of Philosophical Logic, vol. 5, pp. 147–196. Springer, Dordrecht (2002). https://doi.org/10.1007/978-94-017-0458-8_3
8. Blackburn, P.: Representation, reasoning, and relational structures: a hybrid logic manifesto. Log. J. IGPL 8(3), 339–365 (2000)
9. Blackburn, P.: Nominal tense logic. Notre Dame J. Formal Log. 34(1), 56–83 (1993)
10. Blackburn, P., De Rijke, M., Venema, Y.: Modal Logic, Cambridge Tracts in Theoretical Computer Science, vol. 53. Cambridge University Press, Cambridge (2002)
11. Blackburn, P., Van Benthem, J., Wolter, F.: Handbook of Modal Logic, vol. 3. Elsevier, Amsterdam (2007)
12. Borgida, A., Toman, D., Weddell, G.: On referring expressions in information systems derived from conceptual modelling. In: Comyn-Wattiau, I., Tanaka, K., Song, I.-Y., Yamamoto, S., Saeki, M. (eds.) ER 2016. LNCS, vol. 9974, pp. 183–197. Springer, Cham (2016). https://doi.org/10.1007/978-3-319-46397-1_14
13. Borgida, A., Toman, D., Weddell, G.: On referring expressions in query answering over first order knowledge bases. In: Proceedings of KR (2016)
14. Borgida, A., Toman, D., Weddell, G.E.: Concerning referring expressions in query answers. In: Proceedings of IJCAI, pp. 4791–4795 (2017)
15. Bull, R.A.: An approach to tense logic. Theoria 36(3), 282–300 (1970)
16. Chandra, A.K., Kozen, D.C., Stockmeyer, L.J.: Alternation. J. ACM 28(1), 114–133 (1981)
17. Fitting, M., Mendelsohn, R.L.: First-Order Modal Logic. Synthese Library, vol. 277. Springer, Dordrecht (2012). https://doi.org/10.1007/978-94-011-5292-1
18. Franceschet, M., de Rijke, M., Schlingloff, B.H.: Hybrid logics on linear structures: expressivity and complexity. In: Proceedings of TIME, pp. 166–173 (2003)
19. Gargov, G., Goranko, V.: Modal logic with names. J. Philos. Log. 22, 607–636 (1993)

20. Hilbert, D., Bernays, P.: Grundlagen der Mathematik I. Springer, Heidelberg (1968). https://doi.org/10.1007/978-3-642-86894-8
21. Indrzejczak, A.: Cut-free modal theory of definite descriptions. In: Proceedings of AiML, pp. 359–378 (2018)
22. Indrzejczak, A.: Existence, definedness and definite descriptions in hybrid modal logic. In: Proceedings of AiML, pp. 349–368 (2020)
23. Ladner, R.E.: The computational complexity of provability in systems of modal propositional logic. SIAM J. Comput. **6**(3), 467–480 (1977)
24. Lambert, K.: Free logic and definite descriptions. In: Morscher, E., Hieke, A. (eds.) New Essays in Free Logic. Applied Logic Series, vol. 23, pp. 37–48. Springer, Dordrecht (2001). https://doi.org/10.1007/978-94-015-9761-6_2
25. Mazzullo, A.: Finite traces and definite descriptions. A knowledge representation journey. Ph.D. thesis, Free University of Bozen-Bolzano (2022)
26. Neuhaus, F., Kutz, O., Righetti, G.: Free description logic for ontologists. In: Proceedings of JOWO (2020)
27. Orlandelli, E., Corsi, G.: Labelled calculi for quantified modal logics with non-rigid and non-denoting terms. In: Proceedings of ARQNL, pp. 64–78 (2018)
28. Peano, G.: Studii di logica matematica. Carlo Clausen, Torino (1897)
29. Pelletier, F.J., Linsky, B.: What is Frege's theory of descriptions. In: On Denoting: 1905–2005, pp. 195–250 (2005)
30. Pratt-Hartmann, I.: Complexity of the two-variable fragment with counting quantifiers. J. Log. Lang. Inf. 369–395 (2005)
31. Pratt-Hartmann, I.: The two-variable fragment with counting revisited. In: Dawar, A., de Queiroz, R. (eds.) WoLLIC 2010. LNCS (LNAI), vol. 6188, pp. 42–54. Springer, Heidelberg (2010). https://doi.org/10.1007/978-3-642-13824-9_4
32. Prior, A.: Past, present and future (1967)
33. Rosser, J.B.: Logic for Mathematicians. Dover Publications, Dover (1978)
34. Scott, D.: Existence and description in formal logic. In: B. Russell, Philosopher of the Century, pp. 181–200 (1967)
35. Sustretov, D.: Topological semantics and decidability. arXiv preprint math/0703106 (2007)
36. ten Cate, B., Franceschet, M.: On the complexity of hybrid logics with binders. In: Ong, L. (ed.) CSL 2005. LNCS, vol. 3634, pp. 339–354. Springer, Heidelberg (2005). https://doi.org/10.1007/11538363_24
37. Tobies, S.: Complexity results and practical algorithms for logics in knowledge representation. Ph.D. thesis (2001)
38. Toman, D., Weddell, G.: Finding ALL answers to OBDA queries using referring expressions. In: Liu, J., Bailey, J. (eds.) AI 2019. LNCS (LNAI), vol. 11919, pp. 117–129. Springer, Cham (2019). https://doi.org/10.1007/978-3-030-35288-2_10
39. Toman, D., Weddell, G.: Identity resolution in ontology based data access to structured data sources. In: Nayak, A.C., Sharma, A. (eds.) PRICAI 2019. LNCS (LNAI), vol. 11670, pp. 473–485. Springer, Cham (2019). https://doi.org/10.1007/978-3-030-29908-8_38
40. Toman, D., Weddell, G.E.: Identity resolution in conjunctive querying over DL-based knowledge bases. In: Proceedings of DL (2018)
41. Zawidzki, M., Schmidt, R.A., Tishkovsky, D.: Satisfiability problem for modal logic with global counting operators coded in binary is NExpTime-complete. Inf. Process. Lett. **113**(1), 34–38 (2013)

Reasoning About Quantities
and Functions

Data Graphs with Incomplete Information (and a Way to Complete Them)

Carlos Areces[1,2], Valentin Cassano[1,2,3(✉)], Danae Dutto[1,2,3],
and Raul Fervari[1,2,4]

[1] Consejo Nacional de Investigaciones Científicas y Técnicas (CONICET),
Buenos Aires, Argentina
valentin@dc.exa.unrc.edu.ar
[2] Universidad Nacional de Córdoba (UNC), Córdoba, Argentina
[3] Universidad Nacional de Río Cuarto (UNRC), Río Cuarto, Argentina
[4] Guangdong Technion - Israel Institute of Technology (GTIIT), Shantou, China

Abstract. We introduce a modal language for reasoning about data graphs with incomplete information. Such data graphs are formally represented as models in which data value functions are partial—to capture what is unknown. In this setting, we also allow for unknown data values to be learned. Our main result is a sound and strongly complete axiomatization for the logic.

Keywords: Data Graphs · Incomplete Data · Modal/Intuitionistic Logic

1 Modal Logic and Semistructured-Data Query Languages

Nowadays, there is a well established connection between modal logics [13,15] and semistructured-data query languages such as XPath and some of its relatives [20,25]. The main reason is that semistructured data is usually represented in the form of relational structures or graphs (e.g., an XML document), and modal logics are well suited for describing and reasoning over this kind of structures. This perspective enables us to use modal logic tools to reason with (and about) XPath-like languages (see, e.g., [9]), thereby helping us to develop methods to check the consistency of a database and to optimize queries, among other tasks. Some of these ideas have been explored, e.g., in [18,19], and also, in the presence of data comparisons, in, e.g., [1,3,6,8,11].

The connection mentioned above is illustrated in [16]. There, a version of XPath with (in)equality data tests between attributes in an XML document is named Core-Data-XPath, here called XPath$_=$. Models of XPath$_=$ are usually data trees which can be seen as XML documents. A data tree is a tree whose nodes contain a label from a finite alphabet and a data value from an infinite domain. From a modal logic perspective, these data trees are a particular class of *relational models*. Naturally, this view can be extended to more general relational structures, i.e., to arbitrary *data graphs*. Since data graphs are the underlying

S. Gaggl et al. (Eds.): JELIA 2023, LNAI 14281, pp. 729–744, 2023.
https://doi.org/10.1007/978-3-031-43619-2_49

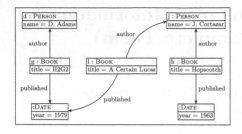

Fig. 1. Graph Database.

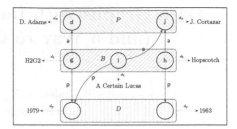

Fig. 2. Concrete Data Model.

mathematical structure in *graph databases* (see, e.g., [4,28,30]), studying the meta-logical properties of languages to query this particular kind of models is important (see, e.g., [1,27]).

Let us provide an example to guide our discussion. Figure 1 depicts a graph database modelling a piece of a library catalog. There, we can see attributes (e.g., "author") as labels on edges; while nodes store data values represented as "tag = value" pairs (e.g., "title = H2G2"). Attributes are usually drawn from a finite set, while data values are assumed to be drawn from an infinite set. Additionally, some nodes may contain keys that uniquely identify a node (e.g., the ISBN number associated to a certain book, or the passport number of a person, indicated, e.g., "d:"). On this kind of graph database, we can state queries such as: "The book with the id l has the same author as the one with the id h". In this way, we can express both properties about the structure of the data graph, and about equality or inequality of the data values contained in it.

To explore graph databases and the possibility of querying them from a logical perspective we need an adequate logical language. We build on [6] and consider a hybrid modal language. In this setting, modalities encode attributes, proposition symbols encode types, and nominals from hybrid logic encode unique identifiers. Figure 2 shows what the graph database in Fig. 1 looks like as a model of the hybrid modal language. In this figure, a and p are accessibility relations associated to their corresponding modalities (for the attributes "author" and "published"); P, B, and D, are proposition symbols (for the types "Person", "Book", and "Date"); and d, j, g, l, and h are nominals (for the unique identifiers appearing in the graph database, representing the passport number of a person or the ISBN of a book). Finally, data values in Fig. 2 are encoded as functions d_n, d_t, and d_y (standing for "name", "title", and "year" values).

To be noted, the model Fig. 2, usually called a *concrete model*, tries to remain as close as possible to the actual graph-database (the similarities between Fig. 1 and Fig. 2 should be obvious). However, depending on the expressive power of our logical language, a simpler, more abstract class of models may be better suited. In particular, many data query languages, like XPath, "abstract away" from the *actual* data values in the graph database, and only care about the result of performing *comparisons* between them (see, e.g., [1,3,6,22,23]). In other words, if the language includes only tests for (in)equality, for example, we can forget about actual data values and define an equivalent model (from the logic standpoint) with data equality relations instead of data value functions. Precisely, two nodes will be related by data equality if and only if they have the same data value. In [6] this connection is made explicit, and the simpler class of *abstract models* is exploited to prove a soundness and completeness result for a Hilbert-style axiomatization of XPath$_=$ extended with nominals and the satisfaction operator. Henceforth, we will refer to this logic as HXPath$_=$.

To tackle the main theme of this article, let us continue with our running example. Suppose that the library catalog from Fig. 1 contains a record of a rare book like the *Voynich Manuscript* [31]. If we treat books uniformly, the catalog will have a book node with data values for the name(s) of its author(s) and its publication year. The problem with the Voynich Manuscript is that neither the author(s) name(s) nor the exact year of publication are known. Notwithstanding, the book certainly has one or more authors, and certainly it was completed at some point in time. It is only that this information is unknown to us at the moment (but nothing prevents us from discovering this information in the future). It seems natural to consider, in this case, that the data values for author and year are undefined for the corresponding node (or, equivalently, to consider that they are assigned a special 'null' value). We call these models "partial data models". Formally, in the above-mentioned set up of concrete models, this calls for the use of *partial functions* for data representation, and to consider *update operators* that would complete the assignment whenever the previously unknown information becomes available. But once this is done, we should reconsider the relation between concrete and abstract data models, as it is in principle unclear how partial data models should be represented in an abstract way, and how are they related by updates. Intuitively, we could think that now abstract partial models would contain "partial equivalence relation" (but we would have to give up reflexivity!). And "learning" the value of an attribute (e.g., the date of edition of a book) may be thought of as "extending" these relations to reflect the (in)equalities that now are obtained. As we will discuss in this article, allowing for this perspective has a huge impact on the logic, and surprisingly at first (and less so after all the work is properly done) it leads to an intuitionistic version of HXPath$_=$. Interestingly, this perspective also points to a fresh connection between modal intuitionistic logics and dynamic logics like those in, e.g., [7, 10, 29].

Our Contribution. We explore a novel approach for treating undefined values on data graphs. We define a notion of update and present it as a partial ordering on a collection of partial data models. To our knowledge this is the first time that these notions have been studied for variants of XPath$_=$. Our work builds on ideas present in [6] about the data-aware language HXPath$_=$. Moreover, we use tools from intuitionistic hybrid logic [17] to model the possibly undefined data values and their possible future definition. The result of putting these pieces together is a new logic that we call IHXPath$_=$. While at the syntactic level, the language of IHXPath$_=$ seems identical to the one of HXPath$_=$, semantics is much more involved (as is the case with classical and intuitionistic propositional logic). *Partial data models*, and the exact correspondence between concrete and abstract models in this new setting is presented in Sect. 2. A variant of the language HXPath$_=$ studied in [6], interpreted over abstract partial data models is given in Sect. 3. Section 4 presents an axiom system for IHXPath$_=$, which is strongly complete for any extension with so-called pure axioms and saturation rules (Sect. 5). Section 6 discusses our results and describes future lines of research.

2 Background and Motivation

The logic HXPath$_=$ in [6] formalizes a fragment of XPath that captures both topological and data (in)equality queries using elements from hybrid modal logic [5]. In HXPath$_=$ data graphs become models of the logic defined in two alternative, yet equivalent, ways. We explain what these models look like and use this explanation to motivate our work. In what follows, we assume Prop, Nom, Mod, and Cmp, are pairwise disjoint fixed sets of symbols for propositions, nominals, modalities, and data comparisons, respectively. Moreover, we assume Mod and Cmp to be finite; and Prop and Nom to be countably infinite.

Definition 1 (The models of HXPath$_=$). *A concrete data model is a tuple*

$$\mathfrak{C} = \langle N, \{R_a\}_{a \in \mathsf{Mod}}, D, \{d_c\}_{c \in \mathsf{Cmp}}, g, V \rangle,$$

where N is a non-empty set of nodes; each R_a is a binary accessibility relation on nodes; D is a non-empty set of data values; $d_c : N \to D$ is a (total) function that assigns data values to nodes; $g : \mathsf{Nom} \to N$ is a (total) function that assigns nominals to nodes; and $V : \mathsf{Prop} \to 2^N$ is a valuation function. In turn, an abstract data model *is a tuple*

$$\mathfrak{A} = \langle N, \{R_a\}_{a \in \mathsf{Mod}}, \{\approx_c\}_{c \in \mathsf{Cmp}}, g, V \rangle,$$

where N, R_a, g, and V are as before; and each $\approx_c$ is an equivalence relation on nodes (representing nodes with the same data value for c).

Remark 1. Notice that concrete and abstract data models are in correspondence to each other. The first yields the second by defining $\approx_c = \{ (n, n') \mid d_c(n) = d_c(n') \}$, while the second yields the first by defining $d_c(n) = [n]_c$.

Figure 2 depicts a concrete data model. More precisely, it depicts only some relevant features of a concrete data model in the context of an example. This is particularly true, e.g., of data values functions such as d_t. In other words, as a total function, d_t must assign a value to each node; yet, only some of these values are present. Though not a technical issue, considering total data values functions is inelegant from a knowledge representation perspective. After all, why must we assign titles to nodes whose values are meant to represent, e.g., dates? This observation takes us to Definition 2.

Definition 2. *A concrete partial data model is a tuple $\mathfrak{C}$ as in Definition 1; with the exception that each $d_c : N \nrightarrow D$ is a partial function.*

What about corresponding abstract data models? On a first glimpse, we may think of them via relations $\approx_c = \{ (n, n') \mid d_c(n) = d_c(n') \}$, which would turn out to be equivalence relations. However, this fails to account for the cases when d_c is undefined. Namely, n and n' need defined data values, i.e., need to belong to the domain of d_c. This forces us to abandon reflexivity and view $\approx_c$ as a partial equivalence relation. This observation takes us to Definition 3.

Definition 3. *An abstract partial data model is a tuple $\mathfrak{A}$ as in Definition 1, except that $\approx_c$ is a partial equivalence relation, i.e., it is symmetric and transitive.*

As a result of these changes, it turns out that now data inequality in abstract partial data models is not the complement of data equality. Namely, two nodes n and n' in an abstract partial data model are taken to have different data if and only if it is not the case that $n \approx_c n'$ and in addition $n \approx_c n$ and $n' \approx_c n'$. This observation will have an important impact in the way we need to define our axiomatization in Sect. 4.

Remark 2. We can still build concrete partial data models from abstract partial data models by setting $d_c(n) = \{ n' \mid n \approx_c n' \}$ if $\{ n' \mid n \approx_c n' \} \neq \emptyset$, and $d_c(n)$ undefined otherwise. Similar to the case in Remark 1, the correspondence between abstract and concrete partial data models is clear.

Now for the last piece of the puzzle. We have established a natural generalization of concrete and abstract data models capable of handling partial information. Let us consider again the case of the Voynich manuscript. It is clear that partial functions are all that we need to represent this book in our models. But suppose that at some point, we do learn the date of edition. This can be formalized as a relation on partial data models reflecting the new 'things' we have learned. One of the possibly different ways in which we can capture this idea is provided in Definition 4.

Definition 4. *Let $\mathfrak{C}$ and $\mathfrak{C}'$ be two concrete partial data model. We write $\mathfrak{C} \preccurlyeq \mathfrak{C}'$, and call $\mathfrak{C}'$ a concrete data update on $\mathfrak{C}$, iff $\mathfrak{C}'$ replaces some partial function d_c in $\mathfrak{C}$ by the partial function $d'_c = d_c \cup \{n \mapsto v\}$ s.t. for all $n' \in \mathrm{dom}(d_c)$*

$$d'_c(n') = \begin{cases} v & \text{if } d_c(n) = d_c(n') \\ d_c(n') & \text{otherwise} \end{cases}$$

and is otherwise equal to $\mathfrak{C}$. Similarly, let $\mathfrak{A}$ and $\mathfrak{A}'$ be two abstract partial data models. We write $\mathfrak{A} \preccurlyeq \mathfrak{A}'$, and call $\mathfrak{A}'$ an abstract data update on $\mathfrak{A}$, iff $\mathfrak{A}'$ replaces some relation $\approx_c$ in $\mathfrak{A}$ by the relation $\approx'_c = (\approx_c \cup \{(n, n'), (n', n)\})^+$, where $n = n'$ or $n' \in \mathrm{dom}(\approx_c)$, and is otherwise equal to $\mathfrak{A}$.

The notion of update in Definition 4 is best explained by making explicit the kinds of updates that are allowed. First, (1) we can add a data value v of type c to an undefined node n. In the concrete case, we have $n \notin \mathrm{dom}(d_c)$. This means that (1) yields a partial function d'_c which adds the pair $n \mapsto v$ to d_c. In the abstract case, we have $n \notin \mathrm{dom}(\approx_c)$. This means that (1) yields a partial equivalence relation $\approx'_c$ which adds the pair (n, n) to $\approx_c$. Second, (2) we can "update" the data value v of type c assigned to a node n. On a first take, we restrict our attention to updates that preserve "data equality". In the concrete case, (2) yields a partial function d'_c that replaces all pairs $n' \mapsto d_c(n)$ in d_c by a corresponding pair $n' \mapsto v$. This kind of update resembles an aliasing situation, i.e., if a data value is accessed through different nodes, then, modifying the data value through one node implicitly modifies the data values associated with all aliased nodes. In the abstract case, (2) captures the idea of partial equivalence classes in $\approx_c$ being "merged" in $\approx'_c$. Interestingly, if $\mathfrak{C}$ and $\mathfrak{C}'$ are concrete partial data models such that $\mathfrak{C} \preccurlyeq \mathfrak{C}'$, then, their abstract counterparts $\mathfrak{A}$ and $\mathfrak{A}'$ are such that $\mathfrak{A} \preccurlyeq \mathfrak{A}'$, and viceversa.

3 Reasoning with Incomplete Information

In this section we introduce a modal logic to reason about collections of abstract partial data models related by updates. We refer to this modal logic as Intuitionistic Hybrid XPath with Data (IHXPath$_=$ for short). We define its syntax in Definition 5 and its semantics in Definition 7.

Definition 5. *The language of IHXPath$_=$ has* path *expressions (α, β, ...) and* node *expressions (φ, ψ, ...), mutually defined by the grammar:*

$$\alpha, \beta := \mathsf{a} \mid @_i \mid [\varphi] \mid \alpha\beta$$
$$\varphi, \psi := p \mid i \mid \perp \mid \varphi \vee \psi \mid \varphi \wedge \psi \mid \varphi \to \psi \mid \langle \alpha \rangle \varphi \mid [\alpha]\varphi \mid \langle \alpha *_{\mathsf{c}} \beta \rangle \mid [\alpha *_{\mathsf{c}} \beta].$$

In this grammar, $p \in \mathsf{Prop}$, $i \in \mathsf{Nom}$, $\mathsf{a} \in \mathsf{Mod}$, and $*_{\mathsf{c}} \in \{=_{\mathsf{c}}, \neq_{\mathsf{c}}\}$, with $\mathsf{c} \in \mathsf{Cmp}$. PE is the set of all path expressions and NE is the set of all nodes expressions.

We abbreviate $\neg\varphi := \varphi \to \perp$, $\top := \neg\perp$, $\epsilon := [\top]$, $@_i\varphi := \langle @_i \rangle\varphi$. We write $*_{\mathsf{c}}$ if it is indistinct to use $=_{\mathsf{c}}$ or $\neq_{\mathsf{c}}$. We refer to path expressions of the form $[\varphi]$ as *tests*; and to node expressions of the form $\langle \alpha *_{\mathsf{c}} \beta \rangle$ or $[\alpha *_{\mathsf{c}} \beta]$ as *data comparisons*. Intuitively, a path expression $@_i\alpha$ indicates an α path which starts at a node named i. Moreover, we read $\langle \alpha *_{\mathsf{c}} \beta \rangle$ as *the endpoints of some α and some β paths have the same/different data value (of type c)*, and $\langle \alpha \rangle\varphi$ as *φ holds at the endpoint of some α path*. We make clear the intuitive role of "box" modalities after introducing what models look like in our logic.

Remark 3. It is worth noting that, on the surface, the language for IHXPath$_=$ is inherently that of HXPath$_=$ [6]. In more detail, however, it contains some important changes. In particular, box data comparisons $[\alpha *_{\mathsf{c}} \beta]$ are introduced as primitive, as are the formulas $\langle \alpha \rangle\varphi$ and $[\alpha]\varphi$. As it will be made clear in what follows, $[\alpha *_{\mathsf{c}} \beta]$ and $[\alpha]\varphi$ are no longer definable in terms of $\langle \alpha *_{\mathsf{c}} \beta \rangle$ and $\langle \alpha \rangle\varphi$ due to the lack of duality between boxes and diamonds in an intuitionistic modal setting. The case of $\langle \alpha \rangle\varphi$ is particularly interesting as its definability in terms of $\langle \alpha =_{\mathsf{c}} \alpha \rangle$ in HXPath$_=$ hinged on the reflexivity of data comparisons, which we gave up to deal with partial data values.

Let us now turn our attention to the structures on which to interpret path and nodes expressions (Definition 6), and to the corresponding notion of satisfiability on these structures (Definition 7). Our definitions combine ideas found in [6] and [17].

Definition 6. *An abstract partial update structure (alias a model) is a tuple*

$$\mathcal{M} = \langle M, \preccurlyeq, \{\langle \mathfrak{A}_m, \cong_m \rangle\}_{m \in M} \rangle,$$

where $\langle M, \preccurlyeq \rangle$ is a poset, and for all m,

$$\mathfrak{A}_m = \langle N_m, \{R_m^{\mathsf{a}}\}_{\mathsf{a} \in \mathsf{Mod}}, \{\approx_m^{\mathsf{c}}\}_{\mathsf{c} \in \mathsf{Cmp}}, g_m, V_m \rangle$$

is an abstract partial data model (Definition 3) and $\cong_m$ is a congruence on $\mathfrak{A}_m$. In addition, for all $m \preccurlyeq m'$:

(i) $N_m \subseteq N_{m'}$, (ii) $\cong_m \subseteq \cong_{m'}$, (iii) $R_m^{\mathsf{a}} \subseteq R_{m'}^{\mathsf{a}}$, (iv) $\approx_m^{\mathsf{c}} \subseteq \approx_{m'}^{\mathsf{c}}$, (v) for all $p \in \mathsf{Prop}$, $V_m(p) \subseteq V_{m'}(p)$, and (vi) for all $i \in \mathsf{Nom}$, $g_m(i) = g_{m'}(i)$.

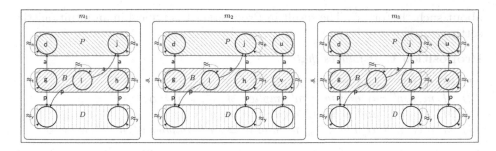

Fig. 3. Abstract Partial Data Update Structure.

Definition 7. *The relation* $\Vdash$ *of satisfiability is defined as:*

$$\mathcal{M}, m, n, n' \Vdash \mathsf{a} \qquad iff \quad n R_m^{\mathsf{a}} n'$$

$$\mathcal{M}, m, n, n' \Vdash @_i \qquad iff \quad g_m(i) \cong_m n'$$

$$\mathcal{M}, m, n, n' \Vdash [\varphi] \qquad iff \quad n \cong_m n' \text{ and } \mathcal{M}, m, n \Vdash \varphi$$

$$\mathcal{M}, m, n, n' \Vdash \alpha\beta \qquad iff \quad \text{exists } n'' \in N_m \text{ s.t. } \mathcal{M}, m, n, n'' \Vdash \alpha \text{ and } \mathcal{M}, m, n'', n' \Vdash \beta$$

$$\mathcal{M}, m, n \Vdash \bot \qquad \qquad never$$

$$\mathcal{M}, m, n \Vdash p \qquad \quad iff \quad n \in V_m(p)$$

$$\mathcal{M}, m, n \Vdash i \qquad \quad iff \quad n \cong_m g_m(i)$$

$$\mathcal{M}, m, n \Vdash \varphi \wedge \psi \qquad iff \quad \mathcal{M}, m, n \Vdash \varphi \text{ and } \mathcal{M}, m, n \Vdash \psi$$

$$\mathcal{M}, m, n \Vdash \varphi \vee \psi \qquad iff \quad \mathcal{M}, m, n \Vdash \varphi \text{ or } \mathcal{M}, m, n \Vdash \psi$$

$$\mathcal{M}, m, n \Vdash \varphi \to \psi \qquad iff \quad \text{for all } m \preccurlyeq m', \ \mathcal{M}, m', n \Vdash \varphi \text{ implies } \mathcal{M}, m', n \Vdash \psi$$

$$\mathcal{M}, m, n \Vdash \langle\alpha\rangle\varphi \qquad iff \quad \text{exists } n' \in N_m \text{ s.t. } \mathcal{M}, m, n, n' \Vdash \alpha \text{ and } \mathcal{M}, m, n' \Vdash \varphi$$

$$\mathcal{M}, m, n \Vdash [\alpha]\varphi \qquad iff \quad \text{for all } m \preccurlyeq m', \ n' \in N_{m'}$$
$$\mathcal{M}, m', n, n' \Vdash \alpha \text{ implies } \mathcal{M}, m', n' \Vdash \varphi$$

$$\mathcal{M}, m, n \Vdash \langle\alpha =_{\mathsf{c}} \beta\rangle \ iff \quad \text{exists } n', n'' \in N_m \text{ s.t.}$$
$$\mathcal{M}, m, n, n' \Vdash \alpha, \ \mathcal{M}, m, n, n'' \Vdash \beta, \text{ and } n' \approx_m^{\mathsf{c}} n''$$

$$\mathcal{M}, m, n \Vdash \langle\alpha \neq_{\mathsf{c}} \beta\rangle \ iff \quad \text{exists } n', n'' \in N_m \text{ s.t.}$$
$$\mathcal{M}, m, n, n' \Vdash \alpha, \ \mathcal{M}, m, n, n'' \Vdash \beta, \text{ and}$$
$$n' \approx_m^{\mathsf{c}} n', \ n'' \approx_m^{\mathsf{c}} n'', \text{ and } n' \not\approx_m^{\mathsf{c}} n''$$

$$\mathcal{M}, m, n \Vdash [\alpha =_{\mathsf{c}} \beta] \ iff \quad \text{for all } m \preccurlyeq m', \ n', n'' \in N_{m'}$$
$$\mathcal{M}, m', n, n' \Vdash \alpha \text{ and } \mathcal{M}, m', n, n'' \Vdash \beta \text{ implies } n' \approx_v^{\mathsf{c}} n''$$

$$\mathcal{M}, m, n \Vdash [\alpha \neq_{\mathsf{c}} \beta] \ iff \quad \text{for all } m \preccurlyeq m', \ n', n'' \in N_{m'}$$
$$\mathcal{M}, m', n, n' \Vdash \alpha \text{ and } \mathcal{M}, m', n, n'' \Vdash \beta \text{ implies}$$
$$n' \approx_m^{\mathsf{c}} n', \ n'' \approx_m^{\mathsf{c}} n'', \ n' \not\approx_m^{\mathsf{c}} n''.$$

For $\Gamma \subseteq \mathsf{NE}$*, we define* $\mathcal{M}, m, n \Vdash \Gamma$ *iff* $\mathcal{M}, m, n \Vdash \gamma$ *for all* $\gamma \in \Gamma$*. Moreover, for* $\Gamma \cup \{\varphi\} \subseteq \mathsf{NE}$*, we define* $\Gamma \vDash \varphi$ *iff* $\mathcal{M}, m, n \Vdash \Gamma$ *implies* $\mathcal{M}, m, n \Vdash \varphi$*.*

Intuitively, models as in Definition 6 can be understood as collections of abstract partial data models related by abstract data updates (cf. Definition 4). These collections capture possible "histories" of updates. Interpreting "box" data comparisons and implications in an intuitionistic way permit us to reason about such "histories". The result in Proposition 1 is typical in an intuitionistic setting.

Proposition 1. *It follows that:*

(1) $\mathcal{M}, m, n \Vdash \varphi$ *and* $m \preccurlyeq m'$ *implies* $\mathcal{M}, m', n \Vdash \varphi$;

(2) $\mathcal{M}, m, n, n' \Vdash \alpha$ *and* $m \preccurlyeq m'$ *implies* $\mathcal{M}, m', n, n' \Vdash \alpha$;

(3) $\mathcal{M}, m, n \Vdash \varphi$ *and* $n \cong_m n'$ *implies* $\mathcal{M}, m, n' \Vdash \varphi$;

(4) $\mathcal{M}, m, n, n' \Vdash \alpha$ *and* $n \cong_m n''$ *and* $n' \cong_m n'''$ *implies* $\mathcal{M}, m, n'', n''' \Vdash \alpha$.

Example 1. We conclude this section with an example illustrating models and node and path expressions in use. For instance, the model in Fig. 3 may be understood as the history of what would occur if we add the Voynich manuscript (m_2) to our original library catalog (m_1), and later on we learn its author(s) and publication date (m_3). This history can be queried using node expressions such as $\langle @_\mathsf{l} a =_\mathsf{n} @_\mathsf{h} a \rangle$, stating that the author's name of *"A certain Lucas"* (l) and of *"Hopscotch"* (h) is the same, and it holds in m_1, m_2, and m_3. We can also write $@_\mathsf{v} B$, stating that *"The Voynich Manuscript"* (v) is a book on the catalog. This new node expression does not hold at m_1, but it holds at m_2 and m_3 –once the book has been added into the catalog. To be noted, adding a new named node is modeled by the addition of a new node together with the association, via $\cong$, of this new node to an already existing named node. Moreover, we can check that $@_\mathsf{v} \langle \mathsf{p} \rangle \top$, stating that v has a publication date, does not hold at m_1, but it holds at m_2 and m_3. Finally, we can check that $@_\mathsf{v} \langle \mathsf{p} =_\mathsf{y} \mathsf{p} \rangle$, stating that the publication date (p) of v is known, holds only at m_3.

4   Axiomatization and Completeness

In this section we present a strongly complete axiom system for IHXPath$_=$. This axiom system takes inspiration from [6,17], and consists of the axiom schemata in Table 1 and the inference rules in Table 2. The axioms under the heading 'Comparisons' in Table 1 deserve a short explanation. These axioms differ slightly from those in [6], since dealing with partial data values forced us to give up reflexivity for data equality. This implies that equality/inequality tests must ensure that they contain actual data. The rules of inference for 'Paths' generalize those from [17] and handle data comparisons. The axiom system for IHXPath$_=$ gives rise to a Hilbert-style notion of deduction of a node expression φ from a set of node expressions Γ, written $\Gamma \vdash \varphi$, defined inductively as usual. Proposition 2 is useful in our proof of completeness.

Proposition 2 (Agree). $\vdash @_i @_j \varphi \leftrightarrow @_j \varphi$.

Soundness and Completeness. The rest of this section covers the adequacy of the axiom system. Soundness is obtained by induction. We prove completeness by showing that every consistent set of node expressions is satisfiable. We use a Henkin-style construction akin to that for Hybrid Logic (see [14,24]). We take NE(Nom'), alias NE', for the set of node expressions with nominals in a set Nom'.

Table 1. Axioms for IHXPath$_=$

Basic	Paths
(IPL) Theorems of Intuitionistic Prop. Logic	(Cat) $\langle\alpha\rangle\langle\beta\rangle\varphi \leftrightarrow \langle\alpha\beta\rangle\varphi$
	(Id$_\epsilon$) $\langle\epsilon\rangle\varphi \leftrightarrow \varphi$
Satisfaction	(Dist1) $@_i\langle\alpha\beta *_c \gamma\rangle \leftrightarrow @_i(\langle\alpha\rangle\langle\beta *_c @_i\gamma\rangle)$
	(Dist2) $\langle\alpha\rangle\langle\beta *_c \gamma\rangle \rightarrow \langle\alpha\beta *_c \alpha\gamma\rangle$
(Distr$_\wedge^@$) $@_i(\varphi \wedge \psi) \leftrightarrow (@_i\varphi \wedge @_i\psi)$	(Dist3) $\langle@_i\alpha *_c @_i\beta\rangle \rightarrow @_i\langle\alpha *_c \beta\rangle$
(Distr$_\vee^@$) $@_i(\varphi \vee \psi) \leftrightarrow (@_i\varphi \vee @_i\psi)$	(Test) $\langle[\psi]\alpha\rangle\varphi \leftrightarrow \psi \wedge \langle\alpha\rangle\varphi$
(Distr$_\rightarrow^@$) $@_i(\varphi \rightarrow \psi) \leftrightarrow (@_i\varphi \rightarrow @_i\psi)$	(Scope) $\langle@_j\alpha *_c \beta\rangle \rightarrow \langle@_i@_j\alpha *_c \beta\rangle$
(Falsum) $@_i\bot \rightarrow \bot$	(Back) $\langle\alpha@_i\beta *_c \gamma\rangle \rightarrow \langle@_i\beta *_c \gamma\rangle$
(Refl@) $@_i i$	$(\langle\alpha\rangle\mathrm{I})$ $(\langle\alpha\rangle i \wedge @_i\varphi) \rightarrow \langle\alpha\rangle\varphi$
	$(\langle *\rangle\mathrm{I})$ $(\langle\alpha\rangle i \wedge \langle@_i *_c \beta\rangle) \rightarrow \langle\alpha *_c \beta\rangle$
Comparisons	$([\alpha]\mathrm{E})$ $(\langle\alpha\rangle j \wedge [\alpha]\varphi) \rightarrow @_j\varphi$
	$([*]\mathrm{E})$ $(\langle\alpha\rangle i \wedge \langle\beta\rangle j \wedge [\alpha *_c \beta]) \rightarrow \langle@_i *_c @_j\rangle$
(T$\langle *\rangle$) $\langle\alpha *_c \beta\rangle \rightarrow \langle\alpha =_c \alpha\rangle$	
(B$\langle *\rangle$) $\langle\alpha *_c \beta\rangle \leftrightarrow \langle\beta *_c \alpha\rangle$	
(4$\langle=\rangle$) $(\langle\alpha =_c @_i\rangle \wedge \langle@_i =_c \beta\rangle) \rightarrow \langle\alpha =_c \beta\rangle$	
(Irref) $\neg\langle\alpha \neq_c \alpha\rangle$	
(CTran) $(\langle\alpha \neq_c \beta\rangle \wedge \langle\alpha =_c @_i\rangle) \rightarrow (\langle\alpha \neq_c @_i\rangle \vee \langle@_i \neq_c \beta\rangle)$	
(Comp) $(\langle\alpha =_c @_i\rangle \wedge \langle@_i \neq_c \beta\rangle) \rightarrow \langle\alpha \neq_c \beta\rangle$	
(EM$_{\langle\neq\rangle}^{\langle=\rangle}$) $(\langle\alpha =_c \alpha\rangle \wedge \langle\beta =_c \beta\rangle) \rightarrow (\langle\alpha =_c \beta\rangle \vee \langle\alpha \neq_c \beta\rangle)$	

Table 2. Rules of Inference for IHXPath$_=$

Basic

$$\frac{\varphi \quad \varphi \rightarrow \psi}{\psi} \; (\text{MP})$$

Satisfaction

$$\frac{\varphi}{@_i\varphi} \; (@\text{I'})$$

$$\frac{@_i j \quad @_i\varphi}{@_j\varphi} \; (\text{Nom})$$

$$\frac{@_i\varphi}{\varphi} \; (@\text{E})^\dagger$$

Paths

$$\frac{\varphi \rightarrow @_i\langle\alpha\beta *_c \gamma\rangle \wedge (\varphi \wedge @_i\langle\alpha\rangle j \wedge @_i\langle@_j\beta *_c \gamma\rangle) \rightarrow \psi}{\varphi \rightarrow \psi} \; (\langle *\rangle\text{E})^\dagger$$

$$\frac{(\varphi \rightarrow @_i\langle\alpha\rangle\chi) \wedge ((\varphi \wedge @_j\chi \wedge @_i\langle\alpha\rangle j) \rightarrow \psi)}{\varphi \rightarrow \psi} \; (\langle\alpha\rangle\text{E})^\dagger$$

$$\frac{(\varphi \wedge @_i(\langle\alpha\rangle j \wedge \langle\beta\rangle k)) \rightarrow \langle@_j *_c @_k\rangle}{\varphi \rightarrow @_i[\alpha *_c \beta]} \; ([*]\text{I})^\dagger$$

$$\frac{(\varphi \wedge @_i\langle\alpha\rangle j) \rightarrow @_j\psi}{\varphi \rightarrow @_i[\alpha]\psi} \; ([\alpha]\text{I})^\dagger$$

$\dagger\, i$ does not occur in φ. $\quad\dagger\, j$ and k do not occur in $\alpha, \beta, \gamma, \chi$ nor ψ.

Definition 8 (Saturated). *Let* $\mathsf{Nom}' \subset \mathsf{Nom}''$; $\Gamma'' \subseteq \mathsf{NE}(\mathsf{Nom}'')$ *is saturated iff:*

1. $\Gamma'' = \{\varphi \mid \Gamma'' \vdash \varphi\} \subset \mathsf{NE}(\mathsf{Nom}'')$;
2. $@_i(\varphi \vee \psi) \in \Gamma''$ *implies* $@_i\varphi \in \Gamma''$ *or* $@_i\psi \in \Gamma''$;
3. *exists* $i \in \mathsf{Nom}''$ *s.t.* $i \in \Gamma''$;
4. $@_i\langle\mathsf{a}\rangle\varphi \in \Gamma''$ *implies exists* $j \in \mathsf{Nom}''$ *s.t.* $\{@_j\varphi, @_i\langle\mathsf{a}\rangle j\} \subseteq \Gamma''$
5. $@_i\langle@_j\mathsf{a}\alpha *_c \beta\rangle \in \Gamma''$ *implies*

$$\text{exists } k \in (\mathsf{Nom}'' \setminus \mathsf{Nom}') \text{ s.t. } \{@_j\langle\mathsf{a}\rangle k, @_i\langle@_k\alpha *_c \beta\rangle\} \subseteq \Gamma''.$$

The conditions above have the following names: 1. $\vdash$-*closed; 2. the disjunction property; 3. named; 4.* $\langle\alpha\rangle$-*pasted; and 5.* $\langle *\rangle$-*pasted.*

Now we are in position to establish Lemma 1, a.k.a., the *Lindenbaum Lemma*. This lemma states a crucial result: consistent sets can be extended to *saturated* sets (enriching the language with new symbols for nominals).

Lemma 1 (Saturation Lemma). *Let* $\mathsf{Nom}' \subset \mathsf{Nom}''$, *and* $\Gamma' \cup \{\psi\} \subseteq \mathsf{NE}'$ *be s.t.* $\Gamma' \nvdash \psi$. *There is* $\Gamma'' \subseteq \mathsf{NE}''$ *s.t.* (1) $\Gamma' \subseteq \Gamma''$, (2) Γ'' *is saturated, and* (3) $\Gamma'' \nvdash \psi$.

Proof. Enumerate all node expressions in NE'' and let $k \in (\mathsf{Nom}'' \setminus \mathsf{Nom}')$ be the first nominal in this enumeration. Define $\Sigma_0 = \Gamma' \cup \{k\}$. Now, suppose that we have defined Σ_n, for $n \geq 0$. Let $\varphi_{(n+1)}$ be the $(n+1)^{\text{th}}$ node expression in the enumeration. If $\Sigma_n \cup \{\varphi_{(n+1)}\} \vdash \psi$, then, define $\Sigma_{(n+1)} = \Sigma_n$. Otherwise, i.e., if $\Sigma_n \cup \{\varphi_{(n+1)}\} \nvdash \psi$, then, define $\Sigma_{(n+1)} = \Sigma_n \cup \{\varphi_{(n+1)}\} \cup \Sigma'$ where:

$$
\Sigma' = \begin{cases}
\emptyset & \text{if } \varphi_{(n+1)} \notin \{@_i(\theta \vee \chi), @_i\langle a\rangle\varphi, @_i\langle @_j a\alpha *_c \beta\rangle\} \\
\{@_i\theta\} & \text{if } \varphi_{(n+1)} \text{ is } @_i(\theta \vee \chi) \text{ and } \Sigma_n \cup \{\varphi_{(n+1)}, @_i\theta\} \nvdash \psi \\
\{@_i\chi\} & \text{if } \varphi_{(n+1)} \text{ is } @_i(\theta \vee \chi) \text{ and } \Sigma_n \cup \{\varphi_{(n+1)}, @_i\theta\} \vdash \psi \\
\{@_i\langle a\rangle j, @_j\varphi\} & \text{if } \varphi_{(n+1)} \text{ is } @_i\langle a\rangle\varphi \\
& \quad \text{and } j \in \mathsf{Nom}'' \text{ does not appear in } \Sigma_n \cup \{\varphi_{(n+1)}\}. \\
\{@_j\langle a\rangle k, @_i\langle @_k\alpha *_c \beta\rangle\} & \text{if } \varphi_{(n+1)} \text{ is } @_i\langle @_j a\alpha *_c \beta\rangle \\
& \quad \text{and } k \in \mathsf{Nom}'' \text{ does not appear in } \Sigma_n \cup \{\varphi_{(n+1)}\}.
\end{cases}
$$

Define $\Sigma = \bigcup_{n \geq 0} \Sigma_n$. It is possible to prove by induction that $\Sigma \nvdash \psi$. The proof finishes if Σ is saturated. We prove only the cases $\langle\alpha\rangle$-pasted and $\langle*\rangle$-pasted.

$(\langle\alpha\rangle$-pasted) Let $@_i\langle a\rangle\varphi \in \Sigma$ and, w.l.o.g., $\varphi_{(n+1)} = @_i\langle a\rangle\varphi$. It follows that, $\{@_i\langle a\rangle j, @_j\varphi\} \subseteq \Sigma_{(n+1)} \subseteq \Sigma$ for j a nominal in $\mathsf{Nom}'' \setminus \mathsf{Nom}'$.

$(\langle*\rangle$-pasted) Let $@_i\langle @_j a\alpha *_c \beta\rangle \in \Sigma$ and, w.l.o.g., $\varphi_{(n+1)} = @_i\langle @_j a\alpha *_c \beta\rangle$. It follows that, $\{@_i\langle a\rangle j, @_i\langle @_k\alpha *_c \beta\rangle\} \subseteq \Sigma_{(n+1)} \subseteq \Sigma$ for $j \in \mathsf{Nom}''$.

Lemma 1 enables us to build the model needed for proving completeness (Definition 9).

Definition 9 (Extracted Model). *Let* $\{\mathsf{Nom}'_i\}_{i\in\mathbb{N}}$ *be a family of pairwise disjoint denumerable sets of nominals. Moreover, let* $\mathsf{Nom}^*_n = \bigcup_{i=1}^n \mathsf{Nom}'_i$; *and* $\mathsf{NE}^*_n = \mathsf{NE}(\mathsf{Nom} \cup \mathsf{Nom}^*_n)$. *For every consistent set* $\Gamma \subseteq \mathsf{NE}$; *define*

$$\mathcal{M}_\Gamma = \langle M, \subseteq, \{\langle \mathfrak{A}_{\Gamma'}, \cong_{\Gamma'}\rangle\}_{\Gamma'\in M}\rangle$$

where: $\mathfrak{A}_{\Gamma'} = \langle N_{\Gamma'}, \{R^a_{\Gamma'}\}_{a\in\mathsf{Mod}}, \{\approx^c_{\Gamma'}\}_{c\in\mathsf{Cmp}}, g_{\Gamma'}, V_{\Gamma'}\rangle$ *and*

1. $M = \{\Gamma' \subseteq \mathsf{NE}^*_n \mid n \in \mathbb{N} \text{ and } \Gamma \subseteq \Gamma' \text{ and } \Gamma' \text{ is saturated}\}$;
2. *for all* $N_{\Gamma'} = \{i \mid i \text{ is a nominal appearing in } \Gamma'\}$;
3. *for all* $\cong_{\Gamma'} = \{(i,j) \mid @_i j \in \Gamma'\}$;
4. *for all* $R^a_{\Gamma'} = \{(i,j) \mid @_i\langle a\rangle j \in \Gamma'\}$;
5. *for all* $\approx^c_{\Gamma'} = \{(i,j) \mid \langle @_i =_c @_j\rangle \in \Gamma'\}$;
6. *for all* $V_{\Gamma'} : \mathsf{Prop} \to 2^{N_{\Gamma'}}$, *it follows that* $V_{\Gamma'}(p) = \{i \mid @_i p \in \Gamma'\}$; *and*
7. *for all* $g_{\Gamma'} : \mathsf{Nom} \to N_{\Gamma'}$, *it follows that* $g_{\Gamma'}(i) = i$.

It can be checked that the structure in Definition 9 is a model in the sense of Definition 6. On this basis, we state the Truth Lemma 2 and the Completeness Theorem 1.

Lemma 2 (Truth Lemma). *Let $\mathcal{M}_\Gamma$ be as in Definition 9, it follows that:*

(1) $\mathcal{M}_\Gamma, \Gamma', i, j \Vdash \alpha$ iff $@_i \langle \alpha \rangle j \in \Gamma'$ (2) $\mathcal{M}_\Gamma, \Gamma', i \Vdash \varphi$ iff $@_i \varphi \in \Gamma'$.

Proof. The proof is by mutual induction on path and node expressions. The inductive hypotheses are

$$(\text{IH}_1) \ \mathcal{M}_\Gamma, \Gamma', i, j \Vdash \alpha \text{ iff } @_i \langle \alpha \rangle j \in \Gamma'; \quad (\text{IH}_2) \ \mathcal{M}_\Gamma, \Gamma', i \Vdash \varphi \text{ iff } @_i \varphi \in \Gamma'.$$

We prove the inductive case for $[\alpha =_c \beta]$ as one of the most interesting. For this case, we need to prove $\mathcal{M}_\Gamma, \Gamma', i \Vdash [\alpha =_c \beta]$ iff $@_i [\alpha =_c \beta] \in \Gamma'$.

($\Rightarrow$) The proof proceeds by contradiction. Suppose: (a) $\mathcal{M}_\Gamma, \Gamma', i \Vdash [\alpha =_c \beta]$ and (b) $@_i [\alpha =_c \beta] \notin \Gamma'$. We prove (c) $\Gamma' \cup \{@_i \langle \alpha \rangle j, @_i \langle \beta \rangle k\} \nvdash @_i \langle @_j =_c @_k \rangle$ for j, k arbitrary in $N_{\Gamma'}$. From not (c), i.e., $\Gamma' \cup \{@_i \langle \alpha \rangle j, @_i \langle \beta \rangle k\} \vdash @_i \langle @_j =_c @_k \rangle$, we get $\Gamma' \vdash @_i ((\langle \alpha \rangle j \wedge \langle \beta \rangle k) \rightarrow \langle @_j =_c @_k \rangle)$; and using ([*]1) we obtain $\Gamma' \vdash @_i [\alpha =_c \beta]$; this contradicts (b). Then, from Lemma 1,

(d) exists $\Gamma'' \supseteq \Gamma' \cup \{@_i \langle \alpha \rangle j, @_i \langle \beta \rangle k\}$ s.t. $@_i \langle @_j =_c @_k \rangle \notin \Gamma''$.

The claim is: (d) contradicts (a). Suppose that exists such a Γ'', using (IH_1), we get that exists $\Gamma'' \supseteq \Gamma'$ and $\{j, k\} \subseteq N_{\Gamma''}$ s.t. $\mathcal{M}_\Gamma, \Gamma'', i, j \Vdash \alpha$, $\mathcal{M}_\Gamma, \Gamma'', i, k \Vdash \beta$, and $j \not\approx^c_{\Gamma''} k$. This means that $\mathcal{M}_\Gamma, \Gamma', i \nVdash [\alpha =_c \beta]$; which is a contradiction. Therefore, $\mathcal{M}_\Gamma, \Gamma', i \Vdash [\alpha =_c \beta]$ implies $@_i [\alpha =_c \beta] \in \Gamma'$.

($\Leftarrow$) Let $@_i [\alpha =_c \beta] \in \Gamma'$. Proving $\mathcal{M}_\Gamma, \Gamma', i \Vdash [\alpha =_c \beta]$ is equiv. to proving that for all $\Gamma'' \supseteq \Gamma'$ and all $\{j, k\} \subseteq N_{\Gamma''}$, if $\mathcal{M}_\Gamma, \Gamma'', i, j \Vdash \alpha$ and $\mathcal{M}_\Gamma, \Gamma'', i, k \Vdash \beta$, then, $j \approx^c_{\Gamma''} k$. Let $\Gamma'' \supseteq \Gamma'$ and $\{j, k\} \subseteq N_{\Gamma''}$ be s.t. $\mathcal{M}_\Gamma, \Gamma'', i, j \Vdash \alpha$ and $\mathcal{M}_\Gamma, \Gamma'', i, k \Vdash \beta$. The proof is concluded if $j \approx^c_{\Gamma''} k$, i.e., $\langle @_j =_c @_k \rangle \in \Gamma''$. From (A) $\{@_i \langle \alpha \rangle j, @_i \langle \beta \rangle k\} \subseteq \Gamma''$. Since $\Gamma' \subseteq \Gamma''$, $@_i [\alpha =_c \beta] \in \Gamma''$. Using ([*]E), we get $@_i \langle @_j =_c @_k \rangle \in \Gamma''$. Thus, $j \approx^c_{\Gamma''} k$.

Theorem 1 (Completeness). $\Gamma \vDash \varphi$ *implies* $\Gamma \vdash \varphi$.

Proof. We prove $\Gamma \nvdash \varphi$ implies $\Gamma \nvDash \varphi$. Let $\mathcal{M}_\Gamma$ be as in Definition 9. From Lemma 1 we know that exists $\Gamma' \supseteq \Gamma$ s.t. $\Gamma' \in \mathcal{M}_\Gamma$ and $\varphi \notin \Gamma'$. From Lemma 2, it is clear that for some nominal $i \in N_{\Gamma'}$, $\mathcal{M}_\Gamma, \Gamma', i \Vdash \Gamma$ and $\mathcal{M}_\Gamma, \Gamma', i \nVdash \varphi$. This proves $\Gamma \nvDash \varphi$.

5   Extended Axiomatic Systems

In this section we briefly cover extensions of IHXPath$_=$ with *pure axioms* and *existential saturation rules*, a family of axioms and rules that enables us to extend our strong completeness result for a wider family of logics. These ideas make use of the ability of hybrid logics to fully internalize the first-order conditions that are needed to characterize many interesting frame classes. Similarly to what is done in [6,14], if we add pure axioms and existential saturation rules into the axiom system for IHXPath$_=$, the completeness proof in the previous section automatically yields strong completeness for the extended axiom systems, with respect to their respective classes of models.

Table 3. Standard Translation into IFOL

Propositional		Paths	
$\mathsf{ST}'_x(\bot)$	$= \bot$	$\mathsf{ST}'_x(\langle\alpha\rangle\varphi)$	$= \exists y(\mathsf{ST}'_{x,y}(\alpha) \wedge \mathsf{ST}'_y(\varphi))$
$\mathsf{ST}'_x(p)$	$= p(x)$	$\mathsf{ST}'_x([\alpha]\varphi)$	$= \forall y(\mathsf{ST}'_{x,y}(\alpha) \rightarrow \mathsf{ST}'_y(\varphi))$
$\mathsf{ST}'_x(i)$	$= x = x_i$	$\mathsf{ST}'_{x,y}(\mathsf{a})$	$= a(x,y)$
$\mathsf{ST}'_x(\varphi \vee \psi)$	$= \mathsf{ST}'_x(\varphi) \vee \mathsf{ST}'_x(\psi)$	$\mathsf{ST}'_{x,y}(@_i)$	$= y = x_i$
$\mathsf{ST}'_x(\varphi \wedge \psi)$	$= \mathsf{ST}'_x(\varphi) \wedge \mathsf{ST}'_x(\psi)$	$\mathsf{ST}'_{x,y}([\varphi])$	$= (x = y) \wedge \mathsf{ST}'_y(\varphi)$
$\mathsf{ST}'_x(\varphi \rightarrow \psi)$	$= \mathsf{ST}'_x(\varphi) \rightarrow \mathsf{ST}'_x(\psi)$	$\mathsf{ST}'_{x,y}(\alpha\beta)$	$= \exists z(\mathsf{ST}'_{x,z}(\alpha) \wedge \mathsf{ST}'_{z,y}(\beta))$

Comparisons
$\mathsf{ST}'_x(\langle\alpha =_c \beta\rangle) = \exists y \exists z(\mathsf{ST}'_{x,y}(\alpha) \wedge \mathsf{ST}'_{x,z}(\beta) \wedge c(y,z))$
$\mathsf{ST}'_x(\langle\alpha \neq_c \beta\rangle) = \exists y \exists z(\mathsf{ST}'_{x,y}(\alpha) \wedge \mathsf{ST}'_{x,z}(\beta) \wedge c(y,y) \wedge c(z,z) \wedge \neg c(y,z))$
$\mathsf{ST}'_x([\alpha =_c \beta]) = \forall y \forall z(\mathsf{ST}'_{x,y}(\alpha) \wedge \mathsf{ST}'_{x,z}(\beta) \rightarrow c(y,z))$
$\mathsf{ST}'_x([\alpha \neq_c \beta]) = \forall y \forall z(\mathsf{ST}'_{x,y}(\alpha) \wedge \mathsf{ST}'_{x,z}(\beta) \rightarrow (c(y,y) \wedge c(z,z) \wedge \neg c(y,z)))$

Partial Equality	
$\sigma_c = \forall x \forall y(c(x,y) \rightarrow c(x,y))$	$\tau_c = \forall x \forall y \forall z(c(x,y) \wedge c(y,z) \rightarrow c(x,z))$

Standard Translation. We will define a *standard translation* of the language of IHXPath$_=$ into the language of Intuitionistic FOL with equality (IFOL). This translation is needed to characterize the frame conditions that the new axioms and rules define. The semantics of IFOL, can be found, e.g., in [21].

Definition 10. *Fix an alphabet of denumerable sets of: unary predicate symbols (*P*), binary relation symbols (*R*), constant symbols (*Con*), and variable symbols (*Var*). The language of IFOL is defined by the grammar:*

$$\varphi, \psi := p(t) \mid r(t,t') \mid \bot \mid t = t' \mid \varphi \vee \psi \mid \varphi \wedge \psi \mid \varphi \rightarrow \psi \mid \exists x \varphi \mid \forall x \varphi,$$

where t, t' are terms –i.e., symbols for constants or variables, $p \in$ P, and $r \in$ R.

Definition 11 establishes a correspondence from the language of IHXPath$_=$ to that of IFOL. Notice that symbols in Prop and P are in a one to one correspondence; that we map each $\mathsf{a} \in$ Mod to a unique $a \in$ Rels; and that $x, y, z, \ldots$ are symbols in Var. Proposition 3 indicates that such a correspondence preserves satisfiability.

Definition 11. *The* standard translation *of a node expression φ is defined as:* $\mathsf{ST}_x(\varphi) = \left(\bigwedge_{c \in \mathsf{Cmp}}(\sigma_c \wedge \tau_c)\right) \wedge \mathsf{ST}'_x(\varphi)$*; where σ_c, τ_c, and ST'_x are as in Table 3.*

Proposition 3. $\mathcal{M}, m, n \Vdash \varphi$ *iff* $\mathcal{M}, m \Vdash \mathsf{ST}_x(\varphi)[x \mapsto w, x_i \mapsto g_m(i)]$.

Pure Axioms and Existential Saturation Rules. We introduce pure axioms and existential saturation rules, and their associated frame conditions. Briefly, pure axioms are formulas that use no proposition symbols; and existential saturation rules are instantiations of first-order formulas with a $\forall\exists$ quantification pattern. These axioms and rules are incorporated to the axiom system from Sect. 4, which contains *unorthodox inference rules*, i.e., rules with side conditions. As discussed in [6,14], unorthodox rules are crucial to obtain a general completeness result.

Notation. We use i_n to indicate a sequence $i_1 \ldots i_n$ of nominals; and $\varphi(i_n)$ to indicate a node expression with no proposition symbols and with nominals in i_n. Lastly, we use $Q i_n \varphi$ to indicate $Q x_{i_1} \ldots Q x_{i_n} \varphi$ for $Q \in \{\forall, \exists\}$.

Definition 12. *A node expression is called* pure *iff it has no proposition symbols. A rule of the form*

$$\frac{\varphi(i_n j_m) \to \psi}{\psi} \ (\rho)$$

is called an existential saturation rule *iff i_n and j_m are disjoint sequences of nominals, and the nominals in ψ are not in j_m. We use* $\mathrm{hd}(\rho)$ *to indicate* $\varphi(i_n j_m)$. *Sets Π and P of pure expressions and existential saturation rules, respectively, define a* frame condition $\mathsf{FC}(\Pi \cup P)$ *defined as:*

$$\bigwedge \{ \forall x \forall i_n (\mathsf{ST}_x(\varphi(i_n))) \mid \varphi(i_n) \in \Pi \} \wedge \bigwedge \{ \forall x \forall i_n \exists j_m (\mathsf{ST}_x(\mathrm{hd}(\rho))) \mid \rho \in P \}.$$

Extending the axiom system of IHXPath$_=$ with pure axioms and existential saturation forces us to revise the definition of saturation and the saturation lemma in Definition 8 and Lemma 1; necessary for completeness. This is done in Definition 13 and Lemma 3, respectively. Theorem 2 states the generalized completeness theorem.

Definition 13 (P-saturated). *Let* Nom$'$ $\subset$ Nom$''$ *and P a set of existential saturation rules;* $\Gamma'' \subseteq$ NE$''$ *is P-saturated iff Γ'' is saturated and*

for all $\rho \in P$ and all nominals $k_n \in \Gamma''$,
    exists $l_m \subseteq ($Nom$'' \setminus$ Nom$') $ s.t. $\varphi[i_n j_m / k_n l_m] \in \Gamma''$ –where $\varphi(i_n j_m) = \mathrm{hd}(\rho)$.

Lemma 3 (P-saturation Lemma). *Let* Nom$'$ $\subset$ Nom$''$; Π *be a set of pure axioms and P a set of existential saturation rules. Moreover, let $\Gamma' \subseteq$ NE$'$ be s.t. $\Gamma' \nvdash \psi$. Exists $\Gamma'' \subseteq$ NE$''$ s.t.: (1) $\Gamma' \subseteq \Gamma''$; (2) Γ'' is P-saturated; and (3) $\Gamma'' \nvdash \psi$.*

Theorem 2. *Let Π and P be sets of pure axioms and existential saturation rules, respectively. The axiomatic system obtained by extending that from Tables 1 and 2 with Π and P as additional axioms and rules, is strongly complete w.r.t. the class of models whose frames satisfy* $\mathsf{FC}(\Pi \cup P)$.

6   Final Remarks

We presented a logic –IHXPath$_=$– that provides an intuitionistic reading of XPath with (in)equality checks for attribute values in the presence of partial data value functions and updates. For this logic, we first identified suitable notions of concrete and abstract models, and characterized a certain class of update functions. This lead us to the definition of abstract partial update structures, which became the models of our logic. To our knowledge, this is the first approach for dealing with incomplete information based on partial orders between data graphs. Other attempts to address similar problems use completely different ideas, such as those presented in [2,12,26]. Moreover, by defining a suitable notion of updates (defining certain cases in which new information can be added to a graph database) we discovered a novel link between dynamic data updates and intuitionistic logic.

We provided an axiomatization and a strong completeness result. Moreover, we showed that our system preserves strong completeness when extended with pure axioms and existential saturation rules (with respect to the corresponding class of models). These extensions allow to characterize several interesting classes of models (cf, e.g., [6,14]).

Much remains to be done. For instance, besides (in)equalities, we would like to explore comparison operators such as less than, greater than, etc. Moreover, we would like to study this logic from a purely dynamic logic perspective, à la [7,10,29]. It would also be interesting to characterize particular classes of models (e.g., the case were the accessibility relations define trees). Other model theoretic questions should also be addressed, e.g., defining a proper notion of bisimulation that captures the expressive power of the logic. Finally, decidability and complexity of different reasoning tasks (e.g., model-checking, satisfiability) should be established. We conjecture, e.g., that the notions of filtration defined in [6] for HXPath$_=$, might be extended and adapted to IHXPath$_=$ to prove decidability of the satisfiability problem, together with upper-bounds to its complexity. These are some initial thoughts that deserve further exploration.

Acknowledgments. We thank the reviewers for their valuable comments. Our work is supported by the Laboratoire International Associé SINFIN, the EU Grant Agreement 101008233 (MISSION), the ANPCyT projects PICT-2020-3780, PICT-2021-00400, PICT-2021-00675, and PICTO-2022-CBA-00088, and the CONICET projects PIBAA-28720210100428CO, PIBAA-28720210100165CO, and PIP-11220200100812CO.

References

1. Abriola, S., Barceló, P., Figueira, D., Figueira, S.: Bisimulations on data graphs. J. Artif. Intell. Res. **61**, 171–213 (2018)
2. Abriola, S., Cifuentes, S., Martinez, M., Pardal, N., Pin, E.: An epistemic approach to model uncertainty in data-graphs. Int. J. Approximate Reason. **160**, 108948 (2023)
3. Abriola, S., Descotte, M.E., Fervari, R., Figueira, S.: Axiomatizations for downward XPath on data trees. J. Comput. Syst. Sci. **89**, 209–245 (2017)

4. Angles, R., Gutiérrez, C.: Survey of graph database models. ACM Comput. Surv. **40**(1), 1:1-1:39 (2008)
5. Areces, C., ten Cate, B.: Hybrid logics. In: Handbook of Modal Logic, pp. 821–868. Elsevier (2006)
6. Areces, C., Fervari, R.: Axiomatizing hybrid XPath with data. Log. Methods Comput. Sci. **17**(3) (2021)
7. Areces, C., Fervari, R., Hoffmann, G.: Relation-changing modal operators. Logic J. IGPL **23**(4), 601–627 (2015)
8. Areces, C., Fervari, R., Seiler, N.: Tableaux for hybrid XPath with data. In: Oliveira, E., Gama, J., Vale, Z., Lopes Cardoso, H. (eds.) EPIA 2017. LNCS (LNAI), vol. 10423, pp. 611–623. Springer, Cham (2017). https://doi.org/10.1007/978-3-319-65340-2_50
9. Arenas, M., Fan, W., Libkin, L.: On verifying consistency of XML specifications. In: 21st ACM SIGMOD-SIGACT-SIGART Symposium on Principles of Database Systems (PODS 2002), pp. 259 270. ACM (2002)
10. Aucher, G., van Benthem, J., Grossi, D.: Modal logics of sabotage revisited. J. Logic Comput. **28**(2), 269–303 (2018)
11. Baelde, D., Lunel, S., Schmitz, S.: A sequent calculus for a modal logic on finite data trees. In: 25th EACSL Annual Conference on Computer Science Logic (CSL 2016), LIPIcs, vol. 62, pp. 32:1–32:16. Schloss Dagstuhl (2016)
12. Barceló, P., Libkin, L., Reutter, J.L.: Querying regular graph patterns. J. ACM **61**(1), 81–854 (2014)
13. Blackburn, P., van Benthem, J., Wolter, F.: Handbook of Modal Logic. Elsevier, Amsterdam (2006)
14. Blackburn, P., ten Cate, B.: Pure extensions, proof rules, and hybrid axiomatics. Stud. Logica. **84**(2), 277–322 (2006)
15. Blackburn, P., de Rijke, M., Venema, Y.: Modal Logic, Cambridge Tracts in Theoretical Computer Science, vol. 53. Cambridge University Press (2001)
16. Bojańczyk, M., Muscholl, A., Schwentick, T., Segoufin, L.: Two-variable logic on data trees and XML reasoning. J. ACM **56**(3) (2009)
17. Braüner, T.: Hybrid Logics and its Proof-Theory, Applied Logics Series, vol. 37. Springer, Cham (2011). https://doi.org/10.1007/978-94-007-0002-4
18. ten Cate, B., Fontaine, G., Litak, T.: Some modal aspects of XPath. J. Appl. Non-Class. Logics **20**(3), 139–171 (2010)
19. ten Cate, B., Litak, T., Marx, M.: Complete axiomatizations for XPath fragments. J. Appl. Logic **8**(2), 153–172 (2010)
20. Clark, J., DeRose, S.: XML path language (XPath). Website (1999). W3C Recommendation. http://www.w3.org/TR/xpath
21. van Dalen, D.: Logic and Structure, 5th edn. Springer, Berlin (2013). https://doi.org/10.1007/978-3-540-85108-0
22. Figueira, D.: Reasoning on Words and Trees with Data. PhD thesis, Laboratoire Spécification et Vérification, ENS Cachan, France (2010)
23. Figueira, D.: Decidability of downward XPath. ACM Trans. Comput. Logic **13**(4), 34 (2012)
24. Goldblatt, R.: An abstract setting for Henkin proofs. Topoi **3**(1), 37–41 (1984)
25. Gottlob, G., Koch, C., Pichler, R.: Efficient algorithms for processing XPath queries. ACM Trans. Database Syst. **30**(2), 444–491 (2005)
26. Grabon, M., Michaliszyn, J., Otop, J., Wieczorek, P.: Querying data graphs with arithmetical regular expressions. In: 25th International Joint Conference on Artificial Intelligence (IJCAI 2016), pp. 1088–1094. IJCAI/AAAI Press (2016)

27. Libkin, L., Martens, W., Vrgoč, D.: Querying graphs with data. J. ACM **63**(2), 14:1-14:53 (2016)
28. Libkin, L., Vrgoč, D.: Regular path queries on graphs with data. In: International Conference on Database Theory (ICDT 2012), pp. 74–85. ACM (2012)
29. Plaza, J.: Logics of public communications. Synthese **158**(2), 165–179 (2007)
30. Robinson, I., Webber, J., Eifrem, E.: Graph Databases. O'Reilly Media Inc., Newton (2013)
31. Schinner, A.: The Voynich manuscript: evidence of the hoax hypothesis. Cryptologia **31**(2), 95–107 (2007)

Computing MUS-Based Inconsistency Measures

Isabelle Kuhlmann[1], Andreas Niskanen[2], and Matti Järvisalo[2(✉)]

[1] University of Hagen, Hagen, Germany
[2] University of Helsinki, Helsinki, Finland
matti.jarvisalo@helsinki.fi

Abstract. We detail two instantiations of a generic algorithm for the problematic and MUS-variable-based inconsistency measures, based on answer set programming and Boolean satisfiability (SAT). Empirically, the SAT-based approach allows for more efficiently computing the measures when compared to enumerating all minimal correction subsets of a knowledge base.

Keywords: Inconsistency measurement · minimal unsatisfiability

1 Introduction

Inconsistency measurement [27,29] aims to provide a quantitative assessment of the level of inconsistency in knowledge bases. However, inconsistency measurement in propositional knowledge bases is highly non-trivial under essentially any reasonable quantitative measure of inconsistency [61]. Despite this, algorithmic approaches to inconsistency measurement have been developed [39–42,57] based on declarative techniques. However, various inconsistency measures based on minimally unsatisfiable subsets (MUSes) of knowledge bases [21,28,32,63] cannot be directly captured with a single call to an NP optimizer due to higher complexity of MUS-based inconsistency measures [61]. Less attention has been paid so-far on developing algorithms for such measures [34].

We develop algorithms for the *problematic* (P) [28] and *MUS-variable-based*[1] (MV) [63] inconsistency measures. Both can be determined by enumerating all MUSes in the knowledge base (KB) in terms of the KB formulas: the former measure is the number of KB formulas that occur in the union of the MUSes, the latter the number of *variables* that occur in the union of the MUSes (relative to the number of variables in the KB). By hitting set duality [60], instead of enumerating all MUSes, the measures can alternatively be computed by enumerating all MCSes of the KB [63] using SAT-based MCS enumerators [6,10,30,58,59] as

---

[1] Not to be confused with the notion of variable minimal unsatisfiability [5,18].

Work financially supported by Deutsche Forschungsgemeinschaft (grant 506604007/IK) and by Academy of Finland (grants 347588/AN and 322869, 356046/MJ).

S. Gaggl et al. (Eds.): JELIA 2023, LNAI 14281, pp. 745–755, 2023.
https://doi.org/10.1007/978-3-031-43619-2_50

extensions of MCS extractors [4,31,48,51,53]; MCS enumeration is known to be often easier than MUS enumeration [7–9,11,45,55]. However, MCS enumeration algorithms are not specifically developed with inconsistency measurement in mind.

We develop a generic algorithmic approach specifically for computing the P and MV inconsistency measures, and detail two of its instantiations: one based on iteratively calling an answer set programming (ASP) solver [26,56] on a sequence of queries under a disjunctive answer set program specific to P and MV, and another based on SAT-based counterexample-guided abstraction refinement (CEGAR) [19,20]. The SAT-based CEGAR instantiation empirically outperforms both ASP and state-of-the-art MCS enumerators.

2   Preliminaries

A *knowledge base* (KB) is a finite set of propositional formulas. The signature At(·) of a formula or knowledge base is the set of atoms (or variables) appearing in the formula/KB. A *(truth) assignment* $\tau : \mathsf{At} \to \{0,1\}$ assigns a truth value (1, *true* or 0, *false*) to each atom in At. An assignment τ satisfies a formula ϕ (and ϕ is satisfiable) iff $\tau(\phi) = 1$, i.e., ϕ evaluates to 1 under τ. A KB $\mathcal{K}$ is consistent if there is an assignment that satisfies all formulas in $\mathcal{K}$, and otherwise inconsistent. Let $\mathbb{K}$ be the set of all knowledge bases. Formally, an *inconsistency measure* is a function $\mathcal{I} : \mathbb{K} \to \mathbb{R}_{\geq 0}^{\infty}$ for which $\mathcal{I}(\mathcal{K}) = 0$ iff $\mathcal{K}$ is consistent for all $\mathcal{K} \in \mathbb{K}$. The *problematic* (P) inconsistency measure [28] counts the number of formulas in a given KB participating in some conflict. Similarly, the *MUS-variable-based* (MV) inconsistency measure [63] counts the number of atoms in the signature of a KB that are involved in some conflict. A conflict is defined by the notion of a *minimal unsatisfiable subset* (MUS). A set of logical formulas $S \subseteq \mathcal{K}$ is a *minimal unsatisfiable subset (MUS)* of $\mathcal{K}$ if S is inconsistent, and all $S' \subsetneq S$ are consistent. Now, let MUS($\mathcal{K}$) be the set of MUSes of a given KB $\mathcal{K}$.

Definition 1. *The* problematic *(P) inconsistency measure* $\mathcal{I}_{\mathrm{p}} : \mathbb{K} \to \mathbb{R}_{\geq 0}^{\infty}$ *is* $\mathcal{I}_{\mathrm{p}}(\mathcal{K}) = |\bigcup \mathsf{MUS}(\mathcal{K})|$. *The* MUS-variable-based *(MV) inconsistency measure* $\mathcal{I}_{\mathrm{mv}} : \mathbb{K} \to \mathbb{R}_{\geq 0}^{\infty}$ *is* $\mathcal{I}_{\mathrm{mv}}(\mathcal{K}) = |\bigcup_{M \in \mathsf{MUS}(\mathcal{K})} \mathsf{At}(M)| / |\mathsf{At}(\mathcal{K})|$.

Example 1. Let $\mathcal{K}_1 = \{x \wedge y, \neg x, \neg y, y \vee z\}$. Then $\mathsf{MUS}(\mathcal{K}_1) = \{\{x \wedge y, \neg x\}, \{x \wedge y, \neg y\}\}$. Hence $|\bigcup \mathsf{MUS}(\mathcal{K}_1)| = |\{x \wedge y, \neg x, \neg y\}| = 3$, so $\mathcal{I}_{\mathrm{p}}(\mathcal{K}_1) = 3$. Moreover, $|\bigcup_{M \in \mathsf{MUS}(\mathcal{K}_1)} \mathsf{At}(M)| = |\mathsf{At}(\{x \wedge y, \neg x\}) \cup \mathsf{At}(\{x \wedge y, \neg y\})| = |\{x, y\} \cup \{x, y\}| = |\{x, y\}| = 2$, and $|\mathsf{At}(\mathcal{K}_1)| = |\{x, y, z\}| = 3$. Therefore $\mathcal{I}_{\mathrm{mv}}(\mathcal{K}_1) = \frac{2}{3}$.

A set $S \subseteq \mathcal{K}$ is a *minimal correction set (MCS)* if $\mathcal{K} \setminus S$ is consistent, and for all $S' \subsetneq S$, $\mathcal{K} \setminus S'$ is inconsistent. In words, MCSes identify fragments of KBs whose removal resolves inconsistency. By hitting set duality between MUSes and MCSes [60], we have $\bigcup \mathsf{MUS}(\mathcal{K}) = \bigcup \mathsf{MCS}(\mathcal{K})$ for any KB $\mathcal{K}$, i.e., the union of MUSes is the same as the union of MCSes. In turn, $\mathcal{I}_{\mathrm{p}}(\mathcal{K}) = |\bigcup \mathsf{MCS}(\mathcal{K})|$. The MV measure is equivalently defined by considering atoms in MCSes [63].

3   Algorithms for the P and MV Inconsistency Measures

Algorithm 1 Generic algorithm for the P and MV inconsistency measures.
Input: knowledge base $\mathcal{K}$, measure $\mathcal{I} \in \{\mathcal{I}_p, \mathcal{I}_{mv}\}$.

1: $Q \leftarrow \mathcal{K}, C \leftarrow \emptyset$
2: **while** $Q \neq \emptyset$ **do**
3:      $mcs \leftarrow$ MCSOVERLAP$(\mathcal{K}, Q)$
4:      **if** $mcs = \perp$ **then break**
5:      **if** $\mathcal{I} = \mathcal{I}_p$ **then**
6:           $C \leftarrow C \cup mcs; Q \leftarrow Q \setminus mcs$
7:      **else if** $\mathcal{I} = \mathcal{I}_{mv}$ **then**
8:           $C \leftarrow C \cup \mathsf{At}(mcs); Q \leftarrow Q \setminus \{\phi \in \mathcal{K} \mid \mathsf{At}(\phi) \subseteq C\}$
9: **if** $\mathcal{I} = \mathcal{I}_p$ **then return** $|C|$ **else if** $\mathcal{I} = \mathcal{I}_{mv}$ **then return** $|C|/|\mathsf{At}(\mathcal{K})|$

The P and MV measures can be computed via the union of MCSes of the input
KB $\mathcal{K}$. This is (naively) achieved by enumerating all MCSes, as suggested for the
MV measure [63]. However, this may result in the extraction of MCSes redundant w.r.t. the measure: for P, an MCS which contains only formulas encountered
in previous MCSes, and for MV an MCS whose signature is in the signature of
previous MCSes, does not affect the inconsistency value. The computation of
irredundant MCSes can be formalized as the *MCS overlap problem*: find an
MCS M of $\mathcal{K}$ which intersects a given query $Q \subseteq \mathcal{K}$ of interest. The corresponding decision problem is Σ_2^p-complete, as it is equivalent to the MUS overlap
problem [37,43] which in turn captures the Σ_2^p-complete problem of deciding
whether a given clause occurs in an MUS [44]. As at most a linear number of
NP oracle calls are needed for extracting an MCS [50], it is not plausible that
MCS enumeration algorithms could avoid computing redundant MCSes.

3.1   Generic Algorithm

Our generic algorithm (Algorithm 1) avoids computing redundant MCSes by
iteratively solving the MCS overlap problem instead of enumerating MCSes.
Assume that a procedure MCSOVERLAP is available, returning for a given KB
$\mathcal{K}$ and query Q an MCS mcs with $mcs \cap Q \neq \emptyset$, or $\perp$ if no such MCS exists.
We start by initializing Q to $\mathcal{K}$ and C (covered elements) to $\emptyset$ (line 1). Then,
while Q remains nonempty, we extract an MCS intersecting Q (line 3). If no
such MCS exists, we exit the loop (line 4). How the query Q and the set C is
updated depends on the measure. For the P measure, we add the MCS to C and
remove it from Q (lines 5–6). For MV, we add the signature of the MCS to C
and remove from Q all formulas whose signature is included in C (lines 7–8).
Finally, we either return the size of C for the P measure, or divide it by the size
of the signature of the KB for the MV measure (line 9).

3.2   Instantiation via Disjunctive ASP

```
1 1{inCs(X): kbElement(X)}.
2 inComplement(F):- kbElement(F), not inCs(F).
3 atomInComplement(A):- atomInFormula(A,F), inComplement(F).
4 validCS:- 1{atomInComplement(A): queryAtom(A)}.
5 :- not validCS.
6 atomInCs(A):- atomInFormula(A,F), inCs(F).
7 1{truthValueCS(A,T): tv(T)}1 :- atomInCs(A).
8 numElementsInCs(X):- X = #count{F: inCs(F)}.
9 csIsSat:- numElementsInCs(X), X{truthValueCS(F,t): inCs(F), kbElement(F)}X.
10 :- not csIsSat.
11 numSupersets(X):- numElementsInCs(Y), numKbElements(Z), X=Z-Y.
12 superset(1..X):- numSupersets(X), X>0.
13 1{addElement(F,S): inComplement(F)}1 :- superset(S).
14 supersetEq(S1,S2):- superset(S1), superset(S2), S1!=S2, addElement(F1,S1),
       addElement(F2,S2), F1==F2.
15 :- supersetEq(S1,S2).
16 inSuperset(F,S):- inCs(F), superset(S).
17 inSuperset(F,S):- addElement(F,S), superset(S).
18 atomInSuperset(A,S):- atomInCs(A), superset(S).
19 atomInSuperset(A,S):- addElement(F,S), atomInFormula(A,F).
20 truthValueSet(A,S,t) | truthValueSet(A,S,f):- atomInSuperset(A,S),
       superset(S).
21 truthValueSet(A,S,t):- isUnsat(S), atomInSuperset(A,S), superset(S).
22 truthValueSet(A,S,f):- isUnsat(S), atomInSuperset(A,S), superset(S).
23 isUnsat(S):- truthValueSet(F,S,f), inSuperset(F,S).
24 :- not isUnsat(S), superset(S).
```

Listing 1.1. Disjunctive ASP encoding for MCS overlap.

First, we detail a disjunctive ASP [17,25,47] approach, directly capturing Σ_2^p, to the MCS overlap problem; see Listing 1.1. Its idea is to guess a candidate set S_{cs} of formulas and check whether it is a maximal satisfiable subset (MSS)—the set-complement of which is an MCS. An MSS must be satisfiable while all of its supersets must be unsatisfiable. Moreover, we enforce that at least one atom from $At(Q)$ (w.r.t. MV) or, respectively, formula from Q (w.r.t. P) must be included in the set-complement of the candidate set, i.e., an MCS. Following [39,40], we encode the formulas in a KB $\mathcal{K}$ by representing each atom x in a formula ϕ as atomInFormula(x,ϕ), and the number of formulas as numKbElements($|\mathcal{K}|$). Atoms and formulas are modeled as atom/1 and kbElement/1, respectively. For MV, we represent each atom $x_q \in At(Q)$ as queryAtom(x_q), and, for P, each formula $\phi_q \in Q$ as queryFormula(ϕ_q). Then, e.g., a conjunction $\phi = \phi_1 \wedge \phi_2$ is encoded as conjunction(ϕ,ϕ_1,ϕ_2). Truth values 1 (t) and 0 (f) are represented by tv(t,f). The evaluation of (sub)formulas is encoded following the semantics of the connectives: e.g., a conjunction $\phi = \phi_1 \wedge \phi_2$ evaluates to 1 by truthValueCS(F,t):- conjunction(F,G,H), truthValueCS(G,t), truthValueCS(H,t). Note that we need to avoid the use of not, due to the use of saturation [23]. To check if supersets of a candidate set are unsatisfiable, we refer to a specific superset, i.e., instead of truthValueCS(F,t), we use truthValueSet(F,S,t), etc. A candidate set S_{cs} containing at least one formula $\phi \in \mathcal{K}$ is guessed (line 1). We check that at least one atom (w.r.t. MV) is in the set-complement (lines 2–5). (For P, line 3 is omitted and atomInComplement (line 4) replaced by inComplement, and queryAtom by queryFormula.) To check S_{cs} for satisfiability, each atom in S_{cs} (line 6) gets a truth value (line 7); S_{cs} is satisfiable iff all $|S_{cs}|$ of its formulas evaluate to 1

Algorithm 2 SAT-based CEGAR for solving the MCS overlap problem. Input: knowledge base $\mathcal{K}$, query $Q \subseteq \mathcal{K}$.

1: $B \leftarrow \top$
2: **while true do**
3:     $(result, \tau) \leftarrow \mathrm{SAT}(\bigvee_{\phi \in Q} \neg\phi \wedge B)$
4:     **if** $result = unsat$ **then return** $\bot$
5:     $S \leftarrow \{\phi \in \mathcal{K} \mid \tau(\phi) = 1\}$
6:     **while true do**
7:         $B \leftarrow B \wedge \bigvee_{\phi \in \mathcal{K} \setminus S} \phi$
8:         $(result, \tau) \leftarrow \mathrm{SAT}(\bigvee_{\phi \in Q} \neg\phi \wedge \bigwedge_{\phi \in S} \phi \wedge B)$
9:         **if** $result = unsat$ **then break else** $S \leftarrow \{\phi \in \mathcal{K} \mid \tau(\phi) = 1\}$
10:    $(result, \tau) \leftarrow \mathrm{SAT}(\bigwedge_{\phi \in Q} \phi \wedge \bigwedge_{\phi \in S} \phi \wedge B)$
11:    **if** $result = unsat$ **then return** $\mathcal{K} \setminus S$
12:    **else** $S \leftarrow \{\phi \in \mathcal{K} \mid \tau(\phi) = 1\}$, $B \leftarrow B \wedge \bigvee_{\phi \in \mathcal{K} \setminus S} \phi$

(lines 8–9). Only satisfiable candidate sets can be derived (line 10). To ensure that each superset of S_{cs} is unsatisfiable, we define $|\mathcal{K}| - |S_{\mathrm{cs}}|$ supersets (lines 11–12), and add exactly one element from the set-complement to each (line 13). No two supersets are equal by lines 14–15. Lines 16–24 check if all supersets of S_{cs} are unsatisfiable. Lines 16–17 and 18–19 determine formulas (respectively atoms) in a given superset. The unsatisfiability check is done by *saturation*: the rule in line 20 allows the atoms in a superset to be both 1 and 0. If both 1 and 0 are derived for each atom (lines 21–22) and the formula evaluates to 0 (line 23), the formula is unsatisfiable. The constraint on line 24 enforces each superset to be unsatisfiable. If the disjunctive ASP program does not have an answer set, no MCS containing at least one formula from Q (w.r.t. P) or at least one atom from $At(Q)$ (w.r.t. MV) exists, and Algorithm 1 terminates. Otherwise, we extract the corresponding formulas or atoms (represented by `inComplement/1` / `atomInComplement/1`), and remove them from Q.

3.3   Instantiation via SAT-Based CEGAR

We detail SAT-based CEGAR as a second approach to MCS overlap. The key idea in SAT-based CEGAR is to overapproximate the solutions to the problem via a propositional abstraction. By iteratively solving the abstraction we obtain candidate solutions, which are subsequently verified. This is done by searching for a counterexample for the candidate solution being a valid solution to the problem. If a counterexample is found, the abstraction is refined by adding constraints which rule out the candidate solution. Our SAT-based CEGAR algorithm is closely related to an earlier-proposed approach that reduces MCS overlap to propositional circumscription [36,37] and employs CEGAR for circumscription [2,3,35] (which in itself is not directly applicable as it only supports computations over sets of individual clauses).

The CEGAR algorithm (Algorithm 2) for the MCS overlap problem takes as input a KB $\mathcal{K}$ and a subset of query formulas $Q \subseteq \mathcal{K}$, with the goal of finding an MCS of $\mathcal{K}$ that intersects Q. This is equivalent to finding an MSS of $\mathcal{K}$

which excludes at least one $\phi \in Q$. As the abstraction, we drop the requirement on maximality, and consider satisfiable subsets of $\mathcal{K}$. To avoid finding assignments which do not correspond to such MSSes, we initialize a set B of blocking clauses (line 1). Since SAT solvers operate on formulas in conjunctive normal form (CNF), each $\phi \in \mathcal{K}$ is encoded in a standard way [62] to a set of clauses $\text{Cls}(\phi)$ and a variable $\text{Var}(\phi)$ so that ϕ is satisfiable iff $\text{Cls}(\phi) \wedge \text{Var}(\phi)$ is. Thus by initializing a SAT solver with $\bigwedge_{\phi \in \mathcal{K}} \text{Cls}(\phi)$, we can query for the satisfiability of any subset $S \subseteq \mathcal{K}$ with additional unit clauses $\bigwedge_{\phi \in S} \text{Var}(\phi)$.

In the main CEGAR loop (lines 2–12), we iteratively ask the SAT solver for an assignment which falsifies some $\phi \in \mathcal{K}$ (line 3). If there is no such assignment, there is no MCS which overlaps Q, and we return $\bot$ (line 3). Otherwise, a satisfying assignment gives a satisfiable subset S of $\mathcal{K}$ (line 5) and $\mathcal{K} \setminus S$ is a correction set. We subset-maximize S iteratively under the constraint that some $\phi \in \mathcal{K}$ is falsified (lines 6–9). Finally, we check if S is an MSS of $\mathcal{K}$ by asking for a counterexample, i.e., an assignment satisfying every ϕ in $Q \cap S$ (line 10). If there is no such assignment, $\mathcal{K} \setminus S$ is an MCS which intersects Q (line 11). Otherwise we block all subsets of the obtained satisfiable subset, including the candidate MSS S (line 12). The number of iterations is bounded by the number of candidate MSSes, and Algorithm 2 terminates. Note that the CEGAR approach allows for several optimizations, in addition to using an incremental SAT solver. Since so-called autark variables cannot be included in any MUS [38], the lean kernel, i.e., the set of clauses not touched by any autarky [12,52], is an overapproximation of the union of MUSes. A *maximum autarky* $\mathcal{A}$ of $\mathcal{K}$ is obtained with an MCS extraction call [49]; $\mathcal{A}$ can be safely removed from every query Q in Algorithm 2. Further, *disjoint cores* can be extracted by iteratively querying the SAT solver for pairwise disjoint MUSes; their union $\mathcal{D}$ is an underapproximation of the union of MUSes and hence the elements (formulas for P, atoms for MV) in $\mathcal{D}$ are known to be covered in the set $\mathcal{C}$.

4   Empirical Evaluation

For implementations of the SAT-based CEGAR and ASP instantiations of Algorithm 1, see https://bitbucket.org/coreo-group/sat4im. We use the ASP solver Clingo [24] 5.5.1, and we implemented the SAT-based CEGAR approach via PySAT [33] 0.1.8.dev3 using the CaDiCaL 1.5.3 [16] SAT solver. We compare the performance of the ASP and SAT-based CEGAR instantiations to mcscache [58] as a state-of-the-art MCS enumerator and umuser [52] computing the union of MUSes. Each KB formula $\phi \in \mathcal{K}$ is encoded into CNF via $\text{Cls}(\phi)$ and $\text{Var}(\phi)$, so that MCSes (resp. MUSes) of $\mathcal{K}$ can be computed as group-MCSes (resp. group-MUSes [46,54]) over $\{\text{Var}(\phi) \mid \phi \in \mathcal{K}\}$ with $\bigwedge_{\phi \in \mathcal{K}} \text{Cls}(\phi)$ as hard constraints. mcscache extracts one MCS of the KB at a time. We keep track of the set of formulas (P) or variables (MV) currently covered by some MCS. We terminate mcscache once all of the elements are covered.

We consider three variants of CEGAR: (i) CEGAR: with subset-maximization, disjoint cores, and autarky trimming. (ii) CEGAR/no CM:

Table 1. Number of solved instances (#solved) and cumulative runtimes (CRT).

	Approach	SRS (90 KBs)		ML (100 KBs)		ARG (100 KBs)	
		#solved	CRT (s)	#solved	CRT (s)	#solved	CRT (s)
P	CEGAR	**87**	1300.16	**55**	2576.94	51	298.78
	CEGAR/no AT	**87**	1302.10	46	19.98	**52**	516.61
	CEGAR/no CM	85	937.42	52	796.21	43	198.07
	mcscache	**87**	1318.20	46	27.86	42	365.05
	umuser	71	699.87	38	11.32	40	455.72
	ASP	21	1783.06	15	651.65	10	203.71
MV	CEGAR	**90**	4.99	**93**	4775.11	**53**	453.82
	CEGAR/no AT	**90**	5.07	46	20.17	52	629.98
	CEGAR/no CM	**90**	5.62	85	2353.93	51	356.5
	mcscache	**90**	6.72	46	29.06	46	387.78
	umuser	71	699.87	38	11.32	40	455.72
	ASP	36	1119.48	17	2645.44	10	339.04

Subset-maximization of candidate MSSes (lines 6–9) is disabled, instead the SAT solver is directly asked for a counterexample (line 10) and instead (line 11), the satisfiable subset for an MSS is maximized. (iii) CEGAR/no AT: No *autarky trimming*.

We use KBs from three sources. (i) SRS [39,40,42]: 90 KBs, generated using *SyntacticRandomSampler* from https://tweetyproject.org/, under 9 parameter combinations, randomly selecting 10 KBs per combination; (ii) ML [39,40]: 100 randomly selected KBs from the *Animals with Attributes* dataset (http://attributes.kyb.tuebingen.mpg.de), interpreting association rules mined with Apriori [1] as implications; (iii) ARG [40]: 100 randomly selected KBs consisting of CNF clauses of a standard SAT encoding [15] for stable extensions of abstract argumentation frameworks [22] from the ICCMA 2019 competition with the constraint that a random subset of 20 % of arguments are in the stable extension. The experiments were run on Intel Xeon E5-2643 v3 3.40-GHz CPUs with 192-GB RAM under Ubuntu 20.04.5 using a per-instance 900-s time limit.

The CEGAR approach performs the best, followed by mcscache and umuser; see Table 1. Default CEGAR performs consistently well, solving significantly more instances in particular on the ML and ARG datasets. Disjunctive ASP solves significantly fewer instances than the other approaches. For CEGAR, disabling autarky trimming (CEGAR/no AT) leads to more timeouts especially on ML benchmarks and MV. Disabling subset-maximization (CEGAR/no CM) also yields more timeouts, especially on the ARG dataset and P. (Disjoint cores did not have a noticeable impact.) Every benchmark instance solved by mcscache is also solved by the CEGAR approach, with the exception of a single ARG instance for the P measure. CEGAR altogether outperforms mcscache on a great majority of the benchmarks.

Overall, the CEGAR approach empirically outperformed ASP as well as state-of-the-art MCS enumerators. Our results motivate the development of specialized algorithms for other computationally notably complex inconsistency measures, such as ones based on counting MCSes [13] and MUSes [12,14].

References

1. Agrawal, R., Srikant, R.: Fast algorithms for mining association rules in large databases. In: Proceedings of the VLDB 1994, pp. 487–499 (1994)
2. Alviano, M.: Model enumeration in propositional circumscription via unsatisfiable core analysis. Theory Pract. Log. Program. **17**(5–6), 708–725 (2017)
3. Alviano, M.: Query answering in propositional circumscription. In: Proceedings of the IJCAI 2018, pp. 1669–1675. ijcai.org (2018)
4. Bacchus, F., Davies, J., Tsimpoukelli, M., Katsirelos, G.: Relaxation search: A simple way of managing optional clauses. In: Proc. AAAI 2014. pp. 835–841. AAAI Press (2014)
5. Belov, A., Ivrii, A., Matsliah, A., Marques-Silva, J.: On efficient computation of variable MUSes. In: Cimatti, A., Sebastiani, R. (eds.) SAT 2012. LNCS, vol. 7317, pp. 298–311. Springer, Heidelberg (2012). https://doi.org/10.1007/978-3-642-31612-8_23
6. Bendík, J.: On decomposition of maximal satisfiable subsets. In: Proceedings of the FMCAD 2021, pp. 212–221. IEEE (2021)
7. Bendík, J., Benes, N., Cerná, I., Barnat, J.: Tunable online MUS/MSS enumeration. In: Proceedings of the FSTTCS 2016. LIPIcs, vol. 65, pp. 50:1–50:13. Schloss Dagstuhl - Leibniz-Zentrum für Informatik (2016)
8. Bendík, J., Černá, I.: MUST: minimal unsatisfiable subsets enumeration tool. In: TACAS 2020. LNCS, vol. 12078, pp. 135–152. Springer, Cham (2020). https://doi.org/10.1007/978-3-030-45190-5_8
9. Bendík, J., Černá, I.: Replication-guided enumeration of minimal unsatisfiable subsets. In: Simonis, H. (ed.) CP 2020. LNCS, vol. 12333, pp. 37–54. Springer, Cham (2020). https://doi.org/10.1007/978-3-030-58475-7_3
10. Bendík, J., Cerna, I.: Rotation based MSS/MCS enumeration. In: Proceedings of the LPAR 2020. EPiC Series in Computing, vol. 73, pp. 120–137. EasyChair (2020)
11. Bendík, J., Černá, I., Beneš, N.: Recursive online enumeration of all minimal unsatisfiable subsets. In: Lahiri, S.K., Wang, C. (eds.) ATVA 2018. LNCS, vol. 11138, pp. 143–159. Springer, Cham (2018). https://doi.org/10.1007/978-3-030-01090-4_9
12. Bendík, J., Meel, K.S.: Approximate counting of minimal unsatisfiable subsets. In: Lahiri, S.K., Wang, C. (eds.) CAV 2020. LNCS, vol. 12224, pp. 439–462. Springer, Cham (2020). https://doi.org/10.1007/978-3-030-53288-8_21
13. Bendík, J., Meel, K.S.: Counting maximal satisfiable subsets. In: Proceedings of the AAAI 2021, pp. 3651–3660. AAAI Press (2021)
14. Bendík, J., Meel, K.S.: Counting minimal unsatisfiable subsets. In: Silva, A., Leino, K.R.M. (eds.) CAV 2021. LNCS, vol. 12760, pp. 313–336. Springer, Cham (2021). https://doi.org/10.1007/978-3-030-81688-9_15
15. Besnard, P., Doutre, S., Herzig, A.: Encoding argument graphs in logic. In: Laurent, A., Strauss, O., Bouchon-Meunier, B., Yager, R.R. (eds.) IPMU 2014. CCIS, vol. 443, pp. 345–354. Springer, Cham (2014). https://doi.org/10.1007/978-3-319-08855-6_35

16. Biere, A., Fazekas, K., Fleury, M., Heisinger, M.: CaDiCaL, Kissat, Paracooba, Plingeling and Treengeling entering the SAT competition 2020. In: Proceedings of the SAT Competition 2020 - Solver and Benchmark Descriptions. Department of Computer Science Report Series B, vol. B-2020-1, pp. 51–53. University of Helsinki (2020)

17. Brewka, G., Eiter, T., Truszczynski, M.: Answer set programming at a glance. Commun. ACM **54**(12), 92–103 (2011)

18. Chen, Z., Ding, D.: Variable minimal unsatisfiability. In: Cai, J.-Y., Cooper, S.B., Li, A. (eds.) TAMC 2006. LNCS, vol. 3959, pp. 262–273. Springer, Heidelberg (2006). https://doi.org/10.1007/11750321_25

19. Clarke, E.M., Grumberg, O., Jha, S., Lu, Y., Veith, H.: Counterexample-guided abstraction refinement for symbolic model checking. J. ACM **50**(5), 752–794 (2003)

20. Clarke, E.M., Gupta, A., Strichman, O.: SAT-based counterexample-guided abstraction refinement. IEEE Trans. Comput. Aided Des. Integr. Circuits Syst. **23**(7), 1113–1123 (2004)

21. Doder, D., Raskovic, M., Markovic, Z., Ognjanovic, Z.: Measures of inconsistency and defaults. Int. J. Approx. Reason. **51**(7), 832–845 (2010)

22. Dung, P.M.: On the acceptability of arguments and its fundamental role in non-monotonic reasoning, logic programming and n-person games. Artif. Intell. **77**(2), 321–358 (1995)

23. Eiter, T., Gottlob, G.: On the computational cost of disjunctive logic programming: propositional case. Ann. Math. Artif. Intell. **15**, 289–323 (1995)

24. Gebser, M., Kaminski, R., Kaufmann, B., Ostrowski, M., Schaub, T., Wanko, P.: Theory solving made easy with Clingo 5. In: Technical Communications of ICLP, pp. 2:1–2:15. OASICS, Schloss Dagstuhl - Leibniz-Zentrum fuer Informatik (2016)

25. Gebser, M., Kaminski, R., Kaufmann, B., Schaub, T.: Answer set solving in practice. In: Synthesis Lectures on Artificial Intelligence and Machine Learning, vol. 6, no. 3, pp. 1–238 (2012)

26. Gelfond, M., Lifschitz, V.: The stable model semantics for logic programming. In: Proceedings of the ICLP/SLP, pp. 1070–1080. MIT Press (1988)

27. Grant, J.: Classifications for inconsistent theories. Notre Dame J. Formal Log. **19**(3), 435–444 (1978)

28. Grant, J., Hunter, A.: Measuring consistency gain and information loss in stepwise inconsistency resolution. In: Liu, W. (ed.) ECSQARU 2011. LNCS (LNAI), vol. 6717, pp. 362–373. Springer, Heidelberg (2011). https://doi.org/10.1007/978-3-642-22152-1_31

29. Grant, J., Martinez, M.V. (eds.): Measuring Inconsistency in Information, Studies in Logic, vol. 73. College Publications (2018)

30. Grégoire, É., Izza, Y., Lagniez, J.: Boosting MCSes enumeration. In: Proceedings of the IJCAI 2018, pp. 1309–1315. ijcai.org (2018)

31. Grégoire, É., Lagniez, J., Mazure, B.: An experimentally efficient method for (MSS, CoMSS) partitioning. In: Proceedings of AAAI 2014, pp. 2666–2673. AAAI Press (2014)

32. Hunter, A., Konieczny, S.: Measuring inconsistency through minimal inconsistent sets. In: Proceedings KR 2008, pp. 358–366. AAAI Press (2008)

33. Ignatiev, A., Morgado, A., Marques-Silva, J.: PySAT: a python toolkit for prototyping with SAT oracles. In: Beyersdorff, O., Wintersteiger, C.M. (eds.) SAT 2018. LNCS, vol. 10929, pp. 428–437. Springer, Cham (2018). https://doi.org/10.1007/978-3-319-94144-8_26

34. Jabbour, S., Ma, Y., Raddaoui, B., Sais, L., Salhi, Y.: A MIS partition based framework for measuring inconsistency. In: Baral, C., Delgrande, J.P., Wolter, F. (eds.) Proceedings of the KR 2016, pp. 84–93. AAAI Press (2016)

35. Janota, M., Grigore, R., Marques-Silva, J.: Counterexample guided abstraction refinement algorithm for propositional circumscription. In: Janhunen, T., Niemelä, I. (eds.) JELIA 2010. LNCS (LNAI), vol. 6341, pp. 195–207. Springer, Heidelberg (2010). https://doi.org/10.1007/978-3-642-15675-5_18

36. Janota, M., Marques-Silva, J.: cmMUS: a tool for circumscription-based MUS membership testing. In: Delgrande, J.P., Faber, W. (eds.) LPNMR 2011. LNCS (LNAI), vol. 6645, pp. 266–271. Springer, Heidelberg (2011). https://doi.org/10.1007/978-3-642-20895-9_30

37. Janota, M., Marques-Silva, J.: On deciding MUS membership with QBF. In: Lee, J. (ed.) CP 2011. LNCS, vol. 6876, pp. 414–428. Springer, Heidelberg (2011). https://doi.org/10.1007/978-3-642-23786-7_32

38. Kleine Büning, H., Kullmann, O.: Minimal unsatisfiability and autarkies. In: Handbook of Satisfiability - Second Edition, Frontiers in Artificial Intelligence and Applications, vol. 336, pp. 571–633. IOS Press (2021)

39. Kuhlmann, I., Gessler, A., Laszlo, V., Thimm, M.: A comparison of ASP-based and SAT-based algorithms for the contension inconsistency measure. In: Dupin de Saint-Cyr, F., Öztürk-Escoffier, M., Potyka, N. (eds.) Scalable Uncertainty Management. SUM 2022. Lecture Notes in Computer Science, vol. 13562, pp. 139–153. Springer, Cham (2022). https://doi.org/10.1007/978-3-031-18843-5_10

40. Kuhlmann, I., Gessler, A., Laszlo, V., Thimm, M.: Comparison of SAT-based and ASP-based algorithms for inconsistency measurement. arXiv p. 2304.14832 (2023). preprint

41. Kuhlmann, I., Thimm, M.: An algorithm for the contension inconsistency measure using reductions to answer set programming. In: Davis, J., Tabia, K. (eds.) SUM 2020. LNCS (LNAI), vol. 12322, pp. 289–296. Springer, Cham (2020). https://doi.org/10.1007/978-3-030-58449-8_23

42. Kuhlmann, I., Thimm, M.: Algorithms for inconsistency measurement using answer set programming. In: Proceedings of the NMR 2021, pp. 159–168 (2021)

43. Kullmann, O.: Constraint satisfaction problems in clausal form II: minimal unsatisfiability and conflict structure. Fundam. Informaticae 109(1), 83–119 (2011)

44. Liberatore, P.: Redundancy in logic I: CNF propositional formulae. Artif. Intell. 163(2), 203–232 (2005)

45. Liffiton, M.H., Previti, A., Malik, A., Marques-Silva, J.: Fast, flexible MUS enumeration. Constraints An Int. J. 21(2), 223–250 (2016)

46. Liffiton, M.H., Sakallah, K.A.: Algorithms for computing minimal unsatisfiable subsets of constraints. J. Autom. Reason. 40(1), 1–33 (2008)

47. Lifschitz, V.: Answer Set Programming. Springer, Cham (2019). https://doi.org/10.1007/978-3-030-24658-7

48. Marques-Silva, J., Heras, F., Janota, M., Previti, A., Belov, A.: On computing minimal correction subsets. In: Proceedings of the IJCAI 2013, pp. 615–622. IJCAI/AAAI (2013)

49. Marques-Silva, J., Ignatiev, A., Morgado, A., Manquinho, V.M., Lynce, I.: Efficient autarkies. In: Proceedings of the ECAI 2014. Frontiers in Artificial Intelligence and Applications, vol. 263, pp. 603–608. IOS Press (2014)

50. Marques-Silva, J., Mencía, C.: Reasoning about inconsistent formulas. In: Proceedings of the IJCAI 2020, pp. 4899–4906. ijcai.org (2020)

51. Mencía, C., Ignatiev, A., Previti, A., Marques-Silva, J.: MCS extraction with sublinear oracle queries. In: Creignou, N., Le Berre, D. (eds.) SAT 2016. LNCS, vol. 9710, pp. 342–360. Springer, Cham (2016). https://doi.org/10.1007/978-3-319-40970-2_21

52. Mencía, C., Kullmann, O., Ignatiev, A., Marques-Silva, J.: On computing the union of MUSes. In: Janota, M., Lynce, I. (eds.) SAT 2019. LNCS, vol. 11628, pp. 211–221. Springer, Cham (2019). https://doi.org/10.1007/978-3-030-24258-9_15

53. Mencía, C., Previti, A., Marques-Silva, J.: Literal-based MCS extraction. In: Proceedings of the IJCAI 2015, pp. 1973–1979. AAAI Press (2015)

54. Nadel, A.: Boosting minimal unsatisfiable core extraction. In: Proceedings of the FMCAD 2010, pp. 221–229. IEEE (2010)

55. Narodytska, N., Bjørner, N.S., Marinescu, M.V., Sagiv, M.: Core-guided minimal correction set and core enumeration. In: Proceedings of the IJCAI 2018, pp. 1353–1361. ijcai.org (2018)

56. Niemelä, I.: Logic programs with stable model semantics as a constraint programming paradigm. Ann. Math. Artif. Intell. **25**(3–4), 241–273 (1999)

57. Niskanen, A., Kuhlmann, I., Thimm, M., Järvisalo, M.: MaxSAT-Based inconsistency measurement. In: Proceedings of the ECAI 2023. IOS Press (2023)

58. Previti, A., Mencía, C., Järvisalo, M., Marques-Silva, J.: Improving MCS enumeration via caching. In: Gaspers, S., Walsh, T. (eds.) SAT 2017. LNCS, vol. 10491, pp. 184–194. Springer, Cham (2017). https://doi.org/10.1007/978-3-319-66263-3_12

59. Previti, A., Mencía, C., Järvisalo, M., Marques-Silva, J.: Premise set caching for enumerating minimal correction subsets. In: Proceedings of the AAAI 2018, pp. 6633–6640. AAAI Press (2018)

60. Reiter, R.: A theory of diagnosis from first principles. Artif. Intell. **32**(1), 57–95 (1987)

61. Thimm, M., Wallner, J.P.: On the complexity of inconsistency measurement. Artif. Intell. **275**, 411–456 (2019)

62. Tseitin, G.S.: On the complexity of derivation in propositional calculus. In: Siekmann, J.H., Wrightson, G. (eds.) Automation of Reasoning, pp. 466–483. Springer, Heidelberg (1983). https://doi.org/10.1007/978-3-642-81955-1_28

63. Xiao, G., Ma, Y.: Inconsistency measurement based on variables in minimal unsatisfiable subsets. In: Proceedings of the ECAI 2012, pp. 864–869. IOS Press (2012)

Towards Systematic Treatment of Partial Functions in Knowledge Representation

Djordje Markovic[1,2]([⊠]) (ID), Maurice Bruynooghe[1,2] (ID), and Marc Denecker[1,2] (ID)

[1] Department of Computer Science, K.U. Leuven, Leuven, Belgium
{dorde.markovic,maurice.bruynooghe,marc.denecker}@kuleuven.be
[2] Leuven.AI – KU Leuven Institute for AI, Leuven, Belgium

Abstract. Partial functions are ubiquitous in Knowledge Representation applications, ranging from practical, e.g., business applications, to more abstract, e.g., mathematical and programming applications. Expressing propositions about partial functions may lead to non-denoting terms resulting in undefinedness errors and ambiguity, causing subtle modeling and reasoning problems.

In our approach, formulas are well-defined (*true* or *false*) and non-ambiguous in all structures. We develop a base extension of three-valued predicate logic, in which partial function terms are guarded by domain expressions ensuring the well-definedness property despite the three-valued nature of the underlying logic. To tackle the verbosity of this core language, we propose different ways to increase convenience by using disambiguating annotations and non-commutative connectives. We show a reduction of the logic to two-valued logic of total functions and prove that many different unnesting methods turning partial functions into graph predicates, which are not equivalence preserving in general, are equivalence preserving in the proposed language, showing that ambiguity is avoided.

Keywords: Knowledge Representation · Partial functions · Non-denoting terms · Guards · Nested function terms

1   Introduction

Partial functions and non-denoting terms have been studied in many different domains: in linguistics and philosophy [20,23], mathematics [8,13,21], proof theory [10,18], and computation [15]. Partial functions enjoy many different treatments in programming languages. They have been studied in the context of formal specification languages [3,12], in declarative constraint languages [5,9], and knowledge representation languages [1,2,4,6]. Good overviews of different approaches are found in [7,24]. In this paper, we look at partial functions from the perspective of modelling and Knowledge Representation (KR).

This work was partially supported by the Flemish Government under the "Onderzoeksprogramma Artificiële Intelligentie (AI) Vlaanderen".

The problem of non-denoting terms arises with applying a function concept to some entity for which the function might be undefined. This problem may occur in a mathematical text, in formal theories, or in programs of declarative or imperative languages. An example made famous by Bertrand Russell is the statement: "The king of France is bald" (since France has no king). In mathematical texts, the problem arises, e.g., in propositions applying division to zero. In practical applications, the problem might appear with variables that are not always defined, e.g., when using attribute *Age* for a deceased person.

In many logics, e.g., first-order predicate logic (FO), it is assumed that function symbols represent *total* functions, which are often used to represent partial functions [7]. In such theories, the problem of non-denoting terms does not formally occur (i.e., every term denotes in every structure). However, problems manifest themselves in a different way. We illustrate this with a FO theory[1] for graph colouring containing the axioms: $\forall x : Ver(x) \Rightarrow Col(colOf(x))$ and $\forall x : \forall y : Nei(x, y) \Rightarrow \neg(colOf(x) = colOf(y))$. The function symbol $colOf/1$ is used to represent the colouring function defined only on vertices, but in first-order logic, it is interpreted as a total function, hence defined on colours as well. As a consequence, there is a *semantic mismatch* between the user's knowledge and its modelling which easily can lead to subtle representation and reasoning problems. For example, applying *model expansion inference* [17] on this theory together with a structure (interpreting all symbols except $colOf$) will return many redundant models $\mathfrak{A}$: groups of models that assign the same colours to vertices but assign different colours to ... colours. Further, to represent that all colours are to be used for colouring, one may write the axiom $\forall x : Col(x) \Rightarrow \exists y : colOf(y) = x$. But this axiom is too weak, it does not exclude models in which some colour is used only for colouring colours. Or perhaps to count the number of different graph colourings, *model counting inference* [11] is applied; but with this theory, the wrong number is obtained. These problems are consequences of the *semantic mismatch* between the correct/intended states of affairs of the application domain (in which only vertices are coloured), and the formal models of this theory (in which also colours are coloured). This problem is caused by the use of the total function symbol $colOf/1$ to model a partial function. One may observe that switching to sorted logic resolves the semantic mismatch problem here, for the base graph coloring problem; however, not for the many variants of it, e.g., when only a subset of vertices is to be colored.

Competent knowledge engineers, logicians, and mathematicians are capable to handle such modelling problems. E.g., by representing partial functions with graph predicates (i.e., using $hasColour/2$ instead of $colOf/1$). Unfortunately, relying blindly on such competences does not progress the scientific state of the art. Moreover, such techniques are well-known to sometimes lead to verbose, unwieldy formulae [7]. In addition, if the goal is to build broadly applicable KR languages, it is important to offer support to less experienced users, e.g., from ICT departments of companies applying declarative methods for representing

---

[1] $Ver/1$ and $Col/1$ are denoting the set of vertices and colours respectively, $Nei/2$ is neighbourhood relation, and function $colOf/1$ is mapping objects to their colour.

business logic. Thus, it seems to us that the development of modelling languages with partial functions is a worthy topic for scientific research in the field of KR.

In natural language, the treatment of non-denoting terms is well-known to be rather unsystematic. E.g., suppose we are told "The king of France is bald". According to Russell, this is an ambiguous proposition which could mean either "*There exists an x which is King of France and x is bald*", or "*For any x, if x is a King of France, x is bald*". Likely, knowing that France has no king, we will protest there is an error, or at least a *false* statement here, taking the existential disambiguation. However, suppose the context was in a discussion of some famous medieval French parliamentary charter in which it is decreed that the king of France is to be bald. In that case, we might very well agree with the statement, taking the universal disambiguation.[2] Also in the mathematical text, partial functions and relations abound (e.g., $\frac{x}{y}$, $\sqrt{x}$). According to good mathematical practice, a potentially non-denoting expression is allowed to appear only in contexts where it is provable that the expression is denoting. Thus, given variable c ranging over the real numbers, one should not write "$\frac{1}{c} > 0.5$" but "$c \neq 0$ and $\frac{1}{c} > 0.5$". However, even mathematical text is not always so rigorous, and often enough the proposition "$\frac{1}{c} > 0.5$" will be used where the *implicature* is meant that $\frac{1}{c}$ is denoting, i.e., $c \neq 0$. In the context of logic, one mainstream view is to interpret atomic formulae containing non-denoting terms as *false*, which provides an easy integration into two-valued logic [21, pp. 39–40]. A more rigorous approach is however that a proposition on non-denoting terms contains a semantic error [13].

In this paper, we develop a logical framework $FO(pf)$ for a logic with partial functions. The leading principle is that the logical treatment of partial functions has to result in formulae that are well-defined (*true* or *false*) and non-ambiguous in all structures. The logic should cope with partial functions with an unknown domain. Moreover, the well-definedness of the logic expressions should be a decidable property. A first basic approach extends 3-valued predicate logic with guards, in which partial function terms are guarded by domain expressions ensuring the well-definedness property despite the 3-valued nature of the underlying logic. Next, to tackle the verbosity of this core language, we propose different ways to increase convenience by using disambiguating annotations and non-commutative connectives. Hence, the main contribution of this work is the syntax of guards that allows a systematic treatment of partial functions. Finally, we show a reduction of the logic to two-valued logic of total functions and prove that many different unnesting methods turning partial functions into graph predicates, which are not equivalence preserving in general, are equivalence preserving in the proposed language, showing that ambiguity is avoided.

The paper is structured as follows: First, the syntax and semantics of the $FO(pf)$ are defined. Next, we propose the language of guards, show its reduction to the total function logic, and present convenient guard constructs. Finally, we

---

[2] Grice's *principle of cooperativity* explains that the human interpretation of a text is influenced by a subconscious desire to make good sense of it.

demonstrate the properties of guarded logic in terms of elimination of function terms. We close the paper with related work and conclusion.

2   *FO(pf)* Syntax

This section describes the syntax of first-order logic with partial functions. We use various meta-variables: τ for terms, ϕ, ψ for formulae, and α for expressions.

Definition 1. *A **vocabulary** Σ is a set of predicate and functions symbols σ, each having an arity $n \geq 0$ (denoted as σ/n). A function symbol $f/0$ is called an **object symbol**, a predicate symbol $p/0$ is called a **propositional symbol**. In addition, for each function symbol f/n, Σ contains a **domain predicate** symbol δ_f/n and a **graph predicate** symbol $\gamma_f/n+1$.*

Intuitively, each function symbol f has an associated *domain predicate* δ_f, expressing the *domain* of the function, i.e., where f is defined, and a *graph predicate* γ_f of f, which represents the set of pairs (x, y) such that x is mapped to y by the function.

We assume the logic possesses an infinite set X of variable symbols, and that all quantified variables have different names.

Definition 2. *Given a vocabulary Σ, a **term** over Σ is defined inductively: if $c/0 \in \Sigma$, then c is a term; if $x \in X$, then x is a term; if $f/n \in \Sigma$ is a function symbol and $\tau_1 \dots, \tau_n$ are terms over Σ, then so is $f(\tau_1, \dots, \tau_n)$. Similarly, **formula** is defined inductively as: true and false atoms t and f are formulae; if $p/n \in \Sigma$ is a predicate symbol and $\tau_1 \dots, \tau_n$ are terms over Σ, then $p(\tau_1, \dots, \tau_n)$ is a formula; if ϕ, ψ, φ are formulae over Σ then so are: $\neg\phi$, $\phi \vee \psi$, **if** ϕ **then** ψ **else** φ **fi**, and $\exists x : \phi$.*

Definition 3. *An FO(pf) **expression** is an FO(pf) term or a formula. An FO(pf) **sentence** is an FO(pf) formula without free variables (i.e., all variables are quantified). An FO(pf) **theory** is a set of FO(pf) sentences.*

2.1   Syntactical Abbreviations

The *FO(pf)* language as defined in Definition 2 is composed of a limited set of language connectives. Other familiar connectives, $\wedge$, $\Rightarrow$, $\forall$, and $\Leftrightarrow$ can be defined in the standard way as shortcuts in terms of the basic ones.

A material implication $\phi \Rightarrow \psi$ is similar in meaning to the conditional **if** ϕ **then** ψ **else** t **fi** but not equivalent. The difference appears in a 3-valued context where ϕ is undefined and ψ true, in which case the material implication is true and the *if-then-else* undefined. The latter statement is equivalent to what is known as the asymmetric or sequential version of the material implication [8,15]. The *if-then-else* conditional will be the building block for *guarded expressions*.

3 *FO(pf)* Semantics

In this section, we define a truth conditional model semantics for *FO(pf)*. Below, D^n denotes the n-ary Cartesian product of the set D.

Definition 4. *Given a vocabulary Σ, a **partial function structure** $\mathfrak{A}$ over Σ is a two-valued structure consisting of:*

- *A non empty set $\mathcal{U}^{\mathfrak{A}}$, called the universe of $\mathfrak{A}$. If $\mathfrak{A}$ is clear from the context, it will be denoted compactly as $\mathcal{U}$.*
- *An assignment of interpretations $\sigma^{\mathfrak{A}}$ to non-logical symbols $\sigma \in \Sigma$: **(i)** Per predicate symbol $p/n \in \Sigma$, a relation $p^{\mathfrak{A}} \subseteq \mathcal{U}^n$. **(ii)** Per function symbol $f/n \in \Sigma$, a set $f^{\mathfrak{A}} \subseteq \mathcal{U}^n \times \mathcal{U}$ such that for all tuples $(\bar{d}, e_1), (\bar{d}, e_2) \in f^{\mathfrak{A}}$, it holds that $e_1 = e_2$. If $((d_1, \ldots, d_n), e) \in f^{\mathfrak{A}}$, we write that $f(d_1, \ldots, d_n) = e$. **(iii)** Per domain predicate symbol $\delta_f/n \in \Sigma$, $\delta_f{}^{\mathfrak{A}}$ is the domain of $f^{\mathfrak{A}}$, i.e., $\{\bar{d} \mid \exists e \in \mathcal{U} : (\bar{d}, e) \in f^{\mathfrak{A}}\}$. **(iv)** Per graph predicate symbol $\gamma_f/n + 1$, the graph relation $\gamma_f{}^{\mathfrak{A}} = \{(d_1, \ldots, d_n, e) \mid ((d_1, \ldots, d_n), e) \in f^{\mathfrak{A}}\}$.*
- *The interpretation[3] $=^{\mathfrak{A}}$ is the identity relation $\{(d, d) \mid d \in \mathcal{U}\}$ on $\mathcal{U}$.*

To be able to evaluate formulas with free variables, a structure $\mathfrak{A}$ need to be extended with a variable substitution denoted here as $[x \rightarrow d, \ldots, y \rightarrow e]$. Thus, $\mathfrak{A}[x \rightarrow d, \ldots, y \rightarrow e]$ denotes a structure extended with a variable assignment.

We now define *evaluation function* of *FO(pf)* as an extension of Kleene's strong truth assignment. It maps expressions to their value; a term is mapped to either an object from the domain of discourse or the special value $\perp_{term}$ representing an undefined term; a formula is mapped to one of $\mathbf{t}$, $\mathbf{f}$, and the special value $\perp_{formula}$ representing an undefined formula. So, while the structure is two-valued, the evaluation function is 3-valued[4]. When clear from the context, we omit subscripts and simply write $\perp$.

Definition 5. *Let α be an FO(pf) expression, $\mathfrak{A}$ a structure extended with a variable assignment over the free variables of α, (all) over vocabulary Σ. The value of α in $\mathfrak{A}$, denoted as $[\![\alpha]\!]^{\mathfrak{A}}$, is defined by induction on the structure of α:*

$$[\![x]\!]^{\mathfrak{A}} = x^{\mathfrak{A}}$$

$$[\![f(\tau_1, \ldots, \tau_n)]\!]^{\mathfrak{A}} = \begin{cases} f^{\mathfrak{A}}([\![\tau_1]\!]^{\mathfrak{A}}, \ldots, [\![\tau_n]\!]^{\mathfrak{A}}), \text{ if } [\![\tau_i]\!]^{\mathfrak{A}} \neq \perp \text{ for all } i \in \{1..n\} \\ \qquad \text{and } \delta_f^{\mathfrak{A}}([\![\tau_1]\!]^{\mathfrak{A}}, \ldots, [\![\tau_n]\!]^{\mathfrak{A}}) = \mathbf{t}; \\ \perp, \quad otherwise; \end{cases}$$

---

[3] Note that every structure with the same domain interpreters "=" as the same relation. All other language built-in relations and functions are to be interpreted in the same way. Note that in the case of partial functions their domain predicate would also be interpreted (e.g., division/would come with $\delta_/$ that is *true* for all pairs of numbers (x_1, x_2) such that $x_2 \neq 0$.

[4] It is also possible to move undefined values into the structure and then just manipulate it in the evaluation function. However, we choose to stay close to the standard set-theoretic implementation of concepts.

$$[\![p(\tau_1,\ldots,\tau_n)]\!]^{\mathfrak{A}} = \begin{cases} p^{\mathfrak{A}}([\![\tau_1]\!]^{\mathfrak{A}},\ldots,[\![\tau_n]\!]^{\mathfrak{A}}), \text{ if } [\![\tau_i]\!]^{\mathfrak{A}} \neq \bot \text{ for all } i \in \{1..n\}; \\ \bot, \quad otherwise; \end{cases}$$

$$[\![\exists x : \phi]\!]^{\mathfrak{A}} = \begin{cases} \mathbf{t}, & \text{if for some } d \in \mathcal{U}^{\mathfrak{A}}, [\![\phi]\!]^{\mathfrak{A}[x \to d]} = \mathbf{t}; \\ \mathbf{f}, & \text{if for all } d \in \mathcal{U}^{\mathfrak{A}}, [\![\phi]\!]^{\mathfrak{A}[x \to d]} = \mathbf{f}; \\ \bot, & otherwise; \end{cases}$$

$$[\![\phi_1 \vee \phi_2]\!]^{\mathfrak{A}} = \begin{cases} \mathbf{t}, & \text{if } [\![\phi_1]\!]^{\mathfrak{A}} = \mathbf{t} \text{ or } [\![\phi_2]\!]^{\mathfrak{A}} = \mathbf{t}; \\ \mathbf{f}, & \text{if } [\![\phi_1]\!]^{\mathfrak{A}} = [\![\phi_2]\!]^{\mathfrak{A}} = \mathbf{f}; \\ \bot, & otherwise; \end{cases}$$

$$\left[\!\!\left[\begin{array}{l} \textit{if } \phi \textit{ then } \phi_1 \\ \textit{else } \phi_2 \textit{ fi} \end{array} \right]\!\!\right]^{\mathfrak{A}} = \begin{cases} \bot, & \text{if } [\![\phi]\!]^{\mathfrak{A}} = \bot; \\ [\![\phi_1]\!]^{\mathfrak{A}}, & \text{if } [\![\phi]\!]^{\mathfrak{A}} = \mathbf{t}; \\ [\![\phi_2]\!]^{\mathfrak{A}}, & \text{if } [\![\phi]\!]^{\mathfrak{A}} = \mathbf{f}. \end{cases} \quad [\![\neg\phi]\!]^{\mathfrak{A}} = \begin{cases} \mathbf{t}, & \text{if } [\![\phi]\!]^{\mathfrak{A}} = \mathbf{f}; \\ \mathbf{f}, & \text{if } [\![\phi]\!]^{\mathfrak{A}} = \mathbf{t}; \\ \bot, & \text{if } [\![\phi]\!]^{\mathfrak{A}} = \bot. \end{cases}$$

According to the Definition 5, undefinedness arises only by application of a partial function to entities outside its domain. In the case of a structure assigning total functions to all function symbols, the truth assignment coincides to the standard two-valued one of first-order logic.

Definition 6. *A **total expansion**[5] of a partial function structure $\mathfrak{A}$ is a structure $\mathfrak{A}^{\uparrow}$ such that, for each predicate symbol $p \in \Sigma$, $p^{\mathfrak{A}^{\uparrow}}$ equals $p^{\mathfrak{A}}$, and for each function symbol $f \in \Sigma$, $f^{\mathfrak{A}^{\uparrow}}$ is a total function expanding the partial function $f^{\mathfrak{A}}$, i.e., $f^{\mathfrak{A}} \subseteq f^{\mathfrak{A}^{\uparrow}}$. This function agrees with $f^{\mathfrak{A}}$ on elements $\bar{d}$ in the domain of $f^{\mathfrak{A}}$ and otherwise assigns an arbitrary domain element.*

The following theorem characterizes the relation between 3-valued and two-valued semantics (where $\|\alpha\|^{\mathfrak{A}^{\uparrow}}$ denotes the value of α according to the two-valued semantics).

Theorem 1. *Let α be a partial function expression and $\mathfrak{A}$ a structure (over Σ) and $\mathfrak{A}^{\uparrow}$ be an arbitrary total expansion of $\mathfrak{A}$, then: $[\![\alpha]\!]^{\mathfrak{A}} \neq \bot \Rightarrow [\![\alpha]\!]^{\mathfrak{A}} = \|\alpha\|^{\mathfrak{A}^{\uparrow}}$.*

Proof (Sketch). Inspection of the rules in Definition 5 shows that, for each rule that does not produce a $\bot$-value, changing a $\bot$-input value into another value cannot affect the outcome.

Kleene [13, p. 334] called this *regularity* of language connectives and expressed it as a property of truth tables, Fitting [8] explored it as a *monotonicity* property of language connectives in an order where $\bot$ is below both $\mathbf{t}$ and $\mathbf{f}$.

4   Guarded *FO(pf)*

In this section, we propose syntactical constraints, *guards*, that will ensure the well-definedness of an *FO(pf)* formula. The *guarded* formula ensures that any

---

[5] The total expansion of a structure does not satisfy the constraints of a partial function structure (Definition 4).

occurrence of a partial function term occurs in the context of a constraint that its argument belongs to the domain of the partial function. For example, to protect the atom $1/x > 0$ against division by 0, one can use **if** $\delta_/(1,x)$ **then** $1/x > 0$ **else** ϕ **fi** where ϕ can be **t** or **f** (or another formula) depending on the desired outcome when $x = 0$; we call such a guard a *conditional guard*. To formalize the notion of a *guarded* formula, we introduce first a guard context. Intuitively, context represents a set of *guards* that are appearing higher in the syntax tree of a formula.

Definition 7. *A **guard context** ω is a set of domain predicate atoms over vocabulary Σ.*

First, we define a syntax of a conservative theoretical language of guards. Namely, a partial function term can occur only in a *"then"* part of a *if-then-else* statement that contains its domain predicate as a condition.

Definition 8. *Given a guard context ω and a vocabulary Σ, a **guarding relation** $\omega \Vdash \phi$ is defined by the following inductive definition (where $\bar{t}$ stands for $t_1, \ldots, t_n$ and $\omega \Vdash \bar{t}$ for $\omega \Vdash t_1 \ldots \omega \Vdash t_n$):*

$$\frac{}{\omega \Vdash \mathbf{t}} \quad \frac{}{\omega \Vdash \mathbf{f}} \quad \frac{}{\omega \Vdash x} \quad \frac{\omega \Vdash \bar{t}}{\omega \Vdash p(\bar{t})} \quad \frac{\omega \Vdash \phi}{\omega \Vdash \neg\phi} \quad \frac{\omega \Vdash \phi \quad \omega \Vdash \psi}{\omega \Vdash \phi \vee \psi} \quad \frac{\omega \Vdash \phi}{\omega \Vdash \exists x : \phi}$$

$$\frac{\delta_f(\bar{t}) \in \omega \quad \omega \Vdash \bar{t}}{\omega \Vdash f(\bar{t})} \quad \frac{\omega \Vdash \phi \quad \omega \Vdash \psi \quad \omega \Vdash \varphi}{\omega \Vdash \textbf{if } \phi \textbf{ then } \psi \textbf{ else } \varphi \textbf{ fi}} \quad \frac{\omega \Vdash \bar{t} \quad (\omega \cup \delta_f(\bar{t})) \Vdash \psi \quad \omega \Vdash \varphi}{\omega \Vdash \textbf{if } \delta_f(\bar{t}) \textbf{ then } \psi \textbf{ else } \varphi \textbf{ fi}}$$

Definition 9. *Formula ϕ is **well-guarded** iff it is guarded in an empty context: $\emptyset \Vdash \phi$.*

The following theorem reflects the main property of well-guarded formulae.

Theorem 2. *Let ϕ be a well-guarded formula and $\mathfrak{A}$ a partial function structure over Σ, then ϕ is well-defined in $\mathfrak{A}$, in symbols: $\emptyset \Vdash \phi \Rightarrow [\![\phi]\!]^{\mathfrak{A}} \neq \perp$.*

Proof (Sketch). Each rule of Definition 8 decomposes the formula into well-guarded parts, all the way to the atoms and terms. Note that a functional term $f(\bar{t})$ is well-guarded only if its domain predicate $\delta_f(\bar{t})$ is in the guarding context ω. This is possible only if term $f(\bar{t})$ occurred in ϕ_1 in formula like **if** $\delta_f(\bar{t})$ **then** ϕ_1 **else** ϕ_2 **fi**; according to the last rule. It is clear that in case $f(\bar{t})$ is undefined its domain predicate $\delta_f(\bar{t})$ is *false* and hence the value of sub-formula ϕ_1 becomes irrelevant.

Every *well-guarded* formula has to contain atoms **t** or **f** or some propositional atom. This is because not all *else* parts of conditional statements can be guarded. In this way, a precise truth value is specified for every formula in case some term turns out not to be defined. This aligns with our principle of well-definedness and non-ambiguity.

Theorem 2 suggests that if all formulae in a theory are well-guarded it is guaranteed that the theory is well-defined. To check well-guardedness of a formula it is sufficient to follow the syntactical rules from the Definition 8, which leads a complete/decidable method, solvable in linear time as characterized in the following theorem.

Theorem 3. *Given an FO(pf) sentence ϕ of length l and with n terms (including all sub-terms), the time complexity of well-guardedness check of ϕ is $O(l)$ and space $O(n + l)$.*

Proof. Counting the number of terms and storing them into an associative array is obviously linear, it requires linear parsing of a sentence. So, we assume that there is an associative array T mapping all terms in ϕ to 0 initially. Intuitively, 0 denotes that the term is not guarded, and 1 that it is. Next we can start parsing the sentence ϕ. When any term t is encountered we check whether $T(t) = 0$, if it is, ϕ is not well-guarded and the procedure terminates, otherwise we continue parsing. Whenever **if** $\delta_f(\bar{t})$ **then** ... **else** ... **fi** is encountered, if $f(\bar{t})$ is in T it is set to 1 for the analysis of the **then** branch, while it remains 0 for the analysis of the **else** branch. If the end of the sentence is reached, the sentence is well-guarded.

The described procedure makes two iterations over the sentence, one to create T, and one for analysing guards. Since the sentence is of length l the time complexity is $O(l)$. The memory used in this procedure is the array T of length n (number of terms in ϕ) and a stack of maximal length l for parsing the sentence. Hence space complexity is $O(n + l)$.

4.1   Conjunctive and Implicative Guards

Writing well-guarded theories using guards as they are defined in Definition 8 would require every single term to be guarded using conditionals, which is by many criteria of Knowledge Representation languages unacceptable. Such a language would be extremely inconvenient and elaboration intolerant; *"A formalism is elaboration tolerant to the extent that it is convenient to modify a set of facts expressed in the formalism to take into account new phenomena or changed circumstances."* [16], whereas in the proposed language adding just a single new function term to a formula would require updating the entire formula. To make guarding more convenient, new guards constructs, based on the principles of well-definedness and non-ambiguity, could be introduced.

The first step towards a compact language of guards is to remove the need for explicit annotations of truth values when terms are not denoting. A well-guarded statement **if** δ_t **then** ϕ **else f fi** can be replaced with a *conjunctive guard* $\delta_t \wedge \phi$ which evaluates to **f** when the guard is *false* and **if** δ_t **then** ϕ **else t fi** can be replaced with an *implicative guard* $\delta_t \Rightarrow \phi$ which evaluates to **t** when the guard is *false*. Notice that the original guarded statement is not equivalent to the proposed replacements. Namely, if δ_t is undefined and ϕ is **f** in some structure, conditional guards would be undefined, while $\delta_t \wedge \phi$ would be **f**. However, this is not possible in a well-guarded statement; for δ_t to be undefined it has to be applied to some term t' which is undefined, but according to the guarding rules, that term has to be guarded too. So, semantically conjunctive and implicative guard connectives are asymmetric, they correspond to connectives in McCarthy's left-sequential 3-valued propositional logic [15] also analysed by Fitting in [8]. In our paper, the semantics of these connectives is not formally needed as they are treated syntactically. Hence, conjunctive and implicative guards should be considered as a shorthand for particular conditional guards (those that have **f** and **t** in the "*else*" part respectively).

However, formulae often contain more than one term and newly proposed guards would often be in a chained form: $(\delta_{t_1} \wedge \cdots \wedge \delta_{t_n}) \wedge \phi$ and $(\delta_{t_1} \wedge \cdots \wedge \delta_{t_n}) \Rightarrow \phi$. In this situation reduction to the primitive conditional guard takes into account the order of domain atoms δ which is important for nested terms. For example, statement like "My husband's mother is a doctor" modeled as $Doctor(mother(mh))$, requires first constant mh to be guarded, and only then $mother(mh)$, i.e., $\delta_{mh} \wedge \delta_{mother}(mh) \Rightarrow Doctor(mother(mh))$. The reason is that $\delta_{mother}(mh)$ is well-defined only if mh is well-defined and hence it has to be constrained first. This means that the conjunction of guards in conjunctive and implicative guards is also a non-commutative connective (e.g., $\delta_{mother}(mh) \wedge \delta_{mh} \Rightarrow Doctor(mother(mh))$ is not a well-guarded statement).

4.2 Implicit Guards

Although expressing guards is slightly more convenient with conjunctive and implicative guards than with conditional guards it is still necessary to guard every single term, furthermore, this has to be done for all nested terms respecting the order of nesting. This is still below the standards of a good KR language. What is necessary for improvement is the support for annotations that can replace a conjunction of guards. Hence, we introduce two new language constructs. The annotation $[[\phi]]$ stands for *implicit conjunctive guards* and the annotation $\langle\langle\phi\rangle\rangle$ for *implicit implicative guards*. When a formula is implicitly guarded it is extended with guards for all the terms, and sub-terms, it contains. For example formula $\langle\langle Doctor(mother(mh))\rangle\rangle$ stands for $\delta_{mh} \wedge \delta_{mother}(mh) \Rightarrow Doctor(mother(mh))$, while formula $[[Doctor(mother(mh))]]$ stands for $\delta_{mh} \wedge \delta_{mother}(mh) \wedge Doctor(mother(mh))$.

Intuitively, these operators will bring all guards of all terms of the guarded statement in front of it in a correct order. For example, with ψ representing the conjunction of guards needed to guard terms inside a formula ϕ, $[[\phi]]$ is translated as $\psi \wedge \phi$ while $\langle\langle\phi\rangle\rangle$ is translated as $\psi \Rightarrow \phi$. Note that $[[]]$ and $\langle\langle\rangle\rangle$, similarly to the modal[6] operators $\square$ and $\diamond$, form a dual pair of operators, i.e., $\langle\langle\phi\rangle\rangle \equiv \neg[[\neg\phi]]$ and $[[\phi]] \equiv \neg\langle\langle\neg\phi\rangle\rangle$.

However, it is not always possible to guard all terms at the same level of the formula, some variables are introduced only deeper in the formula, and they

---

[6] The notation for operators is selected to be aligned with the intuition of modal operators, i.e., $[[]]$ expresses the necessity that all terms are defined, while $\langle\langle\rangle\rangle$ expresses possibility.

do not exist on the top level. Consider the following statement: "If France is coloured blue then there exists a country that is a neighbour of France and is coloured red"; modelled[7] as: $colOf(F) = B \Rightarrow \exists c : Nei(F, c) \wedge colOf(c) = R$.

In this statement, it is not possible to guard $colOf(c)$ outside of the scope of $\exists c$ quantifier. Furthermore, as it is not always the case that the intended guards for the quantified sub-formula are the same as the ones used on the higher level, we require that every quantified sub-formula has its own guard. So, the translation of the implicit guards always puts the guards at the level of the guarded sub-formula. For example: $\langle\langle colOf(F) = B \Rightarrow \exists c : [[Nei(F, c) \wedge colOf(c) = R]]\rangle\rangle$ is translated as: $\delta_{colOf}(F) \Rightarrow (colOf(F) = B \Rightarrow \exists c : \delta_{colOf}(c) \wedge Nei(F, c) \wedge colOf(c) = R)$.

This avoids that the KR engineer neglects that the quantified sub-formula is in a different context, e.g., negated, so that the meaning of an implicit guard changes. Consider as an example statement "if France is coloured blue, no country is coloured red": $[[colOf(F) = B \Rightarrow \forall c : colOf(c) \neq R]]$. If the same guard were propagated to the quantified sub-formula it would imply that all countries are coloured. However the intended meaning is that a country, if coloured, is not red: $[[colOf(F) = B \Rightarrow \forall c : \langle\langle colOf(c) \neq R\rangle\rangle]]$.

For similar reasons we do not allow implicit guarding of terms, for example: $Nei(\langle\langle F\rangle\rangle, [[G]])$, where terms F and G in the atom have to be guarded. The above statement can be translated in two ways depending on which guard is applied first: $\delta_F \Rightarrow (\delta_G \wedge Nei(F, G))$ and $\delta_G \wedge (\delta_F \Rightarrow Nei(F, G))$. These two translations are not equivalent, and hence the language should establish a convention in which way guards are applied. In this paper, we stick with the slightly more conservative approach and require users to be explicit.

We have shown that the basic principles of guarding require tedious modelling and that they are almost always implicit in mathematical texts and natural language statements. Hence, a good KR language has to employ such constructs, and we have demonstrated their principles.

5   Unnesting of Nested Function Terms

Nested function terms are very common in the modelling of human knowledge, e.g., $Doctor(father(mw))$. We demonstrated in the previous section that sentences containing them can carry an ambiguity. Sometimes, there is a need to eliminate functions (e.g., because the preferred solver does not support functions). This can be achieved by *unnesting*, i.e., introducing new quantified variables and replacing functions with their graphs[8] (a good overview of the technique is available in [25]). For example, the constant mw of the above statement could be unnested as: $\exists x : \gamma_{mw}(x) \wedge Doctor(father(x))$ or using universal quantification: $\forall x : \gamma_{mw}(x) \Rightarrow Doctor(father(x))$. Two statements are equivalent, in the case of two-valued logic, because there is exactly one x such that $\gamma_{mw}(x)$.

---

[7] We use constants F for France, B for blue and R for red.

[8] Recall that the graph predicate of a function f is denoted with γ_f.

This is obviously not the case when the term mw might fail to denote. For example, when $\gamma_{mw}(x)$ is *false* for every x, meaning that mw does not exist, the first statement is *false* and the second is *true*.

The unnesting procedure can get very complex, as terms could be unnested higher in the syntax tree. For example, formula $\mathbf{t} \vee c = 10$, which is obviously a tautology, can be unnested in the following way $\exists x : \gamma_c(x) \wedge (\mathbf{t} \vee x = 10)$ which is *false* when c is undefined. This means that not all unnestings are equivalence preserving. Additionally, the problem aggravates because terms can be unnested in a different order, e.g., first $father(mw)$ and mw afterward: $\exists x : \gamma_{father}(mw, x) \wedge Doctor(x)$. This results in an enormous number of unnestings, which potentially leads to different values in case of undefinedness.

The examples from above are suggesting that replacing atoms directly with their unnestings is a safe approach, meaning that if the original formula is well-defined the unnested version will have the same value. This property indeed holds and is not difficult to be proven[9]. However, this method has a major downside as it has to introduce a new variable for each term being unnested, even though the same term might repeat multiple times in a formula. Consider the following example: "My husband is an actor and a pilot." modelled as: $Actor(mh) \wedge Pilot(mh)$. This sentence would be unnested as: $\exists x_1 : \gamma_{mh}(x_1) \wedge Actor(x_1) \wedge \exists x_2 : \gamma_{mh}(x_2) \wedge Pilot(x_2)$. In general, this approach would lead to more complex formulae containing more quantified variables with a strict order (which is known to affect the solving efficiency for QBF [14,19]).

The problem of unnesting is present because potentially non-denoting terms are not used in a disambiguated manner. It is not hard to see that terms in a well-guarded formula are safe to be unnested in the scope of their guards. This justifies the principle of disambiguation imposed by the guarding mechanism. To formalize the described properties we first have to define the two unnestings. We call the one with existential quantifier *strong*, since it approximates a formula to *false* when an undefined term is unnested and the other one *weak*, as it approximates it to *true*. Below, $\phi[t \rightarrow t']$ stands for the substitution of a term t with term t' in formula ϕ.

Definition 10. *Given a formula ϕ containing a term $f(\bar{t})$ such that all variables occurring in $f(\bar{t})$ are free in ϕ, the term $f(\bar{t})$ is **Weak**-ly unnested as: $w(f(\bar{t}), \phi) = \forall x : \gamma_f(\bar{t}, x) \Rightarrow \phi[f(\bar{t}) \rightarrow x]$ and **Strong**-ly unnested as: $s(f(\bar{t}), \phi) = \exists x : \gamma_f(\bar{t}, x) \wedge \phi[f(\bar{t}) \rightarrow x]$.*

For example $w(mh, Actor(mh) \wedge Pilot(mh))$ would result in: $\forall x : \gamma_{mh}(x) \Rightarrow Actor(x) \wedge Pilot(x)$.

Intuitively, a guarded term can be safely unnested as long as it is in the scope of its guard because if unnested inside its guard, a term is always defined. For example, $\delta_{mh} \wedge Actor(mh)$ unnested as $\delta_{mh} \wedge \forall x : \gamma_{mh}(x) \Rightarrow Actor(x)$ is a perfectly safe operation. If the term is not defined, the guard will ensure that the sub-formula where it occurs is not relevant. This is characterized by the following theorem.

---

[9] The proof is omitted due to space constraints.

Theorem 4. *Given a well-guarded formula ϕ, a sub-formula ψ of ϕ, and a term t, if term t is guarded in ψ by some guard (higher in a syntax tree) in ϕ, then for any structure $\mathfrak{A}$ the following holds:* $[\![\phi[\psi \to w(t,\psi)]]\!]^{\mathfrak{A}} = [\![\phi[\psi \to s(t,\psi)]]\!]^{\mathfrak{A}}$.

Proof (Sketch). If $[\![t]\!]^{\mathfrak{A}} = \bot$, values of either $w(t,\psi)$ or $s(t,\psi)$ are not relevant for ϕ as there is (higher in a syntax tree) guard for t. If $[\![t]\!]^{\mathfrak{A}} \neq \bot$ then we should show that $[\![w(t,\psi)]\!]^{\mathfrak{A}} = [\![s(t,\psi)]\!]^{\mathfrak{A}}$. This boils down to the proof that $[\![\forall x : \gamma_t(x) \Rightarrow \phi[t \to x]]\!]^{\mathfrak{A}}$ is the same as $[\![\exists x : \gamma_t(x) \wedge \phi[t \to x]]\!]^{\mathfrak{A}}$. As there can be only one such x (according to Definition 4) it is not hard to see that both formulae reduce to $[\![\phi[t \to x]]\!]^{\mathfrak{A}}$ for such x.

The main motivation in this paper for introducing guards was to create a language capable of disambiguating the meaning of expressions using partial functions. We have shown that the well-definedness property is not enough (e.g., $t \vee c = 10$) to ensure non-ambiguity. However, guards are providing both, well-definedness is reflected in Theorem 2 and non-ambiguity in Theorem 4.

6 Related Work

This section discusses some of the most relevant works for this paper.

The problem of ambiguity, from the Knowledge representation perspective, was already recognized in [6,9]. The work of De Cat et al. briefly discusses the need for disambiguated forms for statements containing partial functions. Inspired by the work of Frisch and Stuckey [9] they adopt the default disambiguation to be the strong one (one with the existential[10] quantifier). While sharing the intuition and base principles, our view is that default assumptions about the language are dangerous and are leading to many pitfalls where users do not understand what is really the meaning of the statements they are making. A distinguishing contribution of our paper is the development of a suitable syntax for a language where no assumptions are made. Another strength of paper [6] is that various other extensions of a good KR language are discussed. Some of these extensions (e.g., aggregates and definitions) require special non-trivial treatment. As our approaches are sharing the base principles, we believe that the language we proposed is flexible and general enough to be extendable with common first-order extensions while preserving the elaboration tolerance [16] of the language.

The constraints that we imposed on the guarded language are strongly related to some special language connectives and constructs as mentioned earlier. The asymmetric connectives from [8,15] were already discussed throughout the paper. A similar idea appears in [18] as a notion of *lazy implication* $[A]B$ and *lazy conjunction* $\langle A \rangle B$. The laziness means that the second proposition B will be ignored when the first one, A, is *false*. In this way, one can write statements

---

[10] Weak unnesting becomes strong when the formula occurs in a negative context (odd number of negations upper in syntax tree). This can cause problems, i.e., some connectives (e.g., $\Leftrightarrow$) contain implicit negations, and hence polarity is not well defined.

in which irrelevant parts are undefined. Also, the authors of [18] perceive ill-defined formulas as *errors*, which is in line with our view. The main difference between both works is that we are focused on the syntactical restrictions of such a language as opposed to the development of a proof system for it. In fact, developing a proof system for our language is not needed due to the result of the reduction to two-valued logic. This means that the standard proof system for first-order logic is sufficient for the language proposed in this paper.

Substantial efforts in the Answer Set Programming (ASP) community have been made when it comes to the integration of partial functions in ASP [1,2,4]. These papers aim at the proper treatment of partial functions and at constructing practical systems for ASP. In the paper [4] by P. Cabalar, the strict approach is followed, namely when an atom contains an undefined term it evaluates to *false*. Initially, this approach substantially differs from ours. However, the derived operators inspired by Scott's existence operator [22] are used in [4] to create convenient language constructs relevant to those discussed in this paper. For example, $t_1 \# t_2$ has a meaning that both t_1 and t_2 are defined and different. Further $[\phi]$ is similar to an implicative guard from this paper, except it operates on the level of atoms, i.e., each atom A containing term t will be replaced with $Et \Rightarrow A$ where E is Scott's existence operator. While being very close to the idea proposed in this paper, the generalized notion of guards is not studied in [4]. This does not mean that the results presented in this paper are beyond ASP, on the contrary, the use of the existence operator would allow the implementation of guards as proposed in this paper in the ASP language. Hence, the main difference between these two works is the goal, the work in [4] focuses on partial functions in ASP, while this paper has guards as language constructs in the first plan.

The approach to partial functions in the theorem prover CVC Lite [3] is that a theory must be provably well-defined (referred to as the *principle of least surprise*), a similar approach appears in the Event-B Modelling Method [12]. This principle aligns with the approach proposed in this paper. However, the difference is that we insist on the additional principle of proving well-definedness on the level of syntax. In CVC Lite, the well-definedness of a formula is established by generating TCC (Type Correctness Conditions) formula out of the original formula and checking its validity. Validity checking is in general undecidable, hence for some formulae, it is impossible to establish well-definedness. We believe that in KR languages this can and should be avoided using the approach proposed in this paper. A good argument for that appears in [3] itself; namely, TCC formulae enjoy the well-definedness property from the way they are constructed, which is exactly the way well-guarded formulae are designed.

Note that one has more "freedom" in guarding partial functions in the formalisms compared so far, e.g., $c \neq 0 \Rightarrow 1/c > 0$ is a two-valued statement accepted by CVC and not by the language we propose (i.e., one has to write $\langle\langle 1/c > 0 \rangle\rangle$). It is true that it is more common in mathematical texts to see guarding like "if $x \neq 0$" or "if $x > 0$", this is because usually guarded functions are rigid (i.e., the same in all structures), like division or square root, and hence always defined on the exact same set of values. Hence, proving that statements guarded in such a manner are well-defined is trivial. However, when it comes to Knowledge Representation it is often the case that functions are not rigid, and guarding them by enumerating all the cases where they are undefined is not possible. For this reason, we believe that guarding techniques proposed in this paper are much more relevant for KR languages. In a sense one does not have to know the value of functions to be able to see that the statement is well-defined; it is inferable from the syntax.

7   Conclusion

We argued the importance and scientific interest in supporting partial functions in KR languages in order to avoid undefinedness errors, ambiguities, and semantic mismatches leading to subtle modelling and reasoning errors.

We started from a logic with expressions in which partial function terms occur in a context guarded by domain expressions. The syntax of the logic is decidable. The logic satisfies the principle of well-definedness: although the underlying logic is 3-valued, guarded formulas are "error-free" in the sense that their truth value is well-defined in all structures. This is so even when no complete knowledge of the domain of partial functions is available. Further, we showed the extensions of the base language reducing verbosity and increasing convenience. Also, we proved that the ambiguity problem of different unnestings does not occur in the defined language. Thus, we argue that the proposed framework is a good core language for partial functions and a good foundation for more convenient languages.

Acknowledgements. Thanks to Pierre Carbonnelle, Gerda Janssens, Linde Vanbesien, and Marcos Cramer for the discussions and for reading this paper.

References

1. Balduccini, M.: A "conservative" approach to extending answer set programming with non-Herbrand functions. In: Erdem, E., Lee, J., Lierler, Y., Pearce, D. (eds.) Correct Reasoning. LNCS, vol. 7265, pp. 24–39. Springer, Heidelberg (2012). https://doi.org/10.1007/978-3-642-30743-0_3
2. Balduccini, M.: ASP with non-Herbrand partial functions: a language and system for practical use. Theory Pract. Logic Program. 13(4–5), 547–561 (2013)
3. Berezin, S., Barrett, C., Shikanian, I., Chechik, M., Gurfinkel, A., Dill, D.L.: A practical approach to partial functions in CVC lite. Electron. Notes Theor. Comput. Sci. 125(3), 13–23 (2005)
4. Cabalar, P.: Partial functions and equality in answer set programming. In: Garcia de la Banda, M., Pontelli, E. (eds.) ICLP 2008. LNCS, vol. 5366, pp. 392–406. Springer, Heidelberg (2008). https://doi.org/10.1007/978-3-540-89982-2_36
5. Cristiá, M., Rossi, G., Frydman, C.S.: Adding partial functions to Constraint Logic Programming with sets. Theory Pract. Log. Program. 15, 651–665 (2015)

6. De Cat, B., Bogaerts, B., Bruynooghe, M., Janssens, G., Denecker, M.: Predicate logic as a modeling language: the IDP system. In: Declarative Logic Programming: Theory, Systems, and Applications, pp. 279–323. Association for Computing Machinery and Morgan & Claypool (2018)
7. Farmer, W.M.: A partial functions version of Church's simple theory of types. J. Symb. Log. **55**(3), 1269–1291 (1990)
8. Fitting, M.: Kleene's three valued logics and their children. Fundam. Inform. **20**(1, 2, 3), 113–131 (1994)
9. Frisch, A.M., Stuckey, P.J.: The proper treatment of undefinedness in constraint languages. In: Gent, I.P. (ed.) CP 2009. LNCS, vol. 5732, pp. 367–382. Springer, Heidelberg (2009). https://doi.org/10.1007/978-3-642-04244-7_30
10. Gavilanes-Franco, A., Lucio-Carrasco, F.: A first order logic for partial functions. Theoret. Comput. Sci. **74**(1), 37–69 (1990)
11. Gomes, C.P., Sabharwal, A., Selman, B.: Model counting. In: Handbook of Satisfiability, pp. 993–1014. IOS press (2021)
12. Hoang, T.S.: An introduction to the Event-B modelling method. Industr. Deploy. Syst. Eng. Methods 211–236 (2013)
13. Kleene, S.C.: Introduction to Metamathematics. North Holland, Princeton (1952)
14. Lonsing, F., Egly, U.: Evaluating QBF solvers: quantifier alternations matter. In: Hooker, J. (ed.) CP 2018. LNCS, vol. 11008, pp. 276–294. Springer, Cham (2018). https://doi.org/10.1007/978-3-319-98334-9_19
15. McCarthy, J.: A basis for a mathematical theory of computation. In: Studies in Logic and the Foundations of Mathematics, vol. 26, pp. 33–70. Elsevier (1959)
16. McCarthy, J.: Elaboration tolerance. In: Common Sense, vol. 98, p. 2 (1998)
17. Mitchell, D., Ternovska, E., Hach, F., Mohebali, R.: Model expansion as a framework for modelling and solving search problems. Technical report, Citeseer (2006)
18. Nivelle, H.: Classical logic with partial functions. In: Giesl, J., Hähnle, R. (eds.) IJCAR 2010. LNCS (LNAI), vol. 6173, pp. 203–217. Springer, Heidelberg (2010). https://doi.org/10.1007/978-3-642-14203-1_18
19. Rabe, M.N., Seshia, S.A.: Incremental determinization. In: Creignou, N., Le Berre, D. (eds.) SAT 2016. LNCS, vol. 9710, pp. 375–392. Springer, Cham (2016). https://doi.org/10.1007/978-3-319-40970-2_23
20. Russell, B.: On denoting. Mind **14**(56), 479–493 (1905)
21. Schock, R.: Logics Without Existence Assumptions. Stockholm, Almqvist & Wiksell, Stockholm (1968)
22. Scott, D.: Identity and existence in intuitionistic logic. In: Fourman, M., Mulvey, C., Scott, D. (eds.) Applications of Sheaves. LNM, vol. 753, pp. 660–696. Springer, Heidelberg (1979). https://doi.org/10.1007/BFb0061839
23. Strawson, P.F.: On referring. Mind **59**(235), 320–344 (1950)
24. Suppes, P.: Introduction to Logic. Courier Corporation (1999)
25. Wittocx, J., Mariën, M., Denecker, M.: Grounding FO and FO(ID) with bounds. J. Artif. Intell. Res. **38**, 223–269 (2010)

Deterministic Weighted Automata Under Partial Observability

Jakub Michaliszyn[ID] and Jan Otop[(✉)][ID]

University of Wrocław, Wrocław, Poland
{jmi,jotop}@cs.uni.wroc.pl

Abstract. Weighted automata is a basic tool for specification in quantitative verification, which allows to express quantitative features of analysed systems such as resource consumption. Quantitative specification can be assisted by automata learning as there are classic results on Angluin-style learning of weighted automata. The existing work assumes perfect information about the values returned by the target weighted automaton. In assisted synthesis of a quantitative specification, knowledge of the exact values is a strong assumption and may be infeasible. In our work, we address this issue by introducing a new framework of *partially-observable* deterministic weighted automata, in which weighted automata return intervals containing the computed values of words instead of the exact values. We study the basic properties of this framework with the particular focus on the challenges of active learning partially-observable deterministic weighted automata.

1 Introduction

Finite automata is a fundamental computational model with a wide range of applications spanning from computational complexity, through AI [17] to formal methods [7]. In some applications, however, the qualitative answers returned by finite automata, i.e., each word is *accepted* or *rejected*, are insufficient. For instance, in formal verification, one can check the existence of execution trances violating a given specification, but violating traces come from a model rather than the actual system and their severity may differ from critical, which are likely to occur in the actual system to one, which are unlikely to be reproduced. Similarly, while checking whether a system has no deadlocks, one can ask whether every request is eventually fulfilled, which lacks performance guarantees involving a bound on the timeframe for fulfilment.

To address these issues, there has been proposed quantitative verification, in which the specification refers to quantitative features of the system. Quantitative verification is based on weighted automata, which return numeric values for words rather than accept/reject words. Weighted automata and their extensions have been extensively studied [5,6,9]. These models can express the severity of errors [11] and various performance metrics such as average response time [6]. The expressive power of such models entails hardness of specification.

S. Gaggl et al. (Eds.): JELIA 2023, LNAI 14281, pp. 771–784, 2023.
https://doi.org/10.1007/978-3-031-43619-2_52

Specifying quantitative properties may be difficult because in addition to describing events (such as a system failure) one has to come up with the associated values. This is especially difficult for properties of an approximate nature such as the aforementioned severity of a failure. Furthermore, the precise values are often not that important as we would be typically interested whether the number is within some acceptable interval, e.g., does not exceed our resources. For instance, the exact value of average response time depends on the computing environment, e.g., its cache size, which is typically not modeled precisely. For the same reason, assigning reasonable values of the average response time to traces is considerably more difficult than specifying a deadlock.

In this paper, we address the issue of construction of quantitative specifications. To ease the specification process, we propose a new framework, in which automata do not reveal the exact values. We study this framework from the specification-synthesis perspective, i.e., we ask whether it is possible to semi-automatically produce quantitative specifications using automata-learning approach. The conditions may be more involved; for example, we may want to express properties stating that the values 0–10 are good, 11–20 are satisfactory, and anything over 20 is bad.

1.1 Our Framework

We introduce partially-observable deterministic weighted automata (PODWA). These automata behave as regular deterministic weighted automata over $\mathbb{Z}$, but return an interval (from a given finite set of possible intervals) that contains the computed value rather than the value itself. The choice of intervals as partial observations is natural. Other choices are possible, but can increase the complexity – even making the membership problem undecidable.

Our motivation comes from the specification-synthesis via automata learning. The idea is that we would like to be able to synthesize quantitative properties without necessarily providing exact values. For that reason, we focus on problems related to active automata learning. First, we study the equivalence problem. It is fundamental in automata learning as one needs to answer whether the learned automaton is admissible. Second, learning algorithms typically construct the structure of an automaton with no weights [2], which leads to the weight synthesis question: given a PODWA Λ_1 and an automaton structure $\mathcal{A}_2$ (a deterministic finite automaton) without weights, is there a weight assignment for $\mathcal{A}_2$, which makes it equivalent (w.r.t. partial observations) to Λ_1? Specifically, assuming that such a weight assignment does exist, is there one such that weights vales are of polynomial order w.r.t. weights from Λ_1? Finally, active automata learning algorithms construct minimal automata [1,2,14]. Thus, to assess feasibility of learning weighted automata in our framework, we study the minimization problem for PODWA.

1.2 Results

The main contribution of the paper is identifying obstacles in developing a polynomial-time active learning algorithm for the new model. We start with the basic properties of the model. We show that the class of PODWA can express more than regular languages and is closed under the complement, but not under the union or the intersection. Then, we show that:

- the equivalence problem for PODWA is CONP-complete in general, and it can be solved in polynomial time if weights are given in unary,
- there is a PODWA Λ with weights $-1, 0, 1$, such that all equivalent minimal-state automata are isomorphic and have exponential weights, and
- the minimization via state-merging for PODWA with unary weights is NP-complete.

These results highlight challenges in learning weighted automata under partial observation. In order to obtain polynomial-time algorithm for active learning of PODWA, we need to focus on automata with unary weights. However, equivalence up to partial observation is too permissive to have an active learning algorithm. One needs a more rigid equivalence notion, which would make minimization decidable in polynomial time, and prevent exponential blow-up of weights in the minimization process.

1.3 Related Work

Typically, the partial observation term applies to equivalence on the set of control states, which has been used to model decisions under imperfect information in Markov decision processes (partially observable Markov decision process [18]), graph games (games with imperfect information [8]), or multi-agent system (multi-player games with imperfect information [3,10]). In contrast, in this work, the state space is intact, and partial observability refers to the returned value. This is related to games with interval objectives [13], in which one of the players objective is to make the numeric outcome of the game fall into a set being a finite union of intervals.

This work is motivated by active automata-learning algorithms, which have been developed for deterministic finite automata [1], deterministic weighted word automata [2] and deterministic weighted tree automata [14] and other types of automata. Similar algorithms have recently been developed for infinite-word automata: deterministic Büchi automata (DBA) [16] and deterministic limit-average automata [15]. These algorithms work in polynomial time even though minimization, closely related to active learning, is NP-complete for DBA. It was made possible thanks to in-depth difficulty assessment of problems related to active learning, which indicated how to extend the learning framework to make polynomial-time learning algorithms possible [16]. We conduct such an assessment in this work to pave the way for the development of active learning algorithms.

2   Preliminaries

A *word* w is a finite sequence of letters from a finite alphabet Σ. By Σ^* we denote the set of all words over Σ. By $w[i]$ we denote the ith letter of a word w, and $w[i, j]$ stands for the subword $w[i]w[i + 1] \ldots w[j]$ of w. The empty word is denoted by ϵ.

Automata and Runs. A *deterministic weighted automaton* (DWA) is a tuple $\langle \Sigma, Q, q_0, \delta, \mathbf{c} \rangle$ consisting of

1. an alphabet Σ,
2. a finite set of states Q,
3. an initial state $q_0 \in Q$,
4. a transition function $\delta \colon Q \times \Sigma \to Q$, and
5. a weight function $\mathbf{c} \colon Q \times \Sigma \to \mathbb{Z}$.

The size of a DWA $\mathcal{A}$, denoted by $|\mathcal{A}|$, is its number of states plus the sum of the lengths of all the weights given in binary.

We extend δ to $\hat{\delta} \colon Q \times \Sigma^* \to Q$ inductively: for each q, we set $\hat{\delta}(q, \epsilon) = q$, and for all $w \in \Sigma^*, a \in \Sigma$, we set $\hat{\delta}(q, wa) = \delta(\hat{\delta}(q, w), a)$. The run π of a DWA $\mathcal{A}$ on a word w is the sequence of states $q_0 \hat{\delta}(q_0, w[1]) \hat{\delta}(q_0, w[1, 2]) \ldots$. We do not consider any acceptance condition here.

The semantics of a DWA $\mathcal{A}$ is a function $\mathcal{L}(\mathcal{A})$ from non-empty words $\Sigma^* \backslash \{\epsilon\}$ into integers. For a non-empty word w of length k, we define $\mathcal{L}(\mathcal{A})(w)$ as the sum of weights of transitions along the run of $\mathcal{A}$ on w:

$$\mathcal{L}(\mathcal{A})(w) = \mathbf{c}(q_0, w[1]) + \mathbf{c}(\hat{\delta}(q_0, w[1]), w[2]) + \cdots + \mathbf{c}(\hat{\delta}(q_0, w[1, k-1]), w[k]).$$

Remark 1. The tropical seminring The weighted automata model considered in this paper is an instance of a more general framrework of weighted automata over semirings [9], where the semiring is the tropical semiring restricted to integers.

3   Our Framework

A *Partially-Observable DWA*, PODWA, is a pair $\Lambda = (\mathcal{A}, S)$ consisting of a DWA $\mathcal{A}$ and a set of a finite number of pairwise-disjoint intervals S covering $\mathbb{Z}$ called *observations*. We assume that intervals are enumerated by $\{0, \ldots, s\}$ according to the order on $\mathbb{Z}$. The *language* of a PODWA Λ, denoted as $\mathcal{L}(\Lambda)$, is a function from $\Sigma^* \backslash \{\epsilon\}$ to $\{0, \ldots, s\}$ such that $\mathcal{L}(\Lambda)(w)$ is the number of the interval containing $\mathcal{L}(\mathcal{A})(w)$.

A *binary PODWA* is a special case of PODWA having only two intervals: $(-\infty, 0]$ and $(0, +\infty)$. We consider words ending in the interval $(0, +\infty)$ as *accepted*. Then, the function $\mathcal{L}(\Lambda)$ is essentially a characteristic function of a set that can be seen as a classic language.

Example 1. Consider a single-state automaton $\mathcal{A}$ over $\Sigma = \{a, b, c\}$. The weights of the transitions over a, b, c are, respectively, $-1, 0, 1$. Consider the set of intervals $S = \{(-\infty, 0], (0, +\infty)\}$ and the binary PODWA $\Lambda = (\mathcal{A}, S)$. Then, $\mathcal{L}(\Lambda)(w) = 1$ if w contains more occurrences of c than a, and 0 otherwise.

Binary PODWA can define all regular languages (without the empty word) and some non-regular languages (see Example 1). All PODWA-recognizable languages are context-free and can be emulated by a deterministic one-counter automaton. On the other hand, deterministic one-counter automata define languages that cannot be expressed by binary PODWA, as the former rely on the counter value at every transition while the latter are agnostic of the counter value. For instance, a pumping argument shows that the language of words that have the same number of (occurrences of) a and b between every pair of c cannot be expressed by a binary PODWA (or any other PODWA with a reasonable language definition).

Binary PODWA can be easily complemented – it suffices to multiply all the weights by -1 and adjust the initial state (for words with value 0). We show that the class of languages recognizable by binary PODWA is not closed under union nor intersection. We will prove the former; for the latter observe that closure under intersection implies closure under union as the union operation can be expressed by the intersection and complement operations.

Let $\mathcal{L}_\cup$ be the language of words w that the number of occurrences of c is greater than the number of occurrences of b or is greater than the number of occurrences of a. Observe that $\mathcal{L}_\cup$ is the union of two PODWA-recognizable languages $\mathcal{L}_a$, $\mathcal{L}_b$, they can be defined as in Example 1. A simple pumping argument shows that $\mathcal{L}_\cup$ is not PODWA-recognizable.

Lemma 1. *$\mathcal{L}_\cup$ is not PODWA-recognizable.*

Proof. Assume a PODWA $\Lambda = (\mathcal{A}, \{(-\infty, 0], (0, +\infty)\})$ with less than N states that recognizes $\mathcal{L}_\cup$.

Consider the word $w = a^N b^N c^{N+1}$. Clearly, $w \in \mathcal{L}_\cup$ because there are more occurrences of c than a.

Since Λ has less that N states, there is $k \geq 0$ and $l > 0$ with $k + l \leq N$ such that the states $\hat{\delta}(q_0, a^k)$ and $\hat{\delta}(q_0, a^{k+l})$ are the same.

Since the automaton is deterministic, for any j the states $\hat{\delta}(q_0, a^k)$ and $\hat{\delta}(q_0, a^{k+jl})$ are the same. Notice that since the automaton is deterministic, this implies that for any j we have $\hat{\delta}(q_0, a^N) = \hat{\delta}(q_0, a^{N+j \cdot l})$.

Let $w_i = a^{k+i \cdot l}$. We argue that $\mathcal{A}(w_1) - \mathcal{A}(w_0) \geq 0$. Notice that for any j we have $\mathcal{A}(w_{j+1}) - \mathcal{A}(w_j) = \mathcal{A}(w_1) - \mathcal{A}(w_0)$. If this number was negative, for a sufficiently large j we would have

$$\mathcal{A}(a^{N+jl} b^N c^{N+1}) \leq 0$$

which contradicts the fact that this words belongs to $\mathcal{L}_\cup$.

Similarly, there is $k' \geq 0$ and $l' > 0$ with $k' + l' \leq N$ such that the states $\hat{\delta}(q_0, a^N b^{k'})$ and $\hat{\delta}(q_0, a^N b^{k'+l'})$ are the same.

Let $w'_i = a^N b^{k'+i \cdot l'}$. As before, we can show that $\mathcal{A}(w'_1) - \mathcal{A}(w'_0) \geq 0$.

Now consider $w_F = a^{N+l} b^{N+l'} c^{N+1}$. The above reasoning shows that $\mathcal{A}(w_F) \geq \mathcal{A}(w)$. However, since Λ recognizes $\mathcal{L}_\cup$, we have $\mathcal{A}(w_F) \leq 0$ and $\mathcal{A}(w) > 0$, which is a contradiction.   □

3.1   Sample Fitting

We briefly discuss the following counterpart of the sample fitting problem, which is related to passive learning: given a set of pairs consisting of a word and an interval, called *the sample*, and a number n, is there a PODWA with n states that is consistent with the sample? The sample fitting problem is NP-complete for PODWA; it is NP-complete even for DFA. However, we discuss it here as the hardness proof is simple and robust.

For membership in NP, observe that if n is larger than the number of letters in the sample (and the sample does not contain a direct contradiction, i.e., a word with different intervals), then such a PODWA always exists (and can be a tree). Otherwise, we can nondeterministically pick a PODWA and check it in polynomial time.

For hardness, consider an instance φ of 3-SAT with variables $p_1, \ldots, p_m$. Consider $n = 1$, $\Sigma = \{q\} \cup \{p_i, \overline{p_1} \mid i \leq m\}$, and $S = \{(-\infty, 0), [0, 1], [2, +\infty)\}$. The sample consists of:

- $(q, [0, 1])$, $(qq, [2, +\infty))$
- $(p_i, [0, 1])$, $(\overline{p_i}, [0, 1])$, $(p_i \overline{p_i}, [0, 1])$ $(p_i \overline{p_i} q, [2, +\infty))$ for each i
- $(xyzq, [2, +\infty))$ for each clause $x \vee y \vee z$ of φ (we identify $\neg p_i$ with $\overline{p_i}$).

If there is a single-state automaton consistent with this sample, then each letter has a value corresponding to the only transition over this letter. The value of each letter is an integer. The first condition guarantees that the value of q is 1. The second guarantees that exactly one letter among p_i, $\overline{p_i}$ has value 1 and the other has the value 0 (we rely on the fact that the weights are over integers). Thus, the values define a valuation of variables $p_1, \ldots, p_m$ from φ. The last condition guarantees that this valuation satisfies every clause of φ, and thus it satisfies φ.

4   Towards Active Learning PODWA

The sample fitting problem is intractable for one-state automata, which is a strong negative result for passive learning. In this section, we now focus on active learning of automata. The classic L^*-algorithm for active learning of DFA asks membership and equivalence queries. While in the PODWA framework, answering a membership query amounts to evaluating the DWA over the input word and returning the interval containing the value, answering equivalence queries is more involved.

4.1   Equivalence

PODWA Λ_1, Λ_2 are *equivalent* if $\mathcal{L}(\Lambda_1) = \mathcal{L}(\Lambda_2)$. The sets of intervals may be different and hence PODWA equivalence is invariant to linear operations, which are consistently applied to all weights and intervals. The *equivalence problem* asks whether two given PODWAs are equivalent. We show its CONP-hardness via reduction from (the complement of) the subset sum problem [12]. Let $a_1, \ldots, a_k$ be a list of integers and T be the target value represented in binary. W.l.o.g. we assume that $a_1, \ldots, a_k$ are even. We construct two binary PODWA $\Lambda_1 = (\mathcal{A}_1, S), \Lambda_2 = (\mathcal{A}_2, S)$ (where $S = \{(-\infty, 0], (0, +\infty)\}$) such that $\mathcal{A}_1$ computes the possible values of sums of subsets of $\{a_1, \ldots, a_k\}$ minus T, and $\mathcal{A}_2$ returns the value in $\mathcal{A}_1$ plus 1, i.e., $\mathcal{L}(\mathcal{A}_2)(w) = \mathcal{L}(\mathcal{A}_1)(w) + 1$. Observe that Λ_1 and Λ_2 are not equivalent if and only if $\mathcal{A}_1$ returns 0 for some word. For such a word $\mathcal{A}_2$ returns 1, which is in a different interval than 0. Thus, the PODWAs are not equivalent if and only if the subset sum problem has a solution.

Lemma 2. *The equivalence problem for (binary) PODWA is* CONP-*hard.*

Proof. We discuss the construction of DWA $\mathcal{A}_1, \mathcal{A}_2$ such that PODWA $(\mathcal{A}_1, S)$ and $(\mathcal{A}_2, S)$ are equivalent if and only if there is no subsequence of $a_1, \ldots, a_k$, which sums up to T.

Without loss of generality, we assume that all values $a_1, \ldots, a_k$ and T are even. The automaton $\mathcal{A}_1$ works over the alphabet $\{0, 1\}$ and input words are interpreted as the characteristic sequence of picked numbers minus T, i.e., the weighted accumulated over a word $w \in \{0, 1\}$ equals the sum of a_i such that $i \in \{1, \ldots, k\}$ and $w[i] = 1$ with T subtracted. One can easily construct such an automaton with $k + 2$ states $q_0, \ldots, q_{k+1}$: it moves from q_i to q_{i+1} regardless of the letter if $i \le k - 1$; the transition over 1 have weight a_{i+1} and the transition over 0 has weight 0. Then, from q_k it moves to q_{k+1} with both transitions of the weight $-T$. Finally, in q_{k+1} it has self-loops of the weight 0.

Next, the automaton $\mathcal{A}_2$ has the same structure as $\mathcal{A}_1$, but the last weight is $-T + 1$ rather than $-T$. Observe that if there is a word w distinguishing $\mathcal{L}((\mathcal{A}_1, S))$ and $\mathcal{L}((\mathcal{A}_2, S))$, then it has to have the value 0 in $\mathcal{A}_1$ and 1 in $\mathcal{A}_2$ — since the values of the two automata differ by 1 and the values of $\mathcal{A}_1$ are even. So the two automata are not observationally equivalent exactly when the word w encodes the solution for the considered instance of the subset sum problem. □

The subset sum problem has a pseudo-polynomial time algorithm and hence the hardness result from Lemma 2 relies on weights having exponential values w.r.t. the automata sizes. Assuming unary weights in automata and the interval endpoints leads to a polynomial-time algorithm for equivalence of PODWA. More precisely, a PODWA $(\mathcal{A}, S)$ is *unary* if weights in $\mathcal{A}$ and interval ends in S are represented in unary.

Theorem 1. *The equivalence problem is* CONP-*complete for PODWA and in* PTIME *for unary PODWA.*

Proof. The lower bound for the binary case follows from Lemma 2. For the upper bound, we show that PODWA equivalence reduces to $\mathbb{Z}$-reachability in 2-dimensional vector addition systems (VASS), i.e., reachability in which values of counters may become negative. The weights in the resulting VASS are from the weighted automata. The $\mathbb{Z}$-reachability problem for fixed-dimension VASS is NP-complete if vectors' values are represented in binary, and it is in PTIME if they are represented in unary [4].

First, consider PODWA $\Lambda_1 = (\mathcal{A}_1, S_1)$ and $\Lambda_2 = (\mathcal{A}_2, S_2)$. If they are not equivalent, then there is $i \neq j$ and a word w such that $\mathcal{A}_1(w)$ belongs to an i-th interval and $\mathcal{A}_2(w)$ belongs to a j-th interval. Without loss of generality, $i < j$ and hence there are values λ_1, λ_2 such that $\mathcal{A}_1(w) < \lambda_1$ and $\mathcal{A}_2(w) \geq \lambda_2$. There are $|S_1| \cdot |S_2|$ candidates for pairs λ_1, λ_2 and one can verify all pairs. Therefore, we assume that λ_1, λ_2 are given and focus on finding w such that $\mathcal{A}_1(w) < \lambda_1$ and $\mathcal{A}_2(w) \geq \lambda_2$.

We construct a VASS $\mathcal{V}$ of dimension 2 such that there is a path from the initial state s_0 with counters $(0,0)$ to the final state t with counters $(0,0)$ if and only if there is a word w such that $\mathcal{A}_1(w) < \lambda_1$ and $\mathcal{A}_2(w) \geq \lambda_2$. The VASS $\mathcal{V}$ is as a product of automata $\mathcal{A}_1$ and $\mathcal{A}_2$, where each transition is labeled by a vector of the weights of the corresponding transitions in $\mathcal{A}_1$ and $\mathcal{A}_2$. The $\mathcal{V}$ has an additional sink state t, which is the terminal state, such that from any other state one can reach t over a transition labeled by $(-\lambda_1 + 1, -\lambda_2)$. Additionally, t has self-loops labeled by $(1, 0)$ and $(0, -1)$. Finally, the initial state s of $\mathcal{V}$ is the pair consisting of initial states of $\mathcal{A}_1$ and $\mathcal{A}_2$.

Formally, for $i = 1, 2$ let $\mathcal{A}_i = \langle \Sigma, Q_i, q_{0,i}, \delta_i, \mathbf{c}_i \rangle$. The VASS $\mathcal{V} = \langle Q, q_0, \tau \rangle$ is defined as follows: $Q = Q_1 \times Q_2 \cup \{t\}$, $q_0 = \langle q_{0,1}, q_{0,2} \rangle$, and $\tau \subseteq Q \times \mathbb{Z}^2 \times Q$ consist of three types of tuples:

- tuples $\langle (q, s), x, (q', s') \rangle$, for all $q, q' \in Q_1, s, s' \in Q_2$ such that there exists $a \in \Sigma$ satisfying $\delta_1(q, a) = q'$, $\delta_1(s, a) = s'$, and $x = \langle \mathbf{c}_1(q, a, q'), \mathbf{c}_2(s, a, s') \rangle$
- tuples $\langle (q, s), (-\lambda_1 + 1, -\lambda_2), t \rangle$, for all $q \in Q_1, s \in Q_2$, and
- tuples $\langle t, (1, 0), t \rangle$ and $\langle t, (0, -1), t \rangle$.

Now, assume that there is a word w such that $\mathcal{A}_1(w) < \lambda_1$ and $\mathcal{A}_2(w) \geq \lambda_2$. Then we construct a path in $\mathcal{V}$ corresponding to w, which leads from s with counter values $(0,0)$ to some state with counter values (a, b), where $a < \lambda_1$ and $b \geq \lambda_2$. Since weights are integers, $a \leq \lambda_1 - 1$. Next, we take a transition to t and the counter values change to (a', b') such that $a' \leq 0$ and $b' \geq 0$. Finally, we can reach counter values $(0,0)$ by taking self-loops over t labeled by $(1, 0)$ and $(0, -1)$. Conversely, consider a path π in $\mathcal{V}$ from s with counter values $(0,0)$ to t with counter values $(0,0)$. Then, let s' be the last state before reaching t and (x, y) be the counter values at that position. Observe that $x \leq \lambda_1 - 1$ and $y \geq \lambda_2$ and hence the prefix of π up to s' with (x, y) corresponds to a word w such that $\mathcal{A}_1(w) < \lambda_1$ and $\mathcal{A}_2(w) \geq \lambda_2$.   □

4.2   Unary Weights

Theorem 1 suggests that restricting the attention to unary PODWA can make learning feasible. However, below we show that minimization of automata with

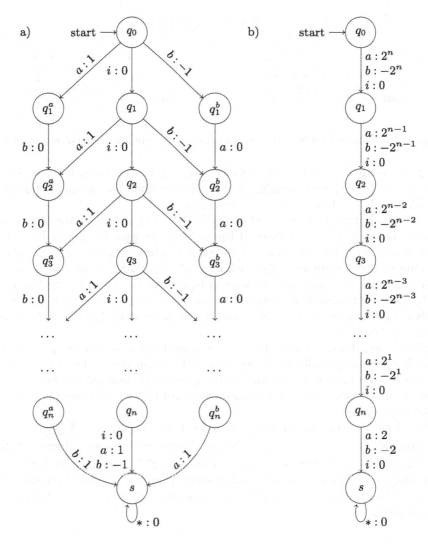

Fig. 1. a) The automaton Λ_n. The omitted edges lead to s with weight 0. b) A minimal automaton equivalent to Λ_n.

bounded weights from $\{-1, 0, 1\}$ may involve exponential-blow up weights, i.e., the decrease in the number of states is possible only through introduction of weights of exponential value:

Theorem 2. *There exists a sequence of PODWA $\Lambda_n = (\mathcal{A}_n, S)$, for $n > 1$, with weights $-1, 0, 1$ such that for all $n > 1$ every PODWA $(\mathcal{B}, S)$ equivalent to Λ_n with $\mathcal{B}$ having the minimal number of states, has exponential weights in n.*

$$S = \{(-\infty, 0], (0, +\infty)\}$$

Fig. 2. Two binary PODWA that are equivalent and minimal but not isomorphic.

Proof. We define, for each $n > 1$, a PODWA $\Lambda_n = (\mathcal{A}_n, \{(-\infty, 0), [0, 0], (0, +\infty)\})$ over $\Sigma = \{a, b, i\}$ with weights $\{-1, 0, 1\}$ such that the minimal equivalent PODWA to Λ_n needs weights exponential in n.

The automaton $\mathcal{A}_n$ is depicted in Fig. 1 a). Intuitively, the value of the word depends on its first $n + 1$ letters. If the word starts with the prefix $i^k a$, where $0 \le k < n$, then it has the value $+1$ unless it is followed by b^{n-k}, in which case its value is 0 (and symmetrically with $i^k b$ and -1). Words i^k have value 0.

An example of a minimal automaton equivalent to Λ_n is depicted in Fig. 1 b). To show its minimality, observe that for $j, k \in \{0, \ldots, n+1\}$ s.t. $j < k$, the words i^j and i^k have to lead to different states, because $\mathcal{L}(\Lambda_n)(i^j i^{n-j} a) = 2$ and $\mathcal{L}(\Lambda_n)(i^k i^{n-j} a) = 0$.

There are infinitely many minimal automata equivalent to λ_n though. For example, one can multiply all the weights of the automaton in Fig. 1 b) by 2. We can show that all automata equivalent to Λ_n with the minimal number of states are structurally isomorphic to the automaton in Fig. 1 b); this proof is relegated to the appendix.

In all such automata for any $j < n$ we have $\mathbf{c}(q_j, a) = -\sum_{k=j+1}^{n} \mathbf{c}(q_k, b)$ and similarly $\mathbf{c}(q_j, b) = -\sum_{k=j+1}^{n} \mathbf{c}(q_k, a)$. Therefore, one can inductively show that for $j < n - 1$ we have $\mathbf{c}(q_j, a) = -\mathbf{c}(q_j, b) = 2^{n-j-2}(\mathbf{c}(q_{n-1}, a) + \mathbf{c}(q_n, a))$. Since $\mathbf{c}(q_{n-1}, a)$ and $\mathbf{c}(q_n, a)$ are both positive (because i^{n-1}, i^n have the value 0 and $i^{n-1}a$, $i^n a$ have positive values), we conclude that the value of $\mathbf{c}(q_0, a)$ is exponential in n. □

4.3 Minimization

The L^*-algorithm relies on the right congruence relation, which has its natural counterpart for DWA. The right congruence relation defines the structure of the minimal DWA (which is unique) and hence the active learning algorithm can be applied to minimize DWA. Observe that minimal-size PODWA need not be unique.

Example 2. Consider the two binary PODWA presented in Fig. 2. They both define the language such that all word have positive values exept for the word a, which has a negative value. Both PODWA are equivalent and minimal; if there was an equivalent PODWA with the underlying DWA of a single state q, then either $\mathbf{c}(q, a) \ge 1$, which would contradict the value for a, or $\mathbf{c}(q, a) \le 0$, which would contradict the value for aa. Clearly, the automata are non-isomorphic.

Remark 2 (The right congruence for DWA). For a function $f : \Sigma^* \setminus \{\epsilon\} \to \mathbb{Z}$, consider a relation $\equiv_f$ defined on non-empty words w, v as follows:

$$w \equiv_f v \text{ if and only if for all } u \in \Sigma^* \text{ we have } f(wu) - f(w) = f(vu) - f(v).$$

The relation $\equiv_f$ is a counterpart of the right congruence relation for DWA and one can easily show the counterpart of the Myhill-Nerode theorem: f is defined by some DWA if and only if $\equiv_f$ has finitely many equivalence classes, and the relation $\equiv_f$ defines the structure of the minimal DWA. This relation cannot be straightforwardly adapted to PODWA as the result $f(wu) - f(w)$ cannot be inferred from observations for wu and w. More generally, Example 2 implies that there is no counterpart of $\equiv_f$ for PODWA as it would imply the uniqueness of the structure of minimal PODWA.

We discuss the complexity of minimization for PODWA, assuming that the set of intervals S is fixed and weights are given in unary. We say that DWA $\mathcal{A}_2$ is *observationally equivalent* to a PODWA $(\mathcal{A}_1, S)$, if PODWA $(\mathcal{A}_1, S)$ and $(\mathcal{A}_2, S)$ are equivalent. The O-minimization problem is to find a minimal-size DWA $\mathcal{A}_2$ that is observationally equivalent to a given PODWA $(\mathcal{A}_1, S)$. We study the decision variant of the O-minimization problem obtained by stating bound k on $\mathcal{A}_2$, i.e., given a PODWA $\Lambda = (\mathcal{A}_1, S)$ and $k > 0$, is there a DWA $\mathcal{A}_2$ with at most k states, which is observationally equivalent to Λ.

Minimization by Merging. A natural approach to minimization of automata is to define an equivalence relation on the set of states of the input automaton $\mathcal{A}$, corresponding to states being *semantically indistinguishable*, and construct the output automaton $\mathcal{B}$ based on the equivalence classes. In that approach, semantically indistinguishable are merged into a single state. Minimization by merging alleviates the problems arising from ambiguity of minimal automata; it guarantees that the input automaton and the minimized one are structurally related. We study minimization by merging for PODWA.

A DWA $\mathcal{B}$ is obtained from a DWA $\mathcal{A}$ by *merging* if there is a surjective (partial) function $f : Q_\mathcal{A} \to Q_\mathcal{B}$ from the set of reachable states of $\mathcal{A}$ onto the set of states $\mathcal{B}$ such that $\delta_\mathcal{A}(q, a) = q'$ if and only if $\delta_\mathcal{B}(f(q), a) = f(q')$.

The unary O-minimization by merging problem is, given an unary PODWA $(\mathcal{A}, S)$ and $k > 0$, is there a DWA $\mathcal{B}$, with at most k states and (the absolute value of) weights bounded by the weights of $\mathcal{A}$, obtained by merging from $\mathcal{A}$ that is observationally equivalent to $(\mathcal{A}, S)$.

Theorem 3. *The unary O-minimization by merging problem is NP-complete.*

Proof. The problem is in NP as one can non-deterministically pick a weighted automaton with unary weights $\mathcal{A}'$ along with the homomorphism witnessing that $\mathcal{A}'$ can be obtained by merging from $\mathcal{A}$. Next, we can check observational equivalence of $\mathcal{A}$ and $\mathcal{A}'$ in polynomial time (Theorem 1).

We show NP-hardness via reduction from the k-coloring problem. Let $G = (V, E)$ be a graph – for readability we assume it is a directed graph. We construct a binary PODWA $\Lambda_G = (\mathcal{A}_G, \{(-\infty, 0], (0, +\infty)\})$, which can be O-minimized to an automaton with $k + 2$ states if and only if the vertices of G can be colored with k colors such that each edge connects vertices with different colors.

Let $\Sigma = \{e^+, e^- \mid e \in E\}$ where $E = \{e_1, \ldots, e_m\}$. The states of $\mathcal{A}_G$ are q_0, q_f and $\{q_v : v \in V\}$. For an edge $e_i = (v, u)$ we define $\delta(q_0, e_i^-) = v$ and $\delta(q_0, e_i^+) = u$, i.e., over e_i^-, e_i^+ the automaton reaches both ends of e. All the remaining transitions lead to q_f.

We define weights function $\mathbf{c}$ so that pairs of states q_v, q_u can be merged if and only if they correspond to vertices u, v not connected in G. For any $e \in E$ we will ensure that in $\mathcal{A}_G$ the values of words $e^- e^-, e^+ e^+$ are negative and the value of words $e^- e^+, e^+ e^-$ are positive. This guarantees that e^+ and e^- cannot lead to the same state. Intuitively, after e^- the state in $\mathcal{A}_G$ has outgoing transitions over e^-, e^+, where the weight of e^+ is strictly greater than the weight of e^-, and for the state reachable over e^+, the order of weights is the opposite.

For every $e_i = (v, u) \in E$ we define $\mathbf{c}(q_0, e_i^-) = \mathbf{c}(q_0, e_i^+) = -3i - 1$. Then, for q_v we define $\mathbf{c}(q_v, e_i^-) = 3i$ and $\mathbf{c}(q_v, e_i^+) = 3i + 2$. For q_u we define $\mathbf{c}(q_u, e_i^-) = 3i + 2$ and $\mathbf{c}(q_u, e_i^+, q_f) = 3i$. For u that is not an endpoint of e_j we set $\mathbf{c}(q_u, e_j^-) = \mathbf{c}(q_u, e_j^+) = 3j + 1$. The weights $\mathbf{c}(q_f, *)$ are all 0.

We show that G is k-colorable if and only if Λ_G can be O-minimized to an automaton with $k + 2$ states. First, observe that the values $e_i^- e_i^-$ and $e_i^+ e_i^+$ in $\mathcal{A}_G$ are -1 and the values $e_i^- e_i^+$ and $e_i^+ e_i^-$ are 1 and hence q_u and q_v cannot be merged. Second, q_0 and q_f cannot be merged with one another or any other state; all words starting from q_0 are negative, and all word starting from q_0 retain their values. No other state has such a property. Therefore, if $\mathcal{A}_G$ is minimized by merging to an automaton with $k + 2$ states, then k is at least equal to the chromatic number of G.

Conversely, assume that $\lambda : V \to \{1, \ldots, k\}$ is a valid coloring of G. We construct a DWA $\mathcal{A}'_G$ with the same structure as $\mathcal{A}_G$, with the property that states corresponding to nodes of the same color have the same values of outgoing edges. Recall that for u that is not an endpoint of e_j we set $\mathbf{c}(q_u, e_j^-) = \mathbf{c}(q_u, e_j^+) = 3j + 1$. Changing any such weight to $3j$ or $3j + 2$ leads to an equivalent automaton. Indeed, the state q_u can be reached with values $-3i - 1$, where $i \neq j$ and hence the values $-3i - 1 + 3j, -3i - 1 + 3j + 1, -3i - 1 + 3j + 2$ are either all positive or all negative. With that observation, we can modify weights in $\mathcal{A}_G$ such that for u, v with the same color, the weights of all outgoing transitions from q_i, q_v are the same and hence the states can be merged. Assume that $u[1], \ldots, u[k]$ have the same color; then for every edge e at most one of these vertexes can be an endpoint of e; if there is such $u[i]$ then we fix weights of all transitions $(q_{u[1]}, e^-), \ldots, (q_{u[k]}, e^-)$ to be the same as the weight of $(q_{u[i]}, e^-)$. If there is no such vertex, we do not change the weights. We fix weights over e^+ accordingly. Observe, the in the resulting automaton states $q_{u[1]}, \ldots, q_{u[k]}$ have all the outgoing transitions to q_f, and transitions over the same letter have the same weight. Therefore, they all can be merged into the same state. $\square$

5 Conclusions

This paper introduces partially-observable deterministic weighted automata, which address the difficulty in specification synthesis originating from the need of feeding the exact values to the specification procedure. We have studied the basic properties of the model as well as problems related to specification synthesis via automata learning: equivalence and minimization. The main contribution of the paper is identifying obstacles in developing polynomial-time active learning algorithm for the new model. While our framework is unlikely to admit such an algorithm, it is possible that restricting the equivalence notion may lead framework admitting polynomial-time active learning algorithm.

Acknowledgements. This work was supported by the National Science Centre (NCN), Poland under grant 2020/39/B/ST6/00521.

References

1. Angluin, D.: Learning regular sets from queries and counterexamples. Inf. Comput. **75**(2), 87–106 (1987)
2. Beimel, A., Bergadano, F., Bshouty, N.H., Kushilevitz, E., Varricchio, S.: Learning functions represented as multiplicity automata. J. ACM **47**(3), 506–530 (2000)
3. Blackburn, P., van Benthem, J.F., Wolter, F. (eds.): Handbook of Modal Logic. Elsevier, Amsterdam (2006)
4. Blondin, M., Finkel, A., Göller, S., Haase, C., McKenzie, P.: Reachability in two-dimensional vector addition systems with states is PSPACE-complete. In: 30th Annual ACM/IEEE Symposium on Logic in Computer Science, LICS 2015, pp. 32–43. IEEE Computer Society (2015)
5. Chatterjee, K., Doyen, L., Henzinger, T.A.: Quantitative languages. ACM Trans. Comput. Log. **11**(4), 23:1–23:38 (2010)
6. Chatterjee, K., Henzinger, T.A., Otop, J.: Nested weighted automata. ACM Trans. Comput. Log. **18**(4), 31:1–31:44 (2017)
7. Clarke, E.M., Henzinger, T.A., Veith, H., Bloem, R. (eds.): Handbook of Model Checking, vol. 10. Springer, Cham (2018). https://doi.org/10.1007/978-3-319-10575-8
8. Doyen, L., Raskin, J.F.: Games with imperfect information: theory and algorithms. In: Apt, K.R., Grädel, E. (eds.), Lectures in Game Theory for Computer Scientists, pp. 185–212. Cambridge University Press (2011)
9. Droste, M., Kuich, W., Vogler, H.: Handbook of Weighted Automata. Springer Science & Business Media, Berlin, Heidelberg (2009). https://doi.org/10.1007/978-3-642-01492-5
10. Guelev, D.P., Dima, C.: Epistemic ATL with perfect recall, past and strategy contexts. In: Fisher, M., van der Torre, L., Dastani, M., Governatori, G. (eds.) CLIMA 2012. LNCS (LNAI), vol. 7486, pp. 77–93. Springer, Heidelberg (2012). https://doi.org/10.1007/978-3-642-32897-8_7
11. Henzinger, T.A., Otop, J.: From model checking to model measuring. In: D'Argenio, P.R., Melgratti, H. (eds.) CONCUR 2013. LNCS, vol. 8052, pp. 273–287. Springer, Heidelberg (2013). https://doi.org/10.1007/978-3-642-40184-8_20

12. Hopcroft, J.E., Ullman, J.D.: Introduction to Automata Theory, Languages, and Computation. Adison-Wesley Publishing Company, Reading, Massachusets, USA (1979)
13. Hunter, P., Raskin, J.-F.: Quantitative games with interval objectives. In: Raman, V., Suresh, S.P. (eds.), 34th International Conference on Foundation of Software Technology and Theoretical Computer Science, FSTTCS 2014, volume 29 of LIPIcs, pp. 365–377. Schloss Dagstuhl - Leibniz-Zentrum für Informatik (2014)
14. Marusic, I., Worrell, J.: Complexity of equivalence and learning for multiplicity tree automata. J. Mach. Learn. Res. **16**, 2465–2500 (2015)
15. Michaliszyn, J., Otop, J.: Minimization of limit-average automata. In: Zhou, Z.-H. (ed.), Proceedings of the Thirtieth International Joint Conference on Artificial Intelligence, IJCAI 2021, Virtual Event/Montreal, Canada, 19–27 August 2021, pp. 2819–2825. ijcai.org (2021)
16. Michaliszyn, J., Otop, J.: Learning infinite-word automata with loop-index queries. Artif. Intell. **307**, 103710 (2022)
17. Millington, I.: AI for Games. CRC Press, Boca Raton (2019)
18. Papadimitriou, C.H., Tsitsiklis, J.N.: The complexity of Markov decision processes. Math. Oper. Res. **12**(3), 441–450 (1987)

Temporal and Spatial Reasoning

Past-Present Temporal Programs
over Finite Traces

Pedro Cabalar[1] , Martín Diéguez[2] , François Laferrière[3(✉)] ,
and Torsten Schaub[3]

[1] University of Corunna, A Coruña, Spain
[2] University of Angers, Angers, France
[3] University of Potsdam, Potsdam, Germany
flaferriere@uni-potsdam.de

Abstract. Extensions of Answer Set Programming with language constructs from temporal logics, such as temporal equilibrium logic over finite traces (TEL_f), provide an expressive computational framework for modeling dynamic applications. In this paper, we study the so-called past-present syntactic subclass, which consists of a set of logic programming rules whose body references to the past and head to the present. Such restriction ensures that the past remains independent of the future, which is the case in most dynamic domains. We extend the definitions of completion and loop formulas to the case of past-present formulas, which allows for capturing the temporal stable models of past-present temporal programs by means of an LTL_f expression.

1   Introduction

Reasoning about dynamic scenarios is a central problem in the areas of Knowledge Representation [6] (KR) and Artificial Intelligence (AI). Several formal approaches and systems have emerged to introduce non-monotonic reasoning features in scenarios where the formalisation of time is fundamental [3,4,13,20,25]. In *Answer Set Programming* [7] (ASP), former approaches to temporal reasoning use first-order encodings [21] where the time is represented by means of a variable whose value comes from a finite domain. The main advantage of those approaches is that the computation of answer sets can be achieved via incremental solving [18]. Their downside is that they require an explicit representation of time points.

Temporal Equilibrium Logic [2] (TEL) was proposed as a temporal extension of *Equilibrium Logic* [23] with connectives from *Linear Time Temporal Logic* [24] (LTL). Due to the computational complexity of its satisfiability problem (EXPSPACE), finding tractable fragments of TEL with good computational properties have also been a topic in the literature. Within this context, *splittable temporal logic programs* [1] have been proved to be a syntactic fragment of TEL that allows for a reduction to LTL via the use of Loop Formulas [16].

When considering incremental solving, logics on finite traces such as LTL_f [12] have been shown to be more suitable. Accordingly, *Temporal Equilibrium Logic*

S. Gaggl et al. (Eds.): JELIA 2023, LNAI 14281, pp. 787–795, 2023.
https://doi.org/10.1007/978-3-031-43619-2_53

on *Finite traces* (TEL_f) [9] was created and became the foundations of the temporal ASP solver *telingo* [8].

We present a new syntactic fragment of TEL_f, named *past-present* temporal logic programs. Inspired by Gabbay's seminal paper [17], where the declarative character of past temporal operators is emphasized, this language consists of a set of logic programming rules whose formulas in the head are disjunctions of atoms that reference the present, while in its body we allow for any arbitrary temporal formula without the use of future operators. Such restriction ensures that the past remains independent of the future, which is the case in most dynamic domains, and makes this fragment advantageous for incremental solving.

As a contribution, we study the Lin-Zhao theorem [22] within the context of past-present temporal logic programs. More precisely, we show that when the program is *tight* [14], extending Clark's completion [11,15] to the temporal case suffices to capture the answer sets of a finite past-present program as the LTL_f-models of a corresponding temporal formula. We also show that, when the program is not tight, the use of loop formulas is necessary. To this purpose, we extend the definition of loop formulas to the case of past-present programs and we prove the Lin-Zhao theorem in our setting.

The paper is organised as follows: in Sect. 2, we review the formal background and we introduce the concept of past-present temporal programs. In Sect. 3, we extend the completion property to the temporal case. Section 4 is devoted to the introduction of our temporal extension of loop formulas. Finally, in Sect. 5, we present the conclusions as well as some future research lines. The full version of this paper can be found in [10].

2 Past-Present Temporal Programs over Finite Traces

In this section, we introduce the so-called *past-present* temporal logic programs and its semantics based on *Temporal Equilibrium Logic over Finite traces* (TEL_f for short) as in [2]. The syntax of our language is inspired from the pure-past fragment of Linear Time Temporal Logic (LTL) [19], since the only future operators used are *always* and *weak next*.

We start from a given set $\mathcal{A}$ of atoms which we call the *alphabet*. Then, *past temporal formulas* φ are defined by the grammar:

$$\varphi ::= a \mid \bot \mid \neg\varphi \mid \varphi_1 \wedge \varphi_2 \mid \varphi_1 \vee \varphi_2 \mid {\bullet}\varphi \mid \varphi_1 \mathbf{S} \varphi_2 \mid \varphi_1 \mathbf{T} \varphi_2$$

where $a \in \mathcal{A}$ is an atom. The intended meaning of the (modal) temporal operators is as in LTL. ${\bullet}\varphi$ means that φ is true at the previous time point; $\varphi \mathbf{S} \psi$ can be read as φ is true since ψ was true and $\varphi \mathbf{T} \psi$ means that ψ is true since both φ and ψ became true simultaneously or ψ has been true from the beginning.

Given $a \in \mathbb{N}$ and $b \in \mathbb{N}$, we let $[a..b] \stackrel{def}{=} \{i \in \mathbb{N} \mid a \leq i \leq b\}$ and $[a..b) \stackrel{def}{=} \{i \in \mathbb{N} \mid a \leq i < b\}$. A *finite trace* $\mathbf{T}$ of length λ over alphabet $\mathcal{A}$ is a sequence $\mathbf{T} = (T_i)_{i \in [0..\lambda)}$ of sets $T_i \subseteq \mathcal{A}$. To represent a given trace, we write a sequence of sets of atoms concatenated with '·'. For instance, the finite trace $\{a\} \cdot \emptyset \cdot \{a\} \cdot \emptyset$ has length 4 and makes a true at even time points and false at odd ones.

A *Here-and-There trace* (for short HT-*trace*) of length λ over alphabet $\mathcal{A}$ is a sequence of pairs $(\langle H_i, T_i \rangle)_{i \in [0..\lambda)}$ with $H_i \subseteq T_i$ for any $i \in [0..\lambda)$. For convenience, we usually represent the HT-trace as the pair $\langle \mathbf{H}, \mathbf{T} \rangle$ of traces $\mathbf{H} = (H_i)_{i \in [0..\lambda)}$ and $\mathbf{T} = (T_i)_{i \in [0..\lambda)}$. Given $\mathbf{M} = \langle \mathbf{H}, \mathbf{T} \rangle$, we also denote its length as $|\mathbf{M}| \overset{def}{=} |\mathbf{H}| = |\mathbf{T}| = \lambda$. Note that the two traces $\mathbf{H}, \mathbf{T}$ must satisfy a kind of order relation, since $H_i \subseteq T_i$ for each time point i. Formally, we define the ordering $\mathbf{H} \leq \mathbf{T}$ between two traces of the same length λ as $H_i \subseteq T_i$ for each $i \in [0..\lambda)$. Furthermore, we define $\mathbf{H} < \mathbf{T}$ as both $\mathbf{H} \leq \mathbf{T}$ and $\mathbf{H} \neq \mathbf{T}$. Thus, an HT-trace can also be defined as any pair $\langle \mathbf{H}, \mathbf{T} \rangle$ of traces such that $\mathbf{H} \leq \mathbf{T}$. The particular type of HT-traces satisfying $\mathbf{H} = \mathbf{T}$ are called *total*.

An HT-trace $\mathbf{M} = \langle \mathbf{H}, \mathbf{T} \rangle$ of length λ over alphabet $\mathcal{A}$ *satisfies* a past temporal formula φ at time point $k \in [0..\lambda)$, written $\mathbf{M}, k \models \varphi$, if the following conditions hold:

1. $\mathbf{M}, k \models \top$ and $\mathbf{M}, k \not\models \bot$
2. $\mathbf{M}, k \models p$ if $p \in H_k$ for any atom $p \in \mathcal{A}$
3. $\mathbf{M}, k \models \varphi \wedge \psi$ iff $\mathbf{M}, k \models \varphi$ and $\mathbf{M}, k \models \psi$
4. $\mathbf{M}, k \models \varphi \vee \psi$ iff $\mathbf{M}, k \models \varphi$ or $\mathbf{M}, k \models \psi$
5. $\mathbf{M}, k \models \neg\varphi$ iff $\langle \mathbf{T}, \mathbf{T} \rangle, k \not\models \varphi$
6. $\mathbf{M}, k \models \bullet\varphi$ iff $k > 0$ and $\mathbf{M}, k-1 \models \varphi$
7. $\mathbf{M}, k \models \varphi \, \mathbf{S} \, \psi$ iff for some $j \in [0..k]$, we have $\mathbf{M}, j \models \psi$ and $\mathbf{M}, i \models \varphi$ for all $i \in (j..k]$
8. $\mathbf{M}, k \models \varphi \, \mathbf{T} \, \psi$ iff for all $j \in [0..k]$, we have $\mathbf{M}, j \models \psi$ or $\mathbf{M}, i \models \varphi$ for some $i \in (j..k]$

A formula φ is a *tautology* (or is *valid*), written $\models \varphi$, iff $\mathbf{M}, k \models \varphi$ for any HT-trace $\mathbf{M}$ and any $k \in [0..\lambda)$. We call the logic induced by the set of all tautologies *Temporal logic of Here-and-There over finite traces* (THT$_f$ for short).

The following equivalences hold in THT$_f$: 1. $\top \equiv \neg\bot$, 2. $\mathsf{I} \equiv \neg\bullet\top$, 3. $\blacksquare\varphi \equiv \bot \, \mathbf{T} \, \varphi$, 4. $\blacklozenge\varphi \equiv \top \, \mathbf{S} \, \varphi$, 5. $\hat{\bullet}\varphi \equiv \bullet\varphi \vee \mathsf{I}$.

Definition 1 (Past-present Program). *Given alphabet $\mathcal{A}$, the set of* regular literals *is defined as* $\{a, \neg a, | \, a \in \mathcal{A}\}$.

A past-present rule is either:
- *an* initial rule *of form* $H \leftarrow B$
- *a* dynamic rule *of form* $\hat{\bullet}\square(H \leftarrow B)$ *where B is an pure past*
- *a* final rule *of form* $\square(\mathbf{F} \rightarrow (\bot \leftarrow B))$

formula for dynamic rules and $B = b_1 \wedge \cdots \wedge b_n$ with $n \geq 0$ for initial and final rules, the b_i are regular literals, $H = a_1 \vee \cdots \vee a_m$ with $m \geq 0$ and $a_j \in \mathcal{A}$. A past-present program *is a set of past-present rules.* □

We let $I(P)$, $D(P)$, and $F(P)$ stand for the set of all initial, dynamic, and final rules in a past-present program P, respectively. Additionally we refer to H as the *head* of a rule r and to B as the *body* of r. We let $B(r) = B$ and $H(r) = H$

for all types of rules above. For example, let consider the following past-present program P_1:

$$load \leftarrow \tag{1}$$

$$\hat{\mathsf{o}}\square(shoot \vee load \vee unload \leftarrow) \tag{2}$$

$$\hat{\mathsf{o}}\square(dead \leftarrow shoot \wedge \neg unload \mathrel{\mathbf{S}} load) \tag{3}$$

$$\hat{\mathsf{o}}\square(shoot \leftarrow dead) \tag{4}$$

$$\square(\mathbf{F} \rightarrow (\bot \leftarrow \neg dead)) \tag{5}$$

We get $I(P_1) = \{(1)\}$, $D(P_1) = \{(2),(3),(4)\}$, and $F(P_1) = \{(3)\}$. Rule (1) states that the gun is initially loaded. Rule (2) gives the choice to shoot, load, or unload the gun. Rule (3) states that if the gun is shot while it has been loaded, and not unloaded since, the target is dead. Rule (4) states that if the target is dead, we shoot it again. Rule (5) ensures that the target is dead at the end of the trace.

The satisfaction relation of a past-present rule on an HT-trace $\mathbf{M}$ of length λ and at time point $k \in [0..\lambda)$ is defined below:

- $\mathbf{M}, k \models H \leftarrow B$ iff $\mathbf{M}', k \not\models B$ or $\mathbf{M}', k \models H$, for all $\mathbf{M}' \in \{\mathbf{M}, \langle \mathbf{T}, \mathbf{T} \rangle\}$
- $\mathbf{M}, k \models \hat{\mathsf{o}}\square(H \leftarrow B)$ iff $\mathbf{M}', i \not\models B$ or $\mathbf{M}', i \models H$ for all $\mathbf{M}' \in \{\mathbf{M}, \langle \mathbf{T}, \mathbf{T} \rangle\}$ and all $i \in [k+1..\lambda)$
- $\mathbf{M}, k \models \square(\mathbf{F} \rightarrow (\bot \leftarrow B))$ iff $\langle \mathbf{T}, \mathbf{T} \rangle, \lambda - 1 \not\models B$

An HT-trace $\mathbf{M}$ is a *model* of a past-present program P if $\mathbf{M}, 0 \models r$ for all rule $r \in P$. Let P be past-present program. A total HT-trace $\langle \mathbf{T}, \mathbf{T} \rangle$ is a *temporal equilibrium model* of P iff $\langle \mathbf{T}, \mathbf{T} \rangle$ is a *model* of P, and there is no other $\mathbf{H} < \mathbf{T}$ such that $\langle \mathbf{H}, \mathbf{T} \rangle$ is a *model* of P. The trace $\mathbf{T}$ is called a *temporal stable model* (TS-model) of P.

For length $\lambda = 2$, P_1 has a unique TS-model $\{load\} \cdot \{shoot, dead\}$.

3   Temporal Completion

In this section, we extend the completion property to the temporal case of past-present programs.

An occurrence of an atom in a formula is *positive* if it is in the antecedent of an even number of implications, negative otherwise. An occurrence of an atom in a formula is *present* if it is not in the scope of ● (previous). Given a past-present program P over $\mathcal{A}$, we define its *(positive) dependency graph* $G(P)$ as $(\mathcal{A}, E)$ such that $(a, b) \in E$ if there is a rule $r \in P$ such that $a \in H(r) \cap \mathcal{A}$ and b has positive and present occurence in $B(r)$ that is not in the scope of negation. A nonempty set $L \subseteq \mathcal{A}$ of atoms is called *loop* of P if, for every pair a, b of atoms in L, there exists a path of length > 0 from a to b in $G(P)$ such that all vertices in the path belong to L. We let $L(P)$ denote the set of loops of P.

Due to the structure of past-present programs, dependencies from the future to the past cannot happen, and therefore there can only be loops within a same time point. To reflect this, the definitions above only consider atoms with present occurences. For example, rule $a \leftarrow b \wedge \bullet c$ generates the edge (a, b) but not (a, c).

For P_1, we get for the initial rules $G(I(P_1)) = (\{load, unload, shoot, dead\}, \emptyset)$ whose loops are $L(I(P_1)) = \emptyset$. For the dynamic rules, we get $G(D(P_1)) = (\{load, unload, shoot, dead\}, \{(dead, shoot), (dead, load), (shoot, dead)\})$ and $L(D(P_1)) = \{\{shoot, dead\}\}$.

In the following, $\varphi \rightarrow \psi \overset{def}{=} \psi \leftarrow \varphi$ and $\varphi \leftrightarrow \psi \overset{def}{=} \varphi \rightarrow \psi \wedge \varphi \leftarrow \psi$.

Definition 2 (Temporal completion). *We define the temporal completion formula of an atom a in a past-present program P over $\mathcal{A}$, denoted $CF_P(a)$ as:*

$$\Box\left(a \leftrightarrow \bigvee_{r \in I(P), a \in H(r)} (\mathsf{I} \wedge S(r, a)) \vee \bigvee_{r \in D(P), a \in H(r)} (\neg\mathsf{I} \wedge S(r, a)))\right)$$

where $S(r, a) = B(r) \wedge \bigwedge_{p \in H(r) \setminus \{a\}} \neg p$.
The temporal completion formula of P, denoted $CF(P)$, is

$$\{CF_P(a) \mid a \in \mathcal{A}\} \cup \{r \mid r \in I(P) \cup D(P), H(r) = \bot\} \cup F(P).$$

A past-present program P is said to be *tight* if $I(P)$ and $D(P)$ do not contain any loop.

Theorem 1. *Let P be a tight past-present program and $\mathbf{T}$ a trace of length λ. Then, $\mathbf{T}$ is a TS-model of P iff $\mathbf{T}$ is a LTL_f-model of $CF(P)$.* $\qquad\square$

The completion of P_1 is

$$CF(P_1) = \left\{ \begin{array}{c} \Box(load \leftrightarrow \mathsf{I} \vee (\neg\mathsf{I} \wedge \neg shoot \wedge \neg unload)), \\ \Box(shoot \leftrightarrow (\neg\mathsf{I} \wedge \neg load \wedge \neg unload)) \vee (\neg\mathsf{I} \wedge dead)), \\ \Box(unload \leftrightarrow (\neg\mathsf{I} \wedge \neg shoot \wedge \neg load)), \\ \Box(dead \leftrightarrow (\neg\mathsf{I} \wedge shoot \wedge \neg unload \, \mathsf{S} \, load)), \\ \Box(\mathsf{F} \rightarrow (\bot \leftarrow \neg dead)) \end{array} \right\}.$$

For $\lambda = 2$, $CF(P_1)$ has a unique LTL_f-model $\{load\} \cdot \{shoot, dead\}$, which is identical to the TS-model of P_1. Notice that for this example, the TS-models of the program match the LTL_f-models of its completion despite the program not being tight. This is generally not the case. Let P_2 be the program made of the rules $(1), (3), (4$ and $(5$. The completion of P_2 is

$$CF(P_2) = \left\{ \begin{array}{l} \Box(load \leftrightarrow \mathsf{I}), \ \Box(shoot \leftrightarrow (\neg\mathsf{I} \wedge dead)), \ \Box(unload \leftrightarrow \bot), \\ \Box(dead \leftrightarrow (\neg\mathsf{I} \wedge shoot \wedge \neg unload \, \mathsf{S} \, load)), \ \Box(\mathsf{F} \rightarrow (\bot \leftarrow \neg dead)) \end{array} \right\}.$$

P_2 does not have any TS-model, but $\{load\} \cdot \{shoot, dead\}$ is a LTL_f-model of $CF(P_2)$. Under ASP semantics, it is impossible to derive any element of the loop $\{shoot, dead\}$, as deriving $dead$ requires $shoot$ to be true, and deriving $shoot$ requires $dead$ to be true. The completion does not restrict this kind of circular derivation and therefore is insufficient to fully capture ASP semantics.

4 Temporal Loop Formulas

To restrict circular derivations, Lin and Zhao introduced the concept of loop formulas in [22]. In this section, we extend their work to past-present programs.

Definition 3. *Let φ be a implication-free past-present formula and L a loop. We define the supporting transformation of φ with respect to L as*

$$S_\perp(L) \overset{def}{=} \perp$$
$$S_p(L) \overset{def}{=} \perp \text{ if } p \in L \text{ ; } p \text{ otherwise, for any } p \in \mathcal{A}$$
$$S_{\neg\varphi}(L) \overset{def}{=} \neg\varphi$$
$$S_{\varphi\wedge\psi}(L) \overset{def}{=} S_\varphi(L) \wedge S_\psi(L)$$
$$S_{\varphi\vee\psi}(L) \overset{def}{=} S_\varphi(L) \vee S_\psi(L)$$
$$S_{\bullet\varphi}(L) \overset{def}{=} \bullet\varphi$$
$$S_{\varphi\mathbf{T}\psi}(L) \overset{def}{=} S_\psi(L) \wedge (S_\varphi(L) \vee \bullet(\varphi\ \mathbf{T}\ \psi))$$
$$S_{\varphi\mathbf{S}\psi}(L) \overset{def}{=} S_\psi(L) \vee (S_\varphi(L) \wedge \bullet(\varphi\ \mathbf{S}\ \psi))$$

$\square$

Definition 4 (External support). *Given a past-present program P, the external support formula of a set of atoms $L \subseteq \mathcal{A}$ wrt P, is defined as*

$$ES_P(L) = \bigvee_{r\in P, H(r)\cap L\neq\emptyset} \left(S_{B(r)}(L) \wedge \bigwedge_{a\in H(r)\setminus L} \neg a\right)$$

$\square$

For instance, for $L = \{shoot, dead\}$, $ES_{P_2}(L)$ and $ES_{P_1}(L)$ are

$$ES_{P_2}(L) = S_{dead}(L) \vee S_{shoot\wedge\neg unload\,\mathbf{S}\,load}(L)$$
$$= S_{dead}(L) \vee (S_{shoot}(L) \wedge S_{\neg unload\,\mathbf{S}\,load}(L))$$
$$= S_{dead}(L) \vee (S_{shoot}(L) \wedge S_{\neg unload}(L) \vee \bullet(\neg unload\ \mathbf{S}\ load))$$
$$= \perp \vee (\perp \wedge \neg unload \vee \bullet(\neg unload\ \mathbf{S}\ load)) = \perp.$$
$$ES_{P_1}(L) = S_{dead}(L) \vee S_{shoot\wedge\neg unload\,\mathbf{S}\,load}(L) \vee (\neg load \wedge \neg unload)$$
$$= \neg load \wedge \neg unload.$$

Rule (2) provides an external support for L. The body *dead* of rule (4) is also a support for L, but not external as *dead* belongs to L. The supporting transformation only keeps external supports by removing from the body any positive and present occurence of element of L.

Definition 5 (Loop formulas). *We define the set of loop formulas of a past-present program P over $\mathcal{A}$, denoted $LF(P)$, as:*

$$\bigvee_{a\in L} a \to ES_{I(P)}(L) \text{ for any loop } L \text{ in } I(P)$$

$$\widehat{\mathsf{o}}\square\left(\bigvee_{a\in L} a \to ES_{D(P)}(L)\right) \text{ for any loop } L \text{ in } D(P)$$

Theorem 2. *Let P be a past-present program and* **T** *a trace of length λ. Then,* **T** *is a TS-model of P iff* **T** *is a LTL_f-model of $CF(P) \cup LF(P)$.*   □

For our examples, we have that $LF(P_1) = \widehat{\circ}\square(shoot \vee dead \rightarrow \neg load \wedge \neg unload)$ and $LF(P_2) = \widehat{\circ}\square(shoot \vee dead \rightarrow \bot)$. It can be also checked that $\{load\} \cdot \{shoot, dead\}$ satisfies $LF(P_1)$, but not $LF(P_2)$. So, we have that $CF(P_1) \cup LF(P_1)$ has a unique LTL_f-model $\{load\} \cdot \{shoot, dead\}$, while $CF(P_2) \cup LF(P_2)$ has no LTL_f-model, matching the TS-models of the respective programs.

Ferraris et al. [16] proposed an approach where the computation of the completion can be avoided by considering unitary cycles. We extended such results for past-present programs in the extended version [10].

5 Conclusion

We have focused on temporal logic programming within the context of Temporal Equilibrium Logic over finite traces. More precisely, we have studied a fragment close to logic programming rules in the spirit of [17]: a past-present temporal logic program consists of a set of rules whose body refers to the past and present while their head refers to the present. This fragment is very interesting for implementation purposes since it can be solved by means of incremental solving techniques as implemented in *telingo*.

Contrary to the propositional case [16], where answer sets of an arbitrary propositional formula can be captured by means of the classical models of another formula ψ, in the temporal case, this is impossible to do the same mapping among the temporal equilibrium models of a formula φ and the LTL models of another formula ψ [5].

In this paper, we show that past-present temporal logic programs can be effectively reduced to LTL formulas by means of completion and loop formulas. More precisely, we extend the definition of completion and temporal loop formulas in the spirit of Lin and Zhao [22] to the temporal case, and we show that for tight past-present programs, the use of completion is sufficient to achieve a reduction to an LTL_f formula. Moreover, when the program is not tight, we also show that the computation of the temporal completion and a finite number of loop formulas suffices to reduce TEL_f to LTL_f.

Acknowledgments. This work was supported by MICINN, Spain, grant PID2020-116201GB-I00, Xunta de Galicia, Spain (GPC ED431B 2019/03), Région Pays de la Loire, France, (project etoiles montantes CTASP) and DFG grant SCHA 550/15, Germany.

References

1. Aguado, F., Cabalar, P., Pérez, G., Vidal, C.: Loop formulas for splitable temporal logic programs. In: Delgrande, J.P., Faber, W. (eds.) LPNMR 2011. LNCS (LNAI), vol. 6645, pp. 80–92. Springer, Heidelberg (2011). https://doi.org/10.1007/978-3-642-20895-9_9

2. Aguado, F., et al.: Linear-time temporal answer set programming. Theory Pract. Log. Program. **23**(1), 2–56 (2023)
3. Baral, C., Zhao, J.: Non-monotonic temporal logics for goal specification. In: Veloso, M.M. (ed.) IJCAI 2007, Proceedings of the 20th International Joint Conference on Artificial Intelligence, Hyderabad, India, 6–12 January 2007, pp. 236–242 (2007)
4. Baral, C., Zhao, J.: Non-monotonic temporal logics that facilitate elaboration tolerant revision of goals. In: Fox, D., Gomes, C.P. (eds.) Proceedings of the Twenty-Third AAAI Conference on Artificial Intelligence, AAAI 2008, Chicago, Illinois, USA, 13–17 July 2008, pp. 406–411. AAAI Press (2008)
5. Bozzelli, L., Pearce, D.: On the expressiveness of temporal equilibrium logic. In: Michael, L., Kakas, A. (eds.) JELIA 2016. LNCS (LNAI), vol. 10021, pp. 159–173. Springer, Cham (2016). https://doi.org/10.1007/978-3-319-48758-8_11
6. Brachman, R.J., Levesque, H.J.: Knowledge Representation and Reasoning. Elsevier (2004). http://www.elsevier.com/wps/find/bookdescription.cws_home/702602/description
7. Brewka, G., Eiter, T., Truszczyński, M.: Answer set programming at a glance. Commun. ACM **54**(12), 92–103 (2011)
8. Cabalar, P., Kaminski, R., Morkisch, P., Schaub, T.: telingo = ASP + Time. In: Balduccini, M., Lierler, Y., Woltran, S. (eds.) Logic Programming and Nonmonotonic Reasoning. LPNMR 2019. LNCS, vol. 11481, pp. 256–269. Springer, Cham (2019). https://doi.org/10.1007/978-3-030-20528-7_19
9. Cabalar, P., Kaminski, R., Schaub, T., Schuhmann, A.: Temporal answer set programming on finite traces. Theory Pract. Log. Program. **18**(3–4), 406–420 (2018)
10. Cabalar, P., Diéguez, M., Laferrière, F., Schaub, T.: Past-present temporal programs over finite traces (2023). https://arxiv.org/pdf/2307.12620.pdf
11. Clark, K.: Negation as failure. In: Gallaire, H., Minker, J. (eds.) Logic and Data Bases, pp. 293–322. Plenum Press (1978)
12. De Giacomo, G., Vardi, M.: Linear temporal logic and linear dynamic logic on finite traces. In: Rossi, F. (ed.) Proceedings of the Twenty-third International Joint Conference on Artificial Intelligence (IJCAI'13), pp. 854–860. IJCAI/AAAI Press (2013)
13. Emerson, E.: Temporal and modal logic. In: van Leeuwen, J. (ed.) Handbook of Theoretical Computer Science, pp. 995–1072. MIT Press (1990)
14. Erdem, E., Lifschitz, V.: Tight logic programs. Theory Pract. Log. Program. **3**(4–5), 499–518 (2003)
15. Fages, F.: Consistency of Clark's completion and the existence of stable models. J. Methods Log. Comput. Sci. **1**, 51–60 (1994)
16. Ferraris, P., Lee, J., Lifschitz, V.: A generalization of the Lin-Zhao theorem. Ann. Math. Artif. Intell. **47**(1–2), 79–101 (2006)
17. Gabbay, D.: The declarative past and imperative future. In: Banieqbal, B., Barringer, H., Pnueli, A. (eds.) Temporal Logic in Specification. LNCS, vol. 398, pp. 409–448. Springer, Heidelberg (1989). https://doi.org/10.1007/3-540-51803-7_36
18. Gebser, M., Kaminski, R., Kaufmann, B., Ostrowski, M., Schaub, T., Thiele, S.: Engineering an incremental ASP solver. In: Garcia de la Banda, M., Pontelli, E. (eds.) ICLP 2008. LNCS, vol. 5366, pp. 190–205. Springer, Heidelberg (2008). https://doi.org/10.1007/978-3-540-89982-2_23
19. Giacomo, G.D., Stasio, A.D., Fuggitti, F., Rubin, S.: Pure-past linear temporal and dynamic logic on finite traces. In: Bessiere, C. (ed.) Proceedings of the Twenty-ninth International Joint Conference on Artificial Intelligence, (IJCAI'20), pp. 4959–4965. ijcai.org (2020)

20. González, G., Baral, C., Cooper, P.A.: Modeling multimedia displays using action based temporal logic. In: Zhou, X., Pu, P. (eds.) Visual and Multimedia Information Management. ITIFIP, vol. 88, pp. 141–155. Springer, Boston, MA (2002). https://doi.org/10.1007/978-0-387-35592-4_11

21. Lifschitz, V.: Answer set planning. In: de Schreye, D. (ed.) Proceedings of the International Conference on Logic Programming (ICLP'99), pp. 23–37. MIT Press (1999)

22. Lin, F., Zhao, J.: On tight logic programs and yet another translation from normal logic programs to propositional logic. In: Gottlob, G., Walsh, T. (eds.) Proceedings of the Eighteenth International Joint Conference on Artificial Intelligence (IJCAI'03), pp. 853–858. Morgan Kaufmann Publishers (2003)

23. Pearce, D.: A new logical characterisation of stable models and answer sets. In: Dix, J., Pereira, L.M., Przymusinski, T.C. (eds.) NMELP 1996. LNCS, vol. 1216, pp. 57–70. Springer, Heidelberg (1997). https://doi.org/10.1007/BFb0023801

24. Pnueli, A.: The temporal logic of programs. In: Proceedings of the Eight Teenth Symposium on Foundations of Computer Science (FOCS'77), pp. 46–57. IEEE Computer Society Press (1977)

25. Sandewall, E.: Features and Fluents: The Representation of Knowledge About Dynamical Systems, vol. 1. Oxford University Press, New York, NY, USA (1994)

Robust Alternating-Time Temporal Logic

Aniello Murano[1] , Daniel Neider[2,3](✉) , and Martin Zimmermann[4]

[1] Università degli Studi di Napoli "Federico II", Naples, Italy
[2] TU Dortmund University, Dortmund, Germany
daniel.neider@tu-dortmund.de
[3] Center for Trustworthy Data Science and Security, University Alliance Ruhr,
Dortmund, Germany
[4] Aalborg University, Aalborg, Denmark

Abstract. In multi-agent system design, a crucial aspect is to ensure
robustness, meaning that for a coalition of agents A, small violations
of adversarial assumptions only lead to small violations of A's goals. In
this paper we introduce a logical framework for robust strategic reasoning about multi-agent systems. Specifically, inspired by recent works on
robust temporal logics, we introduce and study rATL and rATL*, logics
that extend the well-known Alternating-time Temporal Logic ATL and
ATL* by means of an opportune multi-valued semantics for the strategy quantifiers and temporal operators. We study the model-checking
and satisfiability problems for rATL and rATL* and show that dealing
with robustness comes at no additional computational cost. Indeed, we
show that these problems are PTIME-complete and EXPTIME-complete
for rATL, respectively, while both are 2EXPTIME-complete for rATL*.

Keywords: Multi-Agents · Temporal Logic · Robustness

1 Introduction

Multi-agent system verification has been receiving a lot of attention in recent
years, thanks to the introduction of powerful logics for strategic reasoning [4,
10,20,36,40]. Along this line of research, a story of success is *Alternating-Time
Temporal Logic* (ATL) introduced by Alur, Henzinger, and Kupferman [4]. ATL
is a generalization of Computation Tree Logic (CTL) [21], obtained by replacing
the path quantifier ∃ (and its dual ∀), with the modality ⟨⟨A⟩⟩ (and its dual
[[A]]), where A is a set of agents. The interpretation of ⟨⟨A⟩⟩φ is that the coalition
A has a strategy such that the outcome of this strategy satisfies $φ$, no matter
how the coalition of the agents not in A behaves. ATL formulas are interpreted
over concurrent game structures, which extend classical Kripke structures to
represent the dynamism of the agents. The model-checking problem of ATL is
PTIME-complete [4], while the satisfiability problem is EXPTIME-complete [51].

A crucial aspect in multi-agent system design is to ensure system *robustness*,
which should reflect the ability of a coalition of agents to tolerate violations

S. Gaggl et al. (Eds.): JELIA 2023, LNAI 14281, pp. 796–813, 2023.
https://doi.org/10.1007/978-3-031-43619-2_54

(possibly up to some extent) of adversarial assumptions [19]. Numerous studies have shown that reactive AI systems can be very sensitive to intentional or unintentional external perturbations, posing huge risks to safety-critical applications [33]. Notably, the formal methods community has put large efforts in reasoning about system robustness in several specific settings, mainly concerning closed system verification or (two-player) reactive synthesis [15,17,23,25,26,28]. As far as we are aware of, there are no logic-based works dealing with robust strategic reasoning in multi-agent systems. To highlight the significance of this challenge, we describe a few specific contexts in which multi-agent systems act as the natural model and robustness plays a crucial role.

Scenario 1. Climate change threatens people with food and water scarcity, increased flooding, extreme heat, diseases, and economic loss. Human migration and conflict can be a result. The World Health Organization calls climate change the greatest threat to global health in the 21st century. Recently, researchers examining alternative policies to address the threat of climate change have become increasingly concerned about uncertainty and the fact that we cannot predict the future. This requires to develop mathematical models to properly represent the intricate interaction among all decision makers and the ability to define strategies that are robust against a wide range of plausible climate-change futures [37]. For risk-averse policy-makers, such strategies would perform reasonably well, at least compared to the alternatives, even if confronted with surprises or catastrophes. Robust strategies may also provide a more solid basis for consensus on political action among stakeholders with different views of the future, because it would provide reasonable outcomes no matter whose view proved correct.

Scenario 2. The fast-evolving domain of *autonomous vehicles* is one of the best examples of multi-agent modelling, where safety-critical decisions strongly rely on sensor observations (e.g., ultrasound, radar, GPS, Lidar, and camera signals) [50]. It is of primary importance that the resulting decisions are robust to perturbations, which often are treated as adversarial perturbations [39]. A careful evaluation of such adversarial behaviours is necessary to build and deploy safer autonomous vehicle systems.

Scenario 3. Power systems play an important role in all sectors of the national economy and in our daily lives. Ensuring a safe and reliable power supply from the power network is a fundamental requirement. As renewable energy-based smart grid and micro-grid systems rise in popularity, multi-agent system technology has been establishing itself as a useful paradigm of choice for modelling, analysis, control and optimization of power systems [30,45,48]. The model usually consists of several agents competing not only among themselves to get energy resources, but also playing against the unpredictable behaviour of nature. Then, a classical safety requirement amounts to ensuring system robustness, in the meaning that the power system has to keep operating, possibly by rationing resources, despite the loss of any single asset such as lines or power plants at any time [1,14]. This is usually enforced by following a simple guiding redundancy principle while developing the system: designers have to predict the effect of having any line disconnected in any moment and cope with it, in real time and even at larger scales [43]. This may also require the players to coordinate and/or play rational while keeping the system under equilibrium [12].

Our Contribution. In this paper we introduce rATL, a robust version of the logic ATL. Our approach here follows and extends an approach originally introduced for robust Linear Temporal Logic (rLTL) [49] and later extended to robust Computation Tree Logic (rCTL and rCTL*) [42]. To illustrate the robust semantics, consider an invariant of the form $\Box p$ specifying that the proposition p always holds. There are several ways this invariant can be violated, with varying degrees of severity. For example, p failing to hold a finite number of times is less severe than p failing infinitely often. An even worse situation is p holding only finitely often while p not even holding once is the worst way to violate the invariant. The authors in [49] argue that these five degrees are canonical and use them as the basis of a five-valued robust semantics for temporal logics. The semantics of the Boolean operators are then defined to capture the intuition that there are different degrees of violation of a formula while the other temporal operators, e.g., next and eventually, are defined as usual. In particular, the definition of implications captures the idea that, in a specification of the form $\varphi \to \psi$, a "small" violation of an environment assumption φ must lead to only a "small" (proportional) violation of a system's guarantee ψ.

Here, we devise a meaningful robust semantics for the strategy quantifiers to obtain a robust variant of ATL, and show that it is capable to reason about the robustness of multi-agent systems. More precisely, rATL allows to assess whether a strategy f of a coalition A is robust in the sense that, with respect to the outcome of f, small violations of the adversarial team assumptions only lead to small violations of A's goals. We study expressiveness of rATL and show that it strictly subsumes ATL, as rATL can express fairness. We also study the model-checking and satisfiability problems for rATL and show that dealing with robustness comes at no additional computational cost. Indeed, we show that these problems are PTIME-complete and EXPTIME-complete, respectively. This is in line with the results on rLTL and rCTL, for which model-checking and satisfiability are also not harder than for LTL [49] and CTL [42], respectively.

Finally, we also study rATL*, the robustification of ATL*, showing that also in this setting, robustness comes for free: model-checking and satisfiability for rATL* are 2EXPTIME-complete, as they are already for ATL* [4,46].

All proofs omitted due to space restrictions can be found in the full version [41].

Related Work. There are several works done in formal strategic reasoning that have been used (or can be easily adapted) to develop robust systems. Besides those reported above, we recall the works dealing with strategy logics extended with probabilistic [5,31,47] and knowledge (imperfect information) aspects [24]. These works allow to reason about the unpredictable behaviour of the environment. Unfortunately, in both cases, the model-checking problem becomes highly undecidable, unless one restricts strategies to be memoryless. In the imperfect information case, memoryfull strategies with less severe restrictions have been also studied (e.g., hierarchical visibility [13] and public action [11]) although model-checking remains infeasible, i.e., non-elementary, in practice.

Other lines of research have considered quantitative aspects of the logic, in different directions. Bouyer et al. [16] considered a fuzzy extension of ATL*, namely ATL*[$\mathcal{F}$]. The satisfaction value of ATL*[$\mathcal{F}$] formulas is a real value in $[0, 1]$, reflecting "how much" or "how well" the strategic on-going objectives of the underlying agents are satisfied. In [16] a double exponential-time model-checking procedure for ATL*[$\mathcal{F}$] is presented. A careful inspection of that procedure yields, for the special case of ATL[$\mathcal{F}$], an EXPTIME-completeness result by means of an exponential reduction to Büchi games. Faella, Napoli, and Parente [27] and Aminof et al. [6] considered a graded extension of the logics ATL and ATL* with the ability of checking for the existence of redundant winning strategies.

Module checking is another example of a formal method to devise robust systems. Indeed, module checking amounts to checking whether a strategic behaviour of a coalition of agents satisfies a goal, irrespective to all possible nondeterministic behaviours of an external environment [32, 35].

Finally, robustness is also an active field of study in reinforcement learning [44], which treats environment mismatches as adversarial perturbations against a coalition of agents. In the simplest version, the underlying model is a two-player zero-sum simultaneous game between the protagonist who aims to find a robust strategy across environments and the adversary who exerts perturbations. Computational methods have been proposed to solve this game and to find a robust strategy for the protagonist (see Pinto et al. [44] and the references therein).

2   Preliminaries

We denote the nonnegative integers by $\mathbb{N}$, and the power set of a set S by 2^S. Throughout the paper, we fix a finite set AP of atomic propositions.

A concurrent game structure $\mathcal{S} = (St, Ag, Ac, \delta, \ell)$ consists of a finite set St of states, a finite set Ag of agents, a finite set Ac of actions, and a labeling function $\ell\colon St \to 2^{\mathrm{AP}}$. An action vector for a subset $A \subseteq Ag$ is a mapping $v\colon A \to Ac$. Let AV denote the set of action vectors for the full set Ag of agents. The transition function $\delta\colon St \times AV \to St$ maps a state and an action vector to a state. The size of $\mathcal{S}$ is defined as $|St \times AV|$.

We say that a state s' is a successor of a state s if there is an action vector $v \in AV$ such that $s' = \delta(s, v)$. A path of $\mathcal{S}$ is an infinite sequence $\pi = s_0 s_1 s_2 \cdots$ of states such that s_{n+1} is a successor of s_n for every $n \geq 0$. We write $\pi[n]$ for s_n.

A strategy for an agent is a function $f\colon St^+ \to Ac$. Given a set $F_A = \{f_a \mid a \in A\}$ of strategies, one for each agent in some set $A \subseteq Ag$, $out(s, F_A)$ denotes the set of paths starting in s that are consistent with F_A. Formally, a path $s_0 s_1 s_2 \cdots$ is in $out(s, F_A)$ if $s_0 = s$ and for all $n \geq 0$, there is an action vector $v \in AV$ with $v(a) = f_a(s_0 \cdots s_n)$ for all $a \in A$ and $s_{n+1} = \delta(s_n, v)$. Intuitively, $out(s, F_A)$ contains all paths that are obtained by the agents in A picking their actions according to their strategies and the other agents picking their actions arbitrarily.

3   rATL

The basic idea underlying our robust version of ATL, or *rATL* for short, is that a "small" violation of an environment assumption (along the outcome of a strategy) must lead to only a "small" violation of a system's guarantee. This is obtained by devising a robust semantics for the strategy quantifiers and by stating formally what it is meant for a "small" violations of a property. For the latter, we follow and adapt the approach by Tabuada and Neider [49], initially proposed for a robust version of Linear Temporal Logic (rLTL), and use five truth values: 1111, 0111, 0011, 0001, and 0000. Let $\mathbb{B}_4$ denote the set of these truth values. Our motivation for using the seemingly odd-looking truth values in $\mathbb{B}_4$ is that they represent five canonical ways how a system guarantee of the form "always p" ($\Box p$ in LTL) can be satisfied or violated. Clearly, we prefer that p always holds, represented by the truth value 1111. However, if this is impossible, the following best situation is that p holds at least almost always, represented by 0111. Similarly, we would prefer p being satisfied at least infinitely often, represented by 0011, over p being satisfied at least once, represented by 0001. Finally, the worst situation is that p never holds, represented by 0000. Put slightly differently, the bits of each truth value represent (from left to right) the modalities "always" ($\Box$), "eventually always" ($\Diamond\Box$), "always eventually" ($\Box\Diamond$), and "eventually" ($\Diamond$). We refer the reader to Anevlavis et al. [9] for an in-depth explanation of why these five ways are canonical.

Following the intuition above, we order the truth values in $\mathbb{B}_4$ by

$$1111 \succ 0111 \succ 0011 \succ 0001 \succ 0000.$$

This order spans a spectrum of truth values ranging from 1111, corresponding to *true*, on one end, to 0000, corresponding to *false*, on the other end. Since we arrived at the set $\mathbb{B}_4$ by considering the canonical ways of how the invariant property $\Box p$ can fail, we interpret all truth values different from 1111 as *shades of false*. We return to this interpretation when we later define the semantics for the negation in rATL.

Having formally discussed how we "grade" the violation of a property along paths, we are now ready to define the syntax of rATL via the following grammar:

$$\varphi ::= p \mid \neg\varphi \mid \varphi \vee \varphi \mid \varphi \wedge \varphi \mid \varphi \rightarrow \varphi \mid \langle\!\langle A \rangle\!\rangle \Phi \mid [\![A]\!] \Phi$$
$$\Phi ::= \odot\varphi \mid \Diamond\!\!\!\cdot\,\varphi \mid \Box\!\!\!\cdot\,\varphi$$

where p ranges over atomic propositions and A ranges over subsets of agents. We distinguish between *state formulas* (those derivable from φ) and *path formulas* (those derivable from Φ). If not specified, an rATL formula is a state formula.

Various critical remarks should be made concerning the syntax of rATL. First, we add "dots" to temporal operators (following the notation by Tabuada and Neider [49]) to distinguish between the original operators in ATL and their robustified counterparts in rATL—otherwise, the syntax stays the same. Second, many operators of rATL, most notably the negation and implication, can no longer be derived via De Morgan's law or simple logical equivalencies due to rATL's many-valued nature. Hence, they need to be added explicitly. Third, we omit the until and release operators here to avoid cluttering our presentation too much. Both can be added easily, as in rLTL [7,8].

We define the semantics of rATL by an *evaluation function* V that maps a state formula and a state or a path formula and a path to a truth value in $\mathbb{B}_4$. To simplify our presentation, we use $b[k]$ as a shorthand notation for addressing the k-th bit, $k \in \{1, 2, 3, 4\}$, of a truth value $b = b_1 b_2 b_3 b_4 \in \mathbb{B}_4$ (i.e., $b[k] = b_k$). It is worth emphasizing that our semantics for rATL is a natural extension of the Boolean semantics of ATL and is deliberately designed to generalize the original Boolean semantics of ATL (see Subsect. 3.3).

Turning to the definition of rATL's semantics, let us begin with state formulas. For atomic propositions $p \in \mathrm{AP}$, we define the valuation function by

$$V(s, p) = \begin{cases} 1111 & \text{if } p \in \ell(s); \text{ and} \\ 0000 & \text{if } p \notin \ell(s). \end{cases}$$

Note that this definition mimics the semantics of ATL in that propositions get mapped to one of the two truth values *true* (1111) or *false* (0000). As a consequence, the notion of robustness in rATL does not arise from atomic propositions (e.g., as in LTL[$\mathcal{F}$] by Almagor, Boker, and Kupferman [3] or fuzzy logics) but from the evolution of the temporal operators (see the semantics of path formulas). This design choice is motivated by the observation that assigning meaningful (robustness) values to atomic propositions is often highly challenging in practice—if not impossible.

The semantics of conjunctions and disjunctions are defined as usual for many-valued logics in terms of the functions min and max:

$$V(s, \varphi_1 \vee \varphi_2) = \max \big(V(s, \varphi_1), V(s, \varphi_2) \big)$$
$$V(s, \varphi_1 \wedge \varphi_2) = \min \big(V(s, \varphi_1), V(s, \varphi_2) \big)$$

To define the semantics of negation, remember our interpretation of the truth values in $\mathbb{B}_4$: 1111 corresponds to *true* and all other truth values correspond to different shades of *false*. Consequently, we map 1111 to 0000 and all other truth values to 1111. This idea is formalized by

$$V(s, \neg\varphi) = \begin{cases} 0000 & \text{if } V(s, \varphi) = 1111; \text{ and} \\ 1111 & \text{if } V(s, \varphi) \prec 1111. \end{cases}$$

Note that the definition of $V(s, \neg\varphi)$ is not symmetric, which is in contrast to other many-valued logics, such as LTL[$\mathcal{F}$]. However, it degenerates to the standard Boolean negation if one considers only two truth values.

Since our negation is defined in a non-standard way, we cannot recover implication from negation and disjunction. Instead, we define the implication $a \to b$ by requiring that $c \prec a \to b$ if and only if $\min \{a, c\} \prec b$ for every $c \in \mathbb{B}_4$. This notion leads to

$$V(s, \varphi_1 \to \varphi_2) = \begin{cases} 1111 & \text{if } V(s, \varphi_1) \preceq V(s, \varphi_2); \text{ and} \\ V(s, \varphi_2) & \text{if } V(s, \varphi_1) \succ V(s, \varphi_2). \end{cases}$$

Again, this definition collapses to the usual Boolean definition in case one considers only two truth values.

We now provide the robust semantics for the strategy quantifiers, which are the key ingredient in rATL. First, notice that the strategy quantifiers $\langle\!\langle \cdot \rangle\!\rangle$ and $[\![\cdot]\!]$ are not dual in our robustified version of ATL and require their individual definitions. Intuitively, $\langle\!\langle A \rangle\!\rangle \Phi$ is the largest truth value that the coalition A of agents can enforce for the path formula Φ, while $[\![A]\!]\Phi$ is the largest truth value that $Ag \setminus A$ can enforce against A. Formally, we have the following:

- $V(s, \langle\!\langle A \rangle\!\rangle \Phi)$ is the maximal truth value $b \in \mathbb{B}_4$ such that there is a set F_A of strategies, one for each agent in A, such that for all paths $\pi \in out(s, F_A)$ we have $V(\pi, \Phi) \succeq b$.
- $V(s, [\![A]\!]\Phi)$ is the maximal truth value $b \in \mathbb{B}_4$ such that for all sets F_A of strategies, one for each agent in A, there exists a path $\pi \in out(s, F_A)$ with $V(\pi, \Phi) \succeq b$.

Let us now turn to the semantics of path formulas. We begin with the $\boxdot$-operator. This operator captures the five canonical ways an invariant property "always p" can be satisfied or violated, thereby implementing the intuition we have presented at the beginning of this section. Formally, the valuation function $V(\pi, \boxdot\varphi)$ is given by $V(\pi, \boxdot\varphi) = b_1 b_2 b_3 b_4$ where

$$b_1 = \min_{i \geq 0} V(\pi[i], \varphi)[1], \qquad b_3 = \min_{i \geq 0} \max_{j \geq i} V(\pi[j], \varphi)[3],$$
$$b_2 = \max_{i \geq 0} \min_{j \geq i} V(\pi[j], \varphi)[2], \qquad b_4 = \max_{i \geq 0} V(\pi[i], \varphi)[4]).$$

Note that for $p \in AP$ and a path π, the semantics of the formula $\boxdot p$ on π amounts to the four-tuple $(\Box p, \Diamond\Box p, \Box\Diamond p, \Diamond p)$ because $V(s, p)$ is either 0000 or 1111 on every state s along π (i.e., all bits are either 0 or 1). However, the interpretation of $V(\pi, \boxdot\varphi)$ becomes more involved once the formula φ is nested since the semantics of the $\boxdot$-operator refers to individual bits of $V(\pi, \varphi)$.

Finally, the semantics for the $\Diamond$-operator and $\odot$-operator are straightforward as there are only two possible outcomes: either the property is satisfied, or it is violated. Consequently, we define the valuation function by

- $V(\pi, \Diamond\varphi) = b_1 b_2 b_3 b_4$ with $b_k = \max_{i \geq 0} V(\pi[i], \varphi)[k]$; and
- $V(\pi, \odot\varphi) = b_1 b_2 b_3 b_4$ with $b_k = V(\pi[1], \varphi)[k]$.

Again, note that both $V(\pi, \Diamond\varphi)$ and $V(\pi, \odot\varphi)$ refer to individual bits of $V(\pi, \varphi)$.

Example 1. Consider the formula $\varphi = \langle\!\langle A \rangle\!\rangle \boxdot p$. We have

- $V(s, \varphi) = 1111$ if the coalition A has a (joint) strategy to ensure that p holds at every position of every outcome.
- $V(s, \varphi) = 0111$ if the coalition A has strategy to ensure that p holds at all but finitely many positions of every outcome.

- $V(s, \varphi) = 0011$ if the coalition A has strategy to ensure that p holds at infinitely many positions of every outcome.
- $V(s, \varphi) = 0001$ if the coalition A has strategy to ensure that p holds at least once on every outcome.

3.1 rATL Model-Checking

The model-checking problem for rATL is as follows: Given a concurrent game structure $\mathcal{S}$, a state s, an rATL formula φ, and a truth value $t \in \mathbb{B}_4$, is $V(s, \varphi) \succeq t$?

Theorem 1. *rATL model-checking is* PTIME-*complete.*

The proof is based on capturing the semantics of the strategy quantifiers $\langle\!\langle A \rangle\!\rangle$ and $[\![A]\!]$ by sequential two-player games, one player representing the agents in A and the other representing the agents in the complement of A. We begin by introducing the necessary background on such games.

A (sequential) two-player game structure $\mathcal{S} = (St, St_1, St_2, Ac_1, Ac_2, \delta)$ consists of a set St of states partitioned into the states $St_p \subseteq St$ of Player $p \in \{1, 2\}$, an action set Ac_p for Player $p \in \{1, 2\}$, and a transition function $\delta \colon St_1 \times Ac_1 \cup St_2 \times Ac_2 \to St$. The size of $\mathcal{S}$ is $|St_1 \times Ac_1 \cup St_2 \times Ac_2|$. A path of $\mathcal{S}$ is an infinite sequence $s_0 s_1 s_2 \cdots$ of states such that $s_{n+1} = \delta(s_n, \alpha)$ for some action α. A strategy for Player 1 is a mapping $f \colon St^* St_1 \to Ac_1$. A path $s_0 s_1 s_2 \cdots$ is an outcome of f starting in s, if $s_0 = s$ and $s_{n+1} = \delta(s_n, f(s_0 \cdots s_n))$ for all $n \geq 0$ such that $s_n \in St_1$. A two player game $\mathcal{G} = (\mathcal{S}, \mathrm{Win})$ consists of a two-player game structure $\mathcal{S}$ and a winning condition $\mathrm{Win} \subseteq St^\omega$, where St is the set of states of $\mathcal{S}$. We say that a strategy f for Player 1 is a winning strategy for $\mathcal{G}$ from a state s, if every outcome of f starting in s is in Win.

Given a concurrent game structure $\mathcal{S} = (St, Ag, Ac, \delta, \ell)$ and $A \subseteq Ag$, we define the two-player game structure $\mathcal{S}_A = (St_1 \cup St_2, St_1, St_2, Ac_1, Ac_2, \delta')$ where $St_1 = St$ and $St_2 = St \times Ac_1$, Ac_1 is the set of action vectors for A, Ac_2 is the set of action vectors for $Ag \setminus A$, $\delta'(s, v) = (s, v)$ for $s \in St_1$ and $v \in Ac_1$, and $\delta'((s, v), v') = \delta(s, v \oplus v')$ for $(s, v) \in St_2$ and $v' \in Ac_2$, where $v \oplus v'$ is the unique action vector for Ag induced by v and v'. Note that the size of $\mathcal{S}_A$ is at most linear in the size of $\mathcal{S}$.

A path in $\mathcal{S}_A$ alternates between states of $\mathcal{S}$ and auxiliary states (those in $St \times Ac_1$), i.e., it is in $(St \cdot (St \times Ac_1))^\omega$. Thus, when translating paths between $\mathcal{S}$ and $\mathcal{S}_A$, only states at even positions are relevant (assuming we start the path in $\mathcal{S}_A$ in St). Hence, given a property $P \subseteq St^\omega$ of paths in $\mathcal{S}$, we extend it to the corresponding winning condition $P' = \{s_0 s_1 s_2 \cdots \in (St \cdot (St \times Ac_1))^\omega \mid s_0 s_2 s_4 \cdots \in P\}$ of paths in $\mathcal{S}_A$.

The next lemma reduces the (non-) existence of strategies that allow a set A of agents to enforce a property in $\mathcal{S}$ (which formalize the semantics of $\langle\!\langle A \rangle\!\rangle$ and $[\![A]\!]$) to the (non-) existence of winning strategies for Player 1 in $\mathcal{S}_A$. It derives from results of de Alfaro and Henzinger [2] for concurrent ω-regular games.

Lemma 1. *Let S be a concurrent game structure with set St of states containing s, let A be a subset of its agents, and let $P \subseteq St^\omega$.*

1. *There is a set F_A of strategies, one for each agent $a \in A$, such that $out(s, F_A) \subseteq P$ iff Player 1 has a winning strategy for (S_A, P') from s.*
2. *For all sets F_A of strategies, one for each agent $a \in A$, $out(s, F_A) \cap P \neq \emptyset$ iff Player 1 does not have a winning strategy for $(S_A, (St^\omega \setminus P)')$ from s.*

In the following, we consider the following winning conditions for a two-player game played in S_A, all induced by a set $F \subseteq St$ of states:

$$\mathrm{Next}(F) = \{s_0 s_1 s_2 \cdots \in (St \cdot (St \times Ac_1))^\omega \mid s_2 \in F\}$$

$$\mathrm{Reach}(F) = \{s_0 s_1 s_2 \cdots \in (St \cdot (St \times Ac_1))^\omega \mid s_n \in F \text{ for some even } n\}$$

$$\mathrm{Safety}(F) = \{s_0 s_1 s_2 \cdots \in (St \cdot (St \times Ac_1))^\omega \mid s_n \in F \text{ for all even } n\}$$

$$\mathrm{B\ddot{u}chi}(F) = \{s_0 s_1 s_2 \cdots \in (St \cdot (St \times Ac_1))^\omega \mid$$
$$s_n \in F \text{ for infinitely many even } n\}$$

$$\mathrm{coB\ddot{u}chi}(F) = \{s_0 s_1 s_2 \cdots \in (St \cdot (St \times Ac_1))^\omega \mid$$
$$s_n \in F \text{ for all but finitely many even } n\}$$

Again, note that these conditions only refer to even positions, as they will be used to capture a property of paths in S, i.e., the auxiliary states are irrelevant.

Collectively, we refer to games with any of the above winning conditions as NRSBC games. The following result is a generalization of standard results on infinite games (see, e.g., Grädel, Thomas, and Wilke [29]) that accounts for the fact that only states at even positions are relevant.

Proposition 1. *The following problem is in* PTIME: *Given an NRSBC game G and a state s, does Player 1 have a winning strategy for G from s?*

Proof of Theorem 1. Consider a concurrent game structure S with set St of states and an rATL formula φ. We show how to inductively compute the satisfaction sets $\mathrm{Sat}(\varphi', t) = \{s \in St \mid V(s, \varphi') \succeq t\}$ for all (state) subformulas φ' of φ and all truth values $t \in \mathbb{B}_4$. Note that $\mathrm{Sat}(\varphi', 0000) = St$ for all formulas φ', so these sets can be computed trivially.

The cases of atomic propositions and Boolean connectives follow straightforwardly from the definition of their semantics (cp. the semantics of rCTL [42]), so we focus on the case of formulas of the form $\langle\!\langle A \rangle\!\rangle \Phi$ or $[\![A]\!]\Phi$. Note that we only have to consider three cases for Φ, e.g., $\Phi = \bigcirc \varphi'$, $\Phi = \Diamond \varphi'$, and $\Phi = \Box \varphi'$ for some state formula φ'. The following characterizations are consequences of Lemma 1:

- $s \in \mathrm{Sat}(\langle\!\langle A \rangle\!\rangle \bigcirc \varphi', t)$ if and only if Player 1 has a winning strategy for $(S_A, \mathrm{Next}(\mathrm{Sat}(\varphi', t)))$ from s.
- $s \in \mathrm{Sat}(\langle\!\langle A \rangle\!\rangle \Diamond \varphi', t)$ if and only if Player 1 has a winning strategy for $(S_A, \mathrm{Reach}(\mathrm{Sat}(\varphi', t)))$ from s.

- $s \in \text{Sat}(\langle\!\langle A \rangle\!\rangle \boxdot \varphi', 1111)$ if and only if Player 1 has a winning strategy for $(\mathcal{S}_A, \text{Safety}(\text{Sat}(\varphi', 1111)))$ from s.
- $s \in \text{Sat}(\langle\!\langle A \rangle\!\rangle \boxdot \varphi', 0111)$ if and only if Player 1 has a winning strategy for $(\mathcal{S}_A, \text{coBüchi}(\text{Sat}(\varphi', 0111)))$ from s.
- $s \in \text{Sat}(\langle\!\langle A \rangle\!\rangle \boxdot \varphi', 0011)$ if and only if Player 1 has a winning strategy for $(\mathcal{S}_A, \text{Büchi}(\text{Sat}(\varphi', 0011)))$ from s.
- $s \in \text{Sat}(\langle\!\langle A \rangle\!\rangle \boxdot \varphi', 0001)$ if and only if Player 1 has a winning strategy for $(\mathcal{S}_A, \text{Reach}(\text{Sat}(\varphi', 0001)))$ from s.

Analogously, the satisfaction of formulas $[\![A]\!]\Phi$ can be characterized by the non-existence of winning strategies for Player 1, relying on the duality of the reachability (Büchi) and safety (coBüchi) winning conditions and the self-duality of the winning condition capturing the next operator. For example, we have $s \in \text{Sat}([\![A]\!]\odot\varphi', t)$ if and only if Player 1 does not have a winning strategy for $(\mathcal{S}_A, \text{Next}(St \setminus \text{Sat}(\varphi', t)))$ from s.

Now, to solve the model-checking problem with inputs $\mathcal{S}$, φ, s and t, we inductively compute all satisfaction sets $\text{Sat}(\varphi', t')$ and check whether s is in $\text{Sat}(\varphi, t)$. Using Proposition 1 and the fact that each NRSBC game we have to solve during the computation is of linear size (in $|\mathcal{S}|$), these $\mathcal{O}(|\varphi| \cdot |\mathcal{S}|)$ many sets can be computed in polynomial time, where $|\varphi|$ is the number of state subformulas of φ.

Finally, the lower bound follows from the PTIME-hardness of CTL model-checking [22], which is a fragment of rATL (see Subsect. 3.3). Furthermore, let us note that the PTIME lower bound for CTL model-checking already holds for fragment without until and release [34] (recall that we do not include until and release in rATL for the sake of simplicity). □

3.2 rATL Satisfability

This subsection considers the satisfiability problem for rATL, which is stated as follows: Given an rATL formula φ and a truth value $t \in \mathbb{B}_4$, is there a concurrent game structure $\mathcal{S}$ with a state s such that $V(s, \varphi) \succeq t$?

Theorem 2. *rATL satisfiability is* EXPTIME-*complete.*

Proof sketch. The upper bound is proven by embedding rATL into the alternating μ-calculus while the lower bound already holds for CTL, a fragment of rATL. □

3.3 Expressiveness

The main impetus for introducing rATL is to devise a robust generalization of ATL as a powerful formalism to deal with robust strategic reasoning in multi-agent systems. A natural question is to state the expressive power of rATL with respect to ATL and the robust version of CTL (rCTL) [42]. In this subsection, we show that both ATL and rCTL can be embedded into rATL, i.e., rATL generalizes both of these logics. Furthermore, we show that rATL is strictly more expressive than both of them. We begin by comparing rATL and ATL, and show first that rATL is at least as expressive as ATL, witnessing that our robust extension is set up correctly. This fact is formalized in the lemma below, intuitively stating that the first bit of the evaluation function captures the semantics of ATL.

Lemma 2. *Let φ be an ATL formula. Then, there exists an rATL formula $\varphi^\star$ such that for every concurrent game structure $\mathcal{S}$ and all states s of $\mathcal{S}$: $V(s, \varphi^\star) = 1111$ if and only if $\mathcal{S}, s \models \varphi$.*

Proof sketch. We obtain the rATL formula $\varphi^\star$ as follows: First, we eliminate every implication $\varphi_1 \rightarrow \varphi_2$ in the ATL formula φ by replacing it with the expression $\neg\varphi_1 \vee \varphi_2$. Second, we bring the formula into negation normal form by pushing all negations inwards to the level of atomic propositions. Finally, we dot all the temporal operators to obtain the rATL formula $\varphi^\star$. The claim of Lemma 2 can then be shown by induction over the structure of φ.   □

As we have observed above with Example 1, rATL is able to express basic forms of fairness such as "for a given structure $\mathcal{S}$ there exists a strategy for a coalition of agents A such that a certain property p holds infinitely often". Formally this corresponds to the formula $\varphi = \langle\!\langle A \rangle\!\rangle \boxdot p$ with $V(s, \varphi) \succeq 0011$. As shown by Alur, Henzinger, and Kupferman [4], such a property cannot be expressed in ATL, but rather requires the more expressive logic ATL*. Indeed, it corresponds to the ATL* formula $\varphi = \langle\!\langle A \rangle\!\rangle \Box \Diamond p$. So, by using the result reported in Lemma 2, the following holds.

Theorem 3. *rATL is strictly more expressive than ATL.*

Now, we compare rATL and rCTL: The latter logic is obtained by robustifying CTL along the same lines as described in Sect. 3 (see [42] for detailed definitions). Let us just remark that rCTL formulas, as CTL formulas, are evaluated over Kripke structures by means of a valuation function V_{rCTL}. Thus, to compare the expressiveness of both logics, as usual, we have to interpret a Kripke structure as a (one-agent) concurrent game structure. We start by showing that rATL is at least as expressive as rCTL, just as ATL is at least as expressive as CTL.

Lemma 3. *Let φ be an rCTL formula. Then, there exists an rATL formula $\varphi^\star$ such that for every Kripke structure $\mathcal{K}$ the following holds for all states s of $\mathcal{K}$: $V(s, \varphi^\star) = V_{rCTL}(s, \varphi)$.*

Proof sketch. Our construction proceeds as follows: First, we turn a Kripke structure $\mathcal{K}$ into a concurrent game structure with one agent a, having the same states and state labels, a suitable set of actions, and a transition function δ such that there is a transition in $\mathcal{K}$ from s to s' if and only if $s' = \delta(s, \alpha)$ for some action α. Second, we replace each existential path quantifier $\exists$ in φ by $\langle\!\langle \{a\} \rangle\!\rangle$ and each universal path quantifier $\forall$ by $\langle\!\langle \emptyset \rangle\!\rangle$, obtaining the rATL formula $\varphi^\star$. The claim of Lemma 3 can then be shown by induction over the structure of φ.   □

Now, we recall that Alur, Henzinger, and Kupferman [4] have observed that in ATL there are formulas that cannot be expressed in CTL. The reason is that, given a concurrent game structure, CTL can only reason about a single path (with the existential modality) or all paths (with the universal modality). Conversely, ATL can reason about an arbitrary number of paths by means of strategies. The same argument can be extend to rATL and rCTL. Thus, by putting together this observation with the statement of Lemma 3, the following holds.

Theorem 4. *rATL is strictly more expressive than rCTL.*

Notice that the argument that rATL formulas expressing fairness properties such as "infinitely often" cannot be expressed in ATL (used in Theorem 3 for the strict containment of ATL in rATL) can also be applied to rCTL. Similarly, the argument used above to show that rATL formulas cannot be translated into rCTL (used in Theorem 4 for the strict containment of rCTL in rATL) can also be applied to ATL. This leads to the following corollary.

Corollary 1. *ATL and rCTL are incomparable.*

4 Robust ATL*

Just as one generalizes CTL, rCTL, and ATL by allowing nesting of temporal operators in the scope of a single path/strategy quantifier (obtaining CTL*, rCTL*, and ATL*, respectively), we now study rATL*, the analogous generalization of rATL. Again, we will prove that adding robustness comes for free.

The formulas of rATL* are given by the grammar

$$\varphi ::= p \mid \neg\varphi \mid \varphi \vee \varphi \mid \varphi \wedge \varphi \mid \varphi \to \varphi \mid \langle\!\langle A \rangle\!\rangle \Phi \mid [\![A]\!]\Phi$$
$$\Phi ::= \varphi \mid \neg\Phi \mid \Phi \vee \Phi \mid \Phi \wedge \Phi \mid \Phi \to \Phi \mid \odot\Phi \mid \diamondsuit\Phi \mid \Box\Phi$$

where p ranges over atomic propositions and A over subsets of agents. Again, we distinguish between *state formulas* (those derivable from φ) and *path formulas* (those derivable from Φ). If not specified, an rATL* formula is a state formula.

The semantics of rATL* are again defined via an evaluation function V that maps a state formula and a state or a path formula and a path to a truth value in $\mathbb{B}_4$. The cases for state formulas are defined as for rATL and we define for every path π, every state formula φ, and all path formulas Φ_1 and Φ_2

- $V(\pi, \varphi) = V(\pi[0], \varphi),$
- $V(\pi, \neg\Phi) = \begin{cases} 0000 & \text{if } V(\pi, \Phi) = 1111, \\ 1111 & \text{if } V(\pi, \Phi) \prec 1111, \end{cases}$
- $V(\pi, \Phi_1 \vee \Phi_2) = \max\big(V(\pi, \Phi_1), V(\pi, \Phi_2)\big),$
- $V(\pi, \Phi_1 \wedge \Phi_2) = \min\big(V(\pi, \Phi_1), V(\pi, \Phi_2)\big),$
- $V(\pi, \Phi_1 \to \Phi_2) = \begin{cases} 1111 & \text{if } V(\pi, \Phi_1) \preceq V(\pi, \Phi_2), \\ V(\pi, \Phi_2) & \text{if } V(\pi, \Phi_1) \succ V(s, \Phi_2), \end{cases}$

- $V(\pi,\odot\Phi) = b_1b_2b_3b_4$ with $b_k = V(\pi[1],\Phi)[k]$,
- $V(\pi,\Diamond\Phi) = b_1b_2b_3b_4$ with $b_k = \max_{i\geq 0} V(\pi[i],\Phi)[k]$, and
- $V(\pi,\square\Phi) = b_1b_2b_3b_4$ where

$$b_1 = \min_{i\geq 0} V(\pi[i],\Phi)[1], \qquad b_3 = \min_{i\geq 0} \max_{j\geq i} V(\pi[j],\Phi)[3],$$
$$b_2 = \max_{i\geq 0} \min_{j\geq i} V(\pi[j],\Phi)[2], \quad b_4 = \max_{i\geq 0} V(\pi[i],\Phi)[4]).$$

We show that every rATL* formula (w.r.t. a fixed truth value) can be translated into an equivalent ATL* formula of polynomial size. This allows us to settle the complexity of rATL* model-checking and satisfiability as well as the expressiveness of rATL*. Below, $\models$ denotes the ATL* satisfaction relation [4].

Lemma 4. *For every rATL* formula φ and every truth value $t \in \mathbb{B}_4$, there is an ATL* formula φ_t such that $V(s,\varphi) \succeq t$ if and only if $\mathcal{S}, s \models \varphi_t$. Furthermore, the function mapping φ and t to φ_t is polynomial-time computable.*

The rATL* model-checking and satisfiability problems are defined as their counterparts for rATL. Both model-checking and satisfiability for ATL* are 2ExpTime-complete [4,46]. Due to Lemma 4, we obtain the same results for rATL*, thereby showing that adding robustness comes indeed for free.

Theorem 5. *The rATL* model-checking problem and the rATL* satisfiability problem are both 2ExpTime-complete.*

Another consequence of the translation from rATL* to ATL* and the fact that ATL* is a fragment of rATL* is that both logics are equally expressive.

Corollary 2. *rATL* and ATL* are equally expressive.*

5   A Practical Example

Let us consider a smart grid with a set U of utility companies and a set C of consumers. Assume that for every consumer $c \in C$ there is a proposition ℓ_c indicating that c's energy consumption is within the pre-agreed limit. Conversely, c's consumption is higher than the limit if ℓ_c is violated. Furthermore, there is a proposition "stable" that holds true if and only if the grid is stable (i.e., the utility companies coordinate to provide the right amount of electricity).

Let us now consider the ATL* formula

$$\langle\langle U \rangle\rangle [\![C]\!] (\square \bigwedge_{c\in C} \ell_c) \to \square\text{stable}.$$

This formula expresses that the utility companies U have a strategy such that no matter how the consumers behave, the following is satisfied: if each consumer's consumption always stays within their limit, then the utility companies keep the grid always stable. However, this specification is not robust and provides only limited information when satisfied: even if a single consumer exceeds their limit once, there is no further obligation on the utility companies, and the formula is satisfied independently of whether the grid is always stable or not.

So, let us illustrate how the rATL* formula

$$\varphi = \langle\!\langle U \rangle\!\rangle [\![C]\!] (\boxdot \bigwedge\nolimits_{c \in C} \ell_c) \rightarrow \boxdot \text{stable}$$

does capture robustness. To this end, assume for now that φ evaluates to 1111. Then, there is a strategy for U such that for all outcomes π that are consistent with that strategy, the following holds:

- If $\bigwedge_{c \in C} \ell_c$ holds in every position of π, i.e., $\boxdot \bigwedge_{c \in C} \ell_c$ evaluates to 1111 then by the semantics of $\rightarrow$ the formula $\boxdot$stable also evaluates to 1111. This means the proposition "stable" also holds in every position. Therefore, the grid supply is always stable. Hence, the desired goal is retained when the assumption regarding the consumers holds with no violation. Note that this is equivalent to what the original ATL* formula above expresses.
- Assume now that the consumer assumption $\bigwedge_{c \in C} \ell_c$ is violated finitely many times, i.e., finitely often some consumer violates their consumption limit. This means that the formula $\boxdot \bigwedge_{c \in C} \ell_c$ evaluates to 0111. Then, by the semantics of rATL*, $\boxdot$stable evaluates to 0111 or higher, which means that "stable" holds at every state, except for a finite number of times. So, the degree of violation of the guarantee required by U is at most the degree of violation of the assumptions on the consumers.
- Similarly, if $\boxdot \bigwedge_{c \in C} \ell_c$ holds infinitely (finitely) often, then $\boxdot$stable holds infinitely (finitely) often.

If the formula φ evaluates to 1111, then U has a strategy that does not behave arbitrarily in case the assumption $\boxdot \bigwedge_{c \in C} \ell_c$ fails, but instead satisfies the guarantee $\boxdot$stable to at least the same degree that the guarantee holds.

Finally, even if φ evaluates to a truth value $t \prec 1111$, this reveals crucial information about U's ability to guarantee a stable grid, i.e., the premise $\boxdot \bigwedge_{c \in C} \ell_c$ evaluates to some truth value $t' \succ t$ while the conclusion "stable" evaluates to t.

6 Discussion and Future Work

This paper introduces rATL and rATL*, the first logic formalisms able to deal with robust strategic reasoning in multi-agent systems. As we have shown along the paper, rATL results to be very expressive, useful in practice, and not more costly than the subsumed logics ATL and rCTL. Similarly, rATL* is not more costly than the subsumed logic ATL*.

The positive results about rATL represent the foundation for a number of useful extensions, mainly by extending robustness to logics for strategic reasoning that are more expressive than ATL and ATL* such as Strategy Logic [40] and the like. Notably, Strategy Logic is much more expressive than ATL* [4]. Indeed it can express several game-theoretic concepts including Nash Equilibria over LTL goals. Interestingly, the formula expressing Nash Equilibria uses an implication.

In words the formula says that n agents' strategies $\sigma_1, \ldots, \sigma_n$ form an equilibrium if, for every agent, it holds that whenever by unilaterally changing her strategy the goal is also satisfied, then it *implies* that the goal is satisfied with the original tuple of strategies as well. Robustness in Strategy Logic (by means of rLTL goals in place of LTL) then allows to define a stronger notion of Nash Equilibrium.

Another interesting direction for future work is to come up with an implementation of the model-checking procedure for rATL, possibly by extending existing tools such as MCMAS [18,38].

Acknowledgments. This research has been supported by the PRIN project RIPER (No. 20203FFYLK), the PNRR MUR project PE0000013-FAIR, the InDAM project "Strategic Reasoning in Mechanism Design", and DIREC - Digital Research Centre Denmark. Furthermore, this work has been financially supported by Deutsche Forschungsgemeinschaft, DFG Project numbers 434592664 and 459419731, and the Research Center Trustworthy Data Science and Security (https://rc-trust.ai), one of the Research Alliance centers within the UA Ruhr (https://uaruhr.de).

References

1. Afzal, S., Mokhlis, H., Illias, H.A., Mansor, N.N., Shareef, H.: State-of-the-art review on power system resilience and assessment techniques. IET Gener. Trans. Distrib. **14**(25), 6107–6121 (2020)
2. de Alfaro, L., Henzinger, T.A.: Concurrent omega-regular games. In: LICS 2000, pp. 141–154. IEEE Computer Society (2000). https://doi.org/10.1109/LICS.2000.855763
3. Almagor, S., Boker, U., Kupferman, O.: Formally reasoning about quality. J. ACM **63**(3), 24:1–24:56 (2016). https://doi.org/10.1145/2875421
4. Alur, R., Henzinger, T.A., Kupferman, O.: Alternating-time temporal logic. J. ACM **49**(5), 672–713 (2002). https://doi.org/10.1145/585265.585270
5. Aminof, B., Kwiatkowska, M., Maubert, B., Murano, A., Rubin, S.: Probabilistic strategy logic. In: Kraus, S. (ed.) IJCAI 2019, pp. 32–38 (2019). https://doi.org/10.24963/ijcai.2019/5
6. Aminof, B., Malvone, V., Murano, A., Rubin, S.: Graded modalities in strategy logic. Inf. Comput. **261**, 634–649 (2018)
7. Anevlavis, T., Neider, D., Philippe, M., Tabuada, P.: Evrostos: the rLTL verifier. In: Ozay, N., Prabhakar, P. (eds.) HSCC 2019, pp. 218–223. ACM (2019). https://doi.org/10.1145/3302504.3311812
8. Anevlavis, T., Philippe, M., Neider, D., Tabuada, P.: Verifying rLTL formulas: now faster than ever before! In: CDC 2018, pp. 1556–1561. IEEE (2018). https://doi.org/10.1109/CDC.2018.8619014
9. Anevlavis, T., Philippe, M., Neider, D., Tabuada, P.: Being correct is not enough: efficient verification using robust linear temporal logic. ACM Trans. Comput. Log. **23**(2), 8:1–8:39 (2022). https://doi.org/10.1145/3491216
10. Belardinelli, F., Jamroga, W., Kurpiewski, D., Malvone, V., Murano, A.: Strategy logic with simple goals: tractable reasoning about strategies. In: Kraus, S. (ed.) IJCAI 2019, pp. 88–94 (2019). https://doi.org/10.24963/ijcai.2019/13
11. Belardinelli, F., Lomuscio, A., Murano, A., Rubin, S.: Verification of multi-agent systems with public actions against strategy logic. Artif. Intell. **285**, 103302 (2020)

12. Belhaiza, S., Baroudi, U.: A game theoretic model for smart grids demand management. IEEE Trans. Smart Grid **6**(3), 1386–1393 (2014)

13. Berthon, R., Maubert, B., Murano, A., Rubin, S., Vardi, M.Y.: Strategy logic with imperfect information. ACM Trans. Comput. Logic (TOCL) **22**(1), 1–51 (2021)

14. Bevrani, H.: Robust Power System Frequency Control. PEPS, Springer, Cham (2014). https://doi.org/10.1007/978-3-319-07278-4

15. Bloem, R., Chatterjee, K., Greimel, K., Henzinger, T.A., Jobstmann, B.: Robustness in the presence of liveness. In: Touili, T., Cook, B., Jackson, P. (eds.) CAV 2010. LNCS, vol. 6174, pp. 410–424. Springer, Heidelberg (2010). https://doi.org/10.1007/978-3-642-14295-6_36

16. Bouyer, P., Kupferman, O., Markey, N., Maubert, B., Murano, A., Perelli, G.: Reasoning about quality and fuzziness of strategic behaviors. ACM Trans. Comput. Log. **24**(3), 21:1–21:38 (2023)

17. Bouyer, P., Markey, N., Reynier, P.-A.: Robust analysis of timed automata *via* channel machines. In: Amadio, R. (ed.) FoSSaCS 2008. LNCS, vol. 4962, pp. 157–171. Springer, Heidelberg (2008). https://doi.org/10.1007/978-3-540-78499-9_12

18. Cermák, P., Lomuscio, A., Murano, A.: Verifying and synthesising multi-agent systems against one-goal strategy logic specifications. In: Bonet, B., Koenig, S. (eds.) Proceedings of the Twenty-Ninth AAAI Conference on Artificial Intelligence, 25–30 January 2015, Austin, Texas, USA, pp. 2038–2044. AAAI Press (2015)

19. Chaaban, Y., Müller-Schloer, C.: A survey of robustness in multi-agent systems. In: Cognitive13, Fifth International Conference on Advanced Cognitive Technologies and Applications, pp. 7–13 (2013)

20. Chatterjee, K., Henzinger, T.A., Piterman, N.: Strategy logic. Inf. Comput. **208**(6), 677–693 (2010). https://doi.org/10.1016/j.ic.2009.07.004

21. Clarke, E.M., Emerson, E.A.: Design and synthesis of synchronization skeletons using branching time temporal logic. In: Kozen, D. (ed.) Logic of Programs 1981. LNCS, vol. 131, pp. 52–71. Springer, Heidelberg (1982). https://doi.org/10.1007/BFb0025774

22. Clarke, E.M., Emerson, E.A., Sistla, A.P.: Automatic verification of finite-state concurrent systems using temporal logic specifications. ACM Trans. Program. Lang. Syst. **8**(2), 244–263 (1986). https://doi.org/10.1145/5397.5399

23. Dallal, E., Neider, D., Tabuada, P.: Synthesis of safety controllers robust to unmodeled intermittent disturbances. In: CDC 2016, pp. 7425–7430. IEEE (2016)

24. Dima, C., Tiplea, F.L.: Model-checking ATL under imperfect information and perfect recall semantics is undecidable. arXiv:1102.4225 (2011)

25. Donzé, A., Maler, O.: Robust satisfaction of temporal logic over real-valued signals. In: Chatterjee, K., Henzinger, T.A. (eds.) FORMATS 2010. LNCS, vol. 6246, pp. 92–106. Springer, Heidelberg (2010). https://doi.org/10.1007/978-3-642-15297-9_9

26. Doyen, L., Henzinger, T.A., Legay, A., Nickovic, D.: Robustness of sequential circuits. In: ACSD 2010, pp. 77–84. IEEE (2010)

27. Faella, M., Napoli, M., Parente, M.: Graded alternating-time temporal logic. Fund. Inform. **105**(1–2), 189–210 (2010)

28. French, T., Mc Cabe-Dansted, J.C., Reynolds, M.: A temporal logic of robustness. In: Konev, B., Wolter, F. (eds.) FroCoS 2007. LNCS (LNAI), vol. 4720, pp. 193–205. Springer, Heidelberg (2007). https://doi.org/10.1007/978-3-540-74621-8_13

29. Grädel, E., Thomas, W., Wilke, T. (eds.): Automata, Logics, and Infinite Games: A Guide to Current Research, LNCS, vol. 2500. Springer, Heidelberg (2002). https://doi.org/10.1007/3-540-36387-4

30. Hassan, S.R.M., Hasan, N., Siddique, M.A., Fahim, K.S., Rahman, R., Iftekhar, L.: Incorporating multi-agent systems technology in power and energy systems of Bangladesh: a feasibility study. In: ICREST 2021, pp. 342–347. IEEE (2021)
31. Huang, X., Luo, C.: A logic of probabilistic knowledge and strategy. In: AAMAS, pp. 845–852. Citeseer (2013)
32. Jamroga, W., Murano, A.: On module checking and strategies. In: AAMAS 2014, pp. 701–708 (2014)
33. Kaur, D., Uslu, S., Rittichier, K.J., Durresi, A.: Trustworthy artificial intelligence: a review. ACM Computing Surveys (CSUR) **55**(2), 1–38 (2022)
34. Krebs, A., Meier, A., Mundhenk, M.: The model checking fingerprints of CTL operators. Acta Inform. **56**(6), 487–519 (2019). https://doi.org/10.1007/s00236-018-0326-9
35. Kupferman, O., Vardi, M.Y., Wolper, P.: Module checking. Inf. Comput. **164**(2), 322–344 (2001)
36. Laroussinie, F., Markey, N.: Augmenting ATL with strategy contexts. Inf. Comput. **245**, 98–123 (2015). https://doi.org/10.1016/j.ic.2014.12.020
37. Lempert, R.J., Schlesinger, M.E.: Robust strategies for abating climate change. Clim. Change **45**(3–4), 387–401 (2000)
38. Lomuscio, A., Qu, H., Raimondi, F.: MCMAS: an open-source model checker for the verification of multi-agent systems. Int. J. Softw. Tools Technol. Transf. **19**(1), 9–30 (2017). https://doi.org/10.1007/s10009-015-0378-x
39. Modas, A., Sanchez-Matilla, R., Frossard, P., Cavallaro, A.: Toward robust sensing for autonomous vehicles: an adversarial perspective. IEEE Signal Process. Mag. **37**(4), 14–23 (2020)
40. Mogavero, F., Murano, A., Perelli, G., Vardi, M.Y.: Reasoning about strategies: on the model-checking problem. ACM Trans. Comput. Log. **15**(4), 34:1–34:47 (2014). https://doi.org/10.1145/2631917
41. Murano, A., Neider, D., Zimmermann, M.: Robust alternating-time temporal logic. arXiv:2307.10885 (2023)
42. Nayak, S.P., Neider, D., Roy, R., Zimmermann, M.: Robust computation tree logic. In: Deshmukh, J.V., Havelund, K., Perez, I. (eds.) NFM 2022. Lecture Notes in Computer Science, vol. 13260, pp. 538–556. Springer, Cham (2022). https://doi.org/10.1007/978-3-031-06773-0_29
43. Omnes, L., Marot, A., Donnot, B.: Adversarial training for a continuous robustness control problem in power systems. In: 2021 IEEE Madrid PowerTech, pp. 1–6. IEEE (2021)
44. Pinto, L., Davidson, J., Sukthankar, R., Gupta, A.: Robust adversarial reinforcement learning. In: International Conference on Machine Learning, pp. 2817–2826. PMLR (2017)
45. Sampaio, R.F., Melo, L.S., Leão, R.P., Barroso, G.C., Bezerra, J.R.: Automatic restoration system for power distribution networks based on multi-agent systems. IET Gener. Trans. Distrib. **11**(2), 475–484 (2017)
46. Schewe, S.: ATL* satisfiability Is 2EXPTIME-complete. In: Aceto, L., Damgård, I., Goldberg, L.A., Halldórsson, M.M., Ingólfsdóttir, A., Walukiewicz, I. (eds.) ICALP 2008, Part II. LNCS, vol. 5126, pp. 373–385. Springer, Heidelberg (2008). https://doi.org/10.1007/978-3-540-70583-3_31
47. Schnoor, H.: Epistemic and probabilistic ATL with quantification and explicit strategies. In: Filipe, J., Fred, A. (eds.) ICAART 2013. CCIS, vol. 449, pp. 131–148. Springer, Heidelberg (2014). https://doi.org/10.1007/978-3-662-44440-5_8

48. Singh, V.P., Kishor, N., Samuel, P.: Distributed multi-agent system-based load frequency control for multi-area power system in smart grid. IEEE Trans. Industr. Electron. **64**(6), 5151–5160 (2017)
49. Tabuada, P., Neider, D.: Robust linear temporal logic. In: CSL 2016. LIPIcs, vol. 62, pp. 10:1–10:21. Schloss Dagstuhl - Leibniz-Zentrum für Informatik (2016). https:// doi.org/10.4230/LIPIcs.CSL.2016.10
50. Veres, S.M., Molnar, L., Lincoln, N.K., Morice, C.P.: Autonomous vehicle control systems-a review of decision making. Proc. Insti. Mech. Eng. Part I: J. Syst. Control Eng. **225**(2), 155–195 (2011)
51. Walther, D., Lutz, C., Wolter, F., Wooldridge, M.: ATL satisfiability is indeed EXPTIME-complete. J. Log. Comput. **16**(6), 765–787 (2006)

The Universal Tangle for Spatial Reasoning

David Fernández-Duque[1,2]([✉]) [iD] and Konstantinos Papafilippou[1] [iD]

[1] Ghent University, Ghent, Belgium
Konstantinos.Papafilippou@UGent.be
[2] University of Barcelona, Barcelona, Spain
fernandez-duque@ub.edu

Abstract. The topological μ-calculus has gathered attention in recent years as a powerful framework for representation of spatial knowledge. In particular, spatial relations can be represented over finite structures in the guise of weakly transitive (wK4) frames. In this paper we show that the topological μ-calculus is equivalent to a simple fragment based on a variant of the 'tangle' operator. Similar results were proven for transitive frames by Dawar and Otto, using modal characterisation theorems for the corresponding classes of frames. However, since these theorems are not available in our setting, which has the upshot of providing a more explicit translation and upper bounds on formula size.

1 Introduction

Qualitative spatial reasoning aims to capture basic relations between regions in space in a way that is computationally efficient and thus suitable for knowledge representation and AI (see [4,17] for overviews). The *region connection calculus* (RCC8) [6,16] deals with relations such as 'partially overlaps' (e.g. Mexico and Mesoamerica) or 'is a non-tangential proper part' (e.g. Paraguay and South America) while avoiding undecidability phenomena by not allowing for quantification over points or regions.

RCC8 can be embedded into modal logic (ML) with a universal modality [18]. This allows us to import many techniques from ML, including the representation of regions using transitive Kripke frames, i.e. pairs $\langle W, \sqsubset \rangle$, where W is a set of points and $\sqsubset$ is a transitive relation representing 'nearness'. It also tells us that little is lost by omitting quantifiers, due to so-called modal characterization theorems [14], which state that ML is the bisimulation-invariant fragment of first order logic (FOL), while its extension to the modal μ-calculus is the bisimulation-invariant fragment of monadic second order logic (MSO) [12].

However, these results apply to frames where $\sqsubset$ is an arbitrary relation, whereas Dawar and Otto [5] showed that the situation over finite, transitive

Supported by the FWO-FWF Lead Agency grant G030620N (FWO)/I4513N (FWF) and by the SNSF–FWO Lead Agency Grant 200021L_196176/G0E2121N.

S. Gaggl et al. (Eds.): JELIA 2023, LNAI 14281, pp. 814–827, 2023.
https://doi.org/10.1007/978-3-031-43619-2_55

frames is subtle. In this setting, the bisimulation-invariant fragments of FOL and MSO coincide, but are stronger than modal logic. They are in fact equal to the μ-calculus, but this in turn can be greatly simplified to its *tangled* fragment, which adds expressions of the form $\diamond^\infty\{\varphi_1, \ldots, \varphi_n\}$, stating that there is an accessible cluster of reflexive points where each φ_i is satisfied.

Finite, transitive frames are suitable for representing spatial relations on metric spaces, such as Euclidean spaces or the rational numbers [10, 13]. However, for the more general setting of topological spaces, one must consider a wider class of frames called *weakly transitive* frames: a relation $\sqsubset$ is weakly transitive if $x \sqsubset y \sqsubset z$ implies $x \sqsubseteq z$. The modal logic of finite, weakly transitive frames is precisely that of all topological spaces [7], and this result extends to the full μ-calculus [2]. In this spatial setting, Dawar and Otto's tangled operator becomes the *tangled derivative*, the largest subspace in which two or more sets are dense: for example, the tangle of $\mathbb{Q}$ and $\mathbb{R} \setminus \mathbb{Q}$ is the full real line, since the rationals and the irrationals are both dense in $\mathbb{R}$. In the case of a single subset A, $\diamond^\infty\{A\}$ is the *perfect core* of A, i.e. its largest perfect subset, a notion useful in describing the limit of learnability after iterated measurements [1].

Alas, over the class of weakly transitive frames, the tangled derivative is not as expressive as the μ-calculus [2], which is in turn less expressive than the bisumulation-invariant fragment of MSO, so Dawar and Otto's result fails. Gougeon [11] proposed a more expressive operator, which here we simply dub the *tangle* and denote by $\blacklozenge^\infty$, which coincides with the tangled derivative over metric spaces (and other spaces satisfying a regularity property known as T_D spaces), but is strictly more expressive over the class of topological spaces. While this tangle cannot be as expressive as the bisimulation-invariant fragment of MSO, it was still conjectured to be as expressive as the μ-calculus, thus providing a streamlined framework for representing spatial properties relevant for the learnability framework of [1]. This conjecture is supported by the recent result stating that the topological μ-calculus collapses to its alternation-free fragment [15].

In this paper we give an affirmative answer to this conjecture. Moreover, since we cannot use games for FOL to establish our results, our proof uses new methods which have the advantage of providing an explicit translation of the μ-calculus into tangle logic. Among other things, we provide an upper bound on formula size, which is doubly exponential. It is not clear if this can be greatly improved, given the exponential lower bounds of [8].

Despite the spatial motivation for the μ-calculus over wK4, the results of [2] allow us to work within the class of weakly transitive frames; since their logic is that of all topological spaces, our expressivity results lift to that context as well. The upshot is that background in topology is not needed to follow the text.

Layout

In Sect. 2 we review the μ-calculus, present Gougeon's tangle and some basic semantic notions over path-finite weakly transitive (wK4) frames. Section 3 begins with a review of finality as used in [2], as well as establishing additional properties we need. In Sect. 4 we construct some formulae in the tangle logic that peer into the structure of a given Kripke model, which we use to show that the μ-calculus is equivalent to the tangle logic and strictly weaker than the bisimulation invariant part of first order logic over finite and path finite wK4 frames.

2   Preliminaries

As is often the case when working with μ-calculi, it will be convenient to define the μ-calculus with each of the positive operations, including $\nu x.\varphi$, as primitive, and with negation being only subsequently defined.

Definition 1. *The language of the modal μ-calculus $\mathcal{L}_\mu$ is defined by the following syntax:*

$$\varphi:: = \top \mid x \mid p \mid \neg p \mid \varphi \wedge \varphi \mid \varphi \vee \varphi \mid \Diamond\varphi \mid \Box\varphi \mid \nu x.\varphi(x) \mid \mu x.\varphi(x)$$

where x belongs to a set of 'variables' and p to a set of 'constants', denoted $\mathbb{P}$.

Under this presentation of the language, the formulas are said to be in negation normal form. Negation is defined classically as usual with $\neg\nu x.\varphi(x) := \mu x.\neg\varphi(\neg x)$ and $\neg\mu x.\varphi(x) := \nu x.\neg\varphi(\neg x)$. We also write $\Diamond\varphi := \varphi \vee \Diamond\varphi$ and similarly $\boxdot\varphi := \varphi \wedge \Box\varphi$.

The following is the standard semantics for the μ-calculus over frames with a single relation $\sqsubset$ (or $\sqsubset_M$, to specify the frame).

Definition 2. *A Kripke frame is a tuple $\mathcal{F} = \langle M, \sqsubset_M \rangle$ where $\sqsubset_M \subseteq M \times M$. A Kripke model is a triple $\mathcal{M} = \langle M, \sqsubset_M, \|\cdot\|_M \rangle$ where $\langle M, \sqsubset_M \rangle$ is a Kripke frame with a valuation $\|\cdot\|_M : \mathbb{P} \to \mathcal{P}(M)$. In the sequel, we will use $\mathcal{M}$ and M interchangeably. We denote the reflexive closure of $\sqsubset_M$ by $\sqsubseteq_M$.*

Given $A \subseteq M$, we denote the irreflexive and reflexive upsets of A as $A{\uparrow}_M := \{w \in M : \exists v \in A \; v \sqsubset_M w\}$ and $A{\uparrow}_M^* := A{\uparrow}_M \cup A$ respectively. The downsets are similarly denoted as $A{\downarrow}_M := \{w \in M : \exists v \in A \; w \sqsubset_M v\}$ and $A{\downarrow}_M^* := A{\downarrow}_M \cup A$ respectively. We will omit the M in the subscript when we will be only referring to a single model.

The valuation $\|\cdot\| = \|\cdot\|_M$ is defined as usual on Booleans with:

$$\|\Diamond\varphi\| := \|\varphi\|{\downarrow} \qquad\qquad \|\mu x.\varphi(x)\| := \bigcap\{X \subseteq M : X = \|\varphi(X)\|\}$$
$$\|\Box\varphi\| := M \setminus ((M \setminus \|\varphi\|){\downarrow}) \qquad \|\nu x.\varphi(x)\| := \bigcup\{X \subseteq M : X = \|\varphi(X)\|\}$$

Given a Kripke model M and a world $w \in M$ we say a formula φ is satisfied by M at the world w and write $w \vDash_M \varphi$ iff $w \in \|\varphi\|_M$.

A formula φ is valid over a class of models Ω if for every $M \in \Omega$, $\|\varphi\|_M = M$.

We note that $\mu x.\varphi(x)$ and $\nu x.\varphi(x)$ are the least and greatest fixed points, respectively, of the operator $X \mapsto \varphi(X)$.

We will mostly concern ourselves only with weakly transitive frames. A relation R is weakly transitive iff for all a, b, c where $a \neq c$, if aRb and bRc then aRc. A frame or model is *weakly transitive* if its accessibility relation is.

Example 1. Consider a frame $\mathcal{F}$ consisting of two irreflexive points $\{0, 1\}$ such that $0 \sqsubset 1$ and $1 \sqsubset 0$; this frame is weakly transitive since $x \sqsubset y \sqsubset z$ implies $x = z$, but it is not transitive since e.g. $0 \sqsubset 1 \sqsubset 0$ but $0 \not\sqsubset 0$. To extend this frame into a model, we assign subsets of $\{0, 1\}$ to each propositional variable. Assume that our variables are e (even), o (odd), p (positive) and i (integer). We obtain a valuation $\| \cdot \|$ if we let $\|e\| = \{0\}$, $\|o\| = \{1\}$, $\|p\| = \{1\}$, and $\|i\| = \{0, 1\}$. Then, $\|o \vee \Diamond p\| = \{0, 1\}$, since every element of our model is either odd or has an accessible positive point. We may say that this formula is *valid* in our model.

Recall that a topological space is a pair $\langle X, \mathcal{T} \rangle$, where $\mathcal{T}$ is a family of subsets of X (called the *open sets*) closed under finite intersections and arbitrary unions. If $A \subseteq X$, $d(A)$ is the set of points $x \in X$ such that whenever $x \in U$ and U is open, there is $y \in A \cap U \setminus \{x\}$; this is the set of *limit points* of A. The topological semantics for the μ-calculus is obtained by modifying Definition 2 by setting $\|\Diamond \varphi\| = d\|\varphi\|$. This is the basis to the modal approach to spatial reasoning, but the following allows us to work with weakly transitive frames instead.

Theorem 1. ([2]). *For $\varphi \in \mathcal{L}_\mu$, the following are equivalent:*

- *φ is valid over the class of all topological spaces.*
- *φ is valid over the class of all weakly transitive frames.*
- *φ is valid over the class of all finite, irreflexive, weakly transitive frames.*

This extends results of Esakia for the purely modal setting [7]. Next we recall bisimulations (see e.g. [3]), which are binary relations preserving truth of μ-calculus formulas that will be very useful in the rest of the text.

Definition 3. *Given $P \subseteq \mathbb{P}$ a P-bisimulation is a relation $\iota \subseteq M \times N$ such that, whenever $\langle u, v \rangle \in \iota$:*

atoms $w \vDash_M p \Leftrightarrow v \vDash_M p$ *for all $p \in P$;*
forth *If $u \sqsubset_M u'$, then there is $v \sqsubset_N v'$ such that $\langle u', v' \rangle \in \iota$;*
back *If $v \sqsubset_N v'$, then there is $u \sqsubset_M u'$ such that $\langle u', v' \rangle \in \iota$;*
global $dom(\iota) = M$ *and* $rng(\iota) = N$.

Two models are called P-bisimilar and we write $M \rightleftharpoons_P N$ if there is some P-bisimulation relation between them. Given subsets $A \subseteq M$ and $B \subseteq N$, we write $A \rightleftharpoons_P B$ when $M \upharpoonright A \rightleftharpoons_P N \upharpoonright B$, where $\upharpoonright$ denotes the usual restriction to a subset of the domain.

In the sequel we will omit the P in the subscript and assume it to be the set of constants occurring in some 'target' formula φ. As mentioned, bisimulations are useful because they preserve the truth of all μ-calculus formulas, i,e. if $\langle w, v \rangle \in \iota$ and φ is any formula (with constants among P), then $w \in \|\varphi\|$ iff $v \in \|\varphi\|$. As such, since every weakly transitive model is bisimilar to an irreflexive weakly transitive model, we will make the convention that every arbitrary model mentioned in this paper is irreflexive.

As a general rule, the μ-calculus is more expressive than standard modal logic: for example, in a frame (W, R), reachability via the transitive closure of

R is expressible in the μ-calculus, but not in standard modal logic. However, in the setting of transitive frames, reachability is already modally definable (since R is its own transitive closure), which means that the familiar examples to show that the μ-calculus is more powerful than modal logic do not apply. Dawar and Otto [5] exhibited an operator, since dubbed the *tangle*, which is μ-calculus expressible but not modally expressible. They showed the surprising result that every formula of the μ-calculus can be expressed in terms of tangle. In this paper, we will use a variant introduced by Gougeon [11]. When working with multisets[1], if x occurs n times in A then it occurs $\max\{0, n-1\}$ times in $A \setminus \{x\}$.

Definition 4. *Given a finite multiset of formulae $\Gamma \subseteq \mathcal{L}_\mu$, the tangle modality is defined as follows:*

$$\blacklozenge^\infty \Gamma = \nu x. \bigvee_{\varphi \in \Gamma} \left(\Diamond (\varphi \wedge x) \wedge \bigwedge_{\psi \in \Gamma \setminus \{\varphi\}} \Diamond(\psi \wedge x) \right),$$

where x does not appear free in any $\varphi \in \Gamma$.

We can then define the tangle logic $\mathcal{L}_{\blacklozenge\infty}$ whose language is defined by the syntax, where $\Gamma \subseteq_{fin} \mathcal{L}_{\blacklozenge\infty}$ is a multiset:

$$\varphi :: = \top \mid p \mid \neg\varphi \mid \varphi \wedge \varphi \mid \Diamond\varphi \mid \blacklozenge^\infty \Gamma.$$

It can be checked that over transitive frames, $\blacklozenge^\infty \Gamma$ is equivalent to the 'tangled derivative' $\Diamond^\infty \Gamma$ [10], given by $\Diamond^\infty \Gamma := \nu x. \bigwedge_{\varphi \in \Gamma} \Diamond(\varphi \wedge x)$. The two are also equivalent over familiar spaces such as the real line, but not over arbitrary topological spaces or weakly transitive frames, in which case $\blacklozenge^\infty$ can define $\Diamond^\infty$ but not vice-versa [11]. In metric spaces such as the real line (and a wider class known as T_D spaces), $\blacklozenge^\infty \Gamma$ holds on x if there is a perfect set A (i.e., A has no isolated points) containing x such that for each $\varphi \in \Gamma$, $\|\varphi\| \cap A$ is dense in A.

Example 2. Consider a topological model based on the real line $\mathbb{R}$ with $\|r\|$ being the set of rational points and $\|i\|$ the set of irrational points. Then, $\blacklozenge^\infty \{r, i\}$ is valid on the real line, given that the sets of rational and irrational numbers are both dense. In contrast, if we let $\|z\|$ be the set of integers, we readily obtain that $\blacklozenge^\infty \{z, i\}$ evaluates to the empty set, given that the subspace of the integers consists of isolated points and hence we will not find any common perfect core between $\|z\|$ and $\|i\|$.

The tangle simplifies a bit when working over finite transitive frames. In this case, this operator is best described in terms of clusters. A cluster C of a model $\mathcal{M} = \langle M, \sqsubseteq, \| \cdot \| \rangle$ is a subset of M such that $\forall u, v \in C \; u \sqsubseteq v$. Note that we don't define clusters to be maximal (with respect to set inclusion). In contrast, *the* cluster of w in M is the set $C_w = \bigcup\{C : C \text{ is a cluster of M and } w \in C\}$.

It is well known that a transitive relation (and indeed even a weakly transitive relation) can be viewed as a partial order on its set of maximal clusters. To this end, define $w \prec v$ if $w \sqsubseteq v \not\sqsubseteq w$, and for $A, B \subseteq M$, we write:

---

[1] By working with multisets, we can write $\blacklozenge^\infty \{\phi, \phi\}$ instead of $\blacklozenge^\infty \{\phi, \phi \wedge \top\}$.

– $A \prec B$ iff $\forall v \in B \, \exists u \in A \, u \sqsubset v \not\sqsubseteq u$
– $A \preceq B$ iff $\forall v \in B \, \exists u \in A \, u \sqsubseteq v$.

Then, $\prec$ is a strict partial order on the maximal clusters of M. In the sequel, A, B will usually be nonempty clusters. We also define e.g. $w \prec A$ by identifying w with $\{w\}$.

Lemma 1. *Fix a multiset Γ and a finite pointed model (M, w), we have that $w \vDash_M \blacklozenge^\infty \Gamma$ iff there is a cluster C of M such that $w \preceq C$ and a map $f \colon C \to \Gamma$ such that $u \in \|f(u)\|$ for all $u \in C$, and whenever $\varphi \in \Gamma \setminus \{f(u)\}$, then there is $v \in C$ such that $u \sqsubset v \in C$ and $v \in \|\varphi\|$.*

Example 3. Recall the model of Example 1, consisting of an irreflexive cluster $\{0, 1\}$ with $\|e\| = \{0\}$, $\|o\| = \{1\}$, $\|p\| = \{1\}$, and $\|i\| = \{0, 1\}$. We then have that $\blacklozenge^\infty \{e, o\} = \{0, 1\}$, since each point is either even and has an accessible point that is odd, or vice-versa. On the other hand, $\blacklozenge^\infty \{o, p\} = \varnothing$, since we cannot assign any atom $a \in \{o, p\}$ to 1 in such a way that 1 satisfies $\Diamond a \wedge \Diamond a'$, where a' is the complementary atom to a. And if 0 were to satisfy $\Diamond(a \wedge x) \wedge \Diamond(a' \wedge x)$, then 1 would also have to satisfy $\Diamond a \wedge \Diamond a'$, something we have already shown to be impossible. Thus it is not enough for each element of Γ to be satisfied in a cluster in order to make $\blacklozenge^\infty \Gamma$ true: instead, each point w must have an accessible world satisfying all but possibly one element φ_w of Γ, in which case it must also satisfy φ_w.

3   Final Submodels

The technique of *final worlds* is a powerful tool in establishing the finite model property for many transitive modal logics [9], and is also applicable to the μ-calculus over weakly transitive frames [2]. The idea here is that only a few worlds in a model contain 'useful' information, and the rest can be deleted. These 'useful' worlds are those that are maximal (or *final*) with respect to $\sqsubseteq$, among those satisfying a given formula of Σ.

Definition 5. (Σ-**final**). *Given a model M and a set of formulas Σ, a world $w \in M$ is Σ-final if there is some formula $\varphi \in \Sigma$ such that $w \vDash_M \varphi$ and if $w \sqsubseteq u$ and $u \vDash_M \varphi$, then $u \sqsubseteq w$.*
A set $A \subseteq M$ will be called Σ-final iff every $w \in A$ is Σ-final. The Σ-final part of M is the largest Σ-final subset of M and we denote it by M^Σ.

Sometimes we need to 'glue' a root cluster to a Σ-final model. To this end, a rooted model (M, w) will be called Σ-semifinal if $M \setminus C_w$ is Σ-final.

Baltag et al. [2] built on ideas of Fine [9] to show via final submodels that the topological μ-calculus has the finite model property. While final submodels are not necessarily finite (if M is infinite), they do have finite *depth*. Given a model M, a set of formulas Σ and $w \in M$, we define the *depth of w in M*, denoted $dpt^M(A)$, as the supremum of all n such that $w = w_0 \prec w_1 \prec w_2 \prec \ldots \prec w_n$ (recall that $\prec$ is the strict part of $\sqsubseteq$); note that this is finite on finite weakly transitive models but could be infinite on infinite ones. For $A \subseteq M$ we define the depth of A in M to be $dpt^M(A) = \sup(0 \cup \{dpt^M(w) : w \in A\})$. The Σ-depth of w is defined analogously, except that here we only consider chains such that $w_1, \ldots, w_n \in M^\Sigma$ (note that w itself need not be Σ-final). Then we define $dpt_\Sigma^M(A)$ as before. It is not hard to check that $dpt_\Sigma^M(w)$ is bounded by $|\Sigma|$, and thus if Σ is finite we can immediately control the depth of any Σ-final model. From a model of finite depth, it is easy to obtain a finite model.

In order to use this idea towards a proof of the finite model property (and also for our own results), one must carefully choose Σ so that for any $\varphi \in \Sigma$ and $w \in M^\Sigma$, we have that $M^\Sigma, w \equiv_\Sigma M, w$. For example, Σ should be closed under subformulas, but since we are in the μ-calculus, we will have to find a way to treat the free variables that show up in said subformulas. Because of this, we define a variant of the set of subformulas of a given formula where any free occurrence of a variable is labelled according to its binding formula, thus making sure that the same variable does not appear free with different meanings. We also need to treat reflexive modalities as if they were primitive.

Definition 6. *We define the modified subformula operator* $sub^* : \mathcal{L}_\mu \to \mathcal{P}(\mathcal{L}_\mu)$ *recursively by*

- $sub^*(r) = \{r\}$ *if* $r = \top, p, x$;
- $sub^*(\neg p) = \{\neg p, p\}$;
- $sub^*(\varphi \odot \psi) = \{\varphi \odot \psi\} \cup sub^*(\varphi) \cup sub^*(\psi)$ *where* $\odot = \wedge$ *or* $\vee$ *and* $\varphi \odot \psi \neq$ $\Diamond \sigma$ *or* $\Box \sigma$ *for some* σ;[2]
- $sub^*(\odot \psi) = \{\psi\} \cup sub^*(\psi)$ *where* $\odot = \Diamond, \Box, \Diamond$ *or* $\Box$;
- $sub^*(\nu x.\varphi) = \{\varphi(x_{\nu x.\varphi})\} \cup sub^*(\varphi(x_{\nu x.\varphi}))$ *where* $x_{\nu x.\varphi}$ *is a fresh propositional variable named after* $\nu x.\varphi$;
- $sub^*(\mu x.\varphi) = \{\varphi(x_{\mu x.\varphi})\} \cup sub^*(\varphi(x_{\mu x.\varphi}))$ *where* $x_{\mu x.\varphi}$ *is a fresh propositional variable named after* $\mu x.\varphi$.

Given a set of formulae Σ, *we can define a partial order on* $sub^*[\Sigma]$ *by* $\varphi <_{sub^*} \psi$ *iff* $\varphi \in sub^*(\psi)$ *and* $\varphi \neq \psi$.

Observe that if x_ψ is a free variable of φ, then $\varphi <_{sub^*} \psi$. So we will work with these altered subformulas, but we also need to close Σ under some further operations. Given a set $\mathbb{X}$, some $Y \subseteq \mathbb{X}$ and a set $\mathcal{A}$ of mappings $a : \mathbb{X} \to \mathcal{P}(\mathbb{X})$, we define the closure of Y over $\mathbb{X}$ inductively as follows:

- $Cl_\mathcal{A}^0(Y) = Y$;
- $Cl_\mathcal{A}^{\alpha+1}(Y) = Cl_\mathcal{A}^\alpha(Y) \cup \{a(x) : a \in \mathcal{A} \ \& \ x \in Cl_\mathcal{A}^\alpha(Y)\}$;
- $Cl_\mathcal{A}^\lambda(Y) = \bigcup_{\alpha < \lambda} Cl_\mathcal{A}^\alpha(Y)$ *for* $\lambda \in Lim$.

$Cl_\mathcal{A}(Y) = Cl_\mathcal{A}^\alpha(Y)$ where α is any ordinal such that $Cl_\mathcal{A}^\alpha(Y) = Cl_\mathcal{A}^{\alpha+1}(Y)$.

For the remainder of the paper, unless stated otherwise, we will be working with a set of formulae Σ such that $\Sigma = Cl_{\Diamond, sub^*, \neg}(\Sigma)$. Observe that any finite

---

[2] Remember that $\Diamond \sigma$ abbreviates $\sigma \vee \Diamond \sigma$ and similarly $\Box \sigma = \sigma \wedge \Box \sigma$.

set Σ_0 can be extended to a Σ with this property that is finite up to modal equivalence of formulae since in S4 there are only finitely many non equivalent modalities and $\Diamond$ is an S4 modality [3].

Since we have labelled our variables by their binding formula, we can substitute this formula back and obtain a 'closed' version of this formula.

Lemma 2. *Fix a finite set of formulas Σ closed under sub^* and some $\varphi \in \Sigma$, we let $\lfloor \varphi \rfloor$ denote the closed form of φ; that is every instance of x_ψ is substituted by ψ recursively until there are no free variables left.*
It holds that $\lfloor \varphi \rfloor \in \mathcal{L}_\mu$ for each $\varphi \in \Sigma$.

Observe that additionally $\neg \lfloor \varphi \rfloor$ is equivalent to $\lfloor \neg \varphi \rfloor$ for all $\varphi \in \Sigma$. In the sequel, given a model M and a set of formulae Σ closed under sub^*, we will read $w \vDash_M \varphi$ to mean $w \vDash_M \lfloor \varphi \rfloor$. In particular, this means that w is final for φ in M iff it is final for $\lfloor \varphi \rfloor$ in M.

Definition 7. *Fix a finite rooted model (M, w) and a set of formulas Σ, we will write*

$$w \vDash_M \overline{\langle n \rangle} \varphi :\Leftrightarrow \exists v \in M^\Sigma \, (v \sqsupseteq w \wedge dpt_\Sigma(v) = n \wedge v \vDash_M \varphi).$$

Since for a given cluster C of M and $u, v \in C$, $u \vDash_M \overline{\langle n \rangle} \varphi \Leftrightarrow v \vDash_M \overline{\langle n \rangle} \varphi$, we will occasionally make an abuse of notation and write $C \vDash_M \overline{\langle n \rangle} \varphi$ to mean $\exists u \in C \, u \vDash_M \overline{\langle n \rangle} \varphi$.

The formulas $\overline{\langle n \rangle} \varphi$ provide all the information needed to evaluate truth on C:

Theorem 2. *Let $(M, w), (N, w)$ be finite rooted models with root clusters C and C' respectively. Assume that $dpt_\Sigma^M(w) = dpt_\Sigma^N(w)$ and $\forall \varphi \in \Sigma \, w \vDash_M \overline{\langle n \rangle} \varphi \Leftrightarrow w \vDash_N \overline{\langle n \rangle} \varphi$ for all $n < dpt_\Sigma^M(w)$, and*

- *if C is Σ-final then $C' = C$*
- *if C is not Σ-final then $C' \subseteq C$*

then $\forall v \in C' \, \forall \varphi \in \Sigma \, v \vDash_M \varphi$ iff $v \vDash_N \varphi$.

As an immediate corollary, we get the following, where we write $M, u \equiv_\Sigma N, v$ to mean $\forall \varphi \in \Sigma \, u \vDash_M \varphi \Leftrightarrow v \vDash_N \varphi$. In case $M = N$, we may abbreviate this by $u \equiv_\Sigma v$.

Theorem 3. *Given a finite model M, a model N with $M \supseteq N \supseteq M^\Sigma$ and any $w \in N$, it holds that $M, w \equiv_\Sigma N, w$.*

4 Structural Evaluation

The strategy we will follow to obtain an equivalence is to describe the parts of the world and the model that are relevant to Theorem 2. In particular we will define formulae in $\mathcal{L}_{\blacklozenge\infty}$ equivalent to the $\overline{\langle n \rangle}\varphi$ 'formulae', as well as a formula which approximates the statement "w is Σ-final".

Theorem 2 tells us that we need very little information to evaluate truth of formulas on a given cluster, provided we have already evaluated them on clusters of lower depth. This information is recorded by (semi-)satisfaction pairs:

Definition 8. *Given a model M say that $\langle C, \Theta \rangle$ is a semi-satisfaction pair for M if $\exists w \in M$ such that $C = C_w$ and $\Theta = \{\overline{\langle m \rangle}\psi : w \vDash_M \overline{\langle m \rangle}\psi$ for $\psi \in \Sigma \wedge m < dpt_\Sigma(w)\}$. A pair $\langle C, \Theta \rangle$ is called a semi-satisfaction pair if it is a semi-satisfaction pair for some finite pointed Σ-semifinal model. A satisfaction pair for M is a semi-satisfaction pair $\langle C, \Theta \rangle$ such that C is Σ-final in M.*

Given a semi-satisfaction pair $\langle C, \Theta \rangle$ for some model M, we define[3]

$$\Theta^C := \{\overline{\langle m \rangle}\psi : C \vDash_M \overline{\langle m \rangle}\psi \text{ for } \psi \in \Sigma \wedge m \leq dpt_\Sigma(C)\}.$$

We extend the definition of dpt_Σ by saying $dpt_\Sigma(\Theta) = sup\{n : \overline{\langle n \rangle}\varphi \in \Theta$ for some $\varphi \in \Sigma\}$. Let Sat_n be the set of satisfaction pairs $\langle C, \Theta \rangle$ such that $dpt_\Sigma(\Theta) = n$ and let Sat_n^0, Sat_n^1 be the first and second projections of Sat_n respectively. Similarly, $Sat_n^*, Sat_n^{*0}, Sat_n^{*1}$ are the corresponding sets for semi-satisfaction pairs.

We will need to compare clusters and semi-satisfaction pairs. Roughly, $C \not\sqsubseteq C'$ indicates that C is a smaller cluster than C' (up to bisimulation), and $\langle C, \Theta \rangle \lhd \langle C', \Theta' \rangle$ indicates that the two pairs vary only in their root cluster, where C' is larger.

Let us make this precise. Fix $P \subseteq \mathbb{P}$ and clusters C and C' from models $\mathcal{M} = \langle M, \sqsubset_\mathcal{M}, \| \cdot \|_\mathcal{M} \rangle$ and $\mathcal{N} = \langle N, \sqsubset_\mathcal{N}, \| \cdot \|_\mathcal{N} \rangle$ respectively, we write $C \not\sqsubseteq_P C'$ to mean that there is some $C'' \subseteq C'''$ such that $C' \rightleftharpoons_P C''$. Similarly $C \not\sqsubset C'$ is defined for when additionally $C \not\rightleftharpoons_P C'$. As with the bisimilarity notation, the P subscript is omitted in the sequel. Define $\lhd_n \subseteq Sat_n \times Sat_n$ by $\langle C', \Theta' \rangle \lhd_n \langle C, \Theta \rangle$ iff $C' \not\sqsubset C$ and $\Theta' = \Theta$. Let $\unlhd_n$ be the reflexive closure of $\lhd_n$. We will write $\lhd$, $\unlhd$ instead of $\lhd_n$, $\unlhd_n$ when n is clear.

Satisfaction pairs are sufficient to evaluate truth, but our definition of $\overline{\langle n \rangle}\varphi$ in tangle logic will be sensitive to depth (i.e., to n), and thus we need to control the Σ-depth of the model we are working in. This is achieved by considering chains of satisfaction pairs: if a chain of length n lies above a given world, that means that the depth of that world is at least n. Since the property 'there is a chain of length n' will be expressible in $\mathcal{L}_{\blacklozenge\infty}$, this will allow us to have the desired control over depth.

To formally define chains, we need to consider root clusters glued to a model. Fix a finite model M and a cluster C with $M \cap C = \varnothing$, we denote by $\begin{bmatrix} M \\ C \end{bmatrix}$ the model N with domain $M \cup C$, accessibility relation $\sqsubset_N := \sqsubset_M \cup \sqsubset_C \cup (C \times M)$ and $\| \cdot \|_N := \| \cdot \|_M \cup \| \cdot \|_C$.

---

[3] Due to Theorem 2, Θ^C is uniquely determined irrespectively of the chosen model M for which $\langle C, \Theta \rangle$ is a semi-satisfaction pair.

Lemma 3. *For every Σ-final model M of depth n with a root cluster C, there is some chain $\mathcal{C} = \{\langle C_i, \Theta_i \rangle\}_{i \leq n}$ such that*

1. $C_n = C$
2. $\langle C_i, \Theta_i \rangle$ *is a satisfaction pair for M for each $i \leq n$*
3. $C_{i+1} \prec C_i$ *for each $i < n$*
4. *For all $i < n$, if $\begin{bmatrix} C_i \\ C_{i+1} \end{bmatrix} \rightleftharpoons C_i$ then $\Theta_{i+1} \neq \Theta_i^{C_i}$.*

We will call a chain as in Lemma 3 a *witnessing chain of depth n*; witnessing chains will be denoted as $\mathcal{C}, \mathcal{C}'$ or $\mathcal{C}_i$. Let $Chain_n$ be the set of witnessing chains of depth n. We extend $\lhd_n$ to $Chain_n \times Chain_n$ by setting $\mathcal{C} \lhd_n \mathcal{C}'$ iff the following hold:

- $\langle C_i, \Theta_i \rangle = \langle C_i', \Theta_i' \rangle$ for $i < n$
- $C_n \not\in C_n'$
- $\Theta_n = \Theta_n'$

and let $\unlhd_n$ be its reflexive closure. We will identify $\lhd$ and $\unlhd$ to be the appropriate $\lhd_n$ and $\unlhd_n$ respectively. Finally, given n and a formula $\varphi \in \Sigma$, we write

$$supp(\overline{\langle n \rangle} \varphi) = \{\mathcal{C} \in Chain_n : \exists (M, w) \text{ finite pointed } \Sigma\text{-final model where}$$

$$w \vDash_M \varphi \wedge C_n = C_w \wedge \mathcal{C} \text{ is a witnessing chain of depth } n \text{ for } M\}.$$

The definition of witnessing chains can be further expanded to semifinal models, however the analogue of Lemma 3 for semi-witnessing chains will not necessarily hold for any Σ-semifinal model as we cannot guarantee that we can always find a chain in that case for which condition 4 will hold for the root cluster. In this setting, we instead use a weaker notion.

Definition 9. *Given a Σ-semifinal model M of depth n with root cluster C, a semi-witnessing chain for M of depth n (if it exists) is some chain $\mathcal{C} = \{\langle C_i, \Theta_i \rangle\}_{i \leq n}$ such that*

1. $C_n = C$
2. $\langle C_i, \Theta_i \rangle$ *is a semi-satisfaction pair for M for each $i \leq n$*
3. $C_{i+1} \prec C_i$ *for each $i < n$*
4. *For all $i < n$, if $\begin{bmatrix} C_i \\ C_{i+1} \end{bmatrix} \rightleftharpoons C_i$ then $\Theta_{i+1} \neq \Theta_i^{C_i}$.*

We will denote by $Chain_n^*$ *the set of all semi-witnessing chains of depth n. For M an arbitrary finite model, a (semi-)witnessing chain on M of depth n will be a (semi-)witnessing chain on the Σ-(semi)final part of $w \uparrow_M^*$ for some $w \in M$. Finally for $\mathcal{C} \in Chain_n^*$, let $dpt(\mathcal{C}) := n$ denote its depth.*

We can now define formulas equivalent to the "$\overline{\langle n \rangle} \varphi$" in the language of $\mathcal{L}_{\blacklozenge \infty}$. This is done inductively by having the formula α express the existence of a witnessing chain $\mathcal{C}$ with a satisfaction pair $\langle C, \Theta \rangle$ underneath it. Then the formulae β and γ ensure that the extension $\mathcal{C}^\frown \langle C, \Theta \rangle$ is also a witnessing chain (i.e. the pair $\langle C, \Theta \rangle$ is as high as it can possibly be while remaining below $\mathcal{C}$).

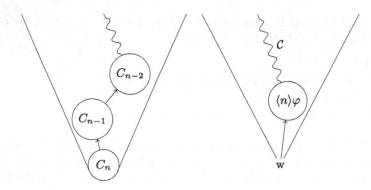

Fig. 1. On the left, a witnessing chain. On the right, a witnessing chain ensures that the Σ-depth of a point where $\langle n \rangle \varphi$ holds is at least n.

At this point it is important to note that if we were to simply use satisfaction pairs, we would run the risk of having the Σ-depth of worlds satisfying $\langle n \rangle \varphi$ being smaller than n; with witnessing chains, we ensure that the depth does not collapse (Fig. 1).

Definition 10. *Fix $w \in M$ and a set of formulae Σ let $\tau_w := \bigwedge_{p \in P(w)} p \wedge \bigwedge_{p \notin P(w)} \neg p$, where $p \in \Sigma$. We will, as a convention, not include the model M and the set Σ in the notation. Below we define the formulas $\langle n \rangle \varphi \in \mathcal{L}_{\blacklozenge\infty}$, along with some auxiliary formulas and notation.*

- $Ir(\mathcal{C}) := \langle C_n, \Theta_n \rangle \trianglelefteq \langle C_{n-1}, \Theta_{n-1}^{C_{n-1}} \rangle \wedge \exists w \in C_n \forall u \in C_n \cap w \!\uparrow\ P(w) \neq P(u)$
  where $n = dpt(\mathcal{C})$
- $A(\Theta) := \bigwedge\limits_{\overline{\langle m \rangle} \psi \in \Theta} \langle m \rangle \psi \wedge \bigwedge\limits_{\overline{\langle m \rangle} \psi \notin \Theta} \neg \langle m \rangle \psi$
- $\tau_w^{\mathcal{C}} := \begin{cases} \tau_w \wedge A(\Theta_{dpt(\mathcal{C})}) \wedge \Diamond\big(\tau_w \wedge \delta(\mathcal{C}{\restriction}dpt(\mathcal{C}))\big) & \text{if } Ir(\mathcal{C}) \\ \tau_w \wedge A(\Theta_{dpt(\mathcal{C})}) \wedge \Diamond\delta(\mathcal{C}{\restriction}dpt(\mathcal{C})) & \text{otherwise} \end{cases}$
- $\alpha(\mathcal{C}) := \blacklozenge^\infty \{\tau_w^{\mathcal{C}} : w \in C_{dpt(\mathcal{C})}\}$
- $\beta(\mathcal{C}) := \Box\big(\bigvee\limits_{\mathcal{C}' \lhd \mathcal{C}} \alpha(\mathcal{C}') \to \alpha(\mathcal{C})\big)$
- $\gamma(\mathcal{C}) := \neg \bigvee\limits_{\mathcal{C}' \ntrianglelefteq \mathcal{C}} \alpha(\mathcal{C}')$
- $\delta(\mathcal{C}) := \alpha(\mathcal{C}) \wedge \beta(\mathcal{C}) \wedge \gamma(\mathcal{C})$
- $\langle n \rangle \varphi := \bigvee\limits_{\mathcal{C} \in supp(\overline{\langle n \rangle} \varphi)} \Diamond \delta(\mathcal{C})$

Here, A describes the $\overline{\langle m \rangle}$-formulas in a given Θ, Ir tells us when a bottom-most cluster in a chain has an 'irreflexive point'[4] which we can use to be able to

---

[4] Whilst by our convention every world w in M is irreflexive, in this context we mean that $C_n, w \neq C', w'$ with w' being reflexive.

jump to cluster in the chain above it, $\tau_w^{\mathcal{C}}$ describes the 'local state' at w, α ensures that the desired chain is present, and β and γ rule out any unwanted chains. By following step by step the definitions above, we can prove the following lemma:

Lemma 4. *Fix a finite model M a set of formulas Σ and $w \in M$, it holds that $w \vDash_M \langle n \rangle \varphi \Leftrightarrow w \vDash_M \overline{\langle n \rangle} \varphi$ for all $\varphi \in \Sigma$.*

Corollary 1. *Fix a finite model M, some $w \in M$ and $C \in Chain_n^* \setminus Chain_n$, then $w \vDash_M \alpha(C)$ iff $C \lceil n$ is a witnessing chain of depth n for M strictly above w (i.e. $w \prec C_{n-1}$) and there is some cluster $C = C_u$ for some $u \in M$ such that*

(a) $w \preceq C \prec C_{n-1}$
(b) $C_n \nsubseteq C$
(c) $C \vDash_M A(\Theta_n)$

The formulas $\langle n \rangle \varphi$ thus defined are the central ingredient in proving our main result. The translation $\chi(\varphi)$ of φ itself into $\mathcal{L}_{\blacklozenge \infty}$ requires a case distinction according to whether we are evaluating on a final world or not. Since a completely accurate definition of finality is impossible to obtain, even in $\mathcal{L}_\mu$, we will instead approximate one with the following. The formula $split(n)$ roughly states that there are two incomparable final worlds of depth n above w, or there is a semi-witnessing chain of depth higher than n above w; in either case, w itself cannot be a final world of depth n.

Definition 11. *We define formulas*

$$split(n) := \bigvee \{ \Diamond \delta(\mathcal{C}) \wedge \Diamond \delta(\mathcal{C}') : \mathcal{C}, \mathcal{C}' \in Chain_n \text{ with } \langle C_n, \Theta_n \rangle \neq \langle C_n', \Theta_n' \rangle \}$$

$$\vee \bigvee \{ \alpha(\mathcal{C}_0) : \mathcal{C}_0 \in Chain_{n+1}^* \setminus Chain_{n+1} \}.$$

Now, suppose we have access to the valuation at w, a chain $\mathcal{C}$ witnessing that w is Σ-final of depth n (with $\mathcal{C} = \varnothing$ if w is not Σ-final), as well as the set Θ of formulas $\langle m \rangle \varphi$ with $m < n := dpt_\Sigma(w)$ which are true on w. For such a tuple $(w, \mathcal{C}, \Theta, n)$, we define a formula $\chi_0(w, \mathcal{C}, \Theta, n)$ stating the above-mentioned properties, depending on whether $split(n)$ holds on w:

$$\chi_0(w, \mathcal{C}, \Theta, n) := \begin{cases} \langle n \rangle \top \wedge \neg \langle n+1 \rangle \top \wedge \\ \neg split(n) \wedge \tau_w \wedge \Diamond \delta(\mathcal{C}) & \text{if } \mathcal{C} \neq \varnothing \\ \langle n \rangle \top \wedge \neg \langle n+1 \rangle \top \wedge \\ split(n) \wedge \tau_w \wedge A(\Theta) & \text{if } \mathcal{C} = \varnothing \end{cases}.$$

We are almost ready to define $\chi(w)$. To do so, we first define $eval(\varphi, n)$ to be the set of all triples $\langle w, \mathcal{C}, \Theta \rangle$ for which there exists a rooted Σ-semifinal model (M, w) such that

1. $w \in M$
2. $w \vDash_M \varphi$
3. $\Theta = \{\langle m \rangle \psi : w \vDash_M \overline{\langle m \rangle} \psi \text{ for } \psi \in \Sigma \wedge m < dpt_\Sigma(w)\}$

4. If $w \notin M^\Sigma$ then $dpt_\Sigma(\Theta) = n$ and $\mathcal{C} = \varnothing$
5. If $w \in M^\Sigma$ then $dpt_\Sigma(\Theta) = n - 1$ and $\mathcal{C}$ is a witnessing chain for M of depth n with $\langle C_w, \Theta \rangle = \langle C_n, \Theta_n \rangle$.

And let $eval(\varphi) := \bigcup_n eval(\varphi, n)$. Since w satisfies φ if and only if we can find $\mathcal{C}$ and Θ such that $\langle w, \mathcal{C}, \Theta \rangle \in eval(\varphi)$, we may define the characteristic formula $\chi(\varphi)$ of φ by

$$\chi(\varphi) := \bigvee_{\langle w, \mathcal{C}, \Theta \rangle \in eval(\varphi)} \chi_0(w, \mathcal{C}, \Theta, dpt_\Sigma(\Theta)).$$

Theorem 4. *Given a formula φ and a finite rooted model (M, w), we have that $w \vDash_M \varphi \Leftrightarrow w \vDash_M \chi(\varphi)$.*

In view of [2], this also applies to the class of topological spaces. Moreover, $\blacklozenge^\infty \Gamma$ can be expressed by a first order formula in all path-finite weakly transitive frames, where path-finite means that the ordering $\prec$ and its inverse $\prec^{-1}$ are well-founded. So we get a first order expressibility of $\mathcal{L}_\mu$ in frames analogous to the ones in [5]. Thus we obtain the following.

Theorem 5. $\mathcal{L}_\mu \equiv \mathcal{L}_{\blacklozenge^\infty}$ *over the class of topological spaces and the class of weakly transitive frames, and so $\mathcal{L}_\mu \subset \mathsf{FOL}/{\rightleftharpoons}$ over finite and path-finite weakly transitive frames.*

In-fact, we fail to get a characterization theorem for the μ calculus over finite and path-finite weakly transitive frames. We show this via a bisimulation invariant formula of FOL whose modal class is not definable via a $\mathcal{L}_\mu$ formula.

Theorem 6. $\mathcal{L}_\mu \subsetneq \mathsf{FOL}/{\rightleftharpoons}$ *over finite and path-finite weakly transitive frames.*

We can obtain a rough estimate of $|\chi(\varphi)| \leq 2^{(14|\varphi|+1)2^{14|\varphi|+6}}$. This upper bound also applies in the transitive setting, whereas it is more difficult to extract from the methods of [5]. This bound is reasonably close to the known lower bound, which is exponential [8]. Finding the optimal size of a translation remains an interesting open problem.

5 Conclusion

We have shown that the topological μ-calculus is equi-expressive to its tangled fragment, provided it's defined in a way that better captures its intended behaviour on arbitrary topological spaces while retaining its original value on metric spaces and other 'nice' topological spaces. Given the much more transparent syntax of tangle logic, this suggests that the latter is more suitable for applications in spatial KR than the full μ-calculus.

This begs the question of whether the topological μ-calculus, or its tangled fragment, can be enriched in a natural way to obtain the full expressive power of the bisimulation-invariant fragments of FOL or MSO. Perhaps something in the spirit of hybrid logics can bridge this gap, but at this point the question remains a challenging open problem.

References

1. Baltag, A., Bezhanishvili, N., Fernández-Duque, D.: The topology of surprise. In: Kern-Isberner, G., Lakemeyer, G., Meyer, T. (eds.) Proceedings of the 19th International Conference on Principles of Knowledge Representation and Reasoning, KR 2022, Haifa, Israel, 31 July–5 August 2022 (2022). https://proceedings.kr.org/2022/4/
2. Baltag, A., Bezhanishvili, N., Fernández-Duque, D.: The topological mu-calculus: completeness and decidability. In: 36th Annual ACM/IEEE Symposium on Logic in Computer Science, LICS, Rome, Italy, 29 June–2 July 2021, pp. 1–13. IEEE (2021). https://doi.org/10.1109/LICS52264.2021.9470560
3. Chagrov, A.V., Zakharyaschev, M.: Modal logic. In: Oxford Logic Guides (1997)
4. Cohn, A., Renz, J.: Qualitative spatial representation and reasoning. In: van Harmelen, F., Lifschitz, V., Porter, B. (eds.) Handbook of Knowledge Representation, Foundations of Artificial Intelligence, vol. 3, pp. 551–596. Elsevier (2008)
5. Dawar, A., Otto, M.: Modal characterisation theorems over special classes of frames. Ann. Pure Appl. Logic 161(1), 1–42 (2009)
6. Egenhofer, M., Franzosa, R.: Point-set topological spatial relations. Int. J. Geogr. Inf. Syst. 5(2), 161–174 (1991)
7. Esakia, L.: Weak transitivity-a restitution. Logical Invest. 8, 244–245 (2001)
8. Fernández-Duque, D., Iliev, P.: Succinctness in subsystems of the spatial μ-calculus. FLAP 5(4), 827–874 (2018). https://www.collegepublications.co.uk/downloads/ifcolog00024.pdf
9. Fine, K.: Logics containing $K4$. I. J. Symb. Logic 39, 31–42 (1974)
10. Goldblatt, R., Hodkinson, I.: Spatial logic of tangled closure operators and modal mu-calculus. Ann. Pure Appl. Log. 168(5), 1032–1090 (2017)
11. Gougeon, Q.: The expressive power of derivational modal logic. Master's thesis, ILLC, University of Amsterdam (2022)
12. Janin, D., Walukiewicz, I.: On the expressive completeness of the propositional mu-calculus with respect to monadic second order logic. In: Montanari, U., Sassone, V. (eds.) CONCUR 1996. LNCS, vol. 1119, pp. 263–277. Springer, Heidelberg (1996). https://doi.org/10.1007/3-540-61604-7_60
13. Lucero-Bryan, J.G.: The d-logic of the real line. J. Log. Comput. 23(1), 121–156 (2013). https://doi.org/10.1093/logcom/exr054
14. van Benthem, J.: Modal correspondence theory. Ph.D. thesis, University of Amsterdam (1976)
15. Pacheco, L., Tanaka, K.: The alternation hierarchy of the μ-calculus over weakly transitive frames. In: Ciabattoni, A., Pimentel, E., de Queiroz, R.J.G.B. (eds.) WoLLIC 2022. LNCS, pp. 207–220. Springer, Cham (2022). https://doi.org/10.1007/978-3-031-15298-6_13
16. Randell, D., Cui, Z., Cohn, A.: A spatial logic based on regions and connection. In: Proceedings of the Third International Conference on Principles of Knowledge Representation and Reasoning, KR 1992, pp. 165–176. Morgan Kaufmann Publishers Inc., San Francisco (1992)
17. Stell, J.: Qualitative spatial representation for the humanities. Int. J. Hum. Arts Comput. 13(1–2), 2–27 (2019)
18. Wolter, F., Zakharyaschev, M.: Spatial reasoning in RCC-8 with Boolean region terms. In: Horn, W. (ed.) ECAI, pp. 244–250. IOS Press (2000)

Author Index

© The Editor(s) (if applicable) and The Author(s), under exclusive license
to Springer Nature Switzerland AG 2023
S. Gaggl et al. (Eds.): JELIA 2023, LNAI 14281, pp. 829–831, 2023.
https://doi.org/10.1007/978-3-031-43619-2